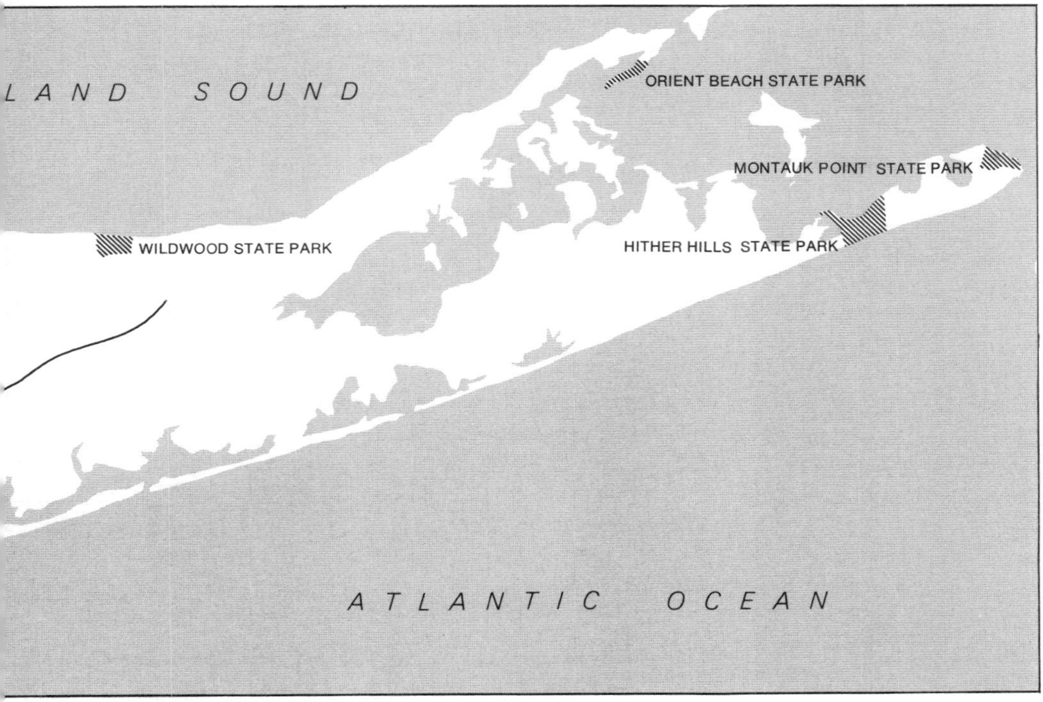
LAND SOUND
ORIENT BEACH STATE PARK
MONTAUK POINT STATE PARK
WILDWOOD STATE PARK
HITHER HILLS STATE PARK
ATLANTIC OCEAN

PRAISE FOR
THE POWER BROKER

'Simply one of the best non-fiction books in English of the past forty years ... There has probably never been a better dissection of political power ... From the first page ... you know that you are in the hands of a master ... riveting ... superb ... not just a stunning portrait of perhaps the most influential builder in world history ... but an object lesson in the dangers of power' Dominic Sandbrook, *Sunday Times*

'One of the great biographies of all time ... [by] one of the great reporters of our time ... and probably the greatest biographer. He is also an extraordinary writer. After reading page 136 of his book *The Power Broker*, I gasped and read it again, then again. This, I thought, is how it should be done ... said to be one of the greatest nonfiction works ever written ... Every MP, wonk and would-be wonk in Westminster has read [Robert Caro's *The Years of Lyndon Johnson*], because they think it is the greatest insight into power ever written. They're nearly right: it's the second greatest after *The Power Broker*'
Bryan Appleyard, *Sunday Times*

'I think about Robert Caro and reading *The Power Broker* back when I was twenty-two years old and just being mesmerized, and I'm sure it helped to shape how I think about politics' Barack Obama

'This is irresistibly readable, an outright masterpiece and unparalleled insight into how power works and perhaps the greatest portrait ever of a world city'
David Sexton, *Evening Standard*

'A stupendous achievement ... Caro's style is gripping, indeed hypnotic, and he squeezes every ounce of drama from his remarkable story … Can a democracy combine visionary leadership with effective checks and balances to contain the misuse of power? No book illustrates this fundamental dilemma of democracy better than *The Power Broker* ... Indeed, no student of government can regard his education as complete until he has read it' Vernon Bogdanor, *Independent*

'The story of how Robert Moses made and broke people and places is astonishing. It comes so highly recommended that it is unignorable' Jeremy Paxman, *Observer*

'Remarkable … we learn as much about the intoxication and addiction of power as we do about the bureaucratic titan whose imprint on New York bears comparison with his only modern equivalent, the smasher and rebuilder of Paris, Baron Haussmann … [with] his detailed reporting and rhythmic prose, his great acuity for understanding and describing the nuances of politics and power … [Robert Caro] has no contemporary rivals' John R MacArthur, *Spectator*

'An epic, meticulously detailed study of power in general: how it's acquired, how it's used to change history, how it ultimately corrupts those who get it ... Masterfully, Caro shows how Moses transformed New York in ways both progressive and backward, benign and cruel ... as an account of how power and ambition shape the urban environment, *The Power Broker* has yet to be beaten' Oliver Burkeman, *Guardian*

'One of the most exciting, unputdownable books I have ever read. This is definitive biography, urban history, and investigative journalism. This is a study of the corruption which power exerts on those who wield it to set beside Tacitus and his emperors, Shakespeare and his kings' *Baltimore Evening Sun*

'Irresistible reading. It is like one of the great Russian novels, overflowing with characters and incidents that all fit into a vast mosaic of plot and counterplot. Only this is no novel. This is a college education in power corruption'
St. Louis Post-Dispatch

'The most absorbing, detailed, instructive, provocative book ever published about the making and raping of modern New York City and environs and the man who did it, about the hidden plumbing of New York City and State politics over the last half-century, about the force of personality and the nature of political power in a democracy. A monumental work, a political biography and political history of the first magnitude'
New York

'The feverish hype that dominates the merchandising of arts and letters in America has so debased the language that, when a truly exceptional achievement comes along, there are no words left to praise it. Important, awesome, compelling – these no longer summon the full flourish of trumpets this book deserves. It is extraordinary on many levels and certain to endure' *Washington Post Book World*

PRAISE FOR
THE YEARS OF LYNDON JOHNSON
THE PASSAGE OF POWER

'Monumental … for many politicians it is the finest book on politics … magnificent … the tension between the fraud and ruthlessness that repulsed political liberals and the reaction of voters to whom he delivered, make Caro's book the ultimate political story'
Daniel Finkelstein, *The Times*

'This extraordinary work will remain essential reading for decades to come'
Richard Lambert, *Financial Times*

'A true story of huge personalities, bloody assassinations, loves, hatreds and betrayals (and the Kennedy family) that renders it by turns gripping, sensational and immensely depressing … a white-knuckle rollercoaster ride … magisterial'
Andrew Roberts, *Telegraph*

'Brilliant … important … remarkable … With this fascinating and meticulous account of Lyndon Johnson, Robert Caro has once again done America a great service'
Bill Clinton, *New York Times Book Review*

'A tremendous story, bursting with colour and character … the sheer wealth of political details keeps you turning the pages … brilliant'
Dominic Sandbrook, *Sunday Times*

'It is not often that I have muttered, "Astonishing", to myself as I close a book. But I see what people were on about now. Caro is a brilliant narrator of recent history … a work of greatness, of such acute observation of politics that its insights are applicable far beyond the time and place of the United States, 1960-64' John Rentoul, *Independent*

'A breathtakingly dramatic story [told] with consummate artistry and ardor … It showcases Mr Caro's masterly gifts as a writer: his propulsive sense of narrative, his talent for enabling readers to see and feel history in the making and his ability to situate his subjects' actions within the context of their times … Taken together the installments of Mr Caro's monumental life of Johnson so far not only create a minutely detailed picture of an immensely complicated and conflicted individual, but they also form a revealing prism by which to view the better part of a century … engrossing'
Michiko Kakutani, *The New York Times*

'My book of the year, by a landslide majority … The adjective 'Shakespearean' is overused and mostly undeserved but not in this case. LBJ emerges from this biography as a fully rounded tragic hero: cowardly and brave, petty and magnificent, vindictive and noble, a man of vaunting ambition and profound insecurities … Caro marries profound psychological insight with a brilliant eye for the drama of the times'
Robert Harris, *Guardian*

MASTER OF THE SENATE

'Regarded by many as the greatest political biography of the modern era. Essential reading for those who want to comprehend power and politics. Compellingly readable … the breathtaking detail makes it impossible to put down' *The Times*

'Quite breathtaking – one of the great political biographies' Gordon Brown

'This books stands out because it brings that pace and drama to life: it makes it almost as exciting to read the book as it would have been to be there – a magnificent history of twentieth-century America' William Hague

'Dazzling ... awesome ... Rarely will you come across a more compelling account of the nature of great power and its entanglement with massive personality. Rarely will you find another biography which is such a fascinating study of how a bad man became a power for the good' *Observer*

'For Caro, writing a biography is writing a thriller – in Johnson's case, a western. You can't stop turning the pages … I can't recommend this book highly enough'
Michael Howard

'A wonderful, a glorious tale … It will be hard to equal this amazing book. It reads like a Trollope novel, but not even Trollope explored the ambitions and the gullibilities of men as deliciously as Robert Caro does … I went back over chapters to make sure I had not missed a word … Caro's description of how [Johnson passed the civil rights legislation] is masterly; I was there and followed the course of the legislation closely, but I did not know the half of it' *New York Times Book Review*

MEANS OF ASCENT

'Monumental … sets a standard by which future political biographies must be judged'
Daily Telegraph

'Thrilling … never has it been told so dramatically, with breathtaking detail piled on incredible development … In *The Path to Power*, Volume I of his monumental biography, Robert A. Caro ignited a blowtorch whose bright flame illuminated Johnson's early career. In *Means of Ascent* he intensifies the flame to a brilliant blue point'
The New York Times

'A white-knuckle hair-raising tale … riveting and explosive'
Time

'A wonderfully detailed, magnificently readable study that gives us not only Johnson's character but also a vivid picture of America in the 1940s'
Literary Review

'Uputdownable … as compulsive as any Hollywood thriller'
Evening Standard

'His depiction of Texas is as brilliant as his account of Lyndon Johnson's driven soul … a richly rewarding book'
New Statesman

THE PATH TO POWER

'A superb and unique biography … Meticulous in research, grand in scale, this is a major work that will remain a tower of its kind'
Barbara Tuchman

'Truly sensational and enthralling … totally original' *Financial Times*

'A book of radiant excellence … at the summit of American historical writing … Proof that we live in a great age of biography'
Washington Post

'Powerful and stirring. A monumental political saga … it is an overwhelming experience to read *The Path to Power*'
The New York Times

'Not only a historical but a literary event. An epic biography … a sweeping, richly detailed portrait … an awesome achievement'
Newsweek

'Wholly fascinating … splendidly enjoyable'
The Times

THE POWER BROKER

Also by Robert A. Caro

The Years of Lyndon Johnson:

The Path to Power (1982)

Means of Ascent (1990)

Master of the Senate (2002)

The Passage of Power (2012)

THE POWER BROKER

Robert Moses and the Fall of New York

Robert A. Caro

THE BODLEY HEAD
LONDON

Published by The Bodley Head 2015

2 4 6 8 10 9 7 5 3

First published in Great Britain in 2015 by
The Bodley Head
20 Vauxhall Bridge Road,
London SW1V 2SA

A Penguin Random House company

Penguin Random House UK

www.penguinrandomhouse.com
www.vintage-books.co.uk

A CIP catalogue record for this book is available from the British Library

ISBN 9781847923646

Printed and bound in Great Britain by Clays Ltd, St Ives plc

MIX
Paper from responsible sources
FSC® C018179

Penguin Random House is committed to a sustainable future for our business, our readers and our planet. This book is made from Forest Stewardship Council® certified paper.

FOR INA

AND FOR DR. JANET G. TRAVELL

CONTENTS

PART IV THE USE OF POWER

PART V THE LOVE OF POWER

PART VI THE LUST FOR POWER

PART VII THE LOSS OF POWER

MAPS

THE POWER BROKER

INTRODUCTION
Wait Until the Evening

One must wait until the evening
To see how splendid the day has been.

—SOPHOCLES

AS THE CAPTAIN of the Yale swimming team stood beside the pool, still dripping after his laps, and listened to Bob Moses, the team's second-best freestyler, he didn't know what shocked him more—the suggestion or the fact that it was Moses who was making it.

Ed Richards knew that Moses was brilliant—even "Five A" Johnson, who regularly received the top grade in every course he took each term, said that Moses could have stood first in the Class of 1909 if he hadn't spent so much time reading books that had nothing to do with his assignments—but the quality that had most impressed Richards and the rest of '09 was his idealism. The poems that the olive-skinned, big-eyed Jew from New York wrote for the Yale literary magazines, sitting up late at night, his bedroom door closed against the noise from the horseplay in the dormitory, were about Beauty and Truth. When the bull sessions got around, as they did so often, now that the Class was in its senior year, to the subject of careers, Moses was always talking—quite movingly, too—about dedicating his life to public service, to helping the lower classes. And just the other evening, in the midst of a desultory discussion about which fraternity's nominee should be elected class treasurer, Moses had jumped to his feet and argued so earnestly that class officers should be chosen on merit rather than fraternity affiliation, that the criterion shouldn't be who a man's friends were but what he could do, that Johnson had said to Richards afterwards, "I feel as if I've had an awakening tonight." And now, Richards realized, this same Bob Moses was suggesting that they get money for the swimming team by deliberately misleading Og Reid.

Ogden Mills Reid was the best thing that had ever happened to swimming at Yale. Since the legendary Walter Camp, athletic director as well as football coach, was hoarding the football receipts for a new stadium, there was no money to replace the dank, low-ceilinged pool, which wasn't even the right length for intercollegiate swimming events. There was no allocation from the university for travel expenses or even for a coach. But Reid, who had been Yale's first great swimmer, not only paid the team's expenses but, week after week, traveled up to New Haven from New York to do the coaching himself. This year, after a long fight, Moses had succeeded in organizing the wrestling, fencing, hockey, basketball and swimming teams into a "Minor Sports Association" which would conduct a general fund-raising effort and divide the money among the teams, in the hope that the existence of such a formal organization would coax new contributions from alumni. The theory was good, Richards had thought at the time, but there was one hitch: any money contributed specifically to one of the teams also had to go into the general fund. Richards doubted that Reid, who was interested only in swimming, would want to contribute to a general fund and he wondered if the swimmers might not end up with even less money than before. But Moses had seemed to have no fears on that score. And now, standing beside the pool, Richards was beginning to understand why. Moses, dressed in suit, vest and a high collar that was wilting in the dampness, had just announced that he was skipping practice to go to New York and see Reid, and when Richards had expressed his doubts that the alumnus would contribute, Moses had smiled and said, "Oh, that's all right. I just won't tell him it's going to an association. He'll think it's the regular contribution to the swimming team."

Now Richards said slowly, "I think that's a little bit tricky, Bob. I think that's a little bit smooth. I don't like that at all."

With astonishing rapidity, the face over the high collar turned pale, almost white. Moses' fists came up for a moment before he lowered them. "Well, you've got nothing to say about it," he said.

"Yes, I do," Richards said. "I'm the captain. I'm responsible. And I'm telling you not to do it."

"Well, I'm going to do it anyway," Moses said.

"If you do," Richards said, "I'll go to Og and tell him that the money isn't going where he thinks it is."

Moses' voice suddenly dropped. His tone was threatening. "If you don't let me do it," he said, "I'm going to resign from the team."

He thought he was bluffing me, Richards would recall later. He thought I wouldn't let him resign. "Well, Bob," Richards said, "your resignation is accepted."

Bob Moses turned and walked out of the pool. He never swam for Yale again.

Forty-five years later, a new mayor of New York was being sworn in at City Hall. Under huge cut-glass chandeliers Robert F. Wagner, Jr., took the oath of office and then, before hundreds of spectators, personally administered the oath, and handed the coveted official appointment blanks, to his top appointees.

But to a handful of the spectators, the real significance of the ceremony was in an oath not given. When Robert Moses came forward, Wagner swore him in as City Park Commissioner and as City Construction Coordinator—and then, with Moses still waiting expectantly, stopped and beckoned forward the next appointee.

To those spectators, Wagner's gesture signaled triumph. They were representatives of the so-called "Good Government" organizations of the city: the Citizens Union, the City Club, liberal elements of the labor movement. They had long chafed at the power that Moses had held under previous mayors as Park Commissioner, Construction Coordinator and member of the City Planning Commission. They had determined to try to curb his sway under Wagner and they had decided to make the test of strength the Planning Commission membership. This, they had decided after long analysis and debate, was Moses' weak point: As Park Commissioner and Construction Coordinator he proposed public works projects, and the City Charter had surely never intended that an officeholder who proposed projects should sit on the Planning Commission, whose function was to pass on the merits of those projects. For nine weeks, ever since Wagner's election, they had been pressing him not to reappoint Moses to the commission. Although Wagner had told them he agreed fully with their views and had even hinted that, on Inauguration Day, there would be only two jobs waiting for Moses, they had been far from sure that he meant it. But now they realized that Wagner had in fact not given Moses the third oath—and the Planning Commission job. And, looking at Moses, they could see he realized it, too. His face, normally swarthy, was pale with rage.

The more observant among these spectators, however, noticed that after the ceremonies Moses followed Wagner into his inner office. They knew all too well what he would be saying to the new mayor; he had said it often enough, publicly and privately, orally and in writing, to Wagner's predecessors, Vincent R. Impellitteri and William O'Dwyer, and, even earlier, to the great La Guardia. "He's threatening to resign," they whispered to one another.

They were right. Behind the closed doors of the inner office, Moses was putting it to Wagner straight: If he didn't get the third post, he would quit the other two. And he'd do it right now.

Wagner tried frantically to stall. The Planning Commission oath? the Mayor said. There must have been an oversight. Some clerk must have forgotten to fill out the appointment blank. Nothing to worry about. He'd see to it in a few days. Moses walked out of the Mayor's office and into the little room down the hall where a deputy mayor and his assistant were filing the appointment blanks. Snatching an unused blank off a sheaf on a table, he sat down at the table and filled it out himself. Then he walked back to Wagner's office and, without a word, laid the paper on the Mayor's desk.

Without a word, the Mayor pulled the paper toward him and signed it.

Robert Moses possessed at the time of his confrontation with Ed Richards an imagination that leaped unhesitatingly at problems insoluble to other men—the problem of financing minor sports had been tormenting Yale deans for two decades—and that, seemingly in the very moment of the leap, conceived of solutions. He possessed an iron will that put behind his solutions and dreams a determination to let nothing stand in their way—to form the Minor Sports Association he, only an undergraduate, had faced up to, and had finally faced down, Walter Camp, who was implacably opposed to its formation. And he possessed an arrogance which made him conceive himself so indispensable that, in his view, his resignation was the most awful threat he could think of.

Robert Moses possessed the same qualities during his confrontation with Robert Wagner. But by then he also possessed something more. He possessed power.

Power is the backdrop against which both confrontation scenes should be played. For power was the reason for the contrast in their denouements.

The whole life of Robert Moses, in fact, has been a drama of the interplay of power and personality. For a time, standing between it and him was an interceding force, the passionate idealism he had expressed in the Yale bull sessions. Dedicating his life to public service, he remained, during the first years of that service, the idealist of those bull sessions, an idealist possessed, moreover, of a vision of such breadth that he was soon dreaming dreams of public works on a scale that would dwarf any yet built in the cities of America. He wandered tirelessly around New York, and a woman who occasionally wandered with him said he was "burning up with ideas, just burning up with them," ideas for great highways and parks circling the city's waterfront and for more modest projects that he thought would also improve the quality of life for the city's people—little shelters, for instance, in Central Park so that mothers could change their babies' diapers without having to go all the way home. And when he argued for his ideas before the Good Government organization for which he worked and before the Board of Estimate, he was very careful always to have his facts ready, never to exaggerate them and always to draw from them logical conclusions, for he believed that Truth and Logic would prevail. When he decided to specialize, the area he chose—civil service reorganization—was one based on the same principle with which he had "awakened" "Five A" Johnson, the principle that jobs should be given and promotions based on merit rather than patronage. And he dedicated himself to that principle with the devotion of the acolyte. Brought into the administration of reforming Mayor John Purroy Mitchel in 1914, Moses devised, in a year of unremitting labor, a system that made every aspect of a city employee's performance—including facets of his personality—subject to a numerical grade. And for three additional years he fought for adoption of his system, battling a Board of Estimate dominated by one of the most corrupt political machines the United States had ever known, speaking night after night—a tall, very slim, very handsome young man with deep, burning eyes, dressed, often and appropriately, in a white suit, clutching a bulging briefcase and introduced to audiences as "Dr. Moses" in recognition of his Ph.D.—into hails of abuse from furious municipal employees who owed their jobs not to merit but to Tammany Hall, and observers said that the viciousness of the jeering crowds seemed to make no impression on him, so deeply did he believe that if only they could be made to understand how good his system was, they would surely support it. In those pre-World War I years of optimism, of reform, of idealism, Robert Moses was the optimist of optimists, the reformer of reformers, the idealist of idealists.

So great a nuisance did he make of himself that in 1918 Tammany Hall decided it had to crush him. It did so with efficiency. At the age of thirty, with the grading papers for his system being used as scrap paper, the Central Park shelters and great highways unbuilt, Robert Moses, Phi Beta Kappa at Yale, honors man at Oxford, lover of the Good, the True and the Beautiful, was out of work and, with a wife and two small daughters to support, was standing on a line in the Cleveland, Ohio, City Hall, applying for a minor municipal job—a job which, incidentally, he didn't get.

When the curtain rose on the next act of Moses' life, idealism was gone from the stage. In its place was an understanding that ideas—dreams—were useless without power to transform them into reality. Moses spent the rest of his life amassing power, bringing to the task imagination, iron will and determination. And he was successful. The oath that was administered to Robert Wagner in City Hall on January 1, 1954, should have given Wagner supreme power in New York. That was the theory. In democratic America, supposedly, ultimate power rests in the voters, and the man for whom a majority of them cast their votes is the repository of that power. But Wagner knew better. The spectators may have thought that he had a choice in dealing with Moses. He knew that he did not. Why, when Moses pushed the appointment blank across his desk, did the Mayor say not a word? Possibly because there was nothing to say. Power had spoken.

With his power, for twenty years prior to the day he strode out of City Hall in triumph (and for an additional fourteen years thereafter), Robert Moses shaped a city and its sprawling suburbs—and, to an extent that would have astonished analysts of urban trends had they measured the implications of his decades of handiwork, influenced the destiny of all the cities of twentieth-century America.

The city in which the shaping by his hand is most evident is New York, Titan of cities, colossal synthesis of urban hope and urban despair. It had become a cliché by the mid-twentieth century to say that New York was "ungovernable," and this meant, since the powers of government in the city had largely devolved on its mayor, that no mayor could govern it, could hope to do more than merely stay afloat in the maelstrom that had engulfed the vast metropolis. In such a context, the cliché was valid. No mayor shaped New York; no mayor—not even La Guardia—left upon its roiling surface more than the faintest of lasting imprints.

But Robert Moses shaped New York.

Physically, any map of the city proves it. The very shoreline of metropolis was different before Robert Moses came to power. He rammed bulkheads of steel deep into the muck beneath rivers and harbors and crammed into the space beneath bulkheads and shore immensities of earth and stone, shale and cement, that hardened into fifteen thousand acres of new land and thus altered the physical boundaries of the city.

Standing out from the map's delicate tracery of gridirons representing streets are heavy lines, lines girdling the city or slashing across its expanses. These lines denote the major roads on which automobiles and trucks move, roads whose very location, moreover, does as much as any single factor to determine where and how a city's people live and work. With a single exception, the East River Drive, Robert Moses built every one of those roads. He built the Major Deegan Expressway, the Van Wyck Expressway, the Sheridan Expressway and the Bruckner Expressway. He built the Gowanus Expressway, the Prospect Expressway, the Whitestone Expressway, the Clearview Expressway and the Throgs Neck Expressway. He built the Cross-Bronx Expressway, the Brooklyn-Queens Expressway, the Nassau Expressway, the Staten Island Expressway and the Long Island Expressway. He built the Harlem River Drive and the West Side Highway.

Only one borough of New York City—the Bronx—is on the mainland of the United States, and bridges link the island boroughs that form metropolis. Since 1931, seven such bridges were built, immense structures, some of them anchored by towers as tall as seventy-story buildings, supported by cables made up of enough wire to drop a noose around the earth. Those bridges are the Triborough, the Verrazano, the Throgs Neck, the Marine, the Henry Hudson, the Cross Bay and the Bronx-Whitestone. Robert Moses built every one of those bridges.

Scattered throughout New York stand clusters of tall apartment houses built under urban renewal programs and bearing color, splashed on terraces and finials, that in the twentieth-century American cityscape marks them as luxury dwellings. Alongside some of these clusters stand college lecture halls and dormitories. Alongside one stand five immense dingy white expanses of travertine that are Lincoln Center, the world's famous, costly and imposing cultural center. Alongside another stands the New York Coliseum, the glowering exhibition tower whose name reveals Moses' preoccupation with achieving an immortality like that conferred on the Caesars of Rome (feeling later that he could make the comparison even more exact, he built Shea Stadium, remarking when it was completed, "When the Emperor Titus opened the Colosseum in 80 A.D. he could have felt no happier"). Once the sites of the clusters contained other buildings: factories, stores, tenements that had stood for a century, sturdy, still serviceable apartment houses. Robert Moses decided that these buildings would be torn down and it was Robert Moses who decided that the lecture halls and the dormitories and the cultural center—and new apartment houses—would be erected in their place.

The eastern edge of Manhattan Island, heart of metropolis, was completely altered between 1945 and 1958. Northward from the bulge of Corlears Hook looms a long line of apartment houses devoid of splashes of color, hulking buildings, utilitarian, drab, unadorned, not block after block of them but mile after mile, appearing from across the East River like an endless wall of dull brick against the sky. Almost all of them—ninety-five looming over the river in the first two miles north of Corlears Hook—are public housing. They—and hundreds of similar structures huddled alongside the expressways or set in rows beside the Rockaway surf—contain 148,000 apartments and 555,000 tenants, a population that is in itself a city bigger than Minneapolis. These buildings were constructed by the New York City Housing Authority, 1,082 of them between 1945 and 1958. Robert Moses was never a member of the Housing Authority and his relationship with it was only hinted at in the press. But between 1945 and 1958 no site for public housing was selected and no brick of a public housing project laid without his approval.

North of the public housing are two immense "private" housing developments: Stuyvesant Town and Peter Cooper Village. Moses was the dominant force in their creation, too (as he was in the creation of an even larger "private" housing development in the Bronx, Co-op City). And still further north along the East River stand the buildings of the United Nations headquarters. Moses cleared aside the obstacles to bringing to New York the closest thing to a world capitol the planet possesses, and he supervised its construction.

When Robert Moses began building playgrounds in New York City, there were 119. When he stopped, there were 777. Under his direction, an army of men that at times during the Depression included 84,000 laborers reshaped every park in the city and then filled the parks with zoos and skating rinks, boathouses and tennis houses, bridle paths and golf courses, 288 tennis courts and 673 baseball diamonds. Under his direction, endless convoys of trucks hauled the city's garbage into its marshes, and the garbage filled the marshes, was covered with earth and lawn, and became more parks. Long strings of barges brought to the city white sand dredged from the ocean floor and the sand was piled on mud flats to create beaches.

And no enumeration of the beaches, parks, apartment houses, bridges, and roads that Robert Moses himself built in New York does more than suggest the immensity of the man's physical influence upon the city. For the seven years between 1946 and 1953, the seven years of plenty in public construction in the city, seven years marked by the most intensive such construction in its history, no public improvement of any type—not school or sewer, library or pier, hospital or catch basin—was built by any city agency, even those which Robert Moses did not directly control, unless Robert Moses approved its design and location. To clear the land for these improvements, he evicted the city's people, not thousands of them or tens of thousands but hundreds of thousands, from their homes and tore the homes down. Neighborhoods were obliterated by his edict to make room for new neighborhoods reared at his command.

And his influence upon New York went far beyond the physical. In twentieth-century America, no city's resources, not even when combined with resources made available by the state and federal governments, came close to meeting its needs. So cities had to pick and choose among these needs, to decide which handful of a thousand desperately necessary projects would actually be built. The establishment of priorities had vast impact on not only the physical but the social fabric of the cities, on the quality of life their inhabitants led. In New York City, for thirty-four years, Robert Moses played a vital role in establishing the city's priorities. For the crucial seven years, he established *all* its priorities.

Out from the heart of New York, reaching beyond the limits of the city into its vast suburbs and thereby shaping them as well as the city, stretch long ribbons of concrete, closed, unlike the expressways, to trucks and all commercial traffic, and, unlike the expressways, bordered by lawns and trees. These are the parkways. There are 416 miles of them. Robert Moses built every mile. Still within the city limits, stretching northward toward Westchester County, he built the Mosholu Parkway and the Hutchinson River Parkway. In Westchester, he built the Saw Mill River Parkway, the Sprain Brook Parkway and the Cross County Parkway. Stretching eastward toward the counties of Long Island, he built the Grand Central Parkway, the Belt Parkway, the Laurelton Parkway, the Cross Island Parkway, the Interborough Parkway. On Long Island, he built the Northern State Parkway and the Southern State Parkway, the Wantagh Parkway and the Sagtikos, the Sunken Meadow and the Meadowbrook. Some of the Long Island parkways run down to the Island's south shore and then, on causeways built by Robert Moses, across the Great South Bay to Jones Beach, which was a barren, deserted, windswept sand spit when he first happened upon it in 1921 while exploring the bay alone in a small motorboat and which he transformed into what may be the world's greatest oceanfront park and bathing beach. Other Long Island parkways lead to other huge parks and other great bathing beaches. Sunken Meadow. Hither Hills. Montauk. Orient Point. Fire Island. Captree. Bethpage. Wildwood. Belmont Lake. Hempstead Lake. Valley Stream. Heckscher. Robert Moses built these parks and beaches.

The physical works of Robert Moses are not confined to New York and its suburbs. The largest of them are hundreds of miles from the city, stretched along the Niagara Frontier and—in distant reaches of New York State known to natives as "the North Country," north even of Massena, a town where frost comes in August and the temperature can be thirty below by November—along the St. Lawrence River.

North from Massena the land rolls barren and empty. Only an occasional farmhouse interrupts the expanse of bare fields and scraggly woods. You can drive for twenty miles without passing another car. But turn a bend in the road and there is the St. Lawrence—and, stretched across it, one of the most colossal single works of man, a structure of steel and concrete as tall as a ten-story apartment house, an apartment house as long as eleven football fields, a structure vaster by far than any of the pyramids, or, in terms of bulk, of any six pyramids together, a structure so vast that the thirty-two bright-red turbine generators lined up on its flanks, each of them weighing fourteen tons, are only glistening specks against its dull-gray massiveness. And this structure, a power dam, is only the centerpiece of Robert Moses' design to tame the wild waters of the St. Lawrence, a design that includes three huge control dams built to force the river through the power dam's turbines. After the dams were built—and the steel forests of transmission towers which distribute the electricity created by water passing through turbines—Robert Moses adorned their bulk with a garland of parks, of campgrounds, picnic areas, overlooks, of beaches built beside lakes that he built, and of miles and miles of more parkways. And at Niagara, Robert Moses built a series of dams, parks and parkways that make the St. Lawrence development look small.

One measure of the career of Robert Moses is longevity. His power was measured in decades. On April 18, 1924, ten years after he had entered government, it was formally handed to him. For forty-four years thereafter—until the day in 1968 when he realized that he had either misunderstood Nelson Rockefeller or had been cheated by him and, in either case, had lost the last of it—he held power, a power so substantial that in the fields in which he chose to exercise it, it was not challenged seriously by any Governor of New York State or, during a thirty-four year period, 1934 to 1968, in which it extended over city as well as state, by any Mayor of New York City. He held this power during the administrations of six Governors—Alfred E. Smith, Franklin D. Roosevelt, Herbert H. Lehman, Thomas E. Dewey and W. Averell Harriman, as well as Rockefeller. He held it during the administrations of five Mayors—Fiorello La Guardia, William O'Dwyer, Vincent Impellitteri, Robert F. Wagner, Jr., and John V. Lindsay. And in 1974, at the age of eighty-five, he was fighting with desperate cunning to get it back.

Another measure of his career is immortality. Men strive for a sliver of it; Robert Moses had it heaped upon him. Not only is there a Robert Moses State Park on Long Island, there is another Robert Moses State Park at Massena. There is a Robert Moses Causeway on Long Island, a Robert Moses Parkway at Niagara. The great dam at Niagara is named for him. And over the entrance to the dam at Massena, in letters of stainless steel each three feet high, gleam the words "Robert Moses Power Dam."

Another measure is in statistics. By the 1960's, expenditures for public works in America were federal-sized, and a federal cabinet officer might have charge of the distribution of billions of dollars. But merely distributing money is not *building*. In terms of true building—personal conception and construction—Robert Moses was unique in America. Without including the cost of schools, hospitals, garbage incinerators, sewers and other improvements whose location and design he approved but which were physically constructed by others, without including the amount of money poured by private sources into construction that also had to be approved by him—including, in fact, only those public works that he personally conceived and completed, from first vision to ribbon cutting—Robert Moses built public works costing, in 1968 dollars, twenty-seven billion dollars. In terms of personal conception and completion, no other public official in the history of the United States built public works costing an amount even close to that figure. In those terms,

Robert Moses was unquestionably America's most prolific physical creator. He was America's greatest builder.

More significant than what Robert Moses built is when he built it. That was how he put his mark on all the cities of America.

When Robert Moses began building state parks and parkways during the 1920's, twenty-nine states didn't have a single state park; six had only one each. Roads uninterrupted by crossings at grade and set off by landscaping were almost nonexistent. Most proposals for parks outside cities were so limited in scope that, even if they had been adopted, they would have been inadequate. The handful of visionaries who dreamed of large parks were utterly unable to translate their dreams into reality. No one in the nation seemed able to conceive of proposals—and methods of implementing them—equal to the scope and complexity of the problem posed by the need of urban masses for countryside parks and a convenient means of getting to them. New York City residents heading for Long Island's green hills and ocean beaches, for example, had to make their way, bumper to bumper, along dusty rutted roads the most modern of which were exactly eighteen feet wide. Those who made it to the Island found that the hills and beaches had been monopolized by the robber barons of America, who had bought up its choicest areas with such thoroughness that there was hardly a meadow or strip of beach within driving distance of New York still open to the public. So fierce was their opposition—and so immense their political power—that New York park enthusiasts had stopped thinking of putting parks on Long Island.

But in 1923, after tramping alone for months over sand spits and almost wild tracts of Long Island woodland, Robert Moses mapped out a system of state parks there that would cover forty thousand acres and would be linked together—and to New York City—by broad parkways. And by 1929, Moses had actually built the system he had dreamed of, hacking it out in a series of merciless vendettas against wealth and wealth's power that became almost a legend—to the public and to public officials and engineers from all over the country who came to Long Island to marvel at his work. When Jones Beach, capstone of the system, opened, it opened to nationwide praise of a unanimity and enthusiasm not to be heard again for a public work until the completion of the Tennessee Valley Authority project a decade later—and the enthusiasm led directly to the creation of scores of state parks in other states, parks built on engineering and philosophic principles that came largely out of the old August Belmont Mansion on Long Island where Robert Moses sat, pounding his palm on what had been Belmont's dinner table and planning out a system far vaster than Long Island's for all New York State. Over the decades, the state park movement developed other leaders, but it was always to be in his debt. And there was never to be any doubt that the breadth of his vision kept him unique within its ranks. At the end of his leadership of the New York system, the total acreage of the state parks in the fifty states was 5,799,957. New York State alone had 2,567,256 of those acres—or 45 percent of all the state parks in the country.

To a few men, young engineers whose passion had been fired by a dramatic facet of their profession—the construction of highways—the Belmont Mansion was Delphi. They came to it to learn, not just the engineering of great roads, for they could learn engineering elsewhere, but rather a secret available at that time nowhere else: the secret of how to get great roads built. For them, the big table at which Moses sat was an altar on which they laid their dreams in the hope of learning the alchemy by which the dreams might be transmuted into concrete and asphalt and steel. And they were luckier than the Greeks, whose journey to their oracle was over narrow mountain paths. They were able to drive to the mansion on the Southern State Parkway and they could still recall, decades later, their awe at first seeing its stone-faced bridges and opulent landscaping. And when they were admitted to the Belmont dining room, they were not spoken to in riddles but in blunt lectures that contained a whole new doctrine on the building of urban public works in a democratic society. As the young men grew older, they became the road builders of America, the heads of state and city highway departments, key officials of the Federal Bureau of Public Roads, caterers of an orgy of public works without precedent in history. And as the roads they built rolled across America, the mark of Robert Moses was as much a part of those roads as the steel mesh on which their concrete pavement was laid. Bertram D. Tallamy, chief administrative officer of the Interstate Highway System during the 1950's and '60's, says that the principles on which the System was built were principles that Robert Moses taught him in a series of such private lectures in 1926.

Parkways were, in general, laid through thinly populated suburbs or open countryside and were designed to carry only cars. Expressways would be laid—after World War II—through cities, and were designed to carry trucks also, to serve as arteries for the commerce as well as the pleasure of a people. When Robert Moses began building expressways, there were plenty of plans for expressways—but few expressways. Politicians boggled at two political problems that would attend the implementation of the plans: their fantastic cost and the necessity of removing from their path and relocating thousands, even tens of thousands, of voters. For years—decades—in every city in the country, the expressways remained on the drawing boards. In every city, that is, except one. In New York, immediately after World War II, Robert Moses began ramming six great expressways simultaneously through the city's massed apartment houses. A decade later, outside New York, there were still only a few stretches of urban expressway in the United States, but Moses' six pioneer expressways were largely completed. When, in 1956, sufficient funds to gridiron America with expressways were insured by the passage of the Interstate Highway Act, an act in whose drafting Moses played a crucial if hidden role, it was to New York that the engineers of a score of state highway departments came, to learn the secrets of the Master. The greatest secret was how to remove people from the expressways' paths—and Robert Moses taught them his method of dealing with people. This method became one of the trademarks of the building of America's urban highways, a Moses trademark impressed on all urban America. Robert Moses' influence on the development of the expressway system in the United States was greater than that of any other single individual. He was America's greatest road builder, the most influential single architect of the system over which rolled the wheels of America's cars. And there was, in this fact, an irony. For, except for a few driving lessons he took in 1926, Robert Moses never drove a car in his life.

In 1949, the federal government enacted a new approach to the housing problems of cities: urban renewal. The approach was new both in philosophy—for the first time in America, government was given the right to seize an individual's private property not for its own use but for reassignment to another individual for *his* use and profit—and in scope: a billion dollars was appropriated in 1949 and it was agreed that this was only seed money to prepare the ground for later, greater plantings of cash.

Most cities approached urban renewal with caution. But in New York City, urban renewal was directed by Robert Moses. By 1957, $133,000,000 of public monies had been expended on urban renewal in all the cities of the United States with the exception of New York; $267,000,000 had been spent in New York. So far ahead was New York that when scores of huge buildings constructed under its urban renewal program were already erected and occupied, administrators from other cities were still borrowing New York's contract forms to learn how to draw up the initial legal agreements with interested developers. When Moses resigned from his urban renewal directorship in 1960, urban renewal had produced more physical results in New York than in all other American cities combined. Says the federal official in charge of the early years of the program: "Because Robert Moses was so far ahead of anyone else in the country, he had greater influence on urban renewal in the United States—on how the program developed and on how it was received by the public—than any other single person."

Parks, highways, urban renewal—Robert Moses was in and of himself a formative force in all three fields in the United States. He was a seminal thinker, perhaps the single most influential seminal thinker, in developing policies in these fields, and the innovator, perhaps the single most influential innovator, in developing the methods by which these policies were implemented. And since parks, highways and urban renewal, taken together, do so much to shape cities' total environment, how then gauge the impact of this one man on the cities of America? The man who was for thirty years his bitterest critic, Lewis Mumford, says:

"In the twentieth century, the influence of Robert Moses on the cities of America was greater than that of any other person."

With his power, Robert Moses built himself an empire.

The capital of this empire was out of public sight—a squat, gray building crouching so unobtrusively below the Randall's Island toll plaza of the Triborough Bridge that most of the motorists who drove through the toll booths never even knew that the building existed. And most of them were ignorant also of the existence of the empire.

But men whose interest in geography centered on the map of power knew of its existence very well indeed. They realized that although theoretically it was only a creature of the city, it had in fact become an autonomous sovereign state. And, realizing that—although its outward form was a loose confederation of four public authorities, plus the New York City Park Department and the Long Island State Park Commission—it was actually a single-headed, tightly administered monarchy, these men described it with a single name, derived from the bridge and the Authority that were its centerpieces: "Triborough."

Anyone who doubted Triborough's autonomy had only to look at its trappings. The empire had its own flag and great seal, distinctive license plates and a self-contained communications network, an elaborate teletype hookup that linked the gray building and the provincial capitals at Belmont Lake, Massena and Niagara. It even had its own island—Randall's—on which it administered every structure and every inch of land. Randall's Island was near the geographic center of New York, but the waters of the East River, Bronx Kill and Hell Gate were a moat between it and the city, and from the air, with its hundreds of acres of lawn, the island appeared separate, a bright green oasis, sharply defined by a blue border, in the midst of the city's vast grayness. And the separateness was more than symbolic: no inhabitant of the city could drive across the island without paying Triborough a tribute in coin.

Triborough had its own fleets, of yachts and motorcars and trucks, and its own uniformed army—"Bridge and Tunnel Officers" who guarded its toll booths, revolver-carrying Long Island Parkway Police who patrolled its suburban parks and roads—responsible to no discipline but that of Robert Moses. To command the army, under Moses, it had its own generals and admirals, senior officers of the United States Army and Navy who, upon retirement, took service under its banner. It had its own constitution: the covenants, unalterable by city, state or federal government, of its bond resolutions. It governed by its own laws: the Rules and Regulations that it promulgated to regulate conduct within its dominions. And, most significantly, it had its own source of revenue: the quarters and dimes that poured in a silver stream into the toll booths at which it collected tribute.

It was a vast empire. In 1960, the year of its furthest expansion, the land area under its direct control—the parks of Long Island and New York City, the highways and highway-bordering playgrounds in the city and the enclaves in which are placed the upstate power dams—totaled 103,071 acres, 161 square miles, an area half as large as New York City. But the best measure of the size of the empire was its wealth; its annual income—the toll-booth revenue, the fees it received for the use of electricity produced at Massena and Niagara, the yearly budgets of the Long Island State Park Commission and the City Park Department—ran as high as $213,000,000; the surplus of just one of its four constituent public authorities, the Triborough Bridge and Tunnel Authority, ran to almost $30,000,000 a year.

The courtiers and courtesans of this empire wallowed in an almost Carthaginian luxury. Favored secretaries, for example, had not only bigger cars than city commissioners (as well as round-the-clock chauffeurs so that they could be on call twenty-four hours a day) but also higher salaries. As for the men closest to the throne, the cadre of Triborough administrators known as "Moses Men," not even his most suspicious critics ever came close to guessing the extent of the wealth he poured into their hands. He made not a handful but scores of men—a low-salaried draftsman who caught his eye, a struggling young hot-dog seller, architects, engineers, contractors, bankers, restaurateurs, concessionaires, developers—millionaires and multimillionaires.

Within this empire, Robert Moses lived like an emperor.

Like an emperor, his every wish was foreseen. On Sundays, when he rested, one of the three boat captains who took turns skippering his favorite yacht waited by a telephone, sometimes for the entire day, just in case he might decide that he wanted to go fishing. Like an emperor, he preferred his own table; people who wanted to dine with Moses had to come to him. And to insure that he could entertain them on an imperial scale, luxurious dining rooms were set up adjacent to the four offices—one at Randall's Island, one at Belmont Mansion and two in downtown office buildings—among which he divided his time. Although only one of them could be used at a time, each of them was equipped with a full-time staff of chef and waiters.

Luncheons were only one aspect of his hospitality. When a dam or park was to be opened upstate, chartered planes flew hundreds of guests not just to the opening but to a whole weekend of lavish receptions. In New York, highly paid Triborough officials had as their principal duty the entertainment of Moses' guests. They conducted tours of the empire, pointing out its principal natural features—the towers of the Triborough Bridge, marching like the façades of twin cathedrals across the East River, the long lawns of Riverside Park—and repeating, at each monument, the legends, burnished by time and constant retelling, of how Robert Moses had created it. And the thousands of guests at the summer capital of the empire, Jones Beach, were entertained—in a million-and-a-half-dollar restaurant whose main purpose, judging from its financial statements, was to entertain them; in a four-million-dollar stadium that he had turned over to his favorite bandleader, Guy Lombardo, virtually as a gift on which Lombardo reaped immense personal profits, so that Lombardo's orchestra would be constantly on call—on a scale and with a sumptuousness that was as close as anyone in America ever got to the entertainment afforded by a monarch.

The wealth of the empire enabled Moses to keep many city officials in fear. With it, he hired skilled investigators he called "bloodhounds" who were kept busy filling dossiers. Every city official knew about those dossiers, and they knew what use Moses was capable of making of them—since the empire's wealth allowed him to create an awesomely efficient public relations machinery. They had seen him dredge up the dark secrets of men's pasts and turn them into blaring headlines. On the occasion of Paul Screvane's appointment as city representative to Moses' 1964–65 World's Fair, Mayor Wagner said to him: "Paul, my experience with Moses has taught me one lesson, and I'll tell it to you. I would never let him do anything for me in any way, shape or form. I'd never ask him—or *permit* him—to do anything of a personal nature for me because—and I've seen it time and time again—a day will come when Bob will reach back in his file and throw this in your face, quietly if that will make you go along with him, publicly otherwise. And if he has to, he will destroy you with it."

There were men whose past contained not even a speck of grist for Moses' mill. This, however, was no guarantee against attack. Perhaps their fathers had committed an impropriety. If so, Moses would visit the sins of the fathers on the children. A respected financier, rising in a City Planning Commission hearing to oppose a zoning change sponsored by Moses, was astounded to hear Moses reply by reading into the hearing transcript newspaper accounts of a scandal, unconnected in any way with zoning, in which the financier's father had been involved—forty years before, when the financier was eight years old.

And if Moses possessed no derogatory information at all about an opponent or his forebears, this was still no guarantee against attack. For Moses was an innovator in fields other than public works. He practiced McCarthyism long before there was a McCarthy. He drove Rexford G. Tugwell out of his City Planning Commission chairmanship—out of New York, in fact—helped drive Stanley F. Isaacs out of his borough presidency and destroyed the public careers of a dozen other officials by publicly, and falsely, identifying them as "Pinkos" or "Planning Reds" or "followers of the Ogpu," the Soviet secret police. There were two widespread Communist witchhunts in New York City, one in 1938 and one in 1958. Both relied heavily on "information"—much of it innuendo or outright falsehood—leaked to newspapers by Moses.

The fear in which Moses was held because of these factors was intensified by his memory. Cross him once, politicians said, and he would never forget. And if he ever got the chance for revenge, no consideration would dilute his venom. For a twenty-year period that did not end until 1968, Moses was given by the State Department of Public Works a secret veto power over the awarding of all state contracts for public works in the New York metropolitan area. No engineer who had ever forcefully and openly disagreed with a Moses opinion ever received even one of the thousands of contracts involved.

Moses was able to shape a city and to build an empire because the supple mind that had conceived of a Minor Sports Association for Yale and innovations in the civil service system for New York City—and also of substantial portions of the New York State Constitution—nad focused on the possibilities of an institution still in its infancy as an urban force when he came to it in 1934: the public authority. He raised this institution to a maturity in which it became the force through which he shaped New York and its suburbs in the image he personally conceived.

Operating through an authority, Moses could keep the public from finding out what he was doing, and this was an important consideration with him. If, throughout his half century and more in the public eye, he displayed an eagerness and a flair for publicizing certain aspects of his career and his life, he displayed an equal eagerness and flair for making sure that only those aspects—and no others—were known. There were, for example, men and women who knew Robert Moses for half a century who never knew that he had a brother, or that in the city in which Robert Moses lived in luxury, that brother spent the last thirty years of his life in a poverty so severe that he lived in a fifth-floor walkup flat in an old tenement huddled against the piers of South Ferry.

The official records of most public agencies are public records, but not those of public authorities, since courts have held that they may be regarded as the records of private corporations, closed to scrutiny by the interested citizen or reporter.

This was very important to Robert Moses. It was very important to him that no one be able to find out how it was that he was able to build.

Because what Robert Moses built on was a lie.

The lie had to do with the nature both of the man and of the public authority. Moses said that he was the antithesis of the politician. He never let political considerations influence any aspect of his projects—not the location of a highway or housing project nor the award of a contract or an insurance commission, he said. He would never compromise, he said. He never had and he never would. That, he said, was the way politicians got things done, but he was no politician. He knew what should be done and he intended to do it the right way or not at all. He said this at the beginning of his career and he said it at the end; in 1961, at the trial of a borough president who had received favors from an urban renewal contractor, Moses, on the witness stand, was asked whether the contract had not been awarded as part of a "deal." Moses' face paled with rage. "In forty years of public life," he said, "I have never made a deal."

Public authorities are also outside and above politics, Moses said. Their decisions are made solely on the basis of the public welfare, he said. They have all the best features of private enterprise. They are businesslike—prudent, efficient, economical. And they are more. They are the very epitome of prudence, efficiency, economy. And they have another advantage over conventional governmental institutions as well. Since they finance their projects through the sale of revenue bonds to private investors, they therefore build these projects without using any public funds. Projects built by authorities, he said, cost the taxpayers nothing.

These statements were believed implicitly for almost forty years by the public to which they were made. And this is not surprising. For Robert Moses repeated his contentions a thousand times and for four decades they were repeated, amplified and embellished by a press that believed them, too.

Because of the forty years of adulation of the newspapers—and of the public that read the newspapers—for forty years nothing could stand in Moses' way. No Mayor or Governor dared to try to breast the wave of public opinion in whose curl Moses rode. One President tried. Franklin Delano Roosevelt, the most bitter enemy that Moses ever made in public life, attempted as President to exact vengeance for humiliations previously received at Moses' hands. But although he made his move at the very zenith of his own popularity and prestige, the President found himself forced to retreat by a storm of acclaim for Moses that rolled not only through New York but across the country and that, ironically, left Moses embedded more firmly than ever in the public consciousness as the fearless defier of politicians. For forty years, in every fight, Robert Moses could count on having on his side the weight of public opinion.

The beliefs on which that opinion was based were never disproved or even seriously questioned, not even during the final, bitter decade of Moses' career, a decade during which his policies were subjected to steadily increasing criticism. For even during that decade, the criticism was of Moses' projects more than of the methods by which he accomplished those projects. The reason for this was simple. The vast majority of the public accepted the legend as fact. And even those skeptics who were disposed to test its truth had no facts with which to make the test, because the records of Triborough and the mouths of its ministers were so effectively sealed. If, however, they had been able to see the records and open the mouths, they would have learned that the legend was a gigantic hoax.

Prudent, efficient, economical? So incredibly wasteful was Moses of the money he tolled from the public in quarters and dimes that on a single bridge alone he paid $40,000,000 more in interest than he had to. Authority projects cost the taxpayers nothing? Covert "loans" made to authorities by the state—loans designed never to be repaid—ran into the hundreds of millions of dollars. The cost of city-purchased land on which authority facilities were built ran into the hundreds of millions. The cost of taxpayer-financed toll roads leading to authority facilities ran into the billions. And the loss in tax revenue because authority-controlled land was removed from the tax rolls drained the city year after year.

Most important, had the records of the authorities been open, they would have disproved another aspect of the lie: the legend that Robert Moses was no "politician," that he operated at a higher level than that implied in the derogatory connotations attached to that noun, that he managed to create his public works at a remove from politics. Actually, as these records prove, Robert Moses' authorities were a political machine oiled by the lubricant of political machines: money. Their wealth enabled Moses to make himself not only a political boss but a boss who in his particular bailiwick—public works—was able to exert a power that few political bosses in the more conventional mold ever attain.

Even had the records been available, of course, the public might not have understood their significance. For Moses was a political boss with a difference. He was not the stereotype with which Americans were familiar. His constituency was not the public but some of the most powerful men in the city and state, and he kept these men in line by doling out to them, as Tammany ward bosses once handed out turkeys to the poor at Thanksgiving, the goodies in which such men were interested, the sugar plums of public relations retainers, insurance commissions and legal fees. This man, personally honest in matters of money, became the locus of corruption in New York City. Robert Moses made himself the ward boss of the inner circle, the bankroller of the Four Hundred of politics. Far from being above the seamier aspects of politics, he was—for decades—the central figure about whom revolved much of the back-stage maneuvering of New York City politics. Triborough's public relations retainers ran to a quarter of a million dollars a year, its legal fees to a quarter million, its insurance commissions to half a million—a total of a million dollars a year. Moses parceled out retainers, fees and commissions to city and state political leaders on the basis of a very exact appraisal of their place in the political pecking order. And an examination of the records of the recipients leads to the conclusion that, year after year, it was the men who received Moses' turkey baskets who fought against any diminution in Moses' power—and for whatever public works project he was pushing at the moment.

Beyond graft and patronage, moreover, Moses also displayed a genius for using the wealth of his public authorities to unite behind his aims banks, labor unions, contractors, bond underwriters, insurance firms, the great retail stores, real estate manipulators—all the forces which enjoy immense behind-the-scenes political influence in New York. He succeeded in mobilizing behind his banner economic forces with sufficient weight to bend to his aims the apparatus so carefully established in City Charter and State Constitution to insure that, in deciding on such projects, the decisive voice would be that of the people. He used economic power for political ends—so successfully that in the fields he carved out for his own, fields in which decisions would shape the city's future for generations if not for centuries, he made economic, not democratic, forces the forces that counted in New York. And because he spoke for such forces, it was his voice that counted most of all.

"He gave everybody involved in the political setup in this city whatever it was that they wanted," one official recalls. "Therefore they all had their own interest in seeing him succeed. The pressure that this interest all added up to was a pressure that no one in the system could stand up against, because it came from the system itself." And since the mayor's power and career rested on this system, he was as helpless to stand against the pressure Moses could exert as was anyone else. When Robert Moses walked into Wagner's office on that Inauguration Day in City Hall and shoved the appointment blank across Wagner's desk, Wagner had no choice but to sign it. Given the circumstances of the Democratic Party in New York City, he *couldn't* let Robert Moses resign. What Moses had succeeded in doing, really, was to replace graft with benefits that could be derived with legality from a public works project. He had succeeded in centralizing in his projects—and to a remarkable extent in his own person—all those forces which are not in theory supposed to, but which in practice do, play a decisive role in political decisions.

Corruption before Moses had been unorganized, based on a multitude of selfish, private ends. Moses' genius for organizing it and focusing it at a central source gave it a new force, a force so powerful that it bent the entire city government off the democratic bias. He had used the power of money to undermine the democratic processes of the largest city in the world, to plan and build its parks, bridges, highways and housing projects on the basis of his whim alone.

In the beginning—and for decades of his career—the power Robert Moses amassed was the servant of his dreams, amassed for their sake, so that his gigantic city-shaping visions could become reality. But power is not an instrument that its possessor can use with impunity. It is a drug that creates in the user a need for larger and larger dosages. And Moses was a user. At first, for a decade or more after his first sip of real power in 1924, he continued to seek it only for the sake of his dreams. But little by little there came a change. Slowly but inexorably, he began to seek power for its own sake. More and more, the criterion by which Moses selected which city-shaping public works would be built came to be not the needs of the city's people, but the increment of power a project could give him. Increasingly, the projects became not ends but means—the means of obtaining more and more power.

As the idealism faded and disappeared, its handmaidens drifted away. The principles of the Good Government reform movement which Moses had once espoused became principles to be ignored. The brilliance that had invented a civil service system was applied to the task of circumventing civil service requirements. The insistence on truth and logic was replaced by a sophistry that twisted every fact to conclusions not merely preconceived but preconceived decades earlier.

Robert Moses was America's greatest builder. He was the shaper of the greatest city in the New World.

But what did he build? What was the shape into which he pounded the city?

To build his highways, Moses threw out of their homes 250,000 persons—more people than lived in Albany or Chattanooga, or in Spokane, Tacoma, Duluth, Akron, Baton Rouge, Mobile, Nashville or Sacramento. He tore out the hearts of a score of neighborhoods, communities the size of small cities themselves, communities that had been lively, friendly places to live, the vital parts of the city that made New York a home to its people.

By building his highways, Moses flooded the city with cars. By systematically starving the subways and the suburban commuter railroads, he swelled that flood to city-destroying dimensions. By making sure that the vast suburbs, rural and empty when he came to power, were filled on a sprawling, low-density development pattern relying primarily on roads instead of mass transportation, he insured that that flood would continue for generations if not centuries, that the New York metropolitan area would be—perhaps forever—an area in which transportation—getting from one place to another—would be an irritating, life-consuming concern for its 14,000,000 residents.

For highways, Moses dispossessed 250,000 persons. For his other projects—Lincoln Center, the United Nations, the Fordham, Pratt and Long Island University campuses, a dozen mammoth urban renewal projects—he dispossessed tens of thousands more; there are available no accurate figures on the total number of people evicted from their homes for all Robert Moses public works, but the figure is almost certainly close to half a million; the one detailed study by an outside agency shows that in a ten-year period, 1946 to 1956, the number was 320,000. More significant even than the number of the dispossessed were their characteristics: a disproportionate share of them were black, Puerto Rican—and poor. He evicted tens of thousands of poor, nonwhite persons for urban renewal projects, and the housing he built to replace the housing he tore down was, to an overwhelming extent, not housing for the poor, but for the rich. The dispossessed, barred from many areas of the city by their color and their poverty, had no place to go but into the already overcrowded slums—or into "soft" borderline areas that then became slums, so that his "slum clearance programs" created new slums as fast as they were clearing the old.

When he built housing for poor people, he built housing bleak, sterile, cheap—expressive of patronizing condescension in every line. And he built it in locations that contributed to the ghettoization of the city, dividing up the city by color and income. And by skewing city expenditures toward revenue-producing services, he prevented the city from reaching out toward its poor and assimilating them, and teaching them how to live in such housing—and the very people for whom he built it reacted with rage and bitterness and ignorance, and defaced it.

He built parks and playgrounds with a lavish hand, but they were parks and playgrounds for the rich and the comfortable. Recreational facilities for the poor he doled out like a miser.

For decades, to advance his own purposes, he systematically defeated every attempt to create the master plan that might have enabled the city to develop on a rational, logical, unified pattern—defeated it until, when it was finally adopted, it was too late for it to do much good.

"*One must wait until the evening* . . ." In the evening of Robert Moses' forty-four years of power, New York, so bright with promise forty-four years before, was a city in chaos and despair. His highways and bridges and tunnels were awesome—taken as a whole the most awesome urban improvement in the history of mankind—but no aspect of those highways and bridges and tunnels was as awesome as the congestion on them. He had built more housing than any public official in history, but the city was starved for housing, more starved, if possible, than when he had started building, and the people who lived in that housing hated it—hated it, James Baldwin could write, "almost as much as the policemen, and this is saying a great deal." He had built great monuments and great parks, but people were afraid to travel to or walk around them.

For all these reasons, this book attempts to tell two stories at once: how New York, forty years ago a very different city from the city it is today, became what it has become; and how the idealistic Robert Moses became what he has become. It must try to be a book about what happened to the city and what happened to the man. For, to an extent few people have really understood, these two stories are one story. Would New York have been a better place to live if Robert Moses had never built anything? Would it have been a better city if the man who shaped it had never lived? Any critic who says so ignores the fact that both before and after Robert Moses—both under "reform" mayors such as John Purroy Mitchel and John V. Lindsay and under Tammany mayors such as Red Mike Hylan and Jimmy Walker—the city was utterly unable to meet the needs of its people in areas requiring physical construction. Robert Moses may have bent the democratic processes of the city to his own ends to build public works; left to themselves, these processes proved unequal to the building required. The problem of constructing large-scale public works in a crowded urban setting, where such works impinge on the lives of or displace thousands of voters, is one which democracy has not yet solved.

Moses himself, who feels his works will make him immortal, believes he will be justified by history, that his works will endure and be blessed by generations not yet born. Perhaps he is right. It is impossible to say that New York would have been a better city if Robert Moses had never lived.

It is possible to say only that it would have been a different city.

I

THE IDEALIST

1. *Line of Succession*

ROBERT MOSES was born on December 18, 1888. He was not given a middle name—because his mother saw no reason for one.

Bella Moses was a strong-willed woman, so strong-willed, in fact, that some of her relatives said she was too much like *her* mother—and not enough like her father. Bella's parents, Robert's grandparents, were first cousins. Both had been born—Bernhard Cohen in 1821, Rosalie Silverman five years later—in the small Bavarian village of Reckendorf to struggling merchant families, two of the tens of thousands of German-Jewish families made highly susceptible to "America fever" by laws that segregated them in crowded *Judengassen* and forced them to pay the humiliating "Jew toll" whenever they made a trip away from the ghetto. The statutes also prohibited Jews from owning any land except that on which their houses stood or from dealing in any goods that could not be carried with them. Bavaria, where German anti-Semitism was most virulent, had even set a limit on the number of Jewish marriages in an attempt to keep the Jewish population down. The Silvermans left Reckendorf for New York while Rosalie was in her teens. Bernhard Cohen had been taken to Frankfurt am Main as a child by parents who hoped that life for Jews in Germany would be better outside Bavaria; when this hope was dashed, they waited until Bernhard was twenty-one, and then sent him and a younger brother, Samuel, to America, where the brothers opened a small dry-goods store in Mobile, Alabama. In 1848, they moved to New York, rented a small office and became dry-goods importers. Bernhard met his cousin and in 1849 they were married.

Business prospered and the Cohen brothers branched out into real estate with such success that they were soon considered millionaires. Their father had been able to send them to America with a little cash in their pockets, so they had never suffered the desperate poverty that had afflicted other German-Jewish immigrants of the 1840's—the brothers Seligman, Abraham Kuhn, Simon Guggenheim and his son Meyer, for instance—who, without enough capital to open stores, had had to earn it trudging through rural Pennsylvania with heavy packs on their backs and sticks in their hands to ward off dogs, peddling merchandise from farmhouse to farmhouse. Perhaps for this reason, the brothers, Bernhard in particular, never displayed the lifelong preoccupation with wealth that flogged the one-time peddlers along a gyre of financial expansion that eventually made them merchant princes, international bankers and mining tycoons—men whom Cleveland

Amory labeled the Jewish Grand Dukes, who were not part of the Four Hundred but rather of their own One Hundred and who created in New York City their own, self-contained society that was known among themselves as "Our Crowd." By the time he was fifty, Bernhard, security assured, was leaving business affairs largely in Samuel's hands and taking an interest, unusual among Jewish businessmen in New York in the 1870's, in civic affairs. Becoming convinced of slum residents' need for more "breathing space," he launched a successful campaign to persuade the city fathers, who were not at all sure that they hadn't already made a gigantic mistake by removing a huge hunk of land from the tax rolls to create Central Park, to set aside other, smaller areas for more parks. Among his friends he gained a reputation as an incisive and visionary analyst of social problems. In 1875, Joseph Seligman resigned from the traditional "Jewish seat" on the City School Commission and Mayor William H. Wickham appointed a non-Jew to fill the vacancy. The German-Jewish community was outraged. "We want the unsectarian character of our public schools preserved," editorialized *The Jewish Times*. "We do not want to be delivered into the hands of disguised missionaries in the persons of principals who smuggle in sectarian prayers and hymns in our public schools." The German Jews decided to unite behind a single man and insist on his appointment to the commission, and the man they chose was Bernhard Cohen, who was appointed in January 1877. If not one of the richer or more famous members of Our Crowd, he was one of the most respected.

Yet, within the circle of his family, Cohen was almost pitied. His grandchildren, years after his death, remembered him as a tall, slim man, handsome with an aquiline nose and pale-blue eyes. They recalled that he was generous, very gentle and mild, a little absent-minded, and so unfailingly courteous in manner that when he visited his granddaughters he would kiss their hands rather than their faces. But what they recalled most vividly about Bernhard Cohen was how unmercifully he was bullied by his wife. "My grandmother had the reputation of being as hard as nails," one says. "She had that reputation because of the way she treated her husband."

Rosalie Silverman had been a beautiful girl, tall, statuesque, with a whiteness of skin that made her black hair and full red lips all the more striking. She aged early, however, and she aged hard, becoming terribly wrinkled and gaunt—her eyes sunken, her long thin nose jutting out sharply from the wrinkles. Only her hair remained youthful, and the fact that it stayed jet black until her death at the age of ninety-three led her family to believe she dyed it. She bore five children—Bella, three other girls and a son, David—but she was not the stereotype Jewish mother. In fact, when two of the girls—Emma, who had married banker Adolph Openhym, and Lydia, wife of Kuhn, Loeb & Co. partner Abraham Wolf—became fatally ill while still in their twenties, wasting away for months before they died, it was Bernhard, not Rosalie, who visited them every day and helped with the nursing. Rosalie, a relative recalls, "seemed to want to forget about them."

Rosalie's bent was intellectual rather than maternal. She was a voracious reader of philosophy and history as well as fiction. Her hobby was crossword puzzles and she made a practice of racing through several of them every day in both English and German newspapers. A sharp mind was coupled with a sharp tongue, which she used on those who disagreed with her opinions. And she was unusually frank for a Jewish—or Gentile—housewife of her era. Once one of her granddaughters was amazed to realize that Old Grannie Cohen was about to give her an unsolicited lecture on sex. "One must be very much in love to enjoy it," Old Grannie began, and she proceeded, with none of the delicacy ladies usually attached to such discussions at the turn of the century.

With underlings, Grannie Cohen was flashingly imperious. After her husband died, she moved with her maid, Susan, into a suite in the fashionable Windsor Hotel, on Fifth Avenue between Forty-sixth and Forty-seventh streets, and sent out invitations to a "suite-warming" luncheon. On the day before the luncheon she decided she didn't like the chandelier in her living room. Marching down to the front desk, she ordered a new chandelier, told the clerk it must be installed by the following day at 10 A.M., cut off his protestations with a curt "I won't take 'no' for an answer!" and swept out the door without waiting for a reply.

Grannie Cohen's definition of underlings, moreover, apparently included the general public. When buying tickets for a railroad trip or a play, her practice was to eye the queue of ticket buyers disdainfully and then stride up to the first man on it and simply elbow him out of the way.

And the definition appeared to include her husband. "The way Grannie Cohen treated Grandfather Cohen was quite striking," the granddaughter recalls. "She absolutely sat on him." Many of the more intellectual members of Our Crowd became impressed during the 1870's with the philosophy of a German rabbi's son named Felix Adler, who was talking about substituting ethics for religious piety. Rosalie Cohen became one of Adler's most enthusiastic supporters. When the Society for Ethical Culture was formed in 1876, with Joseph Seligman as its first president, she became a member—and so did Bernhard Cohen, who previously had been one of the most devout members of Temple Emanu-El, the stronghold of Reform Jewry in New York. On May 13, 1897, after absent-mindedly taking a walk in the rain without an umbrella, Bernhard caught pneumonia and, four days later, died. His funeral services were conducted by Dr. Adler.

Old age did not change Grannie Cohen. In her nineties, she still walked almost every day to public and lending libraries to obtain books, and Robert's college friends who were present when she dropped in on the Moses family were astonished at the range of her knowledge. In summers, at the Moses summer home at Lake Placid, she would arise early, open an imposing stack of German- and English-language newspapers to their crossword puzzles, sit down on a porch overlooking the lake and begin working on puzzles in two languages. Within an hour she would be back inside, chatting with the college boys animatedly about the latest trends in art or science, and one of the boys, happening to glance through the pile of papers she had left on the porch, noticed that every word of every puzzle was completed. Age certainly did not wither her independence. Until she died, she did her own marketing every day. She refused to allow herself to be examined by doctors, even by her grandson Nathan E. Brill, an official of Mount Sinai Hospital and discoverer of "Brill's disease," a form of typhus fever. And, despite the entreaties of her children, she would not allow the bell pull in her hotel room to be moved from the door to a spot near her bed so that she could summon Susan more easily in case of emergency. "I'll never be too sick to walk across the room," she said. In fact, although she became very hard of hearing, she was seldom sick at all—until a night in July 1919, a month after her ninety-third birthday. On that evening, she went to bed with a German crossword puzzle. At midnight, with the puzzle almost completed, she arose, walked across the room, rang the bell pull and, when the maid arrived, said calmly, "Susan, call Dr. Brill. I'm dying." When Dr. Brill arrived, she was dead.

The striking features that had been Rosalie's portion as a girl were passed on to her son and three oldest daughters, all of whom were considered to have made "good" marriages. "Looks ran high in the Cohen family," friends say. But Rosalie's youngest daughter, Bella (she never used her real name, Isabella), was a slim girl and young woman of less than medium height whose features, except for a too prominent, rather high-bridged nose, were, under brown curly hair, exceedingly plain. So were her clothes. Unlike her mother, Bella had a quiet, unassuming manner that combined with her slimness and curls to give her the appearance, even in her twenties, of a sweet little girl. She also possessed a kindliness that is not remembered as one of Rosalie's most noticeable attributes. "Bella was always doing nice things for people, little thoughtful things," recalls one of her cousins, Hilda Hellman. When Hilda's young son Geoffrey broke a leg in an automobile accident and had to spend time in Mount Sinai, he could be sure of an almost daily visit—and present—from his "Aunt Bella."

Nonetheless, of Rosalie's five children, Bella was the one most like her mother. If her looks weren't as impressive, her mind was. Educated by private tutors and then at Charlier, the exclusive finishing school, she could speak both French and German fluently and had a wide acquaintance with the literature of both countries. And if her appearance was that of a quiet and sweet little girl, quite different from her mother, people who bothered to talk to the little girl found that the appearance was deceiving. In discussing her opinions, Bella was mannerly and soft-spoken, but the opinions delivered in that soft voice were direct, forceful—and not particularly susceptible to alteration. In fact, people who tried to alter them came to realize rather quickly that while Bella's voice was soft, the things she might say with it could be sharp indeed. "After you had talked to her," recalls an acquaintance, "you began to observe her more closely. And it didn't take you long to realize that under that quiet manner was an astonishing amount of arrogance. She was her mother's daughter."

In 1886, at the age of twenty-six, Bella married Emanuel Moses, a thirty-five-year-old department-store owner from New Haven. He was a dark, tall, shaggy man, with warm, kindly eyes, a soft mustache and a gentle, slow manner. Born in Cologne of a family in which was mingled blood of both German Jews and Sephardic Jews from Seville, he had started out in America as a lace merchant and then had opened a little department store in New Haven and built it into a successful business. But he was too slow and quiet for the Cohens; they felt that Bella had not made a very good marriage in comparison with her sisters; they felt, in fact, that Bella had married beneath her.

Emanuel and Bella moved to New Haven, which in 1886 was a quiet, charming little town celebrated for its elm-lined streets, a meticulously manicured sixteen-acre Central Green and beautiful public buildings and parks. They settled down in 83 Dwight Street, a big, rambling house with a broad, shaded porch and a generous helping of the gingerbread that characterized the architecture of the period, and it was in that house that their three children were born, Paul Emanuel in 1887, Robert in 1888 and Edna Marion in 1891.

Dwight Street, two blocks from the Yale University campus, was a wide, sleepy, dirt street shaded by some of the biggest of New Haven's elms. The houses along it were substantial, if not elegant, and they were built close to the wooden sidewalk, so that most of the big lots consisted of back yards, and in those yards, because the families on the street were well-off manufacturers and businessmen, were well-tended grape arbors and stables—and inside the stables were horses and carriages. The numerous children of Dwight Street rode up and down the street on those horses, with coachmen or house servants leading them and carefully holding them in to a walk, and played on the shady porches or in the spacious back yards under the tall trees, and there were so many servants in the big houses that mothers didn't scold if boys like "Mr. Paul" or "Mr. Robert," who slept in the same bedroom on the second floor of No. 83, got their Eton collars and Little Lord Fauntleroy suits dirty. To the end of their lives, the three Moses children would remember New Haven with fondness. Searching for an adjective to describe Dwight Street, Robert Moses would say "comfortable"; Paul would say "shady, well-kept, *nice*."

If the Moses children were happy in New Haven, so was their father. His department store was prospering and he had begun to buy up property in the city, including the Chamber of Commerce Building on Temple Street. But Bella disliked New Haven. She felt there was no cultural activity there worth talking about, and she felt she was many cuts above the run of the local matrons. In 1897, the Moses family moved to New York.

Many years later, Robert Moses would say, "I didn't like New York at all. It was too big; the crowds, the noise and the confusion were terrible. I wanted to go back to New Haven, to go to Yale and to become Governor of Connecticut. I felt that way all during my years in New York. . . ."

Emanuel Moses never let anyone know how he felt. In order to move he had to sell his store and his real estate holdings. In 1897, he was forty-six years old, a businessman who had achieved success and who had seemed to be heading for more. Moreover, he had liked running his store. He was a businessman who enjoyed being in business.

He was to spend the rest of his life in retirement.

* * *

In New York, Bella found a cause. It was the Settlement House movement.

In 1897, the year the Moses family moved from New Haven, hundreds of thousands of Eastern European Jews, who had been working eighteen hours a day for a wage of two or three rubles a week, formed *Der Algemayner Idisher Arbeter Bund,* the General League of Jewish Workers, in Russia, Poland and Lithuania, in a last, despairing, foredoomed attempt to improve their lot, which was even harder than that which German Jews like the Cohens and Silvermans had fled a half century earlier. In Czarist Russia, the vast ghetto known as the Pale of Settlement had become a morass of the most bitter poverty. The virtual legalization of discrimination in the May Laws of the 1880's had touched off a series of savage pogroms. When the strikes called by the cobblers, tailors and weavers who had formed the General League were broken—by bloodshed, imprisonment and torture—the Jews of Eastern Europe felt that their only hope was escape to America. They poured into New York at a rate of ninety thousand a year. By 1907, there would be close to a million Jews in the city, by 1915 a million and a half—28 percent of its population. Eastern European Jews arrived in the New World scarred by the lash and the knout, idealistic and socialistic—and dirt poor. Families were shoehorned into blocks of railroad flats, while fathers used their meager savings to stock pushcarts—and learned, all too slowly, that peddling, which had worked so well for the Seligmans, Guggenheims and Kuhns, was no longer the path to riches in America.

To aid these immigrants, the Lower East Side settlement houses sprang up, funded and staffed largely by New York's established German-Jewish community. And Bella Moses, newly returned to New York, soon became an enthusiastic funder and staffer. She worked first at the famous Henry Street Settlement, but soon transferred her allegiance to Madison House, one of the smallest and newest of the settlement houses and therefore one in which she could play a more prominent role.

Two characteristics of Bella's work for Madison House, which was to continue for more than thirty years, soon became apparent.

One was a characteristic shared by many of the German Jews who traveled down to the Lower East Side in carriage and cab from the servanted enclave around Temple Emanu-El. It was a characteristic that moved one of their chroniclers to call their philanthropy "something very close to patronage." For while the motives which impelled the rich Jews to help the poor Jews were certainly in part manifestations of *Zedakah,* the religious principle of charity, historians have also found other motives. They have found that many German Jews—solid, respectable, Americanized—were embarrassed by the gruff, uncouth, shaggy-bearded, conspicuously un-Americanized newcomers. "Those people," the Germans felt, were loud, pushy, aggressive—"the dregs of Europe." They spoke of them in terms others applied to the Yellow Peril, the German-Jewish press lamenting the "un-American ways" of the "wild Asiatics." The German Jews even coined a word for their coreligionists, a word based on the fact that many Russian names end in "ki." The word was "kikes." Yet, despite their efforts to make clear the difference between themselves and the newcomers, they realized that non-Jews were lumping them all together, taking the behavior of the newcomers as the stereotype by which they thought of all Jews.

The solution, many German Jews felt, was to make the shabby immigrants "respectable," to clean them up, dust them off and teach them to act "like Americans." For this reason, the early settlement houses, while working tirelessly to give the newcomers a better life, to provide free lodging, meals and medical care, also emphasized lectures on manners, morals and the dangers of socialism. Many German Jews seemed to feel, as one commentator put it, "as if [they were] assuming the white man's burden"; their philanthropy was that of "patron lords doling out funds to the poor, the miserable, the dependent and the patronized."

If this description was to some extent true of the movement as a whole, it was to a great extent true of Madison House, whose official history says it was established "To help in the Americanization of residents of the Lower East Side." And to some of her relatives, the description fitted Bella's philanthropy. Undoubtedly there ran through her work a strain of genuine idealism. Deeply moved by the plight of the slum residents she met at Madison, she talked of "helping the lower classes" in terms of a holy crusade. "Public service"—service such as Madison House was furnishing—was a phrase which came more and more frequently to her lips, and she said public service was a cause to which one could happily devote one's life. But she also never forgot that the lower classes were lower. Recalls one relative: "Her attitude to these people was 'You're my children; I know best; you do what I tell you and I'll take care of you.' " Rosalie Silverman Cohen began to refer to her daughter derisively as "Lady Bountiful."

The other characteristic of Bella's work for Madison House was one much rarer among the platoons of wealthy German-Jewish matrons on the boards of trustees of the settlement houses. Bella, graying now and often spectacled, could have passed for one of these matrons, although her clothes were plainer than most. Like them, she made liberal financial contributions —Madison House could count on her for an annual donation of about $10,000. But unlike many of the matrons, Bella also began to show an active day-after-day interest in the development of the philanthropy to which she gave money—and as the years went by, the trustees and workers of Madison House became aware that her interest was really in one particular type of development. Bella's concern was not captured by the more philosophical aspects of settlement-house work; she sat back quietly during discussions of lecture content or of the best methods of strengthening ties between immigrant parents and American-born children. But when the discussions turned to the laying out of basketball courts in the back yard of the House or the creation of a summer camp in the country for slum children, the slim little woman would lean forward and her fingers would begin to drum restlessly on the table and her soft voice would begin to inundate the other trustees with a flood of ideas. It was not long before the trustees came to realize that for a gray-haired housewife and mother, Bella Moses had a most unusual interest in physical construction. Behind her spectacles were the eyes of the builder.

The eyes could glitter with enthusiasm over the smallest details. When the board agreed to provide living quarters for House staffers, it was Bella Moses who thought of providing the quarters with a lounge so the young men and women could have a place to chat together during their off hours—and it was Bella who went out and found the perfect centerpiece for the lounge, a heavy table six feet across supported by a pedestal instead of legs so that people could sit around it more easily. When the board decided to set up a temporary summer camp in Pelham Bay Park, it was Bella who thought of putting old rugs under the beds to make the tents warmer. And when, in 1900, Madison House decided to embark on its largest project, the construction of a permanent summer camp, the ideas began to pour out of Bella Moses in a steady stream.

The camp was to be built on an old farm in a beautiful valley near Putnam, New York. Bella began to appear at trustees' meetings with proposed layouts of the camp and then with proposed layouts of interiors of the camp buildings. When the camp was opened, Bella and Emanuel visited it every weekend during the season. Often they would make the sixty-mile trip up from New York with their special friends on the board, Olga and Moritz Kirchberger and middle-aged bachelor Herman Wolff. When the Kirchbergers and Wolff agreed that it would be nice to spend longer periods in the camp, Bella proposed that they should all chip in and pay for the construction of a summer lodge big enough for two couples and a bachelor. And when the comfortable, solidly built structure was completed, it was Bella who suggested an agreement under which the building would become the camp's property, its residence for teen-age girls, when all five owners were dead.

In expounding her proposals, Bella was always a lady. She never raised her voice. But veneered only thinly by her excellent manners was a certain aggressiveness—and if there was a prolonged disagreement with her proposals, the veneer could wear thin indeed. When discussing a project in which she was especially interested, Bella had always displayed impatience with other people's ideas, but in her later years on the Madison House board she seemed more and more unwilling even to consider such ideas—or, in fact, to listen to them. Says one House staffer who sat in on board meetings: "In a quiet way, Mrs. Moses could really be quite . . . impatient. She knew what she wanted and she intended to have it." Says another: "She liked to get things done. And if she had to step on toes to get them done, she'd step on toes."

Some of Bella's proposals were based on generalized theories. You should always buy the best, she would say. Having the best equipment made people respect it—and take care of it. Some of the trustees, feeling that Madison House, perennially broke, should economize, were annoyed, but

Bella brooked no compromise. When the head worker was furnishing the staff quarters, for example, she instructed him: "Now, there'll be no pictures dragged out of people's closets. *Buy* pictures—and buy pretty ones." She was convinced also of the importance of symbols. They were needed, she said, to "give the children a sense of identity," by which she meant a sense that they were part of Madison House. As soon as the camp was opened, she designed a huge "Camp Madison" banner and hung it in the dining hall.

Once Bella got involved in a project, no task was too small for her. Camp counselors saw the slim little matron inspecting the grounds hour after hour. When the inspections disclosed flaws, she was not bashful in bringing them to people's attention. "We had been taught that in social work you should be somewhat permissive," recalls one of the workers. "She wasn't that kind of person. If she saw that the kids weren't cleaning up the bunks properly, she'd say, 'Now get busy! Get that bunk cleaned up!' If she came back and it still wasn't clean, she'd say, 'Didn't I tell you to clean it up?' " And if her hints didn't bring results, she had more direct methods. If a floor remained unswept too long, she'd grab a broom and sweep it herself. Beds were supposed to be made before breakfast, but one bunk never seemed to get them done in time. One morning, Bella said shortly, "I'll make them for you"—and did, all ten of them.

When disputes arose among the trustees, there was one vote Bella could always count on. Emanuel Moses was a member of the board, too, although, as one trustee commented, "he was so quiet you'd hardly know it." The trustees came to know Emanuel as a likable and generous man—but they also learned that his wife did the talking for the Moses family. This was true in the Moses home as well. "The relationship between Mother and Father was simple," Paul Moses would recall. "Father did what Mother directed."

If the relationship seemed similar in general to that of Bella's own parents, there were more specific parallels, too. Like Rosalie, Bella had especially strong feelings about religion: she did not believe in it. She did not want her sons to be circumcised, to be bar-mitzvah—or to have any training whatsoever in the Jewish faith. She wanted her family to be members of the Society for Ethical Culture. Her husband was more religious, but Bella's feelings were the ones which prevailed, as her mother's had prevailed. When Rosalie had joined the Society for Ethical Culture, Bernhard had joined, too. When Bella joined the Society, so did Emanuel.

Bella Moses' children grew up in snug luxury. The family lived at 20 East Forty-sixth Street, just off Fifth Avenue, in the heartland of the German-Jewish elite. The neighborhood was one of lavish private homes. The Seligman house was almost directly across the street from the Moseses', and two doors down lived the Lehmans; their youngest child, Herbert, was a student at Williams College. It was a neighborhood in which the children all knew one another; they visited one another's homes, so alike with the varnished oak and black-walnut paneling, red damask and green repp, heavy-legged, plump-cushioned sofas, gold-fringed lamps and Dresden figurines. They played together in Central Park while private tutors stood sentry duty, and, the boys wearing white gloves, attended Viola Wolff's dancing classes together.

The house in which the Moses children were raised—among oak paneling and red damask—was the one in which their mother had lived when she was a girl; when Bernhard Cohen died, he had left it to Bella in his will, and when she decided that the Moses family would move back to New York, her mother had been happy to move out of the house and into the suite at the Windsor a block away. The house was a large brownstone—five stories and a basement—but there was plenty of money to run it; if the Moseses were not nearly as rich as the Lehmans, the Seligmans or other Grand Dukes such as the Schiffs, they were, in turn-of-the-century terms, rich enough; between Bella's share of her father's estate and the sale of Emanuel's New Haven interests, the family had assets of about $1,200,000. Bella was able to command an establishment that included an extremely talented German cook and three maids, including a long-time retainer known as "Old Annie."

The two Moses boys slept in custom-made beds, six feet six inches long, on hair mattresses woven to order by the most famous mattressmaker in New York, C. P. Rogers. They slept in the same room again, but adjoining their New York bedroom was their own library-study, its walls lined with books. Once Paul counted them; there were more than two thousand. Dinner was served—off the finest Haviland china—in a paneled dining room along one wall of which stood a tremendous sideboard bearing gleaming crystal decanters. After dinner, the family would repair to the library, whose walls were covered with Rembrandt and Dürer prints, and Old Annie would pour coffee from a silver coffeepot into French demitasse cups—each cup a different bright color—that cost twenty-four dollars apiece.

In the summer, there were trips to Europe, or Grannie Cohen might rent a summer place in Elberon, one of the expensive resort towns along the New Jersey shore that had become known collectively as the "Jewish Newport." Grannie's house would be much smaller than the Lewisohns' Elberon castle on a hill, of course, but it would be big and roomy. The Moseses wouldn't travel down from New York by private railroad car as did the Schiffs, but they did have a touring car and chauffeur. And the boys would have a wonderful time.

They always had a wonderful time with Grannie Cohen. If she had, in the opinion of some, not been overly attentive to her own children, she doted on her grandchildren. Every spring, as soon as the weather turned warm, she would take Robert and Paul on a weekend to Atlantic City, purchasing the railroad tickets by the elbowing method while the two little boys watched the imperious old lady with awe. After checking into a hotel, with the manager himself showing her to her room, she would take the boys out along the Boardwalk and cram their pockets full of tickets to the thrill rides at Young's Pier and Hyler's. And when the boys rode the roller coasters or the loop-the-loop, they would not be unaccompanied. Sitting between them, holding tight to her huge hat, would be Rosalie Silverman Cohen, then in her late seventies, laughing with glee.

Bella was strict with her children. Running a taut house, she ordered every aspect of their lives. Their advice was not solicited—even about their own clothes. Once, opening a closet to get their tuxedos for a party, they found that the dress suits had disappeared and new ones had been hung in their places. When they inquired, Old Annie explained that their mother had decided that the old ones were no longer "suitable." On one visit to Brooks Brothers, Paul asked for a green cap; his mother ordered a red one—for no reason that he could see except that he had asked for green.

Bella was particularly interested in the boys' education. She selected as their tutors young men with outstanding credentials; the boys' favorite, for example, had just returned from Oxford, where he had taken a double first in classics and literary humanities. When Paul was thirteen, Robert twelve and Edna nine, the children were enrolled in the Ethical Culture School. After two years, the boys were transferred to the Dwight School for two years and then were sent to board for a year at one of the most expensive of college preparatory schools, the Mohegan Lake Academy near Poughkeepsie, before they went on to college, Paul to Princeton and Robert, who had never forgotten his desire to return to New Haven, to Yale.

Even while the boys were at Ethical Culture and Dwight, Bella hired tutors to give them additional instruction. And she furnished still other instruction herself, assigning them books by Laurence Sterne and other of her favorite authors to read, and then holding long discussions with them—and with Edna when she was old enough—about the books' meaning. Casually reading a passage, she would suddenly turn to one of the children and ask, "What's that mean?" "And when she asked that," Paul would recall more than half a century later, "you had better know." Even while the children were playing, they were reminded of the importance of good English. If one of them mispronounced a word, down the stairs would come their mother's voice saying, "What was that? What was that?"

Edna did not flourish in this atmosphere. An extremely plain, shy girl, she became more and more quiet and withdrawn. But everybody exclaimed over Bella's two boys. Just over a year apart in age, in appearance they might almost have been twins. They were tall—Paul an even six feet, Robert an inch taller—and graceful and very slim, although Robert was wiry and strong and had wide shoulders and wrists that hinted at a frame that would one day be powerful. Their height and the darkness of their hair and skin made them resemble their father, but the father's somewhat broad features had been refined in the boys so that they were stunningly handsome, with high cheekbones and slim, almost aquiline noses to go with full, sensual lips and wide, deep, liquid gray eyes. While the father's skin was dark, the blood of Seville ran even closer to the surface in his sons, making their faces olive-colored, almost swarthy backdrops for smiles that everyone agreed were charming. And where the father's movements were deliberate and calm, theirs were flashing and the set of their heads was haughty. If Paul was quicker to smile, both boys were equally quick to anger; they had tempers that went with the haughtiness. They looked like two young, handsome, passionate Spanish grandees set down by mistake in the stodgy red damask of Forty-sixth Street.

And the boys' minds were as remarkable as their looks. Teachers at the schools they attended told Bella with a unanimity that must have become almost monotonous that her sons were brilliant. And they were popular, not only with girls, who were attracted by their quick wit as well as by their looks, but with the boys with whom they went to school, although Paul was the more popular—Robert was more of a loner. Robert was interested in athletics, but not in sports which required him to be part of a team. He preferred, instead, gymnastics, swimming and track, sports in which the athlete competes alone. In track, he chose the loneliest of events, the cross-country run.

If the handsome, sparkling brothers made quite a picture in the library after dinner, framed by dark wood and Rembrandts, black-uniformed Old Annie hovering behind them with silver service as they chatted with mother, father and sister over demitasse, the picture was complemented by conversation that was the quick play of quick minds, wit striking fire from wit. If there were no visitors present, Edna joined in. The father, of course, was the outsider. It was not that anyone was actually rude to him, relatives and friends would recall. His family's attitude was, rather, amiably patronizing. In the words of one visitor, "It was the kind of thing where, when Emanuel said something, the kids would say good-naturedly, 'Oh, Dad! Oh, Father!' And then they'd go right on with what they had been saying. It was as if everyone, including him, had sort of accepted the fact that he had nothing to contribute." After he moved to New York, Emanuel Moses did a lot of reading. "Reading," he would often say, "is the solace of old age."

Relatives and friends began to notice that within this family circle, an inner circle was forming. It was Robert Moses and his mother. More and more, within the family, they formed a small, increasingly private clique. More and more, it became apparent that Robert was his mother's favorite. This favoritism was expressed with the intensity that characterized everything Bella did. All her children were spoiled, spoiled by maids and cooks and grandmother, spoiled by wealth. But in Robert's case, the spoiling was also done by his mother. Increasingly, Bella Moses began to cater to her younger son's every whim. "You would never think of this word in connection with Bella," one relative says. "But the only word you could use to describe her treatment of Robert was 'doting.' "

No one was sure of the explanation. Relatives speculated that it was because Bella's slashing, incisive mind had found in Robert a mind with like qualities. Perhaps this was part of the explanation, but it ignored the fact that her other son possessed the same qualities. Perhaps another part of the explanation was that when the family discussions grew especially lively, Robert knew where to stop. On issues about which Bella felt especially strongly, Paul would often disagree with his mother. Robert never did. And Bella Moses, after all, was not a woman who liked to be disagreed with.

And part of the explanation, almost certainly, was that Robert tendered his mother the sincerest form of flattery. If Bella cherished the ideal of public service, public service conceived of in idealistic, almost Platonic terms, this ideal was becoming the theme of more and more of Robert's conversation, too. More and more, in the after-dinner chats in the library, Robert began to talk about dedicating his life to "helping people."

The imitation went beyond enunciation of ideals. People who had classified as a manifestation of supreme and deep-rooted arrogance Bella's refusal to be swayed by—or, in later years, even to listen at length to—the opinions of others, now began to notice this same arrogance in Robert. They noticed also that, increasingly, the rhythms of Robert's voice echoed the sharpness of his mother's sallies. The tall, handsome young man even adopted—consciously or unconsciously—a distinctive pose favored by the graying, bespectacled, plain little woman, an unusual tilt of the head. When a person disagreed with Bella, she had a way of leaning her head back on her neck and staring at the disagreer through the bottom of her spectacles with her eyes half closed, quizzical and skeptical. People began to notice that, while Robert Moses did not wear glasses, he was beginning to adopt, in arguments, the same tilt of the head.

In later decades, when Robert Moses was famous almost as much for his personality as for his achievements, observers would marvel at the depth and degree of his outspokenness, stubbornness, aggressiveness and arrogance. They would wonder at the origin of the mold in which he had been formed in so hard a cast. But relatives and friends of the Moses family never wondered. Whatever it was that made Robert Moses the way he was, they knew, whatever the quality that had shaped an unusual—in some ways unique—personality, the quality was one that they had watched being passed, like a family heirloom, from Robert Moses' grandmother to his mother to him. "Robert Moses," these people would say, "is Bella Moses' son."

2. *Robert Moses at Yale*

IF HIS MOTHER spoiled Robert Moses, his college did not. Bella may not have considered him a Jew, but his classmates did, and at Yale University in 1905, this made a difference.

Not in theory, of course. When Robert Moses went back to New Haven, Yale men were proudly proclaiming the university a "democracy of talent" that had spiritually entered the twentieth century by throwing off its traditional social shackles; to prove it, undergraduates made a point of calling every classmate by his first name.

But in fact Yale was still a tightly sealed society. Of the 351 members of the class of 1909 who entered Yale with Moses in September 1905, most had graduated from the "right" Episcopalian private preparatory schools—thirty-three from Andover, for example, twenty-three from Hotchkiss and seventeen from St. Paul's. Moreover, as one of Moses' classmates recalls, "as soon as you got to Yale, you found out that its structure was a social pyramid," its base the select Sophomore Societies, its next step the even more select Junior Fraternities, its apex the three Senior Societies—Skull and Bones, Scroll and Key and Wolf's Head. Sixty years later, surviving members of the class of 1909 could still remember watching classmates burst into tears on Tap Day when they realized that they were not to be selected for a Senior Society.

"The competition that counted at Yale was the competition to get to the top of that pyramid," Moses' classmate says. "If you weren't in at least a Junior Fraternity, you were a nobody." But the competition was not open; it was largely based on family background, social connections and prep-school associations. And to no one was it closed more tightly than to Jews, of whom there were five in Moses' class—listed as "Hebrews" in the Freshman Blue Book and lumped with the class's eighteen Roman Catholics under "Miscellaneous Denominations." In the seventy-three years that the Senior Societies had been in existence they had never tapped a single Jew. And whatever the feelings of Bella's boy about whether he was or was not Jewish, there were no doubts in the minds of his classmates. In his memoir of life at Yale, poet Leonard Bacon, an '09er, would begin a description of Moses with the words "I saw . . . a most attractive Jew."

It wasn't only religion that made Moses an outsider during his first years at college. Not yet seventeen years old when he sat in Dwight Hall listening to President Arthur Twining Hadley's opening address, he was two years younger than most of his classmates. Men from the same prep school generally roomed together as freshmen, but while the five other men in 1909 from Mohegan Lake "were fond of Bob, they kind of regarded him," in the words of a classmate, "as a young boy"—and they didn't invite him to room with them. In his freshman year, he boarded alone in a doctor's house near the campus; if he participated in any extracurricular activities, or linked his arms with classmates to dance down Chapel Street and cheer Ted Coy for his three touchdowns against Princeton, or if he came rushing out of his room at the cry of "Riot!" to help freshmen overturn trolley cars and pelt policemen with water bombs, nobody noticed him. Boys selected their sophomore roommates from the friends they had made at Yale; in his sophomore year, Bob Moses again roomed alone, this time in a dormitory. Lonely, he frequently hung around the suite in another dormitory in which the Mohegan Lake alumni lived. Classmates remember him in his first two years as "diffident," "quiet" and "shy." One of the wealthy prep-school graduates who roomed in the big, friendly suites in Vanderbilt, most prestigious of the dormitories, would recall him as "almost a recluse."

At night, when the other students on his floor began to roughhouse, Moses would quietly close his door. Alone in his room, he would write poems—dreamy-eyed romances and imitations of Walter Pater and Swinburne. And he would read. When he found a subject that interested him, he would clear the library shelves of books on the subject, lug them back to his room, stack them on his desk and read through the stack until it was finished.

Ironically, it was the reading and writing he did behind the door closed against his classmates' shouts that first made them take an interest in him. There was on the campuses of that era a respect for scholarliness and brilliance, and Bob Moses' classmates slowly began to realize the extent to which he possessed these qualities. One of the members of the Mohegan Lake suite says: "I liked Bob from the first, but in the beginning it was a sort of paternal feeling. When he'd come around to the room, he'd seem so young and lost. But then I began to be attracted to him for his mind. I loved Latin; I got very high marks in it, but I knew just enough Latin to know that Bob was on a level way above mine. He *really* knew Latin. I started talking to him—and I became aware of a quality of mind that was exceptional. He was brilliant. I liked talking to him, and I became friendly with him. And that was what happened between Moses and a lot of people; by the end of sophomore year or the beginning of junior year, people were beginning to talk about him. He became admired for his scholarship—and all of a sudden we noticed he was coming around to our suite less and less. He had gotten friends of his own."

Moses began to submit his poetry for publication, not to the famous *Yale Literary Magazine,* where Leonard Bacon and cadaverous, freckle-faced, red-haired Sinclair Lewis were among the classmates competing for places on the board, but to a newer, less prestigious publication—the *Yale Courant.* Encouraged by the acceptance of a poem for the December 1907 issue, he contributed more poems and several short stories, and when, in March 1908, the new *Courant* editorial board was selected, he was on it.

He also joined the Yale swimming team. Swimming occupied approximately the same position in relation to other sports at Yale as the *Courant* did to the *Lit*. Intercollegiate competition in the sport had begun only a few years before, and few colleges had swimming teams. A highlight of meets was still an event called the "plunge for distance," in which the winner was the competitor who, after diving into the pool, could travel the farthest without moving his arms or legs. At Yale, the team practiced—in an ancient, dank, low-ceilinged, too-short pool—only three times a week. The *Yale Daily News* reported the results of the meets—when it reported them at all—at the very end of the list of sports results, after even fencing and wrestling, and thanks to the influence of Walter Camp, who felt that the famous Yale "Y" should be worn only by football, hockey and baseball players—he wasn't too sure about hockey and baseball—swimmers were eligible only for a "Ysa," an insignia standing for "Yale Swimming Association."

Moses joined the swimming team as a sophomore. If he ever won a race, the victory was not reported in the *News*. But he was known as a hard worker in practice and a fierce competitor in meets, and he could be counted upon for second- or third-place points in either the fifty-yard or the hundred-yard crawl. As a junior, Moses was elected manager, an honor which entitled him to arrange meets and buy the team's train tickets.

Swimming and the *Courant* enabled Bob Moses to broaden his acquaintance at Yale. And the classmates who got to know him began to see something special in the tall, slim Jew from New York, very handsome in the required high, rounded collar, who had the huge, emotional eyes and earnest, passionate manner of the idealist, the poet, the lover (in the phrase they learned in a popular course on Walter Pater) of the Good, the True and the Beautiful.

The eyes and the manner, these classmates learned, were not misleading. Not only was Bob Moses a poet but his poems were poems like the dreamy-eyed "Song of the Arctic Nereid, a hymn to the nymphs of the sea," or "Fragments from the French":

Fair night! Fair night!
Afar the day has fled;
Fair night! Fair night!
A torch divine o'erhead
God's goodness flames eternal and abides
Our erring footsteps keeps and, watching, guides,
Fair night! Fair night!

To-morrow!
But is the morrow sure
To-morrow!
The lashes slumber lure;
Ah! Shall we greet the dawning day,
Perchance in vain we longing say,
To-morrow!

And the idealism was deep. Not only had Bob Moses read most of Pater; he believed in what he had read. He loved learning genuinely and for its own sake. If he was competitive in swimming, he wasn't in classroom work. He wasn't uninterested in marks, but he wasn't especially concerned about them either. He spent night after night behind a closed door reading, but his friends began to realize that the reading was not for grades; sometimes they would look at the stack of books on his desk and not one of them had anything to do with the courses he was taking; they were there because they interested him. And their subjects covered a wide spectrum of knowledge; if Moses seemed particularly fascinated by literature and history, he was also reading everything he could find on the history of art. One of his friends was taking German; he came across a phrase one day that seemed to fit Bob Moses—*durstig Geist*. Moses did indeed, the friend said, have a "thirsty mind."

After his sophomore year, one of his new friends went with Moses to Europe. Many college men spent their summers in Europe in the halcyon days before the Great War, but most of them spent their eight weeks abroad in the lobbies of the fashionable hotels of Paris, Rome and Geneva, striking up conversations, under the indulgent eyes of chaperons, with young ladies making their Grand Tours. Moses, the friend reported on their return to Yale, bounded out of bed early in the morning to be at museums when they opened, and he stayed in the museums all day. In Venice, which became his favorite European city, he spent hours in front of the famous Giotto frescoes and Michelangelo statues—and more hours searching out frescoes and statues that his companion had never heard of but about which Moses, in those long nights behind the closed door, had learned every detail.

Moses' greatest enthusiasm was reserved for a more famous work of art—the "Mona Lisa." He seemed riveted to the floor of the Louvre in front of the painting. When he got back to Yale in the fall, he wrote poems about it, including one, apparently done in the style of Swinburne's "Dolores," that called her "Our Lady Divine."

In literature his greatest enthusiasm was for Samuel Johnson. Chauncey Brewster Tinker, a young professor whose empathy for Johnson's era was reflected in an almost eighteenth-century courtesy and insistence on form but whose austerity was burned away on the lecture platform by what one colleague called "the white fire of the poet," made his "Johnson and His Circle" course "a journey in a beautiful and exciting country." Wandering off on his own, Bob Moses explored that country's byways. The assigned reading included excerpts from Boswell's biography of Johnson; Moses read the book complete, became interested in biography and proceeded to read stacks of biographies as well as books on the nature of that genre.

His friends began to see that Moses' idealism was not confined to the printed page. If the more perceptive members of his class realized that "democracy of talent" was a false description of life at Yale, Moses had specific ideas on how to make the slogan a reality. The suggestion that class officers be chosen on merit rather than on the basis of fraternity membership was not the only remedy for Yale's social ossification which Moses proposed, both in late-evening bull sessions and in the *Courant*. He was also, for instance, insistent that some sort of "social recognition" should be given for scholastic achievement. And, in at least one instance, he proved his willingness to fight for his ideals.

Moses not only enjoyed swimming himself; he was convinced that the sport should receive more emphasis at Yale because, as a classmate put it, "he regarded [it] as something in which every undergraduate could take pleasure, as contrasted with the gladiatorial sports like football and baseball." He had the same feeling about other minor sports, such as tennis, track, golf, gymnastics, fencing, shooting and wrestling, all of which had, like swimming, been only recently incorporated into the intercollegiate athletic scene. His enthusiasm about them reached such a peak, in fact, that his friends jokingly began to call him "the minor sport."

Every attempt to upgrade such sports at Yale had run head on into the frenzy over football—it was the era when gridiron heroes like Ted Coy and Tad Jones were the campus gods, when the winner of the Big Three title was national champion, when every victory was celebrated with bonfires and torchlight parades down Chapel Street—and into the personal opposition of Camp, who, in addition to being first among the Eli football pantheon, had the more practical advantage of being treasurer of the Athletic Union. With the Yale Bowl that was his dream drawing ever closer to reality, Camp had been squirreling away the annual surplus of the Union with such enthusiasm that it had already reached $120,000, and he was not about to turn any of it over to the sports he derided.

Bearding Camp in his suite at the New Haven House, Moses suggested a distribution of some of the football surplus among the minor sports. Camp flatly refused to give a nickel.

Another undergraduate might have left quietly. Recalling the scene, Moses was to say: "What you have to understand is what a colossal influence he had; he dominated all of athletics there; his word was absolutely law." But this undergraduate, before leaving, told Camp that someday the minor sports would be just as important on the intercollegiate scene as baseball and hockey. And although Camp treated the prediction as "kind of a joke," he was soon to stop laughing. For Moses refused to let the matter drop.

In editorials in the *Courant* and the *Yale Daily News,* Moses attacked with a directness unusual in college publications of the day. Pointing out that almost as many men participated in minor as in major sports, Moses accused Yale's "football managers"—a euphemism understood perfectly by the Yale community—of being "unjust" to "one-half of Yale athletics."

Camp let it be known that he was personally offended. The editorials continued. Dean "Baldy" Wright called Moses to his office for a friendly but pointed discussion. The editorials continued. And when Moses came up with a plan to create a Minor Sports Association that would hold a single fund-raising drive, raise $3,500, and, through an executive committee composed of the sports' managers, distribute it among the various teams according to their needs, the dean hastily gave the association permission to appeal to alumni for contributions, and also brought back word of a concession from Camp that was small but significant, coming from a man who had previously run Yale athletics without making any concessions at all: if the association raised $3,200, Camp's Athletic Union would contribute the other $300.

Persuading the minor sports to combine into one association, which meant turning over their finances to an outside body, proved almost as difficult as persuading Camp. Hockey and basketball, which were classed among these sports but were popular enough among students so that their managers could generally raise money by a door-to-door appeal on campus, were particularly reluctant. Yet because hockey and basketball were the only two of the minor sports in which there *was* much interest, their participation was essential.

Moses argued that even for hockey and basketball the existence of a formal association would make it much easier to obtain money from alumni and students who had treated as a joke the many separate appeals from the different minor sports. And the idealist also argued on higher grounds. In one editorial, he wrote: "As far as Basketball and Hockey are considered *per se,* they have nothing to gain. But . . . there must be a sacrifice on the part of the Basketball and Hockey teams *for the sake of common good. . . .*"

Hockey and basketball agreed to join. The other sports followed. On June 11, 1908, Moses was able to announce the formation of the Yale University Minor Sports Association.

With Moses organizing its fund drives, the association proved to be more vigorous than Camp had expected. When he realized the extent of its fund-raising efforts among alumni, traditional fountainhead of football funds, Moses was called in by Dean Wright and advised to be "calm and dignified." Any "undue pressure" on alumni, he was warned, would result in the withdrawal of the $300 offer. Moses promptly made the threat public in the *Courant* and announced that the fund-raising would continue.

Moses' friends—and men on campus who had previously hardly noticed him—were impressed by his courage. Sixty years after he graduated, one member of the swimming team could recall that "the report was that he and Camp had quite a go at it. We thought it was quite a thing." Moses' idealism began to be talked about widely in the class—and it was because of this that Ed Richards was all the more surprised when, on a day in January 1909, he climbed out of the pool after doing his laps and heard what Moses was suggesting about Og Reid.

"After I had accepted his resignation," Richards recalls, "he began to put pressure on me to take him back on the team and let him go ahead with his approach to Reid. He managed to work up an amazing amount of pressure. He really was very clever about it. He got the managers [of the other minor sports] to send a delegation to me to talk me out of it. I told them, 'No, it's not an honest way to treat Og Reid. He's always treated us very nicely.' Then Bob went to the man who was the heart and soul of swimming at Yale—Maxie Swartz. Maxie was really just the janitor at the pool, but he was a good old guy. He took a lot of interest in the swimmers, and he was always around the team. Bob got Maxie to ask me to take him back. He had Maxie tell me, 'Oh, Reid has plenty of money. He'll never miss a little of it.' But I talked it over with a few other guys on the team and they said I was right and I refused Maxie too."

Although Richards' firmness terminated Moses' connection with Yale athletics, his activity in more esoteric areas of campus life continued. His interest in art and poetry had made him a member of 1909's little clique of intellectuals and esthetes and, to some extent, he was becoming its leader. He was active on the *Courant*. He may not have been invited to join any of the more "important" clubs at Yale, but he became president of the one he did join, the Kit Cat Club, a new organization which was named after the group of convivial literary spirits who had surrounded Samuel Johnson and which included "Yale men who have shown literary ability and interest in literary subjects." During his senior year, he and a classmate published *Yale Verse,* an anthology of the best undergraduate poetry of the previous ten years.

Moses' academic work continued to be outstanding. A half century after he graduated, a professor said: "I well remember Robert Moses in my classes. He was alert, enthusiastic, very active, always doing 'A' work. . . . He was a model student. It is the energy of the man . . . and his very great intelligence that I remember most clearly. . . ." Seniors were awarded "Premiums," small cash awards established by alumni for outstanding work; Moses won a handful for math and English and Latin, in English composition for an essay on the "Mona Lisa," besides making Phi Beta Kappa.

Though Moses had lived alone during his first two years at Yale, in his last two he had roommates, as a senior Raymond P. McNulty and Elias "Five A" Johnson. "I didn't come to him," Johnson recalls. "He approached me and asked me to room with him. Of course I was glad to. We had been friendly before. But I think the fact that he approached me is an indication of a tendency I noticed in Bob; he selected his friends."

The friends Bob Moses selected were of a specific type: cultured, artistic, interested in the things he was interested in, many of them members of the tight little circle that included members of Kit Cat and the *Courant*. They included Malcolm T. Dougherty, who had already displayed the talent that was to make him a prominent painter of marine life, class poets like Bacon, Carl Thurston and Ed Proctor, and *Courant* and *Lit* contributors like James McConaughy, later Governor of Connecticut, and Harold Phelps Stokes, later chief editorial writer of the New York *Herald Tribune*.

Johnson, a very poor boy from Chicago attending Yale on a scholarship, was perhaps Moses' closest friend. He had already earned a reputation as the class "brain," and if Moses loved to read, "Five A" loved to study. Night after night, the two young men would retire immediately after supper to their living room in White Hall and stay at their desks until midnight or one or two o'clock in the morning, when they'd take long walks which usually ended at a little all-night luncheonette which served the turn-of-the-century equivalent of the late-evening hamburger—a heaping bowl of corn flakes and milk.

In honor of Johnson's slimness—he carried a hundred and twenty pounds on a five-foot seven-inch frame—Moses gave him a new nickname, "Slat." On weekends, he often took Slat home to the apartment Bella and Emanuel had rented in 1906 in a large apartment house at the corner of Central Park West and Seventieth Street, coming down to New York by train and across town from the station by horse-drawn streetcars. To while away time on the trips, the boys would play an early version of Twenty Questions, "Ask Me Another," but Johnson, despite his five "A's," confessed himself hopelessly outclassed. "Bob had the damnedest questions on art and poetry and what not through the ages," he would recall. "His reading was fantastic."

His circle of friends liked and admired Bob Moses. "He was always glad to see you," one says. "He really *liked* you—and you liked him." He might love to read, but he was certainly no "greasy grind." He enjoyed jokes—telling them and hearing them—and he had a quick, infectious laugh. Tall and strong, he enjoyed running and mountain climbing, once leading several friends to the top of Whiteface Mountain in the Adirondacks. He and Johnson might spend most evenings studying, but on some evenings they would walk along Chapel Street, where the "townies," New Haven girls who were not averse to meeting Yale boys, paraded, and Moses was notably successful at striking up conversations, much to the discomfort of the painfully shy Slat. "I remember that one night when we were reading, Bob suddenly jumped up and said, 'Come on, let's take a walk,' " Slat recalls. "We went down Chapel Street and there were a couple of girls ahead of us, and he made some kind of remark and they started laughing. I got afraid and went back to the room, but he walked off with them."

What his friends admired most was his idealism. Sometimes, it took rather odd forms. One night, he and the scrawny Johnson had an argument that escalated into a short but violent fight, and Moses showed no hesitation in knocking sprawling a man so much smaller than he. But once Johnson was down, Moses helped him up and, shaking his hand, congratulated him on his courage in fighting someone bigger and stronger. In discussions about campus life, however, Moses was more consistent. His appeals for true democracy at Yale continued. The argument about which fraternity's nominee should be given the class office was one example. Johnson was trying to convince a group of classmates of the right of his fraternity to the job, when Moses suddenly jumped up and, in Johnson's recollection, "bawled the living daylights out of me. He was saying things like 'What does the fraternity have to do with it? It should be on the basis of ability.' But it wasn't so much what he said as the way he said it. You could see he was speaking from the heart; you could see the honesty coming through in what he was saying. And all of a sudden, I was ashamed. Of course, I saw, he was right. Why *should* money or influence or who a guy's friends were matter?"

When bull-session discussions turned to careers after college, Moses said he was going to "go into public service." He didn't have any specific plans, and even talked occasionally of teaching government. But, more and more, his thinking seemed to his friends to be turning to a more active role. He wanted, he told them, to help the underprivileged, the lower classes, the people ground down by forces beyond their control. These phrases were not unusual ones among college seniors. But Moses' friends were impressed by the intensity, the evident, deep belief, with which he spoke them.

As Moses' acquaintance expanded, moreover, so did the admiration. When, during his senior year, his class held elections for the seven-member Senior Council, the winners were six fraternity men and Bob Moses, who, with fifty-nine votes, came in third.

Other barriers could not be breached, of course. As graduation neared, 1909 elected its socially prestigious Class Day Committees. Moses was elected to neither the Class Supper Committee, the Senior Prom Committee, the Cap and Gown Committee—nor to any of the sixteen other committees selected. By the time the class graduated, forty-five men were in the Senior Societies, one hundred in the Junior Fraternities, fifty-one in the Sophomore Societies—and Moses was not one of them. He never lived in Vanderbilt Hall. And to many of the men who did live in Vanderbilt and who did participate in the secret ceremonies of Skull and Bones or Wolf's Head, the honors that Robert Moses did achieve were unimportant. "Frankly," says one of them in accents ancestral, "I couldn't tell you what the Kit Cat Club *was. Or* the Senior Council." When 1909 voted for its outstanding members, Moses received only a few scattered votes as "Brightest," "Most Scholarly" and "Done Most for Yale." In the official Class History, which listed the rosters of clubs and committees and their outstanding members, his name hardly appeared at all.

But what was, perhaps, significant about Bob Moses and the Class History was not that his name appeared in it infrequently but that it appeared in it at all. His achievements at Yale might be dim beside those of the prep-school Episcopalian leaders of the secret societies, but they were bright indeed for a Jew. If in his first two years at Yale Bob Moses had been a lonely nobody, in his last two years he had become considerably more than that.

And the way in which he had become more was, in the light of his later career, even more significant. He became a campus figure partly, of course, because of the brilliance and idealism that were part of his inheritance. He displayed also, in his refusal to knuckle under to Walter Camp, his inherited stubbornness—and a considerable amount of real moral courage. But, in the light of his later career, what is most interesting is that when he realized that, because of the handicap of his religion, his brilliance and idealism would not take him to the top in the world of Yale, he made, within Yale, a world of his own, and a world, moreover, in which, in collegiate terms, he had power and influence.

He never went out for the *Lit* but he made himself an important member of the staff of a less prestigious publication. He never went out for a major sport but he was active in a minor one. He was never invited to join one of the better clubs but he was president of the lesser club he did join. And if he was not included in the more select social circles of the class, he created a circle of his own, a small coterie of persons with like interests, a coterie within which he was the acknowledged leader. The men in the coterie admired Bob Moses. The men he chose to be his friends were happy to be chosen.

Alongside the massive cathedrals of Yale's traditions, buttressed by prejudice and pride, Bob Moses had erected his own small but sturdy structure. "In our little world . . . ," Bacon was to say, "he made himself a position of power."

In the light of Moses' later career, that was the key point.

3. *Home Away from Home*

As a senior at Yale, Moses had decided to go on to Oxford. He had wanted to go as a Rhodes Scholar, but every third year the prestigious scholarships were not awarded, and 1909 was a third year.* Unwilling to wait until 1910—and with no financial need to—he paid his own way.

Asked in later years why he had chosen Oxford for his postgraduate work, Moses would shrug and say there had been no special reason. But his choice turned out to be an apt one. He was to find in Oxford a spiritual home.

The marriage of Bernhard Cohen and Rosalie Silverman had been a marriage of brilliant mind with brilliant mind—and of idealism, crystallized in a desire to improve the lives of the lower classes, with an overweening arrogance. The strain of brilliance, idealism and arrogance had surfaced in a daughter, Lady Bountiful, and had been passed on through her—undiluted, strong but somewhat formless—to her son Robert. Oxford, using the brilliance as catalyst, was to refine the other two ingredients in the strain. Two years among her spires and statue-crowned columns, her quadrangles and cloisters, her towers that had whispered to Matthew Arnold "the last enchantments of the Middle Ages," would boil the fattiness out of the idealism, rendering out of a vague desire to "help people" not only a clear, definable concept of public service but also a specific means of performing that service. Two years among her richly paneled halls, her ancestral tankards and inlaid croziers, among begowned processions led by bedels carrying silver staves and among gardens tended by a thousand gardeners would distill the arrogance, potent though it already was, and make it still more potent by adding to its essence a philosophical base, the British belief, firm indeed in the early twentieth century and epitomized in the trappings and teachings of Oxford, in the duties—and the rights—of those born to wealth and privilege.

Oxford in 1909 was the castle keep of British conservatism. The key to its ancient gates was wealth; in the year Robert Moses entered Oxford's Wadham College, the university was largely closed to the student whose family was not rich. Conservatism characterized the attitude of its students—including the ninety Americans among them. When, three months after Moses' arrival, an American Club was organized, its first meeting featured two speakers who said, respectively, "We are as much interested as anyone

* The system was changed in 1916.

in preserving Oxford as a home of English conservatism and tradition" and "We should carry into the bustle and stir of the New World, the atmosphere of the Old."

As strong as Oxford's conservatism was its emphasis on public service. Its tone in 1909 had been set for the preceding three centuries by rich young men who were sent to the university as a preliminary to public life and who, from positions in Parliament or the civil service or the learned professions, actually did, after graduation, govern Britain and its vast territories overseas. But the leavening of devotion to public service with an unabashed insistence on the rights and privileges of aristocracy could not help but make that devotion somewhat patronizing, infusing it with a strong air of condescension and *noblesse oblige* in its most obnoxious form. It was a refined, more subtle but also more deeply rooted version of the attitude of the German Jews of New York toward the Russian and Polish late-comers, of Bella toward the children whose parents didn't even know how to bring them up so they would be able properly to clean the cabins Madison House had been kind enough to build for them.

Bella's son was very happy at Oxford. His most frequent companion was Mal Dougherty, his friend from Yale, who was also studying at Wadham. "Bob had a very good time at Oxford," Dougherty recalls. "He liked it very much. It was such a relief after Yale. Yale had that pseudo-democracy, but it was not democratic at all; it was snooty, with all that social tradition. When we got to Oxford, we found all this changed. It was understood by everyone there that by the very fact that you belonged to Oxford, you were the select and the elect. You didn't have to compete for prestige or honors to become one of the elite. Because you were there, you *were* the elite." Moses' understanding of this fact—and his acceptance of it—shone through an article he sent to the *Yale Alumni Weekly*. "There is a moribund institution for workingmen's sons somewhere in Oxford," he sneered. "I have never yet met an undergraduate who knew its exact location, nor have I met anyone who did not become incoherent with rage when it was defended."

Moses liked the gentleman's life that Oxford offered. Breakfast, lunch and tea were served in the students' rooms, and they were encouraged to entertain friends—of whom Moses had plenty. Says one classmate, "Bob was almost universally loved." The first American in history to be elected captain of the Dark Blue water-polo team, he was also swimming captain, although, as at Yale, if he ever won a race, the victory went unrecorded. Taking up debating, he became the first American ever to be elected president of the august Oxford Union, that hardiest of debating clubs.

Oxford's exemption of students from all marks and tests except for a single, all-inclusive examination given after two years appealed to the student who even at Yale had refused to be bound by the confines of his courses. "The Oxford education . . . confers on the average undergraduate independence of mind," he wrote in the *Alumni Weekly*.

Vacations were an especially happy time. Moses and Dougherty spent their "vacs" on walking tours of England or traveling abroad, often with

Moses' roommate, John Gilbert Higgins, a Rhodes Scholar from Newfoundland who sported a long knitted scarf and a thick Irish brogue.

In Switzerland, the youths tried out a sport that was just beginning to attract the attention of American tourists: skiing. In Italy, Moses saw again the frescoes and statues he had loved as an undergraduate and spent hours being gondolaed around Venice, a city with which he had fallen in love. Every summer, his family would sail to Europe and take a large suite of rooms in a hotel overlooking the Lake of Lucerne. There, Moses and Dougherty played tennis, swam and climbed mountains.

In 1911, a Rhodes Scholar named El Allail, the son of an Egyptian bey, invited Moses and Dougherty to visit Egypt. Crossing the Mediterranean on a leaky, shuddering tub named the *Equator,* the youths found themselves in the company of hundreds of Levantine natives and a troupe of women Dougherty describes as "international tarts sailing for the winter season in Cairo and Alexandria." On the first night out of Marseilles, the *Equator*'s captain selected one, disappeared with her into his cabin—and remained there for the rest of the four-day voyage. The same procedure was followed by every other officer except an aged quartermaster. The engines broke down —along with the latrines. But when the ship—and its attendant aroma—arrived at Alexandria, El Allail ensconced Moses and Dougherty in luxury. The three youths spent the days swimming on a magnificent beach at the mouth of the easternmost branch of the Nile and evenings chatting over dinner with the highest British colonial and native Egyptian officials, including the Khedive of Egypt. The Khedive must have been impressed with Moses; he asked him to be his secretary.

The mark of Oxford's influence would be plain on Robert Moses for the rest of his life.

Oxonians habitually wore "bags," old flannel trousers so long unpressed that they were completely shapeless, and sweaters or heavy tweed jackets. The academic gowns required for lectures were often worn along with bedroom slippers. Moses, who had always been exceptionally neat in dress before Oxford, would return to New York affecting a carelessness about attire that at times went to extremes. Insisting he needed only one suit, he would wear it until it was shiny. He had only one pair of shoes, which he never shined; returning home on a rainy day, he would sit in front of the fire in the Moseses' luxurious living room, holding his feet close to the flames, making a point of telling friends that he couldn't go out again until his shoes had dried because he didn't have another pair. He obtained new underwear and socks only when his mother bought them for him. After his marriage, his wife would take over this chore and, since he refused to go to clothing stores at all, would select suits herself, have them brought to their apartment and arrange for a tailor to come and fit them there.

And if Moses was to return from Oxford with a somewhat studied indifference toward clothes, he was to display the same attitude toward money, an attitude which some friends felt, from remarks that Moses made, was an attempt to imitate the scions of British nobility he met at Oxford who never thought of money because they had no need to. His family first saw this attitude on board the luxury liner *Potsdammer* in the harbor at Southampton, where they had just picked up Robert before going on to Lucerne. When Emanuel began to tell his son about money that had been deposited for his Oxford expenses in a London bank account, Robert, who previously had had a normal college boy's interest in his allowance, said loftily, "I don't want to talk about things like that." The affectation that may have underlain this attitude is suggested by another trait that became apparent at Oxford: a seeming compulsion to pick up checks, to be the host at every gathering. Dougherty, who was not in need of subsidy, recalls: "If you went anywhere with Bob—to lunch or dinner or to have a drink—he'd grab the check and just *insist* on paying it. It got so people felt a little annoyed. But if you grabbed one first, you'd have to have sort of a squabble with him about it."

Oxford was also influencing the young man on more significant levels. In long letters to his parents, he said that he had definitely decided to dedicate his life to public service. On his return to the United States, he said, he would make a career in government. He even had his field picked out; he intended to become an expert on the renowned British civil service so that he could inculcate its principles in America. Government pay might not be high, he said, but he didn't care about money. Bella Moses read the letters to relatives with approval.

And while Oxford was refining and strengthening Moses' idealism, it was having the same effect on his arrogance, which, increasingly took the form of galloping Anglophilia. Moses' admiration for things Oxonian broadened into an admiration—strikingly deep—for all things British. Coupled with this feeling was one almost of scorn for things American. Writing to the *Yale Alumni Weekly* in praise of the single-examination Oxford system of education, he went beyond the praise to say: "I hesitate to imagine the introduction of such a scheme in the United States, where intellectual independence is safeguarded by daily recitations . . ."

There was another overtone, too. Under the influence of Oxford's conservative insistence on the rightness of the British system's provisions for keeping the reins of government in the hands of a highly educated upper class, Moses came more and more to admire that system. Such admiration, of course, postulated as a concomitant an amiable contempt for the capability for government found in members of the "lower" classes—which in this context included everyone not a member of the British nobility. And from this attitude, it was a logical step to reserve supreme contempt for those whom the British aristocracy considered most incapable of self-rule—the people of the nations British troops had conquered, which meant, in general, people of color, brown, yellow or black.

Moses took this step.

With agitation for increased self-government rising in Great Britain's colonies, Oxford in 1911 sponsored a World Congress on Race Problems to examine the question—along with the broader question of general discrimination by Great Britain against colored people. Delegations were sent by the colonies and by liberal organizations from many European countries. American students selected Moses to represent their country because of his reputation as a debater.

Previous speakers had pleaded for equality, for fraternity, for "immediate brotherhood." Moses' point of view was somewhat different. Immediate brotherhood, he said flatly, was "not practical." The "subject peoples" of the British Empire were simply not ready for self-government yet. Furthermore, he didn't see any time in the near future when they would be.

As the audience realized what they were hearing, a certain restiveness began to develop. When Moses started explaining—quite clearly—*why* he didn't think the "subject peoples" would be ready for self-government for a long time, several subject people rose and charged at him. One step ahead of them was roommate Higgins. He grabbed Moses, shoved him through a door at the back of the speakers' platform, and hustled him out of the building.

The climax of Moses' academic career was the thesis he submitted for a Ph.D. degree: *The Civil Service of Great Britain.*

The thesis contained no "torch divine o'erhead." The floridness of Moses' Yale poetry and prose style had turned hard, cogent and marvelously lucid at Oxford. Short, hard sentences must have carried his professors through the intricacies of parliamentary in-fighting and regulation rewriting with refreshing ease. He displayed not only a complete familiarity with a bewildering array of bureaucratic technicalities but a gift for the felicitous phrase. Describing Carlyle's appeal to Parliament to muck out the "Augean stables of bureaucracy," Moses wrote that Carlyle appealed with "excremental eloquence." Macaulay's speech on the need for promotion by merit was, he said, "the most masterly vindication of the principles of competition ever left unanswered."

Not only Moses' prose style but what was behind the style had hardened, too. The all-too-conscious revelation in the thesis's pages of what the British civil service symbolized to Robert Moses demonstrated that two years of Oxford had solidified the cast of mind formed in the mold of heredity and upbringing. The youth who had been raised in an atmosphere pervaded by a mixture of idealism and arrogance had found the rationale for such *noblesse oblige* in the British theory of the rights and duties of the upper classes; the thesis with which he laid the capstone of his education focused down on the British civil service as the embodiment of this attitude, the practical result of this theory. And he saw the result as glorious.

The thesis reveals its author as a man convinced that public service is a noble calling and one that must be based on the highest ideals. Moses did not believe that the "perfection" of the British civil service system was an end in itself. Rather, he saw it as an instrument, an indispensable one, for the implementation of great social reforms. Progressive nations, he wrote, had begun creating new departments of government to free mankind from the traditional horrors of old age, disease and unemployment. "These new departments," he said, "must have leaders and a personnel" with outstanding qualifications if they are to fulfill their noble purpose. His idealism is further documented by his admiration, an admiration that approached idolatry, for the uncompromising reformers—Trevelyan, Northcote, "the genius" Macaulay—who had fought to make the civil service system equal to the new demands, and by the vehemence, the sincere, deep passion, of the phrases with which he described the patronage system that had been the reformers' chief obstacle.

Quoting descriptions of the incompetents whom patronage foisted upon the service, he cited a report which concluded, "Patronage is the worst form of bribery," and concurred—with feeling. "The incessant demands of office-seekers, and the contemptible meanness and petty irritations attendant on a distribution of favors," are, he said, "intolerable." Merit, "open competition," Moses said again and again, should be the sole basis of appointment and promotion in public life.

Mingled with the idealism, of course, was the arrogance. It was subordinate to the idealism; if the idealism was displayed in Moses' convictions about what should be done, the arrogance emerged only in his convictions as to who was best suited to do it. But it was every bit as pure and uncompromising. *The Civil Service of Great Britain* reveals its author as the possessor of a depth of class feeling and conservatism more appropriate to a retired Colonel of the Guards than a young progressive from New York City. "Open competition" may be what the young author said he wanted—but the openness was to certain individuals only. "Merit" may be the determinant he said he desired, but it was not merit based on a man's handling of his job. The competition Moses wanted was a competition open only to a highly educated upper class. The merit he was talking about was merit not in public service but in the education given exclusively to members of that class.

What Moses admired in the British civil service was that it had two separate and distinct classes: a very small administrative and policy-making "upper division" reserved for "university men," and a much larger "lower division" consisting of "clerks of ordinary education" selected through examinations on the high-school level who "do the lower and more mechanical work." The class differentiation that Moses admired was a rigid one. Carefully placed technical hurdles made it difficult, almost impossible, for a young man, even one of dedication, industry, ambition and talent, to rise out of the lower division.

"Brilliant," Moses called this setup. "Far-sighted." It attracts into public service precisely the men most needed there, "the most intelligent and capable young men in universities," he said. And it keeps them in government by reserving for them posts from which they can exert real influence and authority.*

* With criticisms of the system Moses had little patience. "The question of admitting natives to the Indian service comes up now and again, but it can hardly be said to be

Was there, perhaps, a question as to the democracy of such a system? Moses' answer was that a civil service with no class differentiation is "one of mediocrity" and "such democracy is false democracy." What about the young man who educates himself, who goes to night school, perhaps, and earns a college degree while he is in the lower division of the civil service? Might not he be considered fit for promotion? Well, Moses said,

> [My] conclusions on this difficult question of democracy versus education in the civil service are these:
>
> In a sense it is a cruel thing to set up class distinctions—even if they only be intellectual . . .
>
> But where does our sympathy lead us? Can the state repair the defects of heredity or of early education? Can it endow the average individual with the intelligence, acuteness and cultivation which economic exigencies have denied him? . . .
>
> There should be no social bar to promotion from the lowest to the highest place—but let us not fool ourselves. When we have made every possible provision for the encouragement of early promise, when we have prepared every child as far as possible for its suitable vocation, the subordinate employees of the government . . . who are fit to rise above the ranks will be few and far between.

As for recent complaints of the lower-class civil servants about wage scales and working conditions, Moses said there was no need to worry about those subjects:

> The writer believes—in spite of Mr. Walling and his socialistic brethren—that the civil servant may safely depend upon the public parliamentary recognition of the justice of his cause, upon the fairness of the Treasury or a minister . . . and upon royal commissions . . . to get real grievances redressed and reasonable demands granted.

What was of more concern to "the writer," in fact, was that the lower-class workers might not understand this and might continue agitating—might, in fact, even form *unions!* Hopefully, a sense of loyalty would stop the workers short of such an act of open rebellion, but if this should not be the case, Moses said, "in the last analysis," there must be "the remorseless exercise of the executive power of suppression and dismissal to solve this question."

The last chapter of Moses' thesis is a plea to his own country to adopt the British system for its own civil service. The chapter is pervaded by contempt for the standards of government service in the United States, where "spoilsmen" and job-hungry politicians lurk everywhere, and "we have been so busy fighting for a full realization of the competitive principle . . . that the great problems of division, of intellectual qualifications . . . and attracting the best men into our government departments have been quite neglected," so that government is staffed by "a very miscellaneous and often ill-educated

---

acute," he said. "Few care to make the trip to England." The suggestion that examinations be held also in India has "been voted down thus far," he noted, and this is "fortunate." "There are as many places open to them now as they are reasonably capable of filling."

division of clerks." Patronage must be eliminated and an upper division created immediately, he said.

To follow Moses' suggestions, the United States would have had to close almost completely the higher ranks of government service not only to all men without a college degree but to all men without a degree from an Ivy League college. In fact, by logical extension of Moses' philosophy, graduates of Columbia, Cornell, Brown, Dartmouth and Penn would be allowed in those higher ranks only by sufferance; in his view, government in America should be ruled, as was football at the time, by men whose birth and breeding had allowed them to attend one of three colleges—Princeton, Harvard or, of course, Yale.

Moses said in his thesis that he feared that America's acceptance of this suggestion would be delayed by its exaggerated concern for equality. Most men are simply incapable of handling the demands of government service, Moses said, and the time has come for Americans to realize it. "We must decide," the young author said, "how much encouragement we may honestly offer to those who expect to rise from the ranks without the almost essential early education of the university man." Moses saw only one real hope for his country—the fact that a man who met his highest standards, Woodrow Wilson of Princeton, had just been elected President. Wilson's writings, Moses felt, "show not only a clear understanding of the defects of our . . . civil service, but also a keen realization of the executive leadership necessary to remedy them."

Moses had begun the thesis after graduation—with honors—from Oxford in June 1911. After a last summer in Lucerne, he spent the fall of 1911 doing research in London. Then he spent a term studying political science at the University of Berlin. Returning to New York in the summer of 1912, he moved back into his old room on Central Park West—it was the height of his one-suit, one-pair-of-shoes period, but Bella at least made sure that the suit was an expensive white tropical from Brooks Brothers—and began writing. He enrolled in Columbia University's School of Political Science, but took no courses formally, spending most of his time on the thesis, which he completed in the summer of 1913. As soon as he finished it, and even before he took the oral examinations for the Columbia Ph.D. he was to receive, he entered public service by getting a job with the Training School for Public Service of the Bureau of Municipal Research, a private fact-finding organization located in an office building at 261 Broadway, which was about to become a virtual arm of the city government.

Robert Moses' education was over. He was beginning the career in public service about which he so often had talked with so passionate an idealism. The quadrangles of Oxford were behind him. Instead of cloisters, there would be the arena. And one day in the summer of 1913, dressed in his clean white suit, Robert Moses carried his bright, shining idealism down to 261 Broadway and flung it on the table to find out what it was worth in the game of life.

II

THE REFORMER

4. *Burning*

IT MUST HAVE SEEMED like a great time to be young and a reformer in New York. In all American history, in fact, it would have been hard to find a better time. The young idealist entered public service in the very year in which there came to crest a movement—Progressivism—that was based, to an extent greater perhaps than any other nationally successful American political movement, on an idealistic belief in man's capacity to better himself through the democratic process.

An outgrowth of the agrarian Populist crusade of the 1880's and 1890's, the Progressive movement had been swelled before the turn of the century by the enrollment of America's urban middle class, its conscience awakened by Lincoln Steffens, Jacob Riis and other muckrakers who dramatized the poverty of the slums, and by the testimony of its own eyes, which could see all too well—in the horrors of child labor and the sweatshop—the problems that flowed from the new industrial order. In searching for the causes of these problems, Progressives settled on the most easily identifiable—the giant corporations and corrupt political bosses who they felt had stolen mythical America away from its people. To exorcise these demons—to force a return to the political democracy and economic individualism that Americans were fond of believing had once existed in their country—they advocated reforms equally simplistic, so simplistic, in fact, that they proved primarily that the old American impulse to do good was still intact. And they were reforms that a young man who wanted to do good, a young man like Bob Moses, could advocate with all his heart. One of the major demands of Progressivism was one that he himself had called for in his Ph.D. thesis: removal of the spoils system from the federal civil service. And if, in the thesis, he had discussed the need for great new departments of government to combat the excesses of industrialism, more and more the reformers were coming to demand intervention by government, the only St. George hefty enough to slay dragons of the size being bred in America. In 1913, the cheers for Wilson's "New Freedom" reform program were ringing from virtually every corner of the country except the bastions of privilege. In the statehouses, it was the era of Altgeld of Illinois, of Pingree of Michigan, of Charles Evans Hughes, exposer of corruption in New York's large insurance companies, and of Robert Marion La Follette, who broke the power of the railroads in Wisconsin and sponsored laws limiting working hours for women and children. It was the very height of an era of optimism and hope for America.

As the time was right for Bob Moses, so, seemingly, was the place. If there was an epicenter of the idealism that was rolling across America, it was the ninth floor of 261 Broadway. The impulse to do good may have been rampant beneath the domes of statehouses and the national capitol, but it reached its zenith in city halls. Perhaps this was because in cities corruption was more visible than in federal politics, issues more succinctly dramatized. Or perhaps it was because the reforming impulse thrived on problems, and it was in the cities, swelling with the immigrant tide, faced with problems of housing, schooling, policing, fire protection, traffic regulation and sewage disposal on a new scale, that America's problems were beginning to loom largest.

Unlike European cities, which also mushroomed in the Industrial Age but which had been built atop previous centuries' strong administrative foundations, America's had sprung into gianthood relatively overnight, often organized around nothing but the factory or the mill, and had no such tested governmental framework. What framework they did have was undermined by blatant corruption, their governments controlled by private interests and by political bosses who, with their Christmas baskets and everything the baskets symbolized, marshaled hundreds of thousands of ignorant voters into vast, seemingly impregnable political machines. "With very few exceptions," asserted historian Andrew D. White, "the city governments of the United States are the worst in Christendom—the most expensive, the most inefficient, and the most corrupt."

To combat these conditions, reform movements sprang up in almost every large city in the United States—and in no city was Progressivism more vigorous than in New York. In New York, its spearhead was the Bureau of Municipal Research. To many observers, in fact, the Bureau was the spearhead of municipal reform not only in New York but throughout the United States; historian Charles A. Beard was later to conclude that its methods constituted "nothing short of a revolution in the . . . approach to such matters."

The three young men who had founded the Bureau in 1907—William H. Allen, Henry Bruère and Frederick A. Cleveland—believed, as did the city's older reformers who had backed them financially, that the growth of forces which had diminished the individual's control over his own destiny had made it incumbent on government to ride to his rescue with increased welfare services. But this trio—known among reformers as "the ABC"—added to the reform ethos new elements derived from two other passions of the era, natural science and scientific management. The emphasis of natural science on empiricism, on firsthand observation, on the obtaining of facts, led them to conclude that it was vain to talk about changing the philosophy of government before learning the facts of government, and they said therefore that the first step toward reform should be analysis of government operations. From scientific management—the age was marveling at the assembly-line techniques introduced by Henry Ford—they concluded that after government operations had been analyzed, the next step should be not a change in philosophy but an improvement in such operations to make them "efficient" and "economic," to insure that the city would get far more for each dollar spent than in the past, and would therefore be financially more able to do what the voters desired.

Their philosophy, seemingly so elementary, was new in 1907. Previously, in New York and in all American cities, reform crusades had been of the "throw the rascals out" variety; stung to fury by particularly blatant corruption, "Good Government" elements would rise up, oust the reigning political bosses and seat in the mayor's chair a hero who they hoped would "save" the city. But salvation was invariably denied because the administrative systems of cities were so chaotic that change in the direction of government was all but impossible. "Budget," for example, was only a dictionary word; in turn-of-the-century America, not a single city possessed one. Allocating money with reference to the total amount available and to the relative urgency of the needs of the various city departments was therefore impossible. Scientific accounting techniques, only recently incorporated into American business, had never been adapted to government, so departmental requests for appropriations were not itemized and therefore items could not be compared with comparable expenditures in the past. In New York, for example, the Board of Estimate made appropriations without even checking to see if there was, or would be, sufficient money available in the city's treasury to cover them; if money ran out, the Board simply issued revenue bonds to make up the difference. Departmental requests to the Board were lump-sum requests which showed in only the most general way how the departments proposed to spend the money they were asking for. Unable to analyze these requests, the Board simply cut each by the same, predetermined percentage, a procedure which some departments circumvented by requesting five times as much money as they really needed.

Given such administrative chaos, the careers of the reform heroes were predictable. In city after city, they failed to make an appreciable dent in municipal problems and, after a term or two, the rascals they had thrown out were back in. In New York, where the businessmen reformers of the Citizens Union had thrust Columbia University President Seth Low into the mayoralty in 1902, Tammany had taken back City Hall in 1904. Said Bruère: "There was the constant futile search for the great administrator, great by instinct and personality. He wasn't found because he doesn't exist. A great administrator needs the tools and techniques of sound administration." The search, he said, "should not be so much for good men as for these good tools and techniques; the idea should be not so much to jail the grafters as to install [in government] business systems which will make grafting difficult." Before government could become humanitarian, he said, it must become businesslike.

The city's businessmen listened to the ABC and put up the money so they could go to work.

Confident that if the citizenry only knew the facts about government it would take the right steps, the three young men decided first to determine and disseminate such facts. Momentarily stymied by the refusal of notoriously corrupt Manhattan Borough President John F. Ahearn to show them his records, they began to check records that could not be hidden—the construction contract specifications that borough presidents were required by law to publish in newspapers—to see if the specifications were being followed. Construction workers began to notice the presence of young men in high collars, vests and bowler hats who spent whole days performing such inexplicable maneuvers as counting bags of cement. When the count was finished, the young men had discovered—and proved—that the city had, in collusion with favored contractors, paid for hundreds of thousands of dollars of supplies—supplies such as bags of cement—that had never been delivered. The Bureau of Municipal Research published its first report, *How Manhattan Is Governed.*

In the time-honored ploy of politicians whose party is in power, Ahearn demanded an official investigation, assuming that it would be conducted by Tammany faithful. Unknown to him, however, Mayor George B. McClellan, Jr., had just decided to break with Tammany. McClellan gave Ahearn the investigation he had asked for—but the man appointed to conduct it was an independent twenty-eight-year-old Yale graduate and lawyer, John Purroy Mitchel. Mitchel confirmed the Bureau's findings. City Club President George McAneny, ignoring Tammany pressures on his business, volunteered to deliver Mitchel's report personally to Governor Hughes with his own endorsement, and Hughes summoned Ahearn to public hearings in Albany. At the hearings, Ahearn said he didn't know anything about the contracts; Hughes said he should have—and removed him from office. As the businessmen reformers hastily established a fund to make the Bureau a permanent institution, the ABC started counting bags of cement in the Bronx and Queens—a mathematical exercise which would result in the removal from office of the presidents of both those boroughs.

The offices of the Bureau were filled with excitement; the ABC, young themselves, gathered around them a group of recent university graduates determined to reform municipal government. They had a sense of mission; one, writing a history of the Bureau, said there was in it "not a little romance." Said another: "The men in training were looking for adventure—and most of them found it."

The young men developed techniques that were to reform every aspect of municipal government and create "a new literature on the science of public administration." They devised the first budget used by any municipal governmental unit, a primitive model employed by the New York City Health Department in 1908. They invented line-by-line itemization to eliminate lump-sum budget requests, and organization charts similar to those coming into use in business to make responsibility easier for voters to pinpoint. When enthusiastic press support forced the Board of Estimate to adopt the Bureau's innovations, city departments, for the first time, had to show what they had spent money for in the past year and which items they wanted increases for—and, for the first time, citizens could understand and could judge a department's record. Tammany Hall called it the "Bureau of Municipal Besmirch"—but its exposés led to the election in 1909 of anti-Tammany reformer William J. Gaynor as mayor. And when reformers McAneny and William A. Prendergast were elected to borough presidencies, they reorganized their offices along lines the Bureau suggested.

In 1911, the Bureau founded its Training School for Public Service, the first educational institution in the United States dedicated solely to preparing young men for work in government. The young idealists of the era of optimism saw in it a chance to obtain training in a field in which their idealism could most easily be translated into effective action. By 1913, there were hundreds of applicants for its handful of places.

Bob Moses was one applicant for whom a place was waiting, since his mother was a cousin of one of the Bureau's trustees, Columbia professor Edwin R. A. Seligman, and a friend of several others. When he finished his thesis, he was allowed to enroll immediately, was told to share one of the tables that served as desks with a student named Meador and was taken on the tour of City Hall that was the students' introduction to municipal government.

In theory—even his own theory—Moses should have been happy at the Bureau. With its concentration on the improvement of the mechanics of government, it was, after all, addressing itself to concerns that he had expressed in his thesis. The admission policy of the Training School, moreover, answered the main demand of the thesis: the need for "university men" in public service. Only applicants of the most impeccable scholastic background were accepted.

Moses understood this. In his thesis, he had written that the Bureau and its Training School were "the system of the future in American cities."

But once he became part of the Training School, it didn't take Moses long to decide that the system of the future wasn't going to be *his* future. In the field of public administration, the Training School was unique in its down-to-earth practicality. Pupils not only were put through intensive reading courses on the theory of budget making, accountancy, scientific management, chart making and the use of forms, summaries and statements, but also spent long days in city offices watching budgets actually being made up and did their scientific management homework sitting in city offices trying to figure out ways to eliminate unnecessary personnel and analyzing projects the city was undertaking, to see if they were really needed. They did the legwork for the Bureau members who were heading the investigations which would result in exposure of corruption or waste in city government.

The students were filled with an *esprit* so strong that it seemed sometimes as if it must surely waft out the windows of 261 Broadway and melt some of the soot from the blackened granite of the Tweed Courthouse below. They believed in the importance of what they were doing; a half century later, rheumy eyes would light up and smiles would curl corners of wrinkled lips as they talked about it, and they talked in terms old soldiers reserve for old battles. "How would I sum up what we were doing?" one would say. "We were fighting to make democracy work, that's what we were doing!" They were very proud of their position in the army of idealism. They idolized their leaders; Allen, Bruère and Cleveland, they knew, were the very men who had charged through a hail of public abuse and private threats to pull down three Tammany chieftains. Who knew what victories over corruption might not be won through the use of the information they were collecting in their daily reconnaissance through the files of City Hall? Watching John Purroy Mitchel stride by their tables to confer with his friend Bruère, they whispered to one another that they hoped the young lawyer would decide to accept the Fusion nomination for mayor. The ninth floor bubbled with excitement. "You couldn't walk in there without getting an assignment," recalls one Training School student. "You'd open the door and someone would yell, 'Hey! Glad to see you! Get up a memorandum on this!' And you'd go back out the door and over to City Hall without even taking your hat off."

For a while Moses seemed at home in this atmosphere. He did the legwork, wrote the memos, joined the other Training School students for twenty-cent lunches at Childs and for their one big splurge of the week, a six-course Sunday dinner at Lüchow's, which might cost as much as $1.25. He didn't interrupt, as they didn't interrupt, when one of the older Bureau staffers was telling again the story of how everybody in the Bureau had jumped to his feet and cheered on the day that a reporter brought the news that Governor Hughes had just announced that the charges against Ahearn merited a public hearing.

At first, he was very popular with the other students. He was pleasant and friendly and had a gift for putting people at ease. Many of the students admired Moses. Those from midwestern universities were new to New York and slightly awed by the big city. Moses obviously knew his way around. Moreover, most of them were struggling along on students' allowances, and they knew he came from a wealthy family; they were thinking about what they were going to do after graduation from the Training School, and they knew Moses would be able to choose his job without regard for financial considerations. In the late afternoons, when they were all heading for the subway for the ride home, they watched him grab a taxicab. Occasionally, they might be talking about an opera they had seen the night before, having been lucky enough to secure standing-room tickets, and they would ask Moses if he had seen it. Oh yes, he would say, his family had a box. But the young idealists admired Moses most for his education. It wasn't just that he had been to Yale; the world's principal centers of education for public service were Oxford and the University of Berlin, and Moses had studied at both. Now he was attending the most advanced school for public administration in the United States; one of his friends wondered, quite seriously, whether Bob Moses was not the man best educated in public administration in the whole country.

Within a few months, however, the students began to notice another quality in Moses, a quality which became more apparent almost day by day. Blazing behind the big gray eyes, they now saw, was a furious impatience. Within months after entering the Training School, Moses made clear that he felt he had learned all it had to offer. He was irritated by the report cards, by the weekly conferences with his Bureau advisers, by all the aspects of school life that made him remember that it was a school and that he was still, at the age of twenty-five, a student.

In particular, he resented the legwork. The Training School men were required to summarize the results of their investigations in memos that had to be written as if they were official Bureau reports but that would actually be seen only by the Bureau men who were writing the real reports that would be published. Moses wanted *his* memos published. He began to press for admission to the Bureau itself, making clear that, because he had an allowance from his mother, he would require no salary; within a year, on that financial basis, he was admitted; his student days were over.

The impatience was not slaked. No sooner was he in the Bureau than he began to make cutting comments about its procedures: the voluminous filing and cross-filing of all information was a waste of time, he said; the weekly staff luncheons were a waste of time; the Bureau's constant emphasis on procedure was a waste of time. The Bureau wasn't "getting enough done," he said. But it was becoming apparent to many of his colleagues that the Bureau would never be able to get enough done to satisfy Moses, no matter how many "technicalities" it dispensed with, simply because the Bureau was merely an agency that investigated and advised government. The way to get things done, Moses was making clear, was to be *in* government. Through Bella, he had a nodding acquaintance with several members of Mayor Gaynor's administration; he began to neglect his work at the Bureau and spend more and more time at City Hall hanging around their offices. His colleagues began to whisper about Bob Moses. The slang of the era contained a phrase that described what they thought he was doing. He was, they whispered, "pushing his acquaintance" at City Hall. There was an adjective heard frequently in the whispers, too. The adjective was "ambitious." Bob Moses, the idealists of the Bureau said, was interested—much too interested—in making a name for himself.

But if there was ambition, that was only a part of what was driving Bob Moses. And the whisperers never saw the other part. For they never saw what Moses did in the late afternoons after he grabbed the taxicabs.

Sometimes, of course, Moses would tell the cab driver to take him straight home. But often he would ask to be dropped off across the West Side, on Riverside Drive, at the end of Seventy-sixth Street near the Hudson River. And as he climbed out of the cab there, he climbed out into a scene far different from the doormanned serenity of Central Park West.

He would be standing on the high bluff that was Riverside Drive; behind him, if he looked up, stately apartment houses would appear to be swaying over him against a backdrop of moving clouds. But he would be looking down. Below him, along the edge of the river, was a wasteland, a wasteland six miles long, stretching from where he stood all the way north to 181st Street. The wasteland was named Riverside Park, but the "park" was nothing but a vast low-lying mass of dirt and mud. Running through its length was the four-track bed of the New York Central, which lay in a right-of-way that had been turned over to the railroad by the city half a century before. Unpainted, rusting, jagged wire fences along the tracks barred the city from its waterfront; in the whole six miles, there were exactly three bridges on which the tracks could be crossed, and they led only to private boating clubs.

The engines that pulled trains along the tracks burned coal or oil; from their smokestacks a dense black smog rose toward the apartment houses, coating windowsills with grit. The smog had an acrid odor, but people who lived in the apartments hardly noticed it; it was scarcely worth mentioning alongside the stench that seemed to hang over Riverside Drive endlessly after each passage of a train carrying south to the slaughterhouses in downtown Manhattan carload after carload of cattle and pigs. When, despite the smell, Riverside Drive residents were driven by the heat to open their windows, they were kept awake at night by the clank of the couplings which hooked the cars together.

Walking in the park was adventure; the walker sank at intervals into the landfill of which it had been constructed, for water had eaten away much of the fill from below. In many spots, it had broken through the crust of the fill to form little lakes. Every year the park grew smaller, as its edge crumbled into the river.

Areas that were still solid had been appropriated by the railroad for wood-lined pits in which coal was piled. Lying along the river were heaps of rotting timbers, stored years before by some city department and forgotten. At Seventy-ninth and Ninety-sixth streets, untreated garbage mounded toward the sky; the Sanitation Department used those areas as dumping grounds from which the garbage was transferred to scows which towed it out to the open sea, but somehow the rate of transfer was never fast enough to clear the refuse away entirely. Other solid spots held human refuse: derelicts who had built tar-paper shanty towns considered so dangerous that the police stayed away from them. At night, the open fires over which the derelicts cooked flickered in the darkness below the Drive.

Looking south, Moses could see the bluff sink and the park narrow until both disappeared, and houses, factories and warehouses crowded close to the waterfront. The railroad tracks wended their way between the buildings, making several sharp curves, and then emerged on Eleventh Avenue, along which, at street level, trains inched their way in a straight line down to the foot of the island. In front of every train, to warn away pedestrians and drivers, rode a cowboy on a horse, waving a large red flag. Since the trains came at frequent intervals and moved extremely slowly along the avenue, traffic was frequently backed up for blocks. Often, a driver would become impatient and ignore the warning flag. For that reason, Eleventh had become known as "Death Avenue." For years, the city had tried without success to find a solution to the problem posed by the presence of the railroad along the West Side.

In the late afternoons, as the sun sank toward the Palisades across the Hudson, Bob Moses walked along Riverside Drive. He walked down the steep paths to the park, over one of the bridges across the tracks and, skirting the dirty tar-paper shacks, along the edge of the clean blue river. And as he walked, he dreamed. One Sunday in 1914, he was crossing the Hudson by ferry to picnic in New Jersey. With him were some college friends and their dates, one of whom was Frances Perkins, later to be United States Secretary of Labor. As the ferry pulled out into the river, Moses leaned on the rail, watching Manhattan spread out behind the boat. Miss Perkins happened to be standing beside him and suddenly she heard Moses exclaim, "Isn't this a temptation to you? Couldn't this waterfront be the most beautiful thing in the world?" As the woman looked at him in astonishment, words began to pour out of Bob Moses and she realized that "he had it all figured out. How you could build a great highway that went uptown along the water. How you'd have to tear down a few buildings at Seventy-second Street and bring the highway around a curve. . . . He wanted places where people could leave their boats safely, public clubs . . . like private clubs." Staring back at the bleak mud flats covered by a haze of smoke from the railroad engines, she heard Moses paint for her a picture of what the scene *could* be like on a Sunday—the ugly tracks completely hidden by the great highway, cars traveling slowly along it, their occupants enjoying the view, and along the highway stretching green parks filled with strollers, tennis players and families on bicycles. There would be sailboats on the river and motor yachts tied up in gracefully curving basins. And the thing that astonished her most, Miss Perkins was to recall, was that Bob Moses had the exact location of tennis courts and boat basins quite definitely in mind; the young Bureau staffer beside her was talking about a public improvement on a scale almost without precedent in turn-of-the-century urban America, an improvement that would solve a problem that had baffled successive city administrations for years. And "he had it all figured out."

Moses was to talk again to Miss Perkins. Every time he did, her astonishment grew. "He was always burning up with ideas, just burning up with them!" she was to say. "Everything he saw walking around the city made him think of some way that it could be better." Happening once to comment that it was too bad that mothers who took infants to Central Park had to leave when diapers needed changing and go all the way home, she saw her idle words strike instant fire in Moses' mind. Why not build diaper-changing shelters? he asked. They could be small structures, used for no other purpose; you wouldn't even need attendants—the cost would be small. Or perhaps they could be additions to comfort stations already built—the cost would be smaller yet. It should certainly be looked into. Moreover, not all the ideas that he told her about required concrete and steel. Bob Moses, she realized, had thought through detailed new concepts of city budget making and social welfare legislation, prison administration and school administration, filing systems and methods of conducting public hearings.

But while Frances Perkins was impressed by Moses' imagination, the Bureau was more impressed by his impatience. Challenged at staff meetings about some details of those of his ideas that he had presented, he responded as Bella did at Madison House board meetings, making it clear that he wasn't much interested in long discussions. The ideas were good; what was needed now was to put them into practice.

Impatience became frustration. Moses wanted the Bureau to take up his ideas officially at once and press the city to adopt them. The Bureau had other projects on which it was already working and which it considered equally important. When it got to Moses' projects, they would have to be thoroughly studied. And as to those suggestions about public works projects like the highway—well, the ABC was not at all certain that the Bureau had the expertise or the responsibility to start suggesting public works.

The frustration boiled over. Moses became more and more critical of some of the Bureau's own procedures, which he felt were keeping it from accomplishing as much as it could. This criticism—offered, with conspicuous lack of tact, by one of the newest members of the Bureau—rubbed senior staffers the wrong way. They felt the procedures had brought the Bureau success; they were particularly incensed at several of Moses' suggestions aimed at speeding up the preliminary work that went into reports. While Bruère felt that some of these suggestions were worth looking into, Cleveland and Allen were more precise, careful men who believed in checking every possible aspect of a situation before writing anything about it, and most of the staffers agreed with this philosophy.

The reaction to rebuff was not graceful. Moses' irritation with the Bureau began to spill over into his work. He didn't feel it was important any more. Investigations didn't accomplish anything. He didn't want to count barrels of concrete; he wanted to pour them. He had said the weekly staff luncheons were a waste of time; the Bureau, believing they were valuable for interchange of ideas, declined to eliminate them—so Moses simply stopped attending. With increasing frequency, sent over to City Hall to get material for a report, he would return without the material and say he had met one of the city officials he knew "and we had a very interesting conversation." Acting as adviser to several Training School students, Moses developed the habit of writing large question marks in the margins of their reports next to statements he questioned—and the papers often were returned with their margins literally filled with these indications of his displeasure. Sometimes, the papers were not returned at all. "I have your memorandum and it's no damn good," he would say to a student. "I threw it in the wastebasket." And the student would find out that Moses meant exactly that; the memo had actually been thrown away; the student would never see it again. He used his tongue as a lash on his advisees. One, considered a brilliant prospect and in fact later to become one of the country's leading experts on police administration, emerged from a conference with Moses so depressed that he gave up his hopes of a public career and resigned from the Bureau. It was only with difficulty that he was persuaded to return. Bruère, who knew Bella and Emanuel Moses socially, stayed tolerant toward their son, but Cleveland and Allen made it clear they were not prepared to put up with his behavior much longer; Moses, they said, just couldn't seem to learn to work as part of a team. Bureau gossip said he would be fired shortly.

* * *

Only one person at the Bureau was sympathetic.

She was a woman who worked as Cleveland's secretary.

Mary Louise Sims was slim, of less than medium height and rather plain, but gay and vivacious. With ash-blond hair and a clear white skin, she looked fresh and clean. She came from Dodgeville, Wisconsin, one of the six children of a Cornishman who worked in the little town's lead and zinc mines. Mary's family didn't consider itself poor, but, as one of her sisters put it, "there wasn't much money to throw around." When Mary decided that she wanted to go to college, she had to earn her first year's tuition as a seventeen-year-old teacher in Dodgeville's one-room little red schoolhouse and then, after she entered the University of Wisconsin, work her way through. After she graduated and began to work full time in Madison, the state capital, a portion of her earnings each week was still put aside for college tuition—for a younger sister.

In Madison, Mary was a secretary, but that was not an adequate description of the work she did. Her employer was Francis E. McGovern, the Governor of Wisconsin, and McGovern noticed that Mary had an instinct for and insight into politics, including the merciless in-fighting that was part of the decor in any statehouse. He used her as confidante and adviser.

But Mary's ambitions were not for herself. She had sought out a job with a politician not because she was interested in politics but because she was interested in what politics could do. She was another of the moths who in the years before World War I hovered so thickly around the flame of idealism. In 1913, Cleveland and Allen visited Madison to study Wisconsin's governmental structure. No one could explain it better than Miss Sims, the Governor said, and delegated her to show the visitors around. She had already become interested in the "efficiency and economy" movement. In the course of the tour, Cleveland and Allen talked to her about how they were trying to make democracy work, about fighting to free government to institute reforms that would really help people. Mary resigned as the Governor's secretary and came to New York to work for the Bureau. In 1914 she was thirty—four and a half years older than Bob Moses—and was known to Bureau staffers and students for her friendliness, her quick wit and the depth of her belief in what they were doing. Bob Moses fell in love with her.

Although women had always been attracted to him, Moses had never before, although he was twenty-five years old, centered attention on any particular one. But now he talked about Mary constantly, and he talked about her in terms that left no doubt that the pedestal he had placed her on was a high one. The lover of the Good, the True and the Beautiful seemed to feel that he had found their embodiment. "He was," a friend said, "very, very much in love."

His devotion was complete. Taking Mary along on his walks around the city, he poured out to her his ideas—and his frustration at the indifference with which they were received by the Bureau. At the Bureau, they would meet in the library, among the books, and they would sit and talk for hours. He introduced her to his friends. They noticed that she was always gay and laughing but that she could also, in a quiet way, deliver a remark that could demolish an opponent's argument—or an opponent.

The Bureau's whisperers soon learned that it was unwise to let Mary hear their criticisms of Moses. If she did, she would not hesitate to let them know where, despite her feelings for the Bureau, her first loyalties now lay. They just didn't understand Bob, she would say. One day he would get a chance to show what he could do.

And, as it turned out, the chance came soon. Having finally accepted the Fusion nomination, John Purroy Mitchel had been elected mayor on November 4, 1913, at the age of thirty-four. Bruère had become his closest confidant, the expert who provided the tinder to fuel Mitchel's zeal; Bruère provided the facts and theories, Allen was to say, and "Mitchel took fire" with them. Now, as mayor, Mitchel made Bruère City Chamberlain. And he asked the Bureau to list the city departments most in need of reorganization and to recommend Bureau experts equipped to advise on the reorganization. Near the top of the Bureau's list was the Municipal Civil Service Commission, and Allen, Bruère and Cleveland found that only one staffer in the Bureau was an expert on civil service. They had no choice but to submit his name to Mitchel, and when, in 1914, the Mayor appointed a new Civil Service Commission, he asked the commissioners to rely for technical assistance on this man and to regard him as if he were in fact on the city payroll.

The new commissioners found the man a more than willing assistant. At last, he was being given a chance to participate in the actual workings of government itself, in workings that could change men's lives, in workings that could make a city a better place to live. Into the work of the Municipal Civil Service Commission, Bob Moses hurled all his energy and all his brilliance, all his zeal for reform, all the long-pent-up enthusiasm and fire of the boundless idealism of his youth.

5. *Age of Optimism*

In setting out to reform New York City's civil service, Bob Moses was setting out to break into the plunderhouse of politics.

The wheels of the Tammany war machine might be greased with money, but the machine was pulled by men, the men who voted Democratic themselves, the men who rounded up newly arrived immigrants and brought them in to be registered Democratic, the men who during election campaigns rang doorbells and distributed literature to those immigrants and to their own friends and neighbors and on Election Day shepherded them to the polls to vote Democratic. And the most succulent of the carrots that lured these men forward, that kept their shoulders braced against the ropes that pulled the Tammany machine, was the carrot of jobs, jobs for themselves, jobs for their wives, jobs for their sons. The only source of jobs on the scale required was the city itself. So the jobs Tammany had to control in order to control the city were the city's jobs—positions as policemen, firemen, sanitation workers, court clerks, process servers, building inspectors, secretaries, clerks. There were, in 1914, 50,000 city employees and this meant 50,000 men and women who owed their pay checks—and whose families owed the food and shelter those pay checks bought—not to merit but to the ward boss. Patronage was the coinage of power in New York City. And reforms of the civil service such as Moses was to propose were therefore daggers thrust at the heart of Tammany Hall.

Tammany understood this well. And Tammany knew how to defend itself. It always had.

Reformers might have forced the adoption of civil service merit systems in one city after another. But in New York, though Tammany might have been forced to make token reforms in other areas of government, civil service was the line at which reform stopped. In New York, in 1914, "merit" was still votes deliverable. The "ability" that determined who got the jobs and which jobholders got promotions and raises was still number of relatives —relatives of voting age—or rightness of connections.

Under such a system, civil service was chaos. Offices were filled with so many clerks and secretaries that supervisors couldn't possibly provide work for all of them. One secretary might be receiving $25 a week. The secretary at the desk next to hers, doing identical work, might be receiving $47 a week. Some city typists were getting $1,200 a year. Others were getting $4,000. When giving tests of the ring-the-gong variety to candidates for jobs requiring physical strength—lifeguard or fireman, for example—the examiner painted over the candidate's side of the dial which registered the force with which the gong was struck, so that only the examiner could see the results, and the results the examiner reported frequently had a relationship less to strength than to amount—the amount of money the candidate pressed into his hand. More than 1,200 employees had been exempted from any competitive examination at all.

No aspect of city mismanagement was more frustrating to reformers than civil service maladministration. What good were campaigns to change the government, if the people running it, administering its machinery, were still the same unqualified, inefficient, indifferent political hacks?

John Purroy Mitchel's announcement that he intended to clean up the civil service therefore was especially cheering to reformers. The impeccability of the reform credentials of the two men he selected to form the majority on the three-member Municipal Civil Service Commission—new chairman Henry Moskowitz, a meek, disheveled social worker who had been the first headworker of Bella and Emanuel Moses' Madison House, and banker Darwin R. James, a natty one-time Princeton track captain and president of the Brooklyn Bureau of Charities—cemented their optimism. Samuel H. Ordway, chairman of the Civil Service Reform Association, said, "We expect great things . . . a real advance in civil service administration."

But generations of Tammany civil service commissioners, masters in their own way of the art of government, had been there first. Anxious to blaze a path straight to the door of rectitude, Moskowitz and James found themselves trapped instead in a maze of technicalities constructed over decades primarily to keep great things from happening. Civil service administration, the two reformers soon realized, was an art and a science—and it was an art and a science they knew absolutely nothing about.

Not trusting long-time commission secretary Frank A. Spencer or Spencer's assistants to lead them out of the maze, Moskowitz and James tried to fire them, learned to their frustration that one of the technicalities prevented this and settled for transferring them to other departments. And they turned to the young man from the Municipal Research Bureau as their guide.

From a technical standpoint, they made a good choice. Two men who had read Moses' thesis—it had been published—were Luther C. Steward, first president of the National Federation of Federal Employees, and H. Elliot Kaplan, later president of the New York Civil Service Commission and executive director of the Civil Service Reform Association. Years later, when Kaplan had read everything there was to read on civil service, he was asked to evaluate the thesis and said simply, "It was a masterpiece." There were, he said, "very few people in the United States in 1914 who knew much about civil service. Bob Moses really knew." Steward's wife, who had been working beside her husband in 1914, was even more emphatic. "Bob Moses wasn't *one* of the men in this country who understood civil service best at that stage," she said. "He was *the* man who understood it best."

James and Moskowitz asked Moses for a plan of action.

Moses said that the first step had to be a reform of the city's efficiency-rating system, the system of ratings given by supervisors to their subordinates to help determine whether to promote a civil service employee or give him a pay raise; under the present method, ratings didn't give the Civil Service Commission enough information for a sound judgment.

Making an evaluation system precise was perhaps the most difficult job in civil service, Moses explained; each job had to be broken down into component parts, so that each part could be graded, and in totaling the grades each part had to be given a mathematical weight corresponding to its importance in the job as a whole. But he knew how to do it, he said. Impressed, James and Moskowitz told him to go ahead—and let it be known that they were considering bringing the Bureau staffer into city employ and starting him off at the top: as Spencer's replacement as commission secretary.

Then, one morning, Bob Moses found his name in a newspaper. ONLY "GENTLEMEN" NEED APPLY, a headline said. THAT IS MOSES' THEORY OF CIVIL SERVICE REQUIREMENTS.

Because he "is being considered as a likely successor to Frank Spencer," said the article under the headline, Moses' Ph.D. thesis, "of which he acknowledges the authorship, and in which he openly advocates that positions in the government service should be open only to university men and 'gentlemen who had inherited breeding and culture,' has caused a mild sensation in civil service circles."

It was a small article, five paragraphs in the Brooklyn *Eagle,* and no other paper bothered to pick it up. But it must have served as a warning to the Mitchel administration of the line of attack that would be used if Moses was appointed—and of Moses' peculiar vulnerability, because of the thesis "of which he acknowledges the authorship," to such an attack. There was no more talk of the appointment.

The article marked the first appearance of Moses' name in a New York newspaper. It was his first direct acquaintance with a newspaper "leak." To the average reader, it would seem that a reporter had discovered the thesis himself, or had been motivated to look for it because of the "mild sensation" he had noticed in civil service circles. But there had been no "sensation," mild or otherwise, over Moses' rumored appointment; hardly anyone in city government even knew who he was. Actually, Tammany had simply done a little research and tipped off a reporter to the existence of the thesis and had told him what he would find if he went up to the public library and looked at it.*

The story could be taken as a "first" of another type, too, a first hint of what was to come, a gentle intimation that politics, in its own way, was rougher than water polo, that the race Bob Moses was entering was not a swimming relay in which judges watched the touch-offs to insure that every-

* After its publication, it became a family joke that only six copies had been sold: three to Bob's mother and three to his grandmother.

thing was fair. It could be taken as a reminder of how important patronage was to Tammany—far too important to let anyone take it away. Disposing of a young man's hopes for a minor city appointment was so simple it was hardly worth mentioning; a little newspaper leak, done offhand by some politician who had more important things on his mind, could take care of that. Were the threat to grow more serious, however, there were other methods.

If it was a hint, however, Moses didn't take it. He would have liked Spencer's job, but the job wasn't what was important to him; reforming the civil service was. He set out to do it.

The Bureau assigned ten men to Moses as assistants. The idea of working under him didn't appeal to the older men, but the younger ones, who hadn't known him before, liked him. "He worked all of us hard," one of them recalls. "But he worked himself harder. He was at the Bureau when you got in in the morning, and he was still there when you left at night. He'd lose his temper, but it was silly to argue with him anyway, because you knew darn well that he had looked the point up before he talked to you and knew it better than you did."

Moses' assistants sat for days watching city workers perform their jobs so that they could break each job down into gradable components. They observed employees of private businesses. They interviewed department heads and civil service commissioners in other cities. Soon memos addressed to "Dr. Moses" were flooding onto his desk. By the spring of 1915, he was able to begin writing the *Detailed Report on the Rating of the Efficiency of Civil Service Employees, Excepting Members of the Uniformed Forces in the Police and Fire Services and in the Lower Ranks of the Street Cleaning Service*. Day after day, he sat in the Bureau, his fine-pointed pen racing over the pages of yellow legal note pads. Often, coming across a point he wanted to check himself, he would fling himself out of his chair and out of the Bureau offices, and stride, sometimes breaking in his haste into a few steps of a run and then self-consciously checking himself and settling back into a walk, over to City Hall or the Municipal Building, where he could see records and officials himself. Soon, to save time, he asked for and was given a desk of his own in the Civil Service Commission offices on the fourteenth floor of the Municipal Building, his first toehold in the halls of power. He wrote and rewrote sections of the report before sending them off to the typist. And when they returned, the fine-pointed pen slashed at the neat pages, crossing out words, putting in others, clarifying, refining, hardening. On July 8, 1915, after nineteen months of work, he typed on a Bureau letterhead: "Dear Commissioner James: I am transmitting herewith detailed report . . ."

Under the present system, Moses reported, most department heads simply gave each of their hundreds of employees "C"—or average—ratings on their "report cards" rather than try to pinpoint outstanding or delinquent workers. To obtain more accurate ratings, he wrote, department heads must be required to give each employee arithmetical grades in dozens of categories. In addition, there must be a complete "reclassification" of the civil service, adding many new levels, to insure that employees would be given the precise salary and authority they deserved. There must be a complete "standardization" of salaries so that employees doing the same type of work would be getting the same pay even if they were working in different departments. The commission should have authority to see that promotions and raises were given strictly on the bases established under the system.

Moses' proposal was a codification of idealism. Omitted, at the insistence of Moskowitz and James, was any mention of "higher division," "lower division" or "university men." There was to be only one standard for promotion in public life: "open competition," how hard and well a man worked and how he performed on examinations. Examination results would be posted in public, and report cards would be open to public inspection so that every city employee would know the basis whereon he and his competitors were judged. Seniority would become unimportant; not experience but ability would be crucial.

The proposal was of a purity, a strength and a scope that was almost more religious than governmental. The system was to be completely new, Moses said. All traces of the old must be washed away. And it must be all-embracing. All government service, he said, could be divided into sixteen categories: executive, legislative, judicial, professional, subprofessional, educational, investigational, inspectional, clerical, custodial, street cleaning, fire, police, institutional, skilled trades and labor. Each category could be divided into specific jobs—custodial, for example, into caretakers, janitors, watchmen, storekeepers and bridge tenders. Each job could be scientifically analyzed to show its "functions" and "responsibilities." Each function and responsibility—and there were dozens of them for most jobs—could be given a precise mathematical weight corresponding to its importance in the over-all job. And the success of the employee in each function and responsibility could be given a precise mathematical grade. These grades would, added together according to weight and combined in service records for each employee, "furnish conclusions expressed in arithmetical . . . terms" and these conclusions and these alone should be "used as a basis for salary increase and promotion."

It was the proposal of a fanatic. John Calvin specifying permissible arrangements for women's hair in sixteenth-century Geneva was not more thorough than was Bob Moses enumerating the "functions" and "responsibilities" of New York's civil servants. No aspect of conduct on the job was too small to be graded. Even personality must be reduced to number. "Personality," Moses said, "includes those intangible elements the existence of which do not readily admit of proof, but nevertheless . . . each employee *must* be rated on personality." Men would have to make sacrifices for the sake of the system: acknowledging that some present employees would not score high enough on his tests for the jobs they held, he had a simple solution—such employees would have to accept demotions and pay cuts. Unnecessary employees, he said, would have to be "eliminated."

The idealism was harsh and uncompromising. In judging the ability of an examining officer, said one of Moses' aides, echoing Moses' views, a "pretty fair clue" is the number of "below standard" ratings given: the more "below standard" ratings, the better the examining officer. If there could be such a thing as a Calvinistic civil service efficiency-rating system, Moses had devised it.

Moses did not deny there was a human element involved; he knew of its existence all too well—it was constantly interfering with the mathematical perfection of his system, and it must be suppressed. "It is essential," he said, "to have a definite, almost a mechanical, program of adjustments in order to avoid personal and political pressure." For some reason, it was hard to make examiners understand this. They were always becoming sympathetic to individuals and talking about the "human factor," and "an examiner who . . . always wishes to take the 'human factor' into consideration is a dangerous man to associate with such work. The consideration of the 'human factor' is entirely a matter of policy for policy-determining bodies in applying salary and grade specifications." The infusion of people, moreover, was always interfering with the work to be done. Annoyed that his recommendations had to be discussed at public hearings, he noted that because of the time he had to spend at such hearings, "it is difficult to . . . keep the field work running smoothly and correspondence up to date." There must, he said, "be some limit to public discussion."

Shining through all Moses' statements was confidence, a faith that his system would work, a belief that the personalities of tens of thousands of human beings could be reduced to mathematical grades, that promotions and raises could be determined by a science precise enough to give every one of those human beings the exact rewards he deserved. Asked once if it might not prove difficult to divide a job like that of janitor into different levels based on different functions and responsibilities, Moses replied flatly that it would not be difficult at all. To the expert, he said, such differences are "clearly discernible." When someone ventured to argue that it might be hard to bring under his system appointees in policy-making posts because policy-making ability was too subtle to measure, Moses could barely restrain his impatience. "There is no reason why it cannot be worked out in that way," he said.

Moses also had confidence that his system would be adopted. It would take "courage and integrity" to push it through, he said, but the city at last had a mayor with such qualities—and with an educational background that would enable him to understand that the system was good and that its adoption would so improve the civil service as to make it truly an instrument for the betterment of the lives of the city's people. Moses talked often about Mitchel; the young mayor was his beau ideal of the public servant, the embodiment of the virtues enumerated in the Ph.D. thesis.

And certainly the first reactions to Moses' *Detailed Report* must have made the confidence seem justified. Terming it "pioneer work," the Civil Service Reform Association said that Moses' efficiency-rating system was the most thorough ever devised. Moskowitz called it "an epoch in the administration of civil service law." James said: "No city, state or national civil service has anything commensurate with this." Mayor Mitchel announced that he would push for the system's adoption. Bella and Emanuel had purchased nineteen acres of land in Lake Placid—Hawk Island—for a summer retreat and had been up there for more than a month. Now, his report finished and praised, their son hurried to join them for what was to be a golden summer. He felt very close to attaining a goal in which was tied up all the idealism of his youth—the accomplishment of a concrete achievement that would truly help people. And now his attention was focused on the girl who seemed somehow a part of that idealism.

"Bob was very much in love that summer," a friend recalls. "We did a lot of swimming and mountain climbing in the Adirondacks, but Bob was talking about Mary all the time." He brought her up to meet his parents, and Bella liked her immediately. On August 15, 1915, one month after he had handed in the report, he and Mary were married. The ceremony was performed at the nonsectarian Labor Temple in New York City by its director, a Presbyterian minister, and the couple honeymooned in a rustic camp near Lake Placid.

Returning to New York in the fall, the couple moved into a small apartment on Ninety-fifth Street near West End Avenue. They had no regular income except Mary's salary at the Bureau, and before the end of the year they knew she was pregnant—a daughter, Barbara, would be born on May 23, 1916—and would have to stop working. But Bella said she would give them enough to get by on; she didn't want Robert to interrupt his work by taking a paying job. Neither Mary nor Bob had much interest in the things that forced other young couples to be concerned with money, anyway; they were perfectly happy, for example, to furnish their living room with only Bella's old sofas and their own shiny idealism.

Every morning—early—Moses would get a call from a young lawyer named George Gove, who lived nearby. "I'm leaving," Gove would say and hang up. Moses would be standing in the street when Gove arrived.

Together, the two young men would walk down Broadway all the way to the Flatiron Building on Twenty-third Street, where Gove had his office—and then Moses would continue alone to the Municipal Building, some six miles south of Ninety-fifth Street.

Gove was a tall, rawboned farmer's son from Wisconsin who regarded himself as a good walker, but he had trouble keeping up with Moses. As they walked, Moses would talk and, as his thoughts raced, his legs seemed to keep pace, so that at times he was almost trotting in his eagerness to get downtown. "We talked about everything under the sun," Gove recalls—art, philosophy, history. The one subject not mentioned was one other young men might have dwelt on: making money. "He just wasn't interested in that," Gove says. The subject that dominated the talk was government and particularly the government of New York City. "He was all caught up in his work," Gove says.

Moses was sure the work was going to pay off. Historians call those last years before America's entry into the Great War America's Age of Optimism; it was Bob Moses' age of optimism, too. His superiors couldn't praise him enough, and took his advice eagerly. When, during a speech, they were asked a particularly sticky question, Moses would lean forward and whisper the answer. They had authorized the printing of the detailed forms on which the arithmetical grades were to be reported, and in the rectangles of heavy yellow paper Moses could see the first tangible results of his years of education for public service. Forms had already been sent to several of the more cooperative departments, and the rest were in boxes stacked in a corner of one of the Civil Service Commission offices, ready to go.

Moses' demeanor revealed his confidence. Openly mocking the weekly staff luncheons and elaborate filing systems, he made no secret of his contempt for the Bureau. Chatting with Bureau staffers, he took care to let them know, in a studiedly offhand fashion, that it was fine to be doing "real work" at last.

He carried himself with an air of vast knowledge. "There was, in his makeup, very little doubt," one of the staffers was to say years later. Another recalls that Moses was the first person he saw on his first day at the Bureau. "Here was this tall, handsome character in a white suit—a summer tropical kind of suit—and he was talking on the telephone to the street-cleaning commissioner. I gathered from the conversation that someone had been advocating some new method of cleaning the streets and the commissioner was saying that he didn't think much of the suggestion. And all of a sudden this character in the white suit raps out, 'Well, we don't think much of it, either.' You should have heard the tone! It was so definite! I thought it was an extraordinary tone for a guy to use who had never been confronted with the problem. I sized him up immediately as self-confident, opinionated and critical." Getting to know Moses, the new staffer found no reason to change his evaluation. "He seemed to regard himself as one of the anointed," he said.

But reality was just around the corner.

Tammany's wily old sachems had probably realized early what Moses' plan would mean for them: it would effectively destroy their control of the civil service. But the sachems, unwilling openly to oppose reform themselves, had said nothing, biding their time. And now the development they had been waiting for was coming to pass; the system's 50,000 members were beginning to realize what the plan would mean for *them*.

The downgrading of seniority in Moses' system would mean that these city employees would lose a large advantage—in many cases their only advantage—over bright young outsiders trying for their jobs. The elimination of unnecessary jobs would mean that some of them would be out of work entirely. Moses' insistence on demotion for men who failed to score high enough on new examinations to qualify for the jobs they presently held would have the most far-reaching effects of all. Men who had run their ward boss's errands for years in return for advancement up the civil service ladder now came to realize that under Moses' system the rewards for which they had waited so long might be snatched from them; in fact, for many of them, "might" was only a euphemism; they knew all too well what their qualifications were and how they would make out on honestly run examinations.

Moreover, Moses' system would effectively bar the simplest path to future raises. Under the old system, once a civil service worker reached Grade Five, the highest grade for clerical employees, he could be given raises, raises without limit as to number or amount, without having to take any examinations at all; all that was necessary was approval from his department head—and since department heads gave raises on the advice of Tammany bosses, the loyal party worker could be assured that his loyalty would be rewarded. Grade Five was, in fact, the biggest carrot that Tammany possessed. More than 10,000 of the 50,000 city employees were at that level, and while the base pay for Grade Five was $3,260 a year—in itself a handsome wage when the average clerical worker in private industry earned $2,100 a year—the earnings of many of the 10,000 had been raised to $6,500 or even $7,500.

Under Moses' system, all civil service workers at Grade Five—all 10,000 of them—would have their pay reduced to $3,260 a year and would have to pass examinations for any future raises. Even if they passed the examinations they would have to climb back up the monetary ladder one step at a time, for promotions were to be given only level by level. And examinations would no longer be given, as they had been, to cozy groups of two or three competitors, or to one man who happened to be the only person who had been notified that the examination was being given. To climb back up to their former salaries, Grade Fivers would be competing with hundreds of applicants.

As the realization of these facts began to seep down to the mass of civil service employees, there was hysteria in the ranks. Protest meetings were arranged.

Young Bob Moses volunteered to speak at the meetings. He wasn't ashamed of his system, he said. He was proud of it. He would be glad to defend it.

But Moses wasn't at Oxford any more. The only effect of his courage was to make things easier for his enemies. Civil service reorganization was a subject so complicated that it was difficult to interest even civil service workers in it. What was needed was a single, visible object on which the workers could focus their hatred. And now Moses had given them such an object—himself.

He was the perfect target. Tall, in a white suit, elegant, haughty, arrogant instead of conciliatory when challenged, he stood before the thousands of sullen, clerkish men like the very epitome of the efficiency expert they feared and hated. And they expressed their hatred and fear in boos and catcalls and vicious, shouted insults.

Moses refused to quit. Night after night, carrying a heavy leather briefcase crammed with facts and statistics he almost never got to use, he stood before civil service employees' associations, speaking into a hail of abuse.

"Once you saw him on those nights, you could never forget him," Kaplan recalls. "Tall, handsome—he'd get up on the platform and go right to bat. He wouldn't pull his punches or try to modify the things he was saying so they'd be less unpopular. Those people had come to hate the word 'efficiency.' Talking 'efficiency' to them was waving the red flag before the bull. But in those speeches it was efficiency, efficiency, efficiency. The more they booed him, the more self-confident, even arrogant, he seemed. In the worst of it, he went right on talking, and with the attitude 'When I say this is it, this is it!' "

But the outspokenness and the courage, along with the arrogance and the lecturing tone, had no effect other than to increase the opposition to his system, to rouse the fury of 50,000 voting men and women to fever pitch.

Tammany knew how to use the opportunity he had given it; while not openly opposing reorganization, it linked the plan with the man the employees hated. Recalls one observer, "Reclassification *became* Moses in these people's eyes." The employees' associations began to circulate petitions calling for the removal of Moses and the men who had appointed him—Moskowitz and James—and those petitions, bearing tens of thousands of names, were submitted to the Board of Estimate. But still Tammany made no overt move. Still the Tiger waited.

Then there began to be doubts about Moses' proposals in the camp of his supporters. Even the most ardent had misgivings about telling men who had become accustomed to making—and supporting their families on—$6,500 to $7,500 a year that they were now making $3,260 a year. Even the adoring Kaplan said "that was a little unfair, really. Put in a new system—okay. But don't adversely affect people who had been working under the old system. Not everyone who was making a good salary in Grade Five was doing so just because of political connections, remember. Some had worked their way up on their own. And a lot of the people who had been given their chance through politics were doing good jobs and deserved the money. You shouldn't suddenly take it away from them." Henry Moskowitz, declaring that "no one can deny [the] soundness and [the] justice of the principle of standardization," said nonetheless that "a ruthless application of the principle . . . is unwise. In my judgment it should be gradually assimilated and *apply to the vacant positions as they arise.*"

But Moses argued against compromise. If the principle behind his system was right, he said, there should be no compromising with it. Making exceptions, he said, would kill the whole plan. If the plan was based on salary standardization, then salaries really had to be standard—all salaries. Moskowitz gave in. Some reformers, considering the commission unreasonable, turned lukewarm in their support.

It was the moment Tammany had been waiting for. The Board of Estimate it controlled scheduled hearings on the standardization proposal.

The support Moses expected from Mitchel seemed forthcoming at first. The Mayor and Fusion Comptroller William A. Prendergast urged the Board to adopt standardization and "cut to the bone" unnecessary positions.

But Tammany packed the hearings with Moses' opponents. Rising to defend his plan, a tall, slim, figure in white among the red-faced, burly, cigar-smoking Tammany politicians in their black derbies that they wore even indoors, he could hardly be heard through the boos. Speaker after speaker related stories of particularly deserving individuals whose standard of living would be reduced, unfairly, under the plan.

Gradually Tammany's strategy became apparent. Each disputed case, the speakers were saying, should be decided on its individual merits by the Board's Bureau of Standards and included as a separate item in the budget, a policy which would not only drag out the hearings indefinitely but would in itself defeat the principle of universal standardization. The Tammany members of the Board said that after careful consideration they didn't see how any other policy could be adopted; humane considerations, fairness, justice—these must not be ignored. They were in favor of standardization, they said, they intended to adopt the Moses plan, but the plan must be modified where individual situations required it. Even pro-Fusion newspapers couldn't find anything to criticize in that.

Mitchel and Prendergast became noticeably silent. When a vote was taken, it was unanimous. Mitchel and Prendergast joined with Tammany to vote for individual consideration.

Moses was disappointed but still hopeful. The Board had, after all, said it intended to adopt standardization. Once the plan was adopted, the exceptions could gradually be eliminated one by one.

But the hearings dragged on and on; there were, after all, hundreds of civil service workers who believed, many with reason, that the proposed reclassification was unfair to them. Their stories made good newspaper copy. Technical arguments for reclassification did not. The Moses proposal began to appear in an unfavorable light.

After weeks of hearings, the Bureau of Standards finally submitted its recommendations to the Board of Estimate, which thereupon adopted a budget including Moses' proposed schedule of civil service grades and salaries, along with hundreds of individual budget items for the individual workers who had persuaded the Bureau of Standards they should be excluded from the schedule. In what was expected to be a matter of routine, the new schedule then went to the Board of Aldermen for approval—and the aldermen vetoed portions of it and added to it dozens of general civil service levels which did not correspond to any levels in the Moses plan. At the end of 1915, the only real result of Moses' effort was still the stacks of yellow form cards.

Nineteen-sixteen was frustration and disillusionment. To meet the aldermen's objections to some of the specific job specifications and salary scales, Moses worked endlessly revising them—only to find when he resubmitted them that the aldermen had still other objections which they had somehow neglected to mention before. There was again no open opposition, nothing that Moses' supporters could seize on as evidence of Tammany opposition to reform; instead, there was again stalling and obfuscation and confusion—and, for Bob Moses, defeat.

Even the efficiency-rating forms of which he had been so proud were turning into symbols of frustration. Attempts to persuade more departments to use them proved fruitless. Roaming restlessly through the commission offices, he had to look every day at the pile of boxes containing the forms—and the pile never got smaller.

The forms that had been distributed were not being used properly. Most of the department heads who had accepted them were reluctant to do the vast amount of work that would be necessary if their many squares and blanks were to be filled in with precise arithmetical grades. Those few who were willing to do the work needed help in using the new system. To provide this help—and to make sure that all departments were using the new salary scales and that employees were doing the work consistent with their salaries—the Civil Service Commission had to rely on its examiners. The enforcement of Moses' system was in their hands. And these were men from the old Tammany regime who, too smart to give Moskowitz and James "grounds for dismissal" by openly defying them, undermined the system by the subtle but effective tactic of slowness in learning and laxness in enforcing the new rules. Moses understood full well that the examiners were making a farce out of his system. "Nothing," he said bitterly, "can make salary standardization more ridiculous than to put it into the hands of [such] men." But it was in their hands, nonetheless, that it remained.

Judges, he learned, were men, too, for all their black robes—and often they were men who had been dressed in those robes by Tammany. When certain department heads refused to hold competitive examinations for elevator-operator positions, the commission ordered the operators dismissed. One, who ran an elevator in the Bronx County Courthouse, brought suit to enjoin the dismissal, arguing that because prisoners rode in his elevator on their way to and from courtrooms, his job was "sensitive" and "exceptional." Of course it was, the judge said reassuringly—and granted the injunction.

The darkening of Bob Moses' optimism occurred against the backdrop of the darkening of America's. A new mood was abroad in the land. "Our country is at peace with the world at war" had been one of Woodrow Wilson's re-election slogans in 1916, but now the War Gods were slogging relentlessly across the Atlantic; the words in the scare headlines were "*Lusitania*" and "U-Boat" and, finally, "Zimmermann." War, not progress, was on the horizon. Aims changed—the world was to be made safe for democracy; that was a large enough order for even the idealism of youth to handle at one time.

In New York City, the fading of idealism on the municipal level had been especially rapid. With reform enthroned in City Hall, not all reformers stayed reformers. Before Mitchel's election, the policy of the Bureau of Municipal Research had been to investigate city government no matter who was running it, but after his election, Cleveland announced, "When its friends are in power, a citizen research agency should not publish unfavorable information." The city's Good Government organizations had become much less active. One reason was that they did not want to hurt what they considered the city's last, best chance against Tammany. But there was also another reason. As Allen himself put it: "One reason for this conspiracy of silent criticism and public applause cannot be too baldly stated or too vividly remembered, namely, almost every agency of outside criticism 'had its feet in the trough'—to use a conventionalized term for sharing in political patronage." Moses could hardly have been unaware that while he was fighting to bring all civil service positions under competitive examination, no fewer than forty-seven Charities Department inspectors had been appointed by reformer John Kingsbury without examination, in clear violation of the law—or that every one of the forty-seven had previously worked for the private organization which Kingsbury had headed. Moses must have known, as all City Hall observers knew, that city offices ranging from clerkships to judgeships were being filled by reformers from lists furnished by pro-Fusion ward leaders.

Moses' idol had developed a case of galloping clay feet. John Purroy Mitchel's elegance had worked against him. Wearer of the dress suit, winner of the one-step contest at costume balls of the Four Hundred, the Boy Mayor had given himself the image of a friend of the wealthy. His independence had worked against him, too. Scornful of public relations, he refused to change his friendships—or even to go to the public with explanations of many of his actions as mayor, so that many of the notable reforms he initiated never got the publicity they deserved. His investigations cut waste in city government but, preoccupied with economy, he did not want to do anything with the money thus saved, but save it. His boasts were not of what was being done to meet the city's needs but of what was being done to save the city's money. Even his admiring biographer would have to admit, "His concern was for the city rather than for its people."

What probably disillusioned Moses most about Mitchel was not the Boy Mayor's elegance but his proposed "solution" of the problem of the railroad tracks below Riverside Drive. Mitchel proposed giving the New York Central exclusive control of the West Side waterfront and allowing the railroad to cure the Death Avenue problem by elevating its tracks below Fifty-ninth Street, a move that would have permanently blighted a large slice of downtown Manhattan. In return for these favors, Mitchel asked the railroad to pay $300,000—an amount not even sufficient to rehabilitate Riverside Park. A furious Citizens Union called the plan a "giveaway" to a railroad owned by Mitchel's social friends—and it was. And the Mayor's plan would have forever deprived the city of the waterfront highway and park Moses had dreamed of.

In the area of civil service, however, Mitchel was Moses' best hope. The Mayor promised to press again in 1917 for standardization and reclassification. After more than three years of unremitting work on the technicalities of civil service, Moses was still fascinated by them and by the potentiality for public good in their improvement. They are not "dry and dull as some may suppose from reading printed salary schedules," he said in 1917. "A student who wishes to see city government as a whole will find no more interesting . . . study than that afforded by a standardization program."

He was still confident. "I believe that the final results of the work in New York City will be regarded as entirely satisfactory," he said. Why shouldn't they be? Hadn't he demonstrated—over and over again, by logic and by science—that his system would improve the city's government? Didn't all the city's top officials now understand this? "A second and revised edition of the standard specifications . . . is about to be published for the Board of Estimate," he said. "Presumably this will be the final edition." The final edition! Galahad thought he was in sight of the Grail.

Bob Moses had done little else but fight for his system for more than three years. Now, in 1917, he fought harder. He made more speeches; he lobbied more editorial writers. He argued with the borough presidents and aldermen whose votes would decide the system's fate.

Getting in to see these officials was never easy. Unless Moskowitz or James knew the official personally, Moses would first have to ask them to speak to some official they knew who did. Then that official would ask the other to see Moses. When the time came for his appointment, he would often be kept waiting—since he was surely among the least important of visitors—in City Hall anterooms, eyed by secretaries who could gauge his unimportance by the length of time their bosses kept him waiting. And when they finally ushered him in, Moses would know that he was talking to a man who regarded the talk only as an irritation. Yet he never stopped trying—and he never stopped hoping.

Unfortunately for his hopes, however, 1917 was an election year and John Purroy Mitchel wanted to be re-elected—and, with 50,000 civil service employees infuriated by Moses' proposals, Tammany nominee John F. "Red Mike" Hylan was making them a major campaign issue. Tammany wanted City Hall back and Tammany speakers were telling mass meetings of city employees, "We do not believe we should have so many efficiency experts"—and the employees were jumping to their feet and bellowing in reply, "A new mayor! A new mayor!" When Moses' system came up before the Board of Estimate, Mitchel was silent. The system was not adopted. Moses' idol, the epitome of the cultured university man in politics, did take one definite step in regard to civil service, however. In October, a month before the election, he fired Henry Moskowitz as Civil Service Commission chairman and replaced him with a man acceptable to the employees.

When Red Mike Hylan swept into City Hall—Mitchel, who had been elected in 1913 by the largest plurality in New York's history, was turned out in 1917 by an even larger plurality—Progressivism in the city was dead. "We have had all the reform that we want in this city for some time to come," Hylan said, and issued an order soon after taking office in 1918: all Bureau staffers who had been working with city agencies were to be dismissed at once.

Dismissed, Moses watched as the handful of civil service innovations that represented the pathetically small accomplishment of his four years of effort were destroyed one by one. The meager measure of standardization that had been enacted was abolished by amendments to the 1918 budget. The few positions that had been removed from the exempt list were placed back on it. Hylan's department heads ended the use of the efficiency records. The yellow forms of which Moses had been so proud were henceforth to be used, if they were used at all, only as scrap paper.

Within months of Hylan's inauguration, in fact, civil service in New York was plunged into depths unknown since the heyday of the Tweed Ring forty-five years before. Non-Tammany employees were forced out of their jobs by humiliating assignments and pay cuts. Hundreds of positions previously competitive were made exempt because of their "exceptional and sensitive" nature. The exemptions covered lifeguards, chauffeurs—and, as a final sprinkle of salt in Moses' wounds, a very highly paid "special examiner" to the Civil Service Commission itself. The special examiner was Frank A. Spencer, the man Moskowitz and James had fired and whom, once, in his days of optimism, Bob Moses had hoped to replace.

In an attempt to help men who might try to reform civil service in other cities, Moses summed up in a speech to a political science convention "certain deductions" which he had made from his experiences. The main deduction was a simple one. "Executive support" was the essential you could not do without. "When a program for standardization work is first made," he said bitterly, "an effort should be made to get the persons who are responsible to pledge themselves to stand squarely behind the program."

At times in his summation, there was an attempt at the old self-confident tone. But it was a sad attempt. Trying to analyze the maneuvers which had bound his system in parliamentary red tape and then, with the red tape holding it helpless, had hacked it to death, Bob Moses finally stopped and said simply, "It is futile to attempt to establish beyond doubt who of the many agencies involved . . . is responsible. . . ." His dream, a dream for which he had fought with all the strength, brilliance and purity of purpose of youth and idealism, was dead—and he couldn't even be sure who had killed it.

The net result of all his work was nothing. There was no civil service standardization, no great highway along the Hudson, no mothers' shelters in Central Park. Intending to reform the city, he had worked hard and mastered with a supreme mastery reform's techniques. Convinced he was right, he had refused to soil the white suit of idealism with compromise. He had really believed that if his system was right—scientific, logical, fair—and if it got a hearing, the system would be adopted. In free and open encounter would not Truth prevail? And he had gotten the hearing.

But Moses had failed in his calculations to give certain factors due weight. He had not sufficiently taken into account greed. He had not sufficiently taken into account self-interest. And, most of all, he had not sufficiently taken into account the need for power.

Science, knowledge, logic and brilliance might be useful tools but they didn't build highways or civil service systems. Power built highways and civil service systems. Power was what dreams needed, not power in the hands of the dreamer himself necessarily but power put behind the dreamer's dreams by the man who had it to put there, power that he termed "executive support." Neither he himself nor James or Moskowitz had had such power. And the man who did, the man on whom he had counted for support, the mayor who was the epitome of his idealization of the public official, had not, in the final test, been willing to use his power on behalf of Bob Moses' dreams.

Bob Moses in 1918 was a man, not so young any more, looking for a job. Offered an army commission as a lieutenant, he decided after some hesitation not to serve in the war. A friend, Benjamin Van Schaick, was an executive of the government's Emergency Fleet Corporation, which had recently been created to build a new American merchant fleet, and Van Schaick got Moses an executive job with the corporation. But when Moses arrived in Washington, he found he had no clearly defined duties. Temper flaring, he demanded a new assignment and was sent to the huge shipbuilding works on Hog Island in the Delaware River. Too late, he realized he had made a mistake. "That was a stupid move," he was to say. "The place to be was with the top people in Washington." Hog Island was booming like a California gold field with the influx of tens of thousands of shipworkers, and the only home he could find for his daughter and his wife, who was pregnant again, was a rather shabby apartment.

The Hog Island operation was being conducted with all the inefficiency that might be expected from a massive production effort thrown together in wartime haste. When Moses complained about the inefficiency—the shipyard often had scores of hulls and not a single keel to attach them to—he was ignored by Hog Island officials. Trying to outflank the officials, he wrote a report detailing the inefficiency and proposing a complete new material-procurement method and persuaded Van Schaick to give it directly to Washington. Washington was impressed and called the local officials on the carpet. Their response was to wait until Washington's interest died down and then call Moses in and fire him.

Van Schaick, who quit voluntarily when he heard what had happened to his friend, procured them both executive positions at a Long Island City factory that was producing airplane engines, but when the war ended in November, the factory was closed down.

Moses had no choice. He had to go back to the Bureau of Municipal Research and ask the men he had scorned for a job. When they finally agreed to give him one, the stipend and duties attached were insultingly small.

Most of Moses' contemporaries were no longer at the Bureau. They had moved on to bigger things. Many, protected by civil service provisions from Hylan's wrath, were deputy commissioners in New York City governmental agencies, some were full commissioners in Philadelphia or Chicago. Some were executive secretaries of private welfare and social work agencies. Others had been hired away by reform groups in other cities to form new municipal research bureaus. Still others, like Raymond Moley, an associate professor at Western Reserve University in Cleveland, were on university faculties. But Moses' continuing attempts to find a niche outside the Bureau brought him only humiliation. One day, Moley happened to be in Cleveland City Hall. As he walked down a corridor, he saw a long line of men waiting to be interviewed for a minor municipal job. One of the men on the line was Bob Moses. And he didn't get the job.

Back at the Bureau, Moses graded students' papers and gave lectures. When the Bureau finally managed to place him with a government agency, the United States Food Commission, he found not only that he was going to be little more than a clerk but that his superior would be another former Bureau staffer, a man several years younger than he. And even this job shortly disappeared. His second child had just been born and it was another daughter, Jane. Moses had desperately wanted a son, but now doctors told Mary she would be unable to have any more children. Bella kept giving the couple money, but she didn't seem to realize how much more was needed now that there were two little girls in the family, and Bob and Mary didn't like to ask for more. They were very short of money. Once Mary worriedly confided to a friend that she had owed a grocery bill for weeks and didn't know how she was going to get the money to pay it. Their apartment, at West End Avenue and Eighty-seventh Street, was too small, and a larger one was out of the question.

The mood of the country, so optimistic when Moses had entered public life five years before, was one of pessimism and disillusionment. As clouds of discord blotted over hopes for an honorable and lasting peace, sunlight ceased to gleam on old illusions and enthusiasms. The star of the man whom Moses had idolized on the national level as he had idolized Mitchel on the local—highly educated university man Woodrow Wilson—was waning. Progressivism was all but dead. There was little talk of reform.

Moses' own mood was one new to him. He seemed confused and worried. With his thirtieth birthday less than a month away, not only dreams but hopes had disappeared. He had been trained for work in government, but with Hylan in control in New York there was obviously no place for him in city government. He had no connections in Washington. There was a new Governor in New York State, elected in an upset—Alfred E. Smith—but Smith was a Tammany man, one of the Tammany men, in fact, who had been most vociferous in scorn of Moses' civil service proposals. Moses had met Smith several years before, when he had been city sheriff, and had not been at all impressed by the short, paunchy Irishman with the red face, gold-filled teeth and loud, rasping voice. "He is a typical Tammany politician," he said to a friend at the time. "What can you expect from a man who wears a brown derby on the side of his head and always has a big cigar in the corner of his mouth?"

Smith was the very antithesis of Moses' ideal of a politician. Whether it was really true that he had never read a book all the way through, the story was plausible; not only had Smith never been to a university, he had never been to a high school—and he boasted about that fact. His remark on the floor of the State Assembly that his only degree was "FFM"—for the Fulton Fish Market, where he had worked as a boy—was already a legend. There seemed as little likelihood of a place for Bob Moses—for his dreams or for himself—on the state level as on the city. There seemed, in fact, to be no place anywhere for him to turn.

And then, one day, Bob Moses got a call from Henry Moskowitz's wife, Belle.

III

THE RISE TO POWER

6. *Curriculum Changes*

She wasn't "Mrs. M" then, or "Moskie," or "Lady Belle." Nicknames would come later when, all but unknown to the public but an almost legendary figure among politicians, she would be possessed of more power and influence than any woman in the United States. She would be called "Mrs. M" by the man who had given her that power and influence, Alfred Emanuel Smith, and by the young social workers and reformers she had recruited to Smith's service. That nickname would be used, in an attempt at familiarity, by politicians who, on favor-seeking visits to Albany, would notice her sitting unobtrusively in a corner of the Governor's office, a short, plump and motherly woman who sat placidly knitting and waiting for the Governor to turn to her, as he did before making any important decision, and ask: "What do you think, Mrs. M?" She would be called "Moskie" by the Irish overlords of Tammany Hall who resented her influence over Smith and who, unable no matter how hard they tried to attribute it to any motive even faintly scandalous, seized in desperation on the fact that she and most of her recruits, men like Joseph Proskauer, were Jewish; in the security of the Fourteenth Street wigwam, they were wont to bellow an anti-Semitic ditty that began with the bitter words "Moskie and Proskie/Are the brains of Tammany Hall." She would be called "Lady Belle" by young social workers who could not persuade her to recruit them and who gave her that nickname—in whispers they were very careful she didn't overhear—because they resented the calmness and assurance with which she sat against the wall at settlement-house tea-and-cookies receptions on New York's Lower East Side, looking over the crowd, and then beckoned to her someone whose work had caught her eye—a Sam Rosenman or a Howard Cullman or a Frances Perkins—and asked them if they would be interested in a nomination to the Assembly or the State Senate, or, perhaps, in a state-agency post she happened to know might shortly become vacant. With that question, she would set the young man or woman she had chosen on the road to the realization of his dreams.

But in late November 1918, when she telephoned Bob Moses, Belle Moskowitz was not a legendary figure—or even an especially impressive one—among the reformers who drifted in and out of the Bureau offices. Everyone knew Belle. Although she was only forty years old, she had been part of the reform movement long before there was a Bureau, ever since she was eighteen, when, slender, dark-eyed, beautiful and passionately idealistic, the daughter of a poor Jewish watchmaker from Eastern Europe, she had begun working, at Madison and other settlement houses, with immigrants even poorer than herself. Writing, producing and directing plays for the Educational Alliance, she was appointed its director of entertainment while she was still a student at Columbia, carrying a schedule that included every course she could find in the university catalogue that she thought might help her to understand, and assist, the underprivileged.

In 1903, she married one of the young men with whom she had been working at the Alliance, an artist and architect named Charles M. Israels. They had three children. In 1911, Israels committed suicide. In 1914, no longer a beautiful girl but an extremely plump and plainly dressed matron, she married social worker Henry Moskowitz. Dozens of reform leaders attended both weddings. Reformers regarded Belle as one of their inner circle.

But had anyone troubled to closely study her career, he would have seen that there was a difference between Belle and the average reformer: Belle Moskowitz's dreams became realities.

In 1909, for example, the Women's City Club, under Belle's direction, began an investigation of the city's so-called "dancing academies." The "academies" were the only easily accessible places of weekday recreation for the poor girls of the Lower East Side who worked in garment-center sweatshops. These girls, many of them in their early teens, were unsophisticated. But the academies served liquor at tables on the dance floor, had rooms ready for hasty rental down adjacent corridors and seemed expressly designed for what reformers euphemistically referred to as "the downfall of young women."

Reformers had been railing for years against the academies but previous clean-up efforts had followed the familiar pattern: investigations which caused newspaper furor and loud demands for change, verbal acquiescence by Tammany, and then, after the furor died down, business as before.

Belle altered the pattern. Instead of loudly denouncing conditions at the academies, she quietly checked incorporation certificates to learn the names of their owners—and found that they included both Tammany leaders and community pillars. Instead of giving the names to the newspapers, which would have brought headlines but not results, since all her ammunition would have been used up, she went to the leaders and pillars and told them she would keep their names secret if they saw to it that regulatory legislation was passed—and strictly enforced. It was. "These laws," the *Times* editorialized, "did more to improve the moral surroundings of young girls" than any other single social reform of the period.

When, in 1913, after years of struggle, garment workers' unions finally forced dress manufacturers to agree to the appointment of an impartial arbitrator to hear workers' grievances, union leaders realized that the appointment of a typical reformer—one ready, with Pavlovian predictability, to side with the workers in every case—would alienate the employers and wreck the system. They suggested Belle Moskowitz for the job. The employers, knowing her only as one of the reform crowd, agreed reluctantly—but they quickly found that Belle decided each case on its merits. The attorney for the employers' association admitted: "She understood the union leaders perfectly. She understood the employers quite as well. No one could fool her." And her recommendations for the improvement of working conditions in the industry were accepted by both sides—and implemented.

But in November 1918, when Mrs. Moskowitz telephoned Bob Moses, no one had studied her career, and none of the young men at the Bureau paid the quiet, matronly woman any special attention when she would drop by, as she sometimes did in the late afternoon, to chat with Bruère or Cleveland. Moses, on the day that she telephoned, didn't even know what activity she was currently engaged in. He wondered what she wanted.

Governor-elect Smith, Mrs. Moskowitz told him, had decided to appoint an official commission to draw up a plan for the complete reorganization of the state's administrative machinery and for the implementation of sweeping social welfare reforms. The Governor-elect, she said, intended to use the report as the basic program for his administration.

The commission, Mrs. Moskowitz said, would be composed of the state's most distinguished citizens, but Governor-elect Smith had appointed her as its executive head, and she was looking for a "chief of staff" to work under her and head its work force, which would include at least fifty persons. This chief of staff, she said, would have a free hand in hiring the fifty and complete charge of the day-to-day work of the commission. Would Dr. Moses be interested in the job?

Dr. Moses said he would.

The next day, Mrs. Moskowitz took Moses to see the Governor-elect in his apartment at the Biltmore Hotel. The meeting was brief and cordial. When Mrs. Moskowitz introduced Moses, all Smith said was that if this young man was her choice for the job, he was sure Dr. Moses would do a good job. From the Biltmore, she took the new appointee straight to the Hall of Records, at the corner of Chambers and Lafayette streets, where a whole section of the third floor had been allocated to the commission, to show him his office, a large, handsomely appointed room that was the first office of his own that Moses had ever had. The commission's work was to get underway immediately, Mrs. Moskowitz said. Bob should start hiring his staff at once.

The Bureau of Municipal Research, where, only a day before, Moses had been working, was just four blocks away from the Hall of Records, but Moses had come in that day a long way from the Bureau by any measurement other than distance. He had been looked down on by his associates there as a loudmouth and a failure. Now, after a single telephone call from a woman he hardly knew, he was suddenly in a position to call those associates —and invite them to apply to him for jobs.

Bob Moses was never to learn why, of all the brilliant, dedicated reformers she knew, Belle Moskowitz had picked him for the first official job she had had it in her power to dispense. Perhaps it was because she had heard about him from her husband. Perhaps it was because, of all those reformers, it was he who had most strongly caught her shrewd and appraising eye. Whatever the reason, he never learned it. But he was able to find out from reformer acquaintances how she had come to be so trusted by Al Smith that the Governor-elect had given her that power.

Most reformers regarded Smith as the epitome of all that they detested in the Tammany politician. Not only was he uneducated and uncouth—his spitting and drinking were legend—but, more important, he took Tammany's orders unquestioningly. For years, he had been Boss Charlie Murphy's chief henchman in Albany, and as president of the Board of Aldermen during Mitchel's mayoralty he had led the opposition that outsmarted and defeated the Boy Mayor at every turn. Al Smith's ethics, according to most reformers, matched his habits.

But a handful of reformers, those who had actually had occasion to work with Smith, had astounded their friends even before his nomination for Governor by arguing not only that Smith was not a typical Tammany politician but that this red-faced, jut-nosed, gold-toothed, harsh-voiced smoker of big cigars and wearer of brown derbies and suits with wide stripes was, in fact, the best hope that existed for the actual enactment into law of the social welfare measures for which they had fought so long with so little real success. One of this handful of pro-Smith reformers, Moses was told by his acquaintances, was Belle Moskowitz. She was, they said, among the most enthusiastic of the group. She had, in fact, come to see in Smith the instrument through which her dreams for the poor people of New York City would become realities.

The gubernatorial election of 1918 had been the first in New York State in which women were allowed to vote. Uncertain how to appeal to the new voters, Smith had felt he needed a woman active in female civic organizations who could sell him to such groups. Most of the female do-gooders around town wanted nothing to do with Smith's campaign. But Belle volunteered eagerly.

However similar their ultimate aims were to turn out to be, Smith had nothing but contempt for typical reformers. Regarding them as wild-eyed, impractical and, most important, incapable of producing results, he called them "crackpots." Women reformers, he had found, were invariably crackpots. Women, he felt, didn't belong in politics anyway. In the tight little tenement Irish world in which he lived, most of them confined their interests to their homes and their children, and that was how it should be. He was prepared to listen to his new adviser with no more than token interest.

He agreed only reluctantly to her suggestion that he address a luncheon of the Women's University Club. Uneducated, he felt he would be out of place before an audience of college graduates. He planned to make a brief talk filled with platitudes—and as hasty an exit as possible.

Sitting on the dais, looking down on the audience of smartly dressed women chattering over fruit cocktail, his misgivings increased. "What the hell am I going to say to a bunch of women like this?" he growled.

"If you're smart," the motherly lady by his side replied, "to this bunch of women you'll make the same speech you'd make to a bunch of businessmen."

Taken aback, Smith decided to give it a try. He spoke on the economic issues of the campaign. A master at gauging crowd reaction, he saw as he spoke that the technique was succeeding, and when he finished, the reception was as enthusiastic as the ones he received in Tammany clubhouses.

Smith had been given almost no chance to win. Tammany's strength was traditionally more than offset in statewide campaigns by the combination of the solid core of educated, independent, anti-Tammany voters in New York City and the solidly Republican, rural, Protestant, Prohibitionist strongholds upstate. Smith realized that he must win over the independent voters, but in the early stages of the campaign he had been having little success. After the luncheon, he began to rely more and more on Belle Moskowitz for advice in handling them. And when, thanks in part to a hefty chunk of their support, he had won the governorship and called a conference at the Biltmore apartment to map out his program, he had invited her to attend.

Smith told the roomful of burly Irishmen that, because of the inefficiency and duplication of effort he had observed during his twelve years as a state assemblyman, he wanted to reform the state's administrative machinery. The plump little Jewish matron sitting among them had long wanted such reform too, because without improvement in the machinery of government, it was useless to talk about the social reforms of which she had long dreamed. When Smith asked for ideas on how to start a drive for administrative reform, Belle had one ready. Even before he took office in January, she said, he should form a Commission for Reconstruction, Retrenchment and Reorganization in the state government.

To the bluff old Irish leaders seated around the little matron, her suggestion had seemed like one they would expect from a reformer. They waited for her to talk about all the benefits that would accrue to mankind from such a commission.

Slipping the word "retrenchment" into the commission title would be a great public relations device, Mrs. Moskowitz had said quietly, connoting as it did economy and prudence.

Smith had been elected because of the support he had been able to draw from independent voters and Republicans, Mrs. Moskowitz had continued. If he wanted to be re-elected, he had to keep such support. The state's Republicans, as they all knew, were divided into two branches. One was the GOP's "regular" organization, bossed by arch-reactionary William ("Big Bill") Barnes of Albany, which ran the state in an atmosphere of such corruption that GOP legislators were known as the "Black Horse Cavalry" because of their looting expeditions against the state treasury. The other branch was the GOP's "federal crowd," which contained most of the party's impulse to public good and had earned its title by the distinguished service rendered in Washington by Charles Evans Hughes and a cadre of stalwarts of the Progressive Republican movement that had swept Theodore Roosevelt to the governorship of the state and then to the presidency—Elihu Root, TR's Secretary of State, Henry L. Stimson, later Secretary of War, and George W. Wickersham, later Attorney General. The "federal crowd" had been pressing for administrative and social welfare improvements for years. They would be enthusiastic about a "Reconstruction, Retrenchment and Reorganization Commission." In fact, they would be happy to serve on it, and they would tend to feel kindly toward the Governor who had asked them to. The "regular" Republicans, who would see in talk of "reconstruction" a threat to their control of the state government, could be expected to oppose the commission's work. Its creation, therefore, would have the dual effect of splitting the Republican Party and lining up with Smith those Republicans who exemplified Progressivism and reform to independent voters. The support of such Republicans would help negate Smith's greatest handicap, the Tammany label he bore. In addition, she reminded the leaders, the "federal crowd" were heavy campaign contributors.

Before the motherly little woman had finished speaking, the roomful of politicians had realized that they were listening to a master politician. Al Smith had bought her suggestion on the spot.

Reorganization of the state government was not a new idea. It had been a basic reform tenet for years, and in 1915 a Bureau of Municipal Research study commissioned by a State Constitutional Convention had found no fewer than 169 separate state departments, bureaus, boards, committees and commissions, many with overlapping functions—taxes, for example, being collected by seven different agencies, public works being carried out by ten. Some agency heads were responsible to the Governor, some to the Legislature and some to officials who were themselves elected by the people and were hence not responsible to either Governor or Legislature. Some agency heads appointed by the Governor were removable only by the Legislature, and there seemed to be almost as many different procedures of removal as there were men who could be removed. His term was only two years, and the terms of some gubernatorial appointees were longer, so that each incoming Governor was forced to entrust the carrying out of some of his policies to men appointed by previous Governors, who might be politically opposed to him. Such nominal members of the executive department as the state engineer, treasurer and secretary of state were not appointed but elected and, therefore, even if they were of the Governor's party, did not owe their primary allegiance to the Governor but to the voters and could, if they wished, ignore his wishes with impunity.

Most important, the study found that the Governor possessed little real authority. Not he but the chairmen of the various committees of the reactionary and corrupt Legislature controlled the state's purse. The document that was called a state budget was actually a collection of appropriations drawn up by these chairmen. No legislator—or any other state official—reviewed the collection, balanced one appropriation against another, cut them down to agreed-upon necessities or measured them against estimated revenue. Even after the document was formally printed, individual legislators continued to introduce their own "private" bills, generally for pork-barrel public works projects, which required public expenditures, and these, when passed, did not even appear in the "budget." No one bothered to add them up, so that, when the Legislature adjourned, no one could be sure how much money it had appropriated. The Governor technically had the power to veto appropriations, but since state law forbade him to veto *part* of an appropriation item, legislators simply made sure that each debatable expenditure was lumped with one too essential to be vetoed.

The Bureau had become convinced that it was this lodging of administrative power in Legislature rather than Governor that, more than any other single fact, explained the utter failure of twenty years of effort by a succession of liberal Governors such as Roosevelt and Hughes to increase the involvement of the state with the new needs of its people. Because the Governor stood at the head of the state and represented all of its people rather than just one assembly or senate district, the Governor must be held responsible if the state failed to move as the voters wanted it to move. But going hand and hand with responsibility, the Bureau said, must be power. If a man was to be held responsible for moving government, he must be given power to move it, "executive power commensurate with executive responsibility" in the Bureau's slogan.

To get power into the hands of the executive, the Bureau recommended a centralization of governmental functions. The 169 agencies should be combined into twelve departments headed by men appointed by, and removable by, the Governor, whose term should be lengthened to four years. An "executive budget" system should be instituted. Under it, department heads would submit financial requests to the Governor, who would weigh the requests against the resources and needs of the state and propose an over-all budget. Only then would the budget be submitted to the Legislature, which would review it, in a series of hearings that would insure that the public could understand it, and then would have the power to reduce it by eliminating items. The Governor would therefore be proposing the way the state was to be run; the Legislature would be reviewing the proposal, and if the differences between Legislature and Governor proved irreconcilable, the public would settle them at the next election. Furthermore, after policy had been established, it was to be administered by the Governor instead of by the Legislature's many committee chairmen.

The Bureau's 1915 report, *Government of the State of New York,* was 768 pages long. With reform leaders taking the floor to argue for its principles, many of its key points were adopted by the Constitutional Convention. But Tammany and the upstate bosses outwitted the reformers by persuading them to combine all the proposed constitutional amendments in a single package, and distaste for one or two unimportant but unpopular amendments, combined with a quiet mobilization of Tammany and upstate machines, resulted in the defeat of the package in a November 1915 referendum.

Bob Moses, who, as a Bureau staffer, had worked on its 1915 report and who now, in his new job, recruited other staffers who had worked on that report, expected at first that the report of the Reconstruction Commission would be practically a duplication. But there was a bigger difference between working for the Bureau and working for Belle Moskowitz than sumptuousness of office arrangements. The Bureau made recommendations; Mrs. Moskowitz made laws. The Bureau got enthusiastic and excited; Mrs. Moskowitz got things done. And no sooner had her chief of staff begun work, two weeks before his thirtieth birthday, than she began to teach him *how* things got done.

The lessons started almost immediately. When Moses submitted a preliminary outline of suggested commission goals, he included a phrase straight out of the reform textbooks and his Municipal Civil Service Commission days: "Elimination of unnecessary . . . personnel." Mrs. Moskowitz struck the phrase out. Personnel, she said, were voters. You didn't antagonize voters. When Moses, copying a 1915 Bureau recommendation, suggested that the unwieldy ten-member "council" which ran the Department of Agriculture be scrapped in favor of a single, professional commissioner, she pointed out that the council memberships were distributed by the Legislature and were among the choicest patronage posts it possessed. The Governor, she said, would need the support of the Legislature if his program were to be approved. The council, she said, would remain.

The lessons were given in daily morning conferences. Moses would arrive brimming over with ideas and impatient for their approval. But the reception they received from Mrs. Moskowitz was somewhat different from the one his ideas had been accorded by Mr. Moskowitz. As Moses excitedly paced around her office, she would sit calmly, attentive but noncommittal. When he finished, she usually would not say anything for several minutes. Often, she would praise the ideas, and break into a smile, full of real pleasure, at Moses' inventiveness. But, equally often, Moses' ideas would be thrown out.

"There was a real divergence of opinion there," staffers recall. "Moses was very theoretical, always wanting to do exactly what was right, trying to make things perfect, unwilling to compromise. She was more practical; she wanted to do the same things as Moses, but she wanted to concentrate on what was possible and not jeopardize the attaining of those things by stirring up trouble in other areas." And her decisions were always final. While Moses paced and argued, trying to change her mind, Mrs. Moskowitz would sit quietly and, when Moses had finished, would quietly repeat her earlier decision. "There was never any question," recalls another staffer, "that she was the boss."

Often, Moses would come bursting out of Mrs. Moskowitz's office cursing under his breath. Striding around the large room in which thirty staffers had desks, he would let the breath out. "He used to call Mrs. Moskowitz all kinds of names which weren't gentlemanly at all," one of the men who sat in that room recalls. "I remember him saying, over and over, 'Do you know what that old she son of a bitch told me this morning?' " Once, lunging across the room in a rage so blind that he thudded into a desk, he paused for a moment, leaned down to the startled man sitting at it, and muttered grimly, "I could have kicked that woman in the shins!"

But, in spite of the cursing, there was a difference in Bob Moses. The man who had not hesitated to criticize to their faces his superiors at the

Bureau of Municipal Research was careful that his cursing of Mrs. Moskowitz was done out of her earshot. "He certainly didn't talk *to* her the way he talked *about* her," a staffer recalls. While he might dispute a decision heatedly, he stopped arguing once she made clear that the decision was final.

Some of the staffers believed this change of attitude was due to a newfound prudence in a man aware that the opportunity he had been given with the commission might be his last chance to make good in his chosen career. One says: "If he had talked to Mrs. Moskowitz the way he talked to Cleveland or Allen—or to Mr. Moskowitz—he would have been thrown out, and if he had been thrown out of that job, that would have been the end of Bob Moses, and he knew it."

Such an explanation, however, failed to take into account the full extent of the difference. For one thing, Moses was not only obeying Mrs. Moskowitz but also obviously studying the lessons that she was teaching, and studying them hard. His conversation began to include the phrases of practical politics as well as those of scientific management textbooks. His analysis of a state job began to take into consideration not only whether the position was necessary for the betterment of mankind but also who had appointed the man who now held the position. He learned to weigh the governmental gains that might be achieved by the position's elimination and by the use for worthier purposes of the salary allocated to it against the political losses the elimination might entail—how much it would antagonize the appointer and how great an obstacle such antagonism might be to Smith's over-all program.

The difference went deeper. It was not just that he obeyed Mrs. Moskowitz and it was not just that he learned her way of thinking; rather it was that, after a while, he seemed almost eager to learn. He had always scorned the considerations of "practical" politics. Practical politicians had crushed and destroyed his dreams and had come near to crushing and destroying him. They had done it with an ease that added humiliation to defeat. And now, given a chance to learn their methods, Bob Moses seemed almost enthusiastic about embracing them.

He was an apt pupil. In his first conferences with Mrs. Moskowitz, they had discussed how the commission would go about obtaining from the Republican-dominated state agencies the information—on salary and internal organization and promotion policy, for example—needed to evaluate the agencies' work. Moses' initial reaction was straightforward. Why couldn't commission staffers simply demand the information? he asked. Smith was Governor, wasn't he? If an agency proved recalcitrant, Smith could simply *order* the agency head to cooperate. Mrs. Moskowitz made clear that the commission wouldn't proceed along any such lines. In the first place, she said, many of the agencies regarded themselves as independent of the Governor; an order he gave them might be disobeyed. Even if it was obeyed, it could cause hard feelings and the Governor didn't want hard feelings; he wanted reform. He had only two years to make a start on it, and he was going to have plenty of trouble no matter how he went about it. He didn't want any more than was absolutely necessary. The commission must be very careful not to stir up any that could possibly be avoided. And not only did Moses, once so impatient and impolitic, become a model of discretion on his trips to Albany, talking only to men to whom Smith's aides could introduce him as a friend; to his staffers he repeated over and over, in urgent, handwritten notes: "Be careful. Remember that we must not embarrass the Governor." And the commission was able to avoid any angry confrontations with agency heads.

The eyes that had picked Bob Moses out of the herd of young reformers were watching his progress. It was as spectacular as it had been at Oxford, where he had learned part of the political science. There, he had graduated with honors. Belle Moskowitz, who taught him another aspect of the science, did not confer degrees, but she awarded him her own type of honor: by the spring of 1919, less than six months after she had taken over Moses' tutelage, she was leaving the supervision of the State Reconstruction Commission almost entirely in his hands.

The commission's work meshed with his personal convictions. Reorganizing government to make it more responsive to social needs was an aim that he had enunciated for himself in his Oxford thesis, and all his work in government thereafter had only strengthened his belief in the urgency of the need for such reorganization. More specifically, the reorganization on which the Reconstruction Commission was embarked was almost certainly going to be designed to increase the powers of the state's chief executive, and power for the executive was another theme that, at least in implication, ran through the thesis.

The commission's work, moreover, was of a scope and an aim consonant with the sweeping, soaring, almost visionary quality of his idealism. For years he had laughed bitterly with other young reformers at the open chicanery of the Black Horse Cavalry, at the inefficiency of the system which sent tax collectors from seven different state agencies to the same factory, at the utter hopelessness of the administrative machinery of New York State. Now, at last, here was a chance to replace that machinery, not just to oil it but to take it apart and haul it away, and then replace it with a new one. Here was a chance to change a state, the most populous and influential in the nation.

If Moses was hopeful of success this time, his hopefulness was not the naïve overconfidence of his Civil Service Commission days. The success or failure of the Reconstruction Commission's efforts, he understood, was not in the hands of the commission but depended on someone else. But he had real hope that this time the someone else might come through.

Moses had been quite prepared to be disappointed by the Governor he had called "a typical Tammany politician." But Al Smith's speech to the prominent liberal Democrats, independents and "federal" Republicans on the commission at its first meeting had certainly not been *pro forma*. Mangled cigar stub stabbing out from his wet lips at the vested, watch-fobbed civic leaders before him, he had rasped, "Is this commission going to do something or is it just going to offer a report? Are you going to have something definite that can be put into effect to benefit the state? Because if you are not, the sooner you report and go out of existence the better." Nor had Smith's actions been *pro forma* when the Black Horse Cavalry refused his request for $75,000 to enable the commission to begin work. Here was a ready-made opportunity to reap political capital. As Mrs. Moskowitz had surmised, the GOP's federal wing raged against their party's legislators, along with most of the state's important newspapers. Without doing anything else, simply by letting the commission die and pointing out that the Legislature had killed it, Smith would have scored a political coup. But Smith did something else. He asked the members of the commission to put up the $75,000 themselves, and when they did, he publicly promised that he would abide by, and sponsor, any recommendations it made when it completed its report.

Often now, in the late afternoon, the Governor would drop by the commission offices. He came primarily to obtain Mrs. Moskowitz's advice on some problem or other. "You could see," says one of the young commission staffers, "that Smith really trusted her. Over and over again, I heard him say, 'Now, Mrs. M, you do so and so or you look into such and such this week and let me know how you feel about it.' " But on his way to the little office in the corner that had been reserved for him—and equipped with a big brass spittoon—the Governor would stop and chat with the staffers, telling them the inside stories of political in-fighting going on in Albany or kidding them about the pretty secretaries in the commission stenographic pool next door. When he finished talking to Mrs. Moskowitz, he would call them into his office and—between well-aimed expectorations toward the spittoon—he would tell more stories. He would talk to them seriously, too. The frank, serious blue eyes that looked so out of place over the big-veined nose and the gold-filled teeth in the flushed face would stare straight into theirs. I won't let you down, he would say. You just get the facts and come up with the recommendations. I'll fight for them. "Nobody could help liking Al Smith," one of the young men said. "You had to like him—and you had to believe in him."

Moses had worked hard before. He worked harder now. Some of his young staffers worked late; when they left, a light was almost always still shining through the frosted-glass top half of the door to Moses' office. In the morning, the staffers would find on their desks long, detailed memos—signed "Robert Moses, Chief of Staff"—outlining new assignments.

Moses would criticize staffers' reports mercilessly. When he returned them, they would be adorned with large, angry double question marks. Sloppy phrasing would be slashed through. "Most essential question not discussed at all," Moses scribbled on one report. "What overhead organization do you propose? Do you believe in a commission or a single commissioner? If the latter, should a rules-making board be attached to him?"

Staffers became accustomed to seeing Moses' handwriting filling the margins and spilling over their type and, scrawled across the top of the first page, heavily underlined: "*REVISE* ALL!"

Activity in the office revolved around the tall, wiry figure with the shock of black hair who worked in shirt sleeves rolled up to the elbow. He had appointed an "assistant chief of staff," reformer Channing Schweitzer, but, too impatient to work through a chain of command, when he had something to say to one of the staffers, he would come out of his office and say it himself.

The tension disclosed in the heavy underlining of the written criticism on the reports would sometimes spill over in short but violent bursts of anger. When a key piece of paper was misfiled one day and a secretary had to report she could not locate it, he glared around the room and shouted, while the staffers discreetly studied the tops of their desks, "Where the hell did it go? Who's got it? Who's got it?"

But if Bob Moses often shouted, he also often laughed, his teeth gleaming in a broad infectious grin, and his laughter was never louder than when it was directed at one of his own mistakes—which he was usually the first to point out. He was friendly with the staffers, seeming to spend as much time during the day out in the big room in which their desks were located as in his office, hunting up luncheon companions with an easy and charming air that brought together large groups to accompany him to the German rathskellers that lined the street back of the Hall of Records. Over lunch, he was a good listener and, with his vivid accounts of his latest hassle with Mrs. Moskowitz, and his vivid descriptions of the big shots on the commission to whom she had introduced him, a good talker.

His personality, his knowledge and his application inspired the young men under him. Many of them would go on to distinguished careers, but they would look back across the decades at the time they spent working for Moses as one of the high points of their lives.

" 'Dedication' has become sort of a phony word," staffer John Gaus said shortly before he died in 1969, "but that's what Moses had. People who are terrifically hard workers you have got to respect anyway, but it was more than just how hard he worked. He was a vibrant and driving person—you just *knew* that if you wanted to work for him, you had to be on your toes, but on the other hand that you would be treated with complete frankness, and you also knew that here was one person who was really thinking of the public interest above everything else. He talked to you hard and direct, but he made you feel that you were both on the same side, fighting for the same things. He made you want to work for him."*

* Moses so fascinated Gaus that for more than two decades, while the young social worker was carving out a reputation as an author of books on public administration and as a professor of government at Harvard University, never seeing Moses during all that time, he collected every newspaper clipping about Moses that he saw, just so he could keep track of his career. After he retired, in 1961, Gaus began collecting clippings on Moses again, filing them in cartons which he kept in the attic of his Utica, New York, home, and he kept filling those cartons until the day of his death.

With the state's coffers closed to the commission by the Legislature, money was constantly tight. Salaries were very low. But the young men said it didn't matter. In the spring of 1919, funds ran out entirely, and while Smith and Mrs. Moskowitz scrounged for private contributions, the young men received neither salary nor expenses for six weeks. Gaus and Morris Lambie, another young reformer, researching in Albany, were able to keep eating only by borrowing money from relatives. Once Gaus wrote Schweitzer, "Since the wolf is approaching so near that I can hear his howls distinctly, I wonder if you can find one of those precious valentines lying around signed by Belle Moskowitz and assuring the bearer that the Guaranty Trust will do its damnedest to trade it in for good U.S. notes. If last month's salary is in the offing, why I want to be there, too." But when Gaus at last got hold of the pieces of information he needed to complete his report on the State Labor Department, money was forgotten. Mailing the report to Schweitzer, with a special-delivery stamp that cost him a substantial portion of the last change in his pocket, Gaus attached to the report a note: "Happy Days! Let the people rule!"

Moses' jubilation matched Gaus's. None of the staffers found any reason to complain about their chief's enthusiasm over their successes. He had, they said, no "side," no pomposity. He was, they said, very "democratic." If they noticed a difference between the manner in which he treated them, men who were almost his equals, and the manner in which he treated men a step lower on the commission's totem pole, they didn't think it important. But the difference was there. The memos Moses addressed to lower-echelon personnel were different in tone from even the most peremptory of those he sent to the staffers. In a memo addressed to a chart maker, for example, Moses laid out his assignment in the tone of an army drill sergeant, unsoftened by a single "please" or courteous adverb. "In connection with your assignment," he wrote, "you will do the following. . . . You will prepare a chart showing the present departments. . . . You will prepare a chart showing the proposed organization. . . . You will keep in touch with Mr. Gaus, Mr. Buck and myself. . . . You will consult other members of the staff before putting the chart in ink."

Moses' energy seemed inexhaustible. For the summer of 1919, he and Mary, along with two other couples with small children, the Henry Bruères and Frances Perkins and her husband, Paul Wilson, rented bungalows near a beach in Douglaston, Queens. Moses never caught any train out from Manhattan but the latest available, which arrived in Douglaston about eight-thirty. Darkness would be falling, but Moses would always go for a swim. Plunging into the water, he would strike straight out Little Neck Bay, his arms windmilling rhythmically and powerfully, his head growing smaller and smaller in the distance. His friends would joke that he didn't seem likely to stop until he had crossed Long Island Sound and reached the shore of Westchester County, which, on clear days, was a low black line on the horizon.

"He was a wonderful swimmer," Frances Perkins would recall. "I never saw a man who could swim so long, so easily, so far, with such confidence and security. We used to get nervous. He'd go way out where you couldn't see him. It being dark, we'd finally lose sight of him entirely. . . . One night he must have been gone an hour and a half before he came back." The watchers thought he had drowned. "Henry was discussing how we should break the news to Mary. 'What shall we tell her?' We were all urging each other, 'Let's wait a little while. Don't call the police yet.' " It wasn't until long after dark that the anxious viewers on the beach saw Moses returning.

On Sundays, Moses didn't go into his office but, as if unable to relax, would spend the days energetically teaching the three sets of children to swim, the evenings telling them stories he made up himself. "He was so good with children," Miss Perkins recalled.

By the latter part of the summer, Moses was forced to work even harder. The commission's funds were running out, and the private contributions which had sustained its work were falling off. With his usual disregard for financial considerations, Moses had paid little attention to this state of affairs. If Gaus and Lambie were living off relatives, so was he —the major part of his income was still coming from his parents—but this didn't seem to bother him, and as for the work of the commission, he vaguely assumed that with all those wealthy men interested in its success, whatever was needed would somehow be raised. They had so much money they'd never miss a little of it, he would say. And anyway, fund raising was not his province but that of the commission's executive committee. In July, however, Mrs. Moskowitz told him that he must begin laying off his staff at once. He had to let some of the young men go with only a week's notice. By Labor Day, the staff had been disbanded. Some sections of the report existed only in recommendation memos, others only in rough-draft form. Only a few sections were actually completed. Lugging the commission's files to his already cramped apartment, Moses wrote the rest of the report alone. By October, it was finished.

The *Report of the Reconstruction Commission to Governor Alfred E. Smith on Retrenchment and Reorganization in the State Government* contained little that was startlingly original. It didn't have to. In that government, little had changed. The Bureau of Municipal Research, in presenting its report to the 1915 Constitutional Convention, had concluded that the state's administrative organization "has nothing in common experience or human reason to commend it." But in the intervening four years, the situation had only worsened. The Bureau's investigators had counted with shock 169 separate and independent state agencies; in 1919, Moses' investigators counted 187. The organization chart of the sovereign state of New York still looked like a web spun by a drunken spider, and the man elected to represent all the people of the state was still trapped in the web, unable to exercise power or leadership.

What made the report written in the small apartment on Eighty-seventh Street a remarkable document was its clarion tone and its clarity. Viewed as part of the long reform movement in New York State, which set much of the tone for Progressivism in the United States, it was the summing up of this movement. The essence of the spirit of reform was captured in its 419 pages, so completely did the words they bore synthesize both its philosophy and its passion.

The prose with which Moses prefaced the report had in particular the ring of the battle trumpet. The 5,200-word opening declaration of "Underlying Principles," written almost entirely by Moses and left untouched by Belle Moskowitz, contained hard, lucid, driving reasoning that reduced complexities to fundamentals. Dealing with a point that reformers generally tried to avoid because of their fear that it was a weak spot in their argument, Moses plunged instead to its heart and found there complete compatibility with the basic reform belief in an increased participation by the citizen in government.

"The only serious argument advanced against . . . [the] proposed reorganization and budget system is that it makes the Governor a czar," he wrote.

> The Governor does not hold office by hereditary right. He is elected for a fixed term by universal suffrage. He is controlled in all minor appointments by the civil service law. He cannot spend a dollar of the public money which is not authorized by the Legislature of the State. He is subject to removal by impeachment. If he were given the powers here proposed he would stand out in the limelight of public opinion and scrutiny. Economy in administration, if accomplished, would redound to his credit. Waste and extravagance could be laid at his door. Those who cannot endure the medicine because it is too strong must be content with waste, inefficiency and bungling—and steadily rising cost of government. The system here proposed is more democratic, not more "royal," than that now in existence. Democracy does not merely mean periodic elections. It means a government held accountable to the people between elections. In order that the people may hold their government to account they must have a government that they can understand. No citizen can hope to understand the present collection of departments, offices, boards and commissions, or the present methods of appropriating money. A Governor with a cabinet of reasonable size, responsible for proposing a program in the annual budget and for administering the program as modified by the Legislature, may be brought daily under public scrutiny, be held accountable to the Legislature and public opinion, and be turned out of office if he fails to measure up to public requirements. If this is not democracy then it is difficult to imagine what is.

As in Moses' Oxford thesis, the tone of "Underlying Principles" was often lecturing and dogmatic. Refusing to debate whether the consolidated state agencies should be under Governor or Legislature, he wrote: "The Constitution says that the executive power shall be vested in the Governor. . . . *There is no other way*." But, as in the thesis, the tone was also evangelistic. "A consolidation of a hundred or more offices . . . affects political patronage vitally," he wrote, "and it requires considerable courage and intelligence"; nevertheless, state after state was taking steps toward such reorganization. A steadily more informed citizenry, demanding efficiency and economy in government, was pushing them forward, he said. It was time for New York to join the march.

In those 5,200 words—and in other sections of the 22,000-word "Summary of Recommendations" with which the report began—was distilled the essence of the philosophy of Progressivism in general and the Bureau of Municipal Research in particular. It was all there, the bywords which New York's reformers had been chanting for twenty years—"executive budget," "longer terms," "consolidation," "responsibility," "commensurate power"—the incantation, like a drum roll underlying the chant, of "efficiency and economy," the idealistic belief that citizen knowledge of the intricacies of government and participation in those intricacies was the panacea for democracy. At one point, defending the imposition of an income tax, Moses wrote, "One of the possible benefits [because of people's interest in the spending of their money] will be the development among . . . citizens of . . . a more vital interest in state organization and expenditures."

In specific recommendations, Moses followed the Bureau's creed, except where practical considerations introduced by Mrs. Moskowitz intruded, commandment by commandment.

The 187 agencies should be consolidated into departments—sixteen instead of twelve because of Mrs. Moskowitz—and each department headed by a single officer except in certain cases where considerations—Mrs. Moskowitz's—dictated the retention of a council or board.

The Governor should be given the power to appoint—and remove—all department heads and key administrative officials, with the exception of the comptroller, whose independence is necessary because his function should be to act as a watchdog on expenditures, including those of the Governor.

The Governor should be given the power to designate certain of his appointees as a "Cabinet," which would meet regularly to advise him.

The Governor's term should be extended to four years.

The long list of elected state officials should be reduced to the Governor, lieutenant governor, attorney general and comptroller.

An "executive budget" system—including not only expenditures but a plan for raising the revenues necessary to pay for them—should be drawn up by the Governor, and only then submitted to the Legislature; it should be safeguarded, at every step, by public hearings to doubly insure that the financial policy of the state would not be decided upon behind the closed doors of either Executive Chamber or committee room.

The commission's recommendations, which took 44 pages to summarize, were backed up with 375 pages of remarkable detail. The governments of other states—every other state—were analyzed. So were every one of New York State's 187 agencies. Included were descriptions of each agency's powers, tabulations of the laws which had, over the years, given them those powers, analyses of how their powers overlapped those of other agencies, descriptions of the power they would be given under the proposed reorganization plan, lists of the personnel of every existing and every proposed agency, the salaries and duties of the personnel, the organization charts (some of which, folded for inclusion in the bound report, opened out to a full five feet in length). Lists were made of the personnel each of the departments should have—down to the precise number of clerks a specific commissioner might need.

For internal changes within agencies or departments—and thousands of them were recommended—only new laws, "statutory changes," would be required, the report concluded. For three of the proposed major governmental changes—creation of the sixteen departments with provision that all existing state agencies and any that might be established in the future would be placed in one of them; institution of the executive budget system; and extension of the Governor's term to four years—the state's constitution would have to be amended, each amendment requiring passage by two Legislatures, elected in different years, and approved by the state's voters in a referendum.

Moses assumed a proprietary attitude toward the report. Certainly he was the driving force in its preparation, wrote its brilliant introduction himself and rewrote many other sections. Yet he was not the only person who had contributed to it, and he seemed unwilling to admit that fact. "I wrote the report, no question about it," he insisted in later years. "I wrote or rewrote everything in it."

It was the practice at the time to list at the beginning of such reports the names of all individuals and organizations who had worked on them, but most members of Moses' staff found that their names were mentioned nowhere. Unhappy about that, they were even more bitter that the Bureau, which they revered and on whose principles and 1915 report on the same subject this report was based, was not mentioned even once in the document they regarded as the historical climax of all its work, not even in those sections for which the Bureau had, at Moses' request, done all the work. Moreover, Moses' boast that he "rewrote everything" in the report was not strictly correct. Comparison of staffers' rough-draft recommendations for two departments—the only such rough drafts available today—with the finished versions published in the report show that they are practically identical.

Moses' attitude led to one particularly bitter episode. Parts of the "Summary of Recommendations," the second half of the introduction, were written, at Moses' request, by Charles A. Beard, then director of the Bureau's Training School and already a noted historian. In particular, Beard wrote the summary of reorganization advances in other states. Whether Moses did any rewriting at all of Beard's work cannot be determined, but Bureau staffers who saw the historian's original copy feel it was included in the final report substantially as written. They were astounded, therefore, to hear that after Beard had written a magazine article on reorganization advances, Moses had accused the author of *An Economic Interpretation of the Constitution* of plagiarism.

"A bunch of us walked into Beard's office one day and there he was, just ready to spit he was so outraged, waving this letter from Moses," recalls one staffer. "The letter said Beard had, in effect, plagiarized from the commission's report. We were astounded; in the academic world, there are few sins as bad as stealing another fellow's work and that was what Moses was accusing Beard of—and we all *knew* Beard had written that section, not Moses.

And as we were reading the letter, Beard kept muttering, 'Well, what do you think of this? What do you think of this?' He was so angry he didn't know what else to say."

Whether Moses wrote all of it or part, the Reconstruction Commission report was something of which a man could be proud. From the moment, on October 10, 1919, that it was published, it was hailed as a historic document, not only by Smith, who had sponsored it, and not only by the reformers, who saw in it the finest exposition of their philosophy, but, more importantly, by the men who Belle Moskowitz had hoped would hail it—the Republican "federal crowd." Charles Evans Hughes—former crusading investigator, Governor, Secretary of State, Justice of the Supreme Court and Republican nominee for the presidency, now returned to private life as a lawyer and "first citizen" of New York State—and Congressman Ogden Livingston Mills, a noted authority on taxation and government finance, volunteered to head a City Club study of the report, which concluded that it was "deserving of unreserved approbation." When a Philadelphia reformer solicited suggestions from Colonel Henry L. Stimson on reorganizing Pennsylvania's archaic governmental structure, Stimson replied with a copy of the report and an attached note that said, "This paper is, I think, the most helpful one that I could put in your hands . . . to give you an idea of . . . what I believe to be the correct principles of state government."

An informal "citizens committee" was formed to back efforts to implement the report, and a little money was raised for the fight. Moses was named secretary of the committee and given a small salary that, with Bella's subsidy, enabled him to continue working full time for reorganization, and, in January 1920, when Smith publicly announced that he would push during the upcoming legislative session for adoption of the report's recommendations, he was assigned the job of making the committee an effective force to assist the Governor.

The first step was to "get the names," to enlarge the committee by adding members whose prestige would lend it political clout. With Hughes, Mills and Stimson already aboard, the job was easy. As the letterhead of the Citizens Committee on Reorganization in the State Government was continually reprinted so that the names of the latest joiners would be on it, the list above "Robert Moses, Secretary" came to include a cross-section of elements of the state who normally would have had nothing to do with a Governor who bore the stamp of Tammany.

The second step was to get money for the fight, and Moses wrote the members of the Citizens Committee for help. Their responses were smaller than their names—Stimson would scribble to his secretary on each of Moses' appeals, "Send $25"—but numerous enough to enable Moses to move the committee's files out of his apartment and into a small office at 305 Broadway. When the three constitutional amendments were introduced in the Legislature on February 9, 1920, Moses wrote again: "The campaign for adoption must now be pushed with the greatest energy. . . . It will be necessary to raise about

$2,000." When, in May, legislative committee chairmen refused to let the amendments come to the floor for a vote and Smith announced that he was considering calling a special session to force a decision, Moses wrote, "We need $1,500." "This budget," he added, "presumes the minimum of expenditures. To date, the expenses of this committee have been kept down by volunteer assistance and maintenance of an extra office at the home of the secretary without expense to the committee." The plea so moved Stimson that he scribbled: "Send $50."

For "executive support," Moses—for the first time in his life—did not have to plead. You just get the facts and come up with the recommendations, Al Smith had told the commission staffers. He would fight for them. And now, he fought, stumping the state to remind the voters that the commission's recommendations were supported by the GOP's most prestigious members and should be treated as nonpartisan proposals instead of as bills being pushed on a Republican Legislature by a Democratic Governor trying to curb its powers.

Al Smith on the stump was a political weapon of the highest caliber. "I believe that I enjoy some little reputation for keeping my word," he said in one speech. "I will give it—I will give it to this Legislature—that if they will come with me, take this report, do the best that they can with it, I am not going to be the fellow who insists on getting his bill the way it is printed [without compromise, in the form it is first introduced] because usually that fellow doesn't want the bill. . . . And I will promise them now that at no time in the future will it ever be referred to by me, or anybody over whom I have any control, as any program of mine. The fact of the matter is: It is not my program. The real truth about it is I could not think that all out myself."

When, at a Women's City Club debate between Smith and Lieutenant Governor Seymour Lowman, a Republican, Lowman charged that the reorganization program was "Governor Smith's attempt to make himself a king," Smith arose and, after alluding—just long enough to bring tears to the women's eyes—to his poverty-stricken youth in an Oliver Street tenement, pointed to himself with a deprecatory gesture and said, with plenty of sarcasm and just the right little touch of bitterness: "Behold the King, the King of Oliver Street."

To get the maximum use out of the big names on the Citizens Committee, Mrs. Moskowitz wanted them—and their support of Smith's proposals—kept in the public eye. But they were under pressure from furious Republican regulars who told them, correctly, that their financial contributions and prestige were being used to build the career of a Tammany man at the expense of their own party. Many, in fact, were on the verge of resigning. Tact had to be used in handling them. Tact had never been one of Moses' long suits, but now he had been taught by Belle Moskowitz. When he arranged luncheons of the committee and asked its big names to make speeches at the luncheons, speeches that the press would report, he made the requests, and pressed for answers, persistently but gently. He displayed a willingness to compromise that was also new to him. When some members of the committee, expressing doubts that all the report's recommendations were correct, threatened to resign, Moses wrote assuring them that "these amendments are not final, but are subject to correction after consultation." There were few resignations—none from significant "names"—and, month after month, Moses directed an almost daily fusillade of support for Smith's position from Hughes, Stimson, Wickersham and even, in what amounted to the most impressive coup for Smith, from former State Republican Chairman Frederick C. Tanner.

Under this onslaught, the Legislature reeled. Republican assemblymen and senators assured the public that they were interested in reorganization too, and introduced bills of their own which they said had the same objectives as the commission's. This put the battle on a technical level. Smith needed rapid analyses of the Republican bills to determine whether their sponsors' claims for them were true. Mrs. Moskowitz summoned Moses to Albany and, with Mary making sure he had the $5.42 for the fare in his pocket, he left the apartment at 6 A.M. to catch the early train to the capital.

At first, Moses worked in a small office in the recesses of the capitol, but as the legislative session moved toward a climax, he was called more and more frequently to the Executive Chamber. Having him at hand saved everybody time. If the Governor and his advisers wanted to know how many jobs a proposed GOP bill would eliminate and whose jobs they were, or whether the wording of a bill conflicted with seemingly contradictory wording in the Constitution, or whether there was any precedent to back up a proposal of their own, or how many secretaries there were in the Public Works Department, or how much was spent annually on printing by the Insurance Department, or under what act the Conservation Commission was empowered to bottle and sell water from Saratoga Springs, it was easier to ask Moses than to try to find out the answer themselves. Because Moses always knew. "He thought fast and he answered quickly," says one who observed him at this time. "He seemed to know the makeup of every department in the state and what its powers were and exactly which sections of law it got those powers from. And he almost seemed to know it all by heart."

Moses' technical expertise gave Smith the ammunition he needed. When Republican legislators introduced bills that appeared to consolidate all public works construction into a single department headed by a "Public Works Commissioner," it was Moses who discovered—and enabled Smith to announce to the press—that the bills did not specifically mention any method of appointment for the commissioner and that, under parallel sections of the State Constitution, he would therefore be an elected official rather than one appointed by and responsible to the Governor. When Republican legislators introduced bills that created the sixteen new departments which the commission had recommended, it was Moses who discovered—so that Smith could announce—that the bills contained no provision that all state agencies be placed in one or another of the departments and, therefore, under existing provisions of the Constitution, all existing agencies would continue to be independent of the departments. A furious Republican senator strode into the Executive Chamber one day and asked Smith, "Who is this fellow Moses anyway?" The Governor leaned back and laughed. "Why," he said, "he's one of your crowd. He's a Republican." (The senator, checking, found that Moses did, indeed, call himself an "independent Republican.") By the time the session ended, the Legislature had been bludgeoned into passing bills incorporating most of the Reconstruction Commission's "statutory changes" and the sixteen-department constitutional amendment, although the amendment would have to be repassed by another Legislature. And although the Legislature voted down the executive-budget and four-year-term proposals, Moses felt confident that the whole program would be passed during Smith's next term.

But the next term was not Smith's. With the backing of many of the old-line reformers, independents and Republicans who normally would have supported his opponent, Nathan L. Miller, the Governor ran 1,090,000 votes ahead of his ticket. But the head of the ticket was presidential candidate James M. Cox, and Cox, along with the Democratic vice presidential nominee, young Franklin Delano Roosevelt, was caught up in the Harding landslide and lost New York State by 1,200,000 votes. In an era in which ticket splitting was far more unusual than it would be a half century later, more than a million New Yorkers had split their ballot to vote for Al Smith. The phenomenon was considered unprecedented in American politics. Elderly reformer William Church Osborn wired Smith, "Even in defeat, you came closer to swimming up Niagara Falls than any man I have ever seen." But the man the wire was addressed to was, nonetheless, a loser—and, Moses was afraid, so was the Reconstruction Commission program.

For a while, dreams had seemed near to realization. Genuine accomplishment had seemed close. Moses had, after all, been the moving force in the drafting of a plan to remake the machinery by which more than ten million people were governed, and he had watched the bills that embodied a substantial portion of that plan move tortuously but steadily along the road to reality. But without at least the sixteen-department constitutional amendment, the statutory changes were meaningless, and, in 1921, Miller opposed the amendment's repassage and the Legislature never let it, or the executive-budget and four-year-term proposals, out of committee. The Citizens Committee on Reorganization in the State Government—with its "extra office at the home of the secretary without expense to the committee" —was disbanded.

To anyone who was, at the time, watching the career of the secretary, these developments must have seemed just another defeat in a life already crammed with defeats. In reality, however, something new had happened, something that would not only insure that the Reconstruction Commission's proposals would eventually become law but that would also change the shape of Bob Moses' life.

Out of public office in 1921 and 1922, Al Smith was back in New York, working as president of a large trucking company. The company's owners were Irishmen from the Old Neighborhood, men who were not only the friends of Al Smith's youth but who, in his maturity, idolized him. Since the company's offices were on Canal Street, only eight blocks from City Hall, a continual stream of city officials, men who had risen through the Tammany organization with Smith, walked the eight blocks to drop in on "the Governor" and pass the time of day. Hoping that Smith would accord them the supreme honor, an invitation to walk home with him across the Neighborhood to his apartment on Oliver Street, the company's owners and the city officials would often find excuses to hang around his office in the late afternoon.

Moses, meanwhile, was working (for a new reform organization, the New York State Association) in a shabby cubicle at 305 Broadway barely large enough for his desk and that of a part-time secretary. He was close to being out of even quasi-official touch with government. Occasionally, he would have lunch with one of the few people he knew in the City Hall area, former Bureau or Reconstruction Commission staffers like Ernie Willvonseder who were now lower-echelon city employees, but more often he had to eat alone. He had few visitors. But, in the late afternoon, the phone would often ring. Moses would pick up the receiver. "Bob," Al Smith would rasp, "how about walking home with me?"

The two men made an odd pair as they walked through the winding, narrow streets of the Lower East Side in the twilight, one of them tall, slim, handsome and aristocratic in bearing, the other, short, potbellied, florid. The taller man, striding out with long, springing steps, continually had to shorten his stride to let the other, who walked with a slow, extremely pigeon-toed gait, catch up. Their progress was further slowed by Smith's popularity. He seemed to know almost every man and woman who passed, and when one of them stopped to chat, he would stop, too, and talk with him without appearance of impatience while his companion would stride restlessly in little circles, or, trying desperately to stand still and listen politely, would nervously clench and unclench his fists.

But between the chats with passers-by, there was plenty of time for talking between Moses and Smith, and not all the talking was done by the former Governor. In fact, as twilight walk succeeded twilight walk, more and more of it was done by Moses. The ideas on government which he had poured forth for almost a decade, the theories, proposals, plans, advice—the dreams—with which he had bored staffers at the Bureau of Municipal Research, examiners at the Municipal Civil Service Commission, borough presidents, park commissioners and a legion of minor city officials, now were poured forth again.

The late-afternoon calls from Smith became more frequent. With regularity now, when the two men had arrived at the old red-brick tenement in which the former Governor lived, he would invite Moses up for dinner.

And one day Bob Moses barged into Ernie Willvonseder's office. He was striding fast, almost running, more excited than Ernie had ever seen him before.

"Ernie," he said, "Al Smith *listens* to me."

7. *Change in Major*

MEN WHO SAW in the bond between Robert Moses and Alfred Emanuel Smith a key to the shape in which the future of New York State and New York City unfolded, as well as to one of the great stories of American politics, never told in its full depth—the blood feud between Smith and Franklin D. Roosevelt—would wonder what had forged between the two men of independence and pride and ambition a tie so strong that, transcending independence and pride and ambition, it would be ended only by death.

Certainly there was nothing in the backgrounds of the two men to bring them close.

Moses' youth was set against a backdrop of Lucerne and Elberon, broad elm trees and leafy arbors, red damask and paneled walls, and coffee streaming from a spout of silver into bright, fragile cups. Smith spent his youth in the Fourth Ward, a wilderness of tenements stretching away from the foot of the Brooklyn Bridge. His grandparents had come to earth in that ward, for no better reason than that they happened to see a "Rooms to Let" sign hung out only a few blocks from the Beekman Street pier where they were deposited in 1841 by the Black Ball Line—along with a shipload of other ragged Westmeath Irish—and they were too hungry and too tired to walk farther. They lived all the rest of their lives in the Fourth Ward. Al Smith's parents lived there, too, and Al Smith, who was born over a barbershop at 174 South Street on December 30, 1873, was to spend all his youth and young manhood in the shadow of the bridge, within an enclave—its borders sharply defined on the south by Water Street, where the tenements were crammed with prostitutes, and on the west by the Bowery, which was lined with flophouses and saloons—held tenaciously by the ward's "respectable" Irish families.

Never leaving it for longer than a day's outing, he grew up in the narrow compass of a neighborhood whose life revolved around two institutions, St. James Roman Catholic Church and the Downtown Tammany Club, and in which, as one who worked there put it, morality was simple, "virtue was virtue, vice was vice," and the views of the parents were the views of the children as to which was which. On summer evenings, the children would sit on the stoops of the tenements and talk until Father Kean rapped on the window of the St. James Parish House as a signal that it was time to go to bed. And they went—as their parents had gone when *they* were children and Father Kean's predecessor, Father Farelly, had rapped for *them.* Bob Moses was neither circumcised nor bar-mitzvah, but young Al Smith was a faithful St. James altar boy, awakening early on bleak, cold winter mornings—with his mother always up even earlier to prepare his breakfast—and trudging up Cherry Hill in the dark to serve at the six-o'clock mass.

At the age at which Bob Moses was being led on horseback along Dwight Street and taken for walks in Central Park, Al Smith was scampering along the hectic Lower East Side waterfront, playing hide-and-seek among the bales and crates that cluttered the East River piers, dangling daringly from the sailing ships' bowsprits that made a line of spears over the horse-drawn trucks clattering along the cobblestones of South Street, playing tag, during an era in which the city didn't build playgrounds in slums, in narrow side streets or in the wider cleared spaces alongside the big, smelly fish market at the foot of Fulton Street, and tobogganing in winter down streets left uncleared of snow by a city that didn't bother to plow the slums. When he learned to swim, he learned in the river, with the spars of the sailing ships looming overhead and garbage floating on the water. Al Smith never went to Central Park; that was regarded by the neighborhood as a preserve for the wealthy—"uptowners," the Fourth Ward called them—who would send their Eton-collared children to its quiet glades with private tutors. His idea of an outing was the Downtown Tammany Club's annual picnic, for which hundreds of sweating neighborhood families—and cases of beer, candy, ears of corn, ice cream and cheap toys—were loaded into huge wagons for the nine-mile trip to Sulzer's Harlem River Park at 126th Street.

At the age at which Bob Moses was being taught by private schools and private tutors, Al Smith was being taught by the good nuns of the St. James Parochial School and trying to avoid Father Kean's stern eye. And while Moses' tutors reported that he was brilliant, the nuns had a very different story to tell about the Smith boy. As one chronicler put it: "The boy had no great fondness for books . . . and showed no inclination to study. . . . He never cared much for school. A passing mark was all he ever desired—and all he ever achieved." And he didn't always achieve that. Al Smith had bright, cheerful eyes and an appealing smile, but there was only one characteristic that set him apart from his classmates—his unusually loud voice. It was no surprise to the nuns that he won medals in citywide parochial-school public-speaking contests.

At the age of thirteen, he didn't have to worry about school any more. Moses' father retired young, but Smith's, a large, powerful Civil War veteran of thundering voice, an inexhaustible supply of funny stories and many friends, had to work too hard. Driving his own truck, loading and unloading heavy cargoes, he would come home no matter how cold the day so wet with sweat that his first move would be to peel off his shirt and undershirt and plunge his face and arms into a tub of cold water to cool off. He worked six or seven days a week and often he got home so late that there would be days and nights on end when Al would not see the father who liked to put his little boy on his knee during family excursions to the beer gardens along the Bowery, regale him with stories and let him sneak sips of his beer. In 1885, the father's health broke, and, unable any longer to do manual work, uneducated and with no skills, he was forced to take work as a night watchman. One by one, he had to sell his horses and finally his truck, but the proceeds of the sales were soon eaten up by doctors' bills and medicine. In November 1886, he died. All he left his son was his self-assurance; it was only through the charity of his friends that funeral expenses were paid. Al's mother was left almost penniless. Walking back from the funeral to the small flat, alone except for Al and his ten-year-old sister, Mary, she muttered, half to herself, "I don't know where to turn." Mary heard her brother say, "I'm here. I can take care of you."

At first, determined to keep her son in school, Al's mother refused to let him work. The very evening of the funeral, holding her children by the hand, she went to an umbrella factory and got a job that she could start the next morning.

Rising before dawn to get breakfast for her children and prepare their lunches, Al's mother would work until dark at the factory, and then come home to make supper and clean the flat. Since the salary she earned at the factory wasn't enough to support three persons, she asked for piecework that she could do at home and, when Al closed the door to his bedroom to go to sleep at night, he would see her bending over the work. A frail woman, within months her own health was affected, and she had to leave the factory. With the help of friends, she opened a tiny grocery and candy store in the basement of the building in which the Smiths lived, but it quickly became obvious that the store would never provide enough to support the family. She could get charity, she knew, but widows who were unable to support their children had the children taken away and placed in institutions. She had heard about the institutions. Anything was better than that. A few months after his thirteenth birthday, a month before he would have graduated from St. James, which had only eight grades, Al Smith left school and went to work.

First he was a newsboy, then a "chaser" for a trucking firm, spending his days on the run, taking assignments for the firm's drivers from the main office and trying to find the drivers in the streets of the Lower East Side so that they would not have to waste time returning to the office. The job paid three dollars a week. In the evenings, he tended counter at the little store while his mother rested. After two years, with income from the store dwindling and the family desperate, he became a shipping clerk—for eight dollars a week. Two years later, with the intake from the store down to almost nothing, he looked for another job and finally found one that would pay him four dollars more. The job was at the Fulton Fish Market.

Al Smith rolled heavy barrels of fish in and out of the market, put the fish on ice, cleaned them and wrapped them. He worked from four o'clock in the morning until five in the afternoon, except on Friday. On Friday, he started work at three. Returning home at night tired and dirty and reeking of fish, he scrubbed off the odor and went downstairs to the store. But in the 1890's twelve dollars a week was almost enough to support a mother and a sister. He stayed at the market for four years. Then, to increase his pay to fifteen dollars, he became a laborer, carrying heavy pipes at a pump works. It wasn't until 1896, when he was twenty-two years old, that he got his first political job.

Moses and Smith came to public service not merely out of different backgrounds, but with different attitudes and for different reasons.

Not even Al Smith's best friends ever said that he went into politics to help the lower classes. He went because, perhaps, he was gregarious and politics for a young man in the Fourth Ward without connections was, in its early stages, mostly hanging around the Downtown Tammany Club or Tom Foley's saloon with other young men, drinking beer, singing around a piano and telling stories while waiting for a contract from Foley. He went because, perhaps, it was a natural course for a young man with little education who wanted to get ahead in the ward's politics-drenched atmosphere—and because, perhaps, he saw no other way out of a life that for most of the years he could remember had been rolling heavy barrels and lifting heavy pipes.

Moses prepared for his career by passing examinations and writing a thesis; Smith prepared for his by executing contracts. A "contract," to Tammany Hall, was something to be done, an assurance to a local undertaker that Tammany would pay for a loyal Democrat's funeral even if his family could not, a discreet visit to a brothel to warn of an upcoming police raid or to police headquarters to ease business-cramping parking restrictions in front of a liquor store belonging to a heavy campaign contributor.

In the Fourth Ward, contracts were given out by Foley, one of the most remarkable of the Tammany district leaders who ran their districts—and looked after the welfare of the straight-ticket-voting Democrats in them—as English squires looked after the welfare of their country villages. "Big Tom" was a square-shaped mustachioed, quiet man who spent most of each day at the Downtown Tammany Club, listening to the cries for help—for a boy who had been arrested, for a process server who had been fired, for a policeman who had been shifted to a Staten Island beat—with unfailing patience. Although his saloons thrived, he was to die a poor man, their profits trickling, along with the payoffs and the campaign contributions, through his fingers into those of his constituents. The only payment he ever asked for the favors he dispensed was a straight Democratic vote—and so heartily were his constituents willing to make this form of repayment that his district regularly rolled up Democratic majorities that made him the most powerful district leader in the city.

Born to wealth that he believed would make him always independent, Moses felt no compulsion to turn associates into friends; arrogance is, after all, one of the coefficients of money. Arrogance would have been an unaffordable luxury to Smith: the equation of politics as he knew it contained a factor of friendship that had at least as heavy a weight as the factor of respect. In the evenings, after work, Smith began to hang around the saloons or the Tammany Club, hoping that Foley would give him a contract, and when he was given one, he executed it with graciousness and tact. Some of the historians who would later analyze his career would speculate that, as one put it, "he made an effort, he trained himself, to be more than ordinarily helpful and obliging." Friends would deny it, saying that there had been something in his nature that had made him, even as a young boy, friendly and eager to assist someone in trouble. Whether it was natural or cultivated, as Al Smith executed the contracts, he displayed a gift for getting along with people that was so highly developed as to be almost genius. Joining the St. James Players, who put on plays to support the parish's orphanage, studying acting from the cheapest seats in the highest balconies at Broadway theaters, he became the parish's star villain, playing Corry Kinchela in Dion Boucicault's *The Shaughraun* so enthusiastically that children began jokingly to hiss him when they saw him on the street. Everyone in the neighborhood seemed to know the slim, clean-cut youth with the soft smile and the loud, happy laugh—and everyone seemed to like him.

Older men were watching him now. Father Kean liked to tell how Smith had tried to refuse to play any more villains. The hisses in the street were becoming louder, he had complained, and in the last production, when he had snarled at the girl who refused him, "You will yet be mine," the boos and catcalls from the gallery had annoyed him. He was going to be a hero or nothing next time, he had said. But all that had been necessary was for the Father to call him in and say, "Alfred, we have over two hundred little girls in the orphanage and it is getting harder every year to feed and clothe and care for these girls," and Alfred had said simply: "Give me the part." When touchy matters—such as visits by respectable parish girls to neighborhood saloons with their dates—had to be brought up with the young people, the Father began to look to Smith to do it; somehow, when Smith handled it, not only did the visits stop but nobody became hurt or angry. He had joined the Seymour Club, a social organization founded by a wealthy old grocer and Tammany financial backer named Henry Campbell. Campbell began looking to Smith to organize club excursions, then he began inviting him home for Sunday dinners—and, in 1896, when there became available a city job as a server of jury notices that paid $900 a year, Campbell saw that Smith got it.

In 1900, after promising her parents that he would never become a professional actor, Smith married Katherine (Katie) Dunn, and the couple took a flat in the neighborhood, Smith's mother moving to Brooklyn to live with Mary and her husband. The children—there would be five—came quickly, and Smith's devotion to his family became a joke, a fond joke, among the people in the ward who saw him wheeling one child and holding the hand of another as he and Katie walked across the Brooklyn Bridge every Sunday after church, rain or shine, to visit his mother.

But in the evenings, after supper, Al Smith left his family and went down to the clubs and saloons. And now another man was watching the youth whom everybody liked—Tom Foley. Signing him up as a campaign speaker, Foley soon saw that even in this heartland of Irish platform eloquence, Smith was something special. And, more important, he saw that

Smith could be counted on; his praise of a Democratic candidate's personal qualifications was just as fervent whether he knew the candidate or not. To the other adjectives with which men described Smith, Foley added one that, in the lexicon of the Democracy of New York City, had a special significance —Smith was, he said, "regular." In 1903, he offered him a nomination for state assemblyman. Proving to be a remarkable campaigner even though, in Foley's districts, remarkable campaigning was not a necessity for Democratic candidates, in November 1903, a month before his thirtieth birthday, Al Smith won his first election.

Katie tied two brooms upright on the iron railings that lined the six steps to the doorway of the tenement in which the Smiths lived. It was a traditional gesture in the neighborhood, symbolizing a clean sweep by Tammany. Inside, in his living room, holding his mother's hand as he accepted congratulations, Alfred E. Smith, red-faced and loud in victory, resplendent in a new suit with wide-set, broad pinstripes, a tie that matched his voice, and a pearl stickpin, a big black cigar tilted cockily up from the corner of his red, wet lips, seemed the typical, "regular" Tammany brave.

Yet what lurked behind the war paint? Al Smith went to Albany unprepared to be a legislator—or even to sleep away from home. On his first night in the capital, he noticed a large fire blazing in the fireplace of his hotel, saw that the room to which he and another new Tammany assemblyman, Tom Caughlan from "Battery Dan" Finn's district, had been assigned was not near any exits, and was so worried that the hotel would burn down and they would be trapped that he made Caughlan spend the night playing pinochle so that they would be awake for any emergency. Arriving in the Assembly Chamber the next morning, he was bewildered by the formalities of the opening session and was shunted by leaders who had no time even to talk to him to a desk so far from the Speaker's podium that he often couldn't hear the rulings. When he did hear, he often didn't understand. Overcome by the intricacies of the legislative process, he sat day after day in the high-ceilinged chamber in silence. During the whole session, he did not make a single speech. He was not appointed to a single committee.

Worst of all were the bills. Every morning when he arrived at his desk, there would be a pile of new ones a foot high. He would try the one that looked simplest, perhaps an act setting the maximum size of vehicles using public highways. "The provisions of this subdivision," he read, "shall not apply to vehicles and implements or combinations thereof not over thirteen feet in width and designed and intended for use solely for farm purposes when owned or in the possession of a dealer in farm implements and equipment and within a radius of fifty miles of the principal place of business of such a dealer, including transportation of such vehicles, implements and combinations thereof as a load on another vehicle, such vehicle or load not to exceed thirteen feet in width, during the same period and under the same conditions and restrictions as hereinbefore in this subdivision provided for such vehicles and implements and combinations thereof when used solely for farm purposes."

This was the simplest. The one underneath it might be eleven pages long, beginning: "Without limiting the generality of the following provisions of this section, property owned by the city and property used for transportation purposes exclusively pursuant to the provisions of a joint arrangement or of a joint facilities agreement or trackage rights agreement shall all be exempt from special ad valorem levies." The next one might be thirteen pages and it might start: "Paragraph (h) of subdivision six of section two hundred thirty-five of the banking law, as last separately amended by chapters forty-six, fifty-one and five hundred eighty-five of the laws of eighteen hundred ninety-nine, is hereby amended to read . . ."

As he sat there staring down at the desk, a page boy would deposit another pile of bills on it. The wording was difficult enough for the expert. It might have been designed to mock a man whose schooling had ended in the eighth grade, who had never liked to read even the simple books of childhood, who, he had said once, had in his entire life read only one book cover to cover: *The Life of John L. Sullivan.*

As far as the course of the Empire State was concerned, it did not seem to matter if Al Smith understood the bills or not. The Democrats, a badly outnumbered minority in the Senate and Assembly, a party that had not elected a Governor since 1893, had no real say in the state's affairs. Most of the Democratic legislators, understanding this, and understanding that in the rare instances in which their votes were important they would be told how to cast them by their leaders back in New York, took their jobs with the lightness they felt they deserved. They spent their evenings in "The Gut," a strip of whorehouses and cheap saloons down the hill from the capitol.

Smith, whose devotion to Katie was—and remained always—legendary as long as he lived, had no interest in the whorehouses, but he loved to sit with his fellow assemblymen in the saloons and drink beer and sing and, when he worked up his nerve, tell a joke or two. As often as they, rousted out of a saloon by the Assembly sergeant-at-arms for a vote, he would appear in the Chamber with his derby over one ear. His clothes were of the same cut, his voice as loud, his language as crude. In appearance, he was one of them.

But late in the evenings, when the parties were still loud, Al Smith would leave the saloons, and as he left his steps would quicken.

Hurrying back to his tiny furnished room in a cheap boardinghouse, he would sit down at a rickety desk. On the desk he would earlier have piled the bills that had been introduced that day. Al Smith would begin reading them. Not only the bills which bore on a subject in which he was interested, and not only the bills which dealt with his Assembly District, and not only the bills which dealt with New York City. Sitting at the rickety desk in the furnished room, Smith read *all* the bills, even those which concerned the construction of a side road or a tiny dam in some remote upstate district. And as he read them, he tried to understand them. Why had one legislator included in a bill a provision that the dam be built by the Conservation Department rather than by the Department of Public Works? What had been in the mind of another that led him to specify that the side road must be surfaced with a specific type of asphalt? Later in the night, Smith would hear bursts of song and laughter as the other legislators left the saloons. One by one, if he looked out the window in his room which faced the capitol, he could see the lights in the huge gray building go out. Still the man who had never liked to read read on.

It must have seemed like the most useless of exercises. In his second term, he was appointed to two committees, but they were the Committee on Banks and the Committee on Public Lands and Forests and, as he remarked in later years, "I had never been in a bank except to serve a jury notice and I had never seen a forest." Again, he did not make a single speech during the entire session. The Democratic leaders had no interest in him except for his nod of assent at the end of a discussion. And the expenses of living in Albany—for which legislators received no reimbursement—ate up an assemblyman's $1,500 salary. By May, all except $250 was gone and seven incomeless months stretched ahead of him. In despair, he told Foley he didn't want to run again. "Meet me at Holtz's for breakfast tomorrow morning," Foley said.

Over ham and eggs, Foley offered Smith another job, New York City Superintendent of Buildings. Smith's eyes lit up.

Foley's were narrow. Watching the younger man closely, he said, If you take the job, of course, you'll never be a big man in this town. I gave you a start toward being one. It's tough for a beginner in Albany. You can't learn what you need to know up there in a couple of years. But you're learning. And you've got great popularity in the district. I think you're on the right track. And I'm willing to stick with you if you want to go back. But maybe you ought to chuck it. "Maybe," Big Tom Foley said, "you're right in thinking that Albany is too tough for you."

Foley said he would give Smith a week to think it over.

In a week, Smith said he wanted to go back.

When he went back, he read harder. Since most of the bills amended or referred back to other bills passed years before—and not described in the new bills—he took to spending evenings in the Legislative Library reading those old bills. Since some of the most confusing wording was based on legal technicalities, Smith began to borrow lawbooks from law libraries and take them back to the furnished room with him. Sometimes, leafing through the thick volumes, he thought wryly that their very appearance would have intimidated him a few years before. Tired of listening to speeches he couldn't understand, he would pay clerks for transcripts and study the transcripts. Near the end of the session, the annual appropriations measure, hundreds of pages long, containing tens of thousands of items, was published. No one, so far as anyone in Albany could remember, had ever read the entire appropriations bill. In 1906, Al Smith read it.

Now, he was to say later, Albany began to make some sense to him. But he kept that fact to himself. Years later, Foley would say, "He would never admit that he knew anything about a subject until he knew everything about it." To his fellow legislators, he was still the typical Tammany regular. He cleared his votes with Foley, never argued with the leaders—

and instead of making speeches saved his voice for the nightly singing in the saloons.

He had many friends in Albany now. He arrived at the capitol each morning with a fresh supply of jokes, hilarious stories told in a variety of dialects, and legislators and clerks would crowd around him to hear them. During a debate on a bill proposing to regulate Chinese laundries, Smith suddenly burst into the Assembly Chamber bearing a huge sign decorated with Chinese characters.

Surprisingly, his friends included Republicans as well as Democrats. No one would have seemed less likely to get along with the aristocratic upstate Republicans, born into families that controlled the great utilities and banks of the state and educated among the Ivy, than Al Smith, but his jokes had them roaring, too. The rising star of a band of reforming Republicans who were trying to unseat the Black Horse Cavalry was young Jimmy Wadsworth, a scion of one of the wealthiest families in Rochester and a former Yale baseball star. Wadsworth soon began to make a regular supper trio with Smith and a slow-talking, forceful, young German-born state senator who had become particularly close to Smith, Robert F. Wagner, Sr. Elected Speaker, Wadsworth handed Smith some choice committee assignments. In 1908, after Smith had swept his district for the fifth time, he found himself, on his return to Albany, one of the capitol's most influential Democrats. He was expected now to use the voice that he had kept silent so long.

And when he did, people began to listen. The years spent reading the obscure minor bills began to pay off. Because no matter what the subject was, the other legislators began to realize, Al Smith understood it. In some way that they were unable to figure out, he had become familiar with their little pet projects, their side roads, the peculiar problems of their districts.

Moreover, when Smith rose to speak, the Assembly Chamber became a place of drama. "His presence electrifies and wins over even his opponents," Dean Christian Gauss of Princeton University was to say. "His . . . voice makes his listeners tingle."

The voice was nasal, grating, harsh and insistent—and unforgettable. One journalist wrote that it had trumpets in it. Coupled with the wit of the man who used it, it could tear an opponent apart or make bored men roar with laughter. (A Buffalo assemblyman once tried to correct Smith's grammar. The Assembly, well aware of Smith's lack of education, waited silently for his reply. Slowly he arose. "I will," he said with dignity, "refer the gentleman from Buffalo to the rule that says, 'When a pluperfect adjective precedes a noun, insert a plus.' ") It could even hold the attention of the legislators during arcane discussions of state finances. One reporter wrote: "Discussion of the annual appropriation bill used to be the signal for a general exodus from the Assembly Chamber. But not so when 'Al' Smith took the floor. He could keep the members in their seats hours on end with his masterly dissection of that measure."

Charles F. ("Silent Charlie") Murphy, the unsmiling Irishman who had risen from saloon keeper to the leadership of all Tammany Hall, had been hearing a lot about Smith. Now he said he'd like to meet him. After the meeting, someone said to Murphy, "He's a nice young fellow. He has a lot of ability. It's too bad he isn't a college man." Murphy looked at the speaker a long moment. "If he was a college man," he said at last, "he wouldn't be Al Smith." In 1911, aided by revelations of widespread corruption among Republican legislators, the Democrats won control of both houses for the first time in eighteen years. Murphy had the Democratic caucus elect Smith majority leader of the Assembly.

In a position of importance at last, Al Smith carried out orders. Using the powers of his office ruthlessly, he rammed through the Assembly, as Bob Wagner was ramming it through the Senate, the notorious "Murphy Charter," which weakened New York City's civil service system and added thousands of patronage jobs to its payroll.

Good Government groups railed at Smith. The Citizens Union called him "one of the most dangerous men in Albany." Identifying him, day after day, as "Smith, the Tammany man," newspapers joined in the outcry. "The Democratic caucus," said a disgusted editorial in the New York *World*, "is Charles F. Murphy at one end of a telephone wire and the Democratic leader at the other end." In all his years in the Legislature, one political observer was to say, Smith had never been anything more than "the brilliant henchman at Albany of the organization housed in the ornate and shabby building on Fourteenth Street."

But such analyses were incomplete. Most legislators spent as little time as possible in Albany, coming to the capital only one or two days a week and spending the rest of their time attending to their outside business interests. Murphy saw to it that Smith was offered a well-paying position with a firm doing business with the city. Finances were still tight for Smith. He could have used the money. But he turned the offer down. Instead, he spent most of every week—all of many weeks—in the capital. Not only did he attend every hearing held by every committee of which he was a member but, legislators began to notice, he would slip quietly into hearings held by committees of which he was not a member and sit in the back of the hearing rooms, following the testimony intently. At night, he would still party loudly and happily—and he would still slip away from most parties early.

Now he would slip away not to a cheap furnished room but to the plush majority leader's suite at the Ten Eyck Hotel. Now the face bent over the pile of bills was considerably fuller than the face that had been bent over the pile seven years before; it was redder and its teeth, once so white, were capped with gold and yellowed by the cigar butts clenched unendingly between them. Now there was a considerable paunch beneath the pinstripes.

But the face still bent over the bills.

And now a new element was added to the background of the picture. Sweatshops didn't close on Saturday, and on the Saturday afternoon of March 26, 1911, hundreds of employees of the Triangle Shirtwaist Company, most of them girls from the Lower East Side, were still bending over swatches of material on the eighth, ninth and tenth floors of a building overlooking New York's Washington Square. Someone in the tenth-floor workroom lit a cigarette and tossed the match away. It hadn't burned out when it fell into the ankle-deep litter around the sewing machines.

There was a puff of smoke, and then a sheet of flame. The exits were inadequate, the doors to many locked. As the terrified girls jammed against them in panic, scores were crushed to death. Others were suffocated by the heavy smoke. As it billowed around them and the flames crept closer, girls leaped from the windows. Bodies smashed against the sidewalks and tore through sidewalk gratings. The death toll was 141.

Reformers had been haranguing against unsafe conditions in the sweatshops for years, but their harangues had thudded without effect against political stockades buttressed with campaign contributions of factory owners. Now they descended on Albany, led by men like Henry Moskowitz, a bunch of near-hysterical women, and one very quiet one, Henry Moskowitz's wife.

Demanding the formation of a commission to investigate factory conditions and to recommend remedial legislation, the reformers brought with them a list of potential commission members. Smith, conferring with them, agreed to most of the names but added one: his own.

At first, the reformers on the State Factory Investigating Commission looked at "Smith, the Tammany man," askance. Then the commission's work began. It took the members to all the major cities of the state. Now and again one or another of the reform members would miss a trip, but they noticed that Smith never did. They watched his face as, day after day, he saw what life in the factories was like. They watched his expression when he saw whole families, mothers with their children, little boys and girls, working all the daylight hours seven days a week in rooms in which there was not a single window, when, after one factory manager had insisted that no children under the age of seven were employed in his plant, commission staffers found such children jammed into an elevator that had been hidden between floors to escape the commission's notice. When the reform members of the commission made their proposals, they waited for Smith's reaction.

You make the proposals, he told them. I'll fight for them.

Even while Good Government organizations were continuing to rail against him—the 1912 Citizens Union summary of his record was even more devastating than its 1911 summary—a few reformers were starting to tell their friends another story.

Al Smith, they said, had absolutely no "general theory." His naïveté in matters of philosophy was ridiculous. When he talked about social welfare legislation, it was in terms of "us" against "them," of the "people" against the "interests," of the Fourth Ward against the factory owners. But the "people," the Fourth Ward, did seem to mean something very special to him. No one could listen to him talk about how doctors' bills could eat up a man's savings and leave his family destitute, about how penniless mothers feared that "the charities" would take their children, about children who grew to manhood without ever having a pair of new shoes, without believing that his determination to help them was real. No one could look at his face when he talked and not *know* it was real. First one and then another of the reformers began to tell their friends that they had really come to believe that maybe, just maybe, after decades of waiting, reform in New York had found at last, in the red-faced Tammany henchman, the instrument for which it had been waiting: the champion who would fight for their dreams in the political arena and turn them into laws. And some of the more romantic among them, examining Smith's long, slow rise through the ranks of Tammany, began to speculate that perhaps all the time he had been executing its dirty work he had been waiting for the chance to do good.

When the commission's recommendations, embodied in bills, came up in the Legislature, Smith fought for them. From their seats in the spectator galleries high up over the Assembly Chamber, the reformers could see him roaming the narrow aisles between the legislators' desks, pleading, cajoling, threatening, bargaining, dealing, trading votes—using every trick he had learned in his years of working for Tammany.

Smith's debating ability was already legendary, but never, observers wrote, had he spoken like this. During a debate on a bill that would have required "one day's rest in seven" for women and children, Republican legislators beholden to cannery interests pleaded for exemptions for canneries. Smith waited until every Republican had finished. Then he rose and walked between their desks down to the well of the Chamber. Whirling to face them, he said quietly, "I have read carefully the commandment 'Remember the Sabbath Day to keep it holy.' I am unable to find any language in it that says, 'except in the canneries.' " Without another word, he returned to his seat. On another occasion, the man whose mother had once feared that her son would be taken from her rose to speak on widows' pensions.

Mr. Speaker, what happens when death takes from the family the provider? The widowed mother goes to the police court or to the charity organization and her children are committed to an institution, and from the moment the judge signs the commitment the people of the city of New York are bound for their support. Let us see what effect that has upon the State itself. The mother stands in the police court. She witnesses the separation of herself and her children. They are torn away from her and given over to the custody of an institution, and nothing is left for her to do but to go out into the world and make her own living. What must be her feelings? What must be her idea of the State's policy when she sees these children separated from her by due process of law, particularly when she must remember that for every one of them she went down into the valley of death that a new pair of eyes might look out upon the world? What can be the feelings in the hearts of the children themselves, separated from their mother by what they must learn in after years was due process of law, when they must in after years learn to know what the State's policy was with respect to their unfortunate condition?

That is the old system. That is the dark day we are walking away from. That is the period that, by this policy, we are attempting to forget.

What new policy does this bill inaugurate? What new system does this bill inaugurate? The State of New York reaches out to them, "We recognize in you a resource of the State and we propose to take care of you, not as a matter of charity, but as a government and public duty." What a different feeling that must put into the hearts of the mother and the children! What better citizens that policy must make! Why? Because it instills into that young heart a love, a reverence and a devotion for the State of New York and its sovereign power.

We are pledged to conserve the natural resources of the State. Millions of dollars of the taxpayers' money, untold and uncounted millions, have been poured into that channel. We have been in a great hurry to legislate for the interests. We have been slow to legislate along the direction that means thanksgiving to the poorest man recorded in history—He who was born in the stable at Bethlehem.

Al Smith's eloquence was useless in the 1912 session, because the Republicans had recaptured control of the Assembly. But in November 1912, the Democrats grabbed it back—and Murphy had the party's caucus elect Smith Assembly Speaker for the 1913 session.

He had never dreamed, Al Smith told friends, that an uneducated Mick from the Fourth Ward could rise so high. That he might rise higher, he was to say later, never crossed his mind. He had, after all, about reached a point beyond which, in America, no Al Smith had ever risen. No Catholic had ever been given a presidential nomination nor, for that matter, any Irish Tammany man a nomination for high statewide office. A Governor or a United States senator was supposed to, in the words of one historian, "present an image—in appearance, speech and manners—appropriate to his high office" and "somehow it was incongruous to think of an Irishman up from the city streets in such a post." Tammany men, while they might not say so, felt that way themselves; they felt unpolished and crude and very uneducated beside the "uptowners"—and they never pushed themselves forward for the top spots.

As Assembly Speaker, Smith was all that Tammany could have desired, building up the organization's patronage and power—and pushing through liquor-law amendments that allowed the sale of alcoholic beverages at hotels that Charlie Murphy favored, and forbade such sales at hotels that Silent Charlie did not.

Some observers bemoaned Smith's lack of dignity. Pounding his gavel with great swings of his arm, bellowing parliamentary rulings in a hoarse gravel voice that one writer called a "Bull-of-Bashan roar," he sometimes seemed to them like a carnival barker. He sometimes ate lunch on the podium. He talked with food in his mouth.

But seldom in the history of the Legislature had its business been transacted so smoothly and expeditiously. Cutting short long-winded speakers, hustling routine bills through at a rate that reporters clocked at eight per minute, Smith was, on the high Speaker's podium, a commanding figure.

And if Smith fought for Tammany's bills, he did not stop fighting for the factory commission's. By the end of the session, many of them had been passed, even a revolutionary workmen's compensation measure. In 1914, the Republicans regained power. Albany was filled with high-priced lobbyists representing insurance companies. Amendments to the compensation measure were introduced that looked innocent but that would in reality tear out its heart. All the amendments did, their sponsors protested, was provide that there could be direct settlements between workmen and insurance companies instead of enforced resort to the machinery provided by the Workmen's Compensation Act of 1913. All that they did was enable the working man to get money sooner.

"And for whom are you doing this?" Smith demanded as he stood in the well of the Chamber and faced the Republicans. Those of them who were his friends saw not a hint of friendliness in his eyes now. "Does the working man want it? No! Does the Legislature want it? No! Does the compensation commission want it? Then what other interested party is there? The Casualty Company! That's who you are working for. . . . The agent can shake the long green before the widow or suffering laborer and tell them if they sign away their rights they can get so much but if they wait they can take their chance on getting something months hence. That carries us back to the good old days when we had no compensation law. Be honest and repeal the whole law and stop faking." A Republican legislator rose to protest, but Smith's voice cracked out like a whip. "You and your Governor have ruined the compensation law," he said. "You have gone the limit for the casualty companies. The people's case is lost."

Up in the high galleries that overlooked the floor, the reformers stood and cheered. The compensation law might be lost but they knew the Republicans would never dare to touch the others now. Great advances had been secured. And, more important, at last they had their champion. Smith, the Tammany man, had made their dreams come true. They hastened to hang others on his lance.

But even when Smith took up the banner of the reformers, he never put down the mace of the practical politician. He himself made no bones about this fact. If cynics said that he had recognized in child labor, disability insurance and workmen's compensation a great political issue, Smith said it too. When someone told him that his views were antagonizing factory owners, he would laugh and say that factory owners lived on Fifth Avenue and "There's no Democratic votes on Fifth Avenue; they're all over on Ninth and Tenth, where I live." Fighting for the working man, for better working conditions for women and children—that, he knew, was an issue on which you couldn't miss. The man who fought for the commission's legislation would be a man fighting on the side of the angels. Supporting its recommendations was more than good politics; it was the best politics.

When he had in some instances to drop either the banner or the mace, it wasn't the mace that fell. In the 1915 Constitutional Convention, he fought for the Municipal Research Bureau's recommended reorganization of the state government. Of all the issues raised by the reformers, reorganization was the one he most eagerly embraced because his years in Albany had allowed him to see for himself the almost incredible inefficiency of the system. But on the morning of August 27, 1915, Smith, who had spent all August 26 fighting shoulder to shoulder with the federal crowd for reorganization, waited in the capitol entrance hall for Progressive Republican Frederick C. Tanner, and when Tanner arrived, he pulled him aside.

"Fred," Smith said, "I've got to pull out on you in this debate." As Tanner recalled it later:

> I said, "What's the matter?" And he said, "Well, I had a telephone call from the old man last night."
>
> I said, "Do you mean Fourteenth Street?" And he said, "Yes." Of course this meant that Mr. Murphy had decided that the Democratic organization would oppose the Constitution when it was finally submitted on Election Day, and that it would not do for . . . Smith to give [his] support to a bill in the convention when the party would oppose it in its submission.

After the convention, Smith campaigned against the proposed new, reorganized Constitution. First and foremost, he was a party man.

Even though Smith felt that times—and people's needs—were changing, he did not try to break away from the party but to change it to meet the times. Every Friday evening, Tammany's sachems would meet for dinner in a private room at Delmonico's Restaurant. Now, in those meetings, Smith began to try to persuade the older men that the party should begin taking a different stance. Tammany had always held the allegiance of the lower classes with the turkey baskets at Christmas and the outings and the civil service jobs, but now people were becoming better educated, he said. Their needs were broadening and increasing. They were beginning to ask for more—and to look to government to provide that more. Tammany should become the champion of social welfare legislation. It should do so because it was the party of the people and the new needs of the people were real needs. And it should do so because it was good politics. Why should Tammany take a chance of losing the massed votes of the Lower East Side to uptown reformers who even now were sponsoring such legislation?

From the head of the table, Silent Charlie listened silently to Smith and other young sachems like Wagner. Murphy knew that Tammany must change. He knew it because of the reasons the young men gave—and he knew it because of a consideration of his own. Never had one of their own kind risen to Governor or senator; never, despite the power of Kelly and Croker before him, never, despite his own power, had a Tammany man ever come even close to the top prize in the Democratic Party for which Tammany supplied so many of the votes. Always Tammany was thought of as the party of Tweed and Kelly and Croker, of the poor from the Old Country who might be fit to sweep the streets but not to sit in the Governor's Mansion or the White House. Becoming identified with Progressivism, becoming known as the party of social progress, would be a way to shatter that image forever. Pushing to the forefront bright young men identified with such causes rather than with the ancient rituals of Tammany would be a way to spawn candidates who would shatter forever the unseen but heavy chains that weighed down the Irish Catholic in America. Why, already, wasn't at least one of his bright young men, as true to Tammany, as loyal, as regular as even he, Charlie Murphy, could wish, also an object of praise by the Good Government organizations which habitually damned anyone who sat around the table in Delmonico's? Hadn't the young man, once assailed by the Citizens Union, recently received one of its highest ratings? Hadn't he been praised in the *Herald?* Charlie Murphy looked down the table at the young man. He gave the okay for Tammany to sponsor the legislation the man wanted. He built up the young man's reputation by running him for sheriff of New York County in 1915 and for president of the New York City Board of Aldermen in 1917. And in 1918, he wrenched from the grip of the upstate Democratic leaders the Democratic nomination for Governor and handed it to Alfred E. Smith.

When Smith won—it was the sixteenth time he had run for public office and the sixteenth time he had won—the inaugural parade up Albany's State Street was led by the Sixty-ninth Regiment of the National Guard, New York City's own Fighting Sixty-ninth. The sidewalks along the route—and the steps of the capitol at its end—were packed with Smith's neighbors from the Fourth Ward. All the night before, arriving by the thousands on trains from New York, they had tramped the streets of Albany and jammed the restaurants, hoisting beer steins in toasts to the new Governor and singing a new, catchy two-step, "The Sidewalks of New York." Their presence was symbolic. Smith's election was the triumph of the immigrants, the oath he took on the capitol steps the next morning, as his mother stood in the place of honor at his side, the first ever taken in America for a state's highest office in the accent of Ireland.

During Smith's first term, it was not that he broke loose from his party but that the party freed him. Shortly after the election, Murphy summoned him to his Long Island estate, Good Ground. Tammany would be asking him for many things, Tammany's leader said, but he had been thinking of what it meant to have a boy from the Old Neighborhood in the Governor's chair. Should Tammany ever ask for anything Smith felt would stand in the way of becoming a great Governor, all Smith had to do was tell him so and the request would be withdrawn. There were to be no strings attached to the job. Smith was to be his own man. And for a start, Murphy said, Smith would not have to worry about patronage considerations. He and Foley would keep the job hunters off the Governor's back.

Smith reappointed deserving Republicans to their judgeships and administrative posts and brought into his inner circle reformers like Belle Moskowitz, Frances Perkins, tall, olive-skinned, mustached Joseph Proskauer, and, to head the Highway Department, that trough of fatty contracts at which Tammany had been hoping to feed, Colonel Frederick Stuart Greene, an urbane engineer who wrote short stories and who displayed a complete indifference to the demands of politics in the administering of his department. The Governor did so not only because he shared Murphy's dream and not only because he genuinely wanted to help the state's urban masses but also because it was good politics. Grover Cleveland, he pointed out to his friends, had become a national figure because "the idea got around the country that he was independent of everybody."

Smith's policies were Progressive—in his first term, he bludgeoned the Legislature into restoring the Workmen's Compensation Law, increased the state's contributions to teachers' salaries by $22,000,000 and fought for governmental reorganization and for shorter hours and better working conditions for women and children—for the same mixture of reasons.

Smith had no patience for those who didn't understand those reasons. He had no patience for reformers who, unlike Belle Moskowitz, didn't understand the importance of practical politics in getting things done, who refused to compromise, who insisted on having the bill as it was written, who raged loudly at injustice, who fought single-mindedly for an unattainable ideal. Their pigheadedness had the effect of dragging to political destruction politicians who listened to them, of ruining careers men had taken years to build. He had seen it happen. And, more important, what was the inevitable result of their efforts? Since they refused to compromise and operate within the political framework—the only framework within which their proposals could become reality—the laws they proposed were never enacted, and therefore at the end of their efforts the people they had wanted to help, the people who *he* knew so well needed help, hadn't been helped at all. If anything, they had been hurt; the stirring up of hard feelings and bitterness delayed less dramatic but still useful reforms that might have been enacted. When the reformers were finished with all their hollering and were back in their comfortable homes, the widows of the Fourth Ward would still be forced to give up their children before they could get charity. What good was courage if its only effect was to hurt those you were trying to help?

So Smith despised the noncompromisers, the starry-eyed idealists. He despised, in other words, most reformers. He coined words to describe them: "mush brains," "double-domes," "crackpots," "Goo Goos." Al Smith despised, in short, what Bob Moses had been.

But he didn't despise Moses.

There were other reformers who were personally friendly to the Governor and who were vital to his political future—men his own age like wealthy Abram Elkus and men Moses' age like Proskauer—but Elkus and Proskauer were seldom if ever invited up to the Oliver Street flat for dinner. For Moses, during 1921 and 1922, the invitations came more and more often. If, after dinner, old cronies from the Neighborhood would drop by and take Smith out to the local taverns for a drink and a song or two around the back-room piano, Smith always insisted that Moses come along. In fact, discovering that Moses had a passable bass to go with his tenor, he insisted that Moses be a part of whatever quartet was hastily arranged for the evening's barbershopping, and when Moses tried to beg off, Smith would drag him out of his seat and make him stand beside him and harmonize.

The reason for the attachment was uncertain. As one of Smith's cronies put it, "They were opposites, two exact opposites, opposites all the way down the line." Was it, as some Fourth Warders, given to cliché, speculated, a "father and son" relationship? Given the affection Smith bore for his own three sons, this seemed too pat an explanation, although it was not difficult to understand why some believed it. Emily Smith would recall how, one night after dinner, her father, who had been making pointed remarks for weeks about the pale-blue Brooks Brothers shirts that seemed to comprise Moses' entire shirt collection, suddenly heaved himself out of his chair at the dinner table and strode into the bedroom. Returning with a large box, he said to Moses, "I'm tired of looking at your blue shirts, so I bought you some." And, opening the box, he spilled out, in striped and silken profusion, a dozen of Sulka's best. The Smiths certainly began to treat Moses like one of the family. "He was like an artist in a way," Emily would recall. "He was dressed, not dirtily, but as if he didn't care. His suits might be okay, but they were obviously quite old or not very well pressed. We always kidded him about his clothes. One night after dinner he started to leave and Dad said, 'Emily, you go down with Bob and see he doesn't take one of my hats and leave his here.' And I can still see Dad and Bob laughing there." Or was the reason for the attachment, as other old acquaintances speculated, that Al Smith, who outwardly laughed at his lack of formal education and never seemed to mind his lack of money, actually felt both lacks keenly and was thus ready to be impressed by a man he thought had such a wealth of both? Was it, as some reformers thought, that, since Smith preferred to get his information from people rather than from books and memos, he needed around him advisers who could talk fluently on concepts of government and who could describe situations and projects so vividly that he could see them in his mind's eye—and that Moses, with his gift for words, was simply the most fluent and descriptive of talkers? Or was it that the man who had worked so hard to learn the art of government was able to tell exactly how hard another man had worked to learn that art—and knew that Bob Moses had, in different circumstances, worked as hard as he? Was it that the man who had learned the art so thoroughly that it must have been boring for him to talk with even the most knowledgeable of his advisers had found a man who had learned it as well as he?

Only one thing was certain. Whatever the reason for the feeling, it was there.

And therefore, if the man who despised what Bob Moses had been liked Moses so much, Moses must have greatly changed.

He had.

For the first part of the Smith interregnum, Moses seemed to be the reformer he had always been.

The Reconstruction Commission, of course, went out of existence with the ouster from power of the Governor it had been advising. Within days after the 1920 election, Mrs. Moskowitz had to tell Moses that there remained in the commission's exchequer only enough funds to pay his very small stipend and the rent on the very small office at 305 Broadway until the end of the year. Moses faced the prospect of being out of a job again on January 1, 1921. But in late November 1920, a tall, elegantly dressed, cheerful and charming man walked into the little office. He was Richard Spencer Childs, whom Moses had heard of but never met, although Childs had graduated from Yale just a year before him.

Richard Childs was the very model of the scientific management reformer. Seeing politics in terms of "good" and "evil"—the latter was a term he used in connection with Tammany Hall—he had determined to remove the possibility of evil from municipal government in the United States and make it efficient, economic and businesslike. Having inherited the public relations genius that had enabled his father to clean up millions with a new soap powder named Bon Ami, he had already succeeded in cheerfully forcing down the throats of more than a hundred astounded municipalities a nonpartisan "city manager" form of government. Finding that a single cause did not quench his thirst for reform, he had become concerned by the fact that while New York City had a Citizens Union to rate the city's legislators, act as a watchdog over city spending and publish a bulletin that gave civic-minded citizens the information they needed to play their proper role in city government, there was no similar organization that covered the state as a whole and could exert a statewide influence for good. Childs decided to put up the money to start one, but found he had a personnel problem. With his own time fully occupied, he would have to leave the new organization almost entirely in someone else's hands, and, reviewing the list of his reform acquaintances, he concluded that none of them could handle the job. Then, one evening, doing his nightly reading of publications dealing with government that poured into his apartment from every part of the United States, he turned to one he had put aside for several months because of its length, the *Report of the Reconstruction Commission to Governor Alfred E. Smith.* Richard Childs had read thousands of such reports; he had written dozens himself. He knew exactly how good this one was. He spent most of the night reading it and, in the morning, walked directly from his breakfast table to 305 Broadway. "I needed no recommendations," he would recall. "I had read the work." Finding Moses at his desk in the little office, Childs introduced himself, announced that he was about to form a statewide Good Government organization and offered him a post, which he explained would unfortunately carry only a small salary, as its secretary and executive officer.

Childs had expected the man across the desk to say that he would consider the offer, that he would let him know in a day or two. At the least, he had expected to be asked some questions. Instead, without even a pause, Moses replied in a single word: "Yes."

Moses' acceptance of the offer elevated him instantly to a position of new importance in the reform movement. A statewide association of leading reformers from both parties would automatically become the rallying point not only for a continued fight for reorganization but for the state's reform sentiment as a whole, which had always dissipated its strength among too many local organizations. Moses dealt on a day-to-day basis with the old giants of the New York City reform movement—Hughes, Root, Stimson, Wickersham, Elkus, the legendary Charles Culp ("CC") Burlingham, Albert S. Bard, and William Jay Schieffelin, fighter against Tammany and the sweatshop, who in 1920 was completing the first decade of a thirty-two-year term as chairman of the Citizens Union (Childs would be his successor). He also dealt with the young lawyers and social workers who were coming up through reform ranks in the city and would one day take the places of the older men: Stanley Isaacs, Morris Ernst, Nathan Straus, Jr., Raymond V. Ingersoll, Henry H. Curran, Robert S. Binkerd, Charles C. Lockwood, three young matrons who stood out from the mass of broad-hatted luncheoneers, Frances Perkins, Mary Simkhovitch and Mrs. William P. (Jen) Earle, and the one of the younger men who had already made a citywide name for himself with his courageous championing of John Purroy Mitchel's first investigative efforts—George McAneny. Joining them on the New York State Association's "advisory council" were upstate reform leaders never before associated with their New York City counterparts in one group.

Inviting these men to contribute to the association's monthly sixteen-page *State Bulletin* or to speak at luncheon meetings at the Whitehall Club on Battery Place or the Ten Eyck Hotel in Albany, soliciting their appearance at public hearings before legislative committees considering bills in which the association was interested, Moses became well known to all of them. And as they heard *him* speak at the Whitehall Club or the Ten Eyck and read his work in the *State Bulletin,* many of these men, old and young, Democrat and Republican, saw in him the embodiment of the finest qualities of the reform spirit. During this period, he stayed true to the aims of reform. Working out of another small downtown office, he campaigned through the *Bulletin* for reform's hallowed causes: social welfare legislation, a "direct primary" system that would end the nomination of candidates by boss-dominated party conventions, the publication of a "state journal" similar to the *Congressional Record* so that interested citizens could study legislative debates and thus obtain information on which to base intelligent judgments of state activities and, of course, for the repassage by the new Legislature of the reorganization amendments that would foster efficiency and economy in state government. He campaigned against special-interest bills, against the subservience of legislators of both parties to their local bosses. Lauding legislators whose work he approved, he did not hesitate to admonish those he felt had strayed from the path of righteousness, lamenting, for example, that "Senator [Frederick M.] Davenport [of Oneida County] seems to us to be losing some of the almost religious fire which made him an unusual and significant figure in state politics. The truth is that the Senator is back on the bandwagon with the regulars. . . . He is not by nature or at his best a rural conservative. To get the most out of himself and for his supporters, a man must act in character." He enshrined the worst of the party hacks in his own "Legislative Hall of Fame." Every issue of the *Bulletin* devoted a full page to the "objects" of the New York State Association: "To press for progress toward responsive, responsible, efficient and democratic government in the state, to increase the number of citizens and local organizations which understand and influence state government . . ." And the *Bulletin*'s other pages were written in the same tone. Denouncing a legislative proposal he felt had been introduced only as a matter of expediency, Moses concluded flatly: "The principle is the important thing."

The association's members approved of that tone. To them, the failure of the association to win even a single major fight was secondary. In the world of these idealists, there were other factors to be considered. "Moses was a very scrupulous researcher," Childs recalls. "He was very reliable. You could always be certain of the facts you read in the *Bulletin*." In 1921, when more than three hundred of New York City's most influential reformers formed a fusion "Coalition Committee" in an abortive effort to prevent Red Mike Hylan's re-election as mayor, they selected Moses as its secretary. He seemed, to most of them, the very model of the reformer, even down to the shabbiness of his tiny office and the fact that, to supplement his salary and Bella's subsidy, he lectured on political science at New York University.

Some of Moses' closest personal friends and at least one member of his family, however, were becoming puzzled.

"When Robert would come over to the house for dinner now," recalled his brother Paul, "it was 'Al Smith this' and 'Al Smith that.' All he could talk about was Smith—what Smith had said that day when Robert walked him home or about some idea Smith had had." The man who had always talked—and who still talked—of most politicians with such scorn talked of Smith with respect and admiration and something that was close to reverence. Moses' brother and friends saw nothing wrong with such a feeling. But they couldn't help noticing that, in discussing Smith, Moses was talking less and less about the great issues of the time with which Smith had been involved and more and more about political maneuvers which the former Governor had described to him. "Why, when he got enthusiastic about something now, and started to really go on about it in that way he had, it was more than likely something that, when you thought about it later, was really nothing more or less than some cheap political trick," one friend said.

And when Smith decided in 1922 to run against Miller for Governor, the puzzlement spread to a broader circle of reformers. They began to feel that the model reformer, presented in the secretaryship of the New York State Association with a great chance for increasing the effectiveness of the reform movement, was instead systematically trying to pervert the association into a tool to further Smith's political career.

In 1922, every issue of the *Bulletin* contained an attack on Miller. Because it was an election year, Moses wrote in one issue, "The Governor's organ is keyed for harmony. The soft pedal will be on, and . . . someone will pull out the Republican *vox humana* stop if it is not jammed from disuse." When Miller claimed that his economy measures had reduced the number of state employees by 2,500, Moses made his own analysis of civil service figures and wrote that the number had actually been increased by 983. A furious Miller called a press conference and declared that "like most all of the statements made by that association, it is untrue, and is a piece of the propaganda that this association is scattering all over the state." He knew where the blame lay, he said. It lay with Robert Moses. Moses' work, Miller charged, was of a "partisan character."

In at least one instance, moreover, Moses' eagerness to attack Miller led him into a mistake inconsistent with the scrupulous, reliable research of the days when his only interest had been in reform. He charged that the Governor had overspent the executive-department budget and then, to conceal the fact, had paid the difference out of his own pocket and had had the state repay him out of "sums set aside for other purposes." Miller replied—and proved—that he had indeed paid the difference, which had totaled over $8,000, but had refused to allow the state to repay him because he felt himself responsible. The discussion, Miller said, was valuable for only one purpose: "It discloses the animus of Mr. Moses and shows how hard put to it he is to find something to criticize." The New York *Herald* editorialized: "Mr. Moses is now engaged, not for the first time, in manifesting his superiority to the facts. . . . Mr. Moses has got a number of things all wrong. Why shouldn't he? He assumes to be a complete censor and impeccable Cato of what is done or undone at Albany. . . . he excites pity and sorrow among all the friends of noble civic objects, the fruitful pursuit of which requires exact knowledge, free from megalomania." The *Herald* was a Republican newspaper. Democratic newspapers, embarrassedly attempting to ignore the dispute, kept silent. So, because there was really no reply he could make, did Moses.

The effect on the association was predictable. "The whole aim was that it would be nonpartisan," Childs lamented. Although many of the younger New York City reformers, both Republican and Democratic, were still sympathetic to Moses, believing that he simply had made a mistake, the older city reformers and the upstaters, Republican almost to a man, were outraged that they were linked with a man who had slandered without cause a Governor of their party. Colonel Stimson, encountering Childs on the street one day, said that he had decided to resign from the association. "You're all right, Childs," the Colonel said, "but that Moses is a rough character."

Other members of the association also resigned. Its growth had been hampered by the differences in viewpoint between liberal New Yorkers and rural conservatives and by the physical difficulties involved in bringing both groups together in a state as large as New York and as short on good roads. But there had been signs of progress. The membership had been increasing, and city and upstate members were beginning to be more understanding of the other's viewpoints. Several of the more wealthy upstaters had even indicated to Childs their intention to become major contributors.

Now, of course, such hopes were dead. The chance to unify reform sentiment in the state and make it a force capable of influencing state decisions was gone. In fact, it was to be gone indefinitely. A half century later, with the sole exception of the single-sex League of Women Voters, New York would still have no statewide Good Government organization. In later years, it was impossible for Childs, who deeply admired Moses, to escape the feeling that Moses' actions had killed the best chance for a Good Government movement that New York State ever had.

Almost as disconcerting to Childs as Moses' sudden partisanship was Moses' attitude. When Childs taxed him about the partisanship, Moses took his protests lightly and seemed amused and not trying especially hard to conceal the amusement. Childs, he said, just didn't understand how politics worked.

Childs received further proof of how much Moses had changed during the latter stages of the 1922 campaign. He and several other reformers familiar with a particular aspect of state government noticed that whenever Smith discussed it, he was making misstatements. The misstatements weren't very important ones; they didn't affect the main thrust of Smith's stand on the issue, with which the reformers thoroughly agreed, but they felt Smith would like to have the facts straight. Knowing that Moses was working on Smith's campaign staff, they pointed them out to him. "We were," recalls one, "absolutely shocked at Bob's reaction. He threw back his head and laughed at us and said, 'Why, we know *that*. But it sounds a hell of a lot better this way, doesn't it?' Bob had always been so truthful. Now Bob was telling us that Smith was telling a deliberate lie—and Bob was condoning it."

Under Belle Moskowitz's tutelage, Bob Moses had changed from an uncompromising idealist to a man willing to deal with practical considerations; now the alteration had become more drastic. Under her tutelage, he had been learning the politicians' way; now he almost seemed to have joined their ranks.

More, he was openly scornful of men who hadn't, of men who still worried about the Truth when what counted was votes. He was openly scornful of reformers whose first concern was accuracy, who were willing to devote their lives to fighting for principle and who wanted to make that fight without compromise or surrender of any part of the ideals with which they had started it.

Bob Moses was scornful, in short, of what he had been.

Moses had transferred his allegiance, and the transfer was appreciated by the man to whom he was now giving it. Al Smith won back the Governorship—by 387,000 votes, the largest plurality any gubernatorial candidate had ever been given in the state, a plurality large enough to pull in behind him every other Democratic nominee for statewide office.

And when, on January 2, 1923, Al Smith went back to Albany, he took Bob Moses with him—and he took him back big.

8. *The Taste of Power*

UNDER A CEILING fifty feet above the floor, walls of marble from Siena, onyx from Mexico, granite pillars from the quarries of New England. Arched windows of stained glass. Facing the presiding officer's dais, a semicircle of fifty-one desks and chairs of oak and burgundy-red leather, set on burgundy broadloom. The Senate Chamber of the State of New York in 1923.

At desk number eighteen on the center aisle, the Democratic floor leader's desk, a short, very slim, very blue-eyed, dark-haired man. Pinch-waisted one-button suit, slenderest of cravats, a shirt from a collection of hundreds, pearl-gray spats buttoned around silk-hosed ankles, toes of the toothpick shoes peeking out from the spats polished to a gleam. Pixie smile, the "vivacity of a song and dance man," a charm that made him arrive in the Senate Chamber "like a glad breeze." Well-timed pauses, head cocked to preface the witticism, brow raised to indicate disbelief, hands tugging at waistcoat or briefly caressing it with upward flicks of expressive palms, forehead dabbed by handkerchief plucked from left-hand breast pocket by left hand instead of by right hand crossing over the chest because a crossed-over hand separates an actor from his audience. The Prince Charming of Politics. The author of "In the Valley Where My Sally Said Goodbye" and "Will You Love Me in December As You Do in May?" slicing through the ponderous arguments of the ponderous men who sat around him with a wit that flashed like a rapier. Beau James. Jimmy. The Honorable James J. Walker strutting his stuff.

And kneeling beside desk number eighteen, one knee on the burgundy broadloom, a tall man, dark-brown, almost black hair receding a little but still slim and handsome with clean-cut and sensitive features, stretching his neck up to whisper to Walker the facts that provided the ammunition for the floor leader's sallies, bending close when the floor leader sat down, murmuring to him urgently.

The fact that Bob Moses had to kneel on the floor in the Senate Chamber was symbolic in ways other than as an indication of his new-found reverence for politics. Just as Moses had no place there that belonged to him—the fifty-one chairs were reserved for the fifty-one elected senators, and officious sergeants-at-arms made sure that no one else, no matter how frequent his presence within the Chamber, sat down in one—so he had no official position in any branch of the state government. His only title—his only salary—was still that of secretary of the New York State Association.

But the fact that he was kneeling next to the floor leader's desk, at the very center of the Senate action, was also symbolic. For in Albany in 1923, Moses was a key figure in capitol maneuvering. Republican senators, cut to pieces day after day by Jimmy Walker's sallies on reorganization or the executive budget but knowing that Walker had no patience to master such subjects himself, knew that it was Moses who was coaching him step by step. And when—during debates in which his continual presence was not required—they saw Moses hurrying at intervals into the Chamber and over to desk eighteen, bending down over Walker, whispering briefly and then hurrying out again, they knew that the messages he bore came directly from Al Smith. The big hand that had pulled Moses out of his chair in Fourth Ward saloons to sing close harmony had now reached out and pulled him into the innermost circle of the Governor's advisers.

Moses was one of the little group which, in the late afternoon, would be swept by Smith out of the Executive Chamber and over to the home of his daughter Emily and her husband, John A. Warner, to chat with him as he bounced the Warners' baby daughter on his knee for an hour. He was one of the group who then followed the Governor over to the "menagerie" he had set up in the rear yard of the Executive Mansion. (The Governor loved animals—he had decided to keep, instead of giving to zoos, the animals bestowed by admirers as gifts. As a result, the menagerie contained tiger and bear cubs, goats, a fox and an elk, and, as permanent residents, six dogs, a mother raccoon with three baby raccoons, and three monkeys.) Moses would be one of the group that several times a week dined with Smith, at a table filled with his children's friends and made merry by the jokes he kept cracking with the servants, and after dinner returned to the Executive Chamber to participate in the legendary bill-vetoing and -signing sessions conducted over bottles of Scotch and Irish whiskey, which featured impromptu skits, songs and soft-shoe routines by the Governor—and his almost uncanny ability to recall details of other bills he had read over the years. "Look at this one," he would growl. "I fought against it six years ago and here it is again, just tricked up a little."

It was a mixed circle: Tammany men like George B. Graves, in his thirty-second year of service to Democrats in Albany, John F. Gilchrist, one of Smith's boyhood friends, and George V. (the Fifth) McLaughlin, a bluff, red-faced banker; and three tall, slim reformers—Moses, Proskauer and the stentorian, Roman-nosed journalistic genius with a thatch of bright red hair and a big, swinging stride, Herbert Bayard Swope. All three were master talkers. Pacing around the room, circling, interrupting, outshouting one another, they made proposals, discussed them, refined them. And interrupting and outshouting them, the Governor, the voice of experience in the quartet of reform, refusing to let anyone agree or curry favor with him, hashing out ideas as an equal. And, always, sitting apart, knitting, saying nothing until the Governor turned to her and asked, "What do you think, Mrs. M?" the plump, matronly little woman—a woman whose qualities astonished the capital more each day. She could mother reporters and bring them chicken soup when they were sick and call them at midnight with the inside tips that they treasured, but when one wrote something about Smith that she didn't like, she knew how to persuade his editor to transfer him from the Albany beat. (When, years later, he again wrote something she didn't like, she could tell the reporter's friends, smiling sweetly, "Well, he had better remember that I got him before.") Her loyalty to Smith was so complete that when, knowing she needed money to raise her children, Tammany leaders offered her a choice of lucrative city posts in an attempt to woo her from the Governor's side, she refused so that she could continue as his unpaid adviser.

It was exciting being part of that circle. It was exciting working for Smith. His enormous plurality made him feel free at last of all constraints, at home in the Governorship. He ran an informal office—when the waiting room was filled with people, the door to the inner office would swing open and Al Smith, ruddy-faced and red-nosed, in shirt sleeves, suspenders and uptilted cigar, would come out and greet each in turn with a wonderful gold-filled smile and the question "What can I do for you?" He was never too busy to see reporters, putting his feet up on his desk as he talked to them, revolving in his swivel chair to spray first one and then the other of the two big brass cuspidors that had been placed at either side of his office. He obviously enjoyed every minute of his banter with them and, giving them his private number at the Mansion, told them to call him day or night.

But underneath the joviality was a rock-hard toughness. The blue eyes could, in the words of one reporter, "turn to steel, absolute steel." Moses and the rest of Smith's inner circle might be free to argue with him but when, after consulting with Mrs. M, he had made his decision, the decision was final. None of them called him anything but "Governor." He could end a telephone call asking for a favor by rasping out the single word "No" and slamming down the receiver. Once he had made up his mind he was inflexible.

It was exciting watching how he maneuvered. If one was close enough to Smith, there was little one couldn't learn about the game of politics—the game that wasn't a game at all—and Moses was close enough. He could watch the Governor twist arms, offer incentives and drop, one by one, with matchless guile, the veils from in front of threats. Watching Smith banter with reporters, seeing how much time he devoted to winning their friendship, Moses learned how important the press was in politics. Seeing that Smith used the banter to cover up the fact that he wasn't telling the reporters anything he didn't want them to know, Moses learned how the press could be used.

He could learn to keep things simple. The Governor wanted no technicalities in his speeches: he himself, with the genius that made him the greatest campaigner of his time, reduced every argument to its most basic terms. During the 1922 campaign against Miller, for example, Smith was scheduled to speak at a county fair in Rochester. Moses had written a draft of a proposed speech that disproved—dollar by dollar, it seemed—Miller's claims that his economies had saved the state $14,000,000. When Smith arose, however, he looked out over the huge crowd of farmers and uttered just two sentences.

"Governor Miller says he saved the state fourteen million dollars," Smith said. "All I want to know is—where is it, and who's got it?" Then he sat down. For a moment the farmers were silent, puzzled. Then Moses, seated by the speaker's platform, heard the crowd begin to murmur, then to laugh, and finally to break into applause and cheers.

Moses was close enough to Jimmy Walker—physically if not spiritually—to learn from him, too, as he coached the mercurial Beau James on the technical aspects of the administration proposals that the floor leader had to steer through a Senate in which the Democrats had a bare one-vote majority. When Ellwood Rabenold, a reformer who had been elected to the Senate on the Democratic ticket and whose independence was continually imperiling the one-vote majority, not only refused Walker his vote on one crucial measure but rose on the Senate floor to chastise the floor leader for "undue pressure," Moses, kneeling beside Walker, heard the dapper little man snarl under his breath, "I'll ruin him, I'll *ruin* him"—and he watched as, in succeeding months, Walker remorselessly drove Rabenold out of politics. Kneeling there on the burgundy carpet, Moses heard the deals by which other Democrats—and Republicans, when needed—were kept or brought into line: the judgeship traded for a senator's vote on a crucial issue, the "campaign contribution" promised for an alteration in a legislator's stand.

Being close to Smith was exciting to Moses for another reason. For a decade, ever since he had entered public service, his mind had been teeming with ideas. But not a single one had become reality.

Now, for the first time, when Moses had an idea, he had a good chance of seeing it implemented. If something was wrong and he knew—just knew—exactly how to make it right, there was a real chance that it would be made right. Ultimately, he had learned through his experience with John Purroy Mitchel, it all came down to a question of power. An idea was no good without power behind it, power to make people adopt it, power to reward them when they did, power to crush them when they didn't. If he still had no position and no power of his own, if his only power was the confidence of one man, still, in Al Smith's Albany, when that one man was Al Smith, that was a not inconsiderable amount of power. "Executive support," he had learned, was the essential that one could not do without if one did not have power of one's own. Now he had that support.

And he got a lot done.

Smith, long angered by the state prison system's complete lack of interest in rehabilitating prisoners for their return to society, asked Moses to study the state's penal machinery. Moses proposed getting youthful offenders into a nonprison atmosphere by turning poorly attended state agricultural schools into minimum-security reformatories. To aid rehabilitation of adult prisoners, he proposed starting small industries in prisons and paying the prisoners for their work. And he proposed abolishing the notoriously repressive State Correction Commission and creating a new, more liberal State Correction Department.

Moses' plan aroused the opposition he had expected from the Correction Commission bureaucrats and the Legislature, but Smith incorporated Moses' prison-industry suggestion in an administration bill, pushed it through the Legislature in 1923, turned the agricultural schools into reformatories by the same method in 1924 and told Moses to draw up the laws creating the new department.

Smith wanted to eliminate grade crossings, the thousands of intersections on the same level of roads and railroad tracks that every year caused not only delays to motorists but deaths running into the hundreds. Other Governors had had the same desire, but the sheer cost of the job—the simplest elimination, in open countryside, cost $60,000—put it beyond the traditional scope of state expenditures. And the subservience of the Republican legislators to the railroads had insured that the railroads would not be forced to pay. Each year, as a gesture, the Legislature would appropriate the funds for a handful of crossing eliminations, but, because of division of responsibility among the many state agencies involved, even these were generally not completed. Smith asked Moses to look into the situation.

Moses recommended that the state and the railroads split the cost and that the state finance its share by selling revenue bonds authorized by a constitutional amendment. Smith accepted the recommendation—and fought for it, campaigning for the amendment across the state. With the press denouncing Republican opposition to such unprecedented governmental expenditure and interference with private enterprise, the 1924 Legislature was forced to pass the amendment, the 1925 Legislature to repass it, and in 1926 the voters ratified it by a margin of more than a million votes. While the amendment was still being debated, Smith asked Moses to see if anything could be done to speed up grade-crossing eliminations already authorized. Moses devised a form that could be sent to Highway Division regional engineers showing the steps in each elimination and the suggested target dates for completion of each step. And these forms were not allowed to yellow in stacks in the corner of some office. Smith ordered Highway Superintendent Greene to send them out to the engineers—and to see that they used them.

Moses had a taste of power now, and he liked the taste—so obviously that, to some observers, it seemed as if he liked the taste in and for itself. Keen-eyed little Reuben Lazarus, who had been brought to Albany from the Old Neighborhood as an Assembly page when Smith was Assembly Speaker and had already become one of the most knowledgeable men in the capitol on the intricacies of bill drafting, remembers that "when I first used to see Moses in Albany, before he had any power, he was a striking figure, dark and handsome, tall and gangly, striding down the corridors with those long strides of his, but he was withdrawn, he was within himself. But then, when Smith brought him up there, he began to be, quite suddenly and quite noticeably, a lot more arrogant, stiff-necked and self-assertive." Belle Moskowitz's son, Carlos Israels, noticed the same transformation when Moses visited the Moskowitzes. "Now he attitudinized when he talked. He would lean back, cross his knees and hold his pipe in an affected attitude."

The man who had had to wait outside so many offices liked being on the inside of everything. He talked—perhaps a bit more than was discreet—about what Jimmy Walker had said to him and about what he had said to Walker. He liked to describe how some assemblyman had refused his instructions on a bill and how he had told the Governor about it and how the Governor had laid down the law, and, thereafter, how the assemblyman had jumped to obey when he, Moses, gave him instructions. If what he was on the inside of was a world he would once have despised, he did not seem to remember those earlier feelings now. Reform work was, more and more, an irritating intrusion on his time. The hours he put in at the New York State Association office each week became fewer and fewer. The gaps between issues of the *State Bulletin,* once a monthly publication, grew longer and longer. And when the *Bulletin* did appear now, it made less and less pretense of being a reform pamphlet. More and more, it resembled a Tammany Hall broadside in support of Al Smith.

Reorganization, of course, was the key to all the hopes of Smith—and of Mrs. Moskowitz and the other reformers around the Governor. No sooner had he been returned to office in 1923 than he hurled down the gauntlet to the Legislature with a special message, drafted by Moses, that restarted the three reorganization amendments down the tortuous road to law. The Legislature passed the amendments consolidating state departments and reducing the number of elected state officials in 1923 and again in 1924, after battles in which Walker and Democratic Assembly leaders fought for every vote—and Moses hurried up and down the marble stairs of the capitol between the Executive Chamber on the second floor and the Senate and Assembly Chambers on the third, bringing them fresh ammunition.

Day after day, during the reorganization fight, Smith had watched Moses drafting the bills that contained the specifics of departmental reorganization: which agency went in which department, which powers were given to each agency. Bill drafting was called by Albany insiders "the black art of politics." An expert bill drafter had to know thousands of precedents so that he could cull out the one, embodying it in the bill he was working on, that would make the bill legal, or so that he could, by careful wording, avoid bringing the new act within the purview of an old one that might make it illegal. He had to know a myriad ways of conferring, or denying, power by written words. He had to know how to lull the opposition by concealing a bill's real content. For years, everyone had known the identity of the best bill drafter in Albany: Alfred E. Smith. And Smith had never been shy about accepting that accolade. But now, when someone brought up the subject, Smith said, "The best bill drafter I know is Bob Moses."

Al Smith was a man who believed in paying his debts. In 1923, he found for Moses a state sinecure with high pay and a low work load: the directorship of a board that would supervise the industries that, thanks to Moses, had been installed in state prisons.

Moses told Smith he didn't want the job.

"What do you want, then?" Smith asked.

"Nothing," Moses replied.

Over and over during 1923 and the beginning of 1924, as Smith watched Moses driving himself in his service, he asked Moses what he wanted. Over and over again, Moses said, "Nothing."

And then, one day, there was something. The something was parks.

9. *A Dream*

PARKS WAS A SUBJECT listed frequently during the 1920's on the agendas of New York City Good Government organizations.

Parks had always been a concern of reformers who were fond of referring to the need for "breathing spaces for the slums" or "lungs for the city," and the agitation for increased respiratory facilities in New York—generally for playgrounds in low-income areas—had been long and insistent.

But other reform causes had been pressed with more urgency. With so much open space then in the city's outlying boroughs, there had seemed no rush to reserve any of it, and the cost of condemning buildings in the slums, so heavily built up that any other method of obtaining space there seemed unfeasible, was so prohibitive that even the most zealous of reformers had found it difficult to suggest such a step seriously. Other matters, it had seemed, should take precedence. There would be time to get to parks.

Now, suddenly, there wasn't any time. The population of New York City had increased from 4,766,883 to 5,620,048 between 1910 and 1920, and now, in the Twenties, the rate of increase was accelerating, and most of it was occurring outside Manhattan. When Bob Moses had returned to the city from Oxford in 1913, some of Brooklyn, most of the Bronx and practically all of Queens had been woods, meadows or farmland. Now red bricks, like those that had imprisoned the Lower East Side in tenements, were being cemented into walls in Brooklyn's remaining green fields, and in the Bronx and Queens great stretches of woodland and field were blossoming hideously with developers' "Spanish stucco haciendas" and "Colonial farmhouses," all available on the new merchandising gimmick: the installment plan. Vacant land, the first and irreplaceable essential for parks, was vanishing in New York City, and it was vanishing fast.

And time had another dimension now. Assembly lines, mass-production techniques—the whole new technology that would make it possible, by 1929, for sixty-nine workers to produce as much as one hundred had in 1920—had given it as a gift to the American working man. Before World War I, a seventy-hour factory week had been common; in 1920, the average was sixty hours; in 1929, just before the Crash, it would be forty-eight. The Saturday half holiday was becoming a part of American life; the full holiday was becoming more common; small-town businessmen who hadn't yet forgotten what was the devil's handmaiden were muttering at Kiwanis Club luncheons about Henry Ford's institution of annual vacations—*with pay!*—

for his workers. Before the eyes of America a bright new world of mass leisure was unfolding.

And along with time the new technology brought a means by which the time could be used to conquer space. In 1909, after sixteen years of experimentation with gasoline-driven vehicles, Ford had announced the invention of the Model T, which could be mass-produced, and, with the unrolling of the unparalleled prosperity of the Twenties, which gave the average American money to spend on luxuries, America beat a path to Ford's door and to the doors of his imitators. The number of automobile-owning families in the country in 1919 was less than seven million; by 1923, it would be twenty-three million.

Their newly acquired leisure time and the mobility to use it to conquer space meant, to the urban masses of America, something very particular. The countryside was no longer inaccessible. For millions of New York fathers, thanks to the machine parked near their door, no longer did a Sunday outing have to be to a Bowery beer garden or a hard-surfaced playground framed by the grimy buildings that they saw every day. Suddenly, it could be to grassy meadows beneath expanses of blue sky, perhaps even to white sand and sparkling surf. They could escape the city, and, more important, they could free their children for a time from its clutches; they could take them boating and hiking and camping, could roam with them through fields and forests, sprawl with them eating picnic lunches on blankets. They could let them do the things that they themselves had done so seldom when they were children. When they taught their sons to swim now, it would not have to be in the East River. Without even a delay for cranking up—self-starters had become standard equipment—they piled into their Fords (or Lexingtons, Maxwells, Briscoes, Hudsons, Templars, Dodges, Buicks, Chevrolets or Cadillacs) on weekends and headed out of New York City.

They headed into disappointment. Most of the land around the city was in private hands and closed to them. To the north, in Westchester County, there were indeed public parks, the rolling hills and green playing fields they sought, but Westchester had barred its parks to anyone not a resident of the county. Fourteen miles north of the city, beyond Mount Vernon, Bronxville, Scarsdale and White Plains, was an unrestricted attraction, Kensico Dam, surrounded by 2,500 acres of trees and meadows, but, since the Bronx River Parkway was still under construction, the only way to get to Kensico—after crossing the Harlem River on the narrow Broadway drawbridge that caused traffic jams even when it wasn't raised (as it was on the average of fourteen times each day) or on the even narrower East River bridges to the south and creeping through the narrow and often unpaved streets of the Bronx—was to take another narrow road that led through the traffic-clogged downtowns of the four Westchester communities. Families who left New York in the morning were lucky to arrive at Kensico by late afternoon.

To the west of New York City, across the broad Hudson River, was a vast preserve open to the city's masses: Palisades Interstate Park. Founded in 1900, funded by the Rockefellers and Harrimans with $15,000,000, it was considered, with its lakes, landscaped drives, herds of elk, and buildings erected "to resemble the eternal hills themselves," the finest park in the United States.

Getting there, however, could be eternal. Since there were no bridges or vehicular tunnels across the Hudson—the Holland Tunnel would not be opened until 1927—the only way across the river was on ferries, the same method the Dutch had used after having purchased Manhattan from the Indians three hundred years before. The Palisades Park Commission operated two that ran to the park itself, but they carried between them only five thousand persons. Every Saturday and Sunday morning in summer, when the ferry ticket takers nailed up the signs that said, in large black letters, FULL, there were thousands of disappointed faces—of fathers carrying picnic baskets and mothers carrying babies, of children who had been so excited about the trip that they hadn't been able to sleep the night before—still in front of them. Privately operated ferries plied the Hudson, but their New Jersey termini were some forty miles south of the park, so families using them had to bring their cars. A ferry carried twenty-four cars at a trip; often, at ten o'clock on a weekend morning, there would be hundreds of cars lined up at the ferry slips in Manhattan. Disembarking in New Jersey, families faced a drive on two-lane roads through the narrow streets of Weehawken, Englewood and Alpine.

So desperate were New York's masses that they made the trip anyway—in steadily increasing numbers. (In 1921, attendance at the park was 3,100,000. In 1922, it topped 4,000,000.) Every year, the Rockefellers and Harrimans built more playing fields and campsites, and nonetheless every year the playing fields and campsites were so jammed that Palisades Park on weekends, for all its beautiful woods and landscaped drives, seemed as crowded as the city its visitors had come to it to escape.

Increasingly, the eyes of the city's masses—and of the reformers interested in providing parks for them—were turning to the east.

The east was Long Island.

Separated from Manhattan only by the East River, it stretched out into the Atlantic Ocean for eighty miles, its bulk about twenty miles wide, and then threw two curving spits of land thirty-nine miles farther out so that its shape reminded Walt Whitman of a whale ducking its great head to plunge beneath the southern tip of Manhattan while its flukes waved behind. Its westernmost sixth was Brooklyn and Queens, crammed in 1920 with two and a half million people, a population greater than that of all but eight states in the Union, but beyond the eastern border of Queens that marked the end of New York City lay, divided into the counties of Nassau and Suffolk, another 1,373 square miles—878,720 acres—inhabited by less than a quarter of a million people, one person to every four acres, an area four times the size of the whole city and with a population less than one twenty-fifth as large, a prodigal extravagance of precisely that luxury of which New York was rapidly being drained: space.

And what space. Once, before the Ice Age, Long Island had been only the easternmost extension of the barren plains stretching out from the new-formed Alleghenies. But the weight of two great glaciers rumbling down from Hudson Bay had pushed under the ocean a wide, deep valley, turning it into a body of water that would one day be called, at different spots along its route, Long Island Sound, Hell Gate, East River and the Narrows, and thereby freeing the land south and east of the valley from the mainland. Then the glaciers had cut into this land hundreds of indentations, so that when the ice had melted, its sharp edges softening and retreating, the north shore of Long Island was fjords and coves, harbors and bays, straits and peninsulas, an endless, beautiful coastline. The melted ice ran south, flooded a huge low-lying meadow on the south side of the Island and left on the ocean side of the meadow just enough low sand bars and dunes to form a barrier beach that checked the force of the Atlantic rollers before they smashed on the Island and then let them continue as gentle waves that washed the Island's shore. The ocean deposited on it gleaming white sand that gave it long horseshoes of beaches, while between the sand bars and the Island, on top of the meadow, a long, narrow, beautiful bay was created. And the tides of eons gently etched into the south shore of the mainland a panorama of incredibly twisting channels and coves and necks, of sandy shoals and tiny bays off the big one, of a marshland catacomb.

Before the two glaciers, the land had been flat, but the glaciers had pushed before them boulders, gravel, sand and clay and, coming to a halt on Long Island and melting there, had left such debris behind as two great ridges that marked the outlines of their farthest advance. The ridges lay along the flatness like a pair of scissors, with the bolt holding the blades in a place called the Wheatley Hills. One blade trailed off along the northern fluke of the Island in a mass of small rocks and pebbles; the other cut down, far out along its length, to the southern fluke and reached out along the fluke in a mass of gravel, clay and rock hills, crowned with gnarled and twisted trees, that ended in a series of steep bluffs. Over the centuries, the ridges had been smoothed and shaped into chains of gently rolling hills that ran to the edge of the whitecapped Sound and the hills had been covered with lush growths of trees—beech, oak, maple and elm, copses of sassafras and dogwood, birch and pine—so that the North Shore of Long Island became "a fresh, green breast of the New World," and, looking at it, F. Scott Fitzgerald would think that "for a transitory enchanted moment man must have held his breath in the presence of this continent, compelled into an aesthetic contemplation he neither understood nor desired, face to face for the last time in history with something commensurate to his capacity to wonder." In summer, to the sweltering masses of New York, the cool green hills and rolling surf of Long Island beckoned like a vast playground filled with the milk and honey of leaves and grass, of sun and sand, that would sweeten the bitterness of city life.

Certainly, the Island seemed open to them. Unlike the Hudson, the East River had been spanned by great bridges—Williamsburg, Queensborough, Manhattan and Brooklyn—and running out from the bridges through Brooklyn and Queens, to the very threshold of the Island, were three boulevards—Northern, Conduit and Queens—one of which, Northern, was perhaps the widest highway in the country. For Brooklyn and Queens residents, moreover, there was no necessity for either bridges or boulevards. Long Island was just down the road.

So was disappointment.

The Island's South Shore, the edge of the meadow that had been transformed into the Great South Bay, offered gentle waves and sandy beaches. But the bay was the haunt of the baymen, a closemouthed, independent breed, some of them descendants of families that had "followed the bay" since the Revolution, others New England Yankees who, hearing about the bay's bountiful harvests of oysters and clams, tommycods and smelts, had left the whaling boats and had moved to Long Island, bringing with them their taciturnity and distrust of outsiders.

Less than thirty miles from the borders of New York City, the baymen lived in a world that resembled nothing so much as the remote fog banks of Nova Scotia. Their lives revolved around the bay. When its tides were flood, no matter what the hour, through the thick, damp mist, hip boots slung over their shoulders, caps pulled low over their eyes, they trudged to their weather-beaten little trawlers and crept out into the fog, returning hours later so heavily laden that only the bows and sterns of the boats were out of the water. They loved the bay's sparkle in summer, its cool breezes; somehow they loved its treacherous shoals and tides and the hidden traps of swamp grass that tangled their boats' propellers. Forced off it by winter storms, they settled down in taverns near the piers that jutted into it, drinking (they were famous for their drinking) and spinning legends about it. Once you were "bay salted," they said, you would never leave.

They were fiercely determined to keep their world for themselves. The bay bottoms, the hell-fire preachers in their weather-beaten little churches constantly reminded them, were "sacred," their "priceless natural heritage," and when it came time each year for the townships that bordered on the Great South Bay—Hempstead, Oyster Bay,* Babylon, Islip and Brookhaven—to sell leases to mine the bay's underwater crops of shellfish, the baymen crowded into town halls to listen while the leases were awarded—and no outsider was ever given a lease. No authority could awe them. In 1892, when the German liner *Normannia* arrived in New York flying the yellow flag that signaled a cholera epidemic on board, the state bought the only hotel on Fire Island so it could quarantine the passengers and crews there. Trawlerloads of armed baymen met the *Normannia* as it tied up to the hotel dock and cut loose its hawsers, and only the dispatch of a National Guard regiment put down the uprising.

Distrusting anyone "from away," the baymen distrusted especially anyone from New York. Hating the city—many boasted that they had never

* The incorporated villages of Hempstead and Oyster Bay are, respectively, in the center and northern part of Long Island but the Townships of Hempstead and Oyster Bay, of which the villages are a part, extend to the South Shore and the barrier beach.

been there—they feared that its "foreigners," hordes of long-haired Slavs, hook-nosed Jews and unwashed Irishmen, would descend on and befoul their beautiful beaches at the first slackening in their vigilance.

And to keep such intruders away, their township boards had created, on every piece of publicly owned waterfront property that might conceivably attract visitors from the city, "parks" whose exclusive use was by statute reserved to township residents.

The baymen's land-locked cousins, the farmers of Long Island, were men of conviction, too. In no part of New York State were the white hoods of the Ku Klux Klan, an organization whose venom was directed in the 1920's not only against Negroes but also against Jews and Catholics, as numerous as in Suffolk County. Three successive chairmen of Suffolk's Republican Party had been members of the Klan, and anyone who needed an additional symbol of its power had only to look at the flagpole in front of the Islip Town Hall: the pole, read the inscription on an attached plaque, had been donated by the Islip branch of the Ladies of the Klan and gratefully accepted by the Town Board. (In 1928, when Al Smith ran for President, fiery crosses would blaze on the hills of Alabama and Mississippi—and, by orders of the county GOP organization, on the hills of Suffolk.) Combining with the baymen to dominate the Suffolk political picture, the farmers had no difficulty persuading the county's supervisors to make sure that there was not a single park in Suffolk open to city residents.

And it was neither the baymen nor the farmers who most firmly barred Long Island to those who hungered for it. The huddled masses of New York City had a far more powerful enemy. It was wealth—vast, entrenched, impregnable wealth—and the power that went with it. For it was to Long Island that the robber barons of America had retired to enjoy their plunder.

These were the men who, during the "Middle Ages of American industry," the half century of unbridled industrial expansion following the Civil War, had harnessed America's vast mineral resources and tapped its long-stored capital to create needed industrial growth but who, to turn that growth into personal wealth, had stationed themselves at the "narrows" of production, the key points of production and distribution, and exacted tribute from the nation. They were the men who had blackmailed state legislatures and city councils by threatening to build their railroad lines elsewhere unless they received tax exemptions, outright gifts of cash—and land grants so vast that, by 1920, the elected representatives of America had turned over to the railroad barons an area the size of Texas. They were the men who had bribed and corrupted legislators—the Standard Oil Company, one historian said, did everything possible to the Pennsylvania Legislature except refine it—to let them loot the nation's oil and ore, the men who, building their empires on the toil of millions of immigrant laborers, had kept wages low, hours long, and had crushed the unions. Their creed was summed up in two quotes: Commodore Vanderbilt's "Law? What do I care for law? Hain't I got the power?" and J. P. Morgan's "I owe the public nothing."

The northern tip of Long Island's Glen Cove peninsula was Morgan's estate, the waters beside it the anchorage for his great black yacht, *Corsair*, and all the northern reaches of the peninsula were "Morgan Country." His son—Morgan the Younger, reporters called him—and four partners of the House of Morgan lived there, their yachts riding to anchor beside that of their father and chief, and so did George F. Baker, the chop-whiskered, taciturn Sphinx of Wall Street who was the president of the First National Bank, the largest single stockholder of both AT&T and United States Steel (his holdings in Big Steel alone totaled $212,500,000 in 1920), and who rode at the right hand of Morgan the Elder in the turn of the century's bloodiest stock-market raids. Baker was old now—eighty in 1920—but not too old to lift his sword; in 1930, when he was ninety and America was in the Depression, he climbed out of bed, pushed aside his doctors, strode to his office and, in a series of incredible stock manipulations, increased his fortune in that year alone by $50,000,000.

To the south of the Morgans lay the demesnes of Standard Oil, where Charles Pratt and Stephen C. Harkness, partners of John D. Rockefeller the First, had carved out adjoining fiefs on either side of a small stream. On his, Pratt built six manor houses for his six sons.

South of the Pratts, around Westbury in the Wheatley Hills, the bolt of the scissors that made Long Island beautiful, there established himself Henry Phipps, full partner of Andrew Carnegie, a man who, while Carnegie drove men to ordeals of sweat, grime and injury in the roaring steel mills of western Pennsylvania, obtained the cash to let Carnegie build more mills by using a talent "for keeping a check in the air as long as any man." Around him, in the hills, Phipps gathered his children and grandchildren. To the west of the Phippses' lands, also in Wheatley, lay "Harbor Hill," the 480-acre holding of Clarence Hungerford Mackay, president, board chairman and major stockholder of the Postal Telegraph Cable Company, precursor of Western Union, who had, during World War I, defied President Wilson's attempts to put the telegraph to use in America's service. North of Mackay lay the principality of Child's Frick, son of Henry Clay Frick, baron of coal and coke, who had gained his legendary wealth during the Panic of 1873 by purchasing for a pittance the land of desperate farmers without telling them that it contained coal, the raw material of the coke essential to steelmaking, then by crushing other rivals in the field and, with a virtual monopoly of the fuel in his hands, by quintupling its price.

To the west of Mackay stretched the fiefs of other barons of American business—the sugar truster Claus Spreckels, for example, and other Standard Oil heirs like Payne Whitney, who in the early 1920's was paying an annual income tax of a million and a half dollars. To the east of the Phippses there were more Whitneys; Ogden Livingston Mills, congressman son of Darius Ogden Mills of the San Francisco "bank ring"; and the lawyers who were the barons' trusted counselors, Colonel Henry L. Stimson, Rockefeller's Robert W. De Forest, Morgan's Joseph E. Davies and Colonel H. Rogers Winthrop, and Francis P. Garvan, the brain behind the Chemical Trust; and, finally, in the eastern outpost of Centerport, the castle of fierce old Commodore Vanderbilt's indolent grandson, Willie. Mingled with the barons were representatives of older wealth—won by gentler means—and of newer. There were six hundred estates on the North Shore, most of them more than fifty acres in size, some of them hundreds of acres, some of them thousands. The turrets of the barons' castles loomed above the trees along the entire North Shore of Nassau County and fifteen miles deep into Suffolk.

The castles reflected the extent of their triumphs. Mrs. John S. Phipps, already mistress of seven other houses, wanted her Long Island residence to look exactly like the great eighteenth-century English manor houses. To make sure that it would, the famous London manor-house architect George Crawley was summoned to the Wheatley Hills to design "Westbury House" and to stay for years until it was completed—a masterpiece of cherry-red brick and limestone, Georgian chimneys and a pale-gold roof rising above the trees, complete with a vault for the family silver, separate rooms for glasses and china and luggage, silver-plated bathroom fixtures and doorknobs, and a cellar so large that in 1960 the Nassau County Office of Civil Defense would designate it as a bomb shelter large enough to hold eighteen hundred persons. To make sure that the mood of England should not be lost in the furnishings, envoys of the Phippses scoured England for furniture made by Chippendale himself. The armoire in Mrs. Phipps's bedroom had belonged to James II. The mantel clock in her study was made by the clockmaker to King George II. The desk in the hall outside it was the desk on which Cromwell had signed the death warrant of Charles I.

And the Phippses were noted for their modesty and restraint. Westbury House, after all, contained only thirty-two rooms. The F. W. Woolworth mansion in Glen Cove contained sixty-two, and included not only solid gold instead of silver-plated bathroom fixtures and doorknobs but a dining-room ceiling gilded with fifteen hundred square feet of fourteen-carat gold. The Tiffany Estate in Laurel Hollow contained eighty-two. The Phippses had a private golf course and two private polo fields, but guests of the Marshall Fields in Lloyd Neck were not forced to limit their activities to polo or golf, since their hosts had also provided them with tennis courts, badminton courts, squash courts, indoor and outdoor swimming pools, sailboats, motorboats, skeet ranges—and a thousand-acre hunting preserve. No extravagance was too great. Finding that all the large hills in the Cold Spring Harbor area, where he wanted to build a chateau, were taken, Otto Kahn built a hill of his own, a small mountain, in fact, and since hauling the necessary earth and stone to the site required a railroad line, he built a railroad line.

The sports of the feudal lords of the Old World were the sports of these feudal lords of the New. The North Shore echoed to the thunder of their horses' hooves, and to the bay of their hounds as, hunting fox and deer, they ranged unchallenged across the estates, riding in a single hunt from one end of Nassau County to the other. And they partied on a scale the New World had seldom seen, outdoing themselves with swimming pools bearing thousands of orchids, diamond tiaras for lady guests, cigarettes wrapped, and designed to be smoked, in hundred-dollar bills, until an awed America named the North Shore "The Gold Coast."

And if their displays of wealth were awesome, so were their displays of selfishness. The robber barons intended to keep their world for themselves.

There was a reason for the size of their fiefs, for their willingness to buy—and, year after year, to pay taxes on—hundreds of acres that they kept in woods and never used. There was a reason for the height and thickness of the walls around those fiefs. There was a reason for their private police forces and armed guards. They needed vast acreage in order that their castles could be set far enough back from public roads so that they would not have to see the public. They needed walls so that the public should understand that it was not wanted on their acres. They needed armed guards to protect their borders from those members of the public who might, on a Sunday excursion to the country, climb a wall to get at the empty green fields beyond. They were willing, they told each other, to spend anything necessary "to keep our privacy"—by which they meant to keep the public out of their demesne.

And in their view this demesne included the whole North Shore.

The officials they controlled allowed all public roads not needed for their own access to their estates to fall into disrepair to discourage public use. Lest the public turn instead to rail transportation, a group of them led by Charles Pratt, who had learned how to handle annoyances from his mentor, Rockefeller, bought sufficient stock in the Long Island Rail Road to control its policies—and saw to it that the railroad's North Shore lines were kept especially antiquated and rickety.

The magnet that most strongly drew the city masses, of course, was their desire to swim in Long Island Sound, and the barons of the North Shore knew what to do about that.

The shore front on the Great Neck peninsula, the first of the series of peninsulas that compose most of the North Shore in Nassau and western Suffolk, was entirely in their hands, except for a few slivers owned by less wealthy individuals who emulated the barons in keeping their property for their own use. So was the shore front on the next peninsula, except for two pieces of property at its tip, Sands Point. One was a small crescent of beach, rather rocky, owned by an elderly widow, a native of Long Island, who liked to see people having fun and had not only resisted entreaties that she bar them from the property but had stubbornly refused, even for an outrageously high price, to sell her beach to those who would; it was in the process of being condemned by a village board controlled by the barons. The other, at the very tip of the peninsula, opposite Execution Rock, where the original, slaveowning settlers of Sands Point had disposed of troublesome slaves by chaining them to the rock at low tide and letting them drown as the tide crept over them, was a sandier five-acre beach owned by the federal government and holding the Sands Point Lighthouse.

The beach could be reached only by a road that crossed an adjacent, privately owned property, but the federal government had purchased an easement for public use of that road. When, however, the adjacent property was purchased by Mrs. Oliver Belmont, a cold-eyed *grande dame* famed for her priceless parure of emeralds and for her "Marble House" at Newport, a white marble structure whose pilasters and capitals were modeled on, although somewhat larger than, those of the Temple of the Sun at Baalbek, she erected across the southern edge of the property, stretching from one side of the peninsula to the other, a wall made of solid concrete three feet thick, twelve feet high, topped with sharp black spikes and iron dragons' heads. Persons who asked the armed guards stationed at the massive iron gate to allow them to pass were informed that the federal government had "surrendered" its easement and that the road could be used only by persons "having official business" at the lighthouse—a fact federal officials brusquely confirmed.

On the next peninsula, Glen Cove, there were five beaches open to the public, two owned privately and three by Oyster Bay Township, rocky and unappealing, pitifully narrow strips of pebbles and weeds for whose use city residents had to pay exorbitant rates, and whose combined capacity was less than ten thousand.

There were long stretches of more appealing beach open to the public in Cold Spring Harbor, the area east of the Glen Cove peninsula, but the barons of Cold Spring had solved that problem; they had built a gate across the only road that led to the beach and stationed armed guards at the gate. Would-be beachgoers who questioned their authority were told that the road was on private property, a legal question somewhat difficult to research on a summer weekend.

Every foot of the two commas of land east of Cold Spring—Lloyd Neck and Eatons Neck—was owned by barons. Huntington Township, just beyond them, contained forty-eight miles of shoreline; 1,250 feet of it were open to the public.

Like those on the South Shore, then, the beaches on the North Shore of Long Island had been effectively closed to city residents. A New Yorker who wanted to take his family for a swim on Long Island could head only for Long Beach on the South Shore, tedious to reach because of inadequate roads and so crowded that it seemed like an extension of the filthy, incredibly jammed Coney Island beach in Brooklyn. The North Shore stood impregnable against the importunings of the masses.

And the barons of the North Shore knew how to keep it impregnable. Accustomed to dealing in the political marketplace (so many of the largest contributors to the Republican Party came from the North Shore that during the 1920's the GOP's National Finance Committee contained forty-nine members—one from each of the forty-eight states and one from Nassau County), they furnished the bulk of the war chest of the state Republican organization—and of the smooth-running Nassau County GOP machine. And they knew how to get value for money spent. They saw to it that key legislative committee chairmen were men who took orders. They sent to Albany as the assemblymen and senators from Nassau County young knights from their own ranks—bright-eyed, enthusiastic F. Trubee Davison, son of Morgan partner Henry P.—or young villagers whom their eyes had picked out as promising men to enlist in their service, such as a handsome, ambitious young lawyer whose father had been Theodore Roosevelt's coachman at Sagamore Hill, Leonard W. Hall. And while state roads of broader width, better paving and improved design might be built elsewhere, they were not built on Long Island. A strangely permissive state law, moreover, allowed the barons to incorporate their estates into self-governing "villages" so that the measures necessary to keep out the city hordes could be legitimatized, given "governmental status"—and enforced by "village police forces," which before incorporation had been their privately employed guards.

So when the families of New York City reached Long Island, they found the milk and honey sour indeed.

If they were heading for the North Shore on Northern Boulevard, 160 feet of smooth macadam shrank to eighteen at the city line. The cars heading east had to cram into a single file. As they crept along, the paving of the boulevard deteriorated, so that each family had to watch the cars ahead jounce, one after the other, into gaping potholes, and then wait for the jolts themselves. More and more frequently, they came to unpaved stretches in which, if there had been a recent rain, cars became mired, bringing the endless line behind them to a halt. If the earth was dry, thick clouds of dust hung over the unpaved stretches, turning dirty the gay dress Mother had worn for the excursion.

As the families drove, they could see on either side of them, through gates set in stone walls or through the openings in wooden fences, the beautiful meadows they had come for, stretching endlessly and emptily to the cool trees beyond. But the meadows and trees were not for them. The gates would be locked and men carrying shotguns and holding fierce dogs on straining leashes would point eastward, telling the families there were parks open to them "farther along." There was no shade on Northern Boulevard and the children became cranky early. In desperation, ignoring the NO TRESPASSING—PRIVATE PROPERTY signs that lined the road, fathers would turn onto the narrow strip of grass between the boulevard and the wall paralleling it and, despite the dust and the fumes from the passing cars, would try to picnic there. But the guards were vigilant and it was never long until the fathers had to tell the kids to get back into the car. Later, in Oyster Bay Town and Huntington, they would come to parks, tiny but nonetheless parks, but as they approached them they would see policemen at their entrances and the policemen would wave them on, explaining that they were reserved for township residents. There were, the policemen shouted, parks open "farther along."

Of those who turned off the boulevard, trying to find a beach, the lucky ones found a spot on the five rocky strips on the Glen Cove peninsula. The others, searching mile after mile for a piece of beach not marked PRIVATE, seldom even got close enough to glimpse the water, for most of the roads down to it had locked gates across them. They would turn south again, heading back to the boulevard.

The more persistent, who determined to head east until they discovered *someplace* to swim or picnic, found the road becoming worse and worse. They would see Long Island villagers sitting on the fences and laughing at the families who, because of engine overheating or in a desperate try at a piece of grass, pulled off the road. The line of cars was so solid, the radiator of one almost touching the tailgate of the one before it, that, once out of the line, it was hard for a car to get back in—and it was fun, the villagers said, to watch them try.

At the head of Hempstead Harbor, the inlet that separates the Sands Point and Glen Cove peninsulas, Northern Boulevard dipped down, curving and winding, rutted and potholed, unpaved in one stretch, and became the Main Street of Roslyn Village. It narrowed as its width was cut by sidewalks in front of little stores, and then, on the other side of the town, wound upward again before resuming its eastern course. Roslynites, watching the endless line of cars, said it took two hours just to get through town, but this was, of course, an exaggeration. In 1923, state officials clocked it on successive Sundays and found you could make it in an hour and a quarter. The officials also determined the length of time it took on an average Sunday to get from the Queensborough Bridge to Huntington, a distance of 32.4 miles. The time was four hours.

If the New Yorkers stayed on Northern Boulevard long enough, there were, indeed, after the estates and guards of the Gold Coast had been left behind—and even if the promised parks "farther along" never materialized—plenty of quiet places with grass and trees in which one could picnic. Why, Smithtown, the township beyond Huntington, alone had 92.5 acres of cemeteries, and fallen tombstones made excellent picnic tables. When the cemeteries were filled, there were always farms, for although the Suffolk farmers were as determined as the barons to keep the foreigners off their lands, they couldn't afford guards to help them do it, and they never seemed to have enough dogs and sons with pitchforks to do the job thoroughly, although they certainly tried. New Yorkers could even swim in Smithtown, if they found a beach whose owner wasn't around. Everyone knew they could, because, every Monday, newspapers would carry stories about the city residents who, swimming in the choppy Sound without the protection of lifeguards, had drowned in Smithtown waters.

Most New Yorkers, however, didn't last to Smithtown. They turned around and slunk home, eating their picnic lunches in their cars, washing them down with bitterness and frustration. If they swam on Long Island, they swam in their cars in their sweat.

Northern Boulevard was not, of course, the only route to the North Shore from New York. There was also Jericho Turnpike. There was one difference between Northern Boulevard and Jericho Turnpike. Jericho Turnpike was two feet narrower.

And the greed of the robber barons had not been satisfied by the riches of the North Shore. Led by Horace O. Havemeyer, the "Sultan of Sugar," a group of them had seized the choicest areas of the South Shore, a series of promontories below East Islip that jut out into the Great South Bay about midway along its sixty-mile length.

They lived there in a splendor equal to that of the North Shore—and they displayed an equal determination to keep their privacy unimpaired. When one of their number, Julian T. Davies, died in 1922, they feared that his estate might be bought by some undesirable or, worse, subdivided. A group of them, led by Havemeyer and his brother-in-law, W. Kingsland Macy, decided to turn it into a private club. The obstacles might have deterred less determined men. Davies had owned only 231 acres and most of them were marshland that was covered by water at high tide, so that there was only enough solid land for a nine-hole golf course. To make the second nine, they were told, dredges would have to work for a year to haul up sand and fill in the marshland with it. They set the dredges to work.

To design the course, they brought over an Englishman who was the most famous golf-course designer in the world. To help the members with their swings, they hired a famous touring professional. They staffed the kitchen with the best chefs they could find. For those members who wanted to sail, they built a large boat basin. And when all was ready, they thought of a name, the Timber Point Club, and opened the club—to exactly one hundred persons.

"You could play golf there on a weekend and if there were two other golfers on the whole course, you considered the place crowded," recalls Robert Hollins, the son of one of the members. "God, that place was empty."

And that was exactly how the members wanted it. As they toured the majestic course that sloped down to the bay, men in caps and knickerbockers and long socks, ladies in long pleated skirts and middy blouses, they considered the lack of people as big an asset as the view. In 1923, Suffolk County established a Mosquito Control Commission and asked various members of the club for contributions. "God, the mosquitoes in the summer were unbelievable on that golf course," Hollins says. "You'd look at the fellow you were playing with and there might be twenty on his face." But most Timber Pointers gave nothing. If the commission got rid of the mosquitoes, Mrs. Hollins explained, more "foreigners" might find the South Shore attractive and try to live there. "I'd rather have the mosquitoes," she told her friends.

To keep the public out was worth any price. When the property adjoining the Timber Point Club, a 1,500-acre estate owned by an eccentric old millionaire who had never been one of them, anyway, George C. Taylor, came on the market after his death, the Timber Pointers raised $250,000 to buy it. Then they hired caretakers, stocked it with herds of deer and flocks of wild pheasant—all for less than ten days of hunting a year and an additional guarantee that they would never have to look over from their golf course and see on the land adjoining it anyone they didn't know.

Thanks to the barons and the baymen, the sandy beaches of the South Shore were as thoroughly closed off to New Yorkers as the rocky beaches of the North. Those New Yorkers who could not afford the exorbitant charges at Long Beach or squeeze into the limited public area of the beach there were shunted along the South Shore from village to village until they reached the flat, unshaded, bleak potato fields of Suffolk County.

And the shunting on the South Shore was along Merrick Road, an artery as narrow as Northern Boulevard and even more congested, which crossed the clogged downtown areas of a dozen South Shore villages and was intersected at half a hundred locations by the tracks of the Long Island

Rail Road, so that every time a train came through, the line of cars, miles long, would have to stop and wait until the crossing gates went up again.

And still, the need was so great that every summer weekend families from New York City flocked to Long Island, trying Jericho Turnpike instead of Northern Boulevard, or the South Shore instead of the North, or a side road they had noticed the weekend before and which would, they felt sure, lead to a beach they could use—an endless eastward-bound stream of baseless hope that lasted from dawn to late afternoon. And all forecasts showed that the need would rapidly grow greater still: the city's population, which had increased by a million persons during the past ten years, was expected to increase by another million during the next ten.

Given the need, therefore, and the possibility that Long Island could meet it, the thoughts of reformers interested in parks had for years turned first to the Island. Here, they all saw, was the land of the greatest opportunity.

But they also saw, even the most unrealistic of them, that the amount of power with which they had to contend on Long Island was such that efforts to create parks there seemed, even to themselves, foredoomed.

In the past, the governments that created parks had been the governments of the areas in which the parks would be located. The township and village governments on Long Island would never create such parks. Conservationists had begun to talk about "state parks," but a state park had to be created by a state, and New York State's Legislature was controlled by the Long Island barons. A dozen proposals by the Good Government organizations for Long Island parks had been introduced in that Legislature; not one had ever made it out of committee.

The scope of the problem discouraged reformers as much as the political difficulties involved.

Parks large enough to serve any appreciable portion of New York City's millions would have to be measured in the hundreds of acres, and since Long Island was run almost entirely by hostile local governments and landowners, how could those acres possibly be obtained? By purchase? Long Island property was valuable, immensely valuable in the hills and along the beach front where parks should be located. By condemnation? Condemnation of valuable property on the scale required would be fantastically expensive—in fact, unheard of in America. And since the barons' battalions of lawyers could be expected to fight condemnation with every tactic available, the proceedings would take years.

And if, somehow, the parks *were* created, how would people get to them? Long highways would be required, and their rights-of-way would necessarily cross hundreds, if not thousands, of different properties, and that meant hundreds, if not thousands, of landowners who would be ready to fight, and that would mean hundreds and thousands of additional condemnation proceedings. The reformers realized that even in the unlikely event that they won on Long Island, that they actually succeeded in unhorsing the powerful barons, they wouldn't know what to do with their victory. The problem was so big, the reformers thought it was insoluble; by 1922, their "park" discussions concerned mainly the creation of more small playgrounds in the city and the improvement of playground equipment.

Often, when Bob Moses went home at night, he would be coming from such "park" discussions, because Smith, trying to maintain his liaison with reform groups in preparation for another run for Governor, frequently asked him to be his "observer" at reformers' conferences.

Moses tendered such discussions only cursory attention. With his attacks on Governor Miller occupying his time, wordy debates over whether a playground site should be on Fourteenth or Fifteenth Street interested him not at all.

But during the summer of 1922, when Bob Moses went home, he went to Long Island. Invited to weekends in Babylon by friends during 1921, he and Mary had fallen in love "with the town, with the bay, with the whole South Shore." In 1922, they rented a bungalow of their own for the summer. So when the discussions on parks ended, he would hurry to the Long Island Rail Road station and catch a train on the South Shore line.

The trips from and to the city took over an hour—forty-five years later, Moses could still reel off without effort the names of the stops as the conductors had chanted them: "*Vall*ey Str*eam, Lyn*brook, *Ocean*side, *Rockville* Cent*re,* Freeport, Merrick, Amityville, *Linden*hurst and *Bab*ylon"—and the train was hot. Moses would try to bury himself in work, but every so often he would look up and glance out the window. And after a while he began to notice that, while most of the route was filled with one-family homes, there were, between some of the villages, thick leafy bands of woods and, gleaming brightly through the trees, the blue water of ponds and streams.

The woods were all to the north of the railroad, the left-hand side of the train going out to Babylon and the right-hand going into the city. Bob Moses began now always to sit on the side nearest them. It was the 1920's; the men around him would be sitting studying the stock-market quotations in their newspapers. Bob Moses sat and stared out the train window.

One weekend he went to Babylon Town Hall and asked what the woods were. An old-timer told him he must be talking about the old Brooklyn water-supply properties, the streams and the areas around them in Nassau and Suffolk counties that Brooklyn, then an independent city, had purchased in 1874, fenced off and kept guarded so that, in case of a water shortage, it would be able to dam the streams and use their water. On Monday morning, Moses stopped by the New York Municipal Building and asked a clerk in the Department of Water Supply if the city used those properties. Why, no, the clerk said, it never had. There had never been any need. And, come to think of it, now that New York had acquired the huge Croton and Ashokan reservoirs upstate and built aqueducts from them to the city, there probably never would be.

And suddenly, the eyes that had looked at the mud flats below Riverside

Drive and seen a great highway and a great park were looking at something else. The eyes that "burned with ideas" were burning again—and they were focused on Long Island.

Most of the water-supply properties were set far enough north of Merrick Road, behind blocks of private homes, to be invisible from it, but Merrick Road was the only way of getting close to them. Moses had never learned to drive, but he obtained from Smith the use of a car and chauffeur and a letter authorizing the guards at the properties to let him enter their gates. And on weekend mornings, as the line of cars from the city crept east along the road, Moses, leaving Babylon, had himself driven west.

Arriving at the spot he had marked from the train, Moses would order the chauffeur to drive north along side streets until there was no more road for a car, and then he would get out and walk through back yards and vacant lots and along footpaths until he reached the gates and could show his letter to the guards. Then he would plunge into the woods.

They contained surprises.

Through the train windows, he had glimpsed in the woods that lay between Merrick and Freeport a small pond. When he got into those woods on foot, he found the pond, but, beyond it, he could see another gleam of water. Reaching that, he found a larger pond and, beyond it, another gleam. Beyond that, there was another. There were four ponds, linked by a stream that ran due north, and each was larger than the one before. Lilies floated in them. Pickerel and trout flickered beneath the pads. Huge oaks, beeches, birches and pines surrounded him. And as he tramped steadily north, there seemed no end to them. He was not in a small woods, he realized, but in a forest—it would survey out at more than seven hundred acres—that lay untouched in the heart of Nassau County.

There were another four ponds—and another wooded seven hundred acres—stretching south from Wantagh all the way to the Great South Bay. There were 595 more acres near Massapequa. Between Valley Stream and Lynbrook, there were only fifty acres, but in the center of them was a lake a quarter mile across. And when he entered the woods between Lynbrook and Rockville Centre, he realized he had come to something that dwarfed the others. The thin band of woods that he had seen from the train at that spot ran north for more than three miles, broadening as it went. Within the woods were long, rolling meadows. He had heard that somewhere in the woods was a reservoir, where a stream had actually been dammed by Brooklyn municipal engineers decades before, that couldn't be seen from the train, and he pushed on, trying to find it. With branches slapping at his face and vines tangling his feet, he came at last to a man-made embankment. Scrambling up, he peered over its top—and there before him lay a body of water almost a mile long and half a mile wide. It was much bigger than the big reservoir in Central Park, he realized. And there was more land around it, he guessed—and he turned out to be right—than there was in Central Park.

Back on Merrick Road, Moses saw the cars from the city still creeping along in the dust and heat, thousands of them, tens of thousands, crammed with people searching desperately for a little patch of green, a spot of clear water, and most of them destined that weekend to find neither.

And behind him, not a quarter mile from the road but unknown to all but one in a thousand of the drivers on it—and closed to even that one—was land, a vastness of land, overflowing with the fruits they sought. Land that didn't have to be purchased. Land that didn't have to be condemned. Land that was owned not by the governments of Long Island, which viewed the masses of New York City as foreigners, but by the government of New York City. Land that could be opened to the city's people merely by turning a key.

Adding together the acreage of the various tracts of woods, Moses could hardly believe the figures. They totaled 3,500 acres. Three thousand five hundred acres just sitting there empty and unused.

And ideally situated. All five tracts were within thirty miles of Manhattan, within eleven miles of the city line. The woods between Valley Stream and Lynbrook, in fact, were only two miles from that line.

And what you could do with those acres! There could be hiking trails through the woods, of course, and picnic sites in the clearings. But there could be more. When reformers, when park planners in general, talked about large parks they talked in terms of keeping them unspoiled and rustic, as close to nature as possible. Even Central Park contained relatively few facilities for any sports other than walking.

But Moses saw a different vision. He had noticed meadows back in those woods that seemed just made to order for baseball diamonds, and level spaces with only a few trees that could be cleared for tennis courts. Why, a portion of the biggest tract, the one between Lynbrook and Rockville Centre, seemed almost made to order for a golf course. And why should people be restricted to looking at the ponds and lakes? Why couldn't they swim in them? That great reservoir alone could cool thousands of sweating youngsters from the city! And there were so many acres available that even after all the facilities were laid out, there would still be vast stretches of woods that could be left untouched except for rustic hiking trails.

Suddenly, the burning eyes were looking at everything on Long Island in terms of parks.

Having fallen in love with the South Shore, Moses had done so with his customary fullness of passion. He kept the Babylon village librarian scurrying to the cabinet in which were locked the ancient, privately printed books that recounted the legends of the Great South Bay. Buying an old bayman's old, broad-bottomed, very slow motorboat, partly covered with a canopy, which Mary named the *Bob*, he putt-putted around the bay following the maps described in the books, sometimes with Mary and his daughters, often alone. Heading out to the pier where the *Bob* was moored, he paused frequently to chat with the sailors who were too old to follow the bay any more and instead spent their days sitting on upturned oyster barrels looking out over it; and, finding him a willing listener to their stories, the old men told him about hidden inlets and about meadows where flocks of wild birds nested, and he spent long days exploring them. Sometimes, in fact, he spent days that were too long; then, as he sat in reverie, the bay's ebbing tide would leave the *Bob* stranded on a sand bar. After a while, Mary knew what it meant when darkness came and her husband still hadn't returned from the bay; she would call a friend, Harry Fishel, whose boat had a shallower draft, and Fishel would go out and bring him in. In the morning, the two men would return to the *Bob*, now refloated by the flooding tide, and Moses would go back on board with a sandwich Mary had prepared—and spend another day on the bay.

Moses' attention had early been caught by the barrier beach, the strip of dunes and beach grass and wild marshes about five miles offshore that from the pier was a long low line on the horizon across the bay. Baymen called it "the strand." Deserted except for a few tiny, scattered summer colonies, an aura almost of mystery hung over it. The baymen told stories of murders and duels to the death on it between sailors armed only with hand spikes. The summer colonies had names—"Short Beach," "Gilgo"—but the names didn't match those on the old maps he found in the library. The very shape of the strand was different. That, the baymen explained to him, was because the ocean was constantly remolding it. Because the "set" of the Atlantic off Long Island was inexorably to the west, they said, sand and pebbles were continually washed up at its western end and the beach grew longer every year. But storms, particularly the howling "sou'easters," also swept away part of the strand each winter, slashed new inlets through its dunes, closed old ones. The name "Fire Island" by which the easternmost section of the strand was known was actually a corruption of "Five Islands," a name given to it in the eighteenth century when it had been divided into five parts by four inlets, all of which have since completely disappeared.*

Fire Island stretches from Bay Shore in Babylon Township east to Moriches. The western section of the strand, separated from Fire Island by a narrow inlet, parallels Long Island from Bay Shore all the way to Freeport. This section was called, vaguely, "Jones Beach." Even the oldest baymen weren't certain where the name had come from, but Moses was. In the old books in the Babylon Library, he had read about Major Thomas Jones, a seventeenth-century Welshman whose valor at the Battle of the Boyne moved King James II to grant him a commission as a privateer. ("That was far from being a pirate," one of the old books emphasized; "it was a *legitimate* business.") Jones made a fortune legitimately plundering ships that did not fly the English flag. In 1695, he purchased thousands of acres of the deserted strand from Long Island's fierce Indian tribes "for a

* Contrary to the belief, held even by some Long Island historians, that Fire Island was named for the signal fires set by whalers and pirates, the old documents in the Babylon Library—they can still be found there—show conclusively that it was originally "Five Islands."

barrel of good cidar," peopled it with crews which dashed out in longboats to capture whales drifting nearby—and made another fortune. Marrying beautiful Freelove Townsend, he erected a house—with thick walls and slits for rifles—on one of the necks of land which at that time linked the strand to Long Island.

After Jones's death, sou'easters tore away the necks, and the strand became an island itself. Between it and the mainland, the underwater reeds grew thicker. The tides tugged at the sand underneath the Great South Bay and the channels between the shoals became more and more crooked and treacherous, sometimes shifting course from week to week. People who tried to sail or motorboat to Jones Beach had to get out and push their boats off sand bars so frequently that one bay captain referred to his week-end journeys as his "walks to the Beach." The summer-cottage colonies grew smaller and smaller. In winter, except for occasional hunters after wild birds and a few hermits who lived in caves hollowed out of the dunes, Jones Beach was deserted.

Sometimes, when Bob Moses stepped out of his boat onto Jones Beach, he could not see another human being. In front of him would be nothing but a wide, straight strip of the whitest sand he had ever seen, stretching unbroken until it disappeared at the horizon, sliding on one side beneath the ocean surf, rising on the other into dunes covered with tufts of beach grass, little gnarled bushes and stunted trees, with, between the dunes, marshes of a peculiar, striking grayish-green color from which swooped up herons and gulls. He had returned to it a hundred times, pushing and pulling his little boat through the reeds, to sit lonely on the beach with wind rustling his hair, drinking in the wild, desolate scene.

Had he been still the poet he had been at Yale, Moses might have looked at this scene and thought of Byron. But now he was thinking of parks. He looked at Jones Beach with eyes that had looked at crowded New York City and had seen a hundred ways of improving it—and he realized that the emptiness of the strand, its endless, untouched vistas, was a clean canvas on which he could draw whatever he chose. And, looking at it that way, he realized that all the landscape needed was the painting in of people to make it a bathing beach, a great bathing beach, a bathing beach such as America had never seen. Moreover, the people, the masses of New York City, were amazingly close. Jones Beach had seemed so cut off from the world, but, he realized with a start, when he stood on its western end he was less than twenty-five miles from Times Square.

The problem, of course, was to get the people out there, and now in the evenings, in his Babylon bungalow, Bob Moses began to study maps of Long Island. One night he suddenly noticed that the water-supply properties off Merrick Road lay in a row. A straight line could be drawn through them. Therefore, so could a road. If a road were built out from New York so that it traversed those properties, a substantial part of the right-of-way would not have to be purchased or condemned. Moreover, the road could give the city masses easy access to the water-supply properties, which he had already determined were themselves ideal for parks. And since one of the properties, the one at Wantagh, ran all the way down to the Great South Bay, another road—connecting with the road leading out from New York—could be built south down to the bay without the necessity of any purchase or condemnation at all. Once it reached the bay, it would be directly opposite Jones Beach. And since the bay was so shallow, it ought to be easy to construct a causeway from the end of the road to the beach. "That was the idea behind Jones Beach and the Southern State Parkway," Moses would recall years later. "I thought of it all in a moment."

As he thought about the road, he thought about the Bronx River Parkway. Although it hadn't yet been opened, the newspapers were full of stories about it. With the exception of a three-mile stretch of the Fenway in Boston and, of course, the transverse roads in Central Park, the parkway would be the first highway in the country to eliminate traffic lights and intersecting traffic by lifting all crossroads above it. The bridges that carried the crossroads would be faced with stone to blend in with the scenery, and the bordering right-of-way would be completely landscaped. Newspapers were predicting that it would be the most beautiful road in America. A road through the Long Island water-supply properties, Moses realized, would, on that portion of it which traversed the properties, be lined with the beautiful trees he had seen. The north-south road running from it to the bay would be lined with trees its entire length, and the causeway across the water would cross the bay panorama. The roads he was thinking of, he realized, could be more beautiful than the Bronx River Parkway.

The line he had drawn on the map through the water-supply properties seemed to point like an arrow into Long Island's South Shore. Looking beyond its point, the easternmost of the properties, Moses saw a series of promontories jutting out into the Great South Bay. He recalled that the promontories were supposed to be beautiful. And on weekends now, Moses had himself driven east.

From the car, he could see that most of the promontories were private estates, but in East Islip he noticed a large piece of property fenced off but overgrown with underbrush and weeds and apparently deserted. A real estate agent told him that it had belonged to an eccentric old millionaire named Taylor and, when he died, had been purchased by a group of wealthy men who allowed it to grow wild because they used it as a game preserve.

There may have been caretakers on the Taylor Estate, but Moses didn't see them when he returned to it. Tramping through the brush and the woods, frightening groups of deer, startling coveys of pheasants, he came to a group of out-buildings, all deserted and all except one, which had been turned into a hunting lodge, crumbling. Looming over them was an old mansion, paint peeling, with broken windows. In front of the mansion was a long meadow of uncut, waving grass that had evidently once been an imposing lawn. Beyond it was white sand and then the dark blue-gray of the bay, and beyond the bay, just a line on the horizon, the dunes of Fire Island. Stirring the trees, the grass and the water was the gentle breeze which Moses had learned from the baymen invariably cooled the bay shore every day from about eleven o'clock in the morning until near sundown. Overhead was a lot of sky. To the east, across a little stream, was an expanse of carefully manicured grass and, on it—the only human figures anywhere to be seen—several foursomes in caps and knickerbockers and long socks striding along with the caddies of the Timber Point Club. Moses had taken to carrying a yellow legal note pad on his excursions. On it now he began to sketch the property, and on the sketch he drew lines, some to indicate where the bathhouses for the bathing beaches would be, others to show a golf course, still others to outline where a public bridle path would wind through the trees and where the fences would be placed to pen the deer and pheasants so youngsters could watch them.

The mind leaped on. Were there similar vacant properties on the North Shore? Soon, through woods and meadows overlooking Long Island Sound, there was striding a tall, athletic figure dressed in corduroy pants, heavy shoes and, usually, an old and stained windbreaker, and carrying in one hand a yellow legal note pad. Within weeks, Moses had discovered in Smithtown a vacant estate magnificently suited to his purpose. As he walked north through its thousand wooded acres, he noticed they sloped steadily downhill and he assumed they were sloping down to the beach, but when the woods ended, he found himself staring at a huge, pale-green expanse of grass that was actually below the level of the beach beyond, and he thought in that instant of a name for the estate: "Sunken Meadow."

The road to Sunken Meadow? It could, perhaps, run from New York along the middle of the Island, where the only opposition would be that of farmers, but Moses knew at once that the road wasn't going to go there. If scenery was an attribute of parkways, why, here was a chance to run a parkway through *real* scenery: the Gold Coast estates. At night, now, Moses began to pore over maps of the North Shore, his pencil sketching out alternate routes. He saw on the map the names across which his pencil was sketching: Phipps, Whitney, Garvan, Morgan, Mackay, Vanderbilt, Otto Kahn. But he saw in his mind a road bordered, beyond the grassy right-of-way, by the magnificent stands of trees the robber barons had imported from Europe and by hedges neatly trimmed by their legions of gardeners.

And the pencil kept sketching.

The mind leaped on. It took as its compass not an island but a state.

The state's other large cities—Albany, Buffalo, Rochester, Schenectady, Syracuse, Troy, Utica—were growing, not as fast as New York but fast enough. So was their need for state parks.

But the State Legislature, considering parks a luxury outside city limits, refused to give them any. In 1922, there wasn't a single state park in New York anywhere east of the Hudson River. West of the Hudson, between the Palisades and Buffalo, there were twenty—nineteen enclaves around famous old mansions or Revolutionary War battlefields that had been purchased by private philanthropists and donated to the state, and one, a thousand-acre tract on the Genesee River, that was New York's only state park of substantial size, donated by Buffalo philanthropist William Pryor Letchworth.

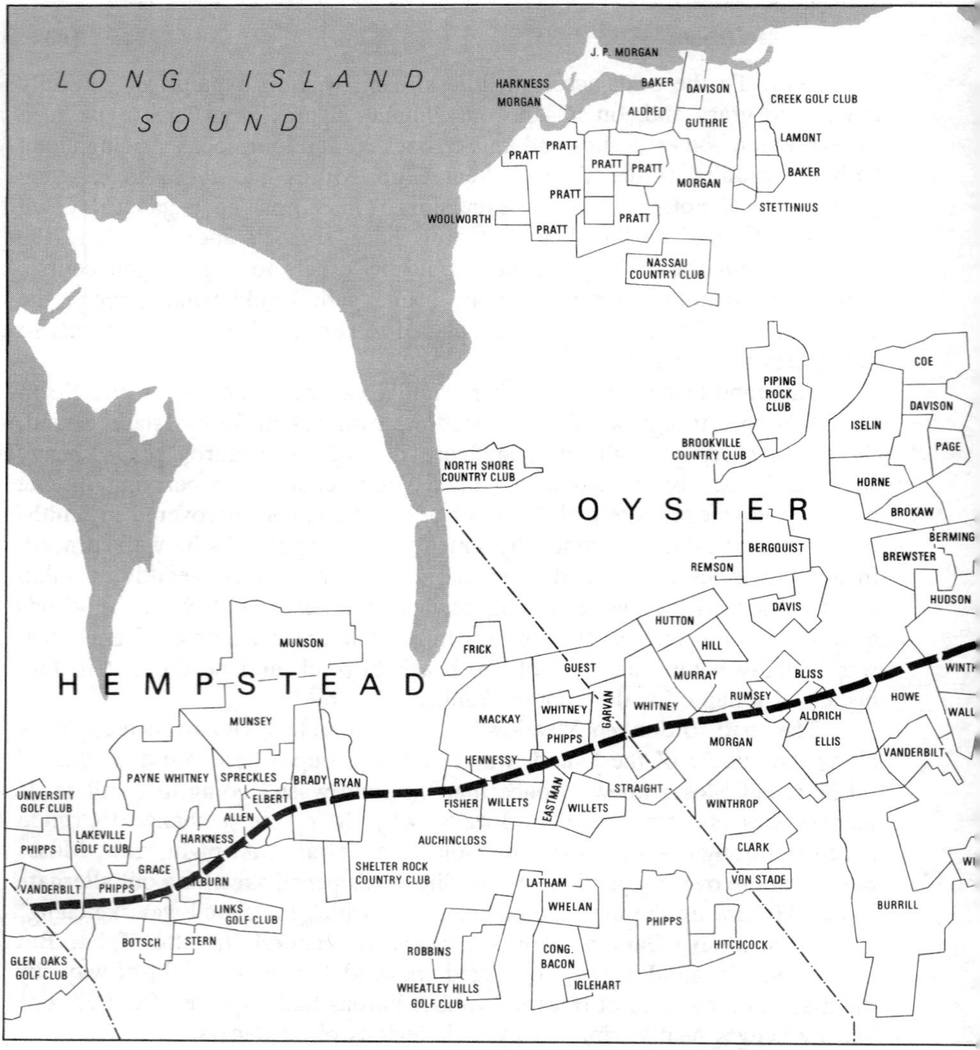

Even when the state was given land, it didn't take care of it. In 1923, the total legislative appropriation for upkeep of state parks would be $30,000. The philanthropists or their descendants or the historical societies designated in their wills to administer the parks had to pay for their upkeep. Permanent improvements—even comfort stations—were all but unheard of. Most parks could not be reached by automobile. In 1922, those state parks that did exist in New York went all but unused.

Part of the difficulty, Moses had learned while running the Reconstruction Commission, went back to the old question of organization. Fearing—*knowing*—that the state would let them run down, the parks' donors had turned their administration over to men or societies dedicated to the preservation of historic or scenic attractions. Montcalm and Spy Island "State Parks," for example, were administered by the Fort Oswego Chapter of the Daughters

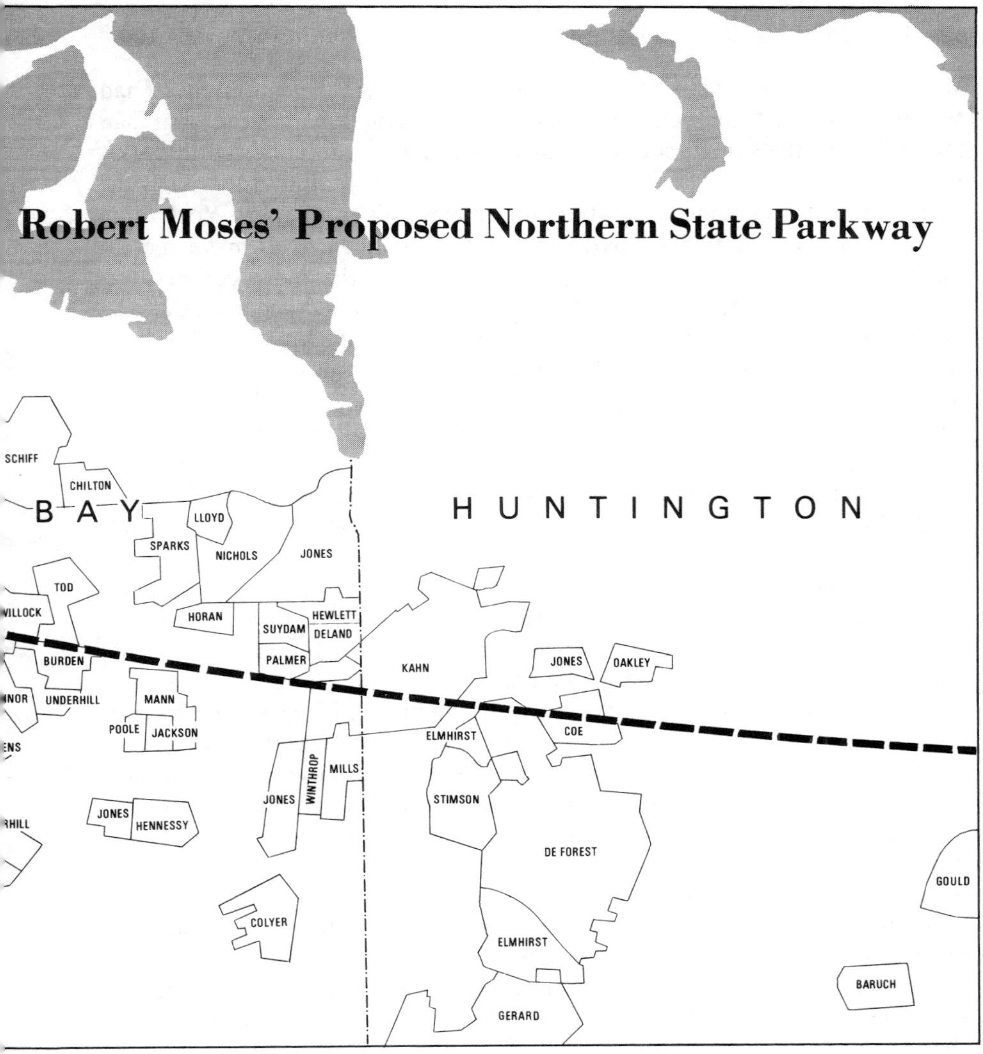

of the American Revolution. Having no authority over private individuals or organizations, the Legislature was reluctant to give them money. And since no central body of any type unified their activities, they presented to the Legislature the spectacle of separate agencies competing with each other for funds.

This lack of unified administration also meant that a considerable potential source of power for parks was dissipated. In many cases, the trustees of the parks were political leaders in the upstate counties in which they lived and from which came many of the Republican legislative leaders. United, the park trustees could have exerted considerable influence in Albany, but, acting separately, they dissipated their influence.

State park administration was one area in which the Reconstruction Commission's recommendations had been ignored. A group of the commission's trustees, including many of the upstate park philanthropists, had begun making a "comprehensive study" of the state's park needs but had stopped when the commission was disbanded. Moses, not interested in parks, had given the report scant attention, anyway. But now he asked the philanthropists to complete the study under the aegis of the New York State Association. He toured their parks with them, urged them to make recommendations for their development, delicately urged the more conservative of them to think in terms of improved roads and enlarged accommodations. And he urged them to start thinking in terms of a unified state park system that would be a formal part of state government. They need not worry about losing control of their beloved parks to faceless bureaucrats in Albany, he assured them; control of each park could be left in the hands of the men then administering it, and to insure that future appointments to the commissions would not become involved in politics, the commissionerships could be unpaid jobs. But if there was a single state body controlling parks, the demands for funds from the different sources interested in parks could be funneled into it and focused, so as to put more heat on the Legislature. When their recommendations for their individual parks came in, he combined them in a report, *A State Park Plan for New York,* which he wrote himself and issued in the name of the New York State Association.

The report was a seminal document in the history of parks in America. Its scope was in itself revolutionary: New York's park needs, it said, were so great that they could not be met by ordinary legislative appropriations; a bond issue would be required—and the amount of the issue should be $15,000,000. But it was not the scope that startled most; New York and other states had floated bond issues for parks before, even if none of the issues had been nearly so large as that Moses proposed. Rather, it was the philosophy. The expenditure of proceeds from previous bond issues had been restricted to land acquisition and in the word "acquisition" was embodied the philosophy that had always in the past governed parks in America, the belief that parks were only land and the trees and grass and brooks on the land, that their sole purpose was to serve as "breathing spaces" for the city masses and to enable them to relax and meditate among beautiful surroundings, to commune with nature, and that they should therefore be kept in their natural state. If the city masses no longer were content with communing, if they wanted space not only to meditate but to swing—to swing baseball bats, tennis rackets, golf clubs and the implements of the other sports that their new leisure time had enabled them to learn—this was a desire that had not yet been translated into governmental action in the United States.

But Moses translated it. The $15,000,000 bond issue, he said, must specifically authorize the Legislature "to provide for permanent improvements as well as the acquisition of land . . . for large facilities which make a park accessible and attractive to people." "Conservation"—the previous park ideal—had to be combined with "recreation," he said. Furthermore, he said, "permanent improvements" did not mean only improvements within parks; it also meant means to get to them—"parkway and boulevard connections between state parks and between state parks and neighboring centers of population." And state parks should no longer be talked of as separate entities; there should be a state park *system*; the state should be divided into eleven regions and all the state parks in each of these regions should be administered by a single regional "state park commission"—the Long Island parks he proposed, for example, by a Long Island State Park Commission. The presidents of those commissions should sit as a State Council of Parks, which would coordinate and unify park policy.

Moses' park report was soon being read—and hailed—by park planners all over the United States. But if its recommendations were to become reality, they would have to become reality through a man who didn't read reports and who seemed highly unlikely to be a parks enthusiast.

Al Smith "somewhat lacked," as one writer put it, "Theodore Roosevelt's zest for 'the strenuous life.' " If there was a sport in which the Governor was interested, his friends didn't know it. He refused to go with them to football or baseball games or even to boxing matches. When he took his family swimming, he watched them from the beach, his little pot belly protruding through his bathing suit, a cigar clenched firmly in his teeth, eyeing the ocean warily. Smith's childhood, moreover, had not prepared him to appreciate Moses' insistence on active sports for the masses.

When Moses began explaining his park plan, the Governor was dubious. Its cost astounded him. "You want to give the people a fur coat when what they need is red flannel underwear," he said once.

But Moses had one advantage. Smith's mind was the type that responded most enthusiastically to what Frances Perkins called "the graphic presentation." The Governor, she said, "wanted you to tell him what it looked like. . . . He got more information out of people who would tell him the exact thing they'd seen, [who] described the detail. . . . Then he saw what it was like." Anxious to improve the lives of the urban poor, he was especially anxious to improve them through things he could actually *see* improving them; his Governorship was distinguished by his emphasis on works of physical construction, solid and visible. Nothing was more visible than the physical entity that was a park, and no one was a more vivid describer, a more graphic presenter, than Bob Moses. After Smith's election in November 1922, Moses persuaded him to visit the New York City watershed properties. They were barren in winter, but with his gift for words Moses made the Governor see them as they could be in summer, with leaves on the trees and people sitting at picnic tables under them. Day after day, pacing restlessly back and forth before the Governor's desk, he poured out his ideas in a continual flow of words. Sometimes the other members of Smith's inner circle had to smile at Moses' vehemence and earnestness. Once, as the torrent of words flowed over him, the Governor gradually began sinking lower and lower in his chair, and, with Moses still talking, disappeared at last under his desk. But when he poked his head up, he was smiling.

Moses persuaded Smith to attend a meeting of the New York State Association park committee at the Whitehall Club and made a lengthy, passionate speech. At its end, Smith arose. "Bob, you win," he said. He directed Moses to draft a special message to the Legislature asking for passage of legislation establishing a State Council of Parks and authorizing submission of the $15,000,000 proposal to the people in referendum. On April 18, 1923, two weeks after Moses finished the message, Smith delivered it.

Under state law, only one bond issue could be submitted to the voters each year. Smith had also proposed an issue for new hospitals and mental institutions. Moses pleaded that parks should come first, but Smith disagreed. When the Governor delivered the message Moses had drafted, he announced he would not push for adoption of its proposals until 1924. It was clear to his advisers that the Governor was worried about public reaction to an expenditure for parks of such unprecedented dimensions.

The reaction was not long in coming. Smith's secretaries reported a most remarkable upsurge in the volume of his mail. It came from the City Club of New York ("Congratulations!" club secretary Raymond Ingersoll wrote delightedly) and from Pomona Grange Number 416 ("God bless you! Sincerely, Matilda Hunt, secretary-treasurer"). It came from slum dwellers and suburbanites. And unlike the mail on most issues, this mail did not contain letters on both sides of the issue. There was, the Governor's secretaries reported, apparently only one side to this issue: *everyone* was for parks.

There was hardly a newspaper in the state, moreover, that did not write an editorial supporting the message. And the praise did not stop at the state's borders. From all over the country, letters were sent to "Governor Smith, Albany" expressing hopes that the writers' own states might follow his example. Wrote the chairman of the National Conference on State Parks: "The New York program . . . will stimulate valuable work in other states. . . . You are rendering a real service not only to your own state, but to other states of the Union which will have the advantage of following your experience."

Mark Antony, shrewd politician, knew the potency of parks as an issue. Rousing the mob to fury against Caesar's "honorable" slayers, he reserved for a climax the reading of Caesar's will. "Let but the commons hear this testament," he cried, "and they would go and kiss dead Caesar's wounds." And it was not the revelation that Caesar had left each Roman citizen, "every several man," seventy-five drachmas that sealed Antony's victory over the citizens' emotions but rather his revelation that

. . . he hath left you all his walks,
His private arbors and new-planted orchards,
On this side Tiber; he hath left them you,
And to your heirs for ever; common pleasures,
To walk abroad and recreate yourselves.

Al Smith, shrewd politician, had risen to the Governorship on great issues, and he was not slow to recognize a new one when it came along. An

Albany reporter watched the awareness grow on the Governor and his circle. "You could see them beginning to realize that doing what Moses wanted would be politically advantageous," he recalls. "One of them told me that supporting parks meant that the Governor would be helping the lower- and middle-class people, and thereby winning their support, and that the intellectuals would be for him because they saw parks as part of the new pattern of social progress. So you'd have all three groups supporting you. And besides, 'parks' was a word like 'motherhood.' It was just something nobody could be against." During the spring of 1923, Smith assured Moses he would push for adoption of the park program in 1924.

And in the summer of 1923, Moses went back to tramping around Long Island.

"I went with him once," a friend says. "We walked all day through one piece of beautiful wild country after another. And he never slowed down. He was tireless." Generally, Moses preferred to be by himself. He walked alone through vast, empty shuttered mansions, through potato fields where farmers worked peacefully, not knowing that the man looking at them was planning to take their fields away. Walls and guards kept him from getting a good look from paved public roads at the route he was considering for the northern parkway, but he discovered unpaved back roads through many of the estates, and he spent days walking along those deserted paths, a solitary figure with a long stride. Through the trees he could see the great castles; at their gates, on little black and gold signs, he could see the names of the great barons who had built them. And the barons, private behind their walls, did not know that staring at those walls was a man determined to tear them down.

Few men had ever viewed Long Island entire. One who had was Walt Whitman, who saw it as a "Sea-Beauty! stretch'd and basking! Isle of sweet brooks of drinking water—healthy air and soil! Isle of the salty shore and breeze and brine!" Now Moses saw it entire, and if he had written poetry once, he wrote park reports now, and brooks, healthy air, salty shore and breeze and brine meant parks. Standing on Montauk Point, where Long Island's southern fluke ends in the steep bluffs plunging abruptly into the Atlantic, Whitman had said, "I stand as on some mighty eagle's beak." Now Moses went to see Montauk, not with the eyes of the poet but with those of the park planner. "The Montauk peninsula," he wrote, "is an extraordinary mass of clay, gravel and rock with high bluffs on the south shore and, back of the bluffs, kettleholes and rolling hills clothed with bayberry, shrubs and gnarled and twisted trees. The irregular shore line and a number of small islands . . . form a veritable patchwork of smaller peninsulas, straits and bays which afford many miles of beaches, dunes and varied waters for cruising, fishing, swimming, golfing and other forms of recreation."

Driving back from Montauk along the southern fluke, Moses discovered endless other miles of unused beaches in Hampton Bays. He found still more on Long Island's northern fluke at Orient Point, where farmers lived in farmhouses built in the seventeenth century. Searching out deserted estates, he found two in the center of the Island, one owned by the son of financier August Belmont, the other by a family named Yoakum. And roaming one day far out in Suffolk County, near Wading River, he stumbled upon a magnificent brick and stone mansion, set upon a bluff overlooking Long Island Sound, that was not only deserted but looked as if it had never been lived in. Inquiring later, he found out it never had. The man who commissioned the famous architect Stanford White to design it and who named it "Wildwood," financier Roland G. Mitchell, had died just as it was being finished in 1906, and the spacious, high-ceilinged rooms had remained shuttered and unfurnished ever since.

Again and again, Moses returned to the lonely strand, not only to Jones Beach but to Fire Island, where a state park, the only one on Long Island, was located, on the two-hundred-acre grounds of the hotel the state had purchased in 1892 to house the passengers from the cholera-ridden *Normannia.*

In 1918, fire had destroyed the hotel, as well as the boardwalks and comfort stations that the state had erected, and when Moses stepped out of the *Bob*, he found "Fire Island State Park" deserted. Charred ruins lay on the sand. The only undamaged structure was the nine-story-high wooden Fire Island telegraph tower, from which the sighting of arriving clipper ships had once been flashed to Manhattan.

Studying maps, Moses was puzzled. They showed the park as comprising the westernmost portion of Fire Island, except for a little enclave on the island's tip which was occupied by an unmanned Coast Guard station. The telegraph tower, which stood on the station, was shown at the very tip. But as Moses stood alongside the tower, the island stretched westward as far as he could see.

Then he remembered what the baymen had told him about the set of the ocean. Since 1892, the waves had been piling sand on Fire Island's western end. He began to walk along the new land—and he walked for four miles. The Coast Guard station wasn't a little enclave any more; its area, he calculated, was at least six hundred acres. And the station was deserted. No one even knew the added six hundred acres were there.

By the end of the summer of 1923, Moses knew that his plans for Long Island had been far too small. Now he wanted not just a state park on Jones Beach but another one, which would include the unmapped six hundred acres, across the inlet on Fire Island. He wanted state parks on the South Shore not just at the Taylor Estate but in Hampton Bays and at Montauk Point. He wanted parks on the Sound not just at Sunken Meadow but at Wildwood, Lloyd Neck and Orient Point. And he wanted two in the center of the Island, at the Belmont and Yoakum estates. He wanted forty thousand acres of parks. He wanted not just a parkway along the South Shore and one along the North Shore but a parkway connecting them far out on Long Island so that families from New York City could drive out on one, loop around and drive home on the other without retracing their path. He wanted another parkway—he wanted two more parkways—linking both the northern and southern parkways with two causeways running to Jones Beach. He wanted still another parkway linking them with Fire Island. He wanted 124 miles of parkways. And he wanted the parkways to be broader and more beautiful than any roads the world had ever seen, landscaped as private parks are landscaped so that they would be in themselves parks, "ribbon parks," so that even as people drove to parks, they would be driving through parks.

Near the latter part of the summer, Alfred E. Smith found himself being chauffeured around Long Island, with Moses sitting beside him, pointing and talking. Smith became enthusiastic about the plans. He asked Mrs. Moskowitz to look into the situation, and Moses gave her the full tour. She approved, and Smith told Moses that when the park program was submitted to the Legislature in 1924, it could be expanded.

"Why don't you take the whole thing over yourself?" the Governor asked. "Why don't I make you president of the Long Island State Park Commission?"

Years later, Moses could recall his thoughts. "I had always had an interest in physical construction, anyhow," Bella's son would remember. "And I had always had an interest in the outdoors; I had done a lot of hiking and fishing and swimming in the Adirondacks, remember. And I was very interested in parks, particularly in the Long Island work."

He said he would like the job.

10. *The Best Bill Drafter in Albany*

DREAMS—visions of public works on a noble scale—had been marching through Bob Moses' mind in almost continuous procession for a decade and more. Not one of them had marched out of his mind into reality.

But during that decade, Bob Moses had learned what was needed to make dreams become realities. He had learned the lesson of power.

And now he grabbed for power with both hands.

To free his hands for the grab, he shook impatiently from them the last crumbs of the principles with which he had entered public service and for which, during the years of his idealism, he had fought so hard.

As a reformer, believing in the principle of centralization in government, he had recommended in the Reconstruction Commission report that all state agencies be included in one of sixteen departments and no longer function as independent bodies. Specifically, Moses had recommended in the report that each agency's budgetary request be submitted to the department head and that the department head have power to act on that request as he saw fit before passing it on to Governor and Legislature. The heads of agencies within departments, he had recommended, should have absolutely no independence in budget making. He had been eloquent on the point. "The more spigots there are in the barrel, the more difficult it is to keep a watch on them," he had written. "There are too many streams and rivulets running out of New York's treasury." As a reformer, Moses had seen no need to make park administration an exception to the principle. The Reconstruction Commission report specified that parks would be administered by a bureau in the Conservation Department, a bureau that would be totally subordinate to the Conservation Commissioner.

But now Moses was interested in parks, and parks were to be an exception. Not on the surface, of course. On the surface, on the face of the bill Moses drafted establishing a State Council of Parks, the council was to be included in the Conservation Department and subordinate to the Conservation Commissioner. The council's budget, in accordance with reorganization principles, could be submitted to Governor and Legislature only by the Conservation Commissioner; a clause in the bill specifically said so. But another clause, further down in the bill, said, "The budget shall be prepared by the State Council of Parks." Precedents had established the statutory meaning of the word "prepared." In this context, it meant that the Council Chairman—not the Conservation Commissioner—had the authority to screen the financial requests of the eleven regional park commissions, weigh one against the other and decide which should be included in the council's budget request. The Conservation Commissioner would get to see the regional commissions' requests only after the Council Chairman had finished with them. He would not even know about the requests made by regional commissions which the Council Chairman had turned down. All he was really empowered to do, therefore, was receive a completed park budget and hand it to the Governor exactly as he received it, and, the bill provided, the Council Chairman from whom he would be receiving the budget would be elected by the council—not appointed by him or by the Governor. Within the reorganized framework of state government, therefore, parks would be a separate, self-governing, very independent duchy.

As a reformer, Moses had fought for the principle of executive power commensurate with executive responsibility, and, believing in the principle, he had recommended in his Reconstruction Commission report that appointed officials should never have terms longer than the Governor's term and that they should always be removable by the Governor if they did not follow his orders. He had been eloquent on the point. "No Governor can be held responsible for the policies and conduct of high officers whom he does not appoint and whom he cannot remove," he had written. "If New York wants . . . efficient government, it must make someone responsible who can be held to account and give him power commensurate with his obligations. There is no other way."

But now Moses was to be an appointed official. And although he could count on Smith's support, Smith would not always be Governor. So there was another way. The bill Moses drafted establishing the Long Island State Park Commission provided that the term of its president—himself—would be six years, three times as long as the Governor's. And it further provided that no Governor could remove the park commission president just because the president was not following the Governor's orders. Removal, the bill provided, could only follow the filing by the Governor of detailed, specific charges of actual misconduct and a formal, public hearing, with both sides represented by counsel, on those charges.

It was not, moreover, the violation of stated principles for the purpose of cementing himself in office that most clearly revealed the change in Moses. Rather, it was the method by which he insured that, once in office, he would have specific powers sufficient for his purpose. For the method was that of concealment and deviousness.

Once, no reformer, no idealist, had believed more sincerely than he in free and open discussion. No reformer, no idealist, had argued more vigorously that legislative bills should be fully debated, and that the debates should be published so that the citizenry could be informed on the issues.

But free and open debate had not made his dreams come true. Instead, politicians had crushed them. And now he was going to make sure that, with the exception of Al Smith and Belle Moskowitz, no one—not citizenry, not press, *not Legislature*—was going to know what was in the bills dealing with parks that the Legislature was going to pass. The best bill drafter in Albany set to work.

First and foremost, parks were land, and land was generally acquired by government through condemnation. But condemnation in 1924 was a slow process, since the state could not take title to property until a condemnation commission set its value. And since the property's owner could appeal to the courts if not satisfied with the commission's evaluation, he could delay the state further. He therefore possessed in his opposition to the state a weapon, even if it was a small one—and in the hands of the barons of Long Island, small weapons could become large.

So one clause within Chapter 122 of the Laws of 1924, "AN ACT TO PROVIDE FOR the location, creation, acquisition and improvement by the state of parks, parkways and boulevards in the counties of Nassau and Suffolk," a clause buried deep within the act, empowered the Long Island State Park Commission to acquire land by condemnation and appropriation "in the manner provided by section fifty-nine of the conservation law."

In 1924, "appropriation" had only one meaning in a legislative context: an allocation of funds by the Legislature. Most legislators—probably all legislators—would, if asked, have said that was the only meaning the word had ever had. And since section fifty-nine of the conservation law had been passed in 1884, most legislators had not read it. But the best bill drafter in Albany had read it—and he knew that in that section "appropriation" had quite a different meaning. Worried in 1883 about incursions by lumbering companies into the Adirondack forests, the Legislature empowered the Conservation Commission to condemn the forests and preserve them. But during that year, between the start of the condemnation proceedings and the actual transfer of title, the lumbermen stripped the parcels being condemned of their trees. In 1884, therefore, the Legislature passed an act—section fifty-nine of the conservation law—empowering the state to "appropriate" forest lands and defining "appropriation" as a procedure in which a state official could take possession of the land by simply walking on it and telling the owner he no longer owned it—and that if he wanted compensation, he would have to apply to the condemnation commission himself.

The "appropriation" method had never been used anywhere except in remote forests. It had never been intended for use in city, suburban or farm areas. Taking a man's land and telling him it would be paid for later was simply unheard of if the land had any substantial intrinsic value, as it always did in settled areas, and not just the value of things on it, such as trees. Moreover, the method had never been used *anywhere* for more than thirty years because of doubts about its constitutionality. But the Legislature had never gotten around to repealing section fifty-nine.

Deviousness was used in other sections of the act he drafted as well. Section eight, for example, entitled "General Powers," supposedly enumerated the powers of the Long Island State Park Commission over its land, and the powers enumerated in this section seemed innocuous enough. But in succeeding sections of the act, each power was "defined," and each successive definition broadened the commission's authority.

The commission had the right to operate parks, section eight said. But section nine said that "the term . . . parks as used in this act . . . shall be deemed to include . . . parkways . . . boulevards and also entrances and approaches thereto, docks and piers, and bridges . . . and such other . . . appurtenances as the . . . commission shall utilize . . ." And the term "parkways" was significant. The Legislature had specifically written into the State Highway Law provision that the supervisors of each county had veto power over the location of highways within its borders. But, because parkways hadn't existed when the provision was written, the Highway Law didn't mention parkways—and there was no local check over *their* location.

The commission had the right to "acquire . . . real estate," section eight said. But section ten said that "the term real estate as used in this act shall be construed to embrace all uplands, lands under water . . . and all real estate heretofore or hereafter acquired or used for railroad, street railroad, telephone, telegraph or other public purposes. . . . " And the words "lands under water" were significant. Under legal precedent, owners of land fronting on the Great South Bay owned the land offshore to the distance of one mile—and if the commission owned land fronting on the bay, it therefore would own part of the bay itself, including the baymen's "sacred" bay bottoms.

By the time the "defining" of the terms used in section eight was finished, the Long Island State Park Commission would be empowered, if the act was passed, to write its own laws, hire policemen to enforce them and prosecutors to prosecute them. By the time it was finished, the commission would, if the act was passed, have over its land, land which if Moses had his way would total forty thousand acres, virtually all the powers granted to the City of New York in the city's charter.

Almost every clause in the act contained a sleeper. Section fifteen ostensibly dealt with the procedure to be used in acquiring property owned by other state agencies. But, apparently tagged on as an afterthought, there was another paragraph: "The . . . Commission shall have power to improve, maintain and use the lands of the municipalities adjoining the parks and parkways of the Commission, with the consent of the local authorities having jurisdiction thereof." The paragraph appeared innocent enough. Since the commission was operating in Nassau and Suffolk counties, what legislator would stop to consider that some lands on Long Island might be owned by New York City and that, once the act was passed, the Long Island State Park Commission would not need the consent of Long Island officials to use that land because "the local authorities having jurisdiction thereof" would not be Long Island officials but New York City officials? Once the act was passed, Moses would be able to use the city's water-supply properties despite the objections of the municipalities in which those properties were located.

Moses concealed his purposes not only from those who, if they knew them, might oppose them—the legislators—but from those who thought they were his allies, the old men who had worked on the New York State Association report and who, through their individual commissions, had been running the parks in the state for so many years. If these men were to oppose his plans, they could, with their control of their local legislators, pose a formidable obstacle to passage. So he didn't tell the old men about the true scope of his plans for the State Council of Parks. In fact, knowing that they were concerned about the fate of the pieces of land they had guarded so long, he assured them over and over that the establishment of the council would in no way affect their control over those lands. "It is," he wrote them, "merely a coordinating agency." Parks in each region, he promised them, would remain under the control of the regional commissioners.

Moses had to know that what he was saying was false. He knew that since regional commissions had to submit their budget requests to the Parks Council, the council, not the commissions, would decide how much money went to each region. The council, not an individual commission, would decide over-all park policies which would affect each commission's parks. And since the commissions would be rivals for funds, there was little danger of them banding together against the man who ran the council. That man would be in complete charge of all the state parks.

Not knowing what was in the bill, believing in coordination and believing in Moses, the old men supported it and him.

Having drafted the bills, Moses looked around for someone to introduce them.

F. Trubee Davison, the son of Morgan partner Henry P. Davison of Glen Cove, had been sent by the barons of the North Shore of Long Island to the State Assembly in 1923, just one year after his graduation from Yale. In 1924, he was only twenty-two years old and, in his own words, "wide-eyed and eager." Not only was he a Yale man but he was, within the limits approved by the barons, interested in reform, and Moses had found plenty to talk to him about. "He was charming," Davison recalls, "and I enjoyed talking with him a lot and I admired his obvious brains." And he was, he recalls, frankly flattered that a member of the Governor's inner circle would spend so much time with a freshman assemblyman.

Moses asked Davison to introduce the bills that would establish a State Council of Parks and a Long Island State Park Commission. He told him nothing about his plans for parks and a parkway on the North Shore. In fact, he told him very little of any of his plans, leaving the impression that the bills were routine measures and that the kind of parks he was talking about were parks in the traditional mold.

Davison was a believer in parks in that mold. He was flattered to be asked to introduce the bills. And when Moses told him that the Governor would like to see him and thank him for his support, he was overwhelmed. His visit to the Executive Chamber with Moses at his elbow was the first time he had ever met Al Smith in person. He didn't think to ask many questions about the bills—and he certainly didn't think to look up section fifty-nine of the conservation law or to study definitions of powers. Just to make sure he wouldn't have much time to even if he wanted to, Moses delayed giving him the bills until the last week of the session. "I never realized what the word 'appropriation' meant," Davison recalls. "I thought it meant what it had always meant, so far as I knew: appropriation of money to be spent. Whenever someone asked me what it meant, I told them that's what it meant."

Not that many people asked him, of course. There was little interest in the bills and when, in the last-minute adjournment rush, they came to the floor, there was not a word of debate about them. On April 10, 1924, on the last day of the session, Assembly and Senate passed them both by unanimous vote.

Moses was in a fever of impatience. On April 12, he wrote George Graves, Smith's secretary: "My dear George: As soon as you get a chance will you ask the Governor, please to sign the bill creating the State Council of Parks so that a meeting of this Council can be held at an early date." On April 18, a pen in the Executive Chamber scrawled across the bills: "Approved—AES." On the same date, Smith appointed to the regional park commissions the men whose names he had previously agreed upon with Moses. He appointed Moses president of the Long Island State Park Commission, a post that gave him automatic membership on the State Council of Parks, and as Moses' co-commissioners on the three-member Long Island Commission the Governor appointed two men Moses knew he could count on to let him run the commission by himself. On April 30, Moses and the other heads of the regional park commissions met in Albany and, with paternal smiles in his direction, the older commission heads elected the youngest member of the State Council of Parks as its chairman.

At the age of thirty-five, Robert Moses had power. And no sooner did he have it than he showed how he was going to use it.

IV

THE USE OF POWER

11. The Majesty of the Law

Law? What do I care for law?
Hain't I got the power?

—COMMODORE VANDERBILT

THE REFERENDUM on the $15,000,000 park bond issue was still seven months away. Even if the vote was favorable, the money would not be available to Moses until the 1925 Legislature made specific appropriations out of the proceeds of the bond sale. But at Smith's request the 1924 Legislature appropriated $225,000 from general state revenues to allow Moses to begin work.

With some of this money, he rented a suite on the fourteenth floor of the Vincent Building at 302 Broadway, diagonally across from City Hall. From the windows of the suite, he could see, beyond City Hall, the Municipal Building, on the fourteenth floor of which he had once watched his civil service rating forms gathering dust in a corner and in which he had considered himself lucky to have even a desk of his own. He could look three blocks down Broadway and see No. 261, where he had worked for the Bureau of Municipal Research first in impatience and later in humiliation. And directly opposite his windows was 305 Broadway, in which had been located the tiny, shabby cubicle in which he had wound up the affairs of the Reconstruction Commission as its money ran out. Now he reserved the large corner room of the suite for his own, laid down expensive carpeting and hung up expensive drapes. He purchased for his own use the most prestigious automobile in America, a black Packard limousine, and hired a chauffeur. He filled the office with his friends, from Benjamin Van Schaick ("I never forgot what he did for me during the war and as soon as I could I dug him out and brought him into the commission as executive secretary") and his Yale roommate, Raymond P. McNulty, its counsel, right down to the secretaries. And then Robert Moses, who had spent four years of his life arguing that personal considerations such as friendship should never be allowed to influence civil service appointments and that no civil servants should be exempt from competitive examinations, worked quietly through Smith's office to exempt his friends from civil service examinations. And he was so lavish in purchasing automobiles for his friends' use and furnishings for their offices that by summer he had spent $63,089 of the $225,000 on such "overhead expenses."

Moses' Yale classmate Harold Phelps Stokes was an assistant to Secretary of Commerce Herbert Hoover. During the first week after his appointment, Moses dashed off a letter informing Stokes of the existence of the six hundred new acres at the Fire Island Coast Guard station and asking him to persuade Hoover to release them as an addition to the adjoining two-hundred-acre Fire Island State Park. When Hoover agreed, Moses had, in a single step, quadrupled the state park acreage on Long Island. During the first week after his appointment, he called on the New York City Commissioner of Water Supply, Gas and Electricity, Nicholas J. Hayes, and asked Hayes to release the 3,500 acres of city watershed properties. Hayes said that his responsibility was to protect the city's water supplies, not to give them away, but he was a good Tammany regular and a call from Al Smith persuaded him to accept a compromise Moses suggested: that the city keep control of the water on the properties and give the commission a "surface easement" that would allow it to use the rest of the land for parks.

Much of the remainder of the route for the envisioned "Southern State Parkway" was farmland. Moses quickly learned not to visit farmers during the day when they were occupied with chores. Instead, in the twilight of Long Island spring evenings, a big black Packard and uniformed chauffeur would be standing in the front yards of neat little farmhouses in Valley Stream, Rockville Centre and Merrick while inside, at the kitchen table, Robert Moses sat, jacket off, tie loosened and shirt sleeves rolled up, drinking what he later remembered as an endless succession of glasses of beer and trading an endless succession of loud jokes with an endless succession of jovial, florid-faced but canny German and Dutch farmers, trying to bargain them down to the price—$1,200 per acre—that he had set for right-of-way. Soon he had obtained options from a dozen farmers from whom he needed infertile land or land on the very edges of their farms, for which $1,200 per acre (payable by June 30, 1925, out of the anticipated legislative appropriation) was a good price. Approaching the socialites who headed the corporation that had purchased the old Taylor Estate next to the Timber Point Club in East Islip and turned it into a hunting preserve, he received a pleasant surprise: they had visited the estate only once in 1923 and were thinking of selling. Talking to them earnestly and winningly of the public service they would perform by selling to the state, he persuaded them to accept $250 and give him an option, subject to approval by the other stockholders, to purchase the estate for $250,000, payable by June 30, 1925. After he worked on the owners of the land he coveted at Hampton Bays and Sunken Meadow, they gave him similar options. The Montauk Point and Lloyd Neck owners seemed ready to follow suit. By the end of the summer of 1924, he seemed well on his way to establishing a state park system on Long Island on the basis of his charm alone.

But the charm could vanish swiftly. He joked and laughed with the farmers, but when one made clear that he would not sell his land, Moses could change in an instant to quite a different approach. P. G. Rasweiler was one of the five burly, thick-necked, red-faced sons of John Jacob Rasweiler, a Brooklyn-born farmer of German ancestry who had gone broke trying to raise lettuce, spinach, cabbage and cauliflower on a farm in Valley Stream and then had sold it and purchased another in Malverne, where, in PG's words, "we all six of us broke our backs to make it pay." PG remembers well the day the "parkway business" started. "The farm was doing good," he recalls. "Then Moses came one day. He introduced himself as 'I'm Robert Moses, representing the State of New York. We're going to put a parkway through this section of Long Island.' He was very polite, very diplomatic, at first. But when he saw my father wasn't going to sell, he stood up in our kitchen and he said: 'You know, Mr. Rasweiler, the state is all-supreme when it comes to a condemnation proceeding. If we want your land, we can take it.'

"Father wanted to make an agreement with him—he didn't want to have to go to the lawyers—but Moses wanted to take twenty acres from us. The whole farm was only eighty, eighty-five acres. The twenty acres was the choice of the whole farm. It had been woodland; we had worked hard to get it cleared off. We had just gotten it cleared, and it was just about ready to begin making money for us. It was right in the middle of the farm; if he took it, all our rows would be cut in half—how could you plow? And he was offering us $1,200—the same price he was offering for bad land on the edges of other farms. That wasn't fair. But when we tried to explain that to him, he wouldn't even listen to us. Father asked him to go on the north boundary line instead. Father said if he'd take it from the boundary and not from the middle, he'd give it to the state for nothing. But Moses said no. His whole attitude was: 'This is where we're going, and that's it.' "

The next day, as John Jacob and his five sons were in the fields, a young engineer Moses had hired, Sidney M. Shapiro, drove up with a surveying crew. "They just walked on the property and set up their things without asking permission," P. G. Rasweiler recalls. "Father asked them if they had papers from a court, and they didn't." John Jacob walked into his house, came out with a shotgun, put it against Shapiro's chest, and said, "I'll blow you to hell if you don't get off my land." Getting off, Shapiro telephoned Moses, who said, "Get the state troopers and go back there."

"They wanted to scare you, I guess," Rasweiler says. "But Father asked the troopers if the surveyors could go on our land without papers, and the troopers asked them if they had papers and they said no and the troopers said to them, 'You can't go on this man's property without papers,' and they went away. So we thought we had won, but the next day, they set up their things on the next farm—Moses only wanted land on the edges of that, so the farmer was friendly to him—and got the survey lines they needed from there and they condemned up the piece of property they wanted. We went to the Court of Claims and got $2,700 an acre—more than twice what Moses offered us. We kept what was left of the farm, but it wasn't the same. Me? I went into the trucking business—worked for my brother-in-law."

The charm could vanish as quickly with a financier as with a farmer. The Timber Pointers were shocked when they learned that Moses planned to turn the adjoining estate into a public park. Pointing to the spot where the proposed park would run alongside the club's golf course, old Horace Havemeyer, "the Sultan of Sugar," growled to his young brother-in-law, stockbroker W. Kingsland Macy: "I tell you, Macy, if they get a park over there, there'll be so much screwing you won't be able to tee up a ball." Havemeyer, Macy and Wall Street trader Buell Hollister had even more reason to be disturbed than the other ninety-seven Timber Point members. Anxious to attract more of "the right kind of people" to East Islip, the trio had recently decided to purchase the Taylor Estate themselves, divide its 1,486 acres into thirty building lots and sell them, at prices ranging from $50,000 on up, to thirty persons so right that they would even be invited to join, on purchase of a lot, the Timber Point Club. The proposition promised to be highly rewarding financially as well as socially. Now, to forestall Moses, Havemeyer, Hollister and Macy hastily persuaded the Timber Pointers in the Deer Range Corporation, the corporation that had turned the Taylor Estate into a hunting preserve, to overrule their officers, deny Moses the option he had been promised and instead sell the estate to them for the same $250,000 he had offered—plus 50 percent of any profit they made on subsequent resales. Learning of these machinations, Moses asked Macy to drop around to his office. When the stockbroker arrived, Moses bluntly ordered him not to consummate the deal. Macy indignantly refused to agree. Then, as he was later to testify under oath, "Mr. Moses told me they were going to take that place away from us and nothing we could do would stop it. . . . Mr. Moses informed me that he had the arbitrary power to seize this property, which was owned by myself and my associates, even though the state did not have one cent to pay for it. . . . Mr. Moses told me that he could take my home away from me. He told me personally that his power was such that he could seize my house, put me out of it and arrest me for trespass if I tried to get into it again. . . . Mr. Moses told me not only that he possessed this arbitrary power, but that he was able to control the press of New York City, so as to hold me up to such obloquy that I would not be able to stand it." And Moses was as good as his word. No sooner had Havemeyer, Hollister and Macy actually purchased the Taylor Estate than, without even a pretense of negotiating with them as the law required, he directed Park Commission attorneys to draw up a Notice of Entry and Appropriation and serve it on the three men—and while it was being served he stationed armed state troopers on the property and instructed them not to allow the three men to enter it even to remove personal property they had left there.

The route Moses had planned for his "Northern State Parkway" ran, west to east, through the estates of Mrs. Henry Phipps, Payne Whitney, Claus Spreckels, Clarence Hungerford Mackay, Henry Carnegie Phipps, Henry Payne Whitney, Francis P. Garvan, E. D. Morgan, Mrs. William K.

Vanderbilt II, Bronson Winthrop, Henry Rogers Winthrop and Otto Kahn.

The Phippses, Whitneys, Spreckelses, Mackays, Garvans, Morgans, Vanderbilts, Winthrops and Kahns refused even to discuss the parkway with Moses. One summer weekend in 1924, as they relaxed in the manor houses which they had so carefully secured against the public, they noticed, outside their gates, surveying crews setting up their telescope-like surveying levels—and pointing the telescopes in their direction. They dispatched servants to inquire what the surveyors were doing—and the servants returned with the information that the surveyors said that they were "laying out the route for the parkway." Astonished, the barons took a closer look at where the telescopes were pointing—and found that it was right at their houses. In some cases, before the guards could chase them away, the surveyors laid out a line of red and white flags to mark the exact route of the parkway—and the flags marched straight across their lawns and right by their front doors.

The barons dispatched their lawyers to Moses, and Moses did not treat those lawyers with the deference to which they were accustomed. The exact nature of his conversation with Colonel Henry L. Stimson is unknown, but Stimson stormed out of the meeting to write Governor Smith: "I believe thoroughly in the importance of improved highway facilities and parks. . . . But, my dear Governor, it cannot be done in this country by Napoleonic methods." Another lawyer told Moses that there was enough power in Wheatley Hills to insure that no parkway would ever run through there. "Well," Moses replied, "we're going to teach the Wheatley Hills people a lesson." To all the barons' lawyers, he spelled it out bluntly: If their clients were willing to donate land for the parkways, its location could be shifted away from their houses to the borders of their huge estates. But if they weren't cooperative, the commission had the power to appropriate the land right next to their houses—and it was going to do so.

"Appropriate?" the lawyers asked one another. What did that mean? In law offices all along Wall Street, pages were hastily turned to section fifty-nine of the State Conservation Law. And then calls were hastily placed to F. Trubee Davison.

"I felt awful, of course," Trubee was to recall. "It's a terrible, high-handed way for a public official to act, to threaten someone with the loss of his home unless he surrenders land. But Moses had the power to do it. He could walk in and take it. And he had the power under the law I had introduced. There was nothing else for me to do but to admit to these fellows who called that I just hadn't studied it thoroughly before I introduced it." One attorney, after studying the law, wrote a friend: "The powers most innocently expressed in Sections Eight and Nine are, when read in conjunction with Section Eighteen, sufficiently broad to permit this Commission to take over the whole of Suffolk County" as long as the Governor was willing to sign the appropriation form.

And even while the lawyers were studying the powers conferred by the act, Moses was giving new evidence of his intention to use them. In August, the owners of the Montauk Point land he wanted learned that Carl G. Fisher, developer of Miami Beach, was planning to transform Montauk into a similar resort area. If he succeeded, their land would become immensely valuable. They notified Moses that they would not sign the option agreement. He promptly appropriated the choicest portion of their land, a 1,700-acre tract called "Hither Hills." A week later, he appropriated twenty-two other acres on Lloyd Neck.

The lawyers told their clients they were in for a fight.

The skirmishers made contact first on the Taylor Estate. The attorneys for Havemeyer, Hollister and Macy's Pauchogue Corporation informed their clients that the powers given to the Long Island State Park Commission by the act Moses had drawn were broad—but that, broad as they were, Moses had overstepped them. He may have written the law, they said, but he had also broken it.

Section fifty-nine of the Conservation Law gave the commission the power to appropriate land, the attorneys said, but section fifty-nine also said that the power could be used only after negotiations with property owners had failed and no price could be agreed upon. Moses had never negotiated; he had never bothered to mention a price to any representative of Pauchogue; he had never even *spoken* to any representative after Pauchogue had purchased the Taylor Estate. Moreover, the State Constitution forbade any state agency to buy, condemn or appropriate land unless it had enough money on hand to pay for it. Moses had appropriated the Taylor Estate on December 4, 1924. The referendum had been passed, but under its provisions the $15,000,000 was not available to acquire land until each specific acquisition had been approved by the Legislature, and the Legislature had, of course, given no such approvals. The Legislature hadn't even *met* since the referendum. Even if Moses contended that the $225,000 allocated to the Long Island Commission by the 1924 Legislature could be used for land acquisition—a contention of extremely doubtful legality—the Taylor Estate was worth more than $225,000. Moses himself had admitted that by offering $250,000 for it. And Moses didn't have even the $225,000 any more. Out of that sum, before the appropriation, he had spent $63,000 on "overhead expenses," not to mention the money he owed the owners of the land he had appropriated at Montauk and Lloyd Neck. The Taylor Estate appropriation, the attorneys said, was clearly illegal. They could surely demonstrate this to Governor Smith, they said, and before an appropriation could take effect, Smith had to sign the appropriation form.

The Timber Pointers did not lack for means to bring their contentions to the Governor's attention. At their behest, visits were paid to his Biltmore Hotel apartment not only by prominent Republican leaders of the Legislature, friends of Smith from his legislative days, and not only by the single most powerful Republican in New York State—GOP national committeeman Charles D. Hillies—but also by Tammany's apple-cheeked ally, Democratic boss John McCooey of Brooklyn. One night, as the Governor relaxed at the Biltmore, there appeared before him, ushered in by a pair of Smith's dearest Tammany friends, W. Kingsland Macy himself, and Macy offered Smith, in this personal appeal, a list of an even dozen other Suffolk County estates closer to the city, beautiful in their own right—a dozen estates whose owners *wanted* to sell. And, he said, if the commission insisted on having an estate in East Islip, why couldn't it buy Willie Vanderbilt's "Idle Hour"? It was as large as the Taylor Estate, as heavily wooded, it had almost as much shore front on the bay—and Vanderbilt's heirs were trying to sell for $150,000, $100,000 less than the price offered for the Taylor Estate, which, he said, was actually worth much more than the price offered.

It was obvious to his advisers that Smith was uncertain. The efficacy of parks as an issue had been proven again in his 1924 re-election campaign. Running against popular young Colonel Theodore Roosevelt, Jr., he had turned his campaign tours into appeals for passage of the park referendum. Although Republican presidential candidate Calvin Coolidge had carried New York State and the Democrats had lost control of the Legislature, Smith had run nearly a million votes ahead of his ticket and won re-election. And, noting that the referendum had carried by nearly a million votes, he felt that no small part of his victory was due to his identification with parks.

Nonetheless, the question of the legality of Moses' appropriation still bothered him. The appropriation form to which Moses was asking him to affix his signature began with the words: "I, Alfred E. Smith, Governor of the State of New York, *being satisfied that there is available a sum representing fair compensation for the land to be entered and appropriated,* do hereby approve . . ." How could he possibly be so satisfied? His advisers, listening to the Governor thinking out loud on the subject, believed he would probably not sign.

After the election, the Governor scheduled a closed hearing on the appropriation. Havemeyer, Hollister and Macy were confident when they arrived at the Biltmore with their attorneys. Moses, arriving with McNulty and two other commission attorneys, was not.

But the outcome of the hearing was not to hinge on legalities. Smith, anxious to learn for himself the basics of both sides' positions, conducted it informally, bantering, telling jokes, encouraging the principals as well as their attorneys to talk. And the Sultan of Sugar talked. Explaining why he didn't want a park in East Islip, Horace Havemeyer said he feared the town would be "overrun with rabble from the city."

In later years, Smith's biographers, describing the hearing, pictured the Governor as laughing at the remark and saying, with a grin, "Rabble? Why, that's me."

The words Smith actually used were similar, but there was no grin. When Havemeyer used the word "rabble," Smith looked up at him. The blue eyes were steel. The laughter in the room died away. "Rabble? That's *me* you're talking about." He reached out a hand and seized the appropriation form. Trying desperately to turn his remark into a joke, Havemeyer said quickly, "Why, where's a poor millionaire to go nowadays if he wants to be alone?" "Try the Harlem River Hospital," Smith said. The Harlem River Hospital was an insane asylum. As Havemeyer flushed, the Governor signed the form.

The hearing was over, but the fight for the Taylor Estate was not. It would be waged without quarter in both regular and special sessions of the New York State Legislature, and in twenty-five separate appellate court proceedings. It would fill the front pages of newspapers across the state for two years, delay for almost that long all expenditures for any of the parks of which Robert Moses had dreamed, and bring to the brink of ruin not only those dreams but Moses' personal reputation and career. But before it was over, Moses would be hauled back from the brink by Al Smith, with a helping tug from Belle Moskowitz, and his reputation, seemingly certain to be tarnished by his actions, would be burnished instead so that he gleamed in the public consciousness with the aura he would bear for the next thirty years: the aura of a fearless, fiercely independent public servant who loved parks above all else and was willing to fight for parks against politicians, bureaucrats and the hated forces of wealth and influence.

The Taylor Estate fight also transformed a quiet, conservative stockbroker and connoisseur of antiques into a major New York State political figure.

The stockbroker was W. Kingsland Macy, a tall, slender former Harvard *Crimson* editor one year older than Moses, who invariably wore starched high round collars and dark-blue suits with vest, and often pince-nez. Not wealthy, but well off, Macy seemed, with his seat on the Exchange, his modest but well-tended East Islip estate and his love of antiques and old houses, the very model of the country gentleman, except that, unlike brother-in-law Havemeyer and the other members of the Timber Point Club, he was noticeably uninterested in making money. As one observer of his career was to write, "All the while he had a vague idea that he would like to enter politics, but he did not know how to go about it." And since he was an unsmiling man with the thin, tight-pressed lips of the ascetic, very reserved even with friends, it seemed unlikely that he would find out. But, as the observer was to write, "No man living excels Macy in the capacity for appreciating an outrage that has been perpetrated against his rights. He cherished and cultivated his wrongs as other men worship Old Masters." And now Macy felt that Moses had wronged him.

The day after the hearing at the Biltmore, new fuel was heaped on Macy's outrage. His lawyers had notified Moses that an appeal was planned, and Moses' lawyers had agreed that the matter was still in abeyance—and that a hunting party of Deer Range stockholders could be held the next day as scheduled. But when the hunters' limousines pulled up to the property, barring their way were men in uniform carrying revolvers, state troopers who refused to allow them even to remove the hunting clothes they had previously left there and that had certainly not been included in any appropriation. The astounded millionaires saw other men in uniform—Conservation Department workers, they were told—rounding up the pheasants and mallards, also unappropriated, that they had raised and that they still owned and putting them in trucks to be hauled away. Within days, Macy was receiving reports that crews of state workmen had begun cutting down trees and tearing down buildings on the property.

Havemeyer and Hollister were businessmen. Smith's action had cost them the opportunity for a large profit, but at least they could, through the Court of Claims, get their money back—with interest. They saw no point in throwing good money after bad by fighting the state. But Macy no longer viewed the situation strictly in business terms. "There is a question of importance . . . because of certain fundamental principles of this Government which are being ruthlessly overthrown by the Long Island Commission," he wrote his partners. "Moses never even tried to negotiate with us. He decided to seize first and negotiate afterward. There was no condemnation, no proceedings, no notice to us. They threw a cordon of state troopers around the property and now they say, 'Your remedy is to go to the Court of Claims for compensation.' " If Moses could do this to us, Macy said, he could do it to anyone. "No one's home is safe." The principles, he said, were too important to be surrendered without a fight. He tried to persuade Havemeyer and Hollister to invest in a legal fight to oust the commission from the property. Hollister refused. Havemeyer agreed to pay half of all legal expenses up to $25,000, but said he would not spend a cent beyond that.

On December 31, 1924, Pauchogue's lawyers began the fight by asking Suffolk County Court to enjoin the Long Island State Park Commission from altering the property until a trial could be held to determine if the appropriation was legal. Judge George H. Furman issued the temporary injunction on the same day it was applied for, allowing the state troopers to remain on the property to insure that its condition was not changed before the trial but prohibiting them from interfering with its use by Pauchogue for whatever purpose the corporation wished—including hunting. And Furman added to his decision a line that seemed to confirm Macy's contentions. The appropriation, the judge said, was clearly illegal.

Hastily striking an alliance with the North Shore robber barons, Macy agreed that the best strategy was to cut off all Park Commission funds until new laws were passed taking from it the right of condemnation by appropriation. Because of the barons' control of the Legislature, there seemed little doubt that the strategy would succeed.

But Macy was handicapped by principles. When a reporter from the New York *Herald Tribune* asked him to show him around the Taylor Estate so that he could see if it was really inaccessible and unsuitable for a park, Macy disdained to seize this opportunity to sway the press. No, he told the reporter, he did not want to influence his thinking. He was sure the truth would be obvious. He would not accompany him. "Macy," Moses was to say, "was the amateur in politics." Once, Moses had been the amateur. But he wasn't any longer. And he knew how to take advantage of someone who was—as became apparent on January 8, 1925, on the front page of *The New York Times*.

A FEW RICH GOLFERS ACCUSED OF BLOCKING PLANS FOR STATE PARK, the headline said. R. B. MOSES OF LONG ISLAND COMMISSION TELLS OF FIGHT FOR SITE ON SOUTH SHORE—INFLUENCE USED, HE SAYS. The story began: "Robert B. [sic] Moses, President of the Long Island State Park Commission, charged yesterday that a little group of wealthy men was obstructing the commission's plan to create a state park on the South Shore, five miles east of Islip, and that legal action had been taken by them only when every avenue of social and political influence had failed." The next two paragraphs were a restatement of that theme. The "wealthy men" were allowed one paragraph—the fourth—for rebuttal; they were not heard from again until paragraph twenty-six, by which point the *Times*'s readers had had spread before them, almost verbatim, Moses' press release, a press release written by a man who had once been the master of "scrupulous, reliable" research but who had become a master propagandist—one who did not let facts stand in the way of his aims.

Moses' release harped on the fact that his opponents were "wealthy residents," "rich residents," "rich people," "possessed of every sort of political and social influence." Nowhere did his release mention the fact that a judge had found his action illegal. And nowhere in the story, which ran for thirty-four paragraphs, did the *Times* see fit to mention that piece of information. Unable to avoid mentioning the injunction, Moses said it had been granted by a "local judge," a phrase with implications. "We will fight it," he said. "Upon its outcome depends whether the public or a small group of rich people can have a playground there."

Any reader who arrived at paragraph twenty-six would begin to notice that there were some other sides to the story. Contrary to Moses' statement, Macy said at that well-buried point, it was not just "a few rich golfers" who objected to the park but a large majority of the residents of Islip Town and Suffolk County. And the point of the injunction, he said, was that Moses had violated the law and seized property without due process. "If the commission can do this," he said, "it can, by passing a resolution and getting the mere formality of the Governor's signature, seize any man's home, dispossess him and put state troopers there to prevent his re-entering. It is for that reason that we have taken the issue to court." But when the *Times* finally gave him a chance to talk, Macy talked too much. Not trying to dodge the "influence" issue, he sought to defend it. "We did use influence," he said. "But we could not go around and see every citizen in the state about the matter. We saw various representative men, and we did go to the Governor. Mr. Moses went to the Governor, too. Well, I am a citizen of the state of New York and I have as much right to see the Governor as Mr. Moses."

Such public relations naïveté, combined with the *Times*'s slanting, made Moses' debut in a headline on the front page of the nation's most respected newspaper a triumph. While Macy had won the first round in a court of law, Moses had won the first round in the court of public opinion.

In the former court, Moses could not evade the facts that the *Times* had relegated to paragraph twenty-six. When, as he had promised the *Times*'s readers, he did "fight" the injunction issued by the "local judge," asking the State Supreme Court to invalidate it, Supreme Court Justice James C. Van Siclen refused. "The defendants have proceeded and are proceeding and threatening to proceed in a manner which tends irregularly, illegally and beyond their powers, under and in violation of the laws and Constitution of the State of New York and of the United States, to invade and seize the property of the plaintiff," Van Siclen said. The injunction would remain in force until a full trial was held. Such a trial, the judge made clear, could result not only in the return of the Taylor Estate to Pauchogue, but also in the assessing of substantial damages against the Long Island State Park Commission, against the individual commissioners, including Robert Moses, against New York State and even, conceivably, against Governor Smith. To indicate his own feelings in the matter, Van Siclen ordered the commission to pay Pauchogue a symbolic ten dollars in court costs.

Now Moses' only hope was the Legislature. If it appropriated—"segregated" was the legal term—$250,000 of the bond-sale revenues for purchase of the Taylor Estate, he could argue that the commission had seized the estate in anticipation of the segregation. This was a weak defense—but at least it was a defense. If the Legislature did not segregate the $250,000, the commission—Moses—would have no legal defense at all. He would have no money to pay for the land he had taken.

The Legislature, however, was controlled by the state's Republican Party, and that party was dominated financially by the barons, philosophically by a concern for the rights of private property, precisely the rights endangered by unstatutory appropriation, and politically by its desire to embarrass Alfred E. Smith, the man who had shattered its control of New York State. Because, in its view, one of Smith's appointees had broken the law, and Smith had, by signing the appropriation form, helped him do it, they saw an ideal chance for such embarrassment if the facts of the case were brought out. On February 11 and 26, 1925, the Senate Finance Committee held hearings in Albany.

Throughout the hearings, despite the efforts of Finance Committee Chairman Charles J. Hewitt to gavel him into silence, Moses was on his feet, berating witnesses. "I never knew of persons to come before a legislative hearing with dirtier hands than the people of East Islip," he shouted at one.

But shouting could not drown out the facts. To refute Moses' contention that only a "few rich golfers" opposed the park, more than a dozen elected officials testified that the majority of Suffolk's 150,000 and Islip Township's 21,000 residents opposed it. The chairman of Suffolk's Board of Supervisors, the county's governing body, testified: "We are opposed to the methods of the Long Island Commission. . . . We are afraid of persons who act as they have." And when Moses himself was summoned to the stand, the questioner was F. Trubee Davison, and Davison had learned a great deal about asking questions since the day, a year before, on which he had agreed to introduce Moses' park bills.

"Did you have the money available at the time [the appropriation was made]?" Davison demanded.

"That is a question for the courts to decide," Moses replied.

"Well, did the commission believe it had the money available to pay a reasonable value on this property?" Davison demanded.

"Yes, we did," Moses said. The money appropriated to the Long Island State Park Commission by the 1924 Legislature.

"Well, let us see about it," Davison said. "The Legislature appropriated $225,000. Did you spend any of that money before the Taylor Estate case came up?"

"Yes, some of it," Moses admitted.

"Well," Davison said, "how did you arrive at your arithmetic? You had only $225,000 to start with and you admit you spent some of it. How could you have enough to cover the Taylor case?"

"We think we had it," Moses said. But Davison had made his point. After the hearing, Moses printed up "transcripts" of the hearing—with his own damaging admissions carefully omitted—and mailed them to state officials and legislators. But the officials and legislators had followed the hearings themselves. The state has "an obligation" to have money available to pay people before taking their property, said Attorney General Albert Ottinger, a Republican. Moses' actions, said the state's chief legal officer, were clearly "illegal." The day following the hearing, Assembly Speaker Joseph A. McGinnies said that the Legislature would strip the power of appropriation from the commission. And he said that the Legislature would certainly not segregate any money at all—ever—for the purchase of the Taylor Estate.

In the Legislature and the courts, then, the issue appeared in February 1925 all but settled: To realize a dream of unprecedented scope, Robert Moses, by use of the law, had armed himself with unprecedented powers—and then, finding that these powers were still inadequate, he had deliberately gone beyond them, beyond the law. "Entry and appropriation" was, even as defined in law, of questionable constitutionality in its negation of the individual's rights when his property was coveted by the state. And Moses had gone beyond the definition to use the power of the state with even less restraint than the law allowed. But both courts and Legislature understood the situation; before both courts and Legislature, Moses stood stripped of all defenses and, it seemed in February 1925, both courts and Legislature would now step in and rectify the situation, the courts by affording redress to the individuals injured by his actions, the Legislature by insuring that he never again had the opportunity similarly to injure any other individual.

But the ultimate court in which the fate of Moses and his dream was to be resolved would be the court of public opinion. And in this court, Robert Moses had close to hand three formidable weapons.

One was the fact that, like motherhood, parks symbolized something good, and therefore anyone who fought for parks fought under the shield of the presumption that he was fighting for the right—and anyone who opposed him, for the wrong.

The second was the fact that it was possible to paint the issue, as Moses had already done, not only as park supporters vs. park deniers, but also as wealth vs. lack of wealth, privilege vs. impotence, influence vs. helplessness, "rich golfers" vs. the sweating masses of the cities.

The third was the ultimate political weapon: Alfred Emanuel Smith.

The Republican majority in the Legislature drafted a bill, introduced by upstate Senator Warren T. Thayer, segregating $6,000,000 of the bond issue for acquisition of various parks but not appropriating any funds for acquisition of the Taylor Estate. The bill also amended the laws Davison had introduced on Moses' behalf the year before. It eliminated appropriation as a method of obtaining park land in developed areas and also provided that all land acquisition for parks or parkways, including acquisition by condemnation, must be approved by the Republican-controlled State Land Board, that all park or parkway construction must be approved by the Republican-controlled State Board of Estimate and Control, that all engineering work on parks and parkways must be carried out by the State Engineer, an elected official who was then a Republican, and that all legal work connected with parks and parkways must be carried out by the office of the Republican State Attorney General, Albert Ottinger. During the last week in March, shortly before adjournment, the Legislature passed the bill. Smith vetoed it. (His veto, said Eberly Hutchinson, chairman of the Assembly Ways and Means Committee, was clearly the work of "that expert and abusive propagandist, practiced in exciting the prejudices of the uninformed and a habitual defamer of the Legislature, Robert Moses," who had boasted to him that if the Legislature did not pass a bill he liked, the Governor would veto it.) But the veto did not help Moses or Smith. They needed $250,000. If it wasn't segregated, Moses' acts would be declared flatly illegal in court, and no Governor would be able to put a good face on such a development, especially a Governor who was, even peripherally and only because he had been misled by an appointee, involved. Early in April, Smith told his advisers that he would summon the Legislature back into special session to try to force it into the segregation.

Moses' only hope of not having to appear in court without money or promise of money for the appropriation was to stall court proceedings until after the special session. Frantically, the commission's attorneys employed every legal stratagem available. They moved to strike certain clauses out of Pauchogue's complaint. Van Siclen denied the motion. They appealed his decision to the Appellate Division of the State Supreme Court. The Appellate Division denied the appeal. They appealed the denial to the Court of Appeals. Then they went back to Van Siclen's court and moved to strike other clauses. Van Siclen denied the motion. They appealed the decision. April dragged into May. The case, the judge commented, should have been tried long ago. But the commission attorneys filed new motions. Then they sought "judgment on pleadings," a device which required the filing of a long series of successive briefs by both sides. Their briefs ran longer and longer. One was 275 pages. Then they appealed the decisions to the Appellate Division. Every appeal was denied—but every one used up time.

Macy raged at the delays. "A speedy determination of the issue is what the public, the county and the state are entitled to," he said. Although his rage did not require new fuel, Moses provided some anyway. Macy, the lover of antiquity, had determined to reserve one of the thirty homesites for himself and to restore the old Taylor mansion, a fantastic mass of pillars, turrets and cupolas, and its outbuildings, to their original condition. But one Sunday in May, strolling around the property, he found the walls of the boathouse riddled with bullet holes. Targets tacked to the walls explained them. The state troopers had been using the building for pistol practice. As he stared aghast at the damage, he heard someone coming through the woods, and turning, saw another Sunday stroller: Robert Moses. Macy protested to Moses, pointing out that the courts had specifically forbade the commission to injure the property in any way. Moses replied with a grin: It's lucky it was this building. We're going to tear it down anyway.

Once let him get Moses on the stand, Macy was sure, and the boasting would stop. He hungered for the court decision which he was certain would vindicate him. But Moses kept stalling.

So did Smith. All through April and May, Moses, anxious, was nudging the Governor to call the special session. So, for less personal reasons, were Smith's other advisers. Since he had a great issue, they said, wouldn't it be best to press it while it was still fresh in the public's mind?

Wait, Smith said. He had thought of something his advisers hadn't. New York City wasn't hot in April. It wasn't hot in May. New Yorkers weren't desperate to get out of the city in April and May, desperate for a bathing beach such as the one the Taylor Estate would provide. In April and May, they hadn't yet reached the point at which they didn't care at all about the legal technicalities of park acquisition; they hadn't yet reached the point at which all that mattered was that someone was trying to provide them with a place to swim—and someone else was standing in his way.

On June 1, a Monday, the first of the inevitable summer heat waves settled over the city like a hot, soggy blanket. By the weekend, the temperature was in the nineties. The city's people fled it. Traffic jams on Long Island were worse than ever. So great was the frustration that when motorists reached a town park in Huntington and found police barring the gates, they assaulted the police in such force that more than forty were arrested. On June 10, Smith announced the special summer session—in a speech that was the first ever carried on a statewide radio hookup.

"There are people in this state who are opposed to parks," Al Smith said. His rasping, friendly, compelling voice sliced through the static of the crystal sets in tens of thousands of steaming living rooms in which sat families who had spent that last weekend in a desperate search for parks. "There are people in this state who are opposed to parks, to the park program, because they do not desire public parks or parkways too close to their private estates, golf clubs and fox-hunting and polo fields."

Smith spoke for two and a half hours. Slowly, painstakingly, he detailed the whole background of his side of the fight, the attempts to remove parks from politics, the Republicans' insistence on injecting into park administration other, politically dominated state agencies, on making the final decision on proposed land acquisition rest not with the State Council of Parks but with the State Land Board.

"Let us compare both bodies," he said. "Let us see who are the members of the Park Council." He listed their names, lingering over several. "Everybody knows Judge Clearwater," he said. "He is one of the leading lawyers of the country. . . . He has been connected with the Niagara State Reservation since its establishment many years ago and has repeatedly been reappointed by Governors of all shades of political opinion. . . . Everyone knows Franklin D. Roosevelt . . . one of the heads of the Boy Scout movement in the country. . . ." Many of these men, he pointed out, were Republicans. All were "serving the state without pay. Many have contributed large sums of money from their personal fortunes for the purchase of lands which they have presented to the state as a gift."

What is the Land Board? he asked rhetorically: "A purely political body." Its entire staff consists of one clerk and two land appraisers, all political appointees in office only since last January. "They don't visit the lands," he said. "They don't know where they are."

"Where," he growled, "did the suggestion come from that this Board be injected into the park program?" From the wealthy people on Long Island who want the program to be controlled by an agency "easily subject to influence and manipulation." The Land Board had never even been mentioned in connection with parks until the Long Island State Park Commission proposed taking a little of their land.

Slowly and carefully, the Governor spelled out his side of the Taylor Estate and Northern State Parkway fights, the need for park land on Long Island, the great natural beauty of the spot selected, the attitude of the opponents, a "few wealthy men," at the Biltmore hearing.

"As between the few and the many to be benefited," Al Smith said, "I cast my lot with the many, and I signed the papers necessary to acquire the property by entry and appropriation. Immediately thereafter, high-priced legal talent was brought in to defeat the purposes of the state." It was from them and from their masters that the suggestion came to place the park program under the Land Board and to paralyze the program until this was done, because they knew that, "before the Land Board, the golf club would probably win."

So, Smith said, "there is a greater question here than Park Councils, Attorney Generals or Land Boards. There is a question of what will ultimately become of the $15,000,000 authorized by the people. Will it buy choice park spots and locate parkways where there is fine air and scenic beauty, or will money, power and influence compel the state to buy for the people that which nobody else wants? The people are either going to get these parks and parkways through the properly organized commissions . . . or this program will be given into the hands of the very men who now desire to weaken it in the interests of the few . . ."

And Al Smith wound up his speech as only Al Smith could. He was willing to leave the question to the people, he said. "I am laying it before them in plain everyday language and I am leaving it to them to serve notice on their servants and representatives in the Legislature just exactly what their wishes are," he said. "The cure for the evils of democracy is more democracy. Let us battle it out right in the shadow of the capitol itself and let us have a decision, and let us not permit the impression to go abroad that wealth and the power that wealth can command can palsy the arm of the state."

In his speech, Smith avoided discussing the legalities or constitutionality of the appropriation. And he avoided, except for a single passing reference, any mention of Robert Moses.

The Republicans tried to shift the focus back to the Governor's controversial appointee and his actions. Replying on the radio the next evening, John Knight, Senate majority leader, said:

> The issue is one of law and order as against lawlessness and a violation of sacred constitutional property rights. With scarcely a dollar in sight or available for payment, Robert Moses, with the written approval of Governor Smith and with the aid of the State Police, seized property of the admitted value of $250,000 and excluded the owners from such property. The question as to the legality of that action is one for the courts, and it appears that the owners of this property have brought an action against Mr. Moses for large damages. That is the big reason why Mr. Moses is so much concerned at this time and why he wants an extra session and funds to pay for this property.

It is, Knight said, because a curb is needed on such wanton abuse of power that a check by an outside body, such as the Land Board, is needed. The Legislature, he said, must "safeguard private property against future unlawful seizure." Attorney General Ottinger issued a statement detailing the "extravagance" of Moses' $63,000 expenditures for cars and office furnishings.

But "sacred constitutional property rights" and the price of office furnishings weren't the issue to the steaming millions of New York City—or of the state's other cities. Twice more before the session Smith took to the air to speak, twice more he pounded on the theme of the few against the many, of wealth, privilege and influence against the masses, of parks against the millionaires' golf clubs. The mailboxes of legislators were situated in 1925 in the "midway," the corridor between Senate and Assembly Chambers on the third floor of the capitol. Each morning, as reporters headed for the legislative chambers, they could see those mailboxes. After each of Smith's speeches, the mailboxes were overflowing with letters and postcards supporting the Governor.

And the press didn't help the Republicans. June 1925 was a hot news month. John Thomas Scopes was being tried in the sleepy town of Dayton, Tennessee, and among the two million words a day being telegraphed out of Dayton were enough to fill endless columns in the New York papers. More page-one columns were devoted to speculation over the fate of Roald Amundsen, whose expedition to the North Pole hadn't been heard from in four weeks, until on June 19 the *Times* could report AMUNDSEN BACK SAFE. But in New York and other cities of New York State, no story was big enough to knock the park fight off page one. The *Times*, for example, carried during the thirty days of June twenty-eight park-fight stories, seven in the lead spot, as well as a long summary in its Sunday magazine, reprints in full of the texts of the long speeches by Smith and Knight, and eight editorials. The editorials of all the big-city papers—with the exception of the New York *Herald Tribune*, notorious during the latter part of the 1920's for its espousal of the upper-class viewpoint—seemed to be vying with one another in whipping up public support for the Governor's stand. The *Times*, in its only direct confrontation with the issue Macy considered important in the fight, said that perhaps Moses *had* broken the law, but that there were more important principles involved than *that*. "It seems not unlikely that Chairman Moses has exceeded his legal authority. But he is acting in the interest of the people at large and of all future generations. . . ."

The support for Smith and Moses spilled off the editorial pages into the supposedly impartial news columns. The paper in which this tendency was most striking was the *Times*, both because the paper strove so diligently for objectivity on other issues and because of its reputation. ("The *Times* was the bible, emerging each morning with a view of life that thousands of readers accepted as reality," its biographer, Gay Talese, was to write. "They accepted it on the simple theory that what appeared in the *Times* must be true.") The slanting in the *Times*'s initial story on the Taylor Estate fight—the verbatim recitation of all Moses' points and the burying of Macy's—was not corrected in succeeding stories. Stories about court developments—which were unfavorable to Moses—were kept short and relegated to inside pages. Van Siclen's flat statement that the appropriation was illegal and a violation of both law and the constitutions of the state and nation was on page twenty-one, and it was exactly five paragraphs long. More favorable stories on political developments were front-paged and allowed to run interminably.

It was not just a case of inequality in space and play. The *Times*'s articles repeated, day after day, as if they were uncontested facts, the key contentions made by Moses and Smith. Story after story, for example, contained some version of the following paragraph:

> Wealthy members of the Timber Point Golf Club used social and political influence to try to get the Commissioners to withdraw. That failing, they created the Pauchogue Land Corporation and bought the estate.

The key contentions of Moses' opponents were almost totally ignored. Only the most diligent readers of the *Times* could understand, for example, that the fact that Moses had appropriated the property without money to pay for it was of importance; the fact was hardly ever mentioned, and the mentions it was given were fleeting. When Ottinger revealed Moses' $63,000 expenditures for "overhead," the *Times* buried the story on an inside page and handled it this way:

> Albany—What is considered here as an attempt at retaliation by Republicans on Governor Smith for his veto of the Thayer State Park bill is contained in a letter of censure sent by Attorney General Ottinger to Robert Moses.

Moses' reply attacked the Attorney General for delays in searching title for proposed park acquisitions; it all but ignored the "overhead." A *Times* editorial said: "Chairman Moses' reply is a model of moderate statement."

As the crucial special session neared, the *Times* began to resemble a Democratic house organ. Its article on the eve of the session said: "The Governor believes in parks. He loves them. . . . The Governor is well aware that he has a stiff battle ahead and is preparing to meet the situation with his usual vigor and undaunted courage." His motives for calling the special session, "a contest that may add a new epic to the annals of the State," the article said, were clear: "an abiding faith that the public can force this legislation in its own interest." Other possible motives—such as an upcoming, all but indefensible court action—were never mentioned.

Part of the explanation for the *Times*'s attitude was the friendship of Adolph S. Ochs, the self-made man from Knoxville who had become its owner and guiding spirit, with the self-made man from the Fourth Ward. During the 1920's, Smith regularly spent summer weekends at Ochs's summer home on Lake George.

Part was the intense interest of Ochs, his only living child, Iphigene, Iphigene's husband, Arthur Hays Sulzberger, Sulzberger's niece-in-law, Mrs. Cyrus L. Sulzberger—of a whole clutch of Ochses and Sulzbergers, in fact —in parks. The old patriarch himself took a particular interest in preserving the Saratoga Battlefield; in 1927, Moses, trying to buy up those portions not yet owned by the state, would find himself short of money—and Ochs would purchase two key parcels and hold them for the state until the money was available. In 1925, Mrs. Cyrus L. Sulzberger was active in the Park Association of New York City. Iphigene, a somber-eyed and idealistic young matron deeply concerned with social problems, had already begun to channel the idealism—and a remarkable amount of enthusiasm and energy that was concealed but not muted by her serene manners and gentle voice—into Park Association work. She had been, she would tell the author forty years later, "thrilled" by Moses' state park work and anxious that the city should also get moving, and in 1925 she was active on a Park Association committee that was mapping a vast city land-acquisition program —and that listened raptly to Moses, who had agreed to help them work it out.

The feeling of the publisher and his family showed up in the news columns of the *Times* probably not as a result of any direct orders to editors or reporters but as the result of their understandable sensitivity to their bosses' feelings. Albert L. Warner, one of the paper's Albany reporters, recalls: "Parks and conservation—they were dear to Mr. Ochs's heart and consequently dear to the hearts of *Times* editors. So I was on the lookout for any attempt to interfere with parks. Not that I had specific instructions to do so, but the editors would react favorably to park and conservation stories, so the reporter naturally keeps his eyes alert for stories of this type." When, in 1931, Ochs received the annual award of the Park Association, the lettering on the illuminated scroll said: "*The New York Times*, under his leadership, has made itself the mouthpiece of friends of the parks, using its great influence to educate the public to an understanding of the place of the parks in modern life."

Whatever the reason, the daily press coverage of the park fight made Smith and Moses look very good—and the Republican legislators look very bad.

The Republican legislators realized this. Faced with an election campaign in November, many of those from New York and downstate districts began to panic. But Hillies and GOP national committeeman George K. Morris, representatives of the powers that ran the party, traveled to Albany and held them in line with naked threats and blandishments. And the upstate legislators didn't have to be concerned about November. One-man, one-vote upstate agitation was decades in the future; these legislators represented New York State's rotten boroughs: districts whose voters numbered in the thousands, not the hundreds of thousands, and who were farmers who had no interest in parks and who were, moreover, fanatically opposed to government spending. The idea of spending millions for parks had appalled them in the first place; the bond referendum might have rolled up a statewide majority of more than a million, but, with a single exception, Ulster, where old park philanthropist Judge Alphonse Trumpbore Clearwater took the stump for it, every upstate county had voted against it. Upstate New York in 1925 was a stronghold of Prohibitionism, of Protestantism, of prejudice, of Ku Klux Klannism—and of Republicanism. Opposing Smith's park policies could only help upstate Republican legislators, not hurt them. As the legislators arrived in Albany for the special session, bitter against being called to the capitol in the summer heat, reporters asked them if there was any chance of a change in their position. "We'll melt in our seats first," one said. When a reporter asked Knight if he might change his mind, Knight replied, "I don't change my mind very often, do I?"

Nonetheless, Smith smote them hip and thigh. The Republicans held a majority of seven in the Senate and forty-two in the Assembly; he had to switch four votes in the Senate and twenty-two votes in the Assembly to win. He sent Moses and other emissaries to the Republican members of the State Council of Parks, the old men who had been fighting for parks for decades, and asked them to intercede with the legislators from their districts. The park philanthropists were men who ordinarily had influence in Republican councils; no legislator from a district anywhere near the headwaters of the Hudson dared publicly to oppose Judge Clearwater's wishes. At a Republican caucus, the park philanthropists spoke one after the other; not a single legislator dared openly to argue against them, but they had their orders; a reporter wrote that, when the speeches were finished, "the Republican leaders sat speechless, until they finally filed their terse refusal to reconsider and quit the conference."

Persuasion having failed, the Governor tried other methods. Westchester, he saw, was a weak spot in the Republican wall: Boss William Ward wanted a new charter for the county, one that would centralize its government under his thumb, and the necessary county referendum on the charter could be authorized only by Legislature—and Governor. A bill authorizing the referendum happened even then to be awaiting Smith's signature or veto. Moses paid a visit to Ward and one of Ward's senators, Seabury C. Mastick. Smith signed the bill—and soon political observers were reporting that Ward had promised Smith the votes of the seven legislators he controlled, and that Mastick might even introduce the park bill Smith wanted.

The Citizens Union and City Club reformers had great influence with Republican legislators from New York City. Smith sent Moses to see them. The younger reformers admired Moses; many of the older men were disenchanted with him, but they believed in the cause for which he was fighting, and they rallied to it: "Park development . . . should be determined by sound principles. These sound principles, the Citizens Union believes, were outlined by the State Council of Parks." With reformers who still had doubts, Smith lent a hand. When, in a chat in the City Club lounge, lawyer Joseph M. Price told Moses that perhaps a central supervisory body such as the Land Board wasn't a bad idea, Moses excused himself, went to a telephone and called Smith in Albany—and hardly had the chat ended when Price received a telegram from the Governor explaining why the Land Board idea was bad. Reformer William B. Roulstone boarded a train to Buffalo, in a single day persuaded the Buffalo Council of Catholic Women, the Buffalo Civic Club and the Buffalo Central Labor Council to pass resolutions supporting Smith's stand—and then headed for Syracuse and a dozen other upstate cities and towns. The upstate park philanthropists were out working, too, old Judge Clearwater himself driving night after night to little villages to talk on their local radio stations, Franklin D. Roosevelt of Hyde Park assailing "the invisible hand behind the . . . Republican . . . policy."

Then Smith and Mrs. Moskowitz conceived a master stroke: they told Moses to call a meeting of the seventy-three regional park commissioners and to hold it in the Executive Chamber at 2 P.M. June 22—just six hours before the opening of the special session—a move that insured that the influential commissioners would be on hand during the session, available to bring further pressure on wavering legislators, and to dramatize to press and public the contrast between the attitude of the Legislature and of men genuinely interested in parks. GOP leaders pleaded with the commissioners not to attend, telling them that they were working against their own party, but the old men were loyal to their parks. They canceled vacation and business trips, and all but nineteen of the seventy-three were present, packed into the visitors' gallery of the Assembly Chamber along with the largest crowd the Chamber had ever held, as Smith, speaking not from the raised Speaker's chair but in the well of the Chamber, a spot where he had stood so many times before, stood so close to the senators seated on folding chairs brought in specially for the occasion that he could touch them. And he told them: You created the State Parks Council. I kept politics out of it by appointing to it these men, mostly Republicans. They include some of the greatest men in the state. And it's their plan, not mine, that you're killing.

Smith's speech brought the packed galleries to their feet cheering. Smith had asked the Legislature for permission to have his speech broadcast; it had not dared refuse. Four microphones had been set up in the Assembly Chamber well, and as the cheers thundered down on the legislators, they could look at the microphones and know that they were being echoed throughout the state.

But when the Republican legislators emerged from behind the closed and guarded doors of their caucus, not a single one—not one from New York City, not even one from Westchester County—was still supporting Smith. Not only would the GOP not segregate the funds Smith had asked for, but by a straight party-line vote, the Legislature repassed the identical bill that Smith had vetoed. With the Legislature confronted by an outpouring of public pressure as great as any in the state's history, the barons of Long Island had laid down the law to the lawmakers—and their orders had been obeyed.

The roll call in the Senate was completed at 5 P.M., in the Assembly at 6:30. At exactly 7 P.M., the Governor again vetoed the bill, in a sequence that a *Times* reporter wrote "is likely to set a mark in legislative history for the record-breaking speed with which it went the route from legislative approval to executive condemnation."

Bitterness roiled over Albany. In a voice "shaking with emotion," John Knight, usually so stolid, stood at his Senate desk and cried, "He [Smith] ought to sign this bill instead of dancing up and down like a spoiled child."

"People on Long Island [are] afraid to go to bed for fear that when they wake up in the morning they would find their property seized by Robert Moses," another Republican senator shouted. Jumping out of his seat, a Democrat replied: "Is it not true that if they don't go to bed on Long Island it is because the bedsheets may be in use elsewhere?"—a reference to the Ku Klux Klan. And Jimmy Walker, his suavity gone for a moment, his cravat for once askew, shook his fist at the Republican senators and shouted, "These millionaires made their millions out of the poor despised kikes and wops of the tenements whom, through you, they are now seeking to shut out . . . from a day in the country."

From the Governor's chambers, Smith thundered that "sealed orders" had been delivered to the GOP. The Westchester delegation had "welched," he said. Seabury Mastick had promised him support—he did not say what he had promised Mastick in exchange—but Mastick later had confessed to him that there had been brought to bear on him "too much pressure" for him to resist. Others quoted Mastick as saying that he had been told bluntly that if he supported Smith, "my career would end."

The facts which confronted Smith and Moses after the special session were as bitter as the shouting: not a cent had been appropriated for park acquisition or development. The option on the two miles of beach front at Hampton Bays was lost, and the land was promptly bought by three developers, who divided it into lots and began to erect bungalows on them. The option on Sunken Meadow was lost, and while the land was not sold, its value had obviously been tripled or quadrupled by the publicity. Other property on Long Island that Moses had coveted was being swallowed up by real estate developments.

More important—politically, at least—there was still no money to lacquer even a veneer of legality over the ugly surface of the Taylor Estate appropriation. An angry Justice Van Siclen had scheduled the Taylor Estate trial for September 1—and had said that no further delays would be tolerated. On that date, Macy was at last going to get Moses on the witness stand, and Moses was going to have to admit that he still didn't have money available to pay Macy for the property he had taken from him. Smith and Moses might have reaped a windfall in the political arenas of Albany, but, they knew, that advantage would be lost when the act they were defending was flatly declared illegal.

"Well," Smith said to Moses one afternoon when the two men and Mrs. Moskowitz were alone in the Biltmore apartment, "can't you get someone to give you the money to make the thing stick?" Who? Moses said. The kind of money they were talking about was too much for his own family even to consider; real wealth was required, and people with real wealth were the people who were angriest at him. No, he said, he didn't know anybody. And they couldn't take a chance on a turndown; if they asked someone who refused, and then spread the story that they were desperate for funds to legalize the seizure, the Republicans would make capital of it—and so would Macy's lawyers. They could make only one phone call—and they couldn't make a mistake in deciding whom it would go to.

The two men turned to Mrs. Moskowitz, who had been sitting quietly in the corner, her head bent over her knitting. "August Heckscher," she said.

Smith was doubtful. He knew that Heckscher, a seventy-six-year-old multimillionaire philanthropist, was a recreation enthusiast who had already donated a playground to New York City. But a playground cost a few thousand dollars; what was required here was a quarter of a million. And Heckscher was an elf of a man—so short that when he sat on a chair his shoes dangled several inches above the floor—with a snow-white goatee, a snow-white fringe of hair around his bald pate, spectacles and a perpetual serene little smile. He would know that he would probably become involved in the lawsuit if he gave the money, and he hardly seemed the type of man who would voluntarily enter so savage a fight. But Mrs. Moskowitz, who had worked with Heckscher on various charities, thought he would, and she telephoned him. He agreed immediately. If it was true—as Moses' opponents were to charge—that the little millionaire demanded in return that the park be named after him, Moses must have considered this a cheap price to pay for the opportunity to be able to say in court that he had money to pay for what he had taken.*

Even with Heckscher's contribution, the court fight did not go well. Commenting that "it would be a pretty state of affairs if a state commission could go about seizing land with gifts provided by private individuals," Macy's attorney, Charles H. Tuttle, later a Republican candidate for Governor, said that if Moses used the money to reappropriate the land, he would be confessing that the first appropriation had been illegal—and Macy and his partners would be entitled to damages for that first appropriation. And the second appropriation would be as illegal as the first because, he said, state law required that the money for a land appropriation come from legislative segregation, not from some other source. Moses apparently feared Tuttle was right. Smith tried privately to persuade Macy to accept Heckscher's $250,000—plus another $12,000 the millionaire had donated to take care of accrued interest—for the first appropriation and drop the fight. Even when Macy indignantly refused, Moses apparently tried to avoid reappropriation: when the formal examination before trial began, the step had not yet been taken.

At times, Moses seemed almost desperate to avoid being put under oath. On the day he was scheduled to be examined, he didn't show up in court. Tuttle asked Justice Selah B. Strong to cite him for contempt, but Strong accepted a commission attorney's explanation that Moses had believed that arrangements had been made for him to be examined at his office.

And when Moses, ordered to appear, finally took the stand, he did not make an impressive witness. Testifying under oath, he swore that he had never been advised by anyone that the Taylor Estate appropriation would be illegal unless the Legislature segregated money for it. Had he not been advised precisely that several times, Tuttle demanded—orally and in a written memorandum—by Deputy State Attorney General Irving I. Goldsmith? No, Moses said. Tuttle thereupon produced the Goldsmith memorandum and waved it in front of Moses as he sat on the witness chair. Before the start of the actual trial, Moses, apparently forced into the act, took the step of reappropriation, and his attorneys began a new series of delaying actions in an attempt to stall the proceedings until January, when there would convene in Albany a new Legislature that just conceivably might give him the appropriation he needed. Assailing the commission's "dilatory tactics," Norman S. Dike, the latest in the relay of judges sitting on the case, said the trial would begin October 18 without fail. On October 18, he called the case—and Moses was not present. "I especially asked Mr. Moses to be here at the opening of

---

* Heckscher was the grandfather of the August Heckscher who was New York City Park Commissioner during the Lindsay administration.

this trial, and he might have had the courtesy to grant the court's request," Dike said from the bench. "It seems as if his absence, unaccounted for, shows a studied effort to affront the court." Tuttle asked that he be punished for contempt, but Dike accepted a commission attorney's explanation that he had advised Moses it would not be necessary for him to appear. The attorney then moved for a jury trial—and when Dike granted the motion, the start of the trial was delayed until December 6. On December 7, the commission attorneys filed more than six hundred pages of briefs asking for dismissal of the case—but Dike peremptorily denied the motion, and there was a note in his decision that the commission could only have considered ominous. As the *Times* reported: "In his decision yesterday [the] judge . . . ruled that the Commission had not had appropriated at the time the Taylor Estate was seized, the funds necessary."

There were ominous developments on another front, too. Jones Beach was owned by the townships of Hempstead, Oyster Bay and Babylon, and while the Long Island State Park Commission could buy, condemn or appropriate land owned by private individuals, state law provided that property owned by a township could be transferred to other ownership only by a vote of the township's residents.

Moses had decided to try Babylon, where he spent his summers, first. On July 18, 1924, he had appeared in the red-brick Babylon Town Hall and asked the Town Board to hold a referendum.

The five board members just stared at him. They had been elected, placed in their seats at the board table, by the votes of the baymen, and they knew that one way to make sure they would not be re-elected would be to demonstrate anything less than complete vigilance over the priceless heritage of the sacred bay bottoms. The Babylon *Leader* reminded them that "Babylon wants this land which has been hers . . . for nearly a century and a half before the State came into existence to keep as a heritage for its children. . . . Keep it—it is a park at present—a natural park swept by breezes from the bay and ocean. Enjoy it as it is or improve it. But keep it—never surrender one inch." Let the commission spend its money elsewhere, its editorials advised Moses, "before it . . . attempts to snatch property that the residents of the Town of Babylon intend to keep for their children's children until the end of time." Within two months after Moses' request for a referendum, not only the Babylon Town Board but the governing board of every village on the South Shore of Suffolk County—as well as the villages' chambers of commerce, boards of trade and civic associations—were lined up against the proposal, and Judge James B. Cooper, editor and owner of the *Leader,* could proclaim with satisfaction that "the project at present has as much chance of carrying as a Great South Bay clam has of growing teeth." When Moses turned to Oyster Bay, furious Oyster Bay citizens formed a "Save Our Beaches" committee that within days had a membership of thousands. In desperation, Moses turned to Hempstead, although he knew that votes in Hempstead Town, as, indeed, in all of Nassau County, went whichever way the county's iron-fisted Republican boss, G. Wilbur Doughty, wanted, and he had been unable to convince Doughty to want Jones Beach development. Doughty allowed the proposition to be placed on the ballot in the November 1925 election, and the vote was 12,106 to 4,200 against it.

Forty years later, Robert Moses would remember how he had felt in 1925 when he heard the Hempstead referendum results. "It looked like we'd lost Jones Beach," he would recall. "It looked absolutely hopeless." More than with any other single project, his dreams had been tied up with Jones Beach. And so had his sense of urgency. He had been hearing with increasing frequency rumors that real estate developers were making deals with Doughty's machine to have the town turn over the land to them for private development. In his mind's eye, he could see those vast stretches of untouched sand covered with shabby bungalows. He knew there would never be another opportunity to create a great beach so close to New York City. "You know," he would recall, "if we lost Deer Range, it would have been bad, but it wouldn't have been the end of the world. But if we had lost Jones Beach . . ." His voice would trail off. And then, remembering, he would say, "And I thought we had lost it."

At the end of 1925, Robert Moses might well have thought he had lost his entire Long Island dream.

The fact that development of Jones Beach could not be begun without approving votes from three townships—and that the one township that had voted had disapproved by a three-to-one margin—was only part of the story.

Not only the options for beautiful Sunken Meadow and for the beach at Hampton Bays but those for the Southern State Parkway right-of-way for which he had drunk beer with farmers had lapsed for lack of money to honor them.

His negotiations with the North Shore barons for right-of-way for the Northern State Parkway had dragged to a complete halt. He had secured easements from New York City for its watershed properties, but he had no money to develop those properties as parks, and there was no money in sight to enable him to do so. There was no money in sight to develop any park on Long Island. The Legislature had refused to appropriate any in 1925, and there was no reason to believe that the Long Island barons would be any less secure in their control of the Legislature in 1926.

Al Smith's loyalty and August Heckscher's money had pulled him back from the edge of the precipice along which he had been tightrope-walking in the Taylor Estate affair, but he was shortly—all too shortly—to stand trial in the affair, and the outcome of the trial might well result in the loss to the state of that property, too. And even if Heckscher's gift let the state keep the Taylor Estate, there was no money in sight to legitimatize the appropriations at Montauk Point and Lloyd Neck.

The only concrete result of all the talk about parkways on Long Island had been an increase in the rate at which real estate promoters were littering the Island with their rows of houses. Every week that winter brought the announcement of another large tract of farmland bought by a developer who was planning to erect model homes on it in the spring.

It had been more than a year since Robert Moses had announced his revised and broadened park and parkway plan, a plan which had, after all, included parks and parkways not only on Long Island but throughout the rest of New York State, along the Niagara Frontier, in the Genesee Valley, in the farmland of the Taconic region, and among the peaks of the Alleghenies, Catskills and Adirondacks. Now, more than a year later, parks and parkways were still located nowhere but in the map of Moses' imagination. After all the talking, all the planning, all the fighting, they simply didn't exist. And at the end of 1925, there seemed little possibility that they would come into existence at any time in the foreseeable future. If one looked ahead a decade, even a generation, it seemed unlikely that any substantial part of the dream would be reality.

Within three years, almost all of it would be reality.

12. *Robert Moses and the Creature of the Machine*

THERE WERE MANY complex reasons for the realization of Robert Moses' state park and parkway plan. But the key reason was simple: the further evolution of Robert Moses.

The construction of parkways—like the construction of conventional highways—was a potential source of great wealth to politicians. Parkways meant construction contracts. Politicians who had a say in which firms received those contracts could expect financial remembrances from a successful firm, if indeed they—or a relative or a trusted associate known in political terminology as a "bag man"—did not actually own a piece of it. Parkways meant real estate transactions, generally either purchase or condemnation, both methods under which landowners could expect to do well financially; state public works officials, anxious to begin construction and not too concerned about price because the money they were offering was not their own, were traditionally more generous than private buyers. If politicians were the landowners—if they bought the land at pre-parkway prices, from owners who didn't know the parkway was coming, and then sold it to the state at right-of-way prices—they could expect a large profit. It took longer to get one's money through condemnation, but the rewards could be even greater; the success of politically well-connected attorneys in winning high condemnation awards from Court of Claims judges who also had risen through the ranks of political machines was an open secret in legal circles in New York State during the 1920's—as it would be in the 1960's. And parkways meant development: sleepy countrysides long static because of their inaccessibility suddenly became desirable locations for factories and housing developments when a parkway brought them close to a city or large town. Land in these areas became suddenly valuable. Land near the parkway's exits, automatic focal points for development, became particularly valuable. The politician who bought this land at pre-parkway prices and sold it as or after the parkway was being built could reap great profit, and the politician who bought the land but instead of selling it developed it himself, building himself the houses and factories, could reap a fortune. Moreover, in terms of development, the impact of a parkway spread in ever-widening ripples: stores and laundries and gas stations and insurance brokerage firms for the residents of the houses, subcontractors and material-supply houses for the factories. This meant a burgeoning in land sales, insurance premiums, legal fees—in all the areas in which politicians grow fat. It meant as well an intangible, but intense, additional attraction for politicians: in a dormant area, opportunities were limited because everything was cut and dried, prices for land, for instance, being well known and firmly established; in an area opened by a road, everything was changing almost on a day-to-day basis; opportunities were wide open.

To take advantage of the financial opportunities provided by a parkway, a politician had to have foreknowledge. If he wanted to be first on line with his recommendations for construction contract awards, he had to know that the highway was going to be built. If he wanted to buy land that was to be acquired for the highway's right-of-way or land strategically near the highway, he had to know where the highway was going to be built, not its general location but its precise route, so that he could buy the exact lots that would be acquired, and he had to know before the owners knew so that, not knowing that their land might be valuable, they would sell cheap. And politicians had a weapon they could use in obtaining such advance information; if they did not get it, they would not approve the building of the highway.

The young Robert Moses, the idealist of Yale and Oxford and the Municipal Civil Service Commission, would not have even considered trading contracts or information for approval. Even the older Robert Moses of the New York State Association, a Moses more admiring of the ways of politicians, would not have done it; that Moses could in 1922 still reserve his bitterest *State Bulletin* sallies for the Nassau County Republican machine because of its link with "political contractors." Even the Moses of 1924, doffing his principles to lighten himself for the pursuit of his greatest dream, wouldn't do it. No sooner had he announced his park plan in 1924 than intimates of the Governor wrote him asking for advance information on parkway location; Moses indignantly refused to give it to them. Senate Finance Committee Chairman Charles J. Hewitt offered to sell the State Parks Council a tract of land he owned in Fair Haven; despite Hewitt's importance to his dream, Moses refused to buy.

Moses apparently took the same attitude in his 1925 attempt to persuade Hempstead Township to cede him its portion of Jones Beach. Hempstead was controlled by Nassau County GOP leader G. Wilbur Doughty. "Today they talk about political bosses," Leonard W. Hall, former national chairman of the Republican Party, would say in the 1960's. "They don't know what a real boss was. Doughty was a real boss. When he spoke, the discussion was over. He always kept his word; he was known for that. But cross him and you were finished. There's no one like him today. We used to call him the Last of the Mohicans." A square-faced man with a walrus mustache, Doughty had an almost visionary concept that rural Long Island would one day be a heavily populated suburban area and was always interested in suggestions for public works that could help open the Island to development. But his vision was heavily mortgaged to practicality: he ran one of the most corrupt political machines in the state—"In Nassau County," one observer said, "zoning was bought and sold like potatoes"—and much of the corruption revolved around public works. Doughty's brother-in-law, "Uncle Andy" Weston, was president of Booth & Weston, the largest contracting firm in the county, and Booth & Weston, along with Hendrickson Bros., Inc., another firm with which Doughty had close ties, were habitually given the lion's share of county contracts. And since many GOP county committeemen happened to be on the payroll of the two construction firms, the firms helped Doughty keep them in line. The link between Nassau politicians and contractors had come close to surfacing in 1922; in that year, a Supreme Court Justice had impaneled a grand jury to investigate it and the investigation had already turned up a loan from Booth & Weston to Assemblyman Thomas A. McWhinney before McWhinney persuaded the Legislature to pass a bill establishing a commission to investigate the judge, a move that effectively stymied the grand jury. Moses had followed the case closely in his *State Bulletin*; calling the bill "legislative brigandry," he had nominated it for his "Worst Bill of the Session" award and had castigated the Nassau GOP machine and McWhinney, whom he termed "the creature of the machine." Moses must have known what it took to get things done in Nassau County, but he apparently wasn't willing to do them; the best proof of that was, perhaps, the defeat of his Jones Beach referendum.

But in late 1925, the dream all but dead, Moses held a series of private meetings with Doughty. There is, of course, no record of what transpired at these meetings, and no proof that any deal was entered into. But certain developments ensued:

• Moses announced that future planning for Jones Beach would be conducted in conjunction with a delegation from Hempstead Township, which would, of course, have access to commission plans showing the precise location of the proposed Meadowbrook Causeway to Jones Beach, and the chairman of the Hempstead delegation turned out to be Assemblyman Thomas A. McWhinney. And Moses was soon meeting regularly with "the creature of the machine" on an extremely friendly basis.

• Within two months after Moses and McWhinney began meeting, a lawyer who was a member of the Nassau GOP's inner circle formed a corporation with a group of associates. The only business the corporation ever transacted was the purchase and sale of land, and the only land it ever purchased and sold was 265 acres of undeveloped, all but worthless meadow and swamp land, 99.5 acres of which would become the right-of-way for the Meadowbrook Causeway, the remaining 165.5 acres of which would, when the causeway had been completed and the land's value enhanced, be sold by the corporation to private developers.

• When the contracts for the causeway, and for other Park Commission projects on Long Island, were awarded, a substantial number went to Uncle Andy Weston and Hendrickson Bros., Inc.

• And the Last of the Mohicans abruptly left the tepee of the commission's opponents and smoked the peace pipe with Robert Moses, supporting every one of Moses' Long Island proposals.

* * *

Doughty's friendship was to give Moses his first real hold on Jones Beach. After the meetings between the two men, the Republican boss told Moses to resubmit, with some minor revisions, the proposal so soundly defeated in the November 1925 referendum. Moses did so in November 1926, and the three-to-one margin against the proposal magically became a three-to-one margin in favor, Hempstead Town voting, 18,872 to 5,076, to cede to the Long Island Park Commission "all right, title, interest and jurisdiction . . . to all that certain town land . . . commonly known as Jones Beach."

More immediately, the friendship altered the balance of power in the over-all state park fight. On December 21, 1925, ten days after Moses agreed to cooperate with McWhinney and the Hempstead Town delegation, the Suffolk County Board of Supervisors passed a resolution asking the Legislature to abolish the Long Island Park Commission. They sent it to the Nassau Board of Supervisors, expecting that body to concur in the request, as it had the year before. To the shock of the Suffolk officials, Nassau declined to do so. The two counties in which the Park Commission was operating were no longer united in opposing it.

The GOP front in Albany was no longer solid, either, because of the votes Doughty controlled in the Senate and Assembly.

Republican ranks were already under severe pressure over parks. In New York City, Al Smith, taking command of Tammany Hall in fact if not in title after Charlie Murphy's death, had snatched the Democratic mayoral nomination away from Red Mike Hylan and handed it to Jimmy Walker, and Walker, at his inauguration on January 1, 1926, had announced support of the vast program of city park-land acquisitions prepared by the city's Park Association with Moses' help. There would be a referendum in November to authorize the necessary bonds, and women's clubs and a reformers' Committee of One Thousand had already launched a mammoth public education campaign. All in all, 1926 was not the year to be opposing parks.

Upstate Republican legislators might be insulated in their rotten boroughs, but it wasn't only legislators whose names would be on the ballot in 1926. Al Smith would be campaigning for re-election, and Republican strategists were determined to knock him out of the Governorship. They had already persuaded the man they regarded as *their* strongest candidate, Ogden Livingston Mills, to leave Congress and run against him. And there was a United States Senate seat up for grabs, too, and the present occupant of the seat was James J. Wadsworth himself, the former Assembly Speaker and one of the state's most powerful Republicans.

No sooner had the Legislature convened, therefore, than Wadsworth summoned the legislative leaders to an Albany hotel suite and told them a compromise on the park fight was in order. The compromise could not be over the Northern State Parkway, he said; the interests of too many of their friends were involved there. But the Taylor Estate was a different story;

Havemeyer, the only Timber Pointer with real influence, didn't seem really interested; Macy did—but Macy had little influence of his own. The Taylor Estate, the Republican leaders agreed, could be sacrificed.

Smith, with his park plans stalled and the threat of the potentially embarrassing Taylor Estate court fight hanging over him in an election year, was not averse to a compromise. In a secret meeting with Hewitt and Hutchinson, the Governor agreed that he would not ask for funds to acquire right-of-way for the Northern State Parkway until Moses came up with a route acceptable to the barons, and he agreed that, even after the right-of-way had been acquired, he would not ask for funds to begin construction until the Southern State Parkway had reached the point at which it would connect with the Jones Beach causeway, a point about fifteen miles into Nassau County. In return, Hewitt and Hutchinson agreed that the Southern State Parkway could be built and that the entire $15,000,000 proceeds of the park referendum would be segregated in 1926; work could therefore begin immediately on Moses' upstate park program and his Long Island projects, including Jones Beach, the causeway leading to it from the Southern State Parkway—and Deer Range (soon to be August Heckscher) State Park.

Since the 1925 Taylor Estate fight had revolved around the question of whether an outside agency, the Republican-controlled State Land Board, should have authority over the State Parks Council, a face-saving device had to be worked out on that point so that it would appear that neither side had surrendered. On January 26, 1926, Smith and the GOP legislative leaders announced that they had agreed that expenditures of the $15,000,000 would be supervised, as the GOP had insisted—but, as Smith had insisted, not by the Land Board. Instead, it was announced, expenditures would be supervised by a committee of three: Smith, Hewitt and Hutchinson.

Macy got his first hint of what was happening when he learned that the segregations of the $15,000,000 included an item of $25,000 for "Deer Range Park, permanent improvement of buildings," and $170,000 to begin the purchase of right-of-way for the Southern State Parkway, that strip of concrete Macy had always been afraid would reach out toward East Islip. Rushing to Albany, he confronted Hutchinson, and the assemblyman answered his questions evasively. The amateur in politics realized that the professionals had betrayed him.

Hewitt and Hutchinson had been pleased with the compromise with Smith. By postponing work on the Northern State Parkway until fifteen miles of the Southern State were built, they thought they were consigning the former road to some far-distant limbo; construction of the fifteen-mile-long Bronx River Parkway, after all, had taken fourteen years. And since they could outvote Smith two to one on the committee set up to supervise park expenditures, they assumed they could keep the pace of construction on the Southern State slow.

Economy, moreover, was as important to them as delay; their upstate conservatism had been affronted by the thought of spending even a million dollars on parks and parkways in a single section of the state; they could see that the actual amount involved would eventually be far higher than the million, but they wanted to keep it down to the bare minimum that they felt was all the state could afford.

But no sooner had they given Moses $170,000 for Southern State right-of-way, confident that that amount would allow him to purchase no more than a mile or two, than the Nassau County Board of Supervisors, now suddenly, and mysteriously, enthusiastic over Moses' projects, purchased additional miles and presented them to the Long Island Park Commission as a gift. Playing on the greed of real estate developers who owned land in the parkway's path, Moses persuaded them to donate right-of-way so that the rest of their property could be opened to development. Suddenly awakened to the fact that the New York City watershed property could be used as right-of-way, Hewitt and Hutchinson realized with a shock that the land for the Southern State was almost all in Moses' hands—all the way out to that magic point where it would trigger the start of work on the Northern State.

Although no funds had been appropriated for surveying and engineering, there were suddenly surveyors and engineers out on the right-of-way, men furnished by the State Department of Public Works—whose Long Island office just happened to be located at the former August Belmont Estate near Babylon that Moses had acquired and turned into a state park, making the old Belmont Mansion his headquarters. And these men, they were told, were drawing up plans with unprecedented speed. Even as they digested this news, a bill was introduced in the Legislature providing for a million dollars for "the construction, reconstruction and widening of highway routes in Nassau and Erie Counties"—including $350,000 for "construction of the Southern State Parkway." They had no trouble understanding why Erie, a Republican stronghold, had been given even more money than Nassau in the bill—Erie's legislators would be even more determined than Nassau's that the bill should pass, and an alliance of the GOP legislators from these two counties with the Democrats would make it impossible for Hewitt and Hutchinson to prevent its passage.

The parks on Long Island were also being developed at a rate they could hardly believe, since they had kept appropriations for such development small. When they checked, they found that park roads were being constructed by DPW crews and park buildings refurbished by Conservation Department crews.

They took a look at the bills Trubee Davison had introduced for Moses in 1924 and found in them a specific provision stating that while the Long Island Park Commission would have final say on the design of parkways—as well as full control of them when completed—their physical construction could be financed out of DPW allocations. They found that the landscaping was being financed out of "routine" 1926 Conservation Department requests for "tree nurseries." The Lloyd Neck lighthouse property was being developed with a Conservation Department appropriation for "oyster culture." When they waxed indignant, they were told blandly that the lighthouse property could certainly be used for oyster culture. There was nothing the slightest bit illegal about anything Moses was doing. The best bill drafter in Albany, they realized, had been at work again.

And when they protested to the Governor, he bourbon-coated the pill he was making them swallow. Inviting them to see for themselves what Moses was doing, he suggested they come to New York City first, sleep over at the Biltmore and then go on to Long Island in the morning. At the Biltmore, as Moses would later recall, "the Governor got Hewitt and Hutchinson to stay overnight in his apartment. They were drinking bozos, you know, and they were really putting it away. As the evening wore on, the Governor put some records on and he was teaching these two fellows to dance. I left at 2 A.M. [Henry] Lutz [a Moses aide] stayed until five and he told me that it was about then that the Governor and he and Hewitt put Hutchinson to bed. Hewitt got up at seven the next morning and ordered a big breakfast for himself and the Governor and they went in to ask Hutchinson what he wanted and Hutchinson sort of groaned, lying there in bed, and said, 'Governor, go away. The stomach revolts at the thought of food.' " During the tour, Smith was at his friendliest. "You see," Moses would say, "in so many cases, things come down to personalities, to the human factor. And they loved the Governor." And even if they hadn't, what, after all, could they do? The Highway and Conservation Department budgets had already been approved. Money was being spent under them. If they tried to reopen the budgets, it would be a mess. And what would the press say? After all, there was the election coming. They decided not to interfere with the program.

The court fight still loomed ahead of Moses, but Smith was able to help him with that, too.

During 1926, Moses continued his technique of stalling the trial while talking as though there were not the slightest doubt about its outcome. In an article he wrote in May outlining the over-all progress of the state park plan, he said blandly, "The state has acquired Deer Range Park." All through May, Moses' attorneys continued filing motions and, when judges overruled the motions, appealing their decisions to higher courts, and when the higher courts threw out the appeals, taking them to still higher courts. Three separate dates were set for trial—and on each of them appeals were still pending and judges had to grant the commission postponements. All through May, Moses' laborers were converting the ballroom of the old Taylor mansion into a cafeteria, the sitting room into a comfort station, setting up tents on the beach to serve as bathhouses and hacking rough roads through the woods so that motorists could reach them. By mid-May, "Deer Range State Park" was opened to the public.

On May 25, State Supreme Court Justice Selah B. Strong received word from Albany that the state's highest court, the Court of Appeals, had thrown out the last of Moses' appeals, in a decision which supported every one of Macy's contentions, even to the point of saying that if the commission's right to peremptory appropriation was upheld, "the conclusion logically follows that it has a charter wide as the wind, withal, and might seize for park purposes all the lands in Nassau and Suffolk counties." Scheduling the trial for June 4, Justice Strong told Walter H. Pollack, who was heading the team of five attorneys handling the case for the commission, that he would not postpone it again for any reason.

On June 4, Pollack was not in court. One of his four colleagues told Strong—falsely—that Pollack was occupied in another courtroom. Strong said the trial was going on anyway. "We will not participate," Pollack's colleague said—and all four commission attorneys walked out of the courtroom, leaving the commission without counsel.

Strong adjourned the trial for a day to give Pollack a chance to appear. On the next day, Pollack and his colleagues were again absent. Strong adjourned it again—and again no attorneys appeared. On the fourth day, the judge allowed a jury to be chosen and told Macy's attorney, Charles H. Tuttle, to present his case. The jury found that both appropriations of the Taylor Estate had been illegal, the first because the commission did not possess $250,000, the second because while it had the money, the money came from a private gift instead of from a legislative segregation, the only legal source of funds for a peremptory appropriation. The jury assessed each of the three commissioners—Robert Moses, Townsend Scudder and Clifford Jackson—$22,000 apiece in punitive damages. Strong "perpetually enjoined" the commission from entering the Taylor Estate and ordered the state troopers removed forthwith. Watching the judge sign the injunction and hand it to the Suffolk County sheriff, watching the sheriff leave the courtroom to serve the injunction on the troopers, Macy thought he had won at last. Declared Tuttle: "The vindication is now complete."

Bella and Emanuel Moses were at their summer lodge at Camp Madison. Every morning a Madison House social worker delivered a *New York Times* to their door. When he handed it to them on the morning after the verdict, and they leafed through it—all the trial stories were on the inside pages now—and learned of the $22,000 judgment against their son, they groaned, and Bella Moses said, "Oh, he never earned a dollar in his life and now we'll have to pay this." The social worker recalls: "It was just assumed that they would pay it. They always paid all his debts."

The day after the verdict, Pollack, suddenly free of other court engagements, appealed on the grounds that the Long Island State Park Commission had not been represented by counsel. A Brooklyn Supreme Court Justice denied the appeal, calling the lack of representation a "deliberate and intentional" attempt to delay the proceedings. But the Appellate Division agreed to hear the appeal—at its fall term—and invalidated Strong's injunction until then. The troopers returned to the property and, during the summer, Moses took reporters on trips to "Deer Range Park," and the reporters rhapsodized about the families enjoying its facilities. In the fall, the Appellate Division upheld Pollack's appeal and ordered a new trial. And this trial, which was to be the closest thing to a legal showdown that was to occur in the case, was to contain a new factor: Al Smith's appearance as a witness for Moses.

Smith's appearance marked the "first time in a generation, probably longer, that a chief executive of the state has appeared in court in the role of a witness." Platoons of reporters followed the Governor as he, Moses and Mrs. Moskowitz boarded a Long Island Rail Road train for the three-hour trip to Riverhead. At the station, he was met by an American Legion band which played "The Sidewalks of New York" as it accompanied him to the courthouse. There, he was escorted to the chambers of Justice James A. Dunne. The Governor talked with Dunne in private and then the judge escorted him into the courtroom so that he could give his testimony—he was on the stand for only fifteen minutes, spent most of the time recounting the Biltmore hearing and was not cross-examined—and as soon as he stepped off the stand, the judge adjourned court. The Governor joined him in his chambers for lunch.

In the newspapers, Smith's appearance dwarfed the legal issues involved in the trial. Whether it had the same effect in the mind of Justice Dunne is unknown, which is unfortunate because the judge, not the jury, decided the case, and his directions to the jury, which precluded it from making a decision on the essential point at issue, were rather sharply at variance with those of the many other judges who had been involved with the case.

Dunne directed the jury to find that the first appropriation of the Taylor Estate had been illegal but that the second had been legal and the property therefore now belonged to the Long Island Park Commission. The only function of the jury, he told it, was to decide whether Pauchogue had suffered substantial financial damages as a result of the first seizure. If it had not, he said, the jury should fix the damages against the commission at six cents. The jury did so. Macy was to believe until he died that Smith's entrance in the case had played a role in the judge's removal from the jury's hands of the right to make a decision on the key point in the case: the legality of the second appropriation. "The Governor came down and took the judge out to lunch—what chance did we have?" he was to say.

Whether Dunne's decision would have remained the binding legal word in the case if both sides had continued the legal battle on equal terms, if both sides had continued to make use of all their remedies at law—if the Pauchogue Corporation had been able to press through higher courts *its* appeals as the Long Island Park Commission had been able to press *its* appeals—is impossible to determine. For both sides weren't equal.

Lawsuits take money. The state's supply of this commodity is comparatively bottomless. The private citizen's is not. And now W. Kingsland Macy was running out of money.

Macy himself was not wealthy. Havemeyer was, but, saying "This . . .

should be considered a business affair," he had told Macy he would have to pay all legal expenses over $25,000.

At the time, Macy had thought that $25,000 would be ample. But as the commission's lawyers began to pile appeal on top of appeal, he wrote Havemeyer that, to a layman, "the ramifications of this litigation are almost beyond belief." And ramifications meant money. If Moses' lawyers were constantly filing new briefs, Macy's had to file briefs in reply. The briefs had to be printed in standard legal form, and they were running into thousands of pages. The printing bill for a single appeal ran to $3,652.63. The stenographic transcript for a single appeal cost $545. And finally, of course, there were the lawyers' fees. Lawyers like Tuttle and the experts required to handle appeals didn't come cheap. The first bill for "services rendered" was delivered to Macy on April 28, 1925. It was for $10,000. Even before the trial in Dunne's court began, the $25,000 mark had been reached. To Macy, the idealist, the case represented something that was more important than money. When Havemeyer wrote, "This . . . is my limit," Macy replied that he would carry on alone. Appeals attorneys told him that if he was willing to press the fight vigorously, he would probably win, although the victory might not come until the case had been transferred out of the state courts and into the United States Supreme Court, which would focus on the basic constitutionality of the use by a state agency of one individual's money to seize the property of another. Macy authorized them to proceed. But Moses' attorneys continued to make motions and file briefs, and when Macy's appeal from Dunne's decision finally reached the Appellate Division in February 1928, his legal costs had mounted to $43,192.61—a burden beyond his financial resources. By April 1928, his attorneys were dunning him for payment of a $1,100 bill. Although the case would eventually be brought before the Court of Appeals, which upheld Dunne's decision, and an attempt was made to bring it to the United States Supreme Court—Justice Louis Brandeis brought the legal fight to an end on January 21, 1929, four years after the Biltmore hearing, by refusing to issue a writ of certiorari which would have enabled the Court to hear the case—it was obviously not pressed vigorously in these last stages, as though the case were really over already.

And, in fact, it was. Moses had never stopped developing the Taylor Estate—as if its acquisition were a *fait accompli*. By the spring of 1927, he had laid concrete for access roads and parking fields, set out scores of stone fireplaces and picnic tables, erected wooden bathhouses with showers and lockers and finished renovating the mansion and outbuildings, at a total cost of hundreds of thousands of dollars. During the summer of 1927, it had hundreds of thousands of visitors. By the time the higher courts came to rule on the question of whether the Taylor Estate was a park, it *was* a park. What was a judge to do? Tell the state to tear up the roads and tear down the buildings, to destroy what hundreds of thousands of dollars of the public's money had been spent to build? Tell the people who had visited the Taylor Estate that they could visit it no more? In theory, of course, judges should not be influenced by such considerations. But judges are human. And their susceptibility to such considerations was undoubtedly increased by Moses' willingness to attack publicly those of them who ruled against him, as he had done to the "local judge," thereby letting the public know exactly who it was who was closing the park to them.

The final hearing before the State Court of Appeals was the twenty-fifth separate appellate proceeding in the Taylor Estate case. The case was, the *Herald Tribune* said, "a landmark in eminent domain."

It was also a landmark in the lifescapes of two men. W. Kingsland Macy, who had possessed before it a vague desire to enter politics, had been precipitated by it into the political arena—and had found he enjoyed fighting there. And Macy had learned in his first bout many tricks. After fighting Robert Moses, he was to say, fighting anyone else was easy. Becoming active in 1927 in the Suffolk County Republican organization, within a year he threw out its leader and seized his place. When the Depression loosened for a moment the barons' stronghold on the state's GOP organization, Macy tore it from their grasp and by 1932 was Republican State Chairman. Although the GOP's Old Guard later re-formed and ousted him from the chairmanship, he was to rule Suffolk County, unchallenged, for more than thirty years. When there came a time when it would be useful to him to be in the State Senate, he sent himself to the State Senate; when he wanted to go to Congress, he sent himself to Congress. Macy's views were liberal, and he introduced progressive governmental innovations in Suffolk County, but to achieve his aims he ruled the county as an old-time political satrapy. Ruthless and cunning, he seemed to know every trick of bending men to his will, and he bent them so successfully that Kingsland Macy was called "the Little King of Suffolk County."

And when, after Macy had fought his way to power, Robert Moses, needing his help, made overtures of friendship, Macy accepted them. Although the strength of their personalities often made them clash, the two one-time "amateurs in politics" were for more than thirty years the closest of political allies, allies so close, in fact, that when, in 1962, cancer-ravaged King Macy knew he was about to die, Moses was the only person outside his immediate family whom he wanted to see.

Robert Moses had also learned from the Taylor Estate fight, his first use of power, lessons that would govern his behavior for the rest of his life.

One, hammered home in his consciousness by the results of his accommodation with G. Wilbur Doughty, was that the simplest method of accomplishing his aims was to use the power he possessed in all its manifestations, even those that as recently as a year previously he had shrunk from using. So thoroughly did he embrace this lesson—and the "creature of the machine" that was its embodiment—that when, in 1927, a vacancy occurred on the Long Island Park Commission, he had Smith appoint McWhinney to it.

The simplicity—combined with the feeling of accomplishment—might well have made Moses ask himself if it really made any difference whether he worked with Tom McWhinney. What difference did it make if the state purchased the right-of-way for the Meadowbrook Causeway from a bunch of farmers or from a bunch of Republican insiders? What difference did it make if he gave a road-building contract to Uncle Andy Weston? What difference did it make to the public—and what difference did it make to him? What did he care if Doughty's friends made money from his dreams? If they did, he had learned, the dream would become reality. If they did not, he had learned, it wouldn't. And the dream was the important thing; the dream was what mattered.

This lesson Robert Moses translated into phrases that began to appear in his letters and, according to associates, his conversation after the Taylor Estate fight: "*The important thing is to get things done.*" "*You can't make an omelet without breaking eggs.*" "*If the end doesn't justify the means, what does?*"

Another lesson Moses learned was that, in the eyes of the public, the end, if not justifying the means, at least made them unimportant. Al Smith had succeeded in blurring in the public's mind the legal technicalities of the fight—by focusing the public's mind on the end of the fight: parks.

The value of parks as an issue was another lesson. As long as you were fighting for parks, you could hardly help being a hero. When the Taylor fight started, he himself had been all but unknown. During the fight, he had been portrayed in a hundred front-page stories and a hundred editorials as a hero, as a man "acting in the interest of the people at large and of all future generations."

This lesson Robert Moses would often recite to associates. He would put it this way: As long as you're fighting for parks, you can be sure of having public opinion on your side. And as long as you have public opinion on your side, you're safe. "*As long as you're on the side of parks, you're on the side of the angels. You can't lose.*"

There were other lessons, too. Whatever the motivation that had impelled him to take the risk of starting to transform the Taylor Estate into a park while the courts had still seemed likely to rule that it was not a park—a fearless determination to do what he knew was right regardless of the consequences, a blind faith in Smith's ability to rescue him from consequences, a desperation to see at last the beginning of the realization of at least one of his dreams, or, perhaps, an insight, the insight of a political genius, that physical development would help rather than hurt his cause—the risk had been magnificently justified. And he had understood the significance of that justification. Once you did something physically, it was very hard for even a judge to undo it. If judges, who had to submit themselves to the decision of the electorate only infrequently, were thus hogtied by the physical beginning of a project, how much more so would be public officials who had to stand for re-election year by year? If he had needed a gift from August Heckscher to make victory certain, what did that prove? Only that once you physically began a project, there would always be some way found of obtaining the money to complete it. "*Once you sink that first stake,*" he would often say, "*they'll never make you pull it up.*"

These lessons had other implications. If ends justified means, and if the important thing in building a project was to get it started, then any means that got it started were justified. Furnishing misleading information about it was justified; so was underestimating its costs.

Misleading and underestimating, in fact, might be the only way to get a project started. Since his projects were unprecedentedly vast, one of the biggest difficulties in getting them started was the fear of public officials—not only upstate conservatives but liberal public officials as well—concerned with the over-all functioning of the state that the state couldn't afford the projects, that the projects, beneficial though they might be, would drain off a share of the state's wealth incommensurate with their benefits.

But what if you didn't tell the officials how much the projects would cost? What if you let the legislators know about only a fraction of what you knew would be the projects' ultimate expense?

Once they had authorized that small initial expenditure and you had spent it, they would not be able to avoid giving you the rest when you asked for it. How could they? If they refused to give you the rest of the money, what they had given you would be wasted, and that would make them look bad in the eyes of the public. And if they said you had misled them, well, they were not supposed to be misled. If they had been misled, that would mean that they hadn't investigated the projects thoroughly, and had therefore been derelict in their own duty. The possibilities for a polite but effective form of political blackmail were endless. Once a Legislature gave you money to start a project, it would be virtually forced to give you the money to finish it. The stakes you drove should be thin-pointed—wedge-shaped, in fact—on the end. Once you got the end of the wedge for a project into the public treasury, it would be easy to hammer in the rest.

Another lesson Moses learned from his first use of power was the latitude given him by its possession.

In the Taylor Estate fight, Moses had broken the law. On this point there had been no judicial disagreement; no court had ruled that his first appropriation of the estate was legal; every court that had ruled on it had ruled it illegal.

But what had happened to him as a result? He had been fined six cents—two cents, actually, if he wanted to insist that the other two Long Island park commissioners pay their share of the fine.

Part of the reason was the Heckscher gift, of course. But a more basic one was that power—specifically, the power that came with the money he could dispose of as a state official—insulated him from the law's retribution. He had been able to employ lawyers numerous enough and clever enough to utilize the technicalities of the law to frustrate the intent of the law, to throw enough sand into the machinery of justice to slow its gears sufficiently so that they could not mesh and produce the conclusion which its spirit demanded. Even an opponent as determined as W. Kingsland Macy—and as well equipped with money as Macy was—had had to abandon his search for ultimate justice. Justice delayed, the Taylor Estate case proved, was truly justice denied. And, Moses must have realized (for he demonstrated the realization in subsequent actions), as long as he had public power, as long as he was representing the state, he would have the means of employing as many lawyers as he needed, of delaying, and thereby denying, justice to his opponents, of shielding himself from its punishments. If there was one law for the poor, who have neither money nor influence, and another law for the rich, who have both, there is still a third law for the public official with real power, who has more of both. After the Taylor Estate fight, Robert Moses must have known—he proved it by his actions—that he could, with far more impunity than any private citizen, defy the law. He gloried in the knowledge; he boasted and bragged about it. For the rest of his life, when a friend, an enemy—or one of his own lawyers—would protest that something he was doing or was proposing to do was illegal, Moses would throw back his head and say, with a broad grin, a touch of exaggeration and much more than a touch of bravado: *"Nothing I have ever done has been tinged with legality."*

There was one more lesson. It was one he had started learning years before, and now it had finally sunk in. Would dreams—dreams of real size and significance and scope—the accomplishment his mother had taught him was so important, ever be realized by the methods of the men in whose ranks he had once marched, the reformers and idealists? He asked the question of himself and he answered it himself. No. The method he had adopted to turn his Long Island dream into reality was the way to accomplish something. It was the way to get things done. It was, he concluded, the only way.

One million dollars was the amount available to Long Island out of the $15,000,000. He had told the Legislature that one million would be the cost of the Long Island program. He knew that actually the million would pay for only a fraction—a small fraction—of the program. But he had learned how to get things done. With the million, he drove a lot of stakes.

Instead of spending the million to complete a few parks, he spent it to acquire the land for many—for Montauk Point State Park and Hither Hills State Park and Wildwood State Park and Sunken Meadow State Park and Belmont Lake State Park and Hempstead Lake State Park and Valley Stream State Park—and to at least begin development of all of them, as well as the Fire Island State Park and Jones Beach State Park he had previously acquired. By the end of 1926, the beaches of Long Island, once reserved for the rich, were dotted with wooden bathhouses open to all. Families who weren't interested in ocean swimming had to travel along Merrick Road only two miles beyond the city line before they came to the Valley Stream Park's wooded ninety-seven acres and calm blue lake, and in the woods hiking trails, picnic tables and fireplaces, and on the lake floats, diving boards, sliding ponds and rowboats were awaiting their use. By the end of 1926, moreover, the road was begun that would free city drivers from the tyranny of Merrick Road. By the time surveying of the route for the Southern State Parkway was completed, it was August. DPW engineers protested that it was too close to the cold, damp Long Island winter to begin construction, but there was plenty of time to drive stakes. To show the public quickly how beautiful his parkways would be, he decided that the first segment would be the 2.78-mile loop around the huge reservoir in Hempstead Lake State Park, the prettiest portion of the whole route.

On August 28, 1926, with only a handful of engineers and an uninterested construction gang as an audience, Robert Moses dug a spade into the soil near the reservoir and jerked it out. The earth that came up with it was the first ever turned for a Robert Moses road. His talk with Frances Perkins about the highway below Riverside Drive had taken place in 1914, a full twelve years before. He had been planning roads ever since. As he stood there still holding the shovel, a foreman gave a signal and laborers began to shovel dirt into the small, spoke-wheeled dump trucks that in the 1920's served as earth-moving machines. Robert Moses stepped back and watched the work begin.

Hutchinson and Hewitt were amazed and angry over Moses' progress in 1926. Counting the DPW and Conservation Department funds he had used, he had already spent on Long Island parks far more than the million dollars that was supposed to pay for the whole Long Island park *and parkway* system, and now he submitted park-improvement requests that totaled a million dollars more. And who knew what innocent-appearing items in 1927 DPW and Conservation Department budget requests concealed additional funds Smith was planning to make available to Moses? A wholly disproportionate share of the state budget was being spent on Long Island. In a private confrontation with Smith and Moses, they said that Moses' plans were too grandiose. Their cost was beyond the ability of the state to pay, they said, and parks were simply not needed on the scale he proposed.

The conflict came to a head over Jones Beach. In 1926, public bathing beaches in America fell into one of two classifications: ill-equipped huddles of shabby, unpainted wooden bathhouses that contained nothing but toilets, showers and lockers; or "boardwalk beaches" such as Coney Island and Atlantic City, which had surrendered the beauty of their seascapes to roller coasters, weight-guessing games, blaring funhouses, bawling barkers and other carnival concessions. But Robert Moses wasn't thinking of unpainted wood or carnivals.

One day, he invited to Jones Beach Gilmore Clarke, landscape architect of the Bronx River Parkway, Harvey W. Corbett, the architect responsible for the design of some of the Long Island barons' most beautiful manor houses, several other famous architects, landscape architects and engineers, and a handful of young commission staffers with whose work he had been impressed. As the little group of men stood on the vast, empty expanse of sand, Moses began pointing.

One bathhouse would be over there, he said, and the other over there. But then they would be almost a mile apart, the men with him pointed out. Yes, he said, and they should understand at once that he wasn't talking about ordinary bathhouses. These were going to contain ten thousand lockers apiece. In addition to bathrooms and shower rooms, they were going to contain wading pools, diving pools and swimming pools, and the swimming pools were going to be large enough to accommodate hundreds of bathers at a time. There were going to be canopied terraces above the pools so people could sit in the shade and watch the swimmers, and there were going to be other terraces on which people could dine at tables set beneath gaily colored umbrellas. The bathhouses were going to contain solaria. They were going to contain restaurants in every price range. Although they were at a bathing beach, they were going to be constructed not of wood but of stone and brick, and the stone and brick were going to be of the finest quality. They were going to be surrounded by landscaped lawns, hedges and flower beds. And he wanted the bathhouses designed with as much care as the finest public buildings in America. With this difference: most public buildings in America were too heavy and stodgy, designed only to impress and awe. The bathhouses would have to be quite large, of course, but they were buildings for people to have a good time in; the architecture must encourage people to have fun. It must be airy and light, gay and pleasant. There must be a thousand little touches to make people feel happy and relaxed. And he didn't want the bathhouses to spoil the panorama. Let them be designed to complement it, not dominate it. The panorama was long, low lines of sand and dunes and the sweep of the ocean. Let the lines of the bathhouses be long, low and sweeping, he said, horizontal rather than vertical. One other thing, he said. The bathhouses were going to have at least one innovation never included in any public or private building in America: diaper-changing rooms. He had designed them himself, he said. They would be divided into cubicles and each cubicle would contain only a diaper-disposal basket, a washbasin, a mirror and a shelf for a mother to lay her baby on. And the shelf shouldn't be table-height, he said. He had watched mothers changing diapers and higher shelves would make it easier.

Frances Perkins would have smiled.

Yanking an envelope from his pocket, Moses began to sketch on its back: Two X's to represent the bathhouses, lines to show how they would be connected on the beach side by a wide boardwalk, on the bay side by an "Ocean Parkway." Midway between the two X's, where the causeway from the mainland would join the parkway, he drew a large circle between two squares. The causeway would end in a circle, he said. People who didn't want to use the bathhouses could drive around it and into the squares, parking lots each large enough to hold ten thousand cars, and then walk with their families to the beach through underpasses under the parkway, or they could drive around the circle, stop on the beach side, drop their families off first, and then park in the lots and walk back to the beach to join them. Or, if they didn't want to go to the beach at all, they could simply keep driving on the parkway east or west. The families that got out at the circle would walk to the beach along a broad mall that ended at the boardwalk, and along the boardwalk would be open-air cafés serving inexpensive meals and a restaurant with cuisine, atmosphere and service equal to the finest in America. And stretching off to either side would be outdoor games: pitch-and-putt golf, table and paddle tennis, shuffleboard, roller-skating rinks, baseball fields set in little stadia. For the evenings, there would be bandstands and dancing under the stars. He sketched in restaurants, parking lots, playing fields and bandstands until there was no more room on the envelope.

One of the famous architects standing around Moses said, "Are you crazy?" The others knew what the architect meant. As one was later to put it: "It was the scale of the thing—nothing on a scale like this had ever been done in public recreation in America. Here we were on an absolutely deserted sand bar—there was no way even to get there but by boat—and here was this guy drawing X's on the back of an envelope and talking about bathhouses like palaces and parking lots that held ten thousand cars. Why, I don't think there was a parking lot for ten thousand cars anywhere in America. And landscaping? Landscaping on a sand bar? We weren't even sure anything would *grow* on a sand bar. We thought he was nuts."

The men gathered around Moses included some of the biggest names in American architecture, but they didn't think big enough for him. When they began drawing up tentative plans, the plans naturally included a water tower; fresh water had to be provided in great quantities in any large park, of course. But their water towers were conventional water towers: aluminum storage tanks set on four spindly uprights, they were exactly like the ones that, in other parks, were invariably the unsightliest feature of the landscape. Moses determined to turn the potentially ugliest part of the park he had planned into its most beautiful. He already knew that he wanted a focal point for the beach, a beautiful centerpiece big enough to be seen from miles away, that would be a symbol of Jones Beach, something that visitors could identify with—he was, after all, the son of the woman who had ordered the huge "Camp Madison" banner—and it might as well be the water tower. But he had a hard time getting the architects to think in his terms. "I was very anxious to have this water tower mean something architecturally," he recalls. "I got the top people out there and I asked them about it. The first suggestion came from our chief engineer and I said, 'That's the goddamnedest stupid thing I've ever heard.' And then someone suggested a lighthouse, and I said, 'No, goddammit, we're not going to have any lighthouse.' We already *had* a lighthouse, for God's sake." (He was referring to the Fire Island lighthouse, which was visible from the eastern end of Jones Beach.) On the next trip to the beach, Harvey Corbett suggested that the water tower be designed as an Italian campanile, or church bell tower. There were many different types, Corbett said, and started to reel them off. As he was reeling, he mentioned the one in Venice. Venice! "I like the one in Venice best," Moses said. According to one of the men there, "he pulled out another one of his envelopes and sketched the campanile in Venice right there—and that's how the water tower was done. And that's the way 'most everything was done. He had the architects and engineers there, but he was the architect and the engineer of Jones Beach. He's more responsible for the design of Jones Beach than any architect or engineer or all of us put together."

Finding the bathhouse designs submitted by the famous architects unimaginative, Moses selected those of an unknown young commission staffer, Herbert Magoon. Magoon had designed two vast pleasure palaces to sit upon the sand. One was a long, low, sweeping expanse of brick and stone and green-tinted glass. Its central portion—a terrace raised just five feet above the beach; behind the terrace, wide expanses of green-tinted glass separated by thin vertical stone columns that held another, set-back terrace surmounted by canopies, and behind that terrace a wall topped with flags—was set off from two wings of glass and brickwork by two simple, square, flat-topped medieval turrets. It was simple, almost austere, from a distance, but Magoon's detail drawings showed Moses that the turrets and walls had been cunningly worked with a thousand little devices of stone and brick. The other bathhouse was, if also of stone and brick, much gayer—Middle Eastern, in fact, almost Moorish. If the first bathhouse, despite its lack of height, resembled a medieval castle like those from which knights rode forth to join the Crusades, the second looked like one of the castles the knights saw when they reached the Holy Land. Each of its two towers, which seemed, at sixty feet, very tall against the dunes, was topped, in fact, with a green turret that swirled upward into a little spear point as did the helmets of the sultan's warriors the knights might have had to fight. Moses was ecstatic over the designs. He loved them, he said. But, the morning after he first saw them, he called in Magoon with endless lists of small changes he wanted to make.

Moses decided himself how he wanted the bathhouses faced. He was determined that the stone and brick of the façades would blend in perfectly with the beach on which they stood. One of the samples brought to him was obviously the perfect type of stone: Ohio sandstone was gray with just enough tinges of tan and blue to catch the colors of sand and sea. Selecting the brick was harder. Nothing seemed exactly right. Then, one day, passing the Barbizon Hotel on East Sixty-third Street, he noticed that it was faced with a random pattern of beige, brown and brownish-red that would catch the color of the sand and complement it. He decided that, to give the Jones Beach development unity, every structure of any size built there would be faced with Ohio sandstone and Barbizon brick.

The architects hastened to explain to him that Ohio sandstone and Barbizon brick were simply not used on public buildings. They were among the most expensive of all facing materials. Why, by using them on structures as large and elaborate as those he had in mind, each bathhouse would cost alone what Moses had originally said would be the cost of the entire Long Island park system: a million dollars.

Ohio sandstone and Barbizon brick it was going to be, Moses replied.

Hutchinson and Hewitt were "guys from the backwoods," recalls one who knew them. "When you said 'water tower' to them, that meant a tank on four skinny poles. A bathhouse was a little wooden thing you put up for fifty or a hundred bucks so the boys couldn't watch the girls undressing.

And here Moses comes along and tells them he wants to spend a million dollars on one." They flatly refused to give him anything like it. Only after Smith had pleaded with them for hours did they consent to appropriate a total of $150,000—for the water tower and both bathhouses.

Moses' architects expected him to tell them to scale down their plans.

"You just go right on the way you were doing," Moses told them. "You forget all about what the appropriation is. I'm *never* going to put up just a tank on poles."

He had already told Smith his plan. "I told him, 'We'll put all the money into the foundation for one bathhouse and then, when it gives out, we'll just go back and tell them they'll have to give us more or leave the foundation just sitting there with no building on top of it.' The Governor thought it was kind of a good joke."

The foundation laid, Moses invited Hewitt and Hutchinson down to see what he had done. To make matters stickier, blowing sand had completely buried the foundation the night before they arrived, and there was not a trace of it visible. All that existed, as far as the two legislators could see, was a god-forsaken sand bar that could be of no possible use to anyone—and the knowledge that, somewhere on it, *on their authorization*, had been spent $150,000 of the taxpayers' money.

They raged. They demanded that Smith fire Moses. In Moses' words, "They went to the Governor and said, 'Get rid of that son of a bitch and we'll go along with something reasonable.' "

But, in Moses' words, "The Governor never backed away from me." So Hutchinson and Hewitt said they would see that Moses was impeached. And they guaranteed the Governor that every appropriation for every park in the state would be cut off until this mess was cleaned up.

But Moses had applied his lessons well. When his antagonists began to think about the situation, they realized they were trapped. What, exactly, for all their power, could they do? Charge that he had misled them—thereby admitting that they hadn't investigated the project thoroughly enough in advance? Deny him further funds—thereby insuring that the $150,000 already spent would be utterly wasted?

And wasn't the overriding issue the same one—Parks vs. No Parks—with which Smith had destroyed them in 1925? Did they want to make him a hero again?

There was, really, very little they could do. Trying to salvage some revenge, they refused, in making the 1927 budget appropriations, to give Moses any money at all for the second bathhouse, for which the foundation had not been laid, and they saw to it that the additional funds they gave him for other Long Island park projects were far less than he wanted even to complete the buildings already begun. But such satisfactions were small ones. They knew that the difference needed to complete the projects to Moses' specifications could easily be made up by Smith out of the appropriations to other state departments.

13. Driving

DESPITE ITS OUTCOME, the battle over the bathhouses filled Moses with a sense less of triumph than of dread, of a need for haste so frantic that it was almost desperation. Time, he was afraid, was running out on his dream—and it was running out fast.

The battle had shown him how little chance he would have of completing his dream without the unflinching support of Alfred E. Smith in the Governor's chair. He knew that he could never hope to receive anything near the full amount he still needed from the Legislature, and the public itself might well waver in its support for his parks if it knew their full cost. He had Smith as Governor now. But he wasn't going to have him for long. Al Smith, he knew, was going to be a candidate for President in 1928, and that meant that he could not, under state law, be a candidate for Governor. On January 1, 1929, there was going to be a new Governor. He probably would be a Republican. Even if he were a Democrat, he would not be Al Smith. January 1, 1929, was less than two years away. And two years was far too short a time for completion of a dream that encompassed three long roads and a score of huge parks. His only hope, he knew, was to complete enough of the roads and parks before Smith left office so that the public could see how great they were going to be and would demand that they all be completed.

So Moses drove himself and he drove his men.

Turning the upstairs bedrooms of August Belmont's mansion into offices, Moses filled the offices with engineers and architects. He himself worked downstairs.

"Belmont had had this tremendous dining room, and there was this huge table there, and Moses made it his conference table," recalls William J. Junkamen, an attorney hired to assist commission counsel Raymond McNulty. "The conferences would start at nine o'clock in the morning and sometimes you couldn't leave until after midnight. And you just worked like hell all day long. Supper was a matter of dashing out and getting a bite to eat as quick as you could." Insisting that the engineers in charge of a project prepare a schedule showing the date on which each of its phases would be completed, Moses would move up the deadlines—by days, by weeks, sometimes by months—until the engineers felt it was absolutely impossible to meet them. And then he insisted that they be met. "The time was never long enough," Gilmore Clarke says. "But that was all the time you were going to get, and he let you know it." James J. Flynn, captain of the State Police troop assigned to the commission, recalls, "If he wanted a job done, he wanted it done. Period. And he wouldn't take any alibis if it wasn't done; he didn't want alibis, he used to say."

Moses knew exactly what he wanted each of his men to do, and he was impatient when they had difficulty grasping that fact. William H. Latham, a young engineer from the Massachusetts Institute of Technology, was also assigned to observe and report on meetings of the Nassau County Board of Supervisors. "I came back from the first meeting and in giving him my report, I generalized," Latham recalls. "He corrected me, but I guess I didn't get it, and the second time, I started to generalize again. Well, he didn't let me get very far. His palm came down on that table of Belmont's and he jumped up and he paced around that table and he told me he wanted facts, no assumptions. All he wanted from me was what had happened at that meeting. He'd draw his own conclusions. And he let me know right there and then that if I couldn't do it that way, he'd have to find another engineer."

And, Latham adds, Moses wasn't "really angry" at him on that occasion. Latham, an athlete and outdoorsman, is a tall, rangy man with huge shoulders and an easy, friendly grin. But the grin fades when he says, "I won't talk about what he's like when he's really angry."

Another technique was the silent treatment. "All of a sudden," a staffer recalls, "you just wouldn't be called in to sit at the conferences any more. He wouldn't talk to you if he passed you in the hall. And then, one day, you'd just be gone."

The men who stayed didn't resent Moses' methods. "If he drove other men hard," says Junkamen, "he drove himself harder."

He was supervising a dozen nonpark projects for Smith, of course, and he was constantly commuting to Albany, a four-hour train trip away. During legislative sessions, he tried to make his trips on Mondays because the Legislature convened each week on Monday evening and it was then that GOP strategy became apparent—and the Governor liked to have his advisers gathered in the Executive Chamber ready to counter it. So that he could get in a full day's work in Albany before the Executive Chamber session, Moses left his New York apartment at 6 A.M. to catch the early train to the capital and avoid a car trip made tortuous by the lack of a through road. When the session broke up, usually well after the last train back had left at midnight, Moses would ask Smith for the use of a state car and chauffeur. He had a lot of work to do back on Long Island, he'd say. If he drove back at once, he'd be able to start in the morning.

Albany wasn't the only duty that pulled Moses from Long Island. To supervise the State Council of Parks, he had to spend at least part of three days a week in New York City. To inspect the regional commissions' upstate projects, he was constantly being driven to or from Watkins Glen or Chittenango Falls or Letchworth Gorge.

But when his car pulled up in front of the Belmont Mansion, Moses never seemed tired. Charging into Arthur Howland's office, he would slam the door behind him and listen to the chief engineer's problems. Then, one by one, he would call in the other top commission officials and, behind the closed door, listen to theirs. Then the door would fly open and he would charge out into the dining room and sit down at the huge table and begin solving the problems. Junkamen recalls: "He might have been working in New York and not arrive out at Belmont until three o'clock in the afternoon, but then he would work from three until ten o'clock or midnight. Another day, I might get there at nine o'clock in the morning and he'd already be there working at the big table. Then I'd go out on some errand and wouldn't get back until supper time, and he'd still be sitting there. And he'd still be sitting there at midnight." Saturdays were no different. "Hours didn't mean anything to him," Latham says. "Days of the week didn't mean anything to him. You worked when there was work to be done, that was all." And there was always work to be done. Since none of the staffers dared leave the mansion until Moses left, they longed for him to get a telephone call from Mary, which usually got him away from the big table and back to his house in Babylon. "Sometimes," Junkamen recalls, "Ray McNulty would slip out and call her and put her up to calling." One Saturday night, repeated telephone calls from Mary failed to bring Bob home, and at ten o'clock she showed up at the mansion. Striding into the conference room, she "just took him by the ear in a very nice but firm way" and pulled him to his feet, Junkamen recalls. "He just laughed and went along—and then we could all go home."

Going home did not, however, necessarily mean a cessation of work for Moses. Giving Howland a key to his Babylon house on Thompson Avenue, he told the chief engineer to stop by every morning on his way to the mansion. Almost invariably, when Howland arrived at about 7:30 A.M., there would be waiting for him on the flat-topped bottom post of the banister a large manila envelope crammed with notes, memos and handwritten letters ready to be typed and mailed, an envelopeful of testimony to what Moses had been doing during the night while his men slept. He tried to keep Sundays free for his family, teaching Jane and Barbara to swim or sail, taking them for picnics, telling them stories. But often the girls would notice that their father had disappeared. When that happened, they knew he was out on the big screened porch on the side of the house, scribbling furiously on a yellow legal pad. And most of the family picnics were held in one of his parks. "Hell," one of the men working under him remembers, "any Sunday at all you could expect to look around and see the boss and his wife and kids and he'd be making notes as he walked along if he saw something he didn't like. So you figured if he was working, why shouldn't you be?"

There were other reasons, too, why the men who stayed didn't resent the driving.

"It was exciting working for Moses," one of the commission staffers recalls. "He made you feel you were a part of something big. It was almost like a war. It was you fighting for the people against those rich estate owners and those reactionary legislators. And it was exciting just being around him. He was dynamic, a big guy with a booming laugh. He dominated that scene in the mansion. He would sit there with people running back and forth around him and he would be banging his hand down on that big table and giving orders—and when he gave orders, things happened! Howland would go hurrying out of the room and twenty-five draftsmen would hurry to their tables and start drawing or surveyors would jump into their cars and head out on the road."

And, men recalled, incongruous as it might seem to use the word "fun" in connection with unremitting work, it was, nevertheless, fun to work for Bob Moses. "There was a very informal atmosphere in the mansion," one engineer says. "Everyone worked in their shirt sleeves—my recollection of Moses is of him sitting with his tie pulled down and over to one side, sleeves rolled up—and there was always a lot of joking going on." And the joking, the engineer says, went both ways. "You weren't afraid to kid him."

He turned the commission staff into a big family. If he couldn't get home to his wife and children as much as he would have liked, he brought them to his work. Commission staffers became accustomed to seeing Barbara and Jane playing on the playground equipment that Moses had brought from all over the United States and set up on the mansion's lawn so that he could test it. Jane was much more adventurous than her quiet, shy, dark-haired sister, who eyed the equipment with distrust, and the staffers laughed to watch the little blonde tomboy scramble around on the top bars of the jungle gyms and swing higher and higher on the swings. Mary was always around. She was the hostess at the little luncheons that Moses would have catered at the mansion if a politician or key landowner was visiting. She was a pleasant, easy friend to the young men working for her husband and a confidante, a sympathetic shoulder for their wives to cry on, who remember her with real affection. Moses was always consulting her; says Mrs. Harold Morse, a friend, "Bob used to say that the only decisions he made that were mistakes were the decisions he had neglected to talk over with Mary first."

He and Mary organized outings and insisted that Howland, Latham, Shapiro, McNulty and Junkamen—and Tom McWhinney, with whom Moses was getting along famously—bring their wives and children along. The outings were very informal—fishing trips on the commission motor launch *Apache* or clambakes—and they were fun. Recalls McWhinney's daughter, Dolie, twenty-eight at the time: "We used to go over to Fire Island for the whole weekend. There was an old frame building at the Coast Guard station there, and we'd sleep in it on cots, all the men in one room and the women and kids in another. There weren't any stores on Fire Island, so we'd bring most of our food along and go trolling from the *Apache* or clamming for the rest." While the women were cleaning the catch, the men would dig a great hole in the sand, cover its bottom with logs and light them for the clambake. There would be bonfires on the beach at night, and singing.

Moses set the tone. His clothes were a constant source of merriment. His pants were khakis faded white or corduroys only some of whose holes had been patched. Possibly because his hairline was beginning to recede, he wore, no matter what the weather, a hat—the same hat. "Robert!" Mary would say. "Take off that hat!" Everyone would laugh. "It was one of those fedoras with a big brim and it was completely shapeless and all stained," Dolie McWhinney recalls. "It was the funniest hat you ever saw. And Bob would never take it off except when he went swimming." He helped arrange the logs for the clambake, helped clean up afterward, helped with the children. Because Charlie Smisek, the *Apache*'s skipper, would be away from home all weekend, Moses insisted that Charlie's wife, Mae, come along, and he went out of his way to make the Smiseks feel at home. "There was no side to Bob Moses at all then," an acquaintance says. The only thing that set him apart was his swimming: hurling himself through the first of the big Atlantic rollers, he would appear on the far side of its tumult swimming and head straight out into the Atlantic, far beyond where even outdoorsman Latham would dare to go.

Of all the reasons why Moses' men didn't resent his driving, the one most frequently mentioned in their reminiscences is that he brought out the best in them. One of Junkamen's duties was to work with Long Island villages on zoning restrictions on the land adjoining the Southern State Parkway. "Mr. Moses wanted five hundred feet on either side of the parkway zoned in the highest residential classifications," Junkamen recalls. "And he didn't want any water tanks or other unsightly structures near them, either. Zoning was a relatively new thing. Hardly a village on Long Island had a zoning ordinance. I had to draw up a lot of what we wanted myself. Then Mr. Moses would have to speak to officials in the municipality and get them to draft over-all zoning ordinances in which our stuff could be incorporated. I'd have to work with the local counsel every step of the way. And then, after the ordinances were adopted, I'd have to work with the local zoning board when people tried to break the restrictions. And I found that at every step of the way, Mr. Moses had ideas that started me thinking along whole new lines."

Constantly, Moses was encouraging his architects and engineers to use their imagination, to make their designs different from and better than any similar designs done before. When the men designing a drawbridge for the Jones Beach causeway submitted their first design, he said, "I know you can do drawbridges. Can you do beautiful drawbridges?" In their second design, the bridge operators' quarters were no longer the standard ugly shacks but turrets faced with stone worked with the silhouettes of sailing ships. Gilmore Clarke thought he had surpassed himself in the design of bridges for the Bronx River Parkway. But he found Moses had some new standards. He wanted variety, Moses told him. Not only were the bridges to be designed to harmonize with the landscape and not only were they to be stone-faced, but every bridge on every parkway on Long Island—all one hundred of them—was going to be different from every other bridge.

Engineers assigned to design guard rails and light poles for the parkways expended tremendous effort making the standard iron poles graceful. But iron wouldn't blend in with a rustic setting, Moses said. Guard rails and light poles would have to be made of wood. But it had been proven that no form of wooden guard rails would resist the impact of a speeding car, the engineers said. Moses sent them back to ponder the problem again, and this time one thought of drilling holes in wooden rails and inserting strong steel cable—and now all the rails on all the parkways could be wood.

As always, it was on Jones Beach that Moses' imagination focused. He thought himself of many little touches to make people feel happy and relaxed there. The dunes, he said one day, were a natural protective wall for an archery range, so archery should be included as one of the sports offered at the beach. And why just have ordinary targets? he said. Why not let kids shooting arrows feel they were really in the Middle Ages, when archers stormed castles? Let some of the targets be cutouts in the shape of enemy bowmen crouching behind castle turrets. Why just have signs directing people to various activities? he asked. Why not decorate the signs with ironwork showing the activities—and showing them in humorous fashion? One day, a designer rather hesitantly showed him a design for the directional signs to the men's rooms. The design was the silhouette of a man, obviously in a desperate hurry, rushing to a bathroom so fast that the little boy he was dragging behind had his feet pulled off the ground. It was, of course, a little daring, the designer began. Daring! Moses said. He wanted his designers to be daring. This was a great design, he said. It would be used.

"Mr. Moses was no lawyer, but he had a great knowledge and grasp of the law," Junkamen would say. "He was not an engineer, but he had a great knowledge of engineering. He knew politics, he knew statesmanship—he was an altogether brilliant man. If you were working with him, you just had to learn from him—if only through osmosis." One of the commission's engineers rhapsodizes: "I don't think there was a man who came into daily contact with him who wasn't inspired to do better work than he had thought he was capable of doing."

If the political difficulties involved in creating a park on Jones Beach were enormous, the physical difficulties were of a size to match. Building on a barrier beach proved to be a very different proposition from building on the mainland. Commission engineers found themselves faced with a succession of problems engineers never encountered on mainland jobs. Cleveland Rodgers, Moses' first biographer, was to write that sometimes it seemed as if Nature herself had "joined forces with the skeptics and obstructionists who had fought Moses all the way from Albany to the beach." But Moses refused to let Nature stand in his way.

None of Moses' engineers had expected work on the barrier beach to continue in winter because drifting ice packs that kept boats off the Great South Bay for days at a time could maroon anyone caught on the strand. But with Smith's time as Governor running out, winters could not be wasted. Moses told the engineers taking surveys for the causeway to cache emergency supplies of food in a shack on the beach and keep working. Even on mornings when wind was whipping the bay into waves and ice was coating the piers, Sid Shapiro led his hip-booted surveyors into boats for the trip across.

One day, while they were on the strand, ice packs closed the bay. It stayed closed for ten days. All the cached food ran out except pancake batter, and the surveyors lived on pancakes. For the rest of his life, Sid Shapiro would never be able to stomach another pancake. But when the ice cleared and the surveyors returned to Babylon, Shapiro could tell Moses, who was standing on the dock waiting for a report, that ten days' more work had been completed.

The completed surveys contained the worst of news. The mean level of the existing barrier beach, Moses was told, was only two feet above mean sea level. During storms, the ocean rose six, seven or even eight feet and covered the strand almost completely. This did not matter as far as the portion of the beach that was to be a *beach* was concerned, but the portion that was to hold Moses' buildings and parking lots and parkway would have to be built up to a mean height of fourteen feet if they were not to be submerged in every storm, and if he wanted a road seventeen miles long along it, it would have to be built up to that height for seventeen miles. The job could be done, of course—floating dredges, huge pumps mounted on barges, could suck up hydraulic fill, which would become sand when dry, from the bay bottom, and pipelines could spill it out over the strand. But approximately forty million cubic yards of fill would be required. The job would take months—and it would be expensive. Even Smith quailed at this, and Moses had to talk fast and hard to persuade the Governor to go along. But he did persuade him, and the largest floating dredges in the United States were brought to the bay as soon as spring cleared the ice off it in 1927. The job could not be completed by the time ice set in again in the winter, but Moses refused to let the dredges leave. Their crews could live on them, he said, and all through the winter of 1927–28 they did, and the pumps kept working. "Night after night," Shapiro recalls, "they kept working to midnight."

When the sand from the bay bottom was spread on the barrier beach, it proved to be the worst problem of all. It was beautiful to look at, dazzling white and fine-grained, but the fineness meant that when it dried, it blew. Even the lightest breeze stirred it into the air in swirls so thick that the strand looked like a desert during a violent sandstorm.

"It was always blowing in your face when you worked," Shapiro remembers. "When it got bad, it would fill your eyes, your ears and your nose as fast as you could clean them out. You'd be choking and coughing. You'd be talking to somebody not three feet away and an especially violent gust would come, and you couldn't even see him any more. You couldn't even see the hand in front of your face." During the day, workmen would dig an excavation. At night, the sand would fill it in—so completely that the workmen couldn't even find its edges. One workman who left his car with its rear end turned into the wind for a few days came back to find the numerals—and all other color—completely erased from its rear license plate.

Moses dispatched landscape architects to other Long Island beaches to find out why the sand on older, natural dunes was more stable. They reported that it was because of the presence on these dunes of a form of "beach grass" (*Ammophilia arenaria*), whose roots, seeking water in the dry sand, spread horizontally rather than vertically and thus held sand around it in place. But to be effective, they reported, the grass had to be planted thickly—hundreds of thousands, even millions, of clumps would be required to hold down the new dunes on Jones Beach—and it could be planted only by hand. In the summer of 1928, on the desolate sand bar on the edge of the ocean, amid half-completed building skeletons that looked like ancient ruins, was a panorama out of the dynasties of the Pharaohs: hundreds, thousands, of men, spread out over miles of sand, kneeling on the ground digging little holes and planting in them tiny bundles of grass.

The peculiarities of man seemed sometimes to join with those of nature to thwart Moses. But he would not be thwarted.

The contract to build the causeway had been awarded to an Atlantic City, New Jersey, firm. In the autumn of 1927, the president of the firm coolly informed Moses that its money had run out and it couldn't meet its payroll. Its laborers wouldn't work without pay, and work would have to stop unless $20,000 was found immediately. Moses drove to Albany, but Smith told him that every cent that could be squeezed out of the Highway Bureau budget—in fact, every cent that could be squeezed out of the budget of any department—had already been squeezed. More money would be available in the 1928 appropriations, of course, but they wouldn't be available until after January 1. Promising to pay her back as soon as the appropriations came through—he did—Moses borrowed the $20,000 from his mother and paid the laborers himself. And they kept working.

To the east of the portion of Jones Beach ceded to him by Hempstead Town, directly in the path of his proposed Ocean Parkway, lay five hundred acres of meadowland owned by Oyster Bay Town and leased as a duck-hunting preserve to a group of wealthy sportsmen headed by Solomon Guggenheim. When Moses appropriated the tract, the sportsmen obtained an injunction and served it on the contractor. But Moses met the contractor on the dredge and, as Cleveland Rodgers put it: "The legal papers somehow slipped off the deck into the swirling waters. . . . When the hunters, in their furlined cloaks and escorted by their formidable legal advisers, arrived a few days later to shoot ducks, under full protection of the law, they found the meadow" slashed through and filled in for the parkway.

And always, day after day, summer and winter, Moses was out on the job, encouraging the men in the field. "People will work harder for you if they have a good time," he told the Morses, and he urged the laborers working on Jones Beach to go swimming during their lunch hour. Organizing softball games on the beach, he umpired them himself. Joking with the men, he made fun about his hat. And he told them what a great project they were building. "He had a gift for leading men," Shapiro recalls. "Those men idolized him. You'd see him walk up to a pickax gang that was tired and talk to them awhile and when he walked away, you could see those pickaxes swing faster."

Hanging over Moses was the realization that every battle he won brought him closer to one there seemed no way of winning—and whose loss would mean that his dream would remain substantially incomplete. Every step he took to develop the land ceded him by Hempstead and Oyster Bay only brought him closer to the day when he must face up to the fact that the rest of Jones Beach was not his. Its eastern half—nine miles long, thirteen hundred acres—still belonged to Babylon Township. Hutchinson and Hewitt might think the park he was laying out was already too big; he knew that, to serve the metropolitan area adequately, it would one day have to be far bigger—and the only place for expansion was Babylon's land. Moreover, if he didn't get that land before the Wantagh Causeway and Ocean Parkway, which would run up to its edge, made it accessible and immensely valuable, he knew he would never get it. And unless he got it, there was nothing to prevent Babylon from building a road to connect with the parkway and lining it with hot-dog stands, gas stations and tiny, ugly summer bungalows that would march right up to the edge of his great park and spoil forever its pristine beauty. Without Babylon's land, moreover, the Ocean Parkway would be only half as long as he wanted it, and it would be difficult to build a causeway and loop it back to mainland Long Island and the Southern State Parkway because he had planned to cut the expense of that causeway by running it over Captree Island, a tongue of land at the eastern end, Babylon's end, of Jones Beach, which extended up toward the mainland. And since it was the eastern end of Jones Beach that almost touched Fire Island, without it he would never be able to build a bridge from Jones Beach to Fire Island and thus enable the Ocean Parkway to continue along Fire Island to the Hamptons.

Babylon's baymen had never forgiven him for his attempt to grab the town's "sacred birthright." When Mary went shopping in town now, the tradesmen eyed her coldly. Sounding out the Town Board members again about a referendum, Moses found them still fully aware of their constituents' feelings.

Moses tried threats. Many of the thousand commission and Highway Bureau employees at Belmont Lake lived in Babylon, and therefore, Moses reminded the town's businessmen, much of the $400,000 monthly payroll was spent in the town. "Doubtless," he said, "more congenial headquarters for the state's work on Long Island can be found elsewhere." But the town was unmoved. The Town Board assured its constituents that there was not going to be any referendum. And without one, there was, under the State Constitution, simply no way in which Moses could get the town's land.

But Moses at last found a weak spot in Babylon's defenses.

"I heard about it by the sheerest kind of accident," he told the author decades later.

"I was thinking then about learning to drive—I never really did—and I was practicing one morning in a Model T in the driveway of this big estate out in Babylon owned by a guy named Willard Reed, whose father, who had been dead for years at this point, had been a Democratic county court judge in Suffolk, the only Democrat on the county court, at the time Grover Cleveland was re-elected.

"I saw Willard sitting on the porch rocking and drinking, and he called to me and said, 'Come on up and have a drink.' So we sat rocking away there and talking and after a while he said, 'I hear you're having some trouble getting some land.' I said, 'Yes, we are.' And he said, 'The Babylon fellows don't want to cooperate?' and I said, 'No.'

"And he said, 'I remember a story my father told me once. You know the whole question of the ownership of the bay bottom in Babylon Town came up a long time ago and my father and another judge, a fellow in Amityville named Samuel Hildreth, were appointed to pass on it. And I think you'd be interested in what was found. You'll never find the decision in Riverhead [the county seat, where court records were kept] because the supervisors will have made sure it's missing. But Hildreth is alive.'

"I said, 'Tell me more, Willard.' He said, 'I think I've told you enough. You go and see this [Hildreth] fellow in Amityville and you tell him I told him to talk to you.' I did, and Hildreth said that way back, in 1848 maybe or 1856, two bills had been introduced in the Legislature. See, before that, the underwater rights in the bay, the bay bottoms, had belonged to the state. But one of these two bills transferred the rights in Nassau County to the various towns in Nassau along the bay and the other transferred the rights in Suffolk to the various Suffolk towns. Well, everyone on Long Island always just assumed that both of these had passed, but Hildreth told me that when he and Judge Reed had looked into it, they had found that for some reason no one seemed to know, maybe just an oversight, only one passed—the Nassau one.

"I said, 'Do I gather then that half the bay bottom belongs to the state? That Babylon doesn't own its bay bottom at all?' And I put all our bloodhounds on it and I found those bills, and I found that Hildreth's story was true.

"Well, in all this time, the supervisors could have gotten the ownership of those lands transferred without any trouble, but I guess they had just decided to let things lie and had kept issuing licenses to fish the bay bottoms when they had no right to. And so I blackjacked them. We told them that we'd trade them the [Jones Beach] land for the bay bottoms. Well, they didn't want to trade. They didn't want to give the land. But we told them that if they didn't, we'd let the people know that the town didn't own the bay bottom after all, that they'd been issuing licenses when they had no right to, that in all the years that had been available to remedy the mistake, they had never taken the simple step of obtaining title to the bay bottoms, that they had been negligent in their stewardship of the town's 'sacred heritage.' " To be convicted in the public eye of such negligence would have been even worse for them than to give away the barrier beach. The bay bottoms were much more important to the baymen; that was what their livelihood depended on. "We blackjacked them, that's all. We threatened to tell. And we said, 'Now, there's one way to adjust this thing.' "

The way—the ultimatum that Moses presented to the Town Board—was to authorize the referendum and to issue a ruling that would give Moses a real chance of winning it: the voting would not be restricted to the town's taxpaying property owners but would be open to anyone who lived there—including the several hundred state employees who had recently moved into apartments. This ruling would violate common sense and common practice—generally, only property owners, a town's taxpayers, were allowed to vote in referenda involving the permanent removal of town property from tax rolls—but Moses did not leave the board members much choice. If the referendum passed, giving the beach land to the state, he told them, the state would in turn quietly give the bay bottoms to the town, and they could go right on issuing licenses; if the referendum passed, he would never tell their constituents about their negligence. And if it didn't pass, he would.

To lull the town's baymen and property owners into overconfidence, the Town Board did not explode the bombshell about voting eligibility until three days before the election. Everything, in fact, was done so fast that the old-time residents never had a chance to organize. Without warning, at a routine meeting held on March 14, 1928, with few residents present, the Town Board, saying for the record that it was opposed to the beach ceding but felt "the people's voice" should be heard, authorized the referendum—and scheduled it for the same day as party primary elections—April 3, 1928, less than three weeks away. "Judases!" Judge Cooper cried.

The Park Commission flooded the local post office with mailings seeking to reassure Babylonians on points that were worrying them. One reassurance concerned a rumor that tolls would be charged on the Wantagh Causeway, that Babylonians would have to pay to use their own land. Absolutely not, Moses said. In a letter he wrote to the *Leader*—and which was printed by Cooper, who made a noticeable effort to give space to his foe's views—Moses promised: "The state causeway and boulevard will be free."

Nonetheless, the judge could not conceive that, even with the voter eligibility ruling, the referendum would pass. No politician, he didn't understand certain other tactics the Town Board had used; he saw, for example, no significance in the fact that while the hours for voting in the primary were noon to 9 P.M., the hours for voting in the referendum ended at 6 P.M.

None of the older residents of Babylon were prepared for election day. As they strolled to the polls, they suddenly noticed cars bearing state shields and crammed with men racing through the streets of the quiet village. They were Park Commission and DPW vehicles carrying employees to vote. Undoubtedly, many of these employees were—under the suddenly relaxed eligibility ruling—eligible to vote. But opponents at the polls said that they recognized many as men who did not have even apartments in the town and were therefore ineligible. When, however, election inspectors tried to check their names against the list of eligible voters in the election registers with which election inspectors were customarily provided, they found that somehow the Town Board had neglected to provide registers this time, and the inspectors were unable to deny the state employees the right to vote. Realtors had cars out, too, rounding up voters known to favor the proposal and transporting them to the polls. But Moses' overconfident—overconfident because hoodwinked—opponents did not have a single car in operation. In addition, many potential "no" voters—one estimate said two hundred—were confused by the fact that the polls remained open until nine; they showed up after six, only to be told that while they could vote in the primary, voting in the referendum had been closed. The final tally showed that "Babylon Town" had ceded its portion of Jones Beach to the state by seven votes. Wrote Cooper: "The verdict was nothing short of a crime and the method by which it was obtained is scandalous." Moses issued a statement, too. He called the referendum results "a vote of confidence in the Park Commission."

The sands were running out on Al Smith's Governorship. Moses' construction crews did not quit for the winter of 1927–28; their grading machines pushed aside snow as well as earth as they smoothed the path for the Southern State Parkway. The Great South Bay froze solid; the men stretching the Jones Beach causeway across it pitched tents on the ice and lived on it.

Early in 1928, an astonished Hutchinson and Hewitt realized that the completion of the Southern State Parkway and Jones Beach causeway, on which they had hinged the beginning of the Northern State and which they had assumed was years, if not decades, away, was rapidly approaching. Frantically, they tried to delay it. In another year, Al Smith wouldn't be Governor. Out of Moses' $4,500,000 1928 budget request, they slashed $626,000. But Smith found the money in the departmental budgets, and the construction crews kept working.

Moses had not been given funds for his Long Island parks and parkways until the spring of 1926. By the end of the summer of 1928, in a period of less than three years, every foot of right-of-way for the Southern State Parkway was in his hands, a seven-mile stretch, from near the New York City line to and around the Hempstead reservoir, was completed. Long rows of newly planted elms and maples lined it and stone-faced bridges, every one different, were carrying crossroads over it so that nothing should interrupt the swift passage of its users. A second seven-mile stretch, from the reservoir to Wantagh, was completed except for the landscaping. A third seven-mile stretch, from Wantagh to Babylon, was graded and ready for paving. And the fill for the Wantagh Parkway had been laid, a pavement placed on top of the fill and three of the four bridges that would carry the causeway across the bay completed.

When Moses had become president of the Long Island State Park Commission on April 18, 1924, there had been one state park on Long Island, the almost worthless 200-acre tract on Fire Island. By the end of the summer of 1928, there were fourteen parks totaling 9,700 acres. Because 6,775 of those acres had been acquired—from Hempstead, Oyster Bay and Babylon towns, the U.S. Department of Commerce, New York City and private individuals—as gifts, the Long Island parks had cost the state a total of about a million dollars. At 1928 land values, they were worth more than fifteen million.

By the end of the summer of 1928, the watershed properties off Merrick Road had been filled with bathhouses, baseball fields and bridle paths. Picnic areas with thousands of tables sat under their trees. Slides, swings and jungle gyms spotted their clearings. Their lakes were decorated with floats, diving boards, sliding ponds, rowboats and canoes. Heckscher State Park contained miles of paved roads for cars and dirt roads for horseback riders, acres of athletic fields, bathhouses holding five thousand lockers, a boardwalk, a bathing pavilion with restaurants and snack bars, an inland canal for row-boating, and a marina at which sailboats could be moored. There were more bathhouses, more boardwalks, more playing fields, more snack bars, more picnic areas, more campsites at Sunken Meadow, Wildwood, Orient Beach, Montauk Point and Hither Hills state parks. On Jones Beach, two years before a desolate sand bar, there stood now, awaiting only the finishing touches that would be added in 1929, a bathhouse like a medieval castle, a water tower like the campanile of Venice, a boardwalk, a restaurant and parking fields that held ten thousand cars each. In the history of public works in America, it is probable that never had so much been built so fast.

During the summer of 1928, park-seeking families heading out of New York City began to feel Long Island open up to them. Week by week, word spread. At the beginning of the summer, the bathhouse at Valley Stream State Park contained a thousand lockers. For a few weekends, these were sufficient. Then they were not. Another thousand lockers were added. Then another thousand. And, even so, by the end of the summer, thousands of would-be bathers were being turned away every weekend. By the end of the summer, attendance at Long Island's state parks had passed half a million.

New Yorkers knew who was primarily responsible for the boon they had been given. It would have been difficult for them not to know. For the press was turning Robert Moses into a hero.

The lionization was on a scale as vast as the achievement. The Twenties was an age for heroes, of course, and if 1927 was Lindbergh's year in the New York press, 1928 was Moses'. Albert Einstein, who announced his theory of relativity in that year, was all but ignored in the city's thirteen daily newspapers, but New York's reporters strove for new adjectives to describe the park builder, one writer concentrating on his physical attributes ("tall, dark, muscular and zealous"), another on the mental ("a powerful and nervous mind"), a third on the moral ("fearless," "courageous") to describe "Rhodes Scholar" Robert A. Moses, Robert B. Moses, most frequently Robert H. Moses (reporters could not seem to reconcile themselves to his lack of a middle initial).

Editorial writers chimed in. "His labors have been unwearied and successful," said the *Times,* "his energy and persistence . . . great." "He has been a faithful, earnest and efficient incumbent," said the *World*. "He has done excellent work." Even the *Herald Tribune* was beginning to look on his works and find them good.

And the praise, on front pages and editorial pages alike, continued day after day. If readers were reminded once during 1928 that Moses was serving the state without pay, they were reminded a hundred times.

Al Smith at the Central Park Zoo.

Belle Moskowitz

Fiorello La Guardia, Al Smith and Robert Moses at the opening of the Belt Parkway, 1938. Behind Moses is Smith's wife, Katie.

PAGEANTRY: The dedication of Moses' seven-block-long Chrystie-Forsyth Park, 1934.

PRESENTATION of award by Park Association president, Iphigene Ochs Sulzberger, and Association official Gustavus Kirby, 1935.

La Guardia speaking—with Moses behind him—at the Chrystie-Forsyth dedication.

THE CANDIDATE:
Above: *1934 GOP gubernatorial nominee Moses arriving at Madison Square Garden for a campaign speech;*
left: *with his wife, Mary, voting on Election Day.*

Herbert Lehman, Al Smith and August Heckscher dedicating Heckscher State Park, 1929. The two girls are Moses' daughters, Jane (left) and Barbara.

Franklin Roosevelt dedicating Jones Beach State Park, 1929, as Smith and Moses sit listening.

Al Smith speaking at the Heckscher dedication on the porch of the old Taylor Mansion. Moses is framed in pillars at left.

Moses receiving an award from children's clubs, 1934.

MOSES AND THE GOVERNORS

Moses and Smith

Moses and Roosevelt

Moses and Lehman

Moses and Dewey

Moses and Harriman (and, left, William Zeckendorf)

Moses and Rockefeller

MOSES AND THE MAYORS

Moses (left) and Walker (third from left)

Moses and La Guardia

Moses and O'Dwyer (third from left; others are Kate Wollman and Hugo Rogers)

Moses and Impellitteri

Moses and Wagner

Moses and Lindsay

Moses welcoming Queen Elizabeth II to the dedication of the Robert Moses Power Dam at Massena, 1959.

Moses presenting the World's Fair Gold Medal to Generalissimo Franco in Madrid, 1964.

Moses posing with Brooklyn B.P. Cashmore, Cardinal Spellman, Manhattan B.P. Wagner, and Mayor O'Dwyer at the opening of the Brooklyn-Battery Tunnel, 1950.

Moses visiting Pope John XXIII at the Vatican, 1963.

MOSES AND THE PRESIDENTS

Moses and Hoover

Moses and Truman

Moses and Eisenhower

Moses and Port Authority Chairman Howard S. Cullman (third from right) at the groundbreaking for the Lincoln Tunnel's third tube, 1952.

Moses, Charles Preusse and George Spargo huddling in the Plaza's Oak Room to discuss plans for the UN building, 1947.

Moses and Harry Van Arsdale at the World's Fair, 1964.

MOSES AND THE POWER BROKERS

Bernard F. Gimbel, Thomas F. Deegan and John W. Hanes watching as Newbold Morris signs the Flushing Meadows Park over to the World's Fair Corporation, 1960.

Moses, Tom Shanahan and Jim Farley.

Moses, Wagner and Samuel I. Rosenman at the Jones Beach Marine Theater, 1960.

J. Russel Sprague, Moses, Smith, Grover Whalen, W. Kingsland Macy, 1932.

Moses with William J. Ronan and William Vermaelen (fourth and third from right), 1968.

Moses, Guy Lombardo and three members of the Jones Beach Marine Theater chorus line, c. 1960.

MOSES AND THE MOSES MEN

Sid Shapiro and "RM" at the Belmont Lake Office.

The Boss in the field with (left to right) aides Darcy, Andrews, Loeser, Ammann.

Mr. Moses and "Mustache" Constable.

Right: *The "Little Soldier" of the Tavern-on-the-Green Battle, 1956.* Below: *Moses, Shapiro and Rockefeller, 1961.*

No. 24,862—DAILY TUESDAY, APRIL 24, 1956 5 CENTS

earst Jr. Reports from Lon

t Leaders 'Drop

hools t Aid

terioriating school ools at the fastest a series of articles some people put s on parents and

ICK D'INCECCO New York City nate looks very the baby with as allowed the at $357,000,000 itions for 140,- d $62,200,000 to ools built before s than half the would earmark that now totals to the fact that ldings is neither gray. effort into new has 54 schools 0 and providing on the drawing

LITTLE SOLDIER IN PARK WAR . . . A "volunteer" in the mothers' war in Central Park, David Newman, 4, sits with toy gun outside fenced in play area as police officer stands guard to prevent women from interfering with workmen constructing parking lot today.

Another photo in Picture Section

ntinued; Rows

NS)—City buses egregation rule—

Actor Robinson's Son Saved After Overdose of Pills

HOLLYWOOD, April 24 (INS)—Edward G. Robinson Jr., 23, son of the actor, took an overdose of sleeping pills to-

Mothers Fenced Out As Bulldozer Digs In

Parks Commissioner Robert Moses early today stole a march on the marching "Central Park Mothers" when work on a new parking lot in the park at 67th st. and Central Park W. got under way behind a snow fence.

IRT Breakdown In B'klyn Delays Rush-Hour Riders

Thousands of morning rush-hour passengers on the IRT Nostrand ave. line in Brooklyn met delays up to 19 minutes

Rockefeller applauding, Moses crying, at the dedication of Robert Moses Plaza at the Lincoln Center campus of Fordham University, 1970.

Moses' lionization in the press had a practical benefit. It insured that he would be allowed to finish the job he had started. No one would dare stop it now.

The Long Island dream was safe.

If the press erred in its description of Moses' achievements, it erred on the side of under-, not over-, statement.

Long Island was only one segment of his state park system. The $14,000,000 allocated for upstate parks in the bond issue was not nearly enough for the system he had in mind. Many of his hurried trips around the state were, therefore, attempts to persuade wealthy men who owned undeveloped land in scenic areas to give their land to the public.

Luckily, many of these men were the old park patriots. The state had never bothered to buy a single foot of Lake George's hundreds of miles of shoreline, and cheap resorts and rooming houses were proliferating on its shores. Lumbermen had stripped the surrounding mountains of their softwood forests and were starting on the hardwoods. The denuded soil was being washed away by rains. But midway along the lake a branch of water jutted out to the northwest, and of the eleven thousand virgin acres on the tongue of land thus formed—most of it called Tongue Mountain—six thousand were owned by a group of wealthy men who were also public-spirited. He persuaded them to donate their land to the state. The remaining five thousand acres on the tongue were owned by a family that was about to sell it to a lumbering company, but the family's attorney was Captain N. Taylor Phillips, a key figure in that stronghold of the park patriots, the American Scenic and Historic Preservation Society. Working through Phillips, Moses persuaded the family to lower its asking price from forty dollars per acre to fifteen—and when he bought the whole tract, he had succeeded in preserving for posterity a substantial part of the Lake George region for a total cost of $75,000.

With the money he had saved, Moses preserved the historic battlefields at Fort Stanton and Oriskany and, with Adolph Ochs's help, at Saratoga. He purchased the 10,692 still untouched acres of Whiteface Mountain, which he had so often climbed as a youth, thus insuring that generations of youths who came after him would also be able to climb it. By the end of the summer of 1928, the scattered little historic reservations that Moses had inherited had been expanded into a system that included seventy parks totaling more than 125,000 acres. And he had used $5,000,000 of the bond issue to beat the lumbermen to great untouched tracts in the Adirondacks and Catskills and build up the state's forest preserve to 2,218,000 acres.

When he had the parks, Moses built roads to link them with the nearest highways, and suddenly families in Rochester and Syracuse and Albany were visiting places they had hardly heard of before—not only Letchworth Gorge and Watkins Glen but Boonville Gorge, Rudd Pond, Roaring Brook and Ore Pit. If they simply wanted to drive through these parks, there were gravel roads they could do that on. If they wanted to hike, there were hiking paths and nature trails through the woods; if they wanted to swim, there were paths down to beautiful, hidden mountain lakes and bathhouses in which they could change into swimming outfits; if they wanted to picnic, there were picnic grounds of which every detail was designed to preserve the fresh, virgin quality of the woods; if they wanted to camp out, there were campsites, designed with equal care, laid out next to cool mountain brooks.

Newspapers in Rochester rhapsodized over Letchworth State Park, newspapers in Albany over Thacher State Park, newspapers in Buffalo over the park on Devil's Island that overlooked Niagara Falls. But these newspapers had little interest in the Long Island parks, and New York City newspapers had little interest in the upstate parks. So no newspaper, no matter how enthusiastic it was over what editorial writers called "Robert Moses' great park program," comprehended the full extent of the program's magnitude—or the full extent of its greatness.

Perhaps the most remarkable characteristic of these parks and parkways that were becoming physical realities in 1928 was that they were, for the most part, the parks and parkways he had proposed in the New York State Association park reports he had written in 1922 and 1923. They were located in the places he had proposed, and the details of their development—down to the façades of their bathhouses and how many lockers and parking spaces each would have—followed the plans Moses had made for them.

Robert Moses had dreamed a dream immense in scope. By the end of the summer of 1928, the dream—all of the dream, even Jones Beach, which had seemed doomed to diminution in reality—was either reality or well on its way to becoming reality.

14. *Changing*

LASHED BY HIS DESIRE for the realization of his dreams, Bob Moses had changed even before he became president of the Long Island State Park Commission on April 18, 1924, from the idealist who put his faith in truth and reason to the pragmatist who put his faith in power. But the acquisition of power in his own name on that date, and his use of power thereafter, broadened the change, accelerated it, intensified it, raised it to an entirely new level.

For once Bob Moses came into possession of power, it began to perform its harsh alchemy on his character, altering its contours, eating away at some traits, allowing others to enlarge.

The potential for these changes had always been there, like a darker shadow on the edge of the bright gold of his idealism. With each small increase in the amount of power he possessed, the dark element in his nature had loomed larger, becoming prominent enough for sharp-eyed men to begin to notice it. Had not Reuben Lazarus said, "When Smith brought him [up to Albany], he began to be, quite suddenly and quite noticeably, a lot more arrogant"? Such men concluded that Moses, even more than most other men, liked power in and for itself; some of them suspected that if Moses ever obtained in substantial measure power of his own, the alteration in his character would become a transformation.

But even sharp-eyed men could not be prepared for the extent of the transformation. For adulthood was, after all, only a part of the pattern of Moses' life, and they had not seen the other part of the pattern. They could not know, therefore, how far back in the over-all pattern the dark thread ran. They could not know how inextricably it was knotted into the pattern's most central design. They had seen Moses' fingers drum impatiently on a table when someone dared to disagree with him, but they had never seen drumming impatiently another set of fingers. They had seen Bob Moses tilt back his head and look down his nose in the prosecutor's stance, but, not having known Moses in his boyhood, they couldn't know where the tilt came from. They may have known Bob Moses, but they did not know Bob Moses' mother. They did not know Bob Moses' grandmother. And therefore they could not know the origin—or the depth—of his susceptibility to the infection of power. They could not know that the susceptibility lay not in Albany but in family—in heredity or upbringing or some combination of the two. He was "Bella Moses' son," the one of her children most like her, the one in whom surfaced most strongly the mixed strain of passionate idealism and overweening arrogance that she had inherited from *her* parents, Grannie and Bernhard Cohen. When the idealism died, the arrogance was already well rooted and strong. If it was given nourishment, it would expand. And power feeds arrogance. As Moses obtained power, therefore, the traits symptomatic of his arrogance became steadily more noticeable. The pattern's hue darkened.

His mother had always displayed—as a Madison House trustee and as a wife—a conviction of her own infallibility and a predisposition to impose her will on others, an unwillingness to listen to others, a burning impatience to see her solutions to problems implemented, to Get Things Done. Moses' imagination seemed most easily fired, as his mother's had been, by physical problems and physical solutions, problems that could be solved by construction, by the shaping of concrete and steel. And the resemblance in traits between mother and son went beyond that. As a staffer at the Bureau of Municipal Research, he had displayed the same dogmatism and the same impatience. Bob Moses had wanted his own way—and he had wanted it when he wanted it.

And now that he had power, he was going to see that he got it.

He had never wanted to listen to people who disagreed with him. Now, in the main, he didn't have to. "When he talked to you," recalls Leonard W. Hall, then a state assemblyman, "he'd just tell you what he was going to do. If you disagreed with him and tried to explain your feelings, or even started asking questions, he would cut right in, slash at you, without answering the questions, making you feel stupid for asking. And if you were talking to him on the phone, he'd just hang up on you. I remember talking to him on the phone and disagreeing with him about something and I was in the middle of a sentence and the damn phone was slammed down."

Moses had always displayed contempt for people he felt were considerably beneath him, the colored "subject people" of the British Empire, for example, or civil servants who hadn't attended Oxford or Cambridge. At the Municipal Civil Service Commission, his irritation at having to interrupt his work for public hearings indicated a tendency to feel that the public he was serving was beneath him, that its suggestions about its own destiny were not worth listening to. Now that feeling about the public was intensified. When the Governor's office received a letter making a suggestion about parks or criticizing one of the regional commissions, the letter was invariably referred by George Graves, Smith's secretary, to Moses for a suggested reply that could be sent back over the Governor's signature. Now, more and more frequently, Moses would suggest that no one bother to reply at all.

His contempt was not limited to the public. It included, apparently, most state legislators. If he wasn't hanging up on them in mid-sentence, he was treating them with extravagant disdain. "They didn't dislike him just because politically he was cutting them to pieces," Hall recalls. "They disliked him personally. He acted with a complete arrogance. He insulted those men to their face." Sniffing at the patronage possibilities at Jones Beach as though they were sea air, Senate Finance Committee Chairman Jeremiah F. Twomey of Brooklyn asked Moses to drop around for a chat before the Finance Committee hearings on a Jones Beach appropriation bill. According to Hall, to whom Twomey told the story:

"Twomey says, 'Bob, it looks like there'll be a lot of jobs out there, and I was wondering if we could get a couple.'

"Bob answers very softly, very gently, very politely. 'What did you have in mind, Jerry?' he asks. Jerry mentions one job, and Moses says very softly, very politely, 'Do you have anything else on your mind, Jerry?' Jerry, completely taken in, thinking that for once this fellow is going to be reasonable, mentions a couple of other jobs, and Moses says, 'Do you have anything else on your mind, Jerry?' Jerry says, 'Well, that's about all.' And Moses says, 'Jerry, you can take that bill and stick it up your ass!' "

Moses had always been impatient. Most men didn't move fast enough for him. Now he could do something about it.

The park philanthropists on the State Council of Parks didn't move fast enough for him.

There were many reasons. For one thing, most of the regional commissions whose chairmen comprised the council were made up of men with a different philosophy of parks from his. This was understandable. They were, in the main, elderly men, men out of the days when parks had meant "conservation" rather than "recreation." Even during the 1920's, of course, parks still meant "conservation" to most park experts; there wasn't one in the country who would lean as heavily as Moses to thinking of parks as baseball fields and tennis courts rather than as glades and forests and hiking trails. The regional commissioners, men of the older era, had become interested in parks to preserve as much of nature's beauties as possible from a ruthless civilization. When they saw the developer's bulldozer imperiling a favorite piece of woodland, they purchased the woodland with their own money and presented it to the state, and when they realized that the state would not provide sufficient funds to preserve it as it should be preserved, they put up the money themselves, year after year, and they put up their time, too, spending weekends and vacations on inspection trips, often making needed repairs with their own hands. In drawing up their wills, they chose carefully the men they wanted to administer the properties after they were gone—and these men, too, felt that preserving the properties in the condition in which they had received them was a sacred trust. Proposals for huge parking fields, for restaurants—these seemed to them to conflict with the ideals they had sworn themselves to preserve. If the state now wanted to "develop" those parks, well, certainly some development was necessary; as long as it was done slowly and carefully, it could be worked out—but they wanted to make sure that the development did not destroy the natural qualities they treasured.

There were other reasons, too, for Moses' impatience with the regional commissioners. At bottom, the philosophy of government on which they had been weaned emphasized the rights of the individual. They believed, therefore, that governmental power should be used with the utmost restraint. They were, frankly, dismayed by the way Moses had used entry and appropriation against Havemeyer and Macy, by the way he had threatened to use it against the North Shore barons. And they didn't intend to use such techniques themselves, even if using slower techniques meant that parks and parkways in their areas wouldn't be acquired as fast as Moses wanted.

A more important source of conflict in their dealings with Moses, however, had nothing to do with philosophy. It was simply that the old men wanted to remain in charge of the parks they loved.

Moses had let them believe that they would remain in charge. He had given them no hint of his true purposes. For Moses had needed them. He had needed their prestige, their reputation (as strong with legislators as with the public) for uprightness, for unselfishness and for devotion to the cause of parks. He had needed the backing of their names.

And they had given him that backing. During the debate over the $15,000,000 bond issue, they had made use of their influence in their home counties to mute upstate resentment toward such a large spending proposal. Judge Ellis J. Staley of Albany had spoken night after night to civic groups in Albany, Troy and Schenectady. Judge Alphonse Trumpbore Clearwater, elderly and ailing, had climbed out of a sickbed in Kingston to tour Ulster County so successfully that that bastion of conservatism had, to Al Smith's astonishment, actually given the referendum a majority. During the Taylor Estate fight, the old park men had let Smith invoke their names—"everyone knows Judge Clearwater"—to dramatize the fact that even these dyed-in-the-wool Republicans could not support the Republican legislative proposals for parks. GOP leaders had told them that Smith was using them to destroy their party. Many of the park men had felt there was some truth in this. But parks came first with them. And when Smith, through Moses, had asked them to come to Albany, they had come.

They had given Moses the help he asked because they believed what he had told them. When he assured them—as he did over and over both in letters and to their faces—that under his park plan they would "continue their duties and powers," that they would continue to administer the parks they loved, that the State Parks Council was merely an "advisory agency," they believed him. And when the bill creating the State Parks Council was signed, their leaders had elected him its chairman.

But now Moses didn't need them any more.

Not a month after his election, Judge Staley, who administered John Boyd Thacher Park near Albany for the American Scenic and Historical Preservation Society, routinely sent to the state a request for $15,000 to build a new caretaker's cottage. State officials told the astonished judge that all such requests now had to go through the State Parks Council, through Moses. And Moses disapproved the request. "The height of impertinence," Staley told the society's trustees. They agreed. "It is highly desirable," they said in the minutes of their meeting of May 26, 1924, "that there be a clear understanding of the difference between the powers of the Council as 'a central advisory agency' and the executive powers of 'the existing commissions, boards and organizations governing the . . . parks.' "

They got their clear understanding. When, during the summer of 1925, they submitted to the council their budget requests for 1926, Moses curtly disapproved many of them. When they tried to circumvent Moses by sending them to state budget officials as they had in the past, the officials sent them back telling them that under the new Parks Council law, all park budget requests had to be transmitted to the state through the council. At a council meeting at 261 Broadway, Judge Clearwater "reminded" Moses that the council's powers were "advisory," not "supervisory." Really? Moses replied coldly. Might he suggest that the judge read the law?

The old park men read the law—and began to realize what they had done.

The realization grew.

Moses had written the Parks Council bylaws. At the first meeting after he had been elected chairman, when he was still charming the old park men, they had approved them, believing them only a formality. Now, reading the bylaws, they realized that all power in the council was centralized in its chairman. The council's finance committee, the key unit which would weigh the requests of the regional commissions, was not elected by them but appointed by him—and he had appointed to three of its five places council staff members hired by and responsible only to the chairman. The whole council staff was responsible to the chairman. And this staff was empowered in the bylaws to draw up the plans for all state parks, including *their* state parks.

The old men reluctantly decided they would have to deny Moses a second one-year term—and suddenly realized, when they tallied up votes, that while their commissions controlled a majority of the state parks, they did not control a majority of the State Parks Council. Six of its eleven votes were in Moses' hands: Moses' own; two cast by Smith appointees not directly connected with parks, the State Conservation Commissioner and the director of the State Museum; three cast by the presidents of three new regional commissions which did not at the moment have any parks to administer but which Moses had insisted—for reasons the old park men now understood—be represented on the council and to which Smith had appointed men who would take Moses' orders. The old park men had many reservations about Moses' over-all park policies as well as about his plans for specific parks. For one thing, they were concerned about his eagerness to develop parks that were far outside city limits—Heckscher was fifty miles from Times Square, Letchworth fifty miles from Rochester—without providing any means of transportation to them other than auto; the truly poor masses of the cities didn't own automobiles, they pointed out; how were they to reach these parks? But every time they raised such points, they were voted down. And Moses was re-elected to the chairmanship in 1925, 1926, 1927 and 1928.

Some of Moses' fights with the elderly park philanthropists could be viewed as conflicts of philosophy—as his determination not to allow his dreams to be thwarted by other men's smaller-scale vision—although the closer one examines their details, the more it appears that the crucial conflict in each was between his demand for speed and their feeling that since once nature was altered by man, it could never be restored to its original condition, any changes in the magnificent gorges and mountains which had been entrusted to them must be considered with painstaking care and designed to blend in with the existing topography; the American Scenic and Historic Preservation Society, for example, did not object to making Letchworth State Park more accessible to the public and to furnishing accommodations for families wanting to stay overnight; they just wanted the proposed inn—and large adjoining parking garage—built on the rim of the beautiful Genesee River Gorge rather than right in its heart, as Moses proposed. On other battles between Moses and the old park men, however, it is more difficult to place any philosophical interpretation. The nature of these fights hints that power was now, for the first time in his life, becoming an end in itself, that he was beginning to crave it now not only for the sake of dreams but for its own sake, that although, through his bill drafting, he had given himself much of the power in the field of parks, he was no longer satisfied with much of the power, that he now wanted *all* the power in the field.

The suspicion is aroused most strongly by his treatment of the commissioners of the state park at Niagara.

There were five Niagara commissioners—all of them elderly men—but the two most active had long been Judge Clearwater and Ansley Wilcox.

"Everyone knows Judge Clearwater," Smith had said, and, in regard to the Central Tier at least, the Governor may have been very nearly right. At seventy-seven Alphonse Trumpbore Clearwater of Kingston was a legend throughout the band of thinly populated counties that stretched three hundred miles across the middle of the state. Tall and thin, with a face that would have been cold were it not for the upward turn of the corners of his mouth, he was a wing-collared embodiment of devotion to the public good. He had been both district attorney of Ulster County and a lawyer who, in an era in which the poor often went unrepresented in court, represented the poor—and as both prosecutor and defender his brilliance and, despite a dry and precise speaking style, his remarkable oratorical ability made him a lawyer other lawyers feared to oppose. While still young, Judge Clearwater had been president of the State Bar Association and a Justice of the State Supreme Court; men said he could, had he wished, been Governor. But he did not so wish. Instead of a politician, he became a historian, and he served his state by studying its history—scholars regarded his knowledge as unequaled—and by selecting from appointments proffered by its Governors not those that would have brought him fame but those that would enable him to help preserve its locales of history and beauty, such as Niagara State Park. His selflessness was widely known; although he had renounced politics, his voice was regarded by politicians as the most influential in the Central Tier. When in 1925 a desperate Moses, assuring Clearwater that the Parks Council would be only an "advisory" body, had asked the judge to help him in the Taylor Estate fight, he had come, old and ill, to Albany to stand before a hostile Republican caucus and argue in Moses' behalf. When legislators had begun criticizing Moses' spending proposals for Niagara as extravagant, Clearwater had written him a letter saying "Your views . . . are just"—and that line of criticism had abruptly stopped. Of all the old park men, Clearwater had been Moses' most effective supporter.

Ansley Wilcox, who had served as a Niagara park commissioner for forty years, was a chubby old gentleman with a white walrus mustache. A successful attorney, he lived in a stately Georgian mansion on Buffalo's fashionable Delaware Avenue. But Ansley Wilcox had been a brilliant student at Yale and after graduation he had gone on to Oxford. Then, attracted by the ideals of the municipal reform movement, he had spent years campaigning, fruitlessly, for a civil service merit system for Buffalo. Then he began to fight for parks. While still in his twenties, he determined to rescue the gorge overlooking Niagara Falls from the factories, mills and cheap rooming houses that were creeping along its edge. Spending two years of his own time appraising the land, he had determined that it would take $1,500,000 to condemn it and, in 1885, after a courageous and bitter fight, had persuaded the Legislature to appropriate the money and create Niagara State Park, which by the 1920's was nationally known, the single most famous park in the country. If Moses had studied Wilcox's life, he might have noticed more than a few resemblances to his own.

But Moses wasn't interested in studying Wilcox's life. And he didn't need Clearwater any more. The two old men—the entire Niagara Commission in fact—were a constant irritant to him. Why? No one could accuse the Niagara commissioners of excessive conservatism or of being too limited in their aims for improving the Niagara Park, long allowed by the Legislature to deteriorate, and for extending the park—along with connecting parkways and bridges—all along the Niagara Frontier. Their aims were, in most important respects, identical with Moses'. So was their insistence on speed.

Ansley Wilcox, in fact, had even more reason to want speed than Moses. In 1925, Wilcox was dying of what his obituaries would call "the wasting disease"—cancer. And Wilcox knew he was dying. He wanted desperately to see before he died at least the beginning of the refurbishment of the park he had created as a young man and had administered, frequently with his own money, for forty years, and at least a start on the park extension and parkway that would preserve forever the gorge he loved.

To speed the refurbishment, which included the acquisition of a new elevator to carry tourists down the cliffs near the falls to the famed Cave of Winds, Wilcox had persuaded another commission member, Paul A. Schoellkopf, president of the Niagara Falls Power Company, to have power-company engineers draw up plans for the elevator so that construction could begin as soon as funds were allocated. And he had done everything he could to enable the commission to get a fast start on the parkway along the edge of the Niagara gorge. Knowing that the $1,000,000 allocated to Niagara in the park referendum would pay for only a fraction of the necessary right-of-way, he asked Schoellkopf, whose power company owned much of the land along the gorge, to agree to donate easements if the commission acquired the rest of the right-of-way. Schoellkopf, who knew the nature of Wilcox's illness and the reason for his desire for haste, agreed. When a small but key parcel came on the market and Wilcox was afraid it would be purchased and developed by private interests, he and Schoellkopf purchased it and presented it to the commission as a gift. When two more key pieces came on the market in 1925, he persuaded Schoellkopf to have the power company purchase them and hold them until the commission received, at the 1926 legislative session, an appropriation to allow it to purchase them in turn. The admiration in which Wilcox was held helped the parkway along; several of his friends said they would buy parcels needed for the right-of-way and give them to the commission in his name, and Schoellkopf advanced money to speed the transactions. The only point of contention between the Niagara commissioners and Moses was that the commissioners wanted to carry out the Niagara development themselves, to keep, as Moses had solemnly promised them they could, power over the park's development and administration, to remain in charge of what was to them a cherished piece of nature instead of turning it over to a faceless bureaucracy in the Parks Council offices in New York City, three hundred miles away. In so wanting, they stood in the way of Moses' absolute control of state parks.

Clearwater, the Niagara Commission's representative on the Parks Council, was a larger irritant for the same reason. When the judge argued that the council was only an "advisory" body and that the regional commissions should be allowed latitude in their work, he was arguing, in effect, against absolute control of all state parks by Moses. And when Alphonse Clearwater spoke, the other council members sitting around the table with him seemed to remember more clearly the promises Moses had given them and the principles of park development that they had once been determined not to surrender. Several times, the judge had even swayed Robert H. Treman, the chairman of one of the three new regional commissions, and the decisive sixth vote had been cast against a Moses proposal.

The refusal of the Niagara Commission to submit to his control had already, Moses complained, made him look "ridiculous." In submitting park spending plans to the three-man committee of the Governor, Hutchinson and Hewitt, Moses, anxious as always to obtain as much money as possible as quickly as possible, had asked for immediate allocation of Niagara's whole million-dollar appropriation. But when Hutchinson asked Wilcox if the commission really needed the whole sum in 1926, Wilcox refused to lie. He said that the commission could use no more than $400,000 of the money in that year.

The Niagara Commission's independence was threatening to cause Moses serious problems. While the commission envisioned a complete parkway system around Niagara Falls, he wanted it to extend all the way to Buffalo, twenty-five miles away. The Niagara commissioners had no objection to the plan, but they didn't want to be responsible for it; they were not trying to build a vast park system; they were interested only in the land they knew and for whose protection they had been fighting for so many years. Furthermore, the parkway Moses wanted would be primarily in Erie County; they felt the newly created Erie County Park Commission should have jurisdiction over it. But the bond issue gave money for improvements on the Niagara Frontier only to the Niagara Commission, and they were afraid that under the law they would be forced to assume responsibility for it. When Moses asked them to give $100,000 of their million for planning of the Erie County section of the parkway, they objected because they felt the whole million was needed around the falls, but they said that they would give it anyway—as long as in return a law was passed making clear that the portion of the parkway in Erie County was not their responsibility. This apparently minor point appeared to worry Moses beyond all relationship to its legal importance, possibly because asking the Legislature to pass new park reorganization laws might give it the opportunity to oust him from control. Furthermore, the existence of open conflict within the Parks Council was a threat to his assertion of absolute dominance over it; as long as maneuverings within the parks empire he was creating were kept quiet, he could quietly work his will within it; let it once become a source of controversy and the Legislature might well begin stepping into it, and the Legislature would not be disposed to allow his dominance to continue.

So Moses moved against the Niagara commissioners. First, although they had a superintendent and an engineer to direct the commission's staff and day-to-day affairs, Moses demanded that they appoint an "executive officer"—who they suspected would be one of his men. They refused.

Then there ensued in April and May 1926 a number of Parks Council meetings at which the commission had no representative present. Clearwater, its authorized representative, was suddenly struck down by an illness so severe that doctors gave him no chance of living. Wilcox, his authorized substitute, was too weak to take his place. And council members who were friends of the two old men reported that in their absence rumors—vicious rumors—were being circulated about them in whispers at council meetings. Someone—Wilcox felt sure he knew who—was hinting darkly that the Niagara Commission, in making its park and parkway plans, had sold out to the interests of Schoellkopf's power company. On June 3, Smith wrote Moses a letter—Wilcox was always to believe that Moses wrote it, and persuaded Smith to sign it—asking Moses to investigate "transactions and relations between the Niagara Reservation Commission and the power companies, including the reservation of easements by the power companies on land sold by them to the commission."

"I also wish to learn," said the innuendo-loaded letter, "whether this park commission has laid out a program which will insure the protection of the Niagara Riverfront . . . or whether they are just buying isolated pieces of land along the banks of the river and leaving the rest of the land in the hands of the power company and other private interests."

Wilcox could hardly believe what he read. Moses, he was sure, was behind the letter, but Moses had known and approved of the commission's arrangements with the power company.

But Wilcox had gotten only a taste of what was in store for him.

Moses called a meeting of the Parks Council for June 26 to consider the Governor's letter. Wilcox, Schoellkopf and the two other Niagara Commission members, Robert W. De Forest and Robert H. Gittins, met and prepared resolutions giving their side of the story and sent them to Moses, asking him to have them read to the council. No Niagara commissioners were present at the council meeting—Clearwater and Wilcox were unable to travel—and they learned after the meeting that Moses had not even told the council about the existence of the resolutions and instead had persuaded it to appoint a five-member committee to investigate the matter at a hearing at the Parks Council office in New York City on July 15. The committee, the Niagara commissioners realized, was packed against them; there was one old park man, Major William A. Welch of the Palisades Commission, on it, and its chairman, Jay Downer of Westchester, although an engineer friendly to Moses and an exponent of the new park theories, was regarded as a man of integrity, but the third member was a representative of Conservation Commissioner Alexander MacDonald, and Moses and his friend and aide, Henry Lutz, were members *ex officio,* so Moses had three votes out of the five.

Whether the only available record of the hearing is complete is impossible to ascertain. The only transcript available was made by Rose Pedrick, Moses' secretary, and Wilcox later complained in a letter to Moses that "several times the stenographer was told to omit things, or portions of the discussion, which were really of the greatest relative significance." These omissions appear at two crucial points in the transcript as "discussions off the record" and once Miss Pedrick refers to an "argument between Mr. Gittins and Mr. Moses" without telling what the argument was about.

Complete or not, however, the transcript is interesting.

What are the specific charges against us? Wilcox demanded as soon as the hearings began. There are no charges, Downer hastily replied. This is not an investigation—"Take that word from the record. This conference; it is a conference. Substitute the word 'conference.' "

You mean there is no one willing to stand up here to our faces and make charges? Wilcox asked. "No, sir. No, sir," Downer replied. "No charges have been made by anybody so far as I know." The only reason the committee was interested in the commission's relations with the power company, he said, was that the Legislature might be reluctant to allocate money for land along the gorge until the power company gave definite written assurances, preferably legal options, that it would give the commission easements over the intervening lands it owned so that the Legislature could be assured that the parkway would be continuous. The only thing the committee wanted was an assurance from Wilcox and Schoellkopf that their informal agreements would be formalized.

Well, Wilcox said, there is a letter written by Governor Smith, "implying that we are handling the thing not for the public interest but for the interests of other people . . . of the power company . . . plainly implying it, so much so that he might as well have charged it in terms . . . just as plainly as if it were put in a little more brutal language, charging us with collusive and improper relations. . . . If the English language has any meaning, it means that." Where did the Governor get his information—false information, outright lies, in fact—on which the letter was based? Moses said hastily, "Mr. Downer, may I interrupt a moment. . . . Personally, I regard the question of where the Governor got his information as something that we have no right to go into." And Downer hastily agreed. Throughout the hearing, which would go on for six hours, at a high cost in pain and weariness to Wilcox and to De Forest—who was seventy-nine years old and so ill that he had been in bed for more than a month—the Niagara commissioners would seek to learn what the charges against them were and why, if there were no charges, they had been summoned to New York City. Throughout the hearing, Downer would evade a direct answer, trying to focus attention on a number of minor matters that had nothing to do with the power company. Near the end of the long day, Downer tried to conclude the hearing. "Just one minute," Wilcox said, and insisted that "the big question that appears in the Governor's letter" be discussed. He made the committee listen while he read into the record Schoellkopf's contributions to the parkway plan, and presented proof that the power company was not getting anything from the informal arrangement and in fact was donating to the state land worth hundreds of thousands of dollars. The Governor's letter talked about "transactions and relations between the . . . Commission and the power companies including the reservation of easements by the power companies on land sold by them to the Commission," Wilcox said. Why, he said, no power company had ever "sold an acre of land to our Commission or made any reservation [easement] whatever on any land whatever." And Downer, as if his sense of fairness had at last won over his loyalty to Moses, said for the record that he had, in fact, toured the Niagara site himself and had been "impressed with . . . the many things that they [the power company] . . . had planned to do for the furtherance of the parkway."

"We have no time to waste in hearing any defense of gentlemen of your reputation as to any collusion with anybody, and this committee will not go into any such question," Downer said. "We are not interested and we do not believe any such things and have nothing in our minds in regard to it. We know your reputations too well to believe you would do such a thing. . . . There is no such thing in the minds of this committee." And when Wilcox insisted that he be formally exonerated of any wrongdoing in his informal argreements with Schoellkopf, Downer said flatly, "I have no fault to find with that transaction," a position with which Welch heartily agreed. Moses, who had repeatedly interrupted Downer and the commissioners during discussions of the other, minor subjects, had been noticeably silent. Now he said, "I would like to ask as a question of fact whether or not the money in the case of the two parcels we discussed before was or was not furnished by the power company." And Downer said flatly, "What if it was, Mr. Moses?"

Downer's anxiousness to avoid discussion of the "big question" raised in Smith's—or Moses'—letter deprived Wilcox of an opportunity to get the committee's approval of acquisition by the power company of a key piece of land that had just come on the market and that Wilcox was eager to have Schoellkopf snap up and turn over to the commission for the parkway before someone else bought it and began to build on it. This, Wilcox was to say, was a bitter disappointment to him. "The opportunity . . . is slipping and my interest and ability to act are waning," he wrote, "and I fear this promising plan may come to naught." But at least the commissioners felt they had been exonerated.

But they had not reckoned with the full extent of the change in Robert Moses. The Niagara commissioners felt sure that Downer's report on the hearing would be fair. And they were right. The committee chairman wrote that Schoellkopf's only relationship with the commission had been to assist it and to have his power company assist it, at considerable expense to both himself and his company. Such criticisms as Downer did make of the commission's operations, based on the minor matters discussed at the hearings, dealt with technicalities, and so did his recommendations for changes in its procedures. But when the Parks Council met on July 24—with Wilcox, exhausted by the earlier trip to New York and the strain of the hearing, again confined to bed and absent—Downer's report was not distributed. Neither was its summary, which contained the exoneration. Instead, its list of "recommendations," which concentrated on the technicalities and did not include the exoneration or even mention the "big question," was read—so hastily that an aide Wilcox had sent to take notes was able to gain only a general idea of its contents—and the innocuous recommendations were adopted.

Wilcox's aide asked Henry Lutz to send a copy of the report to Wilcox, and Lutz promised he would do so. On July 30, Wilcox had not received it, and he sent Lutz a telegram asking for it. Lutz did not even reply.

On August 3, Wilcox, in bed, unable to determine what the report about him said or if it had been sent to the rest of the Parks Council, wrote Lutz. His letter was, considering the provocation, one of remarkable courtesy. The harshest line in it was its last: "If there is a copy of that report in existence or available, I should be glad to have it as soon as convenient."

Lutz did not reply. But Moses did. The first sentence of his letter to Wilcox was: "I will pass over without extended comment the unpleasant tone of your letter. I presume that you have become so accustomed to addressing people in this way that you are hardly aware of its effect on others." He was writing, Moses said, to defend Lutz from Wilcox's attacks. Downer's report, Moses said, was not ready, although the Parks Council had adopted its "conclusions" and "the action taken by the Council has been outlined to the Governor." An astounded Wilcox realized that Moses had sent a copy of his, Moses', letter to the seventy-two other regional commissioners without sending them a copy of Wilcox's letter—and therefore the commissioners could have no way of knowing that Wilcox's letter had not in fact been unpleasant, and they could not know the events that had led up to it.

Since Wilcox's letter was not insulting, why did Moses say it was? In Wilcox's view, Moses realized that the Downer report would not make the Niagara commissioners look bad to the other regional commissioners and would not justify to Smith what he had almost certainly told Smith about them, that he therefore needed another issue to divert attention from the main one, and that he seized on Wilcox's innocuous letter as the whole cloth out of which to manufacture it. In any case, his handling of the letter was consistent with his other actions in the matter. He had sent the seventy-three regional commissioners copies of Smith's letter implying wrongdoing by the Niagara Commission, but he had not sent the regional commissioners —he had not even let them know of the existence of—the Niagara Commission's resolutions that gave its side of the story. He had read at a Parks Council meeting Downer's "recommendations" which seemed to find some fault, however minor, with the commission, but not the summary which exonerated the commission of the major charges. And now he accused Wilcox of writing an abusive letter to a council employee, without allowing the regional commissioners to see the letter for themselves—and to see that it was not abusive. It is impossible to avoid the conclusion that Moses had determined to hound from the state park organization a group of elderly men whose only crime was their refusal to allow him to exercise unbridled power in that organization and to remove them from control of the park they loved, the park that one of them had created, the park to which they had given so much of their lives.

When he received Moses' letter, Wilcox, who had been confined at home, weak and in pain, since his trip to New York, left his bed and went to his office to dictate a reply. He was unable to stay there long or to work in substantial stretches, and it took him five days to finish it. But he finished it. And although its main purport was to exonerate himself from charges of discourtesy and dishonesty, it was also a telling document in charting the evolution of Robert Moses.

"You speak from a high position," Ansley Wilcox wrote.

> Seemingly, this should bring with it a feeling of responsibility and consideration, not merely a sense of dominating authority and a desire to have your own way without opposition in all matters, large and small. It might have led you to show some special consideration to the Niagara Commission and Commissioners, owing to their age and long service and the experience of all of them, giving them an intimate knowledge of many special local problems which you and other members of the State Council, however wise and experienced in general, are only able to guess at; and owing to the desperate illness and disability of Judge Clearwater, our President, and partial disabilities of Mr. De Forest and myself. But it has not produced any such consideration—quite the contrary. . . . Our Commission and its members have been treated by you unfairly and brutally to a degree which cannot be expressed in polite language.

Your rage toward Judge Clearwater and me, Wilcox wrote Moses, is a "poisonous thing." And what, Wilcox asked, is the reason for it? Nothing but the fact that, while supporting in general your park policies, we have "ventured on occasion to speak out in meetings views opposing your policies, and [have] beaten them more than once. This could not be forgotten."

Wilcox denied that his letter to Lutz had been abusive.

"Neither you nor anyone can point out anything offensive in my letter to Mr. Lutz, except to one conscious of trying to play tricks, who finds himself caught and exposed . . . I was feeling indignant, but I had a right to be indignant," Wilcox wrote. You accused us of dishonesty—yes, it was you; you were responsible for the vicious rumors that came up in Parks Council meetings when neither Clearwater nor I were present to repudiate them; you wrote the letter signed by Smith; "the letter does not sound at all like Governor Smith, and it does sound like you"—and then when Downer's report showed us to be innocent, you did not let us or anyone else see the report. Probably the Governor has not seen it either, Wilcox wrote. "You say . . . that 'The action taken by the Council has been outlined to the Governor.' " I am sure it has—"by you, I suppose, and in your own way."

Wilcox's letter, which detailed his "transactions and relations" with the power company, covered ten single-spaced typewritten pages. "That it is too long, I know well," he concluded. "Few will read it and probably none will appreciate it."

The old man was right. His letter lay unread in an unopened folder in a dusty Albany warehouse for forty-two years. And although, in the forty-third year, the folder was opened (by the author) and the letter was read, and although it provided the first detailed account of the changes wrought in Robert Moses by his hunger for power, it could not right the worst of all the injustices Moses perpetrated on Ansley Wilcox. During Moses' long reign as State Parks Council chairman, the plaques previously placed in Niagara State Park by Wilcox's friends to commemorate the contributions to the park made by him and the other old Niagara commissioners were systematically removed—to be replaced with plaques bearing Moses' name. When the parkway along the Niagara gorge was built, it was named after Moses and so was the power dam that became the centerpiece of the park. By the time Moses' reign was over, it would be impossible to find anywhere in Niagara State Park even a single hint that anyone except Moses had been responsible for its creation.

Wilcox's letter had no appreciable effect on Moses. With it, Wilcox sent a request for the names and addresses of the seventy-two other regional commissioners, "to whom you sent your abusive and misleading and unfair and domineering letter," so that he could send copies—along with copies of his letter to Lutz—to them so that they could judge for themselves. Moses never replied. Instead, he continued his assault on the old men, if by more roundabout means. If he could not oust them quickly, his actions seemed to indicate, he would wear them down.

First, a series of charges were filed against the commission's superintendent and chief executive officer, Emil R. Waldenberger. The commissioners investigated and cleared him. Then Moses told Smith that because of the illnesses of Judge Clearwater, Wilcox and De Forest, the commission was "not functioning," and in March 1927 Smith asked De Forest, in the most delicate of terms because of De Forest's great prestige, if he might not prefer a post on the State Housing Board instead. De Forest had, in fact, long wanted to resign. But the old men were loyal to their compatriots. "I would rather not put myself in the position of a deserter," he replied.

In reality, Clearwater had confounded his doctors and recovered—months before. De Forest sent a copy of Smith's letter to the judge, and the judge wrote a letter of his own. He still had the gift of words.

"The Governor's letter . . . seems like a wound in the house of a friend," he wrote. "I have for him a great admiration. He has all the elements of greatness and none of its limitations.

"Unfortunately, some men greatly his inferior have secured access to him and to a considerable extent have his confidence, which unhesitatingly they abuse to gratify their ambitions, their interests and their animosities. By them he at times has been misinformed."

The commission *has* been functioning, the judge wrote. Would the Governor like to know how? And he proceeded to list page after page of extensive land-acquisition negotiations that had been carried out in recent months.

He knew why Moses was lying, the judge wrote. "The situation at Niagara affords opportunities for spectacular publicity not offered by any other of the State Parks, and . . . there are members of the Council of Parks who desire to dominate it in order to capitalize those opportunities for their own glorification." Furthermore, he was not afraid to speak out against those of Moses' policies with which he did not agree. "Now there seems to be a somewhat widespread feeling that because of the Governor's friendship for him, Mr. Moses expects an attitude of abject acquiescence from the members of Council . . . and that unless he receives it, reprisals may be expected."

Moses let the "not functioning" issue drop.

But time is not on the side of old men. The progress of Wilcox's disease was slow but steady. In July 1927, he was forced to resign from the commission, and Smith accepted Moses' recommendation on his replacement. Then Moses convinced the Governor that the activities of the Niagara Commission could not be adequately carried out unless the commission made the new member its executive officer with full powers to act for it. He convinced the Governor not to sign any appropriations for the Niagara Park unless the old commissioners gave the new one this power. In order to realize their dream, in order even to keep functioning the park they loved, the old men were forced to turn it over to someone else. At the end of the fight for control of Niagara State Park, Robert Moses had won.

He won every fight in the State Parks Council. By the end of 1928, most recalcitrant regional commissioners had been replaced, as their terms expired, by men amenable to administration of their parks by the council's central staff, which, through Lutz, took orders from Moses. To further insure that votes within the council would no longer hinge on the changeable margin of a single vote, two new members were named, the State Historian, directly appointed by Smith, and the president of a new regional commission, all of whose members were appointed by Smith.

Parks had never been a source of power before. Since the traditional function of park commissions had been to preserve the land in its natural state, the later developments—construction contracts, jobs—that made parks a source of power had never been a significant consideration. Parks were a source of power now, but the old park men didn't want power. They just wanted to be left alone to preserve and pass on beauty to other generations, and when, as in the case of the Erie County Parkway, the chance for power came their way, they backed away from it.

Politicians failed to grasp the new reality until too late. By the time they finally realized—one can see the realization growing in their correspondence of 1927 and 1928—that a new organ of state government was being created that would dispense yearly millions of dollars in construction contracts and thousands of jobs, Moses had the state park system too firmly in his control for it to be pried loose. He would remain president of the Long Island State Park Commission and chairman of the State Parks Council until 1962, and during the thirty-eight years of his reign over state parks these parks would, even as his activities expanded into other fields, be a constant source of power that he could use to expand his influence in those fields.

In politics, power vacuums are always filled. And the power vacuum in parks was filled by Robert Moses. The old park men saw beauty in their parks. Moses saw beauty there, too, but he also saw power, saw it lying there in those parks unwanted. And he picked it up—and turned it as a weapon on those who had not thought it important and destroyed them with it. Whether or not he so intended, he turned parks, the symbol of man's quest for serenity and peace, into a source of power.

Moses could have done nothing, of course, without Al Smith's constant support.

The old park men pleaded with the Governor for justice. "I am very sure that on the same knowledge of facts there would be no difference at all as to any park matters between you and me," De Forest wrote, and others, too, told him he was being misled. They asked the Governor for appointments so that they could tell him their side of the disputes.

But the appointments they were given were few and far between. And although they didn't know it, most—perhaps all—of the letters they wrote Smith complaining about Moses were sent by Smith's office to Moses for "suggested" replies—and the replies Moses suggested were generally sent out over Smith's signature without a word being changed.

The pattern was the same in Moses' relations with the Legislature. He might have told Jerry Twomey to stick a bill up his ass, but, Twomey told Len Hall, "within two days, Al Smith had me on the phone and I had to put the bill through." The Legislature might rage at Robert Moses—Twomey wasn't the only legislator insulted to his face, Hall not the only one on whom he slammed down the telephone—but no legislator dared to stand up to a Governor who was a master of every method of bending men to his will. As long as Al Smith stuck by Moses, the Legislature could do nothing about him.

And Al Smith stuck. In the midst of the Thayer bill fight, with Smith threatened by political embarrassment because of Moses' actions, a wealthy New Yorker who had been a victim of Moses' insults stormed into Smith's office. According to one Smith biographer, he asked angrily, " 'Do you want to settle this park fight?'

" 'Yes,' the Governor said.

" 'Then I'll tell you how to do it.'

" 'How?'

"The visitor banged his fist on the Governor's desk.

" 'Get rid of Moses!' he shouted.

"The Governor leaped to his feet, his face suddenly purple with rage.

" 'Get out of my office, you idiot!' he roared."

Why Smith stuck was a question that had many answers.

One was that he was a politician. In capitol corridors, Moses may have been a handicap to the Governor, but in voting booths the parks that he built were a priceless asset to Smith. About Colonel Frederick Stuart Greene, the short-story-writing engineer who refused to consider politicians' wishes in awarding contracts but who got roads built that won voters' appreciation, Smith once said, "He may be a devil in May, but he's an angel in November," and the Governor might have said the same thing about Moses. In 1926, desperate to derail the Governor before the 1928 presidential campaign, the state GOP ran against him its strongest candidate, Congressman Ogden Livingston Mills. Campaigning vigorously, Mills tried to focus voters' attention on the unprecedented expenditures of Smith's administration, but the Governor easily diverted them by reminding them, over and over, that Mills was one of the North Shore barons, "that small handful of wealthy millionaires on Long Island [who] said: 'We do not want the rabble from New York coming down into our beautiful country.' " Smith won a fourth term—the first Governor to do so since De Witt Clinton a century before—and he credited a large part of his 257,000-vote plurality to the parks issue.

Smith was not only a politician; he was a Tammany politician. In the simple Tammany code, the first commandment was Loyalty. Smith's loyalty to his appointees was legendary. Once he gave a man a job, he was fond of saying, he never interfered with him unless he proved himself incapable of handling it.

And Smith knew that none of his appointees worked harder for him than Moses. When his daughter Emily, her father's confidante and perhaps the person who best understood him, was asked why her father stuck by Moses, she would begin her analysis by saying simply, "Bob worked so hard for Father, you know."

Beyond politics was the fact that the boy from the Fulton Fish Market wanted so passionately to improve the lives of the people of the Fourth Ward—and of a hundred Fourth Wards throughout the state. And parks were, unlike improvements in teachers' salaries or other highly praised but unmeasurable accomplishments of his administration, an accomplishment that he could *see*, an accomplishment whose visible, concrete existence could prove to him that he had indeed done something for his people. When he saw families picnicking under the tall trees at Valley Stream or swimming at Sunken Meadow, he could feel that he had measurably improved their lives. So many of the things that made him most satisfied with his administration had been the result of Moses' work.

As for his refusal to listen to Moses' opponents, Smith was well aware, as a politician, that every public improvement caused outcries. "You can't get a road built if you're going to listen to every farmer who doesn't want it to go across his land," he often said. Listening to protesters undermined his appointee, and got himself involved in enemy-making situations. Staying out of such situations—leaving responsibility with his appointee—enabled him to stay out of the fights which attended upon the building of public improvements while still allowing him to take full credit for their completion. Moreover, most of Moses' opponents, after all, were upstate legislators or politicians. Smith knew the depth of their reactionism, their narrow-mindedness, their utter inability to understand the needs of the city masses. As Emily put it, "Father wouldn't care what Bob did or said to the GOP legislators. After all, Father was fighting them himself. And Father thought the legislators really were terribly wrong. He felt the things Bob wanted to do were right."

In the opinion of those close to the Governor, he didn't realize how drastic the methods were that Moses was using to accomplish his aims. He didn't understand that Moses was going beyond the actions of other appointees, handling protesters with needless harshness, stirring up protests by his arrogance, creating problems where there need not have been problems. "Particularly with little people," Emily says; "I didn't think that Father really knew how Moses was treating them." And there was, of course, no reason why the Governor would; they didn't have his ear or, since he seldom read even memos from appointees and almost never letters from the public, his eye. And the press, which might have publicized their complaints, was firmly in Moses' corner.

And behind the political considerations there were the personal. Al Smith was a fighter, and he liked fighters. One night Smith heard Richard Childs, introducing Moses at a dinner, smilingly tell his audience: "You all know Bob, of course. He's so forthright and honest that if he saw a man across the street who he thought was a son of a bitch, he would cross the street and call him a son of a bitch, lest by passing him in silence, his silence be misconstrued." Smith roared at the description—and, thereafter, when someone would criticize Moses, the Governor would often give it himself, with evident delight.

And Moses reciprocated. He knew how much he owed Smith for the realization of his dreams. "*We could have done nothing without him*," he would say. He knew how much he owed Smith for rescuing him from a life of obscurity and failure. "Most of what little I know of the practice of government I learned from this remarkable Gamaliel," Moses would write. "Without him I would have been just another academic researcher." After the Governor's death in 1944, Moses wrote, "The few remaining members of the Smith brigade think of him often and at the strangest times, see him in moments of action and relaxation, inspiration and ease. We hear his rough voice. . . ."

Moses may have mocked to their faces men of wealth and influence and insulted the most powerful members of the State Legislature; he treated Al Smith with a respect that to those who saw the two men together was unforgettable. Said Belle Moskowitz's son, Carlos Israels: "When Moses was with Smith, he would always be spouting out ideas, pacing, gesticulating, talking. But it was the talking and gesticulating of an enthusiastic boy with his father, a father whom he admired and to whom he was very respectful." Joseph Proskauer said: "He acted to Smith as he acted to no one else, with deference and respect."

Smith was always "Governor" to Moses. He never addressed him—either in letters or in speech—as anything but "Governor." And this was a fact more significant with Robert Moses than it would be with other men. Moses would, during the forty years after Smith left Albany, serve under five other Governors. He never addressed them—in letters or in speech—except by their first names. He never called any one of them "Governor." For Robert Moses, there would always be only one Governor.

During the final years of Smith's reign, he and Moses became closer and closer. Smith saw that Moses was invited to the most intimate of Tammany soirees, the notoriously boisterous get-togethers at William F. Kenny's Tiger Room. The Tammany bigwigs who had looked at him askance soon came to like him and, when they mentioned this to Smith, the Governor would beam happily. Often, after dinner in the Executive Mansion or, in New York, in the Biltmore suite or a friend's apartment, Smith would say, if Moses had not been present at the dinner, "I wonder what Bob's doing tonight—let's get him." Someone would call Moses. When he arrived, Smith would say, "Bob, let's go to Dinty Moore's," and the two men would sit for hours in a back room specially reserved for the Governor, drinking beer, cracking crabs and talking. "That talk was something," Howard Cullman would recall. "You could tell just listening to the two of them that there were two men with real brains."

Not that the talk was all serious. Often, the Governor and Moses would, to the delight of listeners, go into a sort of rapid-paced comic dialogue on the Albany scene. Says Emily Smith: "It would be more fun to be there listening to Father and Bob than to be out at a theater or dancing somewhere." Or Smith would, if there was a piano handy, jump up, walk over to it and say to Moses, "Come on, Bob, let's show these people what we can do." One of the men who watched Smith and Moses harmonizing on such occasions says, "There was a tie there that was beyond business or politics." Says another: "You could tell just by looking at the two of them together that they liked each other a lot."

15. *Curator of Cauliflowers*

Approval by the Legislature in 1923 and 1924 of the department-consolidating, ballot-shortening amendment—recommended in the Reconstruction Commission report Moses had finished in his little apartment on West Eighty-seventh Street in 1919—permitted its submission to the state's voters, who approved it in November 1925. Henceforth, of the state's top officials, only the Governor, Lieutenant Governor, Attorney General and Comptroller would be elected.

Vicious legislative in-fighting over the laws necessary to implement the consolidation amendment—in-fighting in which Moses was the key behind-the-scenes figure—went on for another year. But the State Department Law of 1926, while establishing eighteen departments instead of the sixteen Moses had proposed, was in most crucial respects a restatement of the report Moses had written for the Reconstruction Commission seven full years before. It consolidated within the eighteen departments every one of the existing 187 agencies, forbade the creation of any new departments and eliminated overlapping agency functions. When the constitutional amendments establishing the executive budget system and the four-year gubernatorial term proposed in the Reconstruction Commission report were repassed, approved in referendum and signed into law—the executive budget amendment in 1928, the four-year-term amendment in 1932—the report written in Moses' apartment became, substantially unchanged, the administrative machinery of the State of New York.

The fight had been a long one for Robert Moses. He had begun working on the Reconstruction Commission report in 1918 and had completed it in 1919. He had written the administration bills, drafted the gubernatorial messages and supplied the technical information for the legislative fights that had resulted in passage of the consolidation–short-ballot amendment in 1920 and repassage, after the 1921 defeat, in 1923 and 1924. Following passage of the referendum in 1925, he had played a key role in the drafting of the State Department Law of 1926. The executive budget proposal did not start down the path to legislative and voter approval until 1926 and it was not enacted into law until 1928. But when it was, at the end of a decade of work for Robert Moses, the Governor of the State of New York possessed at last the power the Governor had always been intended to possess.

Political scientists said so in the patois of political science. The reorganization "released the executive's energy to provide the leadership required in the twentieth century," one said. Al Smith said so in the patois of Al Smith. "When the Governor wants to talk about the state hospitals he will have one man to talk to," he exulted. "When he wants to talk about public parks, he will have one man to talk to, and the same way when he wants to talk about agriculture, charities, education." For the first time, he knew, when he wanted to move the state down a particular path, he could make it move.

Before his fourth term was over, "against the tide of the Twenties" that blinded most of a prosperous nation to the needs of its urban masses, Al Smith had not only forced through a recalcitrant Legislature measures that improved working conditions and reduced working hours for men, women and children, but had also lashed state departments into enforcing the measures. He had not only forced through the first large-scale, low-cost housing program in the United States, increased teachers' salaries tenfold and obtained equal pay for women teachers, but had also moved a dozen state departments into less dramatic but equally vital efforts to meet needs in areas of their jurisdictions. He had not only persuaded voters to approve bond issues of unprecedented size for state hospitals, mental hospitals and prisons but had also geared up the departments responsible for building these institutions to do so with unprecedented speed. He had written on the statute books of New York such a sweep of social welfare statutes that Oscar Handlin could say that they "made the most difficult state the best-governed one in the Union . . . [and] awakened the conscience of the nation to the needs of the urban working people." Franklin D. Roosevelt, as President, was to say that "practically all the things we've done in the federal government are like things Al Smith did as Governor of New York."

Robert Moses himself was conspicuously uninterested in social welfare reforms. But these reforms would have been impossible of attainment without the executive budget and departmental consolidation and reorganization. Even more impossible of attainment would have been another Smith achievement: while expanding manyfold the state's role in helping its people meet their needs, he succeeded, over the course of his four terms, in substantially cutting state taxes. Walter Lippmann called the reorganization of New York's administrative machinery "one of the greatest achievements in modern American politics." Robert F. Wagner, Sr., asked to name Smith's most important achievement, said flatly: "The reorganization." And many other states modeled their reorganizations directly on New York's. Says Leslie Lipson, author of *The American Governor from Figurehead to Leader,* the definitive study of the development of state government in America, "New York is the great classic of the reorganization movement." In that classic, Robert Moses played the leading role. Most of Moses' achievements were highly visible achievements—monuments of concrete and steel—which may be expected to endure in the public consciousness for as long as they stand. But his achievement in reshaping the machinery by which New York State's millions of inhabitants are governed to make it substantially more responsive to the changing and growing needs of those millions is an episode all but lost to history. And it may be that this achievement is at least the equal of any of the others.

Reorganization made the Department of State the "catch-all" repository for scores of minor functions that did not fit logically into any other department. The Secretary of State was made responsible for accepting and filing incorporation papers, compiling election results and county-by-county enrollment figures, supervising the Hell Gate Pilots and the Wardens of the Port of New York and licensing auctioneers, private detectives, real estate salesmen, theater-ticket agencies and poolrooms.

Unexciting as these functions were, they all required manpower—and manpower was jobs and jobs were patronage. The Secretary of State would control a sizable harvest of the carrots that kept political workers straining at the ropes that pulled political machines.

The Secretary of State would, moreover, possess several functions that were not at all minor, including jurisdiction over the state's Athletic, Racing and Land Office commissions. And Smith had announced that he intended to use the Secretary as a coordinator of all state construction work and as coordinator of the Cabinet, that body of department heads which, for the first time, was going to be meeting as a group to advise the Governor—as, in fact, a sort of "Deputy Governor" with power second only to himself.

So politicians of both parties raged when, in January 1927, Smith nominated Robert Moses as New York's first appointed Secretary of State. Democrats raged because Moses was a Republican (an "Independent Republican" according to the press), and Republicans indignantly denied the charge, former GOP State Treasurer—and Nassau County estate owner—Lewis H. Pounds calling him a "political orphan."

The depth and unanimity of the feeling transcended party affiliation. Moses had for years been either insulting or ignoring legislators of both parties. And now the Legislature was being asked—for under reorganization the Senate had to approve key gubernatorial nominations—to approve his elevation to the second most important post in the state. One observer says: "When he walked down a corridor in the capitol and passed a group of legislators, you could see their eyes follow him as he passed, and you could see how many enemies—bitter, personal enemies—he had. I really believe that Robert Moses was the most hated man in Albany."

But Robert Moses didn't have to worry about enemies as long as his friend stuck by him. And his friend stuck. Smith's unprecedented popularity—proven by the ease with which he defeated Mills, a popular Republican running in a heavily Republican state—had given him unprecedented power in the state. And he let the Senate know that he would, if necessary, use every bit of that power on behalf of Robert Moses. He had, the Governor said, been accepting help from Moses for years. Now he wanted to formalize the arrangement.

GOP senators tried to find an issue by saying that no man should hold more than one high-ranking state job at a time. If Moses wanted confirmation, they said, he would have to give up his park posts. But, as a Brooklyn *Eagle* reporter put it:

> . . . None of the objectors forgot for an instant that Alfred E. Smith is still the king, mikado or just plain "boss" of the state.
>
> The Democrats cannot openly object to his course and get away with it. The Republicans know that Smith will politically outjockey them if they don't watch every step taken in opposition to him. The result is that Robert Moses, despite all opposition, in all probability will be confirmed.

The *Eagle*—and other newspapers throughout the state with the notable exceptions of the New York *Herald Tribune* and Hearst's tabloids—helped strengthen the probability with a paean of praise. Said a January 22 front-page *Eagle* headline: PATRONAGE CROWD SORE—KNOWLEDGE THAT MOSES WILL BUCK THEM, CHIEF BASIS FOR FIGHTING HIM. Three days later, it made another point: ATTACK ON MOSES BY G.O.P. LAID TO HIS L.I. PARK FIGHT—PLAN SEEN TO SHELVE HIM TO AID RICH LANDOWNERS.

GOP senators were inundated with pro-Moses missives. In a sprawling hand on the back of a postcard, Howard D. Brown of East Islip wrote Senator George Thompson of Suffolk County: "Mr. Moses did sidetrack the millionaire, so the man on the street could get Parks on Long Island. Your vote for him would be appreciated by all common people." Thompson hastily assured his constituents that his vote would, indeed, be for Moses. When, on January 31, 1927, the Senate clerk called a general voice vote on the nomination there was a loud chorus of "Nays." But when the clerk called the role name by name, only two senators were willing to go on record against it.

The appointment marked a first for Moses as well as for the state. Although he had been working on and off for various governmental bodies for fourteen years, the Secretary's $12,000 per year salary was the first he had received on a regular basis from government. It was, in fact, the first substantial salary he had received from anyone. Although some of his mother's relatives had been commenting pointedly for years that married men ought to at least *try* to support their own families, Bella Moses had always maintained that she was proud of Bob and completely happy in his choice of jobs. Despite her protestations, however, Bella Moses may have been just a little relieved that her favorite child was, at the age of thirty-eight, finally off her dole. When a friend told her, while she was attending a Madison House board meeting, that her son's appointment had just been confirmed, she breathed a sigh of relief and murmured: "At last, *at last,* he's going to start earning a living."

As Secretary of State, Robert Moses was a reporter's dream. If the press thrives on conflict, he provided it with ample nourishment, sallying forth almost daily to "strip the license from" unscrupulous ticket brokers, unscrupulous private detectives, unscrupulous real estate salesmen and inefficient Hell Gate Pilots and Port Wardens. His image, already shiny as a result of newspaper accounts of his park activities, was brought to an even higher gloss.

When Moses announced that he was fighting not only crooks but something that to the American mind loomed as a menace of approximately equal proportions—*politicians*—new highlights were added to his sheen. They didn't fade even when the ringing announcement was followed by a very dull thud—as it was in his attempt to make himself the state's boxing czar.

Before reorganization, the State Athletic Commission had run boxing, and commissionerships had been coveted by Tammany boyos since boxing promoters had learned the wisdom of crossing the commissioners' palms with free tickets, called "Annie Oakleys" because ticket takers punched holes in them similar to Little Sure Shot's bullet holes, to distinguish them in the count from paid-for ducats. By 1927, in fact, sports writer W. O. McGeehan was noting that Annie Oakleys had become "so common that customers of prize fights who wanted to be exclusive insisted upon paying for their tickets and getting them unperforated." In 1927, moreover, the chairman of the commission was James Aloysius Farley and Farley was carrying things to an extreme in cultivating friends, particularly among the contractors and politicians who might have occasion to use the services, or to have the city use the services, of his burgeoning building-materials company; since it cost him nothing to entertain these friends with fight tickets, he cultivated many of them. When Jim Maloney, the Boston Bull, outpointed Bridgeport Jack Delaney in Madison Square Garden on February 18, 1927, more than $30,000 worth of Annie Oakleys were distributed.

Farley, a fast-rising political heavyweight who had never been accused of cramping his style with undue loyalty to the Marquis of Queensbury, was a feared opponent. But less than three weeks after Moses assumed jurisdiction over the Athletic Commission, the new Secretary of State declared that he wanted "to protect the fellow with the thin pocketbook, who is just as much interested in boxing as the millionaire fight fan," and announced that henceforward no commissioner could accept free tickets. Half of all tickets, moreover, would be placed on sale on the evening of the fight, to insure that there would be plenty for the general public.

In vain, promoter Tex Rickard told Moses the plan was unworkable. When the desperate Farley and his fellow commissioners, anxious not to disappoint their friends, *bought* hundreds of tickets for the Dempsey-Sharkey fight and gave them away, Moses ruled that henceforth commissioners could not buy tickets, either. They could not properly regulate a sport "if they are recipients of favors from the people they are supposed to regulate," he said.

But Moses' lack of ring savvy began to show. His swings grew wilder. On one occasion, when there was a row over a decision in a prize fight, he declared: "Any decision should be unanimous. If not, then I will make the decision."

Selling half of Madison Square Garden's 18,000 seats the evening of the fight led only to monumental tie-ups at the ticket windows. Within a year, Moses gave up. "Frankly admitting," as one reporter put it, that he "knows little about the fight game," he announced that the Athletic Commission would be put back in full control of the sport. He was really more interested in parks anyway, he said. No more was heard about unanimous decisions.

In the eyes of the crowd, however, he had chalked up another win. He had, after all, been once again publicly identified as an ally of the "fellow with the thin pocketbook" and as a foe of the millionaire as well as the politician. He even got a title. During his brief but eventful ring career, sports writers, intrigued with his academic background, dubbed Robert Moses "Curator of Cauliflowers."

Though Moses' battles with private detectives and boxing promoters earned him reams of newsprint in 1927 and 1928, the significant accomplishments of his tenure as Secretary of State were accomplishments for which he never received any public notice. And they came in fields in which the Secretary of State supposedly had no power.

Al Smith put him into those fields. When the Governor had said he would put Moses in charge of the Cabinet, he meant *really* in charge. At his direction, Moses assumed responsibility for spurring the heads of other departments into the gallop at which Smith wanted them to move.

The Governor was particularly anxious about public works. Until he came to office, state institutions for men and women convicted of crimes and men and women whose only crimes were mental or physical illness were ancient, crowded and filthy. During his Governorship, against the unwavering opposition of a Republican Party that continually screamed that his financial policies would wreck the state, he persuaded the state's voters to pass referenda allocating not only $15,000,000 for parks and $50,000,000 for hospitals but also $300,000,000 for grade-crossing elimination and $100,000,000 for prisons, mental institutions and other public works. The buildings those bond revenues would buy would symbolize something to him. They would be something he could look at, as he could look at parks, and *know* that he had really done something for the people he had wanted to do something for. Further—and this was no small consideration since he was as much a politician as a reformer and now he had his eye on bigger prizes than a Governorship—they would symbolize something to the voters of other states. He wanted those buildings finished, and when progress on them was too slow, his solution was to make Moses personally responsible for speeding it up.

Running the Department of State, playing a key role in reorganizing the state government and creating, in a space of time unprecedentedly small, a state park and parkway system unprecedentedly large, might seem like a load large enough for one man to handle, but, as Moses drove around Long Island now, pushing his parks, he was haunted by other problems. His secretaries, driving out from New York or Belmont Lake, would be trying to find him to deliver messages from Graves, the Governor's secretary—"The Governor told me to drop you a note and say not to forget about the Long Island hospital situation," one said—and there might be a dozen such messages in a single mail. As Moses paced through a clearing at Sunken Meadow or Valley Stream, a band of aides behind him scribbling furiously while he fired instructions at them, across the clearing would come, trotting, the gray-uniformed, Sam Browne-belted, Stetsoned figure of a state trooper dispatched by the Governor to find him and bring him to a telephone for a message too urgent or too confidential to entrust to the mails. As he stood with his engineers and contractors on Jones Beach, discussing the progress of the causeway across the bay, across the bay would come a boat and in it, standing up as it neared shore so he could jump out and reach Moses the more quickly with the urgent message he bore, would be another Stetsoned figure.

Moses had always possessed tremendous energy and the ability to discipline it. Now he disciplined it as never before, concentrated it, focused it on his work with a ferocious single-mindedness.

Sloughing off distractions, he set his life into a hard mold. Shunning evening social life, especially the ceremonial dinners that eat up so much of a public official's time, he went to bed early (usually before eleven) and awoke early (he was always dressed, shaved and breakfasted when Arthur Howland arrived at 7:30 to pick up the manila envelope full of memos).

The amenities of life dropped out of his. He and Mary had enjoyed playing bridge with friends; now they no longer played. Sundays with his family all but disappeared. He did not golf; he did not attend sporting events; he was not interested in the diversions called "hobbies" that other executives considered important because they considered it important that they relax; he was not interested in relaxing. Since he left to Mary the paying of bills and the selection of his clothes, even the hiring of barbers to come to his office and cut his hair, his resources of energy were freed for the pursuit of his purposes. His life became an orgy of work.

Even so, there was never enough time; minutes were precious to him. To make sure that he had as many of them as possible, he tried to make use of all those that most other men waste.

He had always worked in his car while traveling; now he turned the big Packard limousine into an office. With Howland sitting beside him on the rear seat, three other engineers swiveled around on the jump seats and another two crammed in beside the chauffeur, he held staff meetings in the limousine—while another limousine trailed behind so that when Moses was finished with his men, he could drop them off and they could be driven back to Belmont Lake while he continued on to his destination. The door pockets in the Packard were crammed with yellow legal note pads and sharp-pointed pencils, and he spent his hours alone in the car writing letters and memos that his secretary could type up later.

Often, a secretary was in the car to take his dictation. Usually, it was Hazel Tappan. Miss Tappan was a tall, broad-shouldered Juno whose elaborately marcelled hairdos did nothing to conceal the strength and harshness of her features. "There was," an acquaintance says, "no softness to her." A stenographer fast enough to keep up with the drumfire of Moses' dictation, she also displayed a talent for giving orders—and Moses gave her material on which to exercise her talents. Two secretaries worked full time for Moses at the State Parks Council offices, now occupying an entire floor at 302 Broadway, three more worked at the Long Island Park Commission offices at Belmont Lake. Moses made Miss Tappan his personal secretary and put her in charge of them, demoting Rose Pedrick, his former personal secretary, who was nonetheless to remain on his personal secretarial staff, hating Miss Tappan all the time, for more than a decade.

Wanting Miss Tappan available whenever he needed secretarial assistance, Moses placed at her disposal a car and three chauffeurs, who worked around the clock in eight-hour shifts. On many mornings she arrived at his home at 7:30 A.M., her car pulling up behind that of Howland, who was picking up Moses' night-written memos, and she would get into Moses' limousine so that he could start dictating the minute he stepped in. As she drove with him, her car followed behind so that whenever he was finished with her, she could get out of his car, step into her own, and speed back to Belmont Lake or 302 Broadway to parcel out the work among the subordinate secretaries while he, chauffeured by one of *his* three chauffeurs, continued on to his destination.

Lunches were a constant source of irritation to Moses; he hated to interrupt his work for them. Now he began refusing invitations to lunch. Anyone who wanted to dine with him came to his office, and a secretary would run out for sandwiches.

The annoyances that plague busy executives had to be done away with. One of the worst was the telephone; he was continually being interrupted in the middle of one call by another urgent incoming message. Finally he had a new telephone setup installed. Under it, there were many lines into his secretary's office but only one from hers into his; on the single telephone that remained on his desk there were no buttons. If he was talking on that telephone, all other callers—with the single exception of Governor Smith, for whom all other calls were dropped—had to wait until he was finished. He was very pleased with this stratagem, and he used it for the rest of his life. The five Governors who succeeded Smith and the five Mayors of New York City for whom Moses would work had to get used to being told that Mr. Moses would have to call them back; he could not talk at the moment because his line was tied up.

Then there were intercoms; he liked to see his men face to face when he was giving them orders. His intercom was thrown out and in its place on his desk there was installed a panel with buttons that, when pressed, triggered a harsh buzz in the offices of his top executives. When the buzzer sounded in an executive's office, he was expected to drop everything and get to Moses' office fast. "He didn't want any intercom," says Assembly Speaker Perry B. Duryea, Jr., who, in 1962, succeeded Moses as president of the Long Island Park Commission and moved behind Moses' desk at

Belmont Lake. "When he hit that button, he wanted Shapiro at the door. I tried it and I'll tell you, it certainly throws off an aura of power. You just press a buzzer and you look up and there's a man standing in your door waiting for your orders."

A third feature of Moses' office was his desk. It wasn't a desk but rather a large table. The reason was simple: Moses did not like to let problems pile up. If there was one on his desk, he wanted it disposed of immediately. Similarly, when he arrived at his desk in the morning, he disposed of the stacks of mail awaiting him by calling in secretaries and going through the stacks, letter by letter, before he went on to anything else. Having a table instead of a desk was insurance that this procedure would be followed. Since a table has no drawers, there was no place to hide papers; there was no escape from a nagging problem or a difficult-to-answer letter except to get rid of it in one way or another. And there was another advantage: when your desk was a table, you could have conferences at it without even getting up.

Such techniques stretched his already vast personal resources, but sometimes it seemed as if they had been stretched too far, that they must break under the strain.

There were small signs of the pressure he was under. Often, too rushed to be careful when he was shaving, he would appear for early appointments with nicks still bleeding on his face. As a young man, his handwriting had been well formed, even his signature clear and legible. In the early 1920's, the handwriting began to scrawl; by 1928, it was generally almost totally illegible to anyone not familiar with it. Parts of the scrawls on yellow legal note paper often could not be deciphered even by his secretaries—with the exception of Miss Tappan. "She was," one of the other secretaries recalled, "the only person in the world who could read Mr. Moses' handwriting."

And there were larger signs, too. The fuse, always short, that ignited his temper had been chopped down to a nub. The broad smile with which he greeted underlings could disappear in an instant if their reports displeased him. The hard mask that replaced it would turn pale, almost white, as his rage mounted. And then a wave of deep red, almost purple, would seep up out of his collar and over his face. The palm of his big right hand would begin to smack down on the table as he talked, and his secretaries, listening outside the closed door to his office, trying to smile at each other, would hear his voice begin to rise. Lunging out of his chair, he would stride around the room, bellowing, his eyes wild, and sometimes as he walked he pounded his clenched fist into the walls so hard that the skin was ripped from his knuckles. Oblivious to the pain, he would sit back down at his desk and grab the next batch of papers with bleeding hands.

If Moses' olive-tinted face had been both strong and sensitive during his youth and young manhood, now it was just strong. It had filled out; it broadened downward from the drastically receding forehead. The nose and high cheekbones were fleshed out and the jaw beneath them had become massive, almost prognathous, the dominant feature of the face. Always arresting, the face was still so, but now not because of handsomeness, although the smile was still white-toothed, red-lipped, broad and charming. No longer the face of a poet, it was the face of a man accustomed to command; one could imagine it carved, in all its arrogance and strength, on a sarcophagus to represent a Pharaoh of Egypt. The neck was thick enough to be an adequate pedestal for that face—Moses was constantly yanking his shirt collar open as if it were too tight and thereby exposing a prominent Adam's apple—and so were his shoulders and the wrists beneath his shirt cuffs, which he impatiently rolled up out of his way as he worked. He was a big man—six feet, one inch tall, his weight now about 210 pounds—and when he pulled off his shirt to go swimming, his chest was broad and his arms heavy and muscular. "A big face, a big smile, a big voice—the over-all impression he gave was of bigness, strength, power," recalls a woman who knew him. And his rage could fill a room. Some of Moses' former executives, long retired and out of his reach, were persuaded to discuss certain aspects of their relationships with Moses, but not one of them would discuss what Moses said to him in his rages. "I don't want to discuss what he said to me," one executive said quietly. "I don't want to discuss it ever." But one thing was certain: earlier Robert Moses had led men; now he drove them.

With women, Moses was unfailingly courteous. "He was always a gentleman with us," says one of his secretaries. "You could hear him yelling in his office, but if you went in to take dictation, you found him the same as usual—very fast as a dictater but clear and with a pleasant word for you. And if he had time, he'd be very friendly. He'd start a conversation with you, he'd talk to you. Oh, he could talk you into anything, that man."

But occasionally the strain would tell even with his secretaries. Sometimes, as they typed a long, important letter, they'd glance up and Moses would be standing behind them, reading as they typed, too impatient to wait until they had finished. "Sometimes," one recalls, "when you got to the bottom of a page, he'd actually grab it right out of your typewriter. On a long, complicated letter, he would make a lot of drafts, and he'd stand right at your machine as you did each one, grabbing it out and making corrections."

"When Mr. Moses was around," says another secretary, "you didn't go out to eat. You ate at your desk. And when he buzzed you, you left your lunch and went in." Quitting for the day at five o'clock was unheard of. "When Mr. Moses was around, you just worked. Period. If there was work to be done, you did it before you went home." Despite the courtesy and the friendliness, despite the admiration—too weak a term—they obviously felt for Mr. Moses, his secretaries found themselves awaiting the rasp of his buzzer as nervously as did his male executives.

Water alone slackened the tautness of his existence. Water seemed to attract him. He changed his New York City office because he couldn't see a river from it, and when he moved into his new one, which afforded a sweeping view of the Hudson, he had his desk placed facing the window. When he was able to afford better living quarters in the city, he chose an apartment facing the East River. When he moved from that apartment, his sole requirement for a new apartment was that it also face the river. In the living rooms of both apartments were copies of *Jane's Sailing Ships,* and Moses would look up from his work whenever he heard a whistle from a passing boat and try to identify it. He would spend his evenings walking beside the river. His office at Belmont Lake looked out over the lake. And his Babylon house on Thompson Avenue, of course, backed on a creek that led to the Great South Bay.

Almost every day, sometimes twice a day, no matter how busy he was, Moses would swim. He preferred the ocean; he left time for a swim whenever he was over on Jones Beach; as soon as the causeway was completed, even before it was open to the public, he drove across it to swim in the ocean almost every day during the summer and, indeed, in spring and fall, too, no matter how cold the weather. He would change into a bathing suit in his car, jump out of his limousine and run down across the beach, waving a towel as happily as a boy, plunge through the first breakers, come up on their far side and swim so far out that his men shook their heads in admiration. Sometimes, heading home to Thompson Avenue at midnight, he would tell his chauffeur to head for Jones Beach instead, and there, after running across the deserted beach, he would swim far out to sea, utterly alone under the stars. If he couldn't get to the ocean, he swam in the Great South Bay, or, before it became too polluted, in the creek behind his house. And in winter he used the indoor pool on the estate of a Babylon friend who had given him a key, his arms windmilling him through seemingly endless laps. And no matter where he swam, when he emerged from the water his dripping face was always fresh, smiling and happy.

When he had work that didn't have to be done at his desk, he would take it on board the Park Commission yacht moored at a Babylon dock, even though he would have to spend most of his time on the boat plowing through sheafs of papers while the captain cruised the bay. When he got a day free to spend with his family, the day was spent fishing, swimming, crabbing, sailing—he was good with small sail—off the South Shore. "He just loved that bay," an acquaintance says. "Every time he went out on it, it seemed to invigorate him."

And no matter how thin his remarkable capacity for work seemed stretched in the evening, a night's sleep never failed to restore its resiliency, just as it healed the shaving nicks on his face. No matter how long he had worked the day before, when Miss Tappan pulled up to his house in the morning, he would always come through the front door of his house as briskly as if he had just returned from a vacation—although, all during 1927 and 1928, he did not take a single one of those. Moses' executives learned to try to get appointments with "RM" during the morning. "He wasn't so tense, so wound up, then," one explained. "As the day went on, you could see it getting worse and worse, but the next morning he was fresh again."

As much as any other quality, it was an ability to pick and organize men that enabled Moses to handle so brutal a workload.

He had a gift for picking them out of the throng of draftsmen, engineers and architects at Belmont Lake. "Time and again," one of his top executives recalls, "RM would ask the name of some lower-echelon guy—'Who was that guy you sent in with the bathhouse plans last week?'—that kind of thing. And when you told him, he'd say, 'Why don't you try giving him a little more responsibility and see how he handles it.' Well, it was amazing. The man he picked out might be some guy you yourself had hardly noticed. And RM certainly hadn't had any time to watch the guy at any length at all. But it seemed like every time, he was right; when you gave the guy more responsibility, he was ready to handle it, and you could start moving him up through the organization."

Moses ran the Long Island State Park Commission and the State Parks Council like an army. "Everything was by the 'chain of command,' " an aide recalls. "Everyone had to go through that chain. If you sent him a note with a suggestion or a complaint, he would send it right back to you with a note scribbled on it: 'Have you talked to your superior about this?' " Even with most top officials, he communicated primarily by memo. Only a handful of men in his organization dealt directly with him.

The men who rose through this chain shared a capacity for hard work. Alongside the telephones in his Babylon home and in his New York apartment, Moses kept lists of his aides' phone numbers, and he used that list around the clock, frequently at 2 or 3 A.M. If they went out at night, they had to leave phone numbers at which they could be reached, and they became accustomed to having ushers search them out in darkened theaters to ask them to come to the manager's office for an urgent phone call. Vacations weren't allowed to interfere. If Moses needed a man when the man was in Florida, the man was summoned home, "although," as William Latham put it, "RM was always very good about telling you to go right back and enjoy yourself as soon as you were done with whatever it was he had needed you for." Nor were social obligations allowed to interfere. When Moses called Latham at his Babylon home one Sunday as Latham was broiling steaks for guests gathered around his outdoor barbecue, Moses' only words were: "I'm at 302 [Broadway]. How long will it take you to get here?" Latham's only words in reply: "Forty-five minutes." (He made it in forty.)

They also shared a capacity for subservience. Increasingly, now, Moses showed an unwillingness to be argued with by underlings. His staff became increasingly wary about giving suggestions. An aura of fear began to pervade Moses' relationships with his staff. Colonel William S. Chapin, for example, a tall, powerfully built man of immense engineering capabilities, a key figure during World War II in the building of the famed Burma Road, ate lunch at his desk virtually every day for twenty years because he was afraid RM might call and find him absent.

Absolute loyalty was required of them. As one keen observer of the Moses organization put it: "Once a problem had been explored and discussed, it was what *he* [Moses] wanted that mattered, not what they thought. Once the Moses policy line was adopted, no one ever knew what a Moses deputy thought unless his thoughts were those of Moses himself." They were forbidden to talk to the press; anyone who violated that order was fired. Incredibly hard-working, incredibly loyal—dedicated, faceless—they were already becoming recognized by public officials as an elite cadre within the ranks of the state's civil servants and had already been given the name "Moses Men."

Once they had proven themselves to him, Moses took pains with their training. They were, most of them, engineers and architects, and he was constantly distressed with their weakness in the use of the English language. So he taught them to write. Like a high-school English teacher, he gave them reports to write and letters to draft for his signature and then he corrected the reports and letters and had the authors redo them—sometimes over and over again. In the beginning of this process, he disposed of crude efforts with the single remark "This ain't English!" scrawled across them. When they had learned to write letters in the style he wanted, he let them draft letters for his signature and set them to work teaching their subordinates how to draft letters for their signatures. When his men had mastered a felicity of phrase, he proceeded to refinements. Their purpose was to get public projects built, he would tell them, and to get them built they had to know how to persuade people of their worth—and the key to persuading people was to keep their arguments simple. Down from Buffalo in 1926, without an appointment, long rolls of blueprints spilling from under his arms, came Bert Tallamy, in later years Federal Highway Administrator but then just a young highway engineer, willing to wait a whole day outside Moses' office in the hope of getting the master's advice on how to implement a plan he had conceived for a road from Buffalo to Niagara Falls. When he was finally admitted to the presence, he began to unroll his blueprints on the huge table in August Belmont's dining room. Tallamy had spent days coloring different parts of them so that Moses could more easily study them. But Moses shoved them impatiently aside without looking at them. "The first thing you've got to learn," he said, "is that no one is interested in plans. No one is interested in details. The first thing you've got to learn is to keep your presentations simple."

Moses taught his men not to waste time. He didn't want engineers wasting time debating legal points or lawyers discussing engineering problems. If a legal problem arose at a staff meeting and an engineer ventured an opinion on it, he would cut him short with a curt "Stop practicing law. Leave that to the lawyers."

He even taught them social graces so that they could dine with men in positions of power. When a man from an outside organization such as the State DPW was being considered for a position, Moses would have Howland and Shapiro invite the man to their homes for a "friendly" game of bridge so that they could observe him in a social setting. And Moses had no hesitation about handing out basic tips of social etiquette to his aides. If changes in personality were required, Moses saw that they also were made. Shapiro, for example, was painfully shy. Moses would take him to social gatherings and order him to charm a particular official. Before long, Shapiro was charming.

Some of these men broke under the strain of the demands Moses placed upon them. More than one of the men close to Moses in the 1920's had taken to drink by the 1930's and been dismissed. There were stories of nervous breakdowns within the ranks and of marital difficulties caused by men's inability to work at the pace Moses required and still find time for their families. There was at least one suicide.

But those who didn't break were rewarded. Advancement was rapid. And he had the knack, the knack of the great executive, of delegating authority completely. His men learned that once a policy in their area of authority had been hammered out by Moses, the details of implementing that policy were strictly up to them; all their boss cared about was that they get it done. They therefore had considerable power of their own, and this was incentive to those of them who wanted power.

In rewarding his men financially, Moses was hampered by civil service limits on pay and promotion schedules, but his ingenuity found a hundred ways around those strictures. If a man wasn't making what Moses thought he should be, he would put the man's wife on the payroll in some job that required no work—such as answering the telephone in their home—and pay her an additional stipend. He early hit on the idea of using Park Commission labor and contractors to build homes—generally, comfortable, spacious two-story Colonial houses—for his top executives on park property so that they would be spared the expense of rent, and of using Park Commission personnel to maintain the houses so that they had none of the other expenses of the normal homeowner, either. The Park Commission even picked up the heating and electricity bills for these executives. To make sure that no fuss would be raised about the unusual procedure, the houses were generally built on secluded pieces of park property, so that the public didn't even know of their existence.

The rewards Moses offered his men were not only power and money. If they gave him loyalty, he returned it manyfold. Moses might criticize his men himself, but if an outsider tried it—even if the outsider was right, and Moses privately told his aide so—Moses would publicly defend him without qualification.

And the most valued reward—the thread that bound his men most closely to him—was still more intangible. "We were caught up in his sense of purpose," Latham explained. "He made you feel that what we were doing together was tremendously important for the public, for the welfare of people." The purposes were, after all, the purposes for which they had been trained. They were engineers and architects; engineers and architects want to build, and all Moses' efforts were aimed at building. Men who worked for him had the satisfaction not only of seeing their plans turned into steel and concrete, but also of seeing the transformation take place so rapidly that the fulfillment was all the more satisfying. Moses' men feared him, but they also admired and respected him—many of them seemed to love him.

The increasing illegibility of Moses' signature was one result of the amount of work he was doing for the state. There were others. They were the public works that were completed by the end of Smith's last term. By

December 31, 1928, new hospitals, some specially designed for care of crippled children, for mentally disabled veterans and for the blind, the deaf-and-dumb and tuberculosis sufferers, dotted the state. Great new state asylums for the insane had been completed, as well as an institute for the study of the causes of insanity. Sing Sing and other new prisons had been constructed. So had a State Health Laboratory, a State Teachers College at Albany and a thirty-story building behind the capitol to house previously scattered state offices. During the more than three decades that the Legislature had been ordering the elimination of grade crossings, exactly twelve had been eliminated* before Smith came to office. By the time he left the Governorship, more than two hundred had been eliminated. As for highways, when Smith left he could boast that "We have built since 1919 three thousand miles of new highways and reconstructed two thousand miles."

With the added responsibilities, of course, came added power. Shuffling the offices on the capitol's second floor, Smith gave Moses the one next to the Executive Chamber to use when he was in Albany. The location of the office was symbolic. The capitol's readers of the map of power knew that in governmental matters—Belle Moskowitz was the chief adviser on political matters and there was no rivalry between her and Moses; they liked and respected each other—Moses was next in power to the Governor.

Smith let the capitol know it. He wanted no interference with Moses in the jobs he had been given, he said whenever a cabinet member complained that Moses, in his speeding up of construction projects, was interfering in the affairs of his department. One top departmental engineer repeatedly refused to accept Moses' orders. Smith called the engineer in—and fired him on the spot. The engineer chose a bar near the capitol to drown his sorrows. By the end of the day, many of his friends in other departments and the Legislature had seen him there. To all who approached him he poured out the story of the injustice that had been done him. The engineer may have been looking for sympathy, and to his face, certainly, his auditors gave it, but in the power-conscious capitol what was important to them about his tale of woe was the lesson they learned from it: as long as Smith was Governor, Moses was not to be crossed. By nightfall, the story—and the lesson—had been absorbed by the capitol. When the New York *Tribune,* in an analysis of the capitol scene, headlined in 1927: MOSES SECOND IN POWER TO THE GOVERNOR, the capitol knew that the headline was true.

As to the effect on personality of the infusion of ever larger doses of power, the clearest evidence was in two remarkable extemporaneous speeches that Moses delivered in 1927 before two associations of Long Island real estate brokers.†

* Omitting the cities of Syracuse, Buffalo and New York, where state laws gave jurisdiction over the work to city administrations.

† We have a record of them because W. Kingsland Macy, feuding with Moses at the time, sent a stenographer to take notes.

The speeches dealt with the future of Long Island. The Island was, Moses said, a gigantic cul-de-sac, a body of land with no outlet on its eastern end. Therefore, he said, the Island "is not a commercial community." Instead, it is a place for people to live and play, mostly play. It is "a natural recreational community, the inevitable playground for millions of people in the metropolitan section." New roads, therefore, should be parkways designed to bring people out from New York City for recreation and not for any other reason. The scope of the Island's interlocking problems—water supply, zoning, transportation—can never be solved by the existing system of government; there are simply too many separate and independent municipalities—towns, villages and cities—to allow coordinated planning. "Before you can solve these problems," he said, "you have got to change the system of county and town government. This is an obsolete form; you can't tackle the job with it."

What was remarkable was Moses' tone, his remarkable self-confidence. When he said, "The form of government you have will not solve your problems here," he added: "That is not a theory; I am sure of it." And this was no servant of the people trying to persuade. The opposition to parks on Long Island, he told the Long Islanders, was "stupid opposition." There "has been too much lack of cooperation by [the Island's] public officials, too much tendency to criticize." And it must stop. "The townspeople want to deliberate about park propositions. There is a limit to the amount of deliberation that can be done."

We will do the planning, he said. We don't need your help. We don't need your suggestions. "We don't need so much advice and cooperation as to the general program as we need help and advice with the specific problems as they come up. Theory and plans we take for granted." By specific details, he made clear, he meant only putting pressure on local governing bodies to approve specific sections of parkway or park plans.

And if Long Island didn't cooperate, he said, it would be too bad for Long Island. "The state has a limited amount of money," he said. "It can be spent elsewhere." And if the "stupid opposition" doesn't cease, it will be. "It can and will be used elsewhere if we can't get the cooperation. Somebody else is going to get it."

Some people must be hurt by progress, he said. But that is unavoidable. "You can't make an omelet without breaking eggs."

"There are people who like things as they are," he said. They cannot be permitted to stand in the way of progress. "I can't hold out any hope to them. They have to keep moving further away. This is a great big state and also there are other states. Let them go to the Rockies."

In other extemporaneous statements, Moses showed no hesitancy in displaying his feelings about the importance of law. After he had decided to return the control of boxing to the Athletic Commission, he was busy for a time defending the commissioners, and when a reporter asked him if they had not in some instances violated the law, Moses replied that that really wasn't important. "Whether the commissioners have gone beyond their legal rights, I haven't any idea," he said. "One duty naturally leads to another. Sometimes it happens that in order to do one thing in the right way, it becomes necessary to do something else."

Sometimes Moses' feelings about the law were expressed less ambiguously. While building bathhouses on Long Island, he ran afoul of the State Industrial Commissioner. The commissioner was Frances Perkins, who once, a decade and a half earlier, had stood on the deck of a ferry and listened to a young man with burning eyes talk about a great highway along the waterfront. In the decade and a half since that Sunday, the young man had learned how to build great highways.

"He was building [the] bathhouses in violation of an . . . ordinance," Miss Perkins recalled. The ordinance specified that union labor be used on the job, but Moses had "just hired the local handymen and unemployed laborers to do brick masons' work. . . ."

> I called him up to say, "You mustn't do that. Naughty, naughty, you can't do that. What are you thinking of?"
>
> Well . . . he treated me to . . . vituperation . . . although we were on the most intimate of personal terms. . . . He was building bathhouses for the people of New York. . . . He was going to have bathhouses for the people of New York. . . . He just gave me the devil.
>
> I said, "There's a law about this, Robert. I hate to tell you this, but I shall have to invoke the law about this matter."
>
> Moses said, "Well, go ahead and invoke it! Do anything you think you can do. These bathhouses are going to be built. I'm just going to keep right on building them. You do the best you can to stop it."
>
> He went ahead and built his bathhouses. I invoked all the elements of law enforcement available, but before they got around to making the inspections, issuing the orders, getting him into court and coping with the various postponements that he was able to get, the bathhouses were done and people were going swimming out of them. . . . I think the court rebuked him, but even the court didn't have the nerve to tear them down.

Nor, it was charged, were Moses' feelings about the law confined to bathhouse building. Angry East Islip and Babylon residents had long been complaining about the breakneck speed at which Moses' big Packard limousine sped through the quiet streets of their villages. On July 31, 1927, Moses led sixty members of the State Parks Council on a tour of Long Island. Long Islanders complained that the cavalcade of limousines carrying the council members sped through the streets of those villages at excessive speed while outriders—state troopers on motorcycles—cleared the way by forcing pedestrians and other cars off the road. When the cavalcade arrived at the Babylon Town dock where the Park Commission yacht was moored, the residents complained, the troopers forced everyone except council members off the dock, despite the fact that it was a public dock. As old Judge Cooper editorialized: "We got a taste of what authority in the wrong hands means."

Disregard for law, of course, implies regard for that which law is a barrier against: naked force, power sufficient to bend society or individuals, if not protected by law, to its will. And this, too, now became noticeable in the character of Robert Moses.

Moses was playing by the rules of power now and one of the first of those rules is that when power meets greater power, it does not oppose but attempts to compromise. He had met power invulnerable to him—or even to his champion in the Governor's chair—in the barons of Long Island's North Shore. And where once, in laying out the original route of the Northern State Parkway exactly where he believed it should ideally go, laying it out without compromise, running it right past the massive porticos of the barons' castles, he had spat in the eye of power, now he hastily administered eyewash.

He would not move the parkway route down out of the hills the barons held and onto the plains in the Island's center. This would mean that the parkway could never be truly beautiful. But, within the hills, there were many possible routes, and he was willing to compromise with the barons on which route would finally be chosen. He made deals: with at least a dozen barons he covenanted that he would move the parkway away from the homes to the edges of their property, out of sight of their castles, if they would in return donate the right-of-way so that he would not need a legislative appropriation for it; with a dozen more, where moving it to their estates' borders was impractical, he agreed to move it as far as was practical—and, so the estate would not be sliced in half by the parkway, so that equestrians could proceed unchecked on their rides and hunts, to build, at state expense, bridges, one for each estate, over the parkway for the exclusive use of the baron in residence and his retainers and guests.

The compromising did not stop there. Were the barons afraid that the alien hordes brought to Long Island on the parkway might encroach on their lands? Precautions against this could be arranged. Specifically, he would covenant with the concerned barons that there would be no exits from the parkway within their borders. And he gave his solemn oath that state troopers patrolling the parkway would be under orders to keep automobiles from the city moving, not allowing their occupants to picnic, or even to stop, by the side of the parkway within their borders. Publicly, Moses never stopped excoriating the Long Island millionaires. But in private, many of them were coming to consider him quite a reasonable fellow to deal with.

None found him more reasonable than financier Otto Kahn. In dealing with Kahn, Moses, in his excursions beyond the limits of the spirit of the law, went further than he had ever gone before. The Legislature, subservient to the will of the barons, refused all through 1924, 1925, 1926 and 1927 to give Moses a cent for the Northern State Parkway. Funds were refused even for the surveying of proposed routes—a refusal which made it almost impossible for Moses to work out deals with the barons because he could not be sure whether routes proposed were engineeringly feasible. But in 1926, Kahn learned that Moses intended to run the parkway right through the middle of the eighteen-hole private golf course he had constructed for his pleasure on his Cold Spring Harbor estate.

Kahn, who happened to be a relative of Moses—he was married to the daughter of one of Bella's sisters—offered to secretly donate $10,000 to the Park Commission for surveys, if some of the surveys found a new route for the parkway in the Cold Spring Harbor area, a route which would not cross his estate at all. And Moses accepted the money.

Regard for power implies disregard for those without power as is demonstrated by what happened after Moses shifted the route of the Northern State Parkway away from Otto Kahn's golf course. The map of the Northern State Parkway in Cold Spring Harbor is a map not only of a road but of power—and of what happens to those who, unwittingly, are caught in the path of power.

The parkway was originally supposed to run through Otto Kahn's estate. Since Otto Kahn had power—the power that went with money—he was able to get the route shifted to the south. South of Otto Kahn's estate lay the estates of two other men of wealth and of influence with the Legislature—Congressman Ogden Livingston Mills and Colonel Henry Rogers Winthrop. The Congressman and the Colonel were able to get the route shifted farther south, far enough so it would not touch their estates either. But shifting the route south of the Mills and Winthrop estates meant that it would run through the estates of two other men of wealth and influence, Colonel Henry L. Stimson and Robert W. De Forest. So the route was shifted south again. And south of the Stimson and De Forest estates lay a row of farms, and farmers had neither wealth nor influence.

James Roth was one of those farmers. When he had purchased his forty-nine acres in 1922, much of it had been woodland and all of it had been rocky. Roth had hauled away the rocks and cut down the trees. He owned a team of horses, but they could not budge many of the stumps. As the horses pulled at them, Roth pulled beside them. So did his wife, Helen. So that both would be freed for the pulling, their son, Jimmy, at the age of five, had to learn how to handle the team. As his parents sweated at the ropes, he sat on one of the horses, kicking him forward.

After the farm was cleared, the Roths found that the southern fifteen acres were no good for planting. But the rest of the land was rich and fertile. In the afternoons, during harvest season, James Roth, who had been up since before dawn working in the fields, would load up one of his two wagons and drive to market. While he was gone, his wife and son, who in 1927 was six, would load the other. When Roth returned he would—without pause, since every minute was important to a farmer trying to work thirty-four acres without a hired man—unharness the team, hitch it to the loaded wagon and begin the trip again—while Helen and Jimmy would reload the first wagon. But by 1927 the farm had begun paying. "We felt pretty secure," Jimmy recalls. "We had a nice farm. In those days, a farm wasn't just real estate, like it is now. In those days, a farm was your living. It was your home. And we had a nice farm."

Then, in 1927, a representative of the Long Island State Park Commission—of Robert Moses—drove up to the Roths' farm and told them the state was condemning fourteen acres out of the farm's center for the Northern State Parkway. James Roth argued with Moses' representative. He pleaded with him. All he wanted the commission to do, Roth said, was to move the parkway route about four hundred feet south, less than a tenth of a mile. That would put it in the barren part of the farm. Taking fourteen acres from the center meant that a substantial part of the fertile acreage would be gone. Even more important, it meant that the farm would be sliced in two. How would he get from one side to the other? How would he be able to work it? But Moses' representative refused to listen to the Roths. The route had been decided on the basis of engineering considerations, he said. It could not possibly be changed.

Robert Moses had shifted the parkway south of Otto Kahn's estate, south of Winthrop's and Mills's estates, south of Stimson's and De Forest's. For men of wealth and influence, he had moved it more than three miles south of its original location. But James Roth possessed neither money nor influence. And for James Roth, Robert Moses would not move the parkway south even one tenth of a mile farther. For James Roth, Robert Moses would not move the parkway one foot. Robert Moses had offered men of wealth and influence bridges across the parkway so that there would be no interference with their pleasures. But he wouldn't offer James Roth a bridge so that there would be no interference with his planting.

In years to come, James Roth would talk often about the injustice that had been done him. "My father was really rocked by this; he talked about it until the end of his life," says his son, Jimmy, who had watched his father and mother sweating side by side over their land. "And I don't know that I blame him. I'll tell you—my father and mother worked very hard on that place, and made something out of it, and then someone just cut it in two. To have someone take away something you have . . ." The farm never really paid again. There just wasn't enough fertile acreage left. And the Roths found that it took fully twenty-five minutes to drive their team to the nearest road that crossed the parkway and then to get back to plow the other side of the farm. Each round trip took about fifty minutes, and these were fifty-minute segments slashed out of the life of a man to whom every minute was necessary. "It was quite a ways," Mrs. Roth recalls. "It was quite a ways for a man who was working hard already." The condemnation award "never came to much," Mrs. Roth says. And because there were two separate, rather small pieces of property instead of a single big one, she says, they couldn't even sell the farm.

The situation was the same for the other Cold Spring Harbor farmers whose farms were ruined by the Northern State Parkway. To the end of their lives most of them would remember the day on which they heard that "the road was coming" as a day of tragedy. There was only one aspect of the tragedy that alleviated their bitterness. That was their belief that it was unavoidable, that the route of the parkway had indeed been determined by engineering considerations, and therefore really could not be changed. Forty years later, when the author asked them about the possibility of the parkway being built through the big estates to the north, not one of those farmers thought that such a possibility had ever existed.

Moses was given a further increase in power as a result of Smith's bid for the presidency in 1928.

No associate of the Governor was more enthusiastic about the bid than Moses. On the June night when the Democratic Party was balloting at its convention in Houston and the Executive Mansion in Albany was overflowing with reporters, well-wishers and hangers-on, the porches and the grounds outside filled with throngs, Moses was one of the handful who were invited to join the Smith family in the big second-floor room in which the Governor was trying to listen to the balloting over the static. When Ohio's votes gave Smith the nomination and Emily Smith ran to her father and threw her arms around his neck, it was to Moses that Belle Moskowitz turned and said, almost crying, "Bob, it's over!" And other people in the room were to say that they had never seen Moses happier than at that moment.

Belle's remark was, after all, understandable; Al Smith had run in twenty-two elections and he had won twenty-one, and in the one he had lost he ran almost a million votes ahead of his ticket. She—and Moses and the other members of the Smith inner circle in the room with the Governor—didn't see how he could lose. (Al Smith got up from the big armchair in which he had sat for hours, his attention on the radio, motionless except for the grinding of his lips against his big cigar and the stroking of one hand on the neck of his Great Dane, Jeff, walked over to a small bar, grabbed two handfuls of ice cubes, began dropping them into glasses and said, "Now, all of yez! Come aboard!")

But Moses did not play a major role in the Smith presidential campaign. The Governor had long since stopped using him as a speech drafter—"He had a great respect for Bob's viewpoint on everything except speeches," Howard Cullman says. "The Governor said Bob would just murder him on those. He said Bob had no idea of the public pulse on most issues"—and the campaign was run by Mrs. Moskowitz and by a group of wealthy Irish Catholics who had recently become close to Smith.

So Moses was spared being with his Gamaliel when he went down to defeat in what Oscar Handlin has called "a dark episode in American history." He wasn't with him when, on his tours of a South and a West that he hardly knew, Smith realized that the gay renditions of "The Sidewalks of New York" were being drowned out by whispers that were the surface hissing of what Handlin has called "the dark secret prejudice against the urban foreigners," including Catholics "held in subservience to a foreign despot by an army of priests and bishops." Moses never saw the fiery crosses that burned on the hills of Kansas and Oklahoma—and on the Shinnecock

Hills of Suffolk County—as Smith's campaign train passed. Moses wasn't on the train when the realization spread through it that the prejudice and intolerance could not be licked and that even if it could, 1928, with the "Hoover Market" booming and the nation prosperous and complacent, just wasn't a Democratic year.

Moses' contribution to the Smith campaign was twofold. First, his accomplishments provided the ammunition for the most successful of Smith's speeches, those which concentrated on his record as Governor. Second, while Smith was campaigning, Moses ran the state for him.

This was no minor task; voters in 1928 were far less tolerant than those in 1974 are about officeholders neglecting their duties to seek higher office, and Smith realized that the Republican legislators would take full advantage of any opportunity to charge him with laxness. To make sure that there was no opportunity, Smith gave Moses full authority over all state departments during the months he spent on the campaign trail. He even told Moses to use his office and sit in his big chair in the Executive Chamber. Moses did so. He presided over the drawing up of the 1929 state budget, the first in the state's history to be drawn up under his executive budget plan. He handled the Governor's mail, screening it for important letters that should be sent on to him—and making sure that he never saw the obscene threats that terrified Smith's wife, Katie, when she read them. While Smith was campaigning, Moses ran New York. And the measure of his success in the job was that there wasn't a single Republican charge of laxness in that period.

Moses had no opportunity to take pleasure from either his power or his success as Smith's surrogate. Time, which had for so long panted hungrily at his heels, had drawn close enough to nip them now.

Smith had been prevented by law from running for Governor at the same time he was running for President, and while a new Governor could not oust Moses as Long Island Park Commission head—his six-year term, after all, did not expire until 1930—he could effectively kill any of his park projects that were not well under way when he was inaugurated. And while Moses had accomplished so much during his four years in office, the accomplishments were as nothing beside his dreams. There was, in 1928, so much yet to do. Although the entire right-of-way for the Southern State Parkway had been acquired and construction started on much of it, not a single section had been completed. Without that section, the public would not see how great it was going to be and would not be ready to support him against any Governor who tried to keep him from completing it up to the same—expensive—standards. The Wantagh Causeway to Jones Beach was not completed, and since the public could not see the strand, how could it know he was justified in the expenditure of whatever millions were needed to make it the greatest bathing beach in the world? The Northern State Parkway was not even begun. Unless he could announce that a substantial portion of the right-of-way had been acquired, how could he force a new Governor into building the road? So in November and December of 1928, construction crews were out on the Southern State and the Wantagh, and the surveyors were out along the route of the Northern State.

Those close to Robert Moses knew that there was justification for his urgency, a reason for the desperation which now seemed to underlie his haste. "Without his loyalty to me," Moses was to say about Al Smith, "I could have done nothing." He had had Al Smith—and his loyalty—for ten years. But now he was to have Al Smith no more. And the man who was to follow Moses' greatest friend into the Governor's chair was Moses' deadliest enemy.

16. *The Featherduster*

THERE IS AN EXPRESSION used in Albany to describe the relationship of two men between whom there exists bad feeling when that feeling has existed for years, has resisted every attempt at reconciliation and has only deepened with the passage of time, to a point where "dislike" is not so fitting a name for it as "hatred." In discussing two such men, one assemblyman will say to another, with a knowing shake of his head: "They go back a long way."

Robert Moses and Franklin Delano Roosevelt went back a very long way.

Roosevelt's relationship with the whole circle of advisers around Al Smith was an ambivalent one. They needed him, and they knew it. Any Irish Catholic, city-bred, militantly Wet, Tammany politician, even an Al Smith, needed help with the Protestant, farm-bred, militantly Dry, Tammany-hating upstate New York farmers. Upstate Democrats of stature were in short supply. In fact, Roosevelt was the only one.

And you could hardly ask for a better ally. The tall, handsome, aristocratic Groton and Harvard graduate, who looked exactly like the Hudson River squire he was, had won upstate acceptance of his anti-Tammany bona fides in 1911, during his first State Senate term, by rallying a band of young colleagues and leading them to victory in what had seemed a hopeless cause: their fight against the selection for a vacant United States Senate seat of Silent Charlie Murphy's candidate, railroad frontman William F. ("Blue-Eyed Billy") Sheehan.* Thereafter, upstaters were willing to listen to Roosevelt when he told them, as he did at countless county fairs, that "farmers like you and I" should support Smith because the Governor had risen above the Tammany background from which he had sprung.

If, moreover, Smith had ambitions that went beyond New York State—and he did—he needed an emissary to the Democratic Party's rural-Dry-Protestant wing. And young Franklin bore a name which, throughout the country, possessed the magic that a half century later would infuse the name Kennedy. More than one newspaper, praising his performance as the 1920 Democratic vice-presidential nominee and noting that he had followed

* Until 1913 United States senators were selected by state legislatures.

Cousin Teddy into the New York Legislature and an Assistant Secretaryship of the Navy, had commented that if TR's sons proved unable to carry the old Rough Rider's banner back up the steps of the White House, there was another member of the family who might do it for them.

His every intervention on Smith's behalf had been immensely helpful. Striding, athletic and graceful, to the speaker's podium at the 1920 Democratic National Convention, he had seconded the Governor's token presidential nomination in an effective speech. In July 1922, with Smith, out of office, taking his evening walks home with Moses, Roosevelt, crippled now, got Smith's gubernatorial candidacy off the ground with an open letter calling on him to run. Floor manager for Smith at the 1924 national convention, he had been his nominator, too, swinging to the platform on crutches and delivering a speech that, using a phrase from Wordsworth, dubbed the Governor "the Happy Warrior of the Political Battlefield"—a speech that historian Mark Sullivan called "a noble utterance." Among Smith's happier moments during the convention's interminable 103 ballots were Roosevelt's appearances at the microphone to rally his supporters. So enthusiastic a Smith supporter was he that when the Governor ran in 1926 against Theodore Roosevelt, Jr., the new Assistant Secretary of the Navy, and Franklin Roosevelt found himself physically unable to campaign against his cousin, he sent his wife to do it. (To remind voters of Theodore Jr.'s connection, peripheral at worst, with the Teapot Dome oil scandal, Eleanor Roosevelt constructed a huge cardboard cutout of a teapot blowing steam, tied it on the top of a car and with it trailed her cousin-in-law around the state, a maneuver which she later ruefully admitted had been a "rough stunt.")

But Roosevelt was never really part of the Smith inner circle. As Oscar Handlin put it, he "had been brought up in an atmosphere that stressed the compulsive understatement. . . . It was inevitable that he should feel awkward in Smith's suite at the Biltmore. All those people! He may never actually have dined at the Tiger Room, but he must have heard stories of the goings-on. He could not, without denying his own background, fail to disapprove of the kinds of people Al and his friends were."

And yet, as Handlin added, "mingled with the disapproval was a touch of envy at being left out of the fun." Roosevelt obviously wished he had Moses' gift for blending in easily with the Governor and his hard-drinking, hard-talking friends. Wanting to be part of the Biltmore scene, feeling awkward about going there alone, Roosevelt would, in 1923, often telephone Moses in the late afternoon from his office at 120 Broadway and ask if he might stop by, pick him up and go up to the hotel with him.

Moses took Roosevelt along, but the latter's appearances at the Biltmore were always touched with restraint. Smith appreciated Roosevelt's help and felt a genuine affection for him and Eleanor. Shy about his lack of grammar, the Governor almost never wrote personal letters, but he wrote many to the Roosevelts after Campobello, short, gruff notes full of sympathy and cheer. But, despite the Governor's efforts to erase it, the line between the Fourth Ward contract executor and the Ivy Leaguer—the line which Moses had so thoroughly erased in his own case—always remained drawn between Smith and Roosevelt. Once, with regret in his voice, Smith told a friend: "Franklin just isn't the kind of man you can take into the pissroom and talk intimately with."

Furthermore, Smith and his circle had something less than respect for Roosevelt's abilities. This attitude was understandable. Roosevelt's Harvard classmates had felt the same way. Mocking his propensity for hopping into, and out of, different interests in quick and shallow succession, they called him "the featherduster." After college, because of the same propensity, Roosevelt had not been a particularly successful lawyer or businessman. An acquaintance would recall that when, at the age of twenty-eight, he decided to enter politics, running for state senator from Dutchess County, "everybody called him 'Franklin' and regarded him as a harmless bust." In Albany, his haughty manner, accentuated by "his habit of throwing up his head so as to give the appearance of looking down his nose, his pince-nez—all this, combined with his leadership in the anti-Sheehan fight, stamped him as a snob and branded his ideas, in the outraged language of one regular Democrat, as 'the silly conceits of a political prig.' " Frances Perkins was to remember him arguing with two or three colleagues, "his small mouth pursed up," saying, " 'No, no, I won't hear of it!' " Tammany's Big Tim Sullivan was only summing up the prevailing opinion in Albany when he said, "Awful, arrogant fellow, that Roosevelt." Moreover, as Handlin notes, to the hard, shrewd men around the Governor, who had clawed their way up through a tough world and who knew state government in detail, Roosevelt, with his airy plans, his many hobbies and "his glittering, sweeping discourses, seemed a hopelessly impractical intellectual."

For some reason, Smith's advisers overlooked the fact that not Silent Charlie Murphy but the "political prig" had been the winner of the Sheehan fight. And, after his polio attack in 1921, they did not seem to consider what it had taken for Roosevelt to decide to go back into politics at a time when, Eleanor Roosevelt was later to recall, he was lying in bed and working for hours to try to wiggle one toe. Roosevelt's head had always been tilted at that gay, confident angle; they didn't seem to think of the strength that had had to be found somewhere to keep it tilted now. The agonizing steps he had taken to the podium to give his Happy Warrior speech were the manifestation of an indomitable spirit, but Smith's intimates never thought of the speech without giggling over what had preceded it. The story as they knew it would be somewhat different from that recounted by historians, or by Dore Schary, who in *Sunrise at Campobello* portrayed FDR as saying, when Smith asked him to let Joseph Proskauer help write the speech, "I won't mind the addition of a few phrases. But, Al, what I say will have to be what I want to say." Actually, when Smith and Proskauer walked into Roosevelt's office at Smith campaign headquarters and asked him to make the nominating speech, Roosevelt replied, "I'd like to, but I'm so busy with the delegates—Joe, will you write me a speech?"

"I had already written a speech, the Happy Warrior speech," Proskauer would tell the author. "I waited a few days and then sent it to him. He asked me to come in and talk about it. He said, 'Joe, I can't make that speech. It's too poetic. You can't quote a Wordsworth poem to a bunch of politicians.' "

Proskauer told the author—and so did Smith's daughter Emily and two other Smith intimates—that he kept insisting on retaining the Happy Warrior line while Roosevelt kept insisting that it be removed. Otherwise, Roosevelt said, he would refuse to give the speech. Roosevelt even wrote a speech of his own.

"Finally," Proskauer recalled, "I said why didn't we get a third person to come and take a look and try to reconcile the two speeches. I said, 'I was thinking of [Herbert Bayard] Swope.' He said, 'Fine.' That night we went to Frank's apartment. Swope made a faux pas. We hadn't told him who had written them and he read Frank's speech first, threw it on the floor and said, 'Joe, this is the goddamnedest, rottenest speech I've ever read!' Then he read mine and he said, 'This is the greatest speech since Bragg nominated Cleveland!'* Roosevelt continued to argue and to say he refused to give my speech. Finally about midnight, I got up and said, 'Frank, we're all exhausted. I have just enough authority from the Governor to tell you you'll either make that speech or none at all.' And he said, 'Oh, I'll make the goddamned speech and it'll be a flop!' "

The laughter which boomed out at the Tiger Room or the Biltmore suite when Swope or Proskauer repeated the story—and they repeated it often—helped to blind the men sitting in those jovial watering holes to developing traits in Roosevelt's character. And, more important, it blinded them also to the fact that, while he was completely loyal to Smith, he was using his position as a campaigner for a presidential candidate to keep in touch with key Democrats across the country in preparation for a presidential bid of his own. They never guessed that he even had a timetable—a run for the Governorship in 1932 and the Presidency in 1936. As one Roosevelt biographer put it, the Smith advisers regarded their acquisition as "no more than a showy but harmless piece of window dressing."

All the advisers, that is, except one. Sitting off in a corner of the Biltmore suite, away from the laughter, Belle Moskowitz, who had seen in the thirty-year-old failure Robert Moses something no one else had seen, was watching "harmless" Franklin Roosevelt. And, by 1924, she had come to the conclusion that he was a threat, a very dangerous threat, to her dream that Alfred E. Smith would one day sit in the White House.

The other advisers didn't take this view seriously. For once, they said, Mrs. M was wrong.

---

* At the 1884 Democratic National Convention, General Edward S. Bragg seconded (not nominated) Grover Cleveland for President in a speech that was so eloquent—it included the memorable phrase "They love him for the enemies he has made"—that the galleries stood and urged him on with shouts of: "A little more grape, General! A little more grape!"

* * *

In 1924, when Smith appointed Moses president of the Long Island State Park Commission, the Governor appointed Roosevelt chairman of the Taconic State Park Commission. The thin veneer of friendliness between Moses and Roosevelt thereupon flaked off abruptly and completely.

Moses would attribute the break to a single incident, revolving around gnarled, emaciated little Louis M. Howe, Roosevelt's devoted adviser, whom Smith's circle, because of his habitually dirty, sweat-stained collars and suits dotted with food stains and flecked with cigarette ashes, called "Lousy Louie."

When Roosevelt attempted to appoint Howe secretary of the Taconic Commission, Moses stepped in. If Roosevelt wanted a "secretary and valet," he said, he would have to pay him himself.

Getting Howe the secretary's job, which paid $5,000 per year, was important to Roosevelt. Unable to move around freely, he knew that he would be able to remain in politics only if he was able to delegate most of the tasks he had formerly performed himself. He therefore needed an organization, even if it was only two or three secretaries, but he had to have Howe to direct them and to represent him at political meetings he himself could no longer attend, and he was not financially able to pay Howe an adequate salary. Howe had been about to accept a lucrative offer from private industry when Roosevelt was stricken, but as soon as he had learned of the tragedy at Campobello, he had declined the job. Roosevelt had to find a place for him on some governmental payroll and the only governmental body on which Roosevelt held an official position in 1924 was the Taconic Commission. But Moses was adamant. The State Parks Council would veto any salary for Howe as secretary, he said.

Moses was always to contend that the bad blood between him and Roosevelt flowed from this single incident. Howe never forgave him for the "valet" insult, he said, and took every opportunity to poison Roosevelt's mind against him. "You see," Moses would tell the author, "Roosevelt was in such terrible physical shape that he was home at night a lot, and a person in that kind of condition is very susceptible to the people who are there with him in that house all night. And Howe was always there. And Roosevelt would listen to his stories. It was a result of his illness—he was susceptible to that kind of thing."

But the feeling between Moses and Roosevelt burned too deep to be attributable to a single incident. Personality may have had something to do with it. Moses, after all, was not the only one of the two men whom Albany had found arrogant. Moses was not the only one of the two men who had been given a sip of power, who had liked the taste and who wanted more. And much of the feeling was certainly due to the fact that during the early 1920's Moses was not the only one of the two men dreaming about parks and parkways. During the same years that Robert Moses was tramping the hills and beaches of Long Island, envisioning great parks and parkways there, Franklin Roosevelt was tramping—in his imagination—the hills and rolling farmland of his native Dutchess County, envisioning great parks and parkways there. His ideas were on a scale as big as Moses'. And in the park system that Moses was building, there was room for only one man with big ideas.

Roosevelt had been interested in parks long before Moses, in fact. Both because of his own preoccupations and because of his interest in his famous cousin's campaign to conserve natural resources, he had, from childhood, "cared deeply about nature—about land, water and trees." For years, he had been planting yellow poplar and white pine seedlings by the thousands at the Roosevelt mansion at Hyde Park. Concerned about the destruction of New York's great forests by lumber companies, he proposed in 1922 the formation of a syndicate that would purchase a tract within a hundred miles of New York City and operate it as a park, as private interests operated forests for recreation in Europe.

If Moses knew Long Island as few men knew it, Roosevelt could, in the days when he could walk, say the same thing about Dutchess County and about the other three counties—Putnam, Columbia and Rensselaer—whose gently rolling hills made with Dutchess a continuous soft green border, broken only by the patchwork of cultivated fields, all along the east bank of the Hudson from Westchester to Albany. He had long had his eye on particularly beautiful tracts which he wanted preserved from commercial exploitation—he had, in fact, been negotiating on behalf of the Boy Scouts for one in Putnam County. He was especially enthusiastic about a plan to have New York build a tri-state park, in cooperation with Massachusetts and Connecticut, at the juncture of those three states. The Bronx River Parkway, just opened in Westchester County and a wonder of the world, was pointing at the Taconic region. Even before he was appointed to the Taconic Commission, Roosevelt had envisioned joining to the Bronx River Parkway a new parkway that would head straight north through the Taconic farm counties to parks that could be created there, thereby opening up the lovely Hudson Valley. The parkway as he envisioned it would eventually extend all the way to Albany, and thus make accessible to New York City the beauties of the Adirondack, Berkshire and White mountains. When Smith and Moses—badly needing his name in the Taylor Estate fight—offered Roosevelt the chairmanship of the Taconic Park Commission, whose jurisdiction would encompass the whole east bank of the Hudson from Westchester to Albany, Roosevelt asked if he would be able to build the parkway. Moses apparently gave him assurances on the point—Roosevelt was later to remind Smith that he had—and Roosevelt eagerly accepted.

Within months, he had old Clarence Fahnestock primed to donate his 6,169 acres at Lake Oscawana as a state park and he had completed arrangements for the transfer of three smaller tracts farther north. Having himself driven around the countryside, he had selected sites for "small camping parks" that he wanted built along the parkway. He was sketching himself picnic tables and fireplaces and thinking about which type of rock should be used to face bridges over the parkway so that it would blend in most naturally with the landscape.

Roosevelt was impatient to get this "splendid project" under way; the price of the land for the Boy Scout camp had risen 30 percent in the two years he was negotiating for it. He was driven, as was Moses, by the knowledge that soaring land values were making land acquisition continually more difficult. "The securing of the rights of way for the state should," he wrote, "be immediately put through."

But there was insufficient money in the park allocations made by the Legislature even for Moses' Long Island park plan, and he didn't want any spent on a 125-mile parkway somewhere else. And, it may be, he didn't want within the park system he was so assiduously welding into a monolithic entity responsive solely to his command any opening wedges driven for a project that would be under the command of another vigorous, independent man. Repeatedly, Moses' State Parks Council slashed Roosevelt's budget requests to a level insufficient even to begin acquiring right-of-way for a parkway. The money allowed was not sufficient even for the Taconic Commission to hire an adequate executive staff, and Roosevelt charged that the lack of staff prevented the commission from making plans that would allow it to spend, on small parks, even the meager amount of money it was allotted. In addition, Moses now said a Taconic Parkway should not extend north to Albany but should end only a few miles north of New York City.

Matters came to a head in November 1926.

In submitting during that month his budget request for 1927, Roosevelt asked for funds for engineering plans for the Taconic Parkway, for right-of-way surveys and for salaries for an adequate staff (including Louis Howe). When the State Parks Council met to consider the regional commissions' budget requests (Roosevelt was in Warm Springs, Georgia, where he went every winter to try to coax his dead legs back to life), it disapproved those of the Taconic Commission, on the grounds that it had not spent all the money allocated to it in the past.

Returning north, Roosevelt had at least one bitter face-to-face confrontation with Moses, the details of which can only be imagined. Then Roosevelt tried to go over Moses' head. In December 1926, he wrote Smith asking the Governor to restore the funds he had requested. "It is an absurd and humiliating position to be put in, to be informed that we could have no money because through lack of an Executive we have not been able to properly expend the money we had and then to be informed that we cannot have an Executive because we have not been given more money," he wrote.

But Smith was taking Moses' word as to what was happening in park matters. He asked Moses about the Taconic situation and Moses wrote Smith: "I suggest you write him [Roosevelt] a letter along the line attached." The "attached" said that of course the parkway would go through—it did not say through to where—but that there was so much competition for the limited money available that it must be concentrated on those projects which were moving ahead fastest, and the Taconic Parkway was not one of those.

In fact, the "attached" said, "practically none" of the money already allocated to the Taconic Commission had been spent. Smith sent the letter to Roosevelt exactly as Moses had written it.

A year later, the State Parks Council eliminated from the Taconic Commission's request all funds except those needed for bare maintenance of existing parks. Roosevelt wrote Smith that "the other members of the Commission and I feel very strongly that" the elimination "ends the necessity for the usefulness of the Commission. We have practically no function left." Moses simply used us, Roosevelt said. "The enormous appropriations for . . . Long Island while, perhaps, necessary, prove merely that we have been completely useful [to] other people." And we won't be used any more: "Unless something is done, the Commissioners do not feel it is worth while to continue."

This was serious; there was a presidential election coming up and Smith needed Roosevelt; in fact, he wanted Roosevelt to nominate him again. He apparently intervened; the commission's operating funds were increased. And Roosevelt was assured, apparently by Moses, that when the Parks Council submitted to the Smith-Hewitt-Hutchinson committee requests for additional allocations out of a new $10,000,000 park bond issue that had been passed in 1927, it would ask for $200,000 for Taconic Parkway right-of-way.

But when the three-man committee met, on January 23, 1928, and approved all regional allocations except one, that one was the Taconic. On January 30, 1928, Roosevelt wrote Smith a letter that was as revealing—in the depth of the bitterness it displayed toward Moses—as it was remarkable, coming as it did from the pen of the man who would later shepherd his country through depression and war.

"I wasn't born yesterday!" Franklin D. Roosevelt wrote the Governor. "You see I have been in the game so long that I now realize the mistake I made with this Taconic State Park Commission was in not playing the kind of politics that our friend Bob Moses used. . . . You know, just as well as I do, that Bob has skinned us alive this year—has worked things so beautifully that his baby on Long Island is plentifully taken care of and that all the other Park Commissions up-state, except ours, are getting practically what was approved by the State Council of Parks. When the State Council of Parks approved appropriations to the Taconic State Park Commission of nearly $200,000, Bob knew perfectly well that it would not go through and had his tongue in his cheek when he tried to tell us that he was trying to get it through. . . . As a matter of practical fact, I am very certain in my own mind that we could have got at least some appropriation for acquisition of land this year if Bob and you had gone after it. The money is there—within the total of the budget. For instance, Bob told me himself the other day that on the contract for the New York State Office Building, a couple of hundred thousand dollars will be saved."

As park men like Ansley Wilcox and Judge Clearwater had charged before him, Roosevelt charged that Moses had lied about him to Smith when he was not around to refute the lies. "I am sorry to say it is a fact that Bob Moses has played fast and loose with the Taconic State Park Commission since the beginning," Roosevelt wrote. "I give him great credit for many accomplishments and for his fine vision of a complete State Park system, but he has been guilty of making so many false statements about the Taconic State Park Commission which I have checked up and know all about, that I am very certain that you have been given a very erroneous lot of information about the Commission."

As Wilcox and Clearwater had charged before him, Roosevelt charged that Moses had lied about him to the other members of the Parks Council when he was not around to refute the lies. "One example is sufficient!" he wrote. "Bob told the State Council of Parks that the Taconic State Park Commission had done nothing to cooperate with Massachusetts and Connecticut authorities. As a matter of fact we have not only cooperated with them from the beginning, but are in close touch with them at all times and can tell you or him at any moment just what the situation is in both those states."

Moses will have a chance to lie about me no more, Roosevelt said. "The Commissioners do not want to be the first to make a break in your splendid State-wide Park program, but they have been put in a position where I do not see that they can in any decency" do anything but resign.

Al Smith, who so seldom wrote personal letters, now sat down and wrote one to Franklin D. Roosevelt.

"I know of no man I have met in my whole public career who I have any stronger affection for than for yourself," he wrote. "Therefore, you can find as much fault with me as you like. I will not get into a fight with you for anything or for anybody."

The letter had its effect. Roosevelt did not resign. But the letter did not change the Taconic Parkway situation—or the Moses-Roosevelt situation.

At the 1928 Democratic convention, Roosevelt was again Smith's floor manager. Observers noted that at times during his nominating speech, the cheering seemed to be as much for him as for Smith, and there were some suggestions that Roosevelt—a bearer of TR's name, a Protestant and an attractive vice-presidential candidate even in defeat in 1920—would make a better presidential candidate than the Governor. Belle Moskowitz's comments about Roosevelt began to be more caustic. But Smith himself felt the cheers were no more than Roosevelt deserved—and in September the Governor asked Roosevelt to be his successor in Albany.

Moses had argued against the choice. There are indications that he half-expected Smith to name *him* instead, to try to force him on the Democratic Party. Although he had always identified himself as an "independent Republican" when reporters asked him his political affiliation, he quietly enrolled as a Democrat when he registered to vote in 1928—a bit of opportunism that did him no good, since his name was never seriously mentioned for the Governorship that year by Smith or anyone else. Moreover, among those men whose names *were* seriously considered, Roosevelt was the one Moses least wanted to get the post. He told the conclaves of Democratic leaders to which Smith brought him that Roosevelt did not possess either the mental capacity or the application to be Governor. To Frances Perkins, he said that Roosevelt's only asset was a smile. "It's a pity to have to have him and that Al has set his heart on him," he told her. "It's undoubtedly a good name to carry the ticket with . . . but, of course, he isn't quite bright." The other Smith aides agreed with this view, but mental capacity was not as important to them as political realities. With "Rum, Romanism and Tammany" rapidly becoming the overriding issue of the presidential campaign, they feared that only Roosevelt's name on the ticket could keep New York's upstate Protestant Drys from stampeding into the Republican camp—and denying Smith the forty-five electoral votes of his own state. Estimating that Roosevelt was a full 200,000 votes stronger than any other candidate, they felt that he was the only man with a chance to defeat the attractive GOP gubernatorial nominee, Attorney General Albert Ottinger. As for his ability, Smith's advisers felt he didn't need much; they felt that Moses' reorganization had so streamlined the state government that Roosevelt's lack of administrative experience would not be serious. And Smith himself had a higher opinion of Roosevelt's ability than his aides, and he emphasized that Roosevelt's nomination would assure the party of having a candidate of integrity.

Roosevelt was genuinely reluctant to run—he and Howe had decided that with the nation prosperous under a Republican President, 1928 was not going to be a Democratic year and that their original timetable, calling for a gubernatorial run in 1932, was correct. To stay out of the reach of persuasion while the State Democratic Convention was convening in Rochester, he took himself off to Warm Springs. But he could not escape the telephone, and over it Smith persuaded him to run. The next night, he was nominated by acclamation. Moses turned to Emily Smith and said, shouting so she could hear him above the uproar: "He'll make a good candidate but a lousy Governor."

The man Smith assigned to brief Roosevelt on campaign issues and draft his speeches, Belle Moskowitz's discovery, Samuel I. Rosenman, was at first not altogether enchanted with his assignment. "I had heard stories of his being something of a playboy and idler, of his weakness and ineffectiveness," he recalled. "That was the kind of man I had expected to meet." But he began almost instantly to wonder if such unfavorable views of Roosevelt were correct. "The broad jaw and upthrust chin, the piercing, flashing eyes, the firm hands—they did not fit the description. . . . He was friendly, but there was about his bearing an unspoken dignity which held off any undue familiarity." During the campaign, Rosenman watched Roosevelt pull himself laboriously to his feet as his car arrived in a town, snap his steel braces to hold his body erect, and then, chin up, cigarette holder tilted at the most nonchalant of angles, the cane on which he leaned the only visible sign of any disability, laughingly reassure the crowd that newspaper speculation about his health was exaggerated. By the end of the campaign, Rosenman knew that the Smith camp's assessment of Roosevelt had been very wrong.

But Moses had not changed his opinion. "I don't like him," he told Frances Perkins during this period. "I don't believe in him. I don't trust him."

His comments became more vicious. Miss Perkins recalled Moses saying to her about Roosevelt, " 'He's a pretty poor excuse for a man.' . . . He said so to me in just those words—'He's a pretty poor excuse for a man.'" He never actually mentioned the full extent—or what he imagined to be the full extent—of Roosevelt's disabilities, recalled another member of the Smith entourage, "but he was always hinting around about it in the most vicious kind of way. 'Vicious'—that was the only word for it." His comments took in not only Roosevelt but his wife as well. "I wouldn't repeat what he said about Eleanor Roosevelt," another Smith aide said. "Just say he dwelt on her physical appearance and her voice and was quite insulting."

The comments got back, as comments made in political circles always seem to do, to their targets. And Roosevelt responded in kind. During this same period, *he* told Frances Perkins that, if he was elected, "I'm not going to have Bob Moses around, Frances, because I don't trust him. I don't like him. I don't trust him. . . . There'll be trouble." Roosevelt's feeling for Moses, says one man who knew both, was at least equal in intensity to Moses' feeling for Roosevelt. "You can employ euphemisms to describe the electricity that was present when those two men were in the same room," he says, "but if you are going to be accurate, you have to say there was real hatred there."

Election Day in 1928 was November 6. The dark forces to which Handlin referred had done their work well on the boy who had thought he could rise from the Fourth Ward to be President. Alfred E. Smith received 87 electoral votes to Herbert Hoover's 444. He even lost New York State. But Franklin Delano Roosevelt polled 2,130,193 votes to Ottinger's 2,104,193. The man who hated Robert Moses was Governor.

Al Smith was bitter over the anti-Catholic prejudice that had marked the campaign. But, at first, that was the only bitterness. He seemed reconciled, even relieved, to be out of politics. After twenty-five years in public office, he wanted to settle down with Katie and spend more time with the grandchildren he adored. After twenty-five years, he was still poor—the Governor's salary in 1928 was only $10,000, less than that of his cabinet officers—and he was tired of that, too; he wanted security in his old age and something to leave his sons. John J. Raskob, William T. Kenny and other friends had offered him the presidency of the Empire State Building Corporation, which was erecting New York's tallest skyscraper, at a salary of $50,000 per year. "I have had all I can stand of it. As far as running for office is concerned—that's finished," he said, and at the time he meant it; one proof was his voluntary surrender of the titular leadership of the national Democratic Party; another was his refusal to intervene when his ally Judge George Olvany was forced out as head of Tammany Hall in 1929—if Smith had intended to run for President in 1932 he would certainly have attempted to maintain control of Tammany to keep a base of electoral votes on which to build a campaign. In November 1928, as he packed up so that Roosevelt could move into the Executive Mansion early—and busied himself personally overseeing the installation of the ramps Roosevelt would need to move in a wheelchair around the mansion and the capitol—Alfred E. Smith, the Happy Warrior, was ready to retire, still mostly happy, from politics. He certainly bore no personal animosity toward Roosevelt, and, raised in the Tammany tradition in which men were retired from active service honorably when the time for retirement came (the warriors who had held high political office becoming sachems, assured until they died of a voice in running the Hall) to make room for younger men coming along, "he considered," as Proskauer put it, "that he and Roosevelt were members of the same team."

Moreover, Smith felt that Roosevelt could be trusted to continue his programs. This was important to him. All through 1928, he had been pressing the Legislature for further improvements in working conditions for women and children, for extensions of the Workmen's Compensation Act, for liberalized welfare legislation, for movement in the new field of old-age pensions; and the Legislature had refused to be moved on these issues. Now he wanted Roosevelt to press for them. And certainly there was every reason for him to feel that his successor would. All during the campaign, Roosevelt had pledged himself to continue Smith's policies. His typical campaign speech, the New York *Herald Tribune* said, began with "a few words of fulsome praise for Alfred E. Smith." In the first weeks after the election, Smith was looking forward to helping the younger man get a good start in Albany. When he and Katie moved out of the Executive Mansion, in early December, he took a suite in the De Witt Clinton Hotel at the bottom of the little park in front of the capitol steps, so he would be available if his successor wanted to confer with him, and waited for Roosevelt to call.

And there he waited.

After a week had passed and Roosevelt had not contacted him, Smith swallowed his pride and telephoned the new Governor. He told Roosevelt that he had assumed he would want some assistance with the details of his inaugural address and first message to the Legislature, and had asked Mrs. Moskowitz to prepare a list of items that might be included. Roosevelt replied that the address and the message were almost finished, but he would be glad to show them to Smith and Mrs. Moskowitz when they were. And this, as Arthur Schlesinger puts it, "he 'forgot' to do. When the address was given, it was devoted largely to rural problems and made hardly a reference to what had gone before." When puzzled reporters asked Roosevelt whether he was going to continue the Smith policies, his evasive answer was: "Generally, for that is what we said all through the campaign."

Explanations for Roosevelt's treatment of Smith vary from historian to historian, depending on whether the historian has received most of his information from intimates of Roosevelt or of Smith. Roosevelt-oriented historians say that Smith, whether or not he intended to continue to run the state after he had left office, gave that impression to Roosevelt (they cite his offer of Mrs. Moskowitz's help on the inaugural address as one way he did so). Personal feelings aside, these historians point out, Roosevelt had long viewed the Governorship as a way station on the road to the White House, began planning for a 1932 presidential bid immediately after the election—and knew that if Smith changed his mind and decided to run for the presidency, he would be the man Roosevelt would have to beat. His greatest political problem in Albany, moreover, would be to get out from under the shadow of the man generally acknowledged to have been the state's greatest Governor.

But political considerations alone seem inadequate to account for Roosevelt's actions. One is forced to take into account another side of his complex character, the side which Raymond Moley was to call a "lack of directness and sincerity," and of which Robert Sherwood was to say that "at times he displayed a capacity for vindictiveness which could be described as petty." This side was frequently to be on display when Roosevelt dealt with people he had needed once but needed no longer. "Roosevelt was never at his best in getting rid of people no longer useful to him," Oscar Handlin was to write. "The lack of directness and candor in his actions left a bitter impression of shiftiness, of disloyalty, and of ingratitude." And the impression was to be strengthened in his relations with Smith and Smith's people, in Moley's opinion, because "Roosevelt . . . was deeply sensitive to the fact that so many among the people who knew him . . . believed, for one reason or another, that he lived beyond his intellectual means." Says Moley: "This opinion hurt Roosevelt, but he braced his determination to overcome it. It may be added that with this effort came a not quite Christlike tendency to beat down not only the opinion itself but those who held it. It is not remarkable, therefore, that when he became governor he did not avail himself of Smith's generous tender of help and advice. . . . The mighty engine of governmental power was not destined to spare those who had once deluded themselves with a notion that Roosevelt was a weak man." Of the many books written on Roosevelt, it is significant that every one whose author was an intimate of *both* Roosevelt and Smith—Miss Perkins, Proskauer, Rosenman and Jim Farley, for example—stresses this side of Roosevelt's character in attempting to explain his treatment of Smith.

The final humiliation of Al Smith at the hands of the man he had asked to be his successor revolved around Robert Moses.

Among the subjects Roosevelt was not anxious to discuss with Smith during the period between the election and the inauguration was that of the appointments he would make. Finally, Smith, humbling himself again, went to see Roosevelt at the Executive Mansion. Trying to make the Governor-elect see that they were both members of the same team, he said, "You know, I'll always be ready to help you. I'll always come up any time you want me. I'll talk to anyone you want me to talk to. I'll negotiate with anyone about anything. . . . I know all these people. I don't have anything [to do]." He said he understood that Roosevelt would want to replace most of his appointees with his own men. There were only two members of his administration who he thought were absolutely indispensable. They were Mrs. Moskowitz, whose title was "personal secretary to the Governor," and Moses. Roosevelt, describing this conversation to Frances Perkins, said that Smith told him, "You see, Mrs. Moskowitz knows all about everything. She knows all the plans. She knows all the people. She knows all the different characters and quirks that are involved in everything. She knows who can and who will do this or that." As for Moses, Roosevelt told Miss Perkins that Smith is "very dependent on Bob Moses, as you know, and thinks very highly of him. He feels that nobody else can carry on the parks, or the highways, or even the state hospitals except Moses, because he's got so much ability."

Roosevelt was evasive. And in the days following the Executive Mansion conference, Smith could see which way the wind was blowing. Roosevelt took pains to let reporters know that he had not had a single conference with Mrs. Moskowitz. He dodged their questions about Moses.

Mrs. Moskowitz was, after all, more of a personal adviser to Smith than a state official. He did not again raise with Roosevelt the question of her reappointment. But Smith felt, as one observer recalls, "that it would be a tragedy—a real tragedy—for the state to lose Moses' services as Secretary of State. There just wasn't anyone else with his ability around." Telephoning Roosevelt again, he asked for an appointment. Roosevelt was at Hyde Park, sixty miles from Albany, but, for Moses, Smith made a journey to Canossa. He was rewarded by an end to evasion. As soon as he had finished pleading with Roosevelt to reappoint Moses, the Governor-elect leaned back, puffed on his cigarette for a moment and then said flatly: "No. He rubs me the wrong way."

It is significant that, although Moses held other state positions, the conversation between Smith and Roosevelt concerned only the Secretaryship of State—for the reasons why Moses' other positions were not discussed do much to pinpoint the sources of his power.

Moses' six-year term as president of the Long Island State Park Commission did not expire until 1930; although Roosevelt was Governor and the commission presidency was a gubernatorial appointment, Moses did not need Roosevelt's approval to remain in the post. The chairmanship of the State Parks Council was conferred not by the Governor but by the council. Moses did not need Roosevelt's approval to remain in that post, either.

The only way Roosevelt could remove Moses from either of his park posts was by bringing formal charges against him. But charges of what? If Moses had been guilty of impropriety or illegality, how was a Governor supposed to know it? Moses kept the operation of the commission so secret that no outsider knew where to start looking for proof or could guess whether, if he did look, he would find any. A Governor could, of course, launch a full-scale investigation into the commission, but this would involve the gravest political risks since public opinion was firmly behind Moses. And what if the investigation did not find anything? Then it would look like a malicious attempt to defame a great man. An attempt could be made to defeat Moses at the next State Parks Council election, but his careful stacking of the council membership had made that very difficult. The Governor could, of course, change the membership, but only gradually since the members' terms were also six years. And if word of a council-packing attempt got out, public opinion would again side with Moses. Parks were supposed to be free from politics.

As he had done in the little world of Yale, Robert Moses had erected within New York State a power structure all his own, an agency ostensibly part of the state government but only minimally responsive to its wishes. The structure might appear flimsy but it was shored up with buttresses of the strongest material available in the world of politics: public opinion. A Governor—even a Governor who hated the man who dwelt within that structure—would pull it down at his own peril.

Moses understood this. Asked forty years later why Roosevelt did not oust him from his park posts, he would laugh and say, "He couldn't afford to. The public wouldn't have stood for it. And even if he tried to, it would have been very difficult. See, the law didn't permit it, except on charges. It was set up that way, see. That's the way it was set up." This explanation came at the end of a four-hour interview. All during it, Moses had been serious and guarded in his statements. But when he said this, he suddenly threw back his head and laughed, a laugh of pure enjoyment. "That," he said, still laughing, "was the way it was set up, don't you see?"

Roosevelt apparently saw. Moses pushed matters to a head himself. The duties of Secretary of State included the organization of the inaugural ceremonies—it was the Secretary, in fact, who would administer the oath of office to the new Governor—and Moses had to confer with Roosevelt about the arrangements. At the end of one conference, he raised the subject of his reappointment, and, when Roosevelt dodged, Moses demanded, "You don't want me to stay on, do you?" Whatever Roosevelt's exact reply was, he made it clear that Moses' assumption was not incorrect. But the Governor-elect had then to make it clear that he was talking only about the Secretaryship. He had to ask Moses hastily to stay on his park jobs. Revenge could not have been nearly as sweet as he had hoped.

The aftermath of the conversation must have made it positively sour. Stalking out of Roosevelt's office, Moses immediately composed a curt letter saying that he would resign as Secretary of State "when Governor Smith leaves Albany." Then he released it to the press, embarrassing Roosevelt, who had no successor ready to announce.

Moses, moreover, included in the letter a paragraph saying, "In accordance with our understanding, I shall carry on the state park work." And a flood of editorials greeted this statement with relief. "It is gratifying," said the *World*. "Gratifying," chimed in the *Times*. And Roosevelt, in a hastily composed one-paragraph reply to the resignation letter, had to express gratification, too, saying, "I am, of course, very happy that you will continue to carry on the work . . . You have rendered conspicuous service and I can assure you that I shall often avail myself of your continued cooperation."

The identity of the replacements for Moses and Mrs. Moskowitz could not have been more insulting to Al Smith if Roosevelt had selected them with that aim in mind. As his personal secretary, he chose Guernsey Cross, whose sole qualification was that he was big and strong enough for the Governor to lean on when he walked. As Secretary of State, he chose the Boss of the

Bronx, Edward J. Flynn, whose experience in government, as distinguished from politics, was nonexistent and who didn't even want the job and would not agree to take it until Roosevelt, after Moses resigned, frantically pursued him on a trip around Europe by transatlantic telephone calls and cables. ("The basic reason for my appointment," Flynn later wrote, "was that Roosevelt did not want to appoint Moses.") Flynn's lack of experience in government forced Roosevelt to downgrade the Secretaryship, reducing it mainly to its licensing and ceremonial functions. Flynn never devoted much time to it and it was never again to be a sort of Deputy Governorship, or, in fact, of any real importance in the state governmental setup. What made Roosevelt's refusal to reappoint Moses all the more bitter to Smith was that the new Governor, anxious to avoid any appearance of an open break with his immensely popular predecessor, reappointed sixteen of the eighteen members of Smith's cabinet, every one except Moses, the only one Smith had asked him to reappoint, and the State Industrial Commissioner, a minor official whose dismissal Smith intimates interpreted as a "throw-in" so that newspapers would not be able to comment that Moses had been the only one thrown out.

At the inauguration, however, Smith and Roosevelt put on a show of harmony. When Franklin and Eleanor moved into the Executive Mansion on December 31, Al, who had returned to the mansion for the occasion, met them at the door and, as reporters crowded close to listen, said, "A thousand welcomes. We've got the home fires burning and you'll find this is a fine place to live." Roosevelt, turning to the reporters, said, "I only wish Al were going to be right here for the next two years." One reporter, watching Al depart, waving his brown derby, as the crowd sang "Auld Lang Syne," wrote that Roosevelt was wearing "a smile that had a trace of wistfulness." The next day, at the official inaugural ceremony, the charade continued. In a brief valedictory, Smith praised Roosevelt to the crowd that jammed the Assembly Chamber.

Only Moses would not put on a show. When Roosevelt stood up to take the oath, Moses realized for the first time just how weak his legs were. ("The platform was high above the crowd," he told the author, "and people couldn't see what was going on, but both his legs had to be locked upright, the hinges squeaking and then snapping into place.") But that didn't stop Moses from doing what he had planned. When Roosevelt made his way to the lectern, one arm gripping a cane, the other the arm of his eldest son, James, and placed his hand on the family's two-hundred-year-old Dutch Bible, Moses administered the oath of office—and, as soon as it was finished, without waiting for Roosevelt's inaugural address, stalked off the platform and out of the Chamber.

17. *The Mother of Accommodation*

NOW ROBERT MOSES no longer had behind him a Governor of whose unquestioning loyalty he could, right or wrong, always be certain. "Executive support," about which he had not had to worry for ten years, was a source of concern again. And within three months after Roosevelt had succeeded Smith, Moses was to be reminded how much difference this could mean to him.

The great piece of his business left unstarted at the close of Smith's regime was the Northern State Parkway. In the North Hills, the name given to the terminal moraine near the New York City line, Moses had found a line of small farms that could make a right-of-way—twisting, turning, but still a right-of-way between the holdings of the North Hills barons. Where there was not the slightest crevice between estates, he had introduced into the parkway's route still more curves, so that it would run along the very edges of the barons' estates and not disturb the serenity of their manor houses. He had threaded the route along that portion of the rough at the Links Country Club that could most easily be spared without spoiling the barons' favorite golf course. And by paying them tribute in the form of private bridges and personal entrances, he had persuaded them to donate the right-of-way he needed. The barons of the Dix Hills in the western portion of Suffolk County—Otto Kahn, Stimson, Mills, Winthrop and De Forest—had thrown back with contemptuous ease his attempt to penetrate the fastnesses they controlled, but Kahn's $10,000 had enabled him to snatch from James Roth and other meek farmers of the plains to the south thirteen more miles of right-of-way.

But between the North Hills and Dix Hills stood the Wheatley Hills, the meeting place of the two moraines, the bolt of the scissors that made Long Island beautiful. And in the Wheatley Hills, the estates—identified by black-and-gold signs bearing such names as Morgan, Whitney, Winthrop, Grace, Garvan and Phipps—clustered around the little village of Old Westbury so thickly that there was no path, no matter how tortuous, that could be picked out without running through their holdings. These barons therefore refused to parley and instead hired champions to fight Moses—and the champions included Grenville Clark, whose brilliance as an attorney was not at all dimmed in their eyes by the fact that he had been a Harvard classmate of Franklin D. Roosevelt.

Even before Roosevelt's inauguration, Clark was writing to him at Warm Springs suggesting an alternate route—with a sharp southward dip just before it got to Old Westbury so that it avoided the Wheatley Hills completely.

Dashing off his own letter to Warm Springs, Moses told Roosevelt that Clark was trying to "change the location of about six miles of right-of-way in the center of the parkway, for the sole purpose of avoiding a few people whom he represents." This, Moses said, would involve "torturing the parkway down toward the middle of the island where the landscaping problem is almost insuperable." He would never agree to do so. To brace up Roosevelt, he added that the Wheatley Hills barons are "people of large wealth who have always been able to buy what they wanted or to get what they wanted by influence and pressure. It is difficult for these people to believe there is anyone they cannot reach in some way."

For several months, Moses seemed to be winning the fight. Roosevelt drove over the two routes himself and wrote Clark that he saw no reason to change Moses' plans.

But those plans were soon to be changed nonetheless. For Grenville Clark discovered how Otto Kahn, Moses' relative, had persuaded Moses to shift the parkway route off his private golf course.

Clark relayed the discovery to Hutchinson and Hewitt. The two legislative leaders telegraphed Moses demanding "a complete list of all properties . . . payment for which has been made or is intended to be made by funds from private sources for any parkway or proposed parkway," and "a complete list of persons who have given funds to the Long Island Parkway [sic] Commission." And the telegram demanded: "Please also state whether the route of any proposed parkway was ever tentatively laid out over, through or near the land of any donors of money. . . . If so, after receipt of such gift, was route of any proposed parkway changed so as to run over or through a different part of the land of any donor or donors, or so as not to run at all through or near such land?"

At first, Moses was defiant. Hastily sending an explanation to Roosevelt, he admitted that Kahn had given $10,000, but said that "the idea that we shifted our route to please one man because he gave us some money is too absurd to entertain." The "real reason" for the shift, he said, "was the objection of" Stimson, De Forest and "various others" to the routing of the parkway across their land, and their refusal to donate land unless the route was shifted south—a statement which conveniently ignored the fact that if the route hadn't been shifted off Kahn's land in the first place, it would never have touched their land and their donations would not have been needed.

At first, Moses' new executive gave him support, backing the Wheatley Hills route. But Clark began hinting that any attempt to push that route would result in the disclosure to the public of the Moses-Kahn deal, which, he said, if "finally brought to light will not make a creditable chapter in the history of this State." Various attempts at compromise failed, and Clark—and Hewitt and Hutchinson—made clear to Roosevelt that any attempt to obtain legislative appropriations for the Northern State Parkway until its route had been shifted out of the Wheatley Hills would result in an all-out fight.

The fight over the Taylor Estate—now to be named Heckscher State Park—had been an all-out one, of course, but there would be a significant difference this time. The issue in the first case had been that of millionaires blocking the public; in the Northern State Parkway case, it would be that of a millionaire giving $10,000 to keep his private golf course untouched and the money being used to throw hard-working farmers off their land. It was not the type of issue likely to redound to the credit of the official who had accepted the $10,000 and thrown the farmers off their land—or of a Governor who was placed in the position of defending his action.

Whether Roosevelt was motivated by the threat of public disclosure to prevail on Moses to compromise is not definitely known. But the following sequence of events is clear. On October 23, 1929, Clark gave Roosevelt what amounted to an ultimatum: he and his clients had decided, he said, that it was impossible to reach any kind of agreement with Moses, because he refused to compromise and was highly insulting, and that a full-scale fight would be launched during the 1930 legislative session. Nineteen-thirty was an election year; among those running for re-election would be Franklin D. Roosevelt. Less than two weeks after Clark issued the barons' ultimatum to Roosevelt, Moses agreed to a "compromise." Under the "compromise," the Northern State suddenly altered its eastward course at Glen Cove Road, the western border of the Wheatley Hills, just as it was about to plunge into the estate area, and instead swung south for two full miles, far enough so that when it resumed its course, it would never come near the Wheatley Hills. To make it appear that the "compromise" was really a compromise and that both sides, instead of just the state, had given in, Moses announced to the public with great fanfare that the barons had agreed to pay the state $175,000, which he said would pay for the entire cost of the detour. Actually, however, the cost of the additional right-of-way alone would be $2,250,000, so that more than 90 percent of the bill for the accommodation Moses reached with the barons had to be footed by the state's taxpayers.

The long-term costs to the public of Moses' accommodation include figures that cannot be prefaced with dollar signs. For one thing, the accommodation condemned users of the parkway to a perpetual detour of five miles around the Wheatley Hills. Coupled with the six-mile detour forced on parkway users by Moses' previous accommodation with Otto Kahn and the other Dix Hills barons, it meant that a commuter who lived anywhere east of Dix Hills and who used the parkway to get to his job in New York City was condemned to drive, every working day of his life, twenty-two extra and unnecessary miles. He had to drive 110 unnecessary miles per week, 5,500 per year—all because of Moses' "compromise." By the 1960's there were about

21,500 such commuters, and the cost to them alone of Moses' accommodation totaled tens of millions of wasted hours of human lives.

More important, Moses' great accommodation deprived the public forever of parks in the loveliest part of Long Island. He had once wanted parks on the wooded hills of the North Shore, and his original concept of the Northern State Parkway was therefore of a road leading to parks, as the Southern State Parkway led to parks. But, as part of his "compromise," he had to promise the barons that there would not be a single state park anywhere along the parkway, or anywhere in the section of the North Shore that they controlled—and with a single exception,* acquired in 1967 and still undeveloped in 1974, there are no state parks anywhere in that part of Nassau County or western Suffolk that was known as the "North Shore"

* Caumsett State Park, the former Marshall Field Estate, on Lloyd Neck.

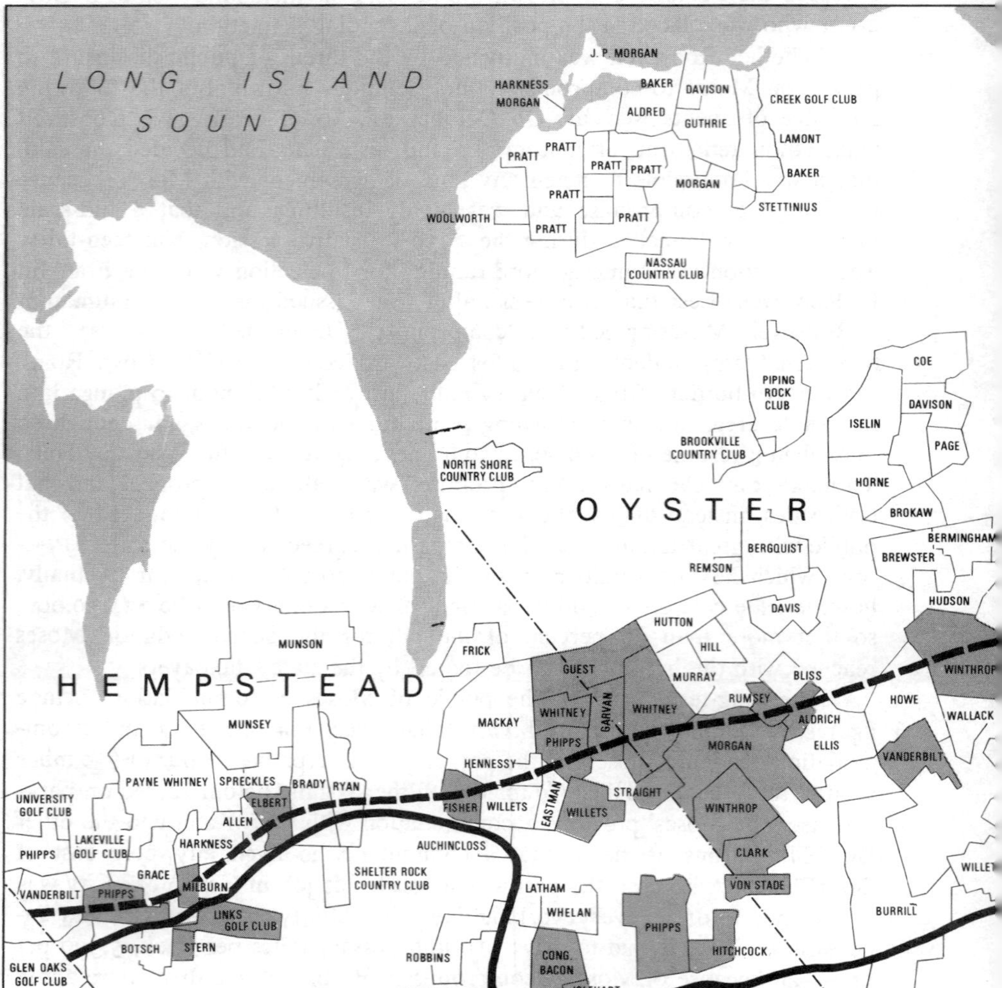

or the "Gold Coast."* Robert Moses' "compromise" with the North Shore barons amounted to unconditional surrender. In later years, most of the barons would have disappeared from the Long Island scene. The names of most of them would be unfamiliar to the new generations using the Northern State Parkway. But every twist and curve in that parkway—and, in particular, the two great southward detours it makes around the Wheatley and Dix Hills—is a tribute to their power, and to the use to which they put it after they discovered the chink in Moses' armor. Farmer James Roth was not the only person who paid for Moses' deal with Otto Kahn.

The completeness of Moses' surrender—coupled with the fact that Moses never surrendered on any park or parkway issue while Smith was

* Motorists using the Northern State Parkway cannot reach any park unless they transfer, forty-one miles from Manhattan, to a spur parkway that leads, after another six miles of driving, to Sunken Meadow.

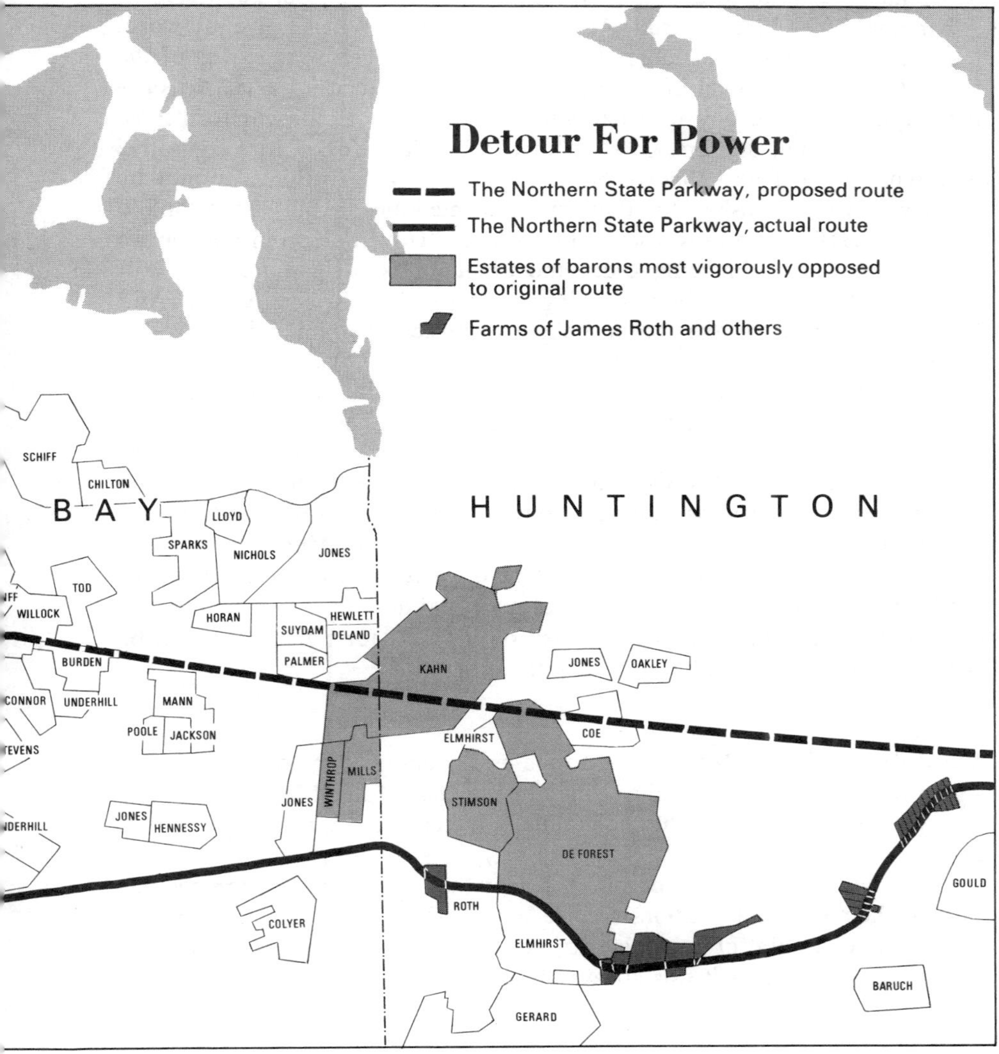

Governor—makes it difficult to escape the conclusion that the change in Governors had something to do with it. By accepting Otto Kahn's $10,000, Moses had presented his opponents with a weapon which they used to club him—and New York State—into submission. But, by illegally appropriating the Taylor Estate, he had presented many of the same opponents in that battle with an equally dangerous weapon. And somehow Al Smith had avoided its swings and beaten them into the ground. Fighting under the Squire of the Hudson was not precisely the same as fighting under the King of Oliver Street.

There were other differences. In Albany, where a legislative session is round after round of hastily formed alliances, trust in a man's word is all-important; when a man promised his support on a bill, he could not later take it back; if he did so, the word on him would soon begin to circulate through the corridors of the capitol, and when discussing their relationships with him, legislators would say, "We deal in writing"—a phrase which, in Albany, was the ultimate insult. Al Smith could say, "When I give my word, it sticks." Now, in the corridors of the capitol, many men were saying of the new Governor, "We deal in writing." Diminutive Reuben Lazarus, the one-time legislative page boy who had since become one of the capitol's most knowledgeable bill drafters, good enough to be New York City's legislative representative, believed that he had been misled twice within a month by Roosevelt when he asked the Governor his intention on bills important to Tammany Hall, and told Roosevelt to his face: "Governor, from now on we deal in writing; and I'm going to demand a bond on your signature."

No man had more bills awaiting signature than Robert Moses. And Roosevelt seemed to take special delight in misleading him. Once Lazarus was sitting in the anteroom outside the Governor's office, "and I heard Moses, inside, shout, 'Frank Roosevelt, you're a goddamned liar and this time I can prove it! I had a stenographer present!' And Moses came storming out of FDR's office without even seeing me, he was so thoroughly angry. I was next and I walked in. The Governor's face was breaking into a grin of real pleasure. He . . . acted as though he had just come out of the bath after a clean shave in the morning." After several such incidents, Moses developed a new routine for his trips to Albany; he would arrive early in the morning for conferences with Roosevelt at the Executive Mansion, but even though the Governor might promise that a bill then on his desk for signature would be signed, Moses would not leave the capitol until it was.

But if Roosevelt gave Moses a hard time before doing so, he did nonetheless sign most of Moses' bills. And although he may have hated Moses, during the four years of his Governorship he gradually increased, not decreased, Moses' power.

He did so, moreover, despite the fact that Moses never trimmed his sails in their personal relationship. He never called Roosevelt "Governor," and he made a point of not doing so; not only in private letters but also in official correspondence it was always "Dear Frank."

He refused to follow conventional lines in their official relations, either. Although his State Parks Council was a part of Roosevelt's administration, the council adopted major new policies without conferring with the Governor about them—sometimes even without notifying the Governor about them. Once, when Moses had the council pass a resolution asking the Legislature to remove all historical state reservations from the council's control and turn them over to the Department of Education, the Governor was reduced to begging Henry Lutz, "Will you be good enough to let me know whether the report is true. . . ."

Moses may have obeyed Al Smith's patronage suggestions without question, but he wouldn't even listen to Roosevelt's. As Jones Beach and other state parks opened during Roosevelt's regime, the number of jobs at Moses' disposal steadily increased. By 1930, the number of lifeguards, special police, gardeners, parking-field and bathhouse attendants, janitors and toll takers at the Long Island parks was more than fifteen hundred. Long Island Democrats eyed these jobs greedily—and expectantly, since Moses was a subordinate of a Democratic Governor. After they had asked Moses for some jobs and had been refused, they appealed to Roosevelt to order him to make some available. Roosevelt gingerly suggested to Moses that he cooperate, and Moses curtly refused. The Governor's personal requests received the same treatment. Roosevelt sent on to Moses a job application with a notation attached—"Dear Bob: This is an old school boyfriend of mine and I would be very glad if you could help him in some way." Moses replied by simply sending the Governor a copy of the official employment regulations of the commission, which included the sentence: "Recommendations based upon merely personal or political acquaintance will not be considered."

And the explanation for the increase in Moses' power during Roosevelt's Governorship certainly wasn't that he gave in like a good subordinate if he had a difference of opinion with his chief over a matter of policy. In fact, if his powers of persuasion were not sufficient to persuade Roosevelt to alter what Moses felt was an unwise decision, he did not hesitate to mobilize forces against the Governor.

For years, Roosevelt, naval buff and lover of the sea, had wanted to transform Fort Schuyler, a little-used fifty-six-acre Army base at Throgs Neck in the Bronx, into a Merchant Marine Academy. The folding chairs set up on the Assembly Speaker's dais for his inauguration had hardly been stored away when he began prodding the Army to close the base and turn the land over to the state. In 1931, the Army finally agreed—but no sooner had it done so than Moses announced that Fort Schuyler should be turned into a park instead. When the Governor refused even to consider that suggestion—Fort Schuyler, he said, was going to be a Merchant Marine Academy; the matter was closed—Moses mobilized his forces.

The Park Association of New York City met to formally endorse Moses' suggestion. So did the Washington Heights Taxpayers Association, the Public Schools Athletic League, twenty-five other civic organizations "of a total membership of half a million" organized into a committee to back the park plea—and the Sulzbergers' *Times*. The influentials who made up the Park

Association's board of directors took the trouble to write personally to Roosevelt on the issue. After conferring with Moses, Nathan Straus, Jr., association president, said, "If it's made an academy it will train three or four hundred boys; if it's made a park, 300,000 to 400,000 people will use it every summer weekend."

Apparently Roosevelt did not realize for some time that it was actually Moses who was behind the opposition. As late as January 8, 1932, Guernsey Cross, obviously under the impression that Moses was on the Governor's side, wrote to ask him for a suggested reply that the Governor could make to a letter from George F. Mand, president of the Bronx Chamber of Commerce. Moses replied promptly: "Attached is suggested reply to [Mand]. 'Dear Mr. Mand: I agree with you . . . that it is much more important to use this area for municipal recreation purposes than to make it the headquarters for the U. S. Merchant Marine Academy, which can well be taken care of with a smaller and cheaper piece of land outside the city limits.' " Cross hurriedly asked Conservation Commissioner Henry Morgenthau to draft the reply instead.

Even after he realized Moses' involvement, however, there was nothing Roosevelt could do. When Samuel Rosenman and Herbert Lehman, contacted by reform leaders, both asked him to forget about the academy, he must have realized that he was surrounded, and he surrendered. (He was able to realize this pet project only after he had been elected President. On December 29, 1932, two days before his term as Governor ended, he signed, on behalf of New York State, a lease proffered by the War Department giving the land to the state for a New York Merchant Marine Academy. And even at this date, Roosevelt did not make any public announcement of the transaction, so that the public did not learn what he had done until he was no longer Governor.)

Part of the explanation for Moses' increased power was simply the breadth and depth of his knowledge of the government at whose head Roosevelt, with little preparation, suddenly had found himself. No one knew the vast administrative machinery the Governor was supposed to run better than this man the Governor hated. To a considerable extent, the machinery was *his* machinery; he, more than any other individual, had drafted the executive budget system, the departmental consolidation and the hundreds of bills that implemented those constitutional amendments. He, more than any other individual, knew the considerations—constitutional, legal and political—that lay behind wording in those laws that was otherwise so puzzling. He knew the precedents that made each point in them legal—and the precedents that might call their legality into question. He knew the reason behind every refinement, every clarification—and every obscuration—in the laws' final versions. When discussing a point of law with some young state agency counsel, Moses liked to let the lawyer painstakingly explain the legal ramifications involved and then say dryly: "I know. I wrote the law." This store of knowledge, coupled with an intelligence capable of drawing upon it with computer-like rapidity, constituted a political weapon which no Governor could afford to let rust in his arsenal.

Roosevelt's very first major administrative hurdle—the compilation of his first budget—taught him Moses' indispensability. The 1929 budget would be the first drawn up under the executive budget system Moses had codified. But no sooner had Roosevelt presented it to the Republican Legislature—a 411-page "complete plan of proposed expenditures and estimated revenues"—than the Legislature struck at its heart, tacking on to the appropriation bills a rider that would give the chairmen of its finance committees, Hewitt and Hutchinson, an equal say with the Governor in determining how each department should spend the lump sums proposed for it by the Governor. The rider was the last desperate challenge of men who saw their power being stripped from them, and they didn't spare the invective; a Syracuse assemblyman, referring to Roosevelt as "that man downstairs," trumpeted that "the very foundation of the State is in danger with this message of avarice, usurpation and presumption."

Roosevelt was unsure how to deal with the challenge. So were his legal advisers, some of whom told him to avoid a test of the issue in the courts since a decision could go either way and since while it was being decided all state expenditures might be paralyzed. The new Governor's initial inclination was to sign the bills, distasteful though their rider may have been.

When, however, he asked Moses' opinion, he was told to veto the bills. The courts, Moses said, would hold that the Governor's budget was constitutional and the Legislature's unconstitutional—and it was perfectly possible to work out a method for financing state activities while the courts were deliberating. Roosevelt sent his former law partner, Basil O'Connor, to see George Wickersham, the reformer and ex-United States Attorney General, and Wickersham said Moses was right. As Roosevelt drafted a veto message, he found himself asking Moses for "suggestions." Moses gave them—and the message as delivered to the Legislature was substantially the one Moses wrote. When lawyers began to draft the Governor's brief, they found themselves relying more and more on Moses for background information. Then they realized they were relying on him for strategy. On November 19, 1929, the seven members of the state's highest court, the Court of Appeals, held unanimously, as Moses had predicted they would, that the Legislature's action was unconstitutional. The principle of executive and legislative separation was at last irrevocably established in New York State—and Roosevelt had learned the truth of a saying of Al Smith's: "If Bob Moses says it's constitutional, it's constitutional."

And then there was Moses' record of accomplishment and his potential for more accomplishment, the fact that Moses had gotten things done and could get things done again. Moses' cleverness in writing laws cementing himself in power helped explain Roosevelt's initial decision not to try to take that power away. But a large part of the explanation for Roosevelt's subsequent willingness to increase Moses' power was not cleverness but accomplishment, the record of what Moses had done with the power he had given himself. For the accomplishment and the potential for more accomplishment had very strong political connotations indeed.

The program for which Moses had so frantically shoveled sod under

Smith came to full bloom in the first of Roosevelt's gubernatorial summers. The summer of 1929 was the summer of the "Hoover Market." It was the summer of General Motors, Radio and Big Steel, of AT&T, of General Electric, which would by Labor Day hit 306, having more than tripled its price in eighteen months. The summer of 1929 was the summer of Big Bill Tilden, who won his seventh American amateur tennis championship, of Bobby Jones and his putter, Calamity Jane, who together carried off the U.S. Open golf championship, of Ernest Hemingway's *Farewell to Arms* and of Thomas Wolfe, whose first novel, *Look Homeward, Angel,* was uncrated at the bookstores in June. It was the summer of Kate Smith, who began in those golden months her career as a radio songstress, and of Gertrude Berg, who in those months first shouted "Yoo Hoo!" across a Bronx airshaft. And the summer of 1929 was the summer of Robert Moses.

Heckscher State Park was formally opened in June and the onlooker who shouted "God bless him!" when Moses was introduced was only sounding the first note of the chorus of hosannas the summer was to bring. "You owe this park . . . to the amazing public spirit of Robert Moses," August Heckscher told 15,000 cheering onlookers, and Lieutenant Governor Lehman, praising Moses for his "vision and courage," agreed.

The Southern State Parkway was opened in July, and fathers driving their families along the lovely tree-shaded road—which, with a width of forty feet, seemed wonderfully wide—were explaining to their wives what "no grade crossings" meant and telling their children as they passed Wantagh that by the end of the summer they would be able to take another parkway there and drive down to the ocean and swim, and every newspaper story on the Southern State coupled its marvels with the name of its creator.

And when, on August 4, 1929, the Wantagh Causeway opened the way to Jones Beach, the hosannas became a hallelujah chorus.

On the day the causeway opened, 25,000 cars rolled across it. In the first month of its operation, attendance at Jones Beach State Park—which legislators had said would never justify its investment because people would never drive forty miles to a park on a sand bar—topped 325,000. The press—not only New York's press but the press of the entire country—spoke of the expanses of surf and sand in tones of awe. Reporters vied with one another in searching for superlatives to describe the parking areas that one said "look as big as a cattle range" and bathhouses "such as you have never seen before."

The praise wasn't only for the size of the park's buildings; it was for the taste with which they had been designed and the ingenuity with which there had been worked into their steel and stone delicate details which the eye, to its delight, was endlessly discovering. Visitors could see that the nautical theme had been carried out everywhere. Walking along the mile-long boardwalk connecting the two bathhouses, they noticed that the boardwalk railing was a ship's railing. Bending down to drink from a water fountain, they found that the fountains were turned on and off by ships' pilot wheels. Looking for trash cans, they found them concealed in ships' funnels. Looking up, visitors saw on the flagpoles crow's-nests and yardarms and halyards decorated with long rows of bright semaphore signals. They saw ships' lanterns swinging on davits from the lampposts. Looking down, expecting the paved walks in the park to be standard gray concrete, they were surprised by mosaics—of compasses, maps and the gay seahorse that Moses had chosen as the emblem of Jones Beach—set into the concrete. The games along the boardwalk were ships' games: shuffleboard, quoits, deck tennis, Ping-Pong. Even the pitch-and-putt golf course was made maritime by the placing near every hole of some reminder of the sea—a rusty anchor, the keel of an ancient boat, old rum kegs retrieved from the Great South Bay. All Jones Beach employees were garbed as sailors, complete with sailor caps, and their supervisors wore officers' uniforms, complete with gold braid. And every button on the uniforms was engraved with a seahorse.

Architects exclaimed over the long, low sweeping lines of the bathhouses and restaurants, their medieval and Moorish cast, the combination of Ohio sandstone and Barbizon brick ("Perfect!" exulted one architect. *"Perfect!"*) with which they were faced. They were startled when, searching for the water tower, they realized that it was concealed in the 200-foot-high campanile. They described with delight the diaper-changing rooms, the cutouts of bowmen crouching against the dune that formed the backdrop for the archery range, the symbolic ironwork cutouts on the directional signs, the gay devices of stone and brick—all the touches that Robert Moses, standing alone on a deserted sandbar, had decided he must have in his great park. "It is in the smaller things that Mr. Moses is at his very best," *Architectural Forum* was to say. "Usually a public institution of any kind in this country has been the occasion for especially dull architecture and walls of cheerless dimensions which invite only the scribbling of small obscenities. But Mr. Moses, being essentially a romanticist, has revived the handicraft spirit in his designers, with the result that the equipment at Jones Beach exhibits irrelevant and endearing good spirits. The architecture has the great virtue of being scaled down to the size of a good time." Even the *Herald Tribune* could only wax rhapsodic over this "most prosaically named, most beautifully landscaped of beaches."

And the letters on the editorial page almost outdid the editorials. Ernest Biehl of Manhattan, just back from a cross-country trip, hastened to take pen in hand to inform his fellow *Times* readers: "I have visited nearly all of the important beach resorts in this country and I must say that nowhere on this continent is there a public or private beach that is even comparable to the one that the State under Robert Moses has built." A thousand letters-to-the-editor echoed Biehl's appraisal. A nation looked at Robert Moses' dream and found it good.

And not just the nation. Delegations of architects and park designers came from France, from England, even from Scandinavia, traditional leader in park development, to learn from Jones Beach. Their comments were summed up by one Englishman who said flatly, "This is the finest seashore playground ever given the public anywhere in the world."

Never, observers agreed, had any park been kept as clean as Jones Beach. College students hired for the summer were formed into "Courtesy

Squads." Patrolling the boardwalk, conspicuous in snow-white sailor suits and caps, they hurried to pick up dropped papers and cigarette butts while the droppers were still in the vicinity. They never reprimanded the culprits, but simply bent down, picked up the litter and put it in a trash basket. To make the resultant embarrassment of the litterers more acute, Moses refused to let the Courtesy Squaders use sharp-pointed sticks to pick up litter without stooping. He *wanted* the earnest, clean-cut college boys stooping, Moses explained to his aides. It would make the litterers more ashamed. He even issued the Courtesy Squaders large cloths so that they could wipe from the boardwalk gobs of spittle. His methods worked. As one writer put it: "You will feel like a heel if you so much as drop a gum wrapper."

The lines of wire trash receptacles on the clean white sand were only a symbol of the emphasis on cleanliness there also. At intervals, loudspeakers sounded a bugle call, and then an announcer, in a carefully modulated tone, "thanked" the visitors for their cooperation in keeping the beach clean. "The effect," as one observer wrote, "is magical. In no time at all, every guilty culprit is doing KP in his immediate area."

Moses' methods extended to his parkways. Stetsoned state troopers stopped every car entering them and gave the driver a card printed with "Rules of the Road," which carefully spelled out rules against roadside picnicking and littering. And the rules were enforced. Littering summonses were issued wholesale. Occasionally, when troopers came across a whole bag of garbage that had been tossed from an automobile window, they would try to identify the driver from the contents. If they could, they would call on him at his home to issue a summons—and Moses would see that there was a troop of newspaper photographers along to record the culprit's expression when he opened his door.

The public praised also the success with which Moses had kept Jones Beach free of the usual amusement-park trappings of other public beaches. "There are no concessions, no booths, no bawling hot-dog vendors," marveled one writer. "You won't see any weight-guessers or three-throws-for-a-dime-and-win-a-dolly alleys or blaring funhouses. For almost the first time in the history of public beaches, this beach is conceived as a spot for recreation, not amusement stimulated by honky-tonk." Whenever Jones Beach was the subject of a magazine article, it seemed, and it was the subject of literally scores in the 1930's, the article contained—at least once—the word "wholesome."

The public beat a path to Moses' door. In 1930, the attendance at Jones Beach would be 1,500,000, in 1931, 2,700,000, in 1932, 3,200,000. The path itself, so recently completed, was jammed to capacity—and then to overcapacity. Although all grade crossings had been eliminated on the Southern State, two, one at Sunrise Highway and one at Merrick Road, remained on the Wantagh because of the refusal of the Legislature to allocate money for the bridges that would carry the two cross roads over the causeway. For the same reason, there was a half-mile gap between the Southern State and the Wantagh. By 1930, traffic was backing up at those spots for more than a mile on summer Sundays. In 1931, the Legislature allocated funds for the bridges and a spur between the two roads. Moses was jubilant. "The traffic capacity of the causeway will be more than doubled," he said.

The facilities at Jones Beach proved inadequate. Both bathhouses were usually filled by noon. The parking lots as big as cattle ranges were jammed as full as sardine tins. Valley Stream, Heckscher and Sunken Meadow state parks were just as crowded. Moses revealed more of the plans he had kept secret, and enlarged them.

There should be an increase in facilities—bathhouses, parking fields and concessions—at all state parks on Long Island, he said. There should be a short parkway—he named it the "Heckscher Spur"—linking the Southern State with Heckscher State Park and a "Sunken Meadow State Parkway" linking the Northern State with Sunken Meadow State Park.

During the fall of 1930, the two-mile-long Ocean Parkway extending along the barrier beach from Jones Beach eastward toward Fire Island was opened. When he had asked the Legislature for money for the parkway, Moses had said that two miles of an ocean drive was all he had in mind. Now he revealed that he actually had been concealing a few other miles—ninety-eight, to be precise. Why, he demanded, shouldn't there be a continuous road, bordered by the rolling Atlantic, all the way from Breezy Point on the Rockaway peninsula in New York City to Montauk Point at the tip of Long Island, a distance of one hundred miles? It would not be difficult to create an Ocean Parkway through the Rockaways and Long Beach by widening existing streets and turning them into an ocean drive, he said. The gap between these two beaches could easily be bridged. So could the gap between Long Beach and the Jones Beach portion of the strand. In fact, he had already broached to Hempstead Town—to G. Wilbur Doughty and Tom McWhinney, to be precise—the possibility of Hempstead's building that bridge, and Hempstead seemed amenable. (Hempstead should have been amenable; some indications of the size of the political boodle involved in such a construction job may be garnered by the fact that one of the contractors involved secured the job by paying $75,000 in cash to the Nassau County Republican organization and—just to insure against any criticism—another $75,000 to the county's Democratic organization.) Thanks to the deeds of land on the Jones Beach portion of the strand that he had accepted from Oyster Bay, wheedled from Hempstead and politically blackmailed from Babylon, the Long Island Park Commission had already in hand the rights-of-way for the parkway along most of this eleven-mile portion, which was called, in order eastward from Jones Beach State Park, High Hill Beach, Tobay Beach, Gilgo, Cedar Island Beach, Oak Beach and Captree. At Captree a causeway would jump a narrow inlet—and the Ocean Parkway would be on Fire Island. There, for fifty miles, it could run along the sand, the ocean stretching broad on one side, the bay beautiful on the other, until the barrier beach swung back at Moriches to join the southern fluke of the whale's tail that was Long Island's eastern end. By pointing out to them that the building of a road along Fire Island would make their land immensely more valuable, he had, he disclosed, already persuaded sixty-seven of the seventy property owners on Fire Island whose lands would be traversed by the parkway to donate the right-of-way, and although two of the three laggards—immensely wealthy and immensely stubborn spinster sisters named Smith—owned so much of the land needed that no public body could afford to condemn it, he was confident that they would sign up shortly. When the Legislature balked, he pointed out that the land deeded to the state by the townships was worth millions of dollars. Did the legislators propose to let it go to waste? The legislators may have considered doing so, but in 1930 the public applause for the two miles of Ocean Parkway already opened made it obvious that such a course would be unwise. During the 1931 legislative session, money was appropriated to extend the road eight miles farther through High Hill, Tobay and Gilgo beaches. The Fire Island portion of the plan had to be dropped when the Smith sisters, for undisclosed reasons, refused to donate, but Moses came up with a substitute plan extending the Ocean Parkway all the way along the Jones Beach portion of the barrier beach to Captree, and then bringing it back to the mainland on a causeway and linking it up to the Southern State Parkway with a spur parkway. There would be time to get to Fire Island later.

Editorials hailed each new Moses plan. The best proof of the universality of their appeal was furnished by Long Island, which for so long had resisted them. At the opening of Heckscher State Park, two shy little girls had been ushered onto the porch of the Taylor Mansion to present Moses with a silver loving cup donated by the East Islip Community Association, a group that had been among the most vocal of W. Kingsland Macy's supporters in Macy's battle against the park. The presentation was symbolic. Long Island's real estate men adored Moses for opening the Island to development and thus further inflating its already ballooning land values. Long Island's people had realized that they had the easiest access to the beaches he had created. A 1930 referendum in Islip Township, stronghold of the baymen and farmers, on a proposition to deed the Long Island Park Commission land on Captree to facilitate the building of the Captree causeway passed by a margin of more than three to one. Long Island politicians, fully aware now of the financial benefits that would accrue to them from Moses' plans, saw the political benefits, too. Immediately following the referendum, both Nassau and Suffolk County Boards of Supervisors spent millions condemning right-of-way for Moses' proposed parkways and presented it to him as a gift.

No Governor would want to be placed in the position of opposing so immensely popular a program—or its creator. Financing Moses' projects placed an immense strain on the state budget. In 1929, with only those announced under Smith under way, their construction, including money spent on them out of the Public Works Department budget, cost the state $5,424,750, more than 70 percent of the entire state expenditure on construction projects in the metropolitan region, including Westchester County. And as the parks were opened, the cost of their maintenance began to be a sore point. Roosevelt was jolted by budget requests for almost a million in "personal service"—salaries—for the Long Island parks alone. Thinking of his national image, not yet aware that liberal public spending might be a way to cushion the effects of the Depression, the Governor was anxious not to give opponents the chance to portray him as a big spender. By the end of 1930, moreover, state revenues had been so slashed by the Depression that the state budget was quiveringly taut. Throughout his second term he was continually pressing his cabinet members to cut costs. There was constant friction over Moses' budget requests.

But in these battles with the Governor, Moses played the popularity that was his trump card for all it was worth. In fact, so sure was he—and he was right—that Roosevelt was afraid he would resign that he began using the technique, when Roosevelt crossed him on major issues, of threatening to do so. Resignation threats begin appearing in Moses' letters to Roosevelt in the middle of 1930; by the end of that year, he had refined the wording. In November 1930, for example, Roosevelt slashed his budget requests for appropriations in the 1931 budget and Moses wrote him: "If proposed cuts . . . stand, I do not want any responsibility for the program."

A similar threat had been strikingly ineffective when made to Ed Richards beside the swimming pool at Yale. But given the fact of his tremendous popularity, it was very effective now. Over the four years of Roosevelt's Governorship a pattern emerged. Moses would submit a budget request far higher than the previous year's; Roosevelt would cut it back almost to the level of the previous request. Moses would tell Roosevelt he would have to resign if he didn't get the funds he wanted. Roosevelt, usually through an intermediary, would back away from the fight, restoring a substantial portion of the cut.

The Legislature was frantic. In 1928, Moses had assured them that the cost of the Ocean Parkway's initial two-mile stretch would be $3,150,000. They had allocated the money, and in 1929 he showed up before them again. The $3,150,000 had been spent, he said, but he had neglected to tell them that the cost of paving the parkway would be extra—$850,000 extra. But they had been trapped. The hydraulic fill for the road had been dredged, the right-of-way graded, the surveying completed, the plans drawn. The $3,150,000 had been spent. Were they now to waste this money by refusing funds to complete the job? Cut as the legislators would, and they always cut, the amount of the annual allocation to the Long Island Park Commission rose steadily, from $3,150,000 in the last year of Smith's regime to $4,000,000 in 1929, $4,700,000 in 1930 and $5,700,000 in 1931. By stake driving and whipsawing, Robert Moses was getting what he wanted from them.

And the projects moved forward. In 1931, the Southern State Parkway was extended from Wantagh to Massapequa, in 1932, from Massapequa to Amityville—the public marveled at the fact that there was a route clear across Nassau County without a single traffic light or intersection. Park facilities were constantly being expanded. A new bathhouse, chlorination plant and playground were built at Valley Stream State Park; ten tennis courts, a miniature golf links and a bridle path at Hempstead Lake; a whole new bathing beach and a spacious stone bathhouse at Heckscher; a causeway to open up new portions of the beach at Sunken Meadow; a loop drive at Montauk Point. And the picnic tables, campfire sites and acres of new parking fields mounted by the hundreds. Some measure of the scope of Moses' achievement is afforded by attendance figures. The number of visits to the Long Island state parks approximated 3,000,000 in 1930; the total number of visits to all national parks in the United States in that year was 3,400,000.

More than not opposing such a program, a Governor would want to be identified with it.

Roosevelt was not present at the first two opening ceremonies Moses staged during his administration, the plaque unveiling at Heckscher State Park and a ribbon cutting on Southern State Parkway. The state representative was Lieutenant Governor Lehman, and at least one source says that the reason was that Moses, to teach Roosevelt a lesson, invited Lehman instead of him. But after a working relationship was evolved between Moses and Roosevelt, all that changed.

When the Jones Beach opening ceremonies were held, Roosevelt was there, having been wheeled up on the boardwalk on a ramp Moses had thought to have constructed. When it came time, during the gubernatorial-election-year summer of 1930, to mortar into place the cornerstone for the West Bathhouse, it was Roosevelt who was invited to wield the trowel—and to tell 75,000 cheering onlookers that the building, which he said would cost $600,000, "would help insure health and happiness" for generations of New Yorkers. Moses also invited the Governor to tour all the Long Island parks. The tour was staged on a Sunday, and the Monday papers were full of pictures of the Governor smiling out over the picnickers at Valley Stream and Hempstead Lake. When he arrived at Heckscher State Park, where bathers had been complaining about overcrowding in the bathhouse, Moses even let him be the one to announce (to cheers and applause) that ground would be broken for a new one by the end of the summer. It was the kind of publicity that money can't buy. Roosevelt was so pleased that, in his speeches, he called Moses "Bob."

In 1931, Moses invited Roosevelt to lay the cornerstone for the monument marking the start of the Northern State Parkway and afterward Moses' limousine led the Governor's to Jones Beach, for lunch in the balcony restaurant in the new bathhouse the construction of which had officially begun the year before. The attendance at Jones Beach that day was 100,000, and as word spread that Roosevelt was present, a great sea of faces pressed close to the restaurant. When the Governor, moved, made his way to a balcony over the bathhouse swimming pool for an impromptu talk, the bathers in the pool shouted happily up at him and cheered. Jones Beach had been an expensive development, the Governor shouted back to them, but "it was the best money the state ever spent." If he recalled in that moment of euphoria that the bathhouse on whose balcony he was standing had cost $1,000,000 instead of the $600,000 he had been told it would a year earlier, he did not mention the discrepancy.

Al Smith was present at every dedication, too—as long as Smith lived,

Moses would never hold a cornerstone laying, a ribbon cutting, or any public ceremony of any type anywhere in the state without inviting the "Governor" and offering him a prominent spot on the program—but Roosevelt couldn't even bridle at this. There was, in regard to the Long Island park system, more than enough credit to go around.

Moses was fond of repeating at this time a quote often used in Albany. "You can get an awful lot of good done in the world if you're willing to let someone else take the credit for it." Certainly Moses was willing at least to share the credit for the work he had done with the man he needed if he was to get more done.

And if accomplishment, and willingness to share the credit for that accomplishment, was part of the explanation for the increase in Moses' power under a Governor who had no inclination to increase it, the accomplishment helped explain this contradiction in other ways, too.

One way is that no Governor could sit in the Executive Chamber long without discovering just how hard—how incredibly hard—it was, even for a Governor, to get things, big things, done. No Governor, having made this discovery, could look at what Robert Moses had gotten done without being impressed, without feeling admiration for his ability, without a recognition of his extraordinary capacity as a public servant. And the proof of this is that through some of the letters and memos written to Moses by Roosevelt during the last two years of his four-year gubernatorial regime, through letters and memos interspersed with others in which irritation and even rage are only thinly glossed over—for Roosevelt's personal animosity toward Moses never lessened—there runs a tone that is unmistakably respect.

Another way is that accomplishment proves the potential for more accomplishment. The man who gets things done once can get things done again. And the potential for accomplishment has very strong political connotations indeed. For political, if not personal, reasons, Roosevelt wanted—*needed*—to get things done. Furthermore, he was trapped, as all politicians in elected executive offices are trapped, by the inexorable equation of democracy and public works. Elections come every two years, or four, and the official who wants re-election needs a record of accomplishment on which to run. Such a record, in the America of the first half of the twentieth century (and perhaps in the America of the second half of the twentieth century, too), from a political standpoint should be most ideally a record of public works and it has to be a record of public works completed—roads opened, bridges built, housing-project apartments occupied, bathhouses crowded with bathers, parks in which the happy shouts of children fill the ear and not just the imagination. It is no good still to be laying cornerstones on Election Day. By then, a public official in executive office must have ribbons he can cut, monuments to which he can point with pride. This is a requirement established by democracy as it has evolved in America, yet the realities of the democratic process in America make it almost impossible to get a road, a bridge, a housing project, a bathhouse or a park approved and built in two years—or four. The Governor who finds a man who can inject into the democracy–public works equation a factor of personality so heavy as to unbalance it and get public works built during the span of a single term of office has little choice, if he is ambitious for political success, but to heap on that man more and more responsibilities, even though the giving of responsibilities carries with it the grant of more power.

In this context, moreover, Moses' arrogance toward opposition was an asset rather than a liability to an elected official. Almost all public works arouse some opposition—roads require land, and some of the citizens from whom the land must be taken do not want it taken—and if the opposition is directed at an elected official, it can be translated into votes against him the next time his name appears on a ballot. But by leaping to deal with opposition himself, and by dealing with it in a way that antagonized the opposition, Moses made himself a lightning rod, drawing the anger at the project onto himself and leaving the elected official unscathed. The official therefore could bask in the credit—at least some of the credit—from the majority of voters, who until the 1960's worshipped public works projects in and for themselves, while escaping the wrath of the minority who opposed it.

In 1930, the president of the Valley Stream Chamber of Commerce asked Roosevelt to inspect the worst grade-crossing problem on Long Island, a spot in the center of the village. Roosevelt agreed, and when his limousine was surrounded by a large crowd of local businessmen and one handed him a petition to Public Service Commission Chairman Milo Maltbie demanding immediate action, Roosevelt, in a grandstand gesture, signed the petition himself.

The gesture showed Roosevelt's gift for public relations, but, having made it, the Governor now had to provide some action—difficult to do because the engineering problems involved were incredibly complex and the railroad had threatened to tie the whole matter up in court for years if the state attempted to force a solution on it.

Having played the ham, Roosevelt needed someone to pull his eggs out of the fire. He selected Moses, who made it very clear that he was doing the job only as a favor. Nonetheless, his first glance at the problem produced a solution. Maltbie turned it down. But when Moses wrote Roosevelt, "Under the circumstances, I must ask to be relieved of any further responsibility," the Governor hastily interceded with Maltbie—and Moses' solution was adopted, immediately eased the traffic situation and brought praise to Roosevelt for "solving" the problem.

No Governor would interfere with an official who could thus spectacularly achieve on his behalf. He wouldn't interfere even when the official actually tried to strangle a colleague.

The incident occurred in Moses' office in the State Parks Council suite. Moses was presiding over a meeting of the council's finance committee when Raymond H. Torrey walked into the room.

Torrey, a pudgy little man, a bird watcher, hiker and lover of the deep woods who spent weekends building lean-tos on Adirondack trails so that other hikers would have shelter, had long been a symbol of frustration to Moses. His very presence in the Parks Council offices was a reminder to Moses that his control of that body, while substantial, was not total. Torrey had long been secretary of the American Scenic and Historic Preservation Society, whose trustees had long been ashamed that they could not afford to pay him an adequate salary, and in the days of the Taylor Estate fight, when Moses had so desperately needed the help of the society's park patriots, he had sought to cultivate them by naming Torrey secretary of the Parks Council at a salary of $6,000 per year. After the fight, when Moses, not needing them any more, was scourging the patriots out of their parks and trying to wrest Letchworth Park from the society's control, he had reduced Torrey's salary as much as civil service laws allowed and made his title a meaningless one by giving his responsibilities to his "assistant," Henry Lutz. But civil service laws prevented Moses from firing Torrey and he was a constant reminder that the society still had some say in Letchworth's administration.

Torrey had proven a thorn in Moses' side in other ways, too. He saw the fight over the Northern State Parkway route through the eyes of the dedicated conservationist; familiar—more familiar perhaps than any other man—with the beauties of the North Shore's glacial moraine, he didn't want a highway, no matter how beautifully landscaped, to run along it. When a newspaper article appeared supporting this view, Torrey reprinted it in the society's monthly newsletter.

On September 12, 1929, Moses learned that Torrey had provided information about Parks Council proceedings on the parkway route to Grenville Clark, the attorney for the North Shore barons, from whom Moses had been attempting to hide his maneuvering. He left word that Torrey should report to his office as soon as he came in. Torrey did so, walking in on the finance committee meeting.

Cursing, his face alternately paling and purpling with rage, Moses began to heap abuse on Torrey. Torrey said that the information he had given Clark was information to which any member of the public was entitled. Moses then launched into a tirade about the reprinting of the newspaper article in the society newsletter. Torrey said that Moses had no right to tell him what he could print.

"God damn you!" Moses shouted. "What do you mean by doing something like that?"

Torrey was mild-mannered, almost invariably soft-spoken. And among his closest friends were Jewish social workers from the Lower East Side settlement houses. "I have endured many verbal assaults from Mr. Moses, and said little, because he is bigger than I am, and because we [the society] have been almost alone in the council in our defense against his aggressions," Torrey was to write. But "his manner and curses irritated me on this occasion beyond further restraint, and I retorted: 'You big noisy kike, you can't talk to me like that.' "

Lunging from his chair, Moses seized Torrey's throat and began choking him. So violent was his rage that when finance committee member Jay Downer tried to pull Moses off, he was at first unable to do so and had to exert all his strength to pry loose first one of Moses' hands and then the other.

As he freed Torrey, Downer grabbed Moses around the waist to hold him and told the smaller man to get away. But as Torrey headed for the door, Moses broke free, picked up a heavy smoking stand and match holder, three-foot steel base and all, and, shouting "You goddamned son of a bitch," hurled it at him. Only the fact that another committee member, DeHart Ames, grabbed Moses' arm as he was letting go the heavy missile made it fall short.

Recounting the incident in a letter to Roosevelt, Torrey said, "I was, of course, at fault for using 'kike,' " but added that Moses' conduct was only one example of his "truculence and violence against anyone who opposes him." Under Moses' control, Torrey wrote, "the Council has lost its original character, as an advisory body of eminent citizens, working amicably together, and has become a vehicle for securing advantages for Moses, for granting favors for his supporters, and for supporting his hostility to any who oppose him." He asked Roosevelt to limit Moses' powers. When the Governor did not reply, Torrey gave his letter to the press. But Moses was not at all abashed. His only regret, he said, was that he had not been permitted to "finish that crackpot." And Roosevelt, pressed for comment by reporters, would say only, "It is a matter for the State Council of Parks and I do not figure in it." The only result of Moses' assault was that Torrey resigned, allowing Moses to appoint Henry Lutz to his place, and the trustees of the American Scenic and Historic Preservation Society, realizing that their conflict with Moses had reached an intolerable pass and that they could not win, in 1930 gave up the society's control of Letchworth Park and its place on the Parks Council, thereby making Moses' control of that body absolute.

Roosevelt wouldn't interfere even when he found out that Moses was discouraging Negroes from using many of his state parks.

Underlying Moses' strikingly strict policing for cleanliness in his parks was, Frances Perkins realized with "shock," deep distaste for the public that was using them. "He doesn't love the people," she was to say. "It used to shock me because he was doing all these things for the welfare of the people. . . . He'd denounce the common people terribly. To him they were lousy, dirty people, throwing bottles all over Jones Beach. 'I'll get them! I'll teach them!' . . . He loves the public, but not as people. The public is just *the* public. It's a great amorphous mass to him; it needs to be bathed, it needs to be aired, it needs recreation, but not for personal reasons—just to make it a better public." Now he began taking measures to limit use of his parks. He had restricted the use of state parks by poor and lower-middle-class families in the first place, by limiting access to the parks by rapid transit; he had vetoed the Long Island Rail Road's proposed construction of a branch spur to Jones Beach for this reason. Now he began to limit access by buses; he instructed Shapiro to build the bridges across his new parkways low—too low for buses to pass. Bus trips therefore had to be made on local roads, making the trips discouragingly long and arduous. For Negroes, whom he considered inherently "dirty," there were further measures. Buses needed permits to enter state parks; buses chartered by Negro groups found it very difficult to obtain permits, particularly to Moses' beloved Jones Beach; most were shunted to parks many miles further out on Long Island. And even in these parks, buses carrying Negro groups were shunted to the furthest reaches of the parking areas. And Negroes were discouraged from using "white" beach areas—the best beaches—by a system Shapiro calls "flagging"; the handful of Negro lifeguards (there were only a handful of Negro employees among the thousands employed by the Long Island State Park Commission) were all stationed at distant, least developed beaches. Moses was convinced that Negroes did not like cold water; the temperature at the pool at Jones Beach was deliberately icy to keep Negroes out. When Negro civic groups from the hot New York City slums began to complain about this treatment, Roosevelt ordered an investigation and an aide confirmed that "Bob Moses is seeking to discourage large Negro parties from picnicking at Jones Beach, attempting to divert them to some other of the state parks." Roosevelt gingerly raised the matter with Moses, who denied the charge violently—and the Governor never raised the matter again.

Roosevelt wouldn't interfere even when Moses (ostensibly to raise money for soaring park maintenance costs) further limited park use by the poor by instituting parking fees at all state parks, fifty cents at Jones Beach, twenty-five at the rest, in violation of the American tradition of free parks.

There was a flood of letters to Roosevelt from Depression-impoverished citizens who said that they had to scrimp to get enough money for the gas to drive to the park, and that the extra quarter would be the straw that would sometimes make it impossible for them to afford the outing. Moses had announced that in some parks "there will be free parking space for those unable to pay . . . somewhat remote from the center." This, protesters said, would only make poor families pay a toll in pride instead of coin. "Who would wish to be classed among those 'unable to pay'?" one asked. "To come walking in from the remote parking fields would be to exhibit the badge of poverty." Roosevelt wrote Moses: "I was a good deal impressed by the complaint . . . I also think fifty cents is too high . . . Frankly, I think the people have a legitimate kick. Won't you seriously take up the question of reducing the Jones Beach charge?"

No, Moses said, he wouldn't. And when Roosevelt pressed again, he brought out his resignation threat. Reducing the charge would force him to reduce Jones Beach maintenance standards, he said. "The entire character of the place would be changed," and if it was, "I do not care to be associated . . ." Roosevelt may have felt that "the people have a legitimate kick," but in the face of such a defense, the Governor punted. Not only did he drop his own request for reconsideration; when the Legislature passed a bill prohibiting fees in state parks, he vetoed it.

Not only does a Governor not interfere with an official like Robert Moses; he heaps on him more and more responsibilities. No matter what the job was, it seemed, if it was difficult Roosevelt turned to the same man. During 1930, 1931 and 1932, Moses handled more than a dozen special assignments for Roosevelt and produced results on every one. And if increasing Moses' responsibilities meant increasing his power—giving him more money to work with, more engineers, architects, draftsmen and police to work with—well, the Governor simply had no choice but to increase that power.

By 1932, with the Governor, running for President, less able than ever to afford a public controversy in his own state with so popular a figure, if one of the two characters in the Moses-Roosevelt drama was dominant, it was not the Governor but his appointee. The hatred between Roosevelt and Moses flared up only occasionally during the four years that the former spent in the Executive Chamber in Albany. But that passion—and the desire for revenge that it engendered—was only banked, not extinguished, and it never stopped smoldering. It was to blaze up into the open later, when Roosevelt was President.

But Roosevelt was not President yet. And he could not yet afford to indulge such a passion. In his dealings with Moses during his gubernatorial years, necessity was the mother of accommodation.

The uniqueness of Moses' relationship to the Governor of whose administration he was at least nominally a member was emphasized when Al Smith finally decided to run against him for the Democratic presidential nomination. Moses calmly informed Roosevelt that he would be taking a few weeks off—to work for Roosevelt's opponent.

The Happy Warrior's last campaign was born, and was to die, in unrelieved bitterness.

Smith had plenty to be bitter about. Roosevelt's systematic—and pointed—disregard of his predecessor had continued. Smith could not reconcile himself to the fact that the younger man, of whom he had been so fond and to whom he had given the gubernatorial nomination, had turned on him. Friends who visited him in New York found that Roosevelt was becoming almost an obsession with him. "Do you know, by God, that he has never consulted me about a damn thing since he has been Governor?" he said to one. "He has taken bad advice from sources not friendly to me. He has ignored me!"

And Roosevelt was not the only younger man who had treated Smith with ingratitude. The treatment he had received from Jimmy Walker had wounded him even more deeply. At the request of Walker's father, an old friend, he had taken Walker under his wing when the young legislator had first come to Albany, rooming with him, steering him up the legislative ladder, helping him time and again out of the scandals in which he was constantly becoming embroiled because of his drinking, his compulsive philandering and his inability to pay attention to the job to which he had been elected. When Smith determined in 1925 to oust Hylan from the mayoralty, Walker had asked Smith to make him Hylan's successor. Smith had told Walker frankly that he felt too worried about his playboy antics to do so. Walker had tricked him into changing his mind. He disappeared completely from the night spots that were his usual haunts and began to be seen in more respectable establishments with his wife. When he told Smith he was on the wagon for good, Smith secured him the nomination. But what Smith didn't know was that Walker had been engaging in all his old activities, but had been doing so in a secluded penthouse rented for him by a friend who had reasons of his own for wanting Beau James to be Mayor. Safely installed in City Hall, Walker had shipped his wife off to Miami for an extended vacation, returned to his public habits—and when Smith had left the Governorship and lost power, Walker had begun ousting Smith's friends from key city posts to make way for his own men, called by one observer "the worst element in Tammany Hall." Then Walker began taking over the Hall. Smith could have stopped him but, determined to stay out of politics, he disdained to do so. When he realized the depth of the corruption pervading city government, he tried to reassert his authority, but by then it was too late. Walker was even able to force out Smith's man, Judge George W. Olvany, as Tammany leader, with Olvany attempting to save face by "resigning" because of "ill health." And then Walker publicly humiliated Smith. At the annual dinner of the Inner Circle, the press-room regulars at City Hall, Walker paused during his speech, turned to Olvany, and with a glance at Smith that no one in the room missed, said, "How's your health, George?" The reporters laughed, and Smith knew they were laughing at him as much as at Olvany. And when Walker hand-picked Olvany's successor, he chose Smith's enemy, John F. Curry. There was no place left for Smith in the party he had loved and led.

All through 1931, Smith refused to run for the presidency. One by one, the state's key Democrats, Farley and Flynn notable among them, came to him and said that Roosevelt was asking them to join his campaign but that their first loyalty was to Smith; all he had to do was ask them to stick with him and they would do so. And all through 1931, Smith told them that he would never be a candidate for the presidency and that they were free to join Roosevelt, which they did.

But in early 1932, Smith's bitterness spilled over. His intimates would long debate whether Smith entered the presidential race because he wanted the nomination himself or because he wanted to deny it to the man who had treated him so cavalierly. Probably both elements were mixed. Certainly, Smith was motivated by personal ambition: in 1932, he was, after all, only fifty-eight years old, still vigorous and bored with the life of a businessman. He was motivated also by the fact that the Depression made election of the Democratic candidate, even a Catholic Democratic candidate, a virtual certainty, and he desperately wanted to prove that being a Catholic and an Irishman did not disqualify a man from the presidency. One visitor, listening to Smith recount how it had been the religious issue that had defeated him in 1928, said, "He felt so terribly hurt, so outraged by that, and the point that he was making was that having been defeated on that issue in a year in which he was bound to be defeated, everybody, including FDR, should have stood aside to let him have the nomination in a year in which he could have been elected! He was very much wrought up about it, he pounded his fists and his voice got loud. He shouted at times in that conversation." But no consideration was stronger than Smith's feelings toward

Roosevelt in pushing him at the last moment into a race foredoomed by the fact that Roosevelt had a four-year head start.

Moses saw at once that the effort was hopeless. "The Smith movement never had a chance," he was to recall. "It started very late, and really had no organization to speak of." He never let himself be deluded by those reminders of past glories which gave Belle Moskowitz, Henry Moskowitz, Judge Proskauer, Herbert Bayard Swope and George McLaughlin flashes of hope: the rallying of Walker and Tammany to Smith's side after Roosevelt had authorized Samuel Seabury to investigate corruption in New York City; the defection to Smith's banner of big-city organizations and the consequent raising of his delegate count to 201; the wild cheers of the tremendous throng that lined his route from the La Salle Street Station in Chicago to the Congress Hotel, where a Smith-for-President headquarters had been hastily established. But practical realities did not weigh with Moses where Al Smith was concerned. Moses was one of those who struggled to the end in convention maneuvering so bitter that Ed Flynn called it "a fight to the death," who fought to hold together an alliance of dark horses that denied Roosevelt the nomination until the fourth ballot, who thought for a few brief hours that they actually had Roosevelt stopped and would be able to force the party to turn to Smith, and whose hopes were finally dashed when the ex-Governor's old adversary, William Randolph Hearst, used his influence with California's William G. McAdoo and John Nance Garner, Governor of Texas, to force the California and Texas delegations to switch to Roosevelt. Moses was one of the small group of friends who sat down with Smith in front of a radio in the Congress Hotel to listen to the last ballot, who watched the former Governor haul himself wearily out of his chair as soon as McAdoo began the speech that signaled the California switch and with a wave of his hand direct them to start packing so they could leave Chicago. He was one of those who sneaked out of the Congress Hotel by a side door with Smith at the moment that crowds were jamming the front entrance to greet the arriving Roosevelt, who listened to the ex-Governor, cornered by reporters, refuse to say he would support his party's choice and who watched anxiously as Smith sat silent on the long train ride home with his face marked by what one observer called a "tired sadness." And if Moses accepted Smith's defeat with his mind, he never accepted it with his heart. A month after the convention, with "Happy Days Are Here Again" drowning out the strains of "The Sidewalks of New York" forever in the Democratic Party's consciousness, Smith's campaign staff held its first and only reunion, complete with a menu featuring "Nuts McAdoo," "Celery Farley" and "Branchless Olives Roosevelt" in the Empire State Club in the Empire State Building. And Moses' contribution to the occasion reflected his bitterness. It was a quotation from Shakespeare that he selected for an epigraph on the menu's cover:

Politics is a thieves' game.
Those who stay in it long enough are invariably robbed.

18. New York City Before Robert Moses

NOW ROBERT MOSES' EYES were turning again to the city around which, as a youth, he had wandered "burning up" with ideas for its improvement.

Nowhere had America's Great Depression struck harder than in America's greatest city.

New York in 1932 was half-completed skyscrapers, work on them long since halted for the lack of funds, that glared down on the city from glassless windows. It was housewives scavenging for vegetables under pushcarts. It was crowds gathering at garbage dumps in Riverside Park and swarming onto them every time a new load was deposited, digging through the piles with sticks or hands in hopes of finding bits of food. New York was the soup kitchens operated from the back of army trucks in Times Square. It was the men, some of them wearing Chesterfield coats and homburgs, who lined up at the soup kitchens with drooping shoulders and eyes that never looked up from the sidewalk. New York was the breadline, "the worm that walks like a man."

New York was the postman handing you the registered letter that you both knew was the eviction notice. It was the long queues that formed in the early afternoon at the Municipal Lodging Houses, and it was the desperate haste of the men turned away to get to one of the nearby bars which allowed customers who purchased even a single drink to sleep on the floor as long as there was space. Subways were truly for sleeping, and when patrolmen walked along station platforms rapping on soles, the men lying there arose without a protest, carefully gathering up their pallets of newspapers, shuffled onto a train and rode to the next station, where they spread their papers and lay down again.

More than 10,000 of New York's 29,000 manufacturing firms had closed their doors. Nearly one of every three employables in the city had lost his job. An estimated 1,600,000 New Yorkers were receiving some form of public relief. Many of those fortunates who had kept their jobs were "underemployed," a euphemism for the fact that they worked two or three days a week or two weeks a month—or, if they worked full time, were paid a fraction of their former salaries; stenographers, earning $35 to $40 per week in 1928, were averaging $16 in 1933; Woolworth's was paying full-time salesladies $7 per week.

Parents skimped for their children—by December 1932 many parents could hardly remember a time when they *hadn't* been skimping—but skimping was only forestalling the inevitable. There was meat on the table twice a week and then once—and then not at all. Then there were no eggs. Parents could make their children feel it was an honor that they didn't have to drink milk any more and could drink coffee instead, but the lack of proper diet took a toll. "Looking back, we can see quite a change," said one schoolteacher. "The children haven't any pep; they don't seem like the same youngsters they were a year ago." They seemed tired; they didn't seem to learn as fast. Said a school nurse: "When you go into a classroom you notice a different expression on [their] faces. . . . There is a strained, anxious look not natural in children at all."

Sometimes the things that outsiders didn't see were worst of all. Teachers didn't see the children whose families were poorest; such children had dropped out of school because they had no money for carfare, lunches or suitable clothes. Staffers at the city's free health clinics were encouraged by the fact that the number of malnutrition cases they handled was rising only gradually (although by 1934 such cases nevertheless would account for 60 percent of all clinic work). Then the staffers realized that many people suffering from malnutrition simply weren't going to the clinics because they knew perfectly well what was wrong with them—and also knew that they would be unable to do anything about it. And no one could see a state of mind; all one could do was try to describe it, as Martha Gellhorn did: "Everywhere there seemed a spreading listlessness, a whipped feeling. . . . I find them all in the same shape—fear, fear . . . an overpowering terror of the future."

The city's government did little to help its people.

The will to help was not the force that drove that government. That force was greed. During the fifteen years in which Red Mike Hylan and then Beau James Walker had been Chief Magistrate of America's greatest city, the Tammany leaders who served under them had seemed motivated primarily by the desire to siphon the city's vast resources into a vast trough on which they could batten.

Former Judge Samuel Seabury's invesigation of corruption in the city, which had begun in 1930, had revealed how successfully this siphoning had been accomplished, exposing the bank accounts, running into the hundreds of thousands of dollars, of literally dozens of city officials, who followed one another to the witness stand in a seemingly endless procession that was dubbed "The Tin Box Parade" after one testified that he had found $360,000 in his home in "a tin box . . . a wonderful tin box." Then Seabury turned to the Magistrates Courts. Witnesses revealed that hundreds of innocent housewives and working girls had been framed as prostitutes and, if they could not raise the cash to buy their freedom, had been jailed, sometimes for months, by a cabal of crooked vice-squad policemen, court clerks and magistrates. Shocked by the strangling in Van Cortlandt Park of one scheduled female witness—her teen-age daughter committed suicide a week later—the city listened in horror to the others Seabury paraded to the stand. One told of helping vice-squad patrolmen trail a young married woman as she inspected houses with a male real estate agent. When they had returned to her home and were waiting for her husband to arrive and conclude the transaction, the police broke in, frightened the real estate agent out of testifying and arrested her. Other witnesses testified that, when business was slow, the vice squad simply "raided" flats in Negro Harlem and made wholesale arrests at random. When Mayor Walker took the stand—"Don't look him straight in the eye," warned a Seabury aide familiar with Beau James's charm, and the former judge stood sideways to Walker as much as possible while questioning him—Seabury revealed that the Mayor had personally accepted more than a million dollars in "beneficences" from firms doing business with the city. On September 1, 1932, while Governor Roosevelt was pondering whether or not to remove Walker from office, the Mayor resigned and sailed for Europe to join Betty ("Monk") Compton, last and loveliest of his paramours, thereby following a traveling precedent established by Robert C. Van Wyck, the first mayor (1898–1901) of the consolidated city, who had died in Paris, and the man who had hand-picked Van Wyck for the job, Tammany boss Richard Croker, who had died in England. Surrogate John Patrick O'Brien won the special election to fill the remaining year of Walker's term, but he proved to be as much a creature of Tammany as his predecessors. While Tammany leaders were trying to persuade the electorate that they had no control over him, O'Brien was replying to reporters who asked him who his Police Commissioner would be, "I don't know. They haven't told me yet." And during O'Brien's administration local Tammany relief administrators would siphon off a big chunk of federal relief payments before they reached their intended recipients—and the city would continue to do nothing to supplement federal programs, although a supplement would have been helpful, since federal payments averaged seventeen dollars per week per family. Tammany would try to use federal payments to build its political power, putting ward heelers on relief payrolls under several different names so that they could draw several salaries for themselves. And the federal payrolls did not show whether the men receiving its money were the men who most needed it. In New York City under Tammany Hall, the test for employment on a federal project was generally politics rather than need; most applicants had to be cleared by their local Tammany leader; one leader boasted, "This is how we make Democrats."

Even had the city wanted to help its people, it would have been unable to. The Depression had forced New York to total up at last the cost of its Rake's Progress under the Hylan and Walker administrations.

When Hylan became mayor of New York on January 1, 1918, the city's population was 5,872,143. Fifteen years later, when Walker resigned, it was 6,930,446—an increase of 15 percent. During that same period, the city's budget rose from $240,519,858 to $631,366,298—an increase of 250 percent. The per capita cost of the budget increased by 200 percent. Year in and year out between January 1, 1918, and December 31, 1932, the city's debt increased at a rate equal to $100,000 per day, until, on the latter date, it had reached the staggering total of $1,897,481,478—a figure that was almost equal to the combined debt of the forty-eight states and that required an annual appropriation for debt service (the payment of interest and amortization) of $209,960,338, almost a third of the entire budget.

Since jobs were the fuel of Tammany's political machine, a disproportionate share of the rest of the budget went to purchase that fuel; between the day Hylan entered office and the day Walker left it, the number of city employees almost doubled, and their salaries, paid as political rewards at levels far above those paid for similar work in private industry, almost tripled. In 1932, they totaled $311,937,199.

City officials acted as if they believed that the budgetary gyre could go on widening indefinitely. They based their optimism on the fact that the value of taxable real estate in the city, the base of the city's tax structure, was increasing almost as fast as city expenditures. As a result, even while the city's budget soared, there was only a slight increase in the real estate tax rate. If the Hylan and Walker administrations had erected a huge superstructure of city expenditures, that superstructure was nonetheless resting on a base that they thought was steadily broadening.

Even before the Depression, however, the rate of increase in the base had begun to slow down ominously. The annual percentage of increase in the value of taxable real estate in the city was 12 in 1927 but only 9 in 1928 and 8 in 1929. The Depression forced this key percentage down to 6 in 1930, 3 in 1931, 1 in 1932. And the Depression forced *up* another key percentage, the percentage of real estate taxes which the city was unable to collect; in the years between 1928 and 1932 this percentage was, successively, 11, 13, 15, 18, 26. The uncollected balance of the 1932 real estate tax, the tax which had to finance the bulk of the city's debt service and current expenditures, was $137,613,213. The base on which the top-heavy superstructure of city finances teetered was shrinking, and it was shrinking fast. The superstructure began to topple.

In desperation the city deferred its required annual payments to the Teachers Retirement Fund and expropriated Sinking Fund surpluses already obligated for small-scale public improvements. Unable despite these expedients to meet even its ordinary day-to-day expenses, it was forced to borrow to pay them—at interest rates set higher and higher by bankers increasingly leery of the city's ability to repay. By 1931, even Jimmy Walker was talking about "economizing."

But the city's economizing capacity was limited because one-third of its budget was allocated for an all but irreducible debt service and because of political realities: the city payroll had become the payroll of the Tammany political machine, and while a city might reduce the number of its employees or their salaries, it was less easy for a political machine to throw its retainers off the payroll or substantially reduce their stipends. City construction contracts had become the main ingredient of the rich swill of graft to which the palate of Tammany leaders—including those party leaders who held high city office—had become accustomed; city officials could reduce a city's appropriations for construction, but men accustomed to feeding at a well-filled trough were far less ready to reduce their own portions. Even while talking economy, city officials made clear that they would not economize on construction appropriations or salaries. (There was one exception: one group of city employees—schoolteachers—were not part of the Tammany machine. In 1930 and 1931, the city fired 11,000 schoolteachers.) The 1932 city budget was the highest ever. The city proposed to finance it with a record increase in the real estate tax rate.

But the day of reckoning for fifteen years of Tammany rule was at hand. When, in January 1932, the city attempted to float new loans to meet the payroll coming due at the end of the month, bankers, convinced that the loans could not be repaid if the city spent money during the coming year at the rate it proposed, refused to make them unless the budget was reduced. The city complied by virtually halting all repairs to its physical plant. It refinanced a quarter-billion dollars of subway bonds, which the city had planned to redeem out of current revenues, by selling long-term bonds in their stead—an expedient which loaded future generations of city taxpayers with a monstrous rapid-transit debt.

Still the city's balance sheet reddened. By December 1932, it was forced to go hat in hand to the bankers again, and when new loans were made contingent on further budget reductions, it had no choice but to cut the salaries of city employees by 6 to 33 percent. And hundreds of millions of dollars in short-term revenue notes would be coming due in 1933 and there was no money in sight to pay them.

Although Walker and O'Brien attempted to do so, it was a misleading oversimplification to blame the Depression for all of New York's problems. The truth was that the city had been falling further and further behind in the race to meet the needs of its people in good times as well as bad, and under reform as well as Tammany administrations.

The city's failure was most apparent, and the problems largest, in those categories of municipal responsibility in which the betterment of its people's lives required the construction of public works on a scale commensurate with the city's size. The concern of the people's tribunes during the Low and Mitchel reform administrations had been for the people's welfare, but that welfare had been conceived of primarily as a lessening of the burden on taxpayers through governmental economy rather than through the construction of civic improvements whose cost would increase that burden. And while Tammany administrations had spent the taxpayers' money with a lavish hand, the taxpayers had received in return surprisingly little increment in life-improving steel and concrete, because the disproportionate amount of the city's budget funneled by Tammany into salaries—into patronage—left little money available for construction contract appropriations.

The quality of men added to the city payroll, moreover, did not match the quantity, thanks to Hylan's destruction of civil service safeguards. If there was a man less devoted to the merit system than Red Mike, it was his successor; when Beau James departed for Europe, he left behind him, on the rosters of the engineering staffs of the borough presidents, the staffs which alone under the existing City Charter were empowered to draw the plans for major public improvements, a group of "engineers" of whom a substantial percentage lacked a high school diploma. And the city's resultant lack of technical expertise crippled its ability to carry out, or even conceive, complicated public works.

So did the amount of graft, the grease which kept the Tammany machine moving smoothly. From condemnation awards—"Every time the city built a school, a politician went into the real estate business," La Guardia growled—to certificates of completion, every step toward a public improvement required a payoff. Since contractors had to include the cost of such payoffs in their estimates of the cost of city construction work, their bids had to be inflated accordingly. The amount of steel and concrete that a city dollar purchased was correspondingly reduced, and the size of contracts the city awarded was not matched by improvements to the civic estate. "The city did not get what it paid for," commented Fusion financial expert Joseph D. McGoldrick. "Although it certainly paid for what it got"—several times over. For its single major public improvement, the construction of the Independent Subway System, the Walker administration paid $800,000,000—approximately twice what outside experts said the job should have cost. And when the $800,000,000 had been spent, substantial portions of the subway were still uncompleted.

And since the hands which city inspectors held out, palms up, to contractors could not easily be doubled into hard fists of regulation, the quality of public works in New York City was more than slightly suspect. No fewer than forty public schools constructed during Walker's administration had to be closed for major repairs—for ceilings that fell, roofs that leaked, stairways that collapsed and plumbing that didn't work at all—within a year of opening.

The gap between the city's physical plant and the increasing needs of its expanding population had, then, been widening in virtually all areas of municipal responsibility. The total accomplishment of the Walker administration in public housing, for example, consisted of the rehabilitation of *some* of the tenements on *one* block, and the number of public hospital beds when Beau James left office was precisely the same as when he entered it. But because of the sudden burgeoning in the use of the automobile and in the desire for active recreation, the city's failure to produce for its people was especially galling in precisely those areas in which Robert Moses had already produced, just outside New York City, so much: highways, bridges and parks.

New York was strangling on its traffic. In 1918, when Hylan took office, there were 125,101 motor vehicles in the city; in 1932, there were 790,173. In all those fifteen years not a single usable mile of arterial highway had been constructed within the city's borders. Motorists were forced to travel through or around New York in 1932 on the same local streets that had existed in 1918, streets complete with intersecting traffic, traffic lights—and traffic jams reporters had long since run out of adjectives attempting to describe.

In 1913, Robert Moses had stood on a high bluff overlooking the muddy wasteland that was Riverside Park and had envisioned a great parkway running through it. In 1932, there was still no highway. The city had begun construction in 1927 of a West Side Elevated Highway running along the waterfront from the Battery as far uptown as Seventy-second Street, the park's southern border. But the pace of construction had been so slow that, when the Depression brought it to a halt in 1931, substantial portions of the highway had not been built—not that that mattered much, since neither had the entrance and exit ramps that would make it usable. And since there were no plans to extend the highway through Riverside Park, motorists heading for Westchester and New England still had to make their way through—and add to—the congenital traffic jams of Manhattan and the Bronx before they could reach the broad Saw Mill River Parkway, which Moses had built down to the city line.

Queens had once been the only borough with adequate through roads. Manhattan families heading for Nassau and Suffolk counties, once past the East River bridges, had not encountered serious delays until they reached the city line and the narrow roads beyond. But with the construction beyond the line of Moses' parks and parkways, the situation was now reversed; the lure of his creations had steadily increased the traffic flow through Queens, and its boulevards were inadequate to handle it. Furthermore, none of the boulevards linked up with a parkway, so drivers wanting to use one had to endure local streets before they got to it.

As for Brooklyn, borough of churches, its inhabitants had been praying for a way out of it for decades. There was, in the entire borough, not a single major through thoroughfare. There was no way out of its vast center, no way to reach Manhattan or Queens or Nassau County, except via local streets. And the streets of Brooklyn, like those of Queens, were becoming more clogged every year; the population of the two boroughs increased by more than a million between 1920 and 1930.

As for connections for automobiles under or over the water which separated the city's boroughs, there hadn't been one built in a quarter of a century.* Manhattan motorists bound for the Bronx, Westchester or New England, after crawling uptown through Manhattan's congestion, found when they reached Manhattan's northern boundary, the Harlem River, that the only way to cross it to get to the congested streets of the Bronx was the

* Two connections had been built, by the Port of New York Authority, between the city and New Jersey: the Holland Tunnel, which opened in 1927, and the George Washington Bridge, which opened in 1931.

Broadway drawbridge, only three lanes wide and so crammed with pillars that traffic tie-ups at either end often extended for blocks. On an average day in 1932, the bridge was raised fourteen times to permit the passage of ships. When one of these raisings occurred at rush hour, the tie-up could extend for miles.*

The population of Long Island, concentrated in Brooklyn and Queens, was more than four million in 1932—greater than all except eight states. But except for a few small and ancient ferries that plied the East River, the only way on or off Long Island for motorists was the same quartet of "East River bridges" that had existed in 1909. Long Island still didn't possess a single vehicular link with the mainland United States. The Island didn't possess a single vehicular link with Manhattan Island north of Fifty-ninth Street, where the Queensborough Bridge touched down. The Queensborough, in fact, was the only link with Manhattan north of Corlears Hook, where the Brooklyn, Manhattan and Williamsburg spans debouched traffic onto the already jammed thoroughfares of the Lower East Side.

On an average weekday in 1933, 238,277 trucks and cars, three times what they were built to handle, poured onto the East River bridges. The Queensborough carried more cars than any other span in the country.

The inadequacy of the approaches to these bridges was matched by the inadequacy of their roadways. Built for horses, not automobiles, they were too narrow for cars and so slippery that, according to a police report, on the Brooklyn Bridge alone, "a dozen accidents were not uncommon on a rainy day."

City officials had been talking for years about repaving the bridges, but no repaving had been done. They had been talking for years about widening their roadways, but no widening had been done. Although in 1932 the Queensborough Bridge had been open for a quarter of a century, the city had not yet gotten around even to marking lanes on it. At either end of the bridge were traffic lights; when they were red, bridge traffic stopped completely. A 1931 police study found that during rush hours the average driver, frantically shifting gears while trying to keep his car in an unmarked lane, spent forty-three minutes negotiating the 1,182 feet of the Queensborough span. The city had created two additional lanes on the Queensborough upper roadway in 1931, but when the lanes were opened, it was discovered that there had been a slight miscalculation: the lanes were too narrow; cars were constantly skinning their tires on the granite curbs. The lanes had to be closed while workmen laboriously chipped away the edges of the curbstones—and the workmen would be chipping, and the lanes would be closed, for three years.

The lack of new interborough bridges and tunnels wasn't due to a lack of ideas; New York was littered with evidence to prove that there had

* Northbound motorists could, of course, cross the Harlem River on one of seven bridges that had been built years before—the newest was finished in 1910—miles to the south. But these bridges debouched into the most congested section of the Bronx, miles from the parkways and other broad roads of Westchester.

been plenty of those. But the evidence also proved how difficult it was, in New York, for ideas to become reality.

In a weed-filled vacant lot in Riverdale just north of the Harlem River stood a marble column a hundred feet high with a strangely unfinished look about its top. There was supposed to be a statue up there, a statue of Hendrick Hudson, for the vacant lot had been purchased by the city as the northern bridgehead of a "Hendrick Hudson Bridge" that was supposed to ease the congestion on the Broadway drawbridge, and a statue of the Great Navigator was supposed to look down on the span that bore his name. But although the lot had been purchased, and the column erected, in 1909, in 1932 work had still not started on the statue—or the bridge.

On the shoreline in Brooklyn's Bay Ridge section, at the edge of the Narrows, stood two rude wooden palisades, rotting from a decade's exposure to sea spray. The palisades had been erected to keep children from falling into two huge holes, each ninety-six feet deep. Directly across the Narrows, dug into the Staten Island shoreline, were two similar holes. The four holes had been the start of the shaft heads for a great "Narrows Tube" designed to link Brooklyn with Staten Island. Work on the tube had begun in 1921. The city had spent more than $7,000,000 on it. But digging had been stopped in 1923 and never resumed, and in 1932 the project was dead—the four empty holes the only evidence of the money spent on it.

And marching across low-lying Ward's Island in the East River were seventeen massive masonry piers, each of them forty feet thick, eighty feet long, more than a hundred feet high. These piers had been erected to support the central span of the "triborough bridge," first proposed in 1910, that would link together at last Manhattan, the Bronx and Queens. But in 1932 the piers had been standing for more than two years, and there was still no bridge for them to support—and hope that there ever would be was rapidly fading.

As for New York's parks, they were scabs on the face of the city.

Parks were the city's legacy from reformers who had fought against long odds for their creation; under Tammany they had become fiefs administered for private gain. The Brooklyn Park Department paid for hundreds of thousands of cubic yards of landfill that it never received. It constructed a large restaurant and for a yearly rental of ten dollars turned over its keys to a restaurateur who was allowed to keep all profits. When a Brooklyn brick manufacturer needed ten acres for a new storage area, the department allowed him to rent ten acres of Dyker Beach Park—for a rental of $2.50 per year. And during his term as Brooklyn Park Commissioner, James J. Browne banked $1,071,713.

Some of the city's choicest public beach front—in Wolfe's Pond Park on Staten Island and at Orchard Beach in the Bronx, for example—was rented to political insiders, who, for a fee of fifteen dollars, were allowed to erect private bungalows on it, and to form "civic associations" that promulgated regulations closing the beaches to the public.

Because parks were a handy place to conceal drunks and loafers, Tammany staffed the park departments with the dregs of its barrel of ward heelers. Because skilled laborers' higher salaries would reduce the amount of patronage that could be distributed, Tammany balked at hiring skilled workers even for those jobs that required skills. So that most of the park department budgets could be devoted to salaries, Tammany scrimped on materials and equipment, spending exactly $225,000 of the total park budget of $8,576,319 on such luxuries in 1932—and in that year 90 percent of park department vehicles were still horse-drawn.

By 1932, the paths, walks and roadways in New York's parks were miles of broken pavement. The lawns, seldom mowed, sometimes looked more like meadows. So many trees were dying that some of the loveliest tree-bordered walks were bordered mostly by stumps—the result of allowing unskilled and unsupervised workers to prune trees by simply climbing up to the top of their ladders and sawing trees off at that height, since they were reluctant to risk their own limbs by climbing out on trees'. According to a Park Association survey, there was not a single structure of any type in any park in the city that was not in need of immediate repair.

What the city called a playground was an open space—equipped with slides and a swing or two, sometimes equipped with nothing at all—around which chicken wire had been strung. Most "playgrounds" were not surfaced; rain turned them into mud holes. Others were surfaced with cinders spread loosely over the dirt, and mothers hated to let their children play in them because they knew the children would come home covered with cuts.

If one of the hundreds of statues in the parks was undamaged in 1932, the Park Association couldn't find it. The faces of the statues were masses of bird droppings. Obscenities had been written on—and never erased from—their chests. Their identifying plaques had been torn off. Swords were missing from sheaths, laurel wreaths from brows. Poets plucked at broken harps, saints stood on cracked pedestals. An Indian hunter had lost his bow. The tiger in Central Park was slipping off his rock. The bayonets had been stolen off the rifles of the soldiers in the Seventh Regiment Memorial on Fifth Avenue.

The ironwork that could be seen in the parks—the fences, benches and playground equipment—was pitted and caked with rust. The condition of the ironwork that couldn't be seen was indicated by the rarity of the comfort stations whose plumbing worked.

Since park concessions were handed out to anyone who could raise the necessary payoff, pushcarts and ramshackle booths crowded park paths—there were nineteen along one short path in Battery Park, each with its own carnival-type barker—and since many sold substandard food, there were recurring reports of sickness among children who ate the hot dogs they sold.

Bryant Park, six priceless acres of green amid the concrete masses of midtown, had been allowed to become a haven for drunks and idlers. In 1932, the city obligingly trucked away two of the park's principal ornaments, eight-foot-high statues of Washington Irving and James Marion Sims, founder of the first women's hospital in New York, and allowed a "George Washington Bi-Centennial Celebration Commission" (debonair Grover Whalen, one of Walker's police commissioners, was chairman) to erect a flimsy reproduction of Federal Hall, the building in which Washington was inaugurated, in the park and then fence it off and place turnstiles at its corners so that the public would be forced to pay admission to see the hall. When the public declined in great numbers to do so, the commission went out of existence without funds to demolish its creation. After picking up the demolition tab, the city discovered that it had managed to lose the Irving and Sims statues. Possibly because the omission of five tons of granite and metal would not be easily concealed in a reconstructed park, Bryant Park was not reconstructed—and in January 1934 it was a weed-filled vacant lot.*

Central Park, most famous and beautiful of the city's open spaces, "the most noble, the most praiseworthy, the most philanthropic of all our public works," according to an 1876 New York *Herald* editorial, had been the creation of Calvert Vaux and the genius of urban landscape, Frederick Law Olmsted, who, in 1857—with Olmsted still an unknown young park department employee—had won a nationwide contest with their design for the park. Olmsted had driven thousands of men to plant half a million trees and shrubs on its 840 rocky, barren and arid acres and to create bowers, mazes, lawns and vistas, revolutionary sunken transverse roads (that were criticized because people said there would never be sufficient traffic across the park to justify them), bridle paths (that were criticized because few New Yorkers

---

* The Bi-Centennial Commission was one of the more hilarious episodes in the city's history. Its "board of directors" contained a number of well-meaning DAR types who had lent their names to what they thought was an attempt to honor the Father of the Country, but the presence of Whalen, an intimate of some of Tammany's most greedy insiders, was the tip-off to the fact that the celebration was intended as a public-scalping party—a suspicion confirmed when food-selling concessions at the "celebration" were handed out to Tammany favorites. First, the commission announced that it would finance the construction of "Federal Hall" by "allowing" citizens to sign a "patriotic roll call"—for a fee of one dollar per signature—designed to raise $150,000. Despite parades beginning, or ending, at Washington Arch, and led by Jimmy Walker himself, that were designed to whip up public enthusiasm, the roll call was answered by only 18,629 patriots. Sears, Roebuck & Co. then announced that it would lend the commission the money against turnstile receipts—but the finished structure into which that firm's money was sunk turned out to be a plaster and papier-mâché structure that swayed alarmingly and looked barely strong enough to withstand a good wind.

On some days total attendance in the park was so low that only twenty persons paid their twenty-five cents to see it. Whalen then conceived the idea of combining the exhibit with "patriotic movies"—which turned out to be Mickey Mouse cartoons. When interest remained low, Italian opera was tried. The commission couldn't even raise enough money to demolish Federal Hall and restore Bryant Park to its original condition, as it had promised to do in its contract with the city. It announced that "a large part of the population feels that this patriotic shrine should be retained" and went out of existence, leaving $76,254 in largely unexplained "expenses," and Sears, Roebuck holding the bag for its contribution. The "Hall" stood, crumbling around the edges, in the huge vacant lot that Bryant Park had become until the city, embarrassed by the screams of rage from the Park Association, tore down the structure at its own—or rather at its taxpayers'—expense.

The Bi-Centennial Celebration did, of course, provide Whalen with valuable experience in running a public exposition. He put it to use in running the 1939 New York World's Fair—which lost $200,000,000.

owned saddle horses), delicate and colorful gardens (that were criticized because people said there would always be enough room in New York for private gardens). Then, his vision completed as he wanted it, Olmsted had fought Tammany for a decade to preserve it, his health and spirit breaking in the fight. Finally ousted as Park Commissioner after a series of worsening nervous breakdowns, he had had to watch hordes of Tammany laborers tear the ivy from the Arsenal walls, "clean up" his beloved "wildernesses," sweep moss and ferns out of all the rocky crevices with house brooms and hack down thousands of trees and shrubs along Fifth Avenue so that park strollers could better view the mansions being built there. And, in 1932, Central Park showed the ravages of the sixty years of neglect that had followed Olmsted's ouster.

The park's lawns, unseeded, were expanses of bare earth, decorated with scraggly patches of grass and weeds, that became dust holes in dry weather and mud holes in wet. Its walks were broken and potholed. Its bridle paths were covered with dung. The once beautiful Mall looked like the scene of a wild party the morning after. Benches lay on their backs, their legs jabbing at the sky. Trash baskets had been overturned and never righted; their contents lay where they had spilled out. The concrete had been stripped off drinking fountains so completely that only their rusting iron pipes remained. And nine out of every ten trees on the Mall were dead or dying.

The red brick of the Arsenal at Fifth Avenue and Sixty-fourth Street had been stuccoed over and painted, and when the stucco had flaked away, the bare spots had been repainted in what was supposed to be the same color but wasn't. The building's turrets, which had made it so quaintly medieval, had been covered with striped wooden cupolas, which were supposed to make it gay, but the wood had broken and caved in and had never been repaired. The ground floor was used as a park department garage; the three upper floors were used mostly as a warehouse to store department records.

Around the Arsenal squatted the twenty-two ancient wooden animal houses of the Central Park Menagerie, crumbling away beneath their yellow paint. So rotted were their walls that park department officials feared that a single charge from a large animal, perhaps maddened by fire, might tear the cage bars right out of them. Instead of rebuilding the animal houses, the department had stationed keepers in front of the lion and tiger cages with rifles and had instructed them to shoot the big carnivores if fire broke out.

The Menagerie was filled with surprises. Because it gratefully accepted any gift that would fill a cage, and people therefore donated their unwanted family pets, it was housing in 1932, alongside the hyacinth cockatoos and the vulturine guinea fowl, several dozen canaries, and, in a cage between the mountain lions and the leopards, an Airedale. Because the Menagerie did not adequately care for its animals or dispose of them when they grew old, its exhibits included such old pensioners as a senile tiger, a puma with rickets and a semi-paralyzed baboon. Its most fearsome exhibits were rats, which roamed it in herds and had become so bold that they were stealing food from the lions' feeding pans. The most vivid memory carried away by many visitors was of the sickening stench that rose from the dung-heaped Barbary-sheep pen.

Almost directly across the park, off Central Park West, was Jacob Wrey Mould's sheepfold, considered by some critics the finest existing example of the full-blown architecture of the mid-nineteenth century, and from a distance the sheep who grazed opposite it on the Green or Sheep Meadow, under the care of a resident shepherd who twice a day held up traffic on the park's West Drive to herd his flock across, made a picture as pretty as Olmsted had envisioned. But a closer look disclosed that, because for generations the sheep had been allowed to inbreed, every one of them was malformed.

Unlovely as the scenery in the parks might be, there was little to do in the parks except contemplate it. Provision for active sports was so inadequate that although Tammany reserved permits for the city's 162 baseball diamonds for teams which had the blessing of its aldermen—Negro teams from politically powerless Harlem seldom got one—there were still 942 teams *with permits* waiting to use the diamonds on a typical Sunday. Waiting time at tennis courts was measured in hours, and the city's one modern golf course was so crowded on weekends that, the *Herald Tribune* reported, "a player standing on line at dawn is lucky if he gets through his rounds by sunset."

New York was a city of islands, a city surrounded by, permeated by, water. But with Orchard Beach and Wolfe's Pond Park handed over to Tammany insiders, the only acquaintance that most of the city's lower-income families, who did not own cars and thus were virtually barred from Jones Beach, made with the ocean surf was at Coney Island, where a million people, treading gingerly among broken glass and filth that seemed never to be cleaned up, jammed the beach so full on a Sunday that one could hardly see the sand. The beach at Jacob Riis Park in the Rockaways was used only sparsely, but there was a reason: there was no way for a family without a car to reach it, and families with cars could reach it only after a tortuous trip. Swimming in one's own neighborhood, moreover, was all but unheard of; in the entire city, there were in 1932 two tiny outdoor swimming pools. Children who wanted to wade and splash in an outdoor shower could wade in the gutters after they unscrewed fire-hydrant covers; no one had ever heard of wading pools in playgrounds.

The men who worked in the parks complemented the scenery. Even in an era in which every city department was staffed through patronage, the five borough park departments were something special. Recalls one observer: "You couldn't tell the difference between a park employee and the bums hanging out in the parks." The weight of the rheumy-eyed drunks who served as lifeguards at Jacob Riis Park, Rockaway Beach and Coney Island was as excessive for their job as were their ages. "The first time I saw those guys lined up in their swimming costumes, I could hardly believe it," recalls Samuel M. White, who was later put in charge of them. "Some of them ran 225 or 250 pounds. And there were guys there sixty years old." Even on summer Sundays, they used the lifesaving dories for fishing. Not all the lifeguards would go out in the dories, of course. Some of them were afraid to; they didn't know how to swim. Parents who took their children to city beaches on Sundays learned not to allow them near the shacks on the beach labeled "First Aid Station." The shacks were invariably filled with prostitutes sleeping off the effects of their Saturday-night parties with the lifeguards. ("Those whores were as unbelievable as the guys," White recalls. "They were some of the ugliest women I have even seen.") The aged biddies in charge of park comfort stations were widows of Tammany ward heelers and they understood that no work was required of them. According to one reporter: "Some had curtained off all but, say, two of the eight toilet compartments, had imported chairs, tables and hangings into the cozy space, and frequently had in their friends to afternoon tea." The lady in charge of the comfort station perched on a rocky bluff overlooking the Metropolitan Museum of Art spent her time there removing much of the plumbing and then building herself a cozy little sitting room, in which she had installed a grand piano. The chords of a Chopin nocturne startled more than one woman who entered the comfort station in good faith.

The Depression added its own touches to the parks: the shack towns named, bitterly, "Hoovervilles," in which homeless men sought refuge. One of the largest was a collection of more than two hundred hovels of old boards, flattened gasoline tins and pieces of sheet iron and cardboard in the dried-out bed of the abandoned Central Park Receiving Reservoir behind the Metropolitan Museum of Art; at night its inhabitants ate birds they caught in the park's bird sanctuary.

It wasn't what the Depression did to existing parks that most worried New York's reformers, however; they were more concerned about its effect on the city's plans to acquire new ones.

Nothing was more disturbing to reformers than the city's lack of park land. In 1932, only 14,827 acres, or 7.28 percent of its area, had been set aside for the recreation of its citizens, a percentage smaller than that set aside for recreation in any of the other ten largest cities in the world or in America. And almost half the 14,827 acres were not really parks but only land intended for parks: 3,256 of those acres, for example, were contained in the two "marine parks" in Brooklyn and Staten Island, and these two parks were nothing but utterly undeveloped marshlands under water part of each day.

There was least park land, moreover, in those areas that needed parks the most. For generations, reformers had been attempting to nerve city officials to buy up tenements, tear them down and thereby shatter with shafts of sunlight the solid shadows of slum streets. But the difficulties of relocating tenement families, the veto power over city policies exercised by powerful Tammany district leaders who didn't want Democratic voters removed from their districts, and the lack of will to civic improvement had kept the Hylan and Walker administrations from taking the leap. And the economy-minded Low and Mitchel administrations, led to the brink several times, had always shied away at the last moment because of the sheer enormity of the cost involved. As a result, after nearly a century of agitation for the creation of "breathing spaces" in slums (Moses' grandfather, Bernhard Cohen, had been one of the agitators during the 1870's), there were on the Lower East Side—in an area a mile wide into which were crammed more than half a million people—exactly two small parks, neither of which contained a single piece of play equipment. With the exception of a block-square dirt- and weed-covered vacant lot owned by the city at Corlears Hook just to the east of this area, there was not another clearing in the wilderness of tenements stretching away from the massive granite piers of the Brooklyn Bridge all the way to Tompkins Square—thirty-one blocks to the north. And if one stood, atop the Upper West Side's high ridge, in Morningside, St. Nicholas or Colonial Park and looked down to where the ridge fell suddenly into an alluvial plain once known as Harlem Flats, which in 1932 contained the city's Spanish, Negro and Italian slum areas, he would see nothing between the end of Central Park on 110th Street down to his right and the beginning of Coogan's Bluff at 155th Street down to his left but a vast expanse of the asphalt gray of streets, the tar-paper gray of tenement roofs and the dingy brick red of tenement walls stretching endlessly eastward until it was at last mercifully cut short by the East River, an expanse in which, except for a poignant hint on the rocky slopes of Mount Morris Park at 124th Street, there did not exist a single patch of green. Wrote one reformer: "In the winter months, when the sun is most needed, it is no uncommon sight to see herds of children blocking the streets in sections where a little sun has been allowed to penetrate because there happen to be a few low buildings on one side of the street."

If slum children could not have parks, reformers had pleaded, at least let them have the tiny, pathetic, chicken-wire-fenced, cinder-paved substitute known as playgrounds. But in 1932, after generations of such pleading, there were only four playgrounds on the Lower East Side and two playgrounds in Harlem. In all Brooklyn, there were only thirty-six playgrounds. In all New York, a city which in 1932 contained approximately 1,700,000 children under twelve years of age, there were only 119, or one for every 14,000 children.

"Children's gardens" in playgrounds were the only places in which most slum children could engage in that most precious of childhood activities: digging. So few were the playgrounds—and their "gardens"—that they could accommodate no more than a handful of those who wanted to use them. Playground supervisors made children stand on line with their pails and shovels until a spot in the gardens was open, and the lines were so long that most of the little girls and boys could see at a glance that they were unlikely to get a turn. Most of them stood on the line anyway; childhood, after all, is the time of hope—and there was, after all, little else for them to do.

Reformers had at least hoped that the difficulty of obtaining park land in areas of the city that had already been built up had taught city officials the necessity of reserving land for parks in other areas before *they* were built up. But all during the 1920's, as they watched with horror, the city allowed developers to devour its open spaces without making more than a few gestures in this direction. Before the reformers' eyes, the red bricks that had walled out the sun in the Lower East Side and Harlem were cemented into place on the hills and meadows of the Bronx and Queens. "It looks as though all sunshine will soon be crowded out and dark shadows take its place," one reformer wrote in despair.

While campaigning for mayor in 1925, Jimmy Walker had promised to spend money lavishly to renovate Central Park. And no one could accuse him of a complete breach of faith. For not four hundred yards beyond the Sixty-fifth Street Transverse Road which formed the northern border of the Menagerie, visible from the Barbary-sheep pen when winter stripped the leaves from the park's trees, was dramatic evidence that, in at least one location in Central Park, Walker had more than kept his word. Not four hundred yards beyond the Transverse Road stood the Central Park Casino, a legend in its time.

The Casino was the brain child of restaurateur Sidney Solomon, front man for a cabal of socialites and Tammany officials who felt the need, as Walker euphemistically put it, of a sanctuary in which they might "entertain visitors without being molested." He asked the Mayor to let him establish one in the Casino, a low, rambling brick-and-stone building that had been built in the park in 1864 as a "Ladies Refreshment Salon" and had since been turned into a quiet little night club.

Walker owed Solomon a great debt. The restaurateur had introduced him to his favorite tailor. Throwing out the night club's previous owner, the Mayor turned it over to Solomon—for a rental of $8,500 a year, a sum which turned out to be equal to one night's receipts.

"The Casino will be our place, Monk," Walker reportedly said to his mistress, Betty (Monk) Compton. (Mrs. Walker's place was apparently Florida, the state to which she had been packed off for an extended vacation.) Although Solomon retained the celebrated Viennese interior decorator Josef Urban, who announced that he would strive for "a feeling of wind among young leaves," none of Urban's sketches was executed until Jimmy and Monk approved. The Mayor, whose disregard of city affairs was legendary, dedicated himself to making the Casino perfect in every detail. When it had been renovated—at a cost to Solomon and his backers of $365,000—and the restaurateur was about to announce its opening, Walker noticed that one of the bandstands blocked the headwaiter's view of the main entrance and thus deprived him of time to screen his guests and decide how important they were and where to seat them. He insisted that a new entrance be constructed—and it was, at a cost of $22,000.

When it opened, the Casino was hailed by one well-qualified observer as "the swankiest restaurant New York has yet seen." The dining pavilion was silver and maroon; the ballroom, except for Urban's flowing golden murals, all black glass; the dayroom fumed knotty pine. Emil Coleman's popular society orchestra played in the pavilion, Leo Reisman's in the Black and Gold Room. Spelling the orchestras were two pianists, the famous Nat

Brandwynne and a handsome youngster, unknown, on whom Solomon had decided to take a chance: Eddie Duchin.

But the Casino was more than a restaurant or a night club. The Casino was Jimmy Walker's Versailles. Friends joked that the Mayor spent more time there than he did at City Hall. When his limousine pulled into view, the doorman would scurry inside and signal the orchestra, so that when Beau James and Betty entered, it would be to strains of "Will You Love Me in December?" Holding hands with Betty, sipping champagne while she sipped beer, the Mayor would receive the parade of visitors to his table with careless ease, and sometimes, when Betty asked him to dance, he would even arise, pinch-waisted and slim in the tuxedo with the shiny lapels that people were beginning to copy, and glide with her around the floor, and the Mayor's friends would know that he was feeling very good indeed, for although he was so graceful a dancer that he had once wanted to be a professional, for years before he met Betty he had refused to dance a step, for reasons he never told anyone.

The regulars at Walker's court played their parts well. They brought their own champagne, their chauffeurs cooling it outside in the Rolls-Royces lined up along the dark paths until the doorman signaled that another bottle was wanted at table. Their wives and girl friends crowded around the bandstands so Reisman and Coleman and Brandwynne could autograph their slippers. Their spending was in character; one insurance man always announced his arrival by handing a thousand-dollar bill to the bandleader. At closing time, the bills fluttering down onto the hat-check girls' little silver trays seemed to one observer to be mostly hundreds. Reisman and Coleman were offered fabulous fees to play on after closing at private homes, and when the society crowd discovered Duchin, there was no limit to their generosity; a member of the Grace steamship family once paid him $20,000 to play at a party. The Depression? What Depression? "Until La Guardia came in, we never had a losing day, panic or no panic," Solomon was to say. And in a duplex upstairs retreat, closed to the public, its very existence concealed by the building's lowering mansard roof, Tammany politicians were entertained by Broadway chorus lines—rushed to the Casino *en masse* by motorcycle escort. And all the while, in a small adjoining office, its walls covered with green moiré and its ceiling with gold leaf, its heavy door carefully soundproofed, Walker held court for favor seekers and politicians, and it was there, insiders said, that much of the city's business was transacted.

Moses' attention had been drawn back to New York even before the Depression. Realizing in 1926 that city officials were not following through on promises to plan a new Queens road network to feed the Long Island parkways he was building, he had, during a solid year of conferences, all but begged the officials to widen Queens, Northern and Conduit boulevards and other major east-west thoroughfares in Brooklyn and Queens, to link Queens Boulevard with the Northern State Parkway, to make good on the promise given to him in 1924 and widen the two-mile stretch of Central

Avenue, the narrow winding farm road that was the only route to the Southern State Parkway. Disturbed that Bronx and Westchester residents could reach his Long Island parks only by driving down into Manhattan and across the Queensborough Bridge, he had persuaded Al Smith to urge a start on construction of the long-talked-about "triborough" bridge.

But in 1932, six years later, not even a start had been made on building these thoroughfares (with the exception of Queens Boulevard, on which work was proceeding so desultorily that its completion was nowhere in sight), and the farms that in 1926 could have been acquired cheaply for the right-of-way had become subdivisions the city could no longer afford to buy. Central Avenue was still unwidened; six years after the opening of the most modern highway in the United States the only approach to it was still a farm road. And as for the Triborough Bridge, the ring of the pile drivers hammering in its foundations after Mayor Walker had broken ground on October 25, 1929, had a distinctly hollow undertone, for while city officials were proclaiming that New York's traffic problems would be largely solved on the day that cars could speed up its mighty ramps, Moses was asking the project's chief engineer, a Tammany hack who had entered city service in 1886 as an axman, where the cars were going to go when they came down—and was learning that no one had thought to plan even a single approach road at any one of the bridge's three termini. And upset as Moses was at that, he soon realized that it was likely to be of no consequence. October 25, 1929, was a Friday, the Friday after "Black Thursday," the day of the stock-market crash. The proximity of the two days proved significant. The city's $5,400,000 initial allocation, largely wasted on extravagant condemnation awards, counsel fees and other items of Tammany graft, ran out after the Ward's Island piers had been built, and the city was prevented by the Depression from raising any additional funds for the project; in 1932 it had been at a complete standstill for two years.

Moses' plans for New York were not confined to Queens. The city's prestigious Park Association, inspired by his Long Island work to attempt again to save the city's fast-disappearing open spaces, had formed the Metropolitan Park Conference and made him its chairman. Assigning selected State Parks Council staffers to city problems (without the knowledge of the Legislature, of course), he furnished the reformers with the ingredient their efforts had been lacking: the expertise of engineers, landscape architects, draftsmen and surveyors experienced in park work. There were plenty of ideas for park acquisition floating around the city; some had been floating around for decades. Now Moses firmed up these ideas, made them concrete, codified them in terms that enabled the reformers to present specific demands to the Walker administration.

And Moses gave the reformers something as valuable as his organization. He gave them his vision. No sooner had he become chairman of the Metropolitan Park Conference than he began driving endlessly around New York. The big black Packard that had once been pulled up in the yards of Long Island farmhouses was parked now at the edge of the lonely marshes on the shore of Jamaica Bay; in the empty, rocky fields on a deserted Bronx peninsula known as Ferry Point; and at the spot on Riverside Drive to which, twenty years before, he had taken taxicabs while he was conceiving his great highway along the Hudson. And while his chauffeur waited in the car, he was walking around, with the same long, restless strides with which he had covered Long Island, lost in concentration, occasionally making sketches on a yellow legal note pad.

On February 25, 1930, before five hundred civic leaders gathered in the Grand Ballroom of the Hotel Commodore for the Park Association's annual dinner, Robert Moses, dressed in tuxedo and black tie (tied by Mary), rose to his feet and tugged a cord which dramatically pulled the drapery from a huge map of New York City hanging behind the dais. Running across the map were heavy red lines. One, which started in Brooklyn at the Brooklyn Bridge, ran along the borough's western and southern shores, skirting Jamaica Bay, and then, in Queens, headed north along the city's eastern boundary. The shore-front portion, Moses said, was a "Marginal Boulevard"—he had not yet named it the "Belt Parkway"—which would provide a quick circumferential passage around Brooklyn. The portion that ran north along the city boundary was a "Cross Island Parkway." A third of the way up its length, it crossed and linked up with the Southern State Parkway. Two-thirds of the way up, it crossed and linked up with the Northern State and with the proposed Grand Central Parkway. And at its end was a bridge—a "Ferry Point–Whitestone Bridge," he called it, not yet having named it the "Bronx-Whitestone"—that would enable motorists to speed across Long Island Sound. And then . . .

The audience's eyes followed the pointer in Moses' hand. At the northern end of the Ferry Point–Whitestone Bridge was another line, heading northeast to link up with the Hutchinson River Parkway that he had already built in Westchester County almost as far north as the Connecticut border. This, Moses said, was a "Hutchinson River Parkway Extension."

The audience, most of whose members had been concerned for years about the city's traffic problems, grasped at once the significance of what Moses was showing them. If the Marginal Boulevard, the Ferry Point–Whitestone Bridge and the Hutchinson River Parkway Extension were built, they saw, motorists would be able to leave Manhattan Island on the Brooklyn Bridge and then proceed over broad modern roads, unhindered by a single traffic light, all the way around Brooklyn to the Long Island parkways and parks. In addition, Manhattan and Brooklyn motorists would be presented with a through route to the Bronx, Westchester and New England—and so would motorists from Nassau and Suffolk counties. And, looking at it in reverse, the Bronx, Westchester and New England would suddenly be brought within easy access of the Long Island parks.

Moses' pointer reversed itself, tracing the Marginal Boulevard backward around Brooklyn. When it got to the Narrows, at a point opposite Staten Island, it stopped. Planners had long dreamed of a crossing between Brooklyn and Staten Island, Moses said; the Narrows Tube had been only one of several abortive attempts to make that dream reality. Now it was time to finish the tube. As soon as it was built, it could be linked with a parkway system on scenic Staten Island—more red lines rimmed the shoreline there—and, via a parkway straight across the island, with the Goethals and Outerbridge Crossing bridges on its western shore. And on the other side of those crossings, the audience realized with a start, was New Jersey! Moses' plan would give the city at last the long-discussed "northeastern bypass," the route, so long vaguely dreamed of by planners, that would enable traffic to and from New England and points south of the city to avoid crowded Manhattan Island and stop jamming its streets, that would free Manhattan forever from tens of thousands of cars and trucks that flooded into it every day although it was not their destination.

And there wouldn't be only one bypass route. The pointer flicked back across the Narrows and then eastward and northward along the Marginal Boulevard until it reached its intersection with the Grand Central Parkway. The western terminus of the Grand Central was no longer Queens Boulevard, the audience saw; now the parkway extended westward all the way to the point where the Triborough Bridge was supposed to touch down in Queens. And from the proposed Bronx terminus of the Triborough, red lines radiated out northwestward along the Harlem River to the Saw Mill River Parkway he was building in Westchester County and northeastward along Bruckner Boulevard to the Hutchinson River Parkway Extension. These, Moses said, would be other parkways—and as he said it, the reform leaders sitting on the dais suddenly realized that the lines behind Moses formed a whole series of rough but concentric rings that would provide a whole series of possible bypass routes around the city and at the same time would make the parks and parkways Moses had built on Long Island easily accessible to any family in the city with a car. Manhattan motorists would be able to drive all the way to Jones Beach without ever being slowed by a traffic light or intersecting traffic. Turn those red lines on Moses' map into concrete, they realized, and motorists in great sections of the city would be largely freed from the trap of local streets in which they had been so long confined.

There were other lines on the map, too. One ran along the western shore of Manhattan Island all the way up to the Harlem River, over the river and up through the Bronx. If the West Side Elevated Highway was extended up through Riverside Park, Moses said, and if it was carried across the Harlem by the Henry Hudson Bridge, and if it then ran north to the city line, its northern terminus would be within three miles of the southern terminus of the Saw Mill River Parkway the state was constructing. If the city built the parkway—the "Henry Hudson Parkway," he called it—he would see that the state extended the Saw Mill River Parkway south to meet it, and there would be a continuous through route from the bottom of Manhattan Island to Westchester County.

A Henry Hudson Parkway would provide further advantages, Moses explained. It would give the city a fast, modern route to the George Washington Bridge. On the other side of that bridge was Palisades Interstate Park. It would no longer be difficult to reach it. All New Jersey, in fact, would be opened to motorists from the west side of Manhattan. And if the

Henry Hudson Parkway was built properly and a great park created alongside it on what was now the mud flats of Riverside Park, the city's residents would not even have to leave the city to find beauty. They would be able to drive along the water, the river stretching to one side of them, the green of the park to the other, above the park the spires of Manhattan. It would be a public improvement unequaled in the world!

Before he finished talking about parkways, Moses said, he had a final point. The plan he proposed was admittedly somewhat ambitious. But it was realistic—and it was realizable. The dream of opening to the residents of New York City the beauty of the lands around it was in reach. After all, he said, much of it was already reality. The Southern State, Northern State and Hutchinson River parkways were already built, the Saw Mill River Parkway begun. Much of the rest of it was begun: the State Council of Parks was committed to building the Saw Mill River Parkway and Hutchinson River Parkway extensions; at least a start had been made on the Triborough Bridge and the West Side Highway. All that needed to be done was to knit these elements together.

Now, he said, he wanted to discuss parks. His listeners, who had noticed that the park along the Henry Hudson Parkway was colored green on the map, saw that much of the land bordering the other parkways Moses was proposing was also green.

All along the parkways, he said, there should be small parks. The parkways' right-of-way itself should be "ribbon parks" similar to those along the parkways on Long Island. Obtaining the necessary land would be easy along much of the Marginal Boulevard and Cross Island Parkway, and along all the parkways in Staten Island, because the areas these parkways ran through were still largely undeveloped and land there was cheap. It would be expensive to buy land along some of the other parkways. But it was never going to become cheaper. It would only become more expensive. It should be bought now.

The larger green areas on the map, he said, represented larger parks. Specifically, he said, they represented a substantial portion of the last areas of natural beauty remaining in the city. The corridor parks he was proposing in eastern Queens, for example, running roughly along the route of the proposed Grand Central Parkway, represented the last undeveloped portions of the heavily forested hills of the glacial moraine. The parks he was proposing along the north shore of Jamaica Bay represented the last chance to preserve from commercial exploitation the bay's wild marshes and abundant animal and bird life. The park he was proposing on the meadows at Flushing Bay represented the last chance to preserve a portion of *that* bay from development. These parks, he said, should be purchased at once. His engineers had compiled estimates of their cost, and it was $30,000,000. A bond issue for that amount should be authorized at once by the Board of Estimate. Admittedly it would take a hard fight to persuade the Board to do what had to be done. He invited the people listening to him to join in that fight.

* * *

The reformers stood up and cheered when Moses had finished, but the reaction of city officials was somewhat less satisfying. For all the cooperation he received from them he might still have been the starry-eyed idealist of 1914 arguing in the language of a Yale bull session for the construction of mothers' shelters in Central Park.

The scale of his plans was too big for them. Not one city official, he would recall, seemed capable of comprehending a highway network on the scale he had proposed—a fact which would not have been surprising even if the officials had been men of vision, since no highway network on that scale had ever been proposed for any city in America, or, for that matter, any city in the world.

The scale of the money involved was too big for them. The total cost would obviously be in the hundreds of millions of dollars, and they felt there was no sense in the city even considering such an amount.

What the city officials could comprehend about Moses' plan they didn't like. The relocations involved for his highways would be on a scale almost unknown in the city: the Whitlock Avenue approach to the Triborough Bridge in the Bronx would alone require the condemnation of buildings containing more than four thousand apartments—voters' apartments.

Moses' general plans for his parkway system were turned over for analysis to city engineers, who, sensing the attitude of their superiors, did not rush to begin working on them. Try as he would, Moses could not get the city to move on them. And once the Depression began to tighten its hold on New York, there was no longer much sense in trying to get the city to move. In 1932, the city had not even begun seriously considering any of the parkways he had proposed at the Hotel Commodore dinner two years before.

Walker's administration did agree in 1930 to issue $30,000,000 in bonds to buy new park land. In 1930, the city acquired 2,530 acres that would be known as Great Kills and Willowbrook parks on Staten Island; Highland, Alley Pond and Kissena parks in Queens; and Owl's Head Park in Brooklyn. But, by the end of that year, it was becoming apparent that the city's people had needs even more pressing than the need for parks, even if there had still been any market for the bonds that had to be sold to buy them. In 1932, with only $4,000,000 of the $30,000,000 spent—and exactly one tenement-area park acquired—even most reformers were agreeing that acquisition of park land was a luxury that New York would have to postpone to some other, happier, decade.

When Roosevelt, under Moses' prodding, agreed to fight the Depression with a state public works program of unprecedented size, Moses saw the agreement as a chance to make the city move. The state had never spent any money on roads in New York City, but Moses persuaded Roosevelt to authorize the state's Temporary Emergency Relief Administration to pay the construction costs of the Grand Central Parkway and the Central Avenue linkup with the Southern State Parkway, and of another, "Interborough," parkway, long proposed but never built, that would provide access into and out of central Brooklyn. The city would have to pay only for the right-of-way. The Legislature, having learned the inadvisability of giving Moses an opportunity to drive the opening wedge for a project that would later turn out to cost many times what he had estimated, gave Moses only $5,000,000, payable at the rate of a paltry $1,000,000 per year. All other expenses, the bill provided, must be paid by the city. But in the city Moses had no political leverage. The Board of Estimate kept delaying approval of the route, the allocations for right-of-way kept getting involved in endless snarls and at the end of 1933 Moses could look back and see that it had taken him as long to build a total of two miles of the parkway projects in Queens as it had taken him to build twenty-two miles of the Southern State Parkway.

Roosevelt's successor as Governor, Herbert H. Lehman, deeply respected Moses. Says one man who served as an adviser to both: "Roosevelt saw Jones Beach in terms both of people swimming and in terms of the political gains that could come from those people swimming. Herbert Lehman thought only of helping people to go swimming and be happy. And he felt that no one could do that job better than Robert Moses."

Within a month after Lehman took office in January 1933, he handed to Moses even more power than Roosevelt had given him. In 1932, Congress, at President Hoover's request, had created the Reconstruction Finance Corporation to help self-supporting public works projects. Lehman set up a State Emergency Public Works Commission to screen such projects and determine which should be submitted to Washington, and named Moses its chairman. This post gave Moses the power to get work under way on his huge park and parkway plan for the Niagara Frontier; a Niagara Frontier Bridge Authority was established, received $2,800,000 in federal funds and constructed bridges that linked both the north and south ends of Grand Island, near Buffalo, to the mainland. A Thousand Islands Bridge Authority built the international bridge to Canada. Under his direction, a New York State Bridge Authority was established to purchase—through agreements he negotiated—the Bear Mountain Bridge from the Harrimans and its other private owners. A Saratoga Springs Authority began refurbishing and expanding the spa. Negotiating in Washington with the RFC, Moses obtained funds for the Port of New York Authority to construct the Lincoln Tunnel and for the city to construct Hillside, Knickerbocker and other housing developments. And he persuaded Mayor O'Brien to ask the Legislature to establish a Triborough Bridge Authority that could issue its own bonds, secured by toll revenues, and that would therefore be eligible for aid from the newly formed federal Public Works Administration, and the PWA granted a $44,200,000 combination loan and grant to the Authority on condition that the city make certain additional token contributions. But hardly had the Tammany-controlled Authority gotten its hands on the first installment of the grant than it blew it on inflated condemnation awards and counsel fees; in addition, the city proved unable to make even the first installment of its token payment. The PWA thereupon cut off funds and announced that no more would be forthcoming until the city paid up and the

Authority cleaned up—and in 1933 there were no immediate prospects of either development.

In vain, Moses pointed out to the Board of Estimate that the money the TERA and PWA were prepared to spend in New York would create vast improvements in the city—at virtually no cost to its taxpayers. In vain, he pointed out that the money would put thousands of hungry men to work for salaries that would feed their families. Such considerations were not of interest to the Tammany-dominated Board. And those that were of interest, Moses, outside the city's power structure as he was, could not offer them.

All through 1933, the city's financial situation worsened. In May, City Comptroller Charles W. Berry informed Mayor O'Brien that the city would be unable to pay $100,000,000 in short-term revenue notes coming due in June. The bankers agreed to extend the notes only after the city agreed to an almost doubled interest rate and budget cuts so stringent that they made it all but impossible for the city to keep its physical plant in repair. And, despite the extension, in September Berry told O'Brien that the city would be unable to meet its October 24 payroll.

After nine days of frantic meetings in which a worried Governor Lehman participated, the bankers agreed on September 27 to further extensions —after the city agreed to accept even more stringent repayment provisions, and to balance its 1934 budget.

The city's worries were still not over. It required legislative authorization to meet the bankers' demands, but the Legislature's Republican majority saw the city's plight as a lever they could use to pry various concessions from Lehman, and a long, tense bargaining session ensued. Not until October 18, just six days before the city would, by all common business definitions, enter a state of bankruptcy, was the authorization given. And a look ahead was hardly reassuring. The amount of short-term revenue notes coming due in the next two years was $500,000,000.

Nevertheless, in the summer of 1933, Moses was convinced that events were moving for, rather than against, him. For during that summer, over a period of several weeks, he was convinced that he was going to get a chance personally to move the city—as its next mayor.

19. *To Power in the City*

In New York City, 1933 was the year of the Goo Goo.

Dormant since debonair John Purroy Mitchel had one-stepped it into the ground nearly two decades before, the city's Good Government movement—"Goo Goos" was the politicians' epithet for the men and women in it—had been hauled back on its feet by stern-visaged, cane-carrying Samuel Seabury. In the early stages of the Seabury investigation, the city had only snickered at the fantastic alibis offered by the participants in the Tin Box Parade. Pretty young women had thrown roses at Jimmy Walker's feet as he left the hearing room after testifying. But as Seabury's quiet, courteous but relentless prodding reached higher and higher and the revelations it uncovered became more and more sordid—not even a $10,000,000 welfare fund for the unemployed went unlooted—and as the deepening Depression made the public less tolerant of the making of illegal fortunes with its money, the laughter faded. In the last weeks of the hearing, when Seabury left the courthouse in Foley Square for lunch, thousands of men and women hung out the windows of surrounding office buildings to cheer him. (The judge courteously raised his hat but did not smile.) Mayor John Patrick O'Brien was proving that his gaffe about the Police Commissioner was in character; a master of the malapropism, he told a Harlem audience, "My heart is as black as yours," and he didn't do much to win the Jewish vote when he told a synagogue audience that he had always admired "that scientist of scientists, Albert Weinstein." O'Brien would be the Democratic nominee in the regular election to be held in November 1933, and obviously he would not be the most formidable of candidates. With Roosevelt, spurned by Tammany at the 1932 Democratic National Convention, moving as President to take control of the city away from the Wigwam, the stars that made Fusion feasible—incontrovertible scandal and Democratic disunity—had never been more favorably in conjunction.

All the reformers needed was a candidate with charisma. Founding a City Fusion Party, they united with the city's Republican Party in a Fusion Conference Committee whose purpose was to select one. And when Seabury, their first choice, refused to run and they began considering other names, Robert Moses' was prominent among them.

New York's reformers considered Moses one of them.

The Old Guard of reform viewed him almost paternally. Darwin James and Henry Moskowitz liked to tell anecdotes about his work for them on the Municipal Civil Service Commission. Henry H. Curran, Fusion candidate against Hylan in 1921, remembered Moses as secretary of his campaign committee. Joseph M. Price, a wealthy dress manufacturer and chairman of the City Club's board of trustees, remembered him pleading earnestly in the City Club lounge for the club's support for the executive budget proposal. And Richard Spencer Childs, who had made Moses secretary of his New York State Association, delighted in telling friends (inaccurately): "I am the man who gave Bob Moses his first job."

Other, slightly younger, reformers—men in their fifties like Stanley Isaacs and Raymond Ingersoll—considered Moses a comrade-in-arms. And he was nothing less than an idol to many of a new generation of reformers, including six-foot five-inch, blond and blue-eyed Newbold Morris, a Yale graduate who at thirty was president of the Silk Stocking Fifteenth Assembly District Republican Club; college professors like Wallace S. Sayre, twenty-eight, of New York University, and Adolf A. Berle, Jr., thirty-eight, and Joseph D. McGoldrick, thirty-two, of Columbia; and young experts in public administration like Rufus E. McGahen, thirty-nine, secretary of the Citizens Union, and Paul Blanshard, forty-one, director of the City Affairs Committee of New York, who were spending enough evenings studying legislative bills and debating municipal policy in the lounges of the City Club and Citizens Union to prove that the Tammany view of man was still, as one historian puts it, "only partially valid; men are moved by things other than just narrow self-interest."

The attitude of the reformers toward Moses was understandable. Not only had he fought in so many causes in which they believed; he had triumphed. Reformers who had learned through bitter, repeated experience the difficulty of translating ideas into realities were almost in awe of his success in doing so. Lillian Wald of the Henry Street Settlement wrote him: "May I . . . tell you how profoundly I admire your genius in designing the parks and procuring them for the community." "His . . . administrative accomplishment at Albany," Rufus McGahen said, was "amazing."

The reformers didn't know the details of those triumphs. They were not, after all, on the inside of state government, where Moses' power plays had been executed, and they knew nothing of his methods. If there had been a change in Robert Moses, none but a handful of them had even an inkling of it, and those who had seen glimpses of the change had, like Childs, been charmed into forgetting them by a Moses who needed their continuing support. They attributed Moses' arrogance to brilliance, his impatience to zeal.

Moreover, reformers, more than slightly addicted to a black-and-white view of morality and life, tended to classify all government officials as either "politicians," who were in public service for power and money, who put those considerations ahead of the common good and who had debased politics into a somewhat questionable way of making a living; or as "public servants," who were "nonpolitical" and therefore good. And they had no doubts about which class Moses belonged to. As a Bureau staffer, no reformer had been more scornful of practical politicians than he. His well-publicized refusal to accept a salary for his services, coupled with his frequent denunciations of patronage and of favoritism in contracts and condemnation awards, convinced reformers, since they had no reason to question his sincerity, that his views had not been changed just because he had obtained power. "The principle is the important thing," he had written. They thought he still believed that. "High purpose," Richard Childs was to tell the author. "And ability. And not interested in getting something for either tne boys or for himself—utterly selfless in all of it. That was how I thought of Moses."

His brilliance was legendary among them. In the field of public administration, they agreed, his mind was unequaled in suppleness and inventiveness. Lillian Wald was not the only reform leader who used the word "genius" in describing Moses. One reformer who maintained a certain detachment about reformers because he was at home not only in the paneled board room of the City Club but also in the bare-walled clubhouses of Brooklyn's Fourth Assembly District—where he had proved himself a canny practical politician by ousting the old-line Republican boss and installing himself in his place—was Paul Windels. Says Windels: "Those people [reformers] could get a little starry-eyed sometimes, and at that time they were very starry-eyed indeed about Bob Moses. They saw in him a man whose ideals were just as high as theirs and who had in addition qualities which enabled him to accomplish things of revolutionary magnitude in the public sphere. The younger men there, and some of the older ones, too, to tell you the truth—they idolized that man. They seemed to consider him the Beau Ideal of what the reformer should be. And to tell you the truth, I thought I was a pretty shrewd cookie —and sometimes I felt the same way."

More practical considerations also recommended Moses to them as a candidate. First, there was the immense favorable publicity he had received. This was no candidate respected in the councils of reform but unknown to the public; this was a candidate about whose virtues the public had been educated for years. More important, there was Moses' relationship with Al Smith. The Brown Derby was still the most popular figure in the city. When, early in 1933, a downtown Tammany club had begun circulating petitions urging *him* to run for mayor, it collected more than 200,000 signatures in one week before Smith issued a statement categorically refusing to make the race. The Fusion leaders knew how Smith felt about Moses. If Moses ran, they believed, Smith would either break with Tammany and support him or, at the least, remain neutral. And either of those stands, they believed, would result in a mass Democratic defection to Moses, a defection essential to victory in a city in which the party registration of enrolled voters was almost four to one Democratic.

Before the Fusion Conference Committee began meeting in March

1933, Moses was contacted by City Club board chairman Price, who had, as chairman of the legendary Committee of One Hundred and Seven, been the prime mover behind John Purroy Mitchel's nomination in 1913, and who wanted now to play the same role for Moses. Moses assured Price that he would accept the Fusion nomination if it was offered to him. As soon as Seabury turned down a renewed offer of the nomination, Price brought Moses' name before the Fusion Committee and received an almost unanimously favorable response.

But Seabury had not been present at the meeting. And Seabury's opinion of Moses was markedly different from that of other reformers.

He didn't like him. Opinionated as well as dedicated, Seabury was accustomed to deference when he presented his views (reformers fondly called him "the Bishop" because of his pontifical air, although they were careful to do so behind his back), and deference was not Moses' strong suit. In 1932 the two men had had a bitter confrontation in Al Smith's Fifth Avenue apartment when Seabury attempted to win the ex-Governor's support for a City Charter revision that would determine membership on the City Council on the basis of proportional representation and would therefore encourage minority parties and help end Tammany's domination of the council. Seabury and Moses, a foe of proportional representation, had argued for hours before Smith, who, ill with a severe cold, was propped up in bed, too hoarse to speak. Exactly what happened at the confrontation is unrecorded, but Moses says, "He [Seabury] didn't stand up very well. He didn't seem to have his stuff [facts] at all. It was a very, very painful session."

More than personality differences lay behind Seabury's hostility to Moses, however. Its root lay in the judge's hostility to Tammany Hall—and in his conviction that Moses' election would allow Tammany to retain control of the city.

A direct descendant of "Speak for Yourself, John" and Priscilla Alden of the *Mayflower*, whose ancestors included Samuel Jones, "the Father of the New York Bar," and a long line of distinguished Episcopalian clergymen, Samuel Seabury had, even as a boy studying in his father's library with the portraits of a dozen famous ancestors peering down, stern and patrician, on his work, been markedly aware and proud of this lineage of law and righteousness, and determined to live up to it.

He was an idealist. In his youth an adoring disciple of single-tax philosopher Henry George, he was elected at the age of twenty-one president of the Manhattan Single-Tax Club. At twenty-four, he gave up his own nomination as Citizens Union Party candidate for the State Assembly to play Sancho Panza in that most gallant of all the Don Quixote rides of New York politics, George's mayoralty campaign of 1897. (When that impossible dream was ended by George's death less than a week before Election Day, Seabury followed on horseback behind the casket—adorned with white roses and the inscription "Progress and Poverty"—as the body of his idol was borne through the streets of the city with half a million citizens watching and the hats coming off as the cortege approached and the whisper going through the great crowds: "Uncover, uncover.")

And his idealism had a target. All his life Samuel Seabury stalked the Tiger. While still in his teens, he took to the street corners—and was stoned by Tammany hooligans—as he spoke against Tammany candidates as an independent Democrat. As a young lawyer, in love with the law, he hated the Tammany-controlled judges who turned New York's courts into instruments of politics rather than justice. Representing, in a hundred cases, men unjustly accused by police who took orders from Tammany and unfairly tried before judges who took orders from Tammany, he knew the bitterness of a hundred unjust defeats.

Just as his idealism grated against Tammany, so did his ambition, which was also strong. His bearing and a rare, stern eloquence made him stand out among the crowd of young reformers. Winning a plurality that for a Citizens Union Party candidate was unprecedented, he was elected a judge over his fellow men at the age of twenty-eight. Soon his fairness and firmness awed even his Tammany colleagues on the City Court into assigning him the most difficult cases. His prematurely white hair, parted in the center, his ruddy complexion, his flowing black robes, his pince-nez—and his bearing—made him a striking figure on the bench. He needed no gavel to quiet spectators, a biographer wrote—"His mien alone served to silence the courtroom." He sat through one long case, according to the New York *World*, "as if his face had been carved out of stone." At thirty-three, he was elected to the State Supreme Court, at forty-one to the Court of Appeals, at forty-three he was running for Governor.

Tammany ordered its braves, in voting for the Democratic state ticket, to ignore the man at its head, and he lost.* He hoped the nomination would come his way again in 1918, but that was the year Silent Charlie Murphy saw that it was handed to Al Smith. Embittered, Seabury retired to private life and a series of monumental legal fees and for more than ten years kept silent on public issues until, suddenly swooping out of the past to take on Tammany Hall in 1930, he revealed that prosperity had not blunted his zeal for reform and that he was still a man against the machine.

There was no telling how far Seabury might have climbed in politics if he had become Governor. The terminus he had in mind was the White House—in 1932, on the strength of the publicity he received from his investigations, he authorized the launching of a try for the Democratic presi-

* Another element in his defeat—which took place in 1916—was Theodore Roosevelt. TR, whose Progressive Party had joined reform Democrats in support of Seabury's run for the Court of Appeals, persuaded Seabury to resign from the bench and run for Governor in the first place, promising to support him against the GOP nominee, Charles S. Whitman. But after Seabury had won the Democratic nomination, Roosevelt, breaking his word, rejoined the GOP and commanded the Progressives to back Whitman. (Seabury paid a visit to Sagamore Hill. Roosevelt started to say something, but Seabury interrupted. "Mr. President, you are a blatherskite!" he said, and stalked out.)

dential nomination—and the hatred for Tammany that had been ignited by his idealism was fueled by the wreckage the Tiger had made of his ambitions. Much of his bitterness centered on Al Smith. While most other reformers felt that Smith had risen above the organization, Seabury felt, as he had always felt, that Smith had simply put a respectable smile on the face of a tiger that was as voracious as ever. If anything, he felt, Smith was more inimical to the public interest than the depredations of the most corrupt ward leaders, because his popularity provided them with protective coloration. And, of course, it was Smith who, by winning five times in a row the Democratic gubernatorial nomination, had insured that Seabury would not be able to follow the gubernatorial road back to the public eye. "He had a real conviction about Smith," Moses told an interviewer. "It amounted to an actual hatred. He felt that Smith had prevented him from being Governor and if he had been Governor he would have been President. Seabury hated the Governor, really *hated* him." By 1933, wrote a Seabury biographer, "his anti-Tammany stand was not merely a cause. It was a mania." The narrowness of his perspective made him feel that the most significant fact about Moses was that he was Smith's protégé. If Moses became mayor, Seabury thought, the ex-Governor would have an opportunity to move Tammany quietly back into control of City Hall. Reform's great opportunity to cleanse the city, the opportunity he had given it, would be lost.

When Joseph Price, following the Fusion Conference Committee meeting, told Seabury its members were for Moses, Seabury refused to approve the choice. And he strongly hinted—he would "reserve all personal liberty of action" was the way he put it—that if the committee nominated Moses, he would enter his own candidate in the race. Recalling his own feelings, Moses said later: "Nobody could be elected without Seabury. With Seabury on his side, anyone running on a Fusion ticket could have won that year. Without him—no, it would have been absolutely impossible to win." Moses issued a statement saying: "I am not a candidate for the Fusion nomination for mayor and should not accept the nomination if it were offered to me."

The Fusion leaders agreed that Seabury's support was crucial. And even if they hadn't felt that way, they would have been reluctant to go against his wishes. They began looking for other candidates. Price drafted an angry statement of resignation from the committee. "The best equipped and most able man considered for the Fusion nomination, a man fearless and independent, was objected to by Judge Seabury upon the narrow-minded reason that he is a close friend of Alfred E. Smith, the most popular man in New York City," the statement said. "The Fusion Conference itself was practically unanimous for Mr. Moses. . . ." But Price was persuaded to withdraw his resignation, to leave unpublished his statement—and to join with the rest of the committee in a search for another candidate.

Five reformers were to be offered the nomination during the hectic weeks that followed.

But these were men to whom politics was something more than an avenue for the realization of personal ambitions. Two of the five—judges—

said that they were happy being judges; a third, a business executive, preferred a career in private life to one in public. And if they did have political ambitions, they subordinated them to principle. Raymond Ingersoll, fifty-eight, a wealthy respected social worker who had served as a park commissioner in the Mitchel administration and as a campaign manager in Smith's 1924 gubernatorial campaign, wanted to be mayor but was afraid his health would not allow him to do the job properly, and so he declined the nomination. Then Seabury and Maurice P. Davidson, chairman of the City Fusion Party, taking a room in the Hotel Commodore to avoid reporters, offered the nomination to Nathan Straus. Wrote Davidson: "I remember how he came into the room; slim, well-groomed, and how he removed his gloves, laid down his hat and cane, and how delighted he was with the offer, and how he said 'nothing has occurred in my lifetime or would ever occur which would bring me greater happiness than the opportunity to serve as mayor of the City of New York, but I ask forty-eight hours to consider.' We met again several days later, and he said that he had discussed the matter with some of his advisers and had decided to decline. . . . The ill-fated star of Adolf Hitler was rising. . . . Jews were accused by Hitler of endeavoring to encompass the control and government of the whole world. Ridiculous and absurd as those charges were, Nathan Straus refused to accept a nomination for Mayor at a time when Herbert Lehman was Governor because it might give credence in some quarters to Mr. Hitler's charges. He felt that in the interest of the welfare of his own people of the Jewish faith and in order not to handicap the success of the reform movement in New York it was up to him to subordinate any and all personal ambition in the interests of the public good and he, too, therefore declined."

There was a politician who wanted the nomination, wanted it desperately. "Fiorello H. La Guardia was standing in the wings—not standing, but moving around very, very rapidly," Davidson was to write. "He would send for me every once in a while and say, 'How are you getting on?' . . . He would say, 'Well, who's your latest mayor?' and I would tell him. He would jump around and shake his fist and he'd say, 'Well, there's only one man going to be the candidate, and I'm the man. I'm going to run. I want to be mayor.' "

La Guardia, a nominal Republican too liberal for most Republicans, had already lunged for the prize twice before. In 1921, president of the Board of Aldermen, he had sought the nomination from the Fusion committee of which Moses was secretary, but the reformers had turned instead to Henry Curran, one of their own, and when La Guardia ran against Curran in the Republican primary, he had failed to carry a single borough. In 1929, the Little Flower had received the Republican nomination, and the only remarkable aspect of his campaign against Jimmy Walker, then at the height of his popularity, was the size of his defeat: failing to carry a single assembly district, La Guardia received only 367,675 votes to Walker's 867,522. Then, in 1932, after five terms as a congressman from Latin East Harlem, where he had constructed an aptly named personal Italian-American political machine—the Gibboni (apes)—La Guardia had been defeated by a Tammany hack. Out of a job at the age of fifty, branded a loser, only by winning the mayoralty could he resuscitate a political career that seemed to be gasping out its last breath.

La Guardia possessed qualifications for making the run beyond the fact that, half Jewish and half Italian, married first to a Catholic and then to a Lutheran of German descent, himself a Mason and an Episcopalian, he was practically a balanced ticket all by himself. Campaigning for mayor in 1929, he had made charges—many of the city's magistrates were corrupt; except for Al Smith, "there isn't a Tammany politician that would care to have his bank account examined"—that the city had thought exaggerated until the Seabury investigations, which began just a month after the election, had proved that most of them were understatements. As the Tin Box Parade swung into full stride, the *Times* commented that La Guardia was the only man with the right "to stand up in New York City today and say: 'I told you so.' "

But La Guardia, son of immigrants, raised in tenements, possessor of neither a high-school nor an undergraduate college degree,* was from a different background than the reformers, and this was not an unimportant point with them. The members of the Fusion Conference Committee, and much of that segment of New York for which the committee spoke, were, as one of La Guardia's biographers put it, "educated at the best colleges, financially secure, eminent in the professions and business, and primarily old-stock American Protestant but also significantly Jewish. . . . The fusionists came, in short, from Gotham's gentry." And the attitude of many of them was, if not bigoted, at least parochial. "They preferred one of their own kind as Mayor or at least a type more like themselves" than the swarthy little Italian-American.

La Guardia's personal style was screaming, ranting, fist-shaking and more than a little irresponsible. (Learning that a family had been burned to death while the mother tried unsuccessfully to telephone the Fire Department, he insinuated that the telephone company was guilty of murder. Testifying before a legislative committee on rent controls, he said, "I come not to praise the landlord but to bury him.") These men who distrusted excess distrusted him. And he did not hesitate to play melting-pot politics, to wave the bloody flag, to appeal, in one of the seven languages in which he could harangue an audience, to the insecurities, resentments and prejudices of the ethnic groups in the immigrant district he had represented in Congress. ("I can outdemagogue the best of demagogues," he told one aide. "I invented the low blow," he boasted to another.) His naked ambition for high office, his cockiness, truculence and violent temper—while he was president of the Board of Aldermen, Curran once had to restrain him physically from striking the City Comptroller—repelled them.

* He had earned an LL.B. from New York University Law School by attending classes, mostly in the evening, from 1907 to 1910.

Furthermore, although the reformers considered themselves liberals, their definition of the term was decidedly pre-Depression, and La Guardia was far too liberal for them. A New Dealer before the New Deal, he made a career for himself as a leader of the have-nots against the haves—and they were haves. His efforts in Congress might have made him, in his biographer's words, "the plumed knight of organized labor," but organized labor, militant, aggressive organized labor, was not precisely what reformers had in mind when they spoke moist-eyed of the working man. La Guardia lashed out, moreover, at the city's businessmen who were Fusion's financial cornerstones, charging, without offering proof, that big property owners were receiving low assessments on their property. When in 1929 he attempted to falsely persuade voters that he was a Fusion as well as a Republican candidate, the Citizens Union replied with a statement characterizing him as an opportunistic, excitable, unpredictable radical. Many reformers, La Guardia's biographers say, were happy that his ouster from Congress had apparently put an end to "an obnoxious career propelled by unstable and dangerous ambitions." The fact that in 1933 La Guardia was "the only professional Republican politician in the city who could dramatize both himself and an issue" did not move them. Moreover, Republican leaders detested this Republican whom they considered a radical. They flatly refused to accept him. Seabury, while not committing himself, noted that La Guardia was an excellent campaigner; the judge wanted to win. But every time La Guardia's name was brought up, it was greeted with open hostility by most other members of the Fusion Conference Committee. Running out of candidates, they began again to lean to Moses. Price asked him to reconsider his withdrawal. Seabury began pushing more strongly for La Guardia, possibly because he saw him as the only remaining viable alternative to Moses, but on July 26 Price took an informal telephone poll of the Fusion Conference Committee. The vote was eighteen for Moses, five for La Guardia. Moses agreed to let Price present his name again. He felt that Seabury, confronted by the *fait accompli* of the nomination, would not split the movement and would back him.

The Fusion leaders felt the same way. A meeting of the committee was scheduled for the following afternoon at the Lawyers Club, 115 Broadway, at 3 P.M. A room was reserved. Reporters were alerted that an important announcement would be made. Everything was in readiness to offer Moses the Fusion nomination for Mayor of the City of New York. As late as noon on July 27, Moses must have felt confident that he had it.

But at noon on July 27, three hours before the meeting was to convene, Seabury invited Davidson to lunch at the Bankers Club and demanded the nomination for La Guardia. When Davidson told him that the committee had decided to give it to Moses, Seabury struck the table with his clenched fist so hard that dishes rattled loudly in the suddenly hushed dining room.

"You sold out to Tammany Hall," the judge shouted. "I'll denounce you and everybody else. You sold out the movement to Tammany Hall." Leaving his guest at the table, he strode out of the dining room to the elevator. Davidson, remonstrating, followed, but Seabury, in the elevator, turned and said, "You sold out. Goodbye"—and the door shut in Davidson's face.

Striding back to his office, which was located at 120 Broadway, directly across from the Lawyers Club where the Fusion Committee was to meet, Seabury issued a statement broadly hinting that he would run another ticket. The Fusion leaders, realizing that they had miscalculated, began to search frantically for a new candidate. Moses, learning of these developments by telephone from Price, told him that he didn't want his name placed in nomination.

In an attempt to placate Seabury while not alienating the Republicans, who still refused to nominate La Guardia, the committee nominated independent Democrat John F. O'Ryan, former member of the City Transit Commission. The reporters covering the Fusion meeting ran across Broadway to Seabury's office to learn his reaction. Seabury hardly knew O'Ryan—and since he knew his ignorance was shared by the voters, he believed O'Ryan could not win. Seeing by now a tiger behind every bush, the Judge told the reporters that this was the reason O'Ryan had been nominated. Tammany, he charged, had forced Republican leaders, some of whom "have long been the owned and operated chattels of Tammany Hall," to nominate a weak candidate. O'Ryan withdrew for the sake of unity. A new "harmony committee" was formed. It included not only Seabury but the one man who could match him in prestige among the reformers, Charles Culp ("CC") Burlingham, who at eighty-two still had the gift of making men forget their differences and remember their common cause. When Seabury began to roar "sellout" during one harmony committee meeting, Burlingham said, "Sit down, Sam, sit down." While the other members goggled at hearing the Bishop called by his first name, he sat down. And after midnight on August 4, CC persuaded the committee members, with the exception of Price and Davidson, who held out for Moses to the last, to authorize Seabury to call a waiting La Guardia and tell him the nomination was his.

The reform movement of New York City had wanted Robert Moses for mayor. Of all the influential reformers, only one had been firmly opposed to him. Given the almost certain success in 1933 of a Fusion ticket headed by so popular a candidate, it is hardly an overstatement to say that only one man had stood between Moses and the mayoralty, between Moses and supreme power in the city. But that man had stood fast; at the last moment, as Moses must have felt the prize securely within his grasp, it was denied him.

During the first two months of the mayoral campaign—which had been turned into a three-way race by the entry, with support from President Roosevelt, James A. Farley and Bronx Boss Edward J. Flynn, of anti-Tammany Democrat Joseph V. McKee—Moses declined to participate. His visceral hatred of Roosevelt had been intensified by his philosophical antipathy to the President's social welfare policies, which he referred to in private as "socialistic." And the liberal La Guardia, who as a lame-duck congressman had introduced in early 1933 several bills favored by the incoming administration, was identified in Moses' mind with the New Deal.

But tough-minded reformer-politician and key Fusion strategist Paul Windels, believing in late October that La Guardia's campaign was losing momentum and needed a lift, asked Raymond Ingersoll to ask Moses to endorse the Little Flower.

Moses agreed. With less than two weeks remaining before Election Day, he suddenly abandoned his role as bystander. And his entry into the campaign had an impact even more dramatic than Windels had foreseen. For Moses' radio speeches and printed statements burst above the murk of the city's political battlefield like a Roman candle whose sparkle, coming from a shower of glittering, sharp-pointed barbs flung off by a graceful and witty malice, was both hard and brilliant.

Assailing Tammany and its mayors in a radio broadcast, Moses urged voters to remember "the strange characters they have seen occupying the places of Judge Gaynor and John Purroy Mitchel in City Hall—Hylan, the ranting Bozo of Bushwick; Walker, half Beau Brummel and half guttersnipe, and John P. O'Brien, a winded bull in the municipal china shop." Is it any wonder, he asked, that younger voters, who could not remember a non-Tammany mayor, "must think of the great office of Chief Magistrate with derision and contempt?"

As for the Farley-Flynn candidate, Moses said, he was a "pious fraud" whose attempt to portray himself as a reformer would forever be known in the city's history as "the strange interlude of 'Holy Joe' McKee." Electing McKee mayor, and thereby giving power to Farley and Flynn, would bring to City Hall only "another kind of Tammany."

"Do you think," he asked, "that the Currys, McCooeys, Farleys and Flynns are in any essential respect different from the Murphys, McCooeys, McCabes and McCalls of the cartoons of a generation ago? Do you think that the McCooey of today, who is the last living link between these two dynasties, is not the same old McCooey of the early 1900's? Let the younger voters ask the older voters this question. There can be no doubt of the answer."

Each of Moses' statements had its own sharp bite. "The Great Statesman McKee," he said in one, "is a synthetic character which never actually existed on sea or land, puffed up by the press . . . and now in the process of deflation. There's a large amount of unfairness to the individual in this process, but in the end it arrives at the truth."

And each statement contained praise for La Guardia couched in a prose that had to it a ring that sounded all the clearer above the dull clangor that is political strife in New York. "No one has ever questioned your independence," Moses told the Little Flower in a public statement. "You have no strings on you. You are not engaged in an obscure struggle for the control of a rotten political machine. You are free to work for New York City. Go to it."

"Moses' statements were no small help," Paul Windels recalls. "His support of La Guardia did more than any other single thing, I think, to give the impression that La Guardia did mean to give the city an independent administration." Moses' statements were front-paged, while others' were buried next to the bra and girdle ads. And their value was further enhanced because newspapers gave their readers the impression that he was speaking not only for himself but also for someone whose name was even more potent a political force in the city than his. Al Smith had not been able to bring himself to back either of his party's candidates. All during the election campaign the press pressed the Happy Warrior for a statement. When it was not forthcoming, reporters drew conclusions from Moses' statements. Pointing out that Moses was "one of Alfred E. Smith's closest friends," the *World-Telegram* said that his endorsement of La Guardia "has invoked a powerful, if silent, reinforcement to help La Guardia win." Moses, who was not speaking for Smith, tried to dispel the impression that he was. But La Guardia's advisers did all they could to foster that impression. When Moses was introduced to the crowd at a climactic Fusion rally at Madison Square Garden, the band played "The Sidewalks of New York." Before beginning his prepared speech, Moses said: "I have no desire to appear on this platform under false colors, much as I appreciate the implications involved in the instructions to the band. I do not come here as an emissary of my distinguished friend and former chief, who remains, in the affections of the people, the first citizen of this city." But at the end of Moses' speech, the band struck up the same tune.

Within a week after the votes were counted, La Guardia invited Moses to join his administration. Whether he had promised, through Ingersoll, to do so in order to obtain Moses' support—the making of such a deal might explain Moses' sudden decision to break his silence on the campaign—is unknown; but there were plenty of other explanations for the invitation.

Some of the explanations were rooted in personality. Fiorello La Guardia had an affection for his city. His wife recalls that when, after twelve years of trying, he finally became its mayor, "it was like he owned the United States. Nobody should do anything to it." With his romantic temperament, he wanted to beautify the city. He had a grand—if vague—conception of a metropolis whose citizens would pass their daily rounds in surroundings that uplifted the spirit. "Too often," he once said, "life in New York is merely a squalid succession of days; whereas in fact it can be a great, living adventure." And he thought of such beautification primarily in terms of public works. "He liked physical accomplishment," recalls Paul J. Kern, La Guardia's first law secretary at City Hall. "He liked to get things built for people; on Sundays, we used to drive around the city trying to think of things that should be built in the city."

La Guardia admired men who built. Lawyers, to lawyer La Guardia, were bad. He often remarked that a lawyer was like a prostitute: a man hired a prostitute to use her body and he hired a lawyer to use his brains and knowledge of the law. And, he would say, he didn't know but that the man who hired the prostitute got the better of the bargain. Engineers were good. "Engineers fascinated him," recalls Joseph D. McGoldrick, his Comptroller. "Lawyers were always getting in his way, telling him things he couldn't do. La Guardia didn't like people who told him what he couldn't do. But engineers could do things. They got things built for people." Says Kern: "He stood like a child in front of the simplest engineering feat." La Guardia's favorite evening watering hole was the Engineers Club at 32 West Fortieth Street, where he was an honorary member. Reuben Lazarus, who often watched him sitting in the club bar listening raptly to the club's non-honorary members talk about their achievements, says, "Engineers were his *gods*." And, although he hardly knew Moses, Moses' achievements especially awed him. He told Windels that he had, more than once, driven over the Long Island parkways "for inspiration."

Other explanations for La Guardia's invitation to Moses were rooted in politics.

La Guardia had won with only 40 percent of the vote; he was still a Republican in a Democratic town, a Republican who had been enabled to win largely because Democratic votes had been split between O'Brien and McKee. He could not count on another split, or on another Fusion-boosting Seabury investigation, in 1937; he knew that his political future depended, as one of his biographers has written, "on his giving New Yorkers the spectacularly good government he [had] promised them."

Specifically, La Guardia had promised to staff the city's government with nonpolitical, nonpartisan experts. To the public, Robert Moses epitomized the nonpolitical, nonpartisan expert. His appointment would prove that La Guardia was keeping his promise. And his immense popularity could not help rubbing off on the mayor who brought his talents to the city.

There were other reasons rooted in politics.

La Guardia feared Al Smith. He well knew that if Smith had been running against him, he would not be mayor, and he knew what would happen if Smith decided to run in 1937, or even to lend his immense prestige to some other candidate who would unify the overwhelming Democratic majority in the city. Making Smith's favorite a part of his administration would do much to keep the Happy Warrior happy—and off the warpath.

La Guardia knew that if he was to produce good government in a bankrupt city, the first requirement was money. "You know," he told a reporter earnestly, "I am in the position of an artist or a sculptor. . . . I can see New York as it should be and as it can be. . . . But now I am like the man who has a conception that he wishes to carve or to paint, who has the model before him, but hasn't a chisel or a brush." The only source of money to purchase a chisel or a brush of the size La Guardia had in mind was the federal government. Its President was not of La Guardia's party. He knew that Moses had enjoyed great success on Long Island in obtaining federal funds—and he did not know of the hatred between Roosevelt and Moses.

Furthermore, La Guardia knew that a key reason for Moses' success in obtaining federal money was that Moses had plans for huge public works ready at the moment the money became available. To get plans, you needed first a large staff of engineers trained in building such works. He knew that the city departments did not have such staffs and he knew that Moses did. Moses needed La Guardia if he was to realize his great park and parkway plan for New York City—but La Guardia also needed Moses.

Moses knew it. To La Guardia's invitation, he replied with conditions. "I told the Mayor," he was to recall, "that I was not interested in taking the city job unless I had unified power over all the city parks and, even then, only as part of the unified control of the whole metropolitan system of parks and parkway development."

"Unified" was the operative adjective. There were five separate, independent park departments in New York City in 1933, one for each borough, each with its own borough park commissioner. If the five commissionerships were abolished and all five departments were consolidated into one, Moses said, he would be willing to be its commissioner—if the commissioner's authority was extended to include not only parks but parkways *and* if he was allowed to keep his state jobs. And since the key to a unified parkway program was the Triborough Bridge, he must also insist on control of the independent agency charged with the construction of that bridge, the Triborough Bridge Authority. He had a plan to finance construction of a "Marine Parkway Bridge" to the Rockaways: the plan was to create another authority to accept the necessary $10,000,000 federal contribution. He wanted control of that authority, too. La Guardia agreed. The Mayor-elect could hardly restrain himself from blurting out the news before the arrangement was finalized. Seated at a dinner party next to Iphigene Ochs Sulzberger, who was bemoaning the state of the city's parks, he told her, "Don't worry. I'm appointing the best man in the United States as park commissioner!" In fact, when Moses suggested that he himself draft the bill consolidating the park departments and setting forth the powers he would possess as New York City Park Commissioner, La Guardia had seen no reason not to agree to that, too. It was the first bill submitted to the Legislature by the La Guardia administration. Neither man considered the Triborough appointment particularly significant; both still considered the Authority nothing more than a toll-collecting agency that would finish building a single bridge and then go out of business as soon as its cost was paid off. But they anticipated opposition in the Legislature, whose permission would be required for a state official to take a city job. The upstate Republicans who were the Legislature's leaders felt that Moses already possessed too much power, and would resist giving him more. Democratic legislators from the city would be opposed to his appointment because of the contracts and patronage it would cost the party. And there were philosophical as well as personal and political objections. Concentrating in a single individual authority over both state and city parks and over most major road-building projects in the New York metropolitan region would give too much power to that individual, no matter who he was, some legislators said. Furthermore, in his state job, that individual would be the Governor's appointee; in his city job, the Mayor's. If the city's elected officials were to veto one of the projects he proposed to them in his capacity as a city official, he would be able to use his influence with the Governor to bring the state's influence to bear on the city officials to force the city into compliance with his will. The situation could also work in reverse. This line of reasoning could be carried on indefinitely, said one state senator: "No man is big enough to serve two masters." This was one reason why there was a law against the simultaneous holding of state and city jobs. And, some legislators attempted to remind the public, there were other, equally persuasive reasons. "Dual officeholding," they said, weakened the constitutional provision that the city should be a separate, independent entity within the state.* There would be plenty of legislative opposition just to his proposed appointment as Park Commissioner; there was no sense in letting the Legislature know that La Guardia actually intended to appoint Moses to *three* city jobs, but permission was necessary for him to take each of them. The best bill drafter in Albany told La Guardia not to worry. Buried deep within the bill he drafted—it was Section 607, to be precise—allowing him to accept the park commissionership was the apparently innocuous phrase "an unsalaried state officer shall not be ineligible to hold any other unsalaried office filled by appointment of the Mayor." The camouflage worked. Unsalaried offices generally referred to meaningless honorary positions; not one legislator appears to have realized that it could also refer to an authority commissionership.

The opposition that boiled down from Albany anyway was blasted by the press—and by reformers who normally would have been the first to oppose a violation of the separation of state and city that they had always viewed as vital, and to oppose giving one man such power. They were not opposed now because the man was the one official they were confident would not abuse that power. And the reformers had considerable influence over the Republican legislators from the city. Soon Herbert Brownell, Jr., already, at twenty-nine, not only a state assemblyman but also a partner in a prestigious Wall Street legal firm, was speaking on behalf of the "Moses bill." Another GOP legislator from the city, Jay E. Rice, was arguing against

* The courts had always emphatically upheld the law against dual officeholding. One memorable case, in fact, had enlivened the political vocabulary with a new phrase. In 1924, Murray Hulbert, the president of the city's Board of Aldermen, had innocently accepted membership on the Finger Lake State Park Commission, believing that because the park post was unsalaried it did not fall within the law's purview. But the City Comptroller, disagreeing, stripped Hulbert of his more important, salary-paying city job and the courts upheld the action—a circumstance which thereafter led Albany wags to refer to any suggestion that a city official be given a state job as an attempt to give the man "the finger."

Brownell when, as the *Herald Tribune* noted, "Mr. Rice was called on the telephone from New York and returned to the Assembly Chamber to withdraw his objection." The string-pulling Long Island barons who had come to see Moses as a friend pulled their strings. La Guardia gave assurances that the city was not surrendering any of its independence. "The city retains complete control through its properly constituted authorities over every cent it spends and everything it does." Governor Lehman, admiring Moses, sent the Legislature an emergency message to rush the bill through. Both the Mayor and the Governor—the two most powerful men in the state—were on Moses' side. So was the most popular; Al Smith publicly supported the appointment. While the press was still playing up the pledges by Tammany legislators to fight the bill to the finish, Moses knew that the fight was already finished—and that he had won. When a reporter called him for comment after one heated debate, Moses said, "There's nothing to get excited about." On January 19, 1934, Lehman signed the "Moses bill." That same day Moses joined a line of minor city officials waiting outside La Guardia's office. When his turn came, he entered the office and was sworn in as New York's first citywide Park Commissioner.

Tammany's three Triborough commissioners held six-year terms, but the financial manipulations of two of them had been so blatant that La Guardia's investigators quickly uncovered them; one resigned and the other was dismissed. On February 4, at 11:57 A.M., a certificate of appointment as Secretary and Chief Executive Officer of the Triborough Bridge Authority, signed by the Mayor, was brought to the city clerk's office by one of the Mayor's secretaries and filed there. The name on the certificate was "Robert Moses." With the appointment to the second vacancy of George V. (the Fifth) McLaughlin, the bluff, red-faced Brooklyn banker and friend of Al Smith's who had long been Moses' friend and ally, control of the Authority was his. As soon as it was, a new bill was introduced, providing for the creation of a Marine Parkway Authority. Its powers were in general the same as those of the Triborough Bridge Authority. But there was one innovation. Those powers would not be exercised by a three-man board; the Authority would have only a "sole member." And that member, the man in whom all the powers of the Authority were lodged, would be "the Park Commissioner of New York City." On April 9, with scarcely any debate, the bill was passed by the Legislature and signed by the Governor.

There were now seven separate governmental agencies concerned with parks and major roads in the New York metropolitan area. They were the Long Island State Park Commission, the New York State Council of Parks, the Jones Beach State Park Authority, the Bethpage State Park Authority, the New York City Park Department, the Triborough Bridge Authority and the Marine Parkway Authority. Robert Moses was in charge of all of them.

The New Deal's attempts to combat the Depression had apparently already given New York an opportunity to refurbish existing city parks. Harry

Hopkins' federal Civil Works Administration, set up in November 1933, had 68,000 men working on park clean-up projects in the city by Christmas. But Moses and his top Long Island park administrators, driving around to the parks to see what those men were doing, found that the city had given them neither adequate tools, materials, supervision nor instructions. Crews were laying asphalt roads and paths without adequate foundations—and even as they laid one section, another, completed a week earlier, was already heaving and cracking behind them from frost action. Six thousand men, assigned to "move ash dumps" in Riverside Park, were standing on the banks of the Hudson pecking at frozen cinders; two thousand were standing on truck beds on a little reef off Staten Island "building up" the reef by dumping out sand—which was washed away, at a cost of five dollars per cubic yard, almost as fast as they could dump it. Fifty-four hundred more were assigned to Brooklyn's Marine Park, purchased during the Mitchel administration and allowed to remain undeveloped for twenty years. Moses' engineers sneaked into the cupola of an old mansion in the park so that they could watch the work unobserved—and found that there was nothing to watch. Spread out over expanses of sand wastes and marshlands, in a scene more reminiscent of a French bivouac during the Retreat from Moscow than a park reclamation project, all but a handful of the fifty-four hundred sat huddled around small fires built against the freezing wind whipping out of Jamaica Bay. Some were passing around wine bottles held in brown paper bags. Others were throwing dice. Most had no tools—and Moses' men understood why when they saw men chopping up shovels and using their handles as firewood. Adding a poignant detail to the scene were a few men who had kept their tools and who obviously wanted to work; they spent hours "raking" the frozen ground or building little fences out of stone they found in the area, "just so," as one of them was later to recall, "I could feel I was doing something to earn my money."

Moses himself spent a lot of time at Orchard Beach, a very low, very narrow sand bar that linked together the eastern edges of Hunters Island and Rodman Neck, two of the little wooded pieces of land at the eastern fringe of Pelham Bay Park that were washed by the water of Long Island Sound. Here, in New York's northeastern corner, so far from any built-up areas in 1934 that visitors could hardly believe they were still within the borders of America's largest city, was located New York's most ambitious park project. When Moses arrived, $346,750 had been spent on bathhouses, a breakwater and a retaining wall running behind the sand bar and designed to turn the bar into a bathing beach convenient to the bungalows of the six hundred families, Bronx Democratic stalwarts all, to whom most of Hunters Island and Rodman Neck had been leased. The engineer who designed the bathhouses, which were constructed of granite paving stones and had cost $84,000 apiece, had apparently been inspired by the Black Hole of Calcutta; the only ventilation in the thirty-foot-high buildings was provided by a few narrow slits near the ceilings. The breakwater had been run out into the Sound through the very center of the beach, thereby splitting it in two and forcing anyone wanting to get from one half to the other to climb over the top—which wasn't easy, since the breakwater designer had neglected to include steps. But the location of the retaining wall made reservations about this splitting of the beach irrelevant. The engineer who designed the wall had apparently seen the sand bar only at low tide; he had placed the wall so close to the water that, for most of the day, the waves lapped right up against it—and there was no longer any beach left to be split.

Moses dispatched teams of engineers to "inventory" New York City's parks—their acreage (incredibly no one knew their exact size), the buildings, paths, roadways, statues and equipment in them, the condition of these items and the type and amount of labor and materials that would be required to renovate them. He filed this information in a loose-leaf notebook kept atop his desk. By the time he was sworn in as Park Commissioner, the notebook was more than a foot thick, and he had a list of 1,800 urgent renovation projects on which 80,000 men could immediately be put to work.

But renovation was only a small part of Moses' plan. Day after day during the bitterly cold November and early December of 1933, while the great city lay inert in the grip of its long malaise, Robert Moses was being chauffeured around it in the big Packard, Hazel Tappan beside him with a stenographer's note pad open on her lap. Twenty years before, as a young staffer at the Bureau of Municipal Research, Robert Moses had wandered around New York City "burning up with ideas, just burning up with them." Now Moses was not young—one of the days he spent in the big Packard was his forty-fifth birthday—but he was still burning. "Sometimes it seemed to me that his voice never stopped," Miss Tappan recalls. "Things just kept pouring out of him. I remember once we were downtown someplace and he wanted to see some underground garage—for sanitation trucks or something—under a city building there to see if it would interfere with some plans he had for putting a park on the street near it and we started to go down this spiral ramp and it was getting darker and darker and he was still dictating. And finally it was almost pitch-black and he was still dictating. To this day I can see it getting darker and darker and that voice going on and on. Until finally I had to say, 'Mr. M! *Mr. M!* Wait a minute! I can't see!' "

By late December, the outline of his ideas for large-scale park construction projects was ready, and now, crowded into the Packard with him and Miss Tappan were his Long Island engineers. They came in relays. One crew would drive with him to certain parks—describing these trips, one engineer echoed Frances Perkins' words of two decades before, "Everything he saw made him think of some way it could be better"—and then that crew would go back to Babylon and translate his ideas into general engineering plans while another would head out with him to other parks.

Relays were needed to keep up with him. "His orders just poured out," recalls the engineer. "Bam! Bam! Bam! So fast that we used to all try to take them down at once so that when we got out to Babylon we could put them together and maybe get one complete list of everything he wanted. You'd start at dawn—hell, sometimes we'd start *before* dawn; I remember driving around Manhattan when everybody was still sleeping except the milkmen, maybe, and the cops on the beats. I remember once a cop really jumping when that big black car filled with men came around a corner in front of him—and by late afternoon, I can tell you, your head would be just absolutely spinning. But he'd still be firing things at you." Didn't they break for lunch? "You didn't break for lunch when you were out driving around with Robert Moses."

Soon the engineers' concepts of his ideas were being presented for his approval.

With few exceptions—City Hall is perhaps the most notable—the public works of New York City were hack work designed by hacks. But the men driving around with Robert Moses were not hacks. They included the unknown young architects, landscape architects and engineers—the Herbert Magoons and Earle Andrewses—responsible for Jones Beach and the other highly acclaimed Long Island parks. And they included Major Gilmore D. Clarke and Aymar Embury II. Clarke, designer of the Bronx River Parkway and other outstanding examples of highway beautification, was in 1934 the most famous landscape architect in the United States; he had been in the process of retiring from public work to accept lucrative private assignments. Embury, an architect, had designed Princeton University's classic Class of 1915 Dormitory and many of Long Island's most beautiful estates—parks in themselves. In 1934, he had waiting for him "more private business commissions than he could handle in a decade." Moses persuaded Clarke and Embury to come to work on New York's parks.

As had been the case with the famous architects who had gathered around him on the barren sand bar called Jones Beach a decade earlier, however, some of the men with him in the big Packard in 1934 had difficulty grasping the extent of his vision. When the plans came in for Riverside Park, where, twenty years before, he had dreamed of a great highway along the water, a highway that would cover the ugly tracks and cleanse the West Side of Manhattan of the smoke and stench from the trains that ran along it, they left the tracks uncovered. The engineers told him that to cover them would add millions to the cost of the park development—for which at the moment there was almost no money at all in sight, not to mention the additional millions that would be needed to build the Henry Hudson Bridge across the Harlem River Ship Canal and a parkway linking the bridge with the Saw Mill River Parkway. Moses told them to worry only about the plans; he would worry about getting the money for them.

Exasperated with their plans for Orchard Beach, he loaded the architects into the big Packard and drove out onto barren, snow-covered Hunters Island.

Standing under winter-stripped trees on a little hill that rose out of the marshes that fringed the islet, he looked across at Rodman Neck, four hundred yards away, at the sand bar, covered now with a thin scum of ice, that held them tenuously together, at the Tammany-built breakwater and Hole of Calcutta bathhouses, and at the six hundred private bungalows.

The sand bar would never be a decent bathing beach as long as those monstrosities were there, he said. He wanted them torn down; he didn't care how much they had cost—*tear them down!* And tear down those goddamned bungalows—yes, all six hundred of them. He had been spending a lot of time wandering around up here in the afternoons, he said, and he had decided

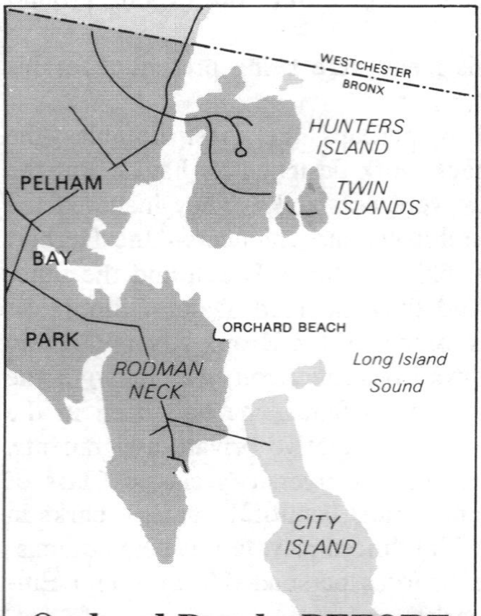

Orchard Beach: BEFORE

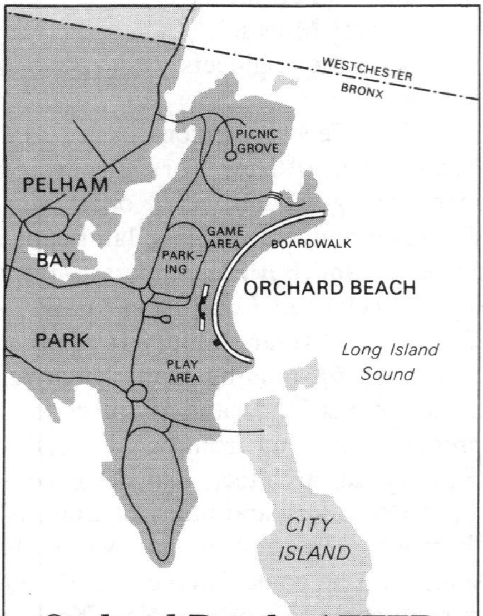

Orchard Beach: AFTER

that the beach should consist of more than just the sand bar. If it extended all the way around the eastern shore of both Hunters Island and Rodman Neck, it would be almost a mile long and almost crescent-shaped. In fact, if it extended over to the Twin Islands—he pointed to two islets to the northeast separated from Hunters Island by two narrow strips of water—the length could be a full mile and the shape of the crescent perfect. He wanted the beach extended to the Twin Islands, he said; the strips of water couldn't be very deep; fill them in. And he wanted the sand on the beach to be gleaming white ocean sand like the kind at Jones Beach and the Rockaway beaches, not their present coarse, pebble-filled gray Long Island Sound sand. The sand could be dredged off the Rockaway beaches and then brought here by barge, up the East River to the Sound. Behind the beach, paralleling its mile-long crescent, he wanted a bathhouse—designed with the same imagination, the same attention to detail, as the bathhouses at Jones Beach, he said; he didn't want it looking like the typical public bathhouse. But that didn't mean it should look like the Jones Beach bathhouses, he said; if his men looked around him, they would see that the setting here was very different from that at Jones Beach. The setting there was the long, low sweep of sand and sea; here it was hills and trees. The Jones Beach bathhouse had been long and low, its lines horizontal; the lines here should be more vertical—perhaps they should start thinking about columns, maybe even a colonnade. He would leave it to them, but he didn't want any of them forgetting that the function of a bathhouse wasn't to impress or overawe; it was to help people have a good time—he wanted it light, airy and gay. And for God's sake, he said, use this kind of imagination on the city's other parks—all the city's parks.

20. *One Year*

On January 19, 1934, Governor Lehman signed the legislation allowing Robert Moses to become the first commissioner of a citywide Park Department. At 5 P.M. that same day, Mayor La Guardia swore Moses into office at City Hall. As soon as his right hand came down from the oath, Moses turned to the assembled reporters and told them he had an announcement to make: the five borough park commissioners and the five borough park superintendents, along with the commissioners' personal secretaries and stenographers, and assorted deputy commissioners and other top-level park aides, were fired—"as of now."

The next morning at 9 A.M., a fleet of chauffeured black Packards roared up to the curb on Fifth Avenue in front of the Arsenal. Out of them stepped Moses and a squad of his top Long Island aides. These men would be running the Park Department from now on, Moses announced. Leading them up the steps of the Arsenal, which he announced would henceforth be departmental headquarters, he assigned them offices.

Moses had given these men their orders. They were to weed out—immediately—those headquarters employees who would not or could not work at the pace he demanded. The weeding out would be accomplished by making all employees work at that pace—immediately.

Unlike the commissioners and their personal secretaries, most headquarters employees were protected by civil service, but that didn't help them much. Men who lived in the Bronx were told that henceforth they would be working in Staten Island; men who lived in Staten Island were assigned to the Bronx. Or they were given tasks so disagreeable they couldn't stomach them. Women were treated no better. One ancient biddy, accustomed to spending her days at the Arsenal knitting in a rocking chair, refused to admit she was over retirement age and gracefully accept a pension. When a search failed to produce a birth certificate to disprove her story, she was ordered to work overtime—all night. Every time she tried to rest, she was ordered to keep working. She retired at 2 A.M.

Down at his State Parks Council office at 80 Centre Street—Moses was never to have an office at the Arsenal and was to visit the building infrequently during his twenty-six years as Park Commissioner because he didn't want to be accessible to departmental employees—Moses was confronting the CWA. Its officials were worried themselves about the demoralization of the 68,000 relief workers in the parks. Moses told them that the first requirement for getting those men working on worthwhile projects was to provide them with plans. Blueprints in volume were needed, he said, and they were needed immediately. He must be allowed to hire the best architects and engineers available and he must be allowed to hire them fast. The CWA must forget about its policy of keeping expenditures for plans small to keep as much money as possible for salaries for men in the field. The agency must forget its policy that only unemployed men could be hired so that Moses could hire a good architect even if he was working as a ditch digger or was being kept on by his firm at partial salary. And the agency must drop its rule that no worker could be paid more than thirty dollars per week. The CWA refused: rules were rules, it said. I quit, Moses said. La Guardia hastily intervened. After seven days of haggling, the CWA surrendered. Moses was given permission to hire 600 architects and engineers without regard to present job status, and to pay them up to eighty dollars a week. So that he could hire them as fast as possible, he was even given an emergency allocation to summon them to interviews not by letter but by telegram.

The CWA capitulated on the morning of January 27. By noon, 1,300 telegrams were being delivered to carefully selected architects and engineers all over New York State, telling each of them that if he was interested in a job, he should report to the Arsenal the next day.

No profession had been hit harder than architecture and engineering. Engineers were particularly reluctant to accept relief. "I simply had to murder my pride," one said. "We'd lived on bread and water for three weeks before I could make myself do it." But *The Nation* estimated that fully half of all engineers were out of work—and six out of seven architects.

These men had been hiding out in public libraries to avoid meeting anyone they knew, or tramping the streets carrying their customary attaché cases although those cases contained only a sandwich. Although the Park Department interviews weren't supposed to begin on January 28 until 2 P.M., on that day, with the temperature below freezing, when dawn broke over the city, it disclosed a line of shivering men outside the Arsenal. The line began at the front door. It wound down the steps, out to Fifth Avenue at Sixty-fourth Street, and along the avenue to Seventy-second Street.

The interviewing went on all day; some of the men who had been waiting on line before dawn didn't get into the Arsenal until late afternoon. But for 600 of them the wait was worth it.

"When you got inside, nobody asked you how much money you had in the bank or what was the maiden name of your great-grandmother," one architect recalls. "All they asked you was: 'What are your qualifications?' " Those whose qualifications satisfied Moses' men were hired on the spot, shown to the Arsenal's garage, in which drafting tables had been set up, handed assignments and told to get to work. In the evening, some started to go home. Those whose assignments didn't have to be finished for a few days were allowed to do so; several hundred whose plans were needed faster were told flatly, "If you go home tonight, don't come back tomorrow." Without exception, these men stayed, catching naps on cots Moses had had set up in the Arsenal's corridors.

Out in the parks, the ragtag ranks of the CWA workers were being shaped up.

Moses had found the men to do the shaping. Out of fear of losing them permanently to rivals, idle construction contractors were struggling to keep on salary their "field superintendents," the foremen or "ramrods" whose special gift for whipping tough Irish laborers into line made them an almost irreplaceable asset. Pointing out that the CWA was not a rival and would probably go out of existence when business improved, Moses persuaded contractors throughout New York, New Jersey, Pennsylvania and New England to give him their best ramrods, "the toughest you've got." And when the new men arrived, 300 in the first batch, 450 more within two months, his instructions to them were equally explicit. CWA workers, he was to say later, "were not accustomed to work under people who drove them. I see to it that my men do drive them."

Arriving at Marine Park on January 31, new superintendent Percy H. Kenah ordered the men away from their bonfires, and when some moved too slowly for him, fired sixty-six on the spot. The men refused to leave. They moved threateningly toward him—and then they noticed that patrol cars crammed with policemen had quietly driven up behind them. On the same day, with patrol cars backing them up, new superintendents fired hundreds of other workers in other parks.

If this method disposed of malingerers and malcontents, it nonetheless proved difficult to whip the relief workers who remained into an efficient work force. Most wanted to work at the pace demanded but were unable to do so. The suits, overcoats and fedoras many wore while wielding shovels were testimony not only to their inability to afford warmer work clothes but also to their lack of experience in performing hard physical labor outdoors. Even in mild weather, they would have had difficulty. In winter, they suffered bitterly from exposure. Since their pay was $13.44 per week, many were still scrimping on their own food so that their children could have more. "I remember guys just keeling over on the job," one laborer recalls, "and you always knew that it was just that they had come to work without anything to eat." And they were scrimping in other ways, too. A worker at Dyker Beach Park at the southern edge of Brooklyn, who had caught a reporter's eye because "the side of his neck is swollen and his breath is from a sick throat," told the reporter that he lived in Manhattan. Shivering in a thin overcoat, he said that to get to work "I walk over four hours. I set the alarm clock for half past two and start walking quarter of four." The reporter asked him why he didn't take a trolley, "Carfare is twenty cents a day," he replied.

Some of the new superintendents quietly handed quarters to laborers whose inability to keep up was due to hunger or frostbite; others fired them. But none of the ramrods stopped driving. If they did, they knew, they would be fired themselves. They were, after all, working for a boss who, when questioned about a new wave of firing that almost touched off riots in several parks, said, "The government and the taxpayers have a right to demand an adequate return in good work, faithfully performed, for the money that is being spent. . . . We inherited men who were working without plan and without supervision. The plans have now been made, the supervision is being supplied, *and we expect the men to work*."

The winter of 1934 was the first of five of the most severe in New York's history. The temperature dropped below zero on five different days—on one day it hit fourteen below—and a steady succession of heavy storms dumped a total of fifty-two inches of snow on the city. The mean temperature for the entire month of February was 11.5 degrees. But all through that winter, the residents of the tall apartment houses rimming Central Park could look down into the park and see, in the snow, thousands of men swinging pickaxes and shovels, climbing ladders set against trees, swarming over scaffolding erected around older structures and building new ones. From behind the park's granite-block walls came the pounding of pneumatic drills, the rumble of concrete mixers, the dull roar of steam shovels and the sharp rapping of hammers.

And to the consternation of those apartment-house residents, this clangor did not stop at five o'clock. At dusk, thousands of men filed into Central Park to replace those who had been working during the day, and when the watchers in the apartment houses retired for the night—for nights that they complained were made restless by the noise—they could take a last look out their windows and see the pickaxes still swinging in the harsh glare of hundreds of high-powered carbide lamps. When they awoke in the morning, the pickaxes were still swinging—and they realized that a third shift had filed into the park during the night. The work was going on twenty-four hours a day. And from behind the granite-block walls of Prospect Park, the high wooden fence left around Bryant Park from the George Washington Bi-Centennial Celebration, and a score of others erected that winter by Moses around other parks, came the same clangor—on the same schedule. Late in the afternoon of February 22, heavy snow began to fall. It continued falling all through the 23rd, dumping a total of eighteen inches on the city. But during those days, the rebuilding of New York's parks never stopped.

Sometimes, now, the laborers were even performing the construction phenomenon known as "working ahead of plans." By February, there were more than 800 architects and engineers in the Arsenal and they had become accustomed to working fourteen-hour days. But often, after they had finished a blueprint and it had been approved by Clarke, Embury, Andrews or some other supervisor and they rushed it themselves out to the project site, they would find that the work crews had already begun, or finished, digging ditches for pipes and foundations, or other preliminary work, and they would have to sit down on the spot and draw new plans to fit in with the work that had already been completed. The team of fifteen architects working at the Arsenal under Embury's personal direction to design a new Central Park Zoo—Moses didn't like the name "Menagerie"—were, Latham recalls, "working [while] looking out the window to see what had already been done." These men, Embury wrote in amazement, "had never seen each other before beginning work." They had to work "with little equipment, crowded together two or three to the table, and moved about from one place to another every few days." They completed the plans for the entire new zoo in sixteen days.

Embury and Clarke themselves, giants of their professions though they were, were caught up in the excitement. Once, going out to lunch together, they stopped at Bryant Park to review the reconstruction work, which was already well under way, and decided they didn't like the plan, already approved by themselves and Moses, on which hundreds of men were already working. Over lunch, they began to discuss new ideas and sketched them out on their tablecloth. When they finished their meal, they asked the headwaiter for permission to take the tablecloth with them, drove straight to 80 Centre Street to show it to Moses and, when he approved, gave it to another team of draftsmen to translate into blueprints.

By March, the economy was beginning to recover and optimism was rising—along with demands from the nation's press, heavily anti-New Deal, that the government begin phasing out the spending of "taxpayers' money" on such "socialistic" practices as work relief. Moses had been led to expect an extension of the act creating CWA, but at the last moment Congress changed its mind, and the agency went out of existence on March 31, on forty-eight hours' notice. With only a limited amount of funds from the Federal Emergency Relief Administration available for park work, half of Moses' men were abruptly dismissed. But he kept the remaining half working.

The harshness of the winter persisted into April, and every weekend was either cold or rainy. But on Saturday, May 1, 1934, the weather turned balmy, and, as they do on the first warm Saturday of every spring, New Yorkers poured into their parks.

Seventeen hundred of the eighteen hundred renovation projects had been completed.

Every structure in every park in the city had been repainted. Every tennis court had been resurfaced. Every lawn had been reseeded. Eight antiquated golf courses had been reshaped, eleven miles of bridle paths rebuilt, thirty-eight miles of walks repaved, 145 comfort stations renovated, 284 statues refurbished, 678 drinking fountains repaired, 7,000 wastepaper baskets replaced, 22,500 benches reslatted, 7,000 dead trees removed, 11,000 new ones planted in their place and 62,000 others pruned, eighty-six miles of fencing, most of it unnecessary, torn down and nineteen miles of new fencing installed in its place. Every playground in the city had been resurfaced, not with cinders but with a new type of asphalt that Moses' engineers assured him would prevent skinned knees, and every playground had been re-equipped with jungle gyms, slides and sandboxes for children and benches for their mothers. And around each playground had been planted trees for shade.

"Generations of New Yorkers," as the *Times* put it, "have grown up in the firm belief that park benches are green by law of nature, like the grass itself." But now, as New Yorkers strolled through their parks, they saw that the benches had been painted a cool *café au lait.* Generations of New Yorkers had believed that the six miles of granite walls around Central Park were a grimy blackish gray. Now they saw that sand blasting had restored them to their original color, a handsome dark cream. Rare was the New Yorker who could remember when the Columbus Circle monument to the men who died in the explosion of the U.S.S. *Maine* in Havana Harbor had not been dingy, or when the boy standing in the prow of the monument's bow had possessed a wreath, or, for that matter, hands to hold it with. As soon as Moses had taken office, he had surrounded the monument with scaffolding and concealed it with drop cloths. Now the scaffolding and drop cloths were removed and the boy had his hands back, and a wreath was in them—and the entire huge monument behind him had been scrubbed clean and white. And a thousand plots in the parks, plots which as long as New Yorkers could remember had contained nothing but dirt and weeds, were gay with spring-blooming flowers.

By midsummer, new construction projects in the parks were being completed. Ten new golf courses, six new golf houses, 240 new tennis courts, three new tennis houses and 51 new baseball diamonds were to be opened to the public before Labor Day. The Prospect Park Zoo was completely rebuilt and a new zoo erected at Barrett Park on Staten Island. Complete reconstruction jobs were done on St. James, Crotona and Macombs Dam parks in the Bronx; Owl's Head, McCarren and Fort Greene parks in Brooklyn; Crocheron, Chisholm and Kissena parks in Queens; and Mount Morris, Manhattan Square and Carl Schurz parks in Manhattan.

On a sunny Saturday, the fence around Bryant Park came down and thousands of spectators in a reviewing stand set up behind the Lowell Fountain saw that the weed-filled lot had been transformed into a magnificent formal garden. Two hundred large plane trees, grown in Moses' Long Island Park Commission nurseries, trucked to the city and then lifted over the fence and lowered into prepared holes by giant cranes, had been planted along its edges, and their broad leaves shaded graceful benches and long flower beds bordered by low, neat hedges. The four acres they surrounded were four acres of lush and neatly trimmed grass, set off by long, low stone balustrades and flower-bordered flagstone walks, that looked all the greener against the grayness of the masses of concrete stores and office buildings around it. As a newly formed sixty-six-piece Park Department band, outfitted in white duck trousers, forest-green jackets with white belts and white caps trimmed with green and gold braid, blew a fanfare, the great-granddaughter of William Cullen Bryant, the poet and journalist for whom the park had been named, and the sister of Mrs. Josephine S. Lowell, in whose memory the fountain had been built, walked together from the reviewing stand to the fountain, escorted by twenty youthful pages and Park Department attendants in uniform, and flung handfuls of petals into it. At that signal, water gushed from the fountain's five dolphin spouts for the first time in a decade, and a speaker said that Robert Moses had outdone his biblical namesake because while the Moses of the Israelites had smote a rock in the desert and brought forth water, Moses of New York had "smote the city's parks" and brought forth not only water but trees, grass and flowers.

In Central Park, Moses' men restored Olmsted's long-defaced buildings, replanted the Shakespeare garden, placing next to every flower a quotation from the Bard in which it was mentioned, and exterminated herds of rats; 230,000 dead ones were counted in a single week at the zoo site alone. While seven hundred men were working night and day to build a new zoo, another thousand were transforming the dried-up reservoir bed that had been called "Hoover Valley"—Moses had torn down the shanty town there—into a verdant, thirty-acre "Great Lawn," were laying flagstone walks around it and planting along them hundreds of Japanese cherry trees. Then, having satisfied those who objected to use of the reservoir bed entirely for active play, Moses constructed a playground and wading pool in the northeast corner of the bed, outside the lawn's borders, for small children and a game field in the northwest corner for older children. On the North Meadow he built handball courts, wading pools and thirteen baseball diamonds. He deported the deformed sheep and turned the old sheepfold into a "Tavern-on-the-Green," an old English inn-in-a-park complete with doormen wearing riding boots and hunting coats and top hats and cigarette girls in court costumes complete with bustles—and with the added touch of an outdoor flagstone terrace on which couples could dance among tables shaded by gaily colored umbrellas to the music of a twelve-piece orchestra costumed in forest green.

And Moses was not merely beautifying the city's parks. He was doing what generations of reformers had despaired of doing: he was creating new ones—in the areas that needed them.

In his first flush of enthusiasm following La Guardia's offer of the park commissionership, Moses had believed that by forcing landlords to dump real estate on the market at a fraction of its former value, the Depression had given the city at last a chance to acquire and tear down slum tenements and use the space thus gained for play space for the slum children who so badly needed it. But then La Guardia disclosed to him the extent of the city's financial crisis and told him that, because of the Depression, even fractions were beyond the city's ability to pay.

"I remember one time he came back from talking to La Guardia and he told us this," said Bill Latham. "And I remember that he said then—I don't remember the words, really, but the idea was: 'All right, then, goddammit, we'll get land *without* money.' "

Moses instructed Latham to set his surveyors to making an "inventory" of every piece of publicly owned land in New York City, every tract or parcel owned by any city department, and to determine, not by asking departmental officials but by personal inspection, whether every piece of that land was actually being used. Within a month, he had learned that on the Lower East Side there were nine long-vacant strips of land along Houston Street that had been acquired by the Board of Transportation to store equipment during subway construction but that had been lying idle ever since the construction was completed, ten elementary schools so old that they had been abandoned by the Board of Education for years and five vacant lots that were owned by the Park Department itself but that the Park Department had somehow not been aware it owned. Alongside the Williamsburg Bridge piers were pieces of land that had been acquired to store equipment used in the construction of the bridge and had been lying idle during the thirty-one years since the construction had been completed. On the other side of the East River, among other tenements, were more piers —and more pieces of land. In the Red Hook tenement slums, Brooklyn's version of Manhattan's "Hell's Kitchen," thirty-eight acres of land had been purchased for a public housing project, but no such project had yet begun. Among the flimsy shacks on the Gravesend Bay side of Coney Island, eight solid blocks of vacant waterfront property was owned by the Dock Department, but the Dock Department had no interest in it. And throughout all the city's slums were scores of small triangular "gores," where streets angled together or bits of land had been left over from street-widening condemnation proceedings, that were now just unnoticed pieces of dirt or concrete and that were too small to be used for play but that were, if planted with grass and a tree or two, large enough to add a touch of green to the drabness around them. Moses asked La Guardia to direct the city Sinking Fund Commission, the body which, under existing charter provisions, held the actual title to all city-owned land, to turn this land over to the Park Department. Often, the other departments involved objected to such incursions into their jealously guarded empires—the Tenement House Commission hastily began drawing up plans for the Red Hook housing project to prove that construction on it was imminent—and sometimes, as in the Red Hook case, La Guardia sided with them. But generally the new mayor backed Moses. Within four months after taking office, the new Park Commissioner had obtained, in slum areas in which there had been no significant park or playground development for at least half a century, no fewer than sixty-nine separate small park and playground sites.

And one that wasn't small. North from the Manhattan Bridge, through the very heart of the Lower East Side, through an area in which tenements were jammed solidly into every block, stretched a row of seven blocks that were completely empty. The "Chrystie-Forsyth Development," as it was known from the names of the streets which bordered it, was another monument to Tammany Hall and to one of its judges, Joseph Force Crater. Forty years later, Judge Crater's mysterious disappearance would still be unexplained, but contemporary speculation linked it with the judge's unexplained generosity to the owners of the disease-breeding tenements which had occupied those seven blocks before the city took them over in 1929. Jimmy Walker had announced with great fanfare that the city would raze the tenements and resell the land at cost to private developers who would erect on it a "model" housing development. But the astonishingly high condemnation awards Crater bestowed on the owners made the cost so high that the private builders who had previously expressed interest now expressed only dismay, and while the razing had been accomplished, the replacement had not. For more than four years, with the lost taxes and interest on the award (the Depression, of course, prevented the city from paying it) costing the city almost half a million dollars per year, the tract had lain between the red brick walls that lined it solidly on either side as flat and featureless as an urban desert. Moses proposed that it be made an oasis of grass, trees, baseball fields, basketball and tennis courts, wading pools and playgrounds. La Guardia, trumpeting "Page Crater!" when reporters asked why the housing development would not be built, agreed.*

While studying the state government for the Reconstruction Commission in 1919, Moses had learned about "unappropriated state lands." A century before, to help tide the country over a time of financial uneasiness, the federal government had made loans to the states, which in turn loaned the money to individuals who pledged farms or other, smaller pieces of property in cities, as security. Some loans had not been repaid, and the states thereupon foreclosed. In most instances, the New York State Legislature later passed bills allowing the municipalities in which the land was located to "appropriate" it. But not, Moses had learned, in *every* instance. Some of the properties involved had seemed too small to bother about in an era in which property was measured in acres rather than feet, and as time passed, these pieces of land had simply been forgotten and had remained "unappropriated." Now Moses sent men to Albany to look up such pieces—and they found several in areas of Brooklyn that were now slums. The city could not afford to buy them, so—hastily, since the Legislature was shortly due to adjourn for the year—he drafted, and got passed, bills turning this land over to New York City.

One day—Sid Shapiro can recall the moment—Moses suddenly remembered that in 1922 the State Division of Canals had filled in swampland near the Gowanus Canal in Red Hook to provide a foundation for a grain elevator it was building there. And he seemed to recall, he said, that there had been some land left over. An investigation proved that he was right: there had, in fact, been eleven acres left over. He had a bill passed in Albany allowing the state to give the land to the city for recreational purposes.

On another occasion, chatting with aides, Moses suddenly asked, "Wasn't there some kind of fund set up about fifteen years ago for a war memorial that was never built?"

There was indeed. In 1918, a public subscription had been held to finance construction of a million-dollar World War Memorial Arch. But the subscription raised only $210,000 and the drive's sponsors, already squabbling over which borough the arch should be located in, were unable to agree on details of a smaller memorial and in 1922 turned the money over to the City Chamberlain's office for safekeeping until the dispute was resolved. It never was, and during the intervening twelve years the sponsoring committee stopped meeting, and the existence of the money, which the Chamberlain had deposited in banks, was all but forgotten—and when Adolf Berle, appointed Chamberlain by La Guardia, looked for it at Moses'

* This park is now known as "Sara Delano Roosevelt Park."

request, he found that accumulating interest had swelled it to $338,395.

The people who had contributed the money had intended it to be used for a war memorial. But Moses persuaded Berle that the definition of "war memorial" could be extended to mean "War Memorial Playgrounds" and he persuaded the surviving members of the sponsoring committee not to oppose the use of the money for this purpose, a persuasion made easier by Moses' agreement that each playground would contain a bronze plaque honoring the memory of World War veterans—and that there would be at least one playground in each borough. With the money, Moses purchased in congested areas of the city eight pieces of property big enough for playgrounds.

He seemed to see opportunities everywhere. While being chauffeured around Harlem, he noticed two tennis courts belonging to a Roman Catholic church on 138th Street. Telling his chauffeur to stop, he jumped out, ran into the church, found the pastor and asked if the courts were much used. When the pastor said they were not, Moses asked him to give them to the city for a playground, and when the pastor told him that such a gift could be arranged only through Cardinal Hayes's office, Moses sent a representative to see a representative of the Cardinal, and the gift was arranged. Noticing a two-acre vacant lot on Eleventh Avenue between Fifty-ninth and Sixtieth streets, he learned it was owned by the Consolidated Gas Company, which had no "present plans" for using it, and persuaded the company to give him a temporary permit to put a playground on the site. In "Middle Queens," the dreary belt of cemeteries, small single-family homes and shabby little factories sprawling northeast from the oily waters of Newtown Creek, there was still one large vacant tract, 127 acres formerly owned by murdered gambler Arnold Rothstein. Learning that Rothstein's estate owed the city $334,000 in back taxes, Moses asked Surrogate James Delehanty if the city could buy the property if it forgave the back taxes and paid $68,000, the difference between the taxes and the assessed valuation. Delehanty agreed, but La Guardia was not able to find even $68,000 that the city could spare. Moses recalled that there was usually several hundred thousand dollars kept in a special "emergency account" of one of the more obscure Sinking Funds. City attorneys informed him that legal restrictions prohibited the expenditure of any of this money except on genuine emergencies. Moses informed *them* that if they restudied the law, they would find there was one exception—money could be removed from the fund temporarily for "first instance" appropriations, appropriations to be repaid out of the next city budget, for a single specific purpose: the purchase of undeveloped real estate. But La Guardia, while agreeing that the acquisition of 127 acres for $68,000 was an unprecedented bargain, was afraid to obligate the city even for that amount. So Moses returned to Surrogate Delehanty and worked out another arrangement under which the city "bought" 74 of the 127 acres for $334,000 but the estate paid the $334,000 back to the city to clear the tax deficiency on all 127 acres, leaving the estate with 53 acres free and clear—and the city with a 74-acre "Juniper Valley" park which it had acquired without a cent of cash outlay.

Moses' charm was as powerful a weapon as his mind. Turning it on John D. Rockefeller, Jr., Moses persuaded the billionaire to donate several other pieces of land to the city. He persuaded his old benefactor August Heckscher to donate a playground in Central Park. When he discovered a well-to-do family with philanthropic leanings but insufficient resources to buy and equip a playground completely, he brought it together with another family in similar circumstances—as he did to give the city the Dreier-Offerman Playground in Bensonhurst, Brooklyn. Learning that a small charitable foundation was unable to meet mortgage payments on a piece of property in Queens and was planning to let it go to the bank by default, Moses appeared before its board of trustees, several of whom were directors of the bank, and talked to them so movingly about the need of slum children for recreation that they agreed to use the foundation's few remaining assets to pay off the small balance remaining on the mortgage—and default instead on the taxes, so that the city could take it over rather than the bank.

And as soon as Moses had his hands on the title to these pieces of land, he filled them with workmen. By July, the eight War Memorial Playgrounds had been finished, by Labor Day, there were fifty-two others, including the Chrystie-Forsyth Street complex, which was really a park but which was dubbed "the finest playground in the United States"—and a city which in its entire history had managed to build 119 playgrounds had seen its stock of that item increased by 50 percent in a single year.

The city cheered. Its thirteen daily newspapers, however divergent their philosophy, united in heaping wreaths of adjectives on his head. The new Park Commissioner was "dynamic" and "brilliant" in the ultra-conservative *Sun*, "able" and "enterprising" in the then ultra-liberal *World-Telegram*, "tireless," "fearless" and "incorruptible" in the sometimes conservative, sometimes liberal Hearst *Evening Journal*.

Headline writers, using topical catch phrases, talked of Moses' NEW DEAL FOR PARKS and the AMAZING ACCOMPLISHMENTS OF MOSES' FIRST 100 DAYS. Editorial writers were more poetic. "Robert Moses has made an urban desert bloom," said an editorial in the *World-Telegram*. The *Herald Tribune*, formally recanting the heresies of which it admitted it had been guilty during his Long Island controversy, dubbed him the "Hercules of the Parks." And the *Times* said:

> . . . Jan. 19 of this year was a red letter day in the history of New York. . . . The time, the place, and the man met in Mayor LA GUARDIA'S appointment of ROBERT MOSES as Park Commissioner on that date. Measured in park progress and development on the scale to which this city had been accustomed, it seems years ago. . . .
>
> The achievements, tangible as well as intangible of the new Commissioner in his first few months of office . . . seem little short of miraculous. It is almost as if MR. MOSES has rubbed a lamp, or murmured some incantation over an old jar, and actually made the jini leap out to do his bidding.

Reporters fought for interviews with him. And when they got them—for he gave them freely—the interviews were very friendly. Murray Davis of the *World-Telegram,* telling readers that "for ten years he has worked long hours, without pay, to give New Yorkers inexpensive outdoor pleasures," added:

> To the suggestion that he was independently wealthy and giving hard work and time to an unremunerative job, he smiled.
>
> ". . . You can't teach an old dog new tricks and I'm 45 now. Ever since I was a kid I was interested in government. My fancy led me into parks and playgrounds and I have nourished those fancies as a hobby, avocation; take your pick.
>
> "The fact remains that I enjoy this work more than any other, so why not stay with it? I have had only two public offices that paid salaries. Now I have my third. It pays—? I don't know. What do commissioners get? $13,000? I don't know. I'm satisfied to make just a bare living if I can realize all my plans for these things I enjoy. I'm interested in cutting down the overhead and getting results, not in pay."

During 1934, Moses was in the New York papers even more than J. Edgar Hoover, who spent the year compiling a highly publicized elite hierarchy of "Public Enemies," and then shooting down Number One on the list, John Dillinger, in a blaze of gunfire. Moses was in the New York papers almost as much as La Guardia. The *Times* editorial on Moses, for example, was only one of 29 praising him in that single newspaper that year. And the *Times* also carried 346 separate articles on his activities, an average of almost one a day.* There were days, in fact, on which there were five separate stories in the *Times.* So many were carried on the "split page," the first page of the second section, devoted in the early 1930's largely to municipal affairs, that there were whole weeks in which this prominent page of the nation's most respected newspaper read like a Park Department press release. There were Sundays on which six separate newspapers were carrying long, uncritically laudatory interviews with Moses or reviews of his accomplishments. His picture stared out from their pages a hundred times during that year.

Each park opening brought forth a new volley of praise. After one, the *Herald Tribune*, under a headline proclaiming: THE PEOPLE OWN THE PARKS, called the event "just another of those triumphs whereby Mr. Moses has almost convinced the public that it really owns the parks. After the long night of Tammany it is an idea difficult to grasp."

The cheers of the press were echoed by the public. While the parks were blossoming with flowers, editorial pages were blossoming with letters from the public praising the man who had planted them. And it was not unusual at park and playground opening ceremonies for children, prodded by their parents, to break into the cheer "Two, four, six, eight—who do we appreciate? Mr. Moses! MR. MOSES!! *MR. MOSES!!!*"

* The *Times* index lists them not only under his name but under "New York City—Parks, Department of," under the names of the individual parks and under other listings given in the index.

* * *

The cheers rose to a crescendo when the Central Park Zoo reopened on December 3, 1934.

Moses had a personal reason for being interested in the zoo. Nineteen thirty-four had been a sad year for Al Smith. The public humiliation to which Jimmy Walker had subjected him at the Inner Circle dinner was only one indication of the fact that there was no longer any place for the old leader in the organization he had led and loved. Only sixty years old, as vigorous as ever, Smith wanted desperately to play a role in the federal government's efforts to end the human misery caused by the Depression. No man was better qualified; Roosevelt himself had told Frances Perkins, "Practically all the things we've done in the federal government are like things Al Smith did as Governor of New York." Roosevelt had asked Smith to campaign for him against Hoover, and Smith had done so. And when Roosevelt had won, Smith had told acquaintances flatly that a man did not feud with the President of his country; he gave him loyalty. He only hoped, he said, that Roosevelt would allow him to work for him. But Roosevelt, another young man of whom Smith had been fond and whom he had helped up the political ladder, refused even to consider him for any federal post. And if Smith considered this the ultimate humiliation, he learned during 1934 that it was not. Worse was to come. When John J. Raskob and the other businessmen who controlled the Empire State Building Corporation had offered him its presidency, they had told him the post was honorary, but, with the skyscraper completed, the Depression made it so difficult to obtain tenants that the corporation was on the verge of bankruptcy, and they told him he would have to do something to earn his $50,000 a year: he would have to go to Washington and beg Roosevelt to throw some government leases his way. For months, Smith refused, but he was finally persuaded that loyalty to his friends required him to help them. Roosevelt responded generously to his entreaty—federal agencies were moved out of offices as far away as Philadelphia to fill up the New York skyscraper—but now in the late afternoons, when Moses dropped by to see him, he would often find the man who had been called the Happy Warrior sitting staring out the windows of his apartment with new lines of bitterness and disillusionment hardening on his face.

Moses knew how much the old Governor loved animals and he knew he missed the little zoo he had maintained behind the Executive Mansion in Albany. The former Governor and Katie now lived at 820 Fifth Avenue, almost directly across from the Menagerie, and Smith spent a lot of time strolling among the cages, feeding and talking to the animals. Saddened by the unsanitary conditions in which they had to live and the lack of care for their physical ailments, Smith was horrified when he learned that in case of fire the animals might be shot. When Moses was appointed Park Commissioner, Smith told him he would regard it as a special favor if the Menagerie were improved.

Moses gave the job top priority. When materials and equipment ran low—because of the CWA's reluctance to spend money on them, they were always running low—what was available was diverted there from other projects. The best ramrods were put on the job to drive the thousand men working around the clock in the fenced-off area behind the Arsenal. Most of the animals had been moved out, but not all, and the lions, shunted from one animal house to another as the buildings were torn down and kept awake by the glow of the carbide flares and the pound of the pneumatic drills, roared through the night, while a reporter who visited the site early one morning found the Menagerie's old polar bear pacing "restlessly up and down in bewilderment, pausing occasionally to peer out at the grimy, torch-lit laborers." The residents of Fifth Avenue apartment buildings near the site roared, too, but Moses refused even to listen to their complaints. Often, in the evenings, he would suddenly materialize on the scene, joking with the field superintendents and with the men, encouraging them, telling them how important their work was, urging them on. All summer and fall, he spurred the job with a special urgency. And when it was finished, on December 2, he turned the reopening into a surprise party for Al Smith.

It was quite a party. Some observers said New York had never seen anything like it. To emphasize that he was trying to make the zoo not so much a great animal museum like its counterpart in the Bronx but a place of delight for young children, Moses had already dubbed it a "picture-book zoo," and when the twelve hundred invited guests filed into the stands set up in front of the Arsenal for the opening ceremonies—twenty-five thousand other persons lined Fifth Avenue waiting to be admitted—they found that in front of the zoo entrance had been erected a six-foot-high wooden replica of an open picture book, with painted green elephants charging across its bright-yellow pages. Flanking the speakers' platform were two huge boxes wrapped in striped and polka-dotted paper and adorned with satin bows like a child's present. As the ceremonies began, four olive-clad trumpeters blew a flourish, the wrapping paper was pulled away—and inside one box was a cage containing a lion, inside the other a cage with a gorilla. Public Welfare Commissioner William Hodson, called to the microphone to give a speech, startled the audience by breaking instead into several choruses, delivered in a rather wheezy tenor, of "Oh, I went to the animal fair." Thousands of balloons were released at intervals to fill the air with color until they were wafted northward by the prevailing breeze. Uniformed, flag-bearing high-school bands and elementary-school fife-and-drum corps came marching, one after the other, up Fifth Avenue. And clattering around the corner of the Arsenal came a team of white ponies drawing a tiny, gaily colored barouche in which sat a little girl holding a large gold key with which La Guardia could "unlock" a door in the middle of the picture book and thus officially open the new zoo.

But before La Guardia got the key, there was something for Smith. Moses had given the former Governor no hint that he would even participate in the ceremonies, simply telling him that there would be a seat for him on the reviewing stand. But when the old warrior walked out the front door of his apartment house to make his way to the stand, he found three hundred schoolchildren from the Fourth Ward lined up in front of the door, cheering and waving balloons, waiting to escort him across Fifth Avenue. He found that his seat was in the place of honor next to La Guardia. (Moses, who had been supposed to sit on his other side, was absent; during the past week he had refused to take a day off despite a severe case of influenza, and doctors summoned over his protests by a worried Mary just two hours before the ceremony began found him in a state of complete collapse and ordered him to bed.) Hardly had Smith sat down when he realized that he was being summoned to the microphone himself, and Earle Andrews, substituting for Moses, pinned to his lapel a large, elaborately engraved medal with a lion's head on its face and announced that he was now, and permanently, "Honorary Night Superintendent of the Central Park Zoo." As Andrews finished speaking, a horse-drawn wagon, reminiscent of those Smith had chased through the Fourth Ward in his youth, rolled around the corner of the Arsenal, and it was jammed with boys—from the Fourth Ward—singing, "East Side, West Side." The horses pulled up in front of him and eleven-year-old Eddie McKeon jumped out and presented him with a large Christmas turkey as the whole reviewing stand stood and joined in his old campaign song.

The old Governor's eyes were tearing, from the cold December wind, no doubt, and it took some time for him to clear them, and even after he did he spent a rather long time chewing on his cigar, which was already in shreds, before he began to speak, but when he did, he knew exactly what he wanted to say. "When Mr. Moses was appointed Park Commissioner, I used all the influence I had with him to get him to work on a new zoo," he said. "And now look at him! In less than eight months, we've got a zoo that's one of the finest of its kind in the world." Smith began then to recite the whole list of Moses' achievements, stopping only when he noticed the children on line trying to peer over the park wall at the cages. Cutting himself short, he said with a smile, "I bid you welcome to this new zoo as night superintendent, and I hope you have a good time," and sat down.

Later that week, when he was well enough to tell him himself, Moses informed Smith that the night superintendency carried with it certain privileges. He gave Smith a master key which unlocked the animal houses and told the Governor that the zoo caretakers had been instructed that he was to be allowed to enter them whenever he wanted, day or night. And until the end of his life, Smith would delight in this privilege. The doormen at No. 820 would become accustomed to seeing him walk out the front door in the evenings and across Fifth Avenue under the street lights, a somewhat paunchy figure with a big brown derby set firmly on his head and a big cigar jutting out from his face, and disappear down the steps of the darkened zoo, not to reappear for hours. The former Governor and presidential candidate would walk through the animal houses, switching on the lights as he entered each one, to the surprise of its occupants, and talk softly to them. He would have in his pocket an apple for Rosie, the huge hippo. And if one of the zoo's less dangerous animals was sick or injured, Smith would enter its cage and stand for a while stroking its head and commiserating with it. When he had dinner guests, he would take them along and, since they were usually Tammany stalwarts unhappy at what La Guardia was doing to the Tammany Tiger, they delighted in a little show he would put on with the zoo's biggest and fiercest tiger, who could be counted upon to respond angrily if anyone growled at him. When Smith and his guests approached, the tiger would be sitting silently staring at them through the bars. Smith would walk up to the cage, thrust his head toward the bars and, in his deepest and harshest voice, roar at the tiger, "La Guardia!" The tiger would snarl, bare its teeth and leap at the bars, growling in what Smith's daughter describes as "obvious disapproval."

While there were cheers aplenty for Smith at the zoo opening, however, there were plenty left over for Moses.

The invited guests on the reviewing stand had been startled by the transformation in the Arsenal. The stucco had been sand-blasted off its walls, revealing handsome dark-red bricks. The cupolas had been torn off its turrets, revealing battlements complete with archer's slits. The newel posts of the banisters on the stairs leading up to its front entrance were now upturned Colonial cannon muzzles, and the banisters themselves were supported by wrought-iron imitations of Colonial flintlock rifles, painted white. Atop the gleaming white doorway, whose lintel had been crenelated to mirror the battlements on the roof above, an eagle glared from between two carved mounds of cannon balls, and on the jambs had been carved crossed swords and Indian spears. The large lamps on either side of the door had been enclosed in wrought-iron replicas of tasseled drums like those carried by Revolutionary War drummer boys. And above the doorway three large flags fluttered colorfully from flagpoles. All in all, the once shabby wreck looked quite like a little fort, a gay little fort that when seen in miniature from the higher floors of Fifth Avenue apartment houses seemed almost to have been set in the park by mistake and really to belong six blocks down the avenue in the windows of F. A. O. Schwarz.

And when La Guardia "unlocked" the door in the bright-yellow picture book, after asking the Honorary Night Superintendent's permission, the crowd followed the two men through the door and through a short corridor erected for the occasion, its walls covered with picture-book inscriptions such as "A is for Ape," "B is for Buffalo." Emerging on the side of the Arsenal, they found there was nothing left of the old Menagerie at all. Where they had been accustomed to see ramshackle wooden animal houses, they found, to their astonishment, neat red brick buildings decorated with murals and carved animal friezes, connected by graceful arcades that framed park vistas beyond—and framing a sea-lion pool set in a handsomely landscaped quadrangle.

Moses had wanted to use distinctive materials as he had used Barbizon brick and Ohio sandstone at Jones Beach, but the CWA's refusal to purchase any but the cheapest materials had forced him to settle for concrete, plain red bricks, and some cheap limestone, and to forgo dozens of imaginative little touches he had planned.

But the eye of the visitor still found plenty to delight it. The sea-lion house in the pool was constructed of unadorned concrete, but it was constructed so that visitors could watch the sea lions even while they were inside. The paths to the pool divided a sunken landscaped quadrangle into four separate, neatly trimmed lawns. Each was surrounded by low hedges. In the center of each was a wonderfully gnarled and twisted Japanese ginkgo tree. The steps leading down to the quadrangle were flanked by fierce-visaged stone eagles big enough to glower eyeball to eyeball at many of the children walking past them. And in its four corners were huge Victorian flying cages from which glowered live eagles.

On the far side of the quadrangle, at the animal-house level, past the cavorting sea lions, the stone eagles, the lawns, the shrubbery and ginkgo trees, the eye was startled by a large lioness proudly holding up for inspection a peacock she had killed, while her two cubs sniffed at the beautiful tail dangling limply to the ground—a bronze statue that had stood in some seldom visited corner of the park for seventy years until Moses rescued it. And behind the statue was a long, low terrace on which little tables topped with gay parasols sat in the shade of a bright, vertically striped awning eighty feet long—an outdoor dining terrace on which diners could sit and be entertained by the sea lions and by the crowds being entertained by the sea lions. And as the eye followed the vertical stripes of the awning upward, it abruptly found itself being stared back at by lions, tigers, elephants and hippopotami gathered under waving palm trees—for the cafeteria's eighty-foot-long clerestory had been covered with a droll animal mural.

Throughout, the zoo was proof piled on proof that Moses had been able, to some extent at least, to make imagination take the place of money.

The CWA had insisted that the animal houses be constructed primarily of common red brick and concrete, but Embury, an architect accustomed to working with the costliest of materials, nevertheless succeeded, under Moses' prodding, in making them attractive. Their proportions were exceptionally well balanced, their lines exceptionally clean. Some of the brick had been used to place charming ornamental chimneys on their roofs. Some more had been used for designs that broke the monotony of the concrete clerestories. Connecting the animal houses with arcades gave the whole scene unity.

And the zoo buildings were adorned with little touches that, as at Jones Beach, scaled down the architecture "to the size of a good time." Tiny, delicate cast-iron birds perched atop the lamps that flanked the doors of the animal houses. Slender rods topped with little white balls held big white globes that cast light over the walk in front of the cafeteria terrace. The lamps hanging in rows in the animal houses were glazed balls, but around each ball was a slanted copper ring that made the fixtures look like a long row of Saturns whirling in the sky.

No one had to wonder what was in each building. Around the top of each wall was a frieze, carved in low relief in limestone panels, depicting its occupants in marvelously lifelike poses; among the figures over the monkey houses, for example, were a monkey chasing butterflies and a gorilla chewing a twig with a wonderfully contemplative expression upon his face. And the weathervanes atop each building were comic depictions of one of the building's inhabitants, done by the unknown designers who had caused architects from all over the world to exclaim at the weathervanes at Jones Beach; the one over the bird house, for example, showing a spindly-legged heron jutting its long bill under water in search of food, was a miniature masterpiece of angularity silhouetted against the sky.

The purpose of a park, Moses had been telling his designers for years, wasn't to overawe or impress; it was to encourage the having of a good time. Wheeling through the park were movable refreshment carts. But these weren't ordinary refreshment carts. They were adorned with painted animals and garlands of flowers in colors that were intentionally gaudy—replicas of gay Sicilian *carretinas*. Their operators were dressed in costumes that were extravagantly Sicilian. Even their wares were special; in addition to the standard peanuts, sodas and candy bars, each carried, prominently displayed on top, whirling silver-foil windmills, strings of brightly colored balloons, flags, banners, braided whips—and stacks of animal picture and coloring books. And to blow up balloons, the zoo was equipped with the latest in balloon-blowing devices—the "Kelly's Rocket," whose windy woosh delighted children. And the decision to build the zoo around a sea-lion pool was the crowning touch; the boisterous barking and slippery antics of these traditional circus clowns, the raucous enthusiasm with which they played tag under water, dove for the fish thrown to them by keepers and playfully slithered big-bellied and long-necked around their concrete home, insured that the central panorama would be one to delight any child—and any adult who had any child left in him. On a summer day, when the animals were all outside, and the central quadrangle in which the sea lions frolicked was lined with black-and-white-striped zebras, tan lions, furry brown monkeys and red-rumped baboons, the central panorama was, as near as any man could make it, given the CWA's stinginess, exactly what Robert Moses had envisioned—a scene out of a child's picture book.

And the zoo was viewed as the triumph it was. Some zoophiles, ignoring the violet-ray baths Moses had installed so that monkeys would get their necessary quota of sun in winter, the specially designed scratching posts set up for the lions and the replacement of Tammany's rifle-toting keepers with trained animal experts and doctors, criticized the concrete floors of the cages, which they said would give the animals tender feet. But architects, as quoted in *Fortune,* found the architecture "gay and amusing and occasionally pointedly absurd." *Architectural Forum* called the view from the cafeteria terrace "the finest eating view in the city." The press cheered, too. And the public gave its own vote of confidence. The crowds that streamed into the zoo behind La Guardia and the Honorary Night Superintendent on opening day numbered 32,000, a figure that Moses found so unbelievable that he ordered the counters he had installed at the entrance double-checked. But the next Sunday, after word of mouth about the new zoo had had a week to spread, attendance was 57,000. By 1935, on an average Sunday, more than 100,000 visitors would come to the picture book in the park.

* * *

And the Triborough Bridge was finally being built.

Here was a project to kindle the imagination.

In size, its proportions were heroic. For all Moses' previous construction feats, it dwarfed any other single enterprise he had undertaken. Its approach ramps would be so huge that houses—not only single-family homes but sizable apartment buildings—would have to be demolished by the hundreds to give them footing. Its anchorages, the masses of concrete in which its cables would be embedded, would be as big as any pyramid built by an Egyptian Pharaoh, its roadways wider than the widest roadways built by the Caesars of Rome. To construct those anchorages and to pave those roadways (just the roadways of the bridge proper itself, not the approach roads) would require enough concrete to pave a four-lane highway from New York to Philadelphia, enough to reopen Depression-shuttered cement factories from Maine to the Mississippi. To make the girders on which that concrete would be laid, Depression-banked furnaces would have to be fired up at no fewer than fifty separate Pennsylvania steel mills. To provide enough lumber for the forms into which that concrete would be poured, an entire forest would have to crash on the Pacific Coast on the opposite side of the American continent.

Triborough was really not a bridge at all, but four bridges which, together with 13,500 feet of broad viaducts, would link together three boroughs and two islands.

One of those bridges, the span over the Harlem River that would connect Manhattan with Randall's Island, would be the largest vertical-lift bridge in the world. Its two steel towers would have to be big enough to support the 2,200-ton steel deck—longer than a football field and wide enough to accommodate a six-lane highway, two sidewalks and a broad median safety island—that would hang between them. The towers would have to be big enough to contain drum hoists capable of raising that deck, together with its highway, sidewalks and median islands, eighty feet, keeping it perfectly horizontal all the time, to permit the passage of large ships.

And the Harlem River span would be the largest vertical-lift bridge in the world only on sufferance from another of Triborough's four bridges, the eight-lane, triple-span, steel-truss affair over the Bronx Kills that would connect Randall's Island with the Bronx. Because the Bronx Kills was not navigable, the Navy had ruled that its span could be a fixed structure—but only if it were built so that its central span could be converted into a lift bridge if the Kills was ever made navigable. And the Bronx Kills span would be so large that if it *were* ever converted into a lift bridge, it would be a lift bridge half again as large as its Harlem River counterpart.

And both the Harlem River and the Bronx Kills spans looked small beside the half-mile-long suspension bridge, one of the largest bridges of *that* type in the world, that would arc 135 feet in the air to carry Triborough's roadway across the turbulent rip tides of Hell Gate, the narrow, twisting, rock-lined passage between Ward's Island and Astoria in Queens. The steel towers of *that* bridge would each be higher than a football field standing on end, and it was *that* bridge's anchorages, in whose concrete would be embedded cables made up of enough wire to circle the globe twice around, that were as big as pyramids.

The last of the four bridges—a causeway connecting Randall's and Ward's islands—would have stood alone as an engineering feat of no mean magnitude, but so huge was Triborough that the causeway was a mere incident in its construction, as was the "flying junction" on Randall's Island, the largest batch of traffic-sorting spaghetti ever concocted, a cloverleaf as big as a railroad switchyard and so ingeniously designed that although twenty-two lanes of traffic converge on, and radiate from, its long lines of toll booths, winding around one another on three decks, no one of those lanes meets or crosses another at grade and every driver using any one of them, no matter what his destination or point of origin, must stop at one, but only one, toll booth. Triborough was not a bridge so much as a traffic machine, the largest ever built. The amount of human energy that would be expended in its construction gives some idea of its immensity: more than five thousand men would be working at the site, and these men would only be putting into place the materials furnished by the labor of many times five thousand men; before the Triborough Bridge was completed, its construction would have generated more than 31,000,000 man-hours of work in 134 cities in twenty states. And the size of the bridge is also shown by the amount of money involved. With $5,400,000 already contributed by the city and $44,200,000 promised by the PWA, the amount promised for its construction was almost equal to the combined cost of all the projects Robert Moses had built on Long Island during the previous ten years.

And size was the least of it.

From the air—and Moses spent hours over New York City as a passenger in chartered small planes in 1934 studying the city's contours—one could hardly fail to appreciate more significant implications of the Triborough project. The built-up streets of Manhattan, the Bronx and Queens rushed together at the bridge site but paused there, held apart by the tangle of water surrounding Randall's and Ward's islands. A procession of piers, erected by the old bankrupt Triborough Authority, was scattered at odd intervals across those islands as if to show how easy it would be to bring those massed streets together by building the Triborough Bridge. But until the bridge was built, the streets would remain separated, their inhabitants condemned to countless wasted hours of needless travel. The man who built the Triborough Bridge would be a man who conferred a great boon on the greatest city in the New World. He would be the man who tied that city together. In fact, since each of the three boroughs was as large as a city in its own right, the man who built the Triborough Bridge could be said to be performing a feat equal to tying together three cities. And he would also, of course, be the man who, patching together the rent torn in the earth millennia before by the glaciers rumbling down from Hudson Bay, reunited Long Island with the mainland of the United States.

Other implications of the project were as dramatic as its size and setting.

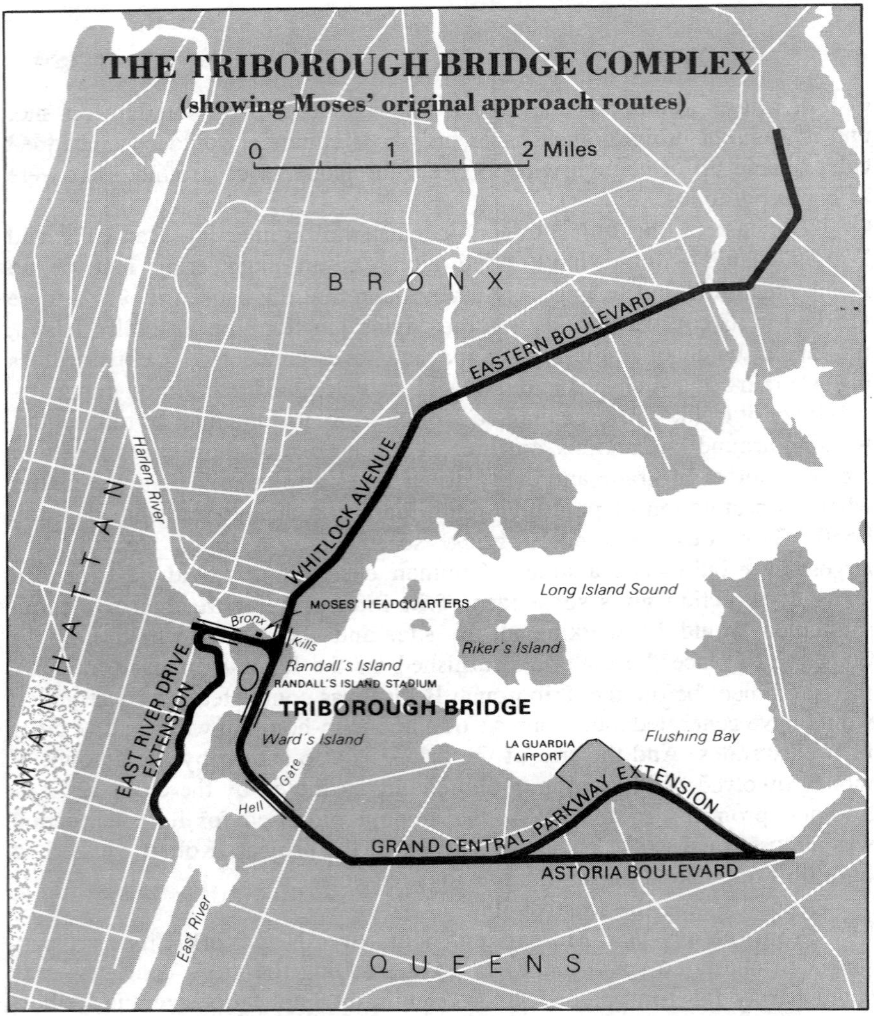

It would slash at a stroke the immense Gordian knot of the East River traffic problem by creating the first direct link between the Bronx and Queens. For Robert Moses, of course, this implication had special significance. He had built his parkways to make accessible Long Island's "healthy air," its "salty shore and breeze and brine," but millions of residents of northern Manhattan, the Bronx and Westchester—and New Jersey—still had no way of reaching those parkways, no way of reaching Long Island, except by traveling into midtown Manhattan, over the East River bridges and along the congested Queens boulevards. The construction of the Triborough Bridge would enable residents of northern Manhattan to reach Queens simply by traveling crosstown and then over the bridge; residents of the Bronx, Westchester, and New Jersey could reach Long Island without ever entering midtown Manhattan at all.

Furthermore, Moses felt confident that, out of the $50,000,000 allocated for the bridge, enough would be left over to link it with the Grand Central Parkway, whose western terminus was stalled at Northern Boulevard because the Legislature would not and the city could not finance its construction any further into the city. Therefore, the Triborough project—and, perhaps, only the Triborough project—could provide the funds to finish the parkway and thereby enable motorists, once they reached the Triborough Bridge, to drive all the way to Jones Beach or the other Long Island state parks on modern parkways on which they would not be delayed by a single traffic light or intersection.

Because the Legislature would not and the city could not extend his Westchester parkways into the city, the Triborough project was the only hope of doing that, also. Moses felt sure that money could be found in the Triborough allocations to link up the bridge at least with the Hutchinson River Parkway. And once *that* link was constructed, the Long Island parkways would be linked with a Westchester parkway. Build Triborough, he felt, and the Long Island parks would at a stroke be made easily accessible from the entire New York metropolitan area.

Randall's and Ward's islands provided large stacks of additional fuel for Moses' imagination.

Throughout the city's history, those islands had been used only as repositories for its refuse, inanimate and human. The site of garbage dumps, potter's fields and almshouses during the eighteenth and nineteenth centuries, in 1934 they held—in addition to a municipal sewage-disposal plant—the City Hospital for the Feeble-Minded and Tubercular, the grim, barracks-like, Civil War-vintage "House of Refuge" of the Society for the Reformation of Juvenile Delinquents, the Manhattan State Hospital for the Insane, complete with black-barred windows, and a military hospital. The rest of the islands' four hundred acres—and an uninhabited fifty-acre sand bar to the east named "Sunken Meadow" that was identified on maps as part of Randall's Island but was actually a separate body of land set apart by a hundred yards of water—was empty and barren marshland.

But Moses didn't care about the condition of the vacant land on the islands. What was important to him was that the land was there—and that there was plenty of it.

Obtaining land anywhere near the center of New York City was extremely difficult. When you talked about new parks in center city, you were talking about tooth-and-claw battles for a vacant lot that might with luck be big enough for half a basketball court. If you found a vacant lot that measured as much as a third of an acre, it was a bonanza. And here, at the city's very heart, were 450 empty acres. Join these islands to the city and you wouldn't have to talk about halves of basketball courts any longer. You could talk about football fields and soccer fields and baseball diamonds. And you could talk about them in the dozens. There could be boat basins and marinas, picnic grounds, tree-shaded esplanades overlooking the river and lined with benches on which people could sit and watch boats passing close by. Join islands to city and you would be creating a moated oasis at the city's core. The building of the bridge would, of course, accomplish the joining automatically. And Moses felt certain that, out of fifty million dollars, he could find enough left over to transform the islands into magnificent parks—especially if the institutional buildings were torn down, as he felt they should be so that they would not interfere with the beauty of the setting. The potentialities of the project, not only for transportation, but for recreation, were awesome.

But the arrangements entered into by the Triborough Bridge Authority during its days of domination by Tammany Hall threatened to make the project as nearly worthless as it was possible for a $50,000,000 enterprise to be.

Before he had taken over the project himself, Moses had told aides that the Authority's refusal to make any semblance of provision for approach roads in Queens and the Bronx was the most glaring example of poor planning that he had ever seen. But now, studying the project more closely, he realized that he had spoken too hastily. What the Authority had done in Queens and the Bronx, he saw, was as nothing compared to what the Authority had done in Manhattan.

The Queens terminus of the Triborough Bridge was directly across the East River from 100th Street in Manhattan. Therefore, the Manhattan terminus of the bridge should have been placed at 100th Street. It certainly should not have been placed any further uptown; the bulk of the bridge traffic—85 percent by one estimate—would be coming from, and going to, destinations south of 100th Street. Placing the Manhattan terminus at 125th Street condemned most motorists traveling between that borough and Queens to drive twenty-five totally unnecessary blocks north and then, once on the bridge, twenty-five totally unnecessary blocks south—to thus add two and a half totally unnecessary miles to their every journey over the bridge. And the complete lack of provision for any approach road from downtown would make the Manhattan portion of the totally unnecessary journey tortuous.

Then there were the plans for the bridge structure itself.

The plans called for a two-deck, sixteen-lane affair. Such a bridge would have a capacity of approximately 16,000,000 vehicles per year, but traffic studies Moses had commissioned had convinced him that it would be forty years before that capacity would be needed. (Moses was, in fact, worried about attracting even the 7,500,000 vehicles per year required to meet amortization and interest payments on the Authority bonds purchased by the PWA; he was convinced that only a network of excellent approach roads that would make the trip via Triborough clearly superior to the old, toll-free, routes would persuade that number of drivers to pay twenty-five cents per trip.) Moreover, building the bridge on two decks would greatly increase its weight, and therefore would require towers, anchorages and piers of enormous size—and cost. And the weight would, under the old plans, be further increased by the fact that the Authority was planning to cover the Triborough's steelwork with great masses of enormously costly ornamental granite. Moses' engineers told him that the two-deck bridge would cost at least $51,000,000 instead of the $44,200,000 the PWA had allocated.

His engineers had another surprise for Moses. They informed him that the Authority's engineers had made Triborough's lanes the same width as the lanes on the Queensborough Bridge which had proved too narrow for cars and had had to be closed while the curbstones were chipped away. Triborough's "eight-lane" decks would hold only six adequate lanes.

After taking over the Authority, Moses took almost no time to find out why the Manhattan terminus had been placed at 125th Street: William Randolph Hearst had owned deteriorating real estate there and he had wanted the city to buy it. And it took Moses little time to learn why the bridge was supposed to be bedecked with costly granite: the quarries that were supposed to furnish the granite were owned by Tammany interests.

Moses had learned how to get things done and one way not to get things done in New York was to pick a fight with Hearst and his three newspapers. He left the Manhattan terminus at 125th Street.

But that was about all Moses left. With George V. McLaughlin admiringly letting him run the Authority as he wished, Moses controlled two of its three votes. The third, he soon learned, was in his pocket, too; its possessor, the chairman and lone remaining member of the original Authority, was an attorney, Nathan Burkan, whose only interest was in protecting Hearst's, and once Moses indicated that he would not interfere with those interests—the publisher received a $782,000 award for his 125th Street holdings—Burkan showed little further concern about the operations of the body of which he was the nominal head and never attempted to contest Moses' assumption of its executive functions. Two years earlier, Moses had called on the Authority's chief engineer, Edwin A. Byrne, the old Tammany man who had entered city service in 1886 as an axeman, and had pleaded with him to strip the granite from the bridge design and to use the money saved for approach roads, and Byrne had refused. Now Moses was Byrne's boss. In his own words: "I sent for the chief engineer and asked him which he thought was more important—adequate approaches or ornamental granite. He unhesitatingly replied, 'Granite.' This ended the conference and I told him to resign and get his pension." And Moses gave similar instructions, after conferences of similar length, to almost all of Byrne's aides.

To head Triborough's new engineering staff, Moses hired the austere, no-nonsense Swiss aristocrat who had designed the graniteless George Washington Bridge: Othmar Hermann Ammann. To head Triborough's new administrative staff, Moses hired a male version of Amelia Clanton, a stern disciplinarian he had met at Hog Island and had hired to shape up the Long Island Park Commission: retired army brigadier general Paul J. Loeser. Loeser had a gift for rubbing almost anyone the wrong way—La Guardia called him "a Prussian and a Nazi"—but Moses had seen in brief encounters with the General qualities that could be useful to him. "He was, no doubt, a martinet," Moses was to recall. "He was tough. . . . He was not popular."

Then Moses set about giving Ammann and Loeser staffs to shape up: a team of the country's most experienced bridge builders. Within weeks, this team had come up with the kind of plans Moses wanted. The granite was eliminated. The two decks were reduced to one, the sixteen lanes were slashed to six on the Manhattan arm of the bridge and to eight on the rest—and the cost of the bridge was cut by 40 percent, from $51,000,000 to about $30,000,000. The Authority was now going to have a surplus of about $14,000,000 from its $44,200,000 PWA allocation.

Moses' plans for using the money to build the roads that would link the great bridge with his Westchester and Long Island parkways raised legal problems: the PWA allocation was for building a bridge, not roads, and while the allocation did permit expenditures for bridge "approaches," that word had traditionally referred only to the ramps leading directly up to the bridge. But Moses persuaded PWA Administrator Harold L. Ickes that "approaches" could be defined as "approach roads." He told him that without such roads the number of motorists who would use the new bridge would be too small to enable the Authority to meet the payments on the bonds the PWA had purchased—an argument that weighed heavily with the thrifty Ickes. In fact, he persuaded him not only to let him use the $14,000,000 for approach roads but to give him an additional $2,000,000 as well.

Sixteen million dollars was an impressive sum, but it wasn't nearly enough for the approach roads Moses had in mind. He persuaded La Guardia to search the corners of the city treasury for additional right-of-way contributions. He persuaded Civil Works Administration officials to permit him to list some of the road-building work as "park" projects—and thereby obtain hundreds of CWA laborers. Then he obtained hundreds more by diverting CWA-paid laborers on other Park Department projects to the Triborough project without CWA permission. (It always took a few days for CWA officials to find out what their laborers were doing, and by then Moses could tell them that since the work had been started, it would be silly not to allow it to be completed. After all, he pointed out, if the laborers were now reassigned, the jobs would be left unfinished—unsightly scars, offending residents of the neighborhoods in which they were located. And if the newspapers got wind of such an example of governmental inefficiency . . . The argument never failed.) And by the autumn of 1934, thanks to the success of his tactics with CWA's successor agencies, work had been begun to widen Whitlock Avenue, the Bronx thoroughfare with which the bridge connected, and Eastern Boulevard, the thoroughfare with which Whitlock Avenue connected, all the way to the Hutchinson River Parkway.

The building of Triborough's Queens approach was a triumph of imagination over seemingly insoluble problems. The four-mile gap between the bridge and the Grand Central Parkway was four miles of Jackson Heights and Astoria, and in those two communities neat one-family homes, garden apartments, stores and small factories were jammed tightly together. Condemning the number of buildings involved would be impossibly expensive, but there was no vacant land left for a parkway right-of-way.

So Moses made land. A hundred yards out from the shoreline of Jackson Heights, giant pile drivers, mounted on giant barges, pounded steel bulkheads into the muck at the bottom of Flushing Bay. Then long strings of barges piled high with sand from the Rockaways made their broad-beamed way up the East River, through Hell Gate and into the bay to dump the sand behind the bulkheads. Long convoys of dump trucks loaded with shale and stone and gravel rumbled across Queens to heave up their backs and slide the shale and stone in with the sand. And the mixture became a mass solid enough to hold concrete, specifically the six concrete lanes that would allow the Grand Central Parkway to circle Jackson Heights for more than two miles and wait until the last possible minute before plunging into Astoria Boulevard for the final run to the Triborough Bridge ramp.

The building of Triborough's Manhattan approach was another triumph of imagination.

Since the Manhattan terminus was to be located at 125th Street, Moses told his aides, there had to be some way of getting up to 125th Street. York Avenue, which presently ended at Ninety-second Street, would have to be extended along the riverfront.

If Charles Dickens had been looking for an illustration for an American edition of *Hard Times,* he could have stopped looking when he got to that riverfront. The stretch between Ninety-second and 125th streets was a catalogue of the unlovely by-products of industrialism; scented by the raw filth pouring from open sewers into the river below was a long row of small, grimy factories, used-car lots, auto-repair shops, junkyards, coal pockets and oil-storage depots. Hogarth could have found a whole gallery of models in the occupants of the bars, whorehouses and tenements that mingled with them. To Moses, however, the panorama possessed less appeal. Unlovely as was the scenery, it would not be cheap to condemn it. On a single factory, the Washburn Wire Works, a large, grimy building that occupied three solid blocks of riverfront, from 116th to 119th streets, the price asked was $3,000,000.

A riverfront highway had been proposed before, but an early Corporation Counsel had announced that he had searched the deeds to the land involved and found that there was no loophole that would allow the city to take title by any procedure other than the unfeasibly expensive one of condemnation. Succeeding city administrations had assumed for decades that that finding was correct. But Moses told his bloodhounds to forget about assumptions and search the deeds again—and to *find* SOMETHING, *goddammit.* And the bloodhounds found something. The title to some of the lots contained a covenant more than a century old, dating back to a time when the lots had been owned by the city itself, they told Moses. And in the covenant the city reserved the right to reclaim a sixty-foot strip along the waterfront in case it ever wanted to build a street there. Moses could have sixty feet of right-of-way along a considerable stretch of his riverfront highway for nothing.

Moses' problems were still far from solved. At least six lanes were required, he figured, and the minimum width for six lanes was not sixty feet but one hundred. And Moses did not intend to waste the waterfront in a park-starved section of the city on a highway. He wanted the river side of that highway to be not a guardrail for the highway but a park from which residents of the area could enjoy the waterfront. There should, he decided, be a tree-shaded esplanade along the waterfront, complete with benches and play areas. And for such a park at least another thirty or forty feet in width were needed, thirty or forty feet that would, if condemnation was required to obtain it, be terribly expensive.

There were other complications. The Washburn company told La Guardia that, if it was forced to move, it would move out of the city altogether and find a cheaper location somewhere else—and the Washburn company employed 1,200 men. The Mayor told Moses that the city could not afford to lose 1,200 jobs—and therefore could not take the chance that the company was bluffing. The Consolidated Edison Company owned large portions of property that were set back from the river and would not have to be condemned. But Con Ed needed access to the waterfront, and that access was now provided by overhead conveyors which crossed the property on which the East River Drive Extension would have to run. If those conveyors were eliminated, Con Ed would be hurt, and the city would have to pay the utility substantial damages.

To keep the amount of land required for the improvement as small as possible, Moses decided to build the park out over the river on a reinforced concrete platform ten feet wide—because a ten-foot-wide platform was the maximum width that could be supported without the construction of expensive pilings. He wouldn't condemn the Washburn Wire Works, he decided. He would chop off its front, run the Drive through the land thus obtained, build additions atop the factory so that its floor space would not be reduced and an underground tunnel beneath the Drive so that it would still have access to the waterfront—and reface the entire shabby edifice with neat brick. This solution would cost a million dollars—two million less than condemnation would have cost. And it saved the city 1,200 jobs.

Moses decided to tear down Con Ed's overhead conveyors and build more underground tunnels to the river so that the company could not claim consequential damages. While he was negotiating with the company about this, he horsetraded—Con Ed's citywide operations required an endless stream of concessions from the city, so, with La Guardia behind him, Moses had plenty of ammunition to horsetrade with—and obtained portions of Con Ed's property along the right-of-way without having to pay for it. Then he made another trip to Washington and asked the PWA to contribute an additional $6,000,000 to acquire land for the Drive so that the bridge would be made more accessible to motorists and more of them would be persuaded to pay tolls to use it. The PWA wouldn't give $6,000,000—but it would give $2,000,000. Moses took La Guardia on a tour of the proposed improvement. La Guardia, who lived in an apartment at 106th Street and Fifth Avenue, was keenly aware of the park needs of the neighborhood. And he was fascinated by the engineering aspects of the work. Moses persuaded him that men paid by CWA and its successor agencies could be reassigned from other city departments to provide the labor needed for the job. This reduced the cost, for land acquisition and materials mainly, to $1,878,500. Scour the city treasury as he would, La Guardia could find no more than about $1,300,000 that could be made available—but this contribution brought the balance down to about $578,000, and Moses said the Authority could afford to pay that itself. And by the end of 1934, the Board of Estimate, under La Guardia's goading, was rushing through the resolutions necessary to obtain title to the area.

Then Moses turned to the question of transforming Randall's and Ward's islands into parks. His Authority had no authorization from the PWA to build parks, it was true, but he convinced PWA officials that the parks would attract to the islands—and to the bridge—enough toll-paying motorists to justify a modest investment. And a modest investment was all he had in mind, he told the officials. The Authority would have to pay for the materials needed to construct baseball diamonds, tennis courts and bench-lined esplanades, but the total cost should not be more than $225,000. The big cost involved, that of labor, would be paid for by the CWA, for he would make the reclamation of the islands a Park Department project.

The old Authority had planned, and had received PWA authorization to build, a Randall's Island municipal stadium with a seating capacity of 10,000. "Wholly inadequate," Moses said. He wanted a stadium seating "at least" 70,000, big enough to hold an annual interborough athletic competition—the competitors to be champions selected in track meets and other athletic events held in each borough—and the big crowds that he was sure would attend. And he wanted it big enough to be the site of Olympic try-outs and great outdoor spectacles. "The stadium must be adequate for big events or it is a failure," he said. "There is ample room on the island for a big stadium." Its components must be of commensurate size, he said. For example, it should have the largest movable outdoor stage in the world. Construction of such a stadium would cost the city millions in ordinary times. But now, the labor, the biggest single item, would be paid for by the federal government. He persuaded the CWA to list the stadium as a Park Department project. A million dollars in materials would be needed for these men to work with, but he persuaded the PWA that the stadium would help attract toll payers to the bridge, and the agency allowed the Authority to increase its previously authorized contribution by $300,000.

There was still an obstacle to the creation of parks and a stadium on Randall's and Ward's islands: the institutional buildings already there. The military hospital was only partly filled and Moses had little difficulty persuading U. S. Army and Navy officials to move the patients to other hospitals and vacate the buildings. But the House of Refuge, the Hospital for the Feeble-Minded and Manhattan State Hospital presented a more difficult problem; city and state reformatories and asylums were already overcrowded. La Guardia's hospital commissioner, Dr. Sigismund S. Goldwater, flatly refused to move patients out of the city buildings on the two islands, and state officials said any moves would have to wait until new state institutions were constructed. But Moses persuaded Lehman to overrule the state officials and La Guardia to overrule Goldwater, and by the end of 1934, with the patients crammed into overcrowded institutions, the House of Refuge had been vacated and demolished and the razing of the Hospital for the Feeble-Minded was under way.

Meanwhile, Moses' eyes had focused on the Sunken Meadow, the fifty-acre sand bar east of Randall's Island. The hundred-yard strip of East River that separated it from the island concealed land that lay only a few feet below the surface. Moses ordered the strip filled in—and Sunken Meadow was thereby made a part of Randall's Island, and another fifty acres was acquired for park space.

The residents of the high-rent apartment houses that lined the Manhattan side of the East River had never gotten much of a view for their money. Opposite them—to the east and dragging off to the south—was scenery done in Early Industrial Era Midlands, the grimy warehouses, factories, tenements, oil tanks and open storage depots of Astoria and Long Island City. Its dreariness broken only by the gaudiness of occasional monster billboards painted large enough so that their messages could be seen clearly across the river, that vista stretched away without a break (there were no housing developments or parks there then) beneath a pall (the word "smog" had not yet gained currency) cast over it by belching smokestacks. And the scene to the north where Ward's Island lay, low in the water with Randall's behind it, had not been any prettier. Dull-colored and lifeless in the distance even when fog didn't shroud them, the two islands had been adorned only by the squat red and gray institutional buildings that failed to block out the scenery behind the islands: the South Bronx, Long Island City's spiritual descendant. Since 1932, the piers erected for the first, abortive attempt to build the Triborough Bridge had been part of the scene, but, dun-colored, featureless and, without a bridge on top of them, seeming in the distance like a succession of walls to play handball against, they did little to relieve its drabness. The view had not been inspiring.

By the end of 1934, that was no longer true.

By the end of that year, the residents of the East River apartments, looking north, could see giant cranes moving about on the islands like long-necked dinosaurs prowling far-off marshes. Around the cranes were stirring masses of men. Over the water came the pound of pile drivers, a sound that was dull and far away, but that never seemed to stop. And rising from behind the little buildings on the left of Ward's Island and curving off to the right across the island in a gigantic curve, a highway was being bolted into place in the sky.

The highway, carried across Ward's Island on the piers, climbed in a long, slow, powerful line. Across the river—to the right as the watchers looked north—they could see its steel roadbed slanting unhurriedly down behind the first line of factories. There was a great gap in the center, but it took little imagination to see how the roadbed would continue to rise there until it was flung across the Hell Gate, for the hulking concrete anchorages that would hold the cables for the Hell Gate suspension bridge were already in place ("Immense things they are," wrote an observer; "beside the Nile they would pass for pyramids"), and so were the bridge's steel towers, which loomed over the river like the façades of twin cathedrals. And even as the watchers watched, new portions of the roadbed paraded past them. Pushing aside the sullen gray of the East River would come a squad of barges, lashed together side by side to bear a weight measured in thousands of tons and pushed along by a whole covey of panting tugboats, bearing to the waiting cranes the specially fabricated steel girders that would hold the bridge roadbed girders—some of which were as big as a ten-room ranch house.

Enormous as the Triborough Bridge seemed to watchers along the East River, moreover, they were seeing only a small portion of the whole project.

Engineers and journalists felt that it was only from a plane that one could get a feel of the project in its three-borough entirety. From the air, one journalist said, "you could see the avenues being widened as if a giant chisel was being rammed between them."

And from the air, more than one journalist said, the project seemed almost too big to grasp.

Robert Moses erected the complex of buildings that was the Central Park Zoo at least partly because of his devotion to Alfred E. Smith. He tore down another building in the park wholly because of that devotion.

He tore down Jimmy Walker's Casino.

Everyone who was interested in the cause of parks in New York City disapproved of the use to which Calvert Vaux's Ladies Refreshment Salon was being put, of course. But none of them wanted the building torn down. As a structure designed by one of the creators of Central Park, it held a special place in the city's history. And for many of the reformers, it was associated with pleasant memories; they could remember accompanying their parents on Sunday bicycle or horseback rides through the park that ended with lunch there in the quieter days before the World War. Moreover, the building possessed a Victorian charm precious in its own right. As a practical matter, although Solomon and his backers had poured almost $400,000 into improvements in the building's interior, he was nonetheless only renting it from the city. The city still owned it. The Park Department could ask him to lower his prices and thereby make the magnificent dining rooms and pavilions more accessible to the general public. If Solomon refused, the city could attempt to cancel his lease and install in his place a more amenable concessionaire. And even if the attempt failed, the lease had only five more years to run; after that, the building, and the improvements, would revert to the city forever. The Park Association had been campaigning for the Casino's conversion into a moderate-priced restaurant, but when the Association's members heard that Moses was planning to raze the building—announcing that it was structurally unsound, that it would cost too much to repair and that luxury restaurants had no place in parks anyway, he said that a playground, complete with wading pool, would be constructed on its site—they were aghast. Such an act, they said, would be wanton destruction. Financially, it made even less sense; a group of restaurant owners had already asked for permission to operate the Casino as a moderate-priced restaurant, abiding by any rules that Moses wished to establish—and pay the city $25,000 annual rental plus a liberal share of the receipts. And finally, as the Casino's chef, Henri Charpontier, put it in a plaintive letter to the *Times*: "Why choose the site of the Casino . . . when there are broad expanses as far as the eye can reach on either side of the Casino, where as fine a swimming [sic] pool as the Commissioner's kind heart urges him to provide could easily be located?"

But Moses refused to compromise. The considerations which motivated him were not historical, aesthetic or financial. To a large extent, they were hardly rational. "It was a case of revenge, pure and simple," says Paul Windels, La Guardia's Corporation Counsel who advised Moses on the case before turning it over, "in disgust," to Assistant Corporation Counsel William C. Chanler. "He never said so straight out, but everyone around him knew why he was doing it—he wanted to get back at Walker for what Walker had done to Governor Smith. God, he wanted to get Walker!" (And the oddest part about the affair, Windels says, was that, "to the best of my knowledge," Moses never spoke to Governor Smith about it—and if he had, Governor Smith "would have told him not to do it.")

Solomon, panicking over his investment, offered to confer with Moses and revise his price list. "I am not going to confer with Mr. Solomon," Moses replied. With La Guardia, advised by Windels against supporting an establishment as notorious as the Casino, refusing to intervene, Chanler served Solomon with an eviction notice that charged the Casino Corporation with a number of technical violations of its lease; a typical charge was that, by allowing fashion shows to be held there, the Casino had violated a regulation prohibiting advertising on park property.

Solomon took the case to court. The trial turned out to be embarrassing for both him and Moses.

Solomon was forced to admit that, during the five years of its existence, the Casino had grossed more than three million dollars and he himself had drawn more than a quarter of a million in salary—while paying the city a total of $42,500 in rent. He had to admit that Park Department officials had been allowed to consume tens of thousands of dollars of free food and liquor. And he had to manage to keep a straight face while maintaining under cross-examination that he couldn't remember the name of a single one of those officials, or of a single one of the Casino's stockholders.

But Moses had some bad moments on the stand, too.

One was reminiscent of the way he had been trapped in an apparent lie the only other time he had found himself under oath. In the Taylor Estate trial, he had testified that he had never been advised that appropriation without funds was illegal, and W. Kingsland Macy's attorney, Charles H. Tuttle, had thereupon produced the paper which had given him that very advice and waved it in front of him. Now, sitting in the witness chair in State Supreme Court in Foley Square, Moses said that he would allow in city parks only restaurants that charged "reasonable" prices, and when pressed for his definition of "reasonable," he said that luncheon should be one dollar or less, coffee no more than a dime—and that "the à la carte system" is a luxury which should not be permitted to exist in a park restaurant. Whereupon Solomon's attorney, the same Charles H. Tuttle, produced a paper, waved it in front of Moses and asked if he recognized it. It was a luncheon menu, approved by Moses, from the Tavern-on-the-Green, the restaurant Moses had installed in the sheepfold after renovating it and turning it over to a favorite concessionaire for a nominal rental, and the attorney read from it a long list of à la carte entrees for luncheon, all priced over a dollar, and concluded by reading the Tavern's price for coffee—twenty-five cents.

The press, which had long used the Casino as a convenient symbol of the abuses of the corrupt "Walkerian Court," treated the trial as an attempt to end those abuses. If there was a principle involved, the press ignored it. But some reformers did not. The Casino case marked the first significant defections from the solid ranks the city's Good Government movement had previously formed behind Moses in every encounter. Not all reformers disapproved of his attempt to demolish the building, of course. Most still believed that anything he did was right—apparently, judging from their comments, because they believed his motives were pure; when he said the building was structurally unsound and repairs were unfeasible, they believed him. And most of those who, having seen the Casino, found his contention difficult to believe, felt sure that he had simply made a mistake, one to which, in view of his past record, he was more than entitled. But some reformers, and among them some of the men and women who had played the most vital roles in persuading the Legislature to allow Moses to assume the city park commissionership, found it difficult to reconcile their idealized image of him with the fact that he was now contemplating "destroying property . . . in Central Park which did not belong to him but to the entire city." And they were certain, they said, that he did not have the power to do so.

But this last group of reformers was in for an awakening, the same kind of awakening that had been undergone ten years before by Trubee Davison, who had introduced a bill Moses had drafted without thoroughly studying it, and by upstate reformers like Ansley Wilcox and Alphonse Clearwater, who had been tricked by Moses into supporting the Davison bill. In outlining the powers of the New York City Park Commissioner, as in outlining the powers of the chairman of the State Council of Parks, Moses had proved again that he was the best bill drafter in Albany.

The city reformers had supported the bill that had allowed Moses to become Commissioner despite reservations about some of its broader provisions. Now they looked at the bill more closely—and found that it was not only its broader provisions that they should have been worried about.

Chanler startled them by arguing in court that the bill granted the City Park Commissioner absolute power "to raze or remove . . . buildings which had been erected as incidental to park uses, such as restaurants, boat houses and similar structures," and that it further provided, as additional insurance against any check on his actions, that "such changes will not be supervised by the judicial power unless palpably . . . abusive of the grant." The inclusion of such language in the bill, they realized, meant that not even the courts could stop Moses from tearing down any structure in the parks that he wanted to tear down. As Trubee Davison had done ten years before, they hurriedly began reading the law—and they found that the language was, buried within a mass of other legalese, indeed in it. And they found that some other language was *not* in it, language that had previously been included in city park laws at their request to insure against willful changes in the parks at the whim of a Park Commissioner. Under the old statute, the approval of a landscape architect, "skilled and expert," had been required for any major alteration in a park. Now there was no longer any such requirement. Moses had skillfully amended it out of the new law. Chanler said in court that the new law gave Moses the right to do whatever he wanted in parks as long as it was for a "proper park use" and that Moses was the only man who could determine what was, and was not, a proper use. And Chanler was right. As the reformers read the law, the law that they had helped pass, they realized that they had helped turn over the parks that were the priceless heritage of the city to the whim of one man.

Before the issue was finally decided, a number of requests for injunctions against the demolition were argued before several different Supreme Court Justices. One, John F. Carew, allowed his emotions to boil over on the bench. Moses' contention that the Casino was in an irreparably bad state of disrepair, Carew said, was "obviously preposterous and contrary to the facts." Having thus called Moses a liar in legalese, Carew went on.

The Casino, he said, "has long been an honorable, useful, beloved, admired, valuable and even historic monument. . . . The Park Commissioner has no more power to destroy the Casino than he has to destroy the Obelisk, to fill in the reservoir, or the lake, to tear down City Hall, the Arsenal [or] the many historic buildings, monuments, structures, statues in the many other parks of the City, the treasured relics of generations here. He is only to hold office for a brief term. He is the passing creature of a day. He will in time, and that not long, be superseded. He may not 'waste' the heritage of New York. In the meantime . . . he must restrain his extravagant, excessive energy and zeal or he must be restrained." He issued the injunction.

But Moses wasn't worried. He knew what was in the law. "I think the higher court will take care of Justice Carew," he told a reporter airily. And he was right. When Chanler appealed Carew's decision to the Appellate Division in Albany, the five justices of that court, sitting together in their high-backed chairs, said that the powers the Legislature had granted to Moses were far too broad and indicated that they wished the Legislature would revoke some of them. But for the present, they said, the law was passed, and it was unfortunately clear; they had no choice but to overrule Carew's decision. If Moses had the power to destroy the Casino, Carew had said, he had the power to destroy the Obelisk, the Arsenal, City Hall or any other structure, no matter how historic, no matter how beautiful, no matter how treasured, in any park in New York City. Carew was wrong about City Hall; it lies just outside the northern boundary of City Hall Park; Moses couldn't tear it down. But Carew was right about everything else.

Moving quickly to forestall any further appeals, Moses had crews of workmen tearing down the Casino within twenty-four hours after he received a copy of the Appellate Court decision. Within two months, the building was gone and its site was covered with a playground. Except for its stained-glass windows, which were used in the new police station being constructed on the Eighty-sixth Street Transverse Road, Robert Moses had succeeded in eradicating every trace of the spiritual home of the man who had publicly humiliated Alfred E. Smith.

21. *The Candidate*

THERE HAD BEEN A DAY in 1934 on which the cheering had stopped. It was the day Robert Moses started running for Governor.

Moses was later to maintain that he had not wanted to run. The Republican nomination "was more or less forced on me," he was to say. He had accepted it only "to hold the party together." Such loyalty to the Grand Old Party is difficult to reconcile with the fact that Moses had spent ten years of his life, the decade during which he worked for Al Smith, fighting it. Such loyalty is difficult to reconcile with the fact that in 1928, when Moses had believed he had a chance to win the Democratic gubernatorial nomination, he had enrolled as a Democrat—he had not re-enrolled as a Republican until 1933, when he needed GOP support for the Fusion mayoral nomination. And in fact no reconciliation is necessary. For if Moses' description of his attitude is based on his memory, his memory played him false. No forcing was necessary at all, says F. Trubee Davison, who first offered him the nomination: "I had a talk with Bob and asked him if he'd be willing to go. He didn't say yes, but he encouraged me." Says another source: "Bob told me Trubee had offered him the nomination and he asked my advice. My advice was not to take it, but I could see he was going to take it no matter what I said. He was hungry for it."

The identity of the man who offered Moses the nomination is perhaps the clearest proof of the inaccuracy of the portrait Moses had painted of himself as the foe of the forces of influence, privilege and wealth. For Trubee Davison was the acknowledged representative of those forces. Son of J. P. Morgan's late partner, Henry P. Davison, heir to Henry P.'s estate, which, behind massive iron gates and thick walls of stone, occupied all 4,000 acres of Long Island's Peacock Point, no longer the naïve young assemblyman who a decade earlier had been tricked by Moses into introducing the bills giving the Long Island Park Commission the right of condemnation by appropriation, Davison was a key figure in the ranks of the Long Island robber barons. And Davison was taking an active interest in the selection of the gubernatorial nominee precisely because the barons felt that their influence and privilege and, to some extent, their wealth, were threatened.

The barons—together with the upstate gas and water-power utility interests—had dominated the state's Republican Party from time immemorial; to a large extent, in fact, the GOP *was* the barons and the "Interests," a fact made clear when H. Edmund Machold, stepping down as Assembly Speaker in 1925, became, simultaneously, state GOP chairman and president of the gigantic utility holding company Niagara-Hudson, and by the fact that among the downstate GOP congressmen were Robert Low Bacon, stipendiary of the House of Morgan, Ogden Livingston Mills, son of Darius Ogden Mills of the San Francisco "bank ring," and willowy millionairess Ruth Baker Pratt, widow of one of the six sons for whom Rockefeller partner Charles Pratt had built manor houses on the Glen Cove peninsula.

It was important to the Interests that they control the state GOP. It was important for business reasons—the party was the Interests' traditional protector in Albany—and it was important for reasons that went beyond business: the conservatism of these men of property, to whom property rights were sacred, was not only financial but ideological, and they viewed their party as a bulwark against heresy, against the increasing emphasis on human as opposed to property rights that characterized the philosophy of the three Democrats—Smith, Roosevelt and Lehman—who had usurped the Executive Chamber. Public reverence for their beliefs might be dying, but they would never surrender them. Not for nothing had journalists dubbed them "the Old Guard."

From the standpoint of both philosophy and pocketbook, in 1934 control of the state GOP was more important to the Old Guard than ever. Their fury at the New Deal—"the purpose of the Roosevelt administration is the imposition of a Russianized form of government," snarled upstater Bertrand H. Snell, House minority leader*—had led them to resolve that the presidential election of 1936 would be a Holy Crusade to oust "that man" from the White House, and they intended to make New York, with its forty-five electoral votes, the crusade's embarkation point. Moreover, most of the Old Guard—"anybody who amounted to anything in the GOP," Warren Moscow said—owned Niagara-Hudson stock, whose value would be immensely increased by the finalization of the scheme that had been the party's grail for almost four decades: the turning over to private utilities such as Niagara-Hudson of the immense water-power resources of the St. Lawrence and Niagara rivers. Smith had established a State Power Authority to keep those resources in the hands of the state's people. Roosevelt had pointed out dramatically that only two heartbeats, his and that of Lieutenant Governor Lehman, separated the "Power Trust" from the state's water power—and millions of New York families from higher monthly electric-light bills. Lehman, as Governor, had proved even more effective, undramatically but stubbornly shoving down the Legislature's throat bills giving the State Public Service Commission authority over utility rates, forbidding the use of

* Snell was only one of a group of reactionary congressmen from upstate which included Hamilton Fish, Jr., John Taber and James W. Wadsworth, who became a congressman after losing his United States Senate seat to Robert F. Wagner, Sr., in 1926 despite his successful mediation in the Taylor Estate fight. (Key reason for Wadsworth's loss: his refusal to temper his opposition to the radical notion of women's suffrage.)

utility funds for political lobbying and—in a step the utilities viewed as particularly ominous—allowing municipalities to construct their own plants and distribute power at low rates. Only the Legislature stood between Lehman and still more radical anti-utilities measures he was proposing; it was vital to the Old Guard, more vital than ever, that the GOP control the Legislature—and that they control the GOP.

But control of the party had been snatched away from the Old Guard—by the former amateur in politics they had once betrayed but who had acquired from his bitter fight with Robert Moses a professionalism that made him their equal: W. Kingsland Macy.

Macy had lost the Taylor Estate fight, his first political battle; he had not lost another one. Having learned the hard way the importance of public opinion, he purchased a string of weekly newspapers that blanketed Suffolk County and by 1927 had ousted the county GOP chairman, installed himself in his place and purged the county organization with a ruthlessness so complete that his control of it would not be seriously challenged for a quarter of a century. Then he turned his attention to wider spheres. Before the barons quite realized what was happening, he had seized the Republican state chairmanship.

Once in power, Macy proved that pince-nez, starched high round collars and blue suits with vests—the outfit he was to affect until he died in 1960—were no guarantee of conservatism. Attempting to reverse his party's blind obstructionism to progressive policies that had been largely responsible for the repeated victories of Smith, Roosevelt and Lehman in a state in which voter registration was heavily Republican, Macy excoriated GOP legislators who opposed Roosevelt's attempt to blunt the effects of the Depression through increased spending and embarrassed enough of them into supporting the state's Temporary Emergency Relief Administration to give the measure the votes it needed to pass. Dismissing the fear of the Old Guard leaders that, if they authorized an investigation of corruption in New York City, Roosevelt would authorize investigations of corruption upstate, Macy called GOP legislators into closed-door caucuses in Albany and, using every ounce of patronage at his command, broke the power of grim old William Ward and forced the tyrant of Westchester to release his legislators to vote as they wished, thereby allowing the passage of the bills initiating the Seabury investigation. And it was pressure from Macy that persuaded Republican fusionists to bow to Seabury's demand and, over Old Guard objections, give the nomination for mayor to the dangerous rabble-rouser La Guardia.

Astounded and antagonized by the course on which Macy was leading their party, the Old Guard was thrown into panic by his next announcement: pointing out—accurately—that the GOP's identification with the Power Trust was a political liability, Macy proposed to end the Trust's domination of the party by making Seabury, who had long attacked utilities as "monopolists and exploiters of the people," its next gubernatorial nominee.

"Well, that was all we had to hear," Trubee Davison would growl three decades later, sitting with one gouty leg propped on a foot stool in the thirty-foot-high study of his mansion on Peacock Point, topping off with cherries jubilee a light lunch served by a white-coated butler and staring out across the Davison compound's half-mile-long terraced croquet court. "Seabury was a Democrat for one thing—that was enough. And he was full of this honesty-in-government thing that was so teeing these guys [Davison's Old Guard colleagues] off. He was calling everybody crooks, just like Macy."

The Old Guard hastily began looking for a candidate of its own to run against the implacable old idealist.

The qualifications required (in addition to respect for the sanctity of holding companies) were quite explicit: What was needed, said an Old Guard-sponsored magazine, was "a candidate who symbolizes the spirit of uncompromising courageous opposition to the whole Roosevelt socialistic program." There was a catch, however. While the Old Guard was determined to have a candidate who shared its views, 1934 was no year to have a candidate who was publicly identified with those views; what was wanted, in short, was a candidate who was actually a reactionary conservative—but who the public believed was a radical liberal. What was wanted was a front man, someone whose reputation would give protective coloration to their attempt. They turned to Robert Moses.

Moses may have antagonized them once, when he threatened to run the Northern State Parkway right past their manor houses. But in the intervening years, they had come to know him better. His aggressiveness had, after all, turned out to be not the hostility of the radical, idealistic reformer to property and power but something quite the opposite, an expression of his regard for power, an acknowledgment of the fact that he had on his side, in the person of that uneducated, practically illiterate demagogue from the Fulton Fish Market, the one man in the state with power equal to theirs and therefore did not have to compromise with them. As soon as he no longer had this power behind him, he had changed, suddenly, dramatically and, to them, satisfyingly. He had proven understanding—sympathetic, in fact—to their desire to keep the rabble away from their estates; he had proven his sympathy, in their view, by his agreement to make the parkway not an accessway to parks on the North Shore but a "traffic bridge," a chute, similar in principle to a cattle chute, on which the public would be shunted across the Gold Coast without being allowed to get off and contaminate it. His receptivity to their demands for private parkway entrances and bridges had proven him to be what they called a "practical man," a man willing to make accommodation with power. His deal with Otto Kahn had been further testimony to this (after all, a man who would turn a highway aside to save a private golf course couldn't be all bad)—as had his relationship with the politician who most directly represented them in state affairs. J. Russel Sprague, G. Wilbur Doughty's nephew, had succeeded the Last of the Mohicans as head of the Nassau County Republican organization and by 1934 had displayed all of his uncle's ability to obtain wampum for his braves. And Sprague told the barons that Moses was a man "you can get along with." Moses had cemented his relationship with the barons by entertaining them in reserved portions of Jones Beach and by displaying during dinner parties at their mansions a hatred for the President equal to theirs. Reported *The North Shore Almanack,* a weekly newspaper that echoed the political views of the Gold Coast: "He is not a New Deal radical. He doesn't believe that the New Deal is working or can work. Finally, his friends say that he doesn't like Mr. Roosevelt at all." Moses' view of the "people," they found, was, in fact, as strikingly similar to theirs as was his view of the people's President.

Just as important to the Old Guard as this facet of Moses' personality was the fact that the public didn't know about it. Thanks to his genius for public relations, to the people he was still the fighter for parks and against privilege. And therefore if he was the Old Guard candidate against Seabury, the press would not be able to charge that the Old Guard—and the scandal-scarred utilities—were trying to keep control of the GOP. No one would believe Macy if he charged that Robert Moses was a front for the "power lobby." Asked three decades later why he had wanted Moses to run, Davison would admit to the author: "No one questioned Moses' honesty. Macy had been calling everybody crooks and he certainly couldn't say this about Moses. My thought was if we could get somebody like Moses they couldn't say that."

There were still some obstacles between Moses and the nomination. A number of Republican leaders simply couldn't stomach the thought of giving it to a man who had spent so many years humiliating them. But the Old Guard knew how to handle such scruples. Relentless economic pressure was applied. When the opposition had been whittled down to a few diehards, Davison called a Sunday-afternoon meeting of party leaders in the Fifth Avenue apartment of his mother, Mrs. Henry P. Davison.

"Well, this meeting was just like an 'Of Thee I Sing,' " Davison would recall. "It was the kind of thing you put on the stage. We had all the leaders there, but some of them—that fellow from Queens [Queens leader Warren Ashmead] and the Syracuse bunch—wanted to run out on us, and I had to tell them they had better come back, and they did, but I knew we had to get this thing wrapped up or the agreement would fall apart. I sent out to the Links Club for sandwiches and I gave the elevator man five dollars not to stop at our floor so nobody could go down, and we wrapped the thing up. Then I wanted Bob up there, so the whole thing would be made final and he was out fishing on the Great South Bay. We got the State Police and they got him off the Great South Bay and brought him to New York. Then Bob and Russ Sprague and I went down to the other end of the apartment to a bedroom and we said, 'Now the fellows are willing to support you and we've got the votes.' He said, 'Well, this is like swimming up Niagara Falls in a coonskin coat,' meaning this was a very hard election to win, but he agreed to accept the nomination."

Davison's strategy worked. Moses' acceptance of the nomination made him the reactionaries' ally but most newspapers responded as did the *Buffalo Evening News*, which said: "None can say that Robert Moses is a . . . tory . . . His every act since entering public life has been dedicated to the best interests of the many." Even Baron Warn of the *Times* could only express puzzlement at the alliance; "one of the odd turns of politics," he mused. Macy was robbed of the chance to portray the nomination struggle as one between an honest liberal and a candidate of the Power Trust. The battle at the GOP convention, held in Rochester in September, was bitter—"The convention will go down in history as one of the most hectic the GOP has ever held," commented the *Rochester Times-Union*—but the result was foreordained and Moses' nomination was cheered by both press and public. "At last! An idealist in politics!" said one typical letter-to-the-editor. Under cover of the cheering, the state committee was able to meet immediately after the nomination and oust Macy as state chairman. (The depth of the misunderstanding of Moses' philosophy was exemplified by an editorial in the *World-Telegram*. Noting that the platform adopted by the convention was "an uncompromising denunciation of the New Deal," the *World-Telegram* said: "Mr. Moses may be able to fit himself to such a platform. We doubt it. With the reputation and record Mr. Moses has as a liberal we don't see how he can." The *World-Telegram* didn't know that Moses had written much of the platform himself.)

If the press was puzzled by Moses' nomination, it was to be dumbfounded by his campaign. For Robert Moses as a candidate was a phenomenon of a type not seen very often on the American political scene.

"It seemed as if he was trying to set some kind of record for antagonizing people," Windels recalls. The time at Moses' disposal was limited—in keeping with the custom of the era the campaign ran for only five weeks—but he didn't waste a day of it. The element of the GOP most enthusiastic about his nomination was the Young Republicans. The very evening after the convention, Davison hosted a cocktail party for them so that Moses could convert their enthusiasm into active support. But things didn't work out quite as Davison expected. "They got into this argument and he started calling them names, and they started calling him names," Davison recalls. "My God, it ended up in a fearful row!"

Having thus rallied young Republicans to his standard, Moses turned his charm on their elders. Davison raised a massive war chest for the campaign—but, he recalls, "Moses wouldn't consult with me. I must have been the most inactive campaign chairman in history as a result. Once the campaign started, we never saw him. He locked himself up in an ivory tower someplace and we never saw his speeches until he gave them. And then he put Ray McNulty in our office [the state committee office]—to keep an eye on us, I think. Well, didn't that just sit well with the boys!"

With his own party taken care of, Moses turned to the opposition. The fact that he was running as a Republican and against Lehman meant that he had to forfeit the support of the men and women he had worked with in government. Most of them, veterans of the Smith, Roosevelt and Lehman administrations, were Democrats. All of them were believers in increased government activity to promote social welfare—precisely the cause most hated by the Old Guard with which Moses had allied himself. Moses should not have expected their backing. But he did. And the way in which he asked for it—or, rather, demanded it—and his reaction when it was not forthcoming, were not particularly gracious.

There were a succession of unpleasant endings to pleasant dinner parties at which Bob and Mary were guests. One occurred at the Manhattan townhouse of Aaron Rabinowitz. Rabinowitz, a fabulously successful realtor turned philanthropist, was Lehman's partner in the state's first limited-dividend housing corporation, which the two men had formed, at a cost to each of them of about $375,000, in an attempt to attract private capital to low-income housing. "I was Moses' friend, too," Rabinowitz recalls. "We were very close. Until one day he was at the house for dinner. He had just been nominated for Governor." As the two men chatted outside the dining room after dessert, Moses asked, "You're going to help me become Governor, aren't you?" Rabinowitz recalls: "I said, 'I can't!' I was Lehman's partner. I was a Democrat. He turned and walked out without a word and for fifteen years, whenever we met, he wouldn't talk to me." Henry Moskowitz, Belle's husband and Moses' old boss on the Municipal Civil Service Commission, traditionally "handled" the foreign-language press for the Democratic Party. Now Moses asked Moskowitz to do the same job for him—the Republican candidate. "Henry said what I said: 'I can't,' " Rabinowitz recalls. "Moses never talked to him again. He owed that man a lot, but the lousy no-good wouldn't even go to his funeral." The friendship of Moses' old associates—men like Joseph Proskauer and Bernard Shientag—might have kept them from taking an active role in the campaign. But after one visit apiece from Moses, all of them were out working for, and lending their powerful names to, Lehman's re-election bid, and thereby emphasizing that Moses was opposing the liberal causes with which he had so long been identified.

Then there was the press.

Most candidates attempt to woo reporters covering the campaign. It took Moses exactly one press conference to turn them icily frigid toward his candidacy.

This might have been surprising to those who had observed his long love affair with the press. But that love affair had endured only because he had never been exposed to the probing questioning to which reporters subject most public officials. His aides, who knew his sensitivity to even the most discreetly implied criticism, could have predicted what would happen when he was.

Moses entered his first press conference smiling broadly and clasping the hands of old acquaintances in the press corps as he strode into the room. But practically the first question asked was the natural one, considering the confusion over how a "liberal" could be nominated by the most conservative elements of the Republican Party: "Mr. Moses, are you a protégé of the Old Guard?"

Said the *World-Telegram* that afternoon: "The gubernatorial candidate drew his breath sharply, and there was a glitter in his eyes." Jumping to his feet, jabbing his finger at the reporter who had asked the question, he "heatedly" declared, "Nobody has any strings on me!" and demanded, "Have you asked the same question of Governor Lehman? Did you ask him if he is a protégé of Tammany Hall?" In what the *World-Telegram* called a "display of temper," he began lecturing the reporters on how to do their job and then "announced belligerently that he would 'not take laying down' anything that was said against him . . . by newspapers." Moses carried out this threat with a vengeance; by the end of the campaign he was spending a substantial part of his press conferences berating the press—and he had completely forfeited the sympathy with which most reporters had been prepared to view his candidacy.

If there was a blunder that could be made, Moses made it. He wanted La Guardia's support and assumed he would have it; after all, he was a member of La Guardia's administration and the Mayor was a Republican. So Moses told the press he had it—and announced a City Hall meeting with La Guardia at which, he told reporters, the Mayor would announce it.

Unfortunately, Moses hadn't bothered to check with La Guardia. The Mayor had been under pressure from President Roosevelt, with whom he was negotiating for federal relief funds, to stay out of the gubernatorial campaign but had indicated to Corporation Counsel Windels that he would campaign for Moses nonetheless. But Moses' taking his support for granted infuriated him. After the City Hall meeting, which lasted almost an hour, La Guardia said blandly, "He'd make a good Governor, gosh, yes," but refused to say he would make a better Governor than Lehman—and he remained seated firmly on the sidelines throughout the campaign. Moses had quietly ducked out of City Hall while reporters were questioning the Mayor, but they cornered him later at 80 Centre Street and he could do nothing but admit that, as the *Sun* put it, "he did not expect Mayor La Guardia to make any campaign speeches in his behalf as the Mayor probably would be too busy with city affairs."

Moses chose a tour of the upstate Republican heartland, where voters were bitterly opposed to any increase in governmental spending or power, to advocate the imposition of a state sales tax. And he didn't make the suggestion in just any upstate city; he did it in Binghamton, where the Chamber of Commerce had just finished collecting tens of thousands of names on anti-sales-tax petitions. He chose Syracuse, center of Onondaga County farm country, as the place to attack Macy, a hero to farmers because of his battle against the utilities that forced them to pay exorbitant rates for hookups to power lines. Then Moses moved on to Rochester. Reported the *World-Telegram*: "Upstate audiences were surprised by the advocacy by Mr. Moses of a sales tax, and startled when he struck at Mr. Macy, but they were left speechless last night at Convention Hall in Rochester, when he casually gave his opinion that . . . Herbert Hoover, still technically the party's national leader, failed to realize the need for action in fighting the Depression and had lost his strength of war days." As Moses moved on to Buffalo, fifth city on his itinerary, the *World-Telegram* reported that he "left behind him a trail of bewildered and frightened party leaders. In four days, the upstate leaders say, he has alienated four large blocs of Republican voters." Senate majority leader George R. Fearon of Syracuse had warned Davison not to nominate Moses. "Don't do it," Fearon had said. "I know Moses." Now he told Davison, "Well, you've done it. Now we're going to lose the Legislature." (Trubee scoffed; the Republicans hadn't done that since 1912.)

When he did deign to discuss campaign plans with the men who had expected to help plan his campaign, Moses was firm. There was going to be no eating of bagels in Jewish neighborhoods or of sausages in Italian while photographers clicked away, he told them—he was determined to eschew the side shows which were a traditional part of political campaigns in the state that possessed the largest collection of ethnic blocs in America.

There was, of course, something admirable in this determination—just as there was something admirable in Moses' enunciation of controversial views before groups hostile to those views. Moses' refusal to take the culinary road to the Statehouse could be interpreted as an indication that he was going to take the high road instead, that he was one candidate who would not pander to the people but who would instead discuss important issues with them freely, frankly and fully, and who would say what he believed—even if what he believed was that the state needed a sales tax.

But such an interpretation turned out to be an inadequate explanation of Moses' campaign tactics. For the candidate, it turned out, was declining not only to pander to the people but, as much as possible, even to talk to them. And while the road he took in the campaign may not have been the culinary, it was certainly not the high, either.

Because Moses was less well known upstate than in and around New York City, his campaign managers suggested a heavier-than-usual "crossroads campaign," the traditional gubernatorial candidate's automobile tour of upstate towns and villages. Moses replied that there wasn't going to be *any* crossroads campaign; he was not going to visit upstate towns and villages; he was not going to appear upstate at all except in large cities such as Buffalo, Rochester and Syracuse—and even in the cities there would be no cocktail receptions, no coffee-and-cake receptions, no walking tours of shopping districts, no attempts at all to meet the public. His only appearances would be formal speeches. Then he told his campaign managers that he was going to follow the same policy in and around New York City; his only public appearances anywhere would be for formal speeches. And there would not be many of *them*. When he finished cutting down the schedule of speeches they had planned, his campaign managers realized that he was going to appear in public exactly twelve times. With the exception of those twelve occasions, his only communication with the voters he wanted to elect him to office would come through press releases.

And if the campaign managers were at first dejected at Moses' insistence on keeping the number of his speeches small, they were soon to count it a blessing. For, as Windels put it, "every time he opened his mouth, he lost ten thousand votes."

Moses' first speech—delivered at the Kismet Temple, a huge auditorium in Brooklyn, after he was escorted to the podium by a steel-helmeted American Legion band and a cadre of the Old Guard, who had dined with him before the rally at their spiritual home, the Union League Club—started the campaign off on the wrong foot.

Moses had always been as much a fanatic on the subject of religion as his grandmother and mother. He had always insisted that he was not Jewish.* He did everything he could to make his feelings clear: he sent his daughters to an Episcopalian school, made disparaging remarks about qualities he felt characterized Jews and, when he learned that the editors of the *Jewish Encyclopedia* were planning to include his biography in its pages, threatened to sue them for libel if they did. To a people that had suffered because of their religion and that was suffering still—in 1934, thousands of New York Jews were agonizing over the fate of relatives trapped in Germany—Moses' attempt to deny it was contemptible. Jews who knew of his feelings regarded him with bitterness; members of Temple Emanu-El, the congregation that included most of the leaders of the Jewish community and therefore most of the men who were familiar with Moses' beliefs, laughed bitterly at the fact that he was seen at many funerals of Catholic Tammany politicians at St. Patrick's Cathedral, but almost never at funerals at Emanu-El.† City Comptroller Joseph D. McGoldrick, discussing Moses with a group of Jewish leaders, was shocked at the intensity of their feelings. "To them," McGoldrick says, "he was a Jew who had renounced his religion and that was worse than anything. He was an apostate to his faith."

But not many Jews were privy to Moses' feelings. Because of his name, they simply assumed he was of their faith. Assumed it, that is, until his first speech, in which, apparently stung by a similar assumption by the press, he brought up the subject of religion himself, and brought it up in a way deeply offensive to Jews. "Moses didn't say, 'I'm a Jew and I'm proud

* He based his assertion on the fact that he had been neither circumcised nor bar-mitzvah, ignoring the fact that, at the time, Jewish theologians generally agreed that Jewishness was a matter of birth rather than conviction, that a Jew is anyone whose mother was a Jew—a definition that meant that Moses' grandmother could not escape being a Jew no matter how hard she tried, that Moses' mother could not avoid it either and that neither could he. ("*Af al pi shechoteh jehudi hu*," the Talmud says—"Even though he has sinned [converted to another faith], he is a Jew.") By 1974, there would be more controversy on the point. Orthodox and Conservative rabbis still held to the strict traditional view, but the Reform rabbinate allowed considerable discretion to its members. Some Reform rabbis held to the traditional view, but others felt that Jewishness was not a matter of birth but of conviction; in the words of Rabbi Daniel Davis of the Union of American Hebrew Congregations, "My standard is whether or not he wants to be a Jew." Said Davis, therefore: "All you can say about Mr. Moses is that he had Jewish forebears but he did not consider himself Jewish."

† "Jim Farley would come, but not Robert Moses," says Emanu-El's funeral director, Samuel Berliner.

of it,' as he should have," recalls Paul Windels. "Instead, he said, 'It's nobody's business what my religion is.' And that got a lot of people very angry." Soon, in shabby *shuls* in the Bronx as well as at Temple Emanu-El, Robert Moses was being called by a term which comes close to being the ultimate insult among pious Jews. Moses, they said, was an *apicoris*, "a man who says he isn't what he is."

Succeeding speeches were worse.

Moses insisted on beginning many of them with an attempt to "dispose of" a "false issue" that he maintained the press was raising: the fact that his candidacy was part of an attempt by the "Power Trust" or "Old Guard" to recapture control of the state.

Actually, the press had scarcely mentioned the issue. It was Moses, unable to endure even a hint of criticism, who kept bringing it up. There were press conferences—at least in the early stages of the campaign, while he was still holding press conferences—at which he was the only person who mentioned the phrase "Old Guard." His method of issue disposal, moreover, was not particularly convincing. It consisted of flat assertions: he was not the Old Guard or Power Trust candidate, he said on one occasion; "neither one of these stuffed shirts has any place in my life or acquaintance"; on another, he stated without qualification, "I am a liberal." Not only were these assertions false—both before and after the election, Moses repeatedly declared without qualification, "I am a conservative"—but they sounded false, since Moses was of course unable to explain who had obtained him the nomination if it was not the Old Guard. His assertion that he would regulate utilities as strictly as Lehman had an equally hollow ring, since he did not offer a single specific regulatory proposal. The only result of Moses' insistence on "disposing of" the utilities issue was to keep it fresh in voters' minds—and to keep himself on the defensive about it.

And Moses on the defensive was a more attractive sight than Moses on the attack.

He had decided that the way to defeat Lehman was to destroy the Governor's image. Unfortunately for this strategy, Lehman's case was that rarity: one in which the image was the man. The Governor's intimates knew him as an individual somewhat less than brilliant and aware he was less than brilliant, but determined to make up for this shortcoming by hard work and dedication, and ambitious not for himself—he had not even wanted to be Governor, accepting the post only when Smith and Roosevelt, admiring his integrity and his dedication to liberal principles, insisted that he succeed them—but for the people. And the voters knew him the same way.

After the campaign, Moses himself would say that Lehman "was essentially a cautious, dependable citizen of the old school" who "carried on the work of Smith and Roosevelt without basic innovation" but who was "enormously conscientious and hard-working. . . . I would classify him as a distinguished Governor." Herbert Lehman, Robert Moses would say after the campaign, was a man of "fine character."

Moses knew even better than most of Lehman's intimates that the only thing that mattered with Lehman was principle; it was Lehman who, running the state while Roosevelt was on vacation, had appointed Moses Moreland Commissioner to head a politically sensitive investigation into the bankrupt City Trust Company without bothering to clear it with the Governor—because he thought Moses was the right man for the job. In a score of quarrels between Roosevelt and Moses, Lehman had stood up—quietly, nervously but unshakably—for Moses, for no other reason than that he thought Moses was right. And Moses knew something that even most of Lehman's intimates didn't know—because Lehman never publicized it; he knew that Lehman, touched by the plight of the small depositors who had lost their savings in the City Trust debacle, had donated a million dollars of his own money in an attempt to save the bank. There were no points at which the image could be attacked—truthfully—and Moses knew it, as his statements after the campaign reveal.

But this was not after the campaign. This was the campaign, a campaign in which, at least for Moses, the prize was power. And the voters were soon reading headlines that said "MOSES CALLS LEHMAN WEAK"; "MOSES CALLS LEHMAN STUPID"; "MOSES CALLS LEHMAN PUPPET FORCED TO SPEAK FOR TAMMANY." And the headlines didn't exaggerate the viciousness of Moses' attacks. In the speech in which he called Lehman "weak," he also said that the Governor had "no guts" and that he "applies to every act the test of personal and political expediency." "Puppet" was one of the more polite terms that Moses employed in his accusations about Lehman and Tammany Hall. The Governor is "the respectable front" for the Hall's crooked politicians, Moses said, "the instrument of consolidating their power and furthering their ends." The Governor, he said, is "a miserable, sniveling type of man . . . contemptible." Repeatedly, Moses challenged Lehman to debate him. Moses was, after all, a past president of the Oxford Union. Just let him get slow, plodding Herbert Lehman on the platform and he would tear him apart, he told aides.

Lehman, advised by men who knew Moses well—Proskauer, Shientag and Moskowitz, for example—handled Moses just right. The Governor ignored the invitation to debate—and, to a large extent, he ignored Moses' charges. In fact, to a large extent, he ignored Moses, sticking strictly to a discussion of the issues and his record as he campaigned earnestly—nine speeches in a single day—through the upstate towns and villages and the streets of New York City in which Moses would not deign to appear. The Governor mentioned Moses just three times in the first three weeks of the campaign—and every mention was devastating. In answer to Moses' charges that he was a puppet of Tammany Hall, the Governor pointed out that he had left Moses in charge of the state park system and had increased his powers in other fields—against the advice of Tammany leaders. Weak? He had fought for Moses' park policies—against the Republican legislative leaders who were now backing Moses. The third time Lehman mentioned Moses was in a speech in Binghamton, whose householders paid monthly electric bills to the Associated Gas and Electric System, a utility which had recently been publicly disclosed to have paid State Senator Warren Thayer $21,600 to kill measures that might have lowered its rates:

"The Republican candidate for Governor undertook . . . to eliminate certain . . . issues from this campaign," Lehman said mildly. "He attempts to dispose of the public utility problem by claiming it is not [an] issue. Surely we can understand his desire to avoid the public utility issue. We can appreciate his anxiety to divert attention from the weakness of the record of his party. . . . Unfortunately . . . however, candidates do not make issues. The people make the issues. It is the people themselves who determine those matters upon which they are entitled to honest report. . . . no candidate can tell the people of the State of New York that it is not important to furnish electricity, gas and telephone service to consumers at low rates."

Newspapers throughout the state agreed. Even the Brooklyn *Eagle*, whose editor, Cleveland Rodgers, was one of Moses' most enthusiastic admirers, had to admit, "He cannot dispose of the so-called 'power issue' by oversimplifying it, as he tried to do."

Moses' response was to increase the violence of his attacks and the wildness of his accusations. He accused Lehman of being responsible for corruption in the Court of Claims—an accusation which ignored the fact that the Court was not under the Governor's control and which was not strengthened by the fact that to document the Court's incompetence, Moses accused of drunkenness a judge who actually had been dead for more than a year. He accused Lehman of discussing the City Trust report with him in advance of its publication in 1929 because he was "anxious to avoid an extension of the . . . investigation," a charge that Moses later admitted in private was not true. Some of his charges had no logic at all. He said flatly that Lehman "created most of the state deficit"—although, as Moses well knew and the press pointed out, when Lehman took office, the deficit had been $114,000,000, and the Governor had since reduced it practically to zero. He implied that Lehman had made an alliance with the O'Connell brothers, Dan and Ed, the Democratic bosses of Albany, because he was "afraid" of them—not only afraid in political terms but physically afraid, because the Governor of the State of New York was worried that the two O'Connell boys might beat him up. Incredible as the statement was, there is no other way to interpret Moses' exact words: "He wants O'Connell votes and he is physically afraid of crossing or antagonizing people who, if they have nothing else, have boldness and physical courage."

Even the Governor's financial integrity was not safe from Moses' tongue and pen. In the campaign's most astonishing charge, he startled dozing reporters at a sleepy Republican Women's Club luncheon in Syracuse by accusing Lehman, who had done more to break the utilities' power than any Governor in the state's history, of being the utilities' secret ally. Waving a sheaf of papers that he claimed documented his charges, Moses stated flatly that the Governor had financial "ties with the utility field." And, as the reporters goggled with amazement, he added that the corrupt "Senator Thayer is a very . . . small factor in public utilities in New York State politics. Why, Governor Lehman is much more a factor than Thayer ever thought of being."

When Moses' "documentation" was examined closely, the "ties" he mentioned with such sinister implication turned out to be nothing more than the underwriting of a utility company bond issue—underwriting that had not even been done by Herbert Lehman but by Lehman Brothers, the family banking firm, in which Herbert Lehman had never played much of a role, and from which he had severed every tie years before. (Such scrupulousness was by no means common among public officials of the day, but, as Lehman biographer Allan Nevins put it, "He was scrupulous about everything. If some decision of his might affect a company in which he owned stock, he whipped off a sale of the stock." During Lehman's long public career, there never had been, and never would be again, even the faintest hint of impropriety.) But Moses did not let these facts deter him. Nor did he let deter him the fact that, hard as he tried, he could not find a single direct link in Lehman's life with any utility company. Lehman's banker brothers had such links—so Moses talked about the brothers ("Robert Lehman is on the board of directors of the American International Corporation. Arthur Lehman is a director in the American International, a holding company—really, a surprising list of utilities stocks and bonds: 77,000 Columbia Gas and Electric; 50,000 American Electric Power and Light. . . . There's a lot of this stuff") and then, attempting to establish the Governor's guilt by association, said, "Now, I have got a lot of other stuff with me along these lines. There isn't time to read it, but it is a very interesting record and I am going to refer to it at length to show you how false the Governor is."

It was on October 23 that Moses really went too far. In a speech in Utica's Majestic Theater before two thousand dairy farmers from the surrounding countryside, he called Lehman a "liar."

"That was a word that was just never used then in campaigns for high office," Paul Windels recalls—veteran political observers could not recall it ever having been used in a New York gubernatorial campaign—"and it really sent a wave of shock through everybody. People had been becoming quite angry at the things he was saying about Lehman—you had to know Lehman to understand why—and this was the last straw."

Moses' use of the word was particularly indefensible. It came in the course of his attempt to link Lehman to inflated milk prices, despite the fact that the Governor had no control over such prices. In the Utica speech, Moses told the audience of dairy farmers, angry over the fact that while the price of milk kept rising, the percentage of the price they received from the middleman dairy interests remained small, that Lehman was also responsible for *that*. The Governor, he said, was linked to dairy interests—because, he said, Lehman Brothers had "traded in the stock of companies interested in the milk business"—and had "simply lied to the people of the state" when he claimed that he did not control the State Milk Control Board, which set both milk prices and the percentage of those prices paid to farmers. "That was a deliberate, cold-blooded evasion," Moses said. "In fact, it was just a lie. . . . He had the authority himself, but lacked the guts to exercise it."

Moses' accusation was a lie: he said that Lehman controlled two members of the board when in fact the Governor controlled only one, the other two being Republicans removable only by the Legislature. But when Lehman pointed this out, Moses' only answer was to repeat the charge the next evening, saying, "I said that Governor Lehman lied about the milk administration; he did lie about it."

Lehman's advisers gathered in a hasty strategy conference to decide what to do about the insult. As it turned out, they didn't have to do a thing. Moses' own supporters did it for them.

General John F. O'Ryan, the respected reformer who, along with Moses, had been blackballed out of the 1933 Fusion nomination for mayor by Seabury, had been backing Moses for Governor. Now the General announced that he wasn't backing Moses any longer. "Mr. Moses," he said, "has indicated by his own acts and words his unfitness for the office he seeks." Even the campaign manager for Moses' own running mate, GOP United States senatorial candidate E. Harold Cluett, publicly announced that he would not vote for the head of the GOP ticket. "He is not the type of man qualified for the leadership of the Republican Party," he said. Running mate McGoldrick, Republican and Fusion Party nominee for Comptroller, kept silent publicly but let anyone who asked privately know how he felt. "The thing was terrible," McGoldrick was to say later. "Those savage attacks on Lehman, personal stuff, just wouldn't wash." Upstate newspapers that for generations had supported every Republican candidate for statewide office announced that they couldn't support this one. Most New York City newspapers rushed into print with editorials like one in the *World-Telegram* which said: "Robert Moses, as was to be expected, has proved a far more aggressive and agile campaigner than the Governor. But aggressiveness cannot in itself inspire confidence. . . . Realities are realities—not to be concealed by curtains of words or by calling Governor Lehman 'weakling' and 'liar.' "

Moses' only response was to keep calling Lehman a liar, to flail out at the Governor more savagely than ever, and to broaden the arc of his wild swings until he was attacking not only the Governor's advisers but men connected only peripherally or not at all with his administration. Within a matter of days, he had attained a novel—and perhaps unique—distinction: he was the first—and perhaps the only—candidate in the history of New York State on whom a radio network demanded nonstop libel insurance; the Mutual Broadcasting System refused to broadcast any of his speeches unless the Republican campaign committee purchased a policy that covered every word that Moses said on the air.

Some of Moses' sallies were reminders of the brilliance of the political invective he had displayed in the La Guardia mayoral campaign of 1933—when he himself had not been personally involved. Jim Farley, still bleeding from his dissection by Moses in the mayoral campaign, wandered into the gubernatorial contest with a quiet little statement of support for Lehman and promptly found himself back on Moses' operating table. Noting that Farley was president of a firm which supplied sand and other building materials to contractors, including some who received government contracts, as well as being Postmaster General and chief patronage dispenser for the New Deal, Moses dubbed him the "sand, mail and bag man of the national administration" and then shortened the description to: "Jim Farley, the big 'bag man.' "

But in most of Moses' attacks, brilliance was made the slave of rage. The scalpel was discarded in favor of the bludgeon—and the swings Moses took with the latter weapon were wild indeed. During its final two weeks, his campaign was almost entirely a campaign *ad homines*, an exercise in wholesale insinuation and vituperation. Seeing his hopes for elective office vanishing, he spewed venom over his opponents—all his opponents, former friends as well as long-time foes, men who were motivated by principle as well as men motivated by politics.

In speeches broadcast across the state by the libel-insured Mutual network, Moses called Roosevelt's former law partner, Basil O'Connor, a "fixer and a chiseler," Seabury a demagogue with a "messianic complex" and the state's senior United States Senator, Dr. Royal S. Copeland, a former eye surgeon, a "professional mountebank."

The closest of former friends—men such as Joseph Proskauer and Morris S. Tremaine, State Comptroller under Smith, Roosevelt and Lehman, with whom Moses had worked closely for years—were not immune. Tremaine, he implied, was senile. "I like Morris Tremaine personally," he said. "He is an old chum of mine, but I think he is getting stale at Albany. . . . Morris ought to get away from statistics for a while. I can guarantee to take care of him in one of our steamer chairs at Jones Beach." He accused Nathan Straus, whose integrity was held in almost as much awe as Lehman's, of using his position as head of the State Housing Board to persuade a low-income housing development to purchase his own property for $200,000 more than it was worth. "If Senator Straus made no claim to be anything more than a very slick trader . . . I should have a good deal more respect for him. When, however, he pretends to be a philanthropist, civic champion and uplifter, it becomes a little disgusting," Moses said.*

If he could not find anything about Lehman's associates to attack, he attacked them for alleged misdeeds of their fathers—even if the fathers were dead. "What is Jack Murray doing at the head of Governor Lehman's campaign committee if power connections are taboo in politics?" Moses demanded in one such charge. As the *Herald Tribune* pointed out, "Mr. Moses did not explain his reference, but it was understood to infer that Mr. Murray's *father*, the late Thomas E. Murray, was connected with the [Consolidated] Edison Company."

If there happened to be any truth in this onslaught of innuendo, Moses did not provide any convincing proof of it. Not one of his more serious charges was documented. Their subjects began treating them almost as jokes. When reporters asked Straus for his reply, he would only say: "Bob Moses

* Straus's friends, who knew that the "slick trader" was so anxious to help provide decent houses for impoverished families that he had once sold a valuable property to the Housing Board for exactly seventy cents per square foot, felt a little disgust themselves.

will be in the limelight for another ten days and is entitled to all the fun he can get out of it. As one of his oldest friends and the man who sponsored his entire park program in the State Senate, I wish him all the luck in the world."

The one victim of Moses' attacks who did reply at length did so in telling fashion. The day after a particularly far-ranging Moses speech, Ed Flynn issued a statement saying, "The emotional instability of this candidate was never better demonstrated than last night, when, without rhyme or reason, he denounced in wholesale lots men who need no defense at my hands. If the campaign were to continue much longer it would reach the point where this candidate would completely satisfy at least himself, if no one else, that he is the only honest and efficient public servant that this state has ever known. Why does he not state publicly the opinion so often privately expressed by him, of his Republican confreres that he now so affectionately takes to his bosom? . . . Because he is now beholden to these members of the 'Old Guard' for his nomination, he does not dare to publicly repeat his real opinion of them."

Only one of Lehman's key supporters was spared the lash of Moses' tongue or pen. He was Alfred E. Smith.

Thirty years after the election, in the midst of a discussion about the former Governor with a luncheon guest, a distinguished historian, Moses suddenly began talking about the day he asked Smith to support him against Lehman. The historian relates that Moses said, "I went to see the Governor and I said, 'Governor, you owe this to me. With your backing, I'm going to go ahead and win this thing. You owe it to me.' And you know what he said to me—after I had worked with him all those years? He said, 'Bob, you know I play this game like a regular.'

"Well, the pain in that man's [Moses'] eyes!" the historian recalls. "Here was a man, the most powerful man in New York State, telling about something that happened thirty years before. And it still really hurt him."

According to Smith's daughter and confidante, Emily, the former Governor had wanted desperately not to hurt Moses. But he had no choice. Moses might deny in public that he was the candidate of the Old Guard, but Smith knew he was. And the "Old Guard" was not just a phrase to Smith—they were the men who had fought against his efforts to cement into place above the heads of the state's defenseless poor a roof of social welfare legislation that would give them some protection against the cold winds of illness, injury, old age and unemployment. He knew that if not held in check by a Democratic Governor, they would begin tearing down that structure brick by brick. No matter how deep his personal affection for Moses, he couldn't let them do that. And if Smith felt he owed Moses a lot—and he did feel that way—he owed Lehman a lot, too, not only for Lehman's cash backing of his own campaigns but for Lehman's vigilant maintenance of, and attempts to add to, the social welfare structure, for Lehman's continual gracious public reminders that he was only continuing Smith's work, and for the considerate requests for advice that had made Smith feel a part of state government again. Smith's personal feelings for Moses were something special, of course, but the former Governor respected Lehman. And he had, after all, played a key role, perhaps *the* key role, in making Lehman Governor; he couldn't try now, without any good reason, to oust Lehman from the post in which he had helped place him. Most important, as he said to Moses, "I play this game like a regular"; he had done so for forty years—his rage and bitterness at Roosevelt had not yet driven him to the point at which he would later, for the first time in his life, break with the party to which he had given so much of it.

When Lehman asked Smith to campaign for him, Smith did. But he campaigned only for the Governor, not against Moses, avoiding any personal attack on him. The press, antagonized by Moses, made capital of Smith's presence in Lehman's camp, but Raymond Ingersoll, one of the few old Smith supporters on Moses' side, was able to reply that "Governor Smith has never said a word against Bob Moses and he never will."

And Moses didn't attack Smith, either. When, moreover, the two men met at a dinner party soon after the end of the campaign, friends who had been apprehensively watching out of the corners of their eyes saw that within minutes they were talking together in as complete a rapport as ever, Moses as respectful and Smith as friendly as in the days before the campaign. "Nothing could disturb that friendship," says the host at that dinner party. "Nothing!" And the proof of how right he was, of course, came with the opening of the Central Park Zoo less than a month after the end of the campaign.

It wasn't what Moses said that most antagonized voters; it was how he said it. He let his contempt for the public show.

"As bad as his speeches read," one observer recalls, "they read a lot better than he read them." The problem was not, observers agreed, that Moses was an unimpressive figure on a podium. On the contrary, he was very impressive. Describing one Moses speech, a reporter wrote: "He stepped up to the 'reading desk' a great bulk of a man, leant comfortably forward and began to speak with the clearest voice and the easiest manner in the world." His broad shoulders, heavy chest, jaw and eyebrows, combined with the physical presence, the sense of poise and self-assurance, he emitted, made him exude strength and power. His voice fit in: it was deep and resonant, just nasal enough to sting.

But if Moses was a powerful figure, he was not a pleasant one. When he was introduced, his smiles as the audience applauded were brief and the look on his face was more one of barely concealed disdain than appreciation. (There was no acknowledgment of the applause.) He generally cut the applause short by stepping abruptly to the "reading desk" and preparing to begin his speech, as if anxious to be done with it so he could depart for some worthwhile activity. As he read his text, he seldom bothered to look up, sometimes going five minutes without a single glance to acknowledge his listeners' presence. When the audience interrupted him with applause, he stepped back with a look that indicated nothing so much as boredom—and resumed reading as quickly as possible. "He made no gestures, he did not vary the note of his voice," wrote one reporter. "He gave no hint of oratory or of rhetorical periods. His only emphasis was a loudening of his voice to drive his points home." "He gave the impression that he was way above them," recalls running mate McGoldrick. "He was alienating them all the way through." He looked like nothing so much as a man dining at a poor relation's home, feeling strongly that it was an act of great condescension and kindness on his part to be there—and determined to let all the people present know he felt that way. The only time that pose was modified was when he got caught up in what he was saying. Then the steady loudening of his voice continued until it was very loud indeed. Loud and harsh. His right hand, which had been resolutely kept in his pocket up until then, would come out—and it would begin to make the pounding gesture his aides had learned to dread. Because there was a microphone on the lectern on which he was pounding, the smack of the palm, thudding down to emphasize each point, would be magnified, and as it rang out over the audience harder and harder, faster and faster, an observer could almost begin to see them squirm, not out of boredom but out of uneasiness, in their seats. As Moses stood before them shouting at them and pounding the podium while not bothering to look at them, he was, all too obviously, not appealing to them for their support but lecturing them, telling them in no uncertain terms what he wanted them to do—and letting them know they had better do it.

The reaction of audiences showed how Moses affected them. Invariably there was more applause at the beginning of a speech than at the end. With each succeeding appearance, the enthusiasm of his audience waned. The number of people who came to hear him fell further and further below the number that had been expected. At a rally in Queens on November 1 that had been expected to be a high spot of the campaign, only one of every five seats in the Jamaica High School auditorium was occupied.

Moses' last appearance showed how little remained of the public enthusiasm that had greeted his nomination. That enthusiasm had persuaded his campaign managers to rent the state's largest auditorium, Madison Square Garden, for a climactic rally on the Saturday night before Election Day. So certain had they been of an overflow crowd that to avoid unseemly jams at the entrance they had printed tickets, to be distributed in advance by local GOP organizations, and had announced that no one would be admitted without a ticket, and that the doors would be closed a half hour before the speeches began.

On the night before the rally, stacks of tickets remained untouched in GOP clubhouses. Despite a frantic last-day effort to persuade loyal Republicans to take them and agree to show up, despite a decision to leave the doors of the Garden open even during the speeches themselves in hopes that passers-by might wander in, far less than half of the Garden's 25,000 seats were filled. The people who were present were so dispirited that when George Everett, a professional cheer and song leader, took the microphone at a few minutes past eight to "warm up" the crowd, he asked them why they were so "downhearted."

When the candidate rose to speak, he saw, looming down on him from the balcony, thousands of empty seats. The arrangements committee had placed a small American flag on each seat on the Garden floor below him to be waved by its occupant and he saw staring at him a sea of flags rather than a sea of faces.

And there, in front of the empty seats, spotlighted in the center of the cavernous, half-empty arena, the candidate stood—pounding his palm hard on the lectern, lashing out in a voice loud and angry, almost ranting, the featured performer of a program that, the *Times* reported, "was marked by more attacks on personalities than any similar meeting in recent political history."

At the polls, the verdict of the people was even clearer. It was Lehman 2,201,729, Moses 1,393,638. Robert Moses, the candidate of the party favored by an overwhelming majority of the state's voters, a candidate for whom, the *Herald Tribune* reported, the GOP waged "the hardest campaign that party has waged for a state ticket in a half dozen years," a candidate who had entered the campaign on the very crest of a wave of favorable publicity that had been ten solid years in building, lost by more than 800,000 votes. His percentage of the votes cast—35 percent—was the smallest percentage polled by a gubernatorial candidate of any major party in the 157-year history of New York State. As George Fearon had predicted, he dragged his party to defeat with him: for the first time in twenty-one years, the GOP lost both houses of the State Legislature. (The GOP won back the Assembly the next year and didn't lose it again for another twenty-nine years;* the year in which Robert Moses headed the Republican ticket was, in other words, the only election in a fifty-year span in which the GOP lost both houses.) He lost upstate communities that no Republican candidate for *any* office had ever lost before; he even ran behind Lehman in the total upstate vote. (This fact so astonished veteran political reporters that they refused to believe the unofficial Election Night tallies that first revealed it.)

The Old Guard which had foisted Moses' candidacy upon the GOP was adequately punished. Its influence would remain strong in the party, but county leaders who couldn't afford to let their local candidates be caught in the undertow of the sinking of a poor candidate and who were determined that one as poor as Moses should never again head the ticket, would never let the Old Guard hand-pick another candidate. His candidacy was its Waterloo.

Moses was in later years to attempt to alibi away his defeat by saying that he had simply been one of many candidates caught in the landslide vote by which the nation in 1934 expressed its approval of Franklin D. Roosevelt. On the day after the election he told an interviewer, "I said when I went into

* Until the Lyndon Johnson landslide of 1964.

this campaign that I did so knowing it was an attempt to swim up Niagara"; no one, he said, could have beaten a New Deal supporter in New York State in 1934.

This is true in part. The New Deal landslide of 1934 swept right-wingers to defeat all across the country. But Moses' explanation does not account for the size of his defeat. His previous popularity; the top-heavy GOP registration in the state; the lavish financing of his campaign—all these factors had led keen political observers like Baron Warn to predict at the time of his nomination a campaign that would be close no matter what the national trend. It was, these observers concluded after Election Day, the reaction of voters to personal, not party, philosophy, as well as to Moses' personality that had eroded the support with which he entered the campaign. Swimming up Niagara was one way of looking at Moses' campaign. In brilliance of strategy and execution, it was perhaps more comparable to the charge of the Light Brigade.

The definitive word comes from Joseph McGoldrick. McGoldrick was running on Moses' ticket—but since he was running for a city office, Comptroller, only in the city. At the beginning of the campaign, he was approached by a pollster named Harry Gordon Lynn whom politicians, including Al Smith, regarded as amazingly accurate.

"Lynn was doing the polling—secretly—for Lehman, but he came to me and said for $2,000, as long as he was doing it for Lehman, he would do it for me at the same time," McGoldrick recalls. "Lynn's first report to me was that Moses would lose the city by 550,000, but I would win it by 75,000. He said, 'Moses is going to be defeated, but don't worry, you'll win.' The second week, he said Moses would lose by 600,000, but I'll still win by 50,000. The third week it was 700,000 and 25,000. And on the Friday before election, he came in and said, 'Boss, you can't make it. Moses is going to lose the city by 800,000 and you can't overcome that: you're going to lose by about 25,000.' And that's approximately what happened. I lost by 23,000." Moses needn't have lost by nearly as great a margin as he did, McGoldrick says; in fact, if Moses had held his deficit in the city to the 550,000 figure at which it stood at the beginning of the campaign and had retained the normal GOP support upstate, he might well have won the election, for GOP candidates normally "came down to the city line"— compiled a margin above the northern boundary of the Bronx—with an edge of more than 600,000 votes. It was his tactics and personality, not national attitudes toward the New Deal, that persuaded tens of thousands of potential supporters to vote against him. "He booted that campaign himself," McGoldrick would say flatly. "If it was a disaster, he made it one."

On Election Night, Moses was careful to show an elaborate disregard of the vote. Reporters ushered into his apartment at 7 Gracie Square saw him poring over a map of the city, "outlining park and playground projects, while he whistled softly" and "giving only perfunctory attention, apparently, to the election returns relayed to him." "I haven't the slightest regrets in any way, shape or manner," he said. "I've done the best I could. I've conducted an honorable campaign and adhered to my convictions. That's all there is to it." And he said that he was planning to return to his park work the next morning.

There was no question about his returning to his city job, of course, but the fact that he included in the statement his state park work showed that he knew Herbert Lehman much better than his campaign attacks on the Governor would have made it appear. For Lehman's treatment of Moses after the campaign was the definitive word on the Governor's character.

No sooner had the landslide aspects of his defeat of Moses become apparent than the *Daily News,* whose publisher was temporarily feuding with Moses, called on Lehman to oust his disloyal subordinate, and so did key legislators and a number of the Governor's most influential supporters—including Farley and Flynn and, according to some sources, President Roosevelt. Now—with Moses' prestige, his previously invulnerable armor against ouster moves, riddled with holes—was the time to bring pressure on the members of the State Parks Council to elect another chairman, they said.

Al Smith heard what was going on and hurried over to Lehman's apartment at 820 Park Avenue to urge the Governor not to move against Moses. He needn't have bothered. Lehman was bitterly hurt by Moses' charges, but he would not allow personal feelings to interfere with his duty. "We have differed in the past and probably will in the future, but in the planning and administration of parks, parkways and recreational facilities, Bob Moses has no superior on the face of the world," the Governor announced. Moses could continue to head the state park system as long as he was Governor, he said. "He was terribly sensitive because he said I called him a liar in the campaign," Moses would recall, but "I found him a very nice fellow to deal with. A very decent, honorable, honest fellow. He always supported me when he was Governor."

Moses should have known that Lehman would support him. After all, the "cowardly, sniveling, lying weakling" had always supported him before.

Why did Robert Moses, previously so talented at public relations, antagonize the public during the episode in his career in which he most needed its support?

In part, because his success in public relations had been due primarily to his masterful utilization of a single public relations technique: identifying himself with a popular cause. This technique was especially advantageous to him because his philosophy—that accomplishment, Getting Things Done, is the only thing that matters, that the end justifies any means, however ruthless—might not be universally popular. By keeping the public eye focused on the cause, the end, the ultimate benefit to be obtained, the technique kept the public eye from focusing on the methods by which the benefit was to be obtained. The technique was also especially advantageous to him because its focus on the cause kept his personality safely blurred.

Moses' use of the technique was a totally conscious one. Knowing precisely what he was doing—"the first rule is to stay on the side of the angels" —he continually urged reporters, under the guise of modesty, to "stick to the parks and playgrounds and bridges, and don't write about me." And he had consistently made sure that his instructions were followed by furnishing only bare, carefully selected facts about himself. From the moment in 1925 when he dramatically propelled himself into the public consciousness by announcing that he was fighting for parks against a "little group of selfish millionaires," he had identified himself so thoroughly with the glowing cause of parks that for nine years the public had seen him always through that glow. Everything he did, he said, was in the name of parks (and, of course, of parkways and bridges that helped people reach parks), and the public believed this. After a while he began—also consciously—to identify himself with related battles against crooked politicians and red-taping bureaucrats—and so cleverly did he make this additional identification that the public accepted it, too. During those years, the public never saw Robert Moses the man.

But in a race for public office, the public focus is more on the individuals involved. Causes championed by a candidate are important to voters, but mainly as they help illuminate his personality and philosophy. It was a man they were voting for, not a constitutional amendment. They wanted to see the man.

And they did. Robert Moses' only campaign for elective office tore away from him the protective coloration in which he had always appeared before the public, and stripped him naked to its gaze. As a candidate for elective office he was no longer only Robert Moses the fighter-for-parks. For the first time, the public got a good look at Robert Moses the man—and it didn't like what it saw.

This explanation, of course, does not answer another question: Why couldn't a man as skilled as Moses at manipulating and charming people he needed, charm the voters now that he needed *them,* conceal from them his philosophy and personality, persuade them—at least for a period of a few weeks—that he understood and sympathized with their aims and aspirations and wanted to help them achieve those aims? Why couldn't he keep the voters from knowing—at least for a period of a few weeks—what he thought of them?

The answer to this question lies somewhere deep in Robert Moses' nature.

In part, it lies in the arrogance that was that nature's most striking manifestation. Robert Moses' arrogance was first of all intellectual; he had consciously compared his mental capacity with other men's and had concluded that its superiority was so great that it was a waste of time for him to discuss, to try to understand or even to listen to their opinions. But there was more to his arrogance than that. Had it been merely a product of a consciously reasoned comparison, it would have been governable by reason, reason that must have informed him that if he hoped to win the prize he so desperately wanted he must for a period of a few weeks conceal his contempt for the public. Had his arrogance been merely intellectual, he could have disciplined himself—this man with a will strong enough to discipline himself to a life of unending toil—for the few weeks necessary to give him a chance at the Governorship. But his arrogance was emotional, visceral, a driving force created by heredity and hardened by living, a force too strong to be tamed by intellect, a force that drove him to do things for which there is no wholly rational explanation. It wasn't just that Robert Moses didn't want to listen to the public. It was that he *couldn't* listen, couldn't—even for the sake of the power he coveted—try to make people feel that he understood and sympathized with them.

And there was something else behind Robert Moses' arrogance, a strange, flickering shadow. For not only could Robert Moses not help showing his contempt for others, he seemed actually to take pleasure in showing this contempt—a deep, genuine pleasure, a pleasure whose intensity leads to the suspicion that, in a way, he *needed* to display his superiority, with a need so great that he simply could not dissemble it. How else to explain the fact that, even when he was appearing before the public to ask for its support, he could not help ostentatiously flaunting condescension and boredom—boredom even at its applause? Robert Moses may, moreover, have understood that he had this need. He may have understood that he would not be able to appear before the voters without having to show them—so clearly that there could be no mistake about it—how much he despised them. For such self-knowledge would explain—and it is difficult to find another explanation—his decision to shun, to so perhaps unprecedented an extent, all public appearances save for a few formal speeches.

Such an explanation also helps to illuminate Moses' otherwise almost inexplicable treatment of the press.

Nobody understood the press and how to manipulate it better than he. And therefore he must have known, intellectually, that he would forfeit its support—support he both needed and wanted—if he attacked reporters personally and directly. Something far stronger than intellect, something stronger than considerations of strategy, stronger even than a chance for the Governorship, was driving him, something that made it simply impossible for him to accept criticism, even the discreetly implied criticism of the reporters' questions at his first press conference.

As for the vilification that he spewed over his opponent and everyone connected with him—former friends as well as enemies—it is difficult to escape the conclusion that the explanation for this, too, lay in character rather than campaign tactics. Since his earliest days in power, Moses had tried not just to defeat but to destroy anyone who stood in his way—by any means possible. The definitive word on Robert Moses' gubernatorial campaign may be an unconsciously revealing remark that Moses made years later to his friendly biographer, Cleveland Rodgers: "I made the only kind of campaign I knew how to make."

22. *Order Number 129*

To THE EXTENT that Robert Moses had lost his popularity, however, it was to be restored to him almost immediately—by his most powerful enemy.

Franklin Roosevelt had said of Moses: "I don't trust him. I don't like him." As Governor, Roosevelt had been forced to ration himself to occasional sips of revenge on the man who had frustrated his dreams for a Taconic parkway, humiliated him and viciously ridiculed not only himself but his wife. But now Roosevelt was President. And he evidently felt it was time to indulge himself.

The President's move against Moses had actually begun in February 1934, months before Moses' gubernatorial race. But it had been kept completely secret from the public for that entire year. Corporation Counsel Paul Windels, one of the handful of men aware of it during 1934, recalls vividly how he first heard about it.

"On February 22—I'll never forget it—I was sitting home reading the Sunday papers in my home on Pineapple Street when La Guardia called. He said, 'What are you doing?' I told him. He said, 'Well, I'm down in Bay Ridge making a talk and I'll be by in about twenty minutes to pick you up.'

"I got in the car and no sooner did I sit down than he cut loose. 'Jesus Christ, of all the people in the City of New York I had to pick the one man who Roosevelt won't stand for and he won't give me any more money unless I get rid of him. Jesus Christ, I had to pick the one that he hated. Jesus Christ!' He was shaking his fists in the air and shouting. 'Jesus Christ! Jesus Christ! Seven million people in the city and I had to pick the one Roosevelt can't stand!' "

La Guardia, unfamiliar with state politics, had been unaware when he brought Moses into his administration—at least partly because he thought Moses could help him obtain New Deal public works funds—of the hatred between Moses and the man who *was* the New Deal. And Moses hadn't bothered to tell him.

But La Guardia hadn't been allowed to remain in ignorance for long. On February 21, Harold Ickes, Secretary of the Interior and Administrator of the Public Works Administration, having summoned the Mayor to Washington on direct orders from the President, informed the Mayor, on direct orders from the President, of the President's feelings, and demanded that La Guardia dismiss Moses from the board of the PWA-financed Triborough Bridge Authority. In Ickes' *Secret Diary,* he wrote that "La Guardia regretted the situation and said that if he had known it existed he wouldn't have thought for a minute of putting Moses on the board. He expressed the highest regard for the President and asked me to give him a few days to see what he might work out."

But in the next few days, La Guardia was able to work out nothing. For Moses did not prove at all cooperative.

The Mayor may have expected Moses to quietly resign. After all, Moses was his appointee and it is traditional in American politics for an appointee to resign when the appointer wishes him to. Moreover, there was so much at stake here: a vital project for the city which could be built only if the federal government was willing to pay for it. One man surely could not think of standing in the way just so he could be in charge of it. And while Moses could not be forced to resign from the Triborough post—he had drawn the Triborough law so that Authority commissioners could be removed only on stated charges after a formal hearing—he held his park commissionership, a post both men then considered much more important, only at the pleasure of the Mayor, and the Mayor therefore possessed a powerful weapon: he could threaten to remove Moses from the more important post unless he resigned from the less important.

But Moses had learned—from his dealings with Roosevelt when FDR was Governor—that he could force a Governor to back down by threatening to publicize certain matters, such as requests for patronage. He had learned that he could force a Governor to back down on more complex issues by simplifying them through a threat to resign over them, a threat which reduced the issue to the question of whether or not the public wanted him to continue in office. And now Moses employed the same technique on a mayor. He told La Guardia that if the Mayor insisted on his resignation, he would resign, all right—but he would resign not just from the Triborough post but from the park commissionership as well, and would issue a public statement disclosing why he was resigning, a statement making clear that the Mayor had bowed to outside pressure to remove a city official who had done nothing to justify such treatment.

La Guardia had picked up Windels on the day after his conference with Ickes to ask the Sage of Pineapple Street for advice. Recalls Windels: "I said, 'Now, look, you've been elected mayor on the theory that you are going to run an absolutely independent administration. . . . You can't start off by knuckling under to outside dictation. If you do, your name is going to be mud.' I told him that if he ousted Moses, the public would believe that he could be pressured in a situation like this and throw out a man who the public thinks is wonderful, and I told him, 'If you do that, you'll never be able to erase that from the public's mind.' " From others—including City Chamberlain and New Deal Brain Truster Adolf A. Berle, Jr., the link between the city and federal administrations—La Guardia received the same advice.*

La Guardia stalled. Repeatedly he promised Ickes that Moses' resignation was imminent—and repeatedly he came up with excuses for new delays. But Roosevelt was, Ickes wrote in his diary, "implacable." The President was determined to have his revenge, and in case that determination flagged—and there is no reason to believe it ever did—little Louis Howe and big Jim Farley were there to keep it fresh, both of them urging him on. He instructed Ickes to take a more forceful tone. The PWA chief, who hardly knew Moses, was to confess later that "from the beginning I had had no stomach for this whole affair. . . . I was in the unhappy position of having to admit to myself that Moses was an efficient administrator and a public-spirited citizen." But, he said, "my loyalty ran to the President and I was determined to work it out to his satisfaction if I could." He told La Guardia that he would not approve new Triborough requisitions until the Mayor had obtained Moses' resignation from the Triborough board. La Guardia stalled. Then Ickes said that he would not approve a single new PWA project of any type in New York City—not hospital, school or subway—until Moses resigned. Still La Guardia stalled. "He would make promises and then he would break his promises," Ickes wrote. "It was 'Give me this payment and I'll get rid of him next week'—that kind of thing," Windels recalled. And the stalling succeeded in keeping payments coming for Triborough and the other projects.

Then came the gubernatorial campaign, with Moses running as a Republican. "Naturally I had to declare a truce during that period in order to avoid a charge that I was playing politics," Ickes said. More requisitions were approved.

But as soon as the votes were counted, the truce was off. On November 7, the day after the election, Moses sent to Washington new Triborough requisitions totaling $8,100,000. The requisitions reached Ickes' desk on November 8, and on that date the PWA Administrator telephoned La Guardia and told the Mayor that they would stay on his desk, unsigned, until Moses' resignation lay there beside them. Furthermore, Ickes said, no new PWA projects would be approved for New York City. And the Administrator apparently made a further threat. In his *Secret Diary* he wrote: "I am considering refusing to honor requisitions for funds" for projects already under way in the city—an action that would throw out of work the tens of thousands of men now employed on them.

---

* Berle telegraphed: THE PRESIDENT: PERSONAL: MOSES MATTER PROBABLY WILL BECOME A NATIONAL INCIDENT WITHIN A FEW DAYS. . . . I THINK THIS IS ONE OF THE THINGS YOU CANNOT DO UNLESS THERE ARE REASONS OTHER THAN PERSONAL GIVING GROUND FOR PUBLIC DEFENSE. MOSES WILL CERTAINLY RESIGN NOT MERELY FROM TRI-BOROUGH BUT FROM CITY ADMINISTRATION STATING HIS POSITION OF WHICH OUR OPPOSITION FRIENDS ARE PREPARED TO MAKE THE MOST. I HARDLY KNOW MOSES BUT SUGGEST THERE MIGHT BE MORE REAL DEVILS TO FIGHT. REMEMBER THE EXECUTION OF THE DUKE [sic] D'ENGHIEN BROKE NAPOLEON.

* * *

All through November and December, the drama of revenge and power played on. Its cast included some of the most colorful characters in American politics. On one side, jaw jaunty, cigarette holder cocked, face open and friendly, the Master Politician in the White House. Beside him the Old Curmudgeon of Interior, the scarred, doughty reformer from Chicago ("almost the incarnation of lonely, righteous and inexhaustible pugnacity," one reviewer was to call him) who in less than two years on the national stage had proven himself a character actor of the first magnitude, winning the public's heart with the dour, skeptical but kindly glare that he flashed at it over the top of the rimless spectacles that were forever slipping down along his nose, and with his flawless performance as the tart-tongued, terrible-tempered but invincibly honest defender of the public interest. On the other side—"a modern Horatius on another unfinished bridge," one reviewer was to call him—Robert Moses, seriously ill and confined for most of the drama to his home with an influenza which had deepened into an illness variously described as "pneumonia" or "nervous exhaustion." In the middle, glowering out from under his big black Stetson, the prickly Little Flower of City Hall. Circling around these stars, spear carriers perfectly type-cast: the burly, bald, gregarious Postmaster General; the lean, sharp-eyed, sardonic City Chamberlain; and the wizened little gnome whose proposed appointment to a minor state park post a decade before had been the drama's prologue. Any audience would have been delighted at the show. But no audience got to see it. It played day after day and week after week behind closed curtains. Not a word of the dispute, not a hint that there was one, was uttered over the airwaves or printed in a newspaper. Moses' grim fight went on in absolute secrecy.

On November 21, the PWA board was scheduled to meet at two o'clock to approve a long list of projects. Shortly before the meeting began, Ickes slashed off the list every one located in New York City. Then he telephoned La Guardia to tell him what he had done. There are indications that Moses' loss of popularity in the gubernatorial campaign was weighing heavily in the scales on which the Mayor was weighing the alternatives; Windels had told him he couldn't oust a man "who the public thinks is wonderful"—but apparently much of the public no longer thought Moses was wonderful. In conversations with him, the Mayor, if he did not ask him to resign in so many words, apparently pressed more forcefully the suggestion that the whole city should not be made to pay for his seat on the Triborough board. In reply, Moses apparently pointed out that there was no way he could be removed from Triborough except on charges. Telephoning Ickes, La Guardia pointed this out. As Ickes recalled in his *Secret Diary:* "I told him that was his funeral not mine."

La Guardia huddled daily with Windels now, and with C. C. Burlingham, the grand old man of the reform movement whose opinion the Mayor valued so highly that "from him and from no one else would he take a scolding." Both men argued—Windels on political grounds, Burlingham on grounds of principle—that he should not knuckle under to Roosevelt. The Mayor was torn. On the one hand, Windels believes, "he realized that it would have painted an indelible picture of him in an unfavorable light." On the other hand, there were his dreams for remaking New York, dreams which would be impossible of realization without the federal funds which Roosevelt alone could provide. Shrewdly calculating politician that he was, Fiorello La Guardia was weighing the alternatives, always weighing.

Then, on December 26, 1934, Roosevelt and Ickes threw on those delicate scales something that weighted them to the President's side. It was an official general PWA order—Administrative Order Number 129 was its title—and it stated flatly: *"Hereafter no funds shall be advanced to any authority, board or commission constituting an independent corporation or entity created for a specific project wholly within the confines of a municipality, any of the members of the governing body of which authority, board or commission holds any public office under said municipality."*

The order obviously applied to Triborough and to Moses. (By coincidence, it also applied to another New York City official, Tenement House Commissioner Langdon W. Post, who was a member of the Municipal Housing Authority, which was also receiving federal funds, but Ickes privately assured La Guardia that the order would not be enforced in Post's case. Post stayed out of the controversy because he was away on an ocean cruise.) It had almost the full force of law. It had the full force of an official regulation of the agency financing Triborough—and, Ickes told La Guardia, it embodied in those official regulations what he had previously said privately: that no more money would be given to Triborough until Moses was off the Triborough board. Most important, it gave La Guardia a public excuse for ousting Moses: an official PWA rule forbade Moses to serve. Its issuance was the move of a fox. "The President helped me draft this order," Ickes diaried.

But the fox was growing reckless. Previously, the President had been careful, always letting Ickes do the talking with La Guardia, not letting himself become directly involved. Now "he discussed it [the order] personally with La Guardia," Ickes wrote. And Roosevelt made another move; either he himself or Ickes—and probably both—told La Guardia that if he felt he could not force Moses to resign, they would be satisfied if the Mayor promised Ickes—in writing—not to reappoint Moses when his term expired on June 30, 1935, well before the bridge would be finished.

This combination of moves stripped La Guardia of excuses that he could make to the President—if in fact he still wanted any. It gave him the public rationale he would need to justify ousting Moses, and it gave him a private rationale to make to Moses. When he received a copy of the order—it had not been released publicly, of course—he showed it to Moses, apparently to prove to him that he had no choice but to give in. Then the Mayor headed for Washington, where he met Ickes, and, on Thursday, January 3, 1935, secretly swore to the PWA Administrator that he would put the promise in writing as soon as he got back to New York.

But the Mayor had miscalculated, as had Roosevelt and Ickes. They may have believed that Moses' loss of popularity had stripped him of his armor, and that Order Number 129 had left him weaponless, but they were wrong. For Moses still possessed a weapon more valuable even than his popularity: his mind. He conceived a masterstroke that simultaneously won him back his popularity and turned the tables on his great enemy. While La Guardia was in Washington, he did the one thing that no one involved in the closed-curtain drama had expected. He leaked the order to the press—and thereby pulled the curtain up.

There, suddenly spotlighted before the public, stood the President of the United States of America—caught in a most unbecoming posture. And the President was only one figure in a tableau that might have been lifted intact out of that traditional melodrama "The Old Homestead." In that melodrama, a villain used the power of money, the mortgage he held on the old homestead, to force the proud beauty to yield to his dishonorable advances. In the drama that Moses suddenly revealed to the public there was also a villain (the President) using the power of money (federal relief funds) to force the Mayor to perform a dishonorable act (ousting from his job a faithful public servant). And this drama had a hero, too—for now that La Guardia had agreed to side with the President, the faithful public servant was seen by the audience as a man standing alone without a single ally and fearlessly fighting for his rights against the two most powerful men in the country. Since, moreover, the critics and the audience didn't know—and never were to learn—the long background of the Roosevelt-Moses feud, their imagination supplied the traditional motive: press and public assumed that the President was attempting to force Moses out of his job simply because he was a Republican and had criticized the New Deal in his election campaign. And just in case anyone missed the point of the drama, Moses supplied a narration—written with the brilliance that characterized his efforts when he had a legitimate point to make.

"There are certain facts which should be known to the public," he said. The sole purpose of Order Number 129 was to force him out of his job; Ickes had admitted as much to La Guardia. And Ickes had also admitted "that I was honest and competent," and that the sole reason for the order was that "I was . . . not sufficiently friendly to the administration."

He had refused to leave quietly, Moses said. "When the Mayor explained this situation to me I told him that I should be glad to retire from his administration entirely if he wanted me to, but that I would not take a back door out of the Triborough Authority merely because there was pressure to get me out for personal or political reasons." He had refused, he said, because he wanted the American people to know what was happening—because there was a principle involved that was more important than himself. "The Federal appropriations for public works and work relief are the funds of all the people of the country. . . . If personal or political considerations are to govern the expenditure of public works and relief funds by the Federal Government, this fact should be known to the public."

Reaction proved as violent as Moses had gambled it would be. Unluckily for Ickes, the PWA Administrator held a press conference every Thursday, and, not knowing that Moses had leaked the story, he held one as usual this Thursday shortly after La Guardia had left his office. To the Administrator's shock, reporters began questioning him about Order Number 129, which he had believed was secret. As he later wrote in his diary: "I was asked whether Farley had ever spoken to me about Moses. To that question I could honestly say No. Then I was asked whether the President had ever done so. There I had to lie, but again I said No." The lie was to force the press to link Roosevelt with the order only in hints for a day or two—although the hints were broad indeed—but it did nothing to cool its ardor for the story. La Guardia had boarded his train back to New York confidently believing that the affair was still secret. Sealed off from the world in a private compartment, he made the trip with that confidence unimpaired. But when he swung off his train at Pennsylvania Station at 9:30 P.M., he saw a pack of reporters running toward him along the platform. Luckily for the Mayor, an aide, Lester B. Stone, had been telephoned by a reporter for a statement, had thus learned that the story had broken and had hurried to the station. Stone reached the Mayor a few steps ahead of the reporters, pulled him aside and told him what had happened, giving him a moment to think. No one ever accused Fiorello La Guardia of needing more than a moment. When the reporters engulfed him, he did not admit that he had agreed to dismiss Moses. Instead, when he was asked, "What are you going to do?" he replied, "I'll think it over." And he decided that night to postpone writing Ickes the letter he had promised.

That proved to be a wise move. For the next day, as one of his advisers was to put it, "the shit hit the fan." The public, that most fickle of lovers, embraced Robert Moses in January as fervently as it had pushed him away in November.

With the exception of the *Daily News*, there wasn't a newspaper in New York that didn't carry an editorial message to the Mayor on Order Number 129 on Friday, January 4, or Saturday, January 5. The ones in the *Herald Tribune* were a fair sample. Friday's said: "If Mayor La Guardia allows one of the ablest of his public servants to be dismissed by a Washington official, without shadow of cause, through a secret ukase so extraordinary and so contemptible that the official himself is ashamed publicly to admit it, then it seems to us that Mr. La Guardia might as well resign his Mayoralty right now." That was Friday's editorial. Saturday's said: "If Mr. La Guardia gives in, he will find that he has sold his soul, sold his administration and sold the people of New York. It is not worth it." Let the federal politicians cancel the city's contracts; show them "who's charged with the conduct of the public business of the people of New York City." Was the *Herald Tribune* a Republican paper? The *American*, the Brooklyn *Eagle*, and the *World-Telegram* were Democratic. "Bureaucracy! Patronage! Politics!" the *American* raged. "If the order stands it will be a lasting stain on the record of the Administration," the *Eagle* said. "Secretary Ickes is jeopardizing public confidence in the nonpartisan honesty of the national Public Works Administration," the *World-Telegram* said. And the independent *New York Times,* normally so dispassionate and restrained, chimed in: "If he [La Guardia] has the backbone of a lamprey, he will stand by Bob Moses, right through to that Judgment Day which he is himself so fond of invoking."

And outrage was not confined to the press. The public was reacting to the press interpretation of the drama—bureaucrats and "patronage politicians" playing politics with *its* money—as the American public always reacts to bureaucrats and patronage politicians. Before his gubernatorial campaign, Robert Moses had been a hero because the public had seen him less as an individual than as a symbol of resistance to politicians and bureaucrats. His conduct during the campaign had, by forcing the public to see him as an individual, stripped him of that cause. But now he was once again basking in its aura—and he was once again a hero. In a display of indignation that proved how completely the Moses masterstroke had restored its author to public favor, on Friday, the day after the storm broke, the Long Island Chamber of Commerce, the Conference on Port Development of the City of New York, the Park Association of New York City, the City Club, the Bronx Board of Trade, the New York Board of Trade and the Merchants' Association of Sheepshead Bay all held separate meetings and passed resolutions backing Moses and denouncing Ickes. On Saturday, it was the Elmhurst Manor Community Council, the Jackson Heights Taxpayers Association, the North Woodside Community Association, the Astoria Property Owners' Association, the Madison Manor Civic Association, the Atlantic Avenue Business Men's and Taxpayers' Association, the Automobile Club of New York, the Corona Community Council and the New York Chapter of the American Institute of Architecture.

The language of the resolutions was indignant, and so was the language of the letters-to-the-editor that flooded into the city's newspapers—the *Herald Tribune* running nine in a single day under the headline "Politicians vs. Public Servant," the Brooklyn *Eagle* running eleven. New York's parks are "the sign and signet of Robert Moses, a man I do not know but whose hand I should be proud to shake," said one. "Our Mayor has repeatedly crawled on his belly before Washington in abject supplication. Are we, as citizens of the sovereign State of New York, to have a political mongrel from the Middle West instruct us as to who shall build our bridges and who shall plant our gardens?"

Confiding in his diary, Ickes blamed the uproar on La Guardia. "La Guardia has followed a crooked course in the whole proceeding," he raged a week after the storm broke. "He let Moses see the letter that I had written him, in which was incorporated my order. . . . I called La Guardia on the telephone on Monday and before I got through with him I told him very clearly and distinctly just how accomplished a double-crosser he in fact is. He equivocated and evaded, but I know that I had him dead to rights. This was a great disappointment to me. I had felt that La Guardia was a man of real courage and substance, but in this matter he has acted like the cheapest kind of double-crossing politician."

The Mayor was frantically steering between the Scylla of losing federal funds and the Charybdis of losing the confidence of his constituency. And he had to steer small indeed. He attempted to make reporters see his predicament; when one asked how Ickes could hold back Triborough Authority funds he had signed a contract to furnish, La Guardia replied, "That's like a lawyer telling his client that he can't be put in jail for something and the client answering that he *is* in jail. I can't build on litigation. I need steel girders and brick, mortar and labor to build." But these attempts only made the storm in his city rage more fiercely. Then the Mayor tried alternately to ignore the controversy and to deny one existed. He avoided reporters as much as possible—once, finding a crowd of them outside his office door when he left one afternoon after a day of refusing their requests for an interview, he shouldered violently through them—and when, on another occasion, they cornered him, he said blandly, "Everything is susceptible of being straightened out by reasonable men. There is complete harmony between City Hall and Washington." But Moses kept the controversy alive with such devices as weekly accountings of the steadily dwindling balances in Triborough bank accounts and tours of the bridge site for platoons of civic leaders—much to La Guardia's displeasure; when a reporter asked "How would Ickes' order affect Commissioner Post?" the Mayor snapped back, "At least Post is on the high seas and he can't issue any statements." The Mayor was stalling; in the face of such a gale of public opinion, he apparently felt, either Moses or Roosevelt would have to turn and run for harbor. Ickes felt the same way, although he felt the man who would have to retreat would be the President. "This enterprise . . . is a great mistake on the President's part," the PWA Administrator diaried. "By making a martyr out of [Moses] we are only serving to build him up."

But it wasn't La Guardia's or Ickes' feelings that counted. It was Roosevelt's and Moses'. And when these two men were dealing with one another, they were not "reasonable men" at all. Not normal political considerations but personal animosity, "real hatred," hatred that had been boiling between them for years, governed their actions. Neither one would give an inch. Chauffeured in from Babylon on January 9 for a two-hour meeting with La Guardia and Windels behind closed doors at City Hall, Moses emerged, noticeably pale and tired, to find reporters waiting. "Are you going to leave the bridge authority?" one asked. "No," Moses snarled. Without another word or a backward glance, he strode out of the building. When Ickes, after a week of trying and, as he put it, "taking it on the chin" on behalf of the President, finally secured an appointment with Roosevelt on January 10, he half expected that, in view of "all the turmoil," the President would try to work out a face-saving compromise. But, the Administrator wrote in his diary the next day, "he told me very firmly that he wanted me to go through along the lines of the order that I have issued." No Triborough requisitions were to be honored "unless the Moses matter is settled to the President's satisfaction."

Apparently confident that he could break La Guardia down and force him to agree not to reappoint Moses in June, FDR told Ickes pontifically that "the thing to do was just to go along, say as little as possible, and let it work out." For a while it seemed that the President was correct. On January 16, he summoned La Guardia to Washington for a private conversation. Returning to New York, the Mayor told reporters, "Nothing is going to happen that will disturb the pleasant relations between the city and Washington. We simply cannot afford to let a break happen. We have too many public projects being financed by federal funds to let such a thing happen." A *Herald Tribune* Washington staffer reported that "at PWA headquarters, Mr. Moses' resignation was confidently expected as a result of Mayor La Guardia's public remark."

But if the President felt he was holding all the cards, he was overlooking the trump: public opinion. And Moses' trump suit was even longer than had previously been apparent.

Roosevelt was forced to admit at a press conference that he had been kept informed of the controversy by Ickes. The President declined to discuss the matter further but even the limited admission made news—PRESIDENT AWARE OF ORDER ON MOSES, the *Times* headlined—and with this opening, newspapers finally told their readers that FDR was not only aware of the order but had directed Ickes to issue it. The public protest rose to hurricane levels, as delegations from 147 civic, business and social organizations met in the auditorium of the State Chamber of Commerce Building at 65 Liberty Street.

The diversity of those delegations—there was one from the Fortnightly Library Club of Brooklyn as well as one from the Manufacturers Association of Bush Terminal—indicated the extent to which the support for Moses extended through every segment of the city. There were delegations from the city's most prestigious civic organizations: the Citizens Union, the City Club, the Women's City Club, the Civic Council of Brooklyn, the Alliance of Women's Clubs, the Civitas Club of Brooklyn and the United Neighborhood Houses—a central body which itself represented forty-nine separate settlement houses and other social work organizations such as the New York Urban League and the Educational Alliance. Sitting on the stage or in the audience at the State Chamber of Commerce auditorium were many of the most respected and influential individuals in the New York City reform movement: Burlingham, Price, McAneny, Schieffelin and other old giants of reform who had been idols at the Bureau of Municipal Research when Bob Moses had been a young staffer there; leaders of the "middle generation" of the movement, contemporaries of Moses like Childs, Stanley Isaacs and Morris Ernst; and leaders of reform's younger generation such as Newbold Morris. Once these men had all been friends and admirers of Moses. Many of them had been alienated from him by his display of vindictiveness and disregard for the truth during the gubernatorial campaign. But now there was a principle at stake and these were men to whom principle was more important than personality; forgetting past differences, they took him again into the shelter of their names and reputations and lent to his fight with the President the ringing phrases of reform. The Triborough Bridge, they said in a letter sent to Ickes on behalf of all 147 organizations, is "an urgently necessary public facility" but "if the price to be paid for the loan of Federal funds is the surrender of control over local government, then we, being unwilling to sacrifice this great principle, would rather wait until such time as some other method of financing will permit its completion."

And just as important in determining La Guardia's attitude as the public expressions of protest were the private expressions. For the men making them possessed not only personal entrée to La Guardia but his respect. As always, the definitive word was Burlingham's:

Dear F.H.

You know my views on the subject; but I think I will put them in writing as my considered opinion, for my own clarification, if not for yours.

You have told me that you do not think one man should be permitted to obstruct or imperil the relief of hundreds of thousands.

That one man, however, has become a symbol. Washington has taken the position the English Kings took toward the American Colonies. The question, therefore, is whether you, as representative not of New York City alone but of every municipality and every state in the Union, will submit to an unreasonable and tyrannical order from Washington.

If you have already committed yourself expressly or by implication, I think you should make it plain to the Secretary and the President that the sentiment of New York is so strong that as its representative you must respect it, and that unless good reason is shown to the contrary you intend to reappoint Moses as Triborough Bridge Commissioner on the expiration of his term.

I have tested public sentiment at all points possible for me, and it is unanimous. Even those who dislike Moses for his bad manners and rough stuff agree that it would be far better to let work on the Triborough cease than to yield to Order Number 129.

Yours,
Burlingham

The flood waters of protest were beginning to creep higher in Washington, too. "Morris L. Ernst, a fine young liberal lawyer from New York, came in to see me today very much worried over the situation and its effect on my reputation," Ickes had told his diary on January 9. "He justly pointed out the fact that my action in the Moses case is at utter variance with any other act of mine. He says I am being criticized by all the liberals of New York. He told me frankly that everybody realized that I was acting for the President but apparently that isn't saving my face or helping my reputation." And Ernst was not the only influential liberal to sit under the stuffed buffalo heads at one end of Ickes' vast walnut-paneled office at Interior, waiting for an audience with the Secretary. Already uneasy in his conscience over what he was doing, Ickes became uneasier still.

Roosevelt tried to ignore the flood—when Joseph Price, an old friend, wrote on January 30 for an interview, the President refused to see him—but by mid-February the waters were beginning to lick at the steps of the

White House. The mail tally that was sent daily to FDR's desk included, day after day, scores of protests from individuals and organizations. On most of them, a presidential aide, probably Colonel Marvin H. McIntyre, scribbled "The usual" and out went a letter, signed by Louis Howe, saying only: "Your letter has been received and will be brought to the President's attention. I want to thank you on his behalf for your interest in sending your views regarding the matter referred to." But some of the mail required more than form replies. For Ernst, Price and Burlingham—and a score of other reform leaders from New York—were personal friends of the President and his wife from Roosevelt's days in New York, and these men were among the writers, Burlingham wiring the President on February 22, a year to the day since FDR had begun the ouster move: "Never have seen such unanimity of feeling. Issue far transcends Moses or New York. . . . Way out can and must be found." And while the protest had at first been confined to New York, with the revelation of the President's direct involvement, it spread. Soon newspapers all over the country, many of which had been looking for proof that federal relief money was being used for political purposes, were finding that proof in Order Number 129 and were treating it accordingly. "I would not have supposed that the country outside of New York would be very interested in this matter," Ickes wrote, "but the newspapers have made it almost a national issue." Arthur Krock, syndicated national political columnist of the *Times,* analyzed the controversy from a political standpoint. Walter Lippmann analyzed it from a philosophical standpoint, concluding that surrender by La Guardia would mean that he has "bartered away not only his independence but the independence of all other local officials" to a centralized bureaucracy in Washington.

There were other developments that Roosevelt could only have viewed as ominous. Conservative elements in the House, led by upstate reactionary Bertrand Snell, began to move for a congressional investigation of Order Number 129. Such an investigation was not likely to redound to Roosevelt's credit—as became evident in a speech by Huey Long. The Louisiana rabble-rouser, already a national figure in early 1935 and intent on becoming more of one, had been bitterly attacking Postmaster General Farley and demanding a Senate investigation of his activities. On March 6, before packed galleries in the Senate Chamber, the Kingfish charged that the "Big Bag Man's" New York-based General Builders Supply Corporation was transacting "matters with which the United States government is identified for the purpose of making private profit." And the Kingfish said that, to prove his charge, "the testimony of Commissioner Robert Moses of New York, and the data which he has assembled will be called. . . ." Whether or not, as was later to be reported, Moses was leaking Long his "data" on Farley as a hint to Roosevelt of the revelations he might make during a congressional investigation, the threat of such revelations was another reason for the President to dread the possibility that another branch of the federal government might intrude into his personal vendetta.

It was not only the legislative branch that might intrude, moreover.

Emphasizing as always their belief that democracy must be a government of laws and not of men, the New York reformers commissioned a legal analysis of Order Number 129. Their attorney concluded in a sixteen-page brief that the order was clearly illegal, "an arbitrary and capricious fiat without any authority in law," that it was a breach not only of express contractual obligations of the government but of "governmental morality," that the records in the case clearly proved that Ickes had issued the order to force from office a single municipal official for no other reason than that that official was not "deemed friendly to the Federal Administration," that Ickes had abused the power given him by Congress and the President and that he had therefore committed an impeachable offense. The attorney said he was prepared to undertake, as a public service for which no fee would be required, an attempt to obtain from the courts a writ of mandamus requiring Ickes to honor his contract with Triborough. And the identity of the attorney made the threat one that could not be laughed off; he was the noted constitutional lawyer William D. Guthrie, senior partner of the celebrated law firm of Cravath, Swaine and Moore, who forty years before had carried a fight against the imposition of a federal income tax all the way to the United States Supreme Court—and had won. (The tax was not reinstituted until 1913, when it was legalized by the passage of the Sixteenth Amendment.*) Roosevelt decided to grant Joseph Price the interview Price had requested, and the reformer returned to New York to report to intimates that he had found the President conciliatory. He told them that Roosevelt had asked him plaintively, "Isn't the President of the United States entitled to one personal grudge?" ("No," Price said he had replied.) Ickes wrote in his diary: "The President, I know, would welcome a way out of this cul-de-sac." But, the Secretary added, "no way offers itself."

Trying to find a way, the President summoned La Guardia to a secret meeting. It was held on February 24 aboard a Pennsylvania Railroad train carrying the President from Washington to a speech in Cambridge, Massachusetts. Although the train stopped in New York, La Guardia drove to Philadelphia and boarded it there to lessen the possibility that he would be spotted by a reporter. When the train stopped in New York, the city's mayor stayed hidden in a compartment behind lowered window shades.

President and Mayor were trying to find a way to retreat and still save face, and La Guardia had brought with him a draft of a letter he thought might do the job. In the letter, which was addressed to Ickes, La Guardia agreed that he would always obey Order Number 129 in the future and would never again appoint a city official to an authority receiving federal funds. But, he said, applying Order Number 129 retroactively to city officials already on authorities created a problem in the case of one particular individual—Housing Authority member Post.

Langdon Post is familiar with the entire city housing program, La

* The main reason for the verdict was the constitutional provision that direct taxes had to be apportioned among the states in proportion to population, a provision struck out by the amendment.

Guardia wrote. "What is more, he is enthusiastic, zealous and energetic in his work. It would be a pity to displace him at this time." Therefore, the Mayor said, could I possibly ask for a "modification" of Order Number 129 that would permit "officials of existing commissions or authorities to continue their work until completion"?

There was also a postscript to the letter. "P.S.," the Mayor wrote. There is one other official who would be affected by the modification. His name is Robert Moses. "I assume the ruling on one will be applicable to the other."

The attempt to cover the retreat on Moses by pretending that the battle was really over Post was so transparent a smoke screen that Roosevelt may have been reluctant to employ it. He did nothing on February 25, 26 or 27. The requisition slips that Moses had sent to Washington on November 8, almost four months before, remained on Ickes' desk, unsigned. The contracts for the next stages of work on the Triborough Bridge remained unlet. Considerations of revenge and politics appear to have been balancing themselves almost evenly in the President's mind.

But on February 27, something happened that tipped the balance.

For weeks, Alfred E. Smith's friends had been urging him to issue a statement on Moses' behalf. Time and again they had told him that he must delay no longer, that Moses could not hold out without help. But while the old warrior was unhappy now and terribly bitter, he had lost none of his wiliness. Wait, he told his friends. The time wasn't right yet. Moses didn't need him to hold out. The newspaper editorials and civic association resolutions would enable him to do that. Moses needed him to *win*. The moment when he should step in was the moment at which the President and the Mayor had been driven to the edge of a decision to give in to Moses and a single push could plunge them over the edge into surrender—if the push was delivered by someone with more influence than a newspaper or a civic association, someone whose name was still a potent force throughout the United States and particularly potent as an influence with La Guardia, who knew that if Smith ever became angry enough to go after his job, he would probably be unable to keep it. Now, Smith judged, the moment had arrived. On February 26, he called reporters to his office on the thirty-second floor of the Empire State Building and said he wanted to make a statement. As usual, he went right to the heart. "Over ten years ago," he said, "Bob was talking to me about a single unified plan for park and parkway development for the state." He has been carrying out that plan ever since. "The Triborough Bridge is the key to the success of the whole system." It was "ridiculous" not to let him finish it. Ickes' order was "narrow, political and vindictive." He could not believe, he said, that President Roosevelt would be a party to it.

As Smith had known it would, his statement made the front pages of newspapers across the country on February 27. The very next day, the President, in Ickes' words, "came to a conclusion that a retreat was in order."

Summoning Ickes to the White House, he called in stenographer Grace Tully and dictated a draft of a reply to La Guardia's letter for Ickes to sign. "Ickes'" reply agreed to solve "the problem created as the result of the expiration of the term of Commissioner Langdon Post" by ruling that Order Number 129 should not apply retroactively and that therefore since Post had been appointed to both his city and authority posts before the order was issued, he could keep them. "Since a like situation exists with reference to Mr. Moses, of the Triborough Bridge Authority, this interpretation shall also apply to him," the letter added. Ickes predated the La Guardia letter to him February 23 and he predated "his" letter to La Guardia February 26—"so as to antedate by one day the blast let out . . . by Al Smith," he noted in his diary. Regardless of the date at its top, however, the letter was a document of unconditional surrender. Moses' great friend had rendered him one last great service.

All but ignoring Langdon Post, the press correctly interpreted the Ickes letter as a personal triumph for the Triborough Commissioner. ICKES BACKS DOWN ON MOSES was the *Herald Tribune*'s three-column lead headline; its editorial noted that Ickes' letter left some questions about the controversy's origin unanswered but said, "No one, we think, will wish to disturb the grandeur of that handsome, outsized white flag now floating above the offices of the PWA by hurling irrelevant questions at it." La Guardia's parting growl—"As I have insisted all along, relations between Washington and City Hall are most cordial and friendly. . . . There was no need for all this 'pro bono publico' business"—was lost in the cheering.

Ickes, who hadn't wanted to become involved in the first place, had suffered not only pangs of conscience but a public humiliation of monumental proportions. "Moses did me more damage than any other one person during my years with Roosevelt," he was to write. But even Ickes could not forbear to cheer the episode's victor. Reminiscing in a letter to Burlingham years later, he said, "There can be no doubt of the porcupinish disposition of Moses. And is he clever! . . . He put it all over President Roosevelt and me in that squabble." Cleveland Rodgers summed up the dimensions of the triumph when he wrote: "The battle of the Triborough Bridge was over. Moses won against the most powerful opponent he ever encountered."

And Moses won more than a battle. For in it, as Rodgers wrote, he "received the most impressive demonstration of public confidence in his career." That was the battle's most significant development. At the conclusion of his gubernatorial campaign, Moses' stock of public confidence had never been lower. But at the conclusion of the Triborough Bridge fight, just four months later, it had never been higher. By placing Moses in a position where he was in fact the opponent of bureaucrats and politicians that he had for so long claimed to be, Franklin Roosevelt had allowed him to screw his halo back on. And so firmly did Moses screw it back on—without ever again making the mistake of running for public office—that in the public's eyes the last of the glow would not fade for almost thirty years. "After that Triborough controversy," Windels was to say, "he couldn't do anything that was wrong in the public's eyes. If you disagreed with him, why you were a public enemy. He was back firmly in the saddle."

The ceremony opening the Triborough Bridge—held on its central span on July 11, 1936—was to add a tinkling little grace note, an inspiration of pure wit, to the resounding triumph Moses had won eighteen months before in forcing Roosevelt and Ickes to allow him to complete the project.

When the invitations were mailed on May 12, one went to the White House. No reply was immediately forthcoming, and the reasons were certainly understandable. Moses, as master of ceremonies at the sumptuous opening, would be introducing the dignitaries present—would, in other words, say a few things about each of them. And Roosevelt, familiar with Moses' gift for invective, could hardly have helped worrying what Moses might decide to say about *him*. A recent incident had provided him with fresh proof of the depth of his foe's animosity: before the opening of the Chrystie-Forsyth park complex, La Guardia, trying to cultivate the President, had suggested naming the park after his mother. Moses had flatly refused. (The name "Sara Delano Roosevelt Park" had been bestowed only after the Mayor outsmarted the Park Commissioner by suggesting the name publicly; Moses did not dare to publicly oppose a chivalrous gesture to an elderly woman.) The President had been forced to eat one large slice of humble pie on the Triborough Bridge issue; he was understandably reluctant to be forced to choke down another helping on the bridge's center span. The Triborough Authority mailroom, alerted to keep an eye out for a response from the White House, reported day after day that none had appeared.

On June 23, Ickes, although himself piqued because the only invitation he had received was one as a "general spectator" ("It is very small indeed. . . . Naturally, I ought to have a place in the program"), advised the President to attend. "I understand that there will be a national hookup and the bridge itself will be featured in newspaper articles and pictures throughout the land. If you go to this affair, credit for the building of the bridge will go to your administration, where it belongs. Otherwise, Mr. Moses can be depended upon to glorify himself. . . ." The dedication, free of political overtones in an election year, "will be of more value to you at this time than a score of campaign speeches," the Administrator said. He added a piece of encouragement: "Mayor La Guardia told me in New York on Saturday that you are the only one who can take this show away from Robert Moses. And you can do it." And he added a warning: ". . . you will be in Hyde Park on the 11th. If you are to be near New York on the 11th, won't your failure to take part in the program be subject to misinterpretation?" But Roosevelt's response was a memo, only two paragraphs long but quite revealing:

I wish much that I could go to the Triborough Bridge opening on July eleventh. It is impossible for me to come down from Hyde Park that day—incidentally, it would be an all day trip to New York and back.

I really think that if you and La Guardia take hold of the ceremony, you will so greatly outshine Brother Moses that we will be able to sing, "Where was Moses when the lights went out?"

F.D.R.

Press speculation over whether the President would attend was mounting, however, and other presidential advisers joined Ickes in pointing out that the bridge was the largest PWA project in the East, that it was in the President's own state, that its location in the country's media capital would insure its dedication nationwide publicity, that credit for it should go to the President's administration—and that the President's absence would arouse press "misinterpretation" that he was afraid to confront Moses again. La Guardia apparently elicited from Moses a promise that he would be on his best behavior. He also elicited a specific promise, insisted on by Roosevelt, that although Moses would introduce all the other speakers, he would not introduce the President but would let the Mayor do it. The Mayor bore the guarantees to Hyde Park, and at the last minute was able to announce that the President was coming after all. Ickes received a "special invitation" to be one of the speakers and at another press conference La Guardia announced that the PWA Administrator was coming, too.

(Leaving the Mayor's office after the announcement about Ickes, Moses was surrounded by reporters. He declined to answer any of their questions, but he could hardly keep from laughing, and he finally said, with a broad grin, "You can say that I'm going to introduce *him*.")

(In a conference in La Guardia's office, at which Windels was present, Moses had shown the Mayor the timetable for the program, which limited the President's speaking time to five minutes. Don't be ridiculous, the Mayor said. Moses gave the President six minutes.)

It was extremely hot on the day of the dedication, ninety-seven degrees on the temporary speaker's platform on the bridge center span, and that may have been the reason why three of the speakers—Roosevelt, Ickes and La Guardia—were sweating. But reporters noticed that Moses was strikingly cool in his white suit.

He was a gracious host when the President's party arrived, letting his charm wash over Ickes in such a great wave that the Old Curmudgeon later confessed to his diary that he had been overwhelmed. Introducing all the speakers—all the speakers except the President—over a nationwide radio hookup while he looked out at the gleaming white bridge roadway stretching out from Randall's Island toward the three boroughs it joined together, and down at the just-completed Triborough Stadium below him, he was expansive and complimentary. And reporters who had hoped for some malice on the center span, a little bloodying of the virgin concrete, were disappointed. All the speeches were standard opening-ceremony inconsequentialities (it was probably an oversight that neither FDR nor Ickes mentioned by name the man who had built the project they were dedicating) and Moses never mentioned the President at all and, in his introduction of

Ickes, was ostensibly all let-bygones-be-bygones, moving the audience to applaud—and the reporters to write that "the feud came to a graceful end yesterday"—when he said that "the Public Works Administrator and I have met face to face and found that neither one of us has horns, hoofs and a tail. . . . At this junction, where traffic from all directions meets, where there are no left-hand turns, no head-on collisions and no sideswipes, it's a genuine pleasure to meet the Secretary of the Interior. . . . I trust that this meeting will be the beginning of a real friendship and regard."

There was, of course, one somewhat unusual note in Moses' introduction of Ickes. "There have been times," Moses said, "when in contemplating our Washington partner, I have been tempted to go back for inspiration to the letter which Dr. Samuel Johnson wrote to Lord Chesterfield about the famous dictionary which the great scholar announced that he had finished with comparatively little assistance. I have always considered this letter to be one of the finest pieces of polite vituperation in the annals of English literature." But no reporter thought to analyze the letter and see its application to Roosevelt and Ickes. Ickes even wrote in his diary that he was quite pleased by the introduction.

If the Old Curmudgeon had attended Yale and had taken Chauncey Brewster Tinker's course on "Johnson and His Circle," his pleasure might have been somewhat diluted.

Professor Tinker had delighted in telling his students—including Robert Moses, president of Yale's version of Samuel Johnson's Kit Cat Club—the story behind the scholar's letter. Setting out on the task of compiling his great dictionary, the scholar had appealed for the financial assistance he desperately needed to Lord Chesterfield, who had encouraged him to expect it, but had then rudely rebuffed him. When, however, after seven years of privation and hardship, the work was completed and acclaimed, Chesterfield had attempted to represent himself as Dr. Johnson's "patron" and thus take some of the credit for it. It was then that Dr. Johnson wrote to him: "Is not a Patron, my Lord, one who looks with unconcern on a man struggling for life in the water, and when he has reached ground, encumbers him with help?" He added: "I hope it is no very cynical asperity to be unwilling that the Publick should consider me as owing that to a Patron, which Providence has enabled me to do for myself."

23. *In the Saddle*

THE LITTLE FLOWER was mastering New York City as no mayor since Peter Stuyvesant had mastered it. Roaming his domain in person like Haroun-al-Raschid, he suddenly appeared on lines in front of municipal lodging houses, checking on the treatment of the luckless, or in police precinct houses, employing the mayoralty's hitherto-unused magisterial powers to mete out swift punishment to arrested gamblers, or at the Bronx Terminal Market before daylight one freezing December morning, assembling an audience of shivering market concessionaires by having two police buglers blow a fanfare and then, clambering up on the tailboard of a truck, announcing an assault on racketeers in the artichoke business by reading a formal proclamation banning the inoffensive vegetable from the premises. Doffing his big Stetson for a big fire chief's helmet, he dashed to fires to make "personal inspections" from which he emerged covered with soot, and he groped through smoke and flames to the side of two firemen pinned under a collapsed wall and knelt by them whispering encouragement until they were freed. He raced to train wrecks in the sidecar of a police motorcycle, battered down doors at the head of police raiding parties, snatched the baton from an orchestra conductor to lead a bravura performance of "The Stars and Stripes Forever" and conducted the Sanitation Department band at a special performance in Carnegie Hall (after instructing a stage manager, "Just treat me like Toscanini"). He gave a city hungering for leadership the impression that there was no part of his domain that he did not dominate.

The Little Flower mastered even the city's most unmasterable element: its government. When Big Tim Sullivan of Tammany Hall, which during most of La Guardia's first term controlled the Boards of Estimate and Aldermen, said, "It is the business of the *majority* to advance a constructive program," La Guardia replied, with a grim smile: "In this administration, I am the majority." Bounding up the front steps of City Hall early on the morning of his Inauguration Day, he had stopped, a roly-poly figure in a ridiculous black hat and a rumpled black suit, and had shaken his little fist at its white Georgian elegance and shouted, *"E finita la cuccagna!"* ("No more free lunch!"), a phrase which, a friend explained, the Mayor was using to promise "The party is over! No more graft!" And to the amazement of reporters who had smiled skeptically at the time, La Guardia kept his promise, slashing thousands of nonessential jobs from city payrolls, slashing the salaries of the employees who remained, balancing the city's budget—and raising the moral tone of government in New York to new heights. Sitting under the portraits of bewigged Colonial Governors with his unruly black forelock down over his forehead, his horn-rimmed glasses pushed up on top of his head, his feet dangling off the floor, sorting through a stack of mail as rapidly as if he were dealing a deck of cards, tossing the letters at three secretaries and shouting, "Say yes, say no, throw it away, tell him to go to hell," the Little Flower made City Hall shake with the pounding of his fists on his desk and echo with the rasp of the six buzzers he had installed there.

But the Little Flower wasn't mastering Robert Moses. The relationship of the two men was the talk, or rather the whisper, of City Hall.

The relationship was kept secret—even, to a large extent, from the newspapermen who prowled the Hall uncovering secrets—because it was known to only a few of the Mayor's intimates and because those intimates, anxious to preserve the Mayor's image as a commander capable of command, a Mayor master of his city, were careful to disclose nothing that would mar this image.* And public knowledge of the Mayor's relationship with Robert Moses would certainly have marred it.

La Guardia was a bullying petty tyrant to subordinates—not only to his secretaries, who came to dread the rasp of his buzzers summoning them into his office, and would sit sobbing at their desks when they came out, but also to his commissioners, the nonpartisan, nonpolitical experts of whose presence in his administration he was constantly bragging. Rexford G. Tugwell, who joined that administration as Planning Commission chairman, recalls bitterly, "He boasted to newspapers [of] his appointees. . . . He did not say that he often treated his commissioners like dogs. . . . We soon discovered that we were expected to do a good deal of humiliating kowtowing, to give many of La Guardia's favorites jobs, and to respect without question whatever capricious notions the Mayor might have about our work." The Mayor moved his desk to the far end of his thirty-two-foot-long office (the Blue Room, formerly used for ceremonial functions because of its size) so that visitors would have a longer walk to reach him, and when a commissioner entered—usually after a long heel-cooling period outside—the Mayor would often further unnerve him by covering his face with his fingers and peering between them so that, as the commissioner approached, all he could see of his boss's face was a pair of button-bright little eyes staring at him. A commissioner who displeased La Guardia by inefficiency—or by showing even a hint of independence—would be abused as if he were a wayward child. And the abuse was not delivered only in private: in his desk the Mayor kept a large bronze bone and at intervals he would call his commissioners together so that in front of them all he could "award" it to

---

* As they were careful to disclose nothing that would hint at the excesses of La Guardia's "colorful" personality. "Everybody talks about the Mayor's temperament—which doesn't exist!" Reuben A. Lazarus blandly assured John Gunther, and the author duly stated in his chapter on the Mayor in *Inside U.S.A.*: "Temperament? There's no time for it—unless it happens to serve a useful purpose."

the one who had pulled the biggest recent boner; once, with a commissioner in his office, the Mayor summoned a secretary and berated her viciously for an imaginary mistake—just so that he could have the pleasure of concluding the tirade by shouting, "If you were any dumber, I'd make you a commissioner." Many commissioners resigned; the turnover in the La Guardia administration, Tugwell says, "must have been unprecedented in municipal history" (although it was later surpassed by the turnover in the administration of New York's next Fusion mayor, John Vliet Lindsay, who succeeded in having seven sanitation commissioners resign on him in four years). Many didn't get a chance to resign, for La Guardia delighted in firing people—he once dismissed a secretary who had worked for him faithfully for years when, for the first time, she showed up at her desk after lunch tipsy—and a La Guardia dismissal was a thorough job: the mayoral pink slip was hand-delivered without any previous warning—by aides bearing also written authorization to seal the hapless commissioner's files on the spot so that he could not remove even personal letters.

La Guardia's relationship with his Park Commissioner was slightly different. Other commissioners might be made to cool their heels outside his office after answering a mayoral summons; when Moses was summoned, *he* would keep the Mayor waiting, showing up late (if he showed up at all; often he sent Earle Andrews in his place). Sometimes the enraged Mayor would accept the proffered excuse that Moses was busy; on other occasions he would refuse to see Andrews and would order an aide to telephone Moses and demand his presence—and while sometimes this demand would produce him, often Hazel Tappan would inform the aide curtly that "Mr. Moses is out in the field" and "can't be reached." Other commissioners might be browbeaten in La Guardia's office, his secretaries hastily jumping up when the furious high-pitched voice began to rise from behind his closed door and scurrying to slam another door to the waiting room outside so that visitors could not hear; when the commissioner behind the door to the Mayor's office was Moses, the secretary knew that if the high-pitched voice began to pierce the door, it would soon be joined, if not drowned out, by another, nasal and resonant.

Men who happened to be sitting behind that door—in La Guardia's office—during confrontations between the Mayor and Moses would speak of those confrontations thirty years later in voices that still contained a tone of awe. "There would be scenes in the Mayor's office that I could hardly believe," recalls Paul J. Kern, La Guardia's law secretary. Another La Guardia aide says, "There were moments when you would have sworn they were going to come to blows—that was how high the feeling ran." The aide who was perhaps present most often was Reuben A. Lazarus, whose expertise in bill drafting, second only to Moses', had earned him the nickname "the walking library" and a reputation for knowing "where the bodies are buried" and who was considered so indispensable that La Guardia had retained him in the same sensitive post in which he had served Jimmy Walker—official city representative in Albany—and had given him extraordinary access to his private office. Lazarus recalls that Moses and La Guardia "used to walk around each other in that office sometimes like a couple of stiff-legged bulldogs. One time Moses was threatening to do something—I don't recall what exactly—to some other commissioner. La Guardia was pleading and pleading with him not to do it. He kept saying, 'Jesus, Bob, look at the trouble you're going to cause me.' Finally Moses said, 'Okay, Major, I won't.' He left and La Guardia turned to me and said, 'Someday I'm going to hit that son of a bitch and knock him through that door!' " "Moses would come out wild—just absolutely wild," says Moses aide Jack Madigan, who was often waiting outside City Hall in Moses' limousine. "He used to say to me, 'Do you know what that dago son of a bitch told me this morning?' "

("That dago son of a bitch," "that wop son of a bitch" and "that guinea son of a bitch" were three of Moses' favorite private descriptions of La Guardia during the Mayor's first term—in letters and to his face, Moses addressed him as "Major," his World War I Army Air Force rank. During his second term, La Guardia, sensitive about his Italian immigrant ancestry and unable to forget that during his youth playmates, seeing an organ grinder, had jeered, "A dago with a monkey! Hey, Fiorello, you're a dago, too. Where's your monkey?," banned organ grinders from the streets. Moses thereupon began referring to La Guardia in private as "the little organ grinder." Later, he took to calling the Mayor "Rigoletto." La Guardia, feeling that Moses' insistence on his own infallibility was comparable at least to an Archbishop's, referred to him in private as "His Grace.")

While La Guardia was constantly severing other commissioners' ties with his administration or threatening to sever those ties, when the Mayor dealt with Moses the shoe was on the other foot. The resignation ultimatum, perfected by Moses during the Roosevelt Governorship, was a heavily utilized weapon in his running battle with the Mayor, a weapon used to win even small points: "I must insist that . . . approval of filling the position be granted forthwith. Otherwise I cannot assume further responsibility for this work." The ultimatum might be delivered in writing by Andrews or orally by Moses himself in face-to-face confrontations—just before he whirled on his heel and slammed out of the Mayor's office. And it invariably worked. When Moses slammed out with the threat hanging in the air, Windels recalls, "La Guardia used to go over to the window [the one in the southwest corner of his office, from which both the front steps of City Hall and Moses' limousine parked there would be visible] and wait to see if Moses really left the building—sometimes he would come back himself, you see. And if Moses did [leave], La Guardia would quickly send someone from the office—a secretary or whoever was with him—after him to try and stop him before he drove away—as if it was the secretary's idea and not his [La Guardia's], see—and get him to come back, or he'd telephone the police booth at the front entrance to get the patrolman on duty there to try to do it. Then he'd stand by the window waiting to see what happened. After a while, it occurred to him that Moses could see him standing there and could see how anxious he was, so he had the lower panes of the window filled with one-way glass so he could look out but Moses couldn't see in."

Baffled by the resignation tactic, which humiliated him by making him back down on the spot, La Guardia at first tried to handle it with mock disdain; once he sent Moses a note saying, "Enclosed are your last five or six resignations; I'm starting a new file." This strategy didn't blunt the weapon, but the wily Windels finally devised one that did: refusing to treat the resignations as anything but a joke. Recalls the Corporation Counsel: "One day I came in and La Guardia was sitting there and he said, 'What the hell am I going to do? Here's another resignation. And Earle Andrews is outside waiting for an answer.' I said, 'What you want to do is kid him.' " Windels suggested that La Guardia print a pad of forms reading: "I, Robert Moses, do hereby resign as ______ effective ______" and simply hand one to Moses whenever the commissioner threatened to resign. The technique worked; the next time Moses made the threat in person, La Guardia simply whipped out the pad, tore off the top form with a flourish and a broad—if forced—grin and handed it to him. Moses snatched the pad off the Mayor's desk, hurled it across the room, stamped out the door—and used the threat more infrequently thereafter. But it remained nonetheless implicit in confrontations between the two men, and while La Guardia won some of those clashes, more often it was the Mayor, rather than his commissioner, who gave way. In one typical episode, La Guardia ordered an investigation of two construction contractors he suspected of defrauding the city. Their attorney, the brilliant Jackson Dykman, recalls that while he was conferring with his clients in Moses' office, "I heard Moses give La Guardia the devil over the telephone." Describing that telephone conversation, Moses gives a wonderful imitation of the La Guardia snarl: "He said, "Yeahhhh, I hear you got a fancy lawyer.' I said, 'Yeahhhh, and he's gonna kick the shit out of you. You better leave him alone.' " And, as it turned out, La Guardia never had the investigation pursued.

On July 23, 1936, readers of *The New York Times* were served with their morning coffee a headline reading MAYOR CALLS POLICE TO HALT RAZING OF FERRY BY MOSES. And as they read on, they found that the headline had not exaggerated. The Mayor of the City of New York had indeed called out the armed constabulary against his own Park Commissioner.

At the beginning of his mayoralty, at the time of the renegotiation of the contract between the Triborough Authority and the PWA, La Guardia had agreed to mothball the ancient city-operated ferry, the *Rockaway,* which for sixteen years had been crossing the East River every twenty minutes between Astoria and the old green municipal ferryhouse at Ninety-second Street in Manhattan, so that the land on which the terminal stood could be used for the East River Drive approach to the bridge and so that the motorists who had been using the ferry would be forced to drive over the bridge instead and pay tolls to the Authority. For months, Moses had been pressing the city's Department of Plants and Structures, which operated the ferry, to discontinue the service so he could begin demolishing the ferryhouse.

But some of the ferry's 1,700 daily riders felt sentimental about the old tub, its fog bell clanging away and its whistle sounding lugubriously to warn off other ships on mist-shrouded early-morning trips. They felt a genuine camaraderie for the men who ran it, contributing seeds to the small garden, divided into tiny plots by fences made of old bedsprings, that the captains and ticket takers cultivated next to the Manhattan ferryhouse, petting and fawning over Red, an Airedale who had wandered into the ferryhouse as a pup ten years before and had lived there ever since. And passengers not given to sentimentality and camaraderie hated to see the ferry go because a round trip cost only a nickel and a round trip on the bridge would cost fifty cents—and those who didn't own automobiles would have no convenient way to get to and from Manhattan. The passengers had petitioned Astoria political leaders to let the ferry remain, and the political leaders had called on the Plants and Structures Commissioner, Frederick J. H. Kracke, an old-line Republican leader and La Guardia supporter—and Kracke had delayed discontinuing the service. Then a new element was added to the picture when the city decided to construct a large low-income housing project on the Astoria waterfront; with the ferry, Housing Authority Commissioner Langdon Post pointed out, residents of the project would have convenient transportation to and from their jobs in Manhattan; without it, since most of them were too poor to possess automobiles, it would be torturous to commute back and forth across the river every day. Kracke had continued to procrastinate. On July 15, La Guardia had personally telephoned and had requested the Sinking Fund Commission to formally turn the ferryhouse property over to the Authority—although the Mayor said that the ferry service should not be stopped for sixty days so that the ferry riders would have time to find other means of transportation. The Sinking Fund Commission concurred.

Moses was not willing to wait sixty days. Defying the Mayor, he decided to stop the service immediately—by tearing down the ferry terminal.

He ordered the contractor building the East River Drive approach, A. N. Hazell, to procure two barges and install a pile driver on one and a wrecking crane on the other. When they were ready, on July 21, he waited until the *Rockaway* had unsuspectingly pulled away from Manhattan for one of its early-afternoon trips to Astoria and then, without warning, ordered the barges towed into the ferry slip and lashed together there so that the *Rockaway* would have no place to dock when it returned. And he ordered the pile driver and the crane to pound and pull the slip to pieces. Attacking simultaneously from the land side, he dispatched crews of workmen to tear up York Avenue's cobblestones in front of the ferryhouse to cut off all access to the terminal by land.

By coincidence, Jack Madigan was in Kracke's office, discussing another matter, when the commissioner received a telephone call about what was happening. "He threw me out," Madigan recalls with a grin, telephoned

City Hall and, while he was trying to contact the Mayor, sent an aide, Deputy Commissioner Andrew Hudson, to the terminal to intercede with the contractors.

Hudson could hardly believe what was happening. The fact that the boat was heading across the river while its dock was being destroyed behind it was the least of it; the ferry could dock at another pier—which, in fact, was what it did when its amazed captain, returning from Astoria, saw what was happening. (Its passengers disembarked at a downtown fireboat landing.) What was more important was that hundreds of regular ferry commuters, who had come to Manhattan by boat that morning, would be left stranded there—with their cars and homes on the other side of the river. But when, assuming there had been some mistake, he pointed this out to the contractors and asked them to stop work until matters could be straightened out, they told him that they had orders from Moses to continue working no matter who tried to stop them—and even while Hudson was arguing with them, the pile driver continued to smash away at the dock.

La Guardia meanwhile contacted Moses and pleaded with him to call the contractors off. If the demolition stopped, he promised the Park Commissioner, he would call the Sinking Fund Commission back into session to shorten the sixty-day waiting period. Moses refused. Telephoning Police Commissioner Lewis J. Valentine, the Mayor—in a voice so choked with fury that it was barely coherent—ordered him to send a squad of patrolmen to the scene.

Expecting the contractors to yield to a direct police order, the Mayor and Valentine had instructed the officer in charge at the scene, Deputy Chief Inspector Edward A. Bracken, not to use force. But the contractors knew whose orders they would have to follow if they wanted to keep working for Triborough. When the Inspector ordered contractor Hazell to quit, Hazell said, "I'm not going to." Moses had told him not to, he said. And the pile driver continued to smash away. By this time, much of the dock had been destroyed and the hundreds of rush-hour ferry passengers standing on York Avenue were watching the workmen on the barges pry away heavy boards that had been loosened on the rest of it. Only force would stop Moses and La Guardia finally realized it. Put through to Bracken on the telephone, the Mayor ordered the Inspector to "drag those men off the boats if they don't quit." Those of the workmen who didn't drop their tools when a fifteen-man police boarding party swarmed over the side had them struck from their hands and were shoved, along with the rest, onto what was left of the dock. Within minutes, a police launch was standing alongside the barges and when a launch carrying the night shift of contractors' men appeared, it was warned away. A city tugboat pushed the contractors' barges away downriver. As night was falling, a procession of barges bearing piles and lumber to repair the slip arrived and workmen worked all night under floodlights to rebuild the terminal and repave York Avenue. By morning, the *Rockaway* was back in service—under the protection of a squad of patrolmen—and La Guardia could tell reporters, with a smile of satisfaction, "All is quiet on the eastern front."

But the last smile was Moses'. La Guardia waited a week for the story to fade from the front pages and then quietly had the Sinking Fund Commission transfer the terminal to Moses in another forty-eight hours. At 11:25 P.M., July 31, with Red gone from the ferryhouse—a night watchman had taken the Airedale home with him—fifty-two Astoria residents who had come down to the Astoria pier for old times' sake (plus twelve other persons who just wanted to get to Manhattan) boarded the *Rockaway* for its last round trip across the river. Mrs. Hattie Arnez of Astoria Boulevard played the accordion and they all sang the plaintive "Where Do We Go from Here?" As the *Rockaway*, having completed the round trip, bumped into the Astoria slip for the last time, they sang "Auld Lang Syne." Then, as the old tub left for the Brooklyn pier where she was to be laid up, her captain blew three long, dolorous whistle blasts of farewell. Hardly had the last note faded when it was succeeded by dull heavy thuds—the pound of Moses' pile driver, tearing the ferryhouse down again.

Within a year—in May 1937—the Mayor would again be forced to call out the cops against his commissioner, in another battle in which the commissioner eventually defeated him anyway. Advised that 2,000 WPA laborers assigned to Park Department projects would be reassigned at the beginning of the month so that work could begin on new nonpark projects (including three ultramodern firehouses for La Guardia's beloved Fire Department) and that 3,000 more men per month would be reassigned thereafter, Moses rumbled that if he had to lay off men, some among them would be playground supervisors; some playgrounds would therefore have to be closed, a step sure to touch off a furious public reaction. About to leave by train for a national conference of mayors in Los Angeles, La Guardia flatly ordered him not to do so, threatening to fire him if he did. Moses defied him. While the Union Pacific Streamliner was speeding the Mayor across country, the Park Commissioner struck: he didn't take some of the 2,000 men from playground duty; he took them *all*, and with them every piece of movable playground equipment, even the seats of the swings. And then he ordered 142 playgrounds padlocked. Telephoning frantically from pay phones at each Union Pacific stop, La Guardia ordered Police Commissioner Valentine to open the playgrounds—by force if necessary. The police were forced to cut the locks when Moses refused to surrender the keys to Valentine, and though the play areas were technically open, the Park Department was empowered by city regulations to hold on to the equipment it had removed, and the city's mothers, confronted by pistol-toting policemen instead of the familiar supervisory personnel—as well as by firmly locked toilets that were usually available to their youngsters—rallied behind the Park Commissioner. By the time the Mayor came home, he was confronted by a hostile public, to whom Moses had already taken his case. "We, mothers of the Chelsea District, want the 17th Street playground reopened and the WPA workers rehired," said one of the countless, hastily drawn petitions delivered to the Mayor. Said one of the letters that poured into his office: "As a mother of three small children, I ask you to take your petty squabble out of the parks and give Mr. Moses enough money to run the playgrounds." Lost in the tumult was the fact that it was the Park Commissioner, not the Mayor, who had designated playground personnel instead of construction workers to be dropped from the Park Department payroll. The public outcry, fanned by the pro-Moses press, forced the Mayor to ask the Board of Aldermen for an extra two and a half million dollars, so that the playgrounds could be properly supervised—and the Park Commissioner's construction projects could go on unabated.

The explanation for Moses' independence of La Guardia was as complex as the Little Flower's many-petaled character and as simple—and ineluctable—as the basic realities of the political game at which the Mayor excelled.

In a way, their vicious confrontations made La Guardia respect and admire Moses. The Mayor's intimates noticed that while he liked to push people around, he only respected those he couldn't push. "I think he put on a great deal of his brutalities to test people out," C. C. Burlingham observed. "If they could stand up against him it was all right, but if they couldn't they were in bad luck." And Moses could stand up against him better than anyone else.

Moreover, if there was much in the characters of the two strong-willed, hot-tempered men to fan antipathy between them, there was also much to produce affection, and if intimates can remember moments when the air between the Little Flower and the Master Builder crackled with anger, they can also remember moments when it glowed with the mutual affection and admiration of two great warriors who felt they were fighting in the same cause.

For, after all, in many respects they were indeed, at least for a while, fighting in the same cause. Against a panorama of politicians interested only in themselves, they stood out as two politicians who were also interested in accomplishments that they believed would benefit others. Robert Moses was, after all, not the only one of the two men who was spending his evenings and his weekends—the time that other men called spare and devoted to private interests—driving endlessly around New York City trying to think of ways to make it more beautiful. Robert Moses was not the only one of the two men to whom the realization of dreams in concrete was desperately important. (When "Fiorello . . . started to build La Guardia Airport," says his wife, "I think he spent every Saturday and Sunday out there watching every bit of sand that was put in. Just nurtured that like a plant.") And because accomplishment was desperately important to both men, while their disagreements may have been made fierce by personal characteristics—their blazing tempers, their arrogance, their dogmatism and their insistence on having their own way—the roots of those disagreements lay not in personal hostilities so much as in differences of opinion about what should be accomplished and how, and therefore their disagreements could always be resolved. So intensely interested were both men in their work, moreover, that often no resolution was necessary. "You'd see the two of them in the goddamnedest argument and then five hours later they could go and have a drink together and you'd never know they had fought," Jack Madigan says. Finally, he says, he came to understand why this was possible: "Other people dealt with personal feelings and emotions, got emotional about personal feelings, see, but these two fellows here, they dealt with subject matter—that was what they got emotional about—and when the subject was over, they could be friends again—unless one of them brought up the subject matter again." Because accomplishment was so important to both of them, when one flew into a fury over opposition, must not the other have understood how infuriating opposition could be? In a posed, formal picture of the top officials of the La Guardia administration, there are thirty-one neatly dressed men—and two, the Mayor and his Park Commissioner, with ties askew and collar points jabbing out beyond their lapels. And their habitual lack of neatness was symbolic, for neither of the two men was at all interested in clothes or other material trappings of life. At times they had exchanges which indicated that although neither would ever admit it, they knew there were respects in which their spirits were kindred. City Court Judge Florence Shientag heard La Guardia shout at Moses, "You can't get away riding roughshod over things!" and Moses shouting back, "That's the way *you* get things done!"

Other aspects of La Guardia's character also made the friendly drinks with Moses as inevitable as the wild altercations. There was the little Mayor's romantic streak, the side of him that was the dreamer, dreaming of making his city beautiful. His dreams for the beautification were vast but vague, and no one appreciated better than he the enormous difficulty in filling in the vague outline of a magnificent metropolis with specific plans and then in obtaining the money—the chisel and the brush—that would allow him to turn the plans into reality. And it was Moses who was enabling him to obtain the plans and the money. An astonishing number of La Guardia's dreams were being realized—by 1936, New York City was receiving one-seventh of the WPA allotment for the entire country—and the Mayor knew who was responsible. He must have known every time he went down to Washington for one of the frequent mayors' conferences called by the WPA. There would be hundreds of mayors there, and most of them would have come with grandiose plans—but when they were confronted with the blunt questions of the Army engineers WPA chief Harry Hopkins had brought in to screen proposed projects, they had to confess that the blueprints weren't ready, or the specifications weren't ready, or the topographical surveys weren't ready. La Guardia watched many of them walk out of the conferences humiliated and without the money they were asking for. But he had blueprints. He had specifications. He had topographical surveys. He had every piece of paper that even the hardest-eyed Army engineer could desire. And he had them because of Moses. Other municipalities were so unequal to the task of planning public works programs of size that in October 1938 the WPA would cancel more than one hundred major grants approved for eleven northeastern cities three years before—because the blueprints for those projects were still not ready. But Moses' engineers would come walking up the front steps of City Hall with blueprints piled high in their arms. President Roosevelt's friendship was indispensable to La Guardia's dreams, but no more indispensable than the tools Moses gave him to make use of it.

And Moses, the skillful manipulator of men, found plenty in La Guardia to manipulate.

There was, for example, the Mayor's boundless enthusiasm for engineering and engineers.

Moses played on this feeling. He was constantly pressing La Guardia to accompany him on inspection tours of construction sites, and, with his great gift for words, his sense of drama, and his squads of engineers who would follow the mayoral limousine in a second car so that they could leap out at a project site, elaborate artists' renderings in hand, and show the Mayor what the project would look like when completed, he made these tours wonderfully exciting to a man who "stood like a child in front of the simplest engineering feat." Once the little Mayor was so anxious to see the work on the Thomas Jefferson Park swimming pool that when he found the gate locked and no one around to open it, he chinned himself on the fence like a little boy so that he could see over the top. "I could always tell when Moses had been taking him around," Windels recalls. "He would be absolutely bubbling over with enthusiasm—he was just thrilled."

If Moses was putting on one of the greatest engineering shows in the history of civilization, moreover, he made sure La Guardia had a ringside seat. For example, on the day that the 2,200-ton vertical-lift span that comprised the Harlem River arm of the Triborough Bridge was to be set into place, the Mayor was standing on Randall's Island in the very shadow of the tower that, along with its twin on the Manhattan shore, would hold the span. And when the span was finally set in place, he said breathlessly, "This is the most thrilling moment I have had since I became mayor. . . . I congratulate the Authority, the engineers, the contractors and every man who has had a part in this magnificent piece of work. Moments like this make up for many heartaches and disappointments." The fact—which astonished him when he learned it—that Moses had never gone to engineering school did not prevent him from gushing on several occasions: "Robert Moses is the greatest engineer in the world."

He wanted Moses' admiration. He was jealous of the only man who really had it. Moses recalls that "when the Mayor was mad at me, which was not infrequent, he would say, 'The only boss you ever had whom you really respected was Al Smith. What's he got that I don't have?' " (Moses recalls that "I always answered that I admired both of them, but thought Smith a better executive" because he always stood behind his subordinates.)

La Guardia's predilection for pageantry, preferably with himself at its center, was obvious to anyone who noticed the yards of gold braid with which the Major outfitted his policeman bodyguard or his penchant for holding full-dress military-type inspections of anything that could conceivably be inspected—police or firemen with motorized equipment, snow plows, new garbage trucks, old garbage trucks—and for preening and strutting as he marched in front of them, literally swelling out his barrel chest as he bounced by at the salute. Moses played on this predilection. He gave the Major pageantry such as no mayor had ever enjoyed in democratic America.

Moses was opening playgrounds at a fantastic rate: 60 in 1934, 71 in 1935, 72 in 1936, 52 in 1937. La Guardia was present at most opening ceremonies. And these were ceremonies with the Moses touch.

For the opening of a small playground on Seventeenth Street between Eighth and Ninth avenues, for example, nearby tenements were draped in red, white and blue—not crepe-paper streamers but immense triangular pennons. Flowerpots containing 25,000 chrysanthemums made a bright ring around the playground fence. Flags were everywhere. The whole scene gleamed with the reflection of the hot summer sunlight off the polished bridles and curried satiny flanks of mounted policemen's horses, the polished brass and buttons of platoons of green-clad Park Department guards, the trumpets and tubas of Park Department and American Legion bands. As the Mayor's limousine pulled up to the curb between rows of rigidly erect policemen at the salute, a smartly uniformed Park Department guard swung open its door and as the Mayor bounced out—followed by the gold braid of his bodyguard—the bands broke into a tune: incredibly, "Hail to the Chief." And when he reached the white-painted, bunting-draped speakers' platform he found he was the only speaker, except for Moses, who confined himself to a very brief recitation of playground statistics and then said, "I now introduce the Mayor of the City of New York"—a performance that led La Guardia to comment later that Moses was the ideal master of ceremonies. At the precise instant at which the applause passed its crescendo and began to fade away after La Guardia's speech, which had been delivered at a lectern custom-built by Park Department carpenters so that the little Mayor wouldn't be forced to stretch to reach the microphone, it was punctuated by a hiss as the center fountain in the wading pool was turned on full blast, dramatically filling the air with sprays of water and eliciting a gratifying "ooooh" from hundreds of children waiting behind a ribbon. And when the Mayor advanced to cut the ribbon and allow the children to rush into the spray, he found that it was no ordinary ribbon but a braided and tasseled strand colored red, white and blue, and the shears held out to him by a little girl from the neighborhood were sterling silver shears resting on a cushion of royal purple velvet.

Then the Mayor jumped back into his limousine for a trip that was an adventure in itself—Fiorello La Guardia's dashes across his city, limousine siren wailing, police on motorcycles clearing the path, were not trips for the fainthearted. And when the Mayor arrived at the other playgrounds, he found again chrysanthemums, flags, men on horseback, polished brass and buttons, bands, "Hail to the Chief"—every detail that had made the first opening so exciting—plus, often, new inspirations: at a playground being opened in Brooklyn's Red Hook section, whose most famous landmark was the "Gowanus House," around which a Revolutionary War battle had been fought, a large painting of the Gowanus House had been placed as a backdrop behind the speakers' platform; the neighborhood was predominantly Italian, and as the Mayor walked onto the platform two aerial bombs were shot into the air, releasing parachutes that floated above the playground site—and attached to one parachute was an American flag, to the other the tricolor of the House of Savoy.

On some days, La Guardia would open as many as fifteen playgrounds scattered across the face of the great city, turning the occasion into a triumphal tour of his domain, speeding behind his helmeted outriders across the reaches of the bridge-connected boroughs and then leaping into a launch to bring his presence even to the colony on Staten Island. Each ceremony would be perfect in every detail. (Or almost every detail: at one dedication in an Italian neighborhood, held before Moses was acquainted with La Guardia's views on organ grinders, Moses had several, along with their hurdy-gurdies and monkeys, on hand to entertain the children, and La Guardia sat on the platform glowering out from under the brim of his big hat.) And the pageantry Moses arranged for the Little Flower was not limited to playground openings. It included the annual Christmas tree-lighting ceremony in City Hall Park, complete with a program of instrumental music and carol singing and a switch that the Mayor threw to light up a sixty-foot spruce. It included the dedication of the baseball diamond complex in Alley Pond Park at which La Guardia, after a series of fantastic contortions on the pitcher's mound, got to throw the first pitch—to a batter who happened to be Babe Ruth. (The Bambino, swinging with something less than his usual gusto, possibly because he was almost doubled over with laughter, hit a pop fly that dropped to the ground in the vicinity of second base.) Moses made a place for La Guardia in every major Park Department event.

Nineteen thirty-six, *Fortune* magazine said in an article on Moses, was "the swimming pool year." The ten giant neighborhood swimming pools were completed that summer, and Moses opened one a week for ten weeks. Of a size previously unimagined in swimming pools—one was 330 feet long and 165 feet wide—they brought the joys of swimming to city-bound children—and parents—by the tens of thousands. Moses' passion for swimming led him to take a special interest in these pools, and he drove the engineers responsible for their design to invent filtering plants of new efficiency and underwater lighting that made them revolutionary developments in recreation—Harry Hopkins called the Astoria Pool "the finest pool in all the world." And Moses exerted all his genius as a showman to make each opening the most memorable event in the history of the neighborhood in which it was located: a parade led by local political leaders and local American Legion, high-school and Knights of Columbus bands would wind through the neighborhood beforehand—generally in the early evening, since the openings were held at night so that the underwater lighting would be more spectacular—attracting tens of thousands of residents. After neighborhood priests had blessed the clear waters—chlorinated—of the pools, there would be swimming races and diving competitions by neighborhood youngsters and by Olympic stars imported from all over the United States, as well as exhibitions by a team of "swimming clowns." Each opening, moreover, would be tailored to the neighborhood in which the pool was located: believing that what Negroes liked to do most was dance and sing, Moses arranged that the opening ceremonies for the Colonial Park Pool in Harlem include an exhibition by Bojangles Bill Robinson (identified by the *Times* as a "negro tap dancer"); a rendition of the Battle Hymn of the Republic by "negro tenor" Roland Hayes, accompanied by the 369th Regiment band; and community singing. But center stage at each opening was reserved for Fiorello H. La Guardia. It was he who pulled the switch that turned on the underwater lighting, an event that never failed to bring a murmur of "oooohs" from the crowd, it was he who gave the word to raise the flag and it was he who got to cut the ribbon and shout to the waiting children: "Okay, kids, it's all yours!"

Moses saw to it that one playground, at the Williamsburg Bridge Plaza, was named the "Fiorello H. La Guardia Playground." ("The best thing about this playground is its name," he wrote the Mayor.)

If there were personal reasons why the Mayor wanted to allow Moses his independence, there were political reasons why he had to.

The most important, of course, was public opinion and Moses' hold on it.

Already predisposed to be friendly toward Moses because he was creator and defender of parks, the city's thirteen daily newspapers had that friendship cultivated with customary Moses thoroughness.

As always, he went directly to the top, giving newspaper owners preopening tours of new bridges and free passes to them thereafter, inviting them to sail on the Long Island Park Commission's yacht, bathe in the reserved section of Jones Beach and dine in the private section of the Marine Dining Room—where he served them lavish helpings of his inimitable charm; Iphigene and Arthur Sulzberger of the *Times*, Helen and Ogden Mills Reid of the *Herald Tribune* (who never found out about Moses' plan to deceive him into making a contribution to the Yale University Minor Sports Association) and Roy W. Howard of the *World-Telegram* regarded him as a personal friend. He spent many weekends at their summer homes.

Moses also lavished attention on top editors. He had easy access to the *Herald Tribune*'s because his Yale classmate Harold Phelps Stokes was one of them, and he used that access; one of the *Tribune* editors was a dyed-in-the-wool reactionary who saw Bolsheviks in every bush, and Moses helped his vision, filling the editor's mail with leaflets mimeographed by left-wingers in the WPA to prove that any dissension among WPA workers in the Park Department was fomented by Communists. The chief editorial writer of the *Times* was Charles Merz, a Yale graduate who lived in the apartment building next to Moses'. "Just by happenstance," remarks Joseph C. Ingraham, a

Times reporter (and later its transportation editor) who became friendly with Moses, "Moses would be waiting in the lobby [of Merz's apartment house] many mornings to ask him if he wanted a lift downtown—so he could plant an editorial."

And while Moses went to the top, he did not stop there, wining and dining reporters as well as publishers, inviting key ones to his elaborate opening-ceremony luncheons, to an annual swimming and dinner outing at Jones Beach, to more intimate, and elaborate, luncheons at Belmont Lake State Park, to the Park Department's Christmas party at the Arsenal and to day-long yacht trips, which often ended with clam and lobster bakes on Fire Island. At all these events the food was superb, the liquor flowed freely and so did the charm.

The most important newspaper in the city—and in the country—was *The New York Times,* and Moses had an especially strong hold over the *Times*: the devotion to parks of the woman who owned approximately two-thirds of its voting stock.

Iphigene Ochs Sulzberger, only living child of the imperious little patriarch of the *Times*, who during the 1920's had purchased key parcels in Saratoga and reserved them for Moses' state park there, had been fighting for years for the expansion and improvement of New York City's inadequate and decaying park system, a fight whose frustration was summed up in one conversation with Tammany Manhattan Park Commissioner Sheehy, who unabashedly told her to her face that until he became commissioner he had never been in Central Park in his life. When La Guardia told her that he was giving Robert Moses power over parks, she had been "happy"—and the adjective had proved inadequate to describe her feelings about what Moses was accomplishing with that power. Elected president of the city's Park Association in January 1935, Iphigene Sulzberger's first official act was to present Moses with the association's annual testimonial award and, as she handed him the illuminated scroll, she said earnestly, "Commissioner Moses, you have made us feel that the projects for which we have striven can be realized." She would serve as president until 1963, heading the Park Association, therefore, for twenty-five of the twenty-six years that Moses served as City Park Commissioner, and during all that time her admiration for him would only increase. In 1963, the association would present him with another illuminated scroll; it closed with the words: "How wondrous are his works; how deep our gratitude."

In private, moreover, Mrs. Sulzberger was, if possible, even more adulatory: in 1967, standing by a window in her Fifth Avenue apartment, looking out over Central Park, the gray-haired, dignified woman would tell the author: "There has never been as great a public servant. . . . He was a man of vision . . . a giant. . . . He saw Nature as a whole. . . . I had a feeling that he liked to fight, that if someone just agreed with him he was disappointed. He liked to beat them. He was a hero of old, always rushing into battle with Excalibur waving above his head. I thought of the Park Association as Aaron and Hur. Do you know who Aaron and Hur were? They were the soldiers in the Bible who stood behind Moses and held up his arms when he got tired [at the battle of Rephidim, at which 'Israel prevailed' so long as Moses held up his hands]. Well, that's how I thought of the Park Association, as upholding the arms of Bob Moses."

Not that she always agreed with him. Mrs. Sulzberger possessed—years earlier than most urban planners—a very acute understanding that the values of engineers were not compatible with the values for which parks were created; "Engineers are straight-line crazy," she would tell the interviewer. She didn't want the unspoiled wilderness of Inwood Hill Park destroyed by the running of a road on a straight line along its crest. A believer in the old theory that the purpose of parks was primarily conservation, not recreation —although she might not have stated the theory in precisely those terms— she didn't like the idea that Moses' plans required the covering over of so many green spaces with concrete for playgrounds, basketball courts and other active play facilities, not to mention roads and parking fields. In particular, believing in the preservation of Central Park as a restful retreat from the abrasions of city life, she didn't want so many active play facilities there. "Iphigene gave us many arguments," Jack Madigan said. "And," he added, "some we walked away from"—a euphemism meaning they surrendered. Moses probably turned the abandoned reservoir site in Central Park into a "great lawn" instead of into the playgrounds and ball fields that he originally wanted there solely because of Mrs. Sulzberger's feelings.

But while Moses may have walked away from some fights with Mrs. Sulzberger, he did not walk away from many; he would not allow—because of his nature, he *could not* allow—anybody, even an individual whose support was so important to him, to criticize his plans. His usual technique with Mrs. Sulzberger was not to walk away but to walk with—to take her himself, or have Madigan or Andrews take her—on a tour of the area in dispute to try to sell her on his idea of how it should be developed. These walks were planned with care; Madigan took her to Inwood Hill on a weekday when the park was deserted and told her that the public wasn't getting any use out of it—guessing, correctly, that she had never hiked up the steep hill on a weekend and hence had not seen the happy picnickers who crowded it then. (Madigan also played shrewdly on her sensibilities, which were firmly Victorian: "I told Iphigene if you walked up there at night you were likely to step on a couple and it might be a good idea to have lights—the headlights from cars, you know—up there.") And the walks usually worked— particularly since Moses' opponents did not know her well enough to take her on walks themselves and show her their side of the argument and did not have the facilities or manpower to compile the facts and figures that might have disproved Moses' facts and figures. Moses persuaded Mrs. Sulzberger to persuade the Park Association to elect Andrews, a native Virginian who could be as courtly with women as he could be curt with men (Mrs. Sulzberger says he was "a remarkable man"), to its board of directors, and thereafter there was someone working for association support of his policies from within.

Mrs. Sulzberger's dedication to the cause of parks was so complete, moreover, that she didn't want to do anything that would interfere drastically with what Moses was doing—even if she felt he was sometimes wrong. This man was rejuvenating parks at a rate she would never have believed possible; she didn't want him hampered by her disagreement with what she regarded as details: "I never did like the concrete floors on the playgrounds," she would tell the interviewer, but, she would note, before Moses came along, there were no real playgrounds at all, "no swings and no jungle gyms . . . hardly anything for children to play on, really."

So sincere was Mrs. Sulzberger's dedication to parks and the new Park Commissioner that this proud and dignified woman even submitted to a public insult—quite possibly the only one she ever received—at his hands.

The quarrel was based on Moses' plan to turn the site of the demolished Central Park Casino into a playground. Mrs. Sulzberger had allowed herself to be reconciled to the creation of "perimeter" playgrounds in Central Park by Moses' argument that small children could not be kept out of the park anyway and the strategic placing of playgrounds next to park entrances would "intercept" them and confine their destructive energy to the park's edge. She had never thought that Moses would begin to lay concrete in the park's interior. Hearing of the plan for the Casino site, she protested publicly on behalf of the Park Association in a letter released to the press on December 23, 1935, in which she stated, "It seems to me that in our desire to establish playgrounds, which are sadly needed in the city, we are completely overlooking the rights and needs of the adult population. Central Park will fail to fulfill its purpose if . . . there is no longer space where men and women can have quiet and relaxation."

Moses' letter of reply, which *he* released to the press on December 24, closed with the words "Merry Christmas." But the rest of the letter was couched in the tone Moses customarily employed with protesters. Your arguments, he informed Mrs. Sulzberger, are "preposterous" and "irresponsible generalizations. . . . It is difficult for me to believe that you seriously contend that the needs of the adult population are being completely overlooked in our parks . . ." The letter even closed with a threat. "This particular question does not seem to me to be important enough to quarrel about, unless you insist on proving your generalizations, in which case I am prepared to refute them by a public exhibition of plans, photographs, maps and supporting figures."

It would have been interesting to see how the *Times,* which buried the exchange of letters on page 25, would have covered such an exhibition. But there was to be no need for one. Mary Moses saw to that. A week later, the Sulzbergers and the Moseses were among the guests at the dance given every New Year's Eve by the "Jewish Gatsby," Adolph Lewisohn, in the great gold-and-white ballroom of his Fifth Avenue mansion. Mrs. Sulzberger recalls that "Mary came over leading Bob by the hand like a little boy and she said, 'You know Iphigene's a good friend. You had no business writing her a letter like that. Now you tell her you're sorry and you kiss her.' " Moses told her he was sorry and kissed her—and at 2 A.M., when the Sulzbergers, as was their custom every New Year's Eve, served friends a scrambled-egg breakfast at their apartment, the Moseses were there as usual.

Mrs. Sulzberger had too deep a sense of her responsibility to the public to take the insulting letter personally, anyway; Robert Moses was too valuable to the city to quarrel with, she felt. And, she was to tell the interviewer, it was "unappreciative" to quarrel with a man who had done so much for New York. On the day after the New Year's breakfast, in an act of selflessness made all the more noble by the fact that her power made it unnecessary for her to perform it, Iphigene Ochs Sulzberger, sacrificing her pride on the altar of what she believed to be the public interest, wrote a public apology to Moses—and ordered it printed in her own newspaper.

. . . I owe you an apology for having said that ". . . we are completely overlooking the rights and needs of the adult population." No such sweeping generalization is warranted. I do, however, believe that we are in danger of paying too little attention to those rights and needs.

You close your characteristically vigorous defense of the Park Department's plans with the remark that the issues raised in this particular controversy do not seem to you to be "important enough to quarrel about." I and other members of the Park Association would dislike greatly any occasion for quarrel with you. You come close to our ideal of what a Park Commissioner should be and we have no desire to be associated, even for a moment, with those who have attempted from time to time to hinder you in your plans for the rehabilitation and development of the parks.

Mrs. Sulzberger's influence on the newspaper of which her father had been, and her husband was, publisher was not overt. Intrusiveness was not her style, which was so reasonable, dignified and soft-spoken that people sometimes mistook her gentleness for timidity. But, as the *Times*'s historian, Gay Talese, has pointed out, "no perceptive editor . . . made this mistake." "Her most casual remark," wrote Turner Catledge, later managing editor, "would be treated as a command."

Mrs. Sulzberger believed that Moses came "close to our ideal of what a Park Commissioner should be"; the *Times* evidently believed so, too. Its reporters and editors may never have been directly ordered to give Moses special treatment but, during the Thirties as during the Twenties, they were not so insensitive as not to know what was expected of them. Moses' press releases were treated with respect, being given prominent treatment and often being printed in full. There was no investigating of the "facts" presented in those press releases, no attempt at detailed analysis of his theories of recreation and transportation, no probing of the assumptions on which the city was building and maintaining recreational facilities and roads. The *Times* ran more than one hundred editorials on Moses and his programs during the twelve-year La Guardia administration—overwhelmingly favorable editorials.

Once, trying in desperation to make sure that Mrs. Sulzberger got to hear both sides of an issue, La Guardia invited her to visit his office to hear Moses argue with the official with whom he was currently feuding, city WPA administrator Victor Ridder. (She was not the only female present; the Mayor for some reason—possibly to create a homey atmosphere—had his adopted daughter, Jean, then eight years old, in the office, too, and she sat on his knee during the ensuing discussion.) La Guardia's ploy worked. At the end of a shouting match between Moses and Ridder—"They really went at it for a while," Mrs. Sulzberger would recall—the Mayor ruled against Moses, and for once there was no *Times* editorial disagreeing with the decision the next day. But such a ploy could obviously not be repeated in every dispute. And in most disputes Moses could count on the *Times*'s support.

Dramatic proof of how popular the press had made Moses was, moreover, available to the Mayor every time he spoke in public. Just as audiences reacted with Pavlovian predictability to every mention of Brooklyn—with laughs—so they reacted with Pavlovian predictability to every mention of Robert Moses—with cheers. At the end of a playground opening, there was almost invariably a "Two, four, six, eight—Who do we appreciate?" for Moses. "La Guardia wanted to fire him often, but he didn't dare," says mayoral law secretary Kern. "The press—*The New York Times* in particular—had babied him like a spoiled child. He couldn't do anything wrong in their eyes. They made him a myth. And a man who had to go to the electorate couldn't fire a myth. He [Moses] was too big to fire." Occasionally Windels would try to brace the Mayor to stand up to Moses. But on those occasions, the Little Flower would wail, "What'll the *Times* say?" If from a personal viewpoint it is not too much to say that La Guardia liked Moses, from a political viewpoint it is not too much to say that he feared him.

At the beginning of his mayoralty, La Guardia attempted to take an interest in the Park Department. When he received protests about Moses' plans for a local playground from a local organization, he would grant its representatives an interview, and if he felt their arguments had merit, he would ask Moses to reconsider. When some individual protested about a Park Department policy or about alleged mistreatment by a Park Department employee, he would send the protest to Moses with a pink slip attached—a slip that in the color code set up by La Guardia to govern his relationship with his commissioners meant the Mayor wanted an immediate reply.

But Moses would either ignore the pink slip or would reply by saying that the Mayor must learn to stop interfering in the "internal affairs of the Park Department." "My policies can't be carried out if the Mayor is going to listen to appeals from individuals," he would write. And if La Guardia sought to press an inquiry, Moses would threaten to resign or to take the issue to the public. "If you disagreed with [Moses], why, you were a public enemy," Windels said. The Mayor had no choice but to let Moses have his way.

By the end of his first term, La Guardia was letting Moses have it. The Astoria Ferry and playground closing fights, which became public knowledge, were exceptions. Most of the disagreements between the Mayor and the commissioner were kept secret—because La Guardia did not press them. When one threatened to become public, the Mayor quickly backed down. He and Moses had been arguing over a twenty-five-acre tract of land in Coney Island owned by the Dock Department but unused. Moses wanted all the land for a park; the Mayor was in favor of a Board of Education plan to use a few of the acres for a school. When he imprudently mentioned to reporters that "the location of a school on the border of a park is ideal," the reporters went to Moses for comment. "I thought this administration wanted playgrounds. Either they do or they don't," he said. And he added what the *Herald Tribune* called "some even more uncomplimentary remarks" about the Mayor. La Guardia hastily scrambled for cover. "I can't believe my Park Commissioner made any such statements," the Mayor said. "No controversy exists and none can be made out of it." And the school idea was dropped. "He didn't want to fight with Moses no matter what," Lazarus says. As long as he didn't fight, La Guardia had learned, Moses would provide him with a seemingly inexhaustible cornucopia of political benefits. If he did fight, Moses would humiliate and defeat him. The little Mayor had learned—the hard way—that it was better not to interfere.

Other political considerations which deterred the Mayor from interfering with Moses in the fields he had carved out for his own were the same reasons that had deterred a Governor—Roosevelt—from interfering: Moses' ability to complete public works fast enough to provide a record of accomplishment for an elected official to run on in the next election; his ability to build public works without scandal; his willingness to serve as a lightning rod to draw off opposition from the elected official—most of all, perhaps, his matchless knowledge of government. Says Judge Jacob Lutsky, who not only served in the La Guardia administration but was a top adviser to Mayors O'Dwyer, Impellitteri and Wagner: "You've got to understand—every morning when a mayor comes to work, there are a hundred problems that must be solved. And a lot of them are so big and complex that they just don't seem susceptible to solution. And when he asks guys for solutions, what happens? Most of them can't give him any. And those that do come up with solutions, the solutions are unrealistic or impractical—or just plain stupid. And those that do make sense—there's no money to finance them. But you give a problem to Moses and overnight he's back in front of you—with a solution, all worked out down to the last detail, drafts of speeches you can give to explain it to the public, drafts of press releases for the newspapers, drafts of the state laws you'll need to get passed, advice as to who should introduce the bills in the Legislature and what committees they should go to, drafts of any City Council and Board of Estimate resolutions you'll need; if there are constitutional questions involved, a list of the relevant precedents—and a complete method of financing it all spelled out. He had solutions when no one else had solutions. A mayor *needs* a Robert Moses." But there were new reasons, too, why La Guardia found it politically unfeasible to interfere with Moses. And these reasons had the deepest—and most ominous—significance for the city.

Some revolved around the federal government's newly expanded role in the city's affairs.

Always before, the city and the city alone had had the power to determine the priority, location and design of public works—because the city and the city alone had been paying for them. Every step in the construction of a school or a bridge or a park—from the initial preliminary study of the project's engineering feasibility to the final use of the power of eminent domain to evict citizens to make way for it—had to be authorized by the city government, by officials elected by the city's people. Therefore, those people retained ultimate control over the public works that did so much to shape their lives. The correspondence between their will and public works was, of course, not at all exact; innumerable factors—chief among them, perhaps, the corruption that under Tammany Hall interposed private gain as an integral factor in the governmental equation—bent off its bias the great drive shaft of the engine of city government, the drive shaft that according to the blueprint for that engine, the City Charter, was supposed to be turnable only by the public will. But there *was* a correspondence. A mayor strong enough to dominate the Boards of Estimate and Aldermen would disturb the balance of the drive shaft, which was meant to rest equally on executive and legislative action, but because the mayor was an official elected by and ultimately responsible to the people, the crucial correspondence still existed.

But although the city's new mayor was dominating the city's government, that mayor was not controlling the construction of public works in the city to a similar extent. Not the city but the federal government was paying for the bulk of those public works, and the federal government was much more interested in speed, in getting something to show for its expenditure, than in the considerations that would at least partially motivate a mayor—priorities, location and design, for example. And, because speed of construction depended upon the existence of detailed plans, the federal authorities were therefore primarily interested in such plans. Because the Mayor needed plans and needed them fast, he had no choice but to give priority not to those projects which were most urgently needed, but to those projects for which plans were available—and to a considerable extent not he but Robert Moses decided which projects those would be. Because not he but Moses had the "large, stable planning force" of engineers trained to design urban public works on the new, huge scale made necessary by the growth of the city and made financially feasible by the new federal involvement, to a considerable extent he could not even evaluate those plans. He could not argue intelligently for changes in the location or the design Moses was proposing. Continually La Guardia sought to overcome this handicap. "He was always prodding other departments to come up with plans," Windels recalls. "But it took them so long." And when the plans were available, the labor often was not; Moses' stake-driving tactics had tied it up on Park Department projects. Moses' popularity, moreover, made it all but impossible for the Mayor to snatch the labor back. The convenient symbol of La Guardia's frustration was the firehouses the Mayor had wanted to build with the 5,000 men he had authorized the WPA to detach from Park Department projects in 1937, the 5,000 men he was unable to detach after Moses forced him to back down by locking the playgrounds: the Mayor had twenty new firehouses in mind; he was able to build three. But firehouses were only a symbol;

schoolhouses, jailhouses and police station houses were also involved—as were hospitals, sewage disposal plants, sewers and subways. La Guardia was forced to cut back his planned programs of construction of almost every type of municipal institution except parks—Robert Moses' parks—and bridges—Robert Moses' bridges—and roads—Robert Moses' roads. The lion's share of the billion-plus dollars poured into New York City by the New Deal was spent on Moses' projects. To a considerable extent, in the planning of large-scale public works in New York City during the 1930's, Robert Moses operated independently of the elected official who had appointed him—and therefore independently of the people's will.

The significance of this fact for the development of New York is heightened by the amount of federal money involved.

Even during the flush years of the Jimmy Walker era, New York's expenditures for capital improvements had run only slightly above $100,-000,000 per year. That figure represented, in dollars, the annual alteration—hopefully, for the better—to the civic estate.

But during the first five years of the La Guardia era, the federal government, through CWA, WPA and PWA, contributed more than $1,150,000,-000 for public works in the city, a figure which, when combined with the city's own expenditures (which La Guardia was, by 1936, able to restore to the Walkerian level), meant that during those five years the civic estate was altered more than it had been altered in the preceding fifteen, that New York was able to effect a far greater and more rapid alteration in its physical public structure than had ever before been possible. And this magnified Moses' influence on the city's destiny. The portion of its remaking carried out independently of the people's will was relatively immense.

Then there were other political deterrents to any interference with Moses by La Guardia.

Some were a result of the continuation—and acceleration—of Moses' evolution from scorner of politicians.

The Legislature hadn't changed much since the days when Robert Moses had been denouncing its corruption and avarice. But Robert Moses had changed.

No longer did he respond to a legislator's patronage request by telling him to "stick it up your ass." The state park system was a vast reservoir of jobs—both year-round jobs and, because of the seasonal nature of park work, summer jobs particularly coveted by politicians who wanted their teen-age children to earn good money in the open air during school vacations. And, because the reservoir had outlets (parks) in every corner of the state, Moses had jobs to distribute not only on Long Island but in the undeveloped, job-poor upstate counties in which the leaders of the Republican legislative majority lived. There was a line, firmly drawn, above which patronage was not allowed to intrude into the state park system; top administrators, the elite cadre known as "Moses Men," still had to work their way up from the ranks, still were promoted strictly on the basis of ability and willingness to work killing hours—and still owed their allegiance solely to Robert Moses. But Moses had proved more and more willing to fill lower-echelon jobs with people recommended by key legislators. As for lucrative construction contracts, the one-time idealist had become known in Albany, according to Saul Kaplan, counsel to Assembly minority leader Irwin Steingut, as "a practical fellow who understands the facts of life and what makes things tick, a fellow who is prepared to cooperate with anybody." There was a point at which "cooperation" stopped: the point at which it would interfere with the completion of a project as Moses had originally envisioned it. He employed practical politics only to further his dreams; he did not allow it to interfere with them. "Sometimes someone would ask him for something and it would interfere with what he wanted to do, and in that case, he'd say it couldn't be done," Kaplan says. "But as long as you weren't a pig—okay. If you put a gun to his head and said 'either-or,' he'd tell you to go to hell. But if you laid the cards on the table and didn't try to kid him, he'd help if he could. And if he said *you* could help *him* in solving a couple of problems—you helped."

This influence was increased by Moses' ideological compatibility with the key upstate or Old Guard Republican legislators. "He was a conservative and they were conservatives," Windels says simply. They distrusted La Guardia, whom they considered a "wild man" and a traitor to their party, a liberal using its label to get elected; they were infuriated by the Mayor's all-out support of FDR and by his general disloyalty: although he would be elected mayor three times on the Republican ticket, not once during his twelve years in that office would La Guardia ever support a Republican candidate for a state or national office. But because of the Legislature's broad control over the city, La Guardia constantly needed favors from it. Moses' influence with it could therefore be an asset to him—if Moses wanted to use that influence on his behalf. Conversely, the possibility that Moses would use that influence against him was a very real threat; at least once an inoffensive bill that La Guardia had thought would be passed routinely was inexplicably held up in committee while he was embroiled in one of his disputes with Moses, and, although he never received any proof that his Park Commissioner was behind the holdup, the Mayor received hints that he was—and saw it as Moses' way of letting him know what Moses could do to him in Albany if he wanted to. Whether or not Moses actually used his power with the Legislature for or against La Guardia, he made himself in many instances the broker between the Mayor and the legislative leaders, often acting as middleman in closed-door bargaining sessions.

Moses' power in state government therefore increased his power over the city government to which he, alone among state officials, also belonged—to a point where it drastically eroded the ability of the city's highest elected official, technically his superior, to control him. This, of course, was precisely what the framers of the state's constitution—and many reformers—had feared when they sought to prohibit the simultaneous holding of state and city jobs by the same individual. But the reformers had sacrificed the principle because they believed that Moses' unique abilities should exempt him from normal considerations and because La Guardia had assured them that his power as mayor made such a prohibition unnecessary. An appointed official not directly responsible to the electorate could never obtain power to defy the official who was responsible for his appointment, the Mayor had said. But Moses had nonetheless obtained a large measure of such power. Coupled with the power he had obtained from his use within the city of federal money, it gave him considerable independence of the city's mayor. He was using forces outside the city to bend its highest elected official to his will. By employing forces outside the city's control, he was remaking the city in certain crucial areas without allowing the city any say in that remaking.

24. *Driving*

ALWAYS TIME HAD PURSUED Moses hotly; now it panted at his very heels. His dream now was to remake a city, but the city itself would obviously never be able to finance its own remaking. Only the federal government possessed sufficient resources, and there was no guarantee that those resources would continue to be made available for the purpose; in fact, there was more reason to suppose they would not, for every upswing in the economy brought a corresponding rise in the outcry for a cutback in work relief from the predominantly conservative press and from conservatives in Congress. The President, whose belief in the balanced budget was dying hard, continually wavered himself—in 1936, during another upswing, he ordered a stretch-out in the spending of already allocated work relief funds. Good news for the nation was therefore bad news for Moses; every upswing in the economy spelled a downswing in his hopes. And the disappearance of CWA on forty-eight hours' notice in 1934 had taught him how quickly those hopes could be dashed altogether. Moses knew that the opportunity presented by the $4.8 billion WPA program might disappear at almost any time, and a similar opportunity might never present itself again; he couldn't allow anything or anybody in the city to stand in his way or to slow him down. And he used the same forces that were so effective in dealing with the city's mayor—influence with state and federal governments, immense personal popularity, tactics he had perfected on Long Island—to make sure that no one would.

The rest of the city's government might have slowed him down. Obeying and following the complex laws and procedures set forth in the city's 3,000-page Charter and Administrative Code would have slowed the pace of Moses' building. But the special powers he had written into the Park Department Unification Act exempted him from many of the Charter's restrictions, and he ignored or circumvented most of the others. (Under the Charter, for example, the design of every public structure had to be submitted to and approved by the Municipal Art Commission. Moses submitted the designs for his structures—on the very day that their construction was beginning, so that by the time the commission got around to considering them, they were finished.)

That government's appointed officials, sworn to uphold a law that

Moses was violating in spirit or letter and determined to live up to their oath, might have slowed him down. But he didn't let them.

His usual technique with an insufficiently compliant departmental official was to demand that he be fired. Moses would attempt to convince the department's commissioner to do so by "confidentially" revealing to him damaging personal information dug up by his "bloodhounds." And if they hadn't been able to dig up any, Moses invented some. He insinuated, for example, that an Assistant Corporation Counsel who had angered him with his refusal to proceed with a legal case against residents of land adjoining a park site, was a drunk.

On more than one occasion, this technique worked. If it did not, Moses simply stepped up the pressure another notch. He refused to deal with the official involved or to allow any of his aides to deal with him. This tactic brought the relationship between the Park Department and the other department involved to a halt until the commissioner agreed to shift his offending subordinate to a post in which he did not deal with the Park Department and to replace him with a more amenable individual. It was a tactic that brought weak-spined commissioners to their knees in short order, and it even worked with Windels. The Corporation Counsel at first refused to fire or shift his "drunk" assistant, but Moses sent him a telegram stating: I HAVE GIVEN ORDERS THAT NO ONE IS TO DISCUSS ANY . . . MATTER . . . UNDER MY JURISDICTION WITH HIM. Windels sent back a telegram of his own: THE MANNER IN WHICH LEGAL MATTERS ARISING FROM THE WORK OF YOUR DEPARTMENT ARE TO BE HANDLED BY MY DEPARTMENT WILL BE DETERMINED BY ME. But Moses refused to relent, and the Corporation Counsel realized that he could not allow park development to be stalled by a dispute over one individual. He shifted the assistant to another assignment.

If a commissioner still resisted, Moses used the public rather than the private smear. "Mr. Moses told me . . . that he was able to control the press of New York City, so as to hold me up to such obloquy that I would not be able to stand it," W. Kingsland Macy had testified a decade before. The smear technique that had been used then was used now—frequently.

In the hands of a man for whom the press acted as a gigantic sounding board, repeating and amplifying his words, the smear was a terrible weapon—particularly when those words were as caustic and cutting as Moses'. At Yale, his poetry had revealed an undeniable gift for language. During the decades since Yale, Moses had turned this gift from imagery to invective, and that invective had been honed by years of use to an edge as cruelly sharp as that of a razor with a jagged edge. And he used that razor to strike straight for the jugular: not an opponent's issues or arguments but his reputation. For most public men, prominent on the list of hurts that pierce the heart, that sear the soul, is the hurt of coming to the breakfast table one morning and seeing harsh black headlines call them fools or liars or hack bureaucrats or crooks—headlines based on charges by a man regarded as a genius who was always right and followed by an article that made the charges seem true, even if they were false.

Herbert Lehman's advisers had been able to laugh off Moses' smears because they were famous men, with established reputations, and because Moses' accusations against them had been specific—and therefore refutable by publication of the facts. But the minor officials on whom Moses now employed the smear technique were more vulnerable—particularly since Moses, having learned, perhaps, from the gubernatorial campaign, usually smeared now not with specific charges but with generalizations, with labels, such as "politician" or "bureaucrat," that conjured up vague but unpleasant connotations in readers' minds—and which, being vague, were difficult to disprove, so difficult, in fact, that his victims were effectively denied recourse even to libel suits.

Deputy Comptroller Douglas Matthewson, for example, was only doing his duty as legal adviser to the Sinking Fund Commission when he informed it in a memorandum that Moses' demand that it transfer to the Park Department a tract of land in Coney Island belonging to the Board of Education was illegal; the Charter, Matthewson pointed out, clearly provided that the commission could make permanent transfers only subject to approval of the Board of Estimate and that even the Board could act only after formally asking all other city departments if *they* needed the property so that it could be guided in assigning land by an over-all view of departmental needs. Unfortunately for Matthewson, however, while he believed that his memorandum was routine, it struck at the heart of Moses' method of operation. The Park Commissioner didn't *want* the Board of Estimate, or anyone else, taking an over-all view of departmental needs, because if they did they would realize that the Park Department was obtaining a wholly disproportionate share of city-owned land and, more important, was obtaining land for which other departments were even then planning uses—as was, in fact, the case with the tract in question: the Board of Education was planning a badly needed school on the Coney Island site. Moses wanted to work—too fast for other departments to defend against his land raids—only through the malleable Sinking Fund Commission.

When, as the result of Matthewson's memo, the commission delayed action on Moses' request, and when Matthewson's boss, Comptroller McGoldrick, refused to obey Moses' demand that he fire his subordinate, Moses called in reporters. Telling them that the only questions involved were procedural, he said: "If Matthewson's theory is to prevail, politics would come in. . . . Can you imagine when the public would have parks if they had to wait for all this red tape. . . . Are the old hacks or red-tape boys going to hold things up?" At the commission's next meeting, the transfers Moses wanted were quickly approved, with McGoldrick voting for them—and thereby against his subordinate. Matthewson sat through the meeting without a word. Shortly thereafter, the "old hack" and "red-tape boy" quietly resigned, one of a score of minor officials publicly ridiculed and humiliated by Moses—and driven out of public service—for no other reason than that they had tried to make him obey the law.

If an official refused to resign and his boss refused to fire him even after Moses' smear tactics had made him a political liability, there was still another notch on the Moses pressure gauge: the liability could be escalated.

By 1935 this was easy, for 1935 marked the height of nationwide hysteria over the "red peril." William Randolph Hearst was hoarsely alerting America to the infiltration of the White House by liberal professors who had made the New Deal "more communistic than the Communists," operatives of the demagogue publisher's *Journal-American* were posing as Columbia University students to entrap professors into radical remarks, the House Un-American Activities Committee was probing WPA theater projects ("Now this [Christopher] Marlowe," demanded the Hon. Joe Starnes of Alabama, "is he a Communist type, too?") and when Diego Rivera refused to remove from his mural in the gleaming new lobby of Rockefeller Center a likeness of Lenin glaring down on a scene of American police clubbing strikers, young Nelson Rockefeller ordered the artist down off his scaffold, handed him a check to wind up his contract and had the half-finished work covered with tar paper. And the nation's hysteria provided Moses with a new set of labels—"Commie," "Bolshie," "pinko," "left-winger"—more damning in the American public consciousness than even "hack politician" or "red-tape boy" and therefore, in the arsenal of the smear, perhaps the ultimate weapon.

Moses applied these labels generously, branding them not only onto labor leaders ("radical, left-wing") and New Deal Brain Trusters (Rexford Tugwell he assailed as a "Planning Red") and urban planners who dared to offer suggestions for the future of New York City ("regarded in Russia as our greatest builder," was how he characterized Frank Lloyd Wright; he called Lewis Mumford "an outspoken revolutionary"; Walter Gropius, he said, was seeking to change the American system by advocating "a philosophy which doesn't belong here"; planners in general, he said, are "socialists," "revolutionaries" who "do not reach the masses directly but through familiar subsurface activity. They teach the teachers. They reach people in high places, who in turn influence the press, universities, societies learned and otherwise, radio networks, the stage, the screen . . .") but onto youthful city officials who dared to stand up to him and who had, his bloodhounds discovered, once allowed enthusiasm and naïveté to lead them into membership in some organization that they later learned was a Communist front. His enthusiasm for these labels was based in part on his conservative belief in the necessity for class distinctions; to a man who had believed the trade unions of "Mr. Walling and his socialist brethren" to be blasphemy, the liberalism of the Thirties was heresy. But he also saw the effectiveness of the labels in wrecking opponents' reputations; he branded with those labels not only opponents whom he may sincerely have believed, no matter how mistakenly, to be Communists, but also opponents he was well aware were not Communists and had never been, men like gentle Stanley Isaacs, the Republican reformer who became Manhattan borough president in 1937, whom Moses had known for twenty years and whose only crime was that he once had been ill-advised enough to appoint brilliant young Simon Gerson to a minor position on his staff without bothering to investigate him and learn that he was an avowed Communist. He branded with the labels young city officials whose dossiers, compiled by his bloodhounds, clearly revealed that while they may once, years before, have belonged to Communist-front organizations, they had long since renounced their membership in those organizations —in applying the labels to them, he simply never bothered to mention the renunciation. If Robert Moses was a pioneer in the fields of parks and highways, he was also a pioneer in McCarthyism, twenty years before McCarthy. And his estimate of the effectiveness of his new weapon was not an overestimation—not even the deep affection of a strong-minded and independent mayor for a young man he seemed to regard almost as a son could stand before it.

The young man—tall, handsome and brilliant—was Paul J. Kern, La Guardia's law secretary and, of all his youthful aides, perhaps the one closest to the Mayor, his companion on his Sunday tours of the city and so frequent a guest at his apartment that he seemed almost a member of the family. Ironically, Kern admired Moses; "I was a Moses fanatic," he was to recall ruefully. But when, early in 1936, La Guardia appointed him, at the age of twenty-seven, to the Municipal Civil Service Commission, he refused—as young, brilliant Robert Moses would have refused during *his* days with the Municipal Civil Service Commission—to allow the older, changed Robert Moses to continue circumventing civil service regulations by firing Park Department employees on whim and paying favorites two salaries at once. And he insisted that employees of Moses' public authorities be brought under civil service regulations.

First, Moses destroyed the source of Kern's power, his friendship with the Mayor. He did so, Kern charges, with a tactic that would have been familiar to Ansley Wilcox and Judge Clearwater, who felt Moses had used it to discredit them with Al Smith. "He lied," Kern says. "He lied about me to La Guardia."

There was, Kern says, a "whole series" of lies that gradually "poisoned" his friendship with the Mayor; once, for example, Moses told La Guardia that Kern had disobeyed La Guardia's specific order to certify a disputed civil service list of authority employees although Kern had in fact done so, and La Guardia, without bothering to check the facts, flew into a towering rage and wrote Kern a letter that stung him deeply. Years later, Kern could recall even the salutation—"My dear Mr. Kern"; "He had never called me 'Mr. Kern' before," he would say.

Proud and angry and hurt—"It was almost like his father disowning him," said Professor Wallace Sayre, a Civil Service Commission member at the time—Kern would not attempt to explain. And, months later, just as the rift between the two men was beginning to heal, Moses widened it beyond any possibility of healing—with a public smear that made Kern a political liability that the Mayor could not afford to keep in his administration.

The commission, with Kern reinforced by the appointment of Dr. Frank A. Schaeffer, a Fordham University Latin professor he had persuaded to take a leave of absence to accept the post of commission secretary (the same post to which Dr. Robert Moses had once aspired), began in 1939 to press harder and harder for complete civil service reform (the same type of reform for which Dr. Moses had once pressed), and, to enforce it, suggested encouraging city employees to report venality and civil service violations by awarding promotion credits for verifiable tips. Terming the commission's actions "un-American," Moses suggested that Dr. Schaeffer "send this communication to the OGPU [secret police] in Russia, whose American representative you seem to be." And when Kern defended Schaeffer—"He was a good Roman Catholic and being called a Communist upset him tremendously; we doubt very much if you would recruit OGPU agents at Fordham"—Moses called *Kern* an OGPU agent.

Kern was vulnerable to such attack. Addicted to overenthusiasm in his liberalism (he wryly describes himself as a "sucker for causes"), years before, while still in his teens, he had joined a number of organizations that later turned out to be Communist fronts. And though by 1939 he had seen through them and resigned in disgust, Moses' attacks on him as a Communist were echoed by the Red- and Jew-baiting Detroit demagogue Father Coughlin, who "revealed" that Kern's insistence on reforming the Police Department's promotion system was really a plot to place over "the cops of New York . . . 90 per cent of them good Christians, *a group of Reds*, an OGPU! . . . who could not tell a night stick from a streak of salami." The Hearst papers were soon yowling for the young man's scalp and a committee of the Tammany-dominated City Council began investigating the commission.

Kern believes that Moses inspired and helped direct from behind the scenes not only the investigation, one of the viler chapters in New York political history (the committee took advantage of the association in the public mind of godless Communism with free love to drag into the hearing insinuations about Kern's love life), but also the public smear campaign against him of which the investigation was the centerpiece—and that the Park Commissioner's bloodhounds kept the investigators supplied with fresh ammunition. This belief was concurred in by Windels and at least one other key La Guardia official, who points out that new revelations about Kern's background were generally aired first by Murray Davis, the *World-Telegram*'s senior political writer, who had been used before, and would be used again, by Moses as a conduit to get before the public "facts" Moses wanted the public to know without letting it know that the facts came from him.

And if there is no evidence to document Moses' continued participation in the public smear campaign against Kern—the key investigators are all dead and Davis, who later became Moses' personal public relations man, isn't talking—there is plenty of evidence to document his continued participation in a private campaign, a campaign to make La Guardia suspect his young friend. Moses reminded the Mayor continually of Kern's "Communist" leanings; once, for example, he wrote him a personal letter that concluded, "Don't let Kern try to set up an OGPU in New York."

The tactic worked with a Mayor who was constantly terrified that his liberal administration would be tarred as "Communist," a charge he felt would alienate irreparably the city's huge block of Catholic voters (in 1941, despite his respect for Stanley Isaacs, the Mayor dumped the reformer from his ticket because of the outcry, which Moses kept alive, over Isaacs' hiring of the young Communist Gerson). By the end of the investigation, he was hardly speaking to Kern, and not long thereafter, in the midst of another dispute, he fired him.

Kern says he understood why Moses wanted him fired. "His hatred of me was not based on the fact that he thought I was a Communist—I'm sure he didn't—but that I represented interference with the way he wanted to run the Park Department," he says.

And from that standpoint, Moses' tactics were wholly successful. Until the end of his park commissionership in 1960, no civil service commissioner ever interfered with the department again.

Moses' fellow commissioners, anxious for a fairer share of WPA funds or a more equitable relationship between their departments and his, might have slowed him down. But he didn't let them.

Moses' normal technique with other commissioners was to bully them. Often this approach worked, for they were well aware that if they attempted to challenge him, he would be backed by the press—and by their mutual boss, the Mayor.

One commissioner with whom this approach did not work, of course, was Windels.

"Paul knew how to handle him, all right," says William C. Chanler, Windels' chief assistant (and, in 1938, his successor as Corporation Counsel). "We'd been in office about six weeks and Paul went up to Albany and left me in charge of the office and while he was up there, Moses called me on the phone. He said he was being held up because we were working too slow on condemnation proceedings in which he was interested. He was really yelling at me. He got ruder and ruder about our not getting his title cleared —'You didn't get this done, you didn't get that done, you haven't got the *certiorari*. What the hell's the matter with you?' I told him we had only been in office six weeks. He said, 'Goddammit, I got *my* office organized in forty-eight hours. If you fellows don't get going, I'm going to call up the press and tell them what a bunch of incompetents you are.' I called up Paul Windels in Albany and he said, 'I'll tell you what you do. There are a lot of cases in which we're being held up by something we need from the Park Department. You get a list of those cases and you have it right on your desk. When Moses calls up the next time, don't take any abuse from him. Just say exactly this—'Listen here, Moses, goddammit, what the hell's the matter with your office? We've got this and this and you're holding us up.' Well, he did call up again and he started being rude and I said even more than Windels had told me to. I said, 'And if you ever come over here I'll kick your ass out of the office!' Well, as soon as I did that, his whole tone of voice changed. He said, 'Well, perhaps'—his whole tone of voice changed—he said, 'well, perhaps you and I'd better talk this over. How about coming over for lunch?' I went over and the door was opened by the most charming, gracious, smiling man. He gave me a very sumptuous lunch—I think we had a bottle of wine, I don't remember—and he said, 'Oh, we're going to get on fine.' A short time later, he called up again on something he was mad about and started to yell again. But by this time I knew how to handle him. I yelled back and immediately it was 'Oh, all right, oh, all right,' and he calmed down."

The lesson wasn't lost on Chanler. "If you stood right up to him, he backed right down," he says. "He was just a natural bully. So whenever he tried something, I'd pretend to lose my temper. And after a while, he didn't try any more." But the other commissioners didn't know Moses as well as Windels and they didn't have the benefit of his advice—and when Moses' harsh voice rasped over the telephone into their offices threatening to take them to the press and the Mayor, they thought the only way to avoid such a fate was to do what he wanted. Many of the other commissioners despised and resented Moses. When they attempted to establish an *esprit* by meeting for weekly "commissioners' luncheons," Moses refused to attend—a gesture that they interpreted, correctly, as an attempt by Moses to show them that he considered himself above them. They considered the plant from a Park Department greenhouse that Moses sent in his place each week a gratuitous insult. But while they might despise and resent Moses, they also feared him. And they generally did what he wanted. Even the more independent among them, moreover, were outwitted by his brilliance in the bureaucratic arts. Pointing out to a recalcitrant commissioner that because of the Park Department's unprecedented activity, its demands on the commissioner's own department were undoubtedly disrupting its normal procedures, Moses would suggest that the commissioner designate one of his aides to do nothing but handle Park Department liaison, perhaps even allowing him to work in the Arsenal. Then Moses, by bullying or by charm, would take the aide into camp—making him an ally of the Park Department and thereby practically freeing himself of the necessity of winning the other department's approval of his actions. Soon Moses had his "own man" in the office of many other commissioners—men loyal to him rather than to their own commissioners and useful to Moses not only as liaison with other departments but as spies within their ranks.

The city's elected officials, motivated by a hundred political considerations, might have slowed his building. But he didn't let them.

The broad powers possessed by the Board of Estimate, the upper house of the city's bicameral legislature, would normally have made ignoring it impossible. But many of those powers rested on the power of the purse and the purse that was financing most of Moses' projects was not the Board's but the federal government's. And the power that remained to the Board he offset with the techniques—stake driving, whipsawing, wedge driving, deception—that he had learned and mastered during a decade of building public works on Long Island.

Because the Charter gave the Board authority over all street closings and Moses wanted to build Chrystie-Forsyth Park across four Lower East Side streets, he submitted his plans for the street closings to the Board for approval. Manhattan Borough President Levy noted that crosstown traffic would be crammed into the two streets Moses was willing to leave open through the park, Grand and Delancey. Although Moses said those two streets were adequate to handle the traffic, Board members said it would overcrowd them, and refused to approve the street closings without further discussion and a full-scale on-site inspection. But when they arrived at the site a few days later, they found the streets already closed—with concrete, hastily laid during those few days by Moses' workers, in which the footings of fences, benches, swings, seesaws and even handball courts were rapidly hardening into immovable reality.

When Board approval of a project was absolutely essential—because he needed city funds to acquire the site, say—he would whipsaw it by stating that the WPA had agreed to finance the project and urging them to grab the money while it was available. (At the same time he would be assuring the WPA that city approval was assured and the land was therefore available, an argument that persuaded the WPA, anxious for fast results, to give *its* approval.) If they did, he would say, the city would get the improvement—and desperately needed jobs—without any city expenditure. If the Board said it wanted time to study the project, Moses would tell them that the delay would cost the city the WPA funds—and this argument, backed by the threat (which was frequently implemented) to tell the press about the threatened loss, was one which almost invariably brought the Board to its knees.

He drove wedges, too. In his 1935 budget request, he asked the Board to allocate $3,600,000 for construction projects in Jacob Riis, Fort Tryon, Pelham Bay and the two Marine parks. The Board did, and the thin edge of the wedge was in. Year after year, thereafter, he returned to the Board for new allocations which he said were necessary to make the improvements built with the previous allocations "usable"; unless the money was given, he would say, the previous allocations would be wasted. Jacob Riis Park would be completed by 1938, after an additional city allocation of $3,500,000, but the others were not. Year after year, the Board would allocate new funds—and then would learn that still more were needed. Marine Park in Brooklyn could be completed for $6,000,000, he assured the Board. When $6,000,000 had been spent on the park, Moses informed the Board that an additional $6,000,000 would be necessary. And when that was spent, the park would still be far from completed.

He deceived the Board constantly. To obtain permission to construct a stadium on Randall's Island, he had assured the Board that the "PWA" project would cost the city "not a penny." Then, with permission obtained and work under way, he announced that he would need $250,000 additional for materials the PWA would not buy, but assured the Board that this was the only contribution the city would have to make for the "whole Triborough Bridge project," in return for which the federal government was making a contribution of $46,200,000. The Board allocated the money. Within a month, he was back again, asking for a special bond issue of $8,000,000 to pay for the right-of-way for the bridge approaches. He blandly told the Board that when he had spoken of the "whole Triborough Bridge project," he naturally hadn't meant the land for the project. He hardly bothered to conceal the technique—one of his press releases on the Central Park Zoo contained two different estimates of the cost—but because the Board had left itself open to political blackmail by approving earlier fund requests without adequately checking them, it was helpless to deny him later requests and thereby allow him to charge that it had wasted the public's money by building only part of a project. Moreover, since the Board's membership was continually changing, just as one borough president or Comptroller learned never to trust Moses' figures, he would lose an election and the man who took over his seat would have to begin the learning process anew. And, most important, while the Board may have distrusted Moses' figures, its lack of adequate engineering assistance prevented it from coming up with any of its own.

Those on the Board who tried to bring him to heel soon wished they hadn't. When they dueled with him, they did so from the dignity of their seats behind the massive raised mahogany horseshoe in the Board chamber, backed by fluted Corinthian columns and wine-red draperies. But their setting couldn't save them from his tongue.

"He would enter the chamber hearty, very hearty, with this broad grin," recalls McGoldrick, who, as Comptroller, sat in one of the seats on the horseshoe. "He was very impressive, tall, handsome, and he'd always come in with a team of his aides behind him—a different team for each project. And he knew his stuff inside and out. He wasn't like [some of] the other commissioners, who had aides with them and every time you asked them a question, they had to turn to them and whisper to get the answer. And this was very impressive. His men didn't seem to have any purpose there, except that one or two always stood behind him to hand him papers when he needed them. When the matter in which he was interested was called he would walk to the railing at which officials stood to address the Board—there was no public-address system or microphone then—with the same grin. He was very breezy and self-confident. I remember his coming up very genially, with his head thrown back and a grin on his face."

But let one of the Board members venture to criticize—or even to question—one of his projects, and the grin could fade in an instant. "[He was] very intolerant of any criticism of anything he wanted to do," McGoldrick recalls. "He wanted to do it. He was going to do it. And withering with his adjectives anyone who opposed him." Says one observer: "When someone else was speaking, he'd begin to pace up and down. He'd turn his back—total boredom. Off to one side a little. Then he'd suddenly whip around without asking permission, walk up and make some sharp remark . . . often out of the side of his mouth, you know, throwing his shoulders around. There was no indication of respect—he seemed to emanate an air of arrogance, of contempt, for the men sitting up there." If he felt called upon to make extended reply, he would do so while rocking slightly on his heels, his large head thrown back and to one side, and the words that rasped out of the handsome, sensual mouth were devastating. "Time and again," said one magazine writer, "he transfixes his opponent with graceful malice."

As for the Board of Aldermen and its successor under the new Charter, the City Council—he treated those worthies, many of whom he told Lazarus he could buy "with a couple of jobs," like men who could be bought with a couple of jobs. Or he simply ignored them. In 1939, he urged the Park Department's 3,000 employees to vote against councilmen who had slashed the Department's budget requests, and when the Council, after hearing a committee report calling Moses' action "one of the most brazen attempts at political intimidation in the history of the city," ordered him to appear before it to explain the action, he simply didn't bother to show up, sending a letter saying he hadn't received "adequate notice."

The complexities of life in a city might have slowed him down. But he didn't let them.

There was a difference between building parks and parkways in the country—on sparsely populated Long Island, where most of Moses' previous projects had been concentrated, or in rural upstate counties—and building them in a city, and the difference was people. When you built a park on a deserted sand bar such as Jones Beach, you didn't have to worry about removing people from the site and relocating them somewhere else because there *weren't* any people. You were building parks and parkways *for* people, of course, and therefore you had to take people's needs into consideration in planning them, but only in a broad, impersonal sense, for you were planning for people in the tens of thousands, humanity in the mass, and the needs of humanity in the mass could be deduced as well from a general knowledge of people as from a specific knowledge of the human beings who made up the mass. When you built public works in a countryside you were painting on a clean and empty canvas—and you could use brush strokes as broad as you chose. If there was a formula for building public works, for Getting Things Done, on Long Island, it was not a simple one—no formula that had to include cooperation with as powerful an oligarchy as the North Shore Robber Barons, as greedy a political machine as the Nassau County GOP and as shortsighted a collection of public officials as the New York State Legislature could be simple—but many factors that would have made the formula vastly more complicated did not have to be included in it. Moses could determine by himself—by his own unaided foresight and insight, his strictly private conception of the public need—what types of projects were needed, where they should be located and how they should be designed.

Things were different in the city. The crucial factor in the building of public works on Long Island was space, vast, endless tracts of uncluttered openness; in the city the crucial factor was lack of space and the fact that space was not merely filled but filled with people, people with their endlessly intertwined, hopelessly snarled tangles of aspirations and antagonisms, hopes and fears, dreams and dreads. People on the site would have to be removed—evicted, dispossessed, thrown out, relocated—and removal would rend the fabric of their lives. The lives of those near the site might not be rent but they would certainly be altered, for the physical environment which did so much to shape their daily existence would be altered, not only in dramatic ways such as the razing of a block of tenements for a bridge anchorage, but in ways subtle and endlessly various: the construction of almost any public work inevitably added to or subtracted from that delicate balance of humanity that was a city neighborhood ingredients that would change that balance forever, change the neighborhood's economic or ethnic composition, make it quieter or noisier, cleaner or dirtier, cut one part of it off from the rest, fill it with new life or drain it of its vitality, turn it into something different—possibly better but also possibly worse—than it was before.

Therefore, unlike a public work on Long Island, a public work in the city had to be planned not only in terms of itself but in terms of its environment, the neighborhood in which it was located. It had to be judged not only in physical terms—highway as highway, park as park—but also in social terms: in terms of its effect on the human beings who had to live around it. If in creating public works on Long Island, one could paint on a clean and empty canvas, in creating public works in New York City one had to paint over an already existing mural, a mural whose brush strokes were tiny and intricate and often, when one looked closely, quite wonderful, lending to the vast urban panorama subtle shadings and delicate tints and an endless variety, so that if it was crowded and confused and ugly it was also full of life and very human, so much so, in fact, that while the painting as a whole might lack beauty, order, balance, perspective, a unifying principle and an over-all effect commensurate with its size, it nonetheless possessed many charming little touches and an over-all vitality, a *brio,* that made it unique and should not be lost. If Moses attempted to employ on the canvas of New York City the same broad brush strokes that he had used on the canvas of Long Island, he would be obliterating the city's intricacies indiscriminately instead of working around those that were worth keeping and preserving them—and while this method might result in the creation of something beautiful and good, adding to the mural new values, it would also almost certainly destroy many existing values. A public work in the city might in terms of itself—Moses' terms—be an excellent public work while in broader terms being a poor public work: a highway, for example, that, however magnificently designed, was damaging either to the adjacent neighborhood—shattering its essential unity, cutting its homes off from its playground or from its churches and shopping areas, filling its quiet residential areas with noise and gasoline fumes that made them no longer nice places to live and to bring up children—or to the city as a whole: a highway, for example, through a hitherto sparsely inhabited area that initiated a sudden influx of subdivisions and apartment houses, loading it with people, before the city had provided the sewers and subways and schools those people needed, and that by boosting land costs made it immensely difficult for a financially hard-pressed city to provide such services—services which could, if installed before the highway was built, have been installed at a price within the city's means.

If one tried to plan public works in New York City by the same simplistic formula by which the public works of Long Island had been planned, the public works thus created might well destroy what was good in New York even while it was supposed to be improving the city.

Part of Moses' Long Island formula—the vision and the viciousness, the imagination and the ruthlessness, the drive, the urgent, savage thrust, the instinct for the magnificent and the jugular that overrode purely selfish opposition, shortsightedness and red tape to turn vision into reality—was needed in the city, needed desperately, for without it the city would never be able to build parks and roads and bridges—or, for that matter, housing or hospitals, sewers or schools—on the scale its citizens needed. But Moses' formula could be successful in the city only as the basis of a new, vastly more complicated and subtle and sophisticated formula, one that would turn public works into a far truer reflection of the subtle and complicated human needs they had to serve in the city. A whole new input—a factor of humanity—would have to be added.

And Moses would not allow it to be added.

Moses had a genius for grasping the needs of people in the mass, of people in the tens and hundreds of thousands, of a city and a state as a whole, and for devising ways to meet those needs. But that genius could not help him grasp the needs of a specific city neighborhood in which he was building a small park or playground, for those needs might be shared by no other neighborhood in the world.

In the first place, the people in the mass that he understood were people of a particular social strata that his own background enabled him to understand: the classes he called "upper" and "comfortable middle." He had never had any interest in—and therefore had little understanding of—classes he considered beneath his own, the classes who made up so many of New York City's neighborhoods. Moreover, even a genius couldn't deduce the needs of a neighborhood—any neighborhood—until he knew and understood it. And the only way of knowing and understanding it was to study and learn about it, to find out how many children lived in it and how old they were, what games they liked to play, what games their parents liked to play with them on weekends, what games their parents liked to play among themselves, to find out whether the parents liked to play games at all or simply to sit quietly and talk, whether the neighborhood's teen-age boys wanted a place to walk after dinner and watch the neighborhood's teen-age girls walk or whether they wanted to spend their time after dinner playing basketball, to find out which streets the neighborhood's mothers considered safe enough so that their children could cross them alone and thus use a playground on the far side whenever they wanted and which streets the mothers considered too dangerous, to find out exactly how far the children were willing to walk to get to a playground in the first place. And there was only one way to learn about a neighborhood: listen to its people, discuss their problems with them. Unless Moses did that—not Moses himself necessarily; his lieutenants or the architect designing the specific playground in question—he simply wouldn't, *couldn't,* know enough about the neighborhood to satisfy its needs.

On a broader scale, that was also the only way to study and learn how to plan larger public works for New York City. It was the only way to plan even those large parks—Central, Prospect, Van Cortlandt, Kissena, Alley Pond—that contained plenty of space in which there lived no people at all. Even these parks could not be developed successfully by a formula as simplistic as that on which the Long Island parks had been developed. For these parks were not just open space but open space within a city—within a city in which open space was becoming terribly scarce—and the space within them was therefore precious and must be utilized not just to advantage but to fullest advantage. And what was that advantage? What was it most important for those big parks to give the city? The city's facilities for active recreation were laughably inadequate. Therefore the park must provide them. They must be filled with baseball diamonds and football fields, tennis and handball and basketball courts, skating rinks and swimming pools. But the city was also growing—growing and spreading; in 1934, most of Staten Island, the entire central portion of Queens and much of southern Brooklyn were still free of intensive development, but real estate developers were already eyeing those areas too. Open space—quiet open space, natural settings in which city dwellers could find relief from gray concrete and congestion and noise—was precious in New York now. Parks must provide that, too. If they did not, there would soon be no place within the great city in which these values could be found. It was particularly vital that these values be preserved within the city because Moses' restrictive policies had made it difficult for the city's poor, who did not have access to private automobiles, to reach his Long Island parks; if these values were not preserved in the city's own parks there would soon be no place at all in which a poor family could find them. The city's parks had to serve both recreational and conservational functions, but designing the parks so that they could provide both functions would be immensely difficult. For the two functions were not compatible. Peace and quiet and solitude were in general obtainable only at a far remove from the shouts and frantic activity of the playing field. And while parks like Kissena in Queens were considered large, Kissena contained exactly 219 acres; 219 acres sounded big, but it sounded a lot smaller when one realized that a single baseball diamond took up two and a half acres and even a small parking field twenty-five. There was room in parks like Kissena either for peace or for parking fields—but not for both. With the exception of the two Marine Parks, which were not really parks at all but only undeveloped marshland, the only park of a thousand acres in the whole city was Van Cortlandt, and even in Van Cortlandt, you could have both active play facilities and natural, peaceful areas only if you exercised the greatest ingenuity and delicacy in laying them out.

Therefore, choices had to be made—hard choices. And they could not be made intelligently without determining, in the case of each park, whether it was going to serve the neighborhood around it or the city as a whole, and which functions were most needed in that park by the people it was going to serve.

There had been so much space on the Island that there had been no need to ask such questions in planning parks. Even after Moses had built all the baseball diamonds and tennis courts and bathhouses and parking fields that he wanted in Heckscher State Park, for example, more than 1,200 of the park's 1,657 acres remained in their natural wooded state, enough for green, quiet woods away from crowds. Moses himself had been uninterested in a park's "natural" functions. His mind saw people in the mass, running, jumping, swinging tennis rackets or baseball bats; one reason he wanted Triborough Stadium so big was that he wanted it large enough for mass calisthenics on the Third Reich scale. His vision never focused on the individual wandering alone through a forest or on the family sprawling in solitude in a meadow; in thinking of parks he did not, except incidentally, think of them as places of forests or meadows or solitude. And if the very breadth of his vision thus made it hard for him to think of parks as untouched nature, so did the very force of his creativity; he was a builder, a molder, a man who yearns to put his hand to and reshape—"improve"—whatever he sees. Therefore to him a park was not open space. The open space was already there. The "park" was that portion of the open space that he had filled with his own creations. (He referred to the portions of the Long Island parks without active play facilities as "undeveloped for park use.") His lack of interest in untouched nature had not mattered on Long Island. But it was to matter greatly in New York.

And how small could a park be? What was the smallest number of square feet it was feasible to supervise and maintain as a public place of recreation? Five acres, the area of a standard city block? Three acres? Two? One? The 100 by 20 feet that was the size of the standard building lot in tenement sections—and that was often the only piece of vacant land anywhere around?

This was a question of desperate importance. The recreational needs of city families that couldn't afford to own a car—and those families comprised a full two-thirds of the city's population—had to be satisfied within their immediate neighborhoods, and because it was too expensive to condemn buildings in these neighborhoods and the only land still vacant was small plots, the only parks that could be built in these neighborhoods were small parks. But even small plots were enormously expensive to maintain and supervise, far more expensive per square foot than large parks. Given the hard fact that the city would never be able to create nearly enough parks for its people, was there any sense in developing a large number of small parks? Where did you sink those resources that were available—into large parks that could be developed relatively economically or into small parks that alone could provide recreation for that portion of the city's people that most needed recreation? The needs of providing recreation for the city's poor must be weighed against the cost of that provision. What a later generation would come to call "priorities" must be established, and it would not be easy to establish them. The hard choices would have to be made. Only by the most intense analysis and discussion—discussion with the people most directly involved, the city's poor—could these choices be made intelligently. And, again, because the success of a neighborhood park depended so largely on intimate knowledge of that neighborhood, once the decision to establish a park in a neighborhood was taken, even more intense discussion with the residents of that neighborhood would be necessary.

Then there was the question of roads in parks. Should there even *be* roads in parks and, if so, where within the parks should they be located?

Once, in the days—a decade or even two decades before—in which the young Robert Moses had been planning parks and roads, the answer to that question had been quite clear. Driving in automobiles had then still been thought of primarily as pleasure, a pursuit for comfortable middle-class or wealthy fathers (the only fathers who could afford automobiles) taking their families for an outing, just as driving horse-drawn carriages had been a pursuit for pleasure. And it had therefore been important to insure that these families had the most pleasant surroundings possible to drive through, and within the city's limits the most pleasant surroundings were those provided by parks. The provision of pleasant scenery for drivers to enjoy was, in fact, a primary function of parks; that was why every great city in Europe had its great driving park, Paris its Bois de Boulogne, Rome its Pincian Hill, Florence its Cascine and London its Hyde Park. Roads had belonged in parks in the nineteenth century—so much so that, if necessary, other values of a park had to be sacrificed to provide the roads with the best of the park's scenery.

But this was the twentieth century now. And the answer to the question —do roads belong in parks?—was no longer clear. For the nature of driving had largely changed. The automobile age, still in its infancy when Robert Moses had stood on Riverside Drive and planned his "great highway going uptown along the water" in 1914, still only in its adolescence when Moses had been planning his Long Island parkways in 1924, had come to full maturity by the time he came to power in New York City in 1934. There had been 273,435 motor vehicles in New York City in 1924; there were 804,620 now. And people no longer used their cars primarily for weekend pleasure trips but, increasingly, to get to and from work and to shop. Cars were part of people's daily lives. And they drove faster now; they had less time for scenery. What implications did these facts have for parkways?

What was a parkway anyway?

Was it still mainly a source of beauty and pleasure, or had it changed into a source of convenience—or at least intended convenience? Were people still interested in parkways primarily because of the scenery they could see along them or were they interested in them primarily as a means of getting from one place to another? And if the latter, what was the significance of that fact? Should the best of scenery still be reserved for the driver?

But Robert Moses wouldn't allow any discussion.

He wouldn't allow discussion because discussion would have slowed down his building programs, and he felt that he couldn't allow them to be slowed down. And he wouldn't allow discussion because he had no respect for the opinions of the public that he would have had to admit to the discussions. And even if he limited discussion to the experts who were interested in the various fields, he had no respect for their opinions, either. Robert Moses had no respect for anyone's opinion but his own.

Once Moses had at least listened to his own aides, allowed them to argue with him, tested his opinions against theirs. But now that had changed, too. In the first days of his power, he had hired aides whose opinions were worth listening to. He had selected men for ability, engineering ability, legal ability. The aides he was hiring now had also to possess an additional ability: the ability to say, "Yes, sir."

"Lunches at Moses' office were really starting to get pretty sickening," recalls one top La Guardia official. "Even if he only had one guest, he would always have six or eight of his 'Moses Men'—'my muchachos,' he used to call them—at the table and it was all 'Yes, sir, RM,' 'No, sir, RM,' 'Right as usual, RM!' When he laughed, they laughed, only louder—you know what I mean. Christ, when he made a statement, you could look around the table and see eight heads nodding practically in unison. It was like a goddamned Greek chorus."

Reuben Lazarus, invited by Moses to become chief counsel for the Triborough Bridge Authority, refused—"I didn't want to be a doormat for any man"—and when Moses asked him to recommend one of his assistants, Lazarus selected the one who, he had noticed, "doesn't answer back," and in the taxi taking William Lebwohl to lunch with Moses, told him what was going to be expected of him: "You're going to have to be able to bend over and take a kick in the ass and say 'Thank you, sir,' with a smile." At the luncheon, Lazarus recalls, "Lebwohl did not answer back." Moses hired him—and kept him on as Triborough counsel for more than thirty years.

The effect of such a hiring policy was predictable. The aides he had hired in the 1920's, the Art Howlands, Sid Shapiros, Bill Lathams, Bill Chapins and George Spargos, became legendary throughout state and city government for their ability, drive and indefatigability. The aides he hired in the 1930's were quite another story. "The older guys—tops!" says William Zeckendorf, who had a keen eye for men himself. "But some of the others he had working for him—I wouldn't have hired them to sweep my lobbies!"

Moses' sensitivity to criticism had impressed itself on such men. They didn't criticize anything he said. They saw he was less than receptive to suggestions—and they didn't make suggestions.

If Moses refused to accept ideas from public, experts or aides—from, in general, anyone at all—the source of his ideas, his concept of public works for New York City, could be only his own mind. The mind was brilliant, but even a brilliant mind is only as good as the material—the input—fed into it. It was at about this time that Lazarus, planning to write a book about government and public figures and keeping a card file of impressions, wrote on a card he filed under the name "Robert Moses":

> Bob Moses has climbed so high on his own ego, has become so hidebound in his own arbitrariness, that he has removed himself almost entirely from reality and has insulated himself within his own individuality.

This difficulty could to some degree have been overcome by sheer mental ability. Robert Moses' mind was supple, resourceful. Even without input of social and human considerations, it could have deduced some of these considerations simply by thinking about the problems involved.

But Robert Moses no longer had much time to think.

Building a state park system had been an immense job, but he had brought to it not only immense energy but immense ability to discipline that energy. He had found time—*made* time, to be more precise, made it by devoting to his work the hours when other men play or relax or sleep, or lunch, made it by working fourteen, sixteen, eighteen, twenty hours a day, seven days a week, fifty-two weeks a year—he had found time to oversee every detail of design, to present his architects and engineers with the basic concepts he wanted followed, to insist during the fleshing out of those concepts on a standard of excellence, of boldness and daring far above that common for public works and to inspire the architects and engineers ("I know you can do drawbridges. Can you do beautiful drawbridges?") to raise their work to that standard. And besides furnishing inspiration, he furnished ideas; many of the most brilliant touches at Jones Beach had been *his* ideas. He had found time—*made* time—to infuse the brick and concrete and sandstone of that park, and of other Long Island parks from Valley Stream to Montauk—and of other state parks from Palisades to Niagara—with his personal genius.

But when Moses expanded his sphere of activity into New York City he did not stop his work on Long Island or in the rest of the state—in 1934, on Long Island alone, he built Bethpage State Park and Bethpage State Parkway; in 1935, he built the Meadowbrook Causeway; in 1936, he built great new bathhouses at Sunken Meadow and Heckscher state parks as well as the Heckscher State Parkway Spur, and during all these years he was extending the Northern and Southern state parkways and building literally scores of smaller park structures. Instead he simply added to his state park work, itself enough to tax the strength of even the strongest of men, work in the city that was not limited to the direction of 80,000 men in the rebuilding of a huge park system but that also included the building of four parkways and three bridges, with each of the bridge-building jobs in itself a job that would have been considered a full-time job for any other man. It was not possible for him to make for himself any more time than he had already made. There were no more days in a week than seven or weeks in a year than fifty-two, and he was working all those days and weeks already. He had already sloughed off all social life and most family life; there was nothing more in his life that could be sloughed off. He was already, with his use of his limousine as an office and conference room, making use of every available minute; there were no more minutes to be found unless he drove himself beyond the limit of his physical and mental and emotional strength—and the "almost nervous breakdown" of December 1934 had shown how close he was crowding that limit.

It was lack of time more than any other single reason that accounted for an astonishing fact about many New York City park projects: they were banal.

Richard Spencer Childs recalls visiting Moses at his office one day and having their conversation interrupted by the arrival of Aymar Embury. "Embury had a bunch of drawings of some buildings for the parks," Childs recalls. "He had brought them to show Moses. Moses went right through them—'Nope.' 'Okay.' 'Nope.' Throwing them to one side or the other if he approved them or not. . . . There were no hard feelings. Moses and Embury were good friends. There was lots of respect between them. But here perhaps $100,000 worth of public business was settled on Moses' offhand taste." And, recalls Childs, when Moses finished with the drawings, Embury pointed to one he had rejected and said, "That one you threw away was the best of the lot."

Embury may well have been correct: the offhand taste even of a genius is offhand taste. Working incredibly fast, Moses had managed to make the Long Island projects public works of genius. Now he was trying to work even faster—and he was working too fast to do even a good job.

When there is no time for the thinking required for original creation, the tendency is to repeat what has proven successful in the past. Many of Moses' New York projects (not all; those in which he was particularly interested—and on which he spent substantial time—would be magnificent additions to the civic estate) began to reveal a conscious effort to duplicate aspects of his acclaimed Long Island parks. In this tendency lies the explanation for the otherwise inexplicable failure to make provision for baby carriages at so many New York parks: no provision for baby carriages had been necessary at the entrances to the Long Island parks because people got to them by automobiles. If there was a difference that should have been obvious to Moses—that the parks he was building now would be used by mothers who walked to them instead of drove—Moses was simply too busy to see it.

At Embury's drawings, Moses at least had time to glance. For more and more small park projects, even a glance could not be spared. Moses found himself forced to delegate all authority for them to subordinates. Authority is delegatable; genius is not. Some of the men to whom the work was delegated were first-rank architects or engineers—many of them, in fact, for the Depression had driven into the Arsenal many brilliant young professionals who in ordinary times would have been making names for themselves in private commissions. But they were not Robert Moses. The further Moses' presence receded from individual small park projects, the less distinguished these projects emerged. In designing the Central Park Zoo, the Seventy-ninth Street boat basin, Jacob Riis Park, Orchard Beach, the ten big neighborhood swimming pools, problems were solved with ingenuity and thoughtfulness. Perhaps if he had been able to take the same interest in all park problems—the problems involved, say, in the location and design of a neighborhood playground—*all* park problems would have been solved with ingenuity and thoughtfulness. But Moses was not taking the same interest in all park problems—and, in fact, as the number of park projects multiplied, spread by the hundreds across the face of the great city, he was able to take a substantial interest in only a very small percentage of them—in, for example, only a handful of the hundreds of neighborhood playgrounds. The inevitable result was made more striking by the need for haste—building hundreds of playgrounds as fast as possible is easier if a single basic design is used—and by the need for design approval by the WPA, an Army-engineer-staffed agency in which simple designs and cheap materials, rather than architectural excellence, were the order of the day. (Moses had to fight for every amenity, no matter how small; every improvement on the basic blocky comfort station design represented a victory, hard-won; because two-story structures required more expensive structural steel than one-story, Moses had to plead with the WPA for weeks for approval of Aymar Embury's masterful classic, colonnaded interpretation of his insistence that the Orchard Beach bathhouse blend in with the hilly, wooded landscape behind it. And when the structure was almost finished, at a cost of a million dollars, the WPA flatly refused to spend $2,500 more for two clocks that Embury had envisioned as grace notes on its towers; Moses obtained that money only by begging La Guardia for it. There was to be no Barbizon brick and Ohio sandstone in New York City parks; concrete—plain, unadorned concrete—and brick—plain, red brick, the cheapest made—were what the WPA had in mind; Moses was able to relieve the blankness of the concrete Orchard Beach bathhouse only by finding a mysterious source of terra cotta tiles, which, while cheap, at least added some necessary color, a chaste blue, to the unrelieved grayness. While Moses was willing to fight—endlessly and ingeniously—to make his big projects as perfect as possible, it was obviously unfeasible to battle over the details of every playground when one was building hundreds, especially since arguing about every design would have cost him his great advantage over other city departments with the WPA: the fact that when new funds became available, his plans were "ready to go.")

A standard Park Department playground design was evolved and architects were given little leeway to deviate from it. If there was to be an indoor playhouse in the playground, there was a standard design for that, too, and if the architect wanted to make variations in it they had better be small ones.

These designs were banal, containing for the most part nothing but benches for mothers and standard "active play" equipment—swings, seesaws, jungle gyms, wading pools, slides—for children. The equipment was surrounded by fences that only a mother could love: either dreary chain-link or high, black bars that made the playgrounds look like animal cages. And they were set in a surface that even a mother had to hate—a surface cheap to lay down and easy to maintain (that was why Moses' engineers had selected it) but hard on the knees and elbows of little boys and girls who fell on it. Comfort stations, squat and unadorned, looked like nothing so much as concrete or brick pillboxes. A neighborhood committee might request some particularly desired facility—a bocci court, for example, for an Italian neighborhood—but few substitutions were permitted.

Then there was the difference in usage accorded parks in the city, a difference complicated by vandalism. Designing for hard usage was not always compatible with designing for beauty—as was demonstrated by the evolution of the marginal playgrounds in Central Park. At first, the playgrounds were equipped, in addition to the swings, slides and jungle gyms, with sandboxes, tunnel segments that children loved to crawl through, and with striped, turreted little toy guardhouses that served as "play booths"—and their peripheries were only a ring of benches backed by trees and shrubs that provided shade for mothers and that screened the noise of playing children from the apartment houses across the street. Dogs wandered into the playgrounds and urinated and defecated in the sandboxes and the sandboxes had to be removed. Drunks crept into the tunnel segments at night and fell asleep, to be discovered by children the next morning sleeping in their own vomit. The tunnel segments had to be removed. Drunks wandered into the striped guardhouse "play booths" during the day and urinated in them. Perverts used them as hiding places from which they could watch the playing little girls and boys at close range and masturbate. Vandals pried loose the light lumber out of which the play booths were constructed. The play booths had to be removed. Then the drunks slept and the perverts hid in the trees and shrubbery behind the benches, so this landscaping had to be removed. Still drunks kept wandering into the playgrounds at night; Moses tried to keep them out first by putting up bars between the bench groupings, and little gates at the playground entrance as a warning to stay out, but the drunks ignored the warning—and finally Moses felt he had no choice but to surround the playgrounds, now reduced to amenity-bare patches of asphalt, with high fences whose high gates could be locked at night; critics might rage that the playgrounds now resembled animal cages; Moses saw that resemblance himself; he just felt that there was nothing he could do about it.

Young architects like Robert Weinberg argued among themselves—their Park Department superiors wouldn't listen to them—that solutions to the difficulties inherent in intensive usage could be compatible with good design. All that was needed, they felt, was imagination, and an understanding of the basic needs of the neighborhoods in which the playgrounds were located. Including a bocci court in a playground instead of a row of swings was not, after all, a task requiring immense creativity. Weinberg was particularly incensed at one design defect that reduced the usefulness of many playgrounds and that could have been cured very easily indeed. Some playgrounds were situated atop hills and their entrances were set with flights of steps despite the fact that the most frequent users of these parks were mothers with baby carriages, which were difficult to maneuver up steps, and entrance to these playgrounds could have been made easier for them by simply making the entrances ramps instead of steps.

But Moses no longer had much time for detail.

His imagination was as vigorous as ever; the big projects in which he took a personal interest were innovative, ingenious, daring and bold, to a considerable extent as carefully thought out in both over-all conception and minute details as his Long Island parks; smaller projects which happened to fall under his gaze, Carl Schurz Park on the East River at Eighty-sixth Street, which he passed on his evening walks from his Gracie Terrace apartment, were just as carefully thought out; there are throughout the New York City park system small touches of beauty—comfort stations, for example, that are proof that even a bathroom can bring beauty to a cityscape—but inquiry reveals that most of these structures are the rare ones in which, for one reason or another, Moses took a personal interest.

In building his state parks, Moses had been uninterested in building for the "lower classes." He was still uninterested—although now he was building parks in the city, where those classes lived.

Moses had begun his park commissionership by enthusiastically gobbling up vacant city-owned lots in the slums with the intention of turning them into tiny parks. But this enthusiasm soon waned.

The effort involved in creating such "vest-pocket" parks was immense. The land acquisition alone involved the approval of countless agencies and officials and, therefore, endless red tape. Designing something that would make a tiny lot attractive or useful was difficult. Because you couldn't afford to keep a full-time supervisor on duty in every vest-pocket park, those small parks located in slums quickly became filled with rubbish and winos.

The rewards involved in creating vest-pocket parks were, moreover, not at all commensurate with the effort required. If the reward was a sense of achievement, what—to the creator of Jones Beach—was the achievement in creating a tiny bit of green space or a few benches or a seesaw or two? Moses had always thought on the grand scale—that was his genius: the ability to grasp the needs of a whole city or state and devise a means of satisfying them—and this quality of mind made it difficult for him to take much interest in something small. There was something inherently good in size itself, he seemed to feel. If the reward was public applause, the size of the reward for building a vest-pocket park was small indeed; editorial writers didn't get nearly as excited about a tiny park as they did about a Randall's Island or Orchard Beach; it was the great projects that awed them: size seemed to signify significance to them, too. Whatever the reasons, "RM," an aide would say, "just wasn't interested in anything small. He used to say, 'That's a little job. Give it to so-and-so.' And that attitude filtered down, so that the fellows weren't interested in small things either." Coupled with his feelings about the people for whom the effort would have to be made—the lower classes who didn't "respect" or "appreciate" what was done for them, in particular the Negroes who were "dirty" and wouldn't keep his beautiful creations clean—his lack of interest in "anything small" made him uninterested in small parks in slums.

Within a year, the vest-pocket park program was all but dead and he was determined that it wouldn't be revived; he flatly refused a 1936 offer of small, abandoned Transportation Board plots, calling them "of no use to this Department . . . because they are all too small." The program never really got off the ground except in two areas—the Irish-Catholic slums of the Lower East Side in which Al Smith, and hence Moses, still took an interest, and La Guardia's old "Little League of Nations" East Harlem congressional district. In other slum areas there was almost no park development at all after 1935, and the lack was particularly marked in Negro Harlem and in the South Jamaica and Stuyvesant Heights tenement districts in Queens and Brooklyn into which a steadily mounting overflow from Harlem had begun to creep.

The protests about this policy from the slums themselves were faint and few: slum dwellers—particularly slum dwellers with black skins—weren't making many protests in the 1930's. But some reformers raised their voices on their behalf.

These reformers were in the main those associated with settlement houses; Stanley Isaacs, president of United Neighborhood Houses, was notable among them. Working in the slums, they knew the needs of their people, and, knowing, they knew that those people, forced to depend for beauty and recreation on what they could find in their neighborhoods, were particularly desperate for precisely those things that parks provided. Trees, a small plot of grass, a few flowers, anything that would provide a contrast to the concrete and red brick that surrounded the slums' people with bleakness, that trapped them in stone—these people hungered for them; one had to do no more than walk along a block of tenements and look up and suddenly notice that fire escapes and window sills were sprouting rusty cans filled with vines and flowers to realize that, as one observer was to put it, "The poor have every bit as much interest in green growing things as the well-to-do, . . . [in] open space or natural beauty." Mothers and fathers in the slums hungered for play space for their children. They couldn't afford to send the children to summer camps; they couldn't afford to take them on weekend or vacation trips: because they didn't have cars, they couldn't take them to the parks Robert Moses had built on Long Island; because they seldom left the slums, they were only vaguely aware that there were large parks in other sections of the city which the children could reach by subway; children who went to these parks often returned to say that the white people there had made them feel unwelcome or that gangs of white teen-agers had chased them away—and they did not go again. Any playing that the children of the slums did would have to be done in the slums; kids have to play: that is what being a kid is—and if there were no parks in the slums for them to play in, they would have to play in the streets; if there were no jungle gyms, they would have to swing on rusty fire escapes; if there were no indoor playhouses in which they could play on rainy days, they would have to find shelter somewhere else, and that meant deserted or burnt-out tenements, the lair of the winos and the junkies and the perverts.

And parks meant more in the slums than even beauty or play space; they had other values more intangible but also more important.

They were a sign to the urban poor, the reformers said, that society cared for them, that the city in which they had been trampled so brutally low was holding out a hand to help them to their feet. In a way they were a symbol of what Alfred E. Smith, who had understood the urban poor because he was one of them, had been talking about when, fighting for widows' pensions, he had stood in the well of the Assembly Chamber, a trumpet in his voice, and asked the legislators to consider the penniless widow whose children were taken away from her—"What must be her feelings? What must be her idea of the State's policy? . . . What can be the feelings in the hearts of the children themselves . . . when they must in after years learn to know what the State's policy was with respect to their unfortunate condition? . . . What new policy does this bill inaugurate? The State of New York reaches out to them, 'We recognize in you a resource of the State and we propose to take care of you, not as a matter of charity, but as a government and public duty.' " If the city didn't provide parks, the reformers understood, that was a sign that society didn't care; the people who lived in the slums might not verbalize that concept, but they would feel it even if they didn't put it into words; and therefore the lack of parks could only increase their bitterness toward society.

This last intangible was even more important in terms of the Negroes, whose influx into New York was beginning to assume the proportions of the previous Jewish, Irish and Italian waves of immigration. (There had been only 60,000 Negroes in the city in 1900, but there were 327,706 in 1930—and by 1940 there would be 458,000.) The society from which the Negro was alienated was the one that kept the black man confined so low on the economic ladder that in 1939 half of all Negro wage earners in New York were receiving less than $850 per year. It was the society that forced black women to line up every morning in the "slave market" in the East 160's in the Bronx so that white housewives could bid for their services (the pay was between ten and fifteen cents an hour, with the cost of lunch deducted). It was the society that made sure that Negroes would have to work for such slave wages by closing to them its trade unions, thus adding to their handicap in competing with white men for better jobs, and by denying them the capital necessary to go into business for themselves (there was not a single bank in Harlem north of 125th Street). And as for that embodiment of society that was government, the city government that was supposed to represent them as well as the white man, the attitude of that government was symbolized by public works. When La Guardia came to office in 1934, there hadn't been a new school built in Harlem in twenty-five years (La Guardia's administration didn't get around to building one for four more years), and in all Harlem the city provided, to serve 300,000 people, exactly one clinic, built—with WPA funds—in 1937, equipped with substantial facilities for child care, and exactly one hospital (on whose executive staff there was exactly one Negro). Mothers and their babies died in Harlem at a rate more than double that in the city as a whole; more than one out of every ten babies born in Harlem died at birth.

Isaacs and other reformers saw that the swelling Negro population was not being assimilated into the city. Such assimilation was necessary, they said; if the influx continued and there was no base—no solid community that was part of the larger society around it—on which it could build, what would happen? "The question of what will happen to the Negro in New York . . . is overlaid with shadows of tragic premonition," one wrote. Isaacs and others begged the city to make an intensified effort to meet the needs of these new immigrants. These people needed help, they said, and the city must give it to them. It was a civic duty to do so, they said. It was a matter of conscience. And if you weren't interested in duty or conscience, well, it was a matter of expediency, too. For neglecting Harlem's needs in the future as they had been neglected in the past could only lead to havoc in the city.

Knowing how important small parks were to the city's poor, the reformers could hardly believe the implications of Moses' policies when they began to discern them. By banning public transportation, he had barred the poor from the state parks. In the same way, he was barring the poor from the best of the city parks, the big parks on the city's outskirts such as Jacob Riis and Alley Pond. And now he was saying that he would not provide the poor even with small parks. He was pouring tens of millions of dollars into creating new parks in New York—but he was creating almost none for the people who needed parks most. The philosophy that parks were only for the "comfortable middle class" had been outdated for at least ten years. But, they began to see, that was the philosophy Moses was following.

The reformers were still influential in the city (although they were becoming less so as La Guardia gathered power unto himself), and, unlike other Moses opponents, they received a hearing for their views from the city's press; Good Government organization resolutions calling for small parks in the slums were at least printed, even if primarily on inside pages.

But Moses simply shouted the reformers down. He replied—in replies that received better newspaper "play" than the statements he was replying to —that he *was* giving the slums parks—great parks. What, he demanded, was the great recreational complex he was building on Randall's Island? The great recreational complex he was building in Riverside Park? They were "easily accessible" to Harlem. As for small parks within the slums themselves, his "experience," he said, had taught him that they were just "too expensive" to be considered. Three acres, he said, was the smallest area that could be "controlled and managed" as a park. And since three acres is 130,680 square feet and land bearing profitable slum tenements was going in the 1930's for about $30 per square foot and a single park would thus cost the city about $4,000,000 for land acquisition costs alone, and since as many as 2,500 people might be displaced by the razing of the tenements involved and would have to be relocated, this was an unanswerable argument—if you accepted it.

Many reformers—far more than had ever disagreed with Moses before—did not accept it. A park did *not* have to be three acres to help a slum, they said. It could be the smallest crevice in the grim wall of tenements; even a space the size of a single 100-foot-by-20-foot building lot—or smaller—could if planted with grass and a few trees or if equipped with a few benches mean so much to the people of the block on which it was located. Something doesn't have to be big to brighten something that is drab, to bring pride to a place without any pride. Because they have nothing else to do, the people of the slums spend a lot of time looking out their windows; if there was a small park, even a tiny park, in the neighborhood, there would be a pleasant little scene to look at, something affirmative; even if there was no grass in the park there could be a few benches—and all at once the neighborhood would have a better place to rest than the fenders of parked cars; a vest-pocket park could be an elegant little plaza, but it could also be just a place for a kid to play or the elderly to relax—or for a pregnant mother to sit down for a minute on a walk home from the grocery store that suddenly seemed longer than it ever had before. The reformers, experts in parks, knew there were good small parks in other cities; they knew that Moses' argument was wrong.

Furthermore, these reformers said, Randall's Island and Riverside Park were not "easily accessible" to the slums. The Triborough Bridge would make the island accessible by car, but the people of the slums didn't have cars. There would, by Moses' edict, be no bus service to the island; the only way to get there would be to walk—from the nearest point in Harlem or the South Bronx a good three-quarters of a mile.* And that was from the nearest point of the slums, the edge on the river. From most of the slums, you would have to walk much farther; from the center of Harlem, then 145th Street, say, more than two miles. Riverside Park along the Hudson River was a hike up a long, achingly steep hill from the nearest point in Harlem. People didn't want to hike long distances to parks; they wanted recreational facilities close at hand, so that every trip to sit under a tree or shoot some baskets didn't have to be an expedition. The people of the slums wouldn't use these parks, they said. Morningside, St. Nicholas and Colonial parks, the three parks which formed the western border of Harlem, were fine, they said, but there was no other park between them and the East River. In the entire three square miles of Harlem, an area which contained 300,000 people, there wasn't a single patch of green.†

But while newspapers printed the reformers' resolutions, they did not support them editorially. And the reform front on the issue was not solid. The prestigious Park Association of New York City was dominated by elderly park fighters who clung to the old view of parks; its insistence that

---

* Distance figured from the point in Harlem at which a pedestrian would mount the Triborough Bridge pedestrian walk to the nearest park facility on Randall's Island. The Ward's Island Pedestrian Footbridge would not be built for another twenty years.

†Mount Morris Park, between 120th and 124th streets, would become part of the Negro slums of Harlem later—when the slums expanded south. In the mid-1930's, their southern border was still 125th Street.

Central Park be kept for passive contemplation was the proof of the way it really felt. And while its president, Mrs. Sulzberger, was more liberal on the point than many of her colleagues, Mrs. Sulzberger was not criticizing Robert Moses.

And Moses was not listening to criticism, anyway. When an alderman from Harlem wrote to Moses appealing for more playgrounds, Moses replied that he was, of course, "in entire sympathy with what you have in mind" but that "the sites you suggest are too expensive. We shall provide one playground in Harlem. . . ." When the alderman ventured to write him again on the subject, Moses declined to continue the correspondence.

In 1930, Moses, as head of the Metropolitan Park Conference, had led the fight to persuade the city to preserve parts of its fast-disappearing woodland in Queens and Staten Island by purchasing huge tracts for park land. Reformers had cheered him for that accomplishment; it had preserved open space—beautiful, wooded open space—for the city forever. But now Moses was filling that space with baseball diamonds and football fields and tennis courts—and the land for them could be cleared only by cutting down trees. And Moses was filling other parks with playgrounds and stadia and parking fields and handball courts. Throughout the city's park system, the reformers suddenly realized, grass was giving way to concrete.

The reformers knew that grass had to be supplanted by recreational facilities and parking lots in many of the city's parks. But not, they were sure, in *all* the city's parks.

But Moses' plans for parks did not include keeping them—*any* of them—in their natural state. His plans were not limited to repairing the ravages made in them by Tammany park commissioners so as to restore them to their natural state. His plans were to cram them—cram *all* of them—with bathhouses and tennis houses, baseball diamonds and tennis courts, restaurants and bicycle paths, zoos and asphalted playgrounds with ugly black iron fences around them, as well as with that essence of the city, concrete—the concrete of access roads, through roads and parking lots—concrete instead of precious grass.

It took a while for the reformers to realize what Moses was doing—first, because he kept his plans so secret that it was difficult for them to discern the over-all pattern beneath them until they had begun unfolding; second, because they had been so thoroughly convinced that he was a fighter for parks that they did not easily accept the realization that his definition of parks was much narrower than theirs, and perhaps not at all compatible with it, that where they saw in a towering stand of oak and elms and white pine a priceless bounty to a beauty-starved city, Moses saw a baseball diamond. Many of them, in fact, never came during the 1930's to realize this because they never took the time to study his over-all park plans and while they were distressed by what he was doing to a particular park in which they were interested, they accepted his assurances that he was preserving nature in the rest of the park system.

But some of the reformers did come to realize the implications of Moses' park philosophy rather quickly, and were anxious to discuss it with him. They were anxious that room be found in the park system—which, after all, was a huge one and included thousands of acres of still undeveloped woods and fields and streams—for their values as well as his. They were sure that in a discussion they would have no difficulty explaining to him—for, they all agreed, he was brilliant; the most brilliant public servant, many of them said, that they had ever met—the crucial difference, which apparently he had not yet grasped, between the implications of his philosophy when applied to Long Island parks and parks within the city. On no point, in fact, were they more anxious for discussion. For the destruction of the natural values of a park was not a remediable mistake; it was one that could never be rectified. Destroy the delicate natural balance of a marshland to make a concrete-lined lagoon and it did not lie with the power of man to restore that balance. Before any changes were made in the parks, therefore, there must be sufficient discussion to insure that the changes made were the right ones.

But Moses no longer had to discuss. He had long had great dreams for the city, and now he had learned how to make dreams come true. He had learned the technique of stake driving and of whipsawing. He had learned how to mislead and conceal and deceive, how to lie to men and bully them, how to ruin their reputations. And he used all these methods to bring the dream to reality.

Or was it all for the dream?

V

THE LOVE OF POWER

25. *Changing*

Because of the arrogance that was so basic to his nature—and to his mother's and grandmother's—Moses' susceptibility to the addiction of power was unusually strong. After he was given substantial power of his own by his appointment in 1924 to the presidency of the Long Island State Park Commission, the doses available to him were massive—but they did not satisfy him, as was noted by Judge Clearwater and Ansley Wilcox, who, charting his symptoms, observed a "sense of dominating authority and a desire to have [his] own way in all matters, large and small." Once Robert Moses had sought power only for the sake of his dreams, only as a means to an end; even then, however, there were signs that he was beginning to seek it for its own sake, as an end in itself. And the avidity with which he sought power—and the lengths to which he went to get it—revealed the depth of his need for it. The need was strong—and it was growing.

And now it had been growing for ten years.

Power is being able to laugh at people who oppose you and to laugh at them with impunity, to antagonize them without fear of reprisal. Now Robert Moses seemed to be going out of his way to laugh at people.

The Community Councils of the City of New York, Inc., and their executive secretary, minister Frank P. Beal, were disturbed by his plan to raze a reproduction of George Washington's Mount Vernon in Prospect Park, but they were not pressing the point particularly hard—or attempting to make a large public issue of it. The Councils had no power; Moses could easily have ignored them and simply have gone ahead with the work. Instead, he gave the opposition publicity—calling in reporters to tell them about it—apparently for no other reason than to be also able to tell them that "the work is going ahead in spite of the Community Council" and so that he could deliver himself of a remark that he wanted to make and have published. He set up the remark by saying, "It's a strange thing, but nothing has been heard from any responsible person on the Community Council." A reporter asked, as Moses had undoubtedly expected a reporter to ask, "What about Mr. Beal?" And Moses could thereupon say, "That's what I mean." On other occasions, he similarly volunteered information about opposition, only so that he could loftily dismiss it; once he volunteered, unsolicited, the information that a group of distinguished architects had presented him with a plan for reconstruction of Bryant Park apparently just so that he could add, with a smile: "Such a plan is not to be carried out."

He seemed to be going out of his way to antagonize people. He could have simply ignored William Exton and Robert Weinberg when they began proposing changes in his West Side Improvement plan; the two young reformers had no chance of making him even consider the changes. But he agreed to the interview with Exton—and Exton recalls that when he arrived at Moses' office, "he said, 'Well, as [city] Park Commissioner, maybe I can see you have a case, but the state park commission says so and so and the Authority says so and so.' Well, he was the state park commission, and he was the Authority, and I knew it, and he knew I knew it. It wasn't particularly subtle. It was just thumbing his nose at you"—and, Exton says, he had the feeling that Moses had given him the interview just so he could have the pleasure of thumbing it.

Once he apparently went all the way to the Rockaways just to antagonize a local civic association which had invited him to speak because they were concerned about the effect his proposed Marine Parkway Bridge might have on Floyd Bennett Field, the airport that was the Rockaways' pride. He could have declined the invitation—he seldom spoke before civic groups—but he accepted and made the long trip across Jamaica Bay, mounted the stage and informed the audience, "That airport of yours isn't so hot. It never should have been built in the first place." And then, as the *Times* reported, "he smacked his hand down [and] glanced up at the ceiling" to indicate that he was through discussing the topic. If Moses had any motive for the trip—to enlighten the audience, educate them, persuade them, convince them, conciliate them, listen to them or answer their questions—other than his enjoyment at insulting them, and showing them that he could thumb his nose in their faces and there was nothing they could do about it, that motive eluded the audience.

Power is being able to ruin people, to ruin their careers and their reputations and their personal relationships. Moses had this power, and he seemed to use it even when there was no need to, going out of his way to use it, so that it is difficult to escape the conclusion that he enjoyed using it.

He may have felt it was necessary to turn the power of his vituperation on men whom he felt posed a threat to his dreams, but he turned it also on individuals who posed no such threat.

Pearl Bernstein, for example, was a young Barnard College graduate whom La Guardia, for some inexplicable reason, had had appointed secretary to the Board of Estimate. "She was a naïve girl and the job was utterly beyond her," Kern recalls; it was common knowledge that she made no decisions on her own but simply carried out La Guardia's orders, relayed through Kern.

Moses must have known this, but when, in 1934, La Guardia, infuriated by the Park Commissioner's cooperation with Democratic members of the Board, issued an order that no matter was to be placed on its calendar at the instance of any commissioner until he had personally approved it, and Miss Bernstein, who was in charge of the calendar, therefore refused to place on it some of Moses' unapproved requests, Moses attacked her, writing Kern a letter—with copies sent simultaneously to Miss Bernstein's associates and to officials throughout City Hall—attacking her "amateurishness, delay and pettiness" and "complete absence of willingness to cooperate with people who are trying to get something accomplished."

Kern, who was at this point still a "Moses fanatic," was startled because he knew that the Mayor, not Miss Bernstein, was the source of the order; Kern had, in fact, heard Moses arguing with La Guardia about it. Just in case the Park Commissioner had forgotten, Kern reminded him of this fact—but to his surprise the attacks continued, escalating in viciousness; one, also circulated throughout City Hall, referred to the order as "one of Pearl Bernstein's new wrinkles" and added, "If it were merely a question of casting swine before Pearl, I should be glad to have a standing order at any slaughter house—but these are really important construction matters with which she is interfering." Kern began to realize—reluctantly—that his idol, angry at the order and unwilling to argue further with its originator, had decided to vent his spleen on Miss Bernstein instead—apparently for no other reason than that she was handy and too small to fight back. Moses' attacks, Kern was to conclude, were "an example of his irresponsible brutality, a wantonness almost, a sadistic joy in hurting other people," as well as of his "willingness to beat little people" on occasions when he was reluctant to "go to the mat with big people" like the Mayor.

The number of defenseless minor officials on whom Moses unleashed his vituperation was legion. The officials least able to fight back were those on his own staff, and to those he was, if possible, even more viciously abusive. Once, when one of his aides, at a luncheon meeting attended by a dozen men, ventured to offer a suggestion which he hadn't cleared with Moses first, Moses whirled on him and said, "Now, you're just a swabbie on this ship—do you understand?" And while the others present squirmed in embarrassment for the man being humiliated, Moses repeated to him, "Do you understand?" "Do you understand?"—refusing to be satisfied with a nod, making the aide say out loud, "Yes, sir."

And the bullying was not just verbal. City Hall was whispering about Moses' physical encounters with other men.

The two-hundred-pound Park Commissioner had had at least two such encounters during his governmental career prior to entering the city administration, and, as in the case of scrawny little "Slat" Johnson, the roommate he knocked down at Yale, neither of them was his physical equal. Raymond Torrey, whom he tried to strangle at a State Council of Parks meeting and at whom he then hurled a heavy smoking stand, was a pudgy little bird watcher. Moses had also staged a fist fight with WPA administrator Hugh Johnson in Bernard Baruch's apartment, and Johnson, at the time, was fifty-two—eight years older than Moses—and exceedingly drunk. Now Moses had additional physical encounters—and the pattern continued.

"This was at the opening of a section of the West Side Highway," Joseph Ingraham of the *Times* recalls. "It was raining and we had to go into some kind of tent. Some little old character—just a minor functionary in government—was there and Moses said to me, 'Wait'll you see what I do to this guy.' He went over and grabbed him and almost literally picked him up by the scruff of the neck and shook him. It was very embarrassing. I said, 'What did he do?' He said, 'He hasn't done anything yet, but I just wanted to head him off.' " Other City Hall observers recall other Moses fist fights but not one with a man to whom he had a chance of losing.

Once, in an executive session of the Board of Estimate, Moses presented the Board with a proposal for a project whose cost, he promised, would be borne almost entirely by the federal government and would cost the city practically nothing. He presented the Board with a set of extremely detailed "facts" to "prove" his point.

Most of the members of the Board were thinking the same thing, one of them recalls, but only Stanley Isaacs had the courage to give the thoughts voice. He said mildly:

"When Mr. Moses says something will cost 3.4 percent, he adds the .4 only to make you think it's accurate. It's really 6.2 percent." Moses' response was to take a violent swing with his fist in Isaacs' direction and say, "I'd like to punch you in the nose!"

"He wasn't close enough to hit him with a baseball bat," says Isaacs' borough works commissioner, Walter D. Binger. "It was just a motion of passion. But Moses was tall and athletic" and the mild-mannered Isaacs was fifty-seven years old. "Everyone in the room was shocked," Binger says.

He wasn't satisfied merely to defeat people who opposed his wishes. He had to try to destroy them, too. He wasn't content with ignoring Exton and Weinberg and he wasn't content with thumbing his nose at them, either; he had to attempt to damage their reputations beyond repair by charging—falsely—that the two young reformers wanted the location of the Henry Hudson Bridge changed because a change would increase the value of Weinberg's property. For years he had been stung by the caustic voice of the "Old Judge," James B. Cooper, whose Babylon *Leader* continued to remind the residents of Moses' summer hometown that Moses had broken his promise never to charge tolls on the Wantagh Causeway—and who in the 1930's was leading the opposition to Moses' proposal to build a highway on Fire Island, although, with scrupulous fairness, he always allowed plenty of room in the *Leader* for Moses' replies. Now Moses did everything he could to silence that voice.

"We had always carried 'legals' [the advertising—of contracts and new ordinances, for example—that governmental bodies are required by law to do in newspapers, and that is often the difference between profit and loss for small-town weeklies] from the state," recalls Cooper's son. "And then they just suddenly disappeared from the paper—he had some and then he had none. They never said anything directly—they'd be far too subtle for that"; the *Leader* was simply no longer included on the list of Suffolk County publications which shared in the legal advertising connected with state projects which were located in Suffolk and had to be advertised in that county. Says Cooper's son: "I grew up in a house where we knew that we weren't going to get any printing from the state because of the way my father fought editorially for what he believed in." There were hints from Long Island State Park Commission executives that Cooper could get the legals back—and lucrative state printing contracts besides. "The inference was 'Behave yourself and you'll be taken care of,' " the son says. "But that sort of thing never appealed to my father. He had on his masthead 'I Have Never Known a Master and I've Never Worn a Muzzle' and he would rather be broke than lose his soul." Soon he *was* broke—the legals had been very important in the touch-and-go financing of the little newspaper (its circulation never reached 4,000 during Judge Cooper's thirty years as publisher), and the paper almost died before he did on May 30, 1940. But "what mattered more than the money involved in the legals," his widow says, "was the principle of the thing. His feelings were hurt that anyone would do such a thing."

A streak of maliciousness and spitefulness seemed to run through Moses' character, and he gave that full play, too.

The sole oasis in muddy and barren Riverside Park was the Columbia Yacht Club, which since 1888 had been occupying an acre at the foot of Eighty-sixth Street, paying only a nominal rental of $300 per year because it had created most of the acre itself by barging in landfill, had spent $50,000 building its own marina and three-story clubhouse, and because it maintained those buildings, and surrounding lawns, hedges and flower beds it had planted, at its own expense. The club's six hundred members had succeeded in making themselves semi-official city hosts to visiting royalty (the club's proudest boast was that the Prince of Wales had made it his headquarters on not one but two visits aboard the *Renown*) and club members seemed to regard themselves as the city's link with maritime glory; naval officers of all nations were always welcome and the club was "official host" for the squadrons of the U.S. Navy which anchored off Manhattan each summer.

In March 1934, three months after he had been sworn in as City Park Commissioner, Moses announced that the Columbia Yacht Club was in the way of his West Side Improvement and would be torn down.

Shocked as the members were, they didn't try to fight the eviction; they understood that the park belonged to the city. Their only request was that they be allowed to remain in the clubhouse through September, so they could fulfill their pledge to entertain the U.S. Navy's Pacific Fleet, which was arriving in July for the summer.

At first, Moses agreed to this request without reservation; he certainly had no reason not to, for there was no prospect that work on the Improvement would have progressed far enough by September so that the presence of a single building in the six miles of park would interfere with it; in March 1934, he wasn't even sure where the Henry Hudson Parkway was going to run, no plans had yet been drawn for any substantial part of it, and money for the job was not yet in hand—or indeed in sight. But then Moses saw an opportunity of obtaining a valuable addition to the Improvement for nothing. He evidently decided to turn the clubhouse into a public restaurant on the waterfront, and he sent Ray McNulty back to the club officials with the message that he would allow the club to remain through September only if it then donated its clubhouse and marina to the Park Department. On April

18, club commodore John A. Harriss telephoned Moses to tell him that the board was agreeable and wanted only enough time to submit the proposition to the entire membership, which he expected would also approve it.

Unfortunately, in talking to Moses, Harriss somehow—he was never to be sure how—managed to irritate him. The next day the commodore received a letter from the commissioner, a letter he later characterized as "brutal," accusing the club of "stalling," ordering it to vacate its site by May 1, in exactly twelve days—and warning that "if your property is not removed by that date, it will be treated as abandoned property" and confiscated.

Anticipating that the matter would become public knowledge, Moses went to the press—and he did so with his usual blend of demagoguery and deception: breaking the story himself to get his side of it before the public first; oversimplifying the basic issue to one of public vs. private interest; identifying the "private interests" with the sinister forces of "influence" and "privilege"; concealing any facts that might damage his own image. "The whole question," he said, "is whether public interest is going to yield to private," whether parks are going to be "for the people." The public needed the land occupied by the yacht club and it needed it immediately so that a great public improvement could be gotten under way, he said; he had advanced the date of eviction because the West Side Improvement was progressing faster than he had thought it would, and any delay in evicting the yacht club would slow the Improvement down. Moreover, the use of the public's property by the club was "a social racket," an "exclusive privilege," successful in the past only because of "the influence of certain members." The club had not the slightest legal right to be on the property in the first place; it has, he stated flatly, "no lease, no permit, no anything." He did not neglect to add a touch of class antagonism: "It is an interesting fact," he said, "that the yacht club in their talk of entertaining yachtsmen and officers say nothing about the entertainment of enlisted men." The tactics worked as successfully as usual. The headline on the *Times* article reporting one of his press releases was PARKS COME FIRST, MOSES DECLARES, while the *Herald Tribune* headlined COLUMBIA YACHT CLUB IS "RACKET," MOSES REPEATS.

The club applied to the State Supreme Court for a temporary injunction restraining Moses from ousting it so quickly. And in that more impartial arena there emerged, as usual, some facts that Moses had somehow neglected to mention. The Park Commissioner had contended that the club had "no lease, no permit, no anything" for the use of the park land. The attorney for the club said that the club had had a permit since 1888, that the permit had been renewed by the Park Department annually each of the forty-six years since, including 1934—and that Moses knew it. And to prove *his* contentions the attorney presented the court with a photostat of a check for $150 for the first half of the 1934 rent, made out to and deposited and accepted by the Park Department.

Moses had also contended that the club had never done anything but occupy the public's property. Obviously, the attorney pointed out, the club had done far more. It had improved the public's property, building $50,000 worth of structures on it. And now it was probably willing to give all those improvements to the public in return for only five more months of occupancy; the board of trustees was agreeable to such an arrangement; it was asking only for enough time to poll the membership. Moreover, even if the schedule for the West Side Improvement required the club to vacate in a hurry, its members, some of whom were in Europe, should be given more than twelve days to remove their property from the clubhouse, or have it confiscated as "abandoned." And the schedule did *not* require the club to vacate in a hurry; it was quite obvious that the Improvement was barely under way, and that even if money was made available, Moses had more than six miles of Riverside Park to work in and did not have to start immediately on the single acre that the club occupied.

Supreme Court Justice Aaron J. Levy found the attorney's statements accurate, noting dryly in the opinion he handed down that "the Commissioner was in error in asserting that the club was occupying the premises without a permit." And the judge went further. Even if Moses' motives were honorable, he said, he had allowed himself to be carried away:

> I must observe that a burning zeal for the public interest should not dazzle a public official—no matter how well intentioned—so as to blind him to individual amenities. Even where the public authority is entirely correct in his legal position, he should maintain it without inflicting undue hardship or injury. Tyranny, whether it consists of oppressive measures or brutal severity, is never necessary.

And, the Justice said, he was not at all sure Moses' motives *were* honorable. His examination of the commissioner's plans for the West Side Improvement left no doubt that the club's land would not be needed that summer at all:

> The precipitate notice gives the appearance of having been prompted by the Commissioner's pique at plaintiff's refusal to accept [his] terms. . . .

He issued a temporary injunction restraining Moses from ousting the club until a trial on the matter could be held.

But Moses was not to be restrained by a judge. Even as the club's attorney had been applying for the temporary injunction, two huge steam shovels were rumbling into Riverside Park and taking up positions north and south of the clubhouse. As club members watched in amazement, they began scooping out trenches all the way from the New York Central Railroad tracks in the middle of the park to the edge of the river. Their operators said they were "testing the fill," but the yacht clubbers realized with a shock that once the trenches were completed, the dirt roads from north and south would be cut, there would be no way for members' automobiles or delivery trucks to reach the clubhouse and the only means of access by foot would be along a narrow footbridge across the railroad tracks. Shouting to make himself heard above the thunderous chug-chug of the shovels, a club official told a reporter he had called to the scene, "They will have us dug out of here before the court can render its decision."

This occurred on a Friday. The next day, with the clubhouse crowded with men and women preparing for some weekend yachting or sipping drinks in the pleasantly shadowy clubhouse bar, the shadows suddenly grew deeper. The club's electricity had been turned off. Hurriedly telephoning the New York Consolidated Edison Company to find out what had happened, the club superintendent was informed by an official there that "someone from the club" had asked that the current be shut off. The superintendent said he was sure there had been some mistake, and when the Con Ed officials checked, he found out that there had indeed. The man who had identified himself as being from the club was actually from the Park Department.

As the club's electricity was being turned on, its water was almost being turned off. Ten men drove up in a Park Department automobile and began digging near the clubhouse. When the club superintendent demanded to know what they were doing, they said they wanted to "repair" a leak in the water main. Only their inability to locate the main kept the club liquid.

"Sheer spite work," the club secretary termed Moses' actions, but reporters who telephoned the commissioner found him unabashed. As the *Herald Tribune* put it:

> Mr. Moses said he knew nothing of this, but that it might easily be true. "I instructed my men," he said, "to go ahead with the construction work for the improvement of that part of the park and not to let anything get in the way. It is perfectly possible they did this."

Some of the city's elected officials attempted to restrain him, the Board of Aldermen passing a resolution demanding that Moses rescind his eviction order. One of the aldermen, Fusionist Lambert Fairchild, called the Park Commissioner's methods "steam-shovel government." But Moses was not to be restrained by elected officials. The Board's action, he said, was "just cheap politics. . . . I don't take their actions seriously. I'm sure they didn't." He filled the press with his side of the story—"The whole question is whether private interest should yield to public interest"—and if the press saw that some other questions were involved, it didn't mention them. And by the time the temporary injunction halted his steam shovels, they had completed the trench to the north of the clubhouse, cutting off all access from that direction, and had completed all of the trench to the south except for a narrow gap described as "perilously close to the river"—and as a final touch Moses had stationed a guard at that gap to charge all vehicles using it a quarter toll. Club members felt that their continued occupancy of a clubhouse that seemed to be under siege was untenable and that they might as well stop fighting. In a stipulation entered into before the trial for a permanent injunction, they agreed to get out if Moses would just give them enough time to remove their property—until June 18. When the fleet docked in July, they were not there to welcome it.

And neither was their clubhouse. Moses had razed it to the ground, as he had the Central Park Casino, the physical structure on which he had vented his malevolence against Jimmy Walker. By destroying the Columbia

Yacht Club clubhouse, he deprived the city of a $50,000 structure which could have been turned into a waterfront restaurant with only the most minor alterations—or, if he didn't want to leave it on the waterfront, could have been moved to any other park in the city and used for any purpose he chose.

And while Moses had maintained that he had harried the club out of existence so mercilessly because its existence conflicted with the public interest, those close to the affair knew differently, knew that his actions were, as the club secretary had said, "sheer spite work." Recalls Assistant Corporation Counsel Chanler, who handled the case for Moses and drew up the final stipulation: "I spoke to Moses about it. He said they had to be evicted at once. I said, 'Why?'

"He said, 'Because they were rude to me.' "

If Moses was indulging his enjoyment at hurting people not in order to help him with his aims but simply because he liked hurting, the indulgence nonetheless helped him achieve his aims. As Judge Jacob Lutsky puts it, "If you know that every time you get in a guy's way, he's going to kick you in the balls, you make pretty damn sure you don't get in his way—right?" Within a remarkably brief time after Moses entered the city administration, word had spread through City Hall and the Municipal Building that any time someone got in Moses' way, Moses kicked him in the balls. So the men who worked in those two buildings were in general exceedingly careful not to get in his way. They went to great lengths to do exactly what he wanted—when he wanted. The great spongy mass of the city's bureaucracy, a mass of inertia and red tape and obfuscation and confusion, had absorbed and smothered the energy and the dreams of a thousand commissioners—but Commissioner Robert Moses sliced through the bureaucracy as if it were soft butter and he were a knife. And when at public meetings of the Board of Estimate, he would stride up to the little lectern reserved for city officials appearing before the Board and extend his hand behind him without looking, like a surgeon extending his hand for a scalpel, and an aide smacked a file folder into the hand, and Moses opened it and began, with the precision of a great surgeon, to dissect a man's character, the members of the Board, watching the reporters' pens and pencils avidly scribbling down his words, knew that those words would be appearing in headlines.

"He was terribly unfair to people," McGoldrick says. But, the Comptroller admits, the attacks served their purpose. Moses' methods "*did* intimidate people from debating with him. And it intimidated us, too, most likely." Soon, in the whole city government, from bureaucracy to Board of Estimate to mayor, there was no one to stand in the way of his dream, no one who would dare to tell the public the truth about the methods that were being used to make it come true, no one who would venture to examine—or to proclaim—its flaws.

* * *

And the dream unrolled.

During the 1930's, Robert Moses reshaped the face of the greatest city in the New World.

He gouged great gashes across it, gashes that once had contained houses by the hundreds and apartment houses by the score. He laid great swaths of concrete across it. He made it grayer, not only with his highways but with parking fields, like the one on Randall's Island that held 4,000 cars, the one at Orchard Beach that held 8,000 and the one at Jacob Riis Park that held 9,000, that together covered with asphalt a full square mile of the 319 in the city. And he made it greener, planting within its borders two and a half million trees, shrubs and vines, bringing a million others back to bloom, reseeding lawns whose area totaled four square miles and creating a full square mile more of new ones. He filled in its marshes and made them parks. He yanked railroad trestles off its avenues, clearing an even dozen from Brooklyn's Atlantic Avenue alone as part of a grade-crossing elimination program he considered so minor that he seldom mentioned it. He brought the stars down to it, arranging, in a brief interval crammed in between more important projects, for the financing of Hayden Planetarium. He changed its very shape: the millions of cubic feet of rock and shale and sand and stone that the long convoys of his barges and the endless caravans of his trucks dumped behind the steel bulkheads that he rammed out away from its shoreline into the muck beneath rivers and harbors hardened into new land, more than 5,000 acres of new land, and thus expanded and transformed its physical contours, adding to Manhattan Island alone an area as large as the island from river to river between Fifty-ninth and Eighty-sixth streets. He joined together small islands within its borders with earth, blending Ward's Island into Randall's and Hunters and Twin Islands into Rodman Neck. He soldered together the larger islands that were its boroughs with steel, linking three of them together at once with the Triborough Bridge, tying the West Bronx to Manhattan with the Henry Hudson, drawing the far-flung Rockaways closer to the rest of metropolis with the Marine Parkway span. In the five years after he became Park Commissioner, in a city in which the parks had been barren for decades, he made the parks bloom. In a city in which there had been only 119 playgrounds, he built 255 new ones. In a city in which not a mile of new arterial highway had been built in fifteen years, he built fifty miles of arterial highway. In a city in which a new bridge had not been built in a quarter of a century he built not only the three new big bridges—Triborough, Henry Hudson and Marine Parkway—but 110 smaller ones to carry local streets across his parkways. *Si monumentum requiris, circumspice,* reads the inscription on the tomb of Sir Christopher Wren. *If you would see his monument, look around.* By 1939, the same advice could have been given to a New Yorker asking to see the monuments of Robert Moses. They were everywhere in the great city.

With his showman's flair for the spectacular, Moses made the opening of each of his creations an event, a colorful civic celebration, and if the celebrations sometimes seemed more like morality plays (for Moses was careful to point out at each one that the creation had been possible because of the victory of the altruistic public servant over "old hack" Tammany politicians and "red tape" bureaucrats) the public was so enthusiastic that it didn't mind the moralizing. New York City cheered what Robert Moses was doing to it—cheered so loudly, in fact, that the thin cries of disagreement, of disagreement and despair, were all but completely drowned out.

Robert Moses built 255 neighborhood playgrounds in New York City during the 1930's.

The adults and children who attended playground dedication ceremonies cheered when, at the end of the speeches, the fountain showers in the wading pools were turned on. And the cheers were echoed and amplified by the press. "Nothing Robert Moses has done is as great as what he has done with playgrounds," the *World-Telegram* said. "He has bestowed an unqualified boon on the neighborhoods of this city."

To dramatize the size of the achievement, Moses gave each playground a number, and the press counted along with him: PLAYGROUND NUMBER 189 OPENS, the headlines said. PLAYGROUND NUMBER 194 DEDICATED . . . PLAYGROUND 204 . . . PLAYGROUND 240 . . . And he had his mapmakers prepare pairs of outline maps of the city, blank except for dots representing playgrounds. The map on the left would be labeled simply "1933," the year before he had become Park Commissioner, the one on the right simply "1937" (or "1938" or "1939"). And the contrast between the two maps was certainly spectacular, the one on the left almost empty, the one on the right covered thickly with dots. And public and press drew from the maps the conclusion that Moses wanted drawn from them: that his playground-building program was an unqualified improvement, an absolutely unalloyed benefit, to all the people of New York City.

A close inspection of the maps would have revealed some rather puzzling characteristics about the pattern formed by the dots.

Their distribution, for example, was not at all even. The areas of the maps on which the dots were clustered most thickly corresponded in the main to those areas inhabited by families that were well-to-do or at least "comfortable." The areas of the maps on which the dots were sprinkled most thinly corresponded in part to undeveloped outlying areas of the city that did not really need playgrounds, but they corresponded also to some of the city's most congested areas, to the tenement neighborhoods and slums inhabited by families that were poor—to areas that needed playgrounds desperately. Most of Robert Moses' neighborhood playgrounds had, in other words, been built in the neighborhoods that needed playgrounds least. Few of the playgrounds had been built in the neighborhoods that needed playgrounds most.

The areas of the maps on which the dots were sprinkled most thinly of all corresponded to those areas of the city inhabited by its 400,000 Negroes.

Robert Moses built 255 playgrounds in New York City during the 1930's. He built one playground in Harlem.

An overspill from Harlem had created Negro ghettos in two other areas of the city: Brooklyn's Stuyvesant Heights, the nucleus of the great slum that would become known as Bedford-Stuyvesant, and South Jamaica. Robert Moses built one playground in Stuyvesant Heights. He built no playgrounds in South Jamaica.

"We have to work all day and we have no place to send the children," one Harlem mother had written before Robert Moses became Park Commissioner. "There are kids here who have never played anyplace but in the gutter." She could have written the same words after he had been Park Commissioner for five years. After a building program that had tripled the city's supply of playgrounds, there was still almost no place for approximately 200,000 of the city's children—the 200,000 with black skin—to play in their own neighborhoods except the streets or abandoned, crumbling, filthy, looted tenements stinking of urine and vomit; or vacant lots carpeted with rusty tin cans, jagged pieces of metal, dog feces and the leavings, spilling out of rotting paper shopping bags, of human meals. Children with white skin had been given swings and seesaws and sliding ponds. Children with black skin had been left with the old broomsticks that served them as baseball bats. Children with white skin had been given wading pools to splash in in summer. If children with black skin wanted to escape the heat of the slums, they could remove the covers from fire hydrants and wade through their outwash, as they had always waded, in gutters that were sometimes so crammed with broken glass that they glistened in the sun.

Negroes begged for playgrounds.

The children begged silently. Recalls Father C. Edward Harrison, who during the 1930's served as assistant to Father Shelton Hale Bishop, rector of St. Philip's Protestant-Episcopal Church on 134th Street: "They wouldn't say they had no place to go. The need was unexpressed, inarticulate. But you knew that in their own way they were begging for somewhere to go, something to do. There weren't even basketball courts then, except at the 'Y' or in the big parks. There was nothing in the neighborhood. And you would see kids improvising basketball baskets, hanging a fruit basket against a lamppost or against a wall—you know, hanging it up on *something*, playing on the sidewalks or in the streets." In 1944, Father Bishop would persuade his parishioners to convert the old four-story parish house, which contained a gymnasium, into a community center with recreational facilities, and, Father Harrison recalls, "you should have seen the kids come in here, just because we had a gym. The very fact that they came here in such numbers and were so happy to have something to do showed us how much they needed recreational facilities."

Not just because of the gym, of course. There were recreation supervisors there who cared about the children—"It's not just recreation that we're talking about, you know," Father Harrison says. "I guess you could call it an involvement of ourselves; they felt they belonged here and that they were wanted here, that someone cared about them; recreation has to go along with other things, you know"—but that was precisely what playgrounds were providing in other areas of the city. "In the Thirties," recalls Park Department official Melvin Daus, the Park Department playground supervisors were "young guys, bright young guys, all college-educated. There were no other jobs available then. We were trained in working with young people, supervising them, giving them leadership, giving them help. And what with WPA and all, there were so many supervisors—there were two or three at even the smallest playground—that we could really get involved with the kids, not just supervise their games but be around so that if one of them needed someone to talk to, he had someone. I mean a kid would never come around and say right out, 'I need some advice,' but kids were saying that in their own way. They were saying it silently, but they were saying it all right. They were begging for it."

Adults begged aloud—in letters-to-the-editor and resolutions to the mayor—and their voices sometimes grew shrill and desperate. "The police just keep the kids moving and there is no place to send them," one Stuyvesant Heights mother said. "Harlem is a poor section," one civic organization wrote La Guardia. "Each day from morning to night those people who are trying to give their children a decent living and make them something in the world to be proud of, are . . . out at work trying to earn a living." It was impossible for them to stay home and care for their children at the same time. Therefore, they wanted to send them to playgrounds. Since there weren't any, the children had little choice but to "roam the streets while their parents are worried half to death wondering where they are. . . . Please realize and understand the conditions of Harlem in order that you might see what the children there have to contend with." Ministers and settlement-house workers attempting to alleviate the problem through their own efforts found a particular poignance in their inability to make any real dent in it—the crowds of children who tried to jam into Reverend Bishop's little parish house only impressed him the more with the fact that only the city could do the job on the scale required. "We knew the need," Father Bishop's assistant, Father Harrison, says. "We couldn't understand why the city didn't. When you have to turn kids away, the feeling is one of anger, frustration—of Why? Why? Why?" And sometimes the anger and frustration would spill over in angry speeches. Reverend Bishop, who was to try for ten years to persuade Robert Moses to build one playground in his neighborhood—reading, almost every time he picked up a newspaper, it seemed, of another new playground being opened in some other neighborhood—addressed himself to the problem of Harlem crime by telling an audience: "The children have no place to go. Day and night they must use the block on which they live for recreation. No wonder they are like caged tigers and, once loose, want to wreak havoc."

But the adults might as well have been silent, too. La Guardia, who was doing so much in other areas for the city's Negroes, was not interfering with his Park Commissioner, and he referred the resolutions to him. And his Park Commissioner flatly denied their contentions. "The fact is that Harlem and its adjacent neighborhoods have not been overlooked and neglected or discriminated against," Robert Moses said. "The tendency has been in just the other direction, that is to give more attention to Harlem than to other sections which are in just as great need of recreation." He had done this with all the Negro slums, he said. And he bolstered his arguments with floods of facts and figures compiled by his corps of statisticians. The facts and figures were misleading, but no one did the work necessary to disprove them; the first full-scale survey of recreational facilities by any organization other than the Park Department—a United Parents Association study which found "plenty of playground space" only "where the rentals are high"—was not conducted until 1941, and it was not until 1943, when a grand jury investigating the causes of the high crime rate in Bedford-Stuyvesant found lack of recreational facilities to be a contributing factor, that any even quasi-official body went on record about the effect of Moses' park policies on the Negro slums. (Moses' reply was the issuance of an eight-page release that termed the jury's report "without the slightest foundation.") The press, the instrument best equipped to investigate the situation and come up with independent facts and figures, never made any such investigation. It buried or ignored the recreation reports of the United Parents Association and the grand jury and the resolutions passed by the Negro community organizations, and reprinted only the barest handful of letters-to-the-editor (it took Reverend Bishop fourteen years to get one printed). In 1950, the *Times* would send a reporter to Harlem to make his own, independent tour, and he would report that playgrounds for many Harlem children were vacant lots, in which "bare-legged children" played "on dumps of broken glass, rusty cans and refuse. . . ." But during the 1930's the press was taking Robert Moses' word for what was being done for the slums. A day-by-day review of the *Times*, *Herald Tribune* and Brooklyn *Eagle*—and a more cursory review of the city's other major dailies—for the entire 1934–39 period did not turn up a single editorial even hinting that Moses' playground-building program might be neglecting the slums. A typical editorial was the one in the *Times* that said that Moses was sowing "playgrounds over the congested areas of the city . . . as a sower might sow magic seed, bidden to flower in the slums."

Robert Moses built ten new community swimming-pool complexes in New York City during the 1930's.

Because of his fascination with water in general and swimming in particular, Moses gave each of the pools, for which he had obtained a special WPA grant of $10,000,000, his personal attention. Under his prodding, his architects adorned them with masterful little touches; over the entrance which divided men from women as they entered the bathhouse at the Corona Pool complex sat a stork wearing an expression that made him look as if he were puzzling over the physical differences in the creatures he had brought into the world. Under his prodding, his architects produced dozens of innovations that would set a new standard for swimming-pool construction, public and private, from pool bottoms of wood-float rough enough to prevent slipping and smooth enough to permit games during the off season, when the pool was drained, to a totally new type of scum gutter wide enough to let in sunlight that would kill the bacteria whose formation had been a problem in older public pools. He himself solved a problem that had always baffled designers—how to force swimmers to wash their feet before entering the pool—by building what the *Architectural Forum* called "tactful depressions"—hollows too wide to be jumped—clear across each corridor leading from the locker room to the pool so that swimmers had no choice but to walk through them and through the special foot-cleansing solution with which they had been filled. Despite the WPA requirements that only the cheapest materials be used, each pool turned out to be a municipal marvel of the first magnitude.

And they were hailed as such. "Simple materials simply disposed" in designs that were "always sound and sometimes brilliant," the *Forum* said. As for their size (the main pool at the three-pool Corona complex is 365 feet long), the *Forum* said, "The openings were marked by the publication of statistics which seemed to the reading public all but incredible. The Astoria Pool, for instance, was reported to have accommodations for 6,200 bathers. Nobody had heard anything like that before, but it turned out to be literally true. The ten new pools erected last year plus two old ones that had been remodeled, now have a combined capacity—as measured by their locker-room facilities—of *49,000!*"

The ingenuity that Robert Moses displayed in building swimming pools was not restricted to their design.

Moses built one pool in Harlem, in Colonial Park, at 146th Street, and he was determined that that was going to be the only pool that Negroes—or Puerto Ricans, whom he classed with Negroes as "colored people"—were going to use. He didn't want them "mixing" with white people in other pools, in part because he was afraid, probably with cause, that "trouble"—fights and riots—would result; in part because, as one of his aides puts it, "Well, you know how RM felt about colored people."

The pool at which the danger of mixing was greatest was the one in Thomas Jefferson Park in La Guardia's old East Harlem congressional district. This district was white, but the pool, one block in from the East River, was located between 111th and 114th streets. Not only was it close to Negro Harlem, but the city's Puerto Rican population, while still small, was already beginning to outgrow the traditional boundaries of "Spanish Harlem" just north of Central Park and to expand toward the east—toward the pool. By the mid-Thirties, Puerto Ricans had reached Lexington Avenue, only four blocks away, and some had begun moving onto Third Avenue, only three blocks away.

To discourage "colored" people from using the Thomas Jefferson Pool, Moses, as he had done so successfully at Jones Beach, employed only white lifeguards and attendants. But he was afraid that such "flagging" might not be a sufficient deterrent to mothers and fathers from the teeming Spanish Harlem tenements who would be aware on a stifling August Sunday that cool water in which their children could play was only a few blocks away. So he took another precaution.

Corporation Counsel Windels was astonished at its simplicity. "We [Moses and I] were driving around Harlem one afternoon—he was showing me something or other—and I said, 'Don't you have this problem with the Negroes overrunning you?' He said, 'Well, they don't like cold water and we've found that that helps.' " And then, Windels says, Moses told him confidentially that while heating plants at the other swimming pools kept the water at a comfortable seventy degrees, at the Thomas Jefferson Pool, the water was left unheated, so that its temperature, while not cold enough to bother white swimmers, would deter any "colored" people who happened to enter it once from returning.

Whether it was the temperature or the flagging—or the glowering looks flung at Negroes by the Park Department attendants and lifeguards—one could go to the pool on the hottest summer days, when the slums of Negro and Spanish Harlem a few blocks away sweltered in the heat, and not see a single non-Caucasian face. Negroes who lived only half a mile away, Puerto Ricans who lived *three blocks* away, would travel instead to Colonial Park, three miles away—even though many of them could not afford the bus fare for their families and had to walk all the way.

The fact that they didn't use their neighborhood pool—and the explanation for this fact—was never once mentioned by any newspaper or public speaker, or at least not by any public speaker prominent enough to have his speech reported in a newspaper.

Moses built an immense park complex on Randall's Island, one equipped with baseball fields, tennis courts and soccer fields. Only one item was needed to make it a great park: people. But this ingredient was not provided. Moses had said that the island was "easily accessible" to the slums. Trekking the two miles to the island once was evidently enough to convince most slum families differently. Even on weekends, the vast new facilities sat almost empty. As for the Randall's Island Stadium, Moses had demanded

70,000 seats. The WPA had allowed him 22,000. Even this number was, during the stadium's first five years of operation, not sold out once. At most events, the attendance was not in the thousands but the hundreds.

The Grand Central, Interborough and Laurelton parkways opened early in the summer of 1936, bringing to an even one hundred the number of miles of parkway constructed by Moses on Long Island and in New York City since he had conceived his great parkway plan in 1924.

At the opening of one stretch of parkway, Fiorello La Guardia lavished praise on everyone connected with its construction except Moses, and then, reaching up and placing his hand on his Park Commissioner's shoulder, said earnestly: "I don't have to say anything to you, Bob. Those who came to cheer have stayed to cheer."

The city's press had stayed. One editorial opined that the new parkways would, by relieving the traffic load on the Southern and Northern State parkways, solve the problem of access to Moses' Long Island parks "for generations."

The new parkways solved the problem for about three weeks. "It wasn't more than three weeks after they opened that I decided to go out to Jones Beach on a Sunday," Paul Windels recalls. "I got on the Interborough and by God it was as jammed as the Southern State ever was."

Moses announced that he had the solution: build forty-five miles of new parkways, including a great "Circumferential Parkway" around Brooklyn and Queens that would provide motorists of these boroughs (and of Manhattan if the proposed Brooklyn-Battery Tunnel was built and linked up with the parkway) with an easier way to reach the Island—and, since the parkway would run for twenty miles along the edge of the Brooklyn waterfront, with a wonderful view.

Some city planners noticed that the traffic pattern on Long Island had fallen into a set pattern: every time a new parkway was built, it quickly became jammed with traffic, but the load on the old parkways was not significantly relieved. If this had been the pattern for the first hundred miles of parkways, they wondered, might it not be the pattern for the next forty-five also? Perhaps consideration should be given to trying to ease Long Island's traffic problem by other means, specifically the improved mass transit that the Regional Plan Association and other reformer-backed groups had been proposing for a decade. The RPA ventured to raise this suggestion again, and it was backed by other planners and by some reformers. But their voices were drowned out by the flood of praise for Moses' idea. Said the *Sun* of the Circumferential proposal: "When it's done, you South Brooklynites can hitch up the old buggy and be in the Bronx before a Harvard man could say Greenpernt."

The Triborough Bridge opened on July 11, 1936.

Even men familiar with large-scale public works were awed by this one. "From the engineering point of view, it is one of the greatest in the world as it is one of the biggest," PWA Administrator Ickes wrote in his diary. General Hugh Johnson wrote in his syndicated column, "The Triborough Bridge in New York City is one of the greatest accomplishments of man in the most fascinating department of civil engineering—bridge building." Harry Hopkins said that "of 70,000 WPA projects in the United States . . . there is none of which we are prouder."

The awe—and the pride—was shared by the city. "The imagination with which the whole project was conceived, and the integrity with which it has been carried out, reaffirms our faith in the ways of democratic government," the *Times* editorialized. City officialdom and press assured the public that the project would, as Moses had promised, provide at a single stroke a solution to most of the traffic problems between Long Island and New York. "A tour over the Triborough Bridge yesterday by two newspaper reporters revealed that the huge structure . . . is up to the expectations of the public and the promises of its builders both in beauty and in usefulness," the *Times* said. Trips from northern Queens to 125th Street in Manhattan, which previously had required "in the best of conditions" forty-five minutes via the Queensborough Bridge, would henceforth be negotiated in as little as sixteen minutes, reporters reported. Police Commissioner Valentine said that the opening of the bridge would sharply reduce traffic on all the East River spans, on the Queensborough "by from 40 to 50 percent."

On August 17, 1936, a little more than a month after the Triborough Bridge opened, Long Island's parkways were the scene of what some observers called the greatest traffic tie-up in the history of the metropolitan area.

Referring to it as a "cross-country traffic jam," the *Herald Tribune* was forced to conclude that the bridge had, at least indirectly, caused it. Apparently, a Monday-morning editorial quarterbacked, the "motoring residents of the Bronx" had all discovered at the same moment that the Triborough "brought them within easy time of Jones Beach and other cool and pleasant resorts on the south shore of Long Island" and had decided "at the same moment to head for the ocean by way of the new bridge and the Grand Central Parkway. And nearly all of them got stuck—as did countless other motorists going to and from . . . Long Island."

Public officials responded with alarm. "The Interborough Parkway, barely opened, was already impossible," Brooklyn Borough President Ingersoll noted.

Moses said he knew what to do: build more parkways in the Bronx and Westchester ("It's time we gave Westchester a break"), including the Hutchinson River Parkway Extension, and on Long Island not only rush the construction of the parkways he had already proposed but also build new roads that would not be restricted, as parkways were, to private automobiles, but would also carry commercial traffic. In particular, he proposed a road down the center of Long Island—the road that would, when finally built, be known as the "Long Island Expressway."

Yes, agreed Ingersoll, that was what was needed. Yes, indeed, said the *Herald Tribune*—and the rest of New York's press.

The Wantagh State Parkway Extension was opened on December 17, 1938, three months ahead of schedule. Reminiscing in the brochure distributed at the ribbon-cutting ceremony, Moses noted that in the nearly fifteen years since he had planned a metropolitan area transportation system, 110 miles of parkway, including 191 grade-eliminating bridges, had been completed in New York City and on Long Island, and so had the Henry Hudson, Triborough and Marine Parkway bridges. The "arterial system" he had created, he said, was "unparalleled"—and it had had to be, for so was the metropolitan area's traffic problem. And, he said, his program had been successful. "Today," he said, "we are well on our way toward a sensible solution of this problem in the metropolitan area." In his speech at a luncheon held afterward at Jones Beach, Moses repeated this theme. A thousand guests applauded enthusiastically.

The Wantagh State Parkway Extension did not receive its first real test of traffic-easing capacity until the first warm weekend morning of 1939. On that morning, it was jammed bumper to bumper for more than three miles. Traffic experts could not understand where those cars had come from. The other Long Island parkways, after all, were just as jammed as ever.

Four months after the Triborough Bridge opened, Othmar Ammann gave a speech on its operation to the American Society of Civil Engineers. In it, Triborough's chief engineer announced that traffic on the span was running considerably ahead of estimates.

The opening of a bridge was big news, but its operation was not. Most newspapers did not even bother to send a reporter to cover the speech. The *Times* did, and Ammann spoke with him after the meeting, and provided him with a further bit of information. Despite the heavy volume on the Triborough Bridge, Ammann said, "the relief of the traffic load on the Queensborough Bridge has not been as great as expected." But the

Times editors evidently did not consider this fact particularly noteworthy. They devoted only four paragraphs to the story and buried it at the bottom of page 26.

But Ammann's statement was a hint, the only published hint New Yorkers were given during all of 1936, of certain developments that were puzzling—and beginning to worry—the city's traffic experts. Traffic on Triborough was indeed running ahead of estimates—far ahead. Before its opening, Moses, on the basis of Jack Madigan's figures, had estimated that eight million vehicles would use the bridge during its first year of operation. Within four months the estimate was increased to nine million. Three months later, it was ten million—and the counts at the Randall's Island toll complex showed that traffic was rising more sharply every month. There began to be reports of traffic tie-ups on the huge new structure.

But traffic on the four other East River bridges was not falling off at anything near a comparable rate. The eight million cars and trucks that Moses had forecast would use Triborough each year were supposed to be cars and trucks that had previously used the other bridges, particularly the Queensborough. Not only Moses but all traffic experts who had studied the problem had agreed on that. Otherwise, where would these cars and trucks come from? Yet traffic on the other bridges, down about 15 percent immediately following Triborough's opening, was creeping higher again month by month—back, within two years, almost to the pre-Triborough level. Traffic between Long Island and New York had, before Triborough's opening, flooded the twenty-two lanes available on the four old bridges; suddenly the traffic between Long Island and New York had become so heavy that it was also flooding eight new lanes, the new lanes of the Triborough Bridge—and it was hardly any lighter than before on the old bridges. Traffic between the Island and the city had been increasing before, of course, increasing steadily. But never had it increased at this rate. If traffic between the Island and the city was a stream, something had suddenly opened the sluice gates much wider than they had ever been before—and the more the traffic experts studied the problem, the more difficult it was for them to avoid the conclusion that the something was the only new element in the situation—nothing other than the Triborough Bridge itself. Somehow, in ways they did not even pretend to understand, the construction of this bridge, the most gigantic and modern traffic-sorting and conveying machine in the world, had not only failed to cure the traffic problem it was supposed to solve—but had actually made it worse.

Moses was convinced he knew the solution to the problem: build another bridge. Within a year after Triborough had opened, he was proposing the construction, a mile to the east, of the Bronx-Whitestone that would, by tying directly into the Hutchinson River Parkway to the north, enable motorists from the East Bronx, Westchester, Connecticut and New England to get to Long Island without using Triborough.

For the first time, one of Moses' transportation proposals met with less than unanimous support from Good Government groups. The Regional

Plan Association said that such a bridge should not be built unless provision was made on it for railroad trains as well as cars—so that a rapid transit tie-in between Long Island and the Bronx, Westchester and Connecticut could be established. The tie-in did not have to be immediate, the RPA said. Construction of the rapid transit system could wait until the need for it had been proven and financing was available. But provision for it should be made immediately. All that was required was to make the bridge wide enough for two lanes of tracks as well as for automobiles or to build a second deck for the tracks—or, if Moses did not want to adopt either of these courses at the present time, to make the bridge foundations and towers strong enough so that, should at some later date the rapid transit link be desired, the bridge could support a second deck that would be built at that time. If provision was made now, while the bridge was being planned, the RPA said, it could be made cheaply, at a minor increase in the cost of the bridge. If it was not made, a whole new bridge would have to be constructed from scratch when the rapid transit link proved necessary, and the cost would be tremendous. It might even prove prohibitive, preventing construction of such a link entirely. Failure to make provision for a rapid transit link as part of the Bronx-Whitestone Bridge, the RPA said, could therefore condemn Long Island forever to be linked to the north only through roads—which would mean that no matter how much population increased in the metropolitan area, the only means of reaching the Island from the north would still be by automobile. And this would condemn Long Island to future inundation by larger and larger numbers of automobiles.

But Moses refused even to consider its proposal, and the RPA received no editorial support. Without opposition from a single city official, he built the Bronx-Whitestone Bridge without any provision for a rail link, opening it three full months ahead of schedule, on April 29, 1939.

During 1940, its first full year of operation, 6,317,489 vehicles passed through the Bronx-Whitestone's toll booths, cramming its four lanes to capacity and causing massive tie-ups on it. Traffic on the Triborough was reduced by 122,519 vehicles. Traffic on the other four East River bridges was reduced not at all. In fact, it rose slightly. Somehow, the new bridge had generated, in a single year, more than 6,000,000 new on-and-off-Island motor trips. It had not improved the traffic situation on the old bridges at all. What had been the net effect of its $17,785,000 construction—or, in fact, of the construction of both it and the Triborough Bridge—on the traffic problem these bridges were built to solve? Before they existed, four bridges had connected Long Island with the rest of the world, and they had all been jammed. Now six bridges connected Long Island with the rest of the world. And *they* were all jammed.

By dumping a tremendous new load on the Long Island parkways, the Bronx-Whitestone Bridge made the traffic tie-ups on them noticeably worse.

Shortly after the bridge opened, Moses completed the road linking the bridge with Westchester County, the Hutchinson River Parkway. Soon, that was jammed too.

The Gowanus Parkway, the elevated highway Moses placed atop the pillars of the old BMT Elevated Line on Brooklyn's Third Avenue, was opened on November 1, 1941, just in time for another mayoral election.

"When Commissioner Moses finds the surface of the earth too congested for one of his parkways, he lifts the road into the air and continues it on its way," the *Times* editorialized. "A busy, crowded, region lay in Mr. Moses' path, too heavily built up for a leisurely, landscaped parkway. The problem was solved successfully. . . . Beginning today . . . Brooklyn reaps a new, incalculable highway benefit." Brooklyn's borough president called Moses an artist who, in his own field, ranked with Leonardo da Vinci.

The canvas on which Moses had drawn the Gowanus creation was a neighborhood known as "Sunset Park." Its residents had pleaded with Moses to build the parkway not along Third Avenue but along Second, one block to the west, near the waterfront; Second Avenue ran not through a neighborhood but through the middle of Bush Terminal, a 200-acre agglomeration of piers, railroad sidings, lofts and factories that was already so noisy with the clatter of trucks and freight cars that the noise generated by a few more lanes of traffic would hardly be noticed. Comptroller McGoldrick, a resident of Sunset Park, had agreed with them; he pointed out that the city had been planning to tear down the elevated line because a new parallel subway had recently been built under Fourth Avenue, and "the elevated at least let some light in. The parkway would be solid and it would be wider than the El. It would come right up to the windows of the buildings." The Comptroller—along with non-Moses engineers—doubted Moses' contention that using the El pillars would be much cheaper than building a whole new parkway, particularly since it would have to swing back to the shore after only one mile—a distance long enough to "permanently blight" a neighborhood but not to make a substantial difference in cost. Moses had replied by telling the Board of Estimate that Sunset Park wasn't particularly worth saving because it was a "slum."

"A slum! That wasn't a slum!" says Cathy Cadorine, who lived in Sunset Park. "That was a very nice neighborhood. It was poor, but clean poor."

Actually, part of the area was dirty poor. Blight spawned in the dirt and noise of the Bush Terminal piers, warehouses, factories and railroad sidings along the waterfront had oozed inland along the side streets, forcing "clean poor" families to flee before it and leaving the old brownstone and red brickfront houses to derelicts, winos and whores.

But that was just part of the area. And it wasn't what families like the Cadorines thought of as "the neighborhood" at all. What they thought of as "Sunset Park"—the area extending from west of Third Avenue all the way to Eighth and from Thirty-sixth Street south to Sixty-third and containing some 70,000 people, half of them Norwegians, the rest Finns, Danes, Irish and Germans—had been menaced by that blight for at least thirty years. But they had always stood it off: although it had spread inland as far as Second Avenue by the time of World War I, that was where it stopped; in 1940 it had not gotten even a foothold on the side streets between Second and Third. And despite the Depression, which hit especially hard at a neighborhood of skilled carpenters and housepainters and plumbers (60 percent of Sunset Park men were members of trade unions), they had made a world of their own.

It was indeed, as Cathy Cadorine said, a "clean" world. The brickfronts and brownstones were immaculate; one could walk by them any morning and see the housewives sanding and scrubbing their stoops; even the sidewalks were swept; the little plots of grass that their owners proudly called "lawns" may have been tiny but they were lush green and neatly trimmed. But it was more than clean. It was quiet and peaceful—there were many trees lining the streets, but few cars; "Not many people around there had cars then," recalls Hertha Smalgo; "when people wanted to go to work or to the city, they took the elevated"—and warm and friendly: every summer brought a round of block parties, street lamps festooned with streamers, women and girls in gay peasant blouses from their native lands, folk singers with their accordions singing the old songs, long tables covered with tablecloths washed and washed again until they gleamed snowy under the lamps, and with heaping bowls of *kalalatikko* and *hernierokka*. In "Finn Town," the section of Sunset Park east of Fifth Avenue and south of Thirty-sixth Street that contained half a dozen public saunas, there were also half a dozen cooperative apartment houses, and many of the same families had been living in them for a quarter of a century. In the evening, families walked together to the bluff of Sunset Park to look out over ship-filled New York Harbor. Girls like Cathy Cadorine who grew up there, married boys from the neighborhood and raised their own families there because "we wouldn't want to live anywhere else."

The heart of the neighborhood—the focal point that gave it unity and a sense of community—was Third Avenue. Lining it, along with newsstands off which 9,000 *Nordisk Tidendes* were sold every day, were seven movie theaters, dozens of tiny restaurants run by couples and featuring recipes from the old countries ("little restaurants, but good and so many you wouldn't know where to go for lunch," recalls Harold Benson, whose hardware store was on Third Avenue at Fifty-fourth Street), and scores of small, friendly "Mama and Papa" stores (the Northland Gift Shop, the Finnish Book Store, a hardware store that looked like a general store out of the Old West, a butcher shop that raffled off twenty-five big turkeys every Christmas) that occupied the ground floor of three- and four-story brickfronts in which Mama and Papa lived upstairs with the children. "The avenue was always busy, people shopping or window shopping or just walking," Benson recalls.

The El overhead was noisy, but, the shopkeepers say, "you got used to the trains and anyway when they built the new subway [under Fourth Avenue] we thought it was going to be torn down." The soot and cinders that wafted down from the El were annoying, but the shopkeepers kept the sidewalks clean—by sweeping them morning, noon and night. "Clean?" Cathy Cadorine recalls. "Those were the cleanest stores you ever saw!" And the El made Third Avenue even more of a focal point for a neighborhood in which "not many people had cars." "The husbands all took it to work," says Cathy Wylde. "So there were always people coming to Third Avenue to take it." This made the avenue even busier. Neighborhood girls didn't hesitate to walk down to the movies at night in pairs or to go shopping in the evening alone. "You would think the El would have been a divider [of the neighborhood], but it wasn't really," says Miss Wylde. "In a way, because everybody used it, it brought it closer together. Third Avenue was never an esthetic avenue. But it was a nice avenue."

If Third Avenue was the heart of the neighborhood, Moses tore it out.

Relocation began the procedure.

The Board of Estimate had approved the Third Avenue route under the impression that because Moses was using an already-existing facility, the old El structure, no new right-of-way would be required—and hence no families would have to be evicted from their homes. But after the approval was given, the Board found that that impression was not quite accurate. It was off, in fact, by some one hundred stores—and 1,300 families.

Some buildings had to be torn down because, while an El did not need entrance and exit ramps, a highway did, and a single entrance ramp took half a block of homes. But this need accounted for only a minor percentage of the relocations. Most of the buildings that were torn down—and every building on one side of Third Avenue between Thirty-ninth and Sixty-third streets was torn down—had to go because Moses would not allow trucks on his parkways, and so that *he* would build it instead of the city, he classified this elevated highway through a densely packed urban area, a highway unadorned by a single tree, as a "parkway." Since Moses' Brooklyn-Battery Tunnel would pour trucks as well as cars into Brooklyn just north of Sunset Park, and since trucks as well as cars would need a route south, he decided to make Third Avenue that route—by making that four-lane street under the parkway into a ten-lane highway.

The El had cast a shadow over Third Avenue, but the El had been forty feet wide. The Gowanus was ninety-four feet wide. Its shadow was more than twice as broad.

And more than twice as dark. The gaps between railroad ties had made the El's shadow a Venetian-blind shadow; sunlight had come through as if through the slats of an opened blind. A highway was a concrete slab, without gaps. The construction of the Gowanus Parkway, laying a concrete slab on top of lively, bustling Third Avenue, buried the avenue in shadow, and when the parkway was completed, the avenue was cast forever into darkness and gloom, and its bustle and life were forever gone.

And through that shadow, down on the ten-lane surface road beneath the parkway, rumbled (from before dawn until after dark after the opening of the Brooklyn-Battery Tunnel flooded the area with freight traffic) regiments, brigades, divisions of huge tractor-trailer trucks, engines gunning and backfiring, horns blasting, brakes screeching, so that a tape recording of Third Avenue at midday could have been used as the soundtrack for a movie of a George Patton tank column. And from above, from the parkway itself, came the continual surging, dull, surf-like roar, punctuated, of course, by more backfires and blasts and screeches, of the cars passing overhead. Once Third Avenue had been friendly. Now it was frightening.

It was made more frightening by the absence of people.

Stores, restaurants and theaters had brought people to Third Avenue. Now half the stores, restaurants and theaters were gone.

The El had brought people through Third Avenue on their way to and from its stations. The parkway did not. Moreover, although the El had been a huge, gloomy structure, it was, as Cathy Wylde puts it, "one that people from the neighborhood related to; they traveled on it, they were familiar with it." The parkway was something unfamiliar and strange. There were no lights underneath it and it always seemed damp there—condensation on the tubular steel supporting pillars caused a constant dripping on the street. "The highway was something different," Miss Wylde says. "It was noise, dirt, accidents, not lighted, a garbage dump, drag races along it in the night, wild kids, something totally negative. It was a tremendous psychological barrier. In a way you could say the people feared the highway." It was something to stay away from. It was a physical barrier, too. Elderly persons and mothers with small children found Third Avenue frightening not only because it was negative but because it was wide. Crossing the ten-lane truck road, wider than a football field, was even more of a problem because the traffic lights never seemed to allow enough time for anyone not in the best of health to get across. Sunset Park families began to do their shopping in stores that were not on Third Avenue. Once the avenue had been a place for people; Robert Moses had made it a place for cars. And as the avenue's roadway became more crowded, its sidewalks began to empty.

The vicious gyre of urban decay began—and widened. Because there weren't as many people shopping on Third Avenue, there weren't enough to support the avenue's stores and restaurants—not even the half of the stores and restaurants that remained after the widening. One by one they began to close. Because there weren't as many stores and restaurants, people began doing their shopping and dining out elsewhere, and then there were even fewer people on Third Avenue. Because the streets in the evening were no longer filled with people, more people who might have gone to Third Avenue in the evening stayed away. Fewer people meant even less business. One by one the shops and restaurants closed. The shop that had raffled off twenty-five turkeys raffled off ten now and then one—and then it was gone. And since the owners of many of the stores had lived in the apartments over them, when they were forced to move their businesses out of the neighborhood, they were forced to move their families out, too, and those families had provided customers for other stores.

Not only Third Avenue was wrecked by the road; so were the side streets between it and the waterfront. With Moses' road and tunnel making Sunset Park more accessible to trucks, industries requiring truck traffic—including two large new plants, one a division of Bethlehem Steel, the other a division of American Machine & Foundry—moved onto Sunset Park's waterfront, already crowded with industrial activity. And the truck traffic for all these factories had no way to get to and from them from Third Avenue except through those narrow streets, between whose parked cars the children of the neighborhood had always played. "There was just so much traffic on those little streets that you wouldn't believe it," Cathy Cadorine recalls. The death of one little boy—hit by a huge tractor-trailer in the street right in front of his house—was enough. Faster and faster, the residents of the side streets began to move out. "The whole area died with the road," a resident would marvel. "And it died so quick." Soon it was, in his words, "a ghost town." Along the avenue and on adjacent side streets, rows of brownstone and brick-front buildings that had held stores and apartments, the stores and apartments that had stood as a bulwark between Sunset Park and the slum to the west, began to be vacated. Their rooms, the rooms that had been kept so clean and neat, stood empty.

And into them came what the neighborhood had always feared.

"Third Avenue became the place you could get sex," Cathy Cadorine recalls. "Everybody knew about it." Drunks as well as whores roamed the avenue, cadging drinks until they fell asleep in doorways. Cheap saloons opened in some of the abandoned stores. Soon there were street gangs, fighting gangs, Irish and Puerto Rican teen-agers, seeping down from the notorious Red Hook section to continue their racial warfare and prey on passers-by. The side streets off Third Avenue—streets whose apartments were now filled with families on welfare, families without fathers, and with poor Spanish-speaking families without clothes adequate for the cold New York winters—became places to dump and strip stolen cars; the streets began to be filled with their ravaged hulks. Rotting litter, rain-sodden mattresses and broken glass filled the sidewalks and gutters. Rats began to grow bold in the rubbish in vacant lots. There were even, to the horror of those residents who remained, drug addicts.

With its heart gone, the neighborhood had no will to resist the invasion. There was nothing to hold its people—and as they saw the blight creeping closer, they simply moved away. For more than thirty years, the blight in South Brooklyn had been confined to the waterfront area. Now, thanks to Robert Moses and his parkway, it was on the loose, spreading across Sunset Park. The world of neat little houses and block parties vanished beneath it along the entire twenty-six-block length of the Gowanus Parkway, as far east as Fourth Avenue and, except for a few isolated blocks, as far west as Sixth—where the parkway was far enough away so that the community put up a stand, and won. Moses' steel and concrete, "lifted into the air" above a neighborhood for the convenience of motorists driving through the neighborhood to get somewhere else, had destroyed the neighborhood.

Convenience? No sooner would Moses open the Brooklyn-Battery Tunnel at one end of the Gowanus Parkway and the Belt Parkway at the other than the Gowanus would be jammed solid with traffic. At rush hours, the traffic trying to get up onto it would be backed up solid, spilling off the ramps and back into the neighborhood for blocks. Because there were no shoulders on the elevated road on which a disabled car could pull off, one disabled car could tie up a whole lane for hours.

Moses knew what to do about that, he said: widen the Gowanus Parkway, creating six lanes instead of four, although there would still be no shoulders. That would bring the road right up to the windows of the apartments that were left along it. The cars would be so close to the buildings that on wet days the spray they kicked up would splatter the apartment windows. No matter, Moses said, the Gowanus would have to be widened.

And he widened it.

Residents of Sunset Park had pleaded with Moses to build the road along Second Avenue instead of Third. After it was built, and they saw what it had done to their neighborhood, they knew their suggestion had been correct. "That was an industrial area anyway. Building it over there wouldn't have changed anything in the area at all," Cathy Cadorine said.

But no newspaper mentioned that fact.

Of all the hundreds of public works that Robert Moses was building in New York City during the 1930's, the one whose creation most clearly manifested the same extraordinary capacities he had displayed on Long Island was the project that arose from the first and longest-held of his dreams, the dream of the "great highway that went uptown along the water" and of the great park alongside that had made him exclaim to Frances Perkins in 1914, staring from the deck of a Hudson River ferryboat at the muddy wasteland below Riverside Drive: "Couldn't this waterfront be the most beautiful thing in the world?"

All the qualities that made Robert Moses a genius of public works were needed for the realization of this dream. Its scope was all but unprecedented in urban America—the "West Side Improvement," as he named it, included not only the completion of the long-stalled, five-mile elevated express highway from the southern tip of Manhattan Island to Seventy-second Street; but also the design and construction of the extension of that highway six and a half miles north to the northern tip of Manhattan Island; the transformation of six and a half miles of muddy wasteland into a park that would make beautiful the city's western waterfront; the throwing of a "Henry Hudson Bridge" across the Harlem River that separated Manhattan from the Bronx; the continuation of the highway through the Bronx to the city line and, beyond the line, to the Saw Mill River Parkway, so that the city would have at last a true outlet to the north. And the problems in the way of its realization were unprecedented as well. At last, twenty years after he had dreamed the dream, he had the power in the city that was half of the elixir needed to transfer the dream into reality. But he still didn't have the other half of the elixir—money.

The amount needed was staggering. The work below Seventy-second Street had been carried out under a 1927 agreement between New York City and the New York Central Railroad, which was anxious for an enlarged freight yard at Thirtieth Street and longer covered train-assembling tracks further uptown because of the introduction of diesel locomotives, which could pull longer trains than steam locomotives. Under the agreement, the city gave the railroad land for an enlarged yard and for depressed tracks leading to it, the railroad in return surrendered its permanent right-of-way through Riverside Park and down Eleventh Avenue, and the railroad and city, under an incredibly complicated arrangement, were to share the cost of constructing a West Side Elevated Highway from the Battery north to Seventy-second Street, the southern border of Riverside Park, as well as the cost of covering the railroad's tracks through the park and through its northerly extension, Fort Washington Park, which ran to 192nd Street.* By 1929, the city, proceeding with the highway in typical Tammany fashion, down to its adornment with millions of dollars' worth of granite, had spent $25,000,000 as its share of the job, and the railroad had spent $84,000,000, for a total of $109,000,000. And when the Depression brought both railroad and city to the brink of bankruptcy and forced the halt of work, the job was not nearly done; out of 120 blocks in the park, for example, the tracks had been covered for only the first seven, between Seventy-second and Seventy-ninth streets. Twenty million dollars might be needed to complete the highway and track-depressing operations below Riverside Park alone, and Moses' preliminary estimates of the rest of the work indicated that the amount of money needed to finish the whole "West Side Improvement" might well equal the $109,000,000 already spent.

And the immensity of this amount was only part of the problem. From a political point of view, what seemed to make obtaining it almost impossible was the 1927 agreement, which provided that a substantial part of the cost of the Improvement was to be borne by the New York Central. The city's taxpayers had been aroused by decades of questionable dealings between the railroad and complaisant city officials, dealings such as the one that

* The public used the name "Riverside Park" to refer to both parks and so, for the sake of simplicity, will this book.

had given the railroad the permanent right-of-way through a city park and down a city avenue in the first place. They obviously would view any attempt to use their money to relieve the railroad of its obligation as another "giveaway." No sensible politician would dare to suggest such an arrangement. The railroad's share of the West Side Improvement was going to have to be paid by the railroad—or there wasn't going to be any Improvement. But the railroad was in no position to pay—and obviously wasn't going to be for years to come.

One hundred and nine million dollars was a terrible obstacle to place between a man and his dream. Since the turn of the century other men had been attempting to obtain just a small portion of that sum—enough to build the bridge over the Harlem River and short approach roads; no one but Moses had come up with a fully-thought-out plan for the reclamation of Riverside Park—and had never come close to obtaining funds for even those limited improvements. On five separate occasions since 1904, the city had drawn up plans for a "Henry Hudson Bridge," and when Moses drove up to the Harlem in 1934, the only trace of the plans he could find was the hundred-foot-high column without a statue on top of it and a number of faded billboards, one, it seemed, for every city administration of those thirty years, proclaiming the imminent start of construction. Couple the amount needed with the fact that a substantial part of it had to be provided by a near-bankrupt railroad, and, even to Moses' aides, who had watched RM work fiscal magic before, the obstacle looked insurmountable.

They watched RM set out to surmount it.

Under one part of the 1927 agreement, the New York Central had agreed to pay the city $5,000,000—and the city had agreed that it would spend that money only on the West Side Improvement. Under another part of the agreement, the railroad had agreed to pay outright part of the cost of roofing its tracks in Riverside Park; $3,200,000 of the track-roofing cost was still outstanding—which meant that the railroad owed the city a total of $8,200,000.

If Moses could get this money from the railroad, he would have taken at least a first step toward the realization of his $109,000,000 dream. But the railroad didn't have it. In order for him to get the money from the railroad, the railroad would have to get it from somewhere else first. Since the Central's own sources of credit were exhausted, Moses would have to obtain the money for the railroad himself—and he would have to give the money to the railroad's hard-eyed directors under conditions that would force them to spend it not on such urgent obligations as weekly payrolls (which the railroad, desperately short of cash, was finding it increasingly difficult to meet) but on obligations that in time of financial crisis the directors might well consider eminently deferrable: the beautification of a city park.

There were, Moses saw immediately, reasons for the railroad directors to want beautification. For one, they, as well as the city, wanted the tracks in Riverside Park covered; that was the only way the long diesel-pulled trains could be assembled without interference from weather. For another, on part of its debt to the city, the $5,000,000 part, the railroad was paying 6 percent interest, compounded annually. The railroad had not been able to meet the interest payments since 1929 and they had therefore been added to the principal. By 1934, the principal—the amount on which the railroad was paying interest—was no longer $5,000,000 but $6,500,000. Its over-all debt was therefore no longer $8,200,000 but $9,700,000. And its 1934 interest payment on the $6,500,000 would be $390,000 for that year alone. Since the Depression had forced the cost of money—interest rates—down to well below 6 percent, the railroad was paying the city much more for its money than it should have been.

Now, in the free moments of many days, Moses began to cover pages of yellow legal note pads with little clumps of figures. When aides looked over his shoulder, they saw that he was multiplying numbers together. The numbers being multiplied were millions of dollars; those he was multiplying by were percentages—the aides realized that they were interest rates. And one day the figures fit together into a pattern—a pattern that enabled him to obtain from the New York Central Railroad not $9,700,000 but $13,500,000.

The key was obtaining new cash for the Central at an interest rate that would make it possible for the railroad to accept it, use part of it to pay off the $6,500,000 debt to the city, use another part of it to pay off its $3,200,000 debt to the city, have enough left over to *give* the city an additional, new contribution for the West Side Improvement, a contribution it was not required to make under the previous agreement—and still be paying an annual interest less than the $390,000 it was now being forced to pay. Such an arrangement would give the railroad the track covering it needed while at the same time saving it money.

Moses needed a source that not only would loan money to a private business in precarious financial condition but would loan it money at a very low rate of interest. There was, he knew, such a source. It was the State of New York.

At first, this source did not look like a promising one. The Depression had made the state's own financial position shaky; even if it were steady, Governor Lehman and the Legislature would shy away from spending money to bail out a railroad whose shadowy hold over public officials was legendary.

But Moses knew that there was one source of state money that had been lying untapped ever since the Depression began: the sizable balance in the $300,000,000 Grade-Crossing Elimination Fund that had been created in 1926. No one had ever thought of using the fund to finance the West Side Improvement—Moses did not think of it himself at first—because "grade crossings" traditionally referred to the lifting of a highway over a railroad track at a single point, and the West Side Improvement, besides being as much a park as a highway project, consisted of building a highway beside or on top of a railroad track—for six and a half miles. But both a railroad track and a highway were involved in the West Side Improvement, and the best bill drafter in Albany found that there were provisions in the legislation establishing the Grade-Crossing Elimination Fund that would, by a broad interpretation, allow use of the fund for at least part of the Improvement. The interest rate on monies from the fund was, he realized, only 2 percent. Two percent of $9,700,000 was only $194,000 per year, almost $200,000 less than the interest the New York Central was now paying on its debt to the city. The railroad could accept far more than $9,700,000 from the state, give the balance to the city—and still be saving money. He suggested this course to the railroad and persuaded it to agree to accept $13,500,000—an amount on which the annual interest would be $270,000, representing a saving to the railroad of $120,000 per year at the same time it obtained its track covering. Then, to reconcile Lehman and the Legislature to the loan by making it apparent to the public that it was no "giveaway," Moses conceived a complicated device which required the railroad to place all interest payments in escrow six months in advance, while making the loan what amounted to a tax lien against all the railroad's properties in the state, properties worth many times the amount of the loan. On a yellow legal note pad, he drafted legislation authorizing the loan and told Jack Madigan to take it up to Albany. If the legislation became law, the city would be getting $13,500,000 in improvements at no cost to itself. And Robert Moses would see his longest-held dream a long step closer to becoming reality.

The legislative session was rapidly drawing to a close. Madigan painstakingly explained the bill's complexities to those legislators who had difficulty understanding them. Others—well, the railroad wanted the bill and the railroad could help persuade some of those others. When some legislators still yelled "giveaway," Moses toughened the tax-lien provision. The bill passed three days before the end of the session.

Then there was the Governor. Moses received word that Lehman didn't want to sign. The Governor, he was informed, was leery about its legality and about the "giveaway" implications. And to make matters stickier, Lehman and Moses were in the midst of a bitter battle over another Moses maneuver. Since the bill was passed during the last three days of the session, it was a "thirty-day" bill. The Governor had to sign it within thirty days of the session's end or the bill was dead. And on the twenty-ninth day after the session's end, Lehman still had not signed it.

"Moses sent me up to see him because he knew he liked me," Madigan recalls. "I was up in the Capitol at nine o'clock in the morning. And the Governor let me sit out in his outer office on my fanny from nine o'clock in the morning until five-ten in the afternoon. Twice I ran out and called Moses because I knew how worried he was. I told him, 'He's letting me sit.' Moses said something like 'Stubborn bastard!'

"Finally I got in to see him. He jumped all over me. I told him how much the city was going to get out of this.

"He says, 'Moses'll get all the credit for this.' I said, thinking fast, 'Governor, you should be able to share the credit.' He said, 'He's not the kind who likes to share much.'

"I said, 'Governor, nobody in the world knows if you're going to veto this bill or not.' His PR man was Joe Canavan,* who was one of the very best. I said, 'Have Canavan write up your own release and give it to the Sunday papers. I have glossies right here that you can use.' I said, '*Governor, tomorrow's the last day!*' "

Madigan was offering to let Lehman instead of Moses announce that he would sign the bill and reveal the benefits it would give to the city, thereby gaining identification with the project and basking in the praise that newspapers would undoubtedly bestow on everybody connected with it. Madigan was reminding the Governor that the story would undoubtedly get a good play because Saturdays are generally slow news days. He was even offering to let the Governor distribute the glossy, ready-for-newspaper-reproduction photographs of the improvements the $13,500,000 would buy.

"The Governor said, 'That'd make Bob so goddamned mad.' He smiled. But then he said, 'I need a memorandum from the Comptroller' [a written opinion, which Lehman could use to justify his signing, that the bill was constitutional]. Bob had briefed Charlie Mullins in the Comptroller's office about the bill because he knew Lehman trusted him. I said, 'Governor, Charlie Mullins is over there right now and he knows all about this.' Lehman called over there and Mullins agreed that the bill was legal. So everything worked out all right."

Of the approximately $109,000,000 that had stood between Robert Moses' dream and reality, $13,500,000 had been acquired.

There was $95,500,000 to go.

The arrangement with the New York Central soon gave Moses $4,000,000 more. As part of his plan to expand Riverside Park, he wanted to sink bulkheads out from the shoreline and fill the water behind them with rock and earth. Such fill was expensive—more than two and a half dollars per cubic foot. But Moses suddenly realized that the excavations that the Central would now be able to finish below Seventy-second Street would provide vast amounts of fill. Inquiring as to what was being done with it, he was told that it was simply being transported "somewhere on Long Island" and dumped there. He pointed out to railroad officials that if they let him send trucks to the excavations and haul it away and use it in Riverside Park, they would save the cost of transporting it. They agreed, and in this fashion he obtained 1,500,000 cubic yards of fill—$4,000,000 worth.

There was $91,500,000 to go.

"RM has this mind—he can read a piece of legislation and remember every darn thing in it," Sid Shapiro recalls. "He seemed to know the wording of every darn bill in Washington and in Albany that had ever been passed relating to public works. We were talking about the Seventy-ninth Street boat

---

* Joseph J. Canavan, former editor of the *World*.

basin and he said, 'Let's build a *real* boat basin,' " the façade of the marina decorated with stone gargoyles and behind it a fountain with jets of water arching from the mouths of brass turtles. "Have you ever heard of a boat basin with gargoyles? Well, I hadn't either. But he remembered some obscure federal statute that had been passed—oh, years before—to encourage the use of artwork on public works." If we put on gargoyles, Moses said, not only would the boat basin be beautified, but the money from the fund could be used to build it. "One day, RM said, 'What happened to some fund I remember that was set up [by a private philanthropist] so that it could only be used to decorate a public project with ornamental friezes? Is there any money left in that?' Well, we looked it up and there was. So RM said, 'Well, then, let's have a frieze.' We told our boat basin guy about this. These guys are usually hard-boiled fellows, think in terms of jetties, groins, sheet metal, riprap. When you tell one of them gargoyles and friezes, he almost falls off his designer's stool." But the two funds contained a total of almost $100,000 for which the boat-basin phase of Robert Moses' dream would be eligible.

And there was $91,400,000 to go.

The Seventy-ninth Street boat basin was, of course, the magnificent structure Moses had envisioned for Riverside Park years before—a combination marina, riverside restaurant and pedestrian promenade. In the plans that Moses finally approved, throwing his arms around chief architectural engineer Clinton Lloyd in joy, the top level was a large traffic circle that allowed cars coming from the city's interior access to the "great highway along the water." The center of the circle was hollow. Down inside it, on the middle level, was a cool, shadowy interior courtyard. The center of the courtyard was the fountain, its murmur just loud enough to drown out the noise of cars and city above it. Around the fountain was a low marble bench for passers-by to sit on. On the river side of the courtyard were three high, wide arches. Beyond them was a broad outdoor terrace, overlooking the marina below it and the river beyond, designed to hold both the gaily canopied tables of the riverside restaurant and the broad, tree-shaded pedestrian promenade. And the bottom level of the structure, completely concealed inside it and reached by access roads circling down around its outside from the traffic circle above, was a two-hundred-car garage for the owners of boats docked in the marina. The structure did not resemble a railroad grade-crossing elimination at all, but by coincidence Harold Ickes, the PWA Administrator, perturbed that PWA expenditures were not generating enough immediate employment, had recently promised quick approval for projects for which plans were ready—and when a reporter had asked what kind of projects the administration had in mind, Ickes "said he thought that elimination of highway grade crossings over railroad tracks offered one means . . . that could be undertaken immediately." There were no highways over the tracks around Seventy-ninth Street to be eliminated, but there were tracks to be covered and roads to be built—and Ickes sounded anxious for plans.

Working night and day, Lloyd and a team of engineers from Madigan's consulting firm completed them in a week, and Madigan headed down to Washington with the blueprints under his arm. The first thing that PWA officials there noticed when they unrolled them was their new, very prominently displayed title: "Seventy-ninth Street Grade Elimination Structure." If the officials noticed that it didn't resemble any other grade-crossing elimination structure ever built, they didn't mention the fact, the only demurrer coming from one narrow-minded bureaucrat who commented that "the brass turtles and comfort stations were a little too much to be tacked on to a grade crossing" and slashed off the $154,000 cost of those items, and Madigan returned with a promise that the PWA would chip in the $1,766,000 that the materials for the rest of the structure would cost. Then Moses told La Guardia that for just $154,000 more the city could have not just a boat basin but a *beautiful* boat basin—and the Mayor scrounged up that money. Then Moses told the CWA that the materials for the project were paid for and he could put men to work immediately, and the CWA contributed more than $3,000,000 for wages on work on the boat basin, bringing the total money raised for the structure to more than $5,000,000.

And there was $86,400,000 to go.

"RM never seemed to run out of ideas," Shapiro would recall. "He said to us, 'We'll build the highway part of the way along the New York Central tracks, so we'll be eligible for state aid to railroads.' Because there were boat basins along a river involved, he found clauses in the [federal] Rivers and Harbors Act under which we could get money. There was federal highway money available, of course, so he said, 'We'll tie it in with the George Washington Bridge, so it'll be an interstate highway and we can get funds that way.' Because he had to demolish some buildings ["You'd have to tear down a few buildings at Seventy-second Street and bring the highway around a curve," he had told Frances Perkins twenty years before, and that was just how it worked out], he even found a way we were eligible for federal housing funds. On that one project, we had housing, interstate highway, rivers and harbors, and railroads." Moses obtained a total of more than $12,000,000 from such sources.

And there was $74,000,000 to go.

Still $74,000,000 to go. And much of this money was needed for materials and equipment which could be obtained in no other way than by putting up hard cash, cash that Moses didn't have. He had to economize.

And he knew where to do it. The cost of the Riverside Park he had envisioned as a young man, a park in which the ugly railroad tracks were covered—covered with lush lawns and trees, a park crammed lavishly with marinas and waterfront promenades and tennis courts and playgrounds—was running about $8,000,000 per mile. He continued to develop the park lavishly for the first two of its 6.7 miles, the two miles bordered by a neighborhood inhabited by the upper and "comfortable middle" classes he liked to develop parks for. But for the rest of its length—from about 110th Street, where the neighborhood was becoming perceptibly poorer—he scrimped, putting in few improvements and doing those in a cheap, slapdash style. One Hundred and Twenty-fifth Street was the southern border of Negro Harlem. Already, in 1934, black faces were appearing on many of the side streets behind Riverside Drive. From 125th Street north, Robert Moses put almost no improvements into Riverside Park, designing its northern 3.3 miles with one aim in mind: to do them as cheaply as possible.

The aim was accomplished. The development of the southern two miles of Riverside Park—the stretch south of 110th Street—cost $16,300,000, or about $8,000,000 per mile. The development of the northern 4.7 miles of Riverside Park—the stretch north of 110th Street that included Negro Harlem—cost $7,900,000, or about $1,700,000 per mile, and thus saved Moses about $6,300,000 per mile, or a total of $29,000,000 less than it it would have cost if he had built it to the same standards as the southern section.

And there was $45,000,000 to go.

Of this $45,000,000, about $15,000,000 represented the cost Moses was figuring for the section of the Improvement above 192nd Street, so that only about $30,000,000 stood between him and the completion of his dream the length of Riverside Park. He informed the Board of Estimate that $20,000,000 of this amount would be for labor, and he could get the labor free from the CWA if only he had the $10,000,000 for the rest of the materials and equipment. Were they going to let the money be wasted for want of $10,000,000? The Board caved in and gave it to him—or, rather, since it didn't have the money to give, it authorized a $10,000,000 assessment on Riverside Drive property owners. At the same time that he was telling the Board that he could get the $20,000,000 worth of labor from the CWA if only they gave him $10,000,000 worth of materials, he was telling the CWA that he could get $10,000,000 worth of materials from the Board if only they gave him $20,000,000 worth of labor. The CWA authorized the rehabilitation of Riverside Park. It authorized the building of the Henry Hudson Parkway through the park; since the CWA was not allowed to build highways or parkways, it called the parkway "a park access road" on the report it submitted to Washington.

And he had the $30,000,000.

He had all the money needed to complete Riverside Park. He had 6.7 miles of the dream, enough to get it all the way up to 192nd Street, in the bag.

There were three miles—and $15,000,000—to go.

North of 192nd Street the shoreline of Manhattan Island climbed steeply away from the Hudson River into the high bluffs of Fort Tryon and Inwood Hill parks. There was a sharp, quick break in the bluffs where the Harlem River sliced through to meet the Hudson and then the bluffs were part of the

Bronx, and perched atop them and on the slopes leading down to the two rivers was the residential community of Spuyten Duyvil, somewhat more thickly settled than Riverdale, which lay between it and 263rd Street, the city's northern border.

All previous plans for a through highway to the north envisioned the highway swinging sharply inland when it got to Fort Tryon Park so as not to disturb the wooded beauty of its hills, which formed a serene setting for the Cloisters that John D. Rockefeller, Jr., was building atop them, or those of Inwood Hill Park beyond, which constituted Manhattan's last piece of unspoiled forest. Under these plans the highway would run along the easternmost edge of the two parks, taking a thin slice from the edge at the point where it sloped down to meet the rest of the city, and obtaining the rest of its right-of-way from the city streets adjoining the parks and from condemning the relatively few single-family houses that had been built along them. Besides leaving the two forest parks unspoiled, this route had the further advantage of allowing the Henry Hudson Bridge to cross the Harlem River not by leaping from high bluff to high bluff, which would require an expensive high-level bridge, but by crossing from the low land east of Inwood Hill Park to a low-lying section of the Bronx opposite it called Marble Hill that was the site of nothing except a filthy shanty town and some boxcars that had somehow been left on the site for years—no one was sure how they had gotten there—and were now serving as the home for about a hundred homeless men. Marble Hill could use a good cleaning up anyway. Once in the Bronx, the highway would run through Marble Hill and a corner of Riverdale until it reached Van Cortlandt Park, where it would take right-of-way from the park's westernmost edge so as not to disturb it any more than necessary.

Moses found that using this route would cause him problems—financial problems.

Avoiding Fort Tryon and Inwood Hill parks meant that Moses would not be able to use the "free" labor provided for him on "park access roads" by the CWA. The parkway would have to run alongside the parks, on city streets. Under existing federal legislation, it would therefore fall under the jurisdiction of the Bureau of Public Roads—and the legislation establishing the Bureau specifically prohibited it from extending any aid, for laborers' pay or any other expenses, on any road leading to a toll facility. Since Moses was planning to finance the construction of the Henry Hudson Bridge through the sale of bonds of the Henry Hudson Parkway Authority he had had the Legislature create, he would have to have tolls on the bridge to pay off the bonds. The city would therefore have to pay for the parkway north of Riverside Park. Furthermore, there was the cost of condemning buildings needed for the right-of-way. Even if a state or federal agency had been willing to pay for the buildings, it could not legally do so; under one of the most fundamental provisions of the City Charter, only the city had the power to condemn property within its borders. Paying for both labor and land north of Riverside Park would cost the city about $5,000,000 more.

Robert Moses decided not to swing inland when he got to Fort Tryon Park.

Running the parkway straight through that park and Inwood Hill solved many of his financial problems at a single stroke. The land acquisition problem was solved instantly and completely; since park land was already owned by the city, no land would have to be acquired. As for CWA-paid labor, it couldn't be used on a road without approval from the Bureau of Public Roads, but it could be used on "park access drives"; in fact, the CWA looked favorably upon the building of such drives because they made parks more accessible to the public. The sections of parkway running into Fort Tryon and Inwood Hill parks certainly met the definition of "park access drives" and who was to say where they stopped; why could not the drive continue into the park itself—and, perhaps, across it? Moses had learned from his previous dealings with the CWA that once he got a project in a park started, once he got the first stake driven for it, it was almost impossible for the CWA to refuse to let him complete it. Run the parkway through Fort Tryon and Inwood Hill parks and the cost of the northern section of the West Side Improvement would be not $15,000,000 but no more than $10,000,000—which happened to be the amount that the Henry Hudson Parkway Authority—Robert Moses, sole member—was authorized to raise by the sale of its toll-revenue-secured bonds. Using the direct route through the parks would, moreover, have other financial advantages as well: Moses' preliminary discussions with bankers had demonstrated to him that they had no great enthusiasm for buying bonds for a toll bridge that would be located only a few hundred yards from a free bridge—the present Harlem River drawbridge on Broadway. They believed that drivers would not pay a toll if a free alternative was so close by, particularly if the parkway's drawbridge also had to be raised—if only occasionally—when a ship came through. Moses didn't feel their argument was correct—he was sure drivers would be willing to pay to get off jammed Broadway and onto a modern parkway—but placing the Henry Hudson Bridge on the high bluff a mile to the west of the Broadway bridge would make the bridge high enough to allow ships to pass underneath it. He was sure that the bankers would then have no possible reason for a lack of enthusiasm for the project. Amortizing the forty-year bonds he wanted to issue could be done if only 2,000,000 of the 14,250,000 cars that came into and out of Manhattan each year over the Broadway bridge used the Henry Hudson instead and paid a ten-cent toll on it—and he was sure that one out of every seven drivers would pay ten cents per trip for the added convenience.

But Moses found that vision was not in plentiful supply on Wall Street. He had felt sure that this $10,000,000, the last $10,000,000, all that was left between him and the realization of his dream, would be the easiest part of the cost of the West Side Improvement to obtain. Instead, it proved to be the hardest.

The Depression had ended the myth that the bonds of public authorities, even public authorities whose credit was backed by a municipality, were risk-free investments. Since Black Thursday, more than two hundred municipalities across the United States had defaulted on their *own* bonds, turning them into worthless pieces of paper. And if the bankers needed an example closer to home—and bankers didn't—they knew how close New York City had come to default. Michael J. (Jack) Madigan, who was trying to persuade investment bankers to agree to purchase the bonds if the Authority put them on the market, had to report back to Moses that the bankers were afraid to make the investment.

The son of an impoverished bartender, Jack Madigan had come out of the Pennsylvania hard-coal country in 1907 at the age of thirteen to enter the construction industry as a waterboy lugging buckets for thirsty work gangs, and by the time, in 1928, he was promoted to supervisor for one of the Jones Beach contractors, he had spent his whole life with the gangs. With his ruddy, square face and grizzled hair he looked like one of them, and he was as boisterous as they as he crowded with them into South Shore taverns after work to wash the sand of the barrier beach out of his throat. His "dese, dose and dem" speech revealed his lack of formal education; he was addicted to awesome malapropisms: "From the standing point of finances," he would say of Tammany's handling of the Triborough Bridge project, "what a terrible finesco!"

But during the tension of the Jones Beach construction—the firm Madigan worked for was the one that went broke on the job—Moses came to know a different Jack Madigan, a deliberate, mild-mannered man who, when his opinion was solicited, would stand very still, his feet close together, his eyes staring into the distance for a long time before he was ready to give it—and who, when he was ready, gave it in a voice that was quiet, firm and precise. When he quit his job and with a friend, Richard V. Hyland, formed Madigan-Hyland, Inc., Consulting Engineers, with "offices" in the furnished room they shared over a Rockville Centre restaurant and files stored in the back seat of Hyland's car, Moses gave them Long Island Park Commission contracts, contracts that made Madigan a millionaire.

And the uneducated Irishman filled an abandoned cigar factory in Long Island City with expensive, college-trained talent—among his employees, whom he called "my Phi Beta Kappa keys," was the brilliant Emil F. Praeger, who during World War II, as chief engineer of the U.S. Navy, would design the floating dry docks that were used in the Normandy landings.

Moses found, moreover, that Madigan was talented with money as well as men—a fact the author learned during a series of three-hour private Madigan lectures on the financing of public works. (One lecture began and ended with the words "Money means *all:* unless you get it, you're going nowhere, brother.") "He had an extraordinary native shrewdness," Moses said, and when Moses had to select a representative for his first attempt to tap the sources of private funds that Wall Street bankers controlled—the sale of Henry Hudson Parkway Authority bonds—he selected the bartender's son. He selected right. A banker was later to say, "He can tailor a bond issue as neatly as an artisan assembles a stained-glass window."

But bankers, burned by the losses they had taken on municipal bonds during the Depression, would not even try on the Henry Hudson bond issue for size. In the preceding twenty-four months, not a single new issue of such bonds had been successfully floated in the United States. The bankers informed Madigan that they were not interested in the Authority's bonds unless the "coverage" of those bonds (the earnings that would enable the Authority to pay interest on and amortize them) was at least 1.75 and preferably 2.00 (twice as much as would be needed for that interest paying and amortization). "They were scared, that's all," Madigan would recall.

Moses' own surveys had convinced him that not merely one out of every seven but one out of every three cars using the Broadway bridge would pay ten cents for an easier trip over the Henry Hudson Bridge. He did not have the slightest doubt of it; in fact, he considered that figure ridiculously conservative. And one-third of the Broadway bridge traffic was 3,560,000 cars per year—or, at ten cents per car, $356,000 in toll revenues. You could subtract the $70,500 annual cost of paying toll collectors and keeping the bridge painted and in repair and still have left over almost twice as much as would be required to pay the yearly interest and amortization on the $10,000,000 bond issue which would provide the funds needed to build a six-lane Henry Hudson Bridge across the Ship Canal, and to continue the parkway north to link up at the city line with the Saw Mill River Parkway.

But Moses' figures were not conservative enough for the bankers. "We were trying to sell them the idea that people would pay ten cents to avoid that terrible route up Broadway," Madigan recalls. "They couldn't see why you would pay ten cents when you could go the other way for nothing. The idea that people would pay for convenience hadn't yet been established."

All through the summer of 1934, Madigan-Hyland counted the cars traveling north and south on Broadway and Riverside Drive to show the bankers the tremendous volume on which the new bridge would be able to draw. But the bankers still balked. "They wanted illustrations of previous situations where a free—if less convenient—bridge was competing with a toll bridge and the toll bridge had been successful, and there weren't many," Madigan recalls. "Most toll bridges were built to give access to a place where there wasn't any other access. We finally found one in Miami [where the toll Venetian Causeway was highly successful although in competition with a free County Causeway]." But the bankers still balked.

Madigan finally had to report to Moses that their final decision was that they would purchase no more than $3,100,000 in Authority bonds, an amount for which the traffic *they* estimated would use the Henry Hudson Bridge would provide 1.75 coverage.

Moses worked frantically to get the cost down to that level. By persuading the CWA that the construction of the parkway through Fort Tryon and Inwood Hill parks could be called in its entirety a "park project," he got the labor for that section of parkway free. When he persuaded La Guardia to pick up the tab for hire of the construction equipment needed, the entire cost of that section—$700,000—could be knocked off the amount of bonds that had to be sold, reducing that amount from $10,000,000 to $9,300,000. On the northern, or Riverdale, side of the bridge, he had already planned the parkway to run along Spuyten Duyvil Parkway for almost two miles, so that only limited condemnation would be needed. Now the Authority could no longer pay for even that condemnation. La Guardia said the city couldn't do it, either; an estimated $2,500,000 was required and there was no money around for it. The only solution was to run as much of the parkway as possible through the only city-owned land in Riverdale: Van Cortlandt Park.

Doing this reduced the cost of the right-of-way to $1,260,000. The Authority had been supposed to pay for the engineering plans for the northern and southern sections of the parkway. Moses persuaded State Highway Commissioner Arthur W. Brandt, one of his admirers, to have state engineers draw the plans. This saved about $200,000 more, and reduced the amount to be raised to $9,100,000. Then Moses got a break. In December 1934, Madigan returned from Washington with word that as soon as the new Congress convened, it would make a new appropriation to the PWA of $400,000,000—on which the agency would be allowed to waive the past requirement that grants for road-related projects had to be matched by state contributions. Rushing to Albany, Moses persuaded Lehman to use part of the new money the state would receive to construct the Riverdale portion of the parkway. Since this section had been expected to cost $2,750,000, the amount to be raised could be reduced to $6,350,000. Moses went back to La Guardia. Was the Mayor going to deny the city this $10,000,000 project for want of $1,260,000 worth of right-of-way? he asked. The Mayor agreed that he could not let that happen. He agreed that the city would purchase the right-of-way needed to widen Spuyten Duyvil Parkway, although at the moment he didn't know where he would find the money. The amount needed to be raised by the bond sale was reduced to $5,090,000.

Try as he would, however, Moses seemed unable to reduce the amount any further. He had already sliced from the Authority's obligation every cost except that of the bridge itself. Federal funds could not be used for the bridge because it was a toll facility; state funds could not be used because the Legislature would never authorize another highway expenditure in the city; the city had no money to help. Time and again, Moses sent Madigan back to his engineers; time and again, Praeger, whom Madigan had assigned to head the team working on the project, gave him the same answer: six lanes of traffic were needed on the bridge; a bridge with six lanes on a single level or deck was so wide that three arches running from one side of the river to the other were needed to support it; and a three-arch bridge could not be built for a penny less than $5,000,000. It certainly could not be built for $3,100,000. Praeger had costed out a narrower, two-deck bridge built on two arches. But the weight of such a bridge was virtually the same as that of the wider bridge; since that weight had to be carried by two arches instead of three arches, the arches had to be made much stronger; the cost of the two-deck bridge was actually a little higher than the single-decker.

"He [Moses] was really totally discouraged," Madigan recalls. "I had never seen him so low." The two men had agreed that Madigan would hold one final meeting with the bankers, and on the Friday morning in December on which that meeting was held, Moses kept looking up from his work in his 80 Centre Street office to ask his secretaries if there was any word from the Irishman.

Madigan arrived at Centre Street shortly before noon and told Moses that the last-ditch attempt had failed and that "we might just as well give up the idea that they would change their minds. Three-million-one was as high as they would go." The engineer recalls that he had been scheduled to have lunch with Moses, but that "we didn't feel much like eating. I went out and got into my car to go back to my office."

But then, Madigan recalls, as "I was driving along, I happened to think of a bridge I had once heard about in Havergrass [Haverstraw], Pennsylvania, across the Schuylkill River. It had been built by the Pennsylvania Railroad, but then the railroad didn't need it any more and gave it to the community, see? It was a narrow two-lane bridge because there was just enough room on it for a couple of railroad tracks. The community put a floor on it and used it for cars. But then, see, they decided they needed more capacity so they just strengthened up the steel and put a second deck on it.

"Well, it came to me just like that. I remember I leaned forward and I said to the chauffeur, 'Step on it, goddammit!' We hurried up to the office and I had a great chief engineer—Emil Praeger—and he was there and I said to him, 'Suppose we left out one of our archways [arches], strengthened up the other two of them and made the bridge only four lanes wide—how much could we possibly reduce the cost?' So the office worked all day Saturday and all day Sunday, and all night, too, see, and by Monday noon we knew that everything was working for us. There was rock on both sides of the river, see, so you could put the weight we had been going to put three arches on on two and the rock would hold it. And we knew that we could build what you know as the lower deck of the Henry Hudson Bridge for $3,100,000, and we were able to show that if the traffic was to be up to our estimates, and we needed more lanes, we would be able to strengthen up the steel on the archways and build a second deck on top of the lower deck at a future date when more money was available.

"When I brought it in to Moses, he studied it a little bit before he said anything. And then he looked up and said, 'Now we have a chance!' "

By the end of that week, the bankers had agreed to purchase $3,100,000 of Henry Hudson Parkway Authority bonds, the money to be used to construct a one-deck, four-lane bridge. And they had agreed to incorporate in the purchase agreement a provision that if traffic on the bridge lived up to Moses' estimates and warranted further expansion, they would, as soon as the traffic reached that point, purchase an additional $2,000,000 of Authority bonds, which would enable the Authority to reinforce the two arches and the steelwork on the bridge and build a second deck on it. Although the lawyers for the Authority and the bankers would not finish dotting the *i*'s and crossing the *t*'s in the agreement until March 1935, Moses and Madigan knew the money was in the bag. The financing of the West Side Improvement was complete.

* * *

In later years, as he grew steadily richer, Jack Madigan would become addicted to the way of life of the rich. The living room of his Fifth Avenue apartment would be furnished in shades of gold—golden carpet, golden loveseats, golden armchairs. But over the long golden sofa, in the place of honor in the room, hung a simple engineer's sketch in black and white: a rendering of the arches—two arches, not three—that support the Henry Hudson Bridge.

Robert Moses had envisioned the West Side Improvement with the eyes of a visionary. He had discerned a way to finance it with the eyes of a banker, a very astute banker. The financing of the West Side Improvement was a supreme example, perhaps *the* supreme example, of the practical side of Robert Moses' genius. For more than half a century, New York City had strained to find a way to build the West Side Improvement and had been unable to find sufficient funds to build it on even the most limited scale. In slightly more than one year, Robert Moses had found the funds to build it—on a grand scale. True, one source of his financing, the federal relief program, had not been available before in the dimensions it was available under CWA and WPA. But that was only one source out of more than a score that he pulled together. The catalyst that finally brought the West Side Improvement to fruition wasn't Washington's largesse but Moses' genius for turning a dream into reality, for accomplishment, for Getting It Done.

But Robert Moses was in the city now, not on the Island. While on the Island his proposals had been opposed most vigorously by selfish interests, in the city his West Side Improvement proposal was being opposed vigorously by people whose interests were not selfish at all, who cared very deeply about the city and who felt that while an Improvement was needed, the form in which Moses was proposing to build it was not the best form—was in fact a form that might even bring the city harm, harm that might outweigh the good—and who also felt that it was not necessary to build it in that form at all.

Among these men were two young reformers, Bill Exton and Bob Weinberg.

Robert C. Weinberg was the Park Department architect whose early admiration for Moses had already been tempered by his refusal to take neighborhood preferences into account in the designing of neighborhood playgrounds. William Exton, Jr., was a witty young man-about-town whose tireless pursuit of romance (his list of girlfriends was legendary among his friends) was constantly being interrupted by his penchant for working night and day for reform causes that caught his eye.

Although Exton and Weinberg were both still in their twenties, both Harvard graduates (the brilliant Exton had graduated at nineteen) and both active members of the Citizens Union, the City Club and the Park Association, they had never been close friends. But the West Side Improvement was to make them close. For Exton loved Inwood Hill Park and Weinberg loved

Spuyten Duyvil. And each of the two young men felt that the "Improvement" would destroy the thing that he loved.

Inwood Hill Park was not a park at all, but a wilderness, a wonderful wilderness, a last reminder, crowded into the craggy hills in the northwesternmost corner of Manhattan Island by the relentless spread of concrete, that once almost all of the island had been covered with lush green forests. To the east, the hills sloped down into a valley that opened on a beautiful, peaceful cove formed by a U-curve in the Harlem River. In the valley, the site of the old Algonquin village of Shora-Kap-Kock* ("in between the hills"), was a little museum operated by an Indian woman and a pottery studio, complete with kilns capable of the most delicate ceramics. In the cove, the last bit of natural waterfront on Manhattan Island and the reputed site of the landing of a longboat from Henry Hudson's *Half Moon* three hundred years before and of a battle between the longboat crew and the Algonquins, stood a giant tulip tree under which Hudson had held a powwow with the Indians. On the opposite, or Hudson River, side of the park's hills, two hundred feet below the steep escarpment that formed their western edge, was a narrow strip of landfill that held a New York Central roadbed. But in the three hundred acres covered by the hills themselves, there was hardly a sign of the hand of man. The Lords of Lord & Taylor had once lived in two mansions on the escarpment, but these had burned to the ground decades before. When Exton turned off the city's asphalt streets and wandered up the steep slopes—it was their steepness that had saved them from development—he found himself in a different world, a world of wild underbrush and towering trees. Hiking up to their crest, under foliage so thick that it all but blotted out the sun, he could pick wild hackberries and blueberries or, in spring and early summer, could stop and look for a while at the fragrant purple- or white-blossomed lilac bushes, some of them three times as tall as he. At the crest, out on the escarpment, was a view that guidebooks marveled over—"perhaps the finest Manhattan offers," said one: the broad sweep of the Hudson below and, looming above the river on its far shore, the endless miles of the Palisades, unmarred north of the George Washington Bridge by a single man-made structure. If Exton sat so that he couldn't see the bridge, there was nothing to remind him of what he had left behind at the foot of the hills except for the occasional passage, far below him, of a little toy New York Central train.

Exton loved that world. "On the top, there was a big outcropping of granite on the north end, and I used to go up there in April and just lie on it in the sun and look down at the water. I was no great outdoorsman, I'm not trying to say that. But when I went into Inwood Hill, I really felt that I had gotten away from the city. And sometimes I needed that feeling."

The idea of altering that world horrified him. "It was the only real woodland left on Manhattan," he would recall years later. "It was the last hunk of primeval forest in the whole metropolitan area. It was unique. It was irreplaceable."

---

* Origin of the name of Spuyten Duyvil's Kappock Street.

And to alter it with a *highway!* "When you were up on top there, you were away from the roar of cars and the smell of gasoline. It was the only place on Manhattan where you could still say that." Moses' proposed Henry Hudson Parkway would bring the roar and the smell right into that beautiful spot. In fact, it would, to a large extent, eradicate it, bury it under six lanes—140 feet in width—of concrete, since Moses' plan was to run the highway right along the escarpment. Moses was saying that running the road through the park would destroy "only a few trees." Exton knew that couldn't be true: so thick were the towering elms, maples and oriental pines that no road 140 feet wide could be picked through them without cutting down hundreds. A highway would have values—Exton, having served on City Club committees studying the traffic problem, was aware of the need for a northern outlet—but this unique, irreplaceable forest offered the city other values that a highway would destroy, and "it just didn't make sense" to destroy them if there was any alternate route available.

Weinberg saw other values in Spuyten Duyvil, the residential community located atop the bluffs that faced Inwood Hill across the Harlem River. The community was not a "prestige" area like Fieldston directly to the north; but it was proof that even within a large city even families without wealth could find peacefulness, seclusion and beauty. Its modest single-family homes—there were only three small apartment houses in Spuyten Duyvil then—were built on small plots. But they were built along ravines that led down to the Hudson and along lanes that rambled among flower gardens and picturesque rock formations and were shaded by lordly oaks and elms. A reporter who visited Spuyten Duyvil in 1935 wrote in surprise that it was a "village," a village in the midst of a city, a village straight out of "some remote part of rural England," complete to its four big, fieldstone- and ivy-covered English country churches. It was a village that possessed a beautiful view—many of its homes enjoyed a magnificent prospect of the Hudson and the Palisades—and an asset that was even more valuable in the city: quiet. Tucked into a corner of the Bronx as it was, it had no through traffic; the only thoroughfare wider than a country lane in all Spuyten Duyvil was "Spuyten Duyvil Parkway," a two-lane road whose right-of-way, lined by trees so big that their branches met over it umbrella fashion, was barely thirty feet. Moses' proposal to turn it into a 140-foot-wide Henry Hudson Parkway by tearing down hundreds of the trees and condemning lawns of the bordering houses horrified the community. The road would split the community in half, make it difficult to get from one side to the other, and would funnel through it a great stream of traffic. "It will be the end of beautiful Spuyten Duyvil," wailed one resident. Weinberg—whose work in city planning at Harvard and, after graduation, with the pioneering urbanologist Werner Hegeman had taught him the importance of human values in a city—was interested in Spuyten Duyvil both because his family owned real estate there and because the community embodied so many human values. He began to study Moses' plan, and his conclusions were the same as Exton's: that "it made no sense" if there was any alternate route available.

And as the two young men began to study Moses' West Side Improvement plan together, they realized immediately that there *was* an alternate route—the one that had been proposed before Moses, a route that, upon reaching the southern border of Inwood Hill Park, swung inland so that it would run not through the most beautiful portion of the park but along its eastern edge and adjoining city streets, that would cross the Harlem River on a low-level bridge, inland from the Hudson, whose northern terminus would not be Spuyten Duyvil but the Marble Hill shanty town in the hollow below it, and that would continue north not through Spuyten Duyvil but through largely uninhabited areas of Marble Hill until it reached Van Cortlandt Park, where it could run just inside the park's edges, taking just a thin slice from it, until it reached the Saw Mill River Parkway.

There were, as Exton and Weinberg saw it, certain obvious advantages to this alternative: it would spare Inwood Hill and Spuyten Duyvil, eliminate the Marble Hill shanty town, and, because a low-level bridge costs less than a high-level, be less expensive than Moses' plan. (Condemnation costs would still be minimal because most of the right-of-way would be taken from the park edge and adjoining streetbeds; only a few single-family homes would have to be condemned.) Their route was only three-quarters of a mile longer, an inconsequential factor when weighed against the preservation of the city's last virgin woodland and a uniquely peaceful residential community.

As Exton and Weinberg had been thinking about the alternatives, moreover, they had come to realize that their route had certain other advantages, not so obvious but, perhaps, even more important. It was difficult for them to define these advantages, because in the early 1930's there was almost no literature to draw upon; it would not be for more than a decade, in fact, that terms to explain what they were thinking would come into common coinage—like "ecology" and "environment" and "human scale." Moreover, the defining might well not bring them much popularity, they knew, because a nation that worshipped the engineer was not yet ready to be told that the engineer's values might not be the last word in highway design. But they struggled to define them nonetheless.

"I remember realizing that he [Moses] was thinking in terms of the view of the river, the view that the motorist would have—he was thinking in terms of the motoring public, of automobiles," Exton says. "Well, a motorist spends a few seconds at a spot and maybe he can't even look at it; maybe he has to be looking at the car ahead of him. But the pedestrian spends a long time at a spot. He can sit down and look at it. So it's the pedestrian we should be thinking of. And then there was the damage to the park itself. Cutting down the trees would probably interfere with the natural drainage system, and then you'd have to start building drains and God knows what else." Weinberg, putting *his* thoughts in writing, wrote Exton that building a parkway through Spuyten Duyvil would, simply by making Spuyten Duyvil more accessible, bring many new residents—and many apartment buildings—to the area and to all Riverdale. Therefore, before the parkway was built, plans to accommodate the new residents should be made. If apartment houses were simply plumped down helter-skelter onto Riverdale's narrow country lanes, their residents' cars would jam them, turning Riverdale into just another extension of the noisy, traffic-jammed city. If a few of the streets were widened, and if apartment-house building was restricted to those streets by zoning, and if areas near them were zoned for stores, the apartment residents would be able to walk to stores and would therefore not have to do so much driving within Riverdale, and the quiet, country serenity of the non-apartment areas could be preserved. But Moses refused to do any advance planning himself—he would not even allow Riverdale civic leaders to tell him where overpasses across the parkway should be built to be most convenient for the community—or to allow anyone else to do any: to minimize community antagonism, he kept the exact route of the parkway secret as long as possible, which made advance zoning changes impracticable. "These are not competition projects, but units in the living life of the people" that will "affect the daily life of the thousands of individuals and families who live within the adjacent neighborhoods," Weinberg wrote. "Before the West Side Improvement is built, its effect on those neighborhoods should receive greater study. . . ."

Analyzing the rest of the West Side Improvement, Exton and Weinberg did what no one else in the city was doing: took a close look at Moses' plans. Moses had stated that the Henry Hudson Parkway would run through only "a corner" of Van Cortlandt Park. Actually, the two young reformers found, it would run through its center. And the location of a giant cloverleaf planned in the center to provide an interconnection with another parkway Moses was proposing—the Mosholu—was near the only fresh-water marsh of any size left in all New York. When biology teachers had protested to one of Moses' aides about the destruction of part of the marsh, the last spot in the city at which students could study marsh plants, birds and animals, the Moses Man had assured them that "destruction" was an inexact term; "beautification" was more suitable, for Commissioner Moses planned to "landscape" the marsh by dredging it to create a series of "lagoons" with formal shrubbery along their edges. And, the aide went on, they needn't worry that the job would be only half done; the Commissioner was always thorough: the marsh was going to be landscaped not only near the cloverleaf but along its entire length. One of the teachers begged Exton to fight for "one of the most beautiful spots, with a riot of plant life and birds. . . . I wondered how shortsighted officials could expect any 'planted shrubs' would equal that dense thicket." The primeval wilderness of Inwood Hill Park was not the only priceless and irreplaceable natural asset that would be lost to the city and its people forever if Moses was allowed to carry out his plan, Exton realized.

And as Exton and Weinberg proceeded with their study, they realized that there was yet another, vastly more important, natural asset that was going to be lost to the city: its waterfront.

"It didn't require much brains to see that running the highway in Riverside Park along the water would have the effect of making sure the waterfront itself could never be used for a park," Weinberg was to recall. It "would forever eliminate for recreational purposes several miles of the most beautiful waterfront in the world." Except at scattered, difficult-to-reach locations, people would no longer be able to stroll beside the broad river, play beside it, fish in it or picnic beside it. They would no longer be able even to look at it in peace; there would be a massive barrier of steel and concrete—and the roar of the motors of countless cars—between the watcher and the water. There should be a highway through Riverside Park—agreed. But why could the highway not run where every other planner wanted it to run—atop the New York Central tracks that ran either up the center of the park or close to the slopes leading up to Riverside Drive? That would leave the rest of the park free for recreation—all the way down to the waterfront—as well as free from automobiles, and overpasses or underpasses could easily allow pedestrians to cross the highway to get to it.

What lay between the two young reformers and Moses was partly a question of values.

Moses' had been formed in a different age, the age, twenty years and more in the past, when *he* had been a young reformer. To understand his dream for the West Side Improvement, one had to understand the age in which he had dreamed it.

In that age, parks had been for the upper and "comfortable middle" classes and one of the things those classes wanted most to do in parks was to drive through them—at the slow, leisurely speeds of the era—and enjoy their scenery. In that age, therefore, it made sense for a road through a park to be placed at its most scenic location—in the case of Riverside Park, at the river's edge.

But things had changed. There had been 125,101 motor vehicles in New York City in 1914; there were 804,620 in New York City in 1934—and additional hundreds of thousands in the Westchester and New Jersey suburbs that would also pour cars onto the Henry Hudson Parkway. Heavy traffic on Moses' Long Island parkways was already beginning to make driving on them less and less a source of pleasure and more and more a source of pain—or at least irritation; their value as a source of beauty and pleasure in themselves was already clearly diminishing.

At the same time, moreover, the need for providing and preserving other values was becoming more important. Cities were growing. Their people were being cut off more and more from nature. They needed every chance they could be given to see it and feel it around them. "Recreation" had been the key word among park enthusiasts when Moses had started building parks; now, "conservation" was being heard more and more. In a New York in which concrete was devouring green grass and trees more hungrily every year, nothing was more necessary of conservation than the last piece of natural woodland on Manhattan, or a beautiful and unique swamp in Van Cortlandt Park—and its waterfront.

Moreover, as Weinberg had pointed out, the highway was going to be, inevitably, a part of neighborhoods. The West Side Improvement could give adjoining neighborhoods a priceless bounty—a great waterfront on which they could, without expense or travel, "walk abroad and recreate" themselves and their families. And if the river were ever cleansed of pollution—and this possibility should be considered, no matter how remote, for a public improvement such as Moses was proposing might well last for centuries and anything could happen in centuries—they could swim in it, swim almost at their very doorstep. Build a highway along that waterfront, erect huge viaducts of steel and pavements of concrete at the water's edge, and that waterfront would be gone, possibly forever, lost to the hungry city until the end of time. Build the West Side Improvement to Robert Moses' specifications and the city would undoubtedly gain in many ways, but it would lose in many ways, too—and it would lose in ways that could never be remedied.

Moses might have seen these truths if he had been willing to listen to those who saw them so clearly. But he refused to listen, granting Exton only one interview, the one in which "he was just sitting there laughing at you."

Other city officials who listened to Exton and Weinberg didn't laugh. From the edge of the high bluff in Fort Tryon Park on the north side of the Cloisters, Comptroller McGoldrick could see Inwood Hill Park and the community of Spuyten Duyvil spread out below to the north as clearly as if they had been parts of a diorama. With his eyes following Exton's pointing finger, McGoldrick could see at a glance how much lay in the path of Moses' route—thickly forested slopes in the park, quiet residential streets in the community—and how little in the path of Exton's. He could see how little harm would be done to the park if a narrow band was sliced off its eastern edge for part of the right-of-way, and how the city street alongside the park would provide most of the rest. Across the river, beyond the northern terminus for the low-level bridge Exton wanted, below the built-up slopes of Spuyten Duyvil to the left, there stretched dramatically straight north a valley occupied only by flimsy tar-paper shacks, a valley which might have been placed there as an ideal parkway right-of-way. "Their route would have added maybe three-quarters of a mile," McGoldrick was to recall, "but what's three-quarters of a mile to a motorist? A flick of the eye, that's all. And it would have saved the park and Riverdale and Fieldston from having a trench run through it."

Some officials found flaws in Moses' plan that Exton and Weinberg hadn't thought of. Moses' ingeniously restrictive laws and ingeniously low-clearance parkway bridges had insured that buses would never be able to ruin the beauty of his Long Island parkways or carry poor people along them to his state parks. The Board of Estimate's Chief Engineer, Philip P. Farley, noticed that Moses was planning to low-bridge the city, too; enough of his Henry Hudson Parkway bridges were going to have a maximum headroom of thirteen feet and a headroom at the curb of eleven feet so that usage of the parkway by buses—which were exactly thirteen feet high—would be impractical. "One-third of the families in the City have automobiles," Farley reported to the Board. "The other two-thirds depend on buses. If they are to get any benefit from this improvement, buses must use [it]." Moreover, while the principal function of Moses' Long Island parkways had been to enable drivers to reach state parks, the principal function of the Henry Hudson Parkway would be to enable drivers from the Bronx and Westchester to commute to their jobs in Manhattan; his earlier roads had been roads for pleasure, but this would be a road for business.

Without buses, commuting on it could be only by car. This might well prove impractical; not only would the parkway increase the flow of cars into traffic-clogged Manhattan, but, with the inevitable increase in the population of Spuyten Duyvil, Riverdale and Westchester, car traffic might well overwhelm the parkway. In some future generation, opening it to buses each able to carry forty or more car drivers might well become imperative. But, as Farley said, "the normal life of the parkway bridges is estimated at 100 years." Rebuilding them after the parkway itself had been completed would be enormously expensive. One of the thirteen-foot bridges, the one at 239th Street, was, by design, the centerpiece of a large traffic interchange, all of which would have to be rebuilt—at a cost of millions of dollars. If Moses was allowed to build low bridges, even if the city might in some future generation want to allow buses on the Henry Hudson Parkway, it might simply be financially impractical to do so.

But Moses wouldn't listen to the city's officials. When McGoldrick tried to talk to him about the alternate route, he cut the Comptroller short. "He would brook no change," McGoldrick recalls. "It had to be straight." When Farley recommended that the Board disapprove the bridge designs, Moses called the recommendation "absurd in the light of the law [the parkway law he had written, of course]" and told the Board flatly that if the bridges weren't built his way, they would not be built at all.

The old reformers who headed the city's Good Government organizations were products of an earlier era—many of them, of the same era as Moses—but they were willing to listen to the two young reformers, and, listening, they were convinced. "Once the Board of the Municipal Art Society had a debate," Exton recalls. "It took a view that Moses was ruining Inwood Hill. Old Electus D. Litchfield, a great and good architect, said what a beautiful view there was from the road. I said that *from* the road there is a beautiful view, but *to* the road there is a lousy view. And I still remember some of the old-time architects and beaux arts boys who were on that board saying, 'Hear, hear!' " Soon the Citizens Union, the City Club and the Regional Plan Association were all asking for a detailed examination of Moses' proposal. Moses stopped laughing. He wrote a letter to the trustees of the City Club charging that the two men were pushing the alternate route because it would increase the value of Weinberg's Spuyten Duyvil real estate.

"There was no truth in what he said, none at all," Exton recalls. "Bob *did* own some real estate in Spuyten Duyvil. But it was a small property he had inherited from his parents, really insignificant when compared to other property he had inherited—he was quite wealthy, you know. And the property was undeveloped and near the route Moses wanted. If the parkway was put along Moses' route, it [the property] would have become quite valuable. Our route would have left it just as it was. Its value would have been increased by Moses' route, not ours. And Moses must have known that the alternate route wouldn't have done what he was saying it would [increase the value of Weinberg's property]. It was obvious. But he said it anyway. His only reply to everything we had proposed was an *ad hominem* attack on us, and it was all a lie, a goddamned lie."

City Club president Eustace Seligman called Exton in, questioned him about the charge and then told the trustees that he was completely satisfied as to the young men's integrity. The City Club's park committee thereupon accompanied Exton to the high bluff at the Cloisters, and saw, as McGoldrick had seen, the advantages of the alternate route. And when Moses refused even to grant the committee an interview, it issued a report—notable in that it was the first formal censure of Moses by any of the Good Government organizations that had long supported him—that called his plan a "violation of the principles of good planning." "While we are for Mr. Moses as a man, having bent over backward in our efforts to get the order [Order Number 129] of Secretary Ickes rescinded, his treatment here is high-handed and not in the best interests of the public," the report said. Other Good Government groups that investigated the West Side Improvement also agreed with Exton and Weinberg; the RPA even commissioned engineers to map out the alternate route.

But the reformers' front was far from solid. The logical group to lead a protest about park plans was the Park Association and the president of the Park Association was Mrs. Sulzberger, and Jack Madigan was telling Mrs. Sulzberger that Inwood Hill was used only for necking. And in the middle of the fight, Mrs. Sulzberger sent Moses a letter which while not specifically mentioning the West Side Improvement said that the association had reviewed "the many developments which are taking place in the parks under your energetic leadership" and "decided that we ought to express to you officially our approval and delight in what you are doing." Even the City Club's board of directors ended up disowning its park committee's report—despite a statement by Director Nathan Straus: noting that "every organization that has studied the project has agreed that the lower route is the only practical one," he accused Moses of treating city parks "as if they were his own private property."

Those reformers who still objected found that the powers they had been so instrumental in persuading La Guardia and the Legislature to give Moses were now turned against them. They appealed to the Board of Estimate to stop the Park Commissioner from chopping down the trees in Inwood Hill Park, but then remembered with a shock that under the Park Department Consolidation Act which they had supported, in violation of their own stated principles, the Board had no authority over the details of work within parks. Since Moses was not using city money for the work, moreover, he did not need Board approval for any work in Inwood Hill.

Then they demanded that Moses hold a public hearing on his plans, and threatened to file a taxpayers' suit to obtain an injunction if he did not agree to hold one. Moses agreed. He set a date two weeks away. And then, during those two weeks, he cut down hundreds of trees for the right-of-way. "He knew how to handle them," Madigan would laugh years later, recalling the reformers' shock when they realized that the park they had wanted so much to save had been ruined. Moses himself regarded his move as a masterstroke; he devoted space in his memoirs to relating how his men invented "a new ingenious tree-pulling device equipped with a sort of electric donkey engine" that cut down trees even faster than he had hoped.

The Board of Estimate did have power over the Riverside Park section of the project—because, despite the federal and state contributions, the city would have to furnish much of the money itself. Borough President Samuel Levy of Manhattan proposed preserving the waterfront for pedestrians by building the Henry Hudson Parkway not along the water but over the New York Central tracks. Moses replied by driving stakes: starting work in Riverside Park on the recreational facilities the public wanted, he asked the Board if they wanted the work wasted. He whipsawed the Board: he announced publicly that his plans were not only ready but approved by the federal government, which was prepared to give the city millions of dollars for them; if the Board accepted Levy's proposal, he said, new plans would have to be drawn up—that would take months; then the plans might or might not gain federal approval; even if they did, federal money might no longer be available; the city should not risk losing the chance of a century to get the job done. He misinformed the Board: he told it at one point that Levy's plan would cost $34,000,000 while his would cost only $6,000,000 (it actually was to cost the city four times that amount). He deluged the Board with attractively printed brochures showing the beauty of his plan. He invoked experience and past successes: when Levy tried to argue for an impartial engineering survey of the two plans, Moses said, "The problem is primarily for park, parkway and landscape experts, and not one of simple engineering"—and he reminded the Board that his men were park, parkway and landscape experts who had built Jones Beach.

Levy was certain that his plan would not cost $34,000,000. And he was certain that Moses' would cost far more than $6,000,000. But without enough technically proficient engineers to cost out Moses' plans, without press support (not only did the press accept Moses' figures as truth, it did not even discuss at length such issues as waterfront preservation), with La Guardia against him (because the Mayor wanted the West Side Improvement built before November 1937, when he would be running for re-election) and exerting pressure on the Board members, the borough president was helpless. Hardly had he completed an acerbic exchange with Moses (Moses: "Do you think you know more about building parkways than I do?" Levy: "I didn't say so." Moses: "Well, this is a parkway") when the Board approved Moses' plan.

If there was any desire for second thoughts, there wasn't time for them. The very day after approval was given, huge pile drivers were hammering bulkheads into the Hudson River off the shore of Riverside Park. Within a week, convoys of dump trucks—five hundred a day—were rumbling over the dirt roads leading into the park. Six thousand WPA-paid laborers were shoveling into place the rock and earth the trucks were delivering, and pouring over them cement that would harden into a new shoreline for Manhattan Island. Progress on the Henry Hudson Bridge was just as rapid. By the time the Board got around to considering whether the Bronx route should go through Spuyten Duyvil (its approval was required for that because its money was required for the condemnation necessary there) the northern bridgeheads were fixed in place, in Spuyten Duyvil. There was no choice but to approve the Spuyten Duyvil route. And Moses did not let the pace slacken; the speed with which the West Side Improvement was driven to completion was symbolized by the construction of the bridge that carried the Henry Hudson Parkway over Broadway at 253rd Street in Riverdale, a job that would normally have taken at least a year to complete. The legislation authorizing construction of the bridge (by the State Council of Parks) was signed at 1 P.M., May 1, 1935. At 5 P.M. that same day, Moses opened bids on the job and let the contract; at 7 A.M. the next morning, laborers were working on the site; one midnight a few weeks later, while most Riverdalians were asleep, the six seven-foot-wide steel spans that would hold the roadbed of the bridge rumbled up Broadway on huge flat floats pulled by tractors and at 5:55 A.M. the last rivet securing them in place over Broadway was set; when Riverdalians went to work in the morning there before them was a bridge where none had existed the night before.

Moses' reluctance to discuss his plans for the northern section of the West Side Improvement was understandable. He could not, after all, tell Exton and Weinberg the real reasons he wanted the approach to the Henry Hudson Bridge to be through Inwood Hill Park instead of along the street at its edge: if word ever leaked out that a six-lane highway was being classified as a "park access road," the CWA and WPA would have to reclassify the project. Moses could not explain to Exton and Weinberg that while it might be better to build the bridge on a lower level near the existing drawbridge and therefore avoid Inwood Hill Park and Spuyten Duyvil, his idea of the proper location didn't matter; only the bankers' ideas mattered because it was the bankers who had to put up the money for the bridge. Moses could not, in fact, allow any discussion of the bridge location at all, because discussion generates controversy, and controversy frightens away the timid, and no one is more timid than a banker where his money is concerned. "The market was so skittish that any little thing could have gotten them to back out," Jack Madigan recalls. "A lesser fellow wouldn't have understood the importance of killing off this agitation right at the start before it began raising up some publicity and getting people arguing," but Moses understood perfectly. The financing of the northern section of the West Side Improvement had been made possible only by remarkable ingenuity on Moses' part, an ingenuity that bent rules and regulations—twisted them, in fact, until they were all but unrecognizable—into a shape that permitted the participation in the financing of the project of bankers and twenty-two separate city, state and federal agencies. Exposure of that ingenuity to the public would tumble in an instant the house of cards he had so laboriously erected. He could not allow it.

And what good would discussion do anyway? The city had been trying to build the West Side Improvement for decades—generations, in fact. It had never, even in the free-spending Walkerian era, been able to find the funds to do the job. It could only be done now because of the federal relief program—and that program might be curtailed at any time. If the job was ever to be done, it had to be done at once, without delay. Discussion meant delay, and therefore discussion could not be permitted. "There was no alternative, see—no alternative," Madigan says.

Madigan's statement was not accurate. There was an alternative—it just was not an alternative that he, or Robert Moses, would even consider. There might be no alternative if the bridge had to be built immediately, but why did it have to be built immediately? If the bankers refused to finance its construction unless it was located on the escarpment, a location which required the destruction of Inwood Hill Park and Spuyten Duyvil, why was it necessary to accept their terms? The city could simply refuse them, and wait until it could build the bridge itself—in the place where it should be built.

And it might not have too long to wait. The situation now was significantly different from the past. Construction of the approach roads was—thanks to Moses—well under way at last, to the south from the Battery to 193rd Street, just a mile from the Harlem River, to the north all the way down through Westchester and into the city down to 249th Street, a point only about a mile from the river. More than sixteen miles of the through route was under construction; only two miles, including the bridge, remained to be built. This was no longer a project not begun. It was a project largely completed. With La Guardia in City Hall, the city's government had the will to complete it. With more than 90 percent of the cost already paid, moreover, this was no longer a project whose cost was $109,000,000. It was a project whose cost—the cost of its uncompleted two miles including bridge—was less than $10,000,000. The city might not have $10,000,000 to spare at the moment, but it was not unrealistic to suspect that, with La Guardia running city finances with an iron hand, it might have it someday—someday soon (as, in fact, was going to be the case; by 1936 the city had sufficient leeway in its capital budget to build the bridge itself).

Such an alternative might well have appealed to Exton and Weinberg. There was an immediate need for the bridge, of course, and there was a risk in delaying its construction, the risk that the city's financial position might worsen, or its will to do the job might fade, and the bridge would never be built. But such risks had to be weighed against the certainties entailed in construction of the bridge at the point the bankers wanted: the destruction of Manhattan's priceless last forest, and of Riverdale's priceless serenity. Weighing the risks, Exton and Weinberg might well have decided on delay. The city, represented by its elected officials, might have so decided, too. But such considerations did not weigh more than a feather on Robert Moses' private scales, unbalanced as they were by his desire for accomplishment, for achievement—for the tangible, physical realization of his dreams. For such dreams, as the man who echoed his thoughts, Jack Madigan, put it, "Money is *all.*" Now, at last, after two decades of dreaming of the West Side Improvement, he had the money for it, and he was not about to let that money slip away. "Yeah, I remember that," Madigan would say thirty years later when asked about the Exton-Weinberg proposal, and the hard, quiet voice would be filled with contempt and disgust. "I remember that as an asinine idea, brother." Robert Moses did not give the city a chance to decide.

The Henry Hudson Bridge opened on December 12, 1936.

The opening ceremony, which Moses combined with a birthday party for La Guardia, was not one of the Park Commissioner's more successful productions. A sudden wild rainstorm forced the celebrants to crowd into the tiny administrative building on the bridge toll plaza into which the bar had hastily been moved, and fierce gusts of wind kept blowing open the windows and dampening the spirits. King Edward VIII picked the same day for his announcement that he was giving up his throne for "the woman I love," and the Mayor insisted, to Moses' rage, on interrupting the ceremonies to listen to a rebroadcast of the abdication speech. In the evening the rain stopped, the skies cleared and Moses, taking Jack Madigan along, drove down to the shoreline below the bridge to view his handiwork by moonlight. Staring up at the slender arch flung across the gap between the two high bluffs, he was struck by its grace, but even this moment was spoiled for him, for the blunt Irishman was not the ideal moonlight companion. When Moses started rhapsodizing about the beauty of the scene, Cleveland Rodgers relates, "Madigan said that all he could think about was the dimes rattling in the toll boxes."

Nothing, however, could dim Moses' pride in the fulfillment of the great dream of his youth. When, on October 12, 1937—in time for Election Day—the whole West Side Improvement was completed, he commandeered Madigan's yacht and ordered its captain to stand out into the Hudson so that he could view his creation in its full sweep. From the deck of a ferryboat in the middle of the river twenty years before, the six miles of Riverside Park had been six miles of garbage dumps and mud, of tar-paper shacks and stacks of rotting timbers, all shrouded in the dirty gray smoke spewed up by the trains that clanked everlastingly through it. Yet he had exclaimed to the woman beside him: "Isn't this a temptation to you? Couldn't this be the most beautiful thing in the world?" Now he felt that it very nearly was. The tracks were gone from the whole lower stretch of the park. So were the mud and the shacks and the garbage. In their place were the things he had seen only in his mind then, "the great highway that went uptown along the water" and the lush park beside it. From the river, the massive retaining walls trimmed with granite and marble, set with loopholes and embrasures, stretching for miles along the water, rising one behind the other up to Riverside Drive, were battlements, a fortification protecting the great city behind it. The loom from Riverside Drive behind the battlements not only of the sheer brick wall of apartment houses but of the turrets and watchtowers of mansions that resembled medieval castles (the central façade of Charles M. Schwab's, which occupied the square block between Seventy-third and Seventy-fourth streets, was reminiscent of the chateau of Chenonceaux, the wings of the castles of Blois and Azay-le-Rideau); the presence behind the battlements of the columns and cannons of the Soldiers' and Sailors' Monument, erected to honor warriors of a civil war, and, farther north, of the massive granite sepulcher of the great general who had led them; the image, life-sized in the distance, of a girl warrior out of the fifteenth century, the bronze mount of the Maid of Orléans rearing at Ninety-third Street from a pedestal set with fragments from Rheims Cathedral, where she waited trial and death; the upthrust of spires out of the thirteenth century, the spires of Riverside Church that were modeled on the Cathedral at Chartres; the stark outline atop a bluff to the north of the simple square watchtower of the medieval monastery of St. Michel de Cuxa that was now called the Cloisters—these only made more complete the effect for which Moses had been striving: that of a wall built to guard a city as walls had guarded cities during the Middle Ages, specifically the German cities whose walls, along with those of the medieval fortress-castles of the *Raubritter,* or "robber barons," had lined the Rhine and fired Moses' imagination when, as a romantic young student, he had so often cruised that river.

Not that the West Side Improvement was just a fortification, of course. It was far more than that. Along its lowest level, at the edge of the water, were lines of moving vehicles and, once one realized they were part of the Improvement, one saw that to call it medieval was to slight it. The towering battlements were combined with an entranceway to the city, an entranceway whose Riverside Park portion alone was six miles long, an entranceway framed in marble and granite and flanked by the tombs of dead heroes—an entranceway of a size and grandeur that could only be Roman, a Via Triumphalis like those along which had ridden the conquering Generals of the Empire, on their way to receive the laurel wreath from the Caesar.

A fortification? An entranceway? The West Side Improvement was also a park—a lovely park. The retaining walls formed a series of terraces rising from the water, and the terraces were lush, green, tree-shaded lawns. Through the shadows of the arches of the Seventy-ninth Street boat basin one could see a fountain splashing coolly. If the West Side Improvement was grandeur, it was also beauty. The scene was just as Robert Moses had envisioned it twenty years before, even to the bright white sails of the boats tied up in the gracefully curving marinas.

Moses was more than satisfied with his handiwork. The sheer cliffs of the forest-topped Palisades, opposite the sheer cliffs of Manhattan's apartment houses, were "the most magnificent river wall anywhere," he felt, and the wall he had created was its match. Now that it was completed, the Hudson vista was the greatest river vista in the world. The Rhine? The Rhine with its "silly, quaint, Wagnerian castles"? Thanks to the West Side Improvement, the Hudson absolutely *dwarfed* the Rhine. Penning an introduction to a brochure describing the Improvement, he sounded like the Bob Moses of his youth.

> This, then, is the Hudson waterfront celebrated by Masefield and O'Neill, where the fabled liners and cargo vessels thrust their prows into the very vitals of the city. . . . Tycoons overlook the upper and lower bays and the Jersey piers. Droves of cars zoom or crawl through Riverside Park and down the West Side Highway and view

the matchless, unspoiled Palisades. By comparison, the castled Rhine with its Lorelei is a mere trickle between vineclad slopes. I wonder sometimes whether our people, so obsessed with the seamy interior of Manhattan, deserve the Hudson. What a waterfront! What an island to buy for $24!

The city's pride matched Moses'. The reporters chauffeured over the Improvement before its opening to the public were all too familiar with the previous route into New York from the north, the wearisome stop-and-go gear shifting over the narrow, bumpy streets of Yonkers, a traffic light on every corner to increase the irritation, the trip through the Bronx down a Broadway made dismal and dingy by the small stores and grimy tenements that lined it and by the shadows and harsh rumbles of the IRT elevated tracks overhead. They, like other drivers, had had to wonder as they approached the Broadway drawbridge whether they would be in for an interminable delay there. And when they crossed the bridge, they had to resume the crawl downtown on Riverside Drive or Broadway in endless lines of traffic. The approaches to New York had been agonizingly slow, and ugly as well, a mean and meager entrance to a great city.

Now they skimmed down to New York along the broad Saw Mill River Parkway, all sweeping curves and spacious straightaways, lined with woods, underbrushy and shadowy and deep, that drenched them in autumn colors, and with clearings in which black boulders sat dramatically in the center of sun-dappled grass. The bridges that carried intersecting traffic over the parkway so that its users should not be disturbed were little Moses masterpieces, each faced with stone carefully selected to blend in with nearby rock formations, each subtly different in design from any other, mere hints in the midst of a natural setting of the shaping hand of man, mere hints of what the parkway was carrying them towards. Yonkers was just something off beyond the trees; slopes shielded motorists from even a glimpse of that unlovely municipality until the parkway had almost reached the Bronx line, where its name changed from Saw Mill River to Henry Hudson (the signs announcing the change were made gay by cartoon silhouettes, done in wrought iron, of Hudson's *Half Moon*), and while at that point there was an unavoidable minute or two of small houses visible atop the slope, the parkway ducked quickly into the shelter of Van Cortlandt Park and was back among trees and grass again. It was not until Van Cortlandt was behind the reporters that houses became a permanent part of the scenery, and then they were at first only on one—the right, or river—side of the road and they were at first just small, private homes, fieldstone-covered, for this was Riverdale, no more than another hint, just slightly broader than the bridges, of what was to come.

Flashing through Riverdale toward the steep cliffs of the Harlem River, the hints became broader still, the private homes flanking the parkway on both sides now, crowding closer to it and closer together, three low apartment houses becoming part of the scene in Spuyten Duyvil, but there were still plenty of trees and grass. Leaping the Harlem on the Henry Hudson Bridge, the reporters saw the Broadway bridge far below them to the left, and, beyond it, a glimpse of the city, but the glimpse, cut short by the approaching bluffs of Inwood Hill, was fleeting and the city was hazy in the distance and hundreds of feet below them, and the bluffs were towering and filled with trees, and while the parkway might be in the city now, it was not yet of the city. Leaving the bridge toll booths, the parkway curved abruptly to the right, down and around a great craggy bluff that towered above it, and even that fleeting glimpse was gone and what was in front of the reporters as their car passed through the bluff's deep shadow was only trees and, seen through the trees, a bright river and beyond the river the Palisades.

And then they were around the curve and there was New York.

First there was steelwork and concrete in the sky, immense towers, thick cables, a roadbed above the water—the George Washington Bridge, looming above the leaves, casting a dark shadow over the parkway so that the reporters' limousine rolled across it as if it were a gigantic welcome mat to a gigantic city. Then, above the parkway to the left, there were apartment houses behind the leaves. And suddenly the city was beside the reporters, looming over them; atop the great cliffs of rock were cliffs of brick, the massed apartment houses of Riverside Drive. Far away to the left, there were the spires of the Empire State Building and the Chrysler Building, their very visibility at such a distance an evocation of the immensity of the canyons of skyscrapers toward which the limousine was headed. Ahead of the reporters was the panorama of the harbor, serene water turned busy, churned by the giant screws of giant ships, dented by piers jutting out from shore.

If there was drama in this entrance to the city, there was, even within the city's confines, beauty, too, and dignity. As the limousine headed downtown toward the reporters' offices, the parkway hugged the river's edge and the water was broad on the road's right hand. The Palisades across the river stayed largely unspoiled for precious minutes. Between the parkway and the apartment houses to the left were the terraces Moses had built and planted with trees and lawn, and the retaining walls of the terraces, the walls that flanked the parkway, were masonry and marble, and their copings were of granite, and above on Riverside Drive were Grant's Tomb and the Soldiers' and Sailors' Monument, friezes and colonnades. And even when there was no more beauty or dignity, there was still convenience. When the Henry Hudson Parkway became the West Side Elevated Highway and there were no more trees or terraces, and the Jersey shore, what could be seen of it through a dense industrial haze, was a panorama of all that was wrong with the Industrial Era, and the view to the left, toward the city, was of railroad yards and warehouses and traffic-jammed streets, the reporters could still realize that they were not on those streets, that they were speeding downtown without having even to pause.

The reporters rhapsodized. "The most beautiful drive in the world," wrote one from the *Daily News*. "Always the man in the car has the river in full view," marveled one from the *Times*. Simeon Strunsky said in "Topics of the Times": "The West Side Highway as a name . . . utterly fails to do justice to the . . . new masterpiece out of Robert Moses' atelier. . . . The traveler comes and goes in a setting of beauty which [it] is not too much to call intoxicating." (Strunsky was also to write: "The poet Wordsworth stood on Waterloo Bridge and said about the Thames view that earth had no finer sight; but Wordsworth should have stood at the north end of the Henry Hudson Bridge and looked south and west.")

Moses had promised that the new road would "eliminate" the West Side's north-south traffic jams. He announced that the trip from Canal Street to the city line, which had previously required sixty-eight minutes, would henceforth take only twenty-six. And none of the journalists had the slightest doubt that Moses was correct. "It is a veritable motorist's dream," said the *Journal-American.* The *Times* marveled that "the gleaming new concrete ribbon" would not only "afford immediate and measurable relief to traffic congestion on Riverside Drive" but would enable motorists to drive all the way from Canal Street "nearly to Poughkeepsie without having to stop for a traffic light or slow up for an intersection."

And journalists understood that Moses' project was not just a view or a road. "The West Side Improvement is much more than that," the *Sun* editorialized. "It gives the island not only a new major highway and a new shore line along part of its length but park land and . . . playgrounds." The *Journal-American* said it provided "a fountain of health and pleasure from which New York's people and their children and guests will be drinking long years to come." The Brooklyn *Eagle* emphasized that "after decades of fruitless effort, the railroad tracks are covered at last." In fact, said the *Times,* "all that has been unsightly along the Hudson—the railroad, the ash dumps, the coal yards—has been swept away or completely disguised."

The statistics in the thick packets of press releases that Moses' men handed to the reporters were, even to men accustomed to press releases filled with statistics, almost too big to grasp. To create the Riverside Park portion of his dream alone, Robert Moses had poured into the six miles of muddy wasteland 1,250,000 cubic yards of stone riprap, 3,000,000 cubic yards of hydraulic fill, 296,400 linear feet of steel and concrete piling, 6,800,000 pounds of reinforcing steel, 1,912,000 bags of cement, 120,000 pounds of lead, 12,500 cubic yards of stone masonry, 1,600 cubic yards of granite and 220,000 cubic yards of topsoil and humus.

But the reporters did their best to make the city grasp them. They pointed out that, as the *Times* put it, Moses had, in "the most extensive alteration of Manhattan's topography in recent history, put . . . a highway . . . through an already overcrowded park with a substantial gain, instead of a loss, of recreational space"—a gain that amounted to the incredible total of 132 acres, an addition to the land area of crowded Manhattan Island worth, at current land values, $23,760,000. They pointed out that he had filled that space with fifteen tennis courts, seventeen playgrounds, twenty-three softball fields, thirty-eight basketball courts, forty handball courts, 13,000 trees, 140,000 feet of footpaths and 350,000 shrubs.

The most incredible statistic of all was not included in the press release. That was the cost of Moses' dream. His press releases stated that the cost was $24,000,000, but this figure bears no discernible relationship to reality, since even the most cursory examination of the cost—all that is possible, since Moses took care never to reveal it and its components are concealed in such a multitude of appropriations, citywide property assessments, borough property assessments, special Board of Estimate appropriations and federal contributions from twenty-two separate sources that thirty-seven years later it is unfeasible to attempt to compute them—reveals that the total cost of the West Side Improvement (including the elevated highway) was at least $180,000,000 and perhaps as high as $218,000,000, an immense figure in Depression dollars. (The famous Boulder Dam, always cited as an example of spectacular New Deal expenditures, cost $76,000,000.) But New York's press did not attempt to analyze the cost, accepting, instead, Moses' $24,000,000 figure—and coupling it with the comment that for this expenditure the city had received in return land worth $23,760,000. Out of thirteen daily newspapers, not one had the slightest doubt that the West Side Improvement was anything but an "improvement," an unalloyed improvement, an absolutely unmitigated blessing, to New York City.

Not a dissenting voice could be heard. One can search in vain through the city's newspapers during the weeks in 1937 in which articles on the Improvement were appearing daily looking for a single hint—even a buried quote in a story or a lone letter-to-the-editor—suggesting that there was the slightest imperfection in the project.

"The railroad tracks are covered at last," an editorial said.

Not exactly.

The railroad tracks were covered until they reached 125th Street—the beginning of Harlem.

Moses had decided to economize on the section of the West Side Improvement, between 125th and 155th streets, that bordered the city's Negro community, and one of the economies was dispensing with the track covering in that section. Uncovered tracks meant a never-ending clanking, from the couplings of railroad cars, and periodic bawling, from the cows and other animals being transported south to the slaughterhouses, unless the people who lived in the apartments above kept their windows closed. And in the summer, when it was too hot to keep windows closed, uncovered tracks meant not only noise but odors, the stench of the animals, and they meant soot and smoke that spread a coat of gritty grime, confined to windowsills in winter, over walls and furniture. Now, thanks to the genius of Robert Moses, the white people who lived along Riverside Drive were freed from these annoyances.

But the black people weren't.

Robert Moses spent millions of dollars enlarging Riverside Park through landfill, but he did not spend a dime for that purpose between 125th and 155th streets. He added 132 acres to the parts of the park most likely to be used by white people—but not one acre to the part of the park most likely to be used by black people.

* * *

Robert Moses ruthlessly removed all commercial enterprises from the waterfront along the entire six-mile length of Riverside Park—except for those commercial enterprises (wharves, small warehouses, coal pockets, junkyards and the like) that were located in the Harlem section of Riverside Park. Those he allowed to remain—to occupy what otherwise would have been park land for Harlem.

Because he did not enlarge Riverside Park in the Harlem section, there was, really, for two-thirds of the Harlem section, the stretch between 125th and 145th streets, no Riverside Park at all. The green of lawns and trees that he laid out with such a lavish hand south of Harlem ends abruptly at 125th Street and the only green that remains is a very narrow, very steep treed slope, too steep for anything except slipping and sliding down it, that, for some of those twenty blocks, climbs from the uncovered tracks to Riverside Drive above. Except for that little ribbon of trees, pathetic when compared to the lush lawns and lavish plantings downtown, the "park" is, for these twenty blocks, only the grim steel of the tracks and the gray concrete of the parkway.

Robert Moses devoted endless ingenuity to making the Henry Hudson Parkway beautiful in and of itself. From Seventy-second to 125th Street, for example, he lined the roadway with trees and shrubs and faced the walls along its sides with granite and marble and expensive masonry. But between 125th and 145th streets, he lifted the roadway into the air—on a gaunt steel viaduct. There is not a tree or shrub on the viaduct. There is not a foot of granite or marble or masonry. The only ornamentation whatsoever on the starkly ugly steel is the starkly ugly cheap concrete aggregate with which it is paved.

And the viaduct is not only unlovely in and of itself. It makes the waterfront over which it runs even uglier than it was before, filling its streets with its shadows and the never-ending rumble of the cars that travel along it. And its presence insures that even should New York City one day decide to give those twenty blocks of Harlem what it has given most of the other residential neighborhoods along the Hudson River, a park below Riverside Drive, the park will have to be one filled with shadow and noise.

There is at least one spot in this twenty-block stretch at which it would have been easy to create a park even without landfill operations.

At the foot of 125th and 126th streets, these mean and narrow thoroughfares slope down and, after running under Moses' viaduct, run right out into a broad wharf that juts out into the river, so that turning it into a park would have made the riverfront a part of Harlem. Of the whole Hudson River waterfront, no area was more intimately a part of the adjoining community and more suitable to be a park for it.

Moses might not have wanted to spend much money on the Harlem section of the West Side Improvement but a park here would not have cost much money. Condemning the wharf would have been cheap, as would also have been placing playground facilities on it to give the children of the neighborhood a chance to play right on the river or laying earth and sod on it to bring a touch of brightness to a neighborhood without brightness. And seeing the park possibilities of the wharf was easy; in fact, it would have been hard not to, for on every sunny day it was crowded with people fishing, staring out over the water or washing their cars in the sun.

But somehow Moses didn't see. He never made a move to turn the 125th Street wharf into a park, and in 1974 it would still be standing vacant, a monument to a city's indifference to the needs of its poorest people.

Harlem does, of course, have a section of Riverside Park, the section between 145th Street, where the Henry Hudson Parkway swings down off the viaduct, and 155th Street—a stretch of land ten blocks long, plenty long enough to provide the playgrounds, ballfields and other facilities that a recreation-starved community so desperately needed.

Robert Moses built seventeen playgrounds as part of the West Side Improvement. He built one playground in the Harlem section of the Improvement. He built five football fields as part of the Improvement. He built one in the Harlem section. He built eighteen horseshoe courts, twenty-two tennis courts, half a mile of roller-skating paths and a mile of bicycle paths in the rest of the Improvement. He did not build a single horseshoe or tennis court or a foot of roller-skating or bicycle path in the Harlem portion.

When the Improvement first opened, in fact, there was not a single recreational facility of any type in the entire "Harlem section"—not so much as a stanchion with a basketball hoop attached. The initial plans Moses had distributed to newspapers when he was persuading La Guardia to approve the Improvement had shown a recreational area between 146th and 148th streets on the river side of the parkway, but while most of the recreational areas above and below Harlem were completed when the Improvement opened, the 146th Street–148th Street area was not even begun. He did move thereafter to build it—hurriedly, because, according to one report, La Guardia suddenly realized the omission and insisted it be rectified and Moses was afraid the Mayor would make it public. But its pitifully inadequate and cheaply built facilities proved remarkably difficult to reach from the community it was supposed to serve. The only way to reach it on foot from Harlem, in fact, was by walking to Riverside Drive, walking down an incredibly long flight of steps to the New York Central tracks, crossing the tracks on a footbridge (which meant climbing up another flight of steps to get on it and climbing down a flight to get off) and then walking down another flight of steps to an underpass under the parkway which led to the recreational area. And reaching it was downhill. Getting back up to Riverside Drive was uphill. On even pleasant summer afternoons, the recreational area Moses had so generously bestowed upon Harlem would be almost empty—except for motorists from other areas who found it remarkably accessible (just pull off the parkway and there you were) by car.

Robert Moses had always displayed a genius for adorning his creations with little details that made them fit in with their setting, that made the people who used them feel at home in them. There was a little detail on the playhouse–comfort station in the Harlem section of Riverside Park that is found nowhere else in the park. The wrought-iron trellises of the park's other playhouses and comfort stations are decorated with designs like curling waves.

The wrought-iron trellises of the Harlem playhouse–comfort station are decorated with monkeys.

Robert Moses had "reclaimed the city's waterfront for its people," an editorial said.

Not exactly.

Robert Moses had indeed built a huge, beautiful Riverside Park. But the park was not on the riverside. The parkway was on the riverside. For much of the six miles of Riverside Park, the road, not the park, occupied the land nearest to the river. And that meant that the park, and the people who used it, were separated from the river by six lanes of concrete filled with rushing automobiles.

If Moses had built the road where other planners and young reformers like Bill Exton and Robert Weinberg had wanted it built—atop the New York Central tracks, at the edge of Riverside Park close to the steep slope below Riverside Drive—the city's people would, after strolling down from the Drive and crossing the road on easy overpasses, have found themselves in a park whose tree-shaded lawns, playing fields and esplanades swept hundreds of yards down to the river's edge unbroken by the concrete of a highway or the rush and smells of automobiles. Because the park would have extended to the Hudson's edge, they would have been able to picnic or play, or simply sit on benches and think, at the very edge of a broad and beautiful river. They would have been able, on the very rim of the city, to escape the city—and to escape it completely.

But Moses had chosen, in much of Riverside Park, to build the road at the water's edge. And therefore, in much of the park, its users were hardly conscious that there was any river there at all. From much of Riverside Park, in fact, they could hardly *see* the water. Robert Moses placed in Riverside Park 5,500 benches offering, he said, "fine views of the river." But from most of those benches the river is hardly visible. They are placed at the same level as the highway and above the highway barrier wall only a thin sliver of water can be seen. Near Ninety-sixth Street, for example, there are hundreds of benches, in long, neat rows, facing the river, but all you can see from the benches is the barrier wall, the tops of cars speeding past behind it, and the very edge of the Hudson on the New Jersey side.

From some of the 5,500 benches, you can see all of the river, but always there are cars, a fierce, never-ending rush of them, long lines of them, cars with their hurry and noise and smell, in front of that river. There are *always* cars in front of the river in Riverside Park. "In place of great parks and terraces and promenades," Peter Blake was to write in the 1960's, "we have built, along almost every single foot of the coastline of this city, gigantic viaducts of steel and concrete that carry streams of automobiles and effectively block our views of the water, a passing steamer, a seagull or, possibly, a sunrise."

"Always the man in the car has the river in full view," wrote a newspaperman. That was true. But to give the man in the car that view, fleeting at best and harried, to let him enjoy a brief glimpse of beauty as he passed by it, hurriedly and with his mind on other things, Moses had taken it away from the man not in the car, the pedestrian walking beside the river or sitting beside it, picnicking or just looking at it, soaking it in for long minutes and hours, the man who would have had time to enjoy and savor the view, the man whose life could have been enriched by it. He had thought that by building a road along the waterfront he was giving the beauty and openness of the waterfront—as he had given the beauty and openness of Long Island—to both the city's cars and the city's people. But he was wrong. It was no longer possible to do both. In building the West Side "Improvement," he had, although he did not realize it, the choice of giving the city's precious Hudson waterfront to either cars or people. And he had chosen to give it to cars. Cars were part of the essence of the city. He had brought cars to the city's very edge. Concrete was part of the essence of the city. He had laid concrete at the city's very edge. With a chance, a wonderful chance, to give the city's people a way of escaping the city, he had, instead, sealed them within it.

Riverside Park was a beautiful park. But it was not a "riverside park." For all the use it made of the six miles of adjoining water, it might, except for a very few points, have been located in the middle of Brooklyn. Robert Moses reclaimed the city's waterfront, all right. By turning six miles of wasteland into the parkway and park he had envisioned, he had added an immense asset to the city. But he had deprived the city of another asset: its waterfront. And alongside the loss of this asset, the gains that did accrue from Moses' development of Riverside Park, from his spending of more than $100,000,000, were, while immense, very tiny indeed.

And the loss may not be replaceable. With his usual thoroughness, Robert Moses had done the job too well. When he finished with the city's Hudson River waterfront, the waterfront was gone. And it was quite possibly gone forever.

Jack Madigan was keeping an ear on the rattle of dimes in the toll boxes on the Henry Hudson Bridge. In an astonishingly short time, the melody had reached a pleasurable volume.

The cautious bankers who had been willing to finance only a single deck had said they would purchase more bonds only when traffic reached approximately 6,000 cars per day.

On the first day on which tolls were collected on the bridge after the Henry Hudson Parkway giving access to it was completed—Monday, December 14, 1937—9,086 cars used it. Madigan was careful not to let himself get too optimistic. The first figure would, of course, include people who merely wanted to say that they had used it on the first day and who might not use it again. His caution seemed confirmed when, on Tuesday, the volume dropped to 8,100. But on Wednesday, it was 9,278; Thursday, 8,504; and Friday, 8,760. And then came the first weekend. On Saturday, 10,215 cars crossed the bridge; on Sunday, 15,644.

Every Monday morning, when Moses arrived at 80 Centre Street, on top of the pile of papers awaiting him was a thermometer-type chart showing traffic—southbound in green, northbound in red. And each Monday the red and green together climbed higher on that thermometer. On the first charts, the peak daily volume allowed for, the top number on the thermometer, was 20,000. If that was the average daily rate, 7,300,000 cars—double what even Moses had calculated—would be using the bridge during a year. But soon the red and green were nearing the top of the thermometer, and then they passed it. Soon traffic on the bridge was running at a rate that made the annual figure not 7,300,000 but 10,322,002.

The bankers were watching charts, too. Three months after the bridge opened, Moses asked for additional financing, not the $1,400,000 originally agreed on but $2,000,000, and they were only too happy to give it to him. Selling the first issue of Henry Hudson Parkway Authority bonds had taken months. The new issue of Authority bonds was oversubscribed within minutes after it was offered. Less than seven months after the bridge opened, a second deck, which would hold three northbound lanes, was being placed atop it, thereby freeing the old deck for three southbound lanes.

"The success of the project," Moses announced, "is established."

With the additional financing, Moses was able to put a statue of Henry Hudson atop the hundred-foot-high column that had been standing in Spuyten Duyvil waiting for it since 1909, and to turn the small plot around it, named "Henry Hudson Memorial Park" in 1909, into a real park, with "a completely equipped small children's play area" and "permanent benches." "These improvements," Moses announced, "carry out the principle we have adopted of establishing increased local park and recreational facilities along a free-flowing traffic artery."

Moses intended the park for "small children" accompanied by their mothers. But it was hard for mothers with small children to get them there. The park was situated on the crest of a little hill and Moses had built up the hill not paths but flights of steps. Moreover, at the time the park was built, the bulk of the population that would use it lay on the opposite, or eastern, side of the Henry Hudson Parkway, and the only way across the parkway in the vicinity was the Kappock Street underpass, which was also set with steps. Unless she walked on the narrow pavement of the underpass roadway, in danger from every car that suddenly swung around its corner, "there is," as Bob Weinberg put it, "no way . . . whereby a mother with a baby carriage or go-cart can use this underpass"—or the park. Residents of the area noted that the park had been used by more mothers with small children before Moses had built the facilities for them than after. And, despite pleas by the Riverdale community for elimination of the steps to Henry Hudson Memorial Park, it would be twenty years before they were removed.

"Motorists launching gaily into the lovely new parkway have been appalled to find that not all traffic problems have been solved," *The New York Times* said. "Because everyone wants to see it, on certain days and at certain hours there [is] a long procession of these eager citizens, enjoying the scenery but not getting anywhere."

"But," the *Times* added, "the public should be of good cheer. . . . When Mr. Moses has got his parkway hooked up firmly to the remainder of the parkway and has double-decked his Spuyten Duyvil Bridge, we may look to see the arterial tension in our traffic arteries diminishing considerably."

By July 1938, the parkway was all hooked up and the double-decking of the bridge was completed. But the hardening of the arteries continued. Traffic on the bridge had been 10,300,000 cars in 1937. By 1939, it rose to 12,700,000; by 1941, 14,300,000; it would finally top out at 26,000,000. In the face of such increases, double-decking a bridge hardly seemed to make any difference at all. Motorists pulling up to pay their tolls found themselves at the end of lines that seemed little, if any, shorter than the lines had been at the old Broadway bridge, whose congestion New York had considered intolerable. And there was another puzzling fact. Although the new bridge had been built to relieve the congestion on the old bridge, congestion on the old bridge had not been noticeably relieved. The lines of cars waiting to cross it were, in fact, almost as long as ever.

And traffic jams were not restricted to the bridge toll booths—or to certain days and certain hours. They extended the length of the West Side Improvement that led to and from the bridge, so that sometimes the three lanes of the Henry Hudson Parkway and West Side Elevated Highway that carried traffic in the direction of the rush—the southbound lanes into the city in the morning, the northbound lanes out of the city in the evening—were three lanes of bumper-to-bumper cars all the way from Canal Street to the city line. The rush-hour jams were just as bad as the rush-hour jams had been on Riverside Drive before the West Side Improvement was built; reporters escorted over the West Side Improvement before it opened had found it reduced the time required for the nine-mile trip from sixty-eight minutes to twenty-six; now one of those reporters made the trip over the

West Side Improvement at two rush hours—admittedly very bad ones—and found that on one trip it took fifty-eight minutes, on the other seventy-three. And looking at the situation that way, the total effect on traffic congestion of the West Side Improvement had been to move the congestion one block west—and yet there was still congestion on Riverside Drive, congestion that had been eased only slightly by the construction of a parallel route. The Improvement had simply provided New York with two congested thoroughfares where only one had existed before—and, of course, had given the motorists using the new congested thoroughfare a nicer view. And, in fact, the drivers on the new thoroughfare were hardly in a position to enjoy the view. Following another car bumper-to-bumper required the focusing of a driver's eyes not on "the Hudson waterfront celebrated by Masefield and O'Neill" or "the matchless, unspoiled Palisades," but on a bumper.

How about drivers using the Henry Hudson Parkway during off hours? Year by year—the situation would not change until 1956, when the opening of the parallel Major Deegan Expressway and the southward extension of the parallel Bronx River Parkway cut traffic on the Henry Hudson Parkway in half—the number of "off hours" on the Henry Hudson Parkway grew smaller and smaller. During daylight, in fact, there was hardly an hour in which traffic on that parkway was not generally heavy. Passengers could enjoy the view, of course. But Saturday and Sunday traffic was heaviest of all. And there must be some doubt whether many passengers were prepared to enjoy the view for as long as it took, stopping and starting, braking and accelerating, sweating under their car's hot tin roof, to negotiate the parkway on those days.

The West Side Improvement had had two purposes: to reclaim Manhattan's waterfront for its people, and to alleviate Manhattan's traffic congestion. It was to achieve these purposes that Robert Moses spent an incredibly large sum of money.

But despite that expenditure—all but inconceivable in terms of urban spending of that era—the first of the two purposes was achieved only in part. The West Side Improvement did create a park, but while it was a great park, it was not nearly as great as it could have been; instead of reclaiming the waterfront for Manhattan's people, the West Side Improvement deprived them of it.

And the second of the two purposes was not achieved at all.

The effect of the West Side Improvement on New York City was not limited to its effect on traffic or on Riverside Park, of course. The Improvement extended through several areas north of Riverside Park.

North of Riverside Park was Inwood Hill Park. On the afternoon on which the opening ceremonies for the West Side Improvement were held, Bill Exton went back to Inwood Hill Park.

"Or what was left of Inwood Hill Park," the young reformer was to recall. "Even before I got up to the top, it was all changed. There were concrete staircases where there used to be dirt paths, and drinking fountains and a whole drainage system—cutting down the trees on top had destroyed the natural drainage, you see, so now they were laying a new one."

At the top, there had once been the wonderful view of the river and the Palisades, and there had been peace in which to enjoy it. "Now," he was to recall, and his voice would turn bitter, "there was a view all right, a view of the road, a great roaring concrete gut through the forest. They still called it Inwood Hill but it wasn't Inwood Hill any more."

Suddenly, Exton recalls, "I don't know, I just wanted to get out of there, I wanted to get out of there as fast as I could." Turning, he walked back down Inwood Hill—and he never went back again.

Years later Exton would recall that "I wished that day that there was a reporter up there with me, someone who would listen to me. I would have given him a little footnote about the great West Side Improvement."

But there were no reporters up on Inwood Hill that day. They were all down at the Seventy-ninth Street Grade-Elimination Structure, listening to the speeches.

As for Spuyten Duyvil and all Riverdale to the north of Inwood Hill, Weinberg had predicted that if the parkway were run through it without planning and zoning for community growth first, it would be turned from a peaceful, quiet place to live, one that could have absorbed a degree of apartment development while still remaining a quiet place to live, into a formless, shapeless mass of high-rise apartment houses with neither adequate nor convenient shopping, jobs or recreational facilities for its residents. World War II staved off this outcome for five years, but after the war, that is precisely what once-beautiful Riverdale became.

North of Spuyten Duyvil, at the north end of Riverdale, was Van Cortlandt Park, where once there had been the only fresh-water marsh left in New York City. When the Henry Hudson Parkway was finished, the marsh was, too. Once botany and biology students by the thousands had come every year to study salamanders and polliwogs and flowers and shrubs and insects—and a dozen species of birds who would nest only in a fresh-water marsh—in their natural habitat. Henceforth, as long as New York City might exist, its botany and biology students would be able to study them only by looking at their pictures in books.

Biology and botany teachers wrote letters-to-the-editor. A few were printed. Aside from them, no public notice was taken of the city's loss.

Robert Moses had spent $109,000,000 of the public's money on the West Side Improvement. Counting the money expended on his advice by other city agencies on the portion of the Improvement south of Seventy-second Street, the Improvement had cost the public more than $200,000,000.

But the total cost of the Improvement cannot be reckoned merely in dollars. The West Side Improvement also cost the people of New York City their most majestic waterfront, their most majestic forest, a unique residential community, and their last fresh-water marsh.

When the Improvement was finished, all these things were gone forever.

Adding them to the cost of the West Side Improvement, one might wonder if the Improvement had not cost New York City more than it was worth. Adding them into the cost, one might wonder if the West Side Improvement was really, on its total balance sheet, an "improvement" at all. One might wonder if it was not, on balance, a tragic and irremediable loss.

But, with a few lonely and unheard exceptions, at the time the Improvement was built, no one was adding.

"Two, Four, Six, Eight—Who Do We Appreciate? Robert Moses! ROBERT MOSES!! *ROBERT MOSES!!!*"

Little children in New York City during the 1930's cheered the Park Commissioner that way—and by parading to 80 Centre Street to present him with tokens of their esteem, such as two scrapbooks containing the names of "thousands" of boys and girls from the summer day camps run in his parks by the WPA and the Board of Education. Older children, many of whose high-school civics and social studies classrooms were decorated with pictures of his bridges and parks distributed broadscale by the Park Department, cheered him at "special assemblies" at which he received their tributes; the president of the Richmond High School Arista, awarding "Commissioner Moses" the honor society's annual medal, called him "the ideal civic leader" because he possessed "the following qualities: Intelligence, efficiency, conviction, personality, culture, incorruptibility, sense of humor, perseverance, foresight, tolerance, knowledgeable unselfishness, idealism and modesty." Children off to college took their enthusiasm along. He was voted "America's most useful public servant" at Manhattan College, "the ideal public servant" at Fordham University.

And the city's children weren't cheering any louder than its adults. Some neighborhoods may have gotten no playgrounds and others may not have liked the ones they did get, but many neighborhoods were thrilled with theirs—and grateful to the man responsible for their creation. The ceremonies opening Greenpoint's McCarren Park were preceded by a mammoth parade during which bluff old Pete McGuiness, a long-time Sheriff of Brooklyn and Boss of his beloved "Greenpernt," insisted that Moses, dressed in the white suit he invariably wore at daytime ceremonies, march at its head. And when, on the speakers' platform afterward, McGuiness pulled Moses out of his seat, raised both of his hands over his head like a boxer's second raising his hands in a victory gesture, and boomed, "Bob Moses—the Champeen Park Commissioner of the world," the crowd was so eager to touch the Commissioner that it surged forward against the park's brand-new wrought-iron fences and knocked them over.

Some young reformers who had had the opportunity to observe Moses' work firsthand had become disturbed by both his policies and practices, but the city's most prestigious Good Government groups were still dominated by the old-line idealists like Richard S. Childs, George McAneny, William J. Schieffelin and Joseph M. Price, whose first impression of Moses had been of a young idealist and who felt, in Childs' words, that "basically he hadn't changed"; during the 1930's Moses received many tokens of their tribute—even the gold medal of the American Scenic and Historic Preservation Society, whose leadership had passed out of the hands of the upstaters who had seen Moses trick them out of their control of their beloved state parks, force them to stop printing their annual report and try to strangle their secretary. So highly did the old-line reformers idolize Moses that they were willing to suffer snubs to be able to present him with an award in person: when he informed the Park Association that he was "too busy" to take time off for a luncheon at which Mrs. Sulzberger was supposed to present him with the association's Testimonial Award for "most outstanding service to parks," Mrs. Sulzberger and fifty other members of the association trooped off to his office with their illuminated scroll (to be rewarded with what one of the fifty recalls as "an attitude that I can only describe as utter contempt"). Joseph M. Price, who had fought so hard for Moses' mayoral candidacy, was reduced to coming to Moses' apartment one evening to present him with the City Club's annual award, a leather-bound hand-illuminated parchment stating that Moses' achievements "constitute the major contribution of our generation to the improvement of the conditions of life in our city." As for businessmen, their admiration for the man whose parkways had boosted real estate values and whose efficiency was giving New York big improvements at small cost, was cast in bronze and silver medallions from real estate organizations and Chambers of Commerce and from the One Hundred Year Association, a group of firms in business in the city that long. Three officers of the Irving Trust Company organized a Committee for Deserved Recognition whose "sole object is to name the West Side Highway the Robert Moses Highway"—an object that failed, as attempts to name Jones Beach after its creator had failed, because politicians were afraid that the public would shorten the name "Robert Moses Highway" to "Moses Highway" in usage and would thereby offend the sensibilities of the city's non-Jewish residents.

If Moses' days were white-suit days, his evenings were black-tie. The city's hotels should have been grateful during those lean Depression years for his popularity; if it would have been difficult selling tickets for a block party honoring Robert Moses in Sunset Park or Harlem or Spuyten Duyvil, there was no difficulty in selling tickets to members of those organizations that honored their heroes in the Grand Ballroom of the Waldorf-Astoria or the Baroque Suite at the Plaza; in fact, when the guest of honor at a formal dinner was the city's Park Commissioner, a full house could always be expected. (His biting "ad hominisms" were worth the price of any ticket, even if they were delivered in a harsh, bored tone by a man who seldom bothered to glance up at his audience; at a dinner celebrating the opening of the $800,000 Hayden Planetarium, whose construction was financed by an RFC loan arranged by Moses with great difficulty and whose star-reproducing, dumbbell-shaped projector was purchased with a $160,000 gift from Charles Hayden, who made it, to Moses' scorn, only on condition that the entire building be named after him, the financier was preening himself on the dais when Moses, rising to speak, turned to him and said: "Charlie, never in the history of philanthropy has anyone earned immortality so cheaply.") On one evening, Moses, in black tie, might be at the Waldorf to be handed a gold medal from the Citizens Union; on another, at the Plaza in black tie to be handed a gold medal from the St. Nicholas Society; on still another, at the St. Regis to have a gold medallion—fourteen-carat, this time—hung around his neck on a blue-and-gold moiré ribbon by the New York Rotary Club; then on to the Pennsylvania, where the plaque awaiting him was only bronze but inscribed with a description that Moses thought apt—"Dreamer-Planner-Doer"—and where the praise heaped on him in front of a thousand diners was so syrupy that Moses, rising to speak, said he was getting up to try and escape from a "Niagara of Molasses." He varied the béarnaise sauce circuit with trips to Carnegie Hall, also in black tie, to pick up medals, medallions, plaques and illuminated scrolls before audiences too large to be crammed into even Grand Ballrooms. So many organizations wanted to hold dinners in his honor that sixteen of them finally decided to combine. (The affair, held in the Rainbow Room at Rockefeller Center by the City Club, Park Association, Regional Plan Association, Architectural League of New York, Art Commission Associates, Central Park West and Columbus Avenue Association, Garden Club of America, Municipal Art Society, National Academy of Design, National Sculpture Society, New York chapters of the American Society of Architects and the American Society of Landscape Architects, New York Society of Architects, Outdoor Cleanliness Association of New York and the Fine Arts Federation of New York, was notable for the fact that the guest of honor did not show up; he was in the midst of a particularly heated battle with La Guardia at the time and when he learned that the Mayor had been invited to speak, refused to come; La Guardia did, and devoted his speech to reminding the audience that "the Park Department . . . could not have accomplished anything if it had not been for the sympathetic understanding and aid of the federal government; never in the history of the world did a Park Commissioner have the amount of funds that have been made available to Mr. Moses . . .") If, with his deceptions and innuendoes and breached promises, Robert Moses was seducing New York City into compliance with his desires, New York was loving every minute of the seduction—and begging for more.

The media, whose amplification of his statements without analysis or correction played so vital a role in making the public susceptible to the blandishments of his policies, carried out the same effective if unintentional propaganda for his personality. Continually, in five- or six-part series or

Sunday-supplement feature stories or long interviews, it said he was totally honest and incorruptible, tireless in working sixteen- and eighteen-hour days for the public, and it allowed him to repeat or repeated itself the myths with which he had surrounded himself—that he was absolutely free of personal ambition or any desire for money or power, that he was motivated solely by the desire to serve the public, that, despite unavoidable daily contact with politicians, he kept himself free from any contamination by the principles of politics. His flaws reporters and editorialists made into virtues: his vituperation and personal attacks on anyone who dared to oppose him were "outspokenness"; his refusal to obey the rules and regulations of the WPA or laws he had sworn to uphold was "independence" and a refusal to let the public interest be hampered by "red tape" and "bureaucrats"; his disregard of the rights of individuals or groups who stood in the way of completion of his projects was refusal to let anything stand in the way of accomplishment for the public interest. If he insisted that he knew best what that interest was, they assured the public that was indeed the case. If there were larger, disturbing implications in these flaws—they implied that he was above the law, that the end justifies the means, and that only he should determine the end—they ignored these implications or joked about them; columnist Westbrook Pegler dubbed Moses' technique of driving stakes without legal authorization and then defying anyone to do anything about them, the "Oops, Sorry" technique.

By the end of the Thirties, praise of Moses was spreading across the country—fostered by the nationally circulated magazines published in New York. If it was possible to be more one-sidedly favorable to the Park Commissioner than the New York newspapers had been, the national magazines, whose readers were not interested in the details of local issues and who therefore provided those readers with only a broad outline of his career, without any close examination of his methods, accomplished the trick. An article in *Harper's* began: "This is the story of . . . the pride of a city in a man who brings beauty to a herded people," and ended: "New York presents an impressive exhibit of one citizen's building for the common good." In the fourteen intervening pages, the reader was assured that Moses was interested only in the people's welfare and that those who opposed him were "obstructionists" and "politicians" and that his temper should therefore be excused—"His rages are against those who would cheat the public interest" —and that he was so absolutely honest and incorruptible that the laws which governed other public officials should not be applied to him in any case:

> Moses knows his way through the mazes of the law. On Flushing Meadow he moved so swiftly that the 600-odd owners, the city, and the State never caught up with him. . . . By May 15th [1936] Moses was in possession of the property, leaving it for the courts to decide later how much would be paid.
>
> . . . The city charter provides that contracts shall go to the lowest bidder . . . It takes a hardy commissioner in New York to reject the low bidder, a commis-

sioner against whom the charge of graft would not stick. . . . The Board of Estimate swallowed hard and approved Moses' plan.

The work of filling and grading was begun on schedule—and finished on schedule. . . . And at any hour of the day or night Moses would appear to make sure that there was no delay. His only heartbreak was the fact that once every twenty-four hours the machinery was stopped twenty minutes for oiling. . . .

Did Moses feel that accomplishment was all that mattered, that the end justified the means? Apparently *Harper's* agreed. "Those familiar with New York's ways would have prophesied that these [600-odd condemnation] cases would keep the courts busy for years; but they would have reckoned without Moses," the article said. "The docket was all cleared within . . . six months." The article did not ask *how* the docket was cleared, or whether the rights of the 600-odd families being evicted from their homes were trampled in the rush.

There was an overblown, romanticized quality to *Harper's* recounting of the Commissioner's life story:

At Yale they remember Robert Moses for his victory over Coach Walter Camp and the football enthusiasts who thought to monopolize the athletic money. . . . At Oxford they still speak of the avid vigor with which he studied the ways of government. . . . "Take a salary," said Smith. "No," said Moses. . . . Moses looked upon the grass, and it was moth-eaten. He brought fertilizer and the soured acres turned green. He turned to the trees. With his own hands multiplied seventy thousand times, he trimmed away the dead branches, cut out the rotted sides, fed the abused roots, watered and tended . . . and brought shade to a dusty people. . . . He saw the streets filled with children, frantically seeking to make ballparks out of thoroughfares. We must bring the playground within reach of the baby-carriage pushers, said Moses. He searched the city for bits of land. . . . It never occurs to him that he is noble. . . . What are the mainsprings of this man's single-mindedness? Why does he drive himself, and others, in the public interest? Why does he forswear private gain for the public weal? . . . Is it human sympathy which drives him? Is it a sense of the misery of the millions who breathe tenement house air? He knows that men must live and that their children should see the grass and sky. And he fights for the grass and sky with the devotion of an Amos.

And there was an overblown, romanticized quality to the prose in which that life story, with its great battles—the Taylor Estate fight against the "selfish interests," the Triborough Bridge fight against the "politicians"—was recounted in *Time* and *The Saturday Evening Post* and *Current History* ("Moses: Idealist in Action") as well as in the *Architectural Forum,* which, naming him its "Man of the Month," confessed that conferring another title on the man who "probably holds as many important jobs as any other living American" was "preposterous" and that *its* title was particularly inappropriate: "What month? It is a lean thirty days on the Commissioner's calendar when he doesn't pop up with a new bridge or a flock of playgrounds or forty miles of parkways or a zoo or a proposed tunnel from New York to Brooklyn or a plan to reshape the Atlantic Ocean," and in *Fortune,* which said, "Other men have built parks and roads and bridges in states and cities other than New York, and there were all of these things in New York before

Robert Moses was born. But it is doubtful if any other man ever built so many of these things and on such a grand scale," and which added, after calculating that he had spent $552,000,000 in public funds, that his success in defeating opponents was due to "his scrupulous and unquestioned honesty" in money matters and "Thus, not only like a boy scout is Bob Moses always prepared; like Galahad, his strength is as the strength of ten because his heart is pure." It was in the national magazines that Robert Moses was first dubbed "the master builder" and "the master planner." If the city's press had made him a hero, the nation's magazines made him a folk hero, a figure larger than life, almost mythical, shrouded in the mist of his own legends, a Paul Bunyan of Public Works, a John Henry of Highways, the man who, in the phrase dreamed up during his gubernatorial campaign by some obscure GOP phrase maker and now spread, complete with capitalization, across the country, Gets Things Done.

As the publicity spread beyond New York, so did the cheering. Life was not all white suits and black ties; it was also academic gowns and mortarboards; it was during the Thirties that Moses began to spend his Junes traveling to out-of-town colleges to receive honorary degrees; he would eventually be a Doctor of Laws eleven times over, a Doctor of Engineering six times over, a Doctor of Humane Letters twice ("I never wrote a humane letter in my life," he protested), as well as Bachelor and Master of Arts (twice each) and a Doctor of Fine Arts and of Public Administration as well as Philosophy. Park and horticultural associations all up and down the eastern seaboard began to give him awards; the Boston-based Trustees of Public Reservations, for example, commended him for "distinguished service in conservation." So fast did the awards flow in, in fact, that he found that if he traveled to each out-of-town event at which he was to receive one he would have little time for work; he therefore made a practice of not attending, and of reading his acceptance speech over the telephone on his desk, which was hooked up at the dais at the event to an amplifying device that enabled the audience to hear it. For a time his wife and secretaries mounted the medals, medallions, plaques and illuminated scrolls on the walls of his office—along with one memento that Moses insisted be placed in a prominent position, a memento that *Fortune* described as "a letter of restrained commendation" dated 1930 and signed Franklin D. Roosevelt. The office walls were soon filled, and Mary Moses covered a long wall in the living room of their apartment with them. But they continued to pour in so fast that his secretaries finally just began storing them in packing cases.

Other cities began to send their planners and engineers to New York to see what all the fuss was about. Buses chartered by the park associations of Boston and Philadelphia brought matrons by the score to see the new playground design. And the response was invariably that of the hundred members of the American Shore and Beach Preservation Society whose reaction following a day-long tour of Moses' works was summed up by a *Herald Tribune* reporter as "amazed." Arriving back at City Hall after a similar tour, Mayor William B. Hartsfield of Atlanta asked a reporter, "Where does New York get all the millions to do this?"* Urban improvements on such a scale had never been seen—had, perhaps, never been dreamed of—in America before; there were, for example, more miles of divided through highways uninterrupted by intersections at grade in the New York metropolitan area in 1940 than in the next five largest cities in the United States—Chicago, Philadelphia, Detroit, Los Angeles and Cleveland—*combined.*

The *Architectural Forum* advised America's urban planners: "If you are thinking of designing a system of parks (and parkways) for your own cities, you might well go to New York for a few pointers." And, the *Forum* concluded, "while you are in New York, for best results kidnap Robert Moses." A score of American cities tried to take the advice, at least on a part-time basis; week after week requests to lay out, as a highly paid consultant if he would not accept a full-time job, highway and park plans for cities large and small poured into 80 Centre Street. During the Thirties, he accepted one such commission, to review plans for arterial highways for the Pittsburgh Regional Planning Association. He dispatched a team of aides to spend two months in Pittsburgh, reviewed their findings himself, and on the basis of their reports, submitted a plan laying out a comprehensive arterial highway program for the city. He had to refuse the others, but his mark was left on them, too, for their engineers came to New York and spent weeks—in some cases, months—watching Moses' men in action and, when they returned to their own cities, applied the principles Moses had taught them in building their own parks and roads.

Nor was the cheering limited to America. Teams of park experts came to New York from countries all over Europe, even from Scandinavia, traditional leader in park design, and went home vastly impressed. As for roads, a survey of public works in America made for the British government by a team of British urban planners said:

> The most important development in American city planning has in recent years been the building of express highways on a large scale. New York City has led the way in the development of an outstanding system of express highways and parkways. These are so good that it would seem almost essential that England should study them. . . . It is probably the outstanding example of democratic city planning in the world.

In the years during which Americans wondered if Roosevelt would run for a third term, there were many media suggestions that Moses be the Republican nominee for the presidency. *Life* selected him as the Republican to write "The Case Against Roosevelt"; *The Saturday Evening Post* commissioned him to give "Advice to My Party." Moses never had any real

---

* Another reaction was voiced by a Latin American diplomat taken on a tour by La Guardia himself. At each bridge and highway that the Mayor pointed out to him, the visitor asked, "And who was in charge of giving the contracts?" Each time La Guardia replied, "I was." "Ah, La Guardia," the diplomat said at last, with real admiration in his voice. "Ah, La Guardia. You must be a very rich man."

chance of obtaining the presidential nomination, of course. But the frequent suggestions were a further indication of the extent of his popularity.

Such popularity left little room for dissent. The press which was turning him into a legend in his own time had scant space to spare for critics. At the Hotel Pennsylvania dinner at which he was deluged with a Molasses-Niagara of sweet praise, a hundred pickets were marching outside the hotel protesting his treatment of WPA workers, but most of the city's newspapers never even mentioned them.

The attitude of the press was reflected in the attitude of the public. At one Kiwanis Club luncheon, held in March 1934, the assembled Kiwanians applauded his speech, but during the question-and-answer period that, under Kiwanian tradition, followed the speech, one member of the audience said that he was disturbed by newspaper reports that Moses was intending to revoke all camping privileges at Orchard Beach immediately. "As one of the campers at Orchard Beach," he said, "will you grant us the privilege for a committee to interview you and put before you our story about the beach?"

"No, sir," Moses replied—"calmly and finally," according to the *Herald Tribune*. "The camps are coming down." The camper tried to protest the arbitrariness of the decision, but he was drowned out—by the strains of the song sung by the rest of the audience to usher Moses out: "For He's a Jolly Good Fellow."

Moses basked in his popularity. He wallowed in it. He boasted to his friends about it.

And he felt it was no more than his due. He understood fully the importance of the press in creating it. In the introduction to the Park Department's 1940 brochure—*Six Years of Park Progress*—he wrote, "We owe much to the press, without whose constant interest and publicity it would be impossible to explain our program and to obtain public support for it." But he had not the slightest doubt that the press's support for his policies would continue. Once, explaining his feeling that a controversial project could be pushed through the Board of Estimate, he ended a conversation with an objecting McGoldrick by saying dryly, "We'll undoubtedly have the cooperation of the press, you know."

No matter how busy he was, Moses always tried to find time in the late afternoon to drop in on Al Smith.

The former Governor was a sad and bitter man now, old long before his time. Retired from public life at the age of fifty-six—too early for retirement for a man accustomed to action and applause and still healthy and strong—he had found in business only humiliation: he felt that all New York must know that he had had to beg Frank Roosevelt for help to rescue the Empire State Building—and that even after Roosevelt had moved federal agencies into the skyscraper, it was still not earning enough to meet the mortgage payments and they were being picked up almost as charity by John J. Raskob and the Du Ponts.

And Al Smith wasn't interested in business anyway. He was interested in helping people. With the Depression, people needed help, needed it desperately. And he wanted—wanted desperately—to have a hand in bringing it to them. He was no businessman. He was the Happy Warrior of the political battlefield. And he yearned desperately, with all the desperation of a man who sees the sands of his life running low, to be part of that battlefield again before it was too late. As realization grew in him that Roosevelt would never allow him to play a part in his administration, that he was to be forever excluded from the public service in which he had spent his life by a man Smith felt owed him his career, he came to hate Roosevelt, with a hatred so unreasoning and blind that it was all too easy for him to hate the things Roosevelt stood for.

The old friends, the friends who would have made him see that the social welfare programs Roosevelt was espousing were only extensions of the social welfare programs he had espoused as Governor, were gone. Mrs. Moskowitz was dead. Others were alive, but he didn't see much of them any more. Their field was politics, and he was no longer part of politics. In their places had come new friends—the ultrareactionary Raskob and William T. Kenny—who hated "that man in the White House." Al Smith had always been loyal to those who helped him, and these were the men helping him now. He had gotten his ideas from interaction with the ideas of associates, and these were the only associates left to him—these and Moses, who spent so much time with him, whom he respected so deeply, and who was as bitter about Roosevelt and the New Deal as any of them. There was no Mrs. M. to counterbalance their arguments. It was easy for Raskob and right-wing financier Jouett Shouse to use his bitterness for their own ends, to help him convince himself, as they were convinced, that the New Deal was "Communistic" and "Bolshevistic," that a spreading red-tinged bureaucracy was taking over America and destroying the principles that had made the country great. By 1936, the man who had once made being "regular" his First Commandment was ready to try to split the Democratic Party by lending his name to the right-wing Raskob-and-Du Pont-financed "Liberty League," and by giving a speech—Moses played a key role in its drafting—assailing Roosevelt and warning that "there can be only one capital, Washington or Moscow."

As soon as he had given the speech, Smith knew that he had made a terrible mistake. But what hurt worse was the attitude of the public, the public of whose support he had once been so confident. The speech had caused a flurry in the press, but the flurry had been brief; Roosevelt had been able to laugh it off. To laugh *him* off! The old Governor knew he was still an immensely popular figure among New Yorkers. The drivers of the Fifth Avenue buses he took to get home every day recognized him, and on rainy days they would make a special stop in front of the awning at No. 820 so that he could get out without getting wet—and often other riders on the bus would stand and applaud the figure in the brown derby as he walked, somewhat stooped and stiff now, down the steps. But he was afraid that popularity no longer meant respect.

When he got upstairs, his daughter Emily Smith Warner, his confidante and friend, would be there—her devotion to her father brightens the gloomy last pages of his life—and often so would other members of his family. But a family's devotion was no substitute for the roar of a cheering crowd or for a late afternoon in the Executive Chamber, with a dozen associates helping him veto bills or waiting to see what the Republican legislative leaders up on the Third Floor were going to come up with so that he could draft the strategy that would confound them. He was a natural genius in the art of leading multitudes of men toward great goals—and he was being given no chance to use that genius. In the late afternoons, when Moses came to Al Smith's apartment, he would often find the old Governor sitting, alone except for Emily, in the darkened living room, sunk deep in an easy chair, a glass of whiskey in his hand, staring in silence out at the sunset behind Central Park.

One afternoon in 1938 or 1939, Moses came in and began discussing some project—Emily cannot recall which one—that he was planning to propose, and Smith pointed out that there would be opposition. Emily recalls vividly Moses' reply. He would "undoubtedly" have the support of the press and of the public, he said, just as he always did. And Emily recalls vividly what her father said then.

"That's a slender reed to lean on, Bob," Alfred E. Smith said. "A slender reed."

"He meant that it could break at any time, that you could lose the public support," Emily explains. "Bob didn't say anything but you could tell by looking at him that he was sure that *he* never would."

26. *Two Brothers*

OFTEN, AT THE REAR of a cheering audience, there would be standing one figure who wasn't cheering, who amid a roomful of men and women gathered to honor Robert Moses stood watching Robert Moses with a face twisted with bitterness and hatred and contempt.

He was Robert Moses' brother.

Paul Moses had a strange story to tell about this hero who appeared particularly heroic because, so the legend went, he had absolutely no interest in money. Robert Moses, Paul Moses said, had cut him out of part of his inheritance.

And, Paul said, his brother had done more: to minimize the possibility of mutual acquaintances finding out what he had done, he had used his influence to keep Paul away from those acquaintances as much as possible—by keeping him out of city posts for which he was eminently well qualified and to which he would have otherwise been appointed.

The truth of Paul Moses' charge about the inheritance will never be determined. His mother, who left it, is, of course, dead, and so, to the last man or woman, are all but one of her friends and relatives who might be in a position to verify or deny his story. The single exception, of course, is his brother. Robert Moses refuses—and has refused for forty years—to allow the subject of his mother's will (a will, signed on her deathbed in his presence, that invalidated an earlier will that Paul says divided her estate equally among the two brothers and their sister, Edna) to be raised in his presence. The truth of Paul's charge is, moreover, clouded further by the personality of the man who made it and by the shadows which surround certain periods of his life. Paul could have dispelled those shadows. For months, the author asked him to do so. He refused, saying it was no one's business but his own. Finally, he said he would, at their next interview. On the day before that interview, he was stricken with his final illness. From the hospital, he telephoned the author and began the story. Before he could get more than a few sentences into it, he collapsed. Several days later, he died, leaving the shadows forever undispelled.

Paul's personality was, to a striking degree, Robert's personality, the mixture of brilliance, idealism and arrogance that flowed in so rich a strain from the two fierce women who dominated their family, their grandmother and their mother. If the strain was clear in Robert, it was just as clear in his brother, born, in 1887, a year before him. If the two "Moses boys" were in their youth a matched pair, a stunning matched pair, physically—both tall, both slim, both graceful, both haughty, their olive-skinned, high-cheekboned faces not only remarkably handsome but so similar they might almost have been twins; two quick-minded, quick-tempered, passionate young Spanish grandees—the passing years, in which, while his brother stayed slim, Robert's neck, and the face above it, became bulky, made clear that the resemblance was more than physical.

Robert Moses was charming. So was his brother. Inquire about Paul Moses of a dozen women who are old now and who have not seen him since they were young, and a dozen wrinkled faces light up with almost involuntary smiles as they remember him. "Paul was a *very* good-looking man," says Mrs. Carl Proper, widow of an official in Ed Flynn's Democratic machine. "He was tall and very elegant and *very* bright—he had a mind. But the big thing about him was that Moses charm—it just washed over you like a wave." His life was to be filled with beautiful, sophisticated women, because, Mrs. Proper says, "they absolutely threw themselves at him. From the moment he walked in the door at a party, you could see women—the most beautiful, elegant women—watching him out of the corner of their eye. . . . He was *scintillating*."

Robert Moses was arrogant, equipped not only with the "Moses charm" but with a spigot that could turn off charm at the mere hint of disagreement. So was his brother. Each of the two Moses boys was totally convinced that he was intellectually superior to others, each was totally contemptuous of the products of others' intelligence. From his youth, Robert Moses seemed driven, moreover, by some need—some compulsion, almost—to demonstrate this contempt to those for whom he held it. With Paul Moses, this compulsion came later, the product perhaps of the tragic circumstances of his life. But it came. Says Mrs. Proper, who knew both the brothers: "[Paul] was opinionated—my God! When someone disagreed with him, you have no idea! He could argue you right back against the wall. And just as often he couldn't even be bothered arguing. There was this disregard of someone else's point of view, this brushing aside. This was from the mother, of course. I never saw this thing so strongly in any other individual as I did in Bob Moses—except maybe for Paul Moses." The brothers' arrogance was, moreover, more than intellectual. Not only Robert but Paul was to reveal throughout his life a feeling that the laws that governed other men were not meant to govern him. The drive to dominate, to relate to others from a commanding position, was strong in both, as a minor but significant characteristic they shared made obvious: even as a youth, Robert insisted on picking up checks for friends, even wealthy friends—he displayed a real need to be not a member of a gathering but the host. So did Paul.

Robert Moses was brilliant and more than brilliant, possessed of a mind not only quick and supple but broad enough in reach to encompass a great metropolitan region and see its thousand diverse parts in a single, unified relationship.

So was his brother, who was fluent in Greek and Latin (he loved to spend evenings with a massive Greek lexicon, leafing through it as if it were a popular novel), and, an electrical engineer by profession, was considered the most knowledgeable man in New York in the complex field of utility property assessments. While interviewing Paul about his brother—who at the time had rejected requests for an interview himself—the author was, by coincidence, simultaneously researching a series of articles on regional planning. He had been searching for a unifying concept of the metropolitan region as a whole, some sort of overview that would bring at least a measure of coherence to its development, that would suggest some vision of the past and present that could contain clues to—and suggestions about—the future. The search had been in vain. He could spend days, he found, interviewing the region's highest elected public officials—mayors, county executives, freeholders and presiding supervisors—and scores of urban planners without ever obtaining even a glimpse of such a vision. In talking with Paul Moses, the reporter wanted to talk about Robert Moses' boyhood; Paul was constantly lapsing into discussions of housing and recreation and transportation. The reporter was irritated by the digressions until, one day, caught despite himself by his companion's eloquence, he started listening. And then he suddenly realized that he was hearing at last what he had been seeking for so long—a shaping vision of how to plan the most heavily populated and densely congested metropolitan region in the world—hearing it pouring out of a man who had never in his life held any official or unofficial planning position. The author continued interviewing planners and public officials. Eventually he was to hear such a vision—conflicting, of course, but of similar grand scale and scope—from two men: elderly Lewis Mumford and young Lee Koppelman, a brilliant planner from Long Island. He was never—in a hundred interviews—to hear it again.

Except when, months later, he finally got to interview Paul Moses' brother.

During his young manhood Robert Moses was the uncompromising idealist, specifically anxious to "help" the "lower classes." So was Paul—although there were differences between his idealism and his brother's. Robert's concept of help was that of the mother he imitated, the patronizing "Lady Bountiful" who never forgot that the lower classes were lower. It was the concept of rigid class distinction and separation that would later be set in concrete by Robert Moses' public works. Paul, doted on by Grannie Cohen (and by her husband, Bernhard; on Saturdays, the gentle old man and the bright-eyed, handsome little boy would walk from the Moses brownstone on Forty-sixth Street down to the tip of Manhattan Island, where the grandfather would reward him with a nickel), understood exactly what the nickname "Lady Bountiful" implied. "Don't you see that settlement-house attitude of hers in everything Mr. Robert does?" he would demand. "This 'You're my children and I'll tell you what's good for you'? " It was not his attitude. His brother wanted class distinctions made more rigid; Paul wanted them eliminated. His brother despised "people of color"; Paul's attitude, in Mrs. Proper's words, was "a genuine feeling of real indignation over the way Negroes were treated, and don't forget, this was at a time when it wasn't fashionable to have such feelings." His brother's attitude toward members of the classes Bella called "lower" was, like Bella's, markedly patronizing; perhaps in reaction, Paul, says a friend, "was a person who would talk to some menial and be on fine terms with him. He could be impossible—opinionated, arrogant—with people on his own social plane. But he would never, *never*, act like that with anyone who couldn't talk back to him. He was very much aware of the moral responsibility to the lower classes—he was like Robert in that. But his attitude towards these classes was genuinely friendly." He had the ability—which Robert did not—to see people not as members of classes but as individuals. When they were well into their seventies, the two brothers would be asked about the maids, cooks and laundresses who had worked in the Forty-sixth Street brownstone. Robert could remember exactly one: "old Annie." Asked to "tell me something about her," he responded by listing her duties—and stopped. About this woman whom he saw almost every day of his boyhood, he knew nothing more—not even whether or not she was married. Paul remembered an even dozen who passed through the Moses household at one time or another—and, fifty years after he had last seen most of them, he could relate details of their personal lives to an extent that revealed he had talked to them as a friendly equal.

Looking back on the youth of these two remarkable brothers, one difference looms large. Robert Moses would bend to his mother's fierce will. Paul Moses would not. Paul says—and relatives agree—that on many issues he and his younger brother shared views that were opposed to Bella's ("She was very conservative, and neither of us was, not in the terms of that time") but that in the face of her displeasure Robert would draw back, hastening to agree with the plain little woman with the steely eyes behind the steel-rimmed spectacles, while Paul would continue to disagree. And Bella Moses, daughter of a woman who bullied underlings, herself a woman who bullied her husband to a point where, to accommodate her own wishes, she forced him to leave the city and the career in which he was happy, was not a woman who brooked disagreement—not even from her own son. Says Mrs. Proper, who saw them together: "It was no joke to that mother that she was a Republican and her son was a Democrat. That was apostasy to her." There was, moreover, Paul's romance at Princeton with a Philadelphia girl who was not only beautiful but first in her class at the University of Pennsylvania, who also had a habit of saying what she thought—and with whom Bella did not get along at all. Relatives say Paul and his mother had a violent falling out over her. Also at Princeton, Paul became leader of a 1910 version of a Reform Democratic club. Whether or not it was because of the romance and/or the political squabble, Paul left Princeton for four years, four years about which he never talked—these episodes are some of those obscured by shadows—and returned to major no longer in classics and literature but in electrical engineering. The conflict between Paul and his mother was more basic than specific issues: it was as fundamental as the fact that when the family discussions grew especially lively, Robert knew where to stop, and his older brother didn't—or, if he did, refused to act on the knowledge. "Paul was always the same—a maverick, a dissenter, based on this sense of social injustice," Mrs. Proper says. "And you only had to meet that mother once to know that that was a house in which very little dissent was tolerated." "She never did succeed in running me—that's what made her mad," Paul says.

Paul paid a high price for his independence. He wanted to go into public service as much as his younger brother did, but instead, in 1913, the year in which Bella secured for Robert a coveted place in the Bureau of Municipal Research, it was announced to Paul one evening that a partnership had been arranged for him with Kuhn, Loeb & Co., the investment banking firm in which Bella's brother-in-law was a partner. Paul declined to follow the pattern his mother had laid down for his life. "What?" he recalls saying. "You don't expect me to go downtown and spend the rest of my life juggling pieces of paper, do you? Well, that's what the banking business is, isn't it? Juggling pieces of paper?" He says his father wanted to help him get started in public service, but did not. "Why?" he would say bitterly. "Because Father did whatever Mother directed, that's why."

Shadows cover the next few years of Paul's life. According to several vague accounts, he spent them in South America, returning only when America followed the President he idolized into the war to make the world safe for democracy. At any rate, at a time at which his brother was declining to serve in the war, Paul enlisted in the Navy. Mustered out in November 1918, he was in no worse shape than his brother, who in November 1918, almost thirty years old, dreams of civil service reforms crushed, was working at a humiliating job as little more than a clerk, with no place to turn for work in his chosen field.

Looking back at this crucial point in the lives of these two remarkable brothers, another difference—an extension perhaps of Robert's willingness and Paul's unwillingness to bend to the woman they could not face down—looms larger. Robert may have previously refused to compromise with the practical politicians he scorned, but when, at the age of thirty, Belle Moskowitz gave him one last chance, he compromised. Having learned he could not beat the Tammany politicians who had crushed him, he was not only willing but eager to join them; he had learned very well indeed the need to compromise. Paul never learned that lesson. Propelled up the Consolidated Edison executive ladder by his engineering brilliance (he was soon assigned, at a salary of $18,000, to find ways of harnessing the vast power of the St. Lawrence River, a plan that would later be thwarted by Al Smith's determination to have the harnessing done by a State Power Authority), he was hobbled by his refusal to tailor his liberalism to the ultraconservatism of the utility's executive suite; once, a top executive asked him if he didn't agree that Woodrow Wilson was a fool; Paul lashed out at him angrily. Robert Moses may have been the idealist who compromised his ideals; Paul Moses was the idealist who didn't.

Looking back on the lives of the two Moses boys, one difference looms largest of all. Robert went into public service, a field big enough to allow his unique vision and drive full range; a field in which funds were available on the same scale as his immense dreams, in which his arrogance was in part excused by the public need he was serving, and in part protected by the public powers that devolved on him, so that when he went beyond the law, the power of the state protected him from retaliation. Paul did not go into public service. Eager to do so, he thought he was going to have his chance in 1925, the year after his brother was appointed president of the Long Island State Park Commission, when, he says, his close friend Colonel Frederick Stuart Greene, the erudite, urbane head of the State Department of Public Works, offered him a top DPW engineering job. But, Paul says, at the last minute, "after everything was set," Greene told him that Al Smith had vetoed the appointment without explanation. (At the time, Paul told the author with his bitter smile, he did not even suspect that the explanation might have something to do with his brother, whom at the time he considered his friend.)

Either through a quirk of fate or because of a spirit of competition with his brother—who was so quickly making a name for himself creating places to swim for the public—Paul purchased a large swimming club in Upper Darby, Pennsylvania. At the same time that his brother was making grandiose plans for Jones Beach, Paul was making grandiose plans for his "Llanerch Pool," planning to turn it into a huge recreational complex by adding additional swimming pools, a huge dance hall, and different restaurants for different pocketbooks. "It would," recalls a friend to whom he enthusiastically broached his ideas, "have been something really unique for the time. He had *some* imagination, I'll tell you."

But imagination on the Moses scale was feasible only on a public scale. Attempting to carry out his plans, Paul spent the pool's revenues as fast as they came in. Robert's grandiose plans cost far more than he had expected, but because his money came from the state treasury, though he spent on an unprecedented scale, overspent his budget, poured funds allocated for an entire bathhouse into its foundations alone, there was always more where that came from. For Paul there wasn't—particularly after his father died. Emanuel had helped with his ambitious project, but when, in 1925, he died he left all his money to his wife. This money was readily available to the younger of her two sons. Although Bella never gave Robert as much as he needed and he was habitually short on cash, she did support him and his wife and daughters for more than ten years; when, in 1927, at the age of thirty-eight, he was named Secretary of State, it was the first job at which he had ever earned more than a token salary. When, desperate for funds to complete the Jones Beach Causeway, he asked her for a loan of $20,000, she gave it gladly. But for her older son, help was limited and grudging, and he was not a man who could beg. Soon, in the midst of a divorce that ended an unhappy marriage, he was being humiliated by the hounding of his Llanerch Pool creditors. He was unable even to pay his lawyer, and was sued by him, too.

In 1929, there was a reconciliation between Paul and his mother. She asked him to handle her business affairs. Con Ed hired him back on a part-time basis as a consultant, the swimming pool began to earn money, and, appearing nightly in winter at the theater or the opera and at New York's most fashionable restaurants, he was again an elegant, cheerful man-about-town.

Between two men as opinionated as Paul and his brother, there were bound to be frequent arguments, but in the past they had always been friendly; Paul had been a frequent visitor at Robert's home. But since his brother had become a powerful man in state government, Paul felt, his attitude had changed. He no longer, Paul felt, would tolerate anyone—even his brother—disagreeing with him. Looking over the aides his brother had selected, Paul recalled thinking: "Why, he's surrounded himself entirely with behind-kissers." During one heated discussion, his brother adopted an attitude that there was no sense discussing the matter any further since he knew best. "By God," Paul said, "I believe you're beginning to believe what these behind-kissers tell you." But, Paul says, there was never any particularly momentous clash with his brother; he believed they were still friends.

Then, in January or February 1930, Paul and his mother had another falling out. He left in a huff for Philadelphia, staying there for several months. The reason for the falling out is not known; but Paul said that it was no more serious than the other fights he had had with his mother, fights after which they had become reconciled.

But this time, something new happened, something he would never be able to understand—although he would spend the rest of his life trying to understand it. When he came home to make up with his mother this time, she refused even to see him. The other relatives on whom he dropped in, always so happy to see him in the past, were suddenly cold and distant. "They all seemed to think I had done something awful, you could tell from the way they were acting," Paul would say. "But I didn't know what the hell it was supposed to be." Much too proud to ask, Paul reacted by avoiding these people who had suddenly turned against him.

In March 1930, Bella Moses learned that she had cancer. Paul did not know at first. Whether he ever knew can no longer be determined. According to one story prevalent in the family, Paul never went to see his mother at Mount Sinai Hospital until the last few days before she died. According to another, he had gone earlier, but she had refused to see him. And when, on May 22, 1930, after weeks in which she lay semi-comatose in intense pain, she died of cancer, her will divided her estate between two of her children, Robert and Edna (although Robert's share was bigger than Edna's because to it was added, in effect, $50,000 for the education of his children). To Paul Moses, her eldest son, Bella Moses left only $100,000, and she left it in trust, so that he would receive only the interest from it, never the principal. He had to receive that income through his brother, who was named a trustee of the trust fund as well as an executor of the will. And there was an additional clause: if Paul ever contested the will, he would automatically lose even the trust fund, whose principal would then be divided between his brother and sister.*

* Upon Paul's death, half the principal was to go to Edna's children, half to Paul's—should he have children. If he did not, that half would go to Robert's children, Barbara and Jane.

* * *

Paul Moses was to be tortured by his mother's will for the rest of his life.

Financially, it changed his life, of course. Previously his earnings had always been supplemented by gifts from wealthy parents. Now he would have only the interest—so meager compared to those gifts—on his trust fund. More, he had always had security, the assurance of protection against any real hardships, as well as the assurance that one day a share of his family's wealth would be his. He had been raised among servants and tutors, in an atmosphere of snug luxury. He had spent his later life in variations of that atmosphere, and he had never had any reason to doubt that he would be able to live out his life against such a background. Now, suddenly, with a single blow, that security had been stripped from him—irrevocably and forever. It was the Depression: consulting engineers were a luxury companies could no longer afford; at the time he learned the contents of his mother's will, he had just learned that his retainer from Con Ed would soon be terminated. The swimming pool had not been doing badly, but its income would never be anything near a substitute for that security, even if it, too, was not affected by the Depression. He had saved nothing; there had never been any reason to save. He had always been a man who had much and the prospect of more. Now, all in an instant, at the age of forty-three, he had nothing.

But it was not financial considerations that hurt Paul most deeply. What his mother's will did to him cannot be computed on any tally sheet. He was to have to live for the rest of his life not only in straitened circumstances but with the question of why his mother had forced him into them. Thirty-seven years later, a man of eighty, he told the author, "I'm trying all this time to divine what was in my mother's mind. What kind of performance was this? Why did she do this thing?"

He was to have to live also with alienation from the rest of his family, an alienation that hurt him the more because he could not understand the reason for it. "I don't know what was in their minds," he would say. "What was I supposed to have done that was so terrible? Nothing that I know of. But they seemed to think I had." He was to spend the rest of his life tormented by these questions. And the conclusion that, after years of wondering, he finally reached was one that would not have been illogical to Ansley Wilcox or Judge Clearwater or Paul Kern—or any one of a score of men who had, in one way or another, stood between Robert Moses and something he wanted. His brother, Paul Moses felt, had lied about him when he was not around to defend himself, had poisoned his mother's mind and the minds of other members of his family against him, had exaggerated the details of his divorce and his financial difficulties until they seemed like vicious, unforgivable misdeeds. Paul even had a specific explanation for his mother's decision to virtually cut him out of her estate. "I wasn't present, but I know that Mr. Robert must have had something to do with that," he would tell the author. There had been another will, Paul would say, one that had divided his mother's estate equally among her three children. "How do I know?" he would say. "Because I saw it. I saw it several times. I was handling my mother's affairs, you know. It was just a simple thing—divided into three parts after charitable deductions." But Robert Moses had gone to the hospital where his mother lay dying, in a drugged state, Paul said, awaiting an emergency operation that was to be performed that night at ten o'clock, with a new will in hand, and, at six o'clock, had persuaded her to sign it. Paul could even advance a reason for his brother to do such a thing: Robert needed money badly, Paul said. And it was also his brother, Paul said, who was responsible for his difficulty thereafter in obtaining either public or private employment in his profession.

One of Paul's charges is demonstrably false. Bella did sign her final will during her last illness in Mount Sinai Hospital, but, according to the date on the will, she signed it on April 4, 1930, seven weeks before she died. The truth of his charge that his brother lied about him to their mother and their relatives cannot be determined—although it is clear, from a series of interviews with surviving relatives, that although they regard Paul almost as a criminal, not one of them has any clear idea of what his crime—if there was one—was supposed to be. Cousin Hilda Hellman, for example, says, "He was bad. I think he must have done something pretty awful." What exactly did he do? "I really don't have any idea at all," she says. Well, then, why does she think he did *anything?* Mrs. Hellman says it was just "an impression" she had. Asked the source of the impression, she was unable to remember. But at least one other relative, searching her memory, believes it was Robert.

Paul insisted that the will be read in the light of Robert's financial situation at the time his mother died—1930.

It was certainly serious. Having been ousted as Secretary of State by Governor Roosevelt in 1929, in 1930, Robert Moses was not earning any salary at all from his remaining jobs. Aside from expenses for which he was entitled to reimbursement, Robert Moses, at the age of forty-one, had no income at all except what his mother gave him. Now, with their two girls growing up—Barbara was thirteen in 1929, Jane eleven—Robert Moses' financial situation was complicated by the fact that for him it was unthinkable that his children attend public school, and he therefore had to pay tuition at St. Agnes'. The family had a nice place to live—Bella had bought him not only the Babylon summer house but a brownstone at 261 West Seventieth Street—but he was so strapped that in 1929 he did not have sufficient funds to pay the next term's tuition, or to make necessary repairs on the Babylon house. Moses had always made a point—both publicly and privately—of insisting that he be a public servant working without pay, refusing Smith's offer of a salary for his Long Island Park Commission job. His disregard for money was a vital part of the public image he had so assiduously cultivated, and the maintenance of this pose in private was no less important to him. But in September 1929, he took what for him was an unprecedented step—in the light of his previous actions, almost a desperate step. On completion of the City

Trust report he had written as Moreland Commissioner, he submitted a bill for his services of ten thousand dollars plus expenses. This was an unprecedented amount to ask for about two months' work, and Roosevelt, of course, would not have been disposed to grant Moses even a reasonable request. He turned Moses down flat. Moses was constantly being offered high-salaried jobs in industry, but that would mean leaving his public career and his public power. In early 1930, with the mother on whom he had always depended for money dying, he needed money desperately.

His mother's own resources, moreover, had been shrinking—largely because she had the same extravagant, prodigal attitude toward money as her two sons. Following her husband's death in 1925, she picked up more checks for Madison House. She made generous contributions to other charities, largely ones that produced some sign of physical accomplishment. How Robert Moses felt about this would be revealed later by a remark he made to La Guardia in a memo about the Children's Aid Society: "Every year my mother contributed *more than she could afford* to this organization because of her interest in playgrounds."* Although about $1,200,000 of her husband's money had been added to her own substantial inheritance, at the beginning of 1929 her net worth was down to little more than $1,000,000. Sometime during this period, moreover, she told Paul to begin entering future gifts to her children on her books as "advances." This, Paul says, was proof of a growing awareness that her resources, while great, were not inexhaustible—and of her determination to be "fair" in dividing up her estate; the purpose of this method of entering "advances," he said, was to make clear that they were advances against her estate, and that, to keep the total amount each child received from her the same, they would be deducted from each one's share of her estate. (At the time she died, the advances to Robert Moses on her books totaled $37,200.†) Half of her assets were in stocks; the 1929 crash further slashed her assets. In mid-1929, the worth of her stocks was about $500,000; when her estate was appraised after her death the next year, the value of those stocks was found to have shrunk to $293,649. Her total net worth was down to $690,422. She made no secret of her intention to leave about $50,000 to charity. In Paul's analysis, there no longer existed a fund of family capital large enough so that there was, as the Moses children had always supposed, plenty for everyone. A "fair"—one-third—share of Bella Moses' estate would, after the charitable deduction and inheritance taxes and the subtraction of $37,200, give Robert Moses about $170,000. The income from $170,000 would certainly never amount to enough to support in any decent style a man, without a cent of other income, with two houses and two children in private school. In Paul's analysis, Robert Moses realized that if he was to continue his precious career and protect his precious image, he needed for himself every cent of his mother's estate that he could get.

---

* Italics added.

† If there were any advances to Paul, the author could find no record of them.

This, of course, is Paul's analysis. Robert will not discuss it, and there is living no one else who is able to. It is not possible, therefore, for anyone ever to know whether or not Paul's analysis is true—although one part of it seems indisputable: apart from what he could get from his mother's estate, Robert Moses, forty-one years old, had no money to speak of at all.

But it is possible to ascertain the truth of Paul Moses' other charge. It is possible to determine whether or not it is true that Robert Moses secretly employed his behind-the-scenes influence in city government to keep his brother from getting jobs he deserved.

It is true.

Six high officials in that government—six in a position to know—say so. They are Fiorello La Guardia's Corporation Counsel, Paul Windels; his Comptroller, Joseph D. McGoldrick; his legislative representative, Reuben A. Lazarus; the chairman of his Civil Service Commission, Paul J. Kern; commission member Professor Wallace S. Sayre; and one other official who would talk only on the guarantee of anonymity.*

Paul, the liberal idealist who had always wanted to work for the public instead of for the giant utilities he felt were defrauding the public, was eager to work for a mayor who felt the same way. He certainly had the qualifications for the work. Anxious to regulate utilities more strictly and to probe the assessment and easement concessions they had obtained from Tammany, the new mayor was having difficulty finding electrical engineers with both expertise and the willingness to antagonize the major employers in their field. Paul possessed both. Highly regarded as an engineer, he was also, McGoldrick adds, "kind of an engineer with a cause—he was very suspicious of utilities . . . like La Guardia, who was also willing to believe that Con Ed was overcharging the city. . . . And there weren't too many engineers on the liberal side because there was . . . much money to be made working for the utility." Just after La Guardia's inauguration, Paul had an interview with Windels, who was at the moment looking, on the Mayor's behalf, for a Commissioner of Water Supply, Gas and Electricity. Windels was impressed. Recalls Kern: "Paul Windels called me and said, 'I want you to show this guy to the Mayor. He seems like just what La Guardia needs.'" Kern was impressed himself. "Paul Moses came in and talked about himself, not too modestly but impressively, and he left his résumé with me. His record looked good." Whether as a commissioner or in some other high-level post, Kern recommended to the Mayor that Paul be brought into the administration.

But there was something standing in Paul's way.

Precisely what his brother was saying to La Guardia about him is not known, although the one reference by Robert to Paul in writing in the Mayor's private files consists mainly of a paragraph that could hardly have helped raise questions in the mind of so sharp a lawyer:

> While it is nobody's business and purely a family matter, I have not seen my brother for a long time and I am hardly on speaking terms with him. My only

---

* No official could be found who said differently.

contact with him is in my capacity as a trustee of a fund of which he is the beneficiary.*

But that he was saying *something* was obvious. "That was quite clear to me—oh, just from little things [La Guardia] dropped," Windels says. "And it also became quite clear to me that for whatever reason—whether Robert made it a condition of his continuation in the administration that his brother not be hired or whether Robert simply made La Guardia believe it would be unwise to hire him—he wasn't going to be hired." Shortly, it also became clear to Kern. Having received no reply to his first recommendation that Paul be hired, he decided to press a bit. "At one of my half-hour sessions with La Guardia," he recalls, "I took a chance and brought this up, saying, 'With the shortage of good engineers, what's wrong with this guy?' La Guardia's reply was:

" 'Don't bother me. I can't have him around as long as Bob is here.' "

The more Windels and Kern saw of Paul, the more their respect for him grew. "Remarkable mind, remarkable," Windels says. "Like the brother. Reaching out for a whole problem and pulling the whole thing in at once." Kern, who frequently ate dinner with him, found in him another quality that characterized his brother. "He was very good at sizing up people," Kern says. "When I was on the Civil Service Commission, I'd often ask him about some guy and he'd tell me he's no damn good for such-and-such a reason. And we'd hire him, and sure enough he'd turn out just that way." Windels saw to it that Paul did get some work, hiring him as an expert witness in condemnation cases involving utilities, and as a consultant to a committee studying transit unification, and later putting him in charge of a thirty-three-man staff reassessing utility properties—at the fee he asked, fifty dollars per day. "Listen," Windels says, "I checked his qualifications. He was a *top* engineering consultant. He was worth fifty dollars a day of anybody's money." In fact, during several years in which Paul held this last job, the utilities' assessments were raised more than $200,000,000 per year.

But these were temporary jobs, and Paul's repeated attempts to obtain a permanent one met with rebuff. He was earning over $12,000 per year from his consulting work for the city, but the Depression was cutting deeper and deeper into the profits from the swimming pool. He needed a job—and he became very bitter over his inability to get one. He did not know, or even suspect, the real reason. (Ironically, he thought it was Windels who was keeping him from getting one.) "Listen, I wasn't asking for a handout," he would say years later. "I was recommended by the engineering societies. I knew more about this stuff than anyone else around. I was entitled to at least one of all those jobs. Windels, Lazarus—all those fellows: they were pretty shabby to me. I wanted to get something in public life, and no one would

* The paragraph is contained in a brief note Moses wrote in the first months after La Guardia's inauguration. It is a reply to a letter about Paul that the Mayor sent to Moses. The letter is not in the files, and its contents could not be learned.

say a word for me." After Windels resigned in 1938, he could not obtain even consulting work. At first, that did not worry him; his services had always been sought by many engineering firms. But now, for some reason he could not understand, even the firms which once sought them most eagerly were totally unwilling to even consider employing him. All through 1939 he hunted for a job in the profession in which he was an acknowledged expert—and could not find one.

His financial difficulties were compounded because he possessed the Moses prodigality toward money. Remarried—to a divorcée with two children—he had undertaken to send them to private school and college. He had moved his new family into an expensive lower Fifth Avenue apartment. Although between 1934 and 1938 he had been earning a substantial income, he had lived to its limit, saving nothing. And he had refused to—perhaps because of his upbringing had been unable to—put financial limits on the Upper Darby recreational complex that may have been his pitiful attempt to rival Jones Beach. He kept pouring money into the Llanerch Pool—for modern locker rooms, a dance hall, another restaurant. In 1938, with finances flush, he had put a $33,000 mortgage on the property to finance the construction of an "amusement building." As his plans for the building grew larger and larger, so did its cost. In 1939, with the $33,000 spent and the building still not finished, he encumbered the property with a second mortgage. The building was still uncompleted, no receipts were yet being earned by it—and suddenly the receipts earned by the pool and restaurant were being gobbled up by interest payments. One morning, the morning on which the last dreams of Paul Moses' life turned to ashes, there arrived at his office a real estate tax bill that he had no money to pay. The banks, learning of the situation, initiated foreclosure proceedings. He was reduced to borrowing from his wife's aunt, and then from her mother, securing a $12,500 loan from the latter by giving her another mortgage. He desperately needed a good summer—instead there was a polio scare in Philadelphia; few people dared to swim in public pools. The $12,500 melted away. Presented with a $7,500 bill from his attorney, he was unable to pay it; the attorney sued him. His wife's mother had died; in desperation, he had his wife assign the mortgage she had inherited from her to the attorney; he fell behind on federal income tax payments, and interest on them was mounting by the day—drawing tighter and tighter around this once gay, elegant free spirit was a net of debts too snarled to permit escape.

The marriage melted away with the money. Moving into a cheaper apartment was too agonizing for a man of Paul's pride to contemplate; by the end of 1938, however, he had no choice but to move; he had no money to pay the rent. He had to move in with his in-laws. Using every cent he could lay his hands on to try to save his pool—for a while he moved with some of his elegant suits into a tiny, bare room behind the pool office so that he wouldn't have the expense of commuting costs to Philadelphia—he let other bills slide. He and his wife were being dunned by the butcher, the grocer, by a department store, and even, for a hundred dollars, by a maid they had let go.

* * *

He lived on twenty-five dollars a week, using every other cent the pool earned to pay off its debts, and in some weeks in which a bill or a demand for taxes became too pressing, he was unable to take even the twenty-five. When he had to come to New York in 1939, the year in which his brother moved into the expensive apartment on Gracie Terrace, he slept in a Salvation Army lodging house. Pride made him conceal his poverty—so well that acquaintances who, meeting him on the street, noticed that the cuffs on his expensive suits and shirts were ragged, thought this was an affectation on the part of this man who had always cared so much about his appearance. To those who invited him to their homes for dinner, however, it was more difficult to conceal the truth. He might forget and cross his legs, and then friends such as the Propers—who were so kind to him that he would often "drop in" on them when he "happened to be in the neighborhood"—saw that there were holes in his socks and in the soles of his shoes. They saw from the way he ate dinner that he hadn't been eating many. Not only did he not have enough money to buy clothes or shoes, they realized, this man, whose brother was host daily at lavish luncheons, did not have enough to buy food. "He got thinner and thinner," Mrs. Proper says. "He was really not getting enough food. We kept him overnight a number of times. I really don't think he had a place to sleep. We offered to lend him some money. He wouldn't take any, not from us at any rate. I used to wish he had. Poor Paul."

Genuine friends such as the Propers, moreover, saw changes in Paul that saddened them more than the changes in his appearance. For, to people who remembered his wit and gaiety, the holes that gaped most glaringly now were not the holes in his shoes but the holes in his spirit. Paul Moses, they realized, was being eaten away by a terrible bitterness. "We had him to some dinner parties, but he was very difficult to handle," Mrs. Proper says. "Bitter, frustrated possibly, opinionated. This was when this Moses side came to the fore—this brushing aside, this arrogance. He was impossible. Paul was his own worst enemy."

At the heart of Paul Moses' bitterness was hatred for his brother.

Its spark was what Paul felt was injustice in the administration of the $100,000 trust fund of which his brother was a trustee. Their mother had intended that Paul get from that fund an annual income of several thousand dollars per year.

But he wasn't getting a cent.

The fund's trustees—Robert, Edna, cousin Wilfred Openhym and a bank—had invested Paul's money in "guaranteed mortgages," a device, common before the Depression, under which a title company, for a fee, "guaranteed" principal and interest payments and undertook the responsibility of seeing to it that the owner paid his real estate taxes. But two of the three mortgages involved were caught in the crash of the real estate market in New York, during which thousands of owners defaulted on payments, and title companies, unable to meet them all, collapsed. In normal times, the bank, which was managing the trust fund for the trustees, would have received notification of the default in taxes and interest payments from the title companies and would have foreclosed, saving the principal. But in the general confusion, the bank somehow did not check on the tax situation until the owners of the two properties had been in default on taxes and other city charges for more than two years. To keep from losing the entire $24,000 investment they had made in one building, the trustees, foreclosing on it, had to sell it for what they could get: $7,500. To keep from losing the $65,000 they had invested in the other, a loft building at 168 The Bowery, they had to pay off $8,000 in taxes, and make repairs costing $7,000—which they did by putting a $15,000 second mortgage on it. During the five years in which they were paying off this mortgage, the trustees deducted the payments from what Paul would have received. There was nothing left for him. Between October 3, 1935, and August 3, 1939—almost four years—he received nothing from his trust fund. By the time the mortgage was paid off, real estate values on the Bowery had plummeted—permanently. The rents earned by the building into which most of his inheritance had been sunk barely met mortgage payments and taxes. His income from the trust was henceforth going to be barely a thousand dollars a year.

If there was negligence involved in the disappearance of his assets, it was on the part of the bank, which had had the responsibility of managing the properties for the trust, not on the part of his brother, who had in fact lost part of *his* inheritance because he had invested it in guaranteed mortgages. Not even the most prudent investors had foreseen the general collapse of the title companies which had turned tens of thousands of guaranteed mortgages into all but worthless paper. Paul would probably have understood this if his brother had sat down and explained the situation to him.

But his brother wouldn't even talk to him. Once, the few thousand dollars a year that the trust fund was supposed to have provided would have seemed like an insignificant sum to Paul Moses. Now it looked as large as a meal to fill his stomach. It might be the means—the only means—of saving his swimming pool. In an attempt to realize something from the dilapidated Bowery loft that now represented almost his entire inheritance, he thought of two ideas. The bank, he learned, was paying a rental agent about $1,000 per year to collect the rents: why, he wondered, could the bank not hire him to do the collecting instead, and pay *him* the thousand dollars? Or, he wondered, why could not the building be sold? He asked its largest tenant if he would be interested in buying. The man said yes, and made an offer on the spot: $40,000. Paul was sure he would go higher, and even $40,000, placed in a bank, would return him more than the few hundred dollars the building was netting him annually now. Paul telephoned his brother to present these ideas to him—and heard with astonishment a secretary say that his brother wouldn't talk to him. When he telephoned his brother's home, Mary gave him the same message. When he contacted his sister, Edna said she would do whatever Robert wanted. So did Openhym, who, Paul says, "seemed to feel I was some sort of criminal or something." So did the bank. Much as he needed the money involved, it wasn't its loss that hurt Paul the most. It was the attitude of his brother. At about this same time, by coincidence, he asked Edna for some pictures or mementos of their parents; she said she did not have anything to spare—not so much as a single photograph. "Oh, I never blamed Edna," Paul was to say. "Whenever something comes up, she asks Mr. Robert what he wants done and then accedes to it." Now he tried to telephone his brother to ask him for a photograph—"You'd think they'd let me have a picture, wouldn't you? You'd think they'd let me have something, the oldest one in the family and all"—and he still would not come to the phone. He had always been fond of his brother's two daughters, Jane and Barbara. Now, he realized, he was not going to see them at all. And he couldn't imagine why his brother and sister and cousin were treating him this way. For a while he thought it must be because of his marital difficulties. "What right have they to sit in moral judgment on me, an older brother?" he said. But that explanation could not account for their attitude. He simply could not imagine what was behind it.

In January 1941, Paul received a letter that fanned smoldering hatred into flame, convincing him that the motive behind all his brother's actions had been the desire to wring for himself out of their mother's estate every last dollar he possibly could—even if those dollars had to come out of the pitifully few that Paul was receiving. For the letter, a copy of one from the trustees to the Surrogate's Court, informed him that Robert Moses was asking that he be paid—out of the trust fund—for his work as trustee.

For almost four years—from October 3, 1935, to August 3, 1939—Paul Moses had received nothing from the trust fund his mother had left for him. During the remaining months of 1939, he had received $1,144.54, in 1940, $444.18. In five years, then, he had received a total of $1,588.72. The letter informed him that the fund's trustees were asking the Surrogate's Court to approve the payment to them—out of the fund—of commissions for their work as trustees at standard trustee commission rates. Each trustee was asking for $750.90. Together, therefore, they were asking for $3,003.60. At the same time, Openhym asked an additional $750 for himself as "attorney for the trustees."

The wealthy lawyer's request enraged Paul. If it was granted, he would obtain from the trust fund Paul's mother had intended for Paul's support $1,500—just about as much as Paul had received from the fund for the previous five years. And Openhym was only a cousin. Robert and Edna were his brother and sister. They lived comfortably. He often literally did not have enough to eat. But they were attempting to obtain from his trust fund as much money as he had obtained during the previous five years. Together, in fact, the trustees were asking for almost $4,000—more than twice as much as Paul had received during those years.

And that was not all the information his brother's letter contained. The trustees now felt, it stated, that money Paul had been given in 1933 and 1934—some $3,484—had been given to him by mistake; it should have been applied instead to the bills for repairs and back taxes, and it must now be returned to the trust to build up the principal. Since he did not have any money to return, it would be returned for him; the trustees would add $3,484 to the principal by adding to it payments that would have been made to Paul until that amount was arrived at. Paul realized that his brother and the other trustees were proposing that, after a four-year period in which he had received from the $100,000 his mother had left him not one cent, he should receive not a cent for another three years.

Paul could take no more. He could not contest the will—the provision that had been placed in it made it too risky for him to do that—but he could contest what the trustees had done with the money left to him in it. Hiring an attorney, he asked the Surrogate's Court to order the trustees to pay him the thousands of dollars of income from the trust that they had put back to build up the principal, thereby, in his view, throwing good money after bad by pouring funds for repairs into the Bowery property whose value was deteriorating yearly, while at the same time insuring that he would get no income from the trust.

In describing what happened, Paul would tell the author: "It was shifted from a judge who would have been fair to me—a judge who had ruled favorably in a case practically four-square with mine—to a judge my brother knew."

Court records show that the case was originally scheduled to be heard before James Delehanty, one of the two judges in Manhattan Surrogate's Court, who had indeed in another case, similar to Paul's, held the trustees responsible for the dwindling away of a fund's assets caused by a failure to monitor taxes and mortgage payments. On July 17, 1941, however, Paul's attorney received a notice stating, without explanation: "The issues in this proceeding . . . will be heard before Hon. James A. Foley." James A. Foley, the other Manhattan Surrogate, was a key Tammany figure and one of Alfred E. Smith's closest friends. Whether the switch was a matter of court routine or whether Paul was correct in seeing his brother's hand in it cannot be determined. All that is known is what happened at the hearing: while Foley upheld Paul on several minor points, he ruled against him on the key issues, approved payment of the trustees' commissions—and gave Paul a tongue-lashing, saying, in words that caused the blood to rush to Paul's face when he recalled them years later: "You got the whipped cream, now you want the milk." ("Now what the hell did that mean?" Paul would say. "What sense was there in that? I don't know to this day.") To add a further soupçon of bitterness to Paul's whipped cream, Openhym, as a result of "extra work" he had had to do because of the hearing, increased his fee request from $750 to $1,000—and added on, to be deducted from the meager remainder of his cousin's trust, $38.47 in expenses.

Robert Moses had been entrusted by his mother with doling out a pittance to his penniless brother. He took part of that pittance for himself.

He took away from a brother who was poor while he was well off, who was walking the streets with holes in his shoes and sleeping in a Salvation Army lodging house, who was almost literally starving for want of a few dollars, $750.90.

Legally, he had a right to that commission. But the morality behind the request for it was the morality of Robert Moses.

Foley's decision—all the circumstances surrounding the will—was unjust, Paul felt. Most of his mother's money had come to her from her mother, his grandmother, and her husband, his father. His grandmother and father would certainly have wanted him to have a fair share of their money: was it not unjust that he was not being allowed to have it? And why had she acted so unfairly? "I wasn't present, but I know Mr. Robert must have had something to do with that." Preying on him constantly, moreover, was the feeling that even if his brother had had nothing to do with his mother's injustice, he had compounded that injustice by his later actions. "What right have they to sit in moral judgment on me?" To refuse him even a photograph of his parents? Right or wrong, the feeling deepened into an obsession. Festering within him constantly now was the conviction that he had been the victim of a monstrous injustice—at the hands of his own brother. A single talk with his brother might have lanced that infection, but his brother would not grant him the favor of such a talk. The poison from the infection began to soak into his whole personality.

He never spoke about the will to friends. He had too much of the need his brother had, to relate to others from a commanding position; he needed to pretend that he was set off from others by the fact that he still had money. Few of his friends and acquaintances knew his true circumstances. Windels and Kern and Lazarus would be shocked when they were told after his death of his poverty. "No, I'm sure you must be mistaken about that," says one acquaintance. "I remember quite clearly him telling me he had some sort of independent income, didn't have to work like the rest of us, you know. He said he had bonds, clipped coupons so he didn't have to pay taxes. And, oh yes, I recall quite clearly that he said he owned some real estate." But Paul talked incessantly about his brother: criticizing his policies and his treatment of the public. "Can't you see the settlement-house attitude in everything he does—this attitude of: 'You're my children and I know what's best for you'?" In hindsight, many of his criticisms would turn out to be perceptive ("You know who it was who first made me realize what this overdependence on highways was going to do to New York?" Lazarus asks. "Paul Moses, that's who") but he put forth the criticisms in a manner so harsh, became so enraged at disagreement, and, when the talk turned to his brother, acted so bitter as to seem almost irrational. (It is his way of talking about his brother that makes even more than the usual caution necessary in weighing his charges.) Acquaintances who saw him at wide intervals saw a man changing. Lazarus, who had once thought so highly of him, says: "He had a fixation. He hated Bob. Paul . . . was a good engineer, but to get him off balance all you had to do was mention Bob." As the symptoms of this fixation deepened, it was no longer necessary for someone to bring up Bob's name; Paul seemed to turn every conversation to his brother. Lazarus says Paul became "unstable"; Kern calls him "quite neurotic," capable of "violent hatred." Men sitting at a banquet at which his brother was speaking or being honored might notice him standing in the rear of the hall—he was standing in the rear, although they didn't know it, because he could not afford to buy a ticket for a seat—staring up at his brother on the dais with that look of contempt and hatred on his face, and they would nudge their friends and point out the lone, bitter figure standing back in the shadows. This too contributed to the impression of an unstable personality, and, ironically, made it easier for the crowd around City Hall to believe those rumors—the rumors whose source was never identified—that Robert Moses' brother was guilty of some heinous, if unspecified, crime.

Fighting to hold on to the Llanerch Pool, needing every cent he could scrape up, Paul Moses was trying desperately to find a job now. But he couldn't. As, day after day, a man in his fifties, turning gray, he made the long, humiliating rounds of the job hunter, he found that although he had for years been a high-salaried, highly respected consulting engineer, now not one of the city's engineering consultant firms would offer him any job at all.

Perhaps the explanation lay in his altered personality, or in the rumors that followed him. But there were those—engineers who had learned for themselves the hard lesson of what it meant to an engineer in New York to incur the displeasure of Robert Moses—who felt that that was not the real explanation. "You don't really think it was, do you?" asks Ole Singstad, a world-famous engineer who defied Robert Moses once and could not get another job in the city or state for thirty years.

Paul did not ask his brother for a job. He would not. But, without his knowledge, friends tried to.

They tried only once. Carl Proper knew Robert Moses well enough to get an interview without having to say in advance what he wanted to talk about. "Carl only went because it was so obvious that Paul wasn't getting enough to eat—we were worried about his health," Mrs. Proper says. But when Robert realized why Proper had come, Mrs. Proper says, "he was just fit to be tied. He was adamant and uninterested. It was a brush-off." And Paul not only was offered no job by his brother but did not find it any easier to find work for a private engineering firm, so many of which were supported by the contracts Robert Moses controlled. In 1942, unable to meet the real estate taxes, Paul lost the Llanerch Pool.

During World War II, Paul obtained a wartime post as superintendent of construction at the U.S. Navy base in Bayonne, New Jersey, dedicated himself to the work so completely that for months he slept on a cot in his office—and became, to a large extent, his old competent, incisive self again.

But when the war ended, so did the Bayonne job—and Paul, upon his return to New York, couldn't find another one in even the most minor consulting or executive capacity in his field.*

Paul's brother would, after the war, be placing with the private consulting engineering firms he controlled scores of engineers, often on the basis of personal or political considerations. His control of public engineering contracts was a byword in the profession. His brother was an engineer. But his brother could not find a job. "It was damned strange that a guy with his ability, a guy who had held really top jobs, couldn't find anything at all," says one engineer. In 1954, Robert Moses would become chairman of the State Power Authority, the body charged with creating hydroelectric power from the St. Lawrence River. This was the field of Paul's particular expertise; he had, in fact, spent months drawing up a St. Lawrence plan years before, as his brother was well aware—they had frequently discussed it at the time. Robert Moses would experience great difficulty finding engineers with expertise in the field, and he could hardly have approached the professional engineering societies involved without getting a recommendation for his brother. Paul Moses expected his brother to contact him about a job this time. But he heard not a word. And, year after year, for ten years, fifteen years, in a city in which his brother was handing out so many engineering jobs, Paul Moses couldn't get one.

Paul Moses did not ask his brother for a job; Paul Moses could not do that. But he did want to ask him again to sell 168 The Bowery, a move that Paul felt would give him more of an income from the trust fund than the $550 he was receiving. (His second wife was, as a result of their separation agreement, receiving the same amount.) But his brother's secretaries told him they had been instructed not to put him through. At one point, he tried for a year and a half without getting him to come to the phone even once. And when his brother finally did consent to talk to him, it was to curtly refuse even to consider Paul's ideas. Then he cut off communications again. In his seventies, Paul had to eke out a living as a salesman. Finally, this gay, gallant man whose natural habitat was the opera and Delmonico's went to ground in an $86.50-per-month "apartment" that was not an apartment at all but a single large room, converted from what had been a storage space, with an area in a corner of the room that served as a kitchen, on the top floor of a five-story walk-up loft building at 105 South Broad Street that could be reached only by climbing long, steep flights of stairs. And there, in the city in which his brother lived in luxury, Paul Moses lived out the last ten years of his life in a terrible poverty brightened only by the last of his women, a small, pleasant, gray-haired lady about his own age whose devotion to Paul impressed everyone who knew them. Paul's friends—she appears to have had none of her own—knew her only as "Millie." Not one person could be

* Why Paul returned to New York, the city in which his brother was in power, instead of trying to make a new life somewhere else, may be explained in part by his age: in 1945, Paul was fifty-eight. There may have been another reason also. When the author asked him why, Paul replied: "What! Let him drive me away?"

found in New York who knew her last name—she and Paul, although they lived together, could not, because of his wife's refusal to give him a divorce, ever get married. But there are indications that she may have been the same woman with whom, decades before, Princeton freshman Paul Moses, in defiance of his mother, had fallen in love during his glittering youth.

The building in which Paul Moses lived out his life, located at the last stop on the subway, was almost at the very end of South Broad Street, almost the very end of Manhattan Island—as if he had almost, but not quite, been driven off it. In the evenings the area was all but deserted, the streets empty. Millie put curtains on the windows of the top-floor loft that was their home, and curtained off the little kitchen, but there wasn't much that could be done to make the big bare space pleasant—particularly without money. (Of all the things that were missing from it, Paul felt most the absence of books. "I had had all sorts of reference books," he told the author. "Now I have no books.") And it wasn't the bareness of the room that was the worst thing about it; it was its location at the top of those steep stairs. The few visitors he invited up there—"It was the kind of place you wouldn't want to invite a lot of company, I'll tell you that," one says—all remarked on those stairs; "it was technically only four flights but they were so long it was like seven or eight, and they were very steep, old wooden stairs," says a friend, Louis Schulman. And Paul Moses, while remarkably vigorous, had his seventieth birthday in 1957. Those stairs were very hard for Paul, particularly at the end of a long day trudging around Manhattan as a salesman. In his late seventies, he would be stricken by a serious illness. Thereafter climbing those stairs would be very hard indeed. Any apartment in an elevator building would have been a blessing to him. His brother was creating tens of thousands of such apartments: low-income, middle-income. He gave out such apartments as favors to innumerable persons. Any politician with a relative who wanted one had only to ask; Robert Moses would provide. But he wouldn't provide one for his own brother. Paul Moses was to struggle up those stairs until 1967, when, at the age of eighty, he died.

Paul's room was within walking distance of City Hall and the Municipal Building, and he seemed irresistibly drawn to those buildings, perhaps because he was drawn to see in public the brother he could not see in private, perhaps because it was the only way he could obtain even an outsider's glimpse of the public life of which, with its concern for great problems, he had always wanted so much to be a part. He not only attended public hearings of the City Planning Commission, but was continually dropping in uninvited to the offices of its staff members, an elderly but erect man still with traces in his bearing of the old arrogance, still dressed, because he carefully preserved the couple of good suits he still possessed and saved them for such visits, with an elegance out of another age, still with a crisp, biting way of talking and an air of impatience when, as so often happened, a commission staffer turned out to know less about a problem under discussion than he did. It was quite obvious that he came because he wanted—needed desperately—to have someone to talk to about these problems that had fascinated him all his life.

Staffers who took the trouble to be courteous to the elderly man found it well worth their while. Schulman, one of the most knowledgeable of all civil servants in the arcane mysteries of municipal finance—he was at the time director of the Planning Commission's Division of Capital Budget—and a kindly man as well, met Paul one evening at an engineering society meeting and realized immediately that he was in the presence of a remarkable intellect. "You don't often get an opportunity to talk to someone like that, so well-versed, so fluent," he says. Thereafter, when Paul dropped in to his office ("He was lonely, you see"), Schulman would find time to talk to him; at lunchtime, they would often walk together in City Hall Park. Schulman found Paul "off his rocker" whenever he talked about his brother. But about any other subject, Schulman found him "a wonderful conversationalist, very bright, brilliant, refreshing. My wife found him that way, too. My wife won't invite anyone to the house for dinner, but she insisted on inviting him. My wife was very fond of him." Another official who was always glad to see him was Charles Hand, the canny old New York *World* editor and later PR man for Jimmy Walker, who in the early 1950's was an adviser to young Robert Wagner, Jr., then Manhattan borough president. "Paul used to hang around City Hall in the corridors," Wagner recalls. "If Hand saw him, we'd say, 'Come along to lunch.' "

But with every passing year, there were fewer men in City Hall who had known Paul when he had been regarded as a brilliant engineer. Busy young planners considered the old man just another one of the "nuts" who hung around the Hall, particularly if he began talking about his brother. "He'd go into other offices and start to yak away and talk and people wouldn't put up with it," Schulman says. "They would throw him out."

Nonetheless, he continued to hang around. He became a familiar, funny, almost pathetic figure around City Hall, an elderly man with an arrogant air and a sharp tongue, wandering the corridors, talking to strangers.

Telling this story about his brother—the hero of New York, the public servant who didn't care about money—that no one believed.

In 1962, Robert Moses got his brother, then seventy-five, a job.

Climbing the stairs to his apartment one day, Paul collapsed. Taken to the Veterans Administration Hospital in the Bronx, he was believed dying, and in some way word was conveyed to his brother, who came to visit him. It was the first time Robert Moses had seen him in about twenty years. He brought Paul, who had been so anxious to work on the St. Lawrence Power Project but whom he had given no chance to do so, two gifts: a recording of the opening ceremonies of the Robert Moses Power Dam on the St. Lawrence and a copy of his memoirs.

When he emerged from the hospital, Paul had two hundred dollars in the world. He had thought he was dying, and he had become terribly frightened that Millie would be left not only alone but penniless. In the most gallant of all his gallant gestures, he did for her what he would never do for himself: he wrote a letter to his brother—who, once he knew Paul was recovering, would not favor him with his presence again—asking him for a job. His brother arranged with the engineering firm of Andrews & Clark to give him one—as little more than an errand boy, at $96.16 a week.

Whether or not his brother had given Robert Moses cause to treat him the way he did no one will ever know for certain. But his sister certainly never gave him cause to treat *her* the way he did.

The plain, quiet, serious, withdrawn girl grew into a plain, quiet, serious, withdrawn woman—utterly cowed by her mother, with whom she lived until, late in her thirties, she married the purser on a British ocean liner on which she was taking a cruise, and by the brother she idolized. According to the testimony of all who knew Edna Marion Moses, she would do whatever Robert Moses wanted.

Yet, when she and her husband, neither of whom had offered the slightest protest when Robert received the lion's share of their mother's estate, moved to Coconut Grove, Florida, in about 1940, she found to her surprise that her brother never telephoned her, not even on her birthday, and was noticeably unenthusiastic about talking to her when *she* phoned. Years passed in which they hardly talked at all. Once, after she had not seen him for years, she asked if they could not get together. Moses' reply was to say that he would shortly be vacationing in Key West and would be setting down, very briefly, at Miami Airport, to change to a smaller plane. If Edna wanted to see him, he said, she could drive out to the airport and see him for a few minutes there. Edna at last got the message. She did not show up.

Paul Moses, in his bitterness, felt that he understood the reason for his brother's behavior toward his sister. "He had no use for human beings," Paul said. "He would just use them up, and then when he had no more use for them, he would throw them away." His brother had needed Edna when their mother's will had first been probated as an ally to insure that the trustees would maintain a solid front against Paul. But thereafter he did not need her any more. And he "threw her away."

Paul may or may not have been correct, but it is difficult to avoid wondering if there is not another reason—one hinted at in a Windels remark: "Robert never discussed Paul with me. He was quite reticent about him. You would almost have thought that Paul didn't exist."

It is difficult to avoid wondering whether that was not what Robert Moses *wanted* the world to think. To any mention of his brother, Robert reacted with rage sufficient to insure that the brother was not mentioned again. In the circle around Robert Moses, "Paul Moses" was so proscribed a name that in 1956 the *Post*, in a six-part series on the Park Commissioner, could report that "many of his associates do not know that he has a brother . . ."

The *Post* series was almost unique in mentioning Paul at all. It is possible to read through hundreds of magazine and newspaper stories without finding another mention. The reason was Moses' attitude. By never mentioning the brother's existence, he led writers to ignore the possibility that there might be one. If—as happened only rarely—a reporter learned of Paul's existence on his own and mentioned it himself, Moses' reaction was striking. As the *Post* reported, he refused even to say whether he was an older brother or a younger. "I'd prefer not to say," he said—"firmly." And of course a man who did not want the world to know he had a brother, and was avoiding the topic by not mentioning him, would steer away also from mentioning that he had a sister, for the mention of her might make it more difficult to avoid mentioning him. He would not even tell the *Post* if *she* was older than he or younger—and he would not say where she could be located.

In a book about his life, necessarily more detailed than newspaper articles, mention of a brother's existence—and perhaps of other details of their relationship—would be more difficult to avoid. For a man so eager for publicity—a man, moreover, who geared his entire life toward insuring himself immortality—Robert Moses' attitude toward books that might help insure that immortality was surprising. A dozen publishers offered substantial sums for his autobiography. The offers were refused. Dozens of writers made preliminary inquiries about writing his biography. Moses informed each one that he would not cooperate—and that none of his records and documents would be made available. That attitude discouraged all but a handful; with those, Moses took a firmer stand, using his influence with publishers to have the idea killed. In 1960, the Harvard-MIT joint School of Urban Studies asked author and former New Deal Brain Truster Rexford Tugwell to write one and offered him a substantial grant—by one report $50,000—for the job. Tugwell says that Moses promised cooperation. The former New Deal Brain Truster hired a research assistant and with him had spent more than six months on what Tugwell considered the first step—drawing up a detailed chronology of his subject's life, including his boyhood. At that point, however, Tugwell says, "I went to Moses and asked him to look it over. . . . I left it with him, and he called me up in a couple of days and, boy, he blew his top. I went out to [his office] and, boy, did he give me hell. I said, 'I don't think I can write this thing without cooperation from you, so I withdraw.' " Tugwell was never able to understand what had so dramatically changed Moses' attitude.

Only one biography of Robert Moses was in existence before this one. Entitled *Robert Moses: Builder for Democracy,* it was written, in 1952, by Cleveland Rodgers, a profound admirer, as his title suggests, of the Park Commissioner, under the closest supervision from Moses and his aides. There is a chapter on Moses' youth, and it does provide a few details, including brief biographical sketches of his father and mother. There are photographs of his father and mother—and of the house in New Haven in which he was raised, with the Park Commissioner posing in front of it. There is no photograph of Robert Moses' brother or sister—and there is no mention of them, not even a reference by name. In this 339-page book on the life of Robert Moses, there is not the faintest hint that he *had* a brother and sister.

He had a father and mother, too, and the picture he painted of them in the public mind is also striking.

He subtly denigrated his father at every opportunity. When one of the *Post* reporters said in 1956 that he had heard Moses' father had been a successful businessman, Moses replied: "Actually, whatever money there was in the family my mother had."

This attitude—while unfair to the prosperous merchant who had in reality left Bella Moses the bulk of her wealth—was, of course, in keeping with the patronizing attitude Moses had always displayed toward his quiet, gentle father. But the attitude he displayed—after her death—toward the mother he imitated so thoroughly was not. When he spoke about his mother publicly at all—which was almost never—it was to downgrade her reputation as well. Here, for example, in a letter he wrote to "correct" a 1946 *PM* biographical series, is his published description—perhaps his only published description—of his parents:

> Thanks particularly for endowing me with a million dollars. The next thing to real wealth is, I suppose, the reputation of having it. My father did not give me a million. He never had it. My mother left me something, which was not much to begin with, and shrank through neglect while I was plugging at unpaid jobs. My father was, in fact, genuinely distressed because respectable friends deplored my antagonizing our Long Island park opponents, and my mother, probably rightly, thought I could take better care of my family if I got out of dangerous and thankless public service and into a big respectable corporation.

The woman thus described was quite unrecognizable to a score of friends and relatives, who recall her great pride that her favorite son had followed the career in "public service" into which she had urged him; who recall that whenever another relative inquired whether it wasn't about time he started supporting his family, she had defended what he was doing, saying public service was much more important than any private job—and that she had backed up her belief not only by lending him $20,000 to help him create Jones Beach but by making it possible for him to stay in public service by supporting him and his family as long as she lived.

Robert Moses' attitude toward his whole family was striking.

The Moses and Cohen clans were numerous; New York City was well stocked with his aunts, uncles, cousins, nieces and nephews. During his youth, it had been a rather close family. After he came to power, it was still a rather close family. But he wasn't part of it. With the notable exception of the cousin involved in the matter of his mother's will, Wilfred Openhym, he generally saw them only on his own terms, in settings he controlled absolutely—at ground breakings and ribbon cuttings at which he was both host and star. He rejected invitations to their homes. Gradually he cut off relations with most of them; almost invariably they ended in acrimony. One of his cousins, Angie Fink, said that she was practically the only member of his extensive family with whom he was still on speaking terms, and that even she spoke with him seldom. It was, Mrs. Fink said, "as if he had tried to deny his father, his mother, and his whole youth."

As for his wife, on those Saturday evenings at the Belmont Mansion, where Robert Moses sat hour after hour at the big table with no apparent intention of leaving, it was, of course, Mary Moses "who was the most welcome person because she was the only one who could drag him out"—a feat she sometimes accomplished by taking him "firmly by the ear" and leading "him away from the table as if he were a little boy."

For years, in all domestic matters, Robert Moses was led by his wife. If, outside, he gave orders, at home, with Mary and their two daughters, Barbara and Jane, he took them. "He was a different man there," says Joe Ingraham. "So different that if you only knew the public Moses, you'd hardly believe this was the same man."

The Moses homes—the big, rambling old Thompson Avenue house and a Gracie Square apartment that he rented after coming into Bella's inheritance in 1930—were both sunny and cheerful (the apartment looked out on the busy East River and the towers of the Triborough Bridge) and casual, with deep, gaily slip-covered chairs and sofas; bright oil paintings; warm, russet drapes; books piled all around; and, in the foyer at Thompson Avenue, rolled-up sails for Jane's sailboats. The atmosphere was as relaxed and casual as the atmosphere in his offices was intense. And the contrast extended to the man who lived in them.

Moses was not home much—he was generally out of the house by nine, usually returned after eight and worked every Saturday—and when he was, a friend recalls, "he always had that yellow pad on his lap." But the friend says, "he never acted busy or rushed at all; he was easy and utterly gracious." When Jane and Barbara were young, he would make up stories to tell them, sit on the floor with them for hours, making animals out of clay, carry them around on his shoulders, teach them to swim and sail, take them on wonderful Sunday clambakes on Fire Island. When they got older, he and Barbara—Jane early developed an anti-intellectual bias—followed the family tradition established by Grannie Cohen by doing crossword puzzles together, including the difficult Double Crostic in the *Saturday Review*. He was always delighted to have their friends in—the house was always filled with children—and Jane says, "I cannot remember him losing his temper at us." It was he who walked the dog, generally took out the garbage—and, often after working until long past midnight, arose at six or six-thirty to make breakfast. "He loved to cook," Mary's sister, Emily Sims Marconnier, says. "No matter how early I got up, Robert would be in the kitchen and he'd like to know what I'd have—bacon or eggs or whatever." He dressed in the shabbiest of old khakis, a plaid shirt hanging out of his pants, sneakers and one of the incredible hats he loved (the battered old fedora was often replaced now by a transparent rain hat which he cherished); there was, as a friend puts it, "absolutely no side to the man at all. He might have been a powerful man, but if you only saw him around his house, you would never have guessed it."

His wife ran his home, and his life, to such an extent that, describing their relationship, many friends use the phrase: "she mothered him."

Mary bought his clothes—even his underwear and socks—bringing home suits until he found some he liked and then calling a tailor over to fit them, gave him pocket money (says one of her friends: "Before he had the limousine she had to see he had carfare every time he went out. She had to make sure he had change for a telephone call and a few dollars for restaurants and whatever. In a restaurant, she would slip him the money for the check under the table"), paid all the bills, even, until he began to use Triborough accountants, handled the income-tax returns, tried to keep his weight down (she would dish out her husband's portion with a crisp: "No gravy"), ordered him home from the office when he was working too hard and protected him from intrusive telephone calls with an acerbity that reminded visitors that she had once been called "the power behind the Governor" in Wisconsin. And she never complained about the financial privations that for years left her constantly worrying about grocery bills or the lack of ordinary social life. (Moses went to no movies, saw no plays, had no hobbies except those connected with the water—swimming, sailing, clamming—although she, as her sister puts it, "did not particularly like the water." Her only concern—deep enough so that some of her friends refer to it as "a real guilt feeling"—was that Robert had badly wanted a son and she had not given him one.) "Mary was the boss in that household," her sister says. "She ran their lives."

She shared more than Moses' home life. In the years before he installed private dining rooms at his offices, she was hostess for his luncheons, a brilliant and witty one. She knew how to handle politicians and reporters. At receptions, she would whisper the names of oncoming politicians in his ear because she was as good at recalling individuals as he was bad. She brought a touch of humanity to his hard-driven men, asking them about their wives and children, arranging for doctors and hospitals when they were ill, and, when her husband's empire burgeoned in resources, seeing that those resources were put at their service. When, for example, the seven-year-old daughter of the captain of the Park Commission's yacht *Sea-Ef* died, Mary saw to it that the grieving parents "didn't," as the captain's sister puts it, "even have to buy a piece of bread. A chauffeured car came over and stood at the door all the time in case they wanted anything. She sent over food—enough to feed an army. And the car stayed there the whole four days the body stayed in the funeral parlor. And later, every now and then a big bouquet of roses would come, with a card, *From Mary and Robert Moses,* for the cemetery." One thing she did that was especially appreciated by Moses' men was to call his office and say, "Bob's on one of his rampages, everybody watch out." Says one of his men: "That would give us just enough time to get out of there before he arrived." For some of the young architects and engineers, she was a matchmaker, and a sympathetic shoulder to cry on. Arnold Vollmer, a young architect introduced to his wife, Becky, a Moses research assistant, through Mary, says: "She was the sharpest, the most wonderful, brightest woman you ever met." She could be devastatingly caustic. Once egoistic Lester Markel, Sunday editor of the *Times*, perturbed because he had been invited as Moses' guest to the Jones Beach Marine Stadium but had not been seated in Moses' box, made some remark that she overheard. Addressing some people around her—in a voice just loud enough for Markel to hear—she said: "The trouble with Lester is that he thinks he's as smart as Robert. But he's not." She knew just what to say to help her husband; when La Guardia asked her, quite seriously, why Moses respected Smith more than him, she replied: "Because he stood behind his commissioners." When her husband publicly insulted Iphigene Sulzberger, it was Mary who healed the breach. And she was awed by no one. Proskauer recalls that the first time she met Smith after he had refused to endorse Moses for Governor, Mary "absolutely withered him" with a cold stare when Smith tried to embrace her as usual, "turned on her heel, and walked out of the room." She was a confidante and adviser, a respected one. "RM never went anywhere without Mary, and he consulted her on everything," Sid Shapiro says. "And boy was she sharp!" Attorney Morris Ernst, who with his wife saw a lot of the Moseses when the two couples were young, says: "Mary gave Bob an awful lot when he was first starting out. Don't forget, she had been the confidential secretary to a Governor. Her political know-how was really quite significant in helping him accomplish his early objectives." Moses himself told Mrs. Marconnier that "every time he pulled a boner it was on something he hadn't consulted Mary about." Says radio commentator H. V. Kaltenborn, who knew the Moseses for years: "Those of us who are privileged to know something about the home life of Robert and Mary Moses realize how much a wife's unfailing patience and unselfish devotion have meant during years of strife and struggle."

But as strife and struggle yielded success, the relationship between Robert and Mary Moses changed. The change was evident at parties. As Mrs. Morse, the friend who admired both of them, put it, "Well, as a young man he didn't dominate the conversation at parties so much. But it grew worse later . . ."

As he grew louder, she grew quieter. Talk to old acquaintances and the adjectives used to describe Mary Moses are "gay," "charming," "warm," "witty," "vivacious." Talk to acquaintances who first met her during the 1930's and the adjective most heard is "quiet." Attorney Monroe Goldwater, who didn't meet her until about 1936, says she was "a nice person but not very brilliant." One woman, who first met her about that year, calls her "a mouse." By the late 1930's, New York hostesses anxious for the presence of Robert Moses at their dinner parties were wondering what on earth to do about Robert Moses' wife. According to elegant Florence Shientag, the bright, brittle wife of key Smith adviser Bernard Shientag and herself an attorney and judge: "When they visited us, we always had to worry about who would sit next to her. She needed bringing out. . . . She never spoke very much. She had nothing to say, I assume. She was a moon whose light was growing less and less. He was going on, a sun, getting brighter and brighter."

Not that Mary seemed to mind. "Mary was a darling and she never got over her wonder that anyone like Bob should want to marry her," Iphigene Sulzberger says. "She never thought that anyone so handsome, so brilliant, would marry anyone but the Queen of England or someone like that. He was absolute perfection in her eyes." If the submersion of her identity in his was causing her conflict, signs of that conflict emerged only obliquely, as in one interview she gave during the only period in which she consented to talk for publication, his campaign for Governor in 1934. (During this campaign, despite her wit and political insight and experience, she delivered exactly one speech, a talk at a small tea.) The reporter who interviewed her wrote that Mary Moses "suddenly inquired": "But why bother talking to the wife of a candidate? I don't think I'm a very interesting person to interview. I'm not spectacular. And, on the other hand, you can't just do me as the home and mother woman, shelling the peas, mending. I can do all those things. I can cook, and I like to. But I don't. What can you say about a person like me? I know government, because Mr. Moses has been a part of it always, but that makes me like a shadow of him—and that's not correct either."

And then, of course, there was another factor, one at which Florence Shientag hints by saying: "Mary became too old, physically, for him, I think. He continued to be so vibrant, so vital . . ."

Mary had what Hilda Hellman, Moses' cousin and a perceptive confidante, describes as "an awful horror of growing old." But she was four years older than Robert, and the difference seemed to increase each year between her and the husband who seemed as impervious to time as the grandmother he so strikingly resembled in other respects (and who remained youthful and vital until her death at ninety-three), still working his incredible daily schedule tirelessly, still swimming far out to sea in all weather, still energetic and dynamic in appearance at forty and fifty, his added weight making him look more powerful only, not older. Mary, on the other hand, aged hard—in the opinion of some friends because of the strain of not only bringing up two daughters and running two households, for years without maids, when money was always tight, but also managing every detail of her husband's life ("I think it drained her," Becky Vollmer says); in the opinion of other friends because of what Mrs. Hellman describes as "the strain of trying to live up to someone like Robert," who was "almost larger than life."

Her husband was, of course, fascinating to women. In part this was because of his charm. Joan Ganz Cooney, later producer of *Sesame Street,* met him in 1954 at the scintillating Sunday talkfests at the Herbert Bayard Swopes mansion at Sands Point. At the time, she was twenty-four and he was sixty-five, but, she says, "after I had spent the evening with him I was in love with him." "It crossed all generational lines—that charm of his," Joan Cooney says. "What he has is this fantastic recall. He'd tell me what he thought of Tom Dewey and FDR . . . He has that ability to tell you a story so you can just see the people in the room . . . And he's just got that magnetism. Everybody in that room was interesting. He was probably the least rich man in these gatherings because he was a public servant and something about that came through that he had spent his life in public service. I saw him mostly with his contemporaries—when their careers were on the wane. And they had changed in physical appearance. But his appearance hadn't changed at all." (His wife? Oh, says Joan Cooney, she didn't talk at all: "she was just like a little bird who tried to worship him.")

In part, Moses' appeal was based on his power and fame. In part, it may have also been based on other considerations. Justice Florence Shientag, talking about Moses in general, stopped in the midst of a thought, sat thinking for a few minutes and then said, musingly, "He must have been a wonderful lover. He's so direct. No underlying doubts . . ." As a young man, he had been in love only once—with the fresh, clean-looking girl, as passionately idealistic as he, whom he met among the books of the Municipal Research Bureau library and whom he loved with an intensity so vivid that his Yale classmates would remark about it decades later. By the 1930's, Robert Moses' affairs were openly gossiped about in New York political and society circles—particularly his friendship with one of the city's most remarkable women, a North Shore baroness with whom his name became linked at the time he was subordinating his idealism to an accommodation with the power of the North Shore barons. She was the witty and sophisticated Ruth Baker Pratt, widow of one of the Standard Oil Pratts of Glen Cove, who was not only an accomplished violinist, golfer and tennis player but a behind-the-scenes power in Republican politics, the first woman ever to sit on New York City's Board of Aldermen, the first woman ever to represent New York in Congress—and possibly the only politician of either sex ever to best Jimmy Walker in repartee. Recalls Paul Windels: "They were rather affectionate in their attitude toward one another in public—to an extent that was rather shocking to me when I saw it. She was quite taken with him. It was well known in those circles that if they didn't get married it wouldn't be Ruth's fault."

Moses still spent as much time with Mary as possible under the circumstances: his scrupulous courtesy toward her was as noticeable as ever. He never went on vacation without her. But the glow from the man she had made her "sun" grew more and more dim. She began to drink—and the drinking rapidly became very heavy, so heavy that people began to refer to her as "an alcoholic." After several embarrassing incidents at parties she had to be forbidden to drink anything but Dubonnet. At one Park Department Christmas party at the Arsenal, obsequious Moses Men, anxious to ingratiate themselves with the boss's wife, kept coming up to her and asking if she'd like one, and she had so many glasses of the light cordial that when Mrs. Hellman arrived and asked where she was, she was told, with a sneer, "Oh, she had to be taken home." She was hospitalized several times—in an attempt to cure either her drinking or the increasingly serious attacks of what Moses aide General Harry L. Meyers refers to as "nervous trouble"—at the Payne Whitney Psychiatric Clinic, once for what Meyers says was "quite a long time."

27. *Changing*

POWER AND PERSONALITY. Interplay.

The young Robert Moses, immersed in his dreams, had been totally uninterested in power. And if he had, later, sought it, he had for years sought it only for his dreams. The seeking had been solely on behalf of the vision. If, at last, monumental power had been sought—and used—it had been sought and used as a means to a monumental end.

But Moses' personality made him particularly susceptible to the addiction of power. And now he had been a mainliner for years. And while he had always before sought power only for the sake of his dreams, now, for the first time, he began to seek power for power's own sake, as an end in and for itself.

That a turning point had been reached became apparent in 1936—when the New York City Tunnel Authority was created.

No sooner had Moses learned that Mayor La Guardia was considering establishing an authority to build a $58,000,000 Queens-Midtown Tunnel than he began hinting, none too subtly, that he would like to be on it, if not in charge of it.

But the tunnel could be financed only with federal funds, and La Guardia, only recently recovered from the Order Number 129 imbroglio, was not about to put himself again in the position of asking for federal money for a man who was personally obnoxious in the extreme to the head of the federal government. Nor did the Mayor see any reason to. The tunnel was not intended to link up with any Moses projects. There were engineers available outside Moses' organization—most notably Ole Singstad, a cocky, hard-driving, table-pounding Norwegian who had designed the then-novel ventilation system that had made the Holland Tunnel feasible, who, after tunnel designer Clifford M. Holland collapsed and died from overwork, had rammed the job through to completion, and who was regarded as the world's leading authority on underwater vehicular tunnels. Directing city legislative representative Reuben A. Lazarus to draft the legislation creating the new authority, La Guardia ordered him: "Leave the son of a bitch off."

That was easy. Lazarus simply left out the phrase that Moses had included in the legislation setting up the other authorities to which he wanted to be appointed—the phrase stating that "an unsalaried state official shall not be ineligible" for appointment—and thereby left Moses, as a state official, ineligible for appointment to the city body.

Recalls Lazarus: "I had a helluva row with Moses over that. It started off very temperate, with Moses asking me why I did it and couldn't it be changed so he could be on it. I said, 'I had direction on it.' He said, 'That guinea son of a bitch asked you to do this, didn't he?' I said, 'Bob, he's my client. You're not.' "

Moses then attempted to have his upstate Republican friends in the Legislature kill the bill, but Lehman, who knew how badly the tunnel was needed, added his support to La Guardia's, and the measure passed. And La Guardia named as Authority commissioners three businessmen—two personal friends, William H. Friedman and Albert T. Johnston; and Alfred B. Jones, a mild-mannered Quaker who not coincidentally was a cousin of RFC chairman Jesse Jones—whom Moses had never even met.

Unable to obtain control of the new authority directly, Moses tried indirection, sending aides to discreetly ask Singstad, who had been appointed the Authority's chief engineer, if he would "cooperate" with Triborough. But Moses was trying his wiles on the wrong man. Singstad, fiercely independent, despised Moses' aides, who he felt violated engineering ethics every time they subordinated their own objective views of an engineering problem to tell the Triborough chairman what he wanted to hear. One morning, after other approaches had failed, millionaire Jack Madigan himself dropped by Singstad's office and invited Ole to the Downtown Athletic Club for lunch. On the way, Madigan said: "Ole, I want to be helpful. You and the Tunnel Authority would both be better off with a strong man like Moses in charge." "I figured Moses was trying to get me on his side as a talking point to La Guardia for a takeover," Singstad says; Moses, he felt, wanted to be able to tell the Mayor that the chief engineer had said his commissioners were not competent to run the job. "I said I was sticking with my commissioners and I was happy with them."

Unable to control the new authority directly or indirectly, Moses set out to destroy it.

It was under tremendous pressure to produce results fast. Nineteen thirty-six was a presidential election year and Harold Ickes, whose PWA was financing the tunnel, wanted the President to be able to break ground well before November. "They didn't want to have $58,000,000 lying idle in an election year," Singstad says. Assembling an engineering and administrative staff from scratch and producing in a matter of a few months plans for a huge and complicated engineering job—Singstad had to draw more than 125 separate studies before he hit on a feasible plan for the Manhattan entrance—was immensely difficult. And Ickes was adamant. If work was not under way well before Election Day, he said, the grant would be rescinded and there would be no tunnel. The PWA Administrator was demanding weekly progress reports, and every week his impatience grew more noticeable. Any delay might kill the project.

And Moses sought delay.

His legislative allies introduced a bill that would have rescinded the Authority's authorization to construct the tunnel and provided instead for a year-long, state-financed study of whether the crossing should be a tunnel

—or a bridge, which, under the terms of the act creating the Triborough Authority, only Triborough could build. Enactment of the new bill into law would have meant the end of the tunnel no matter what the study's result. "Ickes was constantly threatening to take the money away from us if we didn't get started," Singstad says. "Moses knew damn well that if another year was spent [on the state-financed study], the money [the PWA grant] would be gone to some other state."

There was no real chance of enactment, of course, since Lehman would veto the bill if it passed the Republican-controlled Legislature. But Moses didn't need enactment to accomplish his purpose. He needed only delay. And he used all his vast influence in Albany to obtain it, keeping the bill bottled up in committee—and off Lehman's desk, where it could finally be disposed of—week after week. "And all the time," Singstad says, "Ickes was hammering: 'If you don't do it now, I'm going to withdraw the money.' "

But La Guardia understood that he was in a power struggle now, and while the Mayor may have deferred to Moses on questions of park administration, he deferred to no one on questions of power. Traveling to Washington week after week, he kept the grant alive until the last day of the legislative session, when the bill was finally brought to the floor and defeated, and on October 2, 1936, President Roosevelt was able to break ground for the tunnel.

"Why did Moses try to wreck [the Tunnel Authority]?" Singstad says. "Because he couldn't take it over, that's why, dammit. He couldn't take it over so he wanted to wreck the whole damned project." Lazarus and Corporation Counsel Paul Windels, who were on the inside of the battle from beginning to end, thinking it over independently came to the same conclusion. "I kept trying to understand what his reason was [for trying to take over the Authority]," Lazarus says, "and I just couldn't make sense out of it—unless he wanted to take over every construction job in the city."

And in fact Moses' actions in his fight with the Tunnel Authority in 1936—particularly when coupled with his actions in the struggle with the Authority over the next decade—make it difficult to ascribe to them any other motivation. Search as one may through the record—not only the public record, which is scanty indeed, because the fight was carried on largely in secrecy, but through confidential memoranda and letters culled from La Guardia's files and files of other principals involved—one is unable to identify a single real difference of opinion between Moses and the Authority on any point of substance relevant to the planning, construction or administration of the Queens-Midtown Tunnel. Moses agreed that a crossing was needed. His argument that the crossing should be not a tunnel but a bridge was never presented with any of the thoroughness that marked his serious proposals; it was never really presented seriously at all—possibly, in the view of at least one of his aides, because it *couldn't* be presented seriously, since building a bridge at Thirty-seventh Street would have meant condemning so many office buildings and apartment houses that the condemnation cost alone would have been ridiculously high. Moses never even commissioned a preliminary engineering survey of the bridge proposal. His only real difference of opinion with the Tunnel Authority was over who should control it.

And this difference made the 1936 Tunnel Authority fight a watershed in Robert Moses' life. Always before, Moses had conceived a public work, and then had sought the power to bring it into reality. In the Tunnel Authority fight, someone else conceived the public work. Moses sought the power to take it over. Before, his motivation had always been the work—the project, the achievement, the dream. Now the motivation was power.

And the Tunnel Authority fight also revealed the lengths to which Robert Moses was now prepared to go to gain power. Wrecking the Authority would have cost the city not only $58,000,000, money which would provide a lot of jobs in Depression-wracked New York, but also the tunnel, a public work badly needed in terms of Moses' own aims—the elimination of traffic congestion in New York City. But these considerations did not deter him. If he couldn't build the tunnel, his actions said, no one was going to build it. If he couldn't take it over, he would destroy it.

Thwarted by La Guardia in one attempt to grab more power, Moses made another—only to have the Mayor thwart him again.

Money, as Moses was well aware, was a key to power, but, by 1938, the great wellspring of federal work relief money at which he had been drinking for five years was almost dry. A new spring had begun welling out of Washington and Albany, however. Moses set out to bottle it right under La Guardia's nose.

Its sources were the United States Housing Act of 1937 (co-sponsored by Representative Henry B. Steagall of Alabama and Al Smith's old Albany buddy, U. S. Senator Robert F. Wagner) and a New York State constitutional amendment approved in 1938.

Prior to passage of the Wagner-Steagall Act, Moses had never had much interest in public housing. "Public housing" meant, in the terms of the day, housing exclusively for the poor. Moses had never had the slightest interest in building *anything* for the poor. But the amount given by the Wagner-Steagall Act* to the newly created United States Housing Authority for loans to local municipal authorities was $800,000,000. The amount the state constitutional amendment authorized the Legislature to make available to local housing authorities was $300,000,000. Obviously public housing was going to be a great new—perhaps *the* great new—source of outside money for the city. Hastily recruiting architects from the State Housing Board, Moses set them to work secretly drawing up a public housing program for New York and himself secretly drew up a proposal for "reorganization" of the City Housing Authority, under which the Authority would be reorganized right out of existence and replaced with a board

* Together with a subsequent Congressional amendment in 1938.

consisting of himself and six other members, four of whom he believed he, rather than the Mayor, could control.

The Mayor possessed an intense private interest in public housing. Fiorello La Guardia believed that it had been the dampness and congestion of the tenements in which she had been raised that had given his beloved first wife the tuberculosis that had killed her and their baby; he had vowed to friends that one thing he was going to do "personally" as mayor was to make sure that the city started at last to give poor people in the city a decent, healthy place to live. The vast amounts of money and power that were obviously going to be involved made him even more determined to keep the program firmly in his own hands. So Moses drew up his proposal in absolute secrecy—and presented it not to the Mayor but, in a bold attempt to circumvent him, to influential private citizens; the very day after voters approved the constitutional amendment, he persuaded several real estate and reform organizations to jointly rent the auditorium in the Museum of Natural History for an evening ten days later and to invite several hundred key realtors and reformers to hear him give a speech. And he arranged to bring the program dramatically to the public at the same time by persuading WNYC, the city-owned radio station (which, at the time, boasted a considerable audience), to carry the speech live.

All Moses' previous public works had been basically concerned with recreation and parks and with the means—roads and bridges—of getting people to parks. He may have realized that without protective coloration his attempt to move into a new, unrelated field would look like the bare-faced power grab it was. So he gave it protective coloration; he titled his speech "Housing and Recreation," and in asking realtors and reformers to sponsor the speech and WNYC to broadcast it, he told them it was merely a discussion of coordination of public housing and parks. No one in the audience suspected the truth; even such intimates of the Mayor as Adolf Berle and Paul Windels, applauding with the rest of the audience as the Park Commissioner strode briskly onstage, had no inkling of what was coming until Moses' aides began passing out attractive, four-color brochures and, opening them, they saw in amazement that Moses was proposing in detail—ten projects were proposed, sites specific down to precise boundary lines, costs of land and construction for each already figured—a complete new housing program. The unifying principle behind the proposal was spelled out: only "genuine slum clearance" on the "large scale" would make a real dent in the city's housing problem, so La Guardia's efforts to rehabilitate old tenements should be scrapped; whole blocks of slum tenements should be razed to the ground and replaced with new housing; only genuine slum dwellers should be allowed in the projects, and, to insure this, tenants should be selected by the Welfare Commissioner. The financing was worked out: the program would cost $245,000,000 and it should be financed by "large-scale government subsidy" ($200,000,000 from state and federal funds and a sales tax on cigarettes to raise the balance); it should not be financed, as had been proposed, by an increase in the city's real estate tax, for the real estate tax was too high in the city already. Staring at each other in disbelief, the two officials realized that they were witnessing a public relations blitzkrieg—a lightning-like move by Moses to mobilize the opinion of the public in general and of the influentials in the audience in particular (his opposition to a real estate tax increase was a clever move to insure the support of the city's powerful real estate lobby) behind his plan so that the Mayor would not be able to overrule it.

But a copy of the brochure had, that afternoon, somehow fallen into La Guardia's hands, and the Mayor had summoned WNYC director Morris S. Novick to his office.

Unaware of this, Moses had no reason to suspect that anything was amiss when he began speaking. As he spoke, there right in front of him, attached to the lectern, was a WNYC microphone and, looking down below the stage, Moses could see two WNYC technicians sitting at a table full of broadcasting paraphernalia busily twiddling dials and going through all the motions of technicians making a broadcast. When they saw him glancing down at them, in fact, they made him a thumbs-up signal to indicate that all was going well.

One of Moses' secretaries, however, was attempting to pick up the program at home. Unable to do so, or to locate WNYC at all, she finally realized that the station was off the air. She managed to telephone Allyn Jennings backstage at the Museum. Rushing over to the technicians, the Moses aide asked what was going on. They assured him with straight faces that the program was on the air. Running outside to his car, Jennings turned on the radio, dialed WNYC, got only silence and realized that the technicians must be deliberately fooling him. Running back into the auditorium, he handed up a note to his boss, just as he was coming to the end of his speech. The Park Commissioner, who had believed that he had been speaking for the past forty-five minutes to tens of thousands of New Yorkers, learned that he had been speaking to only two hundred—the two hundred right in front of him. The WNYC microphone in front of him was dead. Someone must have ordered WNYC to cut his program off the air—and must have ordered the technicians to go through all the motions necessary to conceal this fact from him. And glaring down at them as they made still another thumbs-up gesture, he realized that only one man would have thought of that touch. That guinea son of a bitch had outsmarted him again.

La Guardia may have been able to keep Moses from reaching the public's ears, but the Mayor could do nothing about the public's eyes. The next day his Park Commissioner's plan was on page one of every newspaper in the city, with support for that plan on virtually every editorial page. But the Mayor, using all of his power and all of his cunning, cut Moses out of the public housing picture as completely as he had cut him off the air.

The arena in which the initial confrontation took place was an eleven-member committee the Mayor had formed some months before—and to which, not suspecting Moses' designs, he had appointed him—to advise him on public housing. Moses attempted to persuade the committee members to endorse at least some of his proposals, but La Guardia, working through Windels, the committee's chairman, made sure they didn't—by employing relentless pressure. Windels would decline, years later, to furnish any details of the in-fighting. "But I'll tell you this," he said. "When it came to things like that, La Guardia was as hard and as shrewd as they come. Whatever it was necessary to do, he did." The committee declined to recommend a single one of Moses' proposed sites or any diminution whatever in the powers of the La Guardia-appointed and -dominated City Housing Authority.

La Guardia handled all negotiations with Federal Housing Authority chairman Nathan Straus personally. He made all announcements of new projects from his own office, and in general made sure that Moses never knew what new public housing project was being planned until the planning was completed and the necessary federal funds allocated. Moses raged, publicly assailing the "secret, surreptitious" program, but he could not budge the Mayor. By the end of 1941, thirteen separate public housing projects containing a total of more than 17,000 apartments had been constructed in New York, far more than in any other city in America, and Moses had had nothing to do with any of them. The Mayor was even able to indulge himself in an additional soupçon of personal satisfaction. The printing bill for the four-color brochure Moses had distributed at the Museum of Natural History was more than a thousand dollars; when Moses submitted the bill to Comptroller McGoldrick, the Mayor smilingly told the Comptroller, "A beautiful printing job"—and ordered him not to pay it.

The tunnel and housing fights convinced La Guardia, according to Windels, Kern, Berle and other top mayoral assistants, that his Park Commissioner was intent on increasing his personal power. And La Guardia, determined to concentrate power in the city in his own hands, acted as he would have acted toward any rival. The unifying motive behind Moses' actions in both fights was his desire to expand his power—in the tunnel fight to attain power to build not just bridges but all interborough crossings; in the housing fight to extend his power, hitherto limited to the fields of parks and transportation, into a wholly new field of governmental endeavor. La Guardia kept Moses' power confined within its traditional spheres.

Following the tunnel and housing fights, moreover, the Mayor began to re-examine the implications of the virtually unlimited power he had given Moses within those traditional spheres—and to conclude that his power should be curbed in those spheres, too.

This was not, according to the Mayor's top aides, a wholly new feeling. For some time, they say, he had been becoming worried about aspects of Moses' park policy, the same aspects, in general, that were worrying reformers like Exton and Weinberg. If he had not discerned before precisely what those policies meant for those of the city's people who most needed parks, he was beginning to discern it now; Windels recalls the Mayor raging when he realized that the prices Moses' concessionaires were charging at such new city-built or -refurbished park restaurants as the Tavern-on-the-Green and the Claremont Inn were so high that they could not be used regularly by poor or even middle-class families. In transportation, La Guardia had had a vague feeling ever since the beginning of his mayoralty that great road-building projects must be accompanied by corresponding improvements in mass transportation, but because he admired Moses' parkways and bridges, he had not pressed the Commissioner to include provision for mass transportation on them. But as new parkways and bridges became jammed as quickly as they opened, the vague feelings hardened; by 1939, La Guardia would be pressing Moses hard indeed as to why he was not paying more attention to the suggestions of the Regional Plan Association. And beyond questions of parks and transportation, the Mayor had for some time been becoming progressively more aware of the question that a later generation would call "priorities." By 1938, he was acutely aware that the great strides made in parks and parkways were not being matched in any other areas of public works—not even in areas like schools and hospitals in which the need was desperate. "His feelings about Moses had subtly and gradually but substantially changed by the time I resigned as Corporation Counsel [in 1937]," Windels says. "He still felt he had matchless abilities and energies, but he also felt now that those abilities and energies must be channeled in the right direction if the city was to benefit from them."

Now, with the Mayor's feelings intensified by the tunnel and housing fights, "he was worried about how much power Moses had in the city," Kern says. "I know because he kept talking about it. He felt [Moses'] power must be reduced. These feelings really became very strong." And this analysis of the Mayor's feelings was documented by the Mayor's actions: in November 1938, shortly after Moses' Museum speech, he cut from the list of WPA projects at least two large park projects he had earlier promised Moses he would include; in December, La Guardia stood up to him, and to *The New York Times*, with a new firmness in cutting the Park Department's budget request; early in 1939, the Mayor made it clear to Newbold Morris and Joseph McGoldrick, his Board of Estimate allies, that they were to take a harder line on Moses' requests to the Board.

But by 1939 the Mayor's feelings were not to be nearly as crucial to Moses as they had been in the past. To a large extent, in fact, he no longer had to concern himself with such feelings. To a large extent, it no longer mattered to him what the Mayor thought.

Of all the remarkable qualities of Robert Moses' matchless mind, one of the most striking was its ability to take an institution with little or no power, and, seemingly, with little or no potential for more power (at Yale, an unprestigious literary magazine; in state government, the Long Island State Park Commission) and to transform it into an institution with immense power, power insulated from and hence on a par with the power of the forces that had originally created it. And now the mind of Robert Moses had begun focusing on the institution known as the "public authority."

28. *The Warp on the Loom*

No State shall . . . pass any . . . law impairing the obligation of contracts . . .

—THE CONSTITUTION OF THE UNITED STATES OF AMERICA, ARTICLE I, SECTION 10

The authority shall have power . . . to make contracts. . . .

—CONSOLIDATED LAWS OF THE STATE OF NEW YORK, CHAPTER 43-A, ARTICLE III, TITLE 3: "TRIBOROUGH BRIDGE AUTHORITY"

THE PUBLIC AUTHORITY was not a new device. The first of these entities that resembled private corporations but were given powers hitherto reserved for governments—powers to construct public improvements and, in order to pay off the bonds they sold to finance the construction, to charge the public for the use of the improvements—had been created in England during the reign of Queen Elizabeth. By the time Robert Moses went to Oxford three hundred years later, there were 1,800 such part-public, part-private bodies in England, including the huge Port of London Authority (named "Authority" because the clauses in the Act of Parliament that spelled out its powers began with the words *Authority is hereby given*) and highway-building boards whose roads were named "turnpikes" because they were blocked with horizontal bars (or "pikes") set into revolving pillars that would be turned aside to let a carriage pass only after the toll was paid.

But the public authority concept was new in the United States. There may (or may not—there exists no reliable history of authorities) have been a few collecting tolls on rural roads (hearing rumors of one in North Carolina, Jimmy Walker contemplated setting one up in New York to enrich his friends), but at the time Moses went to Oxford the only urban authorities in existence on the western side of the Atlantic were a bare handful set up to build small water-supply systems. The Port of New York Authority, the first large authority in America, modeled on its London counterpart and created by an interstate compact between New York and New Jersey, would not be created until 1921, would not float its first bond issue until 1926 and would not become financially successful until 1931, when, after five years of near fiscal disaster, it would persuade the two states to let it take over the highly successful Holland Tunnel, which had been constructed by an independent commission.* It was not until the New Deal, when Depression-strapped municipalities, unable to finance major public works themselves, suddenly realized that RFC and PWA grants were available for self-liquidating projects, that urban authorities began to be established in any number. In 1933 and 1934, when Moses was playing the crucial role in setting up the Triborough, Bethpage, Jones Beach, Henry Hudson, Marine Parkway and Hayden Planetarium authorities—and a lesser but still key role in the creation of seven other authorities—there were only a few handfuls of other authorities in the entire country.

With the lone exception of the Port Authority, moreover, every public authority created in the United States had been created in a single pattern: each had been established to construct and operate one, and only one, public improvement, a single isolated bridge or tunnel or sewer system, to issue only enough bonds to pay for the construction of that improvement, and only bonds with a fixed expiration date, and, when that date arrived—or sooner, if revenue was collected faster than expected—to pay off the bonds, eliminate all tolls or fees, turn the improvement over to the city and go out of existence. The Port Authority, empowered to operate several improvements, had become America's first "multi-purpose" public authority, but each of its projects fit the traditional pattern since each was financed by a separate bond issue and both Authority members and public officials expected that as soon as each issue was paid off, the tolls on the facility financed by that issue would be eliminated.† Motivated by the failure of several Port Authority projects to earn enough to meet the interest and amortization payments on their bonds, the Authority's brilliant general counsel, Julius Henry Cohen, was attempting in 1934 to break new ground

* Moses had played a small but significant role in the tunnel's construction. One of his first assignments for Al Smith was to analyze two conflicting construction proposals, the commission's plan to build the tunnel by conventional methods at a cost it estimated at $28 million and General George W. Goethals' plan to build it by a new method at a cost Goethals estimated at $12 million. The young reformer, unequipped with the slightest practical experience in construction, interviewed the famed builder of the Panama Canal, and gave Smith his verdict: "a great personality, a go-getter, but neither a great engineer nor a financier." Equally unimpressed with the commission's engineers, he talked with independent experts and concluded—and told the Governor—that the Goethals plan "would not work" and that while the commission's would, the cost would be not $28 but $48 million. Smith's reaction, Moses was to recall, "introduced me to his extraordinary head for facts and figures and his immense loyalty to his assistants, no matter how green, young and new at the game." Ignoring protests, the Governor threw out the Goethals plan and accepted the commission's, but allocated for it the $48 million that Moses had suggested. The actual cost turned out to be $49 million.

† Because the facilities would thereafter belong to not one but two states, there were plans to have them run by bistate commissions with members appointed by both legislatures.

by devising a new kind of bond and persuading bankers who held the Authority's outstanding bonds to accept the new one in their place. Under the plan Cohen had in mind, the individual bond issues would be combined into a single general issue supported by the revenues from all Port Authority enterprises, a move which would allow use of the Holland Tunnel surpluses to bail out such money losers as its two bridges connecting Staten Island with New Jersey. And since the new issue would be "open-ended," the Authority could use any over-all surplus to finance new projects. The bankers refused to consider "open-end" bonds for unspecified new projects but, in 1935, did agree to a consolidation of outstanding bonds in a "General and Refunding Bond" that could be used for *one* new project—the proposed Lincoln Tunnel—and it was this bond, rather than any devised by Moses, that was the first bond issue in the United States secured not by a single public improvement but by an authority's general revenues.

But Moses went much further. Originally, he had conceived of his authorities in the traditional mold: the legislation he had drafted establishing the Triborough, Henry Hudson and Marine Parkway bodies, for example, had explicitly authorized each to construct only a single, specific project and to issue bonds only for that project; the bonds were to be paid off as soon as possible, and not only was a time limit (forty years) set on their expiration but that time limit also limited the authority's life—as soon as its bonds were paid off, it was to go out of existence and turn over its bridge to the city government. The legislators who had created Robert Moses' authorities and the mayor who under the State Constitution had had to ask the legislators to create them had conceived of them as mere creatures of the sovereign city. Legislators and mayor, as well as the city's citizens, continually reminded by the press of the long tradition that all its bridges be toll-free, had been assured that the tolls would be removed forever as soon as their cost had been paid for. And there had been no deliberate attempt to mislead them: Robert Moses had thought of public authorities as men had always thought of public authorities.

But Robert Moses' thinking was changing.

The primary factor behind the change was money.

The carrying charges—interest and amortization—on the $5,100,000 in bonds that had been sold to pay for the Henry Hudson Bridge were about $370,000 per year, a sum that could be collected, at ten cents per car, from 3,700,000 cars. But the number of drivers handing their dimes to the bridge toll collectors was not 3,700,000. In 1938, it was 10,300,000; in 1939, 12,700,000. And maintenance costs on bridges were, Moses was learning, gratifyingly minimal. Painting the entire Henry Hudson, for example, cost only $18,000, and painting was needed only once in four years. The salaries of toll collectors, the only operating personnel required, totaled less than $50,000 per year: "Our bridge was fabulously successful," Jack Madigan would say. "We were earning—*after the carrying charges*—$600,000 per year *NET!!!*" And that was just one bridge! The Triborough, on which the annual carrying charges were about $1,800,000, but on which the toll was twenty-five cents for cars and more for trucks, was by 1938 earning per year *NET!!!* $1,300,000. More significantly still, on all Moses' bridges, the traffic volume for each month was higher than the volume for the corresponding month the previous year; clearly, volume—and revenue—was going to be far higher than even those fabulous figures.

Under the laws creating the authorities—the bills that Robert Moses himself had drafted on his yellow legal note pads—unexpectedly high revenues could be used in only one way: to retire an authority's bonds faster than scheduled, to speed the date when the authority would go out of existence and turn its bridge back to the city.

With surpluses of such unprecedented size, the bonds of Moses' authorities would be retired very fast indeed. At the rate the Henry Hudson Bridge was making money, for example, its cost would be amortized not in forty years but in ten years, perhaps, or nine, or eight. In a decade or less, the bridge that the city had never been able to finance would have been built by Robert Moses—built and paid for, to stand for centuries as a great free public improvement for its citizens.

Using the surpluses in the way required by law would therefore make the Henry Hudson Bridge—and the Triborough—spectacular successes, all the more spectacular in a city in which public works always seemed to cost the public more, not less, than anticipated.

But this was not the kind of success in which Moses, obsessed by accomplishment and power, was interested. Money—revenue, surpluses—was the key to accomplishment and power—but only if he could keep it and use it. It was of no use to him if he had to give it to bankers as fast as he got it. It was of no use to him if, as soon as he had paid off the bankers, he had to surrender control of his bridges. Money was of use to him only if, in other words, he was able to use the bridge surpluses for other purposes than bond paying and if he was able to keep control of the bridges instead of turning them over to the city. And under the law this was impossible.

But what if the law was changed?

What if, in some way, he was able to keep the money?

Madigan and others close to Robert Moses saw his supple mind coiling around the possibilities. The actuality of the money, he began to realize, was not its most significant aspect. Its potential was what mattered. The total annual income of his authorities was, by 1938, $4,500,000. This amount was not insignificant to him; it was as large as his total annual Park Department budget. But it was not as significant as $81,000,000. And $81,000,000 was the amount of forty-year, 4 percent, revenue bonds that could be floated—"capitalized" was the word in the bankers' vocabulary that Moses was learning—with an income of $4,500,000. If he was able to keep the authorities' revenues and use them to float bonds, he would be able to float $81,000,000, or $35,000,000 more than the total $46,000,000 in bonds that the three New York City bridge authorities currently had outstanding. He would have $81,000,000 to use to create dreams and power.

Much more than $81,000,000, in fact.

The multiplier factor would be increased by the proven success of his bridges. When he and Jack Madigan had originally been attempting to persuade bankers to invest in the authorities, the ability of toll bridges to attract substantial amounts of traffic had been in doubt, and the bankers had therefore demanded a coverage of 1.75 or 2.00 (anticipated earnings double that required to cover interest and amortization) and a return of 4 percent on their investment. Now toll bridges were a proven commodity. Bankers might settle for a coverage of 1.5 or even 1.4 and an investment return of 3 percent or even 2.75, and any reduction in coverage or interest rates meant an increase in the amount of bonds that the authority income could capitalize. More important, if some of the money raised by the floating of new bonds was used to build new bridges on which tolls could be charged, the authorities' income would be more than $4,500,000. Since each dollar of tolls could capitalize roughly eighteen dollars in bonds, there was therefore an additional built-in multiplier factor at work: the more public works he built, the more money he would have to build still more public works. And this factor would work indefinitely—forever, possibly.

Robert Moses had built public works on a scale unmatched by any other individual in the history of America. But all the highways and parks and bridges he had built were little more than nothing next to the highways and parks and bridges that Robert Moses wanted to build. He had turned into reality his dream of a great parkway along Manhattan's shoreline, but there was still the Brooklyn shoreline, and the Staten Island. He wanted parkways there, too—a "Circumferential" or "Belt" for Brooklyn, a "Shore" for Staten Island—and he had wanted them, and been arguing for their creation, for more than ten years. He had built fifty miles of highways in the city, but there were a hundred more miles that he wanted to build. He had reshaped to his own vision an urban park system that absolutely dwarfed any other urban park system in the United States, but the parks he had created in New York were in their turn dwarfed by the parks that he dreamed of creating; it had been 1930 when he had proposed a Soundview Park and a Flushing Meadows Park and two Marine Parks and a park—the greatest of all urban waterfront parks—in Jamaica Bay, and now it was 1938 and these parks were still only proposals. Where was the Rockaway Improvement? Even those parks that he had been able to create in the city, moreover, had not been created as he wanted; he had been forced to scale them down, to use inferior materials, to compromise. As for bridges, he had built in the city three, including one that was the greatest traffic-moving machine in the history of civilization, but he wanted to build at least four more—including one even larger than Triborough.

And that was just in the city. What about the areas around it? There were parkways on Long Island, all right, but not his greatest parkway—the ocean- and bay-bordered Fire Island masterpiece. There were parks—11,000 acres of parks, the greatest state park system in the country—on Long Island but he could foresee all too clearly the day there would be so many people living in the metropolitan area that 11,000 acres would not be nearly enough. After a decade and a half of building public works, the public works he had not yet built loomed before him larger than ever.

Moreover, the chances of building them seemed to be growing steadily more remote. Only the New Deal had enabled him to make even as much of a start as he had on his plans for New York City. Now, in 1938, the New Deal well was running dry, and La Guardia was insisting with a new firmness that he stop trying to lap up the city's share all by himself. Albany was drying up, too; each year Herbert Lehman was finding it more difficult to obey the law that required him to balance the state's budget. As for the city, La Guardia may have pulled it back from the door of fiscal death, but not even La Guardia could restore it to fiscal health; the corruption that had preceded him had weakened the body politic far too seriously. Political realities, moreover, made it unlikely that health could ever be restored. Existing taxes could support an annual budget—the budget out of which the debt service for new bonds for new public works would have to be paid—of about $575,000,000, and the debt service and salaries loaded on by Tammany ate up $500,000,000 of that even before other necessary expenses were figured in. As for the so-called "capital budget," there was no leeway in that, either: the city was constantly bumping up against the state-imposed ceiling that limited its borrowing capacity to 10 percent of the total assessed valuation of real property; the city's fiscal inability to construct public works was so pronounced that by 1940 La Guardia, who had dreamed of carving out a beautiful new metropolis, would have no choice but to limit new capital spending for the year to a symbolic one dollar. Because the city was a creature of the state, city taxes could be increased and the city budget ceiling raised only by the State Legislature, and not only the Legislature's conservatism but the influence wielded within it by the city's own propertied interests, which wanted the key property taxes kept down and, to protect the bonds they held, as few new bonds as possible issued, made the Legislature as reluctant to take those steps as La Guardia was to ask it to do so; desperately anxious to reshape his city La Guardia might be, but he was not anxious enough to court political disaster by asking for new taxes. Surveying such realities, Moses could see no reasonable possibility, in any foreseeable future, of the city being able to finance his dreams. If he wanted to remake the city, it was clear, he was going to have to do the job without its money.

But if he was able to keep the authorities' revenues, keep them indefinitely, he would have the money.

He would, moreover, have money he would be free to use as he chose.

Tens of millions of dollars had been placed in his hands already, of course—by Governors and Legislatures, by Mayor and Board of Estimate, by federal alphabet-agency administrators. But these had been millions hedged about by all the safeguards—the rules and regulations and established procedures, the technicalities—that had been established by generations of legislators and bureaucrats and that made it so difficult to Get Things Done.

Tens of millions of dollars had been given him to hire men, but he had been required to hire them according to civil service regulations which made it difficult for him—in most cases made it impossible for him—to hire the kind of men he wanted: the *best* men, the best engineers, the best administrators, the best ramrods, the best laborers. Under those regulations, he couldn't pay them enough to attract them to his service. He couldn't even hire whom he wanted of the men available at the salaries he *could* pay; he had to hire off civil service lists. These regulations could sometimes be circumvented, of course—no one circumvented them as cleverly as he, as was proven by the quality of his "Moses Men"—but they could be circumvented only with difficulty and delay, the delay he hated. And they could not be circumvented wholesale: the "Moses Men" were a prize cadre, but a cadre was not an army, and he was constantly raging at the quality of the main body of his troops, noncommissioned officers as well as enlisted men; once the Depression eased, civil service salary limits had made it impossible to keep loyal to his colors more than a handful of the prized seven hundred and fifty ramrods he had recruited during its depth. Civil service regulations made it impossible for him even to drive men as he wished to drive them: to drive men mercilessly you have to have threats to hold over their heads; the ultimate threat—dismissal—was all but denied him by the regulations; and dismissal for even a legitimate cause was a cumbersome and tedious procedure that had none of the efficacious effect on other workers of a snappy "Pick up your time and get out" from Art Howland or Earle Andrews. Civil service regulations had prevented him from using his men flexibly and efficiently; because he had to hire men out of allocations for a specific upstate or Long Island park commission or the New York City Park Department, and civil service regulations required him to use an employee of a public agency only on that agency's work, it was illegal for him to assign an upstater to a city job even if he was best qualified for it. Most important, civil service regulations required him to hire men only for specific purposes approved by Legislature or Board of Estimate, and these purposes had never included the one most vital to his aims: long-range planning. For more than ten years he had been scheming, scraping and saving to build up a "stable planning force"—without success.

But changing the law would give him one. The Legislature had placed public authorities under civil service, of course, but the power of Civil Service Commissions to enforce their edicts rested, as Moses had learned from the bitter experience of his youth, on the power to disapprove salary payments—on the commission's control of the purses out of which municipal and state agencies drew their "personal service" funds. It rested on the power of money. Let *him* have the money—let him keep control of the authorities' revenues—and he, this man who had mastered the intricacies of civil service as well as any man who ever lived, would be able to devise a hundred ways to manipulate Civil Service Commission rulings to his own ends. He would be able to attract to his service the men his sharp eyes had picked out of the herd, to hire and fire them as he pleased, to provide them with material rewards huge enough to make them endure his driving and his demands and to guarantee their absolute loyalty. And he would be able to hire men not only for specific but for general purposes. He would be able to have, at last, his stable planning force. Let him keep the control of the authorities' revenues and he would be able to study transportation needs before elected local officials studied them. He would be able to determine by his own criteria which transportation facilities should be built and in which order. He would be able to determine by his own criteria *how* these facilities should be built—what their design, size and precise location should be. He would be able to translate these general plans into detailed blueprints and specifications. And then, when the time was right—when a large new state or federal grant became available, or when the public was demanding a solution to the transportation problem—he could present these plans to elected officials as the solution, a solution already engineered, already designed, already costed out, a solution feasible engineeringly and economically, a solution whose planning was already a *fait accompli,* a solution that awaited only their approval for implementation, a solution for which, in many cases, money—the money of his public authorities—was already available. What official would then be willing to risk public antagonism by withholding that approval?

And if an official did dare to suggest an alternative, what good would it do him? The city possessed neither an engineering corps capable of planning large-scale public works nor money to hire in sufficient numbers engineers who did possess such capability. For that matter, the city had no money to build an alternate large-scale public work if it wanted to. It would be dependent upon the federal government or upon Moses' authorities to provide the cash. Federal money might well be lost by the delay additional studies would entail; as for the authorities' money, cross the man who was offering it and he might (bearing in mind that the man was Robert Moses, he probably would) withdraw the offer, and the official then could be accused of having cost the city a great public improvement. Let Moses keep control of the authorities' revenues and there would be no more nonsense about the Mayor or the Board of Estimate studying alternate routes for a highway or alternate locations for a bridgehead or alternate methods—mass transportation instead of highways, for example—of solving transportation problems. In the fields he had chosen for his own, the city would have to build public works where and how he chose.

Additional tens of millions of dollars had been given to him for non-salary items—construction costs, mainly—but he had been allowed little leeway in the spending of that money either. Much of it he had had to give to contractors—under strict regulations which not only required him to award contracts to the lowest qualified bidders, thereby preventing him from making awards to firms he personally favored, but also set many conditions designed for economy, a saving of taxpayers' money, rather than for the speed he wanted; strict restrictions on overtime had been especially irritating to this supreme ramrod, this archetypal top sergeant, who wanted his projects driven forward around the clock.

Allocations directly to his agencies allowed him even less leeway; such

Verrazano-Narrows Bridge

LANDSCAPE BY MOSES: Robert Moses' three-armed Triborough Bridge is the center of a cityscape in which the following are other Moses additions: In Manhattan *(left) the East River Drive Extension along the waterfront south of the bridge, and the Harlem River Drive, to the north, and behind these roads, every one of the high-rise low-income housing and Title I urban renewal projects rising out of Harlem.* In the Bronx *(top right) the Major Deegan Expressway running northwest from the Triborough's Bronx bridgehead, and the Bruckner Expressway running northeast; the housing project just north of the bridgehead; Van Cortlandt and Bronx parks at the top.* In Queens *(bottom) Astoria Park, with the giant Astoria pool. Randall's and Ward's islands (center) were almost entirely shaped by Moses.*

Bronx-Whitestone Bridge

Throgs Neck Bridge

Cross Bay Bridge

Robert Moses Twin Causeway

Alexander Hamilton Bridge

Henry Hudson Bridge (before the second deck was added)

Marine Parkway Bridge

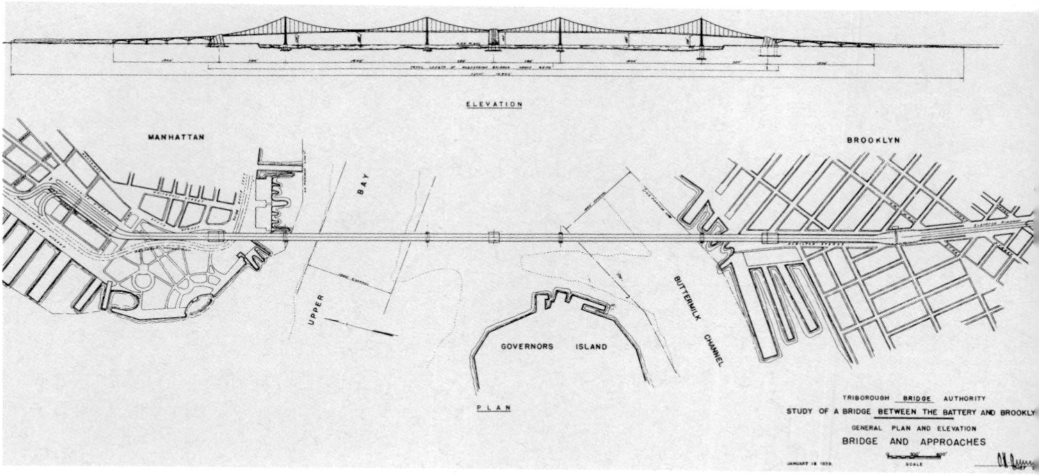

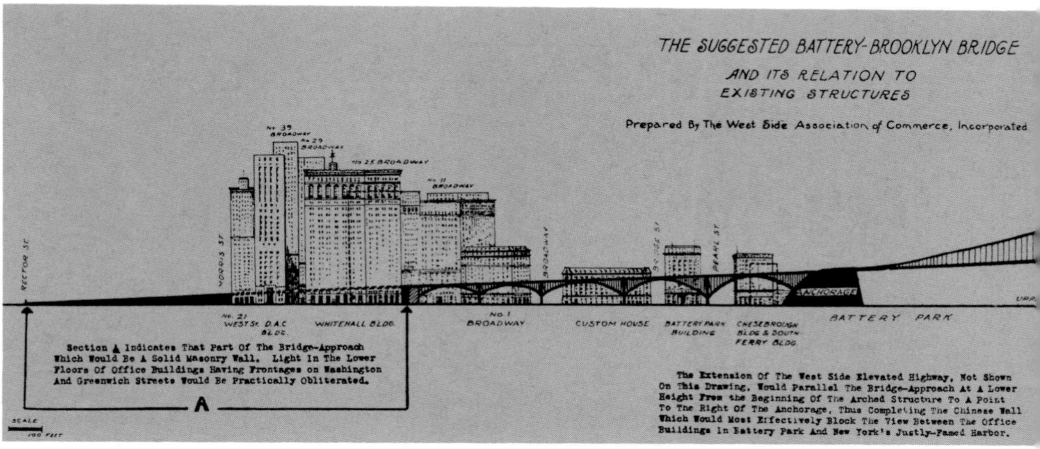

THE BROOKLYN-BATTERY BRIDGE: A Difference in Perspectives. *Moses attempted to persuade the public that the impact of his bridge on Lower Manhattan would be minimal, and had his artists draw the top rendering; others saw the bridge as a "Chinese Wall" that would block the view and blight the area (center); Ole Singstad dramatized these effects in the bottom rendering.*

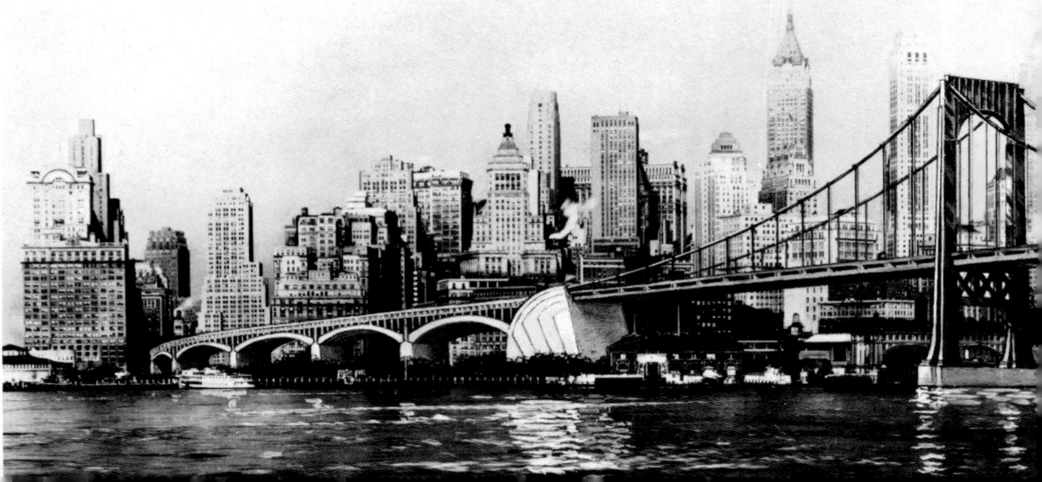

THREE MOSES BEACHES: Orchard Beach (top left), Jacob Riis Park (bottom left), Jones Beach (above).

Stone carvings (the State Seal on the Water Tower), ships' funnels to conceal garbage cans, directional signs complete with wrought-iron figures, and the architectural elegance of the East (below) and West (right) bathhouses and of the famous Water Tower show the effect of Moses' imagination at Jones Beach.

LIGHT
LUNCHES
— AND —
REFRESHMENTS

DO NOT DRESS ON BEACH
TO THE
BATH
HOUSE
USE UNDERPASS

BEACH TOYS
BATHING SUPPLIES
AND ACCESSORIES
IN BATH HOUSE LOGGIAS

SURF
ATHING
ALSO TO
EFRESHMENTS
ND MEN'S COMFORT
STATION

OCEAN FRONT
PARKING
25¢

GAS

Robert Moses Power Dam at Massena

Robert Moses Power Dam at Niagara

Part of the St. Lawrence Power Project: in the foreground, Robert Moses State Park; in the rear, the Moses-built Long Sault Control Dam.

THE WEST SIDE IMPROVEMENT—AND AN ALTERNATIVE. Below: *The Henry Hudson Parkway (left) and Seventy-ninth Street boat basin in Riverside Park (right).* Above: *The Henry Hudson Bridge and Parkway as Moses built them through Inwood Hill Park and Spuyten Duyvil in Riverdale. The dotted line indicates the route that urban planners suggested to avoid harming the park and Riverdale: along the open corridor next to Inwood Hill, across the Harlem River on a less-expensive, low-level span, through Marble Hill Valley (uninhabited at the time except for a shantytown) to Van Cortlandt Park, where it could also have run along the edge. (The Harlem River now follows an essentially straight path to the Hudson because Moses in effect moved the light-colored land jutting into the river to the left, joining it to Inwood Hill Park.)*

LANDSCAPES BY MOSES:
Above: *Moses' 1964–65 World's Fair and the Grand Central Parkway, Van Wyck, Whitestone and Long Island expressways.* Below: *Moses' housing projects in Harlem, East River Drive Extension, Manhattan arm of the Triborough Bridge, Ward's Island Pedestrian Bridge, Downing Stadium, Bruckner Expressway.*

United Nations Headquarters

New York Coliseum

Lincoln Center for the Performing Arts

Shea Stadium

World's Fair

Astoria Pool

Right: *Typical Moses low-income housing project.* Below: *The Alexander Hamilton Bridge (foreground) with ramps and approaches connecting it to the Harlem River Drive and Major Deegan Expressway (along the river) and the Cross-Bronx Expressway (to the right).*

The Grand Central Parkway and the four-level bridge interchange with the Clearview Expressway.

The Cross-Bronx Expressway guts a neighborhood.

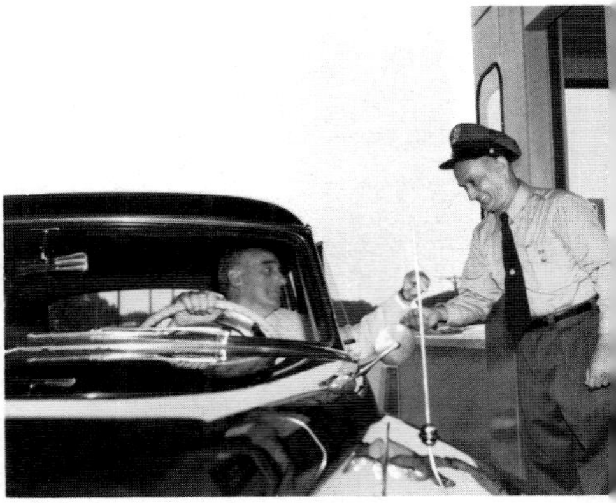

TWO THAT NEVER HAPPENED: One highway Moses did not get to build was his proposed Mid-Manhattan Expressway along Thirtieth Street; Moses, who never learned to drive and who never paid tolls, poses for a photographer.

AMERICAN
BADER BROS.

appropriations were made "line by line" for specific items. And members of the Legislature or Board of Estimate—accountable to the voters and therefore anxious not to make any appropriations that appeared to waste their money (and anxious as well not to let Moses further expand his empire)—resisted especially making any appropriations to him for the PR items which would seem blatantly wasteful to taxpayers but which Moses knew were vital to Getting Things Done: the printing of impressive, persuasive brochures and pamphlets; the creation of large-scale dioramas and scale models ("It never ceases to amaze me how you can talk and talk and talk to some guy about something you've got in mind, and he isn't very impressed, and then you bring in a beautiful picture of it or, better yet, a scale model with the bridge all in white and the water nice and blue, see, and you can see his eyes light up," Jack Madigan says); the hiring of public relations men to visit publishers, editors, reporters and radio commentators as well as nonmedia influentials, sell them on a project in advance, escort them on pre-opening limousine or yacht tours, leak them information that would place Moses' views in a favorable light (and his opponents' views in an unfavorable light); the rental of the necessary limousines; the hiring of the "bloodhounds" to dig up facts about an opponent that could induce him to cease his opposition, or, should he prove stubborn, could be leaked into print to discredit him; and, especially important to Moses because it gave him a chance to exercise his matchless charm as host, the laying on of hospitality—intimate luncheons for key individuals or lavish buffet luncheons for influentials by the hundreds— at which he could drape a big arm over a recalcitrant borough president's shoulders and use the glow induced by good food and fine wine to win him to his cause. He had, of course, used his ingenuity, and his skill at circumvention of the spirit if not the letter of the law, to publish brochures, hire public relations men, purchase limousines and host luncheons in the past. But he had never had enough money to do all this as lavishly and effectively as he wanted. But let him keep the authorities' revenues and he would have enough.

Changing the law might give him more than money. Changing the law might give him power, more power than he had ever attained before. Money itself is power, of course, but the power he was thinking about now was power of far greater dimensions.

A public authority, he had learned, possessed not only the powers of a large private corporation but some of the powers of a sovereign state: the power of eminent domain that permitted the seizure of private property, for example, and the power to establish and enforce rules and regulations for the use of its facilities that was in reality nothing less than the power to govern its domain by its own laws. The powers of a public authority were vested in the board of that authority. If there was only one member of that board in fact (as in the case of the Henry Hudson Parkway Authority: Robert Moses, Sole Member) or in practice (as in the case of the Triborough Authority, whose other members would routinely rubber-stamp Moses' actions), the powers of the authority would be vested in that member—in *him,* Robert Moses.

And there was another dimension to his thinking, too. Keen as always in discerning the potentialities for vast power in humble institutions, he had glimpsed in the institution called "public authority" a potentiality for power whose implications no one else—no one in City Hall or the Albany Statehouse for certain and, so far as research can determine, no one anywhere in the United States—had noticed, but that were exciting and frightening and immense.

Authorities could issue bonds. A bond was simply a legal agreement between its seller and its buyer. A legal agreement was, by definition, a contract. And under the Constitution of the United States, a contract was sacred. No state—and no creature of a state such as a city—could impair its obligations. No one—not Governor, not Mayor, not State Legislature, not City Board of Estimate—could interfere with its provisions. If Robert Moses could write the powers which had been vested in him into the bond contracts of his authorities, make those powers part of the agreements under which investors purchased the bonds, those powers would be his for as long as the authorities should remain in existence and he should control them. If he could keep the authorities in existence indefinitely and could keep his place at their head, he would hold those powers indefinitely—quite conceivably, until he died. The powers might have been given him by the Legislature and the Governor at the request of the Mayor and City Council, but if he embodied those powers in bonds, neither Legislature, Governor, Mayor nor City Council would ever be able to take them back.

Giving public authorities indefinite existence and such vastly expanded powers would not be easy. In proposing to give the institution substantial governmental powers and a lifespan at least of decades, possibly of centuries—in proposing to make it an institution that might endure as long as the Republic endured—Moses was in effect, whether or not he thought in such terms, proposing to create, within a democratic society based on a division of powers among three branches of government, a new, fourth branch, a branch that would, moreover, in significant respects, be independent of the other three.

The public officials whose approval was necessary would never give it. Those who were thinking men would realize that if they gave it they would be adding, without sufficient thought and consideration by themselves or by the public which should have the final say on matters of such significance, a whole new layer to urban government in America. The rest of them, concerned with power and patronage, would realize that to the extent they gave away power, they would be diminishing their own power. The key body whose approval was necessary—the Legislature that under the State Constitution alone had the power to create new authorities—had been fighting for years to keep Moses from gaining more power, from building his own empire within the state government. The Legislature would never approve the bills Moses was drafting if they understood them.

So Moses would have to keep them—and all the other officials involved—from understanding. He would have to persuade Mayor, City Council, Legislature and Governor to approve his bills before they realized what was in them.

In 1924, he had faced a similar problem—and had solved it successfully, persuading a naïve assemblyman to introduce, and hostile Republican legislative leaders to accept, bills that appeared innocuous but gave the Long Island State Park Commission vast new powers. This time, however, the job would be harder. His aims now were far more ambitious, the powers which he wanted now were far broader than those he had wanted then. And in 1924, he had had the Governor on his side. Now he had no one on his side. If a single person in Albany or New York—Democrat, Republican, Governor, Mayor, assemblyman, councilman, any one of the thousand sharp-eyed lawyers who prowled the Capitol and City Hall—caught even a glimpse of his true aims, and sounded the alarm, he would never be able to accomplish those aims. He had to conceal his purposes from everyone.

The safeguards included in all previous New York State legislation on authorities to limit their lifespan were the provisions setting a time limit on their bonds, a date by which each authority must redeem all its bonds, surrender control of all its facilities and go out of existence. Moses, drafting amendments to the Triborough Bridge Authority Act, knew that the Legislature would never agree to the elimination of these safeguards.

So he didn't eliminate them.

He just made them meaningless.

Right at the beginning of the original Triborough Act—in Section One, in the portion labeled "Existence"—the act said explicitly that the Triborough "board and its corporate existence shall continue only for a period of five years and thereafter until all its . . . bonds have been paid in full . . . ," a provision which when coupled with a provision setting the maximum life of the bonds at forty years, was intended to limit the maximum life of the Authority to that span. The amended Triborough Act which Moses was proposing said the same thing—in the same place, right at its beginning, in Section One.

But it also said something else. Not at its beginning and not in the portion labeled "Existence," but long, legalistic pages later, buried deep within the act, in a subdivision of Section Nine, a subdivision and a section that ostensibly had nothing to do with "Existence," there was a new sentence:

> The authority shall have power from time to time to refund any bonds by the issuance of new bonds, whether the bonds to be refunded have or have not matured, and may issue bonds partly to refund bonds then outstanding and partly for any other corporate purpose.

"He had figured out a gimmick," says Reuben A. Lazarus, drafter of the original Triborough Act and himself a master of the gimmick—and as Lazarus spoke a smile broke over his old, wrinkled face despite his attempts to conceal it, and his voice was filled with admiration, the admiration of a master of a difficult craft for a man who was more than a master. "That sentence looked so innocuous. But it changed my whole act completely. With that sentence in there, he had power to issue forty-year bonds and every thirty-nine years he could call them in and issue new bonds, for another forty years. La Guardia had thought that authorities . . . would be temporary creations that would build something and then turn it over to the city and go out of existence as soon as it was paid off. But with that gimmick in there, it would never be paid off."

Never. The existence of the Triborough Authority "shall continue only until all its bonds have been paid in full," the act said. But, because of Moses' amendments, the Authority no longer had to pay its bonds in full. Every time it had enough money to pay them in full, it could instead use the money to issue new bonds in their place. The amendments meant that unless it wanted to, the Authority wouldn't ever have to turn its bridges over to the city. It might, if it so desired, be able to keep the bridges—and stay in existence—as long as the city stayed in existence.

The safeguards included in all previous New York State legislation on authorities to limit their scope were the provisions setting a limit on the amount of bonds each could have outstanding, a limit sufficient to pay only for the specific project or projects the Legislature wished it to build and nothing more. The Triborough Act contained such a provision, a clause stating that the Authority could not have outstanding more than $53,000,000—an amount sufficient only to cover its $35,000,000 share of the cost of the Triborough Bridge and the $18,000,000 cost of the Bronx-Whitestone Bridge. But Moses' gimmick made that restriction meaningless, too. For by authorizing the Authority to issue new bonds not only to pay off old ones but also for "any other corporate purpose," it was authorizing it to keep its indebtedness at $53,000,000 even though it had money available to pay off part, or even most, of that figure. If, for example, the income was high enough to pay all its carrying charges and also accumulate a surplus, which after five or ten years amounted to $20,000,000, the Authority could then call in $20,000,000 of its outstanding bonds, pay them off and therefore have only $33,000,000 outstanding. Its legislatively authorized borrowing capacity would still be $53,000,000. Its revenues would support that amount of bonds. So the Authority would have $20,000,000 of borrowing capacity. It could issue $20,000,000 in new bonds and use the proceeds of the sale for "any corporate purpose."

And what were such purposes?

The original Triborough Act had given the Authority power to build only the two bridges and their "approaches." Moses' success in persuading the PWA that approaches could mean roads leading to the bridges had greatly expanded the Authority's power.

Now he proceeded to expand it further.

The new, amended, Triborough Bridge Authority Act that Moses was proposing still said first that the Authority's powers were to build bridges and their approaches. But, in later sections, it also said some other things.

The act empowered the Authority to acquire land for and construct not only approaches but "new roads, streets, parkways or avenues connecting with the approaches," and to widen existing roads, streets, parkways or avenues connecting with those approaches. The word "connecting" was innocuous—unless one began to think closely about what it would mean if Moses expanded its definition as he had expanded the definition of "approaches." If an approach was miles long—the Queens "approach" to the Triborough Bridge, for example, was six miles long—scores of roads, streets, parkways or avenues intersected ("*connected*") with it. Under the amended act he was proposing, the Triborough Authority would have the right to widen any or all of them. It would have the right to build a new thoroughfare that would connect with the approaches anywhere along their length. And how long could that thoroughfare be? A block? A mile? Five miles? Ten? Could it be a highway that ran clear across the city? Under the amended act he was proposing, it certainly could. And suppose he wanted to build another—third—highway, to intersect with the one he had built to intersect with the approaches? Since this new, third, road would connect with the second, and the second would connect with the approaches, why could not the third be said to connect with the first? Under a liberal definition—a definition such as Moses had long since proven himself adept at making—quite possibly it could. Quite possibly, in fact, one could say that any major thoroughfare in the city "connected" with any other. And if one could say that, one could say that the act that Moses was so carefully drafting would mean that the Triborough Authority would have the right to construct highways throughout the city, in many respects exactly as if it were the city government itself.

And not just highways. Another clause in the act gave the Authority power "to construct and develop for the purpose of public parks" lands acquired "in connection with the Whitestone Bridge project and with new or existing roads, streets, parkways and avenues connecting with such project." Under the act Moses was drafting, the Authority would be able to build parks along any highway it might construct. Since the Authority would be able to build highways throughout the city, it would be able to build parks throughout the city, too.

And not just highways and parks. Buried still deeper within the act Moses was drafting was a clause giving the Authority the right to build and operate *any* "facilities for the public not inconsistent with the use of the project." Not with the *project*. With the *use* of the project. Since the project consisted of bridges, roads and parks, why, under that clause, would it be inconsistent for the Authority to build housing nearby that would allow more members of the public the convenient use of those bridges, roads and parks? Why, for that matter, would the construction of *any* public facility be inconsistent with the use of the project? An aggressive Authority chairman, anxious to stretch the powers in the act to the limit, could well find in that phrase legal authorization to build any type of public facility he chose anywhere along the Authority's bridges, roads, streets, parkways, avenues and parks—anywhere, in fact, in the city.

And the best bill drafter in Albany set to work to make sure that, in building and operating its projects, the Authority, despite the limitations on its power by the State Legislature, would nevertheless possess powers equal to those possessed by the state—or by the city of which, in theory, the Authority was merely a creature.

Legislature and Mayor had sought to insure that the Authority would be subordinate to the city by including in the old act the provision that the City Comptroller should be the Authority's "fiscal agent." The new act included the same provision. In drafting the section entitled "Moneys of the Authority," Moses began it, in fact, with the flat statement: "All moneys of the authority from whatever source derived shall be paid to the comptroller as agent of the authority." The meaning of this sentence must have seemed clear to any legislator who read it. The definition of "fiscal agent" was well established; he was the individual empowered to receive and pay out a corporation's moneys. But later in the section, Moses added another sentence: "The moneys . . . shall be paid out on check of the Comptroller on requisition of the chairman of the authority. . . ." With that sentence added, the Comptroller, while still authorized to receive the Authority's moneys, would be able to pay them out only on Moses' requisition—would, in other words, be able to do with them only what Moses wanted him to do. He was still required to take Moses' money to the bank and deposit it there, but he was now forbidden to take the money out again without Moses' signature on the withdrawal slip. The sentence that Moses had slipped into the act meant that although the Comptroller of the City of New York would be called the Authority's agent, he would really be no more than its errand boy.

Legislature and Mayor had sought to insure that the Authority would be subordinate to the city by including in the old act the provision that the city would "own" all Triborough projects. The new act said that it did—flatly and clearly. But it also said that "the authority shall retain full jurisdiction and control over all its projects. . . ." The city might own the Triborough Bridge, but only the Triborough Bridge Authority could run it.

By the time Moses had finished drafting his amended acts, his authorities had not only all the powers of "bodies corporate" but many of the powers of "bodies politic"—including bodies politic that were sovereign states. His authorities had the right to "do all things . . . that a business corporation can do"—to sue, for example, to make contracts and bylaws, to acquire real estate and use it or lease it or dispose of it, and, of course, to issue bonds—and they had the right to do many things that private corporations could not do. They had the power to own public facilities, to require the public to pay tolls for their use and to prevent the construction of competing facilities so that the public had no choice but to pay those tolls. They had the right to govern their domain by making their own laws ("rules and regulations for the protection of" their property which "shall have the force and effect of law," with violations "triable by a city magistrate and punishable by not more than thirty days imprisonment, or by a fine of not more than fifty dollars, or both") and to maintain their own police force (hundreds of Authority "Bridge and Tunnel Officers") to enforce those laws. They could have their own great seals ("and alter the same at pleasure") and set their own statute of limitations (a private citizen suffering damages by negligence of a private corporation had three years to sue; a private citizen suffering damages by negligence of the Jones Beach State Park Authority had six months to sue). They had the sovereign power of eminent domain, and more—not only could they take a private citizen's property, they could enter the land before it was taken to make the surveys necessary to decide if they wanted to take it (never again would some Long Island farmer be able to ram a shotgun against Sidney Shapiro's chest and keep him off his land). They had, in fact, some powers that sovereign states—at least the sovereign state of New York—did not. They could let contracts without competitive bidding. Their officials could be removed only for cause; they were immune from the pleasure of the Governor.

And Moses made sure that these powers, these powers corporate and politic and, in some respects, greater than both, would be embodied, ultimately, not in the authorities but in him personally. In the case of the single-member authorities, of course, the authority *was* Robert Moses. The Triborough, Jones Beach and Bethpage authorities had three-member boards, but while their enabling acts said, "The power of such corporation shall be vested in and exercised by a majority of the members," it also said, "The board may delegate to one or more of its members . . . such powers and duties as it may deem proper."

Then Moses set to work to make sure that no one would ever be able to take those powers away.

He did it in Section Nine, Paragraphs 2 and 4, Clauses *a* through *i*. Paragraph 2 authorized the Authority to pass resolutions governing the sale of its bonds. The various clauses of Paragraph 4 said, when taken together, that the resolutions could contain provisions dealing with toll rates, Authority rules and regulations and *"any other matters, of like or different character, which in any way affect the security or protection of the bonds."* And Paragraph 4 also said that any such resolution "shall be a part of the contract with the holders of the bonds."

Legislation can be amended or repealed. If legislators were in some future year to come to feel that they had been deceived into granting Robert Moses wider powers than they had intended—the right to keep tolls on a bridge even after the bridge was paid for, for example—they could simply revoke those powers. But a contract cannot be amended or repealed by anyone except the parties to it. Its obligations could not be impaired by anyone—not even the governing legislature of a sovereign state. Section Nine, Paragraphs 2 and 4, Clauses *a* through *i*, gave Robert Moses the right to embody in Triborough's bonds all the powers he had been given in the legislation creating Triborough. Therefore, from the moment the bonds were sold (thereby putting into effect the contract they represented), the powers he had been given in the legislation could be revoked only by the mutual consent of both Moses and the bondholders. They could not be revoked by the state that had created the Authority or by the city whose mere instrumentality it was supposed to be. If he copied into the bond resolutions the legislation giving him the right to charge whatever tolls he wished, for as long as he wished, from the moment the bonds were sold that power could never be revoked without his consent. If he copied into the bond resolutions the legislation giving him his other new, broad powers, those powers could never be revoked. The elected representatives of the state and city might have given Robert Moses those powers. But the elected representatives of the state and city would never be able to take them back.

Previously, Robert Moses had always needed what he termed "executive support." He had learned during his first great effort in public life—his attempt to reform the municipal civil service, an attempt brought to naught by his betrayal by John Purroy Mitchel—that as long as he was an appointed official, he could not accomplish great dreams without the backing of the elected official who had appointed him, and he had never allowed himself to forget that fact. His skill at bill drafting and his hold on the public imagination had gained him a unique insulation from Mayors and Governors in his daily operations, but it had still been only a chief executive who could give him the money and power necessary for the creation of giant public works.

But now he needed executive support no longer. In the fields which he had carved out for his own—transportation and recreation—the passage of his "amendments" to the authority enabling acts had given him resources of money and power independent of Governors and Mayors. Their approval was no longer required. Before Moses, the public authority had been a mere instrument of the city, a body established by the city's duly constituted, elected officials to carry out one of their decisions. His public authorities had been set up to do what they wanted done. Now his authorities would do what he wanted done.

For years, Robert Moses had sought executive power himself, hastily switching his party allegiance in 1928 when he thought he had a chance for the Democratic nomination for Governor, switching back to Republican in 1933 when he thought he had a chance for the Republican-Fusion nomination for Mayor, finally obtaining a nomination and running for Governor in 1934.

Each such clutch at executive office had been an attempt to obtain more power through normal democratic processes. After the 1934 debacle, however, it was obvious that this path to power was forever barred to him. His voter-antagonizing personality meant that he was never going to be able to obtain that supreme power which, in a democratic society, only the people can, through their votes, confer.

But now he needed that power no longer. In many ways, the amendments to the authority acts had given him, in his fields of operation, more power than he would have possessed as chief executive of state or city.

And Moses knew it. Prior to passage of the authority amendments, he had scrounged for elective office. After the passage of those amendments, he disdained it. For the next twenty years he would with regularity be approached by men prepared to back him for a gubernatorial or mayoral nomination, and he would firmly discourage them. Robert Moses was interested in money and power, and he no longer needed elective office to obtain those prizes. After the passage of his authority amendments, he had them already. With the institution he defined as "a body corporate and politic," Robert Moses had, on a broader scale, simply repeated the formula successful for him at Yale and with the Long Island State Park Commission, carving out within the state and city governments but outside those governments' traditional, formal framework a unique, independent niche. Now, thanks to his penchant—his genius—for seeing potentialities for power where no one else saw them, in the future his public authorities as well as city officials would be making vital, city-shaping decisions.

He didn't even need public opinion any more.

"That's a slender reed to lean on," Al Smith had said. Now Robert Moses had something more solid: the firm, precise, unbreakable covenants of the bond resolutions.

Robert Moses still had all his old, immense, popularity. But were he, one day, to lose that popularity, the loss would no longer be nearly as disastrous as it would have been in the past. For no one—not the people, not the people's elected representatives, not the people's courts—could change those covenants.

The institution over which Robert Moses had waved his magic wand was one uniquely suited to be the fairy princess that would bring his dreams to life. It dovetailed neatly with his philosophy and personality.

Moses was driven by the need for tangible, indisputable evidence of accomplishment and achievement—evidence such as a public improvement. He was driven by a need to build. Building—building a public improvement—was an authority's primary function; apart from operating and maintaining that improvement, its *only* function.

Moses had what amounted almost to a horror of ceasing to build; of finishing a bridge, say, and then having nothing to do thereafter but keep it clean and collect tolls on it, of being forced, as he put it, "to be a caretaker, to have nothing to do but sit around and collect nickels and dimes for the rest of my life." If an authority ceased to build, it would die; if all it did was collect tolls, the tolls would pay off its bonds and when the bonds were paid off it would have no choice but to go out of existence. Only by continually embarking on new projects—which would require new bond issues—could an authority remain viable.

Moses' vision was on a scale so grand that it transcended the tangled network of boundary lines of the 1,400 cities, boroughs, counties, townships, villages, sewer districts, fire districts, police districts, water districts in the New York metropolitan area. As he had once seen Long Island entire, now he saw the metropolitan region as a single whole, and as he had once wanted to shape the whole Island, now he wanted to shape the whole region. Of all the region's governmental institutions, only an authority could transcend those boundary lines. The jurisdiction of every one of the 1,400 governmental units ended at that unit's borders, and any attempt by one of them to initiate a development which crossed its borders was jealously—and, invariably, successfully—resisted by its neighbor. The sacred right to "home rule" could not be tampered with even by a county; only by obtaining the consent of every incorporated hamlet that would be crossed by a proposed highway could the Board of Supervisors of Nassau or Suffolk or Westchester County build one. Even the state government violated "home rule" only at its peril. Only an authority could with impunity build a project across or through several jurisdictions.

Moses' methods of Getting Things Done were dictatorial, peremptory, arbitrary, arrogant—"authoritarian," an observer addicted to puns might conclude. An official of a conventional governmental agency had difficulty in employing such methods. An official of an authority did not. Many of the restrictions which gave the public recourse from the decisions of old-line agencies did not even exist for public authorities. The symbol was the public hearing, the exemplification of everything Moses detested about normal democratic processes. Under law and custom, conventional governmental agencies could not embark on any large-scale public improvement without holding public hearings. An authority could.

Moses' methods—the methods with which he swayed politicians to his side—required secrecy. An authority gave him secrecy, for unlike the records of conventional governmental agencies, which were public, subject always to inspection, an authority's records were corporate records, as private as those of a private corporation.

Moses' image—the image he had so painstakingly cultivated—was precious to him, not only because it helped him achieve and accomplish, but because of reasons rooted in the murky depths of his personality. The image could not help being reinforced by his identification with public authorities, for public authorities had the same image.

The image was of the totally unselfish and altruistic public servant who wanted nothing for himself but the chance to serve. A key element in it was his disdain for money—a disdain which he made certain was well publicized and which was symbolized by his refusal to accept a salary for his services. Authority officials were traditionally unsalaried (the tradition had begun in England, where it had been believed that authorities would get better officials—men above politics—if they were not paid), and Moses had eagerly followed the tradition with his authorities—and had made certain that the public knew he was serving as authority chairman "without compensation."

The image was of the fearless independent above politics. The public believed authorities—entities outside the normal governmental setup, entities whose members were unsalaried and appointed to terms long enough in theory to insure their independence from politicians—to be "nonpolitical."

The image was of the relentless foe of bureaucrats, the dynamic slasher of red tape. A key rationale for the creation of authorities was their freedom from the red tape involved in old-line governmental agencies and their ability to function freely and efficiently because they were established outside the governmental bureaucracies.

The image was of the man who Got Things Done, who produced for the public tangible, visible, dramatic achievements. The great bridges, tunnels and piers created by authorities were tangible, highly visible monuments to *their* achievements.

In short, Moses had discovered a governmental institution that was not only uniquely suited to his purposes but was, in institutional terms, an embodiment of his personality, an extension of himself. "An institution," said Ralph Waldo Emerson, "is the lengthened shadow of one man." The institution named "the public authority" was, in the form it took after Moses' eyes focused on it in 1937 and 1938, the lengthened shadow of Robert Moses.

He himself seemed to understand this. His remarks and, sometimes, his published statements, reveal a striking identification of himself with authorities, which he defined as "nonpolitical" organizations headed by "unsalaried" trustees in which "the *speed*, *flexibility* and absence of red tape, traditionally associated with private industry," could be used for public purposes. Composing the introduction to a brochure—expensively bound, wide-margined, printed in full color on paper of a weight and sheen suitable for an invitation to a royal wedding—that he issued in 1941 to mark the fifth anniversary of the opening of the Triborough Bridge, he wrote:

> If I may be permitted a personal note, I would say that it has long been a cherished ambition of mine to weave together the loose strands and frayed edges of the New York metropolitan arterial tapestry. . . . The Triborough Bridge Authority has provided the warp on the metropolitan loom, the heavier threads across which the lighter ones are woven.

"The warp on the loom": the public authority, this new institution—new at least to America—at whose birth he had been present, to which he had served as prescient nursemaid and which he, more than any other individual, had raised to a maturity consonant with a major role on America's urban scene, would be the vehicle which would make his dreams come true.

A series of decisions Robert Moses took in 1937 symbolized his realization of this fact.

Two were financial. Previously, realizing that his dreams would never be funded by state and city governments, he had, through intricate and ingenious financial devices, arranged wherever possible to have revenues collected by the state commission and city department he headed paid not into state and city treasuries but into special "revolving funds" that in effect let him add them to the regular commission and department budgets. Now, in another series of maneuvers, he circumvented his circumventions—and when he had finished, the revenues of the Jones Beach parking fields no longer went to the Long Island State Park Commission but to the Jones Beach State Parkway Authority, and the revenues of the Jacob Riis Park parking field went not to the City Park Department but to the Marine Parkway Authority. He still had the money to spend—but now he could spend it through the authorities.

One was physical. Previously, he had had four offices: the State Council of Parks office at 80 Centre Street; the Long Island State Park Commission's offices at Belmont Lake State Park; 270 Broadway (the New York State Office Building), selected for its proximity to City Hall; and his nominal office in the headquarters of the New York City Park Department in the Arsenal in Central Park.

Four might have seemed adequate, but now he built a fifth, and told his aides it would be "the main office from now on." And this office was located on Randall's Island.

Geographically, Randall's Island was near the center of New York, but the water which surrounded it was a moat which separated it from the rest of the city. Moses' "amendments" to the Triborough Act made that separation more than physical. No inhabitant of the city could use the lawns or stadium or other facilities on Randall's Island—could even drive across it—without paying the Triborough Bridge Authority a tribute in coin, a tribute which Moses exacted from even the highest city officials, generally refusing to give free bridge passes even to borough presidents and sometimes, angry at La Guardia, withholding them from the Mayor. Once on the island, visitors were subject not to the city's laws but to Triborough's—Authority rules and regulations enforced by Triborough's Bridge and Tunnel Officers. Moses' decision to build his main office there was, intentionally or not, symbolic of his independence of the city.

If, moreover, Moses' authorities were becoming an independent empire, the heart's blood of that empire was money: tolls. The bulk of those tolls were collected at the huge Triborough Bridge toll plaza. If the empire had a heart, that was it. Moses built his new office in the very shadow of that toll plaza.

Not only the location of Moses' headquarters but its height was symbolic. Although the squat, gray three-story structure was built directly adjacent to the Triborough toll plaza, its roof was just enough below that plaza so that the building could not be seen by drivers on the plaza or on the bridge roadway. Although tens of thousands of drivers used the bridge day after day, year after year, none but a handful ever realized that there was an office building there. Moses' headquarters was concealed almost completely from public view.

He no longer needed the support of the city's mayor—and he wasted little time letting him know it. Exactly one month after La Guardia, on the strength of his trust in Moses' earnest representations, had assured Governor Lehman that the city was retaining ample control over Moses' authorities, thereby persuading the Governor to sign one of Moses' new authority bills, a dispute arose over the Authority's hiring practices, and Moses wrote the Mayor, "It is silly to force a court test of such a matter, but I shall have to take this up with attorneys for the bondholders and with the trustees unless the matter is adjusted."

The Mayor thought he knew how to handle so outrageous an attempt at intimidation. "Now, there is one matter I want to make absolutely clear," he replied.

> The Authority bondholders have absolutely nothing to say and have no control over purely administrative matters of the City of New York. So, don't talk about a court test on such matters or taking up anything of this nature with the Authority's attorneys or the stockholders. The Mayor establishes the policy for the City as well as the selection of the commissioners of the Authorities, and the Authority bondholders have absolutely nothing to say from the Commissioner down to the last line of attendants. You are a city official and will take matters up with the Corporation Counsel of the City of New York and not with "attorneys for the bondholders."

Moses' reply was more succinct. "I think you had better read the agreements and contracts," he wrote.

As poor Trubee Davison had done years before, Fiorello La Guardia sat down, too late, to study documents drawn up by Robert Moses which he had approved because he had relied on Moses' word as to what was in them. Then he called in his legal advisers to read them.

"Well, that was the day of the great awakening," recalls Windels, who, having resigned as Corporation Counsel, had not previously seen Moses' "amendments." He and Reuben Lazarus told the Mayor that, as Windels was to put it, "of course, under the bond resolution, the Authority *did* have the power to employ its own counsel, and it had all these enormous other powers as well." The Mayor, of course, had powers, too. On some of his authorities Moses served *ex officio* because he was the City Park Commissioner. The Mayor could fire Moses as Park Commissioner, and thereby divest him simultaneously of his membership on those authorities. But this power existed in theory only; political realities made it meaningless. Remove him from the authority undertaking the Rockaway Improvement and he might use his influence with the State Legislature to have state funds cut off from the state-financed part of the project, the Atlantic Avenue grade elimination; the Legislature had agreed to finance the elimination in the first place only because he was heading both city and state agencies involved. The city had no funds to further the work itself; it would have to remain uncompleted; Atlantic Avenue, already torn up, would remain a three-mile-long stretch of rubble. La Guardia would find himself in the same untenable position in which President Roosevelt had found himself when he had attempted to oust Moses as head of another authority—that of sacrificing a great public improvement for the sake of personal revenge on a faithful and immensely popular public servant. La Guardia might, of course, attempt to make clear the fact that the issue was not personal. He might attempt to make the public understand that public authorities had been given too much power. But the Mayor was only too well aware of the futility of attempting to explain the technicalities of bond resolution contracts to an electorate that idolized the Man Who Got Things Done.

More important, while the Mayor could remove Moses from some authorities, he could not remove him from the Triborough Authority—he had no charges of specific wrongdoing to bring against him—until his term expired in three years. During those three years, Moses would still have immense powers in the city. He would still be in charge of huge public works being constructed within the city's borders. Making an open enemy of Moses would lead to an immensely embarrassing situation, a situation, which, moreover, would continue to be embarrassing for what was, in political terms, a lifetime.

And these considerations combined with the others that always hamstrung La Guardia in his dealings with Moses: Moses' immense popularity; Moses' immense influence with a Governor and State Legislature from whom the Mayor constantly needed favors; Moses' ability to ram through the great public works the Mayor, as sculptor of metropolis, desperately wanted rammed through. La Guardia knew that Moses could ram them through—scandal-free and in time for the next election. With good reason, he doubted if anyone else could. The powers that the Mayor possessed over Moses' authorities in theory he did not possess in practice. Political realities gave him no choice but to allow Moses to remain at their head. And he knew it.

Moses knew it, too. After reading the bond agreements and contracts, La Guardia dropped all further discussion of the authorities' powers. Moses never raised the matter again. But thereafter he treated La Guardia not as his superior but as an equal. In the areas of transportation and recreation, Robert Moses, who had never been elected by the people of the city to any office, was henceforth to have at least as much of a voice in determining the city's future as any official the people *had* elected—including the Mayor.

VI

THE LUST FOR POWER

29. "And When the Last Law Was Down . . ."

The weather being fine and spring-like, I walked for an hour before dinner with my wife in the Battery. . . . What a beautiful spot it is! The grounds are in fine order; the noble bay, with the opposite shores of New Jersey, Staten and Long Islands, vessels of every description, from the noble, well appointed Liverpool packet to the little market craft, and steamers arriving from every point, give life and animation to a prospect unexcelled by any city view in the world. It would be worth traveling one hundred miles out of one's way in a foreign country to get a sight of it.

—DIARY OF PHILIP HONE, APRIL 10, 1835

ANXIOUS AS HE WAS to paint onto the great canvas of New York Moses' long-proposed "circumferential" bypass route around the city to the northeast for traffic from both Lower Manhattan and Brooklyn—a Brooklyn-Battery Tunnel, an elevated highway to carry traffic from the tunnel across Brooklyn's congested downtown and, to carry traffic from the highway around the edge of Brooklyn and Queens to the Bronx-Whitestone Bridge, where it could link up with the Westchester parkways beyond, a "Circumferential Parkway" (Moses had not yet been forced by the unwieldiness of the name to call it the "Belt")—La Guardia could see no way of obtaining the money that the Mayor-artist called the "brush": tunnel would cost $65,000,000, elevated highway $12,000,000, parkway $28,000,000—a total of $105,000,000. This was approximately $105,000,000 more than the city could afford, and the city's Tunnel Authority, which had the legislative authority to build the tunnel, could provide little help: with its first tunnel, the Queens-Midtown, not due to open for another two years, it had no revenues to help capitalize new projects, and investors were so leery of buying bonds for another tunnel before the first had proven successful that they were demanding interest rates that would add additional millions to the cost. When La Guardia tried to sell the bonds in Washington, the reception was chilling; RFC Chairman Jesse Jones said that, cousin on the Tunnel Authority or no, he would not consider sinking a cent more than $39,000,000 in another New York tunnel; Ickes, from whom the Mayor attempted to raise the balance as an outright PWA grant, said that New York's share of PWA funds was already so disproportionate that he would not give the city more than $5,000,000 for *any* purpose. And when La Guardia raised the subject of money with the only other source he could think of—Robert Moses—the chill over the whole situation turned to ice. For while Moses told the Mayor that the Triborough Bridge Authority did indeed have money to spare—to the Mayor's utter astonishment, Triborough's chairman revealed that the Authority could, by capitalizing its surpluses, raise immediately more than $30,000,000—and was willing to use that money for the circumferential project, he also told the Mayor there would be a price for its use: the Mayor would have to allow him to do what two years earlier he had prevented him from doing. He would have to allow him to take over the Tunnel Authority.

To a man who valued power as highly as did La Guardia, the price—which would give Moses a monopoly over all new intracity water crossings, tunnels as well as bridges—was outrageously steep. In his files can be found a memorandum from Moses giving details. Across it is scrawled, in huge letters in the Mayor's handwriting, a single word: *LOUSY!*

But the Mayor found that, if he wanted to build the great project, he had no choice but to pay that price. Repeated pleas to Ickes won from the Old Curmudgeon one concession—the PWA had previously approved grants for $7,000,000 for New York schools and hospitals on which construction had not yet begun; if La Guardia so desired, Ickes said, he was welcome to use that money for the tunnel instead. But the limit on new PWA contributions remained firm at $5,000,000, so the PWA's contribution would total only an inadequate $12,000,000. Trekking back and forth to Washington, Stetson in hand, La Guardia told the RFC the city would somehow scrape up a few millions to provide a greater margin of safety for tunnel bonds, but this persuaded the RFC to raise the amount it would buy only from $39,000,000 to $43,000,000. With the total federal contribution thus frozen at $55,000,000, the Mayor could see no way to a thaw. He appears for a time to have contemplated building only the tunnel and highway, hoping that when Moses saw the rest of the bypass going ahead, his passion to complete it would persuade him to build the parkway with Triborough money, but the tunnel and highway alone cost $77,000,000, $19,000,000 more than he could raise. La Guardia then contemplated delaying the project until the Queens-Midtown was open and earning, but that opening was two years away—by that time, the way things were going in Washington, the PWA might no longer have any money to give. The Mayor explored the possibility of *making* Moses—through legislative or some other action—contribute the Triborough surpluses, but found that plan balked by the unalterable bond covenants. Trapped between his dreams for the city and the city's utter inability to pay for them, he had no choice. If he wanted New York to have the great belt system, he would have to hand over to

Moses, already far too powerful, more power still. In a formal "Memorandum of Understanding" and an exchange of letters on September 7 and 8, 1938, Moses agreed to use Triborough's surplus to build the $12,000,000 elevated highway and to add $22,000,000 to the RFC contribution to build the tunnel. In return La Guardia agreed that the city would use the PWA's $12,000,000 for the Belt Parkway and would, over the next three years, complete the parkway with $16,000,000 of its own funds. And the Mayor further agreed to ask the Legislature to allow Triborough to take over the Tunnel Authority's Queens-Midtown Tunnel, the Tunnel Authority's authorization to build the Brooklyn-Battery Tunnel—and the Tunnel Authority itself.

With the Brooklyn-Battery Tunnel firmly in his grasp, Moses made a slight modification in its design: It became the Brooklyn-Battery Bridge.

The change reflected the importance Moses had come to place on bankers' values—a bridge could be built slightly more cheaply than a tunnel, would cost slightly less to operate and could, per dollar spent, carry slightly more traffic—and his eagerness to build impressive monuments to himself; a bridge was, after all, the most impressive of monuments ("the finest architecture made by man") as well as one whose life was "measureless"; a tunnel, he said in public, "is merely a tiled, vehicular bathroom smelling faintly of monoxide"; in private, an aide recalls, "he used to say, 'What's a tunnel but a hole in the ground?'—and RM wasn't interested in holes in the ground." And the change had the additional value of tying La Guardia even more closely to his agreement with Moses because it appealed to the Mayor's romantic, artistic conception of himself as a "painter" of New York—as well as to his own not inconsiderable interest in monuments. "RM took the Mayor out on Jack's [Madigan's] yacht into the harbor off Wall Street at sunset one day—and you know how beautiful it is there at sunset—and told him that he was going to use this setting for the biggest, most beautiful bridge in the world, and the Little Flower really ate it up," the aide recalls. And Moses soon found that he needed every tie on the Mayor that he could get. For the Brooklyn-Battery project aroused more opposition than any previous Moses proposal.

The opposition came first from Joseph D. McGoldrick, the reformer-professor whom La Guardia had drafted out of his Columbia classroom to become City Comptroller, and who had previously been the unquestioning ally of the Mayor he idolized.

"If you don't watch [Moses] he's going to bankrupt the city," McGoldrick's predecessor had warned him. By 1938 the Comptroller felt that that prophecy had been just about fulfilled, at least in terms of the city's ability to finance new large-scale public works or maintain old ones. Increases in the city's obligations for debt service to pay for such construction and maintenance—obligations made necessary to a large extent by Moses—had boosted the city's annual expenses to a level at which its annual revenues barely covered them. The capital budget situation was even more ominous.

Not only was there little margin left under the constitutional debt limit, but commitments made for future public works projects—mostly Moses' projects—had insured that there would be hardly any money available in 1939 or 1940 either. The city would be able to pay its $16,000,000 share of Moses' tunnel-highway-parkway proposal only by eliminating most non-Moses public works and all large-scale maintenance jobs for both years; the canceling of the public works would be bad enough; the cancellation of the maintenance would inevitably saddle the city in later years with even larger bills for major repair work that preventive maintenance would have made unnecessary. McGoldrick felt that such a course did not make sense.

During his interim appointment, in 1934, the Comptroller had listened to local delegations pleading for better hospitals, better schools, better libraries, and for the creation of desperately needed child health care centers in the slums. Now, back on the Board of Estimate after three years, he was listening to the same groups plead for the same things—and it was glaringly apparent to him that the city's progress in building roads and parks had not been matched in other areas in which physical construction was needed. Hospitals, he felt, were "a disgrace." "Many schools were fairly ancient; we had some that had been built right after the Civil War and were still in use. We had schools ninety years old. We had one school—PS 35—that was a hundred years old." In the wealthiest city of the wealthiest nation in the world, 290 schools were not even fireproof. Despite his admiration for La Guardia, he could not help noticing that, despite the Mayor's annual promises, in four years not a single child care center had been built. As for mass transportation facilities, the city's failure to build new subways to service rapidly developing outlying areas was only part of the problem. The subways already in existence were beginning to require extensive preventive maintenance. Without it, their deterioration would accelerate. The imbalance in the spending of city funds must be corrected, he felt, to meet other needs besides roads and parks. Taking $7,000,000 allocated for schools and hospitals and allocating it to a highway was not the way to do it.

La Guardia had told McGoldrick that he agreed with the need for more balance, and that he was planning to act on it. Now, however, when Moses suddenly requested Board of Estimate approval for the Circumferential Parkway, La Guardia supported him. And McGoldrick, who had suppressed previous doubts about Moses' proposals on "an assumption that he was almost always right," found himself, during "some long nights of soul searching," re-examining that assumption. At first he suppressed his doubts; he gave the PWA the certification required from the city's chief financial officer of the city's willingness to pay any unexpected costs on the project. But late on the evening of October 11, less than thirty-six hours before the Board vote, the pudgy, bespectacled mild-mannered little Irishman issued a public statement that was the closest thing to a *cri de conscience* uttered by a top city official since Moses had come to power within its borders:

Reluctant as I am to suggest that we consider postponement of the Circumferential Parkway . . . it is my duty to point out that [if it is built] the city will be brought to the virtual exhaustion of its debt-incurring capacity, with no margin remaining for normal capital growth of its existing facilities. . . . No one can dispute the vital need for keeping the city's plant in efficient condition. We have a stupendous investment in public buildings, bridges and equipment which must be protected. Unless this plant is properly maintained we will undergo a repetition of the era when broken-down equipment and neglected buildings cost the taxpayers many needless millions in increased costs of operation and maintenance.

As for new construction:

Not a single new school, not a single new hospital, not a new police station or firehouse, not even a baby health station, would be provided [in either 1939 or 1940]. . . . These are essentials, and in my considered judgment, we cannot embark upon new ideas until we have met these basic needs.

McGoldrick could cast only three of the sixteen votes on the Board of Estimate. The next day, however, La Guardia's two other Fusion allies on the Board, City Council President Newbold Morris and Manhattan Borough President Stanley M. Isaacs, announced they would vote with the Comptroller. Together the trio could cast eight votes—enough to keep the parkway from being approved.

Employing his usual strategy, Moses attacked not McGoldrick's arguments but McGoldrick. "What has happened since the application [certification] was signed, sealed and delivered by the Comptroller himself?" he demanded the next day. "What is behind the Comptroller's move and his swift change of front?"

It was the kind of attack that McGoldrick was later to admit "*did* intimidate people from debating with him—and intimidated me, too, quite likely." Moses knew perfectly well why he had changed his mind, the Comptroller was to tell the author. He had explained his feelings to the Park Commissioner at length. Moses knew there was no corrupt or sinister motive. But, he says, Moses certainly made it sound as if there was.

Nevertheless, McGoldrick refused to back down. So the next morning, as City Hall bustled with preparations for the crucial Board of Estimate session, cars crammed with Park Department and Triborough Authority employees began pulling up outside. A rumor suddenly swept the Hall: Moses himself was in the building—closeted with the Mayor in secret conference. The Mayor had not attended a Board session in months, always sending a deputy in his place, but now, as McGoldrick, waiting nervously for the meeting to begin, sat in his high-backed, burgundy leather chair near the center of the Board's raised horseshoe, watching Moses' claque pack onto the benches below him, the figure that dropped into the empty chair right beside him at precisely 10:30 A.M., with a fierce sideways glower, and opened the meeting with a pound of the gavel that to McGoldrick's ears sounded like the crash of fate, was that of the Little Flower himself.

Moses had not overestimated the need for the Mayor's presence. With his supporters—overflowing the Board chamber and jamming the corridors outside all the way back to the "hanging staircase"—cheering his every point, he pulled out all the old arguments, telling the Board—falsely—that the $12,000,000 would not be made available by the PWA for any other purpose and that therefore the "real issue" was whether or not the city was going to lose $12,000,000 in federal money. When McGoldrick, his voice almost lost in vicious booing, tried to explain that he was suggesting postponing the project, not killing it, the Park Commissioner, pounding his fist down on the lectern, shot back:

If this thing goes down now, it is dead, and it is dead for a long, long time. I don't know who will revive it. Don't kid yourself about this. You are not putting this off. You are settling it one way or another. No member of this board will see this project started if it is not done now. That is because the federal government has given its promise for a $12,000,000 grant, because the engineering staffs of the city, state and federal government have been sitting up day and night working on the plans and because those plans, approved and in official form, are lying on the Mayor's desk right now.

But McGoldrick refused to yield—and neither would Morris or Isaacs. La Guardia had to call the Board into executive session behind closed doors.

The doors remained closed for more than four hours. When they opened, and the Board filed back onto the horseshoe dais, it approved unanimously the expenditure of $16,000,000 for the Circumferential Parkway—and, to enable the city to spend the money, eliminated from the list of previously approved projects $8,000,000 worth of schools and hospital improvements, $5,000,000 in subway extensions and $3,000,000 in other projects.

What had happened behind the closed doors? Asked years later, McGoldrick said that La Guardia had placed the issue on a personal basis, telling the three Fusion officials flatly: "You've got to go along with me on this." Refusing such an appeal would, McGoldrick said, have meant a complete split with the Mayor, after the new Fusion administration had been in office only ten months. And that, McGoldrick felt, was something New York could afford even less than a Belt Parkway, for such a split would make impossible the truly sweeping reforms which a united Fusion administration might accomplish.

"We changed because—you know, La Guardia was very intolerant of differences. We knew him well enough to know this would blow things right up. [We] knew that we couldn't at that early stage have a break with the Mayor—it would have thrown the whole administration into chaos."

And, McGoldrick admitted, with a quiet candor, there was also "the personal factor." "Both the Mayor and Moses were really angry that day," he recalled. Standing up to Moses in a rage was intimidating enough. Standing up to Moses and La Guardia simultaneously—in a room outside whose doors hundreds of their cheering supporters were waiting—was, when coupled with the other considerations involved, a lot to ask of any man.

Moses' disclosure that the Brooklyn-Battery Crossing was going to be not a tunnel but a bridge came on January 22, 1939, three months after the Board of Estimate's approval of the parkway. (More precisely, according to the announcement, there were to be two bridges, a pair of giant suspension spans in tandem, linked in the middle of mile-wide Upper New York Bay by a joint anchorage pier near Governor's Island, descending to street level in Brooklyn on Hamilton Avenue, near the terminus of the planned Elevated Highway, sloping down in Manhattan into Battery Park, where a series of giant piers planted in the park would carry a low-level causeway above the park to meet a planned southward extension of the West Side Highway.) For three days after the disclosure there was silence; not a word of comment was uttered for publication by any citizen or public official.

And then, on January 25, the storm broke.

This was no protest that was going to go unheard. This was no circulating of petitions by a group of housewives out in Flushing, no attempt by some neighborhood chamber of commerce in the Rockaways to persuade their local assemblyman to use all his influence to induce one of Moses' lower-ranking aides to grant them the boon of a ten-minute hearing. This was a cry, first of disbelief and then of sheer outrage, from New York's most prestigious and influential private citizens, from "Gotham's gentry," the aristocracy—of wealth and talent both—of the greatest city in the New World. This was a cry of outrage, moreover, from that segment of the city's aristocracy which held the city in deepest affection, from those individuals who formed the backbone of New York's legendary Good Government movement, who had proven in long days attending Board of Estimate sessions and long evenings studying statistics or writing reports for the Citizens Union or the City Club that "men are moved by things other than just narrow self-interest," whose influence in city affairs was therefore not only practical but moral—and political, too, since their very names symbolized reform and were, therefore, valuable not only on checks for campaign contributions but in headlines. This was a cry of outrage from men whose influence on New York's affairs could be measured by the fact that, four times since the turn of the century alone, they had, through the "fusion" movements that were the political embodiment of the reforming ethos, defeated an awesomely powerful political machine and had seated a candidate of their own choosing (most relevantly, in the present context, Fiorello Henry La Guardia) in the Mayor's chair; these were men who, in the affairs of the great city, had for decades held power such that they could regard it as no more than a footnote in their story that they had played a vital role, perhaps the decisive role, in making one Robert Moses Park Commissioner.

Exton and Weinberg and other young reformers had attempted to explain to these men that Moses' projects were destroying many of the values that made life in the city livable, but these old generals of reform had, as a rule, not been familiar with many of the locales in question and therefore had not been able to appreciate the objections to projects that were certainly worthwhile according to the theories in which they had been schooled. But many of these leaders—most of them, in fact—worked near the Battery. Many of them had real estate interests in the area. Some lived across the bay in Brooklyn Heights. They were very familiar indeed with the locale of the Battery Crossing—with Battery Park, the Wall Street and Lower Manhattan office-skyscraper complex and the bay—and they were therefore able to see what this Moses project would destroy.

Some of the reasons behind their protest were selfish.

Moses' announcement had been accompanied by an "artist's rendering" of the bridge that created the impression that the mammoth suspension span would have about as much impact on the Lower Manhattan landscape as an extra lamppost. This impression had been created by "rendering" the bridge from directly overhead—way overhead—as it might be seen by a high-flying and myopic pigeon. From this bird's-eye view, the bridge and its approaches, their height minimized and only their flat roadways really visible, blended inconspicuously into the landscape. But in asking for Board of Estimate approval, Moses had to submit to the Board the actual plans for the bridge. Isaacs gave copies to Ole Singstad and to Walter D. Binger, an engineer and reformer whom Isaacs had brought into city government as Manhattan Commissioner of Borough Works. And after they had analyzed the plans, Isaacs called in reporters and told them what the bridge would look like not to a bird but to a human being.

The public might be interested to know, Isaacs said, that the proposed bridge anchorage in Battery Park, barely visible on Moses' rendering, would be a solid mass of stone and concrete equal in size to a ten-story office building. The approach ramp linking the bridge to the West Side Highway, a ramp depicted on the rendering as a narrow path through Battery Park, would actually be a road wider than Fifth Avenue, a road supported on immense concrete piers, and it would cross the entire park—the entire lower tip of Manhattan Island—and curve around the west side of the island almost to Rector Street at heights ranging up to a hundred feet in the air. Not only would anchorage and piers obliterate a considerable portion of Battery Park, they—and the approach road—would block off much of the light not only from what was left of the park but also from the lower floors of every large office building they passed; because the approach ramp was really an elevated highway that would dominate the entire tip of Manhattan, it would depress real estate values throughout the entire area. Many Good Government leaders owned some of that real estate, and they saw Isaacs' prophecy confirmed almost immediately when a corporation broke off negotiations for leasing an entire floor at 21 West Street when it suddenly realized that the view from the windows would no longer be of the harbor but of the underside of a highway.

But even private considerations had public implications. Lower Manhattan real estate, quite possibly the most valuable in the world, was valuable not only to its owners, but to the city. According to some estimates, the portion of the city's total real estate tax paid by Lower Manhattan was as high as 10 percent; large office buildings contributed hundreds of thousands of dollars annually to the city in real estate taxes. Reduce their light and air and they would be entitled to a substantial reduction in taxes. And Moses' bridge would reduce the taxes for dozens of such buildings. Computing the depreciation in real estate values conservatively, Singstad found that, during the next twenty years alone, building the Battery Crossing as a bridge instead of as a tunnel would cost the city more than $29,000,000 in real estate taxes.

And many of the reasons behind the objections were not selfish at all. To these men who loved New York, the locale in which Robert Moses was planning to build his bridge—New York Harbor and Battery Park—contained many of the reasons they loved it.

From the sea New York Harbor was a sight to make authors strain for adjectives. Writers had described the colossal staired and serried mass of towering skyscrapers, which seemed to be rising out of the water, as a giant ship (Melville had been reminded that the very name "skyscraper" had once been used by sailors to describe a sailing ship's topmost canvas); as a "structure of tiered decks," pointing at the watcher and "growing taller and taller" like the prow of a furiously onrushing vessel; as a medieval fortress, whose towers, rising out of swirling tides, at night were "blocked by darkness into a sentinelled medieval keep of enormous height and unscalable defense" that might have been inhabited more fittingly by dead kings than recent bankers; as a mesa, a petrified forest, a "giant's cromlech." And the very number of the metaphors proved the power of the scene to excite the imagination, proved, in fact, the truth of the one image used most frequently to describe it: that the view of New York from its harbor was one of the wonders of the world.

The unique importance of Battery Park to New York City was obvious not from the sea but from the air—from a plane or from the observation platform of the Empire State Building a thousand feet in the sky over Manhattan Island. To the observer looking out over what has been called "the most significant panorama that modern civilization offers," the buildings in which 12,000,000 persons lived and worked in 1939 seemed to stretch out endlessly to the horizon. But from such vantage points it could be seen that they were not only stretching out but closing in, building up, pressing inward, crowding closer and closer together, until, as if the concentrating inward surge of humanity constituted a geologic force, in the epicenter of that surge the buildings of Manhattan were thrust upward and toward the sky. And it was near the island's southern tip, the tip jutting into the harbor, that the colossal upthrust had been greatest. In the upper part of Manhattan the masses of concrete were mostly sixty feet high, or seventy; in the center of the island, they were a hundred and fifty or two hundred. But as the island narrowed toward its southern tip, they were four hundred feet high, five hundred, cramming closer and closer together, bulking up higher and higher as they loomed southward pressing inexorably toward the island's tip—until at the very tip, at the very end of the most crowded island in the world, at the very spot in the entire world in which buildings should have been crowded most closely together, there were suddenly, with the exception of a tiny old fort converted into an aquarium, no buildings at all. At a point at which a single square foot of land was worth thousands of dollars, at which the value of an acre was computed not in the millions of dollars but in the tens of millions, there sat 967,032 square feet of land—22.2 acres—vacant except for grass and trees, pathways between them, benches, and a broad, breezy waterfront promenade.

And it wasn't from either sea or air that the value of park and harbor was most apparent. It was from the ground, from the nearby streets of the city, from the bleak narrow concrete canyons of Lower Manhattan from which towering masses of concrete and steel had crushed sunlight and sky and green grass and trees and, by hemming between them the swirling concentration of humanity (half a million human beings worked in Manhattan's single southernmost mile), peace. If there was ever a place in which a man occasionally needed to be alone for a while, to sit in the open, in the sun, among grass and trees, for a minute or two, to escape from crowds and noise, that place was Lower Manhattan. And in all the streets of Lower Manhattan, there was no place to do so.

There should, moreover, have been a sense of the sea in Lower Manhattan, which was, after all, the tip, the seamost tip, of the island that was the world's largest seaport. But there was no sense of the sea in Lower Manhattan; skyscraper walls blocked that out, too.

There was no sense of history, either.

Of all the qualities that the skyscrapers had crushed out of Lower Manhattan's streets, it was perhaps history whose disappearance was most poignant to New York's reformer-aristocrats. For, familiar as they were with the city's early history, and with the early history of the fledgling nation of which the city had been a part—especially familiar because many of them were direct descendants of the men who had made it—they were well aware how much of it had been made in those streets when those streets *were* the city. It was, for example, in Fort James at the foot of the island that Jacob Leisler in 1689 persuaded his fellow militia captains to sign, on the head of a drum, a document ousting the latest Royal Governor, thereby giving New York two years of self-government, and it was in that fort, with drums rattling, that, two years later, a new Governor hanged Leisler from a gallows. It was in a courthouse in Lower Manhattan that, in 1735, in a case from which the best New York defense attorneys had been barred, the famous lawyer Andrew Hamilton, smuggled in from Philadelphia, rose to startle the court by announcing that he would represent a printer charged with libel, told the jury that their verdict would determine whether men had the right to oppose tyrants by writing the truth, and persuaded them to acquit John Peter Zenger. Those streets echoed to the shouts of throngs led by the Sons of Liberty carrying the "liberty poles" that were erected on the Commons (later City Hall Park) as fast as British soldiers could cut them down; to the tramp of marching men—five dust-stained regiments George Washington had led south from Boston; and to the first public reading—on the Commons, to troops formed into a great hollow square around their general—of the Declaration of Independence.

Those streets had seen despair. One morning the harbor that had been empty the night before was a forest of masts: the British fleet had arrived—130 ships bearing 31,000 redcoat and Hessian soldiers, veterans of a hundred battles; soon the hills of Staten Island were white with their tents. After the raw and ragged Continentals had been routed at the Battle of Long Island, and driven off Manhattan Island (Washington, watching from across the river, wept as the Hessians bayoneted the wounded at the last outpost at Fort Washington), the only troops that walked those streets until the end of the war seven years later were troops wearing the red coats of the oppressor. But those streets had seen triumph, too. At the end of the war, Washington returned. "The troops just leaving us were equipped as if for show, and with their scarlet uniforms and burnished arms, made a brilliant display," wrote one woman. "The troops that marched in, on the contrary, were ill-clad and weather-beaten, and made a forlorn appearance. But then they were *our* troops." It was in those streets—at Fraunces Tavern at Pearl and Broad—that their leader, having just refused a crown, took farewell of his weeping officers, weeping himself as he did so and then walking silently to the barge waiting at Whitehall Ferry. And it was to those streets that George Washington returned six years later—in a barge rowed by thirteen ships' captains clad in white uniforms—to step ashore at Murray's Wharf at the foot of Wall Street as women threw flowers at him (he "read his history in a nation's eyes," wrote one) and be sworn in on the balcony of Federal Hall at the corner of Wall and Broad. And it was through those streets—the streets of the first capital of the new Republic—that there walked the three men—Hamilton, Jay and Madison—who together were "Publius," author of the eighty-five great essays urging ratification of the controversial new Constitution.

To many of the reformer-aristocrats, the history of those streets was family history. The rolls of Citizens Union and City Club—and of groups such as the American Scenic and Historic Preservation Society—were filled with names like Morris and Bayard and de Peyster and Van Rensselaer and Gerry and Hamilton. But as the Age of Skyscrapers had made land so valuable that history could no longer find a place on it, they had had to watch as cobbled slips and lanes had been paved over with asphalt, and as row after row of beautiful, sober, red-faced Federal residences, of buildings that housed sailmakers' shops and ship's chandleries behind Greek lintels and steeply pitched dormers redolent of the harbor's historic sailing age, had crumbled beneath the wreckers' iron balls. Before their eyes, the elegant townhouses that had stood on State Street in a neat, graceful row had been torn down one by one—even No. 9, where Lafayette had lived—until only one remained, the delicate ironwork of its balconies and the slimness of its tall white columns an ironic grace note in a cityscape without grace. By 1939 Fraunces Tavern was the only structure left associated with the hundred moments of triumphs and glory Washington had played out in those streets. In an area dedicated to commerce, in which men spoke in what Henry James called "the vocabulary of thrift," there was no interest in a more epic vocabulary. Once Lower Manhattan had been steeped in history. Now that sense of history was gone, vanished, crushed out of those streets as completely as the sense of the sea.

But turn a corner and there was history and sunlight and sky and, stretching before you, the sea. For turn a corner—the corner at the bottom of Pearl or Front Street, for example, or the bend at the foot of Broadway—and there was Battery Park.

Step into Battery Park and suddenly—remarkably suddenly—the city was all behind you. Walk down one of its winding paths (for its paths *were* winding then) under the leaves of the big old trees that lined them (for they *were* lined with big old trees then) and the clamor of the traffic-jammed streets of Lower Manhattan faded away so quickly that within a hundred paces only an occasional particularly strident car horn remained as a reminder of what you had just escaped.

Sit down on one of the benches under the trees and what you heard first was mostly quiet, as if your ears had become so attuned to the din you had left that for a minute or two they couldn't register more subtle sounds. But then you began to hear the sparrows and the orioles, and the harsh faraway scream of some sea bird. You began to notice the flutter of a waxwing from tree to tree, the soft swoop of gulls across the high sky.

If, sitting there, you looked back at the tall buildings behind you, you saw them through leaves, and they didn't look so tall. They seemed, in fact, rather far away. Only a few steps out of the sunless streets, you had found sunlight. Only a few steps out of their colorless walls, you had found green lawns. Only a few steps out of their tumult, you had found peace.

And if you got up and walked a little deeper into the park, suddenly, before you, there through the trees was the heavy blue-green swell of the sea, and that rhythmic, restless sound, at once peaceful and intense, was the lapping of waves against the shore, and all at once, only steps from the dead gray walls of Lower Manhattan, you were standing at the edge of a broad and busy harbor: crisscrossing the waves were stubby tugboats, freighters with derricks and masts a tall forest on their decks, speedy motorboats skimming from crest to crest, gaily painted ferries, private steam yachts, white-painted and glistening, giant gleaming ocean liners, so big that their sides were moving cliffs. Everywhere there were bright flags—the pennons and burgees of the yachts, the tricolor of the *Normandie* and the Union Jack of the *Queens,* the colors of a dozen other foreign nations—and all fluttering against the blue of the sky. It was a panorama of vastness and beauty in the sun, of drama in storms, when the tossing whitecaps that stretched to the horizon, the howling of the wind that filled your ears and the smash of the waves against the piers at your feet made you remember with a start that Manhattan was only an island and that you were standing at its very tip. And at night, with the towering statue of Liberty Enlightening the World floodlit from pedestal to torch, and the rows of lamps on the ferryboats gliding across the dark waters, the view from the Battery was, as one of the reformers put it, "a thing of beauty never to be forgotten."

Sunlight, serenity, a sense of the sea—and something more. For walk into Battery Park at its Broadway entrance and staring at you, at the end of a long, broad *grande allée*, was an odd-looking building.

If you knew the history of New York City, you could read it in layers on that building. Architects remodeling it to make its appearance harmonize with its present purpose—for the last half century it had been the city Aquarium—had given it a three-story-high façade that made it look like a toy fort, with rounded turrets at each end, a cornice crenelated to resemble battlements and flags along the top, and a white stucco finish that, shining in the sun, would have made it a perfect target. In that gay façade, the massive bolt-studded and iron-reinforced doors, set in an immense stone portal twenty feet high, loomed with an inappropriate grimness. But if you knew the history of New York, you knew why those doors were there—and you knew that if you stripped that layer of stucco away from the lower story, you would find behind it huge, rugged walls of weather-beaten sandstone, walls twenty feet high and eight feet thick, walls thick enough to withstand the bombardment of a fleet, walls through whose barred embrasures had glinted black thirty-two-pounders capable of sweeping the harbor from shore to shore. You knew that if the top two stories of that odd building were a fake fort, the bottom story, behind the façade, was a real fort—Fort Clinton, constructed during the War of 1812 to repel an expected British invasion.

Fort Clinton, named after Erie Canal builder De Witt—the fort that in 1939 stood in Battery Park under a coat of white stucco and two stories of fish tanks—had never fired a shot in anger. The expected British invasion never came (probably, historians believed, because the British were deterred by the presence of Fort Clinton and its sister fort on Governor's Island, Castle William), and no enemy fleet was ever again to threaten New York. The only ships ever sunk by its twenty-eight thirty-two-pounders were hulks sunk for target practice. But the broad circle—a full two hundred feet in diameter—of its massive walls was an evocation in weathered red sandstone of the nearly two centuries when men ran for forts at the news of Indians or the French. Walk down beside it, stand beside one of its embrasures and see where its cannon bore, then look out across the harbor and see, across a mile of water, the massive hulk—unstuccoed, grim, cannon still mounted, so that through its embrasures the sun still glinted off black metal—of its sister fort, and you were back in another, more heroic age. Walk down beside it, and that city behind you, that city without history, had a history again.

And in that building there was the history of still another era to read. For behind that stucco façade was also a domed roof that, built in 1824, transformed Fort Clinton, its guns still in place, into "Castle Clinton," or "Castle Garden," circular auditorium and theater.

If Fort Clinton was heroism, Castle Garden was the glory heroism earned.

It was at Castle Garden on August 16, 1824, that, in the words of one historian, "it was proved that republics are not always ungrateful," for it was at Castle Garden on that date that Gilbert du Motier, Marquis de Lafayette, who as a rich young nobleman had defied his King and fought for America, returned to it, sixty-seven years old and penniless.

"Many of the spectators doubtless had in mind a gallant, boyish figure in the buff and blue of the American Revolution, with powdered hair tied in a queue," the historian wrote. "What they saw was an old civilian, in a short-haired brown wig." But when the old civilian stepped onto the Castle Garden landing stage—after a trip up the harbor on which his ship was escorted by a huge flotilla—to begin a visit on which he was to receive from the government and citizens of the United States gifts of bonds and land worth almost half a million dollars, the Castle's cannon roared out a hundred times. When the old man walked slowly into Battery Park, "to the incessant huzzas of the multitude that packed the waterfront," he walked between the weeping ranks of the Lafayette Guards. When he rode up Broadway, men and women on rooftops threw flowers in his path. A month later, a tall spar was raised in the center of the fort, a vast awning of sailcloth was spread across its entire ceiling, "the white banner of France was entwined with the Stars and Stripes, trophies of arms glittered from the walls"—and when Lafayette appeared at the ball, "the gay sets dissolved" and the dancers formed a long lane, and as the old man walked along it, he saw that each man and woman was wearing a medallion bearing his likeness, the women's entwined with roses.

And it was at Castle Clinton that, ten years later, the handful of Lafayette Guards still alive drew up in a hollow square, in the center of which was a riderless black horse—spurred boots, reversed, slung across its empty saddle—to hear the funeral oration for their dead hero.

Lafayette was only one of a hundred heroes for whom the old fort and Battery Park were the setting for the spectacles honoring them in triumph or in death. Troops were drawn up in the park by the thousands to greet Dewey after he defeated the Spaniards at Manila (the astrakhan busbies of cavalry hussars shook in the sea breeze), Pershing after he defeated the Germans in France, and TR after he returned from safari (conspicuous among the regiments out in full dress to greet the ex-President were a handful of men in khaki and campaign hats: the Rough Riders). Most of New York's great triumphal processions began there; it was at the Battery that Wiley Post came ashore, and Admiral Byrd, and Gertrude Ederle, and Amelia Earhart, and Coste and Bellonte—and, of course, Lindbergh, slim, bareheaded Lindbergh—to be greeted by Grover Whalen and to ride in an open car between mounted policemen "the short, glorious mile" up a Broadway whose canyons were swirling with confetti. The fort's cannon boomed at solemn one-minute intervals as the body of young Captain James Lawrence, who had earned immortality by crying "Don't give up the ship!" as he lay dying on the deck of the *Chesapeake,* was carried ashore and as Washington's riderless horse—and Hamilton's and those of a score of other heroes of the Revolution—were led out from it up Broadway. In New York in which the old was ruthlessly demolished to make way for the new, the fort was pricelessly rich in ghosts of the city's great past.

In 1855, Castle Clinton was transformed into the landing station for the flood tide of immigrants from Europe; for thirty-five years, it would be "the Nation's Gateway," the place at which almost eight million human beings, in flight from persecution or poverty or famine in the Old Country, came ashore in the Land of Opportunity.

Most important, though the old fort was, in 1939, well into the second century of its existence, part of the city's past, it was also, as the Aquarium, part of the city's present, very much part. Its walls were filled with history, but they were also filled with life.

Some idea of the popularity of the Aquarium may be gleaned from its average annual attendance: 2,500,000. It was by far the most heavily attended public institution in New York. It was free, easily accessible to all the city, and with its giant turtles, spear-shaped, hideously spotted morays, grotesque toadfish, mammoth groupers, rainbow-hued tropical fish and sleek, barking seals swimming in its gloomy depths, it had delighted generations of New York children.

Sunshine, serenity, a sense of sea, a sense of history—build the bridge that Robert Moses wanted to build and they would be accessible to the streets of Lower Manhattan no longer. Build that bridge and the vista of New York Harbor would be destroyed, the majestic harbor sweep thrown into shadow, the sheer-rising skyscraper mass slashed in half and blocked, one of the wonders of the world turned into mere, rather unimportant backdrop for just another East River bridge not very different from the three others just behind it. And plunk down in Battery Park a half dozen or more solid masses of concrete each as big as an office building, and set on top of them, on top of the park, a roadbed eight lanes wide (two lanes wider than the bridge), and there wouldn't really *be* a park any more. What had been a place of sunlight and grass would become a place of concrete and steel and shadows. Instead of quiet there would be, directly overhead, the roar of traffic. Instead of vistas of water there would be only glimpses snatched between pillars. There wouldn't even be a sense of history. The old fort would be partially hidden by giant road piers—one would, under Moses' plan, be placed smack in front of it—and thoroughly dwarfed, no longer a monument bulking impressively at the end of a broad mall, filling the park with its presence, but a tiny ornament, cute but unimportant, cowering beside the immense pillar, lost in the shadow of the giant roadway above, its silence not majestic but meaningless among the noises of a new age thundering down from the big highway above.

Build the bridge that Robert Moses wanted to build and "a prospect unexcelled by any city view in the world," would become little more than an extension of the mean streets of Lower Manhattan. The park had once been an escape from those streets—the only escape; now there would be no escape from them at all. Only someone thoroughly familiar with Lower Manhattan could appreciate fully what would be done to the area—and to the half million people who spent their days in it—by the bridge that Robert Moses wanted to build. But New York's reformer-aristocrats possessed that familiarity, and they determined to stop him from building it.

Because they did, the fight over the Brooklyn-Battery Crossing marked the end of Moses' long alliance with New York's Good Government movement, with the reformers in whose ranks he had, as a young man, once marched himself.

The identity of the two men who led the opposition to the bridge spotlighted this aspect of the confrontation.

George McAneny was one of the heroes of Moses' young manhood, the early crusader for civil service reform who in 1909 had risked his hard-won business success (not one of the wealthy reformers, he was a poor boy from Jersey City who had left school at the age of fifteen to become a reporter on the old *World*) to lend the weight of his reputation and that of the City Club of which he was president to a Bureau of Municipal Research exposé, and thus persuaded Governor Charles Evans Hughes to oust corrupt Tammany officials. Borough president himself thereafter, a peppery, tart public official, he, rather than John Purroy Mitchel, could have had the Fusion mayoral nomination in 1917, but declined it because he felt Mitchel, as an incumbent, had a better chance of defeating Tammany. Lack of funds later forced him to retire from public office, but he never retired from public service: an early believer in city planning, he was the moving force behind the city's adoption of the first comprehensive zoning plan in the United States. Some indication of the respect in which he was held was his appointment in 1916 as "executive manager" of *The New York Times*: the title was meaningless, and during the five years he held the job he never had a specific function; *Times* patriarch Adolph S. Ochs hired him, Ochs told friends, to act as "a sort of moral background" for the paper. He aged fast physically—in his sixties, he was strikingly wrinkled and shrunken; he had to hobble on a cane when he came to meetings. But he came. It was he who, in 1935, decided the city should have a World's Fair, and it was he who told Moses the location should be Flushing Meadows Park. ("Bob Moses was very amicable in those days. . . . I said to him, 'We have a great idea and we want your help.' Then I told him what it was, and he thumped the desk, and said, 'By God, that *is* a great idea!' ") And in 1939, at the age of seventy, McAneny was president of the Regional Plan Association and a key member of a dozen other organizations.

Stanley Myer Isaacs, a contemporary of Robert Moses, was born of the same stock: wealthy, Jewish, and dedicated to public service—what Moses' parents were to Madison House, Isaacs' father, a pious Orthodox Jew, was to the Educational Alliance and the Citizens Union. Like Robert Moses, Stanley Isaacs was a hiker, a mountain climber and a brilliant student (top man in his class at Columbia). And, like Moses, he was a leader of men. "I can talk my head off to a roomful of people, and when Stanley walks in, they melt away from me and surround him," a cousin said.

In his youth, moreover, Isaacs apprenticed himself to the same principles to which Moses had apprenticed himself in *his* youth. As a young real estate lawyer, he spent evenings and weekends working for reform, doing legwork not only for his local Republican organization—he was elected district leader at twenty-two—but for a succession of Fusion tickets, as Moses had, in 1921, served as secretary of a Fusion campaign committee. As Moses concentrated on a particular field—civil service—and made himself an expert in it, Isaacs concentrated in his youth on public housing, and made himself an expert in it. And as Moses spent four years of his youth trying to accomplish something significant in his field, only to suffer bitter disappointment, Isaacs spent four years of his youth trying to accomplish something significant in his field—with the same results. From 1925 to 1929, as chairman of the Housing Committee of the United Neighborhood Houses, he led the campaign for a law that would require slum landlords to provide their tenants with such amenities as windows and toilets. When, in 1929, his pleading finally embarrassed the Legislature into passing a new Multiple Dwelling Law, the statute was so watered down that it was virtually meaningless.

But Stanley Isaacs remained true to his stock and his principles. His loyalty to friends and family was legendary; when his brother Julian was desperately ill with tuberculosis, Isaacs spent months in Saranac, cooking his meals and nursing him. Proud of being Jewish, he was active in Jewish philanthropies for forty years. What social worker Helen M. Harris called "his passion for social justice" never burned low; neither private nor political career ever prevented him from working for the causes of his youth; he served as president of United Neighborhood Houses for twenty-five years. By carrying a workload of Mosaic proportions ("He has daily habits that would assassinate another man," a profiler wrote), he was active most of his life in twenty-three separate Good Government or charitable organizations. And he didn't abandon his fight for his first cause as Moses had abandoned the fight for *his;* Stanley Isaacs would be a leader in the fight for better housing for more than thirty years after his 1929 defeat. And although the techniques of the reformer—free and open discussion, persuasion, education—had caused him only disappointment (and were, over and over, to cause him disappointment again), he never abandoned them for the techniques of the politician. Robert Moses may no longer have believed that "the principle is the important thing," but Stanley Isaacs did.

In 1937, after Isaacs had been working for the public for thirty years without ever holding public office, he was nominated—against his wishes—on the La Guardia ticket for Manhattan borough president, McAneny's old post. And when Isaacs was elected, by more than 40,000 votes (after one quietly spellbinding campaign speech, La Guardia, hugging him, exclaimed, "I don't know where you've been so long, Stanley!"), he demonstrated that neither position nor power would change his belief in what was important. He refused—to the point where his feelings became a family joke—to use his official limousine except on official business. He fired scores of political hacks and replaced them with a team of crack engineers. And he proved that there might occasionally be other ways of Getting Things Done than Moses': it was Borough President Isaacs who built—without antagonizing the neighborhood—the East River Drive. Refusing to use his office for patronage himself, he refused to let anyone else use it for patronage, either. He faithfully cleared his appointments with La Guardia—

but rejected the Mayor's suggestions if they were based on political considerations. Declining to fill positions he did not consider necessary, he reduced the borough president's staff by ninety positions, and his budget by more than 25 percent. (To avoid embarrassing the other borough presidents, the Board of Estimate each year gave him more money than he asked for; at the end of each year, he returned the surplus.) George McAneny was a man whom Robert Moses had once admired; Stanley Isaacs was the man whom Robert Moses had once been.

Throughout Moses' career, McAneny and Isaacs had supported him, as had most of the other leaders of New York's Good Government movement—in 1919, when he had needed their money and the prestige of their great names to accomplish his reorganization of the state government; in 1924, when they gave him statewide power by electing him chairman of the State Council of Parks; in 1933, when, after their attempt to make him mayor had failed, they had helped persuade the man who did become mayor to bring him to power in the city; in 1935, when they had supported him against the President. In every great crisis of Robert Moses' twenty-year-long public career, in the face of every threat to his plans or to his power, the reformers had given him their support. They had done so because they had believed that Moses, who had been one of them once, was one of them still, because they believed that his aims were still their aims, that the Things he wanted to Get Done were still the Things *they* wanted to Get Done. They thought of him, in fact, as their champion, as the young recruit who had risen from their ranks to become the one among them capable of leading to victory the causes for which they all marched. They had refused to listen to the handful among them who had tried to tell them what Moses was doing to the city. The American Scenic and Historic Preservation Society had, in fact, just awarded Moses its highest honor, the Society Gold Medal. But the Battle of the Battery Crossing, staged on terrain familiar—and dear—to them, was to give them a close look at Moses' values and thus to show them that those values were no longer their values, that they were, in fact, utterly incompatible with the values they knew must be preserved in the city they loved.

The Battle of the Battery Crossing was, moreover, to show them that the means Robert Moses employed were as incompatible with their principles as his ends.

New York's reformers had never gotten a firsthand look at his methods. Before 1934, he had operated only outside the city; in the five years he had been operating inside, his projects had never directly affected more than a few of them at a time. When those few had tried to tell the others about their experiences, they had not generally been believed. "Maybe," one of the reform leaders was to say, "idolizing him like we did, we didn't *want* to believe."

But they were going to have to believe now. For now Moses' methods were going to be used against them.

Throughout his career, Moses had charmed people he needed—and then, as soon as he didn't need them any longer, had turned on them.

He had always needed the reformers because he had always relied on public support, and they were in many ways the key to that support. But now, thanks to his discovery of the possibilities of the public authority, he didn't need public support any longer, and therefore he didn't need them.

And now, when they decided to fight his bridge proposal, he turned on them.

At first, not yet realizing with what they were dealing, believing that Moses had made an incorrect decision but that he could be made to see that the decision was wrong and would therefore correct it—feeling, in other words, that he would be amenable to reason—they tried to reason with him, requesting meetings at which they could explain their objections.

He did not even reply.

The reformers were disturbed, but not yet worried. The government of their city was, after all, a government of laws, not of men, and there were ample laws to insure against the construction of a public work on the whim of any one man, even if that man was supported by the Mayor. There were laws—procedures and public bodies—established to insure that the will of the public would determine whether a public work was to be built and, if it was, what its design would be. The will of the public might not be heard if the public most directly concerned was some local housewives' group or chamber of commerce, they admitted, but, they believed, *their* will would always receive the fullest of hearings. They had at their command the technical expertise to examine Moses' proposal in detail and determine the facts for themselves, and they had influence enough to insure that these facts would be published.

The facts certainly deserved publication. According to Moses' attractively printed brochure, the Brooklyn-Battery Crossing should be a bridge primarily because a bridge, "with all necessary approaches," would cost less than half as much as a tunnel—$41,200,000 compared to $84,000,000. Thus, the brochure stated, "the bridge with necessary approaches can be financed by the sale of bonds to the public without the contribution of a nickel of City or Federal money." And, according to the brochure, these figures were indisputable because the estimate for the bridge had been prepared by its designer, Othmar Ammann, the estimate for the tunnel by its designer, Ole Singstad.

Singstad had found that last statement interesting. No estimate he had ever prepared showed the cost of the tunnel to be $84,000,000. His estimate—an estimate he had given to Moses when Moses asked for it—showed the cost to be $65,000,000.

The reformers had found Moses' statement incredible. He said the bridge—including "all necessary approaches"—would cost $41,200,000. One approach alone, the Elevated Highway in Brooklyn, was, they knew, going to cost $12,000,000. Even without figuring in the cost of the Manhattan approaches, that left only $29,000,000 for construction of the bridge proper. That figure was ridiculous on its face: the Bronx-Whitestone Bridge, half as long, and four lanes instead of six, had cost $39,000,000. Moses stated he had gotten the bridge estimates from Ammann, designer of the Bronx-

Whitestone. Knowing the famed Swiss engineer's reputation for integrity, the Citizens Union decided to find out if Moses' statement was accurate. Two representatives called on Ammann in his office. The engineer, normally so terse and positive, met their questions with finger-twisting silence. Finally, he told them that while, as one of them put it, "he didn't want to be involved," he would "give us some guidance"—"guidance" which enabled them to report to the Citizens Union's board of directors that the $41,-200,000 figure was not accurate at all. (The board asked Paul Windels, a personal friend of Ammann's, to ask him if he would confirm the report. The report was confirmed.)

Moses' brochure had stated that the bridge and "all necessary approaches" could be built without "a nickel" of city money. Stanley Isaacs had read the brochure with care, and, as a result, he was not worrying about a nickel of city money. He was worrying about 430,000,000 nickels—$21,500,000. Isaacs had noticed that while the attractively drawn map in the attractively drawn brochure showed the indispensable connections between the bridge and the West Side Highway, whose southern terminus at the time was Duane Street, more than a mile away, and with the East River Drive, the cost of these connections was not included in the estimates. Walter Binger estimated the cost of the West Side extension at $11,000,000, that of the East River Drive at $7,500,000. Moses had stated that he would rebuild Battery Park after it had been torn up for the bridge approaches, but had not included the cost of the rebuilding in his estimates, either. Binger said it would be $3,000,000.

The reformers also realized that there were other costs involved, such as the $29,000,000 loss in real estate taxes, that Moses had never mentioned. The land in Battery Park on which Moses was planning to place anchorages and pillars didn't have to be paid for, of course, because the city already owned it, but its worth—in an area in which each square foot of land was worth hundreds of dollars—ran into the millions. "On the basis of real cost," Singstad wrote, "it is obvious that the bridge would be by far the more costly of the two projects when all of the economic factors which should be included are considered." Add economic factors to the non-economic involved—the destruction of the park and the values it represented, the destruction of the once-bustling Syrian Quarter at the foot of Washington Street and the neighborhood values *it* represented, the destruction of the harbor vistas and the old fort—and there was a powerful case to be made for Singstad's tunnel, and against Moses' bridge. The reformers did not say they were unalterably opposed to the bridge. Possibly a full-scale impartial study of all the factors involved would prove that it was a better solution than the tunnel. But, they said, such a study should be made before a project of such magnitude was embarked upon—and such a study had obviously not yet been made, by Moses or anyone else.

The reformers' influence guaranteed that the city's officials—and taxpayers—would hear their side. In the crusty Singstad, they possessed an ally expert not only in engineering but in public relations, and he demonstrated that Moses had no monopoly on misleading drawings. Moses', to minimize the impact of the bridge, portrayed it from directly overhead; Singstad's, to dramatize that impact to the maximum, portrayed it from ground level—possibly, judging from some of the angles, from *below* ground—thus making the structure seem even higher than it was. (There was something funny about the perspective, too. Moses wasn't sure exactly what it was; the best he could do was to rage that the drawings were "completely phony.") By the time the controversy came before the City Planning Commission, in the first step of the process through which the reformers believed the public will was to be expressed, they had the facts and figures—and pictures—ready to go.

The day before the process began, however, the reformers' morning newspapers informed them that at Moses' request bills had been introduced in Albany that would rescind the Tunnel Authority's authorization to build the Battery Crossing and transfer that authorization to the Triborough Bridge Authority. Such bills would, of course, be necessary if the city approved Moses' plans. But by introducing them before the approval had been given, Moses was acting as if it were a mere formality, as if the city had no choice but to give it.

And, the reformers learned the next day, such was in fact the case. At the Planning Commission hearing, the reformers presented their painstakingly prepared facts and figures, maps and drawings. The Regional Plan Association said that if a tunnel proved too expensive the alternative should not be a new bridge that would destroy the harbor and park but a rebuilding of the three old East River bridges and the construction of a link between them, and between the Belt Parkway to the south and the Triborough Bridge to the north (along the lines of the future Brooklyn-Queens Expressway), a solution which the RPA pointed out would detour traffic around Manhattan instead of pouring more of it into its most congested area. The RPA had prepared preliminary plans and cost estimates for its proposal, but the commission did not make even a pretense of giving them serious study. Two weeks later, by a 4–2 vote, it approved the Brooklyn-Battery Bridge. The two dissenting commissioners said that the bridge would destroy values that the city would never be able to replace. The majority opinion did not disagree. The harbor would "undoubtedly be altered" by the bridge, it said. The park would "undoubtedly" be damaged. "There are . . . valid objections to a bridge"; in fact, they too favored a tunnel. But, the majority pointed out, "the commission is not at this time called upon to choose between a tunnel and a bridge." No one was offering to finance a tunnel. Someone *was* offering to finance a bridge. A Brooklyn-Battery Crossing was urgently—desperately—needed. If the only type of crossing available was a bridge, a bridge it would have to be. One of the commissioners who voted for the bridge, Lawrence M. Orton, a former RPA member himself, would spell it out even more plainly to the author years later: "The city didn't have the money for a crossing. Neither did the Tunnel Authority. Only one person had the money—Moses. And Moses wasn't giving us any choice. He just wouldn't build a tunnel. It was the bridge or nothing. Take it or leave it. We didn't have any choice."

* * *

In Albany, meanwhile, Moses' bills—sponsored in the Assembly by Robert J. Crews, brother of Triborough insurance co-broker John R. Crews, and backed by Assembly minority leader Irwin Steingut ("Irwin considered Moses a practical fellow") and by the Republican leadership of both houses—were eating up the legislative track, ordinarily so slow, like thoroughbreds among a pack of Percherons. Passed by the Assembly one afternoon, they were rushed that same afternoon to a Senate committee—and were released that same afternoon to the floor of the Senate for a vote. One upstate senator innocently requested time to consider the measures; he was handed a message asking him to take an urgent telephone call; when he returned to the floor, he dropped the request.

But back in New York, Stanley Isaacs, studying the bills in his quiet way, noticed a point that everyone else had apparently overlooked: there was no home-rule message from the City Council attached to them as the law required. And the arena in which the Battery Crossing fight was being staged was thereupon switched from the State Capitol to the Council Chamber on the second floor of City Hall.

In this arena the reformers had hope of success. Three councilmen were, after all, reformers themselves, nominees of the Fusion Party. Five were members of the American Labor Party, and organized labor favored a tunnel because it would furnish 2,600,000 man-hours of work as against 600,000 for a bridge. And all twenty-six councilmen were susceptible to pressure from civil service organizations angry as always at Moses because of his refusal to use civil service engineers on his authority jobs (he had recently stated it cost twice as much to do so), who wanted the more compliant Tunnel Authority to build the Crossing. Isaacs had, moreover, noticed in the bills a buried clause everyone else had overlooked: a clause specifically prohibiting Triborough from paying for the $11,000,000 West Side Highway link. Surely, the reformers felt, now that this had been pointed out to the councilmen, they would not ask the Legislature to approve the measures and thereby obligate the city, recently obligated to a $16,000,000 expenditure it could not afford for one Moses project, to spend $11,000,000 more.

The reformers were also encouraged by the attitude of the Mayor, whose reaction to Isaacs' discovery of the buried clause was foot-stamping fury; Moses had won his support for the bridge by promising him in so many words that it would cost the city nothing; knowing how Moses worked, the Mayor was sure that the clause was not in the bills by accident but was rather an attempt by Moses to sneak out of his promise—and cost the city $11,000,000. A faint ray of hope was, moreover, beginning to appear on La Guardia's horizon from the direction of Washington. Sentiment was building up in Congress for increased appropriations to the PWA; if the Mayor could grab off a $30,000,000 piece of that action for a tunnel, the cooperative Tunnel Authority instead of arrogant Triborough could build the Crossing. The Mayor considered that "if" big—sounding out

Ickes, he was informed that $30,000,000 more for New York was absolutely out of the question—but La Guardia evidently felt that as long as there was any option at all, he should keep it open. He told key legislators privately that he had had second thoughts about authorizing Moses to build the Crossing; he favored the bill authorizing Triborough to build a Crossing, he said, but not the bill stripping such authorization from the Tunnel Authority, because he wanted both bridge and tunnel options kept alive; if PWA money came through, he could have the Crossing built by the Tunnel Authority; if it did not, Triborough could build it.

The reformers were also hopeful because their aim was modest. They were not, after all, insisting that the bridge proposal be defeated. They were only asking that it be studied. With three competing plans for a solution to Lower Manhattan's traffic problem—and wildly conflicting estimates of the cost and effects of each plan—surely an impartial study was needed to determine the true costs and effects before a decision was made. Moses was insisting on the need for haste, they said, but wasn't the need really for delay, a delay which would provide time for mature consideration? The decision the city took on the proposals would vitally affect it for decades—centuries perhaps. Was it not only rational to take a few more weeks or months to make sure the decision taken was the right one?

Finally the reformers were hopeful because they knew their own strength. United, they felt they could defeat any politician; in the last citywide election, in fact, their victory had been nearly total; Fusion had taken all three citywide offices—Mayor, Comptroller and Council President—as well as the presidencies of the two most populous boroughs in 1937. And never had they been more united. Four years before, the leaders of New York's Good Government organizations had formed a "Central Committee" of civic organizations to support Robert Moses in his fight against Franklin Roosevelt's attempt to oust him from the Triborough chairmanship. Now they formed another "Central Committee," a "Central Committee of Organizations Opposing the Battery Toll Bridge," to oppose Moses. Within a week after its formation, its chairman, eighty-three-year-old Albert S. Bard, had assigned speakers to address every civic-minded body in the city, and every organization concerned with the preservation of beauty and architectural excellence within it; within a week a score of such groups had joined the committee. Under the direction of Eric Gugler, a group of the city's most respected architects were visiting and enrolling other architects in the cause. Famous artists who had held aloof from the issue were contacted by artists of equal stature and persuaded that their participation was needed to preserve a beautiful and majestic scene. Bard was making sure that every reformer who had entree to a politician in City Hall, Albany or Washington was using that entree; a sextet of septuagenarians, for example, spent a week in Washington explaining the situation to New York congressmen. And the most difficult of politicians—Fiorello Henry La Guardia—Bard left to the most respected reformer of them all: the legendary Burlingham, Charles Culp Burlingham, eighty-one years old, almost deaf, but still "the only man from whom La Guardia would take a scolding." "CC" hobbled, gaunt and stooped, up the steps of City Hall one morning, and was ushered in to see the Mayor—as La Guardia hastily shooed a group out of his office, so that the old man would not have to wait a minute. Burlingham emerged to relay to intimates a promise from La Guardia that while he would support a home-rule message for the bill authorizing Triborough to build a Crossing, he would not support—or sign—one for the bill stripping the Tunnel Authority of *its* authorization. The Mayor told Burlingham that he would wait until the War Department, which had jurisdiction over all structures built in or across navigable waters and which had scheduled a hearing on the bridge in April, had formally given approval to build it. The approval was only a formality, La Guardia said, but at least it would give him an excuse to offer Moses for delaying. If, he promised, at any time until the War Department approval was received, money became available for a tunnel, he would see that it, rather than a bridge, was built. And the Mayor promptly proved that he meant what he said by giving the Tunnel Authority permission to lobby in Albany against the bill—and by letting key legislators know that the lobbying had his sanction.

The "Central Committee" did not neglect the public at large. Unlike the usual run of Moses' opponents, the prestigious reformers had entree both to letters-to-the-editor columns and to editors, who usually heard in person only Moses' side of the controversy. Soon, even the *Times* was pointing out that "a brief delay wouldn't hurt the plan. . . . The bridge, if built, will be there a long time. It is worth while taking the time to get it right." The *Herald Tribune* demanded that Moses make public all the facts about the bridge and, urging the Council not to take action until he had done so, and until those facts had been studied, said:

> It seems clear now that a major alteration in the city's design and appearance is involved. No conceivable need for hurry has been suggested. The need is therefore for the carefulest consideration and full public discussion, with every opportunity for alternatives to be reviewed impartially and thoroughly. No possible risk should be run of building in haste and repenting for generations to come.

With the organized construction trades and the civil service organizations backing a tunnel, and with the letters-to-the-editor showing support of the need for further discussion, it was clear that the tide of public opinion was running against Moses' proposal—to an extent it had never run against him before.

Public opinion was the crucial factor in the reformers' philosophy and strategy. Public opinion was democratic government, the government they believed in. If it was not listened to, government was not democratic. "A decent respect for public opinion" had been a key ground for their demand that Roosevelt back down from his attempt to oust Moses. And they repeated that phrase in demanding that Moses back down now, and in insisting that, if he didn't back down voluntarily, the Mayor and councilmen make him.

The reformers felt certain that the Mayor and councilmen would.

They were, after all, politicians, and thus necessarily responsive to public opinion.

But all the reformers' hopefulness proved was that they didn't understand how much power—power over politicians—Moses had been given, or how independent of public opinion he now was. Moses understood. So unconcerned was he about the reformers' efforts that he spent the three weeks before the Council hearing vacationing in Key West, Florida. And the accuracy of his assessment of the situation was proven when, returning from a day fishing among the Keys (he caught two flounders), he received a telephone call informing him of La Guardia's statement that he would delay signing a home-rule message on the Tunnel Authority bill even if the Council passed one. Strolling down to the Key West Western Union office, he wrote out a telegram to the Mayor, addressed to him at his apartment so that the Mayor would receive it that same evening: NO POSSIBLE WAY OF KEEPING BOTH PROJECTS ALIVE UNTIL AFTER WAR DEPARTMENT HEARING STOP THEREFORE REQUEST YOU SIGN BOTH MESSAGES STOP OTHERWISE BRIDGE PROJECT MUST BE ABANDONED AND ALBANY NOTIFIED TO THIS EFFECT.

If the Mayor did not immediately guarantee that there would be no Battery tunnel, Moses was saying, he, Moses, would never give him the money for a Battery bridge. Either guarantee immediately that Moses could build the Crossing—and build the kind of Crossing he wanted—or there wouldn't be any Crossing. The telegram was not a request but an ultimatum, not an appeal from a subordinate to a superior, not a plea from a commissioner appointed by the Mayor that the Mayor change a decision, but a demand from someone who had the money to give the Mayor something he wanted.

La Guardia understood. After all his stalling, Moses' money was still the only money available. If he wanted the Battery Crossing, he would have to do what Moses wanted. The Mayor had no more choice than the City Planning Commission had had. Summoning the Council leaders to his office, he let them know that his feelings in the matter to be discussed at the upcoming hearing had changed.

Robert Moses returned from Florida on the night before the Council committee hearing. The Fine Arts Federation of New York, representing eighteen leading art societies, had that day issued a statement warning that the bridge would "disfigure perhaps the most thrillingly beautiful and world-renowned feature of this great city." A reporter asked Moses about the statement.

"The same old tripe," he said. "We'll take care of it all tomorrow."

Tomorrow was the City Council Chamber.

City Hall filled a gap in the blank-eyed skyscraper wall with the dignity and grace and elegance of another age, and of all its rooms, its

Council Chamber best evoked the values that the reformers had come to see were the real issues in the Battle of the Battery Crossing: respect for the institutions and the law through which, in a democratic society, the will of the people found expression and realization. And that room evoked as well the manner that, in the age which had produced those institutions and laws (and many of those reformers), had been so much more important—the dignity, grace and elegance in speech as well as appearance, the courtliness, the courtesy, the *gentlemanliness;* before its mahogany panels, beneath its delicate wainscoting, the people's elected representatives deliberated under a delicately curving little gallery with an intricately detailed railing, at slanting-topped eighteenth-century desks arranged in a semicircle, before a presidential dais flanked by flags of city and nation, under a ceiling, its details picked out in gold, featuring a huge mural of "New York Receiving the Tribute of the Nations."

If the setting for the drama was apt, so was the casting.

The audience that day was not the typical City Council audience. In the memory of participants, there wasn't even a lone housewife present, not a single claque from a neighborhood civic association to bounce boos and hisses, cheers and the noise of foot stamping off the mahogany-paneled walls and make Jefferson, observing bronze from the back wall, wonder if perhaps Hamilton had been right after all. Instead, sitting rank on rank in the gallery or on chairs set up to handle the overflow, was the very flower of the city's civic leadership, men of wealth and talent devoted to the rule of law and the institutions of democracy that City Hall symbolized, men who had proven that devotion by spending their talent and their time in a dozen great civic battles. For the audience included not only young reformers but elderly men whose first hero had been not La Guardia but Police Board President Theodore Roosevelt—the Burlinghams and Seaburys, Schieffelins and McAnenys, the men who had formed the heart of the Committee of One Hundred and Seven and the Committee of One Thousand—who had been fighting for generations against every threat to the institutions which they felt made their city great. There were starched wing collars in that audience, and vests crossed with heavy gold watch chains, and pince-nez, and walking sticks—and a spirit of reform that went back half a century and more. If New York had an aristocracy of civic leadership, it was assembled in the Council Chamber that day when the long fleet of black limousines screeched up in front of City Hall, and the man whom they had once believed to be the living embodiment of their ideals, dressed in a double-breasted dark-blue suit that only emphasized his burliness and with a close-clipped haircut that emphasized the massiveness of his face and his bull neck, impatiently flung open the door of the first of the limousines without waiting for the chauffeur to come around and, with a full score of aides half running behind him to keep up, stalked into City Hall, pounded up the delicate curve of the hanging staircase, strode past the slender fluted columns on the Rotunda, and burst through the Chamber door.

* * *

The opening presentation by Moses' architects and engineers took two hours but, to the reformers' surprise, provided none of the facts for which they had been asking. Aymar Embury described the bridge with the help of a large-scale model—the same large-scale model Embury had already privately all but admitted to the reformers was misleading. Othmar Ammann, noticeably ill at ease, repeated that the bridge would cost $41,200,000 and the tunnel $84,000,000—but again did not break down the figures, so that the reformers could not determine on what, if anything, they were based (although, with Ole Singstad present, Ammann did not this time attempt to maintain that some of the figures came from Singstad).

Moses' opponents provided facts—in abundance. Stanley Isaacs, directing the opposition presentation, told the councilmen, who goggled over this unprecedented passing up of a chance for personal publicity (didn't he realize that it was only one o'clock, the perfect time for a speech to make the late editions of the PM's?), that he would not speak himself but would simply introduce a series of experts who would prove, through specific facts and figures, that, on almost every point of the bridge-tunnel controversy, a tunnel would provide greater benefits—and cause less harm—to the city.

Major Henry J. Amy, executive director of the Citizens Budget Commission, analyzed Moses' contention that the bridge and its approaches "wouldn't cost the city a nickel," and then simply read the clause of Moses' proposed state legislation that would cost the city $11,000,000. A battery of municipal finance and real estate experts documented—block by block, building by building—Singstad's conclusion that a bridge would cost the city at least $1,500,000 per year in real estate taxes. Regional Plan Association experts testified that everything Moses hoped to achieve by building a new bridge could be achieved—at a small fraction of the construction cost and real estate tax loss—by their alternate plan. Isaacs had even commissioned an analysis of Moses' argument—never before analyzed during the decade Moses had been making it—that civil service architects and engineers were less efficient and therefore cost "twice as much" as the private consultants he employed. The analysis documented that one group did cost "twice as much" as the other—Moses' group. Even Moses' claim that a bridge would have "twice the capacity" of a tunnel was disproven—by Triborough's own traffic counts for its two suspension bridges, which showed that inclement weather (and inclemency for a Brooklyn-Battery Bridge would include not only rain, snow, ice and high winds but the fog which is frequently heavy over the Lower Bay), while not affecting a tunnel's capacity, significantly reduced that of a bridge. As to the relative cost of the two types of crossing, Isaacs' experts gave the detailed breakdowns Moses' had not, proving Singstad's claim that a tunnel would cost $65,000,000, and disproving all Moses' claims; Moses had said that the total cost of the bridge, including approach roads, would be $41,200,000; RPA engineers found that the cost of the bridge proper—without approach roads—would be $56,625,000. Isaacs had insisted that all the figures used be conservative. But even conservative figures were devastating. When Isaacs' parade of witnesses, a parade that lasted more than four hours, was over, every Moses contention subject to factual analysis had been utterly demolished. And as for the side of the controversy not subject to mathematical analysis—the aesthetic side, the effect of the bridge on the beauty of Battery Park and New York Harbor—the old reformers felt the demolition job had been even more devastating. There was a pounding of canes on the Council Chamber's oaken floor and a chorus of "Hear! Hear!" out of another age when George McAneny said of Moses' proposal:

> What all this would do to the values of real estate, some of it the most valuable in the world, I leave to others. But that the city would permit its famous Battery to be dealt with in such fashion seems to me an incredible thing. I am in fact of the opinion that if the plans under discussion are seriously pressed, there will be an uprising of public opinion the like of which has not been known since, forty years ago, some well-intentioned gentlemen in office proposed that City Hall be torn down to make way for something more modern in the skyscraping line.

Wrinkled, stooped old McAneny had lost none of his eloquence. And when he had finished summing up the reformers' arguments and pointed out to the Council that all they were requesting was a study—by impartial experts appointed by the Council itself—to determine the true facts in the case, to study the various alternatives and determine which one would really be best for the city, it was difficult for the reformers, wise though they were in the ways of politicians, to believe that the request would not be granted.

And then, in the seventh hour of the hearing, Robert Moses stood up to speak.

Reading from a yellow legal pad on which he had been scribbling furiously during the opposition speeches, he turned his attention first to the analysis of the relative efficiency of civil service architects and private consultants.

"I want to warn my friends in the civil service that civil service can become a racket," he said. "It's getting to be so that nothing will please them but a Communist state, which we know is so pleasing to Mr. Isaacs. . . ."

There was a moment of shocked silence in the Council Chamber. Then came a storm of boos and hisses, which Moses' lieutenants tried ineffectually to drown out with cheers and applause. But Moses was not to be deterred by boos. He directed his next remarks to the Regional Plan Association proposal.

The RPA had always opposed progress, he said. It had sided with the "fox hunters and estate owners" to oppose the Northern State Parkway, Heckscher State Park and Jones Beach, and many of his other Long Island projects. In New York City, RPA planners "were in a dither about the Henry Hudson Bridge—they asked delay, and advocated a low-level bridge. They said the Henry Hudson Bridge would ruin the finest spot in Manhattan. . . . We built the bridge and a week after it opened the bankers confessed that they had been wrong. We said it would average 16,000 cars, they said 6,000—and we were . . . right." The RPA "has been wrong about all these things," he said, and therefore, "why should we suppose that it is right about this one?" Its current proposal is, in fact, "nonsense"; "every argument applicable to the Battery Bridge is applicable tenfold against the Brooklyn Bridge."

The reformers sat hardly believing what they were hearing. Although the RPA had opposed the Northern State Parkway, it was just not true that the RPA had opposed Heckscher State Park and Jones Beach; it had *supported* them, as it had supported almost all Moses' Long Island projects; moreover, the parkway fight had taken place fifteen years before—what did it have to do with a discussion about the Battery Crossing? The RPA had thought the Henry Hudson Bridge would ruin the finest spot in Manhattan—and the bridge *had* ruined the finest spot in Manhattan; the bridge might be a success in financial terms, but it was a failure in any other terms; the heavy traffic and the resultant congestion proved that, not disproved it; how could "every argument applicable to the Battery Bridge be applicable" to the Brooklyn Bridge?—when the whole point was that the Brooklyn Bridge already existed, and therefore could be rebuilt cheaply and without further destroying real estate values or the harbor view. And then Moses turned his attention to the RPA's president.

Only a man who wasn't going to run for public office would propose "slapping a toll on the Brooklyn Bridge," Moses said. "No man in his right mind would do that." It was, he said, "all right for Mr. McAneny" to make such a proposal. "He's not going to run for public office again." He turned and glanced at the wrinkled old man sitting behind him.

"He's an extinct volcano," Moses said. "He's an exhumed mummy."

This time there were neither boos nor cheers in the Council Chamber. There was only silence, unbroken until Moses began to speak again.

"If there was an argument raised that he answered directly, I don't remember it," says one of the reformers present that day. "We had raised a lot of issues. He hardly mentioned them. All he did was lash out at individuals, at respected, public-spirited men, with a spitefulness, a viciousness, that was almost unbelievable to see." There was no attempt to meet the RPA proposal logically. It was simply "nonsense," Moses said. Or to discuss the effect of a gigantic suspension bridge on the view of the harbor. "The most beautiful architecture wrought by man is a bridge, especially a suspension bridge, and the finest view in Manhattan is the view you get walking across the Triborough Bridge to the Bronx or Queens," he said, and that, apparently, was all that had to be said on that point. As for the argument that the bridge would ruin Battery Park, the park was "no beauty spot" anyway, he said. If McAneny was so interested in it, why hadn't he done "something for it when he was in office"?

Those arguments that he did answer, he answered with lies. The proposal that the Tunnel Authority build the Crossing? Moses said that "the Tunnel Authority" had built the Queens-Midtown Tunnel so incompetently that "the Tunnel Authority will be busted when it is finished. Washington knows that and I know it." The city was going to have to "step in and rescue the tunnel." (The Tunnel Authority was actually bringing in the tunnel far under cost. When it was finished, the Authority would, far from being busted, have a surplus of more than $4,000,000. And Moses, who had been doing detailed analyses of its financing, must have known this.) The need for a city contribution for the West Side Highway and East River Drive extensions? "Colossal effrontery. . . . The Citizens Budget Commission fellow's figures are just beyond me. I don't know where he got them." But Moses must have known precisely where he had gotten them.

The key arguments Moses didn't answer at all. He gave no explanation of where he obtained the disputed figures for the tunnel, and as for the bridge, all he would say was, "I have built many bridges, both over water and over land, and I know what the costs are. We are letting contracts every day for the same kind of work, and when we give you an estimate, it is accurate and our reputation is behind it." The councilmen could take his figures or leave them, he seemed to say.

The councilmen—and the city they represented—could take or leave his whole proposal, he made clear. When one ventured to ask him why he objected to a delay to give time for the alternatives to be studied, he put it to them straight:

"This is a showdown project. Either you want it or you don't want it. And either you want it now or you don't get it at all." He was giving the city an ultimatum. The city could either take his proposal or leave it. He wasn't going to waste his time discussing it.

And the councilmen took it. Without leaving the Council Chamber, hastily putting their heads together, the men who had been contacted the night before by La Guardia or by Steingut or by Crews voted unanimously to release the home-rule message from the committee immediately, without even an hour's study, and to send it to the full Council for a vote the following morning.

Moses snatched his yellow legal pad off the desk and stalked out of the room, his aides scampering behind him. There was a broad smile on his face.

The rest of the audience left the Council Chamber more slowly. As they filed out, many of them came over to McAneny and touched his shoulder consolingly. Burlingham, hobbling over on a cane, put his arm around him and whispered something in his ear.

But consolation was not easy. Years later, Comptroller Joseph D. McGoldrick, explaining why he was "afraid" of Robert Moses, would tell the author, "I was there that day, you know, sitting in the audience, when he said that to George McAneny. Mr. McAneny was old and wrinkled and very shrunken by that time, you know. And when Moses called him an 'exhumed mummy,' I saw the expression on his face. I saw it, you know. So I was afraid of him."

* * *

Other reformers would later describe their overriding emotion at Moses' philosophy and tactics as "shock."

They had no justification for such an emotion. There was nothing new about that philosophy or those tactics. The insistence that his proposals be viewed only in isolation, that each be viewed strictly as an attempt to solve a particular, limited problem by creating a particular structure of concrete and steel, that it not be evaluated in terms of the needs of the city as a whole (the need for a bridge, for example, weighed against the need for schools and hospitals) or even as part of the larger problem of which the specific problem was only a part (a traffic-moving machine like a bridge evaluated in terms of the city's over-all traffic-moving problem) and especially not in terms of its impact on the surrounding neighborhood—was the same insistence that had underlain the public works he had been building in their city for five years. Moses had used these same arguments in arguing for a dozen other projects—most of which the reformers had enthusiastically supported. If they had ever taken a close look at those projects, had ever examined them with the same care with which they examined the Brooklyn-Battery Bridge, they would have seen that this philosophy lay behind them. They were shocked now only because they had never bothered to take such a look.

As for the vicious personal attacks, Moses had been making vicious personal attacks for years. The only difference was that this time the target was *them*—and they therefore saw how unfair the attacks were. Previously they had laughed indulgently at Moses' propensity for personal vituperation, regarding it as a harmless idiosyncrasy; perhaps, when one took into account all the crooked politicians, hack bureaucrats and selfish private individuals with whom Moses had to deal, even admirable. In that laughter and that indulgence was a feeling that Moses' methods, however distasteful, however antithetical to their principles, were justified by the difficulties he had to surmount to Get Things Done.

But in the Battery Crossing fight, the reformers could not avoid taking a good look at one of Robert Moses' controversies—and at Robert Moses. They could no longer avoid seeing precisely what kind of man they had for so long believed in. The Battery Crossing fight was the moment of truth in their relationship with Moses. After supporting him for years in a score of battles, after sacrificing, over and over again, the principles so dear to them in his support, after helping to raise him to power and helping to keep him in power, they saw him at last for what he was—and they realized that he was not the embodiment of everything they believed in but its antithesis. If, for the twenty years before the fight, the Good Government organizations of New York City had supported him, for the twenty years after the fight, those organizations would oppose him.

The Battery Crossing fight was also the moment of truth for the reformers in another respect. It made them see that their opposition no longer mattered to Moses. They had played a vital role in his acquisition of power in the city. Quite possibly, in fact, he could not have acquired that power without their help. But he had taken that power and used it to acquire more and more of it—and now, they suddenly realized, he had enough of it so that they could not take it back from him, could not, in fact, stop him from the absolutely untrammeled use of it. He no longer had to be concerned with their opinions—and he wasn't concerned with their opinions. They were the city's aristocracy. They had always had a voice—an important voice—in decisions vital to the city, a voice that was important to them because they cared about and loved the city. But in the areas that Robert Moses had carved out for his own, they would have a voice no longer.

And neither would the city. For if the Battle of the Battery Crossing was a moment of truth for the reformers, it was also, although no one recognized it as such, a moment of truth for New York.

It was not, of course, only the reformers who opposed Moses' proposal—or at least the haste with which he was trying to ram it through. Also in the opposition were most of the city's most important elected officials—right up to the Mayor—and, speaking with a virtually unanimous voice, the city's press. Always before, elected officials, backed by the press, would have possessed more than sufficient power at least to get a few weeks' time to study a proposal if they wanted to study it. But they possessed such power no longer. The city had a problem that desperately needed solution. It had no money to solve the problem itself. Moses had the money. And if the city wanted a solution, it would have to accept his solution—or none at all. That was the narrow limit of its choices—which was really no choice at all. The ultimatum that Moses had delivered first to the Mayor and then to the City Council symbolized this reality—and so did the reaction of the Mayor and the City Council to that ultimatum.

Less than twenty-four hours after the Council committee hearing, the full Council voted, 19–6, to endorse the Mayor's home-rule request to the Legislature for passage of the bills that would foreclose any possibility of study. (Moses watched the proceeding with what a reporter described as a "happy smile.") Less than twenty-four hours after *that* (with Steingut "wielding the bull whip") the bills were passed, 106–6 by the Assembly, 41–1 by the Senate. ("I'm not surprised," Moses told reporters with a smile.) And less than twenty-four hours after *that*, Governor Lehman announced he would sign the bill (not because he approved the bridge, he was careful to state—"I have no means of forming a sound judgment" on the project—but because it was a city affair and the city's elected officials had asked him to sign it). When the issue—in the form of a Triborough Authority request for Board of Estimate approval of a contract covering the relative city and Authority contributions to the project, a request worded in such a way that Isaacs said it constituted a "blank check" to Triborough—came before the Board, La Guardia ran the meeting with an iron hand, McGoldrick and Morris, despite their preference for a tunnel, voted for the bridge and

Isaacs' two votes were the only ones cast against Moses' project. Only one more step was required before Moses could begin sinking the bridge pilings —War Department approval—and this was regarded as no more than a formality; in fact, Moses had been privately assured by the Army Corps of Engineers that the approval would be forthcoming shortly. "The tunnel is dead," Moses said, and the reformers saw no hope that he was wrong. In *A Man for All Seasons*, Sir Thomas More warns young Roper about the consequences of letting ends justify means. When the young man says he would "cut down every law in England" to "get after the Devil," More replies: "Oh? And when the last law was down, and the Devil turned round on you—where would you hide, Roper, the laws all being flat?" The reformers could have benefited from More's warning. Robert Moses was of course not a Devil, but to give Moses power in the city, they had cut down the "laws" in which they believed. Now those laws no longer existed to protect the city from him. For the reformers and the city they loved, there was no place to hide. There was nothing the city, opposed to the bridge, could do to keep Moses from building it.

When the reformers were in deepest trouble, they always seemed to turn to the same man. Now they delegated Paul Windels to go see him. Windels walked over to 27 William Street and into the office of the senior partner of Burlingham, Veeder, Clark and Hupper, and "CC," after thinking for several long minutes, suddenly smiled ("that wonderful smile," Windels would say. "When you saw that smile you felt everything was going to be all right") and said: "Call Eleanor."

In the April 5, 1939, edition of her newspaper column, "My Day," Mrs. Eleanor Roosevelt was enthusiastically discussing her grandchildren when she switched abruptly to one paragraph on a different topic.

> I have a plea from a man who is deeply interested in Manhattan Island, particularly in the beauty of the approach from the ocean at Battery Park. He tells me that a New York official, who is without doubt always efficient, is proposing a bridge one hundred feet high at the river, which will go across to the Whitehall Building over Battery Park. This, he says, will mean a screen of elevated roadways, pillars, etc., at that particular point. I haven't a question that this will be done in the name of progress, and something undoubtedly needs to be done. But isn't there room for some consideration of the preservation of the few beautiful spots that still remain to us on an overcrowded island?

A single, small paragraph, on a subject she would not raise again. But revealing nonetheless, as the smallest ripple in a pond's still water reveals the hidden trout below. For that paragraph was the ripple, the only ripple, that revealed that far below the surface of the public controversy over Robert Moses' huge bridge, down in the quiet, murky depths, impenetrable to the public gaze, in which real power lurks, private passions were beginning to roil the water—and Robert Moses' great enemy was beginning to move against him.

Ignoring the apparent hopelessness of their cause, the reformers' "Central Committee of Organizations" opposed to Moses' bridge kept filling letters-to-the-editor columns with phrases out of another age. The best, as always, were Burlingham's. "At the risk of being called an extinct fire-cracker, I venture to say that the planning and art commissions have been faithless servants. What justification can there be for men whom we have trusted to preserve the beauty of New York . . . to destroy or risk the destruction of any feature of [that] beauty?" There must be more public hearings and Moses must be made to furnish more information for them, for "a public hearing without specific detailed figures furnished in advance will only darken counsel." Burlingham's were the only letters Moses answered directly: "I see that Mr. Burlingham is back in the papers again. . . . [His] reference to the depressing effect of bridges on surrounding real property . . . is wholly inaccurate. . . . I am sending Mr. Burlingham some pictures of the Bronx-Whitestone Bridge, which most of us think is one of the finest things built by man in New York"; it "will enormously improve" surrounding property. (Burlingham, saying, "It is an honor even to be noticed by Mr. Moses," replied, "To compare the effect of the Whitestone Bridge on the vast swampy regions of the Bronx with that of the Brooklyn-Battery Bridge on lower Manhattan seems a little far-fetched. . . . I'd still like to see a breakdown of his final estimates"—and Moses hastily broke off the exchange.) But it was not written public communications that were to be decisive, but private—and communications too private to be entrusted to writing. Burlingham had told Windels to call Eleanor—and CC himself had written to Eleanor's husband. In a letter across whose top the great attorney, then eighty-one years old, scrawled in longhand, "In graveyard confidence," he wrote:

Dear Franklin:

Now please *stop* and read my letter to the *Herald Tribune*. . . . Nobody fit to have an opinion wants the Battery Bridge except Bob Moses.

. . . The War Department can stop it. . . . *verb. suf. sap.*, especially when the sapient being is a lover of New York, as well as President of the United States and Commander in Chief of the Army.

The Commander in Chief apparently took the hint. The War Department hearing was held under the direction of the Army Corps of Engineers in New York, and Moses was assured by Colonel C. L. Hall, the chief district engineer, that a favorable report would be issued shortly. But the day after the hearing, the colonel's superior, Major General J. L. Schley, chief of the Army Corps of Engineers, received a note from presidential aide Edwin M. Watson asking him to "speak to the President before you make any report on the subject." The report was not issued on schedule, and when Moses asked when it would be, the engineers were suddenly evasive. And Secretary of War Harry H. Woodring suddenly began to take a personal interest in New York Harbor.

Ickes brought up the bridge in a Cabinet meeting one day, saying that he recommended its construction. Frances Perkins recalled what happened then.

> The President pulled down his lip—a sign by which I always knew that something phony was going on inside of him. He'd pull his mouth down over his teeth and say, "Oh, yes" or "Oh, no" as the case might be. It was a curious facial expression. He said, "Well, I don't know. I want to think about that and look into it, Harold."

Some weeks later, the Secretary of the Interior, who hadn't known the President as long as had the Secretary of Labor, brought up the bridge again and, in Miss Perkins' words, "was insistent about its being approved." According to Miss Perkins, "The President said, 'Well, we'll have to consult the military. That's a very important channel.' " Ickes said, "That's all right, Mr. President. We figured out everything. It will not interfere with the operation of ships." But all the President would say was: "Well, I'd like to think about it."

Ickes finally caught on. Miss Perkins relates:

> Ickes said to me, "The President is going to kill this. He's going to kill this wonderful project. I wish you'd speak to him. I wish you'd argue it out with him."
>
> I said, "Well, how is he going to kill it?"
>
> "He's getting the military to condemn it."
>
> I said, "Are you sure?"
>
> "Yes," he said. "I know. I have evidence. He's telling the military to say that it interferes with the navigable streams and it doesn't—not at all. It's all been thought out. It's just that he so hates that Moses. God knows Moses hates him. But I should think that we could build a bridge without regard to that."

Miss Perkins did speak to the President, who, she says, replied, " 'Well, it's no good, Frances. It's just a no-good idea.' Listing the reformers' objections to the bridge, he added, 'Besides, I am reliably informed that though the engineers haven't finished with this, they think it's a very great hazard to navigation. In case of war, we can't have any bridges around there. They'll drop bombs and so forth.'

"I came back and told Harold that I guessed he was right, the President was not going to do it," Miss Perkins recalled. "There was nothing more I could do. There were plenty of other public works projects that were available, and didn't have Moses' name on them." On May 18, 1939, Watson sent the President a memo—which the presidential staff filed in the "Personal and Confidential" file—stating that "the Secretary of War phoned me this morning to please let you know that the War Department had rejected the proposition to build a bridge from the Battery to Brooklyn. . . . He wanted you to have this confidential information, as it has not yet been announced to the public."

The "confidential information" was not announced to the public—or to Moses or even to La Guardia—for two more months. So tight was the lid of secrecy clamped down that Moses, usually so astute, feeling the only reason for the delay was bureaucratic red tape, did not for some weeks realize what was happening, kept his engineers drawing plans for the bridge and, until suspicion began to dawn, spent the two months firing off angry telegrams to the Corps of Engineers demanding a decision on the request for a permit, convinced that the decision could only be favorable. It was not until July 17, 1939, that Secretary of War Woodring announced in Washington that he had decided not to approve the project because "the proposed bridge is seaward of a vital Navy establishment . . . the U.S. Navy Yard at Brooklyn," and if knocked down during a war might block access to the yard from the sea.

The *Herald Tribune* reported that Moses reacted to the decision with "rage and ridicule," and both reactions were understandable. There were already two other bridges, the Brooklyn and Manhattan spans, seaward of the Brooklyn Navy Yard—and other bridges seaward of other naval installations all over the United States. The only way a suspension bridge could be "knocked down," moreover, would be by hitting one of a handful of key cables—if a bomb hit the bridge span itself it would go right through—and Air Force experts queried by Moses prior to the decision had estimated the chances of this happening at 100,000 to 1.

Attempting to repeat his 1935 strategy of bringing Roosevelt's behind-the-scenes maneuvering into the open, Moses issued a statement hinting that the President was behind the decision. When reporters failed to catch the hint, Moses made it broader at another press conference, reminding reporters that Ickes had taken the "blame" for the 1935 ouster attempt and saying, "Why don't you fellows find out if the Secretary of War is willing to take the blame for this?"

But Roosevelt had learned from the 1935 controversy. Then, during a press conference, he had incautiously allowed himself to be identified with "Ickes' " decision. Now, when, at another press conference, reporters questioned him about the "Woodring" decision, the President said firmly that the decision had been that of Woodring and the War Department alone. Pressed to say whether or not he agreed with the decision, he said he had no opinion on it at all. Try as Moses would to link him with it, he could not do so. The fox had left no tracks. And he had planned more cleverly than he had in 1935—as Moses admitted in a formal statement brimming with frustration.

> No doubt this squares up accounts so far as the Triborough Bridge Authority is concerned. The effort to . . . force the resignation of its chief executive officer failed because the public opinion would not stand for it. In the present case the procedure has been a great deal shrewder, because it is assumed that the average person is in no position to argue with military boards of strategy, and must accept their conclusion no matter how silly.

Moses attempted to enlist La Guardia in an attack on Woodring's decision, but the Mayor seemed rather uninterested—and the reason suddenly became clear to Moses when the RFC abruptly decided that it was willing to lend the Tunnel Authority not the $39,000,000 that had previously been its limit, but $59,000,000, and to make the loan at an interest rate so reduced that the cost of the tunnel (which, it now turned out, would in fact have been not Moses' $84,000,000 but Singstad's $65,000,000) could be reduced to $59,000,000. La Guardia's gratification was intense. "This administration is never daunted by anything," he gloated. "We just go on to the next thing."

Moses' rage over what he regarded as his greatest defeat never cooled, not even after the tunnel, years later, was incorporated into his Triborough empire. Any mention of the tunnel—even the most casual reference by a luncheon guest trying to make conversation—would cause the big jaw to jut angrily and the voice of Robert Moses to recite verbatim, as automatically as if the mention had triggered a tape recorder inside his head, the old slogans: "A bridge would have cost half as much as a tunnel, you know, carry twice the amount of traffic, could be built in half the time . . ."

What made his defeat all the more bitter was his belief that Eleanor Roosevelt had engineered it. She denied this, writing (in the only other mention ever made in "My Day" of the Battery Crossing): "Needless to say I have never spoken to anyone in the War Department on this subject. . . . I would like to add that I did not know that Mr. Moses had an interest in this bridge. Which shows how dumb I am!" But Moses, discussing the Crossing controversy years later, would snarl, "Oh, she was in the middle of it, all right—it was her more than anyone else. So now they've got a tunnel, costs twice as much, handles one half of the capacity, took twice as long to build . . ." For years, Mrs. Roosevelt's popularity restrained him from attacking her publicly, although in private his descriptions of her were, in Lazarus' words, "increasingly unprintable." But in the memoirs he wrote long after Eleanor Roosevelt was dead, he said, as if determined to get his feelings on the record for posterity:

> A review of "My Day" discloses an endless succession of noble impulses unsupported by thought or evidence, or naïveté and sophistication, modesty and assurance, the product of confused early education, a cloistered girlhood, and sudden precipitation into world affairs. "My Day" spread the dubious gospel that all problems yield to good intentions. Converting a bridge into a tunnel was a trivial incident in such a record.

There was one more pill for Moses to swallow—a $12,000,000 pill. The RFC's $59,000,000 was enough to build the tunnel and part of the Manhattan approaches, but none of Brooklyn's. La Guardia said the city would pay for the rest of the Manhattan approaches—since it would take four years to build the tunnel, the money would not have to be appropriated until 1943—but he made no announcement about any Brooklyn approaches. When Moses went to the Mayor, with considerably more humility than was his wont, to inquire about the five-mile, $12,000,000 Elevated Highway to Owl's Head Park that had been planned to link the Battery Crossing with his Circumferential Parkway, the Mayor said blandly that the city didn't have the money and that he didn't feel he could ask Washington for it. Perhaps sometime in the future . . .

Without that highway, the "Belt System," the great circle bypass around the city of which Moses had been dreaming since 1927, would still have a five-mile gap. Reluctantly he told the Mayor that Triborough would build the highway if he could charge a ten-cent toll to finance its cost. Blandly the Mayor replied that he didn't think tolls on highways were a good idea. Besides, he went on, hadn't Moses already said—while arguing for Triborough's right to build the bridge—that Triborough had more than $12,000,000 available? Whether or not Roosevelt, working with La Guardia, both men aware how driven Moses was to realize his dreams, had set the RFC loan at a figure exactly enough for a tunnel and nothing else in order to force Moses to cough up the money for the highway is not known, but that is the way it worked out. The Tunnel Authority rather than Moses' Triborough Authority was given the right to build the Battery Crossing and the revenues from it. But Triborough was forced to build the road to get to the Crossing. Obtaining even a soupçon of revenge on Robert Moses—promising to sign a minor bill he wanted and then reneging on the promise—had, Reuben Lazarus said, made Roosevelt, as Governor, look as fresh and happy "as though he had just come out of the bath after a clean shave in the morning." After the Battery Crossing fight, Roosevelt must have looked as if he had just spent a week at a health resort.

On July 20, 1939, the Central Committee of Organizations Opposing the Battery Toll Bridge held a "Victory Luncheon" at the Architectural League.

The taste of victory must have been sweet, for the luncheon did not end until after three. "Rising votes of thanks" were tendered to the heroes of the Goo Goo uprising from McAneny on down. The reformers laughed when Albert Bard recounted details of an Architectural League luncheon that had been held in the same building on the previous day. Aymar Embury had given a speech, and after it, "persistent questioning" by a member of the audience "finally," as the minutes of the Victory Luncheon put it, "elicited the fact that Mr. Embury regarded as approximately accurate the . . . drawing that Commissioner Moses called 'completely phony.' " And when Ole Singstad rose to announce that he had just modified the tunnel plans to remove even the tunnel ventilation shaft from Battery Park—he had found a way to place it north of Battery Place—they cheered in a scene of triumph and jubilation.

If the reformers had looked at the Battle of the Battery Crossing in a broader perspective, however, they would have been holding not a "Victory Luncheon" but a wake. For in such a perspective—the significance of the battle in the history of New York City—the key point about the fight and its significance for the city's future was not that the President had stepped in and stopped Robert Moses from building a project that might have irreparably damaged the city. The key point was that it had taken the President to stop him.

The city's own mayor, the elected representative of the city's people, the personification of the city's will, hadn't been able to stop him. Neither had the city's other elected officials—or its most wealthy, prestigious and influential private citizens, the "in group" or "establishment" that could, when united, usually count on carrying the day on any issue about which it was particularly concerned.

In the governmental institutions—Board of Estimate and City Council—established to insure that the voice of the city's people would be heard and obeyed, their voice had been drowned out by his voice. There were other governmental institutions—Planning Commission, Art Commission—set up to insure that physical changes to the city would be governed by rational, logical planning considerations and that their specific form would be determined by informed and educated aesthetic taste, not by capricious whim and passing fancy, and certainly not by the whim and fancy and personal taste of a single individual. But rational, logical planning considerations and informed and educated aesthetic taste had crumbled before his will. The explanation for the denouement of the Battle of the Battery Crossing was simply personal pique, the fact that a man who for years had hated Robert Moses had finally been given a chance to give that hatred a little venting. The battle had proven that the powers he had obtained as head of a new part-private, part-public entity, a "body corporate and politic," were vast enough so that in his spheres of activity he, not the formal democratic institutions of New York, would henceforth shape New York's destiny.

30. Revenge

A man that studieth revenge keeps his own wounds green.

—SIR FRANCIS BACON

IN VICTORY, Robert Moses had proven himself savage. In defeat, he was to prove himself more savage still. He couldn't hurt Franklin Roosevelt or his wife, but the reformers who had brought Eleanor and Franklin into the Battle of the Battery Crossing and had thus engineered his defeat were vulnerable because they loved the old fort in Battery Park and the Aquarium it housed. He set out to tear the fort down, to raze it to the ground, to destroy every trace that it had ever existed. The fort and the Aquarium were located in a park, and in a park, thanks to the powers they had helped give him, he was sure that not even a President could prevent him from doing exactly what he wanted.

As soon as Moses announced, on February 6, 1941, that the Aquarium was "obsolete" and "unsuitable," that its ventilation and lighting were poor and its roof in need of repair, that the construction of the Brooklyn-Battery Tunnel would require its demolition anyway, and that therefore he was going to demolish it immediately and turn over part of the Bronx Zoological Park to the New York Zoological Society, the Aquarium's administrator, for a new, ultramodern $2,000,000 Aquarium, some reformers who had bumped heads with Moses in the past—notably Bill Exton—suspected that revenge, pure and simple, was one of the primary reasons, if not in fact the only reason, behind the announcement. But most of the older reformers at the Citizens Union and City Club refused at first to believe Exton—until, as they delved into the reasons for the proposed demolition, it became more and more difficult for even the most generous-minded of them to find any reason for it other than the satisfaction of a personal grudge.

Moses said the Aquarium was obsolete and unsuitable. The 2,500,000 visits to the museum each year, the fact that many of these visits were made by men and women who had been taken to it years before by their own parents and who were now bringing their own children to see its wonders, and the almost universal affection for the dark and musty old building in the hearts of New Yorkers made this a rather difficult argument to accept, but even if it was accepted, the answer need not be demolition. As a letter published in the *Herald Tribune* inquired: "If the roof leaks, then it can be repaired; if the ventilation is poor, then it can be corrected, but why remove [the Aquarium] entirely?" The cost of such alterations might be expensive, but they certainly would not approach $2,000,000—even if $2,000,000 was an accurate cost estimate for the new Aquarium, and the reformers' friends in the Zoological Society soon let them know that the figure bore little relation to reality. Moses never attempted to answer this inquiry. Moses said that moving the Aquarium to the Bronx Zoo would "make it attractive to increasing numbers of people." The greatest attraction of the Aquarium was its accessibility; in comparison, the Bronx Zoo was rather inaccessible—what, the reformers asked, was Moses talking about? Moses never bothered to reply.

When a storm of protest arose not only from the reformers but from the public—there were whole columns of letters-to-the-editor day after day; editors trying to "balance out" the selection they printed found it difficult to do so, so scarce were letters favoring Moses' proposal—Moses attempted to give additional reasons. But, upon the reformers' examination of these reasons, each turned out to be invalid.

Moses stated that tunneling under Battery Park would "undermine" the Aquarium and cause its walls to crumble. Bill Exton checked with the two engineers who were *doing* the tunneling—Ole Singstad, in charge of the construction of the tunnel proper, and Walter Binger, in charge of the underpass approach from the West Side Highway—and Singstad and Binger just laughed at this argument; no tunneling—no construction work of any type on either the tunnel proper or the underpass approach—would come within 170 feet of the Aquarium.

Then Moses declared that, whether or not there was any tunneling under the old fort, it was going to fall down. His engineers, he said, had discovered that some of its walls were tilted and in imminent danger of collapse, and that a massive reconstruction job, whose cost he put at $200,000, would be necessary to make it safe. This couldn't be true, could it? asked reformers. The walls of that fort, eight feet thick and solid sandstone, seemed as sturdy a structure as they had ever seen. Of course it wasn't true, said engineers who weren't on Moses' staff. "A joke. I thought it was a joke when he first said that," Binger snorts. "How could it fall down? What was it but an open ring of walls eight feet thick, six hundred feet around and two hundred feet in diameter? An annular [open] ring with a center that's been standing for two, three hundred years [sic—actually for 139 years] isn't going to just fall down. Fall down! Ridiculous! Absurd! . . . And suppose one piece showed signs of falling? You'd just brace it up! . . . A joke, that's what it was, young man! A joke!"

Moses had an aesthetic as well as an engineering rationale for his decision; the fort was not beautiful, he said, but an ugly "large red wart." And as for its historic interest, he said flatly that it "has no history worth writing about." The only people who wanted to retain the Aquarium, he said, were "stuffed shirts." After he announced his plans, "there was not a dry eye at the Knickerbocker Club, all the shades were drawn at the Century

Association and heart-rending sobs issued from the dusty diggings of the American Scenic and Historic Preservation Society. . . . but somehow the great popular uprising against the razing of this structure hasn't materialized."

The proof of the falseness of Moses' statement was on record day after day in the letters-to-the-editor columns; it wasn't only Goo Goos who were writing but men and women who could not possibly be classified as aristocrats but who wanted Fort Clinton saved because, as one put it, he had visited it so often that it seemed "an old friend," because, as another wrote, "without it Battery Park will be lonesome," because it was, in a word found in many of the letters, "beautiful" or because it was the place where they, or their parents or grandparents—where millions—had first stepped onto the soil of the United States. An elderly woman said that there must be many other Americans who, like her, were reminded every time they went to the old fort of how they had, years before, "felt their eyes fill with tears, and their hearts fill with thankfulness as they passed through the doorway of Castle Garden, the doorway to Liberty, a new life, a new world."

All the reasons Moses advanced to justify his decision—engineering, aesthetic, historic—were misleading, not reasons at all but rationales, and transparently false rationales at that. And if the reasons Moses advanced were invalid, what then was the true reason? If, as Exton wrote to the *Times* in one of a series of eloquent letters, the very engineers building the tunnel said that they could build it without disturbing the old fort, "why, then, must this ancient and familiar thing be torn from us?"

More to the point, why did it have to be torn from us *now?* Perhaps Moses did want to build a more modern Aquarium in the Bronx. But the plans were not ready, and the money for construction, as the Zoological Society readily confessed, was nowhere in sight. (As a matter of fact, although the reformers did not know this, Moses was not even certain where he wanted the new Aquarium to be located; he had simply thrown out the Bronx Zoo as the most likely location he could think of without study.) Even if the reformers accepted the argument that there was not room in a city of 7,000,000 for two aquariums, why was it necessary to demolish the existing Aquarium years before the new one could possibly be ready, thereby leaving the city for years without any aquarium at all? What was going to happen to the Aquarium's matchless collection of sea life, amassed over decades at fabulous cost in effort and ingenuity? What was the reason for Moses' insistence that this "ancient and familiar thing" not only be destroyed but be destroyed immediately? If the Aquarium was torn down, moreover, why did the fort beneath it also have to be torn down? Reluctant as the old Goo Goos had been to believe Exton's charge that Moses was motivated by nothing but a mean desire for revenge, many of them eventually concluded that the young man must be right. Years later, the few still alive would be asked about Moses' motivation. "If you knew Bob Moses, you wouldn't have to ask that," Paul Windels would say. "Bob Moses could hate. If you stood up to him, he would hate you forever. If you defeated him, he would try to destroy you. Here were guys he couldn't destroy. So he decided to do the next best thing: destroy something they loved." George McAneny would point out that Moses' claim that tearing down the Aquarium and fort had been made necessary "because of the tunnel" which they themselves had advocated was a particularly apt means of revenge.

To destroy the Aquarium and fort on the spur of a base impulse would be a crime against the city, against history, the reformers felt. They determined to prevent it.

But they couldn't. Moses' possession of unlimited powers over park administrative decisions made it possible for him simply to announce an "administrative decision" on Battery Park and the Aquarium: for the "safety of the public" they would be closed as soon as intensive tunnel work began, on October 1, 1941, the park for the duration of such work, the Aquarium forever. The reformers would have had no opportunity to protest Moses' plans to demolish the Aquarium and the old fort to any official body if the Park Commissioner hadn't needed money—a $20,000 appropriation from the Board of Estimate—for tanks to house the fish in their new home in the Bronx. (The Zoological Society, which Moses had claimed had resources of $2,000,000, proved unable to raise $20,000.) His need for a Board appropriation meant that there would have to be a public hearing and, in theory, a Board decision. But, in reality, what choice did the Board have? The park around the Aquarium was going to be closed shortly, fenced off from the public. Disapproving the appropriation wouldn't keep the Aquarium open; it would only keep Moses from moving the fish to the Bronx Zoo, which would mean either that the fish would stay in the Aquarium for years with the public unable to see them or that Moses would carry out a threat to dump the fish into the sea. When the reformers attempted to raise the demolition question, Moses replied blandly that that wasn't the issue at all; he wasn't asking for approval of the demolition of the structure, he said, but only for moving the fish out of it (he himself had no objection to keeping the fort if the Board wanted to provide for its rehabilitation, he said; and anyway the Board would have a chance to decide the demolition question at some later date, after the completion of a study by Consultant Gilmore Clarke which he had commissioned). The choices open to the Board and the Mayor were further limited by Moses' popularity. In less than two months, the politicians' futures would be in the hands of the voters, and Moses' personal popularity with the voters was far too great to be appreciably damaged by an unpopular stand on a single issue—particularly since the city's press, as if to atone for its heresy in opposing him in the Crossing and Aquarium fights, was laying on the personal adulation in even heavier doses than usual. (It was during this pre-election period that the *Times* commented, on the occasion of the opening of the Gowanus Parkway: "When Commissioner Moses finds the surface of the earth too congested with his parkways, he lifts the road into the air . . .") No politician wanted to make himself the target of the Commissioner's public wrath. Joseph A. Palma, up for re-election as borough president of Richmond County, had stated in May that the Aquarium should not be torn down. "It's a landmark," he had said forthrightly. "We've been destroying too many of our landmarks recently." In September, Palma said not a word—but voted for Moses' proposal. Newbold Morris, up for re-election as Council President, had stated in May that "if two million dollars has to be spent . . . I favor putting it into a tuberculosis hospital in Brooklyn." In September, Morris did not mention any tuberculosis hospital—and he voted for Moses' proposal. As for Fiorello H. La Guardia, who had supposedly mastered the city, he could have swayed Morris and the others if he had wanted to, and for a while he apparently wanted to. The Mayor agreed that the Aquarium's accessibility was a great civic asset, and friends saw that he had more than a little affection for the old building himself. In May, he and Moses had both been speakers at the opening of a new waterhole at the Bronx Zoo; Moses had cockily predicted that the Zoological Society could schedule a "fish chowder" at the Aquarium on October 1, for the valuable specimens would be up at the Zoo by that time; but La Guardia had stunned Moses by stating flatly, "He won't bring the fish to the Bronx." Whether political considerations were influencing the Mayor's thinking on the Aquarium in September is unknown, but the following sequence of events occurred: the right-wingers who dominated the Bronx and Queens Republican organizations—along with some key Republicans in other boroughs also determined to deny the Mayor a third term—offered Moses the nomination. Moses didn't want the nomination—he knew it was worthless without Fusion backing, which only La Guardia could obtain, and his understanding of the power of his public authorities made him uninterested in elective office—but he did not turn down the GOP nod out of hand, telling the leaders he was taking it under consideration. La Guardia felt he could not win without the nomination. Moses turned the nomination down. The old-line leaders then nominated John R. Davies, who would run against La Guardia in the primary election September 16. When the Moses proposal came before the Board, the Mayor's three votes were cast for it. Four days later, Moses announced his support of La Guardia, who won the primary by only 20,000. And a whole wave of park openings, at each of which Moses took pains to praise La Guardia, was then scheduled before the election, in which the Mayor narrowly defeated Democratic candidate William O'Dwyer. (There is no clearer proof of Moses' aura of invincibility than O'Dwyer's reaction to his loud support of the Mayor. Far from attacking the Park Commissioner, O'Dwyer assured the voters that he would continue him in office if he were elected.)

By October 1, after a September in which parents by the tens of thousands had brought their children to the Aquarium one last time, Moses could tell the Board of Estimate, "The fish are gone. . . . The Aquarium, therefore, as such, is a tale that has been told. We don't have to talk about that any more. The only question is . . . Fort Clinton." And, he said, consultant Clarke had found that demolition of the old fort was necessary for the complete reconstruction of Battery Park that he had in mind. The Board approved the demolition by an 11–5 vote. As in the bridge-tunnel controversy, no force in the city had been powerful enough to stand between Moses and his aims. There would, within a matter of months, have been—except for a plaque—no trace of the old fort had it not been for another force outside the city and beyond Moses' control: the Second World War.

To Moses' rage, the war stripped the city of manpower and heavy construction equipment so completely that no demolition company would bid on the job of leveling those massive solid stone walls. He let a smaller contract for the less difficult demolition of the circular sheet-iron roof that covered the fort, and by the fall of 1942 the roof was gone, and the interior of the fort, as well as the ground in front of it, was littered with debris. He was attempting again to get the rest of the job finished when the war gave the reformers another opportunity by halting work on the Brooklyn-Battery Tunnel. The reformers, realizing that neither the executive nor the legislative branch of the city government could stop Moses, made a last, desperate try to persuade the judicial branch to do the job, bringing suit to enjoin him from demolishing the rest of the building on the grounds that he had induced the Board to grant him permission through "false and fradulent representation"—namely, that the demolition was required by work on the tunnel. The judiciary could not restrain Moses—the reformers pressed the appeal to the Court of Appeals, but each court found, in effect, that Moses had virtually absolute power in city parks. But the last appeal was not heard until April 1943, and by that time the equipment and manpower shortage had reached a stage where even Moses realized it was useless to attempt any further demolition until the war was over.

It would be more than five years before work on the Brooklyn-Battery Tunnel was resumed. There was no reason why Battery Park should have been closed during those five years. But closed it was. The gates in the high wooden fences that Moses had erected around it, fences too high for passers-by to see over, remained locked.

The city's press had assumed that the fight over the old fort was ended—had been over, in fact, from the moment Moses had made his decision about it. Commenting on one of his fierce attacks on the reformers, the *Herald Tribune* had said, "With the unleashing of that dread artillery, it is clear that Castle Clinton, along with the traditionalists, are done for." But the writer of that editorial must have been a young man; he must never have seen the "traditionalists"—in particular George McAneny—fighting for something they believed in. The old fort had become even dearer to the old man since Moses had proposed tearing it down. Shortly before his death in 1953, at the age of 84, McAneny was invited to contribute a memoir to the Oral History Research Collection at Columbia University. Most memoirs deal largely with the speaker's own life, and many display a desire for personal immortality. McAneny devoted the bulk of *his* memoir to a painstakingly detailed history of Fort Clinton; the immortality he desired was not for himself. "If I can save [the fort]," he said, "I'll feel I haven't lived in vain." Time and again during the war, the old man led groups of old men down to Washington to try to persuade the city's congressmen to persuade the National Park Service—skeptical of the fort's historic value because

Moses had gotten to them first—to designate the fort a national monument. He laid out the facts of the fort's history to literally scores of federal officials, all the way up to Harold Ickes (and possibly higher: whether Roosevelt personally intervened is unknown, although there are indications that the President may have taken a moment out from the war effort to do so), and the facts were irrefutable. No sooner had the war ended than Ickes told La Guardia that the National Park Service would take over the fort, restore it and maintain it forever if the city allowed it to do so. Moses could no longer argue that the structure would be too expensive to restore and maintain. But, thanks to the high fence, he had a new argument ready. The demolition already accomplished, he said, had left nothing of the fort except two walls, which were caving in. The question of restoring the fort was now academic, he said; there was too little of the fort left to restore. The public could not, of course, determine for itself if this was true; those occasional reporters whom Moses had his aides escort over the site saw no reason to doubt his story—the sheet-iron roof of the Aquarium was gone and so was much of the two-story stucco façade, the pillars that had held up the façade had been torn down, the only remnants of the fish tanks were piles of broken glass, and the debris from the roof and façade had been heaped all around the site (with a particularly large pile in front, blocking it off even more effectively from anyone trying to see it). The scene looked like the site of a typical—and almost completed—demolition job.

But McAneny persuaded Walter Binger to make a personal inspection. A day or two later, Binger was present at a mayoral reception at Gracie Mansion and noticed Moses talking earnestly to C. C. Burlingham. Later, Binger recalls, Burlingham said: "Bob Moses tells me that the fort is already largely demolished. He told me that so much of the fort has already been demolished that it *can't* be saved any more."

"That's a goddamned lie," Binger said.

Burlingham replied, "That is very strong language for you to use, Walter. I'll have to see it myself."

"I got the key [to the fence around the park] and I took him out there the next day," Binger says. "It looked like a battlefield. There were great piles of debris. He must have been all of ninety-five [actually eighty-eight]; he had a walking stick to help him along, but he jumped around like a goat. He was an amazing man. The fort was blocked from view by this pile of debris. He had to climb this high mound, and he looked down and there was the whole damn fort below him! I said to him, 'All that was demolished was the Aquarium.'

"CC was normally a great talker, but he didn't say anything for a while. He had had great faith in Moses; he had believed in him. He was terribly sad." Finally, the old man turned away with a single sentence: "Well, that's not what I was told." And the letter Burlingham wrote Moses the next day also consisted of one sentence:

"Dear Bob: M'avez trompé."

"Two days later," Binger says, "CC gets back a letter: 'Dear CC: Why pull this Anatole France stuff on me? It doesn't make it any better to be called a liar in French.' But he never attempted to deny it or anything." And he couldn't. To conceal his lie, Robert Moses had barred the city from its park for almost five years, but the lie had at last been uncovered. The fort stood—and McAneny's next trip was to the *Herald Tribune*, which sent an airplane over the site and published on its front page a photograph showing the fort intact.

McAneny resumed his trips to Washington. One audience with President Truman was enough to enlist him on the side of the fort, and pressure on the new mayor, Democrat William O'Dwyer, was increased until he agreed to ask the State Legislature for an act enabling the city to deed the fort to the federal government. The Legislature refused. McAneny went to Albany every week for months.

(He recalls: "Everyone up there would say when we approached them, 'Mr. Moses doesn't want this.'

" 'Well, of course he doesn't want it.'

" 'Well, we're going to stick to him,' etcetera and so on. 'He's a great man: he must know what he's talking about.' ")

In 1946, Congress was ready to pass the bill designating Fort Clinton a national monument. But, recalls Binger, "this would take six or eight months." Moses moved faster. At four o'clock one Friday afternoon, he got a new demolition authorization from the Board of Estimate. (O'Dwyer betrayed the reformers; McAneny confided, "He's not a very solid sort of person.") Leaving City Hall, the reformers huddled desperately. Binger had been toying with the idea of bringing a new suit—on the grounds that the fort was a monument and hence permission was required from the Municipal Art Commission for its destruction.

Says Binger: "I went to Paul Windels and I said, 'I have got to have some money right away to get a suit [started].' Paul suggested I call Robert [Dowling, president of the City Trust Company]. I said, 'I need money right away.' He said, 'How much do you need?' I said, 'How do I know? I need money for a top lawyer to take it through two or three courts. It'll cost a couple of thousand dollars.' He said, 'Okay, go ahead.' "

Binger hired Frederick Van Pelt Bryan, who "called Windels and said, 'I'm going to court Monday on this.' And that's when Paul Windels saved the fort. He said, 'Are you crazy? There won't be anything left of this fort Monday morning. He'll demolish it over the weekend.' This was all on a Friday, remember. 'You bring this to court in half an hour.' " Bryan did, and persuaded a Supreme Court Justice to sign an injunction, which was handed to Moses that evening.

How right Windels had been was proven when the reformers rushed to Battery Park the next morning to see if any damage had been done. In the brief hours before the injunction had been served on Moses, Binger recalls, he "had already burned those great doors." But McAneny showed again—year after year, in Washington and in Albany and in City Hall (and in one meeting with O'Dwyer in Gracie Mansion in which, upbraiding the Mayor for breaking his word on the fort, he spoke to him in words so eloquent that, Windels states, "if anything could have recalled that man to a sense of honor, George McAneny would have done it that day")—why young reformers had once stared at him with awe as he strode through the Bureau of Municipal Research. All Moses' lawyers couldn't outfox the old man; the purpose of the suit was delay—delay to stall demolition until Congress could pass a bill ordering the preservation of the fort as a "National Historic Monument"—and McAneny delayed, until, on July 18, 1950, almost ten years after Moses had announced that he was going to demolish Fort Clinton, the bill was passed, along with a $166,750 appropriation sufficient to restore it, including the doors Moses had burned. The old fort was saved.

The successful conclusion of the effort to save Castle Clinton was a victory of wide importance and interest in the cause of historical preservation [said Secretary of the Interior Oscar L. Chapman]. After . . . years of struggle and debate in New York City, in the courts, in the State Legislature and in Congress, the saving of Castle Clinton evidences a new and deeper recognition of the need of preserving the diminishing landmarks of our history as an essential part of our national heritage.

If those words were bitter to Moses, they were sweet to George McAneny. Gentlemen of his school, however, did not forget their manners even in moments of triumph. To a reporter who telephoned him with the news and asked for comment, McAneny gave two words, "Most gratifying"—and a long list, which he asked the reporter to print, of the names of all the men who deserved credit for the victory.

McAneny didn't list himself, but his friends rectified the omission. Stanley Isaacs said it most simply: "McAneny beat Moses."

If the reformers had scored a victory over Robert Moses, however, its dimensions were rather narrow.

Fort Clinton had been saved, but not the Aquarium. And the city therefore had to pay dearly for Robert Moses' revenge.

It had to pay dearly even in dollars and cents. To persuade the Board of Estimate to let him demolish the old Aquarium, Moses had guaranteed that a new one could be built for $2,000,000, and that the New York Zoological Society could and would foot the entire bill. In truth, however, there was never any real chance that the Zoological Society could raise $2,000,000—not that $2,000,000 was the amount that really had to be raised, anyway; the Zoological Society would later disclose that the real figure was $6,500,000. After La Guardia had vetoed the Bronx Zoo site, Moses picked one at Coney Island—and persuaded the Mayor to spend $1,000,000 additional in public funds to acquire it. The Zoological Society still could not raise the cash. When a new Aquarium was finally built, the cost of its construction had risen to $10,000,000—and every cent was paid by the city, so that satisfying Moses' private grudge with the reformers cost the city's taxpayers $11,000,000. Since he placed high admission fees on the new Aquarium—the old one was free, of course—and there seemed no prospect that these would ever be removed, the people of the city would actually be paying for Moses' revenge forever—or at least for as much of forever as the eye could, in 1974, reasonably foresee.

As for costs that could not be measured in money, the people of the city might be paying those forever, too. The Coney Island Aquarium wasn't opened until 1955, fourteen years after the Battery Aquarium was closed, so that an entire generation of New York children grew up without an opportunity of visiting any aquarium at all. As important as the exhibits in the old Aquarium, moreover, had been its ambience—a pungent and warm blend of age and familiarity and long affection and human scale, of busts of old singers and the flash of bright fish, of gloomy corners where one could neck with one's date, of being easy to get to and free, so that people could simply walk in as if it belonged to them. One might admire the new Aquarium; one could never love it.

For many New Yorkers, of course, the atmosphere in the new Aquarium wasn't going to matter very much. For the high admission fees Moses set for it insured that many New Yorkers were going to be able to visit it infrequently if at all. The poignance of this situation was accentuated by the location of the Aquarium at Coney Island, the lone bathing beach reachable by public transportation and therefore the one to which, because of Moses' class-separating policies, the city's poor were herded.

The city's middle and upper classes found it easy to use the Aquarium, of course. Moses had built a large parking field next to it so that they could come without using the subway.

But they didn't come. On weekdays and on non-beach weekends—on days when attendance at the old Aquarium had run, day after day, 7,000 per day—one can walk through bleak echoing halls and see only a handful of other human beings. Out of Robert Moses' grudge, the city got a new Aquarium, for which it paid $11,000,000. It did not, however, get an Aquarium it could use.

The reformers' victory was not even complete in the case of the fort they had saved.

The popular Aquarium within its walls had made the fort a busy, bustling place. Without the Aquarium, it was a circle of walls. As one perceptive observer put it, "Now it is [a monument]: to be looked at, but not used. Having achieved the status of *Art* (Architectural division), it is to be revered as a saintly relic, not involved in the life of the city." It is still history as it sits there in Battery Park, but it is dead history.

In his "Moses-approved" biography of Robert Moses, Cleveland Rodgers wrote that "the ten-year battle was ended, as in the Battery Bridge *vs.* Tunnel fight, by the intervention of the federal government with its long-range guns and superior financial resources." That analysis was correct. No weapon the city possessed—not executive, legislative or judicial—had been powerful enough to stand off Moses' attacks on one of its most beloved institutions. The Aquarium fight only reinforced the conclusion to which some of the most perceptive reformers had come after the Crossing fight: that, in Moses' chosen spheres of activity, the city no longer had much control over its own destiny.

This conclusion was made all the more bitter to the reformers because of their new insight into the character of this creature they believed they had played so large a role in creating.

Some of the old reformers still admired Moses, mainly because they felt that corruption, politics and red tape were so thick in the city that only a man of Moses' almost incredible energy, drive and strength of will could hack his way through it. "Bob Moses is an extremely capable man," Stanley Isaacs, always scrupulously evenhanded, would say in the same oral history in which he detailed so many of Moses' injustices and mistakes. "Properly controlled, he is a great asset to the city."

But these reformers were now in a very small minority. The verdict of other members of the city's Good Government movement on Moses was more harsh. "He is the most unethical man I have ever met," Walter Binger said. "He is a brilliant guy with a highly defective character." "He is the original smear artist," Lawrence Orton said. "Like Hitler," Albert Bard had said of him because of his technique of making one demand, and, as soon as it was met, making another, and, in years in which the name of the dread dictator glared blackly at every American from the front pages of the daily newspaper, this harsh comparison was drawn over and over again. "He is a liar," Walter Binger said. "And he is a liar the way Hitler was a liar. He doesn't lie because he can't help it. He lies as a matter of policy." The very overstatement in such remarks from men generally given to understatement reveals the intensity of revulsion many reformers felt for the man they had once idolized. William Chanler had used a word out of an earlier age—"bullyrag" ("He was just a natural bully")—to describe one of his tactics, and many reformers, men out of an earlier age, now used that expression in talking about Moses. They understood at last the fallacy of believing that his lack of interest in money automatically signified interest in serving the public—and that that was his only interest. They had come to see his other interest, and to understand that in the long run that interest might, when present in a public official with immense, all but uncontrollable power, turn out to be more inimical to the city than financial greed. Al Smith's close friend John A. Coleman, the multimillionaire "Pope of Wall Street" who came out of the Lower East Side with limited education but unlimited shrewdness, said: "Some men aren't satisfied unless they have caviar. Moses would have been happy with a ham sandwich—and power."

31. Monopoly

THE SECOND WORLD WAR gave Robert Moses a second chance to destroy the New York City Tunnel Authority and thus obtain the monopoly he had previously been denied over all revenue-producing water crossings within the city.

He didn't pass it up.

With the Tunnel Authority's continued existence and expansion apparently insured by its victory in the Battery Crossing battle, its twin tubes had hardly begun pushing out toward each other from the Battery and Brooklyn when Ole Singstad was drawing plans for a third Authority project, a seven-story, 1,050-space Battery Parking Garage which would provide a half million dollars' additional annual revenue, and for a fourth, the Narrows Crossing, which would be the largest single public work ever constructed in New York (and which Moses had long wanted to build himself).

Shortly after the war began, however, Moses was appointed director of the "industrial phase" of the city's scrap-metal drive, and before he resigned from the post in just seven weeks (most of his scrapping was done with federal officials), he publicly recommended that the federal War Production Board (WPB) requisition 28,000 tons of "steel" tunnel-lining segments from the Authority, melt them down for scrap and order all work on the tunnel halted for the duration because it would "take four years to build [and] can serve no possible war service."

Not only was that a statement made by a man who was continually arguing that traffic projects were vital for defense; it was as misleading as those he had made in 1939 in his attempt to keep the tunnel from being started. The tunnel would, indeed, take four years to build—but not, as Moses implied, four *more* years. Work had already been under way for two years; two more would finish it. And the tunnel lining was not steel at all but cast iron with a phosphorus content too high to allow its effective use in war production.

In 1942's wartime atmosphere, however, his statement accomplished his purpose. While canceling most large construction projects, the WPB had quietly let the tunnel proceed because there was no other work in their field for the 1,200 sandhogs, most of them too old for military service, employed on the job, because the tunnel tubes on which $15,000,000 had already been invested might be ruined by water seepage if left unlined—

and because the lining segments were not suitable for war production. But the WPB was understandably skittish about public reaction if the continuation of work on the tunnel was spotlighted. After Moses switched on the spotlight, a furious La Guardia declared that his recommendation "does not represent the policy of this administration. . . . In the first place, that 'available steel' is not steel. It is cast iron." But Moses reiterated his recommendation, the press reprinted it and the WPB accepted it. "I'm glad to see that they're doing the right thing," Moses crowed.

All through the war, the tunnel lay empty and unused, a vast, hollow, echoing cavern beneath the waters of the Upper Bay, and its toll booths stood silent, earning no revenue.

And the Tunnel Authority needed revenue. If the war-caused traffic drought could bring even Triborough, with five years of profitable operations behind it and the combined income of six toll-producing facilities to draw upon, to the verge of economic collapse, its impact was even more damaging on an authority whose single usable facility had been completed barely a year before Pearl Harbor. The Tunnel Authority's income did not cover the interest on its bonds. Because the Authority had $4,000,000 (the $4,000,000 Singstad had saved on the cost of the Queens-Midtown Tunnel) in the bank to help pay the interest until the war ended, and because the Reconstruction Finance Corporation, which had purchased the bonds, was willing to wait for the balance ("This is a forty- or fifty-year project," RFC officials told Authority general manager Fearson Shortridge), the interest shortfall would not have been significant—had it not been for Moses. He used it as an opening to employ with La Guardia the technique he had so often been accused of employing against anyone who stood in his way. His own experts' analyses, Moses said, showed that the Queens-Midtown bonds, purchased by the RFC for $48,000,000, would *never* be resalable at face value. Even after the war, no one would pay more than $20,000,000 for them. And when the Brooklyn-Battery Tunnel opened, he told the Mayor, the situation would be even worse; that tunnel, he said flatly, "cannot sustain $57,000,000 in bonds." "Someone, presumably the federal government, will have to stand a loss on the two projects of close to $50,000,000," if, indeed, the second project could ever be finished at all without tremendous new financing, a prospect about which he had serious doubts. And, Moses told the Mayor, he had ascertained that the reason for this impending disaster was Singstad's lack of engineering ability, combined with management so inept that its disclosure would cause a scandal. The Tunnel Authority, he said—hammering home the word repeatedly in confidential memos to the Mayor—was in a real "mess." And by 1944 he was beginning to hint strongly that there was only one way out of the mess: to "rescue" the Tunnel Authority by letting Triborough take it over.

"Mess? What mess?" Ole Singstad demanded when the author used the word during an interview. "I didn't know we were in any mess at all. I didn't hear anything about it." Told about Moses' memos—he had never known of their existence before—he shouted, pounding his desk, "There was no mess! We didn't have to be rescued at all. We were not in financial difficulties! Certainly not!" Though Singstad's statement is an exaggeration, so was Moses'; the Tunnel Authority's difficulties were no worse than Triborough's, were due not to mismanagement—its operations were actually far more economical than Moses'—but to war, and were obviously curable by the same medicine that would cure Triborough's: peace. Letters from RFC Chairman Jesse Jones to Singstad, moreover, indicate that Jones had no doubts about this.

Even had he known about Moses' innuendos, however, Singstad did not possess the entrée to La Guardia that would have enabled him to disprove them, and the Mayor, racing around the country as national civil defense head, had no time to spend learning the truth for himself. Mayoral memos began to display marked irritation with the Tunnel Authority.

And then Moses was presented with even juicier grist for his mill.

Try as they would, his bloodhounds had not been able to come up with even a hint of wrongdoing by Singstad. But in 1941 someone did bring to Moses a hint of wrongdoing by Singstad's brother-in-law—and that was all Moses needed.

Twelve years before, while the Port Authority, for which Singstad was then chief consulting engineer, was considering plans for the Manhattan entrance plaza of the Lincoln Tunnel, the brother-in-law had purchased eight tenements in the area finally selected. Singstad swore that he had no financial interest in the purchase, that he had never heard of the purchase until after it was completed, that when he had learned about it—during a casual conversation—he had violently disapproved, and in fact had forced his brother-in-law to reduce his asking price from $365,000 to $165,000. The conclusive piece of evidence, to an impartial observer, may have been the fact that Singstad did not *want* the plaza located in the area in which his brother-in-law's tenements were located; his recommendation, for which he fought for two years, would have left them uncondemned—and his brother-in-law with no profit at all. The tenements were condemned only because the Authority overruled Singstad and decided to locate the plaza where its chief engineer, Othmar H. Ammann, wanted it. Two intensive investigations—one by the Port Authority, one by the Tunnel Authority—turned up not a single piece of evidence to prove that the peppery little Norwegian's statements were anything less than completely true. The single damaging fact was his failure to tell the Port Authority when he learned his brother-in-law owned the property, and, says Windels, his attorney, the engineer had a reason for not telling: "He was afraid that someone like Moses would find out and smear him with it."

This fear turned out to be justified. The Port Authority found Singstad innocent of every charge except failing to report his brother-in-law's holdings, for which offense, in light of the other exonerating evidence, it gave the engineer only a mild censure. At least one board member expressed "great regret" that the Authority had dignified the accusations even to that extent. The Tunnel Authority's official report not only also absolved Singstad of any wrongdoing but stated that the innuendos which started the investigation were "unjust, unfair and untrue." But Moses, after apparently giving La

Guardia an oral version of the affair, obtained and passed along to the Mayor, "for your confidential information," a transcript of the Port Authority hearings—along with a covering letter of his own that bore the Moses stamp. "This will tell you the Singstad story," Moses wrote. "You will see that in the end, Singstad and his family did not succeed in getting the high price they demanded in condemnation."

No one but Moses, of course, had even suggested that Singstad had demanded a high condemnation price. Two investigations, in fact, had concluded that, whatever price was paid, Singstad was not going to get a penny of it. But to find out how misleading Moses' letter was, La Guardia would have had to wade through the lengthy, complicated hearing transcript. And Moses' letter went further. To undercut the Port Authority's exoneration of Singstad, he quoted his old friend Authority vice chairman Howard S. Cullman as telling him in private: "It is my understanding that [Singstad] more than told untruths throughout the whole situation, and it was finally ferreted out that he himself had approximately $50,000 invested therein."

Whether Cullman actually said this to Moses cannot be determined—Cullman refuses to discuss the investigation—but if he did, his charge is disproven by two separate investigations. Moreover, the best proof of whether Moses himself really believed what he was telling the Mayor is the Park Commissioner's own subsequent actions: in 1944, Jack Madigan, attempting again on Moses' behalf to persuade Singstad to undermine his own commissioners, assured the engineer that if he did so and thereby helped Moses take over the Authority, he could remain its chief engineer as long as he wished. (Singstad refused the offer.) But Moses' letter had the desired effect. The Mayor, who at the time believed that his long campaign for national office was about to be capped with success, was desperate to avoid a scandal. He knew that Moses was capable of creating such a scandal if he was not given his way. "Moses kept wearing him down, talking about a 'mess,' always pressing him, wearing him down, wearing him down," Windels says. And when, in 1945, Moses was presented with an opportunity to take over the Tunnel Authority without public fuss, La Guardia, who had been holding out against such a takeover for nine years—ever since the day in 1936 when he had instructed Reuben Lazarus, "Leave the son of a bitch off"—held out no longer.

The opportunity arose because the Tunnel Authority commissioners—novices in the political arena and unaware of the potentialities for power in their Authority—had not grasped the fact that someone was trying to take it over. Thinking of the Authority only as a builder of public works, they believed that as long as they were building public works competently and honestly, the Mayor would continue them in office. Not seeing the threat posed to them by Moses' ambition, they gave Moses the opening he needed.

Their error was not one of commission but only of omission. It occurred after one of the three members of the Tunnel Authority, Albert T. Johnston, died, in 1943.

With the Authority unable to proceed with any projects during the war, the other two members, Alfred B. Jones and William H. Friedman, saw no necessity for the vacancy to be immediately filled. "I think that if Jones and Friedman had recommended another man, La Guardia would have followed the recommendation," Singstad says. "But they didn't think there was any pressing haste." The only name submitted was submitted—secretly—by Moses: Howard S. Cullman. La Guardia, his defenses not yet weakened to the point of caving in, rejected that recommendation, but no one gave him another, and, in the rush of more pressing affairs, Johnston's seat remained unfilled. And as a result, when, on July 1, 1945, Friedman's term expired, there would be vacant not one but two seats—a majority, enough for a takeover and, moreover, for a quiet takeover that could be accomplished simply by the apparently routine filling of two vacancies and that therefore would not lead, as a more dramatic change in management might lead, to press curiosity that carried the threat of scandal.

Friedman and Jones had no inkling of what was happening until it had happened. With the expiration of his first term on the Authority drawing near six years earlier, Friedman had sent a brief note reminding the Mayor of that fact, and the Mayor had promptly reappointed him. Now, expecting a similar sequence, Friedman on June 15, 1945, sent La Guardia a similar note. But when he received the Mayor's reply this time, the key phrases that jumped out at him were, to his shock: "My dear Bill . . . splendid services . . . You were one of the pioneers. . . . For some time I have been considering the reorganization of the Tunnel Authority and believe that great economies may be effectuated. Therefore I will be able to relieve you of your duties when your term expires. . . ."

"Friedman had been a good friend of the Mayor's," Singstad recalls. "He was the most surprised man in the world." Understanding of the reason behind La Guardia's decision came only when he read (in brief, inside-page articles) that the Mayor had announced that, in the interest of undefined "economies," he had decided to merge the Tunnel and Triborough authorities, and, while the details of the major refinancing and new bond issue required were being worked out, to "interlock" the two bodies by placing them under the same management—Triborough's management, as it turned out, for he appointed to the two Tunnel Authority vacancies Robert Moses and his Triborough sidekick, banker George V. (the Fifth) McLaughlin.

To try to gain the third vote on the board—required on all major contracts—Moses shouted at Jones, a quiet, meek Quaker, at board meetings, and insulted him to his face. When Jones tried to counter this tactic by refusing to attend meetings, Moses wrote him: "There are just two courses open to you." One is resignation, "the sensible thing for you to do. . . . If you decline to do this . . . we shall have to ask the Mayor to remove you . . . on the basis of charges which we shall prefer." And these charges, he said, "will necessarily include reference to . . . the various messes which the Authority was in when the Mayor decided to reorganize it." Jones, no politician—he had accepted the Authority post only because it would give him the opportunity to render a public service—suddenly found that continuing to hold the job would involve his name in scandal; even though no "messes" existed, the Authority's war-caused financial difficulties would make it easy to convince the public that they did, particularly if they were made public in the context of "charges" lodged against him. With his choices narrowed down to two—resignation or dishonor—on April 24, 1946, he resigned, to be replaced by Charles G. Meyer, the other member of Moses' Triborough Board.

Fearson Shortridge, who for years had been meeting Moses on the Gracie Terrace promenade while the two men were walking their dogs in the evening, had believed "we were very friendly personally." Now he found that either he had been mistaken or friendship did not count for much with Moses: Moses fired him, appointing George Spargo in his place, without a word of warning; I "found out about it by reading *The New York Times*," Shortridge recalls. Moses also fired Ole Singstad, of course, replacing him as the Authority's chief engineer with a Yale classmate, Ralph Smillie, and he fired men who had been no more than innocent bystanders in his long feud with the Norwegian—the engineers whom Singstad had recruited from all over the United States.

For nine years, Robert Moses had been seeking control of the Tunnel Authority. Now he had control. He had been unable to prevent the construction of the Authority's Queens-Midtown and Brooklyn-Battery tunnels, but now those tunnels—and their revenues—were his. New York was a city divided by water, split by rivers and bays. Every modern water crossing within the city's borders, not only those above the water but those beneath it, not only every bridge but every tunnel constructed within the city's borders for the use of motor vehicles since 1909, was now under the control of authorities that he controlled. More important, all new water crossings would also be under his control.

The city was obviously not in the foreseeable future going to be able to build new water crossings itself. Only the authorities—his authorities—would be able to build them. He and he alone would be able to decide which crossings would be built and when, what their shape and design would be and where their approach roads would run.

He and he alone, moreover, would decide what tolls would be charged on these crossings. For with his takeover of the Tunnel Authority, he now possessed a monopoly over those public facilities for motor transportation within the city which produced revenue.

America's nineteenth-century robber barons had understood the importance of monopoly, absolute monopoly. They had not been satisfied until they had eliminated all competitors.

Robert Moses, whose aim was not economic but political power but whose power would have to rest not on political but on economic factors, had understood that competition was a threat to his aims. He had schemed for ten years to remove that threat, to obtain over all modern water crossings within New York—the water crossings that were a key to all automobile transportation within the city—an absolute monopoly.

And now he had that monopoly. Henceforth, for the remaining quarter of a century in which he would be in power, no motorist would be able to use a modern bridge or tunnel in New York City without paying his authorities tribute.

The struggles by which the industrial robber barons had built up their empires broke into public view infrequently. For the most part, only the results were announced. The battles which decided the results took place in secret.

So did the battle which cemented Robert Moses' economic power. His public battle against the Tunnel Authority—his campaign of thundering press releases and barrages of statistics designed to persuade the city and its officials that the Battery Crossing should be a bridge and not a tunnel—had failed. The battle in which he destroyed the Tunnel Authority was one shrouded from beginning to end in secrecy. The stakes involved were vast. They included not only control of two of the largest public works projects in America but also the right to build and control a public work that would be far larger than either: the Narrows Crossing. They included the right to award contracts for the completion of the Brooklyn-Battery Tunnel, the Battery Parking Garage and the Narrows Crossing, contracts that would total more than half a billion dollars, with all the immense patronage and power that such a right conferred, and also the right to dispose of the immense annual revenues these three projects and the Queens-Midtown Tunnel would generate, revenues that by 1968 would be running more than $30,000,000 per year. They included the capitalization power of this annual $30,000,000—to build more public works that would generate more cash: capitalization power that by 1968 would amount to half a billion dollars more. And cash—even half a billion dollars in cash—was only a small part of the stakes involved. The significance of the battle went far beyond economics. For at stake also was the issue of whether control of revenue-producing water crossings in the city would in effect be turned over to a single individual, of whether one man would be given a monopoly over all toll receipts paid by motor vehicles in a great city largely dependent upon motor transportation. For concentrating economic power in motor transportation within the city in one man would give that man a voice in all transportation policies within the city at least equal to that of the city itself. But the city itself never was given an opportunity to learn the battle's significance, or to watch it unfold. All during 1942, 1943 and 1944, while Moses and Singstad were maneuvering with RFC officials or La Guardia, while Moses was smearing Singstad and the Tunnel Authority was clearing him, not a single story on the maneuvering appeared in any newspaper. Not a word even hinting at the existence of a behind-the-scenes conflict between the two public authorities was printed.

* * *

Moses had repeatedly ridiculed not only Singstad's honesty but his engineering ability.

He had written La Guardia: "We do not trust Mr. Singstad. We have another man, much more competent and much more reliable, to take his place." Whether he himself believed what he was saying may be judged by his actions. Singstad's plans for the Brooklyn-Battery Tunnel were used with only one modification of any substance. (And this modification—the use of a different method of waterproofing—caused the one engineering flaw in the tunnel, a persistent seepage that eventually had to be corrected—by reverting to Singstad's method.) Moreover, Moses' emissaries asked Singstad to continue with his plans for the Battery Parking Garage, down to the most detailed blueprints and contract specifications. Moses never discussed Singstad's plans with him. He went out of his way to avoid having to meet Singstad face to face. Singstad worked on them alone in his own office. But as each set was completed, Moses' engineers came to the Norwegian and took them, and used them—as drawn.

Singstad took an office—at 17 Battery Place—whose windows looked down on Battery Park, on the portals of the tunnel that was his greatest creation and on Fort Clinton, whose sight he treasured for another reason: "Mr. Moses said it was going to fall down," the fiery Norwegian would laugh to visitors, pointing down at the red walls that looked solid indeed. "Well, it's still standing, isn't it? Its foundations are carried down to solid rock, you know." And then, one palm pounding his desk, he would laugh, a short, harsh laugh that was more like a snort, and say, "Solid rock! I knew that. And Moses' engineers knew it, too."

If Singstad could still laugh twenty-four years later at the recollection of his fight with Moses, the laughs came noticeably hard—and this was understandable. For Moses' revenge on him was thorough.

While Moses was completing the Brooklyn-Battery Tunnel, he and Spargo took care to leave with reporters chronicling its construction the impression that Singstad had had little to do with its final form. Most of the reporters' stories scarcely mentioned him. When preparations for the opening ceremonies—elaborate preparations; not only the gleaming new parking garage and the white tunnel portals and access roads but the façades of adjacent office buildings, including 17 Battery Place, were draped with bunting, flags and mammoth pennons in a display of pageantry that transformed gray Lower Manhattan into a panorama of red, white and blue—were going forward, Singstad had to watch them from his window and know that he had not even been invited to the opening of the tunnel he had designed. (He was invited, on the day before the opening, apparently only because a *Herald Tribune* reporter raised the matter with one of Moses' lieutenants, and Moses did not want any stories on the injustice.) And when he read the brochure, twenty-eight glossy pages, printed in four colors, distributed in the thousands to the distinguished guests who were to ride through the tunnel in a long cavalcade led by the Mayor and Francis Cardinal Spellman, his cup of bitterness must have spilled over. The brochure listed twenty-one separate engineers as designers of facets of the project. The name of its true designer was not among them.

Robert Moses could hate a long time. Ole Singstad was to continue practicing engineering until he died, at the age of eighty-seven, in 1969, twenty-four years after Robert Moses forced him out of the Tunnel Authority. During those twenty-four years, Singstad was to cement his reputation as the world's master tunnel builder, and exhibit a genius for highway design as well. He was to build tunnels and huge highways all over the United States, and all over Europe and South America, receiving knighthoods and medals for his work in Norway and Belgium and Chile. But he was never—during all those twenty-four years—to design or build a mile of highway in New York City or New York State, the city and state in which he lived.

Shortly before his death, he was asked about this anomaly by the author, who mentioned that "at one time you were the most highly regarded tunnel authority in the world." Singstad's head snapped up and the palm of his unusually large right hand smacked down, and he glanced at the interviewer with a look that made it all too easy to see why Ole Singstad had been so dangerous an opponent. "Yeah," he said. "And I still am. And I'll tell you this. In spite of my reputation, since I retired as chief engineer of the Tunnel Authority—I told his Mr. Gumshoer Boy that I wouldn't be happy working with Moses when he tried to talk me into giving up my commissioners—since I retired after thirty-three years in the service of some subdivision of the state government, thirty-three years! Since that time, the state has spent hundreds and hundreds of millions of dollars on work that I have done and could do, but I haven't had a single job from the State of New York. Not one! Just the other day, we were turned down for a highway job on Long Island. And I have been told by a friend in Albany, 'You are wasting your time trying to get jobs there as long as Robert Moses is living.' Ever since I retired, he has been hurting me in the pocketbook. And he has been hurting me in the pride. Ever since!"

Singstad stood up, with astonishing violence for a man in his eighties, walked over to the window and looked down. It was a bleak January day and the wind whipping against the glass from off the Upper Bay was cold and bitter. It had piled snow against the red sandstone walls of the old fort.

But the walls looked mighty solid all the same, and Singstad muttered, half under his breath, "All lies and fabrications. Lies and fabrications." And then, after a while, he said, aloud, "I'm not sorry. A. B. Jones was a Quaker, and Quakers don't fight, but he was a wonderful man. He was a very wonderful man. All my commissioners were wonderful men. I'm not sorry at all."

But then the old man fell silent again, looking out over the Battery and across the Bay toward Brooklyn, and when he finally spoke again, after a long time, he spoke in a very low voice and what he said was: "Ever since. Ever since."

Even after the war, no one would pay more than $20,000,000 for the $48,000,000 in Queens-Midtown Tunnel bonds, Moses had said. As for the Brooklyn-Battery Tunnel, he had said it would "never sustain" the $57,000,000 in bonds it had cost.

Such predictions of financial disaster unless the Tunnel Authority was "rescued" by using the revenues from his profitable bridges to "bail out" its bankrupt tunnels had helped Moses take it over. During the rest of his life, he would, at every opportunity, attempt to prove that this was in fact what had happened.

In reality, the Queens-Midtown Tunnel began earning almost enough to pay all expenses, including the interest on its bonds, practically from the day the war ended; by 1949, it was earning a tidy annual surplus as well. As long as he didn't control that tunnel, Moses had argued that improved access from Queens was unnecessary; as soon as he took it over, he said improved access was imperative—with the opening of his Horace Harding Expressway, forerunner of the Long Island Expressway, tunnel traffic soared, as Singstad had predicted it would, to levels at which its annual surpluses became huge.

Moses had said that the Brooklyn-Battery Tunnel would be lucky to carry 9,000,000 cars per year. In its first full year of operation, the tunnel carried more than 15,000,000 cars. Singstad's tunnel earned Moses $5,485,000 in tolls that year—more than was earned by the Bronx-Whitestone Bridge, more, in fact, than was earned by the Henry Hudson, Marine Parkway and Cross Bay bridges combined. In its first year of operation, in fact, the tunnel earned more than 20 percent of Triborough's total revenues—enough to "sustain" not $57,000,000 but $133,000,000 in bonds.

The two tunnels took off from there. By 1965 they would be providing close to a third of Triborough's total revenue. Moses had predicted financial disaster for them. Instead there was financial triumph. He had said they would have to be "salvaged" by the rest of Triborough's projects. In fact, if there was any salvaging to be done, it was not of but by Singstad's tunnels; their huge surpluses helped Moses' profitable bridges—the Henry Hudson and Triborough and the Bronx-Whitestone—"salvage" ones like the Cross Bay and Marine Parkway which did not earn enough to amortize their bonds.

Not that those facts deterred Moses, of course. In 1969, he wrote in *Public Works: A Dangerous Trade*: "The [Triborough] Authority . . . salvaged the two tunnnel bond issues . . . In effect, this meant pledging bridge tolls after all present bridge bonds were retired . . ."

32. *Quid Pro Quo*

No Tammany man can rise above the local machine. Governor Smith achieved that distinction, but Albany is a long way from the Bowery.

A return to the city of Tammany would be a counsel of despair. People elsewhere would say that water cannot rise above its own level and that the level in New York is contemptibly and irretrievably low.

—ROBERT MOSES, 1941

ON THE BIG DESK in the far corner of the big room in City Hall, among the litter of maps and letters, corncob pipes and spare eyeglasses and the narrow rack holding the six buzzers, there sat now, always, a small bottle of white pills. And more and more frequently now, the little man behind the desk would press both hands hard against his back and hold them there for long minutes, his swarthy face turned gray.

Whether or not Fiorello La Guardia knew in 1945 that he was dying of cancer—and no associate would be able to say for sure later whether he did or not—he was learning that pain could drain even his once-limitless energy (once, talking with a reporter at the end of a long day, he suddenly said, with real surprise in his voice, "Well, I guess I'm tired, too"), and perhaps the sixty-two-year-old Mayor wondered whether he would be physically able to win another victory in the ruthless political arena, where weakness is not pitied but exploited. The odds against victory had never been longer. His frantic grasping for higher office and ludicrous posturing in his wartime jobs had eroded his popularity so deeply that in early 1945 a *Daily News* straw poll showed that only one out of every four New Yorkers favored his re-election. Roosevelt was dead, Truman antagonized by his antics; if he sallied forth again against a Democratic candidate, in a city in which seven out of every nine registered voters were Democrats, he would no longer be able to count on "benevolent neutrality" from the White House. And the candidate would be Tammany-backed William O'Dwyer, who had given him such a tough fight in 1941, who would be able to ride into the arena this time with a brigadier general's stars, bestowed for wartime service that looked good at least on paper, glittering on his shoulders—and who had led him in the *News* poll. The old coalition which he had led out against the Democrats before had dissolved behind him. Republican leaders, incensed because, in his drive for personal power, he had refused them patronage, were determined, once and for all, to deny him their party's nomination. Reform leaders—men interested in principles rather than patronage—felt that he had, in maneuvers such as downgrading the City Planning Commission and ousting Kern and Sayre and Stanley Isaacs, betrayed those principles; the Citizens Union wanted another Fusion campaign, but one with a new knight at its head. And when, in the spring of 1945, the Mayor appealed secretly first to the City Fusion Party and then to GOP leaders for their endorsement and was humiliatingly rebuffed, he announced publicly that he had decided that twelve years as Mayor was enough for any man, that he would not run again and that he would support instead an independent "No Deal" ticket headed by reformer Newbold Morris.

The events that followed that announcement brought the career of Robert Moses full circle. For Moses, who had so long and so violently despised Tammany Hall and all that it stood for, who had called Tammany "a rotten political machine," who had spent the first years of his career fighting it, who had understood so well that the essence of the machine, the motivation of its leaders, men he said were interested only in "dough," in "obscurely making a living out of politics," never changed, who had asked so eloquently in 1933, "Do you think that the Currys, McCooeys, Farleys and Flynns are in any essential respect different from the Murphys, McCooeys, McCabes and McCalls of the cartoons of a generation ago?," who had warned voters in three separate mayoral campaigns that they must never let Tammany return to power, who had said during the 1941 campaign that "a return to the city of Tammany would be a counsel of despair," who had said of Tammany's 1941 candidate, the same William O'Dwyer who was its candidate now, "No Tammany man can rise above the local machine"—this same Robert Moses, during the entire campaign, never once criticized Tammany or its candidate. His lone public statement ostensibly supported Newbold Morris but also mentioned O'Dwyer favorably. And he supported O'Dwyer's running mate, Lazarus Joseph, whom La Guardia called "Flynn's messenger boy."

Men who knew Moses were waiting for the *quid* commensurate with the invaluable *quo* he had bestowed on Tammany Hall. They did not even have to wait until the campaign ended. In a paid announcement over WJZ four days before the election—a date selected to maximize Election Day impact while still allowing ample time for press reaction—O'Dwyer disclosed that "shortly" after his nomination in August, he had conferred with "this valuable public servant" and had asked him to be a part of his administration if he was elected—and not merely as Park Commissioner and Triborough Authority chairman. He had told Moses, O'Dwyer said, that if he was elected he would immediately create a new post to handle a vast program of postwar public works construction, a "Coordinator of Construction" with sweeping powers not only over parks, parkways, bridges and tunnels, but over the construction of public housing, the field from which Moses had been barred by La Guardia—over, indeed, the construction of *all* major public works of any type in the City of New York. He had asked Moses, O'Dwyer said, if he would be willing to accept that post.

"I am happy to announce," O'Dwyer said, "that he has agreed to render this important public service."

Disbelieving reporters telephoned Moses at his apartment. "It's true," he said.

Not that O'Dwyer needed any help—he won in a landslide—but Moses' agreement provided the Tammany candidate with valuable protective coloration. Press reaction was precisely what O'Dwyer's advisers had foreseen it would be. His announcement "was seen today as answering charges of waste should the Democratic-ALP candidate win Tuesday's election," the *Post* reported. "We like . . . the announcement better than any news we've heard yet in connection with the mayoralty campaign," said the *News*. "Big Bob the Builder Moses is one of the ablest public servants in this or any other city. It would be tough to see him step out of the public service picture."

There was, however, puzzlement among the editorial writers: how could Robert Moses—the foe of corrupt machine politicians, the man who would never compromise his principles or make "deals," who would not give politicians inside information or patronage or award contracts to political favorites—manage to run construction in an administration which would be dominated by elements to which construction deals, inside information, patronage and contract favoritism were a way of life. The *Herald Tribune*, which was supporting Jonah J. Goldstein, the Republican-Liberal candidate, and was careful to note that Goldstein had also promised to keep Moses on, said that while "the O'Dwyer statement is good politics and even better, it is good common sense . . . a question still remains: How long? How long would Mr. Moses last under an administration that was dominated by the more raffish and corrupt elements of Tammany Hall? At a good guess we would give him about six weeks."

The guess, off by approximately fifteen years, was about as good as the assumption that underlay it, an assumption revealing only the depth of the misapprehension about Moses' true character. For the Robert Moses about whom the *Herald Tribune* was editorializing hadn't existed for a long time. The Robert Moses of 1945 was not the foe of the practical politician but the essence of that peculiar animal. He was the complete realist. Willing, in order to accomplish his purposes—purposes which in 1945 revolved around the retention and acquisition of power—to throw onto the table any chip he held, he had, in the election of 1945, with a chance to obtain more power than he had ever possessed before, thrown onto the table the most valuable of all his chips: his name.

The drama that was the relationship between Fiorello Henry La Guardia and Robert Moses had been played out for twelve years in the brightest of spotlights. Its last scene was played out in semi-darkness: the gloom of an upstairs bedroom in the small, heavily mortgaged house in Riverdale, the only thing La Guardia owned besides $8,000 in United States War Bonds, in which, nineteen months after he had left office, the wasted little bundle of a man that had once been the Little Flower lay behind drawn shades, waiting to die.

"When the Mayor sent for me late in the summer of 1947," Moses has related, "I was shocked at the change in him. He was in bed, so shrunken, so chapfallen and yet so spunky, and so obviously on the way out. To tell the truth, I felt like crying."

Long after La Guardia died, Walter Binger recalled for the author a conversation he had had with the ex-Mayor in 1946, when La Guardia had still been able to get downtown to his beloved Engineers Club for lunch.

"La Guardia was eating alone in the corner," Binger says. "I was eating at the center table, and I noticed that he was looking very gloomy, and after lunch I went up to him and I said, 'How's things, Major?'

"He said he had just been thinking about the city, and then he said, 'Moses has got too much power up here now.' "

Binger, who hated Moses for what he had done to Isaacs, and who had hoped in vain for years that La Guardia would take a firm stand against Moses at last, says that La Guardia looked so unhappy while he was saying this that he was moved to put his arm around the little Mayor's shoulders. But he couldn't resist asking as he did so, "Well, Major, who gave it to him?"

At that, Binger recalls, La Guardia looked even sadder. Finally, he said, "Yes, but I could control him. Now no one will be able to control him."

The first part of the ex-Mayor's statement was not completely accurate. The second part was.

33. Leading Out the Regiment

The papers and some people are always ready to find wrong motives in what us statesmen do. If we bring about some big improvement that benefits the city and it just happens, as a sort of coincidence, that we make a few dollars out of the improvement, they say we are grafters. But we are used to this kind of ingratitude. It falls to the lot of all statesmen, especially Tammany statesmen. All we can do is to bow our heads in silence and wait till time has cleared our memories.

Just think of mentionin' dishonest graft in connection with the name of George Washington Plunkitt, the man who gave the city its magnificent chain of parks, its Washington Bridge, its Speedway, its Museum of Natural History, its One Hundred and Fifty-fifth Street Viaduct and its West Side Courthouse! I was the father of the bills that provided for all these; yet . . . some people have questioned my honest motives. If that's the case, how can you expect legislators to fare who are not the fathers of the parks, the Washington Bridge, the Speedway and the Viaduct?

—STATE SENATOR GEORGE WASHINGTON PLUNKITT (COMMANDER IN CHIEF OF THE BLACK HORSE CAVALRY), 1905

BEFORE THE WAR, Robert Moses had employed his leverage with a force not responsible to New York City's voters but possessed of considerable influence over the city's government—New York State—to compel the city to give him a free hand in certain areas of public works. Hardly had the war ended when another outside force, the federal government, began to loom larger and larger over the city. And Moses, with his aims for the city now enlarged—enlarged to a point at which they involved in effect the reshaping of its entire public estate—employed that force too to compel the city to accept his aims as its own.

The scale of the new federal involvement in urban America was unprecedentedly massive. Before the war—during the entire Depression—the federal government had financed a total of 200,000 low-income apartments. Within the first four years after the war, the federal government authorized the financing of 810,000 low-income apartments. In 1949, Title I of a new Federal Housing Act codified a new concept—urban renewal—that insured that Washington's role would henceforth be as crucial as City Hall's not only on low-income housing but in most major urban reshapings. Before the war federal aid built mainly highways in the open countryside. The Federal-Aid Highway Act of 1944 authorized arterial routes within city limits as well, and with each postwar federal highway act the proposed urban mileage soared; the Interstate Highway Act of 1956 empowered the government in Washington to trowel down 6,700 miles of roads within the cities of America.

Most Depression-era federal aid had, moreover, been funneled into the cities through the cities' governments or through new agencies such as housing "authorities" set up and controlled by the cities' governments. Nowhere had this been truer than in New York, where La Guardia's alliance with Roosevelt had insured that WPA and PWA grants would be funneled through the city's highest elected official. (Moses had been able to obtain a disproportionate share of such grants, but only by working with and on that official.) As federal grants to cities increased after the war, however, so did the authority of the federal bureaucracy—at the expense of the cities' authority.

In New York, as the city's control over federal grants decreased, Moses' increased.

It increased partly because of Moses' bill-drafting genius, and what that genius enabled him to make out of the new post he had obtained from O'Dwyer.

The post lay outside the established structure of the city's government. Nowhere in the forty-nine chapters of the City Charter was there a single mention of a "City Construction Coordinator." To some men, this might have represented an obstacle. To Moses, it represented an opportunity. For since there was no definition of the position's powers, he could write the definition himself.

As O'Dwyer had conceived the powers, they would be substantial—the Coordinator, while an appointed official, would, in the construction field, possess authority over all other appointed officials, even department heads—but bounded by a strict upper as well as outer and time limit; the Coordinator's authority, limited to construction and temporary—to last only as long as the postwar adjustment period—would be subordinate always to that of the elected officials to whom the voters had entrusted the power to make decisions for the city: he would be merely an instrument to carry out their decisions. The amendment to the city's Administrative Code drafted by Moses to create the position—and delivered to the incoming administration in the midst of the inaugural confusion—ostensibly was faithful to O'Dwyer's conception, providing that "the Coordinator shall schedule and . . . expedite the work of all agencies of the city" but only "upon approval of projects by the Mayor and governing bodies of the city." Not one of the Assistant Corporation Counsels interrupted in the midst of settling into their new offices by a request from O'Dwyer to "take a look" at the draft, saw that it was anything more. When the Citizens Union protested that it "gives too much power to one person and supersedes the Charter," "sources close to O'Dwyer" assured reporters that the Coordinator's job would be "purely administrative and not policy-making." City Council and Board of Estimate passed it unanimously after the most cursory discussion, and O'Dwyer quickly signed it into law as Local Law Number I of 1946, the first legislative act of his administration. (Reporters accepted O'Dwyer's assurance; the press paid as little attention to the code amendment as it had to Moses' stealthy, subtle takeover of the Tunnel Authority a year earlier; its approval by the Board rated exactly one paragraph in the *Times*.)

But, buried within the lines of convoluted legalisms, the amendment also contained an innocuous phrase—concealed, as was the custom of the man who had been the best bill drafter in Albany, at the end of a long sentence whose other clauses all purportedly limited his powers—allowing the Coordinator to "represent the city in its relations with cooperating state and federal agencies." Moses used this phrase, so innocent in appearance, as authorization to write into contracts between the city and these agencies provisions designating himself as the city representative with whom they agreed to deal, thereby making certain that it would be he and he alone who was presenting the city's position—or his representation of the city's position—on the design and relative desirability of construction projects to the two "outside" governments which would be largely funding them. The phrase also empowered Moses to negotiate with federal and state officials, learn their position and present that position—or his representation of that position—to city officials, to be, in other words, the sole broker between the city and the governments on which the city was relying for desperately needed funds. Moses' representations were not always strictly accurate. For twenty years, for example, he falsely told successive mayors that the Federal Bureau of Public Roads was unalterably opposed to building the Lower Manhattan Expressway as a tunnel. But for twenty years—until, in 1964, Mayor Robert F. Wagner, Jr., went to Washington to find out about the expressway for himself—no mayor or other city official investigated any Moses representations. During those years, city officials heard only Moses' version of what the federal government was "insisting" on.

Most of the time, moreover, no misrepresentation was necessary. Moses' relationship with federal bureaucrats helped insure that what they were insisting on was what *he* was insisting on. Their philosophy, of course, was in many ways his philosophy—the road builders in Washington were animated by the same "engineering mentality" that played so important a part in his make-up—and there was a personal factor involved as well: by 1946 he had been dealing intimately with the officials of the Bureau of Public Roads for close to twenty years, wining them, dining them, charming them, persuading them to approve his state parkways and then, when the parkways were finished, thrilling them on elaborate tours that showed them what he had done with their money; Bureau director F. V. Du Pont once wrote Moses: "I know of nothing comparable in the United States, and, I think I can safely say, the world. More power to you!" Du Pont's successor, *de facto* head of the Interstate Highway System, was Bertram D. Tallamy, former superintendent of the New York State Department of Public Works, the same Bertram D. Tallamy who in 1926 had come down from Niagara to sit at Moses' feet for private lectures on the art of Getting Things Done—and who told the author that the Interstate Highway System was built by principles he had learned at those lectures. Moses was not merely the friend of the federal road builders, he was their idol. Lastly, of course, the information on which they based their decisions on what was best for New York was the information that Moses saw fit to give them. If there were other views in the city on proposed highways—as to where they should be located so as to minimize neighborhood disruption, for example—the Bureau of Public Roads didn't get to hear them. The roads that the Bureau approved, roads that would play so large a role in determining the city's destiny, therefore, were Moses' roads; the city officials supposedly responsible for the city's destiny had only two alternatives: to accept the roads offered to them or to turn them down—along with the tens of millions of dollars involved.

It was a position ideal for the whipsaw—and Moses used that technique unmercifully. Says Judge Jacob Lutsky, the gruff, hard-boiled genius of municipal administration who was to be a key behind-the-scenes adviser to all three of the postwar Democratic mayors, O'Dwyer, Impellitteri and Wagner:

> Under federal law, a commitment from the Mayor wasn't enough; you also needed a commitment from the Board of Estimate. But [Moses] would go to Washington and Washington would say, "Okay, as long as you've got Mayor and Board of Estimate approval." Then he would get an "Okay" from the Mayor, with the Mayor saying, "Don't forget you need both Washington and Board of Estimate approval." Then he'd run to Washington and say, "Look, I've got a commitment from the Mayor." They'd firm it up some more, say, "Okay, as long as you've got an approval from the Board of Estimate." And he'd come and say to the Board of Estimate, "If you don't give me a commitment, I'll lose the money." And lots of times we had to give him the commitment because we didn't want to lose it.

Housing, Moses took over by indirection. Faced, as soon as he took office, with an immediate need for competent housing administrators, the harried new Mayor found Moses ready with recommendations. Before the Mayor realized what he was doing, he had filled three of the five places on the City Housing Authority board—and many top Authority staff positions—with men loyal not to him but to his Construction Coordinator. Despite his lack of the slightest formal connection with the Housing Authority, Moses controlled it absolutely for a decade. As late as 1955, Warren Moscow, appointed its executive director by Mayor Wagner, reported to Wagner that its chief engineer regarded Moses, not the Mayor, "as his boss."

In 1948, Moses had a visit from a Yale classmate who wanted to discuss details of a new type of federal slum clearance program—"urban renewal"—that he was considering sponsoring. It was United States Senator Robert A. Taft. Months before Congress approved the Federal Housing Act of 1949—months before the public had even heard the phrase "urban renewal"—Moses had persuaded O'Dwyer to appoint a Mayor's Slum Clearance Committee (Robert Moses, chairman). Through that committee he controlled urban renewal in New York—by far the largest program in any city in America—for a decade, controlled it absolutely. The Mayor and the Board of Estimate, Lutsky says, "never even knew what was going on in that committee until a project was presented to us for approval." Before the war, Moses had used a force outside the city to help him bend the city to his will. Now there was a new outside force. He used that force, too.

And he was to go on using it for some time. O'Dwyer, in creating the position of Construction Coordinator, had envisioned it as a temporary, "postwar adjustment period" job. But *temporary* is a relative term, particularly when applied to a job Robert Moses was holding. And *postwar* is a time limit with a certain elasticity. O'Dwyer would remain in his job for less than five years. Moses would remain in *his* job—signing his letters "Robert Moses, Coordinator"; he preferred that Orwellian title to "Commissioner"—for more than twenty years.

While using the new force, moreover, he did not neglect the old.

His control of the Legislature, cemented by patronage and favors, remained as solid during the postwar as the prewar era. As for the Governor's chair, that was occupied for the first twelve postwar years by Thomas E. Dewey and W. Averell Harriman. Dewey liked to boast that "Bob discovered rather quickly that he couldn't push me around," but the words rang rather hollow to men like the GOP politician who once heard Moses on the phone with the Governor. "I walked in and he was cursing and shouting—'You goddamned son of a bitch! Don't you tell me what to do, you stupid son of a bitch!' Then he hung up and I said, 'Bob, was that the *Governor?*' And he said, with that big grin, 'Yeahhhh.' " Harriman, a crusty aristocrat with a legendary lack of awe even for Presidents, stood in awe of Robert Moses, in part because he had, during the 1920's, been one of the men anxious to create parks for the public but utterly unable to do so until Moses had come along and accomplished what he had begun to think was all but impossible, in part because of sheer force of personality: the Governor was one of the regular guests at the Sunday brunches at Herbert Bayard Swope's Sands Point mansion, and guests recall him sitting silently, not venturing to interject a word, while Moses, another regular, discoursed. But Harriman had some ideas, rather novel in public officials of the time, on the need for increased concern for individuals and for community participation in the planning of public works; noticing on a trip to Monticello early in his Governorship that highway guardrails had been put up within three feet of service stations and restaurants, isolating them from the road that should have brought them business, he issued on the spot an order that they be torn down. Convinced that Moses was not as final a word on the construction of urban expressways as he had been on suburban parkways, he installed a new superintendent of the Department of Public Works, John W. Johnson of Buffalo, gave him several "liberal" young aides, and told them to "get tough" with Moses. But Moses got tough with them—and with Harriman—instead.

Harriman aide James E. Truex describes the Governor's education in the facts of political life. "If you began to fight with Moses," Truex says, "you'd have to fight with him on so many fronts. You'd have to fight with him on parkways and on parks . . . He had so much potential for trouble because of the many directorships he had. And the main threat he had was [to issue press releases]. He could always cause you so much trouble by calling you 'a dirty politician'—he was above politics, of course . . . Governors were always nervous about this. You knew that if he said something, the newspapers would pick it up big." Moses disciplined Harriman not only by using publicity but by withholding it: by not inviting the Governor to speak at ground breakings and ribbon cuttings. In 1957, for example, Moses staged a day-long series of ribbon cuttings to celebrate the completion of a string of grade-crossing elimination projects for which Nassau County communities had long been clamoring. The Democratic Governor, who had authorized the projects and provided the funds for them, didn't even know the ceremonies were being held until he read newspaper stories about them—stories and pictures of Moses and the other official participants, all Republicans. Furious, Harriman ordered that a loyal public relations man be assigned to DPW's metropolitan area headquarters to alert him to future ceremonies—as Truex puts it, "to try to get us some PR." But Harriman found that gubernatorial participation in ribbon cuttings was no guarantee of a gubernatorial share of the publicity. "Moses would put out the announcements, and Moses would put out the summaries of what guys said," Truex explains. Truex put out summaries of the Governor's speeches, of course, but, he says, "the press recognized that Moses' office was running [the ceremony], and they would call his office and not me" for summaries and other information—such as who deserved the credit for the public improvement.

Almost despite himself, moreover, Harriman found himself being influenced by prevailing professional opinion.

When conflicts arose over a Moses project, the old-line DPW engineers would present studies to prove that Moses was right—and it was difficult to find any engineers who felt that Moses was wrong. ("One of the problems," Truex would note, "is that engineers tend to agree on these things.") Harriman, after all, was not an engineer. "When engineers came in and said they agree with Moses and this was the way it had to be done, a Governor had to respect that opinion," Truex says.

Soon the Governor was suing for peace. Harriman had called in Truex and another young liberal aide and, in Truex's words, "said he was getting reports from the local people up on the St. Lawrence that Moses was going to tear out lots of the homes of little people along the St. Lawrence for his parkways, and the little people had to be protected, and we should get right up there [to ascertain if the reports were true]." The two aides found out they were—"there were cottages lining the shore near Massena," Truex says, "nice-looking cottages, too, not luxurious but nice, cottages into which you could tell loving care had gone. Moses was just obliterating them"—but "about ten minutes after we got back [to Albany], there was a letter from Moses [to Harriman]: These people—us—had been up in his territory and we had been talking to people we shouldn't have been talking to, etc. And that was the last we heard of the little people. It was never brought up again." The Governor had backed down. Shortly thereafter, he suggested that the huge centerpiece of the St. Lawrence project be named the "Robert Moses Power Dam." Soon he was being afforded star billing at ribbon cuttings—next to Moses', of course. Truex's tardiness in perceiving the change in the Moses-Harriman relationship cost him a humiliating tongue-lashing. For a Brooklyn-Queens Expressway ribbon cutting in 1958—at which Harriman was to be the main speaker—"I had written a speech kidding Moses," Truex recalls. "We were in the car going toward the ceremony and the Governor looked at [the speech] and he blew up and accused me of seeking to undermine his relationship with Robert Moses." Truex started to argue that "you can score points" by attacking Moses, but Harriman flew into a rage, violently upbraided his aide and told him: "I want you to know Robert Moses is coming out for me in the campaign." (It was small consolation for Truex that Moses' keen eye for political realities saw early on the popularity of Harriman's opponent, Nelson A. Rockefeller, and that the hoped-for endorsement never occurred.)

As important as Moses' relationship with the state's Governor was his relationship with its administrative machinery.

It was, of course, largely *his* machinery, the governmental apparatus his State Reconstruction Commission had designed in 1919. He, more than any other individual, knew which of the tens of thousands of administrative positions in that government were crucial to his purposes, and after a quarter of a century of power in the state, he had "Moses Men" in most of these posts. He had taken measures to minimize the threat to his purposes posed by key officials who were not Moses Men: some of these officials would have been astonished to learn—most of them never did—that their secretaries were on Moses' payroll as well as the state's, and that in transcribing confidential memoranda and minutes of secret meetings devoted to blocking a Moses project or to curbing Moses' power, these secretaries made an extra carbon, which was delivered nightly to Moses' representatives in Albany.

More than twenty years before—while Bill O'Dwyer was still a cop pounding the beat—Robert Moses had laid the groundwork for control of the state machinery that would directly affect his road building, dividing the State Department of Public Works into ten geographical districts, placing the entire New York City–Long Island area, in which most of his road building was concentrated, in a single (and hence easily controllable) district, District

Ten, and writing into state law a unique provision that gave his Long Island State Park Commission a unique veto power over all parkway plans. Moses cemented his control of District Ten's engineers, already firm through identity of interest and philosophy, with stronger mortars. His favor was, for many engineers, the only road out of the tedious progression of the life of a civil service engineer, a life that offered little in the way of either money or power. Cultivate his favor and you could go on luxurious jaunts and be well paid for the privilege—as District Ten chief engineer J. J. Darcy was in being awarded lucrative "consultantships" in Moses' highway studies of other cities. Cultivate that favor and you could be placed in command of great enterprises, as Arthur B. Williams was when Moses plucked him out of a routine middle-echelon engineering civil service job and handed him authority over a hundred middle-echelon civil service engineers by appointing him general manager of the Niagara State Park Commission. Cultivate that favor and when you had had enough of civil service, you might receive a partnership in the consulting engineer firms that received Moses' immensely lucrative contracts: Darcy's successor, Milton E. Goul, became Milton E. Goul of Buckley, Shumavon and Goul. Lose that favor and you would find yourself mired for decades in the same job, or transferred to some other district—as a recalcitrant patrolman is transferred from the Broadway beat to Staten Island—and you would wait out the long years to your retirement sitting in a drab office in Hornell supervising the grading of graveled farm roads in Chemung County. Even during the few months when Johnson was heading DPW, he and the other Harriman appointees teetering precariously atop the huge DPW bureaucracy proved unable to deflect it even momentarily from the course on which it had been gathering momentum for long decades. "The DPW is a tremendous hierarchy," Truex would say years later. "When we got there, it was his hierarchy. When we left, it was still all basically his." Under Tallamy, DPW had given Moses a veto power over all highway projects in the New York metropolitan area. Except for a few months, he retained that veto during Johnson's superintendency, too.

The returns electing Rockefeller Governor had hardly landed on Rockefeller's desk in November 1958 when a hand-delivered letter from Moses arrived there recommending the appointment to the DPW superintendency of J. Burch McMorran, chief engineer of Moses' State Power Authority.

A prototype second-generation Moses Man, McMorran was not as brilliant an engineer as originals like Art Howland or Earle Andrews, but he was competent in his profession and possessed the qualities that Moses now considered more important than brilliance. (The qualities Moses mentions first in his evaluation of McMorran reveal what he was looking for: "McMorran . . . was not an innovator. He was a good soldier, always loyal. . . .") Rockefeller accepted the recommendation—and for at least the first term of Rockefeller's Governorship, Moses still had his veto power. In an arrangement at least tacitly approved by three Governors—an arrangement lasting for at least seventeen years after the war—"Moses had the say," McMorran says, "over who got the contracts on all New York City [area] jobs." And not just on contracts. Moses had the say—absolute authority—

to decide not only who should design and build all highways in the metropolitan area, but which highways would be built, when they would be built and where they would be built. The state had in effect turned over to him—intact and complete—all its authority over the construction of arterial highways in and around New York City.

This authority was extensive. The Interstate Highway System was described by its creators as a "partnership between the state highway departments and the federal government," and that description was accurate. No city was a partner. Federal funds for an arterial highway within a city were handed not to the city but to the state in which it was located. The state—not the city—had the power to spend those funds. The state had the final say on every detail of the plans and specifications, down to the selection of the specific city streets and lots along which the roads would run. They supervised every detail of the actual construction.

And since New York State had turned that power over to Robert Moses, that power was vested in him. His possession of it therefore strengthened the control he already possessed over highways by virtue of his influence with the federal government. Strong already, his power was now stronger still.

Over the planning and building of arterial highways in and around the City of New York—arterial highways which would do so much to shape the future of that city—the federal and state governments had a stranglehold. The hands that implemented that stranglehold were the hands of Robert Moses.

It was not only forces outside the city's government that Robert Moses used in bending the city to his will. He used forces inside that government as well.

He used, for example, the force of greed.

Greed had always been the force that drove the city's five-county Democratic political machine. But Moses' twelve previous years in office in the city had been La Guardia's twelve years, too, and during those years the machine's influence in the city's government had been all but eliminated. Moses, in Getting Things Done, had been able to deal almost entirely with the Little Flower, and only occasionally with the spiritual descendants of Red Mike Hylan.

Now, however, the machine was back in power. It was not, at first, dominated as it had been before La Guardia by the Manhattan Democratic organization housed in Tammany Hall, the Great Wigwam at Union Square. Weakened in relation to its allies by the population exodus from Manhattan, the Manhattan organization had been cut off from patronage and contracts at City Hall by La Guardia, from the Statehouse by Lehman and from the White House by Roosevelt, who, taking revenge for its defiant support of Alfred E. Smith at the 1932 presidential convention, had funneled federal largesse instead through the Boss of the Bronx, Edward J. Flynn, with enough going to Brooklyn to make its Democratic organization as well as Flynn's stronger than Manhattan's. By 1945, the Great Wigwam itself no longer belonged to the Manhattan organization, which, unable to meet the mortgage payments, had had the building sold out from under it,* and neither did control of the city's five-borough Democracy. But journalists, rhetorical traditionalists, were still referring to that Democracy as a whole as "Tammany Hall," and if that catch phrase was misleading in political terms, it was accurate in moral ones, for if the controlling structure of the postwar Democratic machine was different from the pre-La Guardia model, the ethics of the machine were not. As the *Herald Tribune* editorialized in 1945, "A vast, corrupt organization, starved through twelve long years, is panting for its revenge." To the men of the machine, the end of the La Guardia administration, cleanest in the city's history, meant only one thing: the twelve lean years were over. Now was the time for the fat. *E finita la cuccagna!* the Little Flower had promised—and he had kept his promise. But now he was gone. The party was on again. New York was again a city in which *SCANDAL* and *GRAFT* and *FRAUD* glared bold and black out of the headlines stacked on newsstands, in which the newspapers were filled with reports of petty peculation—and in which the reports, no matter how lurid, were no more than a hint of the extent to which the city was again a place in which the badges of governmental authority, the badges of fire inspectors and health inspectors and plumbing inspectors and building inspectors, had become again silver- and gold-plated licenses to extort money from the city's citizens. New York was a city in which the police, every day, sold the law in the streets—sometimes it almost seemed as if being on the force was synonymous with being on the take—and in which sacred justice was sold in the very temples of justice (which was not too surprising, of course, since many of justice's black-robed priests, who presided in those temples, had purchased the right to do so), in which the only law that really counted was the law of the jungle. New York was a city in which public office was, increasingly, a means to private profit. New York was a city in which it sometimes seemed as if there was scarcely an officeholder who didn't demand a slice of the pie—and in which the pie was big enough so that it sometimes seemed as if a slice was available for every officeholder no matter what his party, the Democrats shrewdly making enough key Republicans a part of the arrangements by which the city was governed—putting them on the public payroll, giving them a share of judgeships and a cut of lucrative city contracts, taking them in as business partners—so that the GOP wouldn't try too hard to disrupt those arrangements, and so that when a private citizen, or the Citizens Union, or a newspaper, demanded an investigation of official corruption, no one with the power to conduct a real one was interested in doing so. New York was the city of the Fix, of "protection," of the shakedown. The twelve years of La Guardia had been only an interlude. New York was again what it had been before the Little Flower bounced into City Hall: a city in which everything had its price.

---

* "I never thought I'd live to see the tiger get skinned," Jimmy Walker remarked. The sale was symbolic not only of the loss of power by Tammany but of the rise in power of the city's labor unions: the purchaser was the children's dress unit of the ILGWU.

The price was highest in Moses' fields.

Ever since the post-Civil War years in which the Tweed Ring, authorizing municipal building on a scale that gave New York its own Reconstruction Era, took fixed percentages—5 percent for the Mayor, 20 percent for the Comptroller, 25 percent for William Marcy Tweed, who, with his choice of any post, chose the public works commissionership—of the padding in contractors' padded bills, public works had been the main ingredient in the rich swill of graft on which Tammany battened.

Now the techniques were different: subtler, smoother. Charlie Murphy had taught his sachems that it was stupid to take cash, too easy for some prying reporter or rebel district attorney to trace it, too easy to prove that it had been taken in exchange for a favor, too easy to subpoena a contractor's books and haul the contractor's timid little bookkeeper before a grand jury and frighten him into telling what the items listed as "cash disbursements" really represented. By precept, if not by preachment (for Silent Charlie had not received his nickname for nothing), for example, by having his Board of Aldermen hold up street-closing permits for the construction of Pennsylvania Station until the railroad awarded the excavation contract to a firm in which he had a hidden financial interest, he showed Tammany that there were safer ways of making money from public works. By 1905, Sachem George Washington Plunkitt, who, as a state senator, had ridden at the head of the "Black Horse Cavalry," was sitting, resplendent in handle-bar mustache and gleaming stovepipe hat, on Graziano's bootblack stand in the old courthouse off Foley Square at noon hours expansively explaining how cavalry were obsolete and how he was coining millions out of the "coincidences" surrounding "big improvements," coincidences which he called, in a phrase he may also have coined, "honest graft." (Silent Charlie, who, if he didn't invent "honest graft," refined it to meet the needs of a modern political organization, coined no phrases; he had not received his nickname for nothing.)

Murphy and Plunkitt were uneducated men; they had never been to law school. If they had, they would have found the making of "honest graft" safer and easier still. Al Smith, as always, phrased it best. Strolling through a law-school library one day, the Governor noticed a student poring intently over his books. "There," he said with a smile, "is a young man studying how to take a bribe and call it a fee." By the Twenties, most honest graft was being worked through "fees," mostly through legal fees (more politicians belong to the legal than any other profession), but also through the real estate brokers' fees called "commissions," the insurance brokers' fees called "premiums" and the public relations fees called "retainers." Jimmy Walker's crew, overconfident and careless, forgot Murphy's precepts, but Samuel Seabury, finding the cash in their tin boxes, drummed the teachings of the master into Tammany again strongly enough so that the braves would never forget them again. In the post-La Guardia era, there was no more "Tin Box" Brigade. It was the Retainer Regiment now. Corrupt public officials who were lawyers would support or oppose a bill according to the wishes of a business firm, and later the firm would retain the official in his private capacity as an attorney, paying him a fee for "services"—legal services, of course—"rendered." Corrupt public officials who were insurance brokers would be allowed to write a firm's policies, and thereby to obtain the premiums attached. In the interaction of politics and public works, cash was now the medium of exchange only on the lowest levels. Now if some investigator found that a contractor's books included a $10,000 payment to a city councilman, next to the payment would be the notation "legal fee," and who could prove that the services the councilman had rendered to earn the fee were anything other than legal, that the councilman's vote in favor of a bill the firm also happened to favor was anything but coincidence? The presence of a councilman's name in a contractor's books would, moreover, be unusual, an indication that either the contractor or the councilman was still ignorant of the higher refinements of honest graft, one of which was to have the contractor pay the fee not to the councilman but to another law firm, which would then, taking out a small handling charge for itself, pass it along.

The profit in public works in New York had long been huge; with the postwar building boom, it reached new dimensions. "It's a king's ransom in a city this size," Reuben Lazarus said. And if there was subtlety now in the making of this profit, the making was still, for the machine, the motive. The greed was only refined, not eliminated. The Tiger, starved for so long, was more voracious than ever. Every large-scale public work, it sometimes seemed, had to have its arrangements, its payoffs, its deals—its "coincidences." Until the coincidences were arranged, there would be no public work. If Board of Estimate or City Council approval was required, that approval would not be forthcoming. If implementation of announced policy by a city agency was necessary, that implementation would be endlessly delayed. The great Mayor was dying—almost penniless—in a little house in Riverdale; in the City Hall he left behind him, everything had a price. And to Get Things Done in the city, one had to pay it.

Once Robert Moses would have scorned to pay it. Once he *had* scorned to pay it, refusing for four bitter years to make even the minor compromise over patronage that might have made possible passage of at least some of his proposed civil service reform measures; later, while attempting to realize his Long Island park plan, refusing for more bitter years—refusing even though he saw the possibility that his refusal would doom his great dream forever—to make deals with the Nassau County Republican machine that alone could give him the right to create Jones Beach.

But that Robert Moses no longer existed. The Robert Moses who had taken his place paid the price. And he paid it in full.

He had the money to pay it.

He had the money partly because his control of the City Housing Authority gave him control over close to a billion and a quarter dollars in federal and state funds dispensed through that agency, partly because his control of the State Department of Public Works gave him control over another billion and a quarter dollars in federal and state funds dispensed through that agency, and partly because his control of the Mayor's Slum Clearance Committee gave him control of a billion dollars more dispensed through that agency—a total, during the first fifteen years after World War II, of close to three and a half billion dollars which he dispensed in the city on behalf of federal and state agencies largely beyond the control of the city's government.

But mainly he had the money to pay it because of his control of an agency that was largely beyond the control of *any* government, federal, state or city: the Triborough Bridge and Tunnel Authority.

With the war, and gasoline and tire rationing ended and automobiles pouring off the assembly lines again, the volume of automobile traffic in New York soared.

In 1941, the Triborough Bridge had carried 11,000,000 vehicles. In 1946, it carried 13,000,000; in 1947, 16,000,000; in 1948, 19,000,000; in 1949, 23,000,000; in 1950, 27,000,000; in 1951, 32,000,000—in 1960, fifteen years after the war ended, it was carrying 46,000,000 vehicles per year. And that was just one bridge. Traffic on all Triborough Authority toll facilities had been 43,000,000 in 1941; it was 112,000,000 in 1951 and 154,000,000 in 1960. The Authority's annual income had been $8,000,000 in 1941; in 1951, with the Brooklyn-Battery Tunnel's thirty-five-cent-per-car charge swelling the toll receipts, the Authority's annual income was $26,000,000; in 1960, it was $37,000,000 (in 1962 with the Throgs Neck Bridge open and operating, it would be $43,000,000; in 1967, with the Verrazano-Narrows Bridge open and operating at fifty cents per car, it would be $75,000,000, almost ten times higher than it had been before the war). These receipts were, of course, capitalized through the issuance of revenue bonds. The income he received from bond sales, combined with other Authority income, meant that Robert Moses had available to spend on public works within New York City during the first fifteen years after World War II, more than three quarters of a billion dollars additional.

Part of the significance of that figure emerges when it is combined with the federal and state money Robert Moses spent on public works within the city during those fifteen years, and the total is then compared with what the financially strapped city itself spent. During that period, agencies controlled by Moses and largely independent of any supervision by the city's government spent on public works within the city close to four and a half billion dollars. The city's government—Mayor, Board of Estimate, City Council—was able during that period to spend, through all its separate departments, a total of less than three and three quarter billion dollars. Robert Moses spent on public works within the City of New York more—far more—than the city spent.

But a greater part of the significance of Triborough Bridge and Tunnel Authority revenue—vast in itself—was the secrecy in which its spending could be cloaked.

Federal and state expenditures were public records, subject to public disclosure. But because Triborough was a public authority—unlike the City

Housing Authority, a genuine public authority—its expenditures were not.

Therefore it was safer to take money from Moses than from the city. A politician or public official could accept a legal fee or an insurance premium from Triborough with assurance that no reporter or reformer would ever be able to discover that he had done so. The State or City Comptroller could, in theory, make the discovery; the legislation creating Triborough authorized in-depth audits of its books by these two officials. But there was no precedent for such an audit; none had ever been undertaken. And there were reasons both practical and political to doubt that one ever would. One was the very size of Triborough: auditing the Authority would require a huge staff working for a long time (one estimate was fifty accountants working for a year) and no Comptroller had that kind of manpower to spare, so the job would require a sizable appropriation from either Board of Estimate or State Legislature, a highly unlikely eventuality since any Comptroller seeking to pry open Triborough's books would be asking for the money to do so from the very men whose names were in those books. (The Comptroller's party designation was irrelevant; because members of both parties were in those books, his audit would inevitably embarrass members of his own party.)

The secrecy cloaking Triborough's largesse also protected its recipients because the secrecy protected the man who proffered that largesse.

Since 1924, newspapers had, practically unanimously, been describing Robert Moses as a man above politics and deals, a man whose name it would be ridiculous to mention in the same article with any hint of "payoff" or "scandal." After the war, the New York *Post,* with publisher Dorothy Schiff taking a more active interest in her paper, began to question not only Moses' ends but his means, asked to inspect Triborough's records—and, when Moses refused to open them, took him to court.

But the courts upheld Moses' refusal, and without those records, the *Post* could not document its suspicions about the flaws in the Moses image. And for a solid decade after the war, despite the wishes of an occasional reporter or editor, no other newspaper attempted seriously to dig behind that image.

Moses' personal reputation was reinforced by that of the institution with which, increasingly, it became blended. After as before the war, the public was being informed by Moses and by the press—in a single six-year period, 1946 through 1951, there were more than 1,400 editorials in metropolitan-area newspapers on this theme—that public authorities were not only "prudent," "practical," "businesslike" and "efficient" but "nonpolitical," "outside of politics" and therefore "honest." "Authorities are free from political considerations," the *Times* said. "They are free from the dead hand of partisanship and bureaucracy," the *Herald Tribune* said.

Moses' reputation and that of the institution he did so much to bring to maturity was the final guarantee that the secrecy of its books would remain inviolate. A politician considering accepting a Triborough fee could be assured that should some neophyte legislator ever attempt to open Triborough's books, Moses would assail the attempt as an attempt by a politician to interfere with an agency whose independence he didn't like and to get his hands on some of its funds—that the press would back up that argument, and that the public would be conditioned by years of praise for Moses and for public authorities to accept it. Politicians could be sure that no public official solicitous of his political future would lay that future on the line in a fight with a living legend.* No one could disprove Moses' reputation without first opening Triborough's books, and no one could open Triborough's books without first disproving Moses' reputation. Any public official thinking about accepting a Triborough retainer could feel certain that his own reputation would be safe in the shadow of Moses'. Robert Moses had $750,000,000 of Authority money to spend. In the ultimate analysis, it was the public's money. But Robert Moses was not accountable to the public. He was not accountable to anyone. He had $750,000,000 to give away. And no one would ever know to whom he gave it. And this made politicians and public officials—at least those politicians and public officials interested in retainers—all the more anxious to make sure that he gave some of it to them.

Such politicians and public officials noted another fact about Moses' money which, in their eyes, made it even more attractive than the city's: Moses could give it to whomever he wished.

Expenditure of most federal and state money (slum clearance money was a notable exception) may have been largely free from city control, but it was subject to control by federal and state bureaucrats. Expenditures for highways and low-income public housing, for example, were subject to requirements for competitive bidding and to rigid standards, minimum and maximum, on the work involved, and to constant auditing to insure that those requirements were met. To a certain extent, it was possible to circumvent those requirements—and to the extent it was possible Moses *did* circumvent them—but the extent was extremely limited; the bureaucrats in Washington, in particular, were grimly stubborn about sticking to the letter of the laws they were charged with administering, and the threat of audits to discover violations of federal regulations was a constant inhibiting factor to potential violators. But over the spending of Triborough money Moses enjoyed absolute discretion.

Edward N. Costikyan was a keenly observant reform Democrat who suddenly found himself able to observe the machine as no other reformer had ever observed it: as its leader. New York's political convulsions of the 1960's catapulted him—to his own amazement and that of Tammany Hall—into the Hall's chairmanship and kept him there for more than two years. And Costikyan, upon descending from his unique vantage point, was to report: "The magnet which attracts corrupters . . . the natural locus of corruption is *always* where the discretionary power resides." In New York

* Only a Comptroller who held his duty above his career would conduct the first audit of Triborough—and that Comptroller, Arthur Levitt, would not come along, in either city or state, for almost twenty years. When he did and, unable to secure the necessary appropriations from the Legislature, in 1966 scraped together a skeleton crew of his regular staffers to make at least a limited study, the first in the history of Triborough, of the Authority's books, the findings would, if publicized as widely as the Moses legend, have disproved that legend. But the findings were hardly publicized at all.

City, in the postwar era, the discretionary power resided principally in Robert Moses, and like filings to a magnet—or, more precisely, like flies to a sugar bowl—the corrupters, the men who possessed influence over the city's political or governmental apparatus and who were willing to sell that influence for money, were attracted to Moses, and to the seemingly bottomless sugar bowl for which he possessed the only spoon. And Moses did not send them away disappointed. "Free from political considerations"? Political considerations were in fact the basis—often the *only* basis—on which Moses spooned out his millions. With the power to distribute those millions according to any criteria he chose, during the entire postwar era he chose mainly a single criterion: how much influence an individual had, and how willing that individual was to use that influence on his behalf.

The distribution of the insurance premiums on a single Moses slum clearance project demonstrates the use of this criterion. During the mayoralty of Vincent R. Impellitteri, the insurance was handled by one of Impellitteri's backers, Robert Blaikie. No sooner had Impellitteri lost his bid for re-election (to Robert F. Wagner, Jr., the hand-picked candidate of Tammany boss Carmine De Sapio) than Blaikie lost the insurance account—to a broker associated with De Sapio. And the over-all pattern of the distribution of the Triborough Authority's insurance, a pattern revealed by secret records which the public has never seen, demonstrates the criterion even more strikingly.

The Authority's policies carried premiums of more than $500,000 per year, or a yearly profit to brokers of more than $100,000. And the brokers who received this profit had to do almost no work for it; Spargo was to note in a secret internal Triborough memo that once "the big insurance"—the policies insuring Triborough's bridges and tunnels against collapse or destruction—had been placed with insurance companies, "little if any work on the part of the broker" was required. In 1954, almost twenty years after some of these policies had been written, Spargo could say, "To my knowledge the Authority has spent millions of dollars on premiums and has never filed or collected a claim."

During the La Guardia era, there was little political profit to be reaped through the sowing of such policies. What there was would be reaped through the Democratic machine, and some of Triborough's insurance therefore was given to C. J. Reid & Co., a firm whose office was on Vanderbilt Avenue but whose connections were on Fourteenth Street, and Reid's general practice was to parcel out its commissions to key Tammany figures—but another major hunk of the insurance was given to the State Insurance Fund, without any broker at all being involved, and still another was given to a broker with no political connections, for no other reason than that he had been an old army buddy of Spargo's predecessor, General Loeser.

With the machine back in power, however, all this changed. The Triborough policies formerly held by General Loeser's army buddy and the State Insurance Fund were snatched away and given to a new broker. In a frank—frank because he believed it would remain secret forever—internal Triborough memo, Spargo was candid in explaining a key reason for the choice of the new broker: "because he was a friend of Tom Shanahan's." Shanahan was Tammany's chief behind-the-scenes financial manipulator for close to a decade, until the mid-1950's. For a decade, the policies were left with Shanahan's friend. The Reid company was allowed to keep its policies, but a closer watch was instituted to insure that its farming out of commissions resulted in the maximum political influence for Triborough.

By 1954, Carmine De Sapio had solidified his control of Tammany, centralizing in himself more power than had been enjoyed by any boss since Charlie Murphy. He and he alone called the shots for the machine, and, it sometimes seemed, for Wagner. Sometime in 1954 or 1955, De Sapio was invited for luncheon at Randall's Island. On returning to his office later that afternoon, he told a friend that he had found only two men present when he arrived: Moses and Spargo. And, De Sapio told a friend, after mentioning that they knew he was connected with a certain insurance firm, they had offered that firm *all* Triborough's insurance—the entire $500,000 per year in premiums and $100,000 per year in commissions.

De Sapio told the friend that he had turned the offer down. "He told me," the friend recalls, "that he was not prepared to exert the degree of influence over the administration and the Mayor that he felt would be required of him in return." That he was not unprepared to exert a lesser degree of influence is indicated by the fact that some Triborough insurance began to be given to a new broker, one whom key Democrats considered close to the leader. But De Sapio's refusal to accept it all left a lot of commissions to be disposed of. Steingut, son of Steingut, spiritual heir to McCooey and boss of the Brooklyn organization that the one-time butcher had carved into shape, received some (and, because a "public authority" was not by customary definition a part of "government," could piously tell an inquiring reporter that he never accepted "government business"). So did the Democratic leader of Queens, the Honorable James A. Roe. In 1953, the year in which the *Herald Tribune* was stating that authorities "are free from politics," three of the five county leaders of the machine that dominated the city's politics were therefore on Moses' payroll. There were enough insurance premiums left over for Republicans, and at least one of the GOP county leaders, John R. Crews of Brooklyn, received some of them. As for the Legislature, Moses used insurance premiums to insure that his influence there would be exerted not only indirectly through the influence of Roe, Steingut and De Sapio over the legislators they controlled, but more directly through at least one of the small group of "leaders" who really ran the Legislature, D. Mallory Stephens, a poor farm boy from Putnam County who in 1942 became chairman of the Assembly's key Ways and Means Committee, which controls the flow of legislation to the floor—and in 1943 began receiving Triborough insurance business. Stephens continually pressed Moses and Spargo for more business, telling them frankly that the influence he was using on their behalf entitled him to it, and no matter how much he was given he was never satisfied. So insistent became his demands that in a secret memo in 1953 Spargo told Moses: "The only way you can satisfy Mallory Stephens is to give him the business now handled by [Shanahan's friend]"—the dilemma was resolved by Stephens' decision to leave the Legislature (for a bank presidency).*

A charting of the legal fees and other emoluments that Moses distributed to lawyers during the postwar era—a year-by-year analysis of who got the fees, when they started getting them and when they stopped getting them—provides almost a year-by-year chart of the fluctuations in the political influence of certain key Democratic lawyers.

The influence of two lawyers did not fluctuate. During the entire postwar era, no matter which Democratic factions were in power, it remained, year after year, steady and immense. And, year after year, these two lawyers received a steady flow of legal fees—immense legal fees—from Moses-controlled enterprises. One was Samuel I. Rosenman, who, as a hustling young lawyer a quarter of a century before, had needed a boost from Moses just to stay in public service, but who had then begun drafting speeches for gubernatorial candidate Franklin D. Roosevelt and who in the decades since had become an adviser to Presidents, a small but crucial part of history (in 1970, a political advertisement, seeking to capitalize on Rosenman's endorsement in an election, told voters: *"When Sam Rosenman talks, you should listen. Roosevelt did. Truman did. Lehman did"*), a judge, a president of the Association of the Bar of the City of New York, a figure of prestige so awesome that it seemed to blot from the memory of even old acquaintances the fact that he had once been "Sammy the Rose, Jimmy Hines' assemblyman," a representative in Albany of one of the most notorious of all the old-line Tammany leaders. The other was a less public figure. Monroe Goldwater was a playmate of Ed Flynn's boyhood. When, in 1922, Flynn became Boss of the Bronx, Goldwater, a skilled attorney, became the Boss's law partner.† During the decades in which Flynn made the power, Goldwater

* Anyone wondering why Moses' fellow Triborough Authority commissioners proved so complaisant might perhaps find a clue to part of the answer by looking at Triborough's insurance premiums. The family of Charles G. Meyer, Triborough commissioner from 1945 to 1950, was the largest stockholder in the Home Insurance Company, a major recipient of premiums from the Moses empire. George V. (the Fifth) McLaughlin, Triborough commissioner from 1934 to 1965, was a director and major stockholder of the Equitable Life Assurance Society, another major recipient. For the first twenty-eight years of his commissionership, McLaughlin invariably rubber-stamped Moses' decisions. In 1963, for personal reasons, McLaughlin took the stamp away, showing signs of increased independence. Moses took the premiums away; in 1963, he transferred the policies involved to Hartford Life. (In Triborough's secret records, Moses stated that the reason for the transfer was that Equitable had requested a 15 percent increase in premiums. An indication as to whether or not this was actually the reason may perhaps be found in Moses' reaction to similar Equitable requests in previous years. On March 1, 1959, for example, Equitable was given a long-term Triborough insurance contract for $20,863. Exactly one year later, Equitable requested and received a 35 percent increase in this premium.)

† "Political" law firms traditionally took only a cut of politically connected "fees"—"farming out" most of the work and most of the money, taking $10,000 of a $50,000 fee for their "in" while giving the other $40,000 to a firm that drew the briefs and pleadings, for example—but Goldwater was too sharp for that. A brilliant, shrewd attorney, he did the legal work as well—and Goldwater & Flynn collected the whole $50,000.

made the money—millions, perhaps tens of millions—for both of them. During Roosevelt's presidency, Flynn was forced to spend considerable time on delicate presidential missions. While Flynn was at Yalta or in Moscow, Goldwater kept Flynn's machine in line. Flynn's death in 1953 seemed almost to increase rather than diminish Goldwater's influence, freeing it to spread beyond the Bronx until it permeated every center of power in the New York Democracy. A courteous man with a gentle, benign manner, Goldwater was nevertheless master of any political situation, no matter how rough—a fact that could be ascertained with remarkable speed by a contractor whose campaign contribution did not meet Goldwater's expectations. Wagner selected the quiet, elderly lawyer to manage all three of his mayoral campaigns.

Moses was not interested in Rosenman's prestige or Goldwater's skill with a brief. He was interested in their behind-the-scenes political clout, and he knew that in postwar New York they possessed more of that commodity than any other Democratic attorneys ("enormous," he would say of Rosenman's influence; he never talked about Goldwater publicly if he could help it). And both of them were consistently on his team. Rosenman was his personal attorney—a job for which he may or may not have received a fee—and "Special Counsel" to his Authority (a title Moses modeled on the one, "Special Counsel to the President," under which Rosenman had served Roosevelt and Truman), on a retainer described as "very substantial." And a retainer was only one of the emoluments Rosenman received from public works with which Moses was connected: a single Title I developer, for example, gave his law firm a legal fee of $250,000. Other attorneys—possessed of lesser amounts of political influence—received Triborough legal fees, but smaller fees, handed out in precise ratio to the amount of influence over the city's governmental structure that they possessed. As Charles J. Preusse became closer and closer to Mayor Wagner, for example, he received larger and larger portions of Moses' largesse. If many of the key Democratic politicians in New York City seemed organized now into a Retainer Regiment, it was Robert Moses who was leading the regiment out.

In lockstep. Moses' fees did not come free. There was a price attached. He was buying men's influence—and for each dollar he spent, he made sure he received in return full value.

The price was not demanded outright. Moses did not directly ask recipients of his fees to return the favor by voting in Legislature or City Council for one of his proposals—or by persuading legislators or councilmen to vote for the proposal. He did not ask them directly for support of any kind. Asking would have placed both him and them in violation of the law and of various codes of ethics. And he neither performed himself—nor asked anyone else to perform—any illegal act. Few of the recipients of Moses' fees were as blunt about the services they were expected to render in return as Mallory Stephens, who, asked late one night by his Albany suitemate, Reuben Lazarus, why he invariably supported Moses' legislation while opposing that backed by Austin Tobin, replied, "Because Tobin doesn't give me anything." The exercise of influence was seldom as dramatic as Samuel

Rosenman's hasty plane trip to Albany in 1957 after Harriman announced that he would veto Moses' St. Lawrence power project because of the preferential contract terms it offered big aluminum producers. (On Moses' instructions, Rosenman flew to the Capitol, went to see the Governor—and that same day persuaded him not to veto Moses' proposal.)

Moreover, no evidence has been found of specific fees being given for specific favors. Moses did not operate by demanding direct *quid pro quo*'s. Rather, it was a case of being on his team or not being on his team. Politicians and officeholders who consistently supported his proposals were considered "on the team"—and men who were on the team were generally also on the payroll. And the over-all record is very clear. When a Mayor or a Governor turned to a man on Moses' payroll for advice, often not knowing that the man was on that payroll, the advice given was invariably the advice that Moses wanted given. When a Moses proposal was before city or state legislative body, legislators secretly on Moses' payroll, or controlled by men secretly on Moses' payroll, were generally the legislators pushing hardest for adoption of Moses' proposal. If Moses was purchasing influence, these men were peddling influence.

In terms of money, the terms in which corruption is usually measured, Robert Moses was not himself corrupt. He was, in fact, as uninterested in obtaining payoffs for himself as any public servant who ever lived. In the politicians' phrase, he was "money honest."

But in terms of power, Robert Moses was corrupt. Coveting it, he used money to get it.

And because he had so much money (in his fields, far more than the city) and so much freedom (in his fields, far more than the city) in spending it, within the city he became the locus of corruption: money corruption.

Consider his relationship with Tom Shanahan.

Shanahan's nostrils twitched to a single aroma: the smell of money. Even as a boy at the turn of the century, one of seven children of a poor Irish boilermaker, he had followed that scent to its source: the noses of his Waterbury, Connecticut, playmates may have been flattened against candy-store windows; Tom Shanahan's nose was pressed against the glass front door of Waterbury's Colonial Trust Company; reminiscing forty years later, he would recall vividly passing that building almost every day of his youth and staring inside almost every time he passed; it had been, he would say, a place of "august halls"; from as far back as he could remember, he would say, he had wanted to be a banker.

He followed the scent down to the great city after high school, but for long years he seemed to have followed it into a trap: the tall, strong young man spent seven years behind the barred windows of tellers' cages. He went to NYU at night, in 1926 earned a degree, but five years later still had a job only slightly better—assistant cashier—at one of the smallest and shakiest banks in the city, the eight-year-old Federation Bank and Trust Company. But when, in 1931, the Depression forced the infant institution to shut its doors, it was the assistant cashier who, with Federation's despairing officers ready to liquidate, thought up a complex refinancing plan that reduced the bank's obligations, personally talked a financier into loaning it the money to pay them off, and saved the bank. When it reopened, Shanahan, at twenty-nine, was its vice president and treasurer.

With authority, Shanahan was able to move Federation into a field from which more conservative bankers shied: loans to construction contractors. The age of huge construction companies was still in the future; during the Depression, most of New York's contractors were small and broke. "Tom would take a contractor who didn't have the salary to pay his workers that week, and back him," an associate recalls. "He went on face value, and he very seldom went wrong." He backed Pete Di Napoli (the story around Federation in later years was that when Di Napoli first came in to see Shanahan he had to borrow a nickel for carfare home to Queens) and the Slattery Contracting Company (which was better off, but barely) and a half dozen others, who were to make immense profits—and who deposited those profits with Federation. He proposed giving junior officers of the bank greater responsibility. More cautious elements protested; the bank, after all, had only one office. Shanahan told them not to worry. He'd bring in the business, he said. He just wanted to make sure that there would be people around trained to handle it. He was as good as his word: by 1944, Federation had $30,000,000 in assets. And, increasingly, Federation's assets were his assets. For years, he had been quietly buying up the bank's stock. When, in 1944, the one-time bank teller was elected bank president, he owned shares worth millions of dollars.

Shanahan's rise may have been as dramatic as one of Horatio Alger's heroes', but it was less publicized; he shunned fame with the same diligence with which he had sought wealth. Not a single newspaper or magazine story provides more than the most cursory details of his life. And he had reason to shun fame: since 1941, his activities had involved politics as well as banking, and his political activities were not ones that would appear attractive in the spotlight.

It was not for principle but for profit that he had entered politics. His political philosophy seems to have begun and ended with a violent hatred of "Commies"; the expression on the big Irishman's face would contort into a snarl and the eyes behind the steel-rimmed glasses would glitter with rage when he discussed the "left-wing conspiracy" that he felt was trying to "take over" the city; planning to name him a delegate to the 1952 Democratic National Convention, friends would be embarrassed to learn that he was not eligible because he had not bothered to register to vote. But his dealings with contractors had shown him that their dependence on governmental contracts could be turned to personal financial advantage.

The contractors owed Shanahan much; he transferred part of that debt to the Democratic Party, raising so much money from them for the party's 1941 mayoral candidate, William O'Dwyer, that when O'Dwyer decided to run again in 1945, he made Shanahan his campaign manager. And soon after O'Dwyer was sworn in, a pattern—a pattern in which politics and profit were intertwined—began to emerge on Shanahan's loom: the contractors he had persuaded to contribute to the Democratic Party were being handed lucrative construction contracts by Democratic governmental officials, and were depositing the profits from those contracts in his bank.

In 1948, when Shanahan was forty-six, O'Dwyer appointed him—with an absolute minimum of publicity—to the City Housing Authority. Housing Authority memberships were "nonpaying," but in Shanahan's case that adjective may have applied only to salary. Within a remarkably short time after he was sworn in, the word was out around town, not only among contractors but among architects, landscape architects, engineers, insurance brokers, real estate appraisers—among, in fact, every profession whose members wanted work from the Authority: You had "to do business with Tom Shanahan"—do your banking at Shanahan's bank and kick back a portion of your profits to Shanahan, presumably for the Democratic Party—or forget about your chances. And even after you had obtained an Authority contract, the word went, your business with Shanahan was not finished; when you submitted the bill for your work, further payoffs would be required—or somehow the bill would keep getting lost in the Authority's files, and you would not get paid. The banker quickly became, in the words of one reform Democrat, "one of the most notorious boodle boys around town." Warren Moscow, who was able to do his perceiving from an excellent vantage point—he was executive director of the Housing Authority for two years—could say of the banker:

> He was a very personable guy, but I would say that ethically Tom left something to be desired all the way down the line. . . . It was common knowledge—no, I won't say common knowledge, it was common gossip—that an architect who wanted to get an assignment from the Housing Authority had to turn $15,000 over to Tom Shanahan, theoretically for the Democratic Party.

"Theoretically," Moscow said—and the meaning behind that word was echoed by others who came into contact with Tom Shanahan, for even insiders who took the relationship of money and politics as a matter of course were taken aback by Shanahan's greed; "we all knew what Shanahan was," Monroe Goldwater says, the wrinkles of his aged face forming a pattern of disgust at the recollection.

If little publicity attended Shanahan's rise in banking, less attended his rise in politics. For years, there was scarcely a mention of his name in political stories in New York newspapers; there is no mention at all in the supposedly definitive history of Tammany Hall. But Shanahan was, for more than a decade, Tammany's money man, the individual who, more than any other, greased the wheels of the machine. He was the hub of political payoffs and influence peddling in New York, the center of all those elements in the city's government that lay hidden and festering beneath its façade.

And for most of that time, he was Robert Moses' closest associate in that government.

In a machine oiled by money, the influence of the money man was, of course, enormous. In a machine that danced to the jingle of coins, Shanahan had a large say in calling the tune.

And Moses made sure that the tune was *his* tune.

The insurance premiums to the broker "friend of Tom Shanahan's" were $27,978 per year. But they were a minor item in the list of Triborough fees parceled out to Shanahan. The fees to Shanahan's bank for banking services—fees as paying agent for Triborough bonds, for example, which required little work and which other banks would have liked to have but which other banks were not allowed to bid for—amounted to tens of thousands of dollars on a single issue of Triborough bonds. But these were minor items, too. For the payoffs that really mattered in the Moses-Shanahan relationship were figured not in thousands of dollars but in millions. On Moses' order, in 1948 the Triborough Bridge and Tunnel Authority deposited in the Federation Bank and Trust Company—which at the time had deposits of only $35,000,000—$15,000,000, thereby increasing the bank's capital assets by 40 percent at a single stroke. This money was placed in accounts on which Federation paid no interest, so that the bank had its use—to lend out and earn interest—without paying a cent for it. And it was left in those accounts for the entire decade that Shanahan remained in power, so that the bank had its use for ten years. During the Fifties, on Moses' order, Triborough shipped to Federation $48,963,000 in Authority-owned investment securities—in violation of every prudent business principle because, at the time he did so, the bank did not have enough total resources sufficient to cover that amount if the securities were lost—and left them there, allowing the bank the advantages that accrued from their possession, for years.

Moses placed at Shanahan's disposal not only his money but his power—which Shanahan used to make more money.

During his first five years as Housing Authority vice chairman, Shanahan, with the help of the two Moses Men on the five-member Authority—Chairman Philip J. Cruise and architect William Wilson—dispensed Authority contracts as he wished. When Wagner became Mayor in 1954, however, he wanted the Authority under his control. Naming Moscow executive director, he directed him to inform Cruise, whose term was expiring, that he would be reappointed only on his solemn promise to give his loyalties henceforth to the Mayor instead of Moses—and, Moscow dryly relates, "Cruise made his divorce."

Knowing Shanahan, the Wagner high command, while friendly to the banker, was far from confident that all the kickbacks he accepted as contributions to the Democratic Party were actually reaching the party's coffers. "That was one of the things they put me in to do—quite simply, to take control of the assigning of architects away from Shanahan," Moscow says. Before he could act, however, the banker made a request that would increase rather than decrease his power: for a personal "executive assistant."

Suspicious that Shanahan wanted such a personal representative primarily as a "bag man," an intermediary who could collect the kickbacks and keep the banker's hands clean, Moscow objected to the appointment, and was backed by Cruise and the Authority's two non-Moses members. Shanahan, even more florid than usual, his eyes glaring coldly from behind the steel-rimmed glasses, stalked out of the board room and said he would not return until his request was granted, but for months the Authority stood firm.

Authority members had long dreaded the possibility of an "exposé" by some Red-hunting newspaper of the fact that some Authority social workers had once, during the idealistic Thirties, belonged, even if only briefly, to some organization later labeled as a "Communist front." Early in 1957, with Shanahan's boycott still a failure, Moses Man Wilson raised the question of the vice chairman's "executive assistant" again.

Recalls Moscow: "It was in a meeting of the Authority: the five members of the Authority were there, and me and the assistant to the chairman, and [Wilson] said in so many words: 'I have a message for you from Mr. Moses. You give Tom what he wants or we'll turn the *Daily News* loose on you. You have ten days.' " Tom got what he wanted, and for another two years continued to exercise considerable control over the Authority—and to collect "campaign contributions" from its contractors.

Naming Shanahan vice chairman of the Mayor's Slum Clearance Committee, Moses virtually delegated him absolute power over certain of its projects. Monroe Goldwater found this out when he was retained as attorney by a group of real estate men who wanted to sponsor one. Moses "put it on Shanahan," the attorney recalls. "He said, 'You know I can't do everything myself. I have to let Tom have some of the jobs. This is Tom's job. Go to see him.' "

When Goldwater approached the banker, however, Shanahan reacted as the attorney had suspected he would.

"Shanahan said, 'Well, I don't know about this.'

"I said, 'Don't you think it's your job to take the low bidder, to consider the rate of return they want and the rate of interest they will have to pay, and the quality of the men involved?'

"He said, 'Well, there can be a slight variation.'

"I said, 'Look, cut out the crap with me, Tom—are you committed to somebody?' He said, 'Yes.'

"I said, 'Well, I'm going to make an issue of this with Moses. I'll tell you this right now. Without even knowing what rate of return the other people want, my people will give it to you at half a percent less.' I went to see Moses. [But] he said, 'I can't do this with Tom. Tom is committed to these people' "—and he refused to intervene.

Thus supported by Moses, Shanahan used his vice chairmanship as a lever to force prospective slum clearance sponsors to do business with him. "A part of my deal was that I had to do my banking at Shanahan's bank," one was to relate. Federation's assets, already on the climb, began to climb faster: in 1948, the year in which its president was appointed to the Slum Clearance Committee, they were $35,000,000; in 1959, the year in which he resigned from the post, they were almost $200,000,000—and Shanahan's personal holdings in Federation stock were worth $20,000,000.

Moses put his vast reserves of money and power at Shanahan's disposal; Shanahan put his vast reserves of influence at Moses'. The banker was interested in who got Housing Authority and urban renewal contracts;

unconcerned with the aims and principles of government, he wasn't interested in where Housing Authority and urban renewal projects were located, why they were located there or how they were built: the factors that Moses was interested in. The banker ran the Housing Authority for Moses. The Housing Authority projects built were the projects Moses wanted built—on the sites where Moses wanted them built, to the specifications Moses desired. In 1953, when Shanahan's term expired, Moses wrote Impellitteri: "It is of the utmost importance" that "Tom" be reappointed. It was—to him.

The influence Shanahan exercised for Moses was not limited to housing or urban renewal. Time and time again, on highway proposals by Moses on which the city's officials were divided, the banker's power helped tip the scales in Moses' favor.

In dealing with De Sapio and Shanahan and Goldwater and Rosenman and Steingut and Roe and Preusse, Moses was, as always, going straight to the top.

Charles F. Rodriguez, representing vacationing Bronx borough president James J. Lyons on the Board of Estimate during the controversy over Moses' proposal to construct Shea Stadium, had received no instructions on the matter and, believing that the city had more pressing uses for the $21,000,000 involved, was considering voting against it, when the telephone in his office rang. And the voice on the other end of the line wasn't that of his boss but of his boss's boss. "I think if Jim was here, he'd go along," Charles A. Buckley said gently. "You do it, and if there's any question, ask Jim to see me." Rodriguez did it—and there was never any question. As a state senator would admit privately, describing Moses' methods in Albany, "he wouldn't bother with us at all; he went right to the leaders."

As old-time Tammany ward bosses had distributed Christmas baskets filled with turkeys and sugar plums in decades past, Robert Moses distributed Christmas baskets now. But he distributed them not to voters, and not—at least not primarily—to the men the voters had elected to office, but to the men who controlled the men the voters had elected to office—many of the most powerful men in the city and state. His "ward," his "district," was the uppermost precincts of politics. "There's only one way to hold a district," explained George Washington Plunkitt, who held his for thirty years. "You must study human nature and act accordin'." Moses studied human nature in his district, and acted accordin'. His constituents—the De Sapios and Shanahans and Steinguts—wanted the rich Christmas baskets of "honest graft." Moses handed them baskets. Using the vast wealth of his public authorities, he made himself the ward boss of the highest precincts, bankroller of the inner circle, dancing master of the Four Hundred of politics. And he held *his* district for thirty years.

Doling out sugar plums to such men gave him power over them in another way, too—as Wagner, in a very private talk in 1961 (referred to in the Introduction), tried to explain to Paul R. Screvane. The Mayor was personally fond of Screvane, a younger man he had taken under his wing years before and guided through the political thickets and, just a year earlier, into the City Council presidency. Informing him that he would be city liaison to Moses' World's Fair, the Mayor leaned toward him and said earnestly: "Paul, my experience with Moses has taught me one lesson, and I'll tell it to you. I would never let him do anything for me in any way, shape or form. I'd never ask him—or *permit* him—to do anything of a personal nature for me because—and I've seen it time and time again—a day will come when Bob will reach back in his file and throw this in your face, quietly if that will make you go along with him, publicly otherwise. And if he has to, he will destroy you with it." Screvane admired—"idolized" would scarcely be too strong a word—Moses. He was loath to believe Wagner's warning. "But," he recalls, during a series of battles in the Fair Executive Committee, "I saw it happen time and time again . . . Bob Moses has these files. On at least twenty separate occasions when we were on the same side, I would say about someone, 'I don't think he'll go along,' and Bob would say, 'Well, goddammit, he'd *better* go along! If he doesn't go along, I'll destroy the son of a bitch!' And he'd call for a file, and he would begin to quote chapter and verse. And sure enough [when the vote came], the fellow would go along."

No one could dwell long in the inner circles of New York politics without knowing about Moses' files, the dossiers he had compiled on the men with whom he had to deal. Their existence was so open a secret that *Times* reporter Joseph C. Ingraham, a particular friend of Moses', assigned by an editor to investigate the financial affairs of a Tammany borough president, knew exactly where to start looking. He telephoned Moses and asked for the file on the borough president—and there inside it, documented and photostated, complete down to deeds and incorporation certificates, the reporter found the records of real estate transactions in which the borough president had engaged, transactions based on his foreknowledge, acquired through his official position, of the routes of certain Moses-built highways. Politicians who had accepted favors from Moses knew that the documentation of those favors was in his dossiers—and they knew that Moses would use that documentation to destroy them if they ever refused to go along with his wishes. They had accepted a favor from him perhaps once; he had a hold over them forever.

A politician who had never accepted a favor from Moses knew that this did not grant him immunity from such attack. He knew that Moses' bloodhounds were sniffing, always sniffing, around City Hall and the files in the Municipal Building, and he could be sure that up at Randall's Island there was a file with his name on it—and who knew what might be in it? "Man," as Willie Stark put it in *All the King's Men,* "is born in sin and dies in corruption." Or, in the words of Jack Lutsky, who during his quarter of a century in City Hall earned a reputation as a fearless and honest man: "Is there anyone who, sometime in his life, hasn't done *something* he is ashamed of? Well, you always had the feeling that Moses knew about that something, and that he had the proof of it in those files of his. And that if he needed to, he would use it." Politicians knew what use Moses could make of his dossiers. They had seen him give newspapers leaks—or issue statements—that dredged up for public view and turned into blaring headlines the dark secrets of men's pasts. It was not just the force of greed that Robert Moses used in bending men to his will; in some cases, it was also the force of fear.

If you stayed on his team, moreover, he would take care of you even after you were too old to play—for his own purposes, of course. He would take care of you until you died. William Wilson was, to Warren Moscow, only "Moses' stooge," but he was a well-paid stooge; Wagner kicked him off the Housing Authority in 1954, when he was seventy-three years old; Moses promptly supplemented his city retirement benefits with a $10,000-per-year authority consultantship. When Edwin Salmon was forced out of the $15,000 City Planning Commission chairmanship that Moses had obtained for him, Moses asked Brooklyn borough president John Cashmore to give him a job—and a $15,000 salary—on his personal staff. There was no job open, Cashmore said. Then make a new job, was Moses' reply. (A new job was made.) Paul Screvane remembers running for the 1965 Democratic nomination for mayor after Wagner retired, and losing, and waking up on the morning after the primary wondering what he was going to do with the rest of his life. "Bob had three jobs lined up for me," he says. And these were not just ordinary jobs; Moses offered Screvane his choice of the presidency of a consulting engineering firm whose president had just died, a full, lucrative partnership in another engineering firm, and "he had another authority in mind and I could be chairman and write my own ticket." Says Screvane: "Bob always took care of people who cooperated with him."

If you cooperated.

If you tried, even occasionally, not to cooperate, if you dropped off "the team," if—ever—you exercised your responsibility to the public rather than your responsibility to Robert Moses, you were out in the cold until you died. There would be no consulting jobs, no authority make-work—and, if the rumors were true, when the State Retirement Board met to certify your pension, it would somehow turn out to be less, far less, than you had believed you were entitled to. As Lazarus puts it, "He didn't want anyone who had been on the inside with him to talk about the way he operated. This way, he was buying their silence to the grave." Moses demanded allegiance only in the areas he had staked out for his own, but that allegiance had, in those areas, to be total. And, with most of his constituents, it was. He not only held his district, he controlled it absolutely. He was, in his fields, the boss of the bosses.

He did not extend his field of force only over individuals, of course.

One cannot dip a toe into the water of New York politics without sensing, moving somewhere deep beneath the surface, the presence of an enormous force, a power unseen but immense: the power of banks.

Banks control the dispensing of huge amounts of insurance and they can dispense it to politicians. Their activities generate immense amounts of legal work and they can dispense the least onerous and most lucrative aspects of that work—local real estate closings, for example—to politicians.

They can give politicians access to the inside financial information on which fortunes are made by electing them to their boards of directors, and they can give them fortunes more directly by giving them blocks of their own stock at favorable prices or, more directly still, by giving them unsecured loans which allow them to make investments without the inconvenience or risk of using their own money, and by giving them those loans at interest rates so favorable that the investments can hardly help resulting in a profit. They can give politicians loans of a size that make them rich beyond their dreams.

The acceptance of these—and other—favors puts politicians in the banks' debt. Banks are very good at collecting debts. They collect them with interest. And they collect politicians' debts with interest: the public interest. Decade after decade, what banks wanted from Albany or City Hall, banks got.

Some political analysts speak of the influence of New York's banks as influence exerted almost entirely on the Republican Party, but it is not only Republicans who are interested in money. The power of the great banks of New York crosses party as well as county lines. Within the over-all political structure of New York—city and state—it is all-pervasive and immense. And Moses enlisted it behind his aims.

Banks have one aim: making money. Moses made sure their aim and his coincided. He made sure that banks would make money—quick money, easy money, safe money—from his public works.

Revenue bonds—the key to his authorities' existence and power—were the key to the alliance.

Banks needed authority bonds. Forbidden by federal law from putting the money deposited with them by the public into any but the very safest investments, the very best of what bankers call "good, high-grade paper"—barred specifically from purchasing corporate stock and by inference, inference reinforced by continuous evaluation of their investment portfolios by government regulatory overseers, from purchasing any bonds and notes except those of the most "solid" corporations, of governments and of public authorities—four years of investment-stifling war had left them "loaded with cash," impatient to put it to work earning more cash, and with a drastically insufficient supply of "good, high-grade paper" into which to put it. Jack Madigan, who had spent weeks trying to peddle Henry Hudson Bridge bonds around Wall Street in 1936, was astonished when previously aloof bank presidents began inviting him to lunch in their private dining rooms in 1946—until one, Stewart Becker, president of the Bank of Manhattan, casually remarked over dessert, "You know, Jack, we've got more money than good uses for it." Then he understood. Returning from Becker's table, he told Moses that the banker was asking to be allowed to buy as much as possible of the next Triborough bond issue—and the bartender's son added that he would never have to go hat in hand to bankers again; from now on, bankers would come to him. "It's just supply and demand," he would explain simply. The demand for Triborough's bonds was far greater than the supply.

Of all possible investments legal for banks, moreover, public authority bonds were the most desirable. In selecting investments, bankers had three aims: to keep their money safe, to make as much money as possible with it —and to keep the money they made. Keeping money meant, in postwar America, tax exemption.

Corporate bonds were dependent upon corporate profits, so much more risky than bridge tolls. Their yield was higher—in 1968, 8 percent to about 5 percent—but banks had to pay half of their profits (52 percent, later 48 percent) to the government in taxes, so their yield from a corporate bond would, in terms of money kept, be only 4 percent. So tax-exempt authority bonds had both greater safety and a higher return than corporate bonds.

United States government bonds were as safe as authority bonds, their yield as high, but that yield was subject to state and local taxes; their net yield was lower. State and municipal bonds, exempt from taxes, had net yields about the same as authority bonds. But, in Wall Street's view, they were not as safe since states and municipalities always seemed to be in financial difficulties, and were continually being forced to go to the voters for permission to raise taxes. And who could predict what voters would do? Authorities, on the other hand, grew continually more prosperous, from revenues guaranteed by covenants that were sacred contracts, safe from public whim or will. During the first postwar quarter century, New York City's bonds fluctuated fairly substantially in the ratings they were given for safety. Triborough's held steady, year after year—at AAA, the highest rating given. Ask New York bankers why they are so eager to buy public authority bonds and they begin, as does Dwayne Saunders, vice president of the investment division of the Chemical Bank, by speaking sanctimoniously of "our feeling of responsibility to the community" by financing projects that will benefit it. But the longer one talks to bankers, the less the talk is of responsibility and the more it dwells on more mundane considerations. A Triborough bond "is a very, very high-quality instrument, you know," Saunders says. "And they are paying, say, 5.40, which is [almost] 11 percent. There are corporates out there, but no government stuff. You're always matching yield against safety in this business. Any portfolio manager will try within his limits to maximize his yields—he becomes very, very interested in yield . . . And [authority bonds] are the highest-yielding of any investment-grade security after tax." Higher-yielding than any other safe investment, higher-yielding in fact than most *risky* investments, higher-yielding even than those riskiest of investments, personal loans—a public authority bond is simply the best investment a bank can make. By far.

Of all public authority bonds, moreover, none were more desirable to banks than Triborough's: by design.

Moses wanted banks to be so anxious to purchase Triborough bonds that they would use all of their immense power to force elected officials to give his public works proposals the approval that would result in their issuance. So although the safety of the banks' money was already amply assured by Triborough's current earnings (so great that each year the Authority collected far more money than it spent), by the irrevocable covenants guaranteeing that tolls could never be removed without the bondholders' consent, and by Triborough's monopoly, also irrevocable, that guaranteed them that if any future intracity water crossing were built, they would share in its tolls, too, Moses provided them with additional assurances. He maintained huge cash reserves—"Fantastic," says Jackson Phillips, director of municipal research for Dun and Bradstreet; "the last time I looked they had ten years' interest on reserve"—and when he floated the Verrazano bonds he agreed to lay aside—*in addition to the existing reserves!*—15 percent ($45,000,000) of the cash he received for the new bond issue, and not touch it until the bridge was open and operating five years later. Purchasers of the Verrazano bonds could be all but certain that they could collect their interest every year even if the bridge never collected a single toll. Small wonder that Phillips says, "Triborough's are just about the best bonds there are." Wall Streeters may believe that "any investment is a bet," but Robert Moses was certainly running the safest game in town.

An additional margin of safety, moreover, was provided by Moses' reputation. "Moses never hesitated to give Wall Street the impression that he would go all out to protect their interests," Phillips says. "We all knew," says a banker, "that Moses would fight for his bondholders." During the previous twenty-two years of its existence, the State Power Authority had never been able to interest the Street in even small proposed bond offerings. In 1954, Moses was named its chairman, and he offered for sale an issue of more than a billion dollars, the largest revenue bond offering in history. "There was some caution," Phillips recalls, "but there was the feeling, 'Look, *Moses* is doing this!'" The issue sold out in four days. Holders of Port Authority bonds were perturbed—although without cause—when, in 1960, New York and New Jersey legislatures teamed up to force it to use its surplus revenues to take over the deficit-ridden Hudson and Manhattan Tubes, but holders of Triborough bonds had no such worries; Triborough's annual surpluses may have been huge—more than $20,000,000 per year and climbing—but Moses made sure that every cent was "committed" to future revenue-, not deficit-, producing projects. "Wall Street loved him for this," Phillips says. And, Wall Street knew, Moses had the power to make these commitments stick. The Municipal Forum of New York is a group of extremely conservative municipal finance and bond analysts who generally accord guests no more than perfunctory applause. Whenever Robert Moses appeared before the Forum, its members, those hard-eyed men of finance, stood as one for an ovation.

Moses offered bankers more than safety.

A high return on their money was already assured—in abundance—by the bonds' tax-exempt status. But Moses provided bankers with a still higher return. The interest rates on his bonds were higher than they needed to be to attract buyers—so much higher that, over the life of a single bond issue, the one floated to finance the Verrazano-Narrows Bridge, bondholders would receive the almost incredible amount of $40,000,000 more than they would gladly have settled for.

And favored bankers didn't have to wait for years to make money on Moses' bonds. He made it possible for them to make money in a single day.

Banks make quick profits on bonds through underwriting, a procedure in which they agree to purchase bonds from the issuing agency in the hope of reselling at a profit those they can't afford to keep themselves.

In the case of Triborough's bonds, of course, "hope" was an inaccurate term. No matter what the "state of the market," every postwar Triborough bond issue was sold out—with many buyers still clamoring for them—within twenty-four hours after the underwriting banks offered them for sale. In the case of Triborough's bonds, therefore, the underwriters' "risk"—the possibility that they may not be able to sell the bonds which is the rationale for the profits underwriters are allowed to make—was negligible. And Moses made sure that the underwriters' profits would be huge. He allowed the Verrazano underwriting syndicate, for example, to purchase $300,000,000 worth of bonds from Triborough for $295,760,851. Since these bonds were sold—on the same day they were issued—for $300,570,851, the syndicate reaped a one-day profit of almost five million dollars.

Then there were the smaller morsels.

There were, for example, the "service fees" that Triborough paid banks for authenticating and delivering the bonds; for acting as "paying agents" for the semiannual interest payments; or for acting as "trustee" for the bonds, a job which involved "studying the resolution," collecting an annual "administrative fee" for routine duties connected with it, collecting and cremating the coupons amassed by the paying agents and collecting the bonds when the issue was redeemed. These fees—four cents per coupon for paying agents, for example—seemed small, although Moses' fees were higher than others paid for similar work. But, paid out twice a year, year after year for the forty-year life of the bonds, they mounted up.

Selection as a repository of Triborough deposits was similarly profitable. Moses' agreement to set aside $45,000,000 as a five-year "interest reserve" was in effect an agreement to leave on deposit in banks $45,000,000 on which the banks would not have to pay any interest—but on which they could, by lending it out, collect interest.

Moses' generosity to banks had to be paid for out of the pockets of motorists, of course. If bondholders received tens of millions of dollars extra in interest, drivers would have to pay tens of millions of dollars extra in tolls. The state's Public Authorities Law supposedly keeps the cost to the public of public works as low as possible by prescribing the use of open, competitive bidding on bond sales and all other details of authority operation. But Moses wasn't concerned with the cost to the public. His concern was to enlist in his cause the banks who could use their power to push behind-the-scenes political leaders, as well as state legislators, city councilmen, borough presidents—and Mayors and Governors—into approving a public work that they might otherwise not have approved. Open bidding would have defeated this purpose. Banks would not push hard for a public work if they knew that after it was approved they would have to bid against other banks for its bonds—and might not get them at all. Banks would only push hard if they knew before the work was approved that they would profit from it.

So Moses let them know. He inserted in the Public Authorities Law a section—561—that permitted the Triborough Authority to sell its bonds at either open sales or through "private placement," and, of course, he invariably selected "private placement"—with the banks that had been working with Madigan on the issue since its earliest stages.

And since the aim of the use of private placement was to place power behind his proposals, he selected as the favored banks those that had the most power to place there.

"Chase"—mighty Chase—had the most. The Chase Manhattan Bank, and the Rockefeller family that controlled it. Chase—the principal twentieth-century repository and instrument of the wealth and power of the nineteenth-century Standard Oil robber baron—traditionally, as Theodore H. White notes, "raised the big New York money for Republicans." William O'Dwyer, who tried to buck its power once, found out just how much it had, and later commented bitterly: "There's a dictator in New York City, and I'll tell you who it is. It's the Chase Manhattan Bank." Not that Chase's power was confined to state or city. During the postwar quarter century, the Chase Manhattan Bank was very probably the single most powerful financial institution on the face of tne earth. And the Chase Manhattan Bank was selected by Moses as the trustee of Triborough's bonds and hence was the single largest recipient of the lucrative service fees connected with them.

The Chemical Bank began wheeling and dealing behind the political scenes increasingly during the postwar era, executing an end run around the Federal Corrupt Practices Act by having various officers and directors establish, and contribute heavily to, a "Fund for Good Government" that in its turn made heavy political contributions, notably to the Nassau GOP machine and the Bronx Democratic organization headed by House Public Works chairman Charles A. Buckley. The Chemical Bank was the second-largest recipient of Triborough service fees. A Chemical officer, asked if the bank had ever purchased Triborough bonds, replied: "We bought a ton of them." The remaining service fees—and the lucrative underwriting profits and the right to purchase Triborough bonds direct from the source—were divided up among the Morgan Guaranty Trust, the Marine Midland Bank, the Manufacturers Hanover Trust and the United States Trust, a quartet of banks each of which possessed considerable political clout.

The assets of such banks dwarfed the $200,000,000 of which Tom Shanahan at Federation Bank and Trust was so proud; Chase's assets in 1974 were thirty *billion* dollars. And so did their power. And now this power—the power of the greatest pool of liquid capital in the civilized world—was at the service of Robert Moses. He had a friend at Chase Manhattan, and the friend was its president; "No one will ever be able to thank you adequately for the contributions you have made to the city," David Rockefeller wrote him. He had a friend at virtually every major financial institution in New York. Says one observer of the New York political scene: "Whenever Moses made a proposal—and I mean over a period of years and years and years—you could invariably be sure that behind the scenes, the banks would be pushing for that proposal. Pushing hard."

It wasn't just bankers' grays that Robert Moses had marching behind him; it was blue collars and hard hats, too.

Despising working men and their organizations and desiring to drive men, to hire and fire them as he pleased, to hold their economic fate at his mercy, he had naturally despised labor unions; let her invoke whatever laws she chose, he had told Frances Perkins during the Thirties, no union bricklayer would ever work at Jones Beach.

But by the postwar Forties, labor unions had acquired immense power in New York. Their million-plus members formed the base of the Democratic Party's popular support, and their campaign contributions—contributions not only of money from their seemingly bottomless war chests but of services such as sound trucks and campaign-brochure printing and of manpower to perform the vital doorbell-ringing and Election Day transportation functions once performed by ward heelers—were indispensable. If the banks hid their power, the unions flaunted theirs; thanks to a special legislative privilege granted to no other organization, there was slapped down on the desk of every senator and assemblyman each morning, right next to the official calendar of pending bills, another, "marked," calendar, for his "guidance," a calendar on which was stamped, beside every bill in which organized labor had an interest: "THIS BILL APPROVED (OR DISAPPROVED) BY THE NEW YORK STATE A.F.L.–C.I.O." And they had it to flaunt. No Democratic candidate ran for office without intoning some version of Robert F. Wagner, Jr.'s, oft-repeated incantation: "This is a good, fine union town, and as long as I'm Mayor I intend to keep it that way."

In Moses' fields of operation, the key union figures, Harry Van Arsdale and Peter J. Brennan (later President Nixon's Secretary of Labor), had substantial power to influence government; Moses' contempt for working men and the unions that represented them had not changed, but emotions such as contempt had long since been subordinated to his desire for power; invited to lunch at Randall's Island, "Van" and "Pete," as their host was soon calling them, found themselves the object of all Moses' easy, flattering, gracious charm. Of his earlier hatred for all they represented, they could detect not a trace. "Bob . . . used to have a lot of fights with my predecessor," Pete Brennan says. "But he got to know us and we got to know him." And Van Arsdale and Brennan liked what they got to know. Their background was in the predominantly Irish-Catholic, conservative building trades—Van Arsdale, who ran the city's Central Labor Council, representative of 550 different unions, like a construction foreman ramrodding a gang of laborers, had been a member of the Electricians Union at seventeen; Brennan had worked his way up to president of the 255,000-member Building and Construction Trades Council—and the trades' hard hats were no harder than the prejudices of the men who wore them. There therefore existed areas of ideological agreement with Moses that went beyond his liking for the Irish—including their feelings about Negroes and Puerto Ricans and the necessity of keeping them "in their place"; if there was a labor force in New York with a lower percentage of nonwhites than the building trades locals, it was, after all, the work force at Jones Beach. Van Arsdale and Brennan soon discovered that on Moses' contracts there would be none of the tiresome insistence on "opening up the locals" that eventually became a condition of employment—usually circumventable to be sure, but irritating nonetheless—on city contracts. Moreover, there was another, far more fundamental, identity of interest. The hunger that drove the construction workers could be satisfied only by the satisfaction of the hunger that drove Moses.

Postwar pay in the construction industry was good. But construction workers are paid only when they work. And it takes a lot of construction to keep 255,000 men working. When there is no work, construction workers blame their union officials. When there is no work for too long—and it is remarkable how short a period of time an out-of-work hard-hat can consider too long—they get themselves new union officials. So incumbent leaders are constantly worrying about where next year's work, and the next year's, and the following year's, is going to be coming from. Thinking as they must in terms of employment for tens of thousands of men, they think only peripherally of private construction projects. Even the erection of the largest private office building will require the labor of perhaps a hundred men for a year or so. And, most important, union leaders have little if any influence over private construction.

But the construction of a large public work—a suspension bridge or a highway—will require workers in the hundreds, for substantial periods of time; the Verrazano-Narrows Bridge—just the bridge proper, aside from its access roads—employed a daily average of 1,200 men for *five* years.* And, thanks to their political muscle, union leaders have vast influence over public construction. Union leaders are therefore constantly pressing for the scheduling of new public works. When employment is low, they are pressing for immediate ground breaking for new projects. When employment is high, even when employment is full—even, in fact, when employment appears likely to be full for some years to come—they are pressing, having learned how long a "lead time" a large-scale public work requires, for the scheduling, planning and contract letting for future public works. Of one thing a public official in New York can be sure: the building trades are *always* pressing for public works; in 1959, they were worrying that New York might not get the World's Fair, which, with planned Fair access highways, would employ tens of thousands of men. No sooner had the Fair been awarded to New York than they were worrying about what would happen when, five years hence, the Fair was over; on the very day that the full five-year schedule of Fair-connected highway construction contracts—the biggest, most lucrative

* A total of 10,000 men worked on the bridge at one time or another.

schedule in the history of New York or any other metropolis—was released, a building trades official happened to be talking about another matter to a reporter, who confessed himself puzzled about his lack of glee. "Jesus," the union official said, "just think when this is over—what's going to take up the slack then?" It was just as important to the union leaders as to Moses that government accomplish, build, Get Things Done—on a big scale.

The city government *couldn't* build on that scale. It couldn't afford it. Neither, in general, could the state. And those projects that the city or state *did* decide to build were constantly being delayed by the red tape of bureaucrats and by what the Van Arsdales and Brennans regarded as the timidity of public officials so "scared" of offending voters that they listened to "the nuts, the protesters" instead of "pushing ahead" with the laying of concrete and the erection of steel that meant "progress."

Only Moses—and the Port Authority and the federal government—possessed the financial resources to build on the desired scale. And the Van Arsdales and Brennans knew that Moses, as City Construction Coordinator, controlled the flow of federal funds into the city, and, for almost a decade after the war, possessed enough power so that the Port Authority needed his okay on most major projects within the city. And the Van Arsdales and Brennans were impressed not only by his money but by his will. In Robert Moses, they found a man who understood what was really important. Ask Pete Brennan what he thinks of him and out tumbles the clearest revelation of what he meant to New York's quarter of a million hard-hats.

> I wish he was seventy years younger! We need him! You need guys like him and they're not coming along. Look at his record! It's a very good record in the building field. And the relation with our industry is very good. He always thinks big—I mean, everything he does, nothing's done in a small potatoes way.
>
> Some people might say he's just a coarse old man, but it's just a question of getting things done. Moses always had the opposition—picketing and people lying down in the street and all that garbage—but Moses went ahead and did it. That's the trouble with all those politicians today: they worry about things like that.
>
> Sometimes people have to be tough with you. How the hell else you gonna get it done? Today they have fights over every park, every road, every playground—you say who the hell can be against a playground for kids, but the nuts, the protesters—they're against them. Playgrounds used to be like motherhood, but today they even attack motherhood. The thing about Moses is he's a guy who gets things done. [With him] things are getting done, and we're getting some benefit out of it.

Benefit. On a Moses job it wasn't just fringe. There was little or no double- and triple-pay overtime to be made on city-, state- or federal-financed projects, but Moses not only liked overtime as an institution, since to this driven man the paying of overtime meant that his projects were being built faster, but, wanting all the political help the unions could give, he wanted to maximize their eagerness for his proposals to be approved. With plenty of money to spend and no necessity to account for how he spent it, he loaded his workers down with overtime.

The power of Van Arsdale and Brennan and the construction unions was therefore at his command. And he used this power with his customary astuteness. "He wouldn't call me on something I didn't have any influence with," Brennan says. "He'd call me to exert some influence at the right spot where I could do it. And you knew he was calling other people to put influence on their right spots."

"A construction worker would pave over his grandmother if the job paid $3.50 an hour," Murray Kempton once wrote. The primary concern to the hard-hats—and their leaders—was jobs, and Moses provided jobs. And, in postwar New York, any public official—borough president, Mayor or Governor—who dared to oppose "progress" could be sure that it would not be long before the telephone in his office rang and the voice of the secretary on the other end said, "This is Peter Brennan of Building Trades."

Whether or not, as legend has it, Pete Di Napoli had been forced to borrow a nickel for carfare during the 1930's, by the 1940's, he and his firm, Tully and Di Napoli, Inc., Contractors, were making money by the carload, and so were the cartel of other huge contracting firms—Turner Construction, Mackay Construction, Slattery Contracting, Thomas Crimmins Contracting, Corbetta Construction, Gull Contracting, Sicilian Asphalt Paving, Poirier and McLane—which monopolized mammoth construction projects in and around New York.

The relationship between contractors and politicians was not as blatant in New York as on Long Island, where, whether or not it was true that Nassau Republican boss J. Russel Sprague indeed, as rumor had it, had a personal financial interest in the Hendrickson Brothers Contracting Company, it was a fact that key Republican committeemen were Hendrickson employees, and that their employer threatened to fire them if they did not support Sprague. But the relationship was, nonetheless, crucial in the city, too. There were two organizations to which the Irishmen who ran almost all the giant city contracting firms were the major financial contributors: Cardinal Spellman's Committee for the Laity (Thomas J. Shanahan, chairman, 1945–1960) and the Democratic Party (Thomas J. Shanahan, financial chairman, mayoral elections, 1945–1953).

The hard eyes of these contractors grew starry when they talked of Robert Moses. They thought of themselves as builders, and they thought of him as the greatest builder of all. One had only to sit once under the great chandelier of the Grand Ballroom of the Waldorf-Astoria at the annual dinner of the Building Trades Employers Association, a dinner at which, even in mod 1968, it was difficult to find a single dress shirt that wasn't white (or a single face), to see that to these men he was a hero—as well as to see the frame of reference that, to them, made him a hero. One had only to watch the packed ballroom, previously stirred to enthusiasm only by the rendition of the National Anthem, rise, table by table of burly, white-haired, red-faced men, standing and applauding furiously, after short, squat Roger Corbetta, a bull in a black tie, introducing him as the guest of honor, said: "This great master builder . . . Hundreds of millions of dollars have been poured into the construction business by this great dirt mover as he likes to be called . . . Two power projects . . . one *billion* three hundred million dollars . . . a great man, a great builder, a man of history . . . serving the public for years: the Honorable Robert Moses." One had only to watch them rise, cheering again, time after time, as the guest of honor, graceful and poised and easy in his tux, his presence filling the dais even at seventy-nine, delivered, in a monotonous, hard, harsh, nasal monotone, his diatribe against "crackpots" who oppose "progress."

They admired—idolized—him, and they also needed him: urgently and continually. They had built up big organizations, and big organizations mean big overhead. Their towering cranes and mammoth earth-moving machines were so expensive that the purchase price was often borrowed from banks, using the equipment itself as collateral, so that in effect there was on each earth mover and crane a mortgage, on which payments had to be met every month. New York's big contracting combines needed to keep working and they needed to keep working on big projects. Moses controlled such projects, so he controlled the contractors. And he controlled their political contributions.

As for the big architects, engineers, supply companies, bonding and insurance companies and a dozen other services used by contractors on big jobs, Edward N. Costikyan says:

> I didn't know much about Triborough. That was a pretty closely guarded operation. I did know that when I needed to raise money for the county [organization] I could count on them. At one dinner, before I knew this, I was having trouble selling tickets, and I called [a key Triborough official] and asked if he could help, not hoping for too much. The next thing I knew, people were calling me because of him—saying, "Put me down for two tables" or three or four. These were people like contractors, architects and engineers. You suddenly realized that here was a guy who had access to the people who were used to making contributions.

Fees, retainers and commissions—the goodies of honest graft. Jobs and the endorsements, campaign labor and campaign contributions of organized labor. The contributions, untraceable and untaxable, of banks and contractors. These were the prizes that the individuals in the machine coveted and that the machine itself needed. And Moses controlled those prizes. Asked the secret of Moses' success, Lehman and Wagner adviser Julius Caius Caesar Edelstein replied: "My own theory? He was single-minded in his purpose, undeviating, merciless to those who opposed him—and he bought off everyone who might trip him up. He believed in buying, acquiring, by paying the most . . ." "Moses happened to be in the philosophy of replacing graft," says machine insider Charles Rodriguez. So little understood was Moses' importance to Tammany Hall that a 364-page history of the organization published in 1967 mentioned his name only twice, and then only in passing. But he had centralized in his person and his projects most of the sources of money on which Tammany depended for its very existence. Personally "money honest," he was interested rather in power and accomplishment. But power and accomplishment meant Getting Things Done —and Getting Things Done in New York meant playing ball, paying the price, the money price. He played—and he paid. He gave the machine—the greedy, voracious machine—everything it wanted.

He even gave patronage, the patronage that, as a young man, he had called "the worst form of bribery." Tammany didn't have to ask him for patronage. He offered it himself.

Every spring, the word went out from the Park Department to the Democratic machine's district leaders: "Get the names in." The "names" were those of ward heelers whom the leaders wanted to reward with "temporary" Park Department summer jobs, jobs that numbered in the thousands for which neither civil service examination nor training was necessary; only the district leader's recommendation counted. Costikyan, once a district leader himself, says: "Despite Moses' bullshit about politics, the summer jobs were handled right through the district clubs. We'd get application forms for them, we'd get them filled out and we'd process them through the party, through the county leader. We had some guys who had a lifetime summer job. They were seventy years old."

Honest graft, endorsements, campaign contributions—even patronage. Robert Moses provided the machine with everything it wanted. And as a result, he bent the machine to his ends, mobilized its power and influence behind his plans. For twenty postwar years, almost all the city's elected officials were products of that machine, owing their election to its support and depending on that support for their re-election. Twice during that period, a mayor—O'Dwyer in 1948, Wagner in 1960—attempted to break away from its hold on him and create his own machine. But each found that any new political organization in New York must, if it were to acquire and hold political power, depend upon the same forces as the old machine had depended upon, the forces that Moses controlled.

Moses made allies of other forces which exerted powerful influence on the city's elected officials.

His alliance with the Archdiocese of New York, which spoke so effectively for and to the Irish-Catholic voters who were, for decades, Tammany's most steadfast supporters, was ideologically snug, natural, even had he not come to power through Al Smith. ("I have no more sympathy with Communism than you have and regard your church as our greatest bulwark against it," Moses told the Catholic Youth Organization at the height of the McCarthy era.) There was only one difference between Moses' opinion of Eleanor Roosevelt and that of Francis Cardinal Spellman: the Cardinal's, except for occasional brief outbursts, was secret. The relationship between Church, Irish-Catholic contractors and the Irish-Catholic building trades unions had traditionally been close and directed toward pressuring the city for more public works, which provided simultaneously jobs for Catholic parishioners and, through the contractors' religious contributions, funds for Catholic parishes and charities. Moreover, the Archdiocese, perhaps the largest owner of real estate in the city, constantly needed favors from its government. Moses saw that it got these favors. Moses, in his rebuilding of the city, was continually needing its cooperation. The Archdiocese gave it to him. Sometimes he and the Church swapped pieces of land as casually as if they were playing Monopoly.

Moses' favors to the Church were sometimes immense. In 1955, Fordham University, anxious to relocate and expand its "in-town" college, was unable to afford a big enough piece of land; Moses used his sweeping powers as Slum Clearance Committee chairman to oust hundreds of tenants from six prime acres of real estate adjacent to his Lincoln Center Title I development and turn them over, virtually as a gift, to the university (grateful Fordham named the central square of the Lincoln Center campus "Robert Moses Plaza"). The city's liberals, observing such favors and inferring from them that he would do anything to curry favor with the Cardinal, called him "Spellman's Pet Jew." But they failed to understand that Moses was interested not in favor but in accomplishment and power. His close alliance, cemented by their adoration of Al Smith, with men such as John Aloysius Coleman, William J. Tracy of Tracy Tugboats, Eugene Moran, Sr., of Moran Shipping, George V. (the Fifth) McLaughlin, industrialist John A. Mulcahy, the founding father, Joseph P. Kennedy—and, of course, Tom Shanahan—meant much to New York (one of them alone, John S. Burke, president of B. Altman & Co. and the Altman Foundation, gave Moses hundreds of thousands of dollars for such park improvements as the Central and Prospect Park carousels and the chimes in the Highbridge Park tower) and much to Moses. Time and time again, when a project he was sponsoring was stalled, the Catholic hierarchy—religious or secular—interceded with the politicians, providing the push that was needed to get it rolling again. And when it was completed, and the long line of official limousines rolled across the bridge or through the tunnel, in the first car, along with Moses and the mayor of the moment, would be the tiny, red-robed figure of the chief representative of His Holiness in the greatest city in the New World, gracing the event with his presence at the ribbon cutting, bestowing on Moses' latest work the blessing of Almighty God.

Not only the Prince of the Church but the city's merchant princes, the royalty of retailing, were in Moses' camp—up to and including the inheritors of the great Herald Square rivalry, Bernard F. Gimbel, Jr., of Gimbels and Jack Straus of R. H. Macy & Co. "Growth, development, progress"—the words which meant so much to Moses in terms of his interests, power and accomplishment—meant just as much to these businessmen in business terms. And, again, Moses made certain that this identity of interest was bonded by firmer cement.

Merchandising requires locations and, if successful, expansion, and, in New York, locations and expansion mean zoning changes, and big retailers needed approval from the Moses-controlled City Planning Commission to get them. Zoning considerations aside, locations were not easy to come by, but Moses could be of assistance there, too, as, quite by accident, Traffic Commissioner Henry Barnes learned shortly after coming to New York in 1962. Since one of the worst traffic bottlenecks existed at the Manhattan end of the Queensborough Bridge, he was staggered when he learned confidentially that the Triborough Authority was planning to condemn close to a square block of buildings at the bridgehead, evict their tenants and build a 2,000-car parking garage there. "I couldn't quite figure out why Triborough wanted to do it," Barnes was to recall with a grin several years later. "The traffic would be backed up for miles." But at lunch with Triborough general manager Peter Reidy and Straus on another matter one day, the Traffic Commissioner heard Reidy—according to Barnes, under the influence of one martini too many—mention to Straus "this garage that we're working on with you people."

Warned by a sharp glance from Straus, Reidy stopped talking, but Barnes had heard. "What are you talking about?" he asked. "They both squirmed around," he says, "and finally [Straus] said, 'Well, Bloomingdale's and Alexander's are up there. We feel we ought to have a branch up there, too.' " And then they revealed that atop the garage was to be built a seven-story department store which would be leased to Macy's. To his astonishment, Barnes realized that Moses was planning to use powers and funds of a public authority ostensibly set up to aid transportation to condemn a score of buildings, evict the tenants, and turn it over, complete with Authority-financed parking facilities right in the store, to a private business. And he further realized, as the conversation unfolded, that the planning had advanced to the point at which even the details of the lease—its term was to be fifty years—had been finalized, and that Moses had persuaded Mayor Robert F. Wagner, Jr., to approve.

"I stopped that one," Barnes recalls. Understanding the reason for the secrecy in which the deal had been surrounded—it might arouse even the dulled sense of outrage of the New York public—he returned to his office after lunch, telephoned Wagner and threatened to reveal it to the press unless the Mayor called it off. "I said, 'I'll blow that one right open,' " Barnes recalls. And, within minutes after he had hung up, he recalls, "Wagner called me back and said, 'All right, it's dead.' "

As for Gimbels, Moses pushed through a number of projects that Bernard F. Gimbel, Jr., felt would help business. He was a frequent guest at Bernie Gimbel's Greenwich estate. When the support of the proprietors of Macy's and Gimbels was needed for one of Moses' projects, Moses told them what to do, and they did it.

Several astute observers were to comment that it was through the telephone that power is exercised in New York. Men who felt the impact of Robert Moses' power often described it in terms of the telephone. "Shortly after I arrived in New York, I got into some big hassle with him," Barnes recalled.

"And no sooner had it hit the papers than my phone started ringing. There must have been a half dozen calls stacked up. I remember that two of the first were from Straus of Macy's and David Rockefeller. They called me up and they said to me, 'Don't fight Bob Moses. You can't win. And we need you around this town.' "

The dispute with Barnes was a minor one. That was why there were only a half dozen calls. When an official—commissioner, borough president, mayor—attempted to stand in the way of a major Moses public works proposal, the calls would pour in by the dozen, from contractors, architects, engineers, lawyers, bank presidents, presidents of bonding, title-insurance and building-material-supply companies, union leaders—from all those supporters of the official or leaders of his county organization in the best position to influence him. "It got so all Moses had to do was push that button," says one official. "Each of these groups—bankers, union people, whatever—all had their own interests at heart, but Moses succeeded in combining all these interests behind his own aims. He gave everybody involved in the political setup in this city whatever it was that they wanted. Therefore they all had their own interest in seeing him succeed. The pressure that interest all added up to was a pressure that no one in the system could stand against, because it came from the system itself."

The proof of the irresistibility of this pressure was Moses' relationship with the officials through whom the city's five Democratic county organizations had for decades exercised much of their political influence—the city's five borough presidents—and with the body on which they sat and which was supposed to be the heart of its legislative system: the Board of Estimate.

The borough presidents were, for decades, the keystone of the system by which the county machines held power; the five Borough Halls over which they presided were storehouses crammed with the public works contracts and individual jobs which during those decades could be translated into political clout. With the exception of the parks and parkways which were turned over to Moses by the Legislature in 1934, each borough president controlled virtually every public work in his borough, from bridge to catch basin. In addition to being able to tell contractors whom to hire, borough presidents' control of municipal services, such as snow removal and street cleaning and repair, gave them direct appointive power over thousands of laborers' jobs, as well as additional thousands of administrative and bureaucratic positions. The county machines were embedded in the community. On primary day, Democratic voters would find on the ballot the names of neighbors, for four or five county committeemen would be elected from each election district, and a district might be no larger than a single heavily populated city block: there were, in Tammany's heyday, more than 30,000 Democratic county committeemen in the City of New York. One of the committeemen from the district would be named district captain. At a meeting in the local clubhouse, he and other captains would elect a district leader. The district leaders would in turn elect the county leader, an Ed Flynn or

Irwin Steingut or Jim Roe. This pyramid was, of course, democratic only ostensibly. The county boss at its top could, for example, employ his power to force the district captains to elect the district leader he wanted. Power ran downhill as well as up. The democratic shape of the pyramid was further distorted by the fact that a principal ingredient in the mortar that held it together was graft; public considerations, of which the will of the people was the principal, that should have been the only voice heard at its different levels, were filtered through a host of private considerations. But there *was* a pyramid, and its base *was* the people. And, through the county committeeman–district captain–district leader–county leader–borough president system, the people's voice *was* heard—even on public works. The district captain had to produce votes in his district to keep his job, so he not only had to do small favors for voters—obtaining them jobs or small loans, interceding with a grocer who had cut off credit—but also had to be his district's champion at City Hall, to be able to obtain a neighborhood playground and to see that it was located where the neighborhood wanted it or to kill a plan to run a highway through the neighborhood. The district leader who wanted to remain a district leader had to be responsible to his people and to be willing to fight for them—and he had to be able to win. As Fred J. Cook points out:

> The machine might be totally corrupt, but it had its fingers on the pulse of block and ward and, when the pulse beat stepped up to angry tempo, it heeded the warning—or ignored it at its peril. It is hardly possible to overemphasize the importance of this old, basic relationship. If the people of a ward were aroused about a local injustice, the district leader carried their complaints to the halls of the mighty, and often enough something was done to pacify his constituents.

The borough presidents, the titular heads of the Democratic county machines, had been placed in their jobs by the county bosses—Cashmore, who sat on the Board of Estimate for twenty-one years, by Kelly and Steingut; Lyons, who sat on the Board for twenty-eight years, by Flynn; Jim Lundy by Roe; Hulan Jack by De Sapio; and relying for their support on those bosses and on the district leaders, they had to be just as responsive to the people. Other pressures—private, subtle and strong—were, of course, always working upon them. But the pressure of public opinion was at least as strong as any of the others—and far stronger than most. And in the field of public works, the city's highest legislative body, formed to represent the will of the people of the city, was, to a surprisingly considerable extent, responsive to that will.

For two reasons—a desire for increased governmental efficiency (which backfired) and a desire to curb the powers of the corrupt machines—the reformer-drafted Charter of 1938 shifted the responsibility for many municipal services, notably street cleaning and repairing, from the borough presidents to centralized city departments reporting to the mayor. This shift dealt a body blow to the small contractors who had played so vital a role in providing the jobs and campaign contributions the machine needed. As for large-scale public works, the borough presidents' authority was eroded by the

Charter and by the new scale of construction made possible by the entrance into the field of the federal government, as, under the WPA and PWA, the emphasis shifted continually away from the block to the neighborhood, from the neighborhood to the borough, from the borough to the city. Because the federal programs were so big, they were administered on a citywide basis, so federal officials were predisposed to select as the local administrators of such programs officials who represented the whole city rather than one of its segments. In New York, this predisposition was reinforced by the Roosevelt-La Guardia alliance that resulted in the funneling of all federal public works contracts through City Hall instead of the borough presidents' offices. Handling the new scale of construction required a new scale of contractors, industrial giants with enough financial resources to fulfill cities' bonding requirements, and enough technical expertise to handle previously unprecedented engineering, architectural and construction problems. And since such corporations received their contracts through City, not Borough, Hall, they gave their campaign contributions to City, not Borough, Hall and hired outside architects, engineers and bonding firms that City Hall recommended. The 1961 Charter transferred most of what remained of Borough Hall's power over public works to the mayor, and Charter revisions step by step pared away to a relative handful the number of administrative jobs over which they had direct appointive power. The borough presidents found it increasingly difficult—in the postwar era impossible—to give satisfaction to their constituencies. They could not provide jobs for individuals, could not give work to local architects or engineers, could not oversee the dispensing of orders to local construction-materials suppliers or of policies to local insurance brokers and bonding firms. The imposing façades of the Borough Halls became empty husks behind which dwelt no real power.

The borough presidents' constituents, uninterested in the complexities of Charter revisions, didn't understand that. They thought that a borough president was still what a borough president had always been. They approached him for jobs, contracts and insurance policies as they had always approached him. And when he couldn't provide them, they viewed the failure as that of an individual, not of a system. They resented the failure, so much so that it would have had to be an insensitive borough president indeed not to recognize the danger to his chances for re-election. "They were indicted for a failure," a failure for which they were not at fault, Rodriguez says. There was a gap—a huge gap—between what people expected of them and what they could do.

In theory—the theories about government in New York that were believed, judging by their writings, by political scientists—the borough presidents, by sitting *ex officio* on the Board of Estimate, possessed (at least until the Charter revisions of 1961) substantial legislative as well as administrative powers: the power to control the city's departments and agencies by approving —or disapproving—every single agency expenditure; the power to control city employees by authorizing—or refusing to authorize—their hiring and their individual salaries; the power to make any changes they wished in the mayor's executive budget; as well as all "residual powers" not specifically delegated to mayor, City Council or Planning Commission. The most detailed and comprehensive analysis of the city's government ever written, *Governing New York City,* by Professors Wallace S. Sayre of Columbia and Herbert Kaufman of Yale, concludes that "on the chessboard of the city's politics, the Mayor may be King, but the Board of Estimate is Queen. . . . the Board [is] the single most powerful participant in the distribution of the stakes of city politics."

Over public works, the works which did so much to permanently shape a city and mold the lives of its inhabitants, the Board's powers were, on paper, particularly strong. "The Board of Estimate shall have the control of the streets of the city," the Charter states, and specifically the control—the "exclusive" control—of the street-opening permits for relocation of under-street "conduits or ways" without which, in a city whose underground was laced with a tangled network of sewers and utility mains, no major public work could be built. Moreover, under the theory on which the Charter was framed, a theory which did not take into account public authorities, the Board and the Board alone had control—exclusive control—over all real property owned by the city. It alone could authorize its acquisition; it alone could approve its use; it alone—through its power to draw up the capital budget—could decide what would be built on it. And, because it had the power to regulate the letting of all city contracts, it alone could determine how and when public works would be built.

The votes on the Board jointly controlled by the borough presidents* enabled them, if they stuck together and cast them as a block, to prevent the Board from acting without their consent on the many public works decisions which required a two-thirds or three-fourths majority.

And they did stick together, under an informal agreement by which none of them would vote for a public work unless the president of the borough in which it was to be located approved. So absolutely did they honor this agreement, year after year and decade after decade, that the pledge, which the borough presidents themselves called "borough courtesy," became known to frustrated agency administrators as "the unwritten law." Through both the formal and informal powers of their positions on the Board of Estimate, then, the borough presidents, in theory, enjoyed what Sayre and Kaufman call a "commanding position" in the field of public works.

But new realities in public works made the borough presidents' legislative powers as meaningless as their administrative powers.

One new reality was the wealth of Moses' public authorities and the Board of Estimate's lack of control over that wealth.

The Board's authority over conventional city agencies rested ultimately on the fact that these agencies had no money except what the Board chose to

* From 1938 to 1957, there were sixteen votes on the Board. The three "citywide" officials—Mayor, Comptroller, Council President—cast three each, for a total of nine, and the borough presidents cast a total of seven, two each by the presidents of Manhattan and Brooklyn and one each by the other three. A 1957 Charter amendment raised the number of votes on the Board to twenty-two, twelve of which—four each—were cast by the citywide officials, ten of which—two apiece—by the five borough presidents.

give them, that the Board could dole it out to them item by item, scrutinizing every line in an agency's budget request, and the agency therefore had to obtain Board approval for every expenditure, no matter how small. But Moses' authorities had an independent income. They didn't need the city's money—and therefore they didn't need the city's approval in spending money.

Another new reality was the poverty of the city's government, poverty both absolute (La Guardia's worst nightmares paled before the realities of New York's postwar finances) and relative—relative to the new needs created by its growth and by the fact that the growth consisted of an inpouring of impoverished immigrants in need of more help than the city was accustomed to give, and relative to the new needs of the county Democratic organizations that controlled its politics. The city simply did not have the money to build public works on the new scale required by the public—or by the greed of the political machines. But Moses' authorities—the authorities and the state and federal governments whose expenditures in the city he controlled—had the money. Through their seats on the Board of Estimate, the borough presidents had power—power to withhold street-opening permits, for example—to stop authorities from building. But the borough presidents did not have the power to build themselves. Their power was, therefore, negative only. They could deny, but they could not initiate. They could not provide what the people—and the county machines on which their own careers depended—were demanding. They became, in Rodriguez's words, "incapable of giving political satisfaction to their clientele." The old system by which they had lived was dead. In its place was a vacuum.

And it was into this vacuum that Robert Moses stepped. To a borough president agonizing because he could see no way of providing the action to solve his borough's traffic or housing problem that his constituents were demanding or the jobs that his local unions wanted or the contracts, insurance premiums and "coincidences" of honest graft that his county organization wanted, the Coordinator would suddenly appear bearing wondrous gifts. He would present to him a proposal for a highway or an urban renewal development that would "solve" the problems. He could assure him that the financing was all arranged, that the BPR or FHA or DPW had agreed to provide it as soon as he asked them to. When the borough president asked how long it would take to draw up the plans, Moses could tell him that they were already drawn up, that the project was awaiting only one thing: his okay. The borough president would be able to see that the proposal would provide, at one swoop, jobs, contracts, architectural and engineering fees. Knowing Moses' reputation as a man above politics, he might wonder whom the contracts, jobs and premiums would be going to. But he would soon become aware—if not from Moses himself then from Stuart ("Mustache") Constable or sly little George Spargo—that, reputation or not, the jobs, contracts and premiums would go where he wanted them to go. And if he inquired among politicians who had previously worked with Moses, he would also be told that Moses was, as J. Russel Sprague had commented so many years before, "a practical guy, a guy you can talk to," a guy who, in other words, would have no objection if friends of the borough president began buying up quickly, before even a word of the proposal had leaked to the papers, the land that would have to be condemned, a guy who would accept the borough president's recommendations on who should get the contracts. "What he was doing was giving them a package," Rodriguez says. "He was giving them a finished product. If a borough president accepted the proposal, there would be a resolution of every demand." And when the county organization gave its annual dinner, the borough president would be able to look down from the dais and see that all the tables were filled, and the dinner program lying beside his plate would be satisfyingly thick with ads. What Moses was doing, of course, was creating a new system—one that revolved around him, that substituted his public works for the traditional means by which political machines existed and grew fat. Whether the politicians with whom he was dealing understood this or not is doubtful. "But," Rodriguez says, "they knew it was an advantage." They may have simply seen it as a "package." But they knew it was an attractive package.

It was even more attractive because it would be popular with the public. "There was nothing in the public mind that was unpopular about Moses' performance then," Rodriguez says. "He was a giant." There would be a resolution not only of the demands by the unions for jobs and by the contractors for contracts but of the demands by the press and the public for action. The borough president "would be able to go back to his community as an accomplisher, an accomplisher of really big things." And, perhaps just as important to some men as any of this, they would know that when the time came, during a campaign or at the end of a career, or over a Thanksgiving dinner table, perhaps, with one's grandchildren sitting listening, for summing up one's accomplishments in life, for saying what one had done for his borough, one could say that during his administration had been built this great road.

There was, of course, a price on the package: if you wanted it, you had to take it as is. You couldn't ask for alterations. The borough president knew his borough better than did Moses or Moses' engineers. He knew its people, and where they went to shop, and to worship, and to play and walk in the evenings. He knew the communities in which they lived. Therefore he might know that putting a highway where Moses wanted it would isolate a neighborhood from its shopping area or its churches, while a route just two blocks away would neatly divide two neighborhoods, which had little social intercourse anyhow. Moses didn't know—and he didn't care to learn. He would not even discuss such considerations. He would allow no analysis of community feelings, of planning considerations—no discussion of alternate routes based on such considerations. Moreover, there could be no discussion—although the Board of Estimate on which the borough presidents sat was the key body in which such discussion was supposed to take place—of the worth of the citywide program as a whole or of whether your borough might not need other projects—schools, perhaps, or babies' health clinics, or neighborhood public libraries—and whether those should not be built first. What happened when a borough president sought to raise such considerations is described by an official who spent many years working for one who occasionally did. "All Moses had to do was push a button and the phone calls and telegrams would pour in: You were holding up work, you were holding up progress. 'We need jobs—do you have any other jobs to offer us? Have you got a better idea for solving the transportation problem? Where is the money gonna come from? You're holding up progress.' Let me tell you—until you've sat on the other end of those phone calls for a while, you have no idea how hard it is to stand in the way of 'progress.' "

When, as occasionally happened, a borough president persisted in raising such considerations, Moses used the power of his money to discipline him—so effectively that he was not likely to try it again. In 1953, for example, Moses proposed an elevated expressway along sixteen miles of Bruckner Boulevard. It would cost $23,000,000. Triborough would pay. Bruckner Boulevard, drawing customers from the residents of pleasant residential neighborhoods nearby, was one of the most thriving commercial areas in the Bronx. Businessmen who owned stores along it were aghast. It had been proven that elevated structures brought ineradicable blight to the streets along which they ran; the city had only recently finished tearing down the elevated Third Avenue subway line for that very reason. Could not the expressway be built below the surface of the boulevard, in a tunnel preferably, but, if this were to be shown by engineering studies to be too expensive, in an open cut? There might be some additional cost, but surely it would be worth some to avoid the destruction of one of the borough's most thriving areas. At least, should not the below-surface solution be *considered?*

Under intense pressure from the merchants, who together comprised a formidable lobbying bloc, particularly in an election year, Bronx Borough President Lyons made the mistake of insisting that Moses consider the alternative plan. Moses' response was to call in reporters and announce that he was reallocating $3,000,000 of the $23,000,000 for a highway project in Manhattan, $10,000,000 for a highway project in Queens, the remaining $10,000,000 for a highway project in Brooklyn (the Brooklyn project, ironically, was the widening of Third Avenue beneath another Moses elevated highway, the Gowanus Expressway, which had destroyed another pleasant neighborhood without alleviating any traffic problems; Moses wanted to widen Third Avenue now because traffic along it was worse than ever). "Borough President Lyons lost some $23,000,000" for the Bronx, Moses said. And, he added, "precisely the same thing will happen with" other Bronx highway projects "if Mr. Lyons does not change his tactics."

Lyons, red-faced and sweating beneath his plastered-down shiny black hair, changed them in the very next Board of Estimate executive session. Although he had been delaying approval of the other highways because of local protests, promising consideration of alternate routes, he approved every route Moses wanted—and he never again, during his remaining eight years on the Board, seriously questioned any Moses proposal.

And what if a borough president, despite the advantages that would accrue to him from a Moses proposal, decided to fight it? What would he fight with? His borough had no money to build highways. The city had no money to build highways. The city couldn't get state or federal money without Moses' approval. In effect, only Moses had the money to build highways. Without sufficient engineering expertise on his own staff or sufficient money to hire outside expertise—even if any outside highway expert of stature could have been persuaded to defy Moses—not only couldn't a borough president finance a highway, he couldn't even plan an alternate route. He couldn't even examine Moses' proposal to ascertain its accuracy. He had no realistic choice but to accept it.

Political scientists read the Charter, and they believed what it said. Public authorities, they said—it was not until the late 1960's, more than thirty years after Triborough had been created, that they began significantly modifying their statements—were mere instruments to carry out policy created by the cities' elected representatives. The existence of public authorities growing larger and larger did not in any substantial way lessen the city's control over its own destiny. *Governing New York City*, published in 1960, went far beyond most analyses by admitting that authorities are "insulated" from many of the pressures that influence "line" departments. But the book nonetheless states that "the Board of Estimate occupies the center of gravity in the city's political process" and adds:

> Land use in the City of New York is under the control of the Board of Estimate. The City Planning Commission plays a large part in zoning and land-use regulation, and Borough Presidents individually have important roles also. But the ultimate decisions, the "last say," rest with the Board as an entity.
>
> All the authorities are engaged in construction affected by land-use regulations—particularly the Port and Triborough Authorities, whose bridges and tunnels require elaborate networks of approaches as well as the erection of the central facilities themselves. The Board of Estimate is in a position to obstruct their proposed projects. . . . The Board, a body composed entirely of elected officials, thus possesses a stout stick for its dealings with all the authorities. . . .
>
> The Board of Estimate must approve the acquisition (as well as the use) of property in connection with a large-scale arterial highway program . . . and it is empowered by state legislation to require redemption of Triborough bonds . . . prior to maturity. (The Board promptly used this power to force Triborough reconsideration of some of the approach routes to the contemplated Narrows Bridge.) . . .
>
> There is a chapter in the consolidated laws of New York State called Public Authorities Law. . . . While the legislature may be under some restraints because it is bound by the Constitution of the United States not to violate the obligations of contracts (and bonds are contracts), the authorities are quite vulnerable through their legislation. And legislators, as elected officials, are responsive to the insistent demands of their constituents.

The city's politicians, however, understood the realities of the situation —and acted accordingly (one result of which was that, even as *Governing New York City* was being printed, Moses was refusing, despite protests from large sections of Brooklyn, every city planner who took a position on the issue—and members of the Board of Estimate—to reconsider "some of the approach roads to the contemplated Narrows Bridge," and was forcing the Board to approve the approach routes exactly as he had planned them).

The single most powerful participant in the distribution of the stakes of city politics? In relation to stakes of the size that their constituencies and county machines were demanding, the Board hardly had any to participate in without Moses' generosity.

Require redemption of Triborough bonds? Certainly! All the Board had to do was to raise the money necessary to, in effect, purchase all the Authority's bridges and tunnels, a feat which, by the mid-1960's, would have cost roughly—no precise figure is available—$2,000,000,000, or about $2,000,000,000 more than the city had available, or was likely to have available in this century—or the next.*

The Board of Estimate shall have the control of the streets of the city. An unequivocal statement. But in practice that control ended where Moses' ambitions began.

On paper—the paper on which the Charter was written, the paper on which the press reported the activities of the government established by that Charter, the paper on which professors' theories were enshrined in the form of books—the Board of Estimate possessed many powers over public authorities. But in reality a single power—the power of money—could render all those powers meaningless. And thanks to his public authorities, Robert Moses had the money. A borough president, searching desperately for a means of obtaining large-scale public works for his borough, could find only one way: to cooperate with Moses. He had no choice in the matter. Supposedly the servant of these elected representatives of the sovereign people of the city, Robert Moses was in reality their master.

The proof was in the way he treated them—and in the way they accepted that treatment.

When he attended Board meetings, Moses "was always threatening to resign," Paul R. Screvane recalls. "He used to say, 'I don't need this job.' And then he'd go and stand off in a corner with his arms folded and sort of sulk. And people would say, 'Come on back, Bob,' and it'd be worked around."

When he attended Board meetings. Frequently Moses took the easiest

---

* The chances of the city finding $2,000,000,000 within its perennially exhausted debt limit were so remote as not to be worth considering. So were its chances of obtaining a sizable raise in that debt limit, for a raise of that size would have toppled the city's already shaky credit edifice. And permission to raise the limit to redeem the bonds would have had to come from a State Legislature that had its own, compelling, reasons for not wanting those bonds redeemed. If by some strange concatenation of circumstances—so unlikely as to be unforeseeable—the city had obtained permission to sell so unprecedented an amount of bonds—and had been able to find buyers for them, it would have had to pay in interest, not the 4 percent that Triborough was paying, but 5½ percent, which meant that the city would have to raise $110,000,000 per year just to pay the interest costs.

way of showing his contempt for the authority of the city's dominant legislative body. When it asked him to come to City Hall, he refused.

His refusals with the Board were not as absolute as with the Council—the invitations of whose president he often declined even to acknowledge. In the first years after the war, in fact, while Moses was still testing the limits of his new-found strength, he did, while refusing to appear at public hearings of the Board, attend many of its closed-door executive sessions. But once he had ascertained the extent of his power, he began to make even his closed-door appearances more and more infrequent, notifying the Board that the press of time made it necessary for him to send "delegates" to represent him: Spargo if the matter under discussion concerned the Triborough Authority, William Lebwohl or Samuel Brooks if it concerned urban renewal, Stuart Constable if it concerned parks, Arthur Hodgkiss or Harry Taylor if it concerned arterial highways. By 1950, one Board staffer recalls, "he wouldn't come down to City Hall except on rare occasions. He would communicate by written communication or by telephone, or by sending ambassadors instead—like he was a foreign, sovereign state."

About some of Moses' programs, the Board was vouchsafed no information at all until the planning of the programs had been completed beyond any realistic possibility of alteration. "The Board of Estimate never knew what was going on in the Slum Clearance Committee," Judge Lutsky recalls. "He wouldn't come in there with [a Title I project] until it was all wrapped up"—the site selected, the replacement projects chosen, mapped and blueprinted, the "sponsors" who would be given the projects lined up, the federal financing assured, everything ready to go, in fact, except for their okay. And they had no choice but to give their okay. During the decade and more that Robert Moses ran the Slum Clearance Committee, drawing up without consultation with the Board projects that would throw tens of thousands of the city's people out of their homes and that would transform a substantial portion of the city's face, not one Moses slum clearance proposal was turned down—or even modified in any significant way—by the city's elected officials. In 1954, the Board became aware that Moses was presenting to the Federal Bureau of Public Roads a vast new program calling for the construction of the Verrazano-Narrows Bridge near the southern end of the city, the Throgs Neck Bridge at the northern end, and miles of connecting arterial highways in between—exactly where, the borough presidents did not know and, despite repeated requests to Moses, were not able to find out. And when Moses, having completed the program, slapped it down on the table in front of the Board, they made no attempt to disapprove—or even modify—it. The city's arterial highway program was, in all essential respects, the program drawn up in the privacy of Moses' Randall's Island offices.

Imperfect as New York's old political system may have been, the public will was never insignificant within it. The borough presidents and other elected officials who had exercised power under it were kept in power only by the public's votes, and they were therefore responsible and responsive to the public. Such responsiveness was built into the old system's innermost core.

But Robert Moses was not responsible to the public. Its votes had not put him in office, and its votes could not remove him from office. He despised its opinion. The considerations that he took into account were the considerations that mattered to him personally: the project, in and for itself; the engineering considerations that would Get It Done the fastest and cheapest way; and the considerations—economic considerations, whether the economics of honest graft, or of bonds, or of paychecks to union men—that mattered to the forces he was using to impose his will on the city. By giving the leaders of these economic forces—the bankers, the union leaders, the politicians—what they wanted, he did not have to give the people what *they* wanted. The old system, imperfect as it was, was responsive to the public. The new system—Moses' system—was not. Robert Moses, who replaced corruption in New York City, was worse than corruption for the democratic processes. In the postwar era many forces were coming together to destroy those processes in New York.

But he was the most important force of all.

The building of a public work shapes a city perhaps more permanently than any other action of government. Large-scale public works shape a city for generations. Some public works—most notably the great bridges and highways that open new areas to development and insure that these areas will be developed on the low-density pattern fostered by highways as opposed to the high-density pattern fostered by mass transportation facilities—shape it for centuries if not, indeed, forever.

During Moses' reign over public works in New York—a thirty-four-year reign that not only was significantly long in a city that had, after all, existed as a consolidated entity in its present governmental form only since 1898, but also occurred at the most crucial point of time in the city's history, the decades during which its vast open spaces were filling up and being shaped on a significant scale—it was not the shouts of the people but the whispers of banks, labor unions, insurance companies, big construction combines, big business and, of course, the Retainer Regiment that determined what public works would be built in New York. He centralized in his person and in his projects all those forces in the city that in theory have little to do with the decision-making process in the city's government but in reality have everything to do with it, and by such centralization he made them strong.

What were all these forces? Economic forces. Money—whether in the form of bond-underwriting fees, overtime-loaded jobs, rents from huge apartment developments, contracts, increased department-store grosses or any of the hundred forms of the payoffs called "fees." Under the system as it had existed before Robert Moses, these forces had been present in the decision-making process but had been to a degree subordinated to the force supposedly supreme in a democratic system of government. Moses mobilized these forces—whipped or enticed them into line behind his banner—so effectively that they and they alone were the forces that mattered, the forces that determined how the city would be shaped. He mobilized economic interests into a unified, irresistible force and with that force warped the city off its democratic bias. During his decades of power, the public works decisions that determined the city's shape were made on the basis not of democratic but of economic considerations. During most of his reign —the post-La Guardia portion of it—the city's people had no real voice at all in determining the city's future. He and he alone—not the city's people, not the government officials the people elected to represent them, not the power brokers who dominated some of these officials—decided what public works would be built, when they would be built and to what design they would be built. He was the supreme power broker.

34. *Moses and the Mayors*

O'DWYER

THE BEST PROOF THAT, in the fields Robert Moses had carved out for his own, he and he alone had the final say in New York City, is his relationship with the postwar Mayors of New York under whom he served.

William O'Dwyer, brawny, blue-eyed and from Bohola, County Mayo, had an Irishman's brogue, an Irishman's gift for blarney, an open, friendly, bluff Irish manner, a wonderful Irish grin and what seemed like a typical, bright Irish success story—born in 1890 one of eleven children of two impoverished schoolteachers, he went to the Jesuits in Spain as a lad to study for the priesthood, then, deciding he didn't have the calling after all, took passage to New York and worked his way up: handyman, deckhand on ocean freighter, stoker and fireman on river boats plying the Hudson, longshoreman, hod carrier (hod carrier who at lunchtime would read novels to the other hod carriers; "Little did the boys know that I was practicing my pronunciation"), plasterer's apprentice, bartender at the Plaza Hotel, cop (dissatisfied cop: "When a guy gets along in his twenties he begins to get uneasy; people stare at themselves; and know that they'll be sore as hell at life at sixty if they don't do something to improve themselves"), cop who studied law at night for seven years; then, finally, at the age of thirty-five, a lawyer, then Magistrate, County Court Judge, District Attorney, Brigadier General and President Roosevelt's personal representative to the Allied Control Commission in Italy.

But flickering beneath that brightness were strange shadows. There was O'Dwyer's connection with James F. Moran, a florid, ham-fisted giant with underworld connections, an association that went far back in O'Dwyer's past, how far no one was ever to learn. When O'Dwyer became District Attorney, he made Moran his chief clerk, put him in charge of key investigations and of policemen assigned to the DA's office—and there were people who, overhearing Moran and O'Dwyer talking together, sometimes came away with the funny feeling that the DA's clerk was giving orders to the DA. There was the fact that although O'Dwyer made his reputation as a DA crusading against Murder, Incorporated, he never even called in its kingpin, the notorious Albert Anastasia, for questioning. There was the mysterious disappearance from police files of certain "wanted" cards and arrest sheets, a disappearance that forced detectives to release a waterfront hoodlum who was reportedly willing to testify that Anastasia had murdered a dockworker who had dared to speak up against him at a union meeting, and there was the discovery of the hoodlum's body in a river shortly thereafter—and there was the sworn testimony of a police sergeant that the files had been removed on Moran's orders. There was the mysterious death of Abe (Kid Twist) Reles, another mobster reportedly willing to testify against Anastasia, who was killed when he hit the sidewalk six stories below the window of a hotel room in which he was being held in "protective custody" by six policemen under O'Dwyer's orders. There was the fact that before O'Dwyer received the 1945 mayoral nomination, he paid visits to fifty-two-year-old philanthropist Frank Costello, born Francisco Costiglia, ruler of the eastern underworld, at the Mafia Don's apartment, and there was the fact that contributions for O'Dwyer's mayoral campaign were solicited by a Costello henchman. And there was a fact even more puzzling, a fact known only to a handful of intimates. Under New York election law, a man nominated for office in a primary election cannot thereafter decline the nomination unless he is subsequently nominated for a judgeship. On the very day in 1945 on which O'Dwyer received the mayoral nomination for which he had been working for four years, he suddenly begged Democratic leaders to allow him to decline it by nominating him for a judgeship instead, an appeal that the leaders thought was a joke until he repeated it almost frantically and they realized, to their astonishment, that he was in dead earnest—an appeal that even intimates could not explain, for apparently not one of them conceived at the time of one possible explanation: that the glib, smiling Irishman was being torn inside by the conflicting claims of ambition and fear; that, driven by the ambition to seek the mayoralty, he might at the same time be desperately afraid of what the spotlight in which a mayor must walk might reveal when it shone on those shadowy places in his past.

As mayor, O'Dwyer impressed even the most cynical of observers as anxious to be a good one. He had a real love for New York. Years later, living in Mexico City in what he defiantly insisted was not exile, he would sit for hours listening to Broadway show tunes, talking endlessly of the city he had left behind ("Lovely, dirty, naughty New York . . . Oh, that great big New York up there! Thank God, I've got those memories . . . most of the time I can't get New York out of my head").* He had the qualities to be a great one: powers of intellect and decision, intimate knowledge of the city, capacity for hard work, sophistication about the powers of the office and their use, and an immense popularity, fueled by an instinct for public relations. During and after the election campaign, many of the rumors about

---

* In the bedroom of O'Dwyer's luxurious Mexico City penthouse was an old trunk which contained a faded photograph of a young, handsome patrolman on the beat at Bush Terminal in 1917; Magistrate O'Dwyer's black robe; and a glittering golden badge embossed with the seal of the city, the word "Chief" and five silver stars. Once, with a visitor present, O'Dwyer opened the trunk, put on the black robe and sat staring in silence at the shield. "The badge of the Mayor of the City of New York," he said at last, softly.

O'Dwyer's past were repeated publicly by his opponent, Judge Jonah J. Goldstein, and confirmed by a Brooklyn grand jury, but O'Dwyer shrugged off the charges as "political," and neither press nor public took them seriously. He wanted to be a great mayor, to do things for the city he loved—and Moses, dazzling him with his plans, slapping down on his desk solutions to the city's problems, convinced him that it was only through Moses that those things could be done.

O'Dwyer's relationship with Moses started out as a close alliance. Hardly had he been elected when the city's Pandora's Box of troubles—held shut during La Guardia's last term only by a world war—sprang open. The civic leaders who obtained pre-inaugural audiences impressed on him the need for new schools, hospitals, libraries, sewers and subways whose construction had been deferred by the war and by the prewar Moses monopolization of the city's resources. Idlewild Airport was barely a quarter finished. La Guardia's runways were sinking rapidly back into Flushing Bay, necessitating a mammoth reconstruction job. There existed, of course, a postwar construction program completely outlined and, to a large extent, planned in detail by the Moses-controlled City Planning Commission—it was deposited with O'Dwyer by a Triborough messenger the morning after the election. But the program carried a price tag: $1,565,000,000. O'Dwyer asked Budget Bureau experts to find out how much money he would have available to build public works, and disbelievingly heard the answer: none. Thanks to the wartime moratorium on construction, the city could borrow about $150,000,000 before bumping up against the state-imposed debt limit, but the interest and amortization on such borrowing would have to be paid out of the expense budget, and under the current budget—an austerity wartime budget at that—the city's revenues were already $6,000,000 short of its $763,000,000 of expenditures. There was no sign of any immediate substantial increase in revenues, and expenditures could not be reduced: almost $500,000,000 represented salary paid to city employees, almost $200,000,000 service on already-existing debt piled up layer by layer not only by Tammany crooks but by Moses' vast public works—which he had said repeatedly were not costing the city a cent. Approximately $700,000,000 was, therefore, as good as already spent. The budget requests already submitted by city departments would raise the budget by $153,000,000 if they were granted. When O'Dwyer first heard these figures, he was to say, he sat stunned. And, Budget Bureau experts told him, they hadn't yet talked about subways: in the current fiscal year, every ride a man, woman or child took—for a charge of a nickel—cost the city 6.3 cents, and the subway deficit was more than $50,000,000. Next year, thanks to rising expenses, every ride would cost the city 6.7 cents, which would raise the deficit to $78,000,000. At that very moment, moreover, the militant Transportation Workers Union, whose president, Mike Quill, had hired the Mayor's brother Paul as counsel, was demanding a huge salary increase. If O'Dwyer was not to be branded as the mayor during whose administration New York City went officially bankrupt, new taxes were needed—and they were needed fast. But the city could not impose new taxes without permission from the state—and the state's Governor and legislative leaders, Republicans and up for re-election in 1946, were more interested in embarrassing than assisting him.

The situation had wilted even the hardy Little Flower. It staggered O'Dwyer, who had limited administrative experience, none in dealing with citywide problems and with Albany. Talking to a visitor in Mexico City years later, he would say, "I tell you, there were times when, as mayor, I truly wanted to jump. You would look out over the city from some place high above it, and you would say to yourself, 'Good Jesus, it's too much for me!' "

Then, even before O'Dwyer's inauguration, Moses appeared with a proposal. It listed public works projects which could be deferred—and it spelled out methods of paying for those which could not.

The city didn't have any money for new housing, but the state did: a left-over $80,000,000 from a prewar $300,000,000 housing bond issue. It would be simple to persuade the upstate Republicans who dominated the Legislature to release that money to the City Housing Authority: just remove the "liberals" who now dominated the Authority and who wanted to "give away" housing to the poor, loading it down with "frills" that they would not appreciate, and turn the Authority over to Right-thinking conservatives who could be counted upon to see that housing dollars provided what housing dollars were supposed to provide and nothing more: a roof over the head of people too lazy or ignorant to provide one for themselves.*

The current capital budget included $41,000,000 for Idlewild Airport, a Moses-planned project whose construction he had been directing. It would be simple to free the city from that expense, and from the additional $200,000,000 it might take to complete Idlewild: turn it over to a new public authority that could raise the money by selling its own bonds.

Most important, $425,000,000 of the city's debt limit had been incurred for the subway. In calculating the city's debt, the state did not include self-supporting projects. Therefore, if the subways could be made self-supporting, the $425,000,000 could be lifted out of the constitutional debt limit, and the city would have $425,000,000 more to spend on public works. And the way to make the subways self-supporting was simple: raise the five-cent fare to ten cents.

The last two of these measures would give the city additional borrowing capacity to raise funds for public works. And, Moses said, it would be simple to finance the amortization and interest on such borrowing in the expense budget: just raise taxes. He had a list of proposed new taxes, and the resultant revenues, already worked out. And when O'Dwyer asked him whether or not Albany would approve such new taxes, Moses told him not to worry—that if he accepted the proposal, and gave him authority to negotiate on the city's behalf, he would take care of Albany.

Moses' proposal was a fiscal codification of his philosophy and his lust for personal power. Since a greater proportion of the poorer classes rather than upper rode the subways, doubling the fare was a financial burden that

* Among "frills" Moses specifically objected to: covers on toilet bowls, doors on closets.

would fall heaviest on those of the city's people least able to bear it. Moses' taxing proposals left real estate taxes unraised and income taxes unmentioned, these being taxes that would adversely affect big real estate holders and the city's wealthier citizens, whose welfare Moses equated with the welfare of society. Instead he proposed doubling the 1 percent sales tax and imposing a 5 percent tax on all monthly telephone, gas, electric and other utility bills as well as on admissions to all places of amusement in the city—three regressive taxes that would fall heaviest on the city's poorest inhabitants.

And the new projects that could be financed as a result of this income would be *his* projects. The projects he told O'Dwyer could be "deferred" included scores of schools, public libraries, hospitals and health centers (not to mention firehouses). The "nondeferrable" list included his proposed new highways. Every one of those huge roads would go ahead on schedule.

And there would, at least by some accounts, be a more direct increment to his power, too. According to these accounts, Moses had an associate hint to O'Dwyer that the easiest way to get state money for the Housing Authority would be to appoint as its chairman an official with close ties to the Legislature: namely Robert Moses. Equally important, a threat to his power would be removed. The Port Authority, whose surge for power he had stemmed for a decade at the city's western shore, had seen in the city's inability to finance airport construction a chance to breach his defenses at last—by taking over the city's airports. But, O'Dwyer was to recall, "Bob Moses represented to me that under no circumstances could I go along with the Port Authority"; and under Moses' proposal for a new airport authority, he wouldn't have to.

Liberals were outraged by Moses' tax proposals—"municipal extortion from those who are not in a position to carry such a burden," one called them—and by his proposed fare increase, because it would be regressive, because the five-cent fare, low enough to allow even the city's poor to use subways not only to get to work but to travel to cultural institutions and amusements, was, as Stanley Isaacs put it, the city's "greatest single unifying influence," and because the break in the previously sacred five-cent barrier would establish a dangerous precedent. Operating and maintenance costs were obviously going to keep rising as already-old equipment grew older and TWU salary demands rose. Were the subway riders to pay for every rise? If they were, they would soon find themselves spending a totally disproportionate amount of already tight budgets just for the privilege of traveling around their city.

Not only would Moses' proposal dump a new burden on the poor; the burden would be heavy indeed.

"More than half of those living here have a family income of less than $3,000 per year; many less than $2,000 per year," Isaacs pointed out. If two members of the family were working, it would cost them sixty dollars a year more just to get to work. Isaacs—a wealthy, educated Jewish aristocrat but a product of a home in which the feelings of those less fortunate were considered nightly at the dinner table—understood, as Moses did not, what sixty dollars a year meant. "This is a heavy load," Isaacs wrote the *Herald Tribune*. "It just cannot be met in many cases without cutting the food budget, without providing less milk for the children, depriving them of needed clothing."

Isaacs, moreover, understood the real motive behind Moses' proposal. The Coordinator was claiming that he simply wanted to make the subways self-sufficient, the councilman said. But this was not the truth.

> Commissioner Moses really gave the case away when he . . . explained that he wanted the subways made self-liquidating . . . so as to release $425,000,000 from the debt limit; so that the city can spend a very substantial part of this huge sum on new express highways, throughways and bridges for the motorist, who will not be asked to pay a penny toward the capital cost. These highways are furnished him free of charge. The unfairness of this seems obvious to me.

More important, who would benefit from highways, throughways and bridges? The same upper and middle classes—suburbanites, and the two thirds of a city that could afford to own an automobile—the same classes which, under Moses' proposal, would be freed from supporting the subways through their real estate taxes. The city's wealthier classes—its car-owning classes—would be subsidized at the expense of the poorer classes. If you insisted on increasing the subway fare, at least spend the money from the increase on subways. With $425,000,000 you could, in 1946, have modernized all moving equipment on New York's subways and made possible the construction of comfortable, modern stations—and could, in addition, have sufficient left over to build the more urgently needed new lines. Spending the money from the subway fare on highways would compound the inequities already existing in the city's transportation setup. It was neither fair nor just.

Isaacs and other liberals were also distressed by Moses' airport-financing scheme. Noting that, to offset the lack of other revenues, Moses had suggested that the proposed Airport Authority be allowed to pay interest rates almost 50 percent higher than the Port Authority—or the city—would have to pay, they assailed his scheme as a "giveaway" to bankers. And they knew whose money it was that was being given away: the city's people's. The rates Moses was proposing would raise the interest costs—the bankers' profit—close to $70,000,000 above what the Port Authority or city would have to pay. As it happened, the city had sunk almost precisely that amount into preliminary work on Idlewild and would therefore be subsidizing by that amount any authority that took it over. Why, they demanded, could not the Port Authority be allowed to take it over—on condition that it pay the city back, over the years, the $70,000,000?

The liberals' objections were echoed by La Guardia, who had resisted similar Moses proposals for years. (The sales tax had been imposed only as an emergency measure to finance Depression relief; La Guardia had been determined to remove it as soon as the war ended.) Realizing that Moses' airport plan would turn over even his beloved La Guardia Airport to a public authority, La Guardia attempted in his first radio broadcast after O'Dwyer's inauguration to teach his successor what he had learned—too late—about authorities. You'll find that each is a "super-government," "a wart on your neck," he warned O'Dwyer. "The investment bankers get to be greedy on authority bonds," he said. "Bankers were in control when I took office in this city. They can come back a little at a time. Don't do it!"

The liberals' fears were echoed by at least one high city official: Comptroller Lazarus Joseph. And Joseph added a point that Moses, in his detailed analyses of city finances, had somehow failed to mention: the state, which at that time took from the city each year far more in taxes than it returned to it, had a surplus, due to the wartime moratorium on construction, of $570,000,000. Why could not Governor Dewey and the Legislature ease the city's financial bind by simply giving some of that surplus back? Democratic legislators repeated the question. Pointing out to O'Dwyer that while he didn't have to run for re-election in 1946, *they* did, and therefore did not want to be identified with a tax and fare increase, they demanded that the Mayor throw his prestige behind the demand for more state aid for the city.

Moses' answer was, reportedly, to the point. He threatened, as one reporter put it, to "reveal some facts that would greatly embarrass" the Democratic legislative leaders. The leaders' response was prompt. They swung into line—and, in a naked display of power during a closed-door party caucus in Albany, they whipped other Democratic legislators into line. O'Dwyer did not throw his weight behind the demand for state aid. As for Comptroller Joseph, he had no influence with the men who mattered in Albany—Dewey and the Republican legislative leaders—and Moses did. O'Dwyer gave Moses the authority he had requested, the authority to represent him—to represent the *city*—in the financial negotiations in Albany. And although the Comptroller had been elected by the city's people as the city's chief fiscal officer, at the very moment at which he was appearing before Senate and Assembly fiscal committees on the third floor of the State Capitol, Moses was closeted secretly on the second floor, working out *his* program with Dewey and State Comptroller Frank C. Moore and the legislative leaders who, with Dewey, controlled the Senate and Assembly. O'Dwyer himself never went to Albany. There are those close to him who believe that during the negotiations—which took weeks—he never spoke to Dewey even over the telephone. The city's mayor transacted the city's business entirely through a broker: Robert Moses. Moses was the broker—the middleman—between the Mayor and the Governor, between the city and the state, between Democrats and Republicans.

The deal worked out was the deal the broker wanted. The program that resulted from the negotiations—a program announced, in February 1946, only after an appropriate public show of efforts to find other solutions and to psychologically prepare the public for the load of new taxes that was to be dropped upon it—was, by and large, Moses' program, although the stories on the maneuverings leading up to final adoption that ran day after day in the city's newspapers scarcely mentioned his name.

Moses even played the traditional broker's role of concealing from his principal facts which might have made him pull back from the deal the broker had arranged. Many astute political observers were sure that election-year public reminders from O'Dwyer of the obvious dichotomy of the huge state surplus, obtained from city taxes, and a huge city deficit, would have forced Dewey and the Legislature to make the contribution to the city that Joseph wanted. Some of these observers even believed that Dewey and the legislative leaders were prepared to make such a contribution when Moses arrived in Albany. But Moses did not represent their position to O'Dwyer in this way. He informed the Mayor that his conversations with Dewey and the leaders had convinced him that they would never make such a contribution, and that if O'Dwyer tried to apply public pressure to get it, the only result would be to make them refuse to accept the over-all city program. O'Dwyer had no way of checking Moses' information. He never applied that pressure, never backed his Comptroller's campaign.

In the interests of his deal, Moses misrepresented it not only to his principal but to the public. Fearing public reaction to the fare increase, Dewey apparently entered into an agreement to delay its announcement until after the election—and Moses lulled the public into a false sense of security by stating flatly that if the sales tax was increased, the fare increase would no longer be necessary. On other issues, too, he beclouded and misrepresented the facts—so successfully that, despite reams of press analysis, the full details of the concealed arrangement were never revealed. He may not have been an honest broker, but he was certainly a discreet one.

And, like any broker, he collected a commission—paid in the coinage, power, that he coveted.

A huge commission. During 1946, Albany gave Moses—in addition to the new city taxes whose revenue he could spend, and in addition to the promise that the transit debt would be permanently removed from the constitutional debt limit, so that he would have $425,000,000 more to spend—the necessary approval for his takeover of Ole Singstad's Tunnel Authority; for an increase in Triborough's bond-issuing powers to $360,000,000; for the right to pay interest on those bonds to bankers at the rate he wanted; and for the creation of a New York City Airport Authority. Concerned about the power he was amassing, the Legislature drew the line at allowing him to become chairman of the City Housing Authority, but it authorized the Authority's reorganization along the lines he wanted, lines that would eliminate his "liberal" enemies on it. And it gave the reorganized Authority $80,000,000.

There was even a bonus on top of the commission. On February 19, the same day on which the city-state deal was finalized, Moses, who was not even mentioned in the news stories about that deal, announced, in an apparently unrelated development (it was to keep reporters from spotting the relationship that Moses, not Dewey, made the announcement, and that the announcement was released not in Albany or New York City but at Moses' Long Island headquarters), that the state had authorized $22,000,000 worth of state park and parkway projects on the Island—including an 8,200-seat Jones Beach Marine Theater for huge outdoor stage extravaganzas that Dewey had earlier dismissed as an attempt at grandiose empire building.

Moses got what he wanted, Dewey what *he* wanted: enabled to hold on to the state surplus, he was able to cut state taxes; as part of the deal that Moses engineered, O'Dwyer even praised Dewey's fiscal policies publicly —Dewey won re-election by 687,000 votes. What the city's people got was four new taxes on their heads, plus, although they didn't know it at the time, a subway-fare increase—and their resentment was reflected in the unprecedented meagerness of the Democratic vote in the city in November; even Herbert H. Lehman, running for United States Senator, was defeated in the Republican landslide. But their resentment couldn't touch the men at whom it should have been aimed. O'Dwyer would not be running for another three years; as for the man really responsible—middleman Moses—his fate was beyond the people's control. Even if they had known his role, they would have had no recourse against him. Following his re-election, Dewey gloated that his majority was the largest in the history of the state. The boast was not true. The largest majority had been rolled up, in 1934, against the man who had engineered the deal, on the single occasion in his long career on which that man had submitted himself to the people's verdict.

Their smiling new mayor had gotten what *he* wanted, of course, and he was grateful. "Mr. Moses has been very helpful in this matter, and has gone to a lot of trouble to do things for me he need not have done," O'Dwyer said. "He's done that because he's recognized my plight." The depth of his gratitude was demonstrated at his inauguration (at which Moses, being sworn in as the Park Commissioner and member of the Planning Commission, drew the heartiest applause from the audience). The first official to be sworn in, as O'Dwyer's deputy mayor, was Moses Man George E. Spargo. O'Dwyer let Moses know that when the Housing Authority was reorganized, its new chairman would be the man Moses had recommended, Major General Thomas F. Farrell, a former State DPW engineer who during the war had directed all army construction in the China Theater, including the famed Burma Road. And when the Airport Authority was formed, O'Dwyer's gratitude was demonstrated even more convincingly. "I've put it all in your hands," O'Dwyer told Moses. "Pick your members." Moses picked them without consulting the Mayor; when he telephoned O'Dwyer and told him he was ready to bring them down to City Hall, the Mayor told him to come ahead; he didn't even ask who they were. He didn't know their identity until Moses ushered into his office Harry F. Guggenheim, Laurance S. Rockefeller and Lieutenant General James H. Doolittle. (Guggenheim had been selected because *Newsday,* the newspaper his wife had founded, was becoming a potent political force on Long Island and Moses wanted him drawn into his orbit; Rockefeller was selected because he was a Rockefeller; Doolittle, a hero of the Tokyo air raid, was selected for window dressing.) And then the Mayor simply offered his best wishes, ordered his secretary to bring a Bible, told his press secretary to call the photographers and reporters—and swore the three men in on the spot. After the swearing in, moreover, he kept Moses in command. "I never spoke to Rockefeller, I never spoke to Doolittle, and I never spoke to Guggenheim," the Mayor would recall. "All conversations were had away from the office, between them and Bob Moses. I never talked to them." As for the renamed Triborough Bridge and Tunnel

Authority, here is the transcript of O'Dwyer's conversation with a researcher for the Columbia Oral History Research Project about the Mayor's appointment of George V. (the Fifth) McLaughlin and Queens realtor Charles E. Meyer to serve with Moses on the board:

Q: . . . Could you tell me how you determined that these two men should be selected?

O'D: On the recommendations of Mr. Moses, who knew more about it than any man in the State of New York.

Q: Why did these men want these posts?

O'D: I don't know.

Q: You don't know, but that's how you determined the filling of the posts?

O'D: Yes.

Policy-making posts in other key agencies, ostensibly unconnected with Moses, began filling up with Moses Men.

Q: [There are so many positions to be filled. How do you find qualified men?] Who presents their names?

O'D: I don't know, except that the names would come in. Moses did a lot of it . . .

The new mayor's gratitude was demonstrated more convincingly still when he not only named Moses chairman of the Mayor's Emergency Committee on Housing, but allowed him to name almost all the other members. "We . . . give him about six weeks" in a Tammany administration, the *Herald Tribune* had said. Within six weeks after that administration had taken office, Moses possessed not only more titles than he had ever held before—the construction coordinatorship and the chairmanship of the Emergency Housing Committee, added to his chairmanship of the Triborough, Jones Beach and Bethpage authorities and the State Council of Parks, his presidency of the Long Island State Park Commission, his membership on the City Planning Commission and his city park commissionership, brought the number to nine—but more power. And it was demonstrated most convincingly by O'Dwyer's acceptance of Moses' philosophy. Listening to the Mayor's first annual message to the City Council on January 9, 1946, Jack Lutsky was convinced that while the voice might have been the voice of Bill-O, the hand was the hand of Bob, particularly when O'Dwyer said:

> It is impossible to satisfy everyone in a city as big as this. I welcome suggestions and help from all sources, groups and individuals. But I do not intend to be swayed from the course which has been laid out simply because it does not have unanimous support, or because some toes are trodden on, or some vested interest of one kind or another disturbed. I hope I can proceed with a minimum of disturbance, but progress sometimes involves some temporary hardships.

MOSES EMERGES AS "STRONG MAN" OF THE O'DWYER ADMINISTRATION, the *Times* headlined. ("Mr. Moses, nominally a Republican, is thus viewed as enjoying greater prestige in the O'Dwyer administration than he ever encountered in his long and varied political career," the Warren Moscow article stated. "It has not caused much concern among the patronage-minded in political circles, because Mr. Moses is known to be definitely a policy man, without concern in building up a personal political organization" and because he is "an independent, with a personal fortune that eliminated gain as a possible motive.") La Guardia, raging impotently over the airwaves, said that Moses had been made an "Oberbürgermeister," a "super-Mayor."

Moses agreed with the Moscow and La Guardia assessments. So confident was he of his hold over O'Dwyer, in fact, that he was unable to resist boasting about it—publicly.

"Sure, I'm a conservative. . . . I believe in doing things the conservative way," he told a *Christian Science Monitor* reporter in May 1946. "The dreamers can't get things done. They can't begin to cope with the problems we have. The big prize here, of course, is O'Dwyer. But the Mayor is able to take the pressure. I believe we have won. Last February . . . the radical side tried to get control . . . tried to use the Mayor's brother, Paul, as a lever to swing the Mayor. That force is still at work and is the main avenue through which the radicals would try to swing the city. It was a tough decision for the Mayor. He had that family tie. It was a big temptation for him to waver toward the Left. . . . But after this initial indecision, he swung around." So euphoric was Moses that when a *Post* reporter told him that the interview "made him look like the leader of a city-wide right-wing movement," Moses only laughed and said: "You take the left wing and I'll take the right wing."

Believing he held the Mayor in his palm, he tried to squeeze him. On May 29, a memo from a mayoral aide listing "matters pending" for O'Dwyer's decision included: "Should the housing program be put under Moses as coordinator?"

But Moses had badly underestimated the hardness under the easy Irish smile. Publicly, O'Dwyer laughed off the interview. But Moses' remarks had brought to a boil an Irish temper that had been simmering quietly for weeks. No dummy about bureaucratic maneuverings, he had begun to realize how cleverly he had been hemmed in with men whose first loyalty was not to him. Intellectually capable of grasping citywide problems on the broad scale, he had listened to Citizens Union and City Club deputations explain that the city was heading for disaster unless the burgeoning, surging growth now sweeping across the empty spaces of middle Queens and the upper Bronx and what was left of Brooklyn was shaped by a Master Plan—and the reports that were pouring daily onto his desk brought daily proof that men like Luther Gulick and Lawrence Orton were right. Moreover, no immense intellectual capacity was necessary to see that the problems Moses had promised him would be solved so quickly were not being solved at all; always before, when Moses had stepped into a field, results had been quickly forthcoming; now, months after Moses had accepted responsibility for the emergency housing of veterans, tens of thousands of veterans, more every week, were being forced to live with in-laws, to leave the city entirely—even to bivouac on the streets—because there was no place for them to live; each weekend's traffic tie-up seemed longer than that of the week before. Stating in a speech that "progress sometimes involves some temporary hardships" was well and good; but some of the "temporary hardships" Moses was proposing to inflict were political suicide; thousands—tens of thousands—of families had to be evicted to create the right-of-way for Moses' giant expressways and Moses was proposing to go ahead with the evictions immediately, to tear down tens of thousands of apartments during a desperate apartment shortage. Each Board of Estimate meeting was jammed with hundreds of protesters begging the Board to stop the evictions, and these protesters spoke with a desperation new even to hardened BPs like Jimmy Lyons. Week after week, at these Board meetings, O'Dwyer was forced into the position of defending policies about which—for political if not humanitarian reasons—he was beginning to have doubts.

Spargo, trying as always to out-Moses Moses, began treating O'Dwyer as if he, too, had him in his palm. O'Dwyer fired him on the spot.* Soon City Hall was buzzing with reports that O'Dwyer was creating a "trouble-shooting" squad—with broad authority—of men he knew to be loyal to him. Months earlier, Orton had asked the Mayor for $250,000 to begin work on the Master Plan and a related revision of the zoning code. There had been no reply. Now, in late June or early July, O'Dwyer called back. The Board of Estimate, composed of men who had been listening to Moses' views for years, would not okay a large expenditure for the Plan, he said. But, he added, "I think I can get the money for zoning. Go ahead and make your arrangement." With Edwin Salmon replaced as chairman of the City Planning Commission by Robert F. Wagner, Jr., a rising young star in the Democratic Party, the zoning maps were formulated in a way in which they could form a detailed basis for a Master Plan. As soon as Moses realized what was going on, he fought every move to advance the zoning study, but he lost every vote, the first time he had been on the losing side of an issue since he had joined the commission. (Burlingham and McAneny and Windels and Binger and Isaacs and other old giants of the city's reform movement called on O'Dwyer to express their appreciation—and to raise again the question of the old fort at the Battery and to assure the Mayor that Moses was lying when he said that it could not be restored. They could stop worrying, O'Dwyer told them; they had asked him to stop Moses by ceding the fort to the Department of the Interior—well, he was prepared to do just that.)

It was on Idlewild that the Mayor's boiling temper boiled over. Of all Moses' suggestions, that one had backfired most badly—and, for the Mayor, most embarrassingly. Lulled by Moses' assurances that creation of an authority would end airport-financing problems, O'Dwyer had publicly announced that he had saved New York from the Port Authority and "Jersey politics." But Moses had planned to make the bonds attractive to investors by raising—by as much as 600 percent!—the airlines' rentals for hangar and terminal space, and the airlines, still struggling financially to get off the ground, said they could not afford to pay what Moses asked—and pointed out that they saw no reason why they should, since the old rentals were guaranteed them by contracts they had previously signed with the city. They were willing to re-

* O'Dwyer allowed him to save face by announcing that he was resigning for "reasons of health."

negotiate the rentals, they said, but not to levels anywhere near those Moses was demanding. Over lunch at Randall's Island, Moses, threatening that the city would sue to break the contracts, and pointing out that the suits could drag on for years, depriving the airlines of any landing area in the country's greatest metropolis except for old and antiquated Newark Airport, alternately cajoled and bullied the executives—until Eddie Rickenbacker, the World War II air hero who had become president of Eastern Airlines, said curtly, "I'm going to Newark," grabbed his coat and hat and walked out. Moses had to report to O'Dwyer that the bonds could not be sold. And at this crucial point the Port Authority exerted a crucial bit of pressure, announcing that it would begin immediately a $75,000,000 enlargement that would make Newark Airport the finest in the world. The city's press, already attacking O'Dwyer for the "giveaway" to the bankers, accused him of having surrendered the supremacy in aviation "essential" to the city's future. Removing the city's airport program from Moses' hands, the Mayor turned over Idlewild and La Guardia to the Port Authority. (The Authority promptly canceled an Idlewild design contract that would have given an architectural firm selected by Moses a fee of $1,178,250.)

While Moses' popularity was still overwhelming, it had developed significant gaps on the left; during the same week in which he suffered the Idlewild defeat, and was watching the City Planning Commission slip out of his hands, a committee of liberal organizations was formed with the avowed purpose of forcing O'Dwyer to remove him from office, and 300 delegates representing 28,000 city and state employees supported that demand in a resolution calling him an "anti-Democratic . . . reactionary," and assailing him for cutting the school-building program and for favoring "discrimination in low-cost housing" and in employment. On July 28, *PM* could report that "the biggest story in the City Government today is the apparent decline of Robert Moses as the power behind the throne." And on August 12, the capstone was put on the pyramid of Moses' defeats when President Truman, after checking with O'Dwyer and being told flatly by the Mayor that Fort Clinton should be preserved and restored as a national monument, signed a bill passed by Congress authorizing the Department of the Interior to do so. There were several pointed private developments. Moses heard no more about his suggestion—which O'Dwyer had seemed on the verge of accepting—that General Farrell be appointed chairman of the Housing Authority. He did hear that O'Dwyer was considering enlarging the membership of the City Planning Commission to reduce Moses' influence over it. Most significantly of all, Moses' access to O'Dwyer was restricted—if not in fact all but eliminated. The days of the two-hour chats in which he could "swing" the Mayor were over. Soon City Hall was abuzz with rumors that he was having difficulty even getting in to see the Mayor. Once, attempting to arrange a personal interview with O'Dwyer, Moses used the ploy of asking a deputy mayor to remind his boss that a city program should be agreed upon before the 1947 legislative session and to ask him to appoint—and to meet with—a committee of key city officials—including the City Construction Coordinator—to do so. There was no reply. Moses was reduced to inviting a lower-echelon mayoral assistant, legal aide Harold L. Herzstein, to lunch in an attempt to win the Mayor's ear for the proposal. And the reply from Herzstein, when it came, came in writing and reflected the Mayor's coldness, as well as a desire to return power in the city to the traditional repositories of power. "The Mayor is aware of the necessity for the city's formulation of a program . . . He has a program in mind which he will submit informally to the members of the Board of Estimate for their approval. When he obtains such approval, he will consider the selection of the personnel to effectuate his program in Albany." During this period, even Moses' ultimate weapon failed him—for the first time in decades. A Triborough messenger showed up at Gracie Mansion one day with a letter of resignation from Moses. The Mayor handed it back to the messenger and told him: "Tell the gentleman who sent this that if he wants me to accept it, just send it back again." The messenger did not return.

But Moses used the power of money to bring the Mayor to heel.

O'Dwyer was desperate for money. The city's crises were worsening. Press and public wanted action. He was, moreover, in the midst of a struggle to take over Tammany Hall, a struggle which revolved around his attempts to oust Manhattan borough president Hugo E. Rogers, whose office was a particularly lucrative source of contracts for the machine. He was not unaware, moreover, of the fact that any major public works projects which were not started almost at once would not be finished when he ran for re-election in 1949. His city, his grasp for party power, his personal career—all these required money. And he didn't have any.

Action in the housing crisis was conceived of by press and public as construction of new housing. New housing projects had been planned with the state money Moses had obtained, but the very crisis that made construction imperative—the lack of vacant livable apartments in the city—made construction difficult, because there were no apartments into which to relocate families living on the sites on which planned housing was to be built. The state had agreed to pay $3,000,000 to rehabilitate vacant, boarded-up tenements for the temporary use of such families if the City Housing Authority would also contribute $3,000,000. But while the clamor of the citizenry for housing "action" mounted daily, the city was unable, month after month, to come up with its $3,000,000.

Whether or not—after O'Dwyer's attempt to discipline him, an attempt which included barring him from housing decisions—Moses quietly used his influence with state officials to discipline O'Dwyer instead and force the Mayor to put him into the housing picture, cannot be documented, but during the month of September 1946 the following sequence of events occurred:

• O'Dwyer agreed not to bring to a secret meeting with state housing officials any members of the City Housing Authority—but to bring Robert Moses instead.

• At the secret meeting, the state officials agreed to do what they previously refused to do—to pay the whole $6,000,000 themselves.

• The official announcement of the agreement put out by the state officials said that the agreement had been accepted on behalf of the city by

Robert Moses and Mayor William O'Dwyer—and some informed insiders believed it was no accident at all whose name came first.

Action in the traffic crisis was conceived of by press and public as construction of highways and giant off-street parking garages. The city had no money for garages; the only possible source of funds was Triborough—Robert Moses' Triborough. (In the first flush of his friendliness, O'Dwyer had appointed him for another six-year term.) At O'Dwyer's request he had agreed to spend $40,000,000 building sixteen of them, getting back the money from fees paid by garage users. State and federal money was available for highways—but Moses' hand was on the valves that regulated the flow of state and federal money into the city. State and federal governments, moreover, were forbidden by law to acquire the right-of-way without which the construction of highways could not start. Available city funds for right-of-way were clearly insufficient. A Triborough contribution was necessary. (Moses had promised O'Dwyer such a contribution—of at least $11,000,000 during the next three years—as well as additional contributions, amounting to perhaps another $20,000,000, for planning and, on some stretches, actual construction, to further speed his highway program.) Whether or not Moses told O'Dwyer after the Mayor's attempt to discipline him that he was no longer prepared to make contributions for highway right-of-way, planning and construction—and whether or not he quietly used his influence with the State DPW to delay the awarding of construction contracts—cannot be documented, but during the last six months of 1946, the months of antagonism between Moses and O'Dwyer, there was a noticeable falling off in such awards—and a noticeable slowing down in the construction of highways in the city, to a point where press and public began to complain bitterly about the lack of "action." More pointed were the developments in relation to the giant expressways which Moses had long been planning to construct across Manhattan Island itself. Even before the war, Moses had planned at least three such expressways—all elevated: an "Upper Manhattan Expressway" at approximately 125th Street; a "Mid-Manhattan Elevated Expressway" across either 30th or 36th Street; and a "Lower Manhattan Expressway" that would run across Broome Street and connect the Holland Tunnel with the Williamsburg and Manhattan bridges. Of the three expressways, the Mid-Manhattan would be by far the most spectacular—planned to run at a height of about 100 feet above the busiest streets in the world, through a forest of skyscrapers—and it had captured O'Dwyer's fancy completely; hardly had Moses explained it to him when he was talking enthusiastically (in private, so as not to offend sooner than necessary the powerful real estate interests involved) about "a highway from the Hudson to the East River—through the sixth or seventh floor of the Empire State Building." Such a highway would, of course, be almost incredibly expensive; Moses' public estimate was $43,000,000—at least half of which would be for the condemnation of land occupied by skyscrapers. But Moses had told the Mayor that if it could be a toll road Triborough would build it for him. O'Dwyer had agreed, and, although funds were not immediately available, planning was already under way on Randall's Island and at the giant engineering firms that operated on Moses' orders. Certainly the Mayor had expected that, of the three cross-Manhattan expressways, the Mid-Manhattan would be built first. And he had expected that, when it was built, he would be identified with its building. But on October 14, to O'Dwyer's surprise, Moses and Borough President Rogers issued a joint announcement that studies had been under way for months on the *Lower* Manhattan Expressway, that a route had been finalized, that "it had been incorporated in the federal and state highway systems as eligible for future state and federal highway funds," that preliminary plans—"directed by the Office of the President of the Borough of Manhattan"—"are already under way" by engineering firms, including Madigan-Hyland, that "final plans will follow as soon as all those whose approval is required have given it" and that "it is intended that land shall be acquired and construction started in 1948, and that this crossing shall be completed in 1949."

The announcement was more a pressure tactic aimed at O'Dwyer than a detailed highway plan—the Moses-produced brochure that accompanied the announcement bore uncharacteristic marks of haste—but the pressure involved was heavy indeed. O'Dwyer could hardly miss the hints contained in the fact that Rogers' name and not his was attached to the announcement, and that it was not the Mayor but the borough president who was "directing" the preliminary planning. Completion of the expressway in 1949, he must have realized, would make it the only major highway completed during his term—and it would be a highway identified with one of his opponents, a highway for which the contracts—with all the millions of dollars in patronage and political contributions such contracts entailed—would be distributed not by him but by the organization he was fighting. And given the public demand for traffic "action"—a demand emphasized by the instantaneous press enthusiasm for a proposal that could be "completed in 1949"—opposing the highway was politically unfeasible.

More pressure was applied on December 2. Prodded by O'Dwyer and Lazarus Joseph—and by the protests of school-conscious parents' organizations—the Board of Estimate on that date was meeting in executive session on the second floor of City Hall; Moses was present, but the Board nonetheless shifted more than $21,000,000 in the Moses-dominated Planning Commission's proposed 1947 capital budget from highways to schools. "No details of the five-hour session were available," the *Herald Tribune* reported, "but there were clews to give color to reports that Mr. Moses . . . found the going pretty rough. These hints came from the Mayor. . . ." The Citizens Union rejoiced that "the capital of the city, so far, is still in City Hall."

Reformers who had expected a characteristic Moses explosion were surprised, however. "Taking his defeat gracefully, Moses had no comment to make on the day's proceedings when he left City Hall just before seven o'clock," the *Times* reported. They would have understood the reason for his equanimity—and they would have been less certain of the capital's location—if they had understood the significance of a scene that had taken place on the first floor of City Hall while the Board of Estimate was meeting on the second. At the foot of the graceful hanging staircase a Moses aide had stood handing out copies of a Moses letter stating that a new study of parking garages indicated that such garages would, as the *Herald Tribune* put it, be "losing propositions, too dubious for bondholders' money" and that the Triborough Authority had therefore reconsidered and decided not to finance them. No reporter—or, so far as can be determined, reformer—grasped the relationship between the Board's action and the Authority's, either at the time or later. But O'Dwyer must have—and he must therefore have realized that during his re-election campaign thirty-three months off, he would have no garages to point to with pride.

Moses' most effective use of the power of money came during O'Dwyer's campaign to persuade the United Nations to locate in New York.

The money involved was not so much Moses' own as that of other people. But, of all the city's officials, only Moses had quick access to it—and he used that access so effectively that he not only played the leading role in the Mayor's campaign but made the Mayor like it. And him.

Bringing the newly formed world federation to his city captured O'Dwyer's imagination as did no other project. Reminiscing, he would say, "I felt that this was the one great thing that would make New York the center of the world."

Unfortunately, other cities were also anxious to be the world's center—and they had the money that New York lacked. Before his inauguration, O'Dwyer had appointed Moses chairman of a blue-ribbon committee to grab the prize. Moses had selected the members with an eye to their proven willingness to bow to his leadership (Triborough board member Meyer, Bronx Borough President Lyons, Big "Bag" Man Farley, Al Smith disciple John S. Burke of B. Altman's, old friend Grover Whalen, Arthur Hays Sulzberger) and with an eye also to the wealth they could command (Meyer, Burke, Thomas J. Watson of IBM, Frederick H. Ecker of Metropolitan Life, and not one but two members of the Rockefeller clan, Winthrop W. Aldrich and one of John D. Rockefeller, Jr.'s, sons who had caught Moses' keen eye—the handsome young man had a lively interest in construction—and toward whom he felt almost fatherly, Nelson). As a result, not only the necessary land but the money to produce the items that "sold" projects—architectural and engineering plans, scale models, lavish brochures—were available to "sell" the UNO's Headquarters Committee, and they were available fast, fast enough for New York to steal a march on the other cities: when the UNO's temporary headquarters had opened in October 1946, it had opened in New York—on the site Moses had selected, Flushing Meadows Park, in which the City Building left over (and, since it was located in a park, under Moses' jurisdiction) from the 1939 World's Fair had been transformed at a city-borne cost of $2,200,000 from a skating rink into a General Assembly Building. And Moses and O'Dwyer were prepared to turn over 350 acres of the park to the UNO for its permanent headquarters. But UNO delegates didn't like the site, preferring one in Manhattan. There was no vacant site of sufficient size available there, and acquiring one would therefore require not only an immense expenditure for land acquisition and construction, and not only additional expenditures for the related access and parking improvements for the big "DPL" limousines, but also, the delegates made clear, absolute and permanent exemption from city real estate taxes. The delegates were also insistent on the provision of housing in the housing-short city, not only for themselves but for their staffs and the staff of the UNO Secretariat, which numbered in the hundreds. O'Dwyer felt that asking the Board of Estimate, which was being forced every two weeks to explain that the city had no money to build desperately needed schools, hospitals, libraries and sewers, would be futile—unless he had a "gesture," "something he could show the Board": some sort of private contribution to defray the cost and get the project started. But with the UNO pressuring him almost daily for an answer, he had to confess he had neither the center-city site for a permanent headquarters—nor the money to build one. Meanwhile, San Francisco's mayor was in New York incognito, offering a huge site; Boston had dispatched a team, including its mayor, the Governor and Lieutenant Governor of Massachusetts, and *Christian Science Monitor* editor Erwin D. Canham, to offer not only a site but a guarantee of city funds to build headquarters and housing on it; Philadelphia, many delegates' choice, was offering the world organization its choice of sites. UNO Secretary-General Trygve Lie, himself once a municipal official in Norway, had been personally awed by Moses in their many conferences and was holding out for New York, but on November 9, the General Assembly directed its Headquarters Committee to concentrate on sites in other cities and on December 6, a Friday, with Philadelphia so confident that it was already condemning land for the headquarters, Lie emerged from a committee meeting to telephone O'Dwyer and Moses and tell them "that unless they came up with a new and better proposal the whole thing would be over as far as New York was concerned. I had done all I could." A final decision in favor of Philadelphia was expected the following Wednesday.

O'Dwyer had received another telephone call that Friday—from William Zeckendorf. Zeckendorf, real estate wheeler-dealer on the grand scale, informed the Mayor that for some months his confidential agents had been secretly buying up property in Turtle Bay, an area on midtown Manhattan's eastern shore—occupied since Civil War days by slaughterhouses, packing plants and cattle pens—in which land was cheap. He had succeeded in acquiring an option to purchase the heart of the area, a seventeen-acre tract bounded by Forty-second and Forty-ninth streets and the East River Drive and First Avenue, for only $6,500,000, or seventeen dollars per square foot—a mere fraction of the price of most midtown real estate. He had planned to create a series of huge superblocks there, but plans and financing weren't finalized, the option was running out—and he was willing to sell the tract, the largest land parcel to become available in central New York in twenty-five years, to the UNO.

When O'Dwyer reported the offer to Lie, the Secretary-General said, "Turtle Bay . . . even now, could turn the tide." His remarks, however, did nothing to solve O'Dwyer's cash problem. Zeckendorf recalls that the Mayor "fervently said" that, to keep the UNO in New York, "he'd give an arm, a leg and various other parts of his body . . . but that none of them was particularly salable." The name Rockefeller was suggested as a source of the cash, perhaps because the family had given the UNO's predecessor, the League of Nations, a huge donation. But O'Dwyer had no entree to the Rockefeller from whom, at that time, a gift of the necessary dimensions would have to come—John D. Rockefeller, Jr., John D. Rockefeller who had spent long days riding over the route of the Palisades Interstate Parkway with Robert Moses, John D. Rockefeller who had worked closely with Robert Moses in the construction of the Cloisters and children's playgrounds in Fort Tryon Park, John D. Rockefeller who had, with Moses' cooperation, worked out a land exchange with the city to help along the building of additions to Rockefeller Institute, John D. Rockefeller whose admiration for Robert Moses was well known. In the midst of his feud with Moses, O'Dwyer turned to the Coordinator as a last resort. "This is where Moses came in with Nelson Rockefeller, working on Mr. Rockefeller, his father," the Mayor recalls. There were endless details to be worked out: acquisition of the land that Zeckendorf didn't control, widening of Forty-seventh Street to provide access to the site, city property that had to be included or excluded, a federal gift for construction. And there was only a little over four days—ninety-six hours—to work them out in. When the gavel slammed down to call the UNO Headquarters Committee into session on Wednesday morning, it would be too late.

Saturday and Sunday were among the most tense and exciting that I can recall as Secretary-General [Lie wrote]. Momentous conversations were taking place backstage: steps were being taken that might snatch victory from defeat and crown these fifteen months of effort with success. Ambassador Austin [was] now involved . . . There were secret consultations with the Rockefeller brothers and with their father, John D. Rockefeller, Jr. But what was happening then was known only to a selected few. . . . There was much to be done before so extensive a real estate transaction as this could be assured. Normally it would have taken months of business negotiations with batteries of lawyers.

But in ninety-six hours, it was done. For every snag that arose, Moses had a knife. Teams of lawyers were prepared to research for days the details of city surrender of East River bulkheads; Moses called in a secretary and dictated on the spot without reference to a single law book a memorandum setting out the method—a memorandum lawyers later found to be correct down to the last comma. Legislative permission was needed for the city to close certain streets within the site and give the UNO the land—a few phone calls from Moses to Albany secured a guarantee of the permission. Late Tuesday night—about twelve hours before the Headquarters Committee convened—Zeckendorf, who had taken no part in the discussions following his offer and did not know if there was any chance of its being accepted, was celebrating his birthday in a private dining room at the Monte Carlo when Wallace K. Harrison, the distinguished architect and intimate of the Rockefeller family, walked in with a block-by-block map of the site bulging out of a jacket pocket, sat down at the table, tried to assume an air of nonchalance, failed and blurted out, "Would you sell it for eight and a half million?" Zeckendorf said yes, and the next morning at ten-thirty, as he sat in his office nursing a hangover, the phone rang and he heard Nelson Rockefeller say, "We've been up all night patching up the details, but it's going to work. The old man is going to give that 8.5 million dollars to the UN, and they're going to take your property. See you soon. . . . Good-bye." When, minutes later, the Headquarters Committee convened, Austin arose and announced the gift—which also included, on Rockefeller's insistence, a city commitment of $2,500,000 for property to round out the site and of additional city funds to ease traffic problems by widening Forty-seventh Street and building a half-mile-long north-south tunnel under First Avenue. And within three days, the General Assembly accepted it. A key factor in the acceptance had been O'Dwyer's promise of housing, and, thanks to Moses, O'Dwyer was able to keep that promise, through Metropolitan Life Insurance at Peter Cooper Village, through New York Life at Fresh Meadows Golf Course, through a Moses-conceived "Savings Bank Trust Company" formed to build Parkway Village in Jamaica—all housing projects arranged by Moses in which Moses was now able to reserve whole buildings for UNO personnel.

Some elements in the city—Stanley Isaacs and other "radicals"—objected to a city unable to provide the necessities of modern life for its people spending millions on the UNO and giving tax exemptions on real estate that could bring the city millions more. Some members of the Board of Estimate, notably Lazarus Joseph, seconded those objections.

But O'Dwyer could handle the radicals. He could handle the Board of Estimate, not that much handling of that body was necessary, since they were highly susceptible, as the Mayor had known they would be, to the argument that $8,500,000—and, as journalists were putting it, the chance to be "the permanent capital of the world"—was being given to the city for what was represented as insignificant city contributions. No one on the Board guessed that over the next ten years those contributions would total more than $32,000,000. He could handle the Board because he had the money—and Moses had given him that money.

Letters from key figures in the negotiations revealed deep appreciation of the role Moses had played—and of the personal qualities that had made him perhaps uniquely qualified to play it. "My deepest thanks," wrote Trygve Lie, who was later to say—in the midst of a hot dispute with Moses over construction details: "I understand him and I understand what he has done for New York. . . . It is marvelous. I regard him as one of the greatest men of our time." "My profound thanks," wrote John D. Rockefeller. "Your instantaneous approval of the offer, your broad vision as to the future possibilities, your quick appreciation of the necessary immediate steps, and your prompt action looking toward the city's cooperation, all played a vital role in bringing about the ultimate outcome. It has been a pleasure for me to be associated with you in this matter, so far-reaching in its implications, and I would have you know of my deep gratitude to you. . . ." But Lie and Rockefeller were no more appreciative than the Mayor, and a letter from him expressed gratitude in the way that, to Moses, was most important: the letter, dated January 13, 1947, gave Moses complete power over all details—including those normally handled by other city agencies—relating to the construction of the UNO headquarters. His fall from grace had occurred in

July 1946. By January 13, 1947, it was over. The power of money had not only brought the Mayor to heel, but had made him like it.

Moses not only came back, but came back bigger than ever. Moses Man Farrell was appointed chairman of the Housing Authority, another Moses Man, Philip J. Cruise, was appointed Authority secretary—at double his previous salary. There was no more talk about enlarging the City Planning Commission. A confidential Moses memo told the Mayor which highway sections "we can complete . . . by the Summer of 1949"—in time for O'Dwyer's re-election campaign—"if we . . . tolerate no further delays." O'Dwyer tolerated no further delays. Within weeks, families in the rights-of-way were being evicted and the State DPW was awarding construction contracts—to firms that did their banking with Federation (and that could be expected, through Federation's president, to contribute to O'Dwyer's re-election campaign). Moses was cocky enough to put his dominance over the Mayor who was supposedly his boss on public display. At one Board of Estimate session, Comptroller Joseph refused to approve $144,000 in design contracts for Andrews & Clark, engineers, and Eggers & Higgins, architects, for work on Ferry Point Park, contending that engineers already employed by the city could do the work for $41,000. Turning to O'Dwyer, Moses said, "If I don't have the sufficient confidence of this administration in a matter of this kind I don't want to be Parks Commissioner and I don't want to be Construction Coordinator. I'm tired of this sort of thing, and I mean what I say." O'Dwyer responded to this open threat by angrily lecturing Joseph. When the Comptroller protested, "I'm sorry, General, but it was not my fault," O'Dwyer replied, "It was your fault," and ordered the Comptroller to "patch things up" with Moses. (Joseph did.)

Most important, Moses now had his entrée to the Mayor back—on a regular basis. Every week at least two leisurely Gracie Mansion breakfast conferences were reserved for Robert Moses, who would come over from his apartment a block away. "Tuesdays," O'Dwyer would recall, "it was . . . all United Nations business"—transacted by Moses and whomever he wanted to bring along, Trygve Lie perhaps. On Fridays, Moses would bring along guests who, to O'Dwyer, may have been more important than the Secretary-General of the world organization. "Every Friday morning," John A. Coleman recalls, "he'd set aside for Moses and whatever construction people Moses wanted to bring." There were, in fact, few mornings on which, appointment or not, when O'Dwyer descended the Gracie Mansion staircase at about ten o'clock, Moses wasn't waiting for him.

Moses knew how to make the most of such entrée. Says Lutsky: "He'd see [O'Dwyer] alone, without the Mayor having had an opportunity to hear the other side, and get him committed. And he had another device." By the time O'Dwyer came downstairs at ten, Moses would have been up working for three hours, if not longer. "He would have the papers ready, and if the Mayor said okay, he could get them signed right there." Despite his admiration for Moses, Lutsky saw the danger in this, a danger intensified by the fact that O'Dwyer, naturally friendly, "would always agree with the last man in"—the person right there.

Moses got his commitments from the Mayor now without ever again arousing his ire. Moses' smiling, hearty, arm-around-the-shoulders charm—charm that could disarm a roomful of listeners—was simply overwhelming to an individual who was sequestered alone with him morning after morning, particularly when combined with his intellect and vision and governmental ability. "You know the city's too big. It's too big for one government," O'Dwyer was to recall. "It's a tough battle, and everything falls on your head when you're Mayor. I remember the lonely nights and the snowy nights and the stormy nights up there at Gracie Mansion, and I would walk up and down the porch and look over at Astoria . . . and I would say, 'Good Lord, I'm Mayor of this town!' . . . It was something. The job frightened me at times like that." But Moses, who, despite the bigness of the city, had built the great bridge to Astoria that dominated the view from that porch, would be there to lift the load, with answers, solutions, courses of action for which financing was available, courses of action that could be implemented if only the Mayor would sign right here.

And the Mayor was now increasingly glad to get help from him. "If the two of them were together, it would be Moses doing most of the talking," Paul O'Dwyer recalls. "Bill was a good listener. Moses would be selling, as it were. The scene would be Bill sitting and Moses pacing and talking. My brother was essentially a reader of books, of plays, of history. Bill was essentially an artist. Bill was the dreamer in the larger sense. And Moses was the very practical—the antithesis of that. So from the standpoint of the Mayor and the Coordinator of Construction, they complemented each other very well." However Paul may have felt about Moses, moreover, he had to admit that his brother's feelings for his Coordinator went beyond professional complementation. "He liked Moses, maybe more than Moses liked him, because I don't think Moses liked anybody," he says. Soon, one of Moses' opponents recalls, "all decisions that mattered in the city were being made up at Gracie Mansion, with Moses alone with the Mayor." In December 1947, the *Herald Tribune,* for so long a Moses supporter, felt constrained to comment: "Plans for a future New York are being drawn up on Mr. Moses' personal drafting table and nowhere else. In the absence of adequate planning measures, without up-to-date zoning, without a Master Plan, the city is being re-planned *in camera* . . . A dangerous measure of discretionary power has now been amassed in the hands of a single individual." But O'Dwyer's feelings—the only feelings that mattered—were spelled out in 1962 in his Oral History Reminiscences with a vividness that belied the passage of years.

> On contracts, I'd rely 100,000 percent on Moses, and sometimes on the question of art, the question of repairs to museums and the building of the Aquarium, for instance, and things of that kind—highways, the UN Building . . . that was all well within the Coordinator's job, and that was Bob Moses. Sometimes I didn't agree with him . . . but in the main, I took—paid great attention to the recommendations of Mr. Moses. . . . One sure thing, there are very few people in this town that I think more highly of than Bob Moses. In fact, I don't think there is anyone. . . . He gets the job done, efficiently and without extra cost. . . . I made him the coordinator of all city contracts. I knew that would

keep them clean. I also knew that it would be done with a view to giving the right kind of selection of what to do, you know . . . The thing is, what were the necessary things, and in what order should they be built . . . You have to have the very best brains on selecting what is good—what's the first thing that must be done, and the second and third, in an orderly way. That is where Moses came in. He was wonderful.

And when the interviewer inquired, "Was it his brains? His influence?" O'Dwyer replied:

"He has the brains and he has the influence. He has both."

Early in 1948, Moses apprised O'Dwyer about Senator Taft's plans for a new slum clearance or "urban renewal" program. In December, while Congress was still working out the details, O'Dwyer appointed him to the chairmanship of a new "Mayor's Committee on Slum Clearance"—his tenth post—and allowed him to name most of the other members.

Newspapers, slow to grasp the significance of the pending federal "Title I" slum clearance legislation, were slow to grasp the significance of Moses' appointment. The *Times* buried the story—four paragraphs long—on page nine. But on the landscape of New York's history, that appointment stands out like a mountain. Moses had been campaigning to take over federally funded housing in New York for ten years, to the virtually unanimous dismay of those who believed in the social philosophy which underlay the government's decision to provide shelter for the impoverished among its people, and who feared that Moses' philosophy—so antithetical—would, even while he was in the process of building such housing, undermine the aims for which it was being built. By cutting Moses off the air in 1938, La Guardia had defeated Moses in the first battle of the campaign. A new mayor had, by appointing him Construction Coordinator and naming his aides to the City Housing Authority, given him a measure of the control he coveted, but the control had been indirect and hence incomplete. But now—as of December 17, 1948—his control was complete at last.

Behind the control, moreover, was power of a new immensity. Title I of the Housing Act of 1949 extended the power of eminent domain, traditionally used in America only for government-built projects, so drastically that governments could now condemn land and turn it over to individuals—for them to build on it projects agreeable to government. Under Title I, whole sections of cities could be condemned, their residents evicted, the buildings in which those residents had lived demolished—and the land turned over to private individuals. Here was power new in the annals of democracy. And in New York, that power would be exercised by Robert Moses. "In my opinion," urban expert Charles Abrams was to say, "under present redevelopment laws, Macy's could condemn Gimbels—if Robert Moses gave the word . . ." Once, a quarter of a century before, Moses had, by deceiving the Legislature into giving him the power of condemnation by appropriation, obtained immense power—W. Kingsland Macy had testified, "Mr. Moses told me personally that his power was such that he could seize my house, put me out of it and arrest me for trespassing if I tried to get into it again"—and had obtained an extension of that power, hitherto exercised only in remote mountain forest fastnesses, to Long Island. Now, he had that power not only over farms and private estates but over the massed edifices, crammed with human beings, of a huge city.

A Moses speech in May 1949—"If we can find a man who has a *first-rate program** half-completed and is willing to go through the grueling business for a second term, let us . . . keep him on"—touched off a draft movement headed by John A. Coleman and including Robert Blaikie, John McCarthy, president of the Fifth Avenue Coach Company, William MacCormack, president of the Transit-Mix Concrete Corporation, and Carmine De Sapio, who had just ousted Hugo Rogers as leader of Tammany Hall. Fusion was again in the field—the candidacy of Moses' admirer Newbold Morris was backed by men who had been Moses' allies and who were dedicated to the principles in which Moses had once believed. Moses threw the full power of his name into the scales on Tammany's side—with undisguised eagerness and enthusiasm. He appeared with O'Dwyer on campaign platforms to make campaign speeches, wrote newspaper ads "To Young Voters," issued statements and reports on park, traffic and housing "progress" under O'Dwyer's administration and predicted that the remaining problems in these areas were well on the way to solution. (An angry Paul Windels replied that "perhaps the quickest way to get action would be to take the limousines and chauffeurs away from them and make them go through the subway wringer twice a day like the rest of us.")

The enormous strength of Moses' name and reputation as political weapons had been demonstrated by the prominence given his endorsements of La Guardia in 1933, 1937 and 1941. In 1949, there were a greater number of discordant notes in the chorus that greeted his statements. There were letters-to-the-editor complaining about aspects of his park or highway policies. One candidate, a young reformer named Oren Root running for Manhattan borough president, attacked Moses directly for continuing to build beaches while working against allocations for municipal sewage plants that would keep the water at the beaches fit to swim in; the city's Liberal Party, at the insistence of state chairman Adolf A. Berle, Jr., publicly declared that his power should be "restricted" on planning matters.

But even those few discordant notes were muted by the chorus of praise (the twentieth anniversary of Jones Beach was celebrated in July, with appropriate pageantry). Interrupting a diatribe on water wastage in New York—"For every pint saved by a good citizen, a Communist will waste a dozen bathtubs and there are hordes of Communists"—Westbrook Pegler bemoaned the fact that the two nominees were "inferior men" and then turned to one who he felt wasn't: "There is available in New York one of the greatest administrators of public office that we have ever had who can't get nominated. That is Robert Moses. . . . He would even make a good President of the United States. But there is no sense to labor the point, because the conspiracies and rivalries of sinister men and stupid, paltry hacks will deny us the benefit of Moses' ability, integrity and honesty. He has

* Italics added.

been ruled out for years on the ground that he can't 'get along' with people. He can get along with honest and competent men all right, but not with parasites and grafters and fumbling slobs." Then there were the editorials. Most treated Moses' endorsement of O'Dwyer as proof of the Mayor's integrity and progressiveness. The *Herald Tribune,* supporting Morris, hastened to assure readers that Morris would also keep Moses in office. "If there is anything certain in the Mayoralty scrambles, it is this: no candidate on any ticket will risk announcing before election that he has plans to oust Robert Moses."

Moses' support was probably not needed by O'Dwyer. The Mayor was immensely popular, and as had been the case in 1929, when La Guardia accused Jimmy Walker's administration of underworld ties, no one was listening when Morris made the same charges about O'Dwyer. But it was helpful. The Mayor's answer to these charges was to point to his programs—Moses' programs—as he did once when a reporter questioned him about Morris' latest attack and he replied scornfully, "While we are talking about housing . . . he's talking about bookmakers."

Moses' help to the machine was, moreover, not limited to statements. The New York City campaign of 1949 was the quintessential ribbon-cutting campaign—with the ribbon cut by the Mayor and by the borough president candidates on his ticket. When Moses ran out of expressways at which opening ceremonies could be staged, he opened sections of expressways. There were frequent announcements of future public works that would "solve" the city's problems. Morris criticized the lack of recreational facilities in Harlem; Moses announced that the Triborough Authority would construct a footbridge across the East River to Ward's Island, thereby opening that island's recreational facilities to Harlem residents. Moses regarded O'Dwyer's re-election almost as a personal triumph. He had plenty of obvious reasons—and one known only to himself, O'Dwyer, Spargo and, at most, one or two others. Shortly after the election, Spargo had written to remind the Mayor that "during your first term in office, we stayed away from the projects and sections of projects where the tenant relocation problem was most difficult"—and to ask the Mayor if, with the election safely out of the way, those relocations could now begin. And the Mayor had said they could. Even as the inaugural ceremonies were under way, they were being carried out—with typical Moses dispatch. Many tenants were already out, their buildings already demolished. Once you get that first stake driven, Moses was fond of saying, no one could stop you. Now, with the evictions and demolitions, the first stake was driven—and driven deep—for the system of mighty highways he planned to lay across the face of the city. No one could stop them any more.

There was one source of irritation at the inaugural.

O'Dwyer had a thirty-three-year-old friend, a young, fast-talking reformer on the make named Jerry Finkelstein. Finkelstein understood that O'Dwyer's natural friendliness, his tendency "to go along with the last guy in to see him," made the Mayor a man easily swayed, or, as Finkelstein put it, "played"—and, as he says, "I knew how to play Bill O'Dwyer"; he had already played the Mayor into the vending machine concession for the city's subway stations.

Now the Mayor promised that at his inauguration he would appoint Finkelstein to succeed Robert F. Wagner, Jr., just elected Manhattan borough president, as chairman of the City Planning Commission.

When Finkelstein arrived for the swearing in, however, "a newspaperman who was a friend of mine showed me the list—and my name wasn't on it." Finkelstein rushed in to see O'Dwyer and learned that Moses, wanting the commission under the gavel of a chairman he controlled, had had a chance to play him after Finkelstein.

"I walked in to see Bill O'Dwyer," Finkelstein recalls. "My wife and family were outside . . ."

"He said, 'Jerry, Bob thinks it ought to be a great engineer or a great architect and I'll get you the biggest job . . .'

"I said, 'The only job I want is the chairmanship of the City Planning Commission.'

"He said, 'Oh, you want that?'

"I said, 'That's right.'

"He said, 'You have it.' " He took out a pencil and wrote in Finkelstein's name at the bottom of the typed list, and Moses, confident that everything at the ceremony was going his way, saw with a shock the dark, balding, bespectacled young Jew he hardly knew walking up to take the oath.

Within days, Finkelstein was proving much more than an irritation.

Finkelstein knew little about city planning, but his first move—after redecorating his new office: "it looked cheap; it wasn't at all commensurate with the chairman of the City Planning Commission"—was to follow the advice of friends at the Citizens Union and call in Lawrence Orton to ask him about the Master Plan. Out came the huge maps that had been lying rolled up and out of sight behind Orton's desk for seventeen years, and out came the explanations of interim developments in the city's growth that proved so clearly the need for the Plan.

It didn't take much intelligence to see that Orton was right, and no one ever accused Jerry Finkelstein of being stupid. And if he needed more proof, it flooded across his desk daily. One city department was planning for an eventual city population of 8,000,000; another for a population of 15,000,000. One department was spending hundreds of thousands of dollars drawing plans for a sewage-treatment plant on a city-owned lot; another was planning to build a public library on the same lot; a third was planning a school—each in ignorance of what the others were doing. While schools in older areas of the city were half empty, schools in newly developed areas, due to lack of planning, were terribly overcrowded: forty or even fifty students being crammed into classrooms designed to hold twenty-five or thirty, and double and even triple sessions for hundreds of thousands of students. Many newly developed areas didn't have *any* schools—because no one had planned schools. Children from these areas had to spend part of each school day being bused—on crowded buses—to the nearest schools available, often already overcrowded themselves. Studying the reports which crossed his desk, Finkelstein could see all too easily how simple and cheap it would have been to acquire vacant land for schools in these areas before they had been built up—and how hard and expensive, perhaps prohibitively expensive, it would be to acquire school sites there now. And he could also see—one could hardly help seeing—how, as the tide of development continued to flow outward toward the city's outskirts, the same mistakes which were costing the city so dearly were being repeated, day by day.

Taking up Orton's ideas, Finkelstein fought for them. A month after he had taken office, he asked for a 350 percent increase in the Planning Commission budget from $328,000 to $1,149,000—the bulk of the increase for an expansion in the commission staff to begin work on the Master Plan.

Finkelstein accompanied his request with a statement that revealed that Moses wasn't the only public official who understood that public statements must be simple to be effective. The few figures it contained stood out all the more starkly: Detroit spent 18 cents per capita on city planning, Los Angeles 24 cents, Philadelphia 25 cents, San Antonio 39 cents, New York 4 cents; even with his proposed increase, New York would be spending less than 12 cents—about .001 of the city budget. Its brief summary argued the need for a Master Plan—the preparation of which, Finkelstein pointedly noted, was a duty specifically placed on the commission over ten years before but never carried out—as cogently as anyone ever had, both on economic grounds (duplication of planning by city departments was costing the city far more each year than the $800,000 increase that would provide a Master Plan and end the duplication) and on grounds that went beyond economy:

> New York is at present in a critical stage of its development. The precipitous increase in population since the beginning of the war, the rapid spread of development in the outlying areas, the demand for schools, traffic relief, slum clearance, housing, hospitals and transportation, all argue for effective planning now. . . .
>
> There is need for competent review of the work of all agencies by the one. . . . A city cannot be built economically without coordination . . .
>
> Without a Master Plan, there is no real hope left for the city. . . .
>
> We cannot go on hauling more and more people greater and greater distances to work and back again, each morning and evening. If the city is ever to catch up with these problems, and have any money left for other purposes, some more fundamental solutions must be found. . . .

With a plan, there was hope—thanks to Title I urban renewal funds so unprecedentedly generous that with them a city could make a good start on reshaping itself—"if we take the fullest possible advantage of them" by planning the reshaping under a comprehensive, citywide development plan rather than on a haphazard, project-by-project basis. But the opportunity was fleeting. "In default of action now, the golden opportunity will be lost."

Moses attempted to fight—using his customary tactics. "He invited me up to one lunch," Finkelstein recalls. "I didn't go along with him, and I was never invited again. If I was a part of his team, I could have had *anything*. But I wasn't on his team." (Orton, who at a recent Moses lunch had rejected a lucrative Moses "consultantship," would have been proud of him.) Moses tried to work behind the scenes, first sending Hodgkiss to try to persuade the Mayor's budget advisers to eliminate some of the proposed additional personnel, then going directly to the Mayor: "I want to make a last protest against not only a waste of City funds but an accumulation of crackpot planners . . . whose appointment lends color to the stories which have been put out that we have no intelligent planning at present, that all our improvements are hastily and ill conceived, located at the wrong places, and therefore prodigiously stupid and wasteful." Then he went public, writing, mimeographing and distributing to his vast mailing list, and to the press, a letter charging that Finkelstein's statement "that he would save a great deal of money if his budget were trebled, belongs in the funny papers." Finkelstein's suggestion that he "needs a new staff to advise him on arterial improvements is a piece of impudence. . . . What is needed is to get some work out of the present staff," the Coordinator said.

A lot of old men around New York, however, still remembered the Master Plan and what it was supposed to do, and the days when the Charter in which the Master Plan was embodied had been the banner behind which they marched toward their dreams for the city they loved. A traitor from their own ranks, a traitor they had helped to raise to power, had knocked the banner from their hands and, for ten years and more, had been trampling it into the dust. But now a young Lochinvar—or at least Finkelstein—had appeared and had snatched it up. They fell into rank behind him. Finkelstein's supporters represented a cross-section of Moses' past—and an index of individuals who had helped raise him to power in the city, and to keep him there. They included Burlingham, ninety-one, with the exception of the senile Seabury the last of the old giants of the reform movement; Isaacs, who embodied in his courtliness and integrity and devotion to principle everything that was fine in the movement; Bruère, the "B" of the "ABC's" of the Bureau of Municipal Research in which Moses had begun his career; Proskauer, the "Proskie" of "Proskie and Moskie," who had been one of Al Smith's inner circle along with Moses; Nathan Straus, who had fought for many bills giving Moses power; McGoldrick, who had entered the Fusion administration with him during the days when Fusion thought Robert Moses was a Fusionist; and, of course, George McAneny. These men had once believed that Moses was New York's great hope. Now they believed that he was the greatest threat to the city's future—and they formed a committee, "A Committee for an Adequate City Plan," to save New York from the power they had helped to give him. Within a week, letters from them were pouring in to the press, including one with Burlingham's old clarity of logic and succinctness of phrase: "Much as we may admire great buildings and engineering works as monuments to the ingenuity and ability of man, we can now recognize that they cannot perform their functions properly unless they are related to their developments."

Planning was, moreover, rapidly becoming almost as much a "motherhood" issue as parks; prestigious civic organizations and the press lined up behind the proposed budget increase; the logic behind it was so clear that even the *Times* managed to grasp it; while managing to avoid criticizing Moses, a *Times* editorial stated: "The noble purpose set forth in the Charter of 1938 . . . has never been realized. The 'primary duty' of preparing a Master Plan for the city has never been performed, although more than a decade has passed. We support without reservation the principle involved. . . . City Hall just cannot allow itself to accept without investigation conflicting demands of various departments." Finkelstein was constantly at pains to identify O'Dwyer with every favorable planning development, and to flatter the Mayor; introducing O'Dwyer at a public hearing on the completed zoning study, he gushed, "The final result will be a tribute to Mayor O'Dwyer. . . . Mayor O'Dwyer's legacy to the City. Time will prove that it is the richest legacy any mayor could have bestowed on the people." O'Dwyer pushed the Board of Estimate into giving Finkelstein a hefty chunk of the additional funds he had requested to hire scores of talented young planners, and publicly went on record in support of the Master Plan, promising that "everything will be integrated within it."

Finkelstein made the most of his opportunity.

"O'Dwyer loved Moses," Finkelstein would recall. "He respected Moses. But I knew how to play Bill O'Dwyer. Moses would go to see him on something and win him around to his way of thinking, but after he left, I went up there. I'd say, 'Bill, the Citizens Union is behind me on this, the papers are behind me. I know how you feel about Bob Moses, but on this, Bill, I'm right.' " O'Dwyer would agree. And Finkelstein would race straight back to his office, and write and distribute a release announcing O'Dwyer's approval—so that before Moses had heard about the Mayor's switch, and could get him to switch back, O'Dwyer's pro-Finkelstein stand would be on the record, and therefore almost impossible for Moses to change.

Time and again, Finkelstein took on Moses in this way—and won. In a series of clashes in the Planning Commission the vote was 6–1, with Moses, who no longer showed up at any commission meetings, casting his lone vote through Hodgkiss. Orton proposed a study of proposed developments around the UN site. "Irresponsible . . . ill-conceived," said Hodgkiss, reading his master's words. "Mr. Moses is not the Planning Commission but only one member," Finkelstein replied, and the 6–1 vote proved him right. Soon, to Moses' rage, the commission was even embarking on a study of criteria for playgrounds to insure that they were built where they were most needed.

But, with one exception, these were only studies—no immediate threat to Moses' plans. And in the exception—the single study which posed such a threat, the only confrontation of immediate, practical significance between Moses and Finkelstein and the forces Finkelstein represented—Moses used the power of money on O'Dwyer again.

The crunch came over the Mid-Manhattan Elevated Expressway.

On December 30, 1949, the Board of Estimate authorized Triborough to apply in the name of the city for federal funds to study the "most feasible plan" for an express crossing of the middle of the most crowded island in the world. On June 2, 1950, O'Dwyer announced that Triborough's study had been completed, that it had "proven" the most feasible plan to be the highway among the skyscrapers proposed by Triborough's chairman, that the chairman had already persuaded the federal government to pay the cost—the first installment alone would be $900,000—of plans for the 160-foot-wide road, which would run in the air along Thirtieth Street, using the 60-foot street width and 100 feet created by tearing down the buildings lining the south side of the street, that the chairman had persuaded the Port Authority to pay the cost of planning and building a linkup with the Lincoln Tunnel, that Triborough had agreed to pay $26,000,000 for the rest of its construction—and that the preparation of detailed blueprints would begin at once.

There was ecstasy in the editorial columns—the *Herald Tribune*: "New York shows again the capacity of doing things in a big way . . . Those big builders, Bob Moses and Howard Cullman, sat down with Mayor O'Dwyer in staff session at Gracie Mansion, and the result is that New York is moving ahead at once. . . . Big men got together and made a big decision for the common good." But there was agony among trade and civic associations; they charged that the Board of Estimate had directed Triborough to study all proposals—including one for a tunnel less destructive to Manhattan real estate and aesthetics—but that Triborough had studied only its chairman's. Representatives of twenty associations, along with Finkelstein and Manhattan Borough President Wagner, visited O'Dwyer to ask that the tunnel study be made—by Finkelstein's Planning Commission.

O'Dwyer's response was frank. He himself would prefer a tunnel, the Mayor said; "I don't like overhead structures." But his preferences were not important. "I'm sure you can draw me a satisfactory plan for a tunnel, but all the talk in the world is no good if there isn't anyone to build it. . . . You've got to show me someone who'll put up the money to build it." There was only one man who had that kind of money—and he would put it up only for an overhead crossing, not for one underground.

Pressed hard by his visitors, the Mayor finally said that he would permit the Planning Commission to make its own study, but, he said, such a study would be a useless waste of money—and he wasn't going to provide any city money for it. Finkelstein pointed out that the Mayor's "permission" was therefore meaningless, since the commission had neither personnel capable of making such a study nor the funds to hire such personnel. He and his allies were not saying that an overhead crossing should not be built, Finkelstein said. They all agreed that some solution to the mid-Manhattan traffic problem was necessary. All they were asking was a chance to find out which solution would really be best for the city. Could not he have even $50,000? The Mayor simply threw up his hands without even replying.

No reply was necessary, of course. He was mayor of a city which couldn't afford to build a crossing. Moses could. Moses would have to be allowed to build whatever type of crossing he wanted.

The Mayor's stand certainly seemed pro-Moses—much too pro-Moses—to Moses' opponents. But it wasn't pro-Moses enough for Moses. Angered that O'Dwyer had dared to give "permission"—even meaningless permission—for an independent study, he decided to teach the Mayor a lesson. The Triborough board approved a resolution stating that the Authority was no longer willing to build a mid-Manhattan crossing of any type and formally withdrawing the Authority's request for federal planning funds.

O'Dwyer pleaded with Moses to reconsider. Moses refused. He had made the lesson all the harsher by communicating Triborough's change of plans to O'Dwyer privately. It was the humiliated Mayor who had to make the announcement that the expressway he had announced with such pride just three weeks before was now dead. It was all very well for Jerry Finkelstein to call Moses a spoiled "cry-baby" who, if other boys wouldn't let him play by his own rules, would take his money and go home. It was the Mayor who was still faced with the mid-Manhattan traffic crisis—and with the realization that he had absolutely no way to solve it. All he could do was try—angrily but lamely—to pin the blame on others, saying: "I do hope that the actions of the opponents of the elevated highway study will be a lesson to them that they can't push Bob Moses around. Thirtieth Street and the surrounding area will have the same traffic congestion for a long time to come. The next time a tried-and-true outfit proposes a $40,000,000 traffic improvement, without expense to the city or cost to the taxpayers, I hope the Hate Moses Club will keep away from City Hall. I shall have very little welcome for them." Summoning Finkelstein to his office, he gave him an hour-long tongue-lashing so violent that when reporters crowded around Finkelstein as he left the Mayor's office, the normally ebullient young man pushed past them without a word.

Finkelstein still had O'Dwyer's support on the Master Plan, however, and the rezoning study that was to be its basis pushed ahead, with each step approved by the Planning Commission—by a 6–1 vote. By August, the zoning was completed—two years of work and $325,000 embodied in a 290-page study and ready for public hearings scheduled to begin in September.

They would be *real* hearings, Finkelstein promised. Some would be held in outlying sections of the city—bringing City Hall to the people instead of making the people come to City Hall. And, Finkelstein promised, the hearings would continue "until everyone has been heard who has something to say."

Finkelstein had already provided convincing proof that public participation could be constructive. The main source of opposition to rezoning had been expected to be the real estate industry, which had been Moses' main ally in killing the Tugwell-Orton-spearheaded 1939 Planning Commission try for a Master Plan. Finkelstein had invited some of the industry's more public-spirited leaders to meet quietly with the commission, their objections had been taken into account, some compromises—which Orton and other Planning Commission members felt on balance had actually improved the zoning plan—had been made and the realtors' support for the Plan obtained. Finkelstein had demonstrated that public participation could be constructive on small as well as large issues. Residents of Washington Square had been alarmed by builder Sam Rudin's plan to tear down the old Rhinelander houses on its north border and construct a twelve-story apartment house that would destroy the scale of the square, with its park and arch bordered by low, gracious brownstones. Broad Finkelstein hints about commission zoning powers persuaded Rudin to meet with the residents, and a solution—almost unique in New

York history—was worked out under which both sides got what they wanted: Rudin was allowed to build higher in the rear of the plot—away from the square—than he would otherwise have been allowed to do, and in exchange kept the front of the building lower than the cornices of the private homes.

Other work on the Master Plan was also progressing. By August, the commission was well on its way to a division of the city into smaller areas which would each have a voice in planning its own local improvements—an extension of Isaacs' "arrondissement" proposal of 1939 to keep the city livable by preserving its neighborhood fabric. O'Dwyer, increasingly unhappy with the growing seriousness of the housing and traffic crises that Moses was supposed to be alleviating, convinced that part of the reason for the crises was past lack of planning, was impressed with the commission's progress, so impressed, in fact, that City Hall began to speculate about another split between the Mayor and his Coordinator.

But O'Dwyer had not been able to escape his past. Press and public focus on his administration may have centered on appointees like Robert Moses, but the Mayor had also appointed to public office other men, less visible perhaps, but just as much a part of that administration: friends of Frank Costello and Thomas (Three Fingers Brown) Luchese and other racketeers. And he had appointed to public office Big Jim Moran, who had been using his new job in the Fire Department to extort $500,000 a year from businessmen needing departmental permits, and who had also acted as the conduit for huge contributions to O'Dwyer's 1949 re-election campaign; the president of the United Firemen's Association was later to testify (this testimony was, admittedly, never substantiated) that to assure the Mayor's support of legislation benefiting firemen he had handed Big Jim an envelope containing $55,000 in cash. (The president also testified that in 1949 he had given the Mayor himself a $10,000 "campaign contribution.")

And now the spotlight of which Bill O'Dwyer had so long been afraid was swinging inexorably in his direction. Hardly had he been sworn in for his second term when a pudgy, flashily dressed bookmaker named Harry Gross, arrested in Brooklyn, said that he was ready to testify that he had also been a big O'Dwyer "contributor," that since the Mayor's first inauguration he had been paying a cool million dollars a year in "ice," part to high-level police officials who were close personal friends of the Mayor—and that Moran had once invited him, along with seven other top bookmakers, to attend a meeting with the Mayor himself, a meeting Gross said he had not attended because of illness but which Moran subsequently assured him had indeed taken place.

O'Dwyer's efforts to escape the spotlight had been becoming more and more desperate. During the summer of 1949, he had insisted almost frantically that he would not run for a second term, an insistence from which he could not be budged until, at a last-minute conference at midnight in Gracie Mansion, Ed Flynn brought what one observer was later to describe as "real pressure." Not a month after his election victory, before he had even been sworn in for the new term he had won, he had tried quietly to file his retirement papers, an attempt which failed when Moran found out about it, retrieved the supposedly irrevocable documents from the retirement board, took them to the hospital room in which O'Dwyer was recuperating from "exhaustion"—and burned them before the Mayor's eyes.

In the first years of his administration, New York had loved Bill-O and believed his blarney. With the city's Good Government organizations giving him dinners honoring him for, among other things, keeping corruption out of city government, those years had been years for speeches.

The last year of Bill-O's administration was a year for whispers, whispers that the Mayor was trying to find a graceful way to retire, whispers about why he was trying to retire. To still them, eight separate times he denied that he was thinking of leaving office—once, on vacation in Florida, personally telephoning a *New York Times* editor to do so. But by August, every swing of the spotlight brought it closer and closer to those shadowy places in his past. There was a grand jury in Brooklyn investigating racketeering in that borough, and there were all sorts of rumors flooding City Hall about what that grand jury was learning—and preparing to reveal—about the man who had once been the borough's crusading District Attorney. United States Senator Estes Kefauver's Senate committee investigating organized crime was preparing to hold hearings in New York, hearings that would concentrate on the links between the city's underworld and the city's politicians—and television cameras were preparing to focus on the nervously twitching fingers of key witness Frank Costello. The time for denials was past; now was time for flight. On the eve of a mass Police Department trial for bribery, more than one hundred policemen resigned, so did the Police Commissioner and his two top aides—and so, as the spotlight swung at last full force on his handsome, charming face, did William O'Dwyer. Ed Flynn dropped in on Harry Truman to pass the time of day, Bill-O was appointed Ambassador to Mexico and on August 31, 1950, almost eighteen years to the day after Tammany's most popular mayor had fled the country, Tammany's second most popular mayor crossed the border into Mexico.

IMPY

All during August, Moses had been in South America, drawing up a Rockefeller-financed plan of improvements for São Paulo, utterly unaware of the events crushing in on O'Dwyer. But O'Dwyer's resignation was to place the city in his power more completely than ever before.

By law, the successor to a retiring mayor is the President of the City Council. By fate, the Council presidency was held in 1950 by an individual who, during the entire forty-five utterly undistinguished years of his life prior to his nomination to that $25,000-per-year post, had never been deemed worthy of holding any job more responsible than that of secretary, at $6,500 per year, to a judge named Schmuck.

The nomination of this totally unknown minor Tammany ward heeler to the city's second-highest elective office, the position of succession to the mayoralty, had "staggered," in Warren Moscow's words, "even the most imaginative among political reporters." And so had the explanation of how he had obtained the nomination. At a last-minute reshuffling of the 1945 Democratic ticket, the leaders finally agreed on Lazarus Joseph for Comptroller, and then realized that since O'Dwyer was Irish and from Brooklyn, while Joseph was Jewish and from the Bronx, the slate could have ethnic and geographic balance only if its third member was an Italian from Manhattan—and were unable to think of a single Manhattan Italian official they could trust. After hours of impasse, one leader reasoned that since legal secretaryships to State Supreme Court justices carried a respectable salary for which little or no work was required, they would have been given only to the "safest" of Democratic workers. Pulling out a little "Green Book," the official directory of city employees, he turned to the list of legal secretaries, ran his finger down it looking for a name that even the dumbest voter would be able to tell was Italian—and came to *Vincent R. Impellitteri.* "No one knew who the hell he was," Reuben Lazarus was to recall, but, looking up Impellitteri's address, the leaders determined that he lived in Manhattan, telephoned his district leader and were assured: "You don't have to worry about him. He's a good boy."

Although attested to privately by members of Tammany's hierarchy (and by Moses, whose presence at the crucial ticket-making session—he was the only "outsider" there—reveals his standing with that hierarchy), this explanation seemed almost unbelievable—until one met Impellitteri. If he had a single qualification for the job other than the length of his name and the fact that it ended in a vowel, he kept it carefully hidden during his five-year tenure (he was re-elected with O'Dwyer in 1949) as Council President. "The perfect Throttlebottom," Moscow called him. "He voted as the mayor told him to, on matters he did not necessarily understand, and spent most of his waking hours shaking hands at public dinners, political clambakes, and cornerstone layings too unimportant to merit the mayor's presence." Amiable but slow-witted, he was a joke among political insiders. But now he was mayor—and the joke was on the city.

Impellitteri's wits may have been slow, but he had two fast wits—ex-O'Dwyer aide Bill Donoghue and a young sharpie named Sydney S. Baron—as PR men. Impellitteri had to run in a special election in November if he wanted to hold the office he had fallen into, which meant that he had less than ten weeks in which to create an image and a record, and his PR men quickly hit on two ways to do it: first, take advantage of the fact that no one knew him, that he was therefore not identified with any political bosses, that his opponent, Ferdinand Pecora, was backed by Tammany boss De Sapio and that, unable to get Impellitteri the Democratic nomination, the clique in Tammany that pulled his strings had him running as an independent, and portray him as the "anti-boss," "anti-politician," "anti-corruption" candidate (one of Baron's better lines: "If Pecora is elected, Frank Costello will be your mayor. But the voice will be that of Pecora"); second, identify him with Robert Moses.

The price of that identification came high, both in specifics—Moses made Impellitteri pledge publicly that if he was elected, he would not reappoint Finkelstein—and in generalities: Impellitteri privately promised Moses even more of a free hand than he had enjoyed under O'Dwyer in setting all city construction policies. But Impellitteri paid it. He got full value in return. Refusing an offer of the Republican nomination (time had dimmed at least some GOP leaders' memories of 1934), Moses gave him his endorsement. "Even I, who thought that by this time I knew Bob and the lengths to which he would go, never thought he would go that far," says Lazarus. Remonstrating, he said, "But, Bob, he hasn't any capacity for the job at all!" Moses' response? "He laughed at that." Publicly, the Coordinator declared that Impellitteri "has shown extraordinary courage and independence." And, as always, a Moses endorsement made almost every front page in town. (The *Herald Tribune* article stated: "It was not a political endorsement, Mr. Moses basing his support on his opinion that the [Impellitteri] administration was carrying out the city construction program as planned.") Moses led Impellitteri around to officiate at openings of—and share in the credit and front-page pictures for—highways and housing projects with which he had had nothing to do except to affix his signature as Council President to documents his aides say he often had not even bothered to read. Most observers, noting that the campaign consisted mainly of charges and countercharges of bossism and corruption, felt that the endorsement from an official characterized as "independent" and believed above corruption was an important factor—almost as important as the decision by newspaper headline writers to call him "Impy" and thus give him a lovable public image—in Impellitteri's victory, the first in the city's history by a candidate running on an independent line without the support of either major party. And after his election, Impellitteri continued to pay the price—eagerly.

Thanks to his PR men and his physical appearance—his addiction to the blue suit and the boutonniere, combined with his iron-gray hair, deeply earnest mien and stolidity that during the campaign was mistaken for dignity, made him the very model of a modern mayor; at the approach of a camera his brow would furrow, his lips would purse, his jaw would jut and his eyes would focus on whatever piece of paper happened to be handy just as intently as if he understood the words written on it—Impy had run a great race, but once in possession of the prize he had won, he proved to have not the slightest idea of what to do with it.

He disclaimed any influence over the Board of Estimate, telling reporters, "All I have is three votes on it, you know." Mayors were always telling reporters that—but City Hall insiders soon realized, to their astonishment, that this mayor *believed* it. Says one of his aides, Victor F. Condello: "Impy never understood that he had any power at all." Once Condello suggested that the Mayor call the five borough presidents to an executive session to discuss a thorny issue. "Yeah," the Mayor said, "that's a good idea." Pause. "You think they'll come?"

He was too timid to confront even his own subordinates. Once, a newspaper leveled detailed charges against one. The next time they met, the Mayor asked him if the charges were true. Of course not, the appointee said firmly. Impellitteri never mentioned the matter again. He would take orders from whoever happened to be talking to him at the moment.

Even his enemies had to confess that Impellitteri "personally" was "a very nice man." No one could watch him, childless himself, chatting warmly with the groups of children who visited City Hall, and doubt that; the warmth of his greeting for all delegations, in fact, was beyond affectation, if occasionally a cause for snickers: once, hearing the sound of singing from behind Impy's office door, an aide walked in to find a choir in action—and the Mayor standing with them, wearing a contented if somewhat vacant expression, humming merrily away. But he was a man simply unequal to meeting the duties that had been thrust upon him. The responsibilities he was charged with carrying out utterly bewildered him. At times, he presented an almost pathetic figure as he groped his way through the intricacies of government. Says Warren Moscow: "My God, at Board of Estimate executive sessions, he'd sit there and some problem would come up, and the poor bastard would say, 'I got no answer on this, boys. You got any ideas?' " And if no one had any, the 101st Mayor of the City of New York would sit there with his gavel before him, literally wringing his hands in agitation while long minutes passed in painful silence. He was desperate for someone to turn to, almost frantically anxious to drop his enormous powers—and responsibilities—into someone else's hands.

And the biggest hands around were those of Robert Moses.

Within weeks of Impellitteri's inauguration, Lazarus was noting in his diary that "Robert Moses is actually running this town today. There's no important act Impellitteri takes or does that he doesn't consult Mr. Moses." Soon the town's other top political insiders were saying the same thing. The consultations were held at Gracie Mansion—almost every morning, with Moses dropping by at about nine or nine-thirty, or even earlier. And these were private consultations: when Moses was closeted with Impellitteri in the Gracie Mansion drawing room, no one else was allowed to be present. (Asked why years later, Impy would say, "I considered those very important sessions for me and the city, and I didn't want them interrupted.") Sometimes the Mayor saw no one else until eleven. "He would always come with a big envelope," Impellitteri would recall, and the envelope would be filled with papers Moses wanted him to sign—and invariably by the time Moses drove away in his big limousine, they would *be* signed. One top official says that Impellitteri never left the Mansion in the morning until Moses had given him "his marching orders for the day." Papers that were prepared for signature later in the day were delivered by messenger to the Mayor's office at City Hall—with peremptory Moses covering notes ("There is no use boring you with figures"). And the papers were invariably signed—and the marching orders were invariably obeyed. "Moses' word was law with him," Condello says. "All Impy wanted was to keep him happy. I had written a letter to several" department heads. "Moses got pissed off about it—I never did figure out why—and he wrote to the Mayor: 'Dear Vincent: What is this all about?' And the Mayor called me up and said, 'For God's sake straighten this out with Moses!' I tried to explain to him that there was nothing for Moses to get angry about, but he didn't even want to listen to what it was. He was in a real panic. He just didn't want to do anything to irritate Moses. Moses' word was law in the city."

One proof that Moses' word was law was in the appointments Impellitteri made—and in those he didn't make.

Tammany kingpin Frank J. Sampson, Impellitteri's old district leader, distributed the bulk of the administration's routine patronage, but for high-level jobs in departments whose responsibilities in any way touched on Moses', Impellitteri almost invariably asked Moses for a recommendation—and should Impellitteri neglect to ask, Moses gave a recommendation anyway, submitting so many that the Mayor's files were crammed with them. They were dutifully followed. By the end of Impellitteri's term, there existed within the upper echelons of the city government an extensive network of men whose first loyalty was not to that government but to the man who ran the independent government on Randall's Island.

Off Randall's Island flowed, moreover, not only recommendations but disapprovals. Time and again, men being considered for key city posts were quietly blackballed by Moses—in most cases without their ever knowing about it—in cutting phrases ("Is there any evidence that he is worth $25,000?" "Not heavy enough for the job." "Would certainly not impress . . . the Albany educational authorities . . . to whom the city looks for additional aid") that concealed the real reason for his disapproval: that they had not proven themselves sufficiently ready to swallow their pride and their independence, abandon their own theories and beliefs and unquestionably accept his. And Moses' negative counsel was followed by Impellitteri as slavishly as his positive.

Another proof was in the policies to which Impellitteri put his signature.

They were Moses' policies. During the Impellitteri administration, through a secret "understanding" with Governor Dewey largely engineered by Moses, the city was allowed to adopt a series of financial measures whose common denominator was the fact that they fell hardest on those least able to afford them. The city sales tax, earlier raised from 1 to 2 percent with Moses' backing, was now raised from 2 percent to 3; the subway and bus fare, earlier raised from five cents to ten cents with Moses' backing, was now raised from ten cents to fifteen—by a Transit Authority, created to bear the public's blame for the increase and thereby insulate politicians, whose creation, combined with a legislative mandate to run mass transit on a "self-supporting" basis, removed from the city's constitutional debt limit the $425,000,000 in transit debt service Moses had so long wanted removed so that the borrowing capacity could be freed for his own projects.

And proof lay in the speeches the Mayor made. The voice was the voice of Impy, but the words were the words of Moses. By the time Impellitteri was running in the Democratic primary in 1953, Moses was giving point-by-point "suggestions" for his major television talks (one list was headed by the suggestion that the Mayor make "reference to records of heads of several important departments"—including, prominently, the head of the Department of Parks).

Moses liked to keep the strings on his puppet short. During the summer, which he spent in Babylon, he kept the Mayor convenient to hand, inviting him to vacation in the handsomely furnished Shelter Cottage at Fire Island State Park just across the bay.

More proof that "Moses' word was law in the city" was in what happened to the City Planning Commission and its Master Plan.

When O'Dwyer retired, Jerry Finkelstein had four months remaining before his term expired. During those months, the young commission chairman fought for the Master Plan, pushing the consultants to finish the crucial rezoning proposal, issuing press releases trying to explain the value of establishing local neighborhoods as the basis for studying planning needs. But he was fighting against a master.

The rezoning study—290 pages long, profusely illustrated, crammed with detailed maps and charts—was completed in September, ready for detailed study by city officials and the public, and for public hearings leading to its adoption. But, Orton says, "like dopes, we hadn't gotten enough money to publish the darn thing when we got our appropriation, and we had to go back to the Board of Estimate" with a new mayor sitting at its head. Trying to force Impellitteri's hand before the election, Finkelstein wrote the Mayor in October appealing for his support. There was no reply—and when, after he had written again, an answer did come, it came in the words of Moses. A letter over Impellitteri's signature said that the Mayor would "have no objection" to having the $9,750 printing item brought up for consideration at the next Board meeting—if copies were sent to him and other members of the Board "immediately" to give them time to study them. "Well, of course, we couldn't do that," Orton was to recall. "We didn't *have* copies. It was to *make* copies that we were asking for the money." Finkelstein, in a hospital suffering from exhaustion, attempted to take his case to the public by issuing a release stating that the failure to appropriate $9,750 for printing the report would mean that the $325,000 already spent preparing it would be completely wasted. Orton appeared before the Board in executive session to press the point. But when Orton finished, Moses got up and, Orton recalls, "argued that the whole thing was a bunch of tripe, nonsense, what a lousy job it was, waste of money, all the things that lawyers say—incompetent, irrelevant"—and the Board, with Impellitteri nodding placidly at its head (when Finkelstein had sent the Mayor a copy of the "local neighborhoods" proposal, he had sent it to Moses for an explanation, and Moses had sent it back with a note stating, "Dear Vince: Here's the answer—the attached is a silly idea"), refused to vote the additional funds, and the report for which Finkelstein had fought so hard had still not been seen by anyone outside the commission when, while still in the hospital, his term ran out on December 31.

At Moses' request, Impelliteri moved into Finkelstein's job—and into the office Finkelstein had so optimistically redecorated only a year before—Colonel John J. Bennett, who was shortly to be in the process of organizing, with Moses' approval, a Title I project that was to reap its organizers enormous profits. Orton hoped against hope that the new chairman, who certainly had a distinguished career résumé (former State Attorney General, Democratic candidate for Governor, judge, noted attorney), would carry out the duties of his job. But he saw at the very first meeting that such hopes were useless. "Bennett was totally subservient to Moses."

The two members of the commission who had strayed briefly from Moses' fold at the enticement of O'Dwyer and Finkelstein soon were back among the flock. Why cannot be said, but it was at about this time that Moses gave Cleveland Rodgers permission to do his biography and it was also at this time that Moses had Impy give John Reidel, chief engineer of the Board of Estimate, a hefty salary increase. Reidel and Rodgers, who had supported the Master Plan before, now switched their votes, combining with Bennett—and the caster of the decisive fourth vote: Robert Moses—to overrule the commission's three liberals, Orton, Francis J. Bloustein and Goodhue Livingston, and defeat all proposals to advance it.

Under Bennett, the Planning Commission was in Moses' hands as firmly as it had been in the days when $15,000-per-year Edwin Ashley Salmon wielded its gavel. Many of the eager young planners Finkelstein had brought in were forced out. Work on the Master Plan all but stopped. Eventually, the consultants' zoning report was printed, but the four-man majority on the commission saw to it that the public hearings Finkelstein had dreamed of were never held—and that the commission never adopted the report as its own, so that it remained without official status.

The $325,000 spent on the rezoning was wasted completely. But $325,000 was an almost infinitesimal item compared to the real cost to the city of the return of Moses' control of its Planning Commission. In his one year as chairman, Finkelstein had—in compromises like that at Washington Square—subtly employed the commission's inferential powers to persuade large real estate developers to sit down with local residents and work out plans that would, while allowing the developers their projects, save the fabric of the neighborhoods in which they would be built. He had moved to preserve neighborhoods from city as well as private "improvements" by establishing the principle that "local neighborhoods" must be the basis around which planning works. He had gotten the commission to work on a study of the UN area that might save the city from the enormous costs of having to expand the site if it were found too small, and that would have insured that surrounding private development would be not haphazard but based on some rational guidelines. He had started the commission developing playground criteria that might save the city the immense wastage of building and maintaining playgrounds that no one used. He had personally saved the city—even if accidentally—from the Mid-Manhattan Elevated Expressway. Most important, in that one year he had started the commission down the road—an astonishingly long way down the road—to the formulation of a rational plan for the development of the city as a whole. Manhattan might be largely lost—as O'Dwyer was to say: "Now the city's built up around the mistakes that were made . . . it's too late to tear down skyscrapers to put in things that you would have, if properly planned"—but there was plenty of almost empty canvas (most of Staten Island, the great central belt of Queens, huge expanses of Brooklyn, even bits of the Bronx) on which to draw from scratch, to insure that the people who moved into these areas would have schools, colleges, public libraries, parks, playgrounds—and shopping areas and jobs—close enough so that they would not have to waste a substantial portion of their lives getting to and from them. In all those areas of the city, the rule of reason could have been allowed to operate substantially unfettered—and Jerry Finkelstein had, by recruiting a master planning staff, organizing it and assuring it of his support, inaugurated a program that would have done just that. But now Finkelstein's year was over. Robert Moses was back in control. The rule of reason was over. The rest of the city was going to be built by the law which had governed the building of the earlier parts: the law of the jungle.

And proof lay in Moses' relationship with the city's legislative bodies—the City Council and the Board of Estimate—already so effectively dominated by him through his use of the power of money. Council President Rudolph Halley, a liberal concerned with the social implications of governmental policies, began to question some of Moses' proposals; Moses' attitude—expressed at a lunch at Randall's Island to which Mrs. Halley was also invited—was, she says, "Oh, little boy, sit down. Father knows best."

Halley did not believe so, but he found that most of his fellow councilmen were reluctant to challenge Moses, and that he could do little to influence them. "It was a terribly frustrating period for Rudy," Mrs. Halley says. "He felt so strongly about things—the same things that people feel strongly about today. But then he was ahead of his time, and he couldn't get anything done." The Council President has no real power. When Halley persisted in closely questioning Moses, or, more usually, since Moses himself seldom deigned to appear, Moses' deputies, during their appearances before the Council, Moses adopted a simple solution: he not only refused to discuss his programs with the Council himself but would not allow his aides to discuss them. And to Halley's frustration, the Council's Tammany majority approved those programs anyway.

Halley and Wagner, busy trying to ingratiate himself with the city's liberals in preparation for his own upcoming try for the mayoralty, offered opposition on the Board of Estimate. Moses adopted the same tactics there. Bronx Borough President Lyons, raging publicly, said: "We've seen very little of Mr. Moses at Board meetings, either open or executive. He does all his business at Gracie Mansion." Says Moscow: "Under Impellitteri, it was taken for granted that Moses was Mayor. There was no question about it." If Impellitteri didn't know how to exercise a mayor's powers to whip Board members into line, Moses did—and the Board members knew it, well enough so that none of them dared with any seriousness or regularity to challenge him.

During the forty months of the Impellitteri administration, the trends Moses had caused during the last forty-four months of the O'Dwyer administration—the forty-four months beginning in January 1947 in which Moses exercised near-absolute power over the construction of all public works—intensified. During the O'Dwyer administration, the city spent $3,102,000 on the construction of colleges, $1,169,000 on the construction of libraries—and $80,826,000 on the construction of highways. Before the war, the city's hospital situation had been desperate; $80,000,000 was more than twice as much as the city spent on hospitals during the O'Dwyer administration. It was more even than it spent on elementary and high schools.

During the Impellitteri administration, the city spent $16,176,000 on colleges, $4,118,000 on libraries, $70,314,000 on hospitals, $137,290,000 on schools—and $172,294,000 on highways.* It built eighty-eight miles of new highways, but not one mile of new subways. Near the end of the Impellitteri administration, more than eight full years after the city had announced the start of a "crash program to replace all non-fireproof schools," there were still 182 non-fireproof schools in use. Some 38,777 elementary-school pupils were failing to get a full day's schooling because lack of new construction had caused such severe overcrowding that double or triple sessions were necessary. One out of every three of the city's schoolchildren sat in classrooms that were overcrowded by any educational standard. The four free municipal colleges—City, Hunter, Brooklyn and Queens—had a combined capacity so inadequate that a study showed that 46,000 students per year who would have gone to college had a municipal institution been available were unable to do so.

Taylor had warned McGoldrick and McGoldrick had warned Joseph that Moses would "bankrupt" the city. One way in which the Comptrollers were afraid Moses would do this was by forcing the city to issue long-term revenue bonds to pay for the "negligible" city share of the costs of his public works, costs which, he assured the press and public and city officials not as familiar with city finances as the Comptrollers, were being almost entirely borne by state and federal government. Since most of these facilities were not revenue-producing—those that produced revenue he built under the auspices of his authorities so that they, rather than the city, would get that revenue—the only method of paying the interest on

* The highway construction figures represent, of course, only the city's expenditures—not expenditures on highways by the federal or state governments or the public authorities.

those bonds was to take the money out of the city's current revenues, to include debt service in the expense budget. Thanks to the wartime curtailment on construction and hence on new bond floatings, at the beginning of the O'Dwyer administration the city's debt was down to $2,194,000,000—on which the annual debt service charges were $118,000,000. By 1952 annual service charges were $211,000,000—up 78 percent in seven years. Another, more subtle but, in the long run, more damaging way, was in draining away for new construction so much of the city's resources that it could not pay to keep up maintenance on its existing $12,000,000,000 physical plant. Not only subways but highways fell into this category; even Moses' own roads could not be kept up. And the cost of neglected maintenance is astonishingly high: the West Side Highway, for example, could have been kept in perfect repair during the 1950's for about $75,000 per year; because virtually no repairing was done, by the 1960's, the cost of annual maintenance would be more than $1,000,000 per year; and in 1974 the highway had begun literally to fall apart—a condition that would take tens of millions of dollars to repair. By the time Moses left power in 1968, the city would be utterly unable to make even a pretense of keeping its physical plant in repair.

There was a skewing of expenditures away from service *functions* and toward public works *construction*. This was especially unfortunate because the nature of the city's population was changing; each year, more of the comfortable middle class, which required a minimum of services, left the city to be replaced by families from underprivileged Puerto Rico and from underprivileged southern states who required more services if they were to become truly part of the city and not just live within its borders as unassimilated, hostile, bitter aliens.

Instead, here is what happened.

Just to make the most minimal repairs on the outmoded school plants required between $15,000,000 and $20,000,000 per year. During the O'Dwyer administration less than $5,000,000 per year had been allocated for this purpose, with the result that by the end of that administration, the backlog in minimal repairs, a staggering $30,000,000 at the beginning of that administration, had mounted to $75,000,000. During the Impellitteri administration, thanks largely to the real possibility of disasters in the schools, the amount for maintenance was increased—but only slightly. By the end of that administration, the backlog of minimal repairs to the city's schools was about $100,000,000.

Bridges were painted every three years. Rare was the school that was painted that often. Rare was the school that was painted every five years. At the end of the Impellitteri administration, there were five schools in the city that had not been painted in twenty years.

More important than what the city's own government spent on shaping its future was what the state and federal governments spent, for their resources dwarfed the city's.

During the Impellitteri administration, $498,000,000 was poured into the city for highway and housing construction by the state and federal governments. Every cent of this money was spent under Moses' command. What was built was what he wanted built. There were, for example, twenty-four huge public housing projects constructed during the Impellitteri era by the City Housing Authority whose members and staff were subservient to him. Not a brick of one of those housing projects was laid without his approval. Eleven huge superhighways were begun during this era. Not a mile was laid out without his express O.K.

The public never knew the extent of Moses' influence. One can search through the daily issues of the city's nine remaining daily newspapers—issues crammed, day after day, with "inside dope" on City Hall—without finding a single accurate analysis of that influence. There were, for example, hundreds of stories about the Housing Authority's construction plans and over-all policies. But because he had no direct connection with the Authority, in all these stories there is hardly a mention of Robert Moses, the man whose approval was needed for every plan and who personally set most of its policies and approved the others. The forty months that Vincent R. Impellitteri sat in the mayor's chair were a crucial forty months for the city. It was during them that—with the exception of those on Staten Island—the city's last vast open spaces disappeared. New York filled up, assumed a new shape. The shape Moses dictated.

And Moses' forty months of absolute power enabled him to shape the city for far longer than forty months. The appointments Impellitteri made at his recommendation would extend his influence for years after Impellitteri was no longer mayor. Protected in general by civil service, the appointees would remain in their key, sensitive posts as new mayors sat in City Hall, knowing that mayors come and go, but that Moses remained—and that, therefore, in conflicts between Moses and a mayor, it was in their interest to give their loyalty to the former.

There was, moreover, the momentum effect. Qualified administrators were scarce. Mayors were constantly engaged in a search for men with real experience in handling large-scale problems. The only way to get experience was to handle such problems, and since it was Moses' men who had been placed in positions to handle them, it was Moses' men—and sometimes only Moses' men—who were qualified.

More important than the men he installed, of course, were the stakes he drove. Once you get the first stake driven for a project, he had learned, no one would be able to stop it. During those forty months of Impy, he drove a lot of stakes. He selected the routes for a dozen expressways, had thousands of families evicted from them and demolished their residences. What public official—even if he did not like the route of one of the expressways, even if he did not want any expressway built in the area at all—could thereafter say it would not be constructed, that the evictions made and money spent had been made and spent for no purpose? He selected the sites—and evicted the tenants from—a dozen Title I projects. What public official could then cancel a project—and simply say that the blocks of debris would remain untouched?

No political observer was in any doubt why Impellitteri was defeated by a resounding 2–1 majority in the Democratic primary when he ran against Robert F. Wagner, Jr., in 1953. "Wagner did not merely have one issue, he had all of them—the rent, tax and fare increases to which Impellitteri had been a party, plus continued overcrowding in the schools," says Warren Moscow, at the time Wagner's Borough Works Commissioner. With the exception of the rent increase, the policies that led to Impellitteri's defeat were Moses' policies.

But the people couldn't strike back against Moses—even if they had wanted to, which they didn't since they didn't know that he was responsible for those policies. His state positions, and his authority chairmanships, put him beyond their reach. The result of Moses' policies was, for Impellitteri, defeat. The result of Moses' policies was, for Moses, more power.

To a man to whom power is all-important, other men are judged by how much they give to him. So it was with Robert Moses and Vincent R. Impellitteri. Moses' final evaluation of the bumbling little man who had presented such a pathetic figure in his high office: "He was a good mayor."

To a man to whom power is all-important, other men matter only as long as they possess power.

So it was with Robert Moses and Vincent R. Impellitteri. Years after his retirement, the one-time mayor would sit for an interview in the law offices where he was kept, with little work to do, as window dressing by a much younger man who liked window dressing around him: Joseph F. Carlino, the best-tailored Speaker in the history of the New York State Assembly.

The one-time mayor was almost pathetically glad to have someone to talk to about his days as mayor. And he was very glad indeed to talk about Bob Moses, once he had taken care to make sure the interviewer understood that it had always been he, not Moses, who had given the orders during the old days. ("He would get to Gracie Mansion early in the morning. He had what he called an agenda." Pause. "And sometimes I had an agenda.") "Let me put it this way—I think Mr. Moses will go down in history as the most brilliant, the most imaginative and certainly the most er, er, certainly a man whose integrity is always beyond question . . . the leading public figure in America, not only in New York City but in America. He spent billions of dollars of public funds without anyone ever putting a question mark."

He went on for some time reminiscing about how close he and Moses had been. Then, however, he was asked when he had last seen Moses. And the sincere, friendly face turned sad as he tried, in vain, to recall the last time he had seen the big, charming, brilliant man who had once been so friendly to him.

"I haven't seen him recently," he said at last.

WAGNER

On those unforgettable evenings so long ago on which Al Smith's "Court of Appeals" had convened over cracked clams and cold beer, Moses, singing at the piano with the Governor's big arm around his shoulders while Jimmy Walker played, had often seen, sitting silent and wide-eyed in that room filled with loud, boisterous men, as close to his father as he could get, a shy little boy, for Robert Ferdinand Wagner, Sr., who had been the Governor's roommate when they had both been young legislators in Albany, made a point, ever since young Robert's mother had died when he was nine, of taking the boy with him whenever he could. Moses had given the Senator's son a helpful boost onto the first rung of the political ladder; in his first race for political office—for an Assembly seat from his father's old Yorkville district in 1937—he had enabled him to promise a swimming pool for John Jay Park on Seventy-eighth Street. "Bob Moses was very nice to me," he would recall. "He was going to build it anyway, I'm sure, but he gave me an opportunity to tell my constituents that I had gotten it there. And I was always very grateful to him for that." In his climb up the ladder, however, young Wagner, while strikingly "regular" in all other respects, had displayed what Moses regarded as an infatuation—especially disappointing in one from so sturdy a background—with the "radical" notion of city planning. As chairman of the City Planning Commission, he had pushed the Master Plan, and had even supported Stanley Isaacs' "silly" notion that the plan should preserve and protect the city's neighborhoods. Moses' relationship with the younger man had worsened during his Manhattan borough presidency, in part, perhaps, because Wagner, aware as was his patron, Carmine De Sapio, of the importance of contractors in the new political scheme of things, insisted on using his own, not Moses'; once, in fact (after Wagner Senior was safely in retirement), Moses had written a letter, distributed as usual to a mailing list of hundreds, calling Wagner Junior a "bubblehead." Wagner, for his part, had kept his own counsel (Wagner always kept his own counsel), but while he never attacked Moses directly, publicly or privately ("Wagner never makes derogatory remarks about people," Lutsky says. "Nobody ever heard him say a bad word about anybody: maybe he learned that from his father"), he left with intimates such as Lutsky the impression that "he didn't like Moses." During his campaign for the Democratic nomination for mayor—in which, of course, he was opposing the man Moses was supporting—and in the course of wooing the Good Government groups embraced by De Sapio, who had hand-picked him for the job and was directing his campaign, he led them to believe that he would curb the Coordinator's power. And after his election, he had brave words to the same effect. "I'm not going to let Moses come over to Gracie Mansion and give me my marching orders, like he did Impy," he told Warren Moscow, whom he had drafted from the *Times* to be a mayoral assistant. Shortly after the election, "a source close to the Mayor-elect" was leaking to reporters the information that "Robert Moses will continue to serve in the Wagner city administration, but his powers are likely to be severely restricted," probably to those of Park Commissioner.

Another leak soon followed, however: there was no longer any thought of removing Moses as Coordinator. The Good Government strategists thereupon decided to try to hold the line on the sole remaining post to which he needed reappointment at Wagner's inauguration: his Planning Commission membership, which expired on December 31, 1953.

The site of battle seemed choice. There were stronger arguments against his holding the Planning Commission post than the other two: as Park Commissioner and Construction Coordinator, he proposed public works projects and the Charter had surely never intended the proposer of projects to sit on the body which passed on their merits. Moreover, the Mayor-elect, as a former commission chairman himself, should be able to understand the logic of such arguments.

At first, Wagner did in fact seem to understand that logic. Meeting with the reformers before his inauguration, he told them he understood their views and agreed with them. The reformers left the interview believing that there would be only two jobs waiting for Moses.

On inauguration day, their efforts seemed for a while to have been crowned with victory. As they sat among the hundreds of spectators crowded into the City Council Chamber at City Hall, watching the new mayor summon his appointees forward one after another, administer their oath of office and hand them their official "oath blanks," which he had signed before the ceremonies, they saw him call up Robert Moses, swear him in as Park Commissioner and Construction Coordinator and then, with Moses still standing beside him waiting expectantly for the third oath and blank, beckon the next appointee forward. Watching Moses' face pale, the swarthy skin turning almost white, and then seeing the telltale reddish, almost purple, flush rising out of his collar up along his neck, they whispered happily—in some cases, gloatingly—among themselves.

As each commissioner was sworn in, he walked out of the Council Chamber and into an adjoining room, where he was supposed to leave the "oath blank" as proof—required under the city's Administrative Code—that he had sworn the required oath of loyalty to the Constitution, and where he was supposed to sign the city's massive, gray-bound "Oath Book," the official record of appointments, which was resting on a small table in front of Lutsky and an aide, Philip Shumsky. (City appointments are not official until "certificates of appointment" are issued, but in practice they become official as soon as both the mayor's signature and that of the appointee are on the oath blank, and the appointee's is in the Oath Book.) As Lutsky and Shumsky recall it, Moses stalked in and demanded, "How about City Planning?"

Lutsky, who knew the Mayor had decided not to make the third appointment, shrugged his shoulders as if he knew nothing, saying, "These are the only titles on the list. I just do as I'm instructed."

Without another word, the two men recall, Moses stalked into the Mayor's private office, to which Wagner had repaired alone before the official reception that was to follow. Neither Moses nor Wagner, the only two persons present, will discuss the confrontation in detail. But Moses was to tell aides—and Wagner, asked about the confrontation many years later, was, with an extremely pained expression, to indirectly confirm Moses' account*—that he had put it to the Mayor "straight"; either he got the third job, or he'd quit the other two. On the spot. He'd march right outside and tell the press. As the aides relate it, Wagner tried frantically to stall, saying that there must have been some oversight, that some clerk must have forgotten to fill out the appointment blank, that there was nothing for Moses to worry about, that he'd see to it in a few days.

Returning to the room where Shumsky and Lutsky were sitting, Moses snatched an unused blank off a sheaf Shumsky had placed on the table in case some appointee lost a blank and needed another. Sitting down at a typewriter that had been placed on another small table nearby, he typed in the date, his name, in the space marked "length of term"—eight years—and, in the space marked "position"—"Member, City Planning Commission." Then, carrying the blank, he stalked out of the room and back into the Mayor's private office and—without a word, according to his aides' recollection of the story—laid the paper on Wagner's desk. Without a word, Wagner pulled the paper toward himself and signed it. And, relates Warren Moscow, "Moses increased the dimensions of his victory by relating the story of the hand-typed oath to only fifty or so of his most intimate friends, all in city government."

Four days later, there was another victory, quieter but more significant. Because the powers of the City Construction Coordinator had never been spelled out by law, they were what each mayor chose to make them. Reappointment to that post by Wagner did not mean much to Moses—unless he could obtain from Wagner what he had obtained from O'Dwyer and Impellitteri: authority to "represent" the city in negotiations with state and federal governments. On January 5, he wrote Wagner asking if the Mayor wanted him to do so. "Certainly," the Mayor wrote back.

Moscow got a very close view indeed of Moses' next victory. Abrasive but clever, the former newspaperman decided, even before Wagner's inauguration, "to create for the incoming administration some of the atmosphere of the First Hundred Days—you know: action."

In no field was that commodity needed more than housing: the city's crisis was entering its ninth year. "I asked [Wagner] if we had a housing

* Before the author had had an opportunity to ask Moses about the confrontation, Moses had stopped talking to him. When, in 1972, the author asked Wagner about it, the pained expression came over the ex-Mayor's face and he refused to meet the author's eyes as he said, "I don't remember. I know there was one reason I might not [have wanted to reappoint him]—he was never there. He always sent a substitute [to Planning Commission meetings]." Pressed for a more definite answer—the version Moses had given his aides was read to him—Wagner finally said: "I think that may have happened. I probably thought, 'Let's not get into a big row to start out with.' "

program, if anyone had been assigned to do a housing program, and he said No and I said, 'Would you like me to take it on?' and he said, 'Okay, but make sure you keep in touch with Moses.' "

That stricture should have been a warning, but Moscow was as short on an understanding of people as he was long on an understanding of public relations. In two or three work-crammed weeks during December 1953, he drew up the program for state-assisted middle-income housing that would, with only minor changes, later be named "Mitchell-Lama" after the two legislators who would be permitted to introduce it in Albany. He discussed it not only with Cruise and other Moses Men on the Housing Authority but with Moses, who said he liked it—"He said, 'Good, that'll bring the union treasuries in.' " But then, shortly after the inauguration, Moscow, in a secret memo, presented it to the Board of Estimate himself instead of letting Moses do it.

"Moses blew his top," Moscow recalls. "He wrote a memo to the Mayor—one of those mimeographed things that goes around to 205 people —pretty much denouncing me" and denouncing the program that he had privately told Moscow he liked.

At the same time as the denunciations were flying, however, Spargo and Lebwohl kept telling Moscow to ignore them. "They kept coming to me and saying [here Moscow would whisper to show how the two Moses Men talked], 'Don't answer him. Don't blow your top. It's going to be all right. He's not really angry at you.' " Moscow was understandably puzzled—until he figured out that he was just a substitute target. Their boss, he realized, was angry at Wagner for what he thought was the Mayor's authorization to Moscow to interfere with his control of housing, but, not wanting to alienate a mayor who had otherwise proved so agreeable, had decided to make his views known to him by attacking one of his assistants instead.

And the strategy worked. Despite Wagner's previously professed enthusiasm for the proposal, the Mayor allowed it to languish in the Board of Estimate. Then, three weeks later, Moses dropped in on a Board executive session. He presented his "own" housing program. It bore an amazing resemblance to Moscow's, except that now it was identified with Moses instead. Wagner quickly obtained the Board approval that allowed it to be sent to Albany.

On February 23, 1954, a black-tie dinner in the Grand Ballroom of the Waldorf-Astoria brought to a climax the year-long celebration of New York City's three-hundredth anniversary. The principal speakers were the Mayor and Robert Moses. And Moses, in his speech, went out of his way to praise "My friend, Bob Wagner."

Moses' relationship with Wagner would not always be so friendly. He was still a frequent early-morning visitor at Gracie Mansion, and he still arrived with the large manila envelope filled with documents, but now he often went away without the Mayor's signature on them. One observer reported:

He has been heard to say that he looks back with particular wistfulness upon the term of William O'Dwyer, having found him to be a mayor who would sign almost anything placed before him on the breakfast table, provided that it was accompanied by a reasonably persuasive argument. . . . Wagner is more likely to say, "Splendid, Bob, splendid. Before I sign this, though, let me take it along to the office and think the thing over."

The Port Authority found city approval of its projects obtainable again, more easily obtainable, in fact, than ever before. During Wagner's entire twelve years in office, its power grew. As for the Housing Authority, Moscow's conversations with Cruise and Authority staffers had opened his eyes to the completeness—hitherto unguessed at, keen though those eyes were—of Moses' control of a body to which he ostensibly had no direct relationship. "Theoretically, he had no connection with [public] housing, except in his capacity as Construction Coordinator, which gave him the over-all right to stick his nose into anything," Moscow says, "but, Christ, Cruise wouldn't go to the bathroom unless he asked Moses first." Wagner "became a little worried about the Authority," Moscow says—presumably about the possibility that its activities would result in a full-scale scandal which would reflect on his administration—and seriously considered ousting Cruise (unlike the other four members of the board, who were appointed for fixed five-year terms, Housing Authority chairmen served at the mayor's pleasure), a possibility which delighted liberals who felt Cruise was handicapped by "an inability to stand up to Moses when property rights interfere with human rights." But Moses pressed the buttons, and the calls—calls that no mayor could refuse to take—flooded in. "I want to publicly thank Commissioner Moses, Thomas Shanahan, David Rockefeller and others who said a good word for me," said Cruise, as he was sworn in at a ceremony attended by Moses and Big "Bag" Man Jim Farley; when newspaper photographers sought to pose him with the Mayor, Cruise asked Moses to get in the picture, too. Wagner told Deputy Mayor Paul O'Keefe, "Well, I made my deal. I'm putting my man in to keep an eye on things." The Mayor created a new executive directorship over the Authority's staff and appointed to it Joseph P. McMurray, his father's former administrative assistant. But McMurray turned out to be more friendly to Tom Shanahan than to the Mayor. During 1954, Wagner's worries increased, and by the spring of 1955, he decided that more direct action was necessary. McMurray was replaced by Moscow—"quite simply, to take control of the assigning of architects away from Shanahan"—and Cruise was called in for a very confidential chat.

The former $9,000-per-year Park Department clerk loved his $22,500-per-year chairmanship. He was informed that if he wanted to keep it, some small adjustments in his loyalties would be necessary. "Cruise had a switch," Moscow would say privately years later with a faint, mocking smile. "He, of course, had grown up in the Park Department and was very close to Moses. He was Moses' protégé. But Cruise made his divorce. Thereafter, in matters of controversy, Cruise took his views from the Mayor."

All this maneuvering went on backstage, without any direct confrontation between Moses and the Mayor. It—and other subtle tests of will and strength between the two men—led, however, to constant tension between them, as did more trivial incidents.

"Bob [Wagner] was no less jealous of his prerogatives than any other mayor," Paul R. Screvane says. "And [Moses] didn't come to Bob enough and consult him." Wagner occasionally attempted to assert his authority over his commissioner by asking him to come down to City Hall. Generally, Moses made some excuse, but occasionally Wagner insisted and Moses, needing something from the Mayor, had no choice but to go. When he was forced to make the trip, however, he invariably disciplined Wagner by showing up late. At receptions at Gracie Mansion, Wagner, moving quietly from one guest to another—"He does a lot of his work in whispers at parties," one observer wrote—was remarkably inconspicuous. When Moses entered the room, generally trailed by enough aides to make his entrance conspicuous, women patted their hair to make sure it was in place and discreetly took out pocket mirrors to check their lipstick, and men watched him out of the corners of their eyes. His physical presence and vitality as he stood, head thrown back, teeth gleaming in his dark face, handsome, charming, physically overpowering his listeners, perhaps with a big arm around the shoulders of one, recounting fascinating anecdotes about Smith or Roosevelt or La Guardia, made him, as always, the focal point of the room, and sometimes Wagner, seeing his guests' attention slipping away from him just a bit, could be observed watching the Coordinator from across the room with an expression on his face that could only be described as enigmatic.

But if there was strain, most of the tension on the line was put there—or relaxed—by Moses. It was he—not the man who was supposedly his superior—who dominated the relationship. And in policy he proved as dominant as in personality. If there were points of contention, they were almost always resolved in his favor.

Wagner wanted Moses' dominance in public housing eliminated, but Moscow, assigned to the task, found it somewhat more difficult than he had believed. Charging onto the scene with visions of new brooms sweeping clean, the ex-reporter was encumbered by the fact that he was genuinely affected by the plight of the city's poor—and by his painful realization that Moses' near-monopoly of the engineering and architectural talent experienced in tenant relocation, slum clearing and construction on the immense scale required (and in dealing with state and federal bureaucracies) made it difficult to find qualified replacements—or even to keep from adding new Moses Men to the staff. "We needed a new chief engineer in charge of construction," he recalls. "The best qualified man around was Jim Dawson, who had been in charge of the UN job for Moses. Well, you're not going to turn him down just because Moses recommended him." (Analyzing in later years the sources of Moses' power, Moscow would say that one "stemmed simply from the fact that his enterprises developed people.")

Even with Cruise's conversion, Wagner's control of the Authority board was not assured. The antipathy of its only Negro member, Frank R. Crosswaith, to Moses' philosophies and methods, assured the Mayor of another vote, but Shanahan and "Moses' stooge," William Wilson, gave Moses two, so that the vote of the fifth member would be decisive.

Wagner's first attempt to gain that vote—the appointment of a loyal supporter—had backfired when the appointee died. Then, Moscow says, "I arranged for James Felt to be appointed. I thought he would be ours. Instead, he was Moses'." (Moscow might have been alerted to this possibility had he been aware of the identity of the real estate company that had been handed the lucrative site-assemblage contract for Stuyvesant Town and Peter Cooper Village: James Felt & Co.) In 1956, Felt was eased over to the chairmanship of the Planning Commission and replaced by builder Abraham Lindenbaum, who, Moscow says, "we *knew* was 100 percent for what the Mayor or I wanted." Shanahan and Wilson were finally a minority.

But even a minority—when maneuvered by a master—can have considerable strength. His 1957 threat, delivered through Wilson, to "sic the *Daily News* on the Authority," was only the most dramatic method Moses employed to bend that body to his will. And while Cruise, after his conversion, might take "his views from the Mayor," most of the Authority business did not involve controversy, and in those matters Moses' wishes frequently prevailed. The day-to-day activities of the Authority, moreover, were run by the staff, still so largely Moses-dominated. It was not until 1958, when Wagner reorganized it completely, that Moses' domination of the New York City Housing Authority—then in its thirteenth year—was really ended.

And while Moses' domination of the Authority may have ended in 1958, he still possessed considerable influence, if not over its day-to-day operations, then over its larger planning and construction proposals. The money for the Authority's construction came, of course, largely from the state—specifically from the Legislature and the body that administered the Legislature's wishes, the State Division of Housing, headed by the State Commissioner of Housing. And Governors generally followed Moses' recommendations in appointing the commissioner. As late as 1968, during the administration of John V. Lindsay, liberals like Julius Edelstein would still be complaining about Moses' "influence with State Housing."

And public—low-income—housing was the only area in the vast housing field in which Moses' power was reduced at all. During the first six years of Wagner's administration, the Title I program was to grow to a point at which it was larger than public housing. Wagner never made the slightest attempt to interfere with his control, exercised through his chairmanship of the group misnomered "The Mayor's Slum Clearance Committee."

If Moses' power was reduced only slightly in housing, moreover, it was reduced not at all in parks or transportation. For the first six years of Wagner's administration, his word was as much "law" in those fields as it had been in Impellitteri's. The Coordinator didn't get his way with Wagner as routinely as he had gotten it with Impy—there were more confrontations —but he got it. There were many times when the Mayor announced to friends that he was going to refuse a Moses demand, but the pattern following the announcement was always the same. William F. R. Ballard, a chairman of the City Planning Commission, recalls vividly Wagner "agreeing to back me—told me he would—and then he ended up backing Moses." And some version of Ballard's words are repeated by dozens of officials caught in tugs of war between the two men. "I saw it over and over," Condello says. "Wagner would tell me he was really going to lay down the law this time, show this guy Moses who's mayor. And then they'd meet, and afterwards, Wagner would say, 'Well, I guess I showed that guy.' And I'd have to laugh. [Moses] would go out with about 98 percent of what he wanted—every time."

When Wagner proved especially recalcitrant, the resignation threat would be used. Since there had been little need of it, Moses' ultimate weapon had fallen into disuse during the Impellitteri administration, but he worked it hard indeed during Wagner's. "Sometimes it seemed like he was resigning about one thing or another about twice a day," one high Wagner aide says.

Wagner had no Windels to show him how to defuse the weapon by turning it into a joke, and so when he had to surrender to it, he had to make the surrender a straightforward one, which must have been humiliating to him. But surrender he did—over and over again. Under Wagner, as under O'Dwyer and Impellitteri, not the Mayor but Moses shaped the city.

35. "RM"

THE MAN WHO RULED the empire called "Triborough" ruled it absolutely. There were other members on the boards of its four constituent public authorities but the decisions were all his. Visiting Moses on Randall's Island one day, Cleveland Rodgers rose to leave when two men came into his office, but Moses said not to bother. "There was an exchange of questions and answers"—a very brief exchange—after which the two men quickly departed. Asking who they were, Rodgers "learned that he had been sitting through a monthly meeting of the Triborough Bridge Authority."

The passion that fired that man—who in 1948 celebrated his sixtieth birthday—was the passion that had fired that man at thirty: the passion for tangible, physical accomplishment, and for the power which that accomplishment produced. And if age had not slaked his appetite for power and achievement, neither had it slaked his appetite for the means to power and achievement: work.

No strictly rational explanation could account for the voraciousness of that appetite. In his early days of power, he had sloughed off all hobbies and relaxations save swimming. Now, twenty-five years later, he still had no other hobbies or relaxations. He still did not golf, did not play bridge, did not attend sporting events or the theater—in 1960, Ernie Clark gave him tickets to the musical comedy *Fiorello!*; because of its subject, Moses went, and in thanking Clark mentioned to him that it had been the first Broadway play he had seen in years. Guests at his home can recall no single day that he spent with his family—with the two daughters he loved and the grandchildren on whom he doted—on which he did not disappear for hours into his study and shut the door behind him. He still refused to allow any of the chores that consume chunks of other men's lives—buying clothes and getting haircuts, for example—to consume chunks of his. As she had been doing since the day she married him, Mary still ordered his socks and underwear, bought his suits, carried them home, if they weren't the correct size took them back and brought home others, and when she got one that fit, arranged for a tailor to come to his office and make minimum alterations, when she saw he needed a haircut, had a barber brought in, and, if he was going out to dine, placed money in his pocket. (If she forgot, he would have to ask his companion for a dollar or two for the waiter.) He still invited "friends" for weekends at the rambling old house on Thompson Avenue in Babylon, went clamming with them and his family on Fire Island, was the most charming and gracious of hosts—but the more perceptive among them knew always that they were there not because of friendship but for a purpose, and that before the weekend was over, Moses would be putting his big arm around their shoulders and working for the vote, or the administrative decision, that he needed from them. A quarter of a century before, he had sloughed off the last remaining amenities of living and set before himself a life that would be a feast of work. In 1958, at the age of seventy, he would be still sitting before that feast—with undiminished appetite.

During the 1920's, Moses had established a routine under which, whenever he was living in Babylon, the chief engineer of the Long Island State Park Commission, Arthur Howland, called every morning at 7:30 at Thompson Avenue to pick up a big manila envelope bulging with the memos, letters, press releases and directives to his executives that Moses had written since leaving the office the night before. Now, after twenty-five years of picking up that envelope, Howland was gone. But the envelope was still there. Every morning, without fail, Howland's successor, Sid Shapiro, would call at Thompson Avenue—and every morning, without fail, he would find it sitting there on the newel post at the bottom of the banister. "My God!" says one of his secretaries. "He was a dynamo! Every morning there would be a manila envelope this thick, and six girls would be working all day to do the things he had done overnight." Working, that is, after Hazel Tappan had deciphered his handwriting—unintelligible except to his Junoesque chief secretary.

The mail, a huge stack of it, would be waiting for him on the desk of whichever one of his four offices he was using that day. Summoning three secretaries to ring his desk, he would plow through the letters so rapidly—scribbling instructions on some, snapping off orders about others, dictating replies, tossing the letters to the three women in rotation—that within thirty minutes the huge stack of paper would have melted down to the bare desk top.

During the 1920's, Moses had turned the big black Packard in which he had to spend so much time into an office, holding conferences in it with aides whose own limousines trailed behind, waiting to take them off when the conferences were finished, carrying with him always a supply of legal note pads and sharpened pencils and using the time in the limousine for work. Now the limousine was a Cadillac instead of a Packard. But it was still an office.

Age withers the output of most men, but as decade succeeded decade in the career of Robert Moses, his output seemed only to increase. The flow of broadsides delivered daily to a thousand desks never slackened. "Every morning when you came in, there on your desk would be [the mimeographed] memos that Moses had sent to someone and circulated to everyone else," Lawrence Orton says. They had been on Orton's desk from the day of his appointment to the City Planning Commission in 1938; they were on his desk in 1948 and 1958—and there seemed to be more of them than ever. Orton, who read the memos—out of a fearful fascination—says, "It took the first half to three quarters of an hour every day to catch up on your Moses correspondence." Says Latham: "During the time I knew him—and I knew him for forty-five years—hours didn't mean anything to him. Days of the week didn't mean anything to him. When there was work to be done, you did it. That was the way he was then and that's the way he is now."

If age could not wither his passion for work, sun—even tropical sun—could not bleach it. For years he had not taken vacations; now he did, if infrequently (generally in winter to the Caribbean), although it is notable that most of these vacations were to the luxurious island retreats of Bernard Gimbel or Robert Blum of Abraham and Straus or of other powerful men whose support he needed. But as his male secretary, Harold Blake, sorted through each day's mail during his boss's "vacation," out would tumble envelope after envelope addressed in his boss's scrawl and crammed with memos and orders.

Wind could not cool that passion. Tearing himself away from his desk, he would on some afternoons head for the *Sea-Ef* and his beloved Great South Bay. In the afternoons, the breeze on the bay would be fresh and crisp. Beneath the big cruiser the flounder might be running. But on more days than not his only catch would be another full manila envelope. The captain would cruise back and forth over the bay hour after hour; hour after hour the figure sitting silently in the deck chair at the stern would be hunched over memos and maps and blueprints. Late in the afternoon, he might take the wheel himself, but the charts his mind would be seeing would not be charts of the bay; once Captain Pearsall forgot to keep watch for a few minutes and Moses ran the boat straight onto a clearly visible sand bar.

Illness could not sap it. His were few and far between, and even the most serious of them—an eye operation in 1955, when he was sixty-six—did not slow him down; on the morning after the operation, he was dictating in his hospital room at seven o'clock. The colds and flus and viruses that deflect other men from their work did not deflect him from his. Meeting Moses at home after Shapiro had told him that "RM" was running a 104-degree fever, Tallamy found him propped up in bed surrounded by mounds of documents. "He was writing a speech," Tallamy recalls. "He put it down and plunged right into the subject of my visit" without a minute's break.

He had lost none of the furious urge that made him work. It was too strong to allow him to keep seated for long. "He would drive me crazy with his pacing," says Joe Ingraham of the *Times*. "I have a back condition and I'd be sitting there and all of a sudden Moses wouldn't be there in front of me any more; he'd be pacing around the room as he talked. I'd have to keep twisting around to follow him, and he'd keep pacing and pacing, and I'd have to keep twisting and twisting." Sometimes Tallamy, major supplier of the money for Moses' dreams, would arrive at Randall's Island to find Moses waiting for him outside the front door as if he had been unable to wait the extra minute until Tallamy reached his office on the second floor. As soon as the federal highway administrator stepped out of his car, Moses would begin talking about some project. "Once, I remember, he grabbed my lapels and put his face right up to mine, he was so anxious and so impatient."

And Tallamy not only was a man from whom Moses needed something but, as a federal employee, was not dependent on him for his salary. With men who were—the "Moses Men" who were his top executives and who were now virtually the only part of his empire with which he now dealt personally—Moses' impatience took other forms.

"If your answer wasn't fast enough for him, he'd get up and pace," Ernie Clark says. "If you told him you didn't know [the answer], he might say, 'Well, why don't you?' " And he didn't want to be bored with statistics; "he wanted conclusions and how you had gotten them." Once, a new engineering consultant began reading off page after page of statistics. Clark recalls that "Mr. Moses started pacing, almost like a caged tiger. And then he turned around and said: 'I never heard so much horseshit in my life.' " More and more frequently now, when he heard a report of some delay or obstacle, the big powerful face would turn pale, almost white, and a wave of purple, rising up the thick neck, would sweep across it. More and more frequently, the palm of the big right hand would begin to smack down on the table as he talked, and his secretaries, sitting in their office outside trying to smile at each other, would hear his voice begin to rise. Whirling on Triborough chief engineer Joseph A. Vermaelen one day in front of a roomful of Vermaelen's associates and outsiders, after Vermaelen had made a suggestion dealing with a matter that Moses did not regard as his province, he snarled: "You're just a swabbie on this ship. Now get out of here!" And Vermaelen was lucky. For the voice could cut as well as bellow, slashing at a man with an aim that seemed to find unerringly that vulnerable point at which the man could most be hurt. More and more frequently, he would lunge out of his chair and begin to pace the room, pounding his clenched fist into the walls hard enough to scrape the skin off them, in a rage beyond the perception of pain. Retired Army General Harry L. Meyers, director of the Long Island State Park Commission police force, who says, "My admiration for Mr. Moses is without limit; it's beyond anything," admits: "I've seen him when he wouldn't be himself—waving his arms, just wild." Says Peter J. Brennan: "When he got mad, he was a raving maniac. I've seen him say to an employee of his—'Now, dammit, you get this done or don't come back!' Steel-eyes-like, he'd stare at you and he'd raise the arms . . ." If there was a sudden crash of shattering glass from behind his door, the secretaries knew what it was; he had snatched up his old-fashioned glass inkwell and hurled it at an underling whose report had displeased him.

Tireless at thirty, he was tireless at seventy.

Up in the morning at six or seven, he often made breakfast for his wife and brought it to her in bed. In the evenings, at the far side of twelve or fourteen hours of unbroken toil, he would head not for home but for the swimming pool. One weekend, he invited Ingraham to Babylon and told the reporter to come up to Randall's Island Friday evening and drive out with him. Arriving at five o'clock, Ingraham found Moses in conference, and settled down in the Commissioner's waiting room. An hour later, he was still waiting; the conference was still on. When it broke up around six-thirty, Ingraham was invited in, and Moses told him he still had a few things to attend to. He was still attending to them at seven o'clock and eight o'clock, and nine o'clock and ten. Rising finally, he said, "Let's stop off at Earle Andrews' place on the way out." The "place" turned out to be Andrews' glass-enclosed swimming pool in Huntington. Letting himself in with his own key, Moses changed, plunged into the water and began swimming. Watching the muscular arms windmilling endlessly up and down the pool, the drowsy reporter dozed off. Some time later, he awoke. The windmill was still turning; if anything, Ingraham realized with a start, Moses was swimming faster than before. It was, he says, "late" when the Commissioner clambered out of the water, looking as fresh as a youth, and very late indeed when the two men finally arrived at Thompson Avenue. As Ingraham climbed the stairs to the guest room, he saw the Commissioner's broad back disappearing not into his bedroom but into his study, yellow legal note pad in hand. When Ingraham fell asleep, he knew his host was still working. And what awakened the reporter the next morning—"at some ungodly early hour"—was the smell of bacon and eggs. Hearing him stirring, Mary called up the stairs: "Come on down. Bob's cooking breakfast."

His physical strength was awesome to his associates. Concerned as he grew older for his safety during the swims he took far out into the ocean off Jones Beach or Gilgo, they agreed among themselves that, whenever possible, as Latham puts it, "as long as he was in the water, one of us was with him . . . without making it obvious." But they had to perform this chore in relays; in his sixties and seventies, Robert Moses could tumble around in the surf, diving through and riding the South Shore's big breakers, far longer even than the tall, broad-shouldered Latham, twenty years his junior and himself an exceptionally strong swimmer.

The racing pen seemingly could not brake itself. For money or to get his views into print, he was constantly indulging in the "fugitive scribbling" of commissioned magazine articles; he was the author of a total of 51 articles for *The Atlantic, Harper's, Saturday Review* and other national magazines; of 32 more for *The New York Times Magazine*; of an additional 19 for the *Herald Tribune Sunday Magazine*—and of several score more for other newspaper Sunday supplements. It had "always been his ambition to write cheap pulp stuff," Moses Man Arnold Vollmer recalls; in the mid-1950's, short on cash as usual, he announced to aides that he was going to write "a trashy piece of pulp" that he was sure would sell. Ironically, when he finished it—a reportedly sex-filled novel titled *From Palms to Pines*—and sent it to various publishing houses under a pseudonym, not one would publish it. He had, however, managed to write a full-length novel while simultaneously holding down eight full-time executive jobs. Letters—not only the mimeographed daily broadsides but graceful personal notes of condolence or congratulations—poured from his pen in the thousands, each to be delivered by hand by one of a battalion of liveried Triborough messengers, and they were letters graceful enough to be treasured by their recipients. One to Newbold Morris, delivered on the death of his father-in-law, Judge Learned Hand, said:

. . . To millions who knew little of his profession but had become familiar with his leonine head and brow of Jove, he was the embodiment of righteousness in a mad world. Today beyond the Straight Gate and along the aisle on the other side are massed thousands of cheering lovers of justice as this great exemplar of Law comes marching in.

He giveth His beloved sleep.

(Anyone who thought it strange that the condolence note was addressed not to Mrs. Morris, the late judge's daughter, whom Moses also knew, but to her husband, didn't understand Moses; Moses didn't need the daughter.) Said one man who didn't meet Moses until he was sixty years old and who worked with him frequently for twenty years thereafter: "He never got tired. Never that I saw. He seemed to relax when he was working the hardest. He'd come out of a meeting or conference that had high tension and be completely relaxed, where the ordinary person would be exhausted. Work seemed to make him stronger."

In 1950, Hetty Green, an eccentric millionairess who had long felt grateful to Moses for building the Hutchinson River Parkway, which gave her "such pleasure" driving to and from her homes in Manhattan and Greenwich, Connecticut, died, and, on the reading of her will, it was discovered that her gratitude had taken practical form: a $10,000 bequest to Robert Moses. Not a year later, however, one of the large, unexpected expenses that were continually bedeviling Moses arose—this time a needed re-roofing of his Babylon house—and he discovered that he again had no money in the bank. It had all been spent, and, Moses confessed to Jack Madigan, he didn't know on what.

It wasn't that Moses didn't want money, of course. He wanted it desperately, as is proven by the commissions he continually accepted from magazines for articles he loathed writing, and by the eagerness with which he accepted $100,000 fees for arterial highway plans for other cities. But he had the Moses prodigality with money, the prodigality that had helped make his brother a pauper. He always accepted the $100,000 commissions with an idea of keeping a substantial portion for himself, but he always ended up using the money to buy other men who could help him in his New York work. Detractors who knew the amounts of these commissions and who judged Moses by the standards they applied to other public officials, assumed —understandably—that he was becoming a rich man from them. This conclusion was natural—but it was wrong.

If he created an empire, he roamed it in imperial style.

His car, the most luxurious Detroit could provide (the richness of its leather upholstery gave one guest the feeling that he was not in a motor vehicle but the library of a fine men's club, an illusion reinforced by the placement of the limousine's side windows so far forward that occupants of its deep rear seat could see out only by leaning forward—"There was a feeling of isolation; normally when you ride in the back of a car people are able to look in and you're able to look out, but here it was as if you were insulated from the outside world"), rushed to him by Detroit at his command ("I remember when air-conditioned cars were first coming out and it was a big thing to get one," says an O'Dwyer aide. "The Mayor couldn't get one. But Moses had one"), stood at his call day and night; to insure that it would, he had not one but three personal chauffeurs. Of the tens of thousands of cars that passed daily through the empire's toll booths, that car alone did not stop. (When a new Director of Public Safety was appointed for the empire, he was briefed by Sid Shapiro: everyone else granted free passage—Governor, Mayor, even police cars and the cars of Moses' top aides—was required to swerve out of line and outside the booths so as not to complicate the treadle count; "only one car goes through.") And when the big black limousine with the row of shields on its bumper and the license plate "2000" roared through a booth, not even slowing down, the uniformed officer inside jumping to salute and then staring after it, straining vainly to catch a glimpse of the living legend riding in the rear seat, the lieutenant or captain in charge at the toll plaza would hastily pick up his telephone—as hastily as the commission trooper, miles down the road, seeing the long black limousine looming out of the distance, would reach for his radio microphone—to keep the empire's capital on Randall's Island apprised, minute by minute and mile by mile, of its ruler's progress, so that urgent messages could be delivered to him at the next toll plaza. If, in reply, he wanted to make a call—he would not allow a telephone in his car so that he could work in it uninterrupted—his chauffeur would pull in to the next police barracks, troopers springing up to escort him to a phone.

The empire's gleaming white flagship—and one of its captains—stood at his call. Even on days on which there was no real possibility that he would be able to get out on the bay, the *Sea-Ef,* kept constantly gassed and provisioned, would be held ready at the dock near his Babylon house, just on the off chance that his schedule might change. The captain on duty on Sunday could not relax just because there had been no call for his services in the morning or afternoon or early evening. He was under orders never to be out of earshot of his telephone—just in case RM should call—until 10 P.M. Was it RM's wish to swim? There was a network of swimming pools at his disposal. Keys to Earle Andrews' pool in Huntington, and to the luxuriously decorated, glass-enclosed pleasure dome of commission member and millionaire Landon Thorne in Bay Shore—among others—had been pressed upon him so that he could use these facilities at any time without even having to greet their owners. Did an emperor employ generals and admirals? Moses did, too; Farrell of the Burma Road was not the only one who upon retirement took up service under the flag of Triborough. And Moses could promote men over generals. In the United States Army, Farrell had been William Chapin's commanding officer; in Triborough's, Chapin was Farrell's.

Even as a youth, he had been anxious—eager—to entertain, insistent on picking up checks even for wealthy friends. Now, as the silver stream pouring into the empire's coffers swelled, and swelled, and swelled again, he diverted enough of it to entertain on a truly imperial scale.

At three of his offices—Randall's Island, Belmont Lake State Park and 270 Broadway—complete, separate staffs of chefs and waiters were on hand daily so that, wherever he might be, he could serve lunch to invited guests.

There was a ceremonial to even the smallest lunches.

Waiting to lunch with Robert Moses, a guest would be ushered at Randall's Island into an anteroom lined with pictures of Robert Moses' bridges, Robert Moses' parks, Robert Moses' parkways, of Robert Moses posing with Hoover, of Robert Moses posing with Roosevelt, of Robert Moses posing with Truman, with Eisenhower (and, later, with Kennedy and Johnson—and Pope John); at Belmont Lake into an anteroom with walls covered, literally from wall to ceiling, with Robert Moses' plaques and trophies. There might be a gleaming white scale model or two, of past or future achievements, lying carelessly about. And to insure against the guest's not being sufficiently reminded of his host's achievements, as he was being served drinks by a white-coated waiter, he would probably be joined —by design—by one of Moses' aides who would regale him with anecdotes about RM's triumphs. Finally, RM himself would appear—at the head of a procession of eight or ten aides, for if emperors had courts, so, of course, did he. (If by chance he was called out of the room to take a telephone call, when he returned his aides would jump to their feet, and would not sit down until he sat down.) The doors to the dining room—Randall's Island's lined with more pictures of Moses achievements; Belmont Lake's, a sun-filled, airy room fifty feet long atop a wing of the new Belmont Mansion Moses had built, lined, on all sides, with windows overlooking the lake and stands of magnificent trees—would be thrown open, and Moses would lead the guest inside, with his aides filing after them. Moses sat at the head, his aides—after Moses had sat down—on his right, in seats preassigned in order of rank and favor in his eyes, so that an observer who attended several meals could judge, by how far away from Moses Shapiro or Chapin or Latham was sitting that day, their current standing in Moses' organization. The food at lunches at Randall's Island—not special luncheons, just the typical lunch served by white-coated waiters to groups ranging in size from half a dozen to half a hundred perhaps 150 times a year—was spoken of by guests in tones of awe. At Belmont Lake, they were more informal—but culinary standards were just as high.

No aspect of lunch with Moses was more imperial than the attitude of the host. There was little conversation at these lunches; there was, instead, a dramatic monologue, anecdotes about his struggles, about political in-fighting in which he had engaged, about the Mayors and Governors and Presidents he had known, about his plans for the future. And these were usually not brief monologues. Once, when Moses was attempting to persuade *Newsday* to investigate another state agency with whose cooperation he was not pleased, he invited to lunch reporter Bob Greene and the paper's bull-voiced managing editor, Alan Hathway, possessor of considerable raconteurial ability in his own right and a man accustomed to holding the center of whatever stage he happened to find himself on. During the appetizer, Moses began relating anecdotes about himself. ("He told us that one of the favorite ones that had ever been written about him was: 'Nothing he has ever done has been tainted by legality.' He chortled at that. He obviously relished it.") Greene was an investigative reporter who never lost his presence of mind; when the main course arrived and Moses was still going strong, Greene glanced at his watch, and, upon returning to the city room, was able to report that Moses had talked nonstop for an hour and twenty minutes. "Alan," he told unbelieving colleagues, "couldn't get a word in edgewise."

Moses' court completed the aura. No emperor's was more simpering.

When the calls from the toll booths and the troopers out on the parkways indicated that Moses was heading toward one of his offices, that office would erupt into frenzied excitement. Grown men—men who were themselves in positions of authority over hundreds of men, men who were making forty or fifty or sixty thousand dollars a year—would shout to each other: "RM is twenty-four minutes away!" "He's twelve minutes away!" "The boss will be here in one minute!" They would hurriedly recheck one last time to make sure that any map or blueprint for which he might ask was ready for his perusal. Scurrying back and forth, secretaries would put a dozen freshly sharpened pencils in the pencil holder on his desk, straighten the pile of letters there, dust his office one last time. "Worst of all," says one, was when he headed first from his Babylon home to Belmont Lake, for that trip took only about five minutes. "Everyone would start shouting: 'The boss is coming! The boss is coming! He's on his way over from Thompson Avenue!' And everyone would start rushing around in little circles as if they were crazy." A reporter who arrived early at an auditorium in which Moses was to give a speech listened to his aides "refer to him as if he was God. 'I hope RM likes the podium.' 'I hope RM likes the lighting.' 'How do you think RM will be feeling this morning?' " At luncheons, their role was limited to laughing at his bons mots, scowling along with him when he mentioned his enemies, and occasionally uttering an affirmative "Yes" or "Definitely." Generally they uttered a complete sentence only in answer to a direct question he put to them—and generally that question was only to elicit their confirmation of some point he was making. If some guest was not sufficiently reverent, they quietly took him aside. Henry Barnes' first face-to-face encounter with Moses on coming to New York as Traffic Commissioner in 1962 was at a lunch in Moses' new office at the World's Fair site. "He was telling a story about Grover Whalen and the first fair, how Grover had always had a bunch of cuties around him and how one would say, 'Grover, we ought to have a dress shop' and there'd be a dress shop at the fair, and another would say, 'We ought to have . . .' Moses said something about how he didn't want 'no goddamn babes around me.' Just as a joke I said, 'I think that's a very narrow-minded viewpoint.' He looked very startled. His head jerked around in complete amazement. All the others sort of gasped. After the meeting, Stuart Constable [Park

Department executive officer] came up to me and he said, 'You know, Mr. Moses is a very busy and a very important person and it isn't proper to be facetious with him.' " Says reporter Joe Kahn: "He used to crack jokes; he had a great pride in his sense of humor, and these guys would watch him, waiting for their cue, and laugh. It was a regular Greek chorus, like a choral group—they nodded when he wanted them to nod, they laughed when he wanted them to laugh. Watching them, you got disgusted with your fellow man."

It was not at Randall's Island that Moses entertained most lavishly. For his empire had a summer capital.

At Jones Beach, on that sand bar he had filled with bathing pavilions and deck games and solariums and boat basins and dance floors and restaurants (restaurants operated by concessionaires to whom he had granted franchises so lucrative that their liquor cabinets and wine closets and larders, and their chefs and waiters and bartenders, were at his command); that sand bar operated by a consortium of agencies and authorities with a budget of $12,000,000 for whose spending he did not have to account, and with more than 3,000 employees he could allocate to whatever duties he chose; on that sand bar governed by laws he had written himself, policed by troopers in his pay and responsible only to him, Robert Moses could entertain as Robert Moses had always wanted to entertain.

At Jones Beach, Robert Moses could offer his guests cruising or fishing from his yacht, swimming at his private beach (the section then reserved for his use), and not only paddle tennis and shuffleboard and archery and roller skating but horseback riding, tennis and golf—the livery stables, rows of tennis courts and magnificently groomed golf courses of Bethpage State Park were only twelve minutes away by chauffeured Park Commission limousines. He could offer them the finest food and liquor; having built a $300,000 Boardwalk Restaurant, he turned it over, without competitive bidding, to a young concessionaire who had caught his eye—on terms so liberal that the people of the state might as well have given it to the young concessionaire as a gift.* In return, the concessionaire gave Moses one: he entertained Moses' guests, so many guests and so lavishly that the annual cost can only be guessed at; no complete tabulation has ever been made, but one incomplete tabulation (discovered in the concessionaire's files) shows that during one six-year period, *at least* $179,215—and probably considerably more—was spent on such entertainment.†

* During the 1960's, the Boardwalk Restaurant burned down. Moses built a new one, at a cost of $1,500,000, and, without competitive bidding, turned it over to the same concessionaire—at a rental of $18,000 per year, an amount which, an auditor noted, was "not even enough to amortize the construction cost."

† Each year, the concessionaire made $80,000 available to be mingled with $75,000 from the Park Commission in a separate bank account for "Alterations" and "Special Events"—which included meals for Moses' guests. During the six years between July 1, 1961, and September 30, 1967, $930,000 was spent from this account. The $179,215

At Jones Beach, he could entertain in what was, in effect, his own theater, built with the $4,200,000 in state cash he had collected as broker in the 1950 deal between New York State and New York City that produced the New York Thruway. Erected on a lagoon he carved out of the bay side of the barrier beach, the "Jones Beach Marine Stadium" was built to peculiarly Mosaic specifications, displaying both his delight in the grandiose (it was designed for the presentation not of plays but of spectacles, for the stage was located on a man-made island separated from the nearest seats by a broad moat, so that only the biggest, most lavish productions were feasible) and his belief in the separation of the aristocracy from the common herd (the front rim of the semicircular amphitheater consisted of a row of twelve-person boxes—separated from the rest of the stadium's 8,200 seats by an exceptionally wide and deep aisle; those boxes were offered for sale—on a season-long basis—only to banks and large corporations for the entertainment of their clients; those that were not purchased were kept empty; the boxes, Shapiro told the author blandly, were "not for the general public"). In some ways, in fact, the stadium seemed designed for Moses' personal use. Several boxes were reserved—permanently—for the use of his guests, the big center box for himself and the most favored among them. The aisle behind those boxes was deep enough so that men could stand in it without blocking the view of those behind, and in it, at every performance, stood commission staffers ready to supply his guests with drinks, snacks, warm blankets if the breeze blowing off the bay became uncomfortably chilly, and any other comforts they might wish. These functionaries referred to the center box as "The Royal Box," a fitting name because, as an emperor entertains visiting foreign potentates and their ministers, Moses, close to the world of the United Nations, did the same; on one typical evening, its occupants, in addition to Moses and Governor Dewey, included Prime Minister Menzies of Australia, and the heads of the UN missions of three European nations. (Moses of course paid special attention to the ministers of the nation he reverenced; British Ambassador Sir Michael Dixon Hoare was an especially frequent guest.) Would an emperor, sitting in his royal box, be introduced to the audience? Moses would, too—with drum roll and trumpet fanfare; whenever he was in attendance, the pre-show rendition of "The Star-Spangled Banner" would be preceded by such an introduction by Guy Lombardo, standing in the orchestra pit, as a spotlight played on the royal box. (Moses would act ostentatiously bored during these introductions, often continuing to talk to his guests and glancing up at the applauding crowd above him with only the briefest nod, rising from his seat at last as if it were almost too much trouble to do so, indicating with every gesture the fact that public acclaim interested him not in the least; how difficult, then, to reconcile this attitude with the fact that on many evenings when he was too busy to attend the

---

includes only expenditures specifically marked for "meals"; according to one source, other meal expenditures were concealed as expenditures for "publicity," "recreational activities," etc.

play, when, in fact, he had appointments elsewhere, he would arrange his schedule so he could stop by the theater just long enough for the introduction.) Not public taste but Moses' alone (which considered suitable for public consumption only bland musical comedies with an absolute minimum of sex) determined what plays would be presented—one per season—on that huge stage; once, trying to hypo meager attendance by creating the illusion of public selection of the following year's production, Lombardo had the audience "vote" by applauding for its favorite as he read off the names of several, carefully pre-selected, popular Broadway shows of years past. The vote was clearly in favor of *The Unsinkable Molly Brown.* Moses preferred *Song of Norway.* Watching the vote from a darkened alcove at the side of the amphitheater, Shapiro smiled slyly, snickered and said: "Well, maybe we won't be guided by the results of the poll after all." (The following year's production was *Song of Norway.*) The productions mounted in the stadium by the three Lombardo brothers, Guy, Carmen and Lebert, were as vast as even Moses could have wished, distinguished by immense casts and trappings big enough to be seen from the seats of the hoi polloi some hundreds of feet away. But there was no public enthusiasm. In only two of the theater's first fifteen years of operation were even half the seats filled over the course of a season; in some years, fewer than one out of three was filled. But public enthusiasm was not the primary aim, as was proven by the fact that every production was presented two years running—and attendance in the second year always fell to about half that in the first year.* Unlike other, more centrally located, theaters, the one at Jones Beach drew its audience not from the whole metropolitan area population but, primarily, from Jones Beach-goers. Since few people want to see a show twice, showing only one every two years helped insure that most beachgoing families would go to the theater only once every two years. Such a policy makes sense only if the primary purpose of the show was to provide entertainment for a relatively small, constantly changing audience—an audience such as was provided by Robert Moses' personally invited guests. On many weekday nights, no more than a few hundred of the 8,200 seats were filled—and most of these were the box seats filled with guests invited by Moses

* It has been possible to obtain attendance figures for only seven years of the theater's operation. Here are those figures:

Year	*Production*	*Total Attendance*	*Average Attendance*	*Percentage of Capacity*
1961	*Paradise Island*	375,488	5,007	61.0
1962	" "	179,203	2,597	31.6
1963	*Around the World in Eighty Days*	365,404	5,075	61.8
1964	" " "	165,989	2,305	28.1
1965	*Mardi Gras*	272,504	3,785	46.1
1966	" "	180,706	3,063	37.0
1967	*One Thousand and One Nights*	190,406	2,929	35.7

and by his banker allies. On those nights, the grandstand of the big amphitheater was practically empty. Endless rows of empty seats glared blankly down—on a vast, expensive production and a small select audience. The crowds of actors, sometimes seemingly outnumbering the audience, seemed to be performing almost exclusively for the guests of the man on whose stage they were performing.

He even had his own court musicians, an orchestra whose banal, rigidly traditional arrangements complemented his personal philosophy—Guy Lombardo's red-coated Royal Canadians, who had, fittingly, first become famous the year Jones Beach opened and who still adhered faithfully to the musical style of those prewar decades in which Moses had been so popular and in which he sometimes seemed still to be trying to live. All summer—every summer—"The Sweetest Music This Side of Heaven" was his to command.

Lombardo, the sweetness of whose music was matched by the shrewdness of his business sense, put a high price on his services. But Moses paid it, not only paying the orchestra leader, through a complicated method of cash "advances," more than $100,000 a year to produce the Marine Theater shows (when other producers, not allowed to bid for the right, would have paid *him* to produce them, had they been allowed to produce a new show every year), but also turning the whole theater, a theater built with public funds, over to the three Lombardo brothers virtually as a private concession to be operated for their private profit, allowing them to keep most of the ticket receipts, as well as the revenue from the advertising billboards in the theater and from advertising in the theater programs, even from the rental of seat cushions. To make sure the profit was not diluted, Moses even maintained the theater for them, paying the bills for cleaning, repairing and staffing it right down to the ushers. He even paid the salaries of some of Lombardo's personnel. He even paid for most of the advertising for the show from which Lombardo was reaping most of the profit. He even allowed the Lombardos to use the theater to lure patrons to the family restaurant in nearby Freeport; for $29.90, a couple was offered dinner at the East Point House followed by an after-dinner cruise ("On Guy Lombardo's Yacht") right into the theater, where they could disembark and take their seats.

The $4,200,000 state subsidy for the theater had been a "first-instance" legislative appropriation, an appropriation the Legislature had expected would be paid back out of theater revenues. Moses never paid it back. To all inquiries, he replied that he couldn't afford to; the theater, he said, was losing money. Mentioning the "vicissitudes of outdoor theater productions . . . the gambles . . . ," he implied that the Lombardo brothers had undertaken the productions only as a public service and were also losing money. Guy took care to reinforce this impression, moaning loudly about the sacrifices his Jones Beach productions entailed. In only one year, he says in his biography, did he and his brothers break even, and in that year, to celebrate, they used up the profit buying three bottles of Scotch. "We pay ourselves no salary, we give ourselves no Cadillacs; why, even when we take a taxi to the show, we pay for it out of our own pocket. So the most we've gotten out of ten years of putting on shows at Jones Beach is one bottle of Scotch apiece." Actually, the three Lombardo brothers reaped from their Jones Beach shows hundreds of thousands of dollars in profit. And in return, of course, in addition to putting on the shows that were so largely for the entertainment of Robert Moses' guests, their Royal Canadians were available night after night to play so that Moses' guests could dance afterwards.

Not only did the state—the state's taxpayers—not get back the $4,200,000; the additional costs of theater operation that Moses made them bear so that the Lombardos' profit would not be diluted had, by 1967, passed the $5,000,000 mark.

At Jones Beach, Robert Moses could offer his guests not only a royal box but royal treatment.

Chauffeured limousines could be placed at their disposal; he had so many that on a typical day big black cars and liveried men would be stacked up in the car pool at Belmont Lake waiting for something to do; coming to the Park Commission, Perry Duryea would learn in astonishment that one executive did nothing but handle logistics—"who's riding in what car; it was almost a military-like operation." Human beings could be placed at their disposal; he had so many available to him that he could deploy them in force; any of his guests above a certain minimum level of importance would be met at the entrance to a reserved parking lot; executives dressed in mufti or staffers dressed in the navy-blue and white seahorse-emblazoned uniforms of Jones Beach would escort them on a tour of the park, show them to private dressing rooms, wait while they undressed, escort them to the reserved beach, wait for them while they swam and dressed, escort them to dinner and then to the Marine Theater—where they, or fresh men who took their place, would stand hidden in the dimness of the wide, deep aisle behind their boxes during the entire play to bring them blankets if they were cold, coffee or hot chocolate if they were thirsty, and to escort them backstage during intermission to see the sets—or simply to baby-sit with their children; needing the cooperation of Representative Stuyvesant Wainwright one weekend, Moses was distressed to learn that he was out cruising off Montauk with his two small children; when the Congressman neared shore that evening, there waiting on the pier beside his own car was Sid Shapiro, accompanied by two limousines, three chauffeurs and a secretary. One chauffeur was to drive Wainwright's car home, in order, Shapiro explained, that he and the Congressman could follow behind in one of the limousines and confer; the other limousine was to follow behind with Wainwright's children so that the conference would not be disturbed by childish chatter; the secretary had been brought along as baby-sitter.

"And when there's some big event," Duryea says—a visit to the New York area, for example, by visiting park enthusiasts or planners from another city or Europe or the Orient (Japanese urban planners displayed an endless capacity for viewing and reviewing Moses' works)—"My God!" Duryea says. "The planning that went into it!" Buses or limousines would meet the tourists at their hotel; in each would be one or more of Moses' executives; as the tour unrolled, a tour planned down to the minute (a typical one, given for ten visiting German journalists in 1951, picked them up at 9:20 A.M. at Columbia University, took them over or gave them a view of the following brief sampling of Moses creations: the Henry Hudson Parkway, Fifty-ninth Street Powerhouse, United Nations, Bellevue Medical Center, Peter Cooper Village and Stuyvesant Town, Jacob Riis, Lillian Wald and Governor Smith Houses, Battery Park Underpass, Battery Parking Garage and Brooklyn-Battery Tunnel, Brooklyn-Queens Expressway, Gowanus Parkway, Owl's Head Sewage Disposal Plant, Shore Parkway, Ullmer Park Veterans Emergency Houses, Van Wyck Expressway, Idlewild Airport, the Southern State Parkway and Meadowbrook Parkway, Wantagh State, Northern State, Grand Central and Cross Island parkways, the Triborough Bridge, Ward's Island Sewage Disposal Plant, Ward's Island Pedestrian Bridge, Ward's Island Park, and Abraham Lincoln and Riverton Houses on their way back to Columbia University), the executives would supplement elaborate mimeographed fact sheets with descriptive anecdotes. And at the end of these tours, the guests would arrive at Jones Beach for food, drink, entertainment and perhaps a brief word with the creator of all they had seen.

A day as Robert Moses' guest at Jones Beach was a day to remember.

The chauffeured limousine to take you there would be waiting for you and your family at your door. (If you were an especially important guest, waiting for you where the parkways crossed the city line and Moses' jurisdiction began would be an escort of commission troopers.) When the limousine pulled up to the side door of the West Bathhouse, there would be a respectful, uniformed guide waiting to take you to lunch in a reserved section of the Marine Dining Room, where a waitress would be assigned exclusively to your table. After lunch, the guide would show you around, take you to the dressing room—"Commissioner Moses' private dressing room"—take you to the beach—a private beach—be standing at the water's edge waiting to hand you a towel when you emerged. Then there would be an afternoon of sun and servant; your guide would discreetly drop by every now and then to inquire if there were any refreshments you would like brought to your blanket.

Dressed again, and dinner. Red-coated Royal Canadians making music under a bright red-and-white-striped pavilion. Whole roast beefs and turkeys and hams, cold lobsters in stacks, shrimps pilaf and plain, stacked in great heaps, shrimp and crabmeat salad piled high on huge trays. Sid Shapiro or one of his suave aides coming over to say hello and make conversation and see if you had everything you wanted. After dinner, if you had a small boy or girl, Shapiro would explain to you that Guy Lombardo entered the theater every night by speeding up to the stage in his famed, trophy-winning powerboat, *Tempo,* and getting out to lead the orchestra in "The Star-Spangled Banner" from that spot. Would your little boy or girl like to ride in *Tempo* with Guy as he entered the theater?

The theater. These seats that were so conspicuously the best in the house. *Tempo* roaring in and your son or daughter stepping out into the spotlight, and Guy Lombardo himself leading your child, dazzled, over to you, dazzled, in your seat. Glancing back during the first act and seeing your escort in the dimness of the aisle below you—and the guide darting forward just in case your glance meant that you desired something. Is your wife chilly? Would she like a blanket? Would anyone like a drink? A soda? How about the young man? At intermission, a boat waiting to take the whole family across the lagoon onto the stage and behind it to see the actors and the sets. And after the performance, dancing—under the stars or to a Lombardo band in the pavilion—or a drink with the orchestra leader and the stars of the show and beautiful showgirls in his suite under the theater.

And, most especially, the host.

Unless you were at least a Governor, you would probably see him only for a few minutes at dinner and after the show; he had had a small office, little more than a cubicle, built into the stadium, below the stage, so that he could work without leaving: as soon as the lights dimmed after he had been introduced to the audience, he would slip out, back to his blueprints and his maps and his progress charts; while his guests relaxed for three hours above, he would be toiling for three hours below. But a few minutes were enough. "He was the most gracious host in the world," says one ex-legislator. "He'd put his arm around you, give you that great smile of his, talk to your kids—just put you right at your ease." At the informal nightly buffets in the pavilion, he was regal but charming. At more formal dinners at Jones Beach, he was more regal—but still charming. "You liked him, he liked you." And if he had time to spend with you, a whole extra, unforgettable dimension was added to an already memorable day. For he would probably talk about his accomplishments, telling the "inside story" behind them, about how he had found out the secrets of the ownership of the bay bottoms, for example, and thus wrested the ownership of this marvelous beach from the Babylon baymen. Robert Moses telling the story of his successes was a minstrel spinning a saga so heroic, so filled with vivid personalities and fierce duels, that listeners hearing it for the first time (admittedly they lost some of the savor on the fourteenth—or fortieth—go-round) were left entranced as well as charmed.

And when you were ready to go, the limousine would be waiting again, ready to whisk you back through the darkness, along the causeways and parkways and expressways and bridges that this man had built. He wanted to awe—and he succeeded. "Carol and I and the two kids were overwhelmed by our treatment last night and are most sincerely grateful," wrote Staten Island Borough President Bob Connor. "Sometimes I am not quite sure why you built the Verrazano-Narrows Bridge since there are a number of us who believe that you could have walked across."* Thousands

---

* The full text of Moses' reply:

Dear Bob:

Walking on water is a solitary business.

Cordially,
Robert Moses
Chairman

—perhaps over the decades tens of thousands—of persons remembered these days at Jones Beach and the Marine Theater provided by the man who had built Jones Beach and the Marine Theater as among the most memorable days of their lives. Moses' Yale class came every year for twenty years, in a fleet of limousines leaving from the Yale Club in the morning. Says class secretary Ralph Clark: "There was a beach reserved for the day—no one else could use it; we had the pavilion—like a clubhouse—to ourselves. Lunch, a seafood buffet, generally would be on the patio. Everything was very well organized. There would be a piano, and one of the class would play things like 'Auld Lang Syne' and Yale songs and the Whiffenpoof, which was written by a member of '09. Carolus Clark used to bring his guitar until he died, and he would accompany or play by himself. There would be a photographer there to take class pictures. That was how thoughtful he was. In the middle of the afternoon—or later—sometimes, not until five—Bob would come. He would stop, talk to everyone, moving around, and then would say, 'I'm going to have my swim.' He used to swim out farther than anybody else . . . with a nice crawl stroke . . . nice, easy shoulders and powerful and shake his head, he'd be so happy in the water. We'd have dinner—a formal (sit-down) dinner—in a section of the big Jones Beach dining room. There might be two hundred other people in the dining room, but they always made it seem like a family affair. If he was late, we'd wait dinner. But when he came, the party always sparked up. He kidded everyone, and there were nice discussions. He had this sense of putting people at ease. Mr. and Mrs. Moses would make a point of seeing everyone. They wouldn't sit at the same table at dinner, and they'd get up and move around, leaning over people, asking if everything was okay, if they'd had everything they wanted. . . . After supper, we could go to the show. They'd hustle us into blankets, and we always sat in the first row. Bob would disappear, usually as we were being hustled into the blankets, but there were cars going back at different times so you never had to worry about anything."

Moses liked to pick up checks, to be host, in order to dominate. He certainly succeeded with his class. At Yale, he had been an outsider. Now, says Clark, "the class revolved around him."

His guest list was by no means exclusive, for Moses wanted to impress as many influential people as possible. So many limousines and guides and hostesses had been laid on for guests that Shapiro had trouble finding enough guests to keep them busy—to fill up those theater and restaurant seats. The Park Commission general manager had to lie in wait for every passing covey of visiting municipal officials or urban planners. In 1967, for example, the International Federation of Housing and Planning was holding its annual convention in Philadelphia. Lee Koppelman, executive director of the Nassau-Suffolk Regional Planning Board, thought it would be a good idea for the planners to take a post-convention bus tour around New York and asked Shapiro if it would be possible for them to stop at Jones Beach and have a Park Commission official show them the principal features of the park. "Well," Shapiro said, "wouldn't it be nicer if . . ." The next thing Koppelman knew, the planners were being given not the brief tour he had had in mind but a full-dress presentation, complete with wall charts and elaborate maps, of the history of Jones Beach, followed by a swim, cocktails at the Boardwalk Restaurant, and a buffet dinner so lavish that Koppelman described it as "a setup like you'd expect to find at the Waldorf. Sid circulated at the tables, introduced Guy Lombardo—they were very gracious. He invited some to sit in his box. Seats were waiting for us at the box office—marked 'Paid.' " And at the conclusion of the evening, Shapiro asked Koppelman if there were any other planning groups he could think of to invite out; if there were, Shapiro said, all Koppelman had to do was ask—any time would be all right, any number. Every state or municipal official, newspaper publisher, key corporate executive, key columnist or reporter or other influential with whom Moses was not currently actively feuding was invited annually to some version—its elaborateness depending on which of Moses' hospitality lists the guest was on at the moment—of this tour. And these guests could bring along as many other guests as they wanted. The engraved invitations that went out to groups such as his Yale class for its annual reunion, for example, always said, "And family." "Oh, 'family' could mean anyone, you know," one of the class says. "Quite a few of the class brought quite a few guests down. One fellow from Boston used to come down every year with his wife, two daughters and a whole carload of people."

A host on an imperial scale, Robert Moses was also a host with an imperial style. Formal luncheons for organizations he headed were held in a suite of two rooms at the west end of the second floor of the West Bathhouse. One of those rooms was a comfortably furnished sitting room in which a large dining table could be placed, and it was in that room that the rest of the organization dined. Next to the large room was a small one. Often it was in that room that Robert Moses dined—behind a closed door and alone except for a waiter and an aide who would summon into his presence whatever member of the group outside he wanted to talk to at the moment. At State Council of Parks meetings, for example, the council members would eat outside, waiting to be summoned, one by one, behind that door.

Most lavish of all Moses' entertainments, of course, were those celebrating the completion of new public works.

Even a minor work merited major celebration. The emperor of Triborough could invest with imperial lavishness the opening of even a row of toll booths: *Newsday* reporter Bernie Bookbinder, assigned to cover the 1953 opening of the Southern State Parkway booths in Valley Stream, suddenly found himself standing before a buffet table forty feet long piled high from end to end with platters heaped with magnificent food while waiters carrying hors d'oeuvres and glasses of champagne bore down on him in platoons. (Moses lost no time in putting those booths on the previously free parkway to use. Within minutes after the politicians had moved out of them, his toll collectors had moved in; by the time the party was over late that afternoon, enough dimes had probably been collected to pay for it—if, of course, payment was required; many concessionaires were only too eager to cater the affair for nothing.)

For the large public works—the Brooklyn-Battery Tunnel or the Throgs Neck or Verrazano-Narrows bridges or Captree Causeway, or the Robert Moses Power Dams at Niagara and Massena, for example—the celebrations were on a scale seldom witnessed in a democracy. The invited guests numbered not in the hundreds but in the thousands; the official limousines of the more important among them, lined up at the ramp to a bridge waiting for the ribbon to be cut so they could proceed across it, might stretch for a mile or more. Every detail had been worked out, of course, from the huge, heavy silver-plated ribbon-cutting shears or cornerstone-laying trowels resting on royal purple cushions to the intricate bronze replicas of bridge or dam that would be distributed in the hundreds—even the types of hors d'oeuvres to be served. The interest Moses took in every detail of these celebrations is revealed—as is the still acrid pungency of even his most casual prose—by a memo he wrote to Constable after one concessionaire, Arnold Schleiffer of the Tavern-on-the-Green, anxious to keep in Moses' good graces by making the buffet more elaborate than ever, had gone too far in the matter of hors d'oeuvres.

> Last night's Schleiffer version of Balshazzar's feast was contrary to all instructions. The catering crew was all right, the hat chicks were Belles Amies and the barkeepers upheld the finest traditions of the craft, but the hors d'oeuvres were disgusting—tray after tray of indigestible insides, cows eyes on mushrooms, squid in its own ink, pastry costume jewelry, mounted dog food, mayonnaise rococo and gaudy gook.
>
> Hit Schleiffer over the head for me. We are not celebrating a gangster wedding. . . . Mr. Schleiffer can't seem to get through his noggin that nothing exceeds like excess. We don't want this vulgarity at cocktail parties or buffet lunches. We want a few simple appetizing things, not a pastry competition to be judged by Pretzel Varnishers Union Number 3. . . . If Schleiffer can't grasp this, we can't use him.

And there was so much food. "At the Verrazano opening," one guest recalls, "half of Brooklyn and Staten Island wandered in and there were still mounds left over." At most ribbon cuttings, no provision is made for officials' chauffeurs. At Moses', a whole tent, with its own elaborate buffet, was set aside for their use.

When the openings took place in the empire's more remote reaches, the distant provinces at Massena and Niagara on the far-flung Northern Frontier from which his legions had cleared the savage Tuscaroras, Moses flew north with his whole court from courtiers to chroniclers (PR men and reporters like Ingraham of the *Times* and Murray Davis of the *World-Telegram*)—"fellow" authority commissioners, consultants, engineers, administrators down to the seventh level, even secretaries—to see the new dam or road or park named after him, as Peter the Great had taken his court on an "excursion" to see the new capital he was building on piles in the Baltic marshes at the mouth of the Neva River that was to be named after *him*.

Officials of a dozen governments, Vice President Richard Nixon and other representatives of the federal administration, state officials, county officials, relatives, acquaintances, acquaintances of acquaintances, were flown north, too (and the Canadian Prime Minister flew south), as were scribes to send word of the new wonders back to metropolis. The excursion marking the opening of the Robert Moses Power Dam at Niagara in 1961, for example, lasted three full days. It became a legend among the reporters lucky enough to go along. Says Harvey Aronson of *Newsday*:

It was the plushest junket I was ever on. We flew up on a chartered plane. There were about forty people on it, and most of them were celebrities. I heard this voice behind me extolling the virtues of Robert Moses, and you couldn't help but recognize it: it was H. V. Kaltenborn himself. The pilot made special passes over Niagara Falls for us so that the guests could see the panorama of the dam, and the adjacent Robert Moses Parkway and Robert Moses State Park from the air. For three days, there were all kinds of free trips and excursions in and around Niagara Falls. The receptions—at one, I remember, there was a fountain of martinis. I just couldn't believe it. You just held up your glass, and it was filled up with a martini. If you didn't like martinis, there was a fountain of Manhattans. I never saw anything like it.

Hospitality has always been a potent political weapon. Moses used it like a master. Coupled with his overpowering personality, a buffet often did as much for a proposal as a bribe. "Christ, you'd be standing there eating the guy's food and drinking his liquor and getting ready to go for a ride on his boat, and he'd come up to you and take both your hands in his or put his arm around your shoulders and look into your eye and begin pouring out the arguments in that charming way of his and making you feel like there was no one in the whole world he'd rather be talking to—how could you turn the guy down?" Ingraham knew what it meant when he was invited to a weekend in Babylon or a night at the Marine Theater: "He wanted to plant a story." To other reporters, too, his hospitality was used as a subtle reward, and its withdrawal as a subtle punishment. Write a story that he liked and you would find yourself on one of his lists—and, even on the "C" list, suddenly the need for paying causeway tolls would disappear and you would be able to bring your wife or girlfriend to lavish parties. Continue the good work and you might make the "B" list—or even the "A." Cross him once, and you were off all lists. Every summer, Bookbinder received in the mail, unsolicited, a pass to Jones Beach. One spring, he was assigned to do a story on the fact that the Long Island State Park Commission insisted on planting grass under its highways' steel center dividers, where lawnmowers couldn't get to it. That summer, his pass did not arrive.

Beyond such considerations, moreover, the whole aura that Moses created at his entertainments—in particular at his "working" lunches—was designed to help his work.

The setting at such luncheons was relentlessly social: friendly, easy, gracious. For most men, this setting made disagreement difficult. It is more difficult to challenge a man's facts over cocktails than over a conference table, more difficult to flatly give the lie to a statement over a gleaming white tablecloth, filet mignon and fine wine than it would have been to do so over a hard-polished board-room table and legal pads. It was more difficult still to disagree when most if not all of the other guests agreed: there was strategy as well as ego in Moses' stacking his luncheons with a claque of yesing assistants; he may have felt that their presence heightened his stature but he also knew that their presence created an atmosphere in which the dissenter felt acutely that he was representing a distinctly minority view. To crack an especially tough opponent, Moses might invite him to a lunch at which he would be the only person present besides the Coordinator and his aides: then, if the guest tried to argue, he would be in the position of trying to argue alone against a whole platoon of "informed opinion." It was even more difficult to disagree when the man with whom you were disagreeing was your host. Manners set limits on such disagreement; even if convention was disregarded, the host had the not inconsiderable psychological advantage of fighting on his home grounds, grounds to which, in fact, the guest might even have been transported by his limousine, which he needed to take him home again. It was especially difficult to disagree when disagreement would touch off an argument, possibly a violent argument, with that host—and most guests were well aware of the fact that the slightest disagreement with the host at Triborough was sure to start such an argument. If a guest still ventured to hold his opinion, there would be impatience. The attitude was: "Well, well-informed opinion doesn't agree with you, does it? Does it, Sid? Does it, Earle? How about that, Stuart?" If the guest still did not back down, there would be not the uncontrolled, wall-pounding, inkwell-throwing rage that could fill a room, but a mordant scorn that could slash across a dinner table like a carving knife. "He had a way about him, even strong men stayed away from him—he was the great intimidator," Joe Kahn says. Nowhere was he more intimidating than over his luncheon table. In such a setting, surrounded by pictures of his past successes, scale models of his future successes, by a retinue of supporters and all the trappings of achievement and power, his scorn and anger were at their most awesome. An Austin Tobin might get up from his host's table, say, "I don't have to sit here and be insulted like this," and stalk out. Not many men had Tobin's courage, presence of mind—or the support of a board powerful enough to make courage and presence of mind feasible. In the setting Moses created at his luncheons, most men allowed themselves to be bullied, even if only by not openly disagreeing with some Moses proposal in the hope that they could disagree later in the friendlier confines of their office—only to find that before they could get out of his, Moses was virtually forcing them to ratify their acquiescence by presenting for their signature the necessary document, which an aide just happened to have with him, or to find out by the time they got back to their own office that Moses had already notified the Mayor or other department heads of their acquiescence and that the project in question had already been moved ahead to the next step, making an attempt to call it back awkward if not unfeasible. Casual, friendly, social occasions were not the best arenas in which to confront Robert Moses.

And Moses carefully kept the atmosphere social, even while using it for business ends. He would present a problem and his proposed solution to it, and then call on various of his engineers to present facts and figures supporting his arguments. Then he would say, with an easy, charming smile, "Well, since we're all agreed about this . . . ," and move on to the next item. "Well, maybe everyone there didn't agree," Orton says. "But in that setting, who could get up and start arguing? This was an exercise of power by assumption or inference. And it was damned effective." "So much got done at those lunches," says one of his aides. "He'd have a whole agenda—a whole list of items—and he'd go right through it. You might have two or three disparate groups there—each there about another item of business. And he would move from one to the other so easily, never letting one group know something that another group wanted kept secret. And at the end there would have been a dozen decisions [made]"—made as he wanted. "The city was supposed to be run from City Hall," Orton says, "but let me tell you I watched it year after year and I know: for years the big decisions that shaped New York were made in that dining room on Randall's Island." Hospitality—hospitality on an imperial scale—was one of Moses' most effective tools.

The working lifespan of the elemental force that was Robert Moses defied comparison with the working lifespan of other men. Robert Moses had been in power, shaping Long Island, in 1924. He was in power, tirelessly shaping not only Long Island but the great city stretching out toward it, in 1934, and 1944, and 1954, as he would be in 1964—until 1968, in fact. Other men hold real power—shaping power, executive authority—for four years, or eight, or twelve. Robert Moses held shaping power over the New York metropolitan region for forty-four years.

Was the tirelessness of his work and its duration comparable to a natural force? So was the result of that work—the sum total of the accomplishment, the Things he Got Done. As natural forces shaped the city and its suburbs east of the Hudson, the 2,100-square mile region on which by 1974 dwelt more than 12,000,000 human beings, so did he.

He changed the course of rivers, filling in the beds of the Harlem and the Bronx and cutting new channels for them, shoving to one side the mighty St. Lawrence, making new curves in the swift Niagara. He filled in the city's frayed edges, transforming into solid earth Great Kills on Staten Island, the Flushing Meadows in Queens, a dozen other vast marshes. Nature gave the region one shoreline; he gave it another, closing inlets in the barrier beaches, cutting new inlets, reshaping miles of beach dunes. For mile after mile, the earth and rock that constitute the shoreline of Brooklyn and Queens, and of Manhattan's Hudson shore, are his, the cement and steel that hold them in place are his, the grass and shrubs and trees that adorn them are his—as are the concrete and steel of the marinas, the shoreline overlooks, the parking fields, the bicycle paths, the runways and airport terminals, and, of course, the shoreline parkways. Not nature but he put them there. His bridges bound together Long Island and the mainland of the continent, torn apart by glaciers eons before. His causeways reunited the Island with its barrier beach. He hacked out lagoons, filled lakes, made beaches, welded islands together, cut, at Inwood Hill, through a primeval forest substantially unaltered by the hand of man since the dawn of time. He altered the region's skyline, leveling great areas of the low, regular tenement foothills and replacing them with slim, tall spires two hundred, three hundred feet high—civic and cultural edifices, great groves of apartment houses. By the close of the Age of Moses, for example, the skyline along much of the eastern shore of Manhattan Island that was the heart of metropolis—a skyline that was, to a great extent, Governor Smith Houses, La Guardia Houses, Corlears Hook Houses, Baruch Houses, Lillian Wald Houses, Jacob Riis Houses, Stuyvesant Town, Peter Cooper Village, Bellevue Hospital, NYU-Bellevue Medical Center, the United Nations, Rockefeller Institute, New York Hospital, East River Houses, Woodrow Wilson Houses, Senator Robert F. Wagner, Sr., Houses, Abraham Lincoln Houses, Riverton Houses, North Harlem Houses, Harlem River Houses, Colonial Park Houses—was, for miles at a time, a Robert Moses creation. Do forces of nature—volcanoes, earthquakes, avalanches—destroy whole towns and villages, forcing populations to flee? What force destroyed Spuyten Duyvil, Sunset Park, the Syrian Quarter near the Battery, a dozen other neighborhoods as big as towns?

Robert Moses believed his works would make his name immortal, and he may well have been right—and not just because some of them were named after him. "What will people see in the year 1999?" he predicted. "The long arteries of travel will stand out [and the parks]." Fly over New York in 1974, and the prediction seems likely to be true, not only for the year 1999 but, if New York endures in anything like its present shape, far, far beyond. For so many of the dominant features of the landscape are his—and those features seem likely to endure indefinitely. Some of his highways will probably be covered with housing—the sale of air rights above them, just beginning in the 1970's, seems an innovation likely to gain favor—and thus invisible, no longer part of the landscape. Some may be rerouted or widened beyond recognition, although, given the cost and complexities of condemnation, the length of time it would take to cover or to reroute or reshape even some substantial fraction of the 627 miles of these arteries would have to be calculated not in decades but in generations and perhaps centuries. The roads of Rome stood for two thousand years and more; who would predict less for the roads of Moses? Who would predict less for his Shea Stadium, a structure consciously shaped to resemble Rome's Colosseum because he was afraid that his convention center–office tower "Coliseum" didn't make the comparison clear enough? As for the parks he created, fly over New York in the year 1999, and the two thousand acres of Brookhaven Park and the four thousand acres of Connetquot on Long Island, and the 21,000 other acres of park that Robert Moses wrested away from the developer's bulldozer to insure that the people of New York would always have green space will still be green, a tribute to his foresight. For how long will the great bridges that he built—the Verrazano, the Triborough, the Whitestone, the Throgs Neck, the Henry Hudson, the Cross Bay, the Marine—endure? The life of a suspension bridge, engineers tell us, is measureless. Atomic attack or natural catastrophe could render all New York shapeless. Barring such monumental calamity in centuries to come discerning historians will, if they look for it, be able to see writ plain throughout the great city and its suburbs evidence of the shaping hand of Robert Moses.

Other great builders left their mark on physical New York. But the achievement of even the greatest—a Zeckendorf or a Helmsley or a Winston or a Lefrak, the Rockefellers of Rockefeller Center—is dwarfed by the achievement of Robert Moses. Not even the greatest of the public officials who, while not builders themselves, shaped the growth of the city—the almost forgotten "father of New York," Andrew H. Green, and "the greatest mayor New York ever had," Fiorello H. La Guardia—had a fraction of Moses' influence on the shape of New York. The shapers closest to him in total influence are probably the robber barons who built the railroads into the city and out through its suburbs and who erected monuments to themselves in great skyscrapers and terminals, but the influence of any one of them is dwarfed by his.

To compare the works of Robert Moses to the works of man, one has to compare them not to the works of individual men but to the combined total work of an era. The yardstick by which his public housing and Title I feats can best be measured, for example, is the Age of Skyscrapers, which reared up the great masses of stone and steel and concrete over Manhattan in quantity comparable to his. The yardstick by which the influence of his highways can be gauged is the Age of Railroads. But Robert Moses did not build only housing projects and highways. Robert Moses built parks and playgrounds and beaches and parking lots and cultural centers and civic centers and a United Nations Building and a Shea Stadium and a Coliseum and swept away neighborhoods to clear the way for a Lincoln Center and the mid-city campuses of four separate universities. He was a shaper not of sections of a city but of a *city*. He was, for the greatest city in the Western world, the city shaper, the only city shaper. In sheer physical impact on New York and the entire New York metropolitan region, he is comparable not to the works of any man or group of men or even generations of men. In the shaping of New York, Robert Moses was comparable only to some elemental force of nature.

But if in the shaping of New York Robert Moses was an elemental force, he was also a blind force: blind and deaf, blind and deaf to reason, to argument, to new ideas, to any ideas except his own.

He made himself blind. He possessed vision in a measure possessed by few men. But he wouldn't use it. The arrogance which had been his characteristic from youth, the arrogance which was a most striking characteristic of his mother and grandmother, the arrogance that had led relatives to call him "Bella Moses' son," the arrogance that had gorged on power, swelling with each increase, had, now that his power in his chosen fields of activity was so absolute, become absolute itself.

No rules, not even the most innocuous, could apply to him. Making one of his rare appearances at a public hearing on one of his projects—this one, in City Hall, before the Board of Estimate, on his proposed Verrazano Bridge—he declined to identify himself for the record by name and address as all other speakers had been required to do.

"Make him give his name," a woman shouted, and then several men picked up the shout, and then the audience, which had filled the Board chamber to overflowing and had crammed the corridor outside full, turned it into a chant: "Make him give his name! Make him give his name!" Wagner, presiding, looked at Moses appealingly, but the Coordinator crossed his arms, locked his hands around his biceps, tilted back his head and, with his prognathous jaw jutted out, stood in the face of that chant like some haughty Rameses, finally saying to the Mayor, who was, Shapiro was to recall, "shrinking down behind his microphone so you could hardly see him": "Well, what are you going to do about it?"

"Now if you people can't be quiet, I'll have the room cleared," Wagner said. "You people know who this is; this is Robert Moses."

With the name in the record, Wagner motioned for Moses to proceed, but when the Coordinator began his presentation, the crowd began to chant: "Make him give his address! Make him give his address!" Again Wagner looked at Moses, again Moses stared him down, and again Wagner had to intercede: "You all know where he lives; he lives across the street from me." And Moses was so furious that the Mayor had not ousted from the room this rabble trying to make him abide by the same rules that governed other men that despite a previous promise to the Mayor that he would this once give at least the appearance of participating in a public hearing—it was only because of that promise that he was present in the first place—he talked only briefly, describing a $365,000,000 project, for which an hour-and-a-half presentation had been prepared, in about ten minutes, snatched up his papers and stalked from the room, leaving the Mayor to sit alone listening to protests until four o'clock the next morning.

As he was above rules, he was above the law. He had always felt himself above it, ignored its spirit whenever possible, but now there was a new depth to this feeling, a new intensity to this particular manifestation of arrogance.

Confronted in building up the base for Idlewild Airport by the same problem by which he had been confronted in building up the base for Jones Beach—the sand he imported blew away because it was not anchored, as were Long Island's natural dunes, by the horizontally growing roots of beach grass—Moses, without bothering to obtain anyone's permission, dispatched teams to obtain the grass from public beaches owned by Suffolk County and from the beaches of summer homes owned by private families. W. Kingsland Macy, an ardent conservationist who knew the value of beach grass—and what would happen to dunes suddenly denuded of it—was enraged when he learned that scores of Long Island State Park Commission employees were out on their hands and knees illegally yanking it out of beaches that Macy wanted preserved in perpetuity for the people of his county. He ordered County Attorney Edgar L. Hazleton to order Moses to desist, on pain of arrest and imprisonment of any commission employee caught—and of Moses himself. Moses' reply was not long in coming. The next weekend, when the Hazletons arrived at their summer home at Westhampton, they discovered Moses' men yanking out the grass on *their* beach. (The practice was finally ended when Macy ordered local police to arrest thirteen of Moses' grass pullers.)

The measure of his arrogance was taken by a dictator. Rafael Leonidas Trujillo Molina was considering commissioning Moses to propose public works for his Dominican Republic when, after one long afternoon's discussion with Moses, he abruptly told him he had decided not to hire him after all. According to Moses, the dictator told him: "You'd want my job."

His ego had become as titanic as his imagination. How did he think of his works? Let him answer in his own words. Jones Beach is "the finest public beach in the world," the Bronx-Whitestone Bridge "the most beautiful suspension bridge in the world." On "the saga of city waterfront reclamation . . . I think it may be stated without fanfare or frantic boasting that no other city, faced with anything like our problems, has set about with so much boldness and determination to meet and down them." How did he think of himself? Let him answer in his own words. "The City Builder must have an odd mixture of qualities. He must have a basic affection for his community, he must hate what is ugly, barren and useless. He must have an instinctive dislike of things which are built or run wrong. He must have a healthy contempt for the parasite, the grafter, the carpetbagger, the itinerant expert, the ivory tower planner, the academic reformer and the revolutionary. He must have the barge captain's knowledge of the waterfront, the engineer's itch to build, the architect's flair for design, the merchant's knowledge of the market, the local acquaintance of a political district leader." He was fond of proclaiming, as he did in 1948, "the ancient truth that it is not knowledge but action which is the great end and objective in life, and that for every dozen men with bright ideas there is at most one who can execute them." Did detractors liken him to Hitler? He had another comparison in mind. Sometime around 1949, visitors first noticed in his office a bust of Abraham Lincoln, and talks with his aides soon made it apparent why he had selected it. "To me," Sid Shapiro would say at every opportunity, "Mr. Moses is a lot like Abraham Lincoln—a philosopher and a doer."

Moses' body expressed his feelings about himself more eloquently than his words. With his first taste of power, he had begun to strike poses. Now, with more power, the poses were more striking. When the *Sea-Ef* was heading back into the Babylon dock, for example, he was given to standing at the very point of its prow, arms folded across his chest and jaw outthrust. A Bay Shore history teacher, seeing him one day, thought he looked "very impressive"—strikingly similar to pictures the teacher had seen in history books, pictures of Napoleon Bonaparte. His most frequent pose, of course, was the one he had first adopted during the 1930's and now used on every public occasion to express his lofty indifference to public acclaim; while introducing public officials at one of his ribbon cuttings, watching them cut a ribbon, or before speaking himself at such a ceremony or at a luncheon or dinner at which he was being honored, he would stand, while waiting for the applause to die down, with his arms folded across his chest, each hand grasping the opposite biceps, with his head tilted back. Taking a particularly important guest on a tour himself, he would speak in the imperial "we," but it was his gestures, sweepingly expansive, as, perhaps from a yacht offshore, he indicated the Belt Parkway sweeping off to the right and left, the park areas alongside, and then pointed upward to the Verrazano Bridge towering over the boat ("And then we built . . ."), that most strikingly suggested an emperor who looked on all he saw as his creation; standing on the deck of that yacht, he might have been Claudius looking proudly at Ostia.

The most definitive measure of his egotism, of course, was the men with whom he had chosen to surround himself. The last of those who dared even occasionally to voice even a faintly independent opinion were gone now; perhaps the last had been Allyn Jennings, who, serving in the Coast Guard during the war, had dared to put his country ahead of his public authority. Regarding the war as he did, as no more than an irritating interruption to his plans, Moses was infuriated by Coast Guard orders which were designed to protect the Atlantic Coast from the threat of German attack but which Moses considered meddling in the beaches in whose control he had always allowed no meddling—he was, for example, enraged when the Coast Guard ordered the Jones Beach boardwalk lights dimmed; whether or not he ever complied with this order is a question to which Moses' aides reply only with chuckles—and Jennings reportedly remarked to another Moses Man who had chosen to remain in RM's service during the war: "Doesn't RM know there's a war on?" The remark was eagerly repeated to RM; "that," chuckles Shapiro, "was the end of Allyn Jennings." In the postwar years, Moses was surrounded by a solid wall of sycophancy—the only opinions voiced were his opinions, the only facts and figures presented those that would confirm those opinions.

This, of course, need not in itself have been an insurmountable handicap. Genius—the innovative, creative, shaping impulse that was Robert Moses' form of genius—is to a great extent personal, internal, intuitive, subjective. The inspiration that led Moses to envision in an instant the great Long Island park and parkway system was not the facts and figures that he had to listen to at the endless reform conferences, but the creative flash.

But genius—in particular, public works genius—must have *some* roots in reality. The purpose of public works is to meet public needs; the first requirement of public works genius—an inescapable requirement for which even vision, foresight and drive are no substitute—is a knowledge, an understanding of those needs, of, in fact, the public, of the realities of the life led by the public for which the works are being built. Moses had had that knowledge when he created his great park and parkway system; he had had no choice but to have it; the role of liaison with reformer groups to which

Al Smith had assigned him required him to sit through reform meetings; he could not have helped grasping the nature of the problem, the needs of the metropolitan area public. But Moses' position now in the center of a palace guard that walled him off from all contact with new opinions and facts meant that he did not have that knowledge any more. Reality had changed; the reality of the 1920's was not the reality of the 1950's. The metropolitan area that Moses was now attempting to shape was not the metropolitan area that he had begun shaping; there were more people in it, so many more that the very fact of their numbers alone changed all the dimensions of life in the area; they covered so much more of its land surface with their homes; they were, moreover, a different people: the population of the area had been transformed; to mention just one change, there had been fewer than 200,000 nonwhites in the area when Moses had begun his public career, there were more than 2,000,000 now; embarking on a recreational policy that deliberately excluded nonwhites from most parks may have had in Moses' mind some sort of rationale in 1923; it is difficult to believe that that mind would formulate the same policy in 1953; Moses was nothing if not realistic, and excluding so large a part of an area's population from parks was not realistic. Quality, Hegel said, changes with quantity. Automobiles had meant weekend excursions to the country, leisurely drives, pleasure, freedom, in the 1920's, when there had been relatively few automobiles. Automobiles meant something very different now.

But Robert Moses did not see these changes. He did not see that reality had changed. Not only the sycophancy with which he had surrounded himself but also three hard physical facts of his existence insured this.

Robert Moses had never, aside from a few driving lessons thirty years before, driven a car. He didn't know what driving was. His chauffeured limousine was an office, to him a peculiarly pleasant office, in fact, since in it he was away from secretaries and the telephone and in its upholstered confines he could bury himself in work without interruption. Traveling by car had been pleasant for him in the 1920's; it was still pleasant for him in the 1950's. The nature of driving might have changed immensely for the people of the metropolitan area; it had changed not at all for him.

Robert Moses had never, since he had first come to power, allowed himself any time for reflection, for thought. Reflection, thought, is in a sense no more than the putting to use of a mind, and the unique instrument that was Robert Moses' mind could conceive wonders when it was put to work in that way. As a youth, he had never had enough to do; frustrated at the Bureau of Municipal Research, he had spent his evenings walking the city and thinking—and gradually his steps had led him more and more frequently to Riverside Park, and he had conceived a solution for problems for which no other man had been able to conceive a solution. As only a part-time aide to Al Smith, he had a lot to do—but not nearly enough to use up all his restless energy, and he had had time to sail and walk around the South Shore of Long Island. Living in Babylon and working in New York, he had had to ride the Long Island Rail Road for two hours and more a day; attempting an overview of Moses' career, it is difficult not to ascribe some of the credit for the stroke of genius that led him to see the potential for parks in the New York City watershed properties to the fact that the railroad not only carried him past those properties but trapped him on it for two hours and more a day so that he had to think about them. The following year, Robert Moses had come to power. In the years since, he had had piled upon him, and had grasped for, more and more power with each succeeding decade; the workload of executive responsibility he was carrying in the 1930's was too great to allow time for reflection—a fact he mentioned worriedly to his aides. But in the 1940's he had far greater executive responsibilities than in the 1930's, and in 1954, with his assumption of the chairmanship of the State Power Authority, he undertook in that one job, piled atop all his others, so much work that quiet, reflective thought was a luxury in which he could quite literally indulge almost never. Given a chance to work, Moses' mind might, despite all the handicaps, have come to grips with the new realities and fashioned a shaping vision to deal with them. But now it had no time to deal with the reality at all.

Robert Moses was going deaf.

His lieutenants first noticed about 1950 that the boss was having difficulty understanding what people were saying to him. His hearing deteriorated rapidly thereafter, and doctors apparently told him there was nothing to be done for the condition, a simple result of age—Moses was, after all, in his sixties—except for him to wear a hearing aid.

Robert Moses wear a hearing aid?!? He refused even to consider the suggestion. The condition grew worse. More and more frequently, if he was asked a question at his big conference table, his reply would not be responsive—he would be answering the question he *thought* had been asked. In discussions over lunch with public officials he would misunderstand the thrust of their arguments, sometimes grasp only fragments of what they said. Several times, driving away with Shapiro from conferences with Wagner or Dewey or Harriman, Moses began exulting over some promise he believed he had wrung from Mayor or Governor—and Shapiro, who had been sitting in on the conferences, was certain, heartsick, that no such promise had been made. When it became unfeasible for him to talk over the telephone at all, he consented to have a powerful amplifier placed in the instrument. General Meyers took inspiration and attempted to install an amplifying system in Moses' offices—in such a way as to conceal it from visitors and thereby leave the precious legend of indestructibility intact. On the desk–conference table were placed two small microphones, which would pick up everything said in the room; the amplifier to which the microphones were attached was concealed in a small box and placed on a small table near his left ear, which was slightly better than his right. Any visitor who inquired about the microphones was told that they were there so that if the office was crowded for large conferences, the man speaking could use one and be heard more clearly. Ingenious as the device was, however, its utility lessened, for Moses' hearing degenerated to a level at which even the amplifier was of little use to him.

In a way, of course, Moses' deafness was symbolic. He had, in a way, been deaf all his life—unwilling to listen to anyone, public, Mayor, Governor, deaf to all opinion save his own. But this new, physical deafness contributed in a nonsymbolic, very real way to his divorce from reality. As always, he would not attend public hearings or in any other way place himself in a situation in which he could hear the public's views. His insulation inside a circle of men who would offer no views that were not echoes of his own further insured that no outside voices would become a part of his considerations. Now, thanks to the deafness, he was unable to hear the views, get the thinking of those administrators and public officials who were invited to lunch with him or who sat with him in conferences. Surrounded by men who would not give him the new facts and figures he needed, with no time left to rethink solutions to changing problems—most important, with no feeling that there was any *reason* for him to rethink—the deafness made it impossible for him to learn about the new realities even if he had wanted to.

The proof is a statement he made about golf. If there was any area in which the Robert Moses of the 1920's had been truly expert it was in the area of recreation, in the active games which adults liked to play. But now he mentioned offhandedly that golf was not a game in which the masses were interested; it was, he said, played only by the "privileged few." Golf was now a game played by millions in all walks of life. But Moses didn't know this. His statement would have been true in the Twenties and he thought it was still true in the Fifties.

Because he didn't know anything had changed.

It was in transportation, the area in which Robert Moses was most active after the war, that his isolation from reality was most complete: because he never participated in the activity for which he was creating his highways—driving—at all. Insulated in the comfortable rear seat of his limousine, unable to experience even once the frustration of a traffic jam, unable, unless he made an effort and put his work aside and leaned forward to look out the window, even to *look* at a traffic jam, Robert Moses did not know what driving in the modern era was. He did not know that the sheer weight of numbers of new cars had changed the very nature of the activity for which he was creating facilities, had introduced—or, to be more specific, re-emphasized, since even before the war planners had seen the first signs of the change—new realities into the outlook for metropolitan transportation. He was making transportation plans based on beliefs that were not true any more. He was making plans that had no basis in reality.

But because of the enormous power he controlled, power that was close to absolute in fields he had carved out for his own, such as transportation, he could impose these plans on the metropolitan region, and on its 12,000,000 residents.

36. The Meat Ax

THE TREMENDOUS EXTENT of Robert Moses' power, and the extent to which, with that power, he shaped the greatest city in the New World and the great suburbs stretching out from it, is demonstrated by the roads he built during the quarter of a century following World War II.

These were roads like no other roads in history, for these were roads through a city.

Most of the great roads of antiquity—the 1,500-mile Royal Road of Persia, laid across three mountain ranges and lined with artificial oases at which relays of horses were kept shaded and fresh so that the royal couriers of Darius could cross Asia Minor in nine days instead of three months ("There is nothing in the world that could be faster than these couriers," Herodotus exclaimed); the three "silk roads," the longest roads ever built, laid out centuries before the birth of Christ so that caravans emerging from a gate in the Great Wall of China could carry bales of the material all the way to Europe, where it was valued so highly that it was weighed against gold; the post roads with which Genghis Khan tied together the vast Mongol empire; the twenty-nine military highways of Rome which, built by "the greatest men of the republic" ("None but those of the highest rank were even eligible to the office of superintending them") and radiating from Rome to which all roads led, ran with Roman directness (to avoid curves, mountains were cut through at enormous expense, marshes were bridged or simply filled up with solid masses of concrete) to the most remote provinces ("Even seas did not stop their progress, for the roads were built up to the water's edge and then continued upon the opposite shore") to speed the marches of the legions and engines of war which kept Rome mistress of the known earth—were roads through open country. Their builders may have had to contend with mountains and marshes, with the snow of the Alps and the heat of deserts, but they did not have to evict from their homes tens of thousands of protesting voters, demolish those homes, tunnel under or cut across subways and elevated railroads, sewers and water mains and gas mains and telephone and electric conduits and cables, all of which, providing a city with essential services, had to be kept in operation during construction. They did not have to solve these problems in space almost unbearably constricted because to obtain a single extra foot of width would require additional thousands of evictions. A few major roads were built within ancient cities (some of the Roman highways ran right up to the golden milestone in the Forum, for example), but ancient cities did not have subways and gas mains. These were, moreover, cities on a different scale from modern cities—imperial Rome was one-eighth the size of New York; Athens at the height of its glory was never larger than Yonkers—so the problem of eviction was on a different scale. And since the traffic for which these roads were designed was different from modern traffic—not only in volume but in size and speed—they were constructed on a different scale. The major roads in Rome, the widest paved highways in any ancient city, were, even including their "service roads," the *margines* to which carriages were restricted to keep the central portion free for infantry and pedestrians, only sixty-five and a half feet wide at their widest point; the highways Moses was proposing to build were two hundred feet wide. A horse-drawn carriage can turn fairly sharply; the monster tractor-trailers of the twentieth century require a turning radius so great that a single interchange connecting one highway to another can cover eighty acres. Not only did these roads of antiquity have no underpasses or overpasses to carry intersecting roads across them—access to these roads was not controlled; they could be entered from any intersecting thoroughfare—their very dimensions were so much smaller than those of modern highways that they were really comparable not to those highways at all but only to modern streets or avenues. Nor were the roads even of modern times—of the swollen cities of the nineteenth century and the Industrial Revolution. The greatest intracity road development of modern times before Robert Moses was the boulevarding of Paris envisioned by Emperor Napoleon III and carried out by his Prefect of the Seine, the "brawny Alsatian" Georges-Eugène Haussmann, between 1852 and 1870. But the roads of Haussmann, impressive though they were, were nonetheless still roads designed for the carriage rather than the car.

The automobile age created in the twentieth century a need for roads of a new dimension, roads a hundred feet or more across, roads with underpasses and overpasses and with interchanges so immense that to create them hundreds of acres of earth must be covered over with concrete—gigantic roads, not highways but superhighways. But the greatest of these roads—Mussolini's *autostrade* and Hitler's *Autobahnen* and the Long Island parkways (which predated *autostrade* and *Autobahnen*), Belt Parkway and West Side Highway of Robert Moses—had been built around the edges of cities and between cities. Except for rare instances and short stretches, no superhighways had been built within cities. And even those short stretches of superhighways that *had* been built within cities had almost invariably followed open paths within them—undeveloped river banks, for example, or sparsely populated corridors—as if their creators had shied away from pushing huge roads through the city's dense fabric. The most noticeable exception had been the Triborough Bridge approach highways Moses had built through Astoria and the East Bronx—but the total length of these highways had been no more than eight miles. Now Moses was proposing to build through the heart of the city more than a hundred miles. No one had dared lay superhighways through a heavily populated modern city on anything like such a scale: lump together all the superhighways in existence in all the cities on earth in 1945, and their mileage would not add up to as many miles as Robert Moses was planning in 1945 to build in one city.

The immensity of the physical difficulties in Moses' path could be grasped only "on the ground," and on the ground they made even engineers accustomed to immense difficulties quail.

One of his proposed superhighways, for example, was the "Cross-Bronx Expressway," a seven-mile-long road that would run straight across that densely populated borough. The Cross-Bronx Expressway would be a huge trench gouged across a city. And it would have to be gouged across the city without disturbing the city's lifelines, the water and gas mains, electric cables and telephone wires, sewers and steam pipes, streets and subways, that supplied hundreds of thousands of residents of the Bronx with services too essential to be interrupted for the long months it would take to build each section of the expressway. General Thomas F. Farrell, builder of World War II's legendary Burma Road, did not fully comprehend what that meant until, now a Moses consultant, he was sent out to look over the proposed route.

Standing on a bluff in Highbridge Park in Manhattan looking across the Harlem River at the Bronx, Farrell saw staring back at him from the top of the bluffs across the river a wall, a wall sixty and eighty and a hundred feet high, a wall of apartment houses. And crossing the river, entering the Bronx, Farrell saw that the wall was seven miles deep. Athwart the route Moses had chosen for his road stood literally hundreds of buildings, close to half of them apartment houses.

And an engineer like Farrell, accustomed to grasping at a glance the essentials of even the largest engineering problems, could see on his first tour of the route that apartment houses were the least of those problems.

Stepping out of his limousine at a high spot on Jesup Avenue to look out over a half-mile valley to the east, the general saw that apartment houses crammed that valley solid—a staggering panorama of massed brick and mortar and iron and steel. Looking down at the map Moses had given him, he saw that the Coordinator was preparing to gouge the huge trench of the expressway straight across the valley's heart. But what staggered Farrell most was not what was in the valley but what was on the other side of it, glaring down at him from the high ridge on its far side, a ridge even higher than the one on which he was standing.

On top of that ridge was not only a wall of apartment houses, big, luxurious buildings of a notable sturdiness, for on top of that ridge was the Grand Boulevard and Concourse, the "Park Avenue of the Bronx," but, running along the top of the ridge, a steady stream of automobiles, toy-sized in the distance. For the Concourse—built at the turn of the century in imitation of Haussmann's boulevards with separate, tree-shaded lanes for pedestrians, bicyclists and horse-drawn carriages—was now a major automobile thoroughfare. Construction of an expressway would take years, Farrell knew; the stream atop the ridge could not possibly be dammed for that long: the Cross-Bronx Expressway could not cross the Grand Concourse at grade. A glance told the general that carrying the expressway over the Concourse on a gigantic viaduct was unfeasible; the ascent up from the valley floor would be almost three hundred feet, far too steep for the big trucks that would be using the expressway. The expressway would have to avoid the Concourse by diving beneath it, by diving down through the ridge, tunneling through with dynamite while not disturbing the apartment houses and road above. And, from a cross-section map he had been given, Farrell knew what was inside that ridge—not merely a huge storm sewer and a maze of smaller utility mains, but another utility somewhat more formidable. What was inside that ridge was a railroad, the Concourse line of the Independent Subway. Tens of thousands of persons rode that subway every day; it, too, would have to be kept in operation. And its triple tracks lay sixty feet below the top of the ridge; to get beneath them while going through the ridge, the expressway would have to dive deep indeed. And "deep" in the Bronx, Farrell knew, as all New York engineers knew, meant Fordham gneiss, a rock that combined layers of unusual hardness, requiring intensive and prolonged blasting, with frightening instability that caused sliding and slipping of the rocks on even the simplest engineering jobs. The engineers building the expressway would have to blast it through the ridge while holding up above it—holding absolutely steady even while igniting dynamite blasts that would shake a mountain—not only a tangle of sewers and mains but a boulevard, a subway and a row of apartment houses. And they would have to hold boulevard, buildings and subway steady while trying to find a footing for the necessary massive supports in unstable rock.

Because the expressway had to dive under the subway, it couldn't go over the valley on a viaduct; that would make the dive beneath the subway too steep. It couldn't cross the valley at grade; that would mean closing the north-south streets in it that cut across the expressway's path, and among those streets in the valley were no fewer than five major thoroughfares that couldn't be closed for long. It would have to burrow across the valley, and that meant holding up those streets while struggling through another maze of mains. And atop one of those streets, Farrell saw a distant skeleton of steel, the girders and tracks of the Jerome Avenue elevated rapid transit line, that would have to be kept running. While building the expressway under Jerome Avenue, Farrell realized, Moses would somehow have to hold up, for months if not for years, not only the broad, heavy avenue but the spindly elevated structure above it—and hold it steady enough for the trains to run along it in safety.

The ridge and valley, in fact, were only a microcosm of the physical difficulties in the way of the Cross-Bronx Expressway. The path of the great road lay across 113 streets, avenues and boulevards; sewers and water and utility mains numbering in the hundreds; one subway and three railroads;* five elevated rapid transit lines,† and seven other expressways or parkways, some of which were being built by Moses simultaneously.‡ All had to be kept in operation while the expressway ran below or above them. This would be a difficult enough engineering task if the engineers had sufficient space in which to work. But on the Cross-Bronx Expressway, there was, Farrell could see, never going to be enough room. Blasting a tunnel and building a road while holding up above it a major street that itself is holding up a transit line is difficult enough. But holding it up when the girders which held up the transit line turned out to be resting on the spots—seemingly the only spots—capable of holding the weight of the tunnel required the fastening to those girders of "needle beams" of immense strength, beams built with legs stretching out to either side that could be sunk into the next available firm rock to hold the weight. The rock was blasted and chiseled out from under the girders so carefully that the road's designer, Ernie Clark, would recall years later that "we took the stuff out with a teaspoon." In one 466-foot section, the expressway ran under four major avenues and an elevated rapid transit line. Working with girders some of which were a hundred feet long and weighed nineteen tons, the engineers were constantly hemmed in on either side by the foundations of apartment buildings that could not be condemned because the condemnation would add additional millions to the cost and that were in constant danger of being damaged—some of them *were* damaged—by the blasting. Blasting a tunnel under a rapid transit line is difficult enough. Building a viaduct over the street and under the rapid transit line is less difficult—if there is thirty feet, the required clearance for streets and expressway, between the top of the asphalt of the street and the bottom of the steel of the transit line. When there isn't, the room can be created only by lifting the rapid transit line into the air—so delicately that its operation is not disturbed—by jacking it into the air, three-tenths of an inch at a time, with immense hydraulic jacks and holding it solid, until new girders of the right height can be installed, with timbers so huge that one man who lived near the Third Avenue jacking operation said, "I never knew there were trees like that in the world before." Throughout the construction of the massive superhighway, Ernie Clark says, "we were always figuring in inches and tenths of inches." In the face of such difficulties, moving a river five hundred feet, a job required where the expressway crossed the Bronx River, was a feat so insignificant that in the speeches Clark made to the delegations of engineers who came from all over the United States and Europe to hear him describe the expressway's engineering, he hardly bothered to mention it.

* The subway, of course, is the Concourse line of the IND under the Grand Concourse. The railroads are two branches of the New York Central and one of the New York, New Haven and Hartford.

† The Pelham, Lenox–White Plains Road, Dyre Avenue, Third Avenue and Jerome Avenue rapid transit lines.

‡ The Harlem River Drive, the Major Deegan, Bruckner, Sheridan and Throgs Neck expressways, the Hutchinson River Parkway Extension and the New England Thruway.

If building the huge new highways was tough, tying them together was tougher—for the knots, the interchanges between them, required so much space that even what looked like immense amounts turned out to be insufficient.

So immense was the mass of swirling, intertwined lanes of links between great roads that had to be built between and up the sides of those rocky 170-foot-high cliffs along the Harlem River that the unassuming Clark once ventured to suggest to an engineering convention, in his quiet way, that a new word would have to be invented to describe it: " 'interchange' does not adequately describe the construction in this area."

Two great north-south roads—the Major Deegan Expressway and the Harlem River Drive—were being built by Moses along the two banks of the Harlem. They would have to be linked up with the Alexander Hamilton Bridge, which Moses was building 170 feet above them to carry the expressway across the river valley—and both the bridge and the two river-bank highways would have to be linked as well to local streets on both sides of the river, as well as to the old Washington Bridge which crossed the river a few hundred feet to the north of the Hamilton. A total of twenty-two separate ramps and eighteen separate viaduct structures would be required to carry the thirty-one lanes of roadway necessary for the links. Making the rise in the links shallow enough so that huge tractor-trailers could negotiate them would have been simple if there had been sufficient room to work in: just start the climb far enough away so that the rise in grade could be gradual. But there wasn't nearly enough room. Two thousand feet south of the Washington Bridge was another nineteenth-century structure, the Highbridge Aqueduct, and the massive steel and stone piers of both these structures plunged down to the river banks, so the Hamilton Bridge—and its connecting links—would have to be built between those piers, and two thousand feet was a pittance in terms of the size required. On the Manhattan side of the river, moreover, was an existing roadway resembling an ancient Roman aqueduct, rising from the river to a tunnel cut beneath 178th Street as a connection under Manhattan to the George Washington Bridge. That roadway was supported on columns one hundred feet high. Knock out one of those columns and the roadway might collapse. The Cross-Bronx Expressway would have to be fitted between them, and the expressway's width was only five feet less than the space between the columns; there was practically no room for maneuver at all in the placing of those twenty-two ramps with their thirty-one lanes. The grades could not be kept shallow; to keep them from being impossibly steep, they would have to wind around and around each other; visualizing it in his mind's eye, Clark knew that the interchanges with which Moses would be filling the air on both sides of the deep valley would be the largest bowl of concrete "spaghetti" cooked up to that time by any highway builder in history. Some of the strands in the bowl would have to be almost incredibly thin and long. Because of the space limitations, normal-sized columns could not be used; the diameter of some, in fact, could be no more than 78½ inches. And some of these slender columns, needed to support immense weights, would have to be 100 feet high! Radically new column designs would have to be evolved, Moses' engineers saw. The ingredients in the sauce, moreover, would have to be varied, indeed; as it turned out, no two strands of spaghetti curved exactly alike, so that each piece of steel for the dozens of columns involved, for the girders supporting the roadbeds which sat atop the columns, for the beams which formed the floor of those roadbeds, for the brackets which held those beams and girders in place, had to be fabricated individually.

The Cross-Bronx was one of thirteen expressways Robert Moses rammed across New York City. Its seven miles were seven out of 130. The physical problems presented by its construction were by no means unique. Even for the "easiest" of those monster roads, those traversing relatively "open" areas of the city, there were always private homes, small apartment houses—and whole factories—which had to be picked up and moved bodily to new locations. For most of these roads, Moses had to hack paths through jungles of tenements and apartment houses, to slash aqueducts in two and push sewers aside, to lift railroads into the air or shove them underground. For one expressway, the Van Wyck, he had to hold up in the air the busiest stretch of railroad in the world, the switching yard through which thirteen tracks and sidings of the Long Island Rail Road pass over Atlantic Avenue in Jamaica—hold it up and hold it steady enough so that during the seven months it took to slide the huge expressway underneath, the 1,100 train movements which took place daily in that yard could continue uninterrupted.

None of Moses' previous feats of urban construction—immense though they had been—compared with the roads he was planning now; as is demonstrated by the cost. Highways had always cost millions of dollars. In the whole world, only a handful had cost as much as $10,000,000. These new highways would cost $10,000,000 per mile. One mile, the most expensive mile of road ever built, cost $40,000,000. Their total cost would be computed not in tens but hundreds of millions of dollars. The total cost of the roads Robert Moses built within the borders of New York City after World War II was over two *billion* dollars.

The roads, of course, were not the largest elements in his transportation program. They were, in fact, in one sense only links between the water crossings he was planning to carry their users over or under the water that divided the city into boroughs.

The scale of these crossings made the mind boggle. No suspension bridge anywhere in the world would be as long (or expensive) as the Verrazano-Narrows Bridge; it would be the longest such bridge ever built, its towers so far apart that in designing them allowance had to be made for the curvature of the earth: their tops are one and five eighths inches further apart than their bases. There would be enough wire in the Verrazano's cables to circle the earth five times around at the equator or to reach halfway to the moon, enough concrete in its anchorages to pave a single-lane highway reaching all the way from New York to Washington, and more steel in its towers—taller than seventy-story skyscrapers—and girders than was used in the construction of the Empire State Building. No underwater vehicular tunnel in the Western Hemisphere—and only one underwater vehicular tunnel anywhere in the world—would be as long as the Brooklyn-Battery Tunnel. The tile used to line it would have tiled 4,500 bathrooms; to ventilate it adequately against the fumes of 60,000 cars and trucks per day, air would have to be driven through huge ducts at the velocity of a Force Twelve hurricane, and the fans which drove that air would consume daily as much electricity as is used daily by a small city. Among such marvels even a huge suspension bridge like the $92,000,000 Throgs Neck—itself an engineering feat that would make most cities proud—would hardly be noticed by New York. Comparisons among public works of different types are difficult. In terms of size, however, Moses' road-building program was certainly comparable to any public works feat in history. In terms of physical difficulty, his program would dwarf them all.

Immense as were the physical obstacles in Moses' path, however, the Coordinator was equal to them.

A technological system—engineering and construction techniques and equipment—capable of solving those physical problems was already in existence. The methods and machines required to build mammoth highways even within a congested city had been perfected, even if they had never been used to the capacity Moses was planning to use them.

As for the tangle of red tape in his way—every main and cable and sewer relocation, for example, required approval by several city departments—that was sliced through with his customary directness. Moses' aides were under standing orders to go straight to the department head at the first sign of resistance from any underling. Most city agencies closed up tight at five o'clock—or earlier. Working weekends was unheard of. But hours and weekends meant nothing to men who knew that when their boss wanted something done, "he wanted it done—period—he didn't care how it was done." Commissioners were routed out of bed at midnight—and long after midnight—by their telephone calls. Watching a Broadway play, a commissioner would feel a tap on the shoulder, and, in the flickering darkness of the theater, would see the tall form of Arthur Hodgkiss or Bill Chapin beckoning him peremptorily to the rear of the theater. One refused to leave his seat; he found himself signing forms on his lap in the third row of a darkened theater. And if some commissioner balked at overruling an underling who had refused, say, to O.K. a Chapin-proposed sewer relocation, his secretary would soon be telling him: "Commissioner Moses is on the line—himself!" And if—as almost never happened—some commissioner remained recalcitrant, the next call his secretary would announce would probably be from the Mayor. Frustration might be piled on frustration; Moses faced them all down. After he had whipped into line behind the vast over-all expressway program—after years of effort that can only be guessed at—Mayor, Governor, Legislature, Board of Estimate, City Council, Federal Bureau of Public Roads, State DPW and an army of city bureaucrats, after all agreements were signed and the bidding for contracts under way, inflation of unforeseen dimensions raised the bids to levels beyond the state's ability to pay its share. Painstakingly, he worked out and obtained legislative and voter approval for a $500,000,000 bond issue which allowed him to get many of the expressways under way and even to finish a few. But costs continued to soar. He had underestimated the city's share so drastically that it could not even assume those minor costs that, by law, neither state nor federal government could assume. For years the expressways lay stalled—until the Federal Interstate Highway Act of 1956 allowed the feds to pick up 90 instead of 50 percent. Working through his banking allies, Moses persuaded Congress to include in the Act—despite the fact that it would circumvent its drafters' original intent of creating a toll-free system—clauses allowing roads linked to toll bridges to be included in the system, thus making his expressways eligible. Then, through a dozen ingenious subterfuges, he persuaded the state to use some of its own highway building funds, freed by the reduction in the share of the costs it was to assume, to pick up some of the city costs. There were other minor—but irritating—inconveniences: wars, for example. The Korean conflict was a source of real irritation. Steel was the precious metal to the highway builder, and the National Production Administration was obstinately insisting that available steel should go first to the war effort. Other cities accepted the situation without protest; Moses fired off telegrams to and pulled strings in Washington. Federal officials believed they would placate him by allocating his highways well over 10 percent of all steel available for civilian use, but they didn't know their man. Moses fired his next shot on the front page of *The New York Times,* charging that the officials were turning civilian defense efforts into a "monstrous joke" by sabotaging construction of arterials needed "to prepare for bombing evacuation, troop and supply movements." When federal officials tried to counter his charges with facts, Moses termed their statements "gobbledygook," the *Times* editorialized that roads are "essential in wartime . . . [the federal decision] mustn't be the last word"—and New York's allocation was quickly increased by another 10,000 tons. Next it was copper. Another attack, another victory. Then a strike kept the copper he had been allocated in the warehouses. But he intervened—and the warehouse doors opened.

To obtain his precious rights-of-way, Moses dealt with other giant city real estate holders—insurance companies, railroads, banks, the Catholic Church—as if the city were a giant Monopoly board, shuffling properties as casually as if they were playing cards, giving the Catholic Church, for example, space for an addition to a Fordham campus in the Bronx in exchange for an easement in Queens, handing Con Ed half a square block for a new gas storage tank (complete with guarantees of Board of Estimate easements for the concomitant underground pipeline) in exchange for two hundred feet of right-of-way through a Con Ed open storage area. At Randall's Island luncheons he made himself the broker between a dozen disparate interests, reaping, always, the commission in right-of-way that he wanted. At one location near Fordham Road, for example, the path of the Major Deegan Expressway was blocked by both a housing development being built by the Equitable Life Assurance Society and a 217-foot-tall Con Ed gas storage tank. Negotiations were stalled—until a luncheon. By dessert, in a complicated land exchange, Equitable had been served up even more land for its development, Con Ed had agreed to "rearrange its distribution facilities" to "eliminate the necessity of the tank," and Moses was savoring the taste not only of the necessary right-of-way but of sufficient additional land adjoining it to create a park and playground for the residents of the Equitable development.

Robert Moses didn't merely solve these "physical" problems. He gloried in solving them. A reporter who was permitted to drive around with him on one highway inspection tour saw Moses "mentally readjusting houses as though they were so many toy building blocks." One of the blocks was a three-story factory—Moses turned it around and reset it on the same plot at a different angle. Another was a church—he turned it sideways. Another was an apartment house six stories high, which—with highway officials who had flown in from all over the country watching in awe, most of them expecting the structure to collapse—was inched a hundred yards out of the Van Wyck Expressway right-of-way with the possessions of thirty-five families still inside it. It cost at least as much—and possibly more—to move the building than it would have cost to demolish it, and in later years, Moses was quite frank about why he had decided to move it. "I moved it because everybody said you couldn't do it," he would tell the author. "I'll never do that again, broke a lot of gas mains . . . That was an absolutely crazy stunt, you know." But at the recollection, a broad, genuine grin spread across Moses' face, a grin of achievement and pride. He was overflowing with pride at his construction feats. The reporter painted a picture of a man happy as he played with his toy blocks. When the limousine reached Van Cortlandt Park, the reporter wrote, Moses began chuckling over reminiscences of the attempt by "the bird lovers" to stop him from running the Major Deegan Expressway through a swamp in the park that they had wanted preserved as a bird sanctuary. They had tried to obtain an injunction, he said, "but we just filled in a little faster." During construction of the Brooklyn-Queens Expressway, Moses rented the penthouse floor of the Marguerite Hotel—an old, sedate establishment right next to the expressway's route—and used it as an office. It had two advantages: only a very few people knew of its existence, so he was interrupted by few telephone calls, and he could look down on the construction as he worked. And he spent a lot of time looking down at it, watching the cranes and derricks and earth-moving machines that looked like toys far below him moving about in the giant trench being cut through mile after mile of densely packed houses, a big black figure against the sunset in the late afternoon, like a giant gazing down on the giant road he was molding. "And I'll tell you," says one of the men who spent a lot of time at the old hotel with him, "I never saw RM look happier than he did when he was looking down out of that window."

* * *

It was not the physical problems that were the most difficult to solve, however, but the political.

A technology for solving the physical problems had been perfected, but not the methods and machinery for the creation of large-scale urban public works in a democratic society; the American system of government almost seemed designed to make such creation as difficult as possible.

It is no coincidence that, as Raymond Moley puts it, "from the pyramids of Egypt, the rebuilding of Rome after Nero's fire, to the creation of the great medieval cathedrals . . . all great public works have been somehow associated with autocratic power." It was no accident that most of the world's great roads—ancient and modern alike—had been associated with totalitarian regimes, that it took a great Khan to build the great roads of Asia, a Darius to build the Royal Road across Asia Minor, a Hitler and a Mussolini to build the *Autobahnen* and *autostrade* of Europe, that during the four hundred years in which Rome was a republic it built relatively few major roads, its broad highways beginning to march across the known earth only after the decrees calling for their construction began to be sent forth from the Capitol by a Caesar rather than a Senate. Whether or not it is true, as Moley claims, that "pure democracy has neither the imagination, nor the energy, nor the disciplined mentality to create major improvements," it is indisputably true that it is far easier for a totalitarian regime to take the probably unpopular decision to allocate a disproportionate share of its resources to such improvements, far easier for it to mobilize the men necessary to plan and build them; the great highways of antiquity awaited the formation of regimes capable of assigning to their construction great masses of men (Rome's were built in large part by the legions who were to tramp along them); at times, the great highways of the modern age seemed to be awaiting some force capable of assigning to their planning the hundreds of engineers, architects and technicians necessary to plan them. And most important, it is far easier for a totalitarian regime to ignore the wishes of its people, for its power does not derive from the people. Under such a regime it is not necessary for masses of people to be persuaded of an improvement's worth; the persuasion of a single mind is sufficient.

This last point has especial significance for the construction of public works in a city. For in a city such construction requires the eviction of people from their homes. Even when the public agrees in theory that a work is needed, no members of the public want to lose their homes for it. People never want *their* neighborhood disturbed by it. If it is to be built, they inevitably feel, let it be built somewhere else. A totalitarian regime can ignore such feelings, which is why the great city rebuildings of history—not only Haussmann's of Paris but St. Peterburg's by Peter the Great, and Rome's first by Nero and later by Augustus—have almost invariably been carried out by such regimes, the notable exceptions being cases (such as the great London fire of 1666 or the saturation bombings of the German cities in 1944) in which a monumental catastrophe destroyed so much of a city that it had no choice but to rebuild—and in which the catastrophe had removed from the scene the people who might have objected.

But Moses was not building under a totalitarian regime. Moses was building under a system in which permission to build could be granted only by officials who derived their power from the people. And, in that light, what was most significant about the Cross-Bronx Expressway was not that seven miles of brick and mortar and steel and iron had to be removed from its path but that seven miles of people had to be removed, removed from homes which in a time of terrible housing crisis in New York were simply irreplaceable. "People said that [the route] was so built up that you'd never get the politicians to say okay," Ernie Clark would later recall, and engineers who had built bigger roads even than Ernie Clark agreed. Farrell and Chapin's legendary Burma Road would symbolize to history the epitome of difficulty in construction. But Chapin understood political as well as engineering problems. Years later, he would recall the feeling that had swept over him when he had stood on Jesup Avenue staring down at that valley in the Bronx packed edge to edge with voters' homes. "I said to myself: 'The [Burma] Road was tough. But that was *nothing* compared to this son of a bitch.' " People—the people whose homes stood in the path of all Moses' urban expressways—were the most difficult problem of all.

But Moses solved this problem, too.

Democracy had not solved the problem of building large-scale urban public works, so Moses solved it by ignoring democracy.

Critics who said the Coordinator simply ignored the people in his path oversimplified; he may have wanted to, but political considerations, the considerations that mattered to other public officials, made it impossible for him to do so—at least until after Bill-O had been safely returned to office in 1949, Moses *tried* to take the people into account—tried hard. It was he who, to persuade apartment dwellers (hitherto uncompensated for eviction since they did not own the land involved) to move, persuaded the Legislature to provide for their reimbursement: $100 per room and $100 for moving expenses. Finding that they still balked—for middle- and lower-class families in New York, no few hundreds of dollars could compensate for the loss of a comfortable apartment they could afford—he even moved a few apartment houses smaller than the one on the Van Wyck. He moved entire blocks of private homes—263 homes on the Van Wyck Expressway alone—where there was room to move them. But along most of his routes, there was no room. And, as even his admirer Jacob Lutsky puts it: "He thought about people. But if it came to a project or people, he'd take the project."

He had the power to do so—to ignore or override the procedures democratic government establishes to govern the planning of public works. Was it mostly dictators who had built great urban public works of the past? In road-building in and around New York, he had a dictator's powers. And he used them.

He enjoyed using them—for using them gave him what was his greatest pleasure: the imposition of his will on other people. One evening, he was sitting with Sid Shapiro and several other aides in his limousine parked on a side street in Queens, studying possible locations for the Clearview Expressway. Suddenly there appeared at the end of the street hundreds of citizens bearing torches and a scarecrow effigy labeled, in large letters, ROBERT MOSES. The aides realized that they had happened upon an anti-expressway torchlight rally. The big black car sat at the end of the street unnoticed in the dusk by anyone in the crowd as the effigy was hoisted to a lamppost and set afire. "I didn't dare look at RM," Shapiro recalls. But to his surprise, his boss threw back his head and roared with laughter. And when someone suggested they drive away, RM said no. He wanted to stay for a while. He didn't want to miss a thing. He sat there all through the speeches comparing him to a "dictator," "a Hitler," "a Stalin." And, says Shapiro, "he laughed and laughed. RM really got a kick out of it."

When he replied to protests about the hardships caused by his road-building programs, he generally replied that succeeding generations would be grateful. It was the end that counted, not the means. "You can't make an omelet without breaking eggs." Once, in a speech, he said:

> You can draw any kind of picture you like on a clean slate and indulge your every whim in the wilderness in laying out a New Delhi, Canberra or Brasília, but when you operate in an overbuilt metropolis, you have to hack your way with a meat ax.

The metaphor, like most Moses metaphors, was vivid. But it was incomplete. It expressed his philosophy, but it was not philosophy but feelings that dictated Moses' actions. He didn't just feel that he *had* to swing a meat ax. He *loved* to swing it.

37. *One Mile*

ROBERT MOSES built 627 miles of roads in and around New York City. This is the story of one of those miles.

There is something strange about that mile. It is one of seven that make up the great highway known as the Cross-Bronx Expressway, but the other six, like most of the other miles of Moses' expressways, are—roughly—straight, on a road map a heavy red line slashing inexorably across the delicate crosshatch of streets in the borough's central expanse. There is logic—the ruthless, single-minded logic of the engineer, perhaps, but logic—in that line. When it curves, the curves are shallow, the road hastening to resume its former course. But during that one mile, the road swerves, bulging abruptly and substantially toward the north.

A closer look does not explain that bulge. It makes it not less puzzling but more. Detailed maps show the entire area blanketed with rectangles that represent city blocks—except for one open space, running east-west, parallel to the expressway, that represents an unusually wide avenue, and, directly adjacent to and below that open space, another, colored green, that represents a 148-acre park. And these empty spaces lie directly in the path that the expressway would have followed had it just continued on its former straight course. All it had to do to take advantage of that corridor—to utilize for right-of-way the avenue roadbed, together with a very narrow strip at the very top edge of the park—was to keep on the way it had been going.

If the location of that one mile of expressway was puzzling on maps when Moses first proposed it in 1946, it was more puzzling in reality. For while the maps showed rectangles, reality was what was on those rectangles: apartment houses lined up rank upon rank, a solid mile of apartment houses, fifty-four of them, fifty-four structures of brick and steel and mortar piled fifty, sixty and seventy feet high and each housing thirty or forty or fifty families. Walk through the area, the proposed route of the expressway and the blocks around it, and it was impossible not to see that keeping the road straight would hurt little. Only six small buildings—dilapidated brownstone tenements—would have to be torn down. Most of the right-of-way—the park and the avenue—was already in the city's possession. While turning the road to the north would destroy hundreds upon hundreds of homes, homes in which lived thousands of men, women and children.* And

* The only figures available are Moses'. He said his route would, during the one-mile stretch, require the demolition of 1,530 apartments housing 5,000 persons. These figures are almost certainly far too low.

it would cost millions upon millions of dollars—in condemnation costs for fifty-four apartment houses, in demolition costs for the tearing down of those buildings, in tax revenue that would otherwise be paid, year after year for generations, into city coffers by the buildings' owners.

If the bulge in the expressway was puzzling to anyone studying it, it was tragic to those who didn't have to study it, to the people who lived in or near that right-of-way. For to these people, the fifty-four apartment buildings that would have to be destroyed were not just buildings but homes. That mile of buildings was the very heart of the neighborhood in which they lived, a section of the Bronx known as "East Tremont."

The people of East Tremont did not have much. Refugees or the children of refugees from the little *shtetls* in the Pale of Settlement and from the ghettos of Eastern Europe, the Jews who at the turn of the century had fled the pogroms and the wrath of the Tsars, they had first settled in America on the Lower East Side. The Lower East Side had become a place to which they were tied by family and friends and language and religion and a sense of belonging—but from whose damp and squalid tenements they had ached to escape, if not for their own sake then for the sake of their children, whose every cough brought dread to parents who knew all too well why the streets in which they lived were called "lung blocks." Jews from the Lower East Side who made enough money to escape in style escaped to "the Jewish half-mile" of Central Park West, "the Golden Ghetto." Jews who made enough money to escape—but not that much—escaped to the Grand Concourse. The Jews of East Tremont were luckier than those who had to stay behind on the Lower East Side, but not so lucky as the Grand Concourse Jews. They were not the milliners or the cloak-and-suiters but the pressers, finishers and cutters who worked in the bare workrooms behind the ornate showrooms of the garment district. They were a long way from being rich, and their neighborhood proved it. There were no elevators in most of the five- and six-story buildings into which they began to flood (stopping at 182nd Street, southern border of an Italian neighborhood, as abruptly as if a fence had stood there) after the extension of the IRT elevated line just before World War I linked East Tremont to the downtown garment district. By the end of World War II, the buildings' galvanized iron pipes were corroding, causing leaks and drops in water pressure; a few still had bathtubs that sat up on legs. With some 60,000 persons living along its narrow streets, its "population density"—441 persons "per residential acre"—was considered "undesirable" by social scientists. "In moving through East Tremont one senses a feeling of crowdedness brought on by the lack of open space and close location of buildings," one wrote.

But the neighborhood provided its residents with things that were important to them.

Transportation was important to the fathers who worked downtown, and the neighborhood had good transportation. With the Third Avenue El and the IRT White Plains Road line running right through it, it was only a few easy blocks from anywhere in East Tremont to a subway that took you right down to the garment district.

Jobs were important to the fathers who didn't work downtown, and the neighborhood had jobs available—good jobs by East Tremont standards—in a miniature garment and upholstery manufacturing district that had sprung up around Park Avenue, just ten minutes away.

Shopping was important to the mothers who stayed home and took care of the kids, and the neighborhood had good shopping. East Tremont Avenue, which ran conveniently right across its center, was a bright, bustling mile of bakeries which didn't bother advertising that they baked only with butter because all of them did, of groceries where your order was sliced and measured out and weighed ("You didn't get everything in packages like you do now"), of kosher butcher shops ("We weren't, but I bought kosher for my mother's sake. And it's the kind of meat you know in the pot"), of mama-and-papa candy stores, of delicatessens, filled always with the pungent aroma from the pickel barrels, whose owners got up before dawn to mix olives and pimentos and chives—or dates or caviar—into manufactured cream cheese to create individualized loaves they named "Paradise" or "Dark Jewel." You might go to Alexander's on the Concourse for clothes, but you didn't have to; Janowitz's on Tremont was just as good. You didn't even have to leave the neighborhood for a dress for a real "fancy" affair; "they had *high-priced* stores on Tremont, too; Held's [at the intersection of Southern Boulevard] was very expensive—as good as any store on the Concourse." If you didn't feel like going out, the "better" stores on Marmion delivered, and the stuff they delivered was just as good as if you had been there to feel it yourself, and for many items you didn't even have to pick up the telephone: a few pushcart peddlers still roamed the streets of East Tremont as if to remind the residents of where they had come from.

Parks were important to the mothers, too. There were no playgrounds in the neighborhood—mothers' delegations had attempted in the past to talk to the Park Department about the situation but Moses' aides had never even deigned to grant them an appointment—but running down its length was Southern Boulevard, whose broad center mall had grass plots plenty big enough for little children to play on, and surrounded by benches so mothers could keep their eyes on them to make sure they didn't run into the street. And the southwestern border of the neighborhood was Crotona Park. "Beautiful. Lovely. Playgrounds. There was a lake—Indian Lake. Nice. We used to sit there—under the trees. We raised our children in Crotona Park." Social scientists, who had never lived on the Lower East Side, might consider East Tremont "crowded." The people of East Tremont, who had, considered it open and airy, wonderfully open and airy.

Thanks to Crotona Park, young adults as well as children didn't have to leave the neighborhood for recreation. "It was a *great* park. Twenty tennis courts right *there*. Where you could walk to them. Baseball diamonds, magnificent playgrounds with baskets—three-man games would be going on all weekend, you know. A big swimming pool that Moses had built during the Depression. Indian Lake. And kept really clean then, you know. And safe. *Sure* people walked there at night. You never worried then. A *great* park!" And thanks to Tremont Avenue, you didn't have to leave the neighborhood for entertainment. On the avenue's one mile in the neighborhood were seven movie houses. The Bronx Zoo—with its animals roaming behind moats instead of bars—was one stop away on the White Plains El, the New York Botanical Garden was three; you could *walk* with your children to those two perfect places to spend a Sunday with the kids.

The neighborhood provided the things that were important to its old people. "The benches over on Southern Boulevard were beautiful, gorgeous. On sunny days, you could always find the girls over there, just chatting, you know, and having a good time. On weekends, they'd be so crowded, you couldn't sit down." Old men would sit there in the sun playing chess with men with whom they had been playing chess for thirty years. (Kibitzers had to stand.) There was a place to play chess—or cards—or just sit and talk over a cup of coffee in cold weather, too. The "Y"—the East Tremont Young Men's Hebrew Association—listed more than four hundred "senior citizens" on its active membership roles. "There was no reason for an older person to be lonely in that neighborhood," says one who lived there.

"You knew where your kids were at night, too," says one mother. They were at the Y, which had 1,700 families as members. "There were so many programs out of the Y for kids. At night—before—you never used to know where they were, what they were doing. You always used to hear about gangs—you had to worry, was he with a gang? Now you always knew where your kids were at night." Children who lived on Central Park West might be sent to expensive day camps and, when they got older, to sleep-away camps in the Adirondacks; the Y provided inexpensive day-camp and sleep-away programs—the largest run by any single institution in New York City—for children who lived on Crotona Park North.

Schools were terribly important to the people of East Tremont (a quarter of a century after their kids had graduated, some parents could still remember the precise student-teacher ratio in their classes), and East Tremont had good schools. They were old—PS 44, at 176th and Prospect, the neighborhood's junior high school, had been built in 1901, and the city said there was simply no money to replace it—but there were no double sessions and standards were high. PS 67, off Southern Boulevard, was the first elementary school in New York to offer lessons—and supply instruments—for any child who wanted to learn to play the violin. And all the schools were close, close enough for kids to walk to.

To the people of East Tremont, East Tremont was family. In its bricks were generations. Raised in the neighborhood, Lillian Roberts married a boy from the neighborhood. They made their first apartment in a supposedly "nicer" section over on Fordham Road. When their first child was born, they moved back. "Why? Because my husband had—oh, we both had, I guess—nostalgic feelings. The reason we moved back to that area was that we loved it so much." Lillian and her husband moved into an apartment on the third floor of a walkup at 845 West 176th Street. On the first floor of that building, Lillian's mother, Ida Rozofsky, born in Russia, was living—with Lillian's grandmother. East Tremont was friends—real friends, not just acquaintances you happened to meet because they took their children to the same playground to which you took your children, or because they belonged to the same PTA as you, but friends whom you had grown up with and were going to grow old with, boys and girls—turned men and women—who knew and understood you and whom you knew and understood. Says Mrs. Helen Lazarcheck: "Everyone seemed to help one another. If there was trouble, everyone would do something for you if they could. They were always coming in and sharing what they had. If they were going away, they would give you food that you could use and they couldn't." East Tremont was a feeling of being known—in the streets and in the stores, where shopkeepers like big gruff Saul Janowitz, "the Mayor of East Tremont," had been selling to neighborhood families for decades. (The owner of one Crotona Avenue vegetable stand had been selling vegetables in Tremont when it still largely consisted of the three large "mount" farming estates—Mount Hope, Mount Eden and Fairmount—that had given "Tremont" its name; he had gone from house to house with a horse and wagon then.) East Tremont was a sense of continuity, of warmth, of the security that comes—and only comes—with a sense of belonging. Even families that could afford to have their "simchas"—weddings and bar mitzvahs—in the Concourse Plaza, generally had them instead in the neighborhood's little, somewhat shabby, social halls. No one would have called East Tremont a *united* community. It possessed, one study observed, a "myriad of social systems covering religious *Landsmannschaft* groups, fraternal, educational, political and fund-raising groups" engaged in "a constant and shrill competition for loyalty," a competition which was not even resolved in the two areas where East Tremont might have been expected to be solid: politics and religion. FDR's hold was absolute—but only so far as FDR was concerned; in nonpresidential elections, men who once, long ago, had preached from soapboxes were loyal to an older faith: Socialist, Communist, American Labor and Progressive parties could all count on substantial votes in East Tremont. "In East Tremont," the study noted, "the Yiddishist and Hebraist each had his following with a supporting system of cultural clubs, bookstores, debating societies, etc." The neighborhood's seven synagogues were constantly competing for members and prestige. East Tremont may have been a loud community, a shrill community, a materialistic, money-conscious community. But it was a community.

Robert Moses didn't think much of the apartments of East Tremont. The buildings were old, the plumbing was bad, most of them didn't even have elevators—he referred to them as "tenements," as "walkups" or, if those nouns didn't seem to be eliciting the desired horror from his listeners, as "slums." But Moses had never lived on the Lower East Side.

"Tenements?" says Mrs. Silverman. "Listen, I *lived* in tenements. These were not tenements at all." If the apartments' plumbing was not modern, neither—happily—was the size of their rooms, large—huge by postwar standards—and high-ceilinged. They had foyers—real foyers, L-shaped some of them—as big as rooms themselves. "I served dinner for eighteen in my foyer, that's how big it was," Mrs. Silverman says. They had dining rooms, not dining areas. The apartment houses might not have had elevators, but

they had—almost all of them—courtyards, and there were enough small frame houses interspersed among them to let sunlight in. "Those apartments were light and airy and cheerful," Mrs. Roberts says. Sunken living rooms were not uncommon, the sills on the windows were broad and wood, the walls were not postwar plasterboard but thick and solid, the lines where walls met ceiling were softened with ornamental moldings. "I had what they called four rooms," says Mrs. Silverman. "Besides that big foyer, we had a kitchen with a dining area, two bedrooms—of course, they each had a bathroom, what else?—and a living room; I don't know how big the living room was, but it was a real nice size. When my girlfriend's daughter was engaged, I served dinner for sixty in the living room and foyer, and it wasn't even crowded, that's how big it was. We all loved our apartments."

They loved them—and they could afford them. If the water pressure was low, so was the rent, scaled originally to their ability to pay by landlords who could afford to do so because they had bought land in East Tremont for as little as two dollars per square foot, and kept at that scale by city-instituted rent control. Mrs. Silverman was paying $100 per month for her four rooms, and that was high. Lillian Roberts was paying $62 for her four rooms. Cele Sherman had a six-room apartment—three bedrooms, a living room, kitchen with large dining area, and a foyer with a recess large enough to be a full-scale dining room—and for that apartment Mrs. Sherman was paying $69.

The rents had to be reasonable for these people to afford them. Weekly take-home pay in the garment industry—the pay on which most of these people lived—averaged well under a hundred dollars. And while the generally accepted rule of thumb held that a family could afford to pay a monthly rent equal to about a week's income, this was not a rule accepted by the families of East Tremont, who had their own rule of thumb: that when you had children, you sent them to college, no matter how much scrimping and saving you had to do. The rents they were paying—low as they were—were, in all too many cases, the absolute maximum they could afford. They lived—many of them—on the thin edge of disaster. "Clara Wertel—her husband got sick so they had to move out," recalls Mrs. Sherman. "And Mrs. Aronofsky—her husband died. Same thing. One thing could do it, and so fast. Boom, and you were gone. Your friends never saw you again."

Happy therefore to have those apartments, the people of East Tremont were made desperate to keep them by the harsh realities of New York's housing crisis. Finding an apartment at any price was difficult in a city whose postwar vacancy rate was an habitual 1 percent. Finding an apartment at a rent they could afford to pay, in a neighborhood they felt they could live in, was all but impossible. They knew how difficult it was to obtain an apartment in East Tremont; one could wait for years even after one had promised a "schmear" to any super who let you know about an upcoming vacancy. Similar "middle-class" Jewish neighborhoods with low rents in which they would be comfortable—Washington Heights, for example—were rented up just as solidly. Public housing, overwhelmingly inhabited by Negroes and Puerto Ricans, was unthinkable even for those relatively few East Tremont families whose income was low enough to qualify; no one, moreover, wanted "the stigma" involved in having everyone know you qualified. Huge as was the low-income housing program, moreover, the waiting list was huger still. They had no hope of ever being able to afford the apartments in the new buildings being built in the Jewish neighborhoods around Pelham Parkway, where a "two-bedroom" might rent for $350 per month. As for living in one's own home on Long Island or in Westchester, that was a dream reserved for the children they were sending to college. The apartments generally available in New York for the $75 or $80 per month they could afford were apartments in the black or Puerto Rican slums—or back on the Lower East Side.

If it was desperately important for the people who lived in East Tremont that their neighborhood be saved, it was also desperately important for the city of which that neighborhood was a part. For a hundred years, East Tremont had been performing a vital function for New York, as an "urbanizing" area, a place in which families from European farms or small villages could become accustomed to living in a city, where a common consciousness began to evolve, a man from County Cork learning that the families next door from County Mayo weren't really such a bad sort, a housewife from a Latvian *shtetl* learning that the woman she met at the market who came from the Kiev ghetto was someone she could talk with—a consciousness that translated itself into a feeling of belonging in the city, and (more quickly in the case of the Irish and Italians than the Jews, who were always arguing among themselves) into political organizations that gave them a share of power in the city. It had been a "staging area," a place where newcomers who had lived previously in America only in slums, successful at last in their struggle to find a decent place to live, could regroup, and begin to devote their energies to consolidating their small gains and giving their children the education that would enable them to move onward and upward—to better, more "fashionable" areas. In 1848, it was Rhineland farmers fleeing revolutionary chaos; during the 1870's, it was the Irish, fleeing famine or the Lower East Side. Just after the turn of the century, with the more prosperous among the Irish moving on to Fordham or University Heights or Riverdale, it was the Italians, many of them just off the boat, who followed the new IRT subway to what was then the end of the line and seeped westward to fill up all of the "Belmont" area north of 182nd Street. Then it was the Jews, filling up the area between Belmont and Crotona Park. And East Tremont—with the exception of Belmont, which the Italians held for their own—had been an *integrated* urbanizing and staging area. All the Germans didn't move out when the Irish arrived, all the Irish didn't move out when the Jews arrived—in 1950, there may have been 44,000 Jews in the area south of Belmont, but there were also about 5,000 Irishmen and about 5,000 Germans and Slavs.

There was ample proof in 1950 that East Tremont was serving just as efficiently as an urbanizing and staging area—an integrated urbanizing staging area—for the city's newest immigrants.

In some other areas of the city, the approach of Negroes and Puerto Ricans—part of the great wave of dark-skinned immigrants who had begun flooding into the city just before World War II, a flood that had mounted every year since—had meant flight. But not in East Tremont.

Morrisania, just on the other—south—side of Crotona Park, had become a predominantly Negro slum about 1930. But the people of East Tremont had not fled.

Since about 1940, the less desirable tenements in the shadow of the noisy El along Third Avenue—right on the neighborhood's western edge—had been filled with Negroes. But the neighborhood had held.

The same spur that had roweled the Jews into East Tremont—the hope of a better life for their children—had roweled Negroes there, right into the neighborhood itself. The first was Charles Smith, traffic manager for a fabric company, whose wife, a white Jewish girl who kept a strictly kosher home in Harlem, said to him in 1929, when their son turned six: "Over my dead body my son is going to the 135th Street School." "Negroes in '30 or '31 who came up to the Bronx, they stopped at Prospect [in Morrisania]," Smith recalls. "We didn't want no Prospect. We came all the way up to Tremont." For a while, Smith's son was the only Negro child in PS 44 (then an elementary school), but soon more Negroes—doctors, lawyers, working men whose wives also worked to help make their families a better life—were following them into the neighborhood, some purchasing private homes, some moving into apartments. By 1933, there were seven Negro families in Elsmere Gardens, one of the neighborhood's "best" buildings. There were quite a few along Crotona Park North, the avenue facing the park that was considered East Tremont's most desirable location. But East Tremont took into its bosom the newcomers with black faces as it had taken in newcomers with white faces.

"People here were good with us," Smith says. And they were good with the pioneers who followed Smith. There were Negro women on the executive committee of neighborhood organizations. "My daughter used to walk to school with two Negro boys," says Cele Cohen. "We used to have Negro children over for dinner, and they used to have my daughter over. To tell the truth, we didn't think that way—you know, the way it is now—then."

After the war, the influx of Negroes into East Tremont increased. An influx of Puerto Ricans began. But the influx stayed slow and no whites left because of it. By 1950, there were approximately 11,000 nonwhites in East Tremont, 18 percent of the neighborhood's 60,000 population. And the neighborhood was still holding just fine. Standing astride its whole southern border, Crotona Park provided East Tremont with a natural shield, a comfortably wide—and, at that time, heavily policed—dike against the decay flooding up from the south. Its brunt broken on the park's slopes, the decay oozed around its sides, searching for an opening into the clean streets beyond, but against it the park flung upward, at both its northern corners, extensions that were protecting arms. And there were social, perhaps even moral, reasons as well as physical for the neighborhood to hold. The Jews of East Tremont—liberals, utopianists, socialists, fiery radical labor unionists, men and women who had held on to their ideals even under the lash and the knout, and the children of those men and women—said they believed in the equality of men, including those with darker skins than they. One could argue about how deep that belief really ran, but in 1952 they certainly acted as if they meant it. The neighborhood was still the neighborhood. No one felt the need to move out of it just because a few more Negroes were moving in.

But the strongest reasons were economic. Even if they had wanted to move out, the people of East Tremont couldn't afford to. In the 1970's, it would become a cliché to say that a neighborhood like East Tremont couldn't hold. But that cliché ignored the reality of rents that people could afford, and their inability to find such rents anywhere else. The influx of impoverished Negroes and Puerto Ricans might have been steadily increasing in 1952. The pressures on the neighborhood might have been growing stronger and stronger. But so were the economic realities that had kept it solid. Decent housing at affordable rents was becoming steadily scarcer. The income of East Tremont's older residents, now beginning to retire on inadequate pensions and social security, was falling.

In 1951, with the nonwhite population of East Tremont already substantial and clearly going to increase further, the Association of Young Men's and Young Women's Hebrew Associations of New York—considering building a new Y to replace the Clinton Avenue building—had decided to determine whether or not the investment would be worthwhile, and had conducted the most detailed survey of East Tremont residents ever made. Its conclusions were clear. Negroes might come. The Jews would stay. For more than twenty years, the pressure of urban decay and blight had been pressing on the neighborhood, but for twenty years, the neighborhood had held.

Leave it alone, and it would continue to hold.

By 1952 there were 775,516 Negroes and nonwhite Spanish-speaking people—a full 10 percent of New York's residents—in the city. And, as the Irish had done a century before and the Italians and Eastern European Jews half a century before, these immigrants from the South and from the Caribbean were continuing to pour into the city by the thousands and tens of thousands. For its own sake as well as theirs—if the city was to prosper or if it was even to endure as a place in which people, white or nonwhite, would want to live—it would have to offer the newcomers the same chance it had offered their forerunners: would have to absorb them by providing neighborhoods in which they could learn to cope with urban life, in which they could consolidate the gains that had enabled them to move out of the real slums in the first place and prepare for an assault on even better places to live, neighborhoods which would serve as urbanizing and staging areas. And it would have to provide urbanizing and staging areas that were integrated. If it did not, if these newcomers to New York were forced to live in ghettos, compounded with their resentment at their inability to provide a decent place for their children to live would be an alienation from the society which had isolated them. These people—who were making up more and more of the city—would be an alienated, hostile, hating force within it.

If the city was going to endure, neighborhoods like East Tremont were going to have to endure.

And if it was left alone, this neighborhood would.

The letters came on December 4, 1952.

For years, East Tremont had been vaguely aware that one of Robert Moses' highways was going to run through the neighborhood, that part of it was already under construction over in the East Bronx somewhere. But there had been no hard facts available, and, as Mrs. Lillian Edelstein says, "it had gone on so long, and you keep hearing and hearing and nothing happens, and after a while it doesn't mean anything to you." When they thought about it—if they thought about it—they were sure it would run along the edge of Crotona Park; "I mean, it was so obvious—you just figured it was going to go there," Mrs. Edelstein says. "It was in the wind for a long time that he was going to come through the apartment houses. But we just didn't believe it."

But on December 4, a Tuesday, the letters were there—in hundreds of mailboxes, letters signed by "Robert Moses, City Construction Coordinator," informing each recipient that the building in which he or she lived was in the right-of-way of the Cross-Bronx Expressway, that it would be condemned by the city and torn down—and that they had ninety days to move.

"It was like the floor opened up underneath your feet," Mrs. Edelstein says. "There was no warning. We just got it in the mail. Everybody on the street got it the same day. A notice. We had ninety days to get out. I remember it was a nice day, too, for that time of year. We all stood outside —'Did you get the letter?' 'Did *you* get the letter?' And 'What does it mean?' Three months to get out! Some people had gone out early and hadn't heard. We told them. And then we all waited for our husbands to come home. And my husband said, 'You can't do anything.'"

The ninety-day figure was meaningless, of course. At the time Moses sent out his letter the money to build the East Tremont stretch of the expressway was nowhere in sight; months, if not years, would be required to obtain it. The city had not even acquired title to the property yet, and there were months of procedures necessary before it could do so—and before demolition could begin. Privately, Moses was figuring not on three but eighteen months to clear the area. The use of the ninety-day figure was a scare tactic—"to shake 'em up a little and get 'em moving," a Moses aide explains.

The tactic accomplished its purpose. As the full implication of their position began to dawn on the tenants, they became very scared indeed.

"The first thing you do, naturally, you look to see what else is available," says Mrs. Roberts. "My husband and I looked in the papers and asked around. And when we first found out the type of rents!" Says another East Tremont housewife: "We had been thinking before—for years—about moving to Pelham Parkway—you know, not really seriously, but just talking about it from time to time. Pelham Parkway was a very, very nice area. But now we went over there. My God! On Pelham Parkway they wanted a hundred dollars a room."

Priced out of other "decent" neighborhoods, they turned to a task they knew before they started was almost hopeless: finding a new apartment in their own. The Y was inundated with requests for information about local vacancies. "Occasionally we'd hear about one," says Y director Barney Lambert. "But this was fifteen hundred families that needed them."

A subsequent notice from Moses said that "tenant relocation operations" were already planned, and promised that "we shall cooperate in every possible way so as to avoid hardships and inconveniences." On the "completed," easterly "Section 3" of the expressway, he stated, tenant relocation had "proceeded in an orderly manner."

This notice proclaimed that its purpose was reassurance: "We are issuing this . . . honest schedule for acquisition," because "most Americans prefer to be told just what is in store for them. They dislike uncertainty." Its result was panic. For East Tremont had formed a tenants' committee and, heading over to Section 3, it found out what "orderly tenant relocation operations" meant when carried out under the direction of Robert Moses.

The expressway had been completed over part of Section 3. A great swath of concrete, 225 feet wide, grayish white, unmarked by the treads of a single car, had been laid neatly to within about two and a half miles of East Tremont. But those two and a half miles were a scene of desolation and destruction such as the committee members had never seen. Some of the right-of-way had been cleared: where once apartment buildings or private homes had stood were now hills of rubble, decorated with ripped-open bags of rotting garbage that had been flung atop them. Some of the right-of-way was being cleared; giant wreckers' balls thudded into walls; mammoth cranes snarled and grumbled over the ruins, picking out their insides. Huge bulldozers and earth-moving machines rumbled over the rubble; a small army of grime-covered demolition workers pounded and pried and shoveled. A thick layer of gritty soot made the very air feel dirty. ("I took out a handkerchief and wiped my forehead, and it came away black—absolutely black," Mrs. Edelstein says.) Over the rumble of the bulldozers came the staccato, machine-gun-like banging of jackhammers and, occasionally, the dull concussion of an exploding dynamite charge. And in the midst of this landscape of destruction, a handful of apartment buildings still stood. From the outside, the East Tremont committee saw that most of their windows were boarded up. Going inside, they found the lobbies littered with shards of broken glass that once had been big ornamental mirrors and with the stuffings from the armchairs and sofas that had once been their decoration, and smeared with excrement not only animal but human, from winos and junkies who slept in them at night. Stumbling upstairs, the committee found the doors to many apartments ajar; through them, they could see empty rooms, walls ripped open by vandals who had torn the plumbing pipes out of them. Other doors, however, were closed and locked; on them, especially around the keyholes, were scratches and gouges that showed where someone had tried to break through them. And behind these doors the committee found people, not winos but respectable Irish or Jewish families like themselves.

Some of the apartments were furnished, nicely, for the families living in them were the families who had always lived in them. In others, the families were living out of suitcases, and the only decorations were cheap curtains placed on the windows in the hope that proof that someone was living behind them would deter vandals from breaking them as they broke the windows of unoccupied apartments. And the horrified East Tremont housewives heard the housewives in these apartments inform them that they were living there only temporarily, that they had been moved into them "by the city" when their old homes were demolished and that they expected to be moved out of them—into other temporary quarters—when it came time for the city to demolish *them.* The expressway had pushed up to the very wall of one apartment building, concrete bellying right up to the brick. Going inside, the committee found one family—a middle-aged couple with two children—who had been moved into the building only a few weeks before, and who were obviously going to have to be moved out of it in another few weeks. Standing shivering in cold rooms—for in most of the remaining apartment buildings in Section 3 there was of course no heat—the committee from East Tremont heard women—respectable housewives like themselves, women who had always been proud of the homes they made for their families—state that they had been shunted ahead of the path of the expressway over and over again, forced to move—"like gypsies," one said—from one condemned building to another, each one further along the expressway's route, for years. Disbelieving, the committee heard the topper: these dispossessed families were forced to pay rent for their heatless hovels, and each time they were moved they were hit with a 15 percent rent increase.

Section 3 had received the same assurances that Moses was now making to Section 2, they said—back in 1946, when the city had taken title to that section. "The city" had even set up a Tenant Relocation Bureau—supposedly to find them new, comparable living quarters. They were still living in Section 3 because the Tenant Relocation Bureau (an agency closely allied with Moses) had not found them such quarters. The only apartments she had been shown were apartments "not fit for rats," one bitter, middle-aged housewife said. And the rents asked for those apartments had been double what she had been paying for a nice, two-bedroom apartment—double what she could afford. One elderly widow, one of three tenants left in a twenty-family apartment house, had been ordered to put her furniture in storage and move into a single furnished room. She was desperately holding on to the apartment in the hope of something better because her son, an Air Force flier in Korea, was expected home soon. When he had left her, he had had a home, she said. "He has a right to expect a home" when he gets back, too.

The *Post* had inquired about tenant relocation in Section 3. Moses had replied: "None of the families living in the path of the Cross-Bronx Expressway has been turned into the street. The city, through its Real Estate Bureau, has treated every family involved in a considerate, humane manner." From the tenants still living in Section 3—and from families who had moved out—the East Tremont committee heard about the Real Estate Bureau (another agency closely allied with Moses).

When you first went to the office the Bureau had set up at 1 Hugh Grant Circle, the committee learned, you were told that you had better try to get an apartment yourself. As an inducement to do so—and thus save the Bureau any work at all—you were offered $200 per room, little more than enough to cover moving expenses.

When you returned to the office and said you had been unable to find one that you were willing to live in and that you could afford, the Bureau's first reaction was to tell you that there was nothing more it could do, implying it had washed its hands of your case entirely, and leaving you with a feeling that there was no help available for you from anyone in the city government. If you persisted, and insisted on being shown other apartments, you would be taken—eventually—to inspect, along with other people who had insisted, "comparable" apartments. Apartments that were indeed comparable—and you had to be one of a lucky few to be shown any of those, anyway—bore rents three and four times those you were currently paying. And there were hardly any of those available, anyway. Most of the apartments you were shown were ancient, filthy, cold, dark tenement and slum warrens.

When, in desperation, driven to willingness to accept the "stigma," you asked if "the city" which was destroying your home could not give you another one in one of its public housing projects, you were told that there were tens of thousands of people ahead of you on the waiting list; one resident of the condemned buildings in Section 3 said she had been on the list for six years.

And what if you tried to hold out, to insist on the comparable apartment that the city had promised you? When the time came, the city's Bureau had methods for discouraging you. It would set a deadline, and inform you that the $200 per room they were offering for moving expenses would be reduced to $100 if you did not get out by that date. Then, if you still had not moved, they might set another deadline—on which the amount would be reduced to $50, or to nothing. Then there was the barrage of threatening notices and directives, designed to make you feel that you might return home one day to find your belongings out on the street. One, sent out in 1949, told the recipients that the city required their premises "for the immediate purpose of demolishing. . . . You will please take further notice that upon your failure to remove from the premises within the time specified legal processes will be instituted to recover possession of the premises." When you protested—when you formed a committee to protest; yes, the DP's of Section 3 said, they had formed committees, too—all protests were referred to Moses, and Moses would never even reply to them. Insisting did no good. After interviewing the tenants left in Section 3, Mrs. Edelstein reported that "they knew of *no one* who was relocated by Mr. Moses." Some 325 tenants had moved out—been forced out—of the area by his tactics. But when the committee from East Tremont arrived in 1952—six years after "orderly tenant relocation operations" had begun—there were still living in those doomed, half-empty hulks in the expressway's path no fewer than 250. It was no wonder that when Mrs. Edelstein reported the results of the committee's investigation at a neighborhood mass meeting, they "were received as a nightmare."

But East Tremont's panic was soon replaced by hope.

The hope was based on faith in Robert Moses, or, more accurately, in the Moses mystique. East Tremont's pious Jews still held the campaign of 1934 against him—"I hated him since the time he said he wasn't Jewish," one says—but they still believed in his image as a man above politics and bureaucrats. Believing in that image, the people of East Tremont were sure that if they could only present Moses with an alternate route through their neighborhood that was truly better than the route he had chosen, he would accept it. And it did not take them very long to find out that such a route was indeed available.

Bronx Borough President James J. Lyons; Lyons' chief engineer, Moses' old Planning Commission ally Arthur V. Sheridan; and Sheridan's veteran aides had all been in on the laying out of the route Moses had chosen. But when the East Tremont committee asked for an appointment with Lyons, Lyons aide Charles F. Rodriguez recalls, "Lyons fobbed them off to Sheridan, and Sheridan fobbed them off to someone else"—and the someone else happened to be a recent addition to the staff named Edward J. Flanagan, who was, Rodriguez admits, "a capable engineer" but who had never, during a long engineering career, been associated with Moses and who was "very cocksure of himself" (by which Rodriguez apparently means he was not afraid to say what he thought). And when the housewives mentioned the possibility of an alternate route, Flanagan, without letting them finish, said of course there was, took out a pen, said, "There's no reason the route couldn't go this way," and sketched on a map before him the route through Crotona Park that was precisely what they had had in mind.

Flanagan was silenced—no one from East Tremont ever got an appointment with him again—but he had given the housewives conviction that the alternate route was feasible. The Bronx County Chapter of the New York State Society of Professional Engineers agreed to make a formal study of it. And one member of the society had enough experience with large-scale highway construction to do so—experience garnered working, indirectly, for Robert Moses. Bernard Weiner, a refugee with a heavy accent, was the brilliant engineer who, after working during the 1920's on the Westchester parkway system, had gone to work for Madigan-Hyland and designed, among other Moses projects, all the concrete bridges on the Circumferential Parkway—although he could not pronounce "Circumferential"—and the revolutionary three-span skew frame interchange that carries the Whitestone Expressway and Grand Central Parkway across each other in Queens.

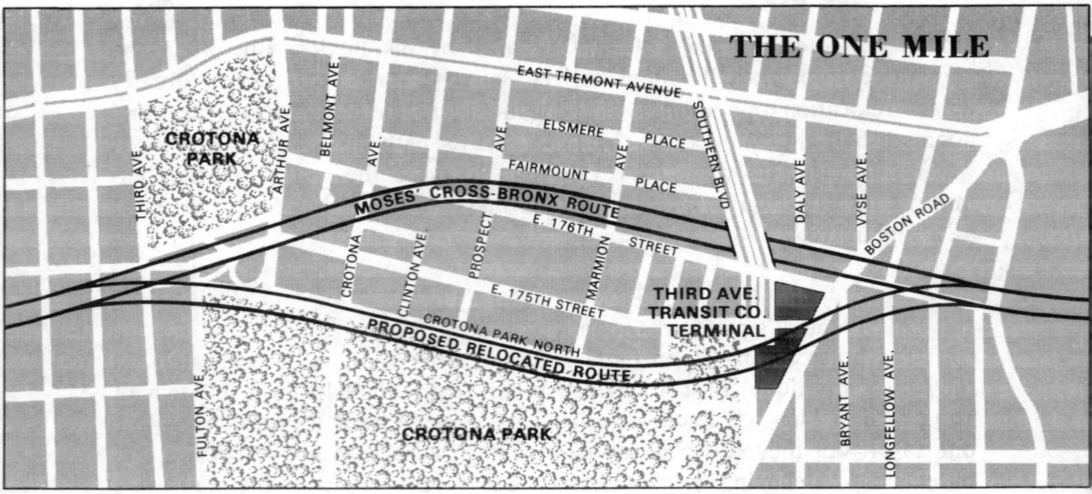

Then his independent outlook—he kept insisting that if Moses did not increase the grades on the Circumferential, it was going to flood in heavy rains—got him dropped from the team. Weiner, who had found it impossible, despite his experience and acknowledged brilliance, to get a good job since, had learned the price of opposing Moses, and he was not willing to pay it in full any more, but he was willing to pay part of it. When the Bronx Chapter asked him to do studies of the alternate route, he agreed only "on condition that I would be anonymous" (another engineer's name was signed to them), but he did do them—with his usual thoroughness, drawing up not just a sketch but a complete engineering study that demonstrated that the route through the park was not only feasible but met every federal and state standard for expressway design.

The arguments in favor of the park route were clear. By making only a gentle alteration in the road's route—swinging it just two blocks (one block in some places) to the south, 1,530 apartments would be saved at no cost to anyone: the road would not be made longer, its curves would not be made sharper—its efficiency as a traffic-moving device would not be harmed in the least. "We were happy then," recalls Lillian Edelstein. "We had been worried, but when we found there was a feasible alternate route, we figured we were in business." The arguments in favor of the alternate route were so clear. Believing in the myth of Moses, the housewives of East Tremont were sure he would accept them. And it wasn't until they tried to present them to him that panic set in again. For neither he nor any of his aides would even listen to those arguments. There would be no point in any meeting, Moses' office told Mrs. Edelstein when she telephoned after letters and telegrams had gone unanswered. The Coordinator had already decided on the route. It would not be changed.

Even then, East Tremont felt it had recourse. "I mean, we felt that Robert Moses might be powerful, but he wasn't the final say, was he?" says Mrs. Edelstein. Most of the money for the expressway was coming from the federal government. In some vague way they didn't understand, the state was involved, too. They had elected officials in the city to represent their views. The informal tenants' committee had by now become a formal group: ETNA, the East Tremont Neighborhood Association. And ETNA had found a leader.

Sam Edelstein's wife Lillian had never led anything. Ask her to describe herself and she says, "I was just a housewife"—and that was what she was, at thirty-nine a strikingly handsome one. But Lillian Edelstein had a big stake in the fight. Not only would she lose her apartment—which she loved and whose $56 rent she could afford even on the $75 per week Sam brought home from his job as a blocker of women's hats—if Moses' route was chosen, but her mother and her sister would lose their apartments, too: they all lived at 867 East 176th Street, Lillian in 2F, her sister in 3F, her mother in 3G. It was important to Lillian Edelstein that she be close to her mother. Her father had died just a little more than a year before, leaving Anna Cohen, born in Russia and able to speak English only haltingly, alone. It was all right as long as her children were close by. "But what if we were separated? What would Mom do?" And it was wonderful that she could be close to her sister—and to all the East Tremont girls with whom she had grown up. Her younger daughter, Janet, was only five, but her older girl, Carol, was fifteen and a junior at Roosevelt High School, and when she heard she might have to leave all her friends, she began to cry. "I was fighting for my home," Lillian Edelstein says. "And my mother. And sister. And daughter. I had a lot to fight for." In fighting she displayed not only energy and determination but an indefinable quality of command. Soon ETNA was turning to her for leadership, and she was providing it. She organized mass meetings and rallies and invited East Tremont's elected officials to them, and, refusing to be turned away by secretaries and assistants, secured appointments to talk to them in person.

And their reaction was encouraging. East Tremont's congressman, Isidore Dollinger, pledged his support. East Tremont's legislators, State Senator Jacob H. Gilbert and Assemblyman Walter H. Gladwin, pledged theirs. Most encouraging of all was the reaction of the city officials who would play the most direct role, not only of East Tremont's councilman, Bertha Schwartz, but of higher-ups, men who to these housewives had been only names in the newspapers—names they associated with enormous power. When ETNA's executive committee went down to City Hall for the first time, more than a little in awe of their surroundings, Comptroller Lazarus Joseph put them at their ease, told them that Moses' new highways "are making a jigsaw out the Bronx," said that their alternate route was certainly worthy of a full study, promised to vote against condemnation of their homes until such a study was made and said that if the study showed the alternate route to be feasible, he would vote for it. Borough President Lyons received the delegation "cordially and warmly," one member wrote. He promised that his engineering staff would make a formal study of the alternate route. "The delegation left feeling that he was very much on their side." Two weeks later, those feelings were seemingly confirmed. Lyons told the *Post* that his engineers had decided that the tenants' route was not only "humane" but "feasible," that it would "save the city money, and that he was in favor of it." Noting that Lyons had previously approved *his* route, Moses angrily charged that the borough president was raising objections now only because it was an election year and there was "local opposition." Any local hardship will be "mitigated," if not entirely removed, "by the elaborate steps which we have taken to move tenants in an orderly way into public, quasi-public and other housing," and should be disregarded anyway, he said. "This route will be the backbone of traffic for centuries after a few objecting tenants have disappeared from the scene. . . . You have from time to time remarked that I do not have to be elected to office. Perhaps that is why I am in a position to protect the really long-range public interest." He used his old threat—"Only recently you lost a substantial amount of . . . money in the Bronx" by "blocking the Bruckner Expressway"; the Cross-Bronx "will cost more than thirty million dollars additional. . . . Would you like to see the project, now half completed, abandoned and remaining state and federal monies spent elsewhere?"—and then escalated it by threatening to resign as Construction Coordinator ("I should not care to carry this responsibility any further if borough politics are to be injected into it"), but Lyons replied that any insinuation that he would allow himself to be influenced by the imminence of an election was "a damnable lie." "This is not Russia. Here we have democracy, and the people should be able to speak out in order to save their homes." Councilman Schwartz had told the tenants about the "Borough Presidents' Union," and they understood that, if Lyons stood firm, Moses' route would not be approved. And so it was with a sense of victory in a righteous cause that, on Thursday, April 23, 1953, more than two hundred East Tremont housewives—East Tremont husbands could not afford to lose a day's pay by skipping work—traveled by chartered buses down to City Hall, to hear the Board of Estimate decide whether to give Moses' draft damage maps the approval that would be the first step toward condemnation, and saw the Board members file out of a door on the raised platform—and then saw, striding out among them, right behind Mayor Impellitteri, the legendary Coordinator.

"He came in and everybody hushed," says Lillian Roberts, "even the men around the Board of Estimate. He wielded power, you could see, a powerful man and you could see it. Arrogant. The big 'I am. Me!' Chest out. He came out of the private room and stood behind the Mayor, and behind him were two of his men. And the way he talked to the Mayor! He practically ordered him around. And when it came time for him to talk" (Mrs. Roberts wrinkles up her face to indicate the disdain and scorn on Moses'): " 'This is going through, and this is going through, and that's all there is to that!' —that's the way he talked." Says Barney Lambert: "He *dominated*—it was like he had inherited a crown. This sense of superiority was there." It took Lillian Edelstein only a few moments to start losing the hopes with which she had come to City Hall. "Handsome, tall, dark—a distinguished-looking man he is. But a mean face. A mean person. When you looked at him, you saw he was a sour person. He looked right at us—like we were little people. He made you feel you were little. And then he looked away. A horrible man. He was talking to each one of the borough presidents. He had Lyons first. He had each one of them separately. And the horrible thing was they were all listening to him. Whispering. No one was listening to us when we talked. When we were up there [speaking], they talked among themselves or with their assistants. They're having a ball. You're talking and presenting your case, and they're laughing about something else. They didn't even have the courtesy to show an interest." She had pinned her hopes on her borough president, and his promise. Therefore, Lyons' statement surprised her. He favored Moses' route, the borough president said. He had always favored it.

Mrs. Edelstein was sitting beside Councilman Schwartz in the first row: "Everybody's poking me in the back and saying, 'Hey, Lil, what's going on here?' I said, 'I don't know.' I had reassured them—that was why they came down the way they did, because we had a possibility of winning. We had a meeting on Tuesday, and I said, 'Come down. He's with us. Show him we're behind him.' So I said to Bertha, I said, 'I think he's pulling a double-cross. Blast him.' She said, 'I can't, I'm a public official. But when you go up there, you blast him.' "

She did. At the conclusion of her short, carefully prepared speech at the lectern at which speakers stood, the housewife looked up, pointed at Lyons and said, "As for you, Mr. Lyons, I have this to say: You've double-crossed the people."

What happened then? "Flashbulbs. Impellitteri starts yelling, demanding that I apologize. I said I'm not apologizing." Jumping to his feet, red face redder than usual, Lyons bellowed that all he had promised the tenants was "a right to their day in court"; he had never, he said, given them any reason to believe he was on their side. Rudolph Halley then disclosed that the Board had held an executive session the day before at which Moses had been present—and that at that session Lyons had attempted to have the Board approve Moses' route secretly, so that the day in court would be meaningless. Whirling on the borough president, the Liberal Council President shouted: "Stop putting on a show!" "Demagogue!" Lyons shouted back.

The uproar changed nothing, of course. Halley and Joseph stuck by their promise to the tenants, and their six votes kept Moses from mustering the twelve necessary to approve the maps on initial submission, but at the Board's next meeting, a simple majority of its sixteen votes would suffice. Three hundred housewives showed up at that meeting, bringing a new nickname for Moses' route—"Heartbreak Highway"—and a copy of the Bronx engineering society's detail map of the alternative. Impellitteri announced that the Board's chief engineer, Robert G. McCullough, would "study" the map. McCullough must have been a quick studier indeed. Within a few minutes, he announced that the alternate route was "unfeasible." William Chapin pointed out to the Board that great sections of the Bronx had already been torn up for other sections of the expressway and for other highways, which, the Moses Man said, had been approved by federal and state governments on the premise that they were all part of a single system—of which the Cross-Bronx Expressway, with the route drawn by Moses, was a vital part. If the Board refused to approve the route, he said, Washington and Albany would refuse to put any more money into the expressway—or, possibly, into the other Bronx highways. State DPW chief Tallamy had already sent Moses a letter threatening to do just that. If there was no money, the highways would remain unbuilt, and "somebody will have to put the Bronx back together." Halley accused Chapin of trying, on Moses' behalf, to "blackmail" the Board. "Demagogue!" Lyons shouted again. By a vote of 10–6, Moses' route was approved.

"It was a farce," Lillian Roberts says. "It was like Mr. Moses runs the city."

Understanding this, when the housewives of East Tremont fought now, it was with a sense of desperation. The poverty of their community made fighting all the harder. Years later, an acquaintance casually remarked to Lillian Edelstein that another group of housewives, Central Park West housewives, had, in a battle over expansion of the Tavern-on-the-Green parking lot in 1956, won a victory over Robert Moses—and was startled to see the eyes of the tall, dignified woman filling with tears of remembered frustration. "Do you know why?" she said bitterly. "Because they had the money for an injunction, that's why."

Mrs. Edelstein had been informed at the very beginning of her fight that there were ample grounds for a full-scale legal, court battle, a battle which would, even if not successful in changing the expressway route, force the city to give tenants comparable new apartments. But, she was also informed, the legal fees could run to ten thousand dollars. Had a single one of the threatened tenants been a lawyer, with a personal interest in the case, legal help might have been available free, but not one was. In the Bronx of Ed Flynn and Charlie Buckley, there were no political dividends—and quite a few political disadvantages—to be reaped from opposing a project that Ed Flynn and Charlie Buckley favored. Several young attorneys did come forward with offers of legal assistance, but invariably their interest waned quickly.

Ten thousand dollars? Lillian Edelstein had difficulty raising amounts far smaller than that. "The feeling among people was, what's the use," explains Arthur Katz. "You can't lick City Hall. And even if you could, you certainly can't lick Robert Moses. We were told by the politicians we saw that when Robert Moses wanted his way, that was it. For a while at the start—with Lyons, when he promised—they had hope. But now . . ." "You'd think people would fight for their homes," says Saul Janowitz. But Mrs. Edelstein had to beg and plead to persuade families to chip in a dollar bill at a time, and each time the dollar bills were harder to come by.

Nonetheless, a small band fought. Most of its members were businessmen who knew the mass evictions of their customers would destroy their businesses, but it was more than businessmen. Among the men and women of East Tremont were the sons and daughters of the revolutionaries who had preached socialism and Zionism in the Pale of Settlement, and on the Lower East Side, and some of them hadn't lost their faith in justice. "At that time there were a lot of lefts around here," recalls Saul Janowitz.

But mostly, it was Lillian Edelstein who fought.

Finding engineers willing to defy Moses, the housewife put them to work drawing maps detailed enough to prove from every engineering standpoint that their route was technically feasible. Then she put them to work obtaining hard figures: exactly how much more Moses' mile would cost than theirs. When they came up with those figures—Moses' route would require the demolition of fifty-four apartment houses, ninety one- or two-family homes and fifteen one-story "taxpayers" housing sixty stores, for a total of 159 separate buildings; condemning and demolishing them would cost more than $10,000,000 more than would be required if the road ran where they wanted it to, even without the cost of relocating 1,530 families and the loss of the real estate taxes (close to $200,000 per year at current rates) from the demolished buildings, income the city would be losing year after year forever—she undertook the harder fight of bringing those maps and figures to the attention of the public and of public officials.

The press didn't help much. She took the maps to every daily newspaper in the city; exactly two—the *World-Telegram* and, of course, the *Post*—printed them. Only the *Post* displayed the figures with any prominence. She always found a sympathetic ear at the *Post*; Joe Kahn and Abel Silver dramatically documented the conditions in Section 3. But no other paper portrayed those conditions in any detail. The three papers that counted most in the city—the *Times,* the *Herald Tribune* and the *Daily News*—never mentioned them, and gave the whole Cross-Bronx Expressway fight scanty —and slanted—coverage. In attempting to enlist the support of other sections in the fight her own was making, she ran into the selfishness that Tallamy knew was one of Moses' greatest assets in New York (and that Moses of course fostered by releasing details of his projects only one section at a time). The East Tremont section of the Cross-Bronx Expressway—Section 2 —was the expressway's middle section. The eastern section—Section 3—had already been almost cleared. But there was a western section, Section 1. Another 1,413 families were scheduled to be displaced there for the expressway. But Section 1 might have been in South America for all the interest it showed in her pleas for support.

But she fought anyway. Teaching herself to type, she typed onto stencils and cranked out on the Y's mimeograph machine tens of thousands of handbills, as well as postcards and form letters to public officials. She persuaded the seven neighborhood movie theaters to show slides advertising the next rally or City Hall hearing. "They let us stand outside their lobbies for days with petitions and trying to raise money—we were grateful for that." She organized card parties—"Subscription $1." Learning that local radio stations such as WBNX were habitually in need of programs to fill up air time, she filled up that time with programs whose scripts she wrote herself.

It was Lillian Edelstein who arranged the rallies and mass meetings to pressure public officials, who chartered buses to take East Tremont housewives down to City Hall for every official hearing on the expressway. Most difficult of all, it was she who persuaded the housewives to take those buses. The people of East Tremont, who believed as gospel that "you can't fight

City Hall," had made one trip down to City Hall on the assurance that, if they went, they would win—and their loss had convinced them that the gospel was gospel. Trying to keep up enthusiasm, Lillian Edelstein scheduled weekly meetings at the Y but found that now, "if you got twelve tenants coming every week, you were lucky." As for spending more days traveling down to City Hall and sitting there for hours waiting for the Board of Estimate to get to the Cross-Bronx Expressway item, "that was torture," she says. "If the bus left at ten o'clock, at nine-thirty you had to go around and kick in the doors," Janowitz says. But, time after time, she kicked them. In an era in which picket lines in front of City Hall were not yet commonplace she even managed to have picket lines of middle-aged Jewish housewives marching outside City Hall, carrying signs she lettered herself at night.

And after a while, it appeared that Lillian Edelstein's efforts were paying off. For one key public official seemed to be listening.

During the committee's earlier interviews with members of the Board of Estimate, Robert F. Wagner, Jr., had appeared receptive; to their argument that motorists' convenience should not be put ahead of people's homes, the plump young Manhattan borough president had responded with a nod that seemed to indicate agreement, saying sincerely, "So they'll get to the Catskills twenty minutes faster." He had left the stormy public hearing early, leaving his two votes, two votes that, if added to Joseph's and Halley's, would have killed Moses' route, to be cast by his Borough Works Commissioner and key strategist, Warren Moscow. Although he had voted in favor of Moses' route, Moscow had stated before voting that although Wagner was voting for the first step toward condemnation, he would not vote for the last—authorization for the city actually to take title—until "every one" of the 1,530 families was properly relocated. Now, running hard for mayor, Wagner had Moscow put that promise in writing in several letters to ETNA and, on August 5, himself put in writing an even stronger promise. In a letter to ETNA signed by Wagner and released to the press, Wagner wrote:

> As you know, I have consistently taken the position that I would not vote for the acquisition of the property for the Cross-Bronx Expressway. I want to assure you that I will vote against any resolution before the Board of Estimate seeking to authorize acquisition of that property.

On October 14, he made the promise in person, repeating it in essentially the same words—"I will vote against any resolution"—to more than a thousand cheering and applauding East Tremont residents packed into the assembly room at PS 44 for one of Lillian Edelstein's rallies.

October 14, 1953, was quite a night for East Tremont. Lazarus Joseph, retiring as Comptroller, was present, and said movingly that "human values" were more important than a highway. The Democratic candidate for Joseph's position, the Bronx's own Lawrence Gerosa, agreed. Bertha Schwartz, running not for the Council this time but for a Municipal Court judgeship, moved the audience to cheers and delighted nods by reminding them of Moses' threat to resign and then slyly adding: "Well, no one is indispensable, you know." When Halley, Wagner's Liberal Party-backed opponent, vowed his determination to continue the "fight to save the homes," both of the two favorites for the mayoralty were firmly on record against Moses' route. "Wagner *promised*," Katz would recall. "There was nothing vague about that." It was no wonder that Lillian Edelstein was confident. Writing to thank Wagner, she said the tenants would like him to get together with the engineers who had drawn up the alternate route so he could see it was truly feasible. Why, certainly, Wagner replied—just as soon as the hubbub of the campaign was over. There seemed little reason to worry about a remark one of Joseph's aides had made to her as he stood beside her listening to the speeches: "Will they love you in December as they do in October?"

Wagner may have intended to keep his promise. According to at least one of the aides familiar with his thinking at the time, he did. Meeting with a few ETNA representatives shortly after the election, he repeated it—along with his crack about the Catskills. But Wagner was a politician who dealt in realities, and as mayor he was to have a better look than as borough president at the over-all realities governing politics in New York City. No mayor who wanted to continue his political career could buck Robert Moses, and Robert Wagner badly wanted to continue his political career. Just as Moses hadn't bothered bargaining with the new mayor on his Inauguration Day over the question of reappointment to the City Planning Commission, so Moses didn't bother bargaining with him now. He gave him a direct order. In his memoirs, Moses recalls what happened when Wagner protested that he had promised East Tremont that he would move the expressway.

> . . . I said, "I am sorry, Bob, but you will have to tell them you can't move it. The city is not going to make that decision. The city pays only half the cost of land. It is federal and state money that's involved and I represent these officials. If you try to move this Expressway you'll never get another nickel from us. You will have to explain that it was all a mistake."

Wagner was not a man to move quickly. It took him almost a year to come around. But he came around.

When, now, ETNA asked for the interview he had promised them, he was suddenly evasive. And when, finally, the housewives and storekeepers, awed, were ushered into the Mayor's office at City Hall and reminded him of his promise, Wagner, in Katz's words, "said he didn't remember saying exactly that, and he turned to someone and asked him to look it up." Recalls Lillian Edelstein: "He tried to tell me Robert Moses knows what he's doing because he's an engineer. We argued, and his aide said, 'Excuse me, Your Honor—he's not an engineer.' He was always the same —friendly, very polite, a good listener, he said he would look into it and let you know." But, says Katz, "we knew by the time we had left the office that he was not going to be supporting us." Halley and Joseph, East Tremont's allies, were gone from the Board of Estimate. Halley's replacement, Abe Stark of Brooklyn, indicated he would go along with whatever Moses and the Mayor wanted. Gerosa, of the Bronx Chamber of Commerce, "as a public official seemed less dynamic than Gerosa as a businessman," Katz was to write. "As far as the . . . Tenants Committee was concerned, he seemed never to have heard of them." Bertha Schwartz, a Municipal Court judge now, was no longer active in politics. Lyons would not grant them another audience. They had no one to whom they could turn.

Proceedings dragged, however. Possibly because Wagner, in his anxiety for election, had made a rare, flat promise and Joe Kahn persisted in reminding the *Post*'s readers of it—once reprinting prominently the letter stating "I will vote against any resolution . . . seeking to authorize acquisition of that property," in other stories conceding that while Wagner had sometimes modified that promise by stating only that he would not vote for acquisition until all tenants had been relocated, so far no tenants had been relocated. Possibly because Wagner, taking even a cursory look at the problem now, could not understand what the tenants could not understand: why the route couldn't be changed—at one hearing before the Board of Estimate, when Moses Man Hodgkiss was answering all questions about the possible route change by saying flatly and arrogantly, "It's impossible," the Mayor, with an unusual overtone of irritation in his normally placid tones, demanded curtly: "*Why* is it impossible?" (Hodgkiss replied that Moses felt "it's just impossible"; Wagner did not press the point.) Possibly because the state had temporarily run out of highway funds, so that no new contracts could be let—and Wagner therefore had both an excuse to offer the Coordinator for not speeding relocation proceedings as well as an opportunity to allow the exact wording of promises to grow a little vague in the public's mind. A key element was the attitude of the aide the Mayor had delegated to deal with the tenants, Deputy Mayor Henry Epstein, a distinguished attorney and older man whom the Mayor respected. Epstein—a former Moses ally for philosophical, not financial, reasons—now, moved by the tenants' plight, made the mistake of making his own survey of the two proposed routes. There was, he told Wagner, not the slightest rational reason why the expressway could not be moved over two blocks.

The City Planning Commission gave the tenants the type of public hearing that might have been expected from a body controlled by a man who, if given his way, would have abolished public hearings. A large delegation had taken the day to ask the commission not to approve the Moses route—a long day. Commission chairman John J. Bennett, at that moment secretly negotiating a Title I transaction for which he needed that man's approval, refused to let even one tenant speak, saying that no public hearing was required. But there was a whole series of hearings before the Board of Estimate. Sometimes Moses was present himself. "He always looked surprisingly young and vigorous," Katz recalls. "He was very cool and detached. He didn't say anything. He had his assistants to do the talking for him. He sat and listened. He made some notes. My greatest anger at him was that he didn't seem to be affected by all this—people were getting up and telling these stories of hardship." But, despite Moses' presence, the Board kept postponing a final vote on his request to have the city authorize condemnation proceedings. After an emotional meeting with the ETNA group and several Bronx councilmen in Wagner's office at which the Mayor was visibly moved (and at which he said, "Every member of the Board will want to know the difficulties facing each family in the path of the expressway"), the Mayor interrupted one Board session—at which Moses had confidently expected the issue to be resolved—to order McCullough, who had done a "study" of the tenants' alternate route for Impellitteri in a matter of minutes, to give it a little more consideration. The engineer returned a month later with a report stating that while the alternate route would spare the protesters' homes, it would require the condemnation of almost as many homes belonging to other people. You see, Moses told the Board, it was just as he was always trying to explain to them: changing a route would just "trade in" one group of protesters for another; no matter where you tried to build a highway in the city, there would be protests, so the only way to handle them was to ignore them. ETNA's leaders, who had been certain that not a single home would have to be touched for the alternate route they had proposed, were shocked by McCullough's findings—until they realized the trick that the engineer had played. He had studied an alternate route, all right, but not *their* alternate route. Instead, he had selected a route that would require large-scale condemnation and studied that instead. Epstein explained this to Wagner. Over Hodgkiss' violent objections, the Mayor ordered McCullough to study the right alternate route this time, to let Epstein oversee the study to make sure it was fair, and to complete the study before the Board's next meeting when a final decision would be made.

"A defeat for Moses," the *Post* reported. The tenants felt it was. "We felt we had won," Lillian Edelstein recalls. Epstein, trying to reassure her, had told her, in her words, "It's like a jury trial. If they stay out long enough, they won't convict you. Because it was dragging so—month after month, I figured something is happening to hold him and his crew."

On the day of the final hearing before McCullough, assembled in his office in the Municipal Building was a full panoply of Moses Men: Arthur S. Hodgkiss, assistant general manager of the Triborough Bridge and Tunnel Authority; Stuart Constable, acting executive officer of the New York City Department of Parks; W. Earle Andrews and Ernest J. Clark of Andrews, Clark and Buckley, consulting engineers; Milton Goul, district engineer, State Department of Public Works District Number 10, designated to represent the State Department of Public Works by Bertram Tallamy, Superintendent; Arthur B. Williams, liaison engineer, New York State Department of Public Works—and, representing Lyons, Edward J. Flanagan, who, during the entire proceedings, would utter not one word. These engineers and a dozen assistants had been assembled for the occasion on the orders of Robert Moses.

Moses had been active in other ways, too. He had no doubt that Wagner would fall into line—years later, asked if there had been no chance at all that the Mayor would overrule him, he would, with a touch of surprise in his voice that it should be necessary to ask such a question, say flatly, "Not the slightest"—but Epstein was delaying the Mayor's compliance with his marching orders. The Deputy Mayor had to be whipped into line. During the week before the McCullough hearing, he was.

Arriving at 10:30 A.M., the time they had been told the meeting would start, the five engineers representing the tenants were surprised to find it already under way. McCullough, they noted, seemed "very uncomfortable." Although there were fifteen Moses engineers in his office, the city engineer said that he would allow in only two of theirs, backing down only after an angry protest.

Having learned something about Moses' methods, the tenants had hired a court reporter to make a verbatim transcript. Convinced that any reasons given for turning down their alternate route could easily be disproved, they wanted once and for all not only to find out what those reasons were but to get them on the record. McCullough ordered the reporter out of the room. Angrily the ETNA engineers demanded to know why, pointing out that the city engineer had his own stenotypist present, and that they were entitled to their own record. McCullough refused to give a reason. (Later, in his official report of the proceedings, he said, "We were holding an engineering conference and not a public meeting"; his own stenotypist, he said, would record any "pertinent facts which might develop.") "We said, 'If you're telling the truth, you should have no objection to its being recorded,' " one ETNA engineer recalls. They refused to participate in the meeting unless their reporter was allowed to be present; McCullough said flatly that there would be no meeting as long as the reporter remained in the room. The ETNA engineers asked him to get a ruling from Epstein. Certainly, McCullough said. He telephoned the Deputy Mayor—and to their shock Epstein ruled that they had no right to have a reporter present.

The ETNA engineers held a hasty huddle.

"We were afraid to go on the record without a stenographer," one, Leonard Swarthe, would say. "It seemed peculiar that [the] others seemed to be afraid of" having what they said set down in black and white; "it was obvious the cards were stacked," said Daniel J. O'Connell. They decided to walk out. Once they were safely gone, the meeting was held—"as scheduled," McCullough blandly stated in his report to Wagner—and its participants arrived at the conclusion that "the original plan was the only acceptable one" and that it would be "impossible to accept the alternate route," a conclusion which may possibly be explained by the fact that the Moses Men again managed to avoid discussing the true—ETNA—alternate route by discussing again the phony "alternate" Moses had put out as a smoke screen.

(Epstein was soon to give the tenants who had trusted him another shock. Repeatedly, month after month, after carefully examining the two routes, the Deputy Mayor had said theirs was the better. Now, he suddenly changed his mind—and he put his new opinion in writing in a letter to Wagner.)

The tenants sent a telegram to Wagner appealing for an engineering discussion under "proper circumstances." There was no reply—and of the showdown Board of Estimate meeting, Katz was to write:

> Dr. Swarthe reported the results of the fiasco in the City Engineer's office. The Board was silent. They made no comment. They permitted all to talk. They made no interruptions or comments, asked no questions. The Mayor set a

time limit for public debate and, at the end of it, called for the question . . . for acquisition of funds to acquire property and for building demolition.

Lyons moved the question, saying, "This is an engineer's problem, not a layman's problem, and all the engineers unanimously support this route." One by one the Board members voted—in the affirmative. The last man to vote was Robert F. Wagner, Jr. He voted in the affirmative, too.

"It was so fast," Lillian Edelstein would recall years later. "I was positive at that last hearing that we would win. Because of Wagner. He had said so straight out that he would never let them do it. He had *promised.*" Lillian Edelstein wanted to ask the Mayor what care had been taken for the families, what the relocation plans were. But she couldn't. She was crying. Katz asked instead. Lyons tried to stop him from speaking, but he went ahead anyway. Quoting Wagner's words that he would not vote for acquisition until he had been satisfied as to the relocation plans, he asked the Mayor what those plans were. The Mayor said he did not know.

Turning to Hodgkiss, Wagner asked about the plans. Hodgkiss said a new approach had been decided on: instead of the city's own Real Estate Bureau handling the job, it had been decided to let the job to a private firm, the "highly efficient" Nassau Management Company, Inc. As Katz was to write: "The Mayor was assured that there would be few problems and that all families would be well provided for."

Mayor Wagner asked [Katz] if this was satisfactory. [He] said no. [Katz] asked the Coordinator's representative if that office would publicly agree to meet with the tenants' committee as a group and instruct the Relocation Bureau to do the same, if the need arose to resolve problems. The Coordinator's representative pledged to do so. Wagner, at any time of difficulty in resolving problems around relocation, wanted the tenants' committee to know that they could personally call upon the Mayor's office to help. He made this last statement for the record.

And why did Henry Epstein change his mind, and, at the very last moment, betray the neighborhood which had counted on him for support?

Years later—Epstein long dead now, his widow not even knowing what the author was talking about when he raised the subject of her late husband's change of mind—Robert Moses, sitting in a cottage he had rented at Oak Beach, staring out the big window from which one could see the Robert Moses Causeway and Robert Moses State Park, would be asked that question.

Charm flooded away from that window. Dressed in the L. L. Bean corduroys, a larger size now to cover the ample paunch, and an old button-down plaid shirt, the papers that signified completed work already piled high by his armchair although it was only 9:30 A.M., a big cabin cruiser waiting down the Ocean Parkway at the Captree Basin for an afternoon's fishing, he was the easy and gracious host. The powerful face—still so young at eighty—was relaxed. Oh, that's not important, he said easily. Let's talk about something else.

The author said he had come to talk about Henry Epstein. The expression changed only slightly, the head swung just a little, but all of a sudden the author saw not the paunch but the big shoulders and the big jaw and, beneath the big eyebrows, the eyes. Then he could see Robert Moses remember that the author was a guest in his home. Moses began to talk, seemingly at a tangent, at first choosing his words, with pauses, and then, warming up, as fast and fluid as usual.

"It happened to be a very, very complicated thing. . . . A lot of personal stuff got into it. . . . They had a couple of agitators up there . . . including a woman who was running for judge . . . and Epstein got personal and nasty about it and he finally got licked. . . . I said, 'This woman, this chum of yours.' He said, 'She's not my chum.' I said, 'Oh, yes she is. She's your chum all right.' I said, 'What's going to happen if we change the route—which we'll never do as long as I'm alive—we'll just be turning in these objectors for another set.' And you know what he said? He said, 'Well, that's in the next district [not Miss Schwartz's].' He made an issue of it with the Mayor to see who had more influence. . . ."

He stopped as if that was all there was to say. The author prodded him.

"Epstein was a very able lawyer," Moses said. "Outstanding lawyer. I had known him a long time."

Well, the author said, prodding some more, he did write that letter saying your route was best.

"Sure," Moses said. "After he was hit over the head with an ax."

What kind of an ax? the author asked. What exactly did you do to him? But there are limits to even a host's obligations. "I won't tell you what we did to him," Robert Moses said.

Reviewing the conversation carefully, however, it is possible to wonder if—without meaning to—Robert Moses had.

About the Cross-Bronx Expressway as a whole, Moses was more expansive. Asked if he had not felt a sense of awe—of difficulties of a new immensity—when, beginning active planning of the great road during the war, he had first seen the miles of apartment houses in his way, he said he had not. "There are more houses in the way [than on Long Island]," he said, "there are more people in the way—that's all. There's very little real hardship in the thing. There's a little discomfort and even that is greatly exaggerated. The scale was new, that was all that was new about it. And by this time there was the prospect of enough money to do things on this scale." Asked if he had ever feared that the tenants might defeat him, he said, "Nah, nobody could have stopped it." As a matter of fact, the East Tremont opposition hadn't really been much trouble at all.

"I don't think they were too bad," Robert Moses said. "It was a political thing that stirred up the animals there. Jim Lyons didn't know which way to turn. But I just stood pat, that's all."

New York's press also didn't see much significance in the East Tremont fight. The *Post* gave it complete coverage, of course, and the *World-Telegram* occasionally devoted a fairly detailed story to it, but, aside from Moses' single personal appearance before the Board of Estimate (on the occasion of which the *Times* put his picture on page one), the rest of the city's big dailies all but ignored it. When they did devote space to it—a paragraph or two at the bottom of a round-up of Board activities—the attitude they displayed is of interest. This, for example, was the *Times*'s description of the final, climactic hearing at which Lillian Edelstein sat crying in City Hall.

> Five years of opposition and delay to the Cross-Bronx Expressway came to an end when the Board of Estimate unanimously voted to acquire land for a one-quarter [sic] mile segment of the middle section. The fight put up by the tenants resulted in a virtual stalling of the overall Cross-Bronx Expressway project, since the two ends of the artery are now finished.

Why *wouldn't* Moses shift the route of the Cross-Bronx Expressway slightly, thereby saving 1,530 apartments, millions in state and city money, months of aggravation and delay—and making his expressway straighter as well?

"I asked George Spargo that," says Joseph Ingraham, the *Times* reporter who was occasionally on Moses' payroll and who spent so much time socializing with the Moses team that he sometimes seemed to be one of its members. "On the day of the ribbon cutting they were opening a whole bunch of sections of different expressways, and it was raining, really pouring. George said, 'Let's sit this out, and we'll catch up to them at the next stop.' We went into a small bar in the Bronx and I asked him there. He said, 'Oh, one of Jimmy Lyons' relatives owns a piece of property up there and we would have had to take it if we used that other route, and Jimmy didn't want it taken, and RM had promised him we wouldn't.' At the time, George even told me the piece of property involved, but I've forgotten."

The people of East Tremont also wondered why Moses wouldn't shift the route. "I mean, we heard lots of rumors about the bus terminal," Lillian Edelstein recalls. "The politicians were always trying to tell us that was the reason. But we could never find out anything about it. And, I mean, I never believed that. I could never believe that even Robert Moses would take fifteen hundred homes just to save a bus terminal."

Spargo's statement may have been untrue. So may the rumors. If any relative of Bronx Borough President James J. Lyons owned property along either the alternate or actual expressway route, the author was unable to find evidence of that fact—although, since, in the Bronx, politicians' ownership of property was habitually concealed through a many-layered network of intermediaries and bag men, a network baffling even to contemporary investigators and all but impenetrable twenty years later, his failure is not conclusive. Moses' refusal to alter the route—unexplainable on the basis of his given reasons, all of which are demonstrably false—may have had nothing to do with the fact that the "bus terminal" of which Lillian Edelstein speaks —actually the "Tremont Depot" of the Third Avenue Transit Company, at the northeast corner of Crotona Park—lies in the path of the alternate route and would have had to be condemned if that route was adopted. It is possible that Moses' selection of the original route—it was he, not any engineer, who selected it—was based on no more than whim, and that his subsequent refusal to alter it was due to nothing more than stubbornness, although if so it was a whim quite inconsistent with Moses' customary whims: almost invariably over a period of forty years, whenever he had a choice of routes, he selected the one that would keep his road straight, not the one that would make the road curve.

However, in attempting to find an explanation for Moses' refusal to change the route, the Third Avenue Transit depot stands out. With the exception of six old, small, dilapidated brownstone tenements, housing a total of nineteen families, it was the only structure of any type that would have had to be condemned if the alternate route was used. (See map, page 864.) In effect, for whatever reason, Robert Moses elected to tear down 159 buildings housing 1,530 families instead of tearing down six buildings housing nineteen families—and the terminal. It is a fact that the Third Avenue Transit Company secretly told Moses it was very anxious not to have the terminal condemned, for its location was strategic for its buses. And it is also a fact that for twenty years it was considered an open secret in Bronx political circles that key borough politicians held large but carefully hidden interests in Third Avenue Transit. And it is also a fact that, in Bronx politics of the period, what Third Avenue Transit wanted, Third Avenue Transit got.

But the unfortunate element in searching for the explanation of Moses' refusal is that in the perspective of the history of New York City it is unimportant. Whether Moses refused to change the route for a personal or political reason, the point is that his reason was the only one that counted. Neighborhood feelings, urban planning considerations, cost, aesthetics, common humanity, common sense—none of these mattered in laying out the routes of New York's great roads. The only consideration that mattered was Robert Moses' will. He had the power to impose it on New York.

"Highly efficient" was the only description of the Nassau Management Company given at the Board of Estimate hearing. A more detailed description would have been instructive.

Nassau Management had been founded three years before on a shoestring with virtually no financial resources behind it. But it was almost immediately to obtain immense tenant relocation contracts for several Robert Moses highway and housing projects. One contract alone netted the firm more than two million dollars.

The men who owned stock in Nassau Management thus made fortunes without risking more than a token investment. The ostensible key men behind the company—its founders of record—were two low-echelon City Housing Authority employees who quit the Authority to form the firm. But they were only front men. The key figures behind Nassau Management, men who would profit from the relocation of the East Tremont tenants,

Emanuel and Bella Moses

Robert Moses in front of his boyhood home on Dwight Street in New Haven

Yale Senior Council, 1909. Far left, Robert Moses.

Yale Swimming Team, 1907–1908. Robert Moses, top row center.

1934

Circa 1936

The candidate with his wife Mary and his daughter Jane, 1934.

With Mary, 1956

1938

1948

© ARNOLD NEWMAN

The Power Broker

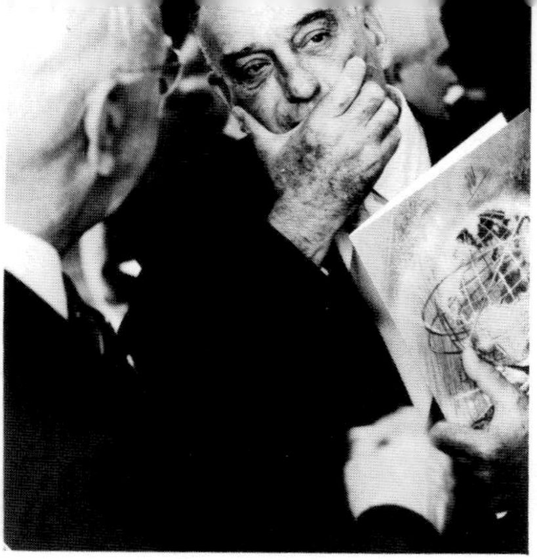

1963

1963

1960

With Mary II, circa 1969

On the St. Lawrence, 1958

In his Randall's Island office, with the Triborough toll plaza in the background, 1960's.

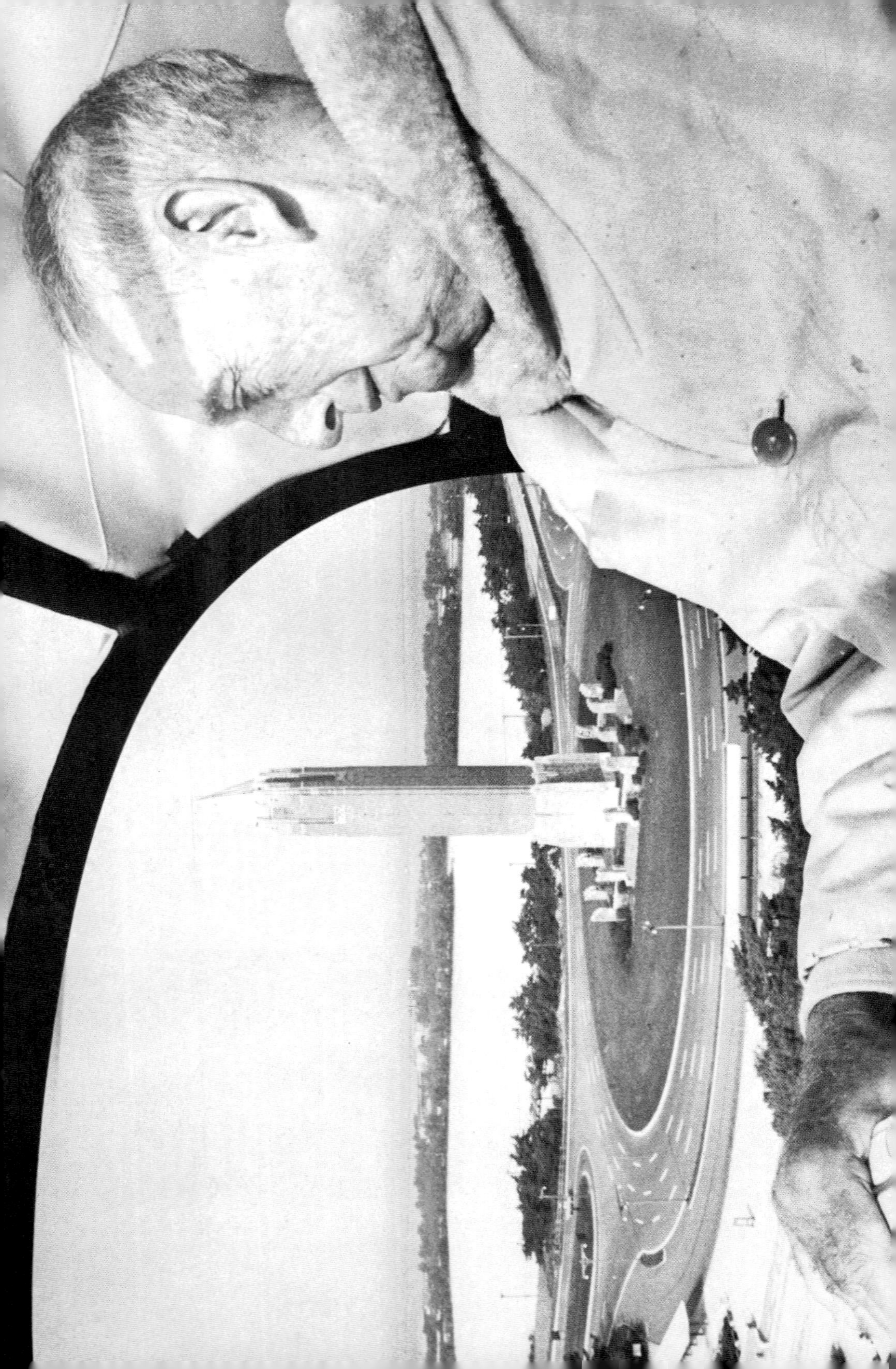

were William S. Lebwohl, counsel of the Triborough Bridge and Tunnel Authority; Samuel Brooks, assistant director of the Mayor's Slum Clearance Committee; and Housing Authority chairman Philip J. Cruise—three of Moses' key aides.

FIRST MAN: *After a lifetime, a piece of paper, an edict from the authorities, and we must all leave our homes.*

MENDEL: *Rabbi, we've been waiting for the Messiah all our lives. Wouldn't this be a good time for him to come?*

RABBI: *We'll have to wait for him someplace else. Meanwhile, let's start packing.*

—FIDDLER ON THE ROOF

It must have been an accident that the "East Tremont" office opened by the "highly efficient" Nassau Management Company was located not in East Tremont but in West Farms, another neighborhood, inconveniently far away for the 1,530 families the office was supposed to serve. It must have been an accident that the office was open only a few hours a day, that those hours were constantly changing, that no notice was ever given of what those hours were going to be, and that inquiring about them by telephone was almost impossible since the single phone number listed for the office seemed to be always busy—so that often East Tremont housewives, having made the long trek over to West Farms, found waiting for them only a locked door. It must have been an accident that there were never enough company representatives in the office, so that the housewives waiting for help had to wait on long lines.

But East Tremont's housewives soon found, as one put it: "They didn't want to help you, they just wanted you out. And they wanted you out fast." A series of incentives was placed before the tenants to accomplish this end. On her first trip to the office, a housewife was not offered any help in finding a new home. Instead, she was told that if Nassau Management had to find her one, she would receive only a hundred dollars for moving expenses, far less than would be needed to cover those expenses. If she found one herself, she was told, she would receive a hundred dollars for each room in her present apartment. If she found one *fast,* she was told, she would receive a flat "fee" of eight hundred dollars. And if she found one *real fast*, she would get not only eight hundred dollars but reimbursement for moving expenses—actual moving expenses. It was only if you refused to accept these incentives and insisted on the help that had been promised that you were given two cards, each bearing an address of an "available" apartment—"comparable" to the one you now occupied.

"I went to one," a housewife recalls. "This was in the West Bronx. It was a walkup—four flights of stairs. The apartment was on the top floor. And there was already a line there of women that had been sent over. People were standing on the staircase—all down the four flights—and outside. What was the sense of standing on line? If the apartment was decent at all, someone else would have taken it. What was the sense of sending hundreds of women to look at one darn apartment? I went home."

Lillian Roberts waited on such a line. "When I finally got to the apartment, it wasn't comparable at all. It was so dark and crummy. It was only three rooms, and I had told them I had four. And they wanted twice as much rent as I was paying. For that filthy thing! I still remember it. Horrible. I wouldn't go back to that office again." Some housewives were so desperate that they did go back. Women who would never have believed that they would ever be in such a position found themselves standing around a bare storefront office, hour after hour, day after day—"like beggars," one says bitterly—hoping that someone would give them a home.

Sometimes, when a woman got to the address Nassau Management had given her, there was no one around to let her in. If she was lucky enough to find a superintendent or a janitor, he sometimes told her that the apartment was not vacant—hadn't been for months. Back they went, day after day, from the apartments they had been sent to see in the West Bronx or Riverdale or Throgs Neck, back to the Nassau Management office and then out again in a search of something they knew now they were never going to find. "I remember that winter," says one of those women. "I got old that winter."

If you still refused to accept either the apartments that were offered or the cash, other incentives were applied.

"As soon as the city took over, the superintendents moved out," Lillian Edelstein recalls. "They got other jobs. You couldn't blame them. But you couldn't get any kind of services. The halls got dirty. There was garbage to take out. . . . I went to fight," Mrs. Edelstein says, but Nassau Management said the city Real Estate Bureau was responsible for maintaining the buildings. The tenants protested to the Real Estate Bureau, but the only result, as Mrs. Edelstein recalls it, "was that they assigned one man to take care of six or eight buildings, and soon he was gone, too." And always the final answer was that on all matters pertaining to the Cross-Bronx Expressway the "final say" had to come from Robert Moses. Katz had asked Moses' representative "if that office would publicly agree to meet with the tenants' committee . . . if the need arose to resolve problems," and Hodgkiss had made that agreement. Now they called Moses and Hodgkiss. "We never even got a reply." They telephoned Wagner's office. Wagner had "wanted the tenants' committee to know they could personally call upon the Mayor's office to help." "Ah, we never got him on the phone, or anyone else but a secretary," one ETNA member says. "They started bouncing us back and forth to the agencies again."

The city formally took title to the 159 buildings in Section 2 on

January 1, 1954. Almost simultaneously, the heat and hot water in many of the buildings was mysteriously cut off. Eleven days later—eleven days of getting the same run-around from the city, and the same lack of response from Moses' office—they told their story to the *Post*. The *Post* got an answer from Benjamin Cymrot, executive officer of the Real Estate Bureau ("Repairs take time, and we are working as quickly as we can. . . . Essential services" will be maintained), but Cymrot's definition of "essential services" was evidently different from the tenants'. For many of them—for much of the winter—the only warmth in their apartments was provided by the little, inadequate electric heaters they purchased themselves, or by gas ranges they kept turned on all the time, and the only hot water was the water they heated in pots. There were a few desultory attempts at repairs, but many of the buildings had no heat or hot water for weeks at a time. One had none for three straight months.

Incentive to get out was provided also by mortification of the mind. "[Nassau Management] said they were only obligated to show you two apartments," Mrs. Edelstein recalls. "If you turned down two apartments that they offered you, they said they were through with you. They said either you get out on your own, or they dispossess you. They said they'd put you out in the street." The threat was backed up by dispossess notices, all designed to look like court orders although they were not, each couched in language more urgent and ominous than the last. On May 1, a Friday, every tenant remaining in the area received one ordering him to vacate or be evicted by the end of the month. After a weekend of hysteria, a tenants' committee accompanied by Councilman Louis Peck was able to see Percy Gale, director of the city Real Estate Bureau. Luckily for them they had brought a *Post* reporter along; Gale hastily explained that the notices were only "a necessary legal prerequisite" (to what he didn't say) and that "no one will be evicted if they do not vacate at the end of thirty days."

The escalation of incentives produced the desired results. More than a thousand of the 1,530 families had stuck it out through the terrible winter because the alternatives were so shattering. "What choices did most of them have?" Lillian Edelstein asks. "Either to move to apartments for the same rent they were paying—which meant for most of them moving to the slums—or to move above their means, which would be a great, great hardship for these people." In the spring, however, they began to move out faster and faster.

The old people clung hardest. "They were the ones I really felt sorry for," Lillian Roberts says. These were very poor old people—Social Security had come too late for many of them—and many of them were alone in their little apartments, the parents or wives or husbands who had come with them from the little *shtetls* of their youth gone now. "There were a lot of widows in East Tremont." But as long as they could stay in their tiny apartments—on the first or second floor, mostly, because stairs are hard on old people—they had something: the Senior Citizens program at the Y, familiar places to sit and stroll in the sun and, most important, companionship. If they had to move, they would have nothing. Impoverished elderly couples were eligible for apartments in City Housing Authority projects. But although there were at the time a number of Authority projects under construction, the Authority's Moses-dominated board was deaf to these couples' pleas that a substantial number of them be allowed to move into the same project, so that they could stay together. Couples eligible for apartments in projects had no choice but to take them; they could not afford decent living accommodations anywhere else. Impoverished elderly men and women who were alone in the world were not eligible for Authority projects; the Moses-controlled Authority made no provision for single people. Such men and women had no chance at all to stay together. "Do you know how poor they were?" Lillian Roberts says. "They didn't have the carfare to visit each other." The old people of East Tremont were terribly frightened of moving. But Robert Moses had made certain they would be more frightened of staying. One by one, faster and faster, the old people moved out, too. By June, half the 1,530 apartments were vacant.

Their emptiness made possible the application of new incentives.

"As soon as the top floor of a building was empty, they'd start tearing off the roof and the top stories, even," says Mrs. Edelstein. "While people were still living in it, they were tearing it down around their heads!" As soon as an apartment was vacated, moreover, its windows were boarded up, which advertised to vandals defenseless premises available for the plundering. Watchmen were apparently a luxury neither the city nor Nassau Management could afford. The other tenants could hear the vandals at night, tearing the plumbing out of the walls for money, ripping the boards off the windows and breaking the glass for sheer malice, throwing bricks and other debris off the roofs to hear the crash when they hit the ground. "Then," Mrs. Lucille Silverstein says, "started the muggings." Soon the people living in those half-empty buildings—lonely, scared, many of them old and alone—weren't safe in their own lobbies or on the flights of stairs which suddenly seemed terribly long and dark. Terror, that most efficient of eviction agents, stalked through that boarded-up, half-empty neighborhood.

Along that mile, now, most of the one- and two-family frame houses had been demolished. As the demolition crews worked, they had piled the lumber they were tearing apart in the back yards of those houses, and when they left, they had left the lumber there in piles twenty-five and thirty feet high, stacked as if for a bonfire. Soon, thanks to vandals, the bonfires blazed and the remaining apartment houses stood not only among these heaps of lumber but among gaping, debris-filled pits, some thirty feet deep—the basements of what had once been other apartment houses. Into one, someone had driven an automobile, and it lay there, stripped and abandoned, for months. To mark the site of other apartment houses there were jagged-topped brick walls, ten or twelve feet high, and the space between those walls was filled with bricks, sharp-edged shafts of steel and shards of broken glass. "The rats were running like dogs and cats in the street," Lillian Edelstein says. So thick was the grime hurled in clouds into the air by the demolition that Dominick Tesone, hanging desperately on to his three-family frame house, spoke of living in "dust storms."

Unsupervised children walked single-file along the tops of those brick walls, trying, as children do, to see who could keep longest from falling—but if they fell, it was onto those shafts and shards. There were no fences around those gaping pits; parents lived in fear that their kids would fall into them. One mother, who normally picked her two little boys up at school every day, was late one day, and, hurrying along the route they took home, saw them jumping back and forth across a hole in the street. Rushing up to them, she saw that the hole was perhaps twenty feet deep.

The people still left along the mile were the last holdouts against what they regarded as injustice. Tesone was informed that he could receive only $11,000 for his three-family frame house because Moses had established that as the price for all the frame buildings along that mile. "They gave $11,000 for a one-family shack, they gave the same to all the houses along the way," Tesone says. "Mine was a good house. It wasn't fair." The appraisal he commissioned set its value at $18,000; the city representative said that appraisal might well be fair, but that didn't matter; $11,000 was the price. Tesone had hired a lawyer and was going to fight on. Other people were still left along the mile because they had no place else to go. The family with eleven children, for example, had been unable to find any landlord—at any price—who would give them an apartment. The City Housing Authority had promised them one, but kept saying that no apartment large enough was yet available. The people who were left were still hoping that the city, and Robert Moses, would keep the promises they had made.

They tried to protest. They called the city agencies pleading that watchmen be assigned to the area, and that fences be erected to keep children from falling into the pits. Surely, they said, with hundreds of workmen in the area, a few could be spared to put up fences. But always, after being shunted from one agency to another, they were eventually told that the State Department of Public Works was in charge of all physical arrangements in the area, and when they called the State DPW, the answer was that while the DPW was technically in charge, the actual work was being carried out under the direction of the City Construction Coordinator, and he was the only one who could help them. And when they called the Coordinator's office, they were never able to speak to anyone except secretaries who told them that someone would call back, and no one ever did. Water and electricity were suddenly and mysteriously cut off and when, after protests to city agencies were publicized by the *Post,* they were restored, they were suddenly and mysteriously cut off again. Tesone's home shared a fire wall with the adjoining building. One day, while Tesone was still living on one side of that wall, demolition began on the house on the other side of that wall. He could see his wall being weakened by vibrations. "One day, it'll come right down on us," he said. Telling his lawyer to drop his appeal, he moved out.

And always, there were the threats. Speed was essential, the Nassau Management Company kept saying. Work on the expressway itself was going to begin any day. And as soon as it did, anyone left in the area would be put out in the street with no further warning. "That was all I heard," one holdout remembers. "If you don't get out, we'll put you out in the street." Out in the street! Out in the street! As the Tsar had harried them—or their fathers or their grandfathers—out of the *shtetls* of the Pale, the Coordinator harried them out of East Tremont. By November, the Nassau Management Company could proudly announce: "In less than ten months, we have relocated 90 percent of the 1,530 occupants of Section 2."

38. *One Mile (Afterward)*

AFTER THE TENANTS had been rushed out of their homes, it turned out that there had been no real need to rush after all.

To obtain the initial state consent to build the Cross-Bronx Expressway, Moses had, as usual, drastically underestimated its cost—which inflation was pushing higher by the month, anyway. By the time—November 1955—that Nassau Management boasted that almost all the tenants were gone, so was almost all the state's highway construction fund, which had to bear half the expressway's cost. Passage of a referendum authorizing a new bond issue for highways would, in 1956, give the state another $400,000,000, but the state was not anxious to spend this new money on the Cross-Bronx: with congestion on Moses' Bronx-Whitestone Bridge worsening, by 1955 he was allocating Triborough funds for another, Throgs Neck, span on the east and the expressway would have to be extended eastward to reach it; with congestion on the George Washington Bridge at the expressway's western end also worsening, and with two intersecting Moses expressways already under construction (the Sheridan, named after engineer Arthur Sheridan, and the Bruckner, named after long-time Bronx borough president Henry Bruckner) obviously going to dump even more traffic onto the Cross-Bronx, it was apparent even before its tragic mile through East Tremont had been cleared that traffic on the Cross-Bronx was going to be immensely heavier than expected—too heavy to possibly be accommodated on the old Washington (not the George) Bridge (constructed in 1888 under the sponsorship of George Washington Plunkitt), on which the road had been expected to cross the Harlem River. Moses decided to build a new bridge—the Alexander Hamilton—right next to the Washington. Designing the expressway extension and the Hamilton Bridge—particularly the bridge, for immense curls of cloverleaf spaghetti would be required to link it to the Deegan and Harlem River highways flanking the river more than a hundred feet below—would take an estimated eighteen months. Obviously, the Cross-Bronx Expressway was not going to be finished—or anywhere near finished—for years. There were other highways around the state that could be finished sooner—in time, say, for the 1958 gubernatorial election for which Averell Harriman was so anxious to be able to cut ribbons—and the money might better be spent on them. Moreover, the colossal true cost of the Cross-Bronx could no longer be concealed; before it was finished, the highway, including its interchanges with other highways and the bridge carrying it over the Harlem, would be the most expensive road constructed in all history, would cost not the $47,000,000 that Moses had originally "estimated" but $250,000,000. Now that Moses had cleared the right-of-way for the expressway, he had no money to build it—and, in fact, was not able to get it under way again except on a token construction scale until 1957, after the Federal Interstate Highway Act of 1956 had authorized an increase in the federal contribution from 50 to 90 percent. Even then, moreover, there would be continual delays. Bids came in far over contract estimates; new estimates would have to be prepared and new rounds of bidding held. Construction of the final segment of the Cross-Bronx Expressway—the Bruckner traffic circle near its eastern end—would not be completed until 1973. The rest of the Cross-Bronx Expressway would not be completed until 1963. And the one mile of the expressway in East Tremont would not be completed until 1960—five years after Moses had removed from that mile the people who lived in it.

Five thousand people had been removed from East Tremont, but that was 5,000 out of 60,000. There were still 55,000 left. Chance, moreover, had spared East Tremont the fate of other communities disemboweled by a Moses highway operation—the heart of this community, bustling East Tremont Avenue, had escaped the Coordinator's scalpel.

But the thuds of the "skullcracker," the huge swinging wrecking ball, the crash of crumbling walls and the rumble of trucks carrying the walls away had been merely a prelude, the rattle of rifle fire from a skirmishers' picket line before the battle is fully joined and the big guns come into play. For Moses' Cross-Bronx Expressway had been designed by a single criterion: its efficiency as a traffic-moving device. This meant keeping the expressway as level as possible, and East Tremont was a neighborhood of hills. "To keep the grade down, we had to go down," Ernie Clark explains. Going down meant going under the surface of East Tremont. And under that surface was solid rock, and there is only one way to get rid of solid rock.

"First you heard the sound, and then, a few seconds later, you felt the tremor, like a rumbling in the earth, a shaking under your feet," recalls Barney Lambert, whose office was seven blocks away. The sound of the explosions of the huge masses of dynamite required "was a boom, a real *boom*—like a bomb." Says Mrs. Silverstein: "The whole neighborhood seemed to be shaking."

It *was* shaking. The blasting found out every flaw in the earth under East Tremont. It caused the bed of a subterranean river beneath Southern Boulevard to shift. Mortar and brick were jarred loose from one end of the neighborhood to the other. As apartment houses settled or were pushed up as the earth beneath them heaved, huge gaping fissures began to appear in their walls and ceilings. Tenants were hastily evacuated—some in the middle of the night.

Lambert and Mrs. Silverstein lived blocks away from the blasting. People who lived closer felt as if they were at ground zero in an air raid.

The scene in the great excavation—a deep gash in the earth 120 and more feet wide and a mile long—was fantastic. Looming through the clouds of dust were a mile of tall cranes, huge earth-moving machines, batteries of bulldozers, battalions of trucks—and an army of men, their helmets glinting through the dust stretching away as far as the eye could see.

At intervals, red flags would be unfurled and men in pairs would carry them up to the streets crossing the excavation and, standing well away from the excavation, wave traffic to a halt. Then, at some signal that could not be discerned from above, the men down in the pit would all run to take shelter behind their equipment. There would be a pause and then the explosion would come, and the giant steel-mesh mats that had been placed over the explosion areas would rise in the air and fly several feet away as if they were bits of carpet. Sometimes long black limousines would pull up to the edge of the embankment, and men carrying rolls of maps and blueprints under their arms would clamber out and scramble down the embankments with their aides, and even if the residents did not know that these were the general staff of the campaign—Colonel Chapin and General Farrell, who had built highways through jungles; Captain Praeger, who had built the Normandy invasion drydocks—there was no mistaking the commander in chief, for sometimes, in the late afternoon, the longest black limousine of them all would pull up, generally at one end of the mile, and out, to see the job "on the ground," he would jump and, barking orders and questions at map-carrying aides, he would stride through the dust and the grime, seemingly oblivious to it, until he reached the other end of the mile, where the limousine, having crept around the side streets, would be waiting for him.

The blasting was only intermittent, and it went on no more than a year. But from the huge pit came also the harsh, staccato, machine-gun-like yammer of the jackhammers, the deep rat-tat-tat of the drills cutting holes for the dynamite, the clank and grind of the treads of the bulldozers, the hoarse bellow of the huge earth-moving equipment, and the heavy, jarring pound of the pile drivers driving down the shafts of steel called "long rock anchors" to strengthen unstable formations and, where the ground was soft, piles that would last for centuries—all combining in a roar that made the air shudder. The blasting was bad enough but the roar was unbearable. "It was the drilling, the constant drilling. You just heard it constantly through the day hours. You never got used to it."

Worst of all, to these people for whom cleanliness was so important, was not the noise or the danger but the dirt. One of the by-products of blasting or drilling in solid bedrock is rock dust, an extremely fine-grained, abrasive grit. The grit—East Tremonters called it "fallout"—arose from the excavation in a continual fine mist. "It just filled the air," Lambert recalls. "If you closed your windows and put towels in to seal them up, it was there anyway. I don't know how. You got up in the morning, and you felt like you had slept in dust. When you came home from work, you couldn't sit down without sweeping it out of the chair. It was impossible to live cleanly—you felt like you were covered with silt. All the time."

Many of the stores nearest the area around the excavation—those on Southern Boulevard and Marmion—had been torn down. Reaching the others was difficult because they had been fenced for the duration of the construction work. Getting to East Tremont Avenue from the area on the south side of the expressway was difficult. When the expressway was completed, there would be overpasses to get across it, but the overpasses would not be built until it was finished. And many of the streets that would be left across it were closed for weeks at a time during various stages of construction. "To go shopping and come back with bundles was like going to Brooklyn," one housewife recalls. Families on the north side found it difficult to get across to the amenity on the south that was also an important part of their lives: Crotona Park. And, worst of all, there was the uncertainty about when the construction work would be over. "It went on year after year, you know," explains Lambert. "Sometimes it would stop for a month or two or three months without any explanation being given, and then it would start up again. After a while, it seemed to have been going on forever." There were perhaps 10,000 people living right next to the excavation. They began to move out.

Some of East Tremont's landlords, trapped for years in the squeeze between rising costs and rents that could be raised only when a tenant moved out, and cursed with tenants who seemed never to move out, welcomed the opportunity of replacing them with tenants whose poverty and lack of family stability insured a higher turnover and more 15 percent increases, and whose lack of big-city sophistication in dealing with landlords made it easier for landlords to skimp on services. The people moving into the vacated apartments were mostly Negroes—not the middle-class or lower-middle-class Negroes with whom East Tremont's middle-class and lower-middle-class Jews had found it easy to be compatible, but impoverished Negroes—many on welfare, many newly fled to New York from the rural slums of the Deep South—to whom the Jews found it impossible to relate, even had they wanted to. Frightened because the newcomers seemed the advance guard of the ravaging army that had previously been kept at bay on the far side of Crotona Park, they didn't want to.

"The vandalism started then all over the neighborhood," one housewife recalls. Furniture in apartment-house lobbies was slashed, urinated on and finally simply lugged boldly out, to be replaced perhaps once, perhaps twice, but finally not to be replaced, so that the lobbies stood empty and bare. The walls of the elevators were marked by things sharp, were painted, were marked again—and finally not painted any more. Break-ins began. New, stronger locks appeared in apartment doors, and then strips of steel to keep intruders from prying under the door jamb. The break-ins increased. Then there began to be the first, terrifying, reports of muggings.

Still, most of East Tremont's people stayed; their apartments were simply too precious to them for even fear to scare them away. In 1960, the year the expressway's East Tremont section opened, there were still—four years after demolition in the area had begun—an estimated 25,000 Jews in that neighborhood.

Because most of the East Tremont section of the expressway runs through a deep cut, all one sees of the great road from adjoining streets is a gap in the ground. There is nothing visible rising out of that gap. But sit next to that gap—in one of the playgrounds that Moses built on "excess condemnation" parcels—or open the window in one of the apartments—approximately 3,000 apartments—whose windows face the gap during rush hour, when, down below, the expressway is packed solid with cars and trucks six lanes across, and one soon realizes that something *is* rising from that gap, filling the air above and around it, filling it with something that, if one touched a match to it, would make it burn with a pale-blue flame—the flame emitted by burning carbon monoxide.

The human constitution apparently adapts itself to such fumes. One can sit next to the expressway for five days, observing it, and notice that by the fifth day, the nausea and headache and dizziness one felt at first are gone. But no one knows what the inhalation of carbon monoxide—and assorted hydrocarbons emitted by automobile motors—in diluted form produces, for no study has ever been done on the effect of prolonged exposure to such gases.

Rising out of that gap in the ground also—concentrated by its high walls—is the noise of herds of cars and trucks. And that noise is much harder to get used to than the fumes. Talk to people who live in the 3,000 apartments next to the Cross-Bronx Expressway and one hears applied to that noise, over and over again, a single adjective: "unbearable."

At rush hours, the sound of a great expressway on the flat is the sound of the sea, a steady, surging roar. But the Cross-Bronx Expressway in East Tremont is not flat. As the huge diesel tractor-trailers, the monsters of the highways, come to each incline, they are forced, having been unable to maintain speed because of the creeping rush-hour traffic, to shift gears and inch their way up the hill, accelerator pedal jammed hard to the floor. So the sound of the Cross-Bronx Expressway at rush hour is a roar, punctuated by the snarl and grind of shifting gears and the snort and growl of acceleration, and, of course, the sudden, loud harsh backfires—and all of this sound, magnified by the underpasses and the high brick walls that line the sides of the expressway cut, comes out of that cut and over the neighborhood as if out of a gigantic echo chamber. "At nights, you should hear those trucks," says a man who lives a full block from the expressway. "You should hear those trucks at four o'clock in the morning. It's noisy all the time, but you usually wake at about that time, and you can't get back to sleep."

More people moved out of the buildings bordering the expressway. Some of the vacancies were filled by the type of family that would have filled them in the days before there was an expressway, for there were still tens of thousands of Jewish families in New York struggling to get out of the Lower East Side and other slums. But, with the noise, most moved out again—as fast as they could. And the families that replaced them were the families from the other side of the park. Muggings increased, and there began to be reports of robberies, thieves breaking right into your home. Before long, the old residents of the 3,000 apartments bordering the expressway were gone, moved away. Then the residents of the apartments next to those began to move, and then the residents of the apartments next to *those*.

The demolition for the expressway had taken 5,000 of East Tremont's

60,000 residents. Now the expressway had forced out 10,000 more. The new, predominantly nonwhite residents, Saul Janowitz says, "shopped to the south"—in Morrisania, where they had always shopped. They didn't patronize East Tremont's stores. As break-ins increased, insurance premiums began to soar. Merchants who had barely been making a living before weren't making one any more. Storekeepers who had been in East Tremont for decades began to look for a way out. Many could find no buyers; when they moved out, their stores were simply boarded up. Each year, reports of muggings increased. Sometime in 1962 or 1963, exactly when isn't clear, a young, pretty teacher took her third-grade class to the park for the "nature trip" that East Tremont youngsters had been taking for generations. Details of the crime vary—it was never reported in the newspapers—but the neighborhood believes that a man with a knife forced her away from her class, took her to a deserted area of the park and raped her. If there was a last straw, that was it. When word of the crime circulated, undoubtedly exaggerated in the telling, the people of East Tremont stopped using the park, and the young families that had always been attracted to East Tremont, moving into its big, roomy apartments when the older people who had lived in them died, moved in no longer. The people of East Tremont—particularly the young families whose breadwinners were not "in cloaks and suits" but in the professions, and who could afford to live in the suburbs or at least in Riverdale—moved out. Faster and faster they left, and faster and faster, wider and wider, spread the urban decay.

Still, what was left of the people of East Tremont tried to fight. They attempted to regroup in the community's northern reaches, a natural defensive position possessed of the strategic asset—a big and beautiful park, Bronx Park—from which they had been driven in the south, and to which the forces of decay had not yet penetrated. There was one major weakness in the position. This northern section, immediately adjacent to the 180th Street station of the White Plains elevated, had filled up about fifteen years earlier than the southern. Its apartment houses were even older. And, since at the time they had been constructed, landlords had not been convinced that families moving up to the Bronx could afford significantly higher rents than they had been paying on the Lower East Side, those apartment houses were of cheaper construction. By 1960 they were in far worse condition than those in the southern Section 2 that Moses had destroyed. Couples already living there were used to it, but it would not attract younger couples—a consideration important to East Tremont, which felt, as Barney Lambert put it, "that if young people want to move into the same area in which they grew up, they ought to be able to do it." But, the community felt, this weakness could be remedied: the papers were full of new programs for the city—"Title I," "Mitchell-Lama"—which, the papers said, were designed to provide housing at rents that people could afford to pay.

Lillian Edelstein was gone—as were most of ETNA's old leaders, who, having lived in the destroyed southern section of the community, were no longer part of it. But the community found new leaders, including Lambert and Vivian Dee, an eager, vivacious young housewife. Under the auspices of the East Tremont Neighborhood House, they worked up a plan for a Title I development called "Bronx Park South," brought Lyons and every other politician who seemed interested in on the planning from the beginning, and one day in 1959 found themselves—to their shock—accompanying the borough president to Randall's Island for an appointment—a personal appointment—with the Mayor's Committee on Slum Clearance, Robert Moses, chairman. "In a smaller room, his personality was even more overwhelming [than in the Board of Estimate chamber]," Lambert recalls. But this time, he was cordial. With a grin that filled the room, he began the meeting by saying to Lyons: "Well, Jim, what can I do for you?"—and when Lyons told him, he said he would do it. Knowing his power, Lambert and the rest of the committee were optimistic. "It was refreshing to have him on our side," he would recall.

But Moses' concept of the project soon expanded. While ETNA had conceived of it as one of limited size, limited to an area of run-down tenements so as not to hurt sound housing in the area, under Moses it was, to their dismay, expanded into a huge concept of 5,400 units—that would destroy no fewer than twenty-four of the best remaining apartment houses in the area. Moses' concept of middle-income rents, moreover, proved to be higher than ETNA's—so much higher that the people of East Tremont, who had proposed the project, realized that they were not going to be able to afford to live in it. One resident vividly recalls the ETNA meeting at which the Moses-proposed scale of rents was announced: "A groan of despair went up from the room."

ETNA tried Mitchell-Lama, over which, by 1959, Moses had little control. After weeks of effort—Janowitz, taking time away from his store, personally canvassed every vacant site of any size in the neighborhood—they came up with one that seemed perfect: a vacant tract next to the Bronx River, large enough for a 200-unit development. Officials of the Housing Redevelopment Board told them the tract was already owned by the city, so that there would be no problems with acquisition. In innumerable meetings with city departments, they plowed their way through masses of red tape. They found a developer who would build the project at a cost that would keep rents down to the level they wanted, and the developer's plans were approved by the Housing Redevelopment Board. And then it turned out that the board's original description of the ownership of the tract was not complete. The city did, indeed, own it—but only in the technical sense that it owned all land under the control of the Triborough Bridge and Tunnel Authority. Moses had acquired the tract some years before for another of his highways, the proposed Sheridan Expressway. "We found out who had title, and we were in despair when we heard it was Moses," Mrs. Dee says.

Mrs. Dee learned that only part of the land was needed for the expressway, and that if its route was shifted from the center of the tract to the side, plenty would be available for the housing project. Even if it wasn't moved, there would be enough land available for a smaller, but still feasible, project. "I asked [Triborough] for an appointment," Mrs. Dee says. "They said it would take time and they would be in touch with us. They weren't." When she pressed for an answer about moving the expressway, "they just said 'impossible.' "

Then how about the rest of the tract, the part not needed for the expressway? she asked. "I mean, this was something we could have gone ahead and done ourselves. Everything was ready. Triborough said that the Park Department had jurisdiction over anything left over. So I spoke to [Park Department executive officer John Mulcahy]. He said it would be okay if Triborough would say okay. Triborough said the Park Department had to decide. This went on for about a year." What happened at the end of the year, basically, was that the community gave up the fight. "You know, there wasn't one hell of a lot of fight left in it any more," Ed Korn says. "They had taken our best housing. Our best people were gone." And Moses "had taken the heart out of" those who were left. "The manner, the style, in which he operated affected them. The way he changed Bronx Park South. It was the same way he had operated with the expressway. Waking up Monday morning and finding out that he had announced something, and there was nothing you could do about it. It wasn't just that this [the 159 structures torn down for the Cross-Bronx Expressway] was very good housing stock. And that it was just torn down. It was the manner in which this was done. The manner had a major impact on how the community reacted to change thereafter. He left them with feelings of being isolated, left alone—that no one cared, no one listened to them. When they tried to protest, they were powerless. No one seemed to be interested in their problem. This does generate a feeling of helplessness, of resentment. We're abandoned! The manner, the implementation, of the highway affected the area as much as the highway. They had had their licks [on the expressway]. They had had their big community thing. And they had found out you couldn't do anything against him. There was a feeling of letdown, of discouragement, that nobody cared about them. Certainly he didn't care, and nobody else in the city interfered with him. The city just wouldn't listen. Downtown wasn't interested. People threw up their hands. What was the use?" Mrs. Dee and her associates had been begging the young couples who wanted to stay in the community to hold on "for another year or two," until the new housing was available. "We got them to stay on for a while," she says, "but after a while we just couldn't keep telling them to wait—or, if we told them that it wouldn't be long now, they didn't believe it. To tell you the truth, we didn't believe it, either." With each month that passed, of course, the young couples could see the blight creeping closer to them. They began to move out, faster and faster, and into the apartments they vacated moved the tenants East Tremont feared. Some of the older people in the area began to leave.

As they left, the chief reason for staying in the neighborhood left with them. "To me, East Tremont was friends," Cele Sherman says. "When there was a Jewish holiday, you met your neighbors on the street, walking. Well, one Rosh Hashanah, I walked down from my house down Clinton Avenue to Southern Boulevard, crossed over and walked back, and didn't meet one person I could say 'Hello' to. What was the sense of staying?" Thanks to the middle-income housing programs of the mid-1960's, there were now at least apartments—rentals and low-priced cooperatives—in "decent areas" that couples such as the Shermans could afford to rent or buy. Says Cele Sherman: "We left, too."

The one mile of the Cross-Bronx Expressway through East Tremont was completed in 1960. By 1965, the community's "very good, solid housing stock," the apartment buildings that had been so precious to the people who had lived in them, were ravaged hulks. Windows, glassless except for the jagged edges around their frames, stared out on the street like sightless eyes. The entrances to those buildings were carpeted with shards of glass from what had been the doors to their lobbies. In those lobbies, what remained of the walls was covered with obscenities. And not much remained. Plaster from the walls lay in heaps in corners; the bare wood which had been exposed was shattered and broken. The pipes which had been behind the wood were gone, ripped out, melted down and sold for the few dollars that would buy the next fix. Elevators no longer worked. Staircases were broken and shattered. Banisters had been ripped from their sockets, for scrap and a fix if they were iron, for malice, an expression of hatred and revenge on an uncaring world, if they were wood. Raw garbage spilled out of broken bags across the floor. The stench of stale urine and vomit filled the nostrils. One tried to look down only enough to avoid stepping on the piles of feces, whether mercifully dried or reeking fresh—animal and human. There was no heat in those buildings; if they were homes, they were homes as the cave of the savage was a home. And yet they *were* homes—homes for tens of thousands of people. They were homes for welfare tenants and for the poorest of the working poor, for families that drift from one apartment to another without, seemingly, ever paying a month's rent in full—urban gypsies—for mothers who say desperately to the stranger, when they can be induced to talk to the stranger: "I got to get my kids out of here," and for children who come to the door long after the knock is heard and peer around and ask the stranger, with fear in eyes and voice: "Are you the man from the welfare?"

After seven o'clock, the residential streets of East Tremont are deserted, roamed by narcotics addicts in gangs like packs of wolves. Even on East Tremont Avenue, by nine o'clock most of the stores are closed, the lights out, huddled behind steel gates and iron bars.

The streets of East Tremont are carpeted so thickly with pieces of shattered glass that they shine in the sun. Garbage, soaked mattresses, bits of broken furniture and, everywhere, small pieces of jagged steel fill the gutters. The sidewalks are full of holes, the streets—particularly the streets overlooking the expressway, for the expressway has made them dead-end, reducing traffic on them to a minimum—with the hulks of stripped automobiles. Once East Tremont, while the expressway was being built, had had the look of blitzkrieged London; now it looked as London might have looked if, after the bombs, troops had fought their way through it from house to house. It had the look of a jungle.

Of the people who had lived in East Tremont, who had found in that neighborhood security, roots, friendship, a community that provided an anchor—friends and synagogue and Y—a place where you knew the people and they knew you, where you could make a stand against the swirling, fearsome tides of the sea of life, only the very old, too poor to move, still lived, almost barricaded in their freezing apartments. As for the rest of the people who had lived there, they were gone.

39. The Highwayman

ON JULY 3, 1945, with the end of the war obviously near, flashbulbs popped as a gray two-door sedan, the first civilian passenger car to be produced in the United States since February 1942, was driven off the assembly line at the Ford Motor Company's River Rouge plant to signal the resumption of automobile production. Within the month, River Rouge and a dozen other giant assembly lines were debouching 25,000 cars per day onto the nation's highways. And on the very first weekend after V-J Day, gasoline rationing ended and America took to the road, with editorial writers cheering "the seemingly endless procession of automobiles" as a welcome return to normalcy.

It took just two weeks for the cheers to turn to groans. Streets and highways, so empty for forty-four months, filled up with astonishing speed; mounting day by day, by the end of those two weeks traffic was back practically to its December 1941 levels. Nowhere did it mount faster than in New York, and New Yorkers who may have forgotten that in December 1941 traffic jams had ceased to be a joke had their memories harshly jogged. The city's consternation was echoed by its press, which detailed the jams in the type of page-one scare headlines that for forty-four months had been reserved for war bulletins (AVENUE TRAFFIC IS TIED UP BY CROSS-STREET CONGESTION, read one *Times* headline. "North-South Arteries Jammed 3 Times in 2 Hours as Lines of East-West Vehicles Extend Across the Intersections"). By August 23, the *Herald Tribune* was demanding to know why the city had not, during the long breathing space afforded by the war, come up with congestion "remedies."

Moses' response—a letter, four times longer than the editorial, sped to the *Tribune* by limousined secretary—accused the newspaper of "ignoring and playing down what in other less busy and sophisticated communities would be hailed as great achievements."

> What has New York done about street congestion? Bless your little journalistic hearts—a hell of a lot. And why sit we idly by without further plans for the big jam singing "Who Threw the Whiskey in the Well?" while up in the Roaring Forties editors are cutting up tires into rubber heels? Tush, tush! The blueprints are oozing from our files and spilling over the floors. Every day sees visiting firemen in New York not only from the hinterland of America but from the four corners of the emancipated globe, examining our work and asking for copies of our plans. Why are they here if there is nothing to see?

Let's see. We have built and are building wide parkways and expressways, bridges and tunnels, without crossings and lights, with service roads for local use and parking, belt and crosstown systems which take through traffic off ordinary streets and enormously cut down congestion. . . . Then we have great new parking spaces in parks, at beaches and along parkways. . . . We have eliminated railroad grade crossings which blocked traffic for miles on Atlantic Avenue and Rockaway, and substituted boulevards for tracks. Trolley tracks are being ripped up all over town to promote the flow of traffic. . . .

Stick around, Mr. Editor, and continue to give us your support. Traffic will run pretty smoothly here within three years, the time needed to carry out our plans.

Soon Moses was documenting the extent of those plans. Blueprints were ready, he said, for widening the city's old boulevards—Horace Harding, Queens, Conduit, Northern, Eastern—and his old parkways—the Belt, the Gowanus, the Cross Island, the Laurelton—and for building close to a hundred miles of new, broader roads, "expressways" to carry not only automobiles but trucks and buses. Soon New York's newspapers began to be filled with names like "Bruckner," "Van Wyck," "Major Deegan,"* "Cross-Bronx," "Brooklyn-Queens," "Harlem River," "New England," "Richmond," "Willowbrook," "Clove Lakes." Also on the agenda, he disclosed, were three monumental "crossings" of Manhattan Island: "Lower Manhattan," "Mid-Manhattan" and "Upper Manhattan" elevated expressways. And that was just within the city. On Long Island, the old parkways whose names were synonymous with his—the Southern State, the Northern State, the Wantagh, the Ocean—were to be widened and extended, the Northern State deep into Suffolk County, and new parkways—the Meadowbrook, the Captree—were to be built. In Westchester, the Cross County and Sprain Brook parkways were to be built, the Taconic, Bronx River and Saw Mill widened. The blueprints may, indeed, have been spilling over the floors. What Robert Moses was proposing was the widening or construction from scratch of no less than two hundred miles of roads. And the agenda did not include merely roads. There were also the facilities to carry traffic under and over the waters that divided the city. While completing Ole Singstad's huge Brooklyn-Battery Tunnel, he had begun preliminary planning for two huge bridges, a "Throgs Neck" span two miles east of the Bronx-Whitestone, and a "Narrows Crossing" to Staten Island.

During the 1920's, Robert Moses had announced a program—his statewide state park and parkway program—that had dwarfed any plan for the recreation of vast urban masses conceived anywhere in the world in recorded history.

During the 1930's, Robert Moses had announced a program—of New York City bridge and arterial highway construction and park reconstruction —which, taken as a whole, as the single, coordinated system it was, dwarfed

* Major William F. Deegan was City Tenement House Commissioner and a former state commander of the American Legion. He died in 1932.

any public work or coordinated system of public works built in any modern city, and, perhaps, in any ancient city as well.

The program Robert Moses was announcing now—during the 1940's—would, if completed, dwarf those earlier programs. And, he said, there was no reason why it shouldn't be completed; it was, he said, no mere visionary dream; not only blueprints but money—mostly state and federal money, reserved during the war years through his efforts in Albany and Washington—were largely in hand; "the postwar highway era is here."

But, strangely, the troops did not respond to this ringing trumpet call as they had to his trumpet calls of the past.

Even before the war, of course, some urban planners had begun to see—largely because of the effects of Moses' creations—that building more traffic facilities would not in itself cure traffic congestion.

These planners had said—the Regional Plan Association had been saying it since 1929 and, after the opening of Moses' creations during the 1930's, with increasing urgency—that the movement of people and goods in a great metropolitan region required a *balanced* transportation *system*, one in which the construction of mass rapid transit facilities kept pace with the construction of roads. During the last two or three years before the war, a few planners had even begun to understand that, without a balanced system, roads not only would not alleviate transportation congestion but would aggravate it. Watching Moses open the Triborough Bridge to ease congestion on the Queensborough Bridge, open the Bronx-Whitestone Bridge to ease congestion on the Triborough Bridge and then watching traffic counts on all three bridges mount until all three were as congested as one had been before, planners could hardly avoid the conclusion that "traffic generation" was no longer a theory but a proven fact: the more highways were built to alleviate congestion, the more automobiles would pour onto them and congest them and thus force the building of more highways—which would generate more traffic and become congested in their turn in an inexorably widening spiral that contained the most awesome implications for the future of New York and of all urban areas. The only remedy that could check that vicious spiral was the coordination of new highways with new mass transit facilities—and not only was New York's Coordinator not planning any such facilities himself; his monopolization of construction funds and his hold over the city's government were making it impossible for anyone else to plan them either. He was, in fact, destroying some of the old facilities, not only the trolley tracks which he was boasting about "ripping up all over town" but the Third Avenue elevated mass transit line, which he was moving to have torn down. Viewed in this light, tearing tracks up and elevateds down was not an achievement but a disaster. And tearing them down was only one method of destroying mass transportation facilities. Moses—whether by design or out of ignorance of the effect of his policies—was employing other methods with equal effect. Highways competed with parallel mass transit lines, luring away their customers. Pour public investment into the improvement of highways while doing nothing to improve mass transit lines, and there could be only one outcome: those lines would lose more and more passengers; those losses would make it more and more difficult for their owners to sustain service and maintenance; service and maintenance would decline; the decline would cost the lines more passengers; the loss in passengers would further accelerate the rate of decline; the rate of passenger loss would correspondingly accelerate —and the passengers lost would do their traveling instead by private car, further increasing highway congestion. No crystal ball was needed to foretell such a result; it had already been proven, most dramatically perhaps in New Jersey, where the Susquehanna Railroad had lost over two-thirds of its passengers in the ten years following the opening of the George Washington Bridge, but also in New York, where the New York Central had been hit hard by the Triborough Bridge, and the Long Island Rail Road had watched more passengers drift away each time a new Moses parkway opened. No crystal ball was needed, therefore, to foretell the end result of Moses' immense new highway construction proposal, coupled as it was with lack of any provision whatsoever for mass transit: it could not possibly accomplish its aim, the alleviation of congestion. It could only make congestion, already intolerable, progressively worse. His program was self-defeating. It was doomed to failure before it began. It just didn't make sense.

It made less sense still, these planners felt, because of certain implications peculiar to the Moses style of highway building.

Roads opened new areas to development. (Moses' prewar parkways had caused a vast upsurge in population on Long Island before the war, both in Brooklyn and Queens, and in the suburban counties of Nassau and Suffolk.) Subways opened areas to development, too, but development in a different pattern. Because people arrived home from the subway on foot and didn't want to walk too far after they reached their stop, subway-inspired development was development close to subway stations: high-density, predominantly apartment-house development. There were suburban-type, single-family-home communities in New York City served by the subway—Sunset Park was one—but the single-family homes in these communities had been placed on small plots by developers who knew that to make these homes attractive to prospective purchasers, they would have to keep the radii of the communities, and the required walking distance within them, reasonable. People arriving home on parkways arrived home in automobiles. It was relatively easy for them to travel far longer distances from their "stops," the parkway exits. Realizing this, developers were able to take advantage of people's growing desire for open space to build on larger plots of land, to spread out the communities in which people lived. Even in Queens and southern Brooklyn, communities created by the opening of Moses' Cross Island and Belt parkways were characterized by larger lot sizes and lower population densities than those created by the opening of subways. Development beyond the city line, freed from the inhibition against large lots inherent in the city's rigid gridiron block pattern, spread more loosely—and widely—still, and as the open spaces of Nassau began to fill up and developers looked for fresh stretches of land to subdivide, they found themselves looking

—and building new communities—much farther away from the center of the city than would have been the case if the impetus to such development had been not roads but railroads. Once, growth in the New York metropolitan region had been, to a great extent, upwards—people being piled on top of people in apartment houses. Now the growth was outwards. Not only was the population of the region growing rapidly (9,000,000 in 1920, it was 11,000,000 in 1930, and, despite the braking effects of the Depression, 12,000,000 in 1940), but it was spreading away from the traditional center of the region even more rapidly.

Had jobs followed the people out into the suburbs, the implications of this spread might not have been so serious. Given the advantages of "open space," they might in fact have been desirable. And normally, because land was relatively so cheap on Long Island, businesses and industries *would* have followed the people out.

But Moses' policies made it impossible for them to do so. Most roads foster commercial as well as residential development, but his parkways were barred to commercial traffic. His behind-the-scenes persuasion of Long Island politicians to zone residential almost all the adjacent land may have kept the parkways pristine and beautiful, but it also kept the land most desirable for commercial development on Long Island closed to such development. Industries and businesses which could have imported raw materials and shipped out finished products by rail instead of truck shied away from Long Island because the Long Island Rail Road, whose lines should have formed the hub of industrial development, was a rickety "Toonerville Trolley" line, and because without a rail connection to New Jersey the rail lines which brought the goods and commerce of the nation into New Jersey could transport it to Long Island only by expensive lightering. So industry and business stayed back in New York City.

In the decade after Moses opened the Southern State Parkway in Nassau County, 200,000 new residents—about 50,000 families—moved into the county, but only 12,000 new jobs were created in the county. This meant that about 38,000 family breadwinners plus tens of thousands of others from the parkway-opened areas of Brooklyn and Queens had to come back into the city to win that bread. Hardly had the war ended when the surge to the suburbs resumed its prewar pace, leaped beyond it and soared to hitherto undreamed-of proportions, spilling beyond Nassau into rural Suffolk. Every projection made by planners showed that hundreds of thousands of families would be moving to Long Island within the next few years. The vast majority of the family breadwinners were going to have to travel into the center city every day to work. To the drivers who had already crammed to capacity and beyond capacity all Moses' roads would be added tens of thousands of additional drivers. How could you possibly build enough roads to accommodate them?

And what about city streets? Once these tens of thousands of additional cars reached the center city, how were they supposed to move around in it? Above the streets? The blighting effect of elevated structures had long since been documented; "We did not tear down the . . . elevated [mass transit] lines to have them replaced with a maze of overhead motor highways which would rob the city of light and air," said Manhattan Borough President Edgar J. Nathan, Jr., a reformer. Below the streets? The maze of underground subways and utility lines made underground construction prohibitively expensive. On the streets? The streets were already crammed with all the vehicles they could possibly hold.

And where were these cars supposed to park? To Moses' highway trumpet call Nathan quickly added a low-key but penetrating counterpoint: "Mr. Moses explains everything beautifully but not where the motorists are going to put their cars." Planners and reformers picked up the theme. Curbs in the city's central business district were already crammed bumper to bumper—and so were off-street private parking garages. Long Island, of course, was not going to be the only source of additional cars. What about the cars that would be attracted into the city by the new roads Moses wanted built in Westchester County—and by the new roads being built in New Jersey, roads leading to the Lincoln Tunnel, to which the Port Authority was planning to add a third tube, and the George Washington Bridge, to which it was planning to add a second deck? Moses' answer was municipal construction of off-street, multistory parking garages; the answer caught the fancy of headline writers, but planners, costing them out, saw at a glance that no expenditure the city—or even a new public parking authority—could possibly afford could build enough garages to accommodate more than a small fraction of the load Moses was planning to dump on them.

Planners and reformers were raising other questions about Moses' policies.

The Coordinator's proposed highways and garages were designed to help automobile-owning families. But in 1945 two out of three residents of New York City belonged to families that did not own automobiles. Many of these families did not own them because they could not afford to. The Coordinator's subway-fare-increase proposals being advanced at that very moment in Albany would force poor New Yorkers to devote more—in many cases, more than they could afford—of their slender resources to getting around the city. The Coordinator's grabbing of the lion's share of public funds for highways and garages meant that public resources would be poured with a lavish hand into improving the transportation system used by people who could afford cars. Only a dribble of public resources would go into the transportation system used by people who could not—and who therefore rode subways and buses. While the city and state were providing car users with the most modern highways, they would be condemning subway users to continue to travel on an antiquated system utterly inadequate to the city's needs. While highways were being extended into "suburban" areas of the city in which highways were needed—and, in fact, into areas of the city in which highways were not needed, in which the need for highways would be created by the highways—subways would not be extended into areas of the city in which subways were needed. There were subway plans, too, just as there were highway plans; some, such as the proposals for a Second Avenue subway (for Manhattan's far east side and the Bronx) and the Hillside

Avenue subway extension (for northeastern Queens), were advanced enough so that construction could have been begun immediately if funds were provided. But the Coordinator's monopolization of public funds made subway construction impossible. By building transportation facilities for the suburbs, he was insuring that no transportation facilities would be built for the ghettos. Therefore, planners saw, in the transportation field, the portion of the public helped by the use of public resources would not be the portion of the public that needed help most.

For the well-to-do residents of the "suburban" areas of northeastern Queens, not having a subway nearby meant having to take a bus or drive a car to the end of the line in closer to Manhattan or having to drive all the way into Manhattan and back every working day. This was a hardship. But for the impoverished residents of the southeastern Bronx, not having a subway nearby and not owning a car meant taking a bus to the subway and that meant paying a double fare each way—twice a day, five days a week—and that meant paying money that many of these residents simply could not afford. And *that* meant that often these residents walked to the subway, walked a mile or more, in the morning and home in the evening when they were tired. And it meant that on weekends, families that would have liked to take their children on trips—to a museum or a movie downtown or Coney Island or some other park (particularly to a park, since Moses had built few in "lower-class" neighborhoods) or to visit a friend who lived in another neighborhood—stayed home instead. The Coordinator's policies were doing more than simply not helping these people. They were hurting them.

They were even limiting their freedom to choose a place to live. His denial of funds for the extension of mass transit lines into outlying sections of the city and into the suburbs meant that the new homes and apartments there would be occupied only by car-owning families. Whether by design or not, the ultimate effect of Moses' transportation policies would be to help keep the city's poor trapped in their slums. They were in effect policies not only of transportation but of ghettoization, policies with immense social implications. "We knew we had to do something to halt this trend," reformer Leigh Denniston said in a letter-to-the-editor. "And we were asking how best to do it."

The answer to all the questions raised about Moses' transportation policies was, of course, mass transportation. The problems involved in moving tens of thousands of commuters into and out of the center city in a couple of peak hours every weekday—problems so unmanageable in terms of highway lanes whose peak capacity was 1,500 cars per hour—were reduced to manageable size by rapid transit lines, a single track of which could carry between 40,000 and 50,000 persons per hour, and could bring them into the city without their cars, so that they wouldn't require parking spaces.

Mass transportation was, moreover, the *only* answer. New highways had a vital function to fulfill: the transportation of people and goods that, for whatever reason, had no choice but to use highways, at a reasonable rate of speed. If you had a viable mass transit system in the region—fast, clean, reasonably inexpensive, modern subways and suburban commuter railroads —you would attract to it a substantial share of the traffic that *did* have a choice, and by removing it from the highways, you would free the highways so that they would be able to fulfill this function. If residents of the region, particularly commuters, did not have a choice, if they were forced by the inefficiencies, inadequacies of service and high fares of mass transit to use highways whether they wanted to use them or not, the highways would never be able to fulfill their function. Build railroads at the same time that you were building roads, and solving the metropolitan transportation problem would be greatly simplified. Pour all available funds into roads without building railroads, and that problem would never be solved.

Public exposure to this point of view was limited. Editorials such as the one in the *Herald Tribune* that so aroused Moses' ire were rare—nonexistent in the two newspapers most decisive in shaping public opinion in New York, the *Times* and *Daily News*; the *News* cheered Big Bob the Builder's "greatest highway plan." Watching traffic pile up in the city, New York's press was screaming for action—and Moses' plan promised plenty of what it considered action.

The public, conditioned by prewar decades of acclaim for road building, accustomed to equating the value of a public work with its size, unaccustomed to critical analysis of public works programs, desperate for action, showed no greater understanding, no comprehension that there might be drawbacks to the biggest road-building plan ever. Writing in *PM* in May 1946, Lewis Mumford tried to explain some of the social implications of building without planning. "A large part of the money we are spending on highways right now is wasted because we don't know whether we want people where the highways are going," he said. But Mumford confessed to despair that the public would understand. "Highways are an impressive, flashy thing to build. No one is against highways."

One did not have to be a Mumford, however, to grasp the fact that Moses' policies might be self-defeating. All one had to do was think about those policies for a while. And, sitting in their cars day after day in ever-lengthening traffic jams, New Yorkers were finding themselves forced to indulge occasionally in that activity. While Moses' plans enjoyed public support through the 1940's, there were signs that it was not as unanimous after the war as it had been before. Denniston's letter was only one of many in which people were trying to articulate new, disturbing thoughts. Within two months after the war's end, editorial pages—not the editorial columns but the letters-to-the-editor columns, in a number which strongly suggests that on this issue the public was ahead of the press—began to contain suggestions like that published on October 22, 1945, in the *Times*: "Why not bar all private cars from Manhattan?" By 1946, such letters were common.

The more informed sections of the public—businessmen exposed at their weekly Rotary or Kiwanis or Chamber of Commerce luncheons to guest speakers familiar with the problem, for example—were even better exposed to analyses of Moses' policies. It was no longer unusual to find in the back pages of the *Times* or *Tribune* articles like the one reporting that on January 23, 1947, Leslie Williams, of the American Transit Association, had, in an address to the New York City Safety Council, expressed the view that "it would be a whole lot cheaper for a community to subsidize public transit than to spend enormous sums for downtown expressways with no assurance even then that these expressways will relieve congestion."

Rebuffed by O'Dwyer, who summarily referred their inquiries and suggestions to Moses, and forced to admit to themselves that they could suggest no immediate method of financing new mass transit lines, these planners pleaded for the city to take at least one simple, inexpensive step that would make construction of new lines possible in the future.

Building transit lines underground was wildly expensive. Building them at ground level was cheap, so far as construction costs were concerned. It was only when the ground was filled with people that the cost of acquiring it became financially and politically prohibitive. And, planners said, there existed at that very moment an opportunity for obtaining the right-of-way for train tracks quickly, cheaply and with an absolute minimum of public hostility.

The city was about to begin acquiring close to a hundred miles of strips of land between 150 and 250 feet wide, the right-of-way for the Coordinator's new highways. Some of these highways were to run through areas either empty or containing only single-family homes, in which land was relatively inexpensive; in 1945, 21 percent of the city was still undeveloped. Simply obtain another fifty feet of right-of-way, add it to the center malls of Moses' highways, and there would be enough room on those malls for a double-track surface mass transit line, a subway running at ground level. Build the six-lane highways just as you had been planning to do, they urged Moses, but make the center mall wide enough to accommodate those tracks. Then when, sometime in the future, the city was ready to build the subway lines, there would be no problem in acquiring the right-of-way. It would be already available, just sitting there waiting for the tracks to be laid atop it.

Seizing this opportunity would slash at a stroke the Gordian knot of difficulties in the way of providing mass transportation in New York.

Residents of adjacent buildings naturally opposed the construction of noisy, dirty rapid transit lines, often in numbers sufficient to make construction a political impossibility. Build rapid transit lines in the middle of highways, and there wouldn't *be* any adjacent buildings. The nearest buildings would be cushioned from the trains' impact by a good hundred feet of space —and in the case of expressways depressed in open cuts, by their location below ground level as well. Highways caused noise and dirt and objections, too, of course, but the highways were going to be built anyway; trains on their center malls would add to such inconveniences only minimally. As long as the city must be provided with new mass transportation facilities, and as long as these facilities could not be built underground, building them on highway center malls was surely not only the cheapest way to build them but the easiest way to minimize political and aesthetic fallout.

If there was any long-range prediction that could be made with any certainty about a city as volatile as New York, these planners felt, it was that such an opportunity would never come again. Expressways spawned intensive development—apartment houses, factories, office buildings—where there had been before only open fields or private homes. The city could afford to acquire open fields or private homes, even the long miles of fields and homes required for Moses' highways. It would probably never be able to afford to acquire long miles of apartment houses, factories and office buildings. And even if it were in some future decade to find the cash to do so, would it be able to find the will? Would not the protests of thousands of voters make the acquisition politically unfeasible? Acquisition of rapid transit right-of-way, so easy in conjunction with the current expressway program, would never be easy again. It might, in fact, be impossible. Fail to grasp the present opportunity and the city might never be able to build sufficient mass transit to significantly improve transportation.

There were no logical reasons not to grasp this opportunity. No federal approval was necessary; the cost of land acquisition was split by state and city. The state was leaving absolute discretion over the design of Robert Moses highways to Robert Moses. The city's share would be so small that even impoverished New York would be able to afford it. The suggestion was not even revolutionary: plans were already under way for the placing of a mass transit route down the center mall of the proposed Congress Street Expressway in Chicago. The suggestion was so logical that it did not even require much imagination to grasp it. All that was required was common sense.

F. (for Francis) Dodd McHugh asked Moses to grasp it in planning the Van Wyck Expressway.

McHugh, a little, bright-eyed Scotsman, had, as chief of the Office of Master Planning of the City Planning Commission, previously aroused Moses' hostility by objecting to his refusal to make provision for schools, libraries and transportation facilities for the residents of his huge housing projects. Call ing McHugh a "smart aleck," and his objections "stupid, long-winded, contentious and impractical," Moses told his boss, Edwin Ashley Salmon, "We had better get rid of staff work of this kind." But McHugh had declined to take this subtle hint. Assigned to draw up a *pro forma* "Master Plan of New York City Airports," he ventured beyond the assignment and asked himself how people were going to get to these airports—and came up with some rather striking figures.

By the most conservative estimates, when the immense new airport under construction on the marshes at Idlewild Point in southeastern Queens was in full operation, 40,000 persons would be employed there, and 30,000 passengers would pass through it every day—most of them during morning and evening "peak period" rush hours. If traffic patterns conformed to those at other major airports, during peak periods 10,000 persons would be trying to get to Idlewild every hour, some of them in multi-passenger buses but enough of them in taxis and private automobiles so that they would be traveling in 3,220 separate vehicles. And heading for Idlewild at the same time would be hundreds of trucks carrying air mail, express and freight.

Most of these vehicles would undoubtedly be using the Van Wyck Expressway; Moses' stated purpose in proposing it was to provide a direct route to the airport from mid-Manhattan. But the Van Wyck Expressway was designed to carry—under "optimum" conditions (good weather, no accidents or other delays)—2,630 vehicles per hour. Even if the only traffic using the Van Wyck was Idlewild traffic, the expressway's capacity would not be sufficient to handle it.

And Idlewild traffic was going to be only a fraction—a small fraction—of traffic using the Van Wyck. The new expressway would be the most direct route not only to the airport but to all southeastern Queens and to the Southern State Parkway leading to fast-growing Long Island. During highway rush hours—which coincided with airport rush hours—the Van Wyck was going to be flooded with thousands of cars heading for *these* destinations. The new road Moses was building could not—even under optimum conditions—possibly come anywhere near fulfilling the purpose for which Moses was building it. And McHugh, who estimated all this traffic conservatively, could not help knowing that his conservatism was not realistic. The air age was just beginning: air traffic was obviously going to boom to immense dimensions. If the Van Wyck Expressway could not come anywhere near handling Idlewild's traffic when that traffic was 10,000 persons per hour, what was going to happen when that traffic increased to 15,000 persons per hour? To 20,000?

Moses' answer was that he was going to widen two other routes to southeastern Queens, the Belt Parkway and Conduit Boulevard. But parkway and boulevard were already jammed far beyond capacity; widen the two roads and they would still be jammed—even without Idlewild traffic. Widening roads could not possibly solve the Idlewild access problem. You'd have to pave over most of southeastern Queens to do that. Building the Van Wyck Expressway was going to cost $30,000,000. The principal result of the expenditure of that staggering sum would be the condemnation of most of the drivers using the Van Wyck—of generation after generation of drivers using it—to the frustration of being trapped, some of them twice a day for every working day of their lives, in staggering traffic jams.

Building the Van Wyck would raise other questions. Once the cars using the expressway got to the airport, how were they supposed to get around in it? An internal road network of enormous cost and size would be required—and even then congestion inside Idlewild might be even worse than the congestion outside. Where were they supposed to park? Parking lots covering hundreds of acres, *thousands* of acres, expanses of concrete stretching endlessly over the marshland, would be required. Since the marshland would have to be filled in before it could be paved, the construction of such lots would be enormously expensive. If the lots stretched for miles, parts of them would be miles from the airline terminals. How were the drivers—and their luggage—supposed to get to the terminals after they parked?

Only by building the Van Wyck with rapid transit could all these questions be answered. Three lanes of this particular expressway (not engineered up to later design standards) could, under optimum conditions, carry each hour 2,630 vehicles, most of them bearing a single passenger. One lane of rapid transit could, under optimum conditions, carry 40,000 persons per hour. And with rapid transit, conditions would be optimum far more often than on a highway, whose capacity was reduced far more severely by rain or snow or fog or by blockage by an accident or breakdown. Build the Van Wyck with rapid transit, and you would be insuring that, for generations, persons traveling to Idlewild would be able to get there with speed—an express trip from Pennsylvania Station in mid-Manhattan to the airport would take exactly sixteen minutes—and comfort. And, since the long lines of cars would melt off the expressway, those drivers who still wanted to get to Idlewild by car would also be able to get there with speed.

Building the Van Wyck with rapid transit would, moreover, be easy. The north-south expressway was going to cross Queens Boulevard in Kew Gardens. A subway—the IND east-west line running out from mid-Manhattan eight miles away—crossed that very intersection. When it reached the intersection, moreover, it slanted south—by coincidence, toward Idlewild—for about a mile before heading east again. During that mile, its tracks lay almost precisely beneath the right-of-way that Moses was even then acquiring for the Van Wyck. For a mile of its four-mile length, therefore, the expressway would be running almost right on top of the subway. All that was needed to complete a rapid transit link between mid-Manhattan and Idlewild was to bring that subway up to the expressway's center mall and extend it for another three miles. Nine miles—nine expensive miles—of rapid transit link between mid-Manhattan and Idlewild were already completed. All that was needed to complete the link were three miles—three inexpensive miles—more. Moreover, another subway—the IND's Fulton Avenue line, coming out from lower Manhattan through downtown Brooklyn—ran close to Idlewild's western edge. Build a branch of *that* line into the airport, a simple, inexpensive job, and travelers from lower Manhattan—including the Wall Street business district from which would come so large a proportion of the airport's users—would also be able to reach it by train.

Within the airport, McHugh noticed, the two subways would be running within a few hundred feet of each other—in fact, might even intersect. This, he saw, would enable the city to solve a problem which had plagued it for generations: providing a subway link between downtown Brooklyn and central and northern Queens, two areas connected only by automobile. Link up the two subways within the airport, and the connection between the two areas, so long sought but so long despaired of because of the large expense, would be accomplished at small expense. Rapid transit on the Van Wyck Expressway would solve not only the Idlewild access problem but a host of other transportation problems.

And it would be so easy to make provision for that rapid transit.

Building rapid transit on the Van Wyck would provide advantages not only for New York City but for all Long Island.

The expressway ran right underneath the Jamaica Terminal of the Long Island Rail Road; it was that terminal that Moses was planning to hold aloft while he slid the highway beneath it. Put rapid transit on the Van Wyck and Long Island residents would be able to get to Idlewild simply by taking the Long Island Rail Road to Jamaica and transferring to the rapid transit line below.

Perhaps the city could not afford at the present time even the relatively small cost of the construction of three miles of surface rapid transit. McHugh doubted that this was true: the cost would be no more than $9,000,000; it made no sense to say that a city that was planning a $280,000,000 expressway program—of its own money, not counting federal and state contributions—could not afford $9,000,000 for an improvement that would make the expressways so much more pleasant to use. But even if it was true, he said, even if the city did not construct the rapid transit lines now, at least make provision for their future construction.

The cost of providing the additional fifty feet of right-of-way would be less than two million dollars—about $1,875,000, McHugh estimated. The Van Wyck Expressway, whose function was to provide reasonably fast, convenient access to Idlewild Airport, was going to cost $30,000,000, anyway. For that amount, that road would probably never be able to fulfill its function properly. For less than two million dollars more, it would.

Spend the two million now, McHugh saw, and the right-of-way would be available whenever the city wanted to use it. Don't spend it now, and if the city should want to acquire the necessary right-of-way for rapid transit in the future, after the expressway opened, the land would be many times more expensive than it was now. Nor would the cost be limited to the price of the land needed for the right-of-way. Because the land the city would have to acquire would no longer be within the expressway, it would abut three miles of buildings. Their owners would be entitled to substantial damages to compensate them for the noise and dirt of the trains. And land would have to be acquired not only for the tracks but for stations. If provision was not made now for right-of-way along the expressway center mall, the cost of that right-of-way would be not two, but tens of millions of dollars—so high that even if the city were to resolve to bear the enmity of thousands of protesting voters and build a rapid transit line, it might be financially unfeasible for it to do so. Reserve those three miles of right-of-way now, and it would be possible in future years for the city to solve the enormous problem of congestion on the Van Wyck Expressway—and a host of other transportation problems—quickly, simply and cheaply. Fail to reserve it now, and those problems might never be solved.

McHugh was planning to include his suggestion in the airport "Master Plan," but he made the mistake of mentioning it first to his boss, Planning Commission chief of staff Colonel William J. Shea, from whom Moses always received close cooperation.

"I was called into [Shea's] office, and Spargo was there raising hell, that I was impeding progress, that this thing had to go through and stop this crap, that I was going to cost the city millions in federal money. The whole effect was, 'Why don't you shut up?' I was asked not to write any memo."

Declining to accept that recommendation, McHugh wrote that rapid transit access should be provided for Idlewild and predicted what would happen if it wasn't. But his statements had been deleted when the commission approved the "Master Plan of New York City Airports." The only future on which his memo had any effect was his own. Although he was under civil service protection, there was a salary range to his position, and he had been at its upper limit. When the next city budget was adopted, he found he was at its lower limit: his salary—previously, he says, "just about enough to get by on" —had been reduced. He had, moreover, been fighting Moses for eight years now, and he was well aware he wasn't getting anywhere. His report on the rapid transit reservation might as well have not been written. He resigned.

As for the Mumfords and other farseeing planners, Moses treated their predictions of disaster with the disdain he felt they deserved. Opponents who charged that he was unaware of the social implications of his transportation policies—that the ghettoization they caused and the commercial development they prevented on Long Island, for example, was inadvertent—underestimated him. He knew precisely what he was doing. He had formed his own vision of Long Island long ago, and all he was doing now was holding true to it—and that vision did not include poor people or jobs. In a 1945 speech before the Nassau Bar Association, which included most of the county's political leaders, he said:

> There seems to have been a good deal of sentiment in Nassau in favor of attracting more industry and business into the county. Let me warn you against too much enthusiasm for commercializing what nature has given you. Nassau should always be largely residential and recreational. Your land lies between the Bay and the Ocean. [These] are your greatest natural assets. Figure out what sort of people you want to attract into Nassau County. By that I mean people of what standards, what income levels and what capacity to contribute to the source of government.

He did not give the slightest indication of understanding that his transportation policies were doomed to failure.

His thinking had been shaped in an era in which a highway was an unqualified boon to the public, in which roads were, like automobiles, sources of relaxation and pleasure. Changing realities could have changed his thinking, but he was utterly insulated from reality by the sycophancy of his yes men; by his power, which, independent as it was of official or public opinion—of, in fact, any opinion but his own—made it unnecessary for him to take any opinion but his own into account; by, most of all, his personality, the personality that made it not only unnecessary but impossible for him to conceive that he might have been wrong; the personality that needed applause, thereby reinforcing the tendency to repeat the simplistic formula that had won him applause before; the personality that made it possible for him to relate to the class of people that owned automobiles and that was repelled by the class of people that did not own automobiles; the personality whose vast creative energies were fired by the vision of cleanliness, order, openness, sweep—such as the clean, open sweep of a highway—and were repelled by dirt and noise, such as the dirt and noise he associated with trains; the personality that made him not only want but need monuments and that saw in highways—and their adjunct, suspension bridges ("the most permanent structures built by man")—the structures that would have a clean, clear ineradicable mark on history; the personality that, driven now by the lust for power, made him anxious to build more revenue- (and power-) producing bridges and parking lots (and highways to encourage their use) and that made him either indifferent or antagonistic to subways and railroads which would compete with his toll facilities not only for users but for city construction funds. He was insulated from experience. Most of the millions who used his roads were now using them primarily not for weekend pleasure trips but back and forth to work twice a day, five days a week, and driving was therefore no longer a pleasure but a chore; but for Moses, comfortable in the richly upholstered, air-conditioned, soundproofed rear seat of his big limousine, driving was still as pleasurable as it had always been. Robert Moses, who had never had to drive in a single traffic jam, really believed that his transportation policies would work. "Traffic will run pretty smoothly within three years," he had said in 1945. During those three years—and afterward—he repeated that prediction often, repeated it without hedging or qualification, spread it on the public record with the assurance of a man sure that he was right. He was confident that his roads would earn him applause now as they had always earned him applause before. Writing on "traffic relief" in a *New York Times Magazine* article, he said, "If we give this to our people, we shall deserve their gratitude." Applause not just of the age but of the ages; he was confident that his roads would bring him immortality. He had read Statius. He knew that, "in gratitude for the benefits bestowed upon them by" the construction of the Domitian Way, the Senate and the people of Rome had raised a triumphal arch to Domitian. He knew that the Via Appia had brought immortality to its builder, the blind Censor Appius Claudius, who, when public funds to build the road ran out, had advanced the difference from his private fortune. Democracies raised no triumphal arches to road builders. The Wantagh Causeway was still named the Wantagh Causeway, despite the fact that *its* builder had also advanced funds from his private fortune, or at least from his mother's. But he was confident history would remedy such oversights. In 1949, *Times* Sunday Editor Lester Markel commissioned him to forecast the city in the year 1999. "The great arteries . . . will stand out," he wrote.* On another occasion, he wrote: "Those who aim and plug away

* The 1949 article was brief—1,140 words—but it provided ample evidence of the extent to which Moses identified his own works with the city as a whole. To the

at limited, near-by objectives and reach them, may in fact build better than they know. Their works may even last longer than those fashioned by more ambitious geniuses for immortality." If he was capable any longer of rethinking his policies, he gave no evidence of it. And because of his power, of course, there was nothing that could force him to rethink.

Within weeks of the opening of the Van Wyck Expressway—at which Moses proudly boasted that "no network of major urban vehicular arteries comparable to the one on which we are busily working here in New York City . . . will be found anywhere else on this or any other continent"—the road was as jammed as F. Dodd McHugh had predicted. At rush hours, when—as McHugh had predicted—10,000 travelers trying to get to Idlewild were forced to share the road space with tens of thousands of commuters trying to get home, the four miles of roadway which Moses had hacked across Queens looked like a four-mile-long parking lot, so closely were the vehicles on it packed together and so slowly were they moving. "Traffic will flow freely," Moses had promised. Inappropriate adverb. Drivers were chained to the Van Wyck; men who, commuting daily to jobs at the airport or in New York, had taken twenty minutes to cover the four miles paralleling the Van Wyck, had looked forward to the opening of the publicized new road; now, clocking their first trips on it, they could hardly believe their watches; where it had taken twenty minutes to cover the four miles on local streets, it took thirty minutes on the expressway—if conditions were good. And, so often, they were bad. The new road had not freed them from the trap of daily travel; it had closed the trap on them more firmly than ever, for new traffic, generated by the new road, was also jamming the local streets.

With every passing year, congestion on the expressway worsened. Mc-

---

question "What Will New York City Look Like in the Year 1999?" he replied mainly by listing his own works, writing: "Nature, not man, will still be predominant, and the air photographer in his blimp or helicopter will still see the rolling ocean, the relatively unspoiled ocean beaches, Jamaica Bay, the Long Island Sound, the lordly Hudson, and their tributaries, and Liberty guarding the magnificent harbor. The great arteries of travel will stand out. The hills of Revolutionary fame will still boast their monuments and citadels; the parks, large and small, will still be conserved for all the people. The great Palisades reservation will still be five times as large as all of Manhattan Island; Jamaica Bay and its shores, reclaimed and dedicated to recreation and air travel, will constitute one-third of Brooklyn; a fourth of the Bronx will remain field, forest and stream. Queens will still be suburban, and Staten Island largely rural. . . . In ten years, one person out of ten will be living in public or other subsidized housing. In fifty years, it may be one out of six or seven—not an altogether pleasant prospect for those who must pay not only their own way but that of their less fortunate or hard-working brothers. Traffic will flow freely in 95 per cent of the city and suburbs. . . ."

The article also provided ample proof that Moses was failing utterly to comprehend that his policies might not be working for the city. "As to the spirit, the enterprise, the magnetism which made the metropolis great," he wrote, "there is not a shred of evidence that their force will lessen. There is no sign of decrepitude, decay or resignation."

Hugh had calculated that during "peak periods" 10,000 persons would be trying to reach Idlewild every hour. As air traffic burgeoned, that figure became 15,000, and then 20,000. New parking fields were built within the airport at a frantic rate: 500 acres of marshland were paved over, then 1,000, then 2,000, then 4,000, then 8,000. And still there was never enough room to park. At peak periods, the paved space within Idlewild—parking fields and internal roadways—was often so jammed that the torrent of vehicles oozing down the Van Wyck could enter the airport only at a trickle; sometimes, the airport had to be closed to new traffic—it was not infrequent for vehicles waiting to get into Idlewild to be backed up on the expressway for a solid mile.

Inside the airport, of course, the scene was chaos. Drivers searching for parking spaces milled around and around on the roadways, mingling with drivers trying to get to the airline terminals. By one estimate, at a normal weekday rush hour, a traveler arriving at Idlewild by private car had to allow a full thirty minutes for travel *after* arriving at the airport.

Other roads were jammed, and created by their opening more traffic than had existed before. The Brooklyn-Battery Tunnel opened on May 25, 1950, with blessings from Cardinal Spellman ("one of man's greatest achievements!"), what may have been the longest cavalcade of official limousines ever assembled outside Washington (338 long black Cadillacs), the highest toll ever charged on a Moses project (thirty-five cents)—and a traffic count almost twice as high as Madigan-Hyland had predicted. Moses' engineers had forecast that the tunnel would carry 8,400,000 cars during its first year of operation. By the end of a month, it was carrying traffic at a 13,000,000-vehicle-per-year rate, 64 percent above their predictions. George Spargo explained that the count had been swelled by an influx of tourists who had come from all over the eastern seaboard to see this new wonder of the world, and that the influx was over now. By the end of three months, the tunnel was carrying traffic at a 14,000,000-vehicle-per-year rate. At the end of six months, it was carrying traffic at a 15,000,000-vehicle-per-year rate, and not only the increase but the rate of increase was increasing every month. "Another pleasant surprise," Spargo said. But the tunnel was engineered for a capacity, rush hour, load of 2,000 vehicles; by 1952, it was being asked during rush hours to handle 5,000, even 6,000 vehicles per hour. Traffic backed up for blocks at its entrances. Moses had expected it to draw off traffic from the parallel Queens-Midtown Tunnel and three free East River bridges. But traffic on the bridges remained "normal," which meant jammed. And traffic through the Queens-Midtown Tunnel, fed now by the widened Queens-Midtown Expressway, increased instead of decreasing. In 1951, while the Brooklyn-Battery Tunnel was carrying cars at a rate of 79.3 percent above estimates, traffic through the Queens-Midtown Tunnel was 26.3 percent higher than ever before. Previously, 10,967,000 cars per year had been trying to use one tunnel. Now there were two tunnels—and 28,445,668 cars were trying to use them. The situation at the southern portion of the East River was duplicated at the northern. In Triborough's annual report for 1951, Spargo wrote happily, "The Triborough Bridge had its fifteenth birthday on July 11th. There were no birthday cakes, presents or ceremonies, just more automobiles." In 1946, the first postwar year, the bridge had carried 13,000,000 vehicles. In 1947, it had carried 16,000,000 vehicles; in 1948, 19,000,000; in 1949, 23,000,000; in 1950, 27,000,000. The count in 1951 had been 32,000,000. And the trend was more striking than the figures. The increase had been two million in 1946, three million in 1947 and 1948, four million in 1949 and 1950, five million in 1951. And this situation was being duplicated on the Bronx-Whitestone Bridge, which Moses had built to drain off traffic from the Triborough. While traffic was increasing 138 percent on the Triborough between 1946 and 1951, it was increasing 129 percent on the Bronx-Whitestone. And traffic volume on the free Queensborough Bridge was also increasing. In the last prewar year, cars had been crossing the East River into Manhattan at the colossal rate of 122,500 per day; in 1951, they were pouring across the river into Manhattan at the rate of 135,000 per day. And what of the roads leading to and from these facilities? Four lanes of Belt Parkway had been jammed before the war. Now six lanes of Belt Parkway were jammed. Prewar congestion on old Atlantic Avenue had been intolerable. Postwar congestion on a new—widened, modernized—Atlantic Avenue was more intolerable. And it wasn't only bridges and highways that were jammed. As seen from the air, at rush hours, every street in neighborhoods near the approaches to the East River crossings was a crawling mass of cars. (On the other side of Manhattan, where, since 1930, the Port Authority's George Washington Bridge and Holland and Lincoln tunnels had been opened to vehicular traffic while New Jersey railroads had been allowed to deteriorate, this situation was being duplicated. Since 1930, railroad commutation from Jersey had declined slightly; commutation by motor vehicle had quadrupled. In the evenings, when 80,000 daily commuters were heading home to Jersey, all of Manhattan between 175th and 181st streets was solid with cars, trucks and buses moving toward the George Washington Bridge. Downtown, the typical line of cars waiting to enter the Holland Tunnel plaza was, at 5 P.M., eight blocks long. The *Times,* clocking travel time to the Lincoln Tunnel, found on one evening that it took a truck twenty-seven minutes to make a one-block-square circuit to the entrance plaza.) Within the city, it seemed that there was not a crevice into which cars did not cram; traffic was piling up everywhere; on the crosstown side streets in midtown Manhattan, the *Times* found, motorists frequently spent forty minutes traversing the two and a half miles from one side of the island to the other.

The clockings themselves were of less significance than the fact that the *Times* was making them. "We learn to tolerate intolerable conditions": press and public reaction to motor-traffic congestion in New York City documents the truth of Barbara Ward's statement. It was during the early 1920's that such traffic first overwhelmed New York; in 1924 and 1925 and 1926, the public reacted with indignation and protest against the jams in which—seated in the vehicles that had promised them new freedom—they found themselves imprisoned instead. Traffic was news, big news; clockings were a front-page staple. By the late 1920's, however, a kind of numbness—measurable by a slackening in angry letters-to-the-editor and campaign statements by both-ears-to-the-ground politicians—was setting in. Psychologists know what happens to rats motivated by mild electric shocks or the promise of a food reward to get out of a maze when the maze is made excessively difficult to get out of; for a while, their efforts to find an escape become more and more frantic, and then they cease, the creatures becoming sullen, then listless, suffering apathetically through shock or hunger rather than making further efforts that they believe will be useless. People caught in intolerable traffic jams twice a day, day after day, week after week, month after month, began after some months to accept traffic jams as part of their lives, to become hardened to them, to suffer through them in dull and listless apathy. The press, responding to its readers' attitude, ran fewer hysterical congestion stories, gave fewer clockings. A city editor seeing a couple of reporters with their feet up on their desks on a slow Friday afternoon found other make-work than sending them out to discover how long it took to get from the Queens-Midtown Tunnel to the Lincoln Tunnel. Only in editorial columns—written, it sometimes seems, by men selected through a Darwinian process in which the vital element for survival is an instant and constant capacity for indignation and urgency—did the indignation and urgency endure. Traffic was still news, but it was no longer big news.

The same process was repeated during the middle and late 1930's, not because a new wound had been inflicted but because the scab on the old one had been ripped off. Moses' unprecedentedly ambitious traffic devices, together with his highly publicized promises that they would solve the traffic problem (and the easing in that problem that occurred for a few months every time a new facility was opened), raised hopes; with hope, motorists dared to look again at what they were being subjected to. And when, a few months after each new facility opened, the jams began to build up again, their consciousness, newly reopened, was rubbed all the more raw. In the last two or three years of that decade, with the Triborough Bridge and the West Side Highway and the Interborough and Grand Central parkways open and congestion worse than ever, there was another howl of public anguish.

In contrast to the Twenties, however, in the Thirties the anguish was beginning to be coupled with awareness. As new bridges jammed up without easing the jams on the old, as every lane of gleaming white concrete was filled with cars as soon as it was opened to traffic, Lewis Mumford and the Regional Plan Association were no longer lone voices crying that no number of bridges and highways could alone solve the traffic problem. Before World War II, the numbness set in again. The howls died down. Motorists sank back into apathy. But before they did, letters-to-the-editor, speeches and articles by urban planners and resolutions of civic associations revealed a greatly increased understanding that something more—something different—was needed.

The war kept people off the roads. It made them forget the pain. And when, after gasoline and rubber rationing ended, New Yorkers took to the highways again, the numbness had worn off. When the pain returned, it seemed sharper than ever. Even in late 1945 and early 1946, when it was no worse than it had been in 1941, people were complaining, and editorial writers calling for "action," far louder than they had in 1941.

After a short while, they had, in fact, more to complain about. The pain didn't only *seem* worse; it *was* worse. Postwar traffic congestion was congestion escalated to an entirely new level. The problem was so immense now that it was difficult even to comprehend its dimensions. How come to grips in one's imagination with a situation in which a mighty expressway, a gigantic superhighway of dimensions literally almost unknown to history, could be opened one month—and be filled to absolute capacity the next, in which expressways opened in 1952 were by 1955 carrying the traffic load that had been forecast for 1985, in which, in this city and metropolitan area already congested to the breaking point, every indicator of traffic—auto registrations, commuting trips per day—was increasing in more than arithmetical, *in almost geometrical,* progression? The press did not in general come to grips with it, at least not in its deeper implications, but it did report thoroughly on its more superficial—and more dramatic—manifestations. Traffic was news again. The *Times,* which had once sent its reporters over the West Side Highway so that it could tell its readers how incredibly fast it made travel, now sent its reporters onto it to report that "at a peak period of evening travel, northbound vehicles took thirty-four minutes to cover four-and-a-half miles." Editorials argued in the *Times* and *Tribune* and screamed in the *News* and *Mirror* for "Action!"—now! As for the individuals caught in this colossal traffic trap twice a day, any psychologist knows that if he turns up the voltage of the electric shock enough, the rats will be shocked out of their apathy and begin frantically scurrying back and forth through the maze again, searching desperately for a way out; newspaper stories of this period document an almost frantic search by drivers for a way out of *their* trap; grim U-turns in the face of oncoming traffic to avoid huge jams seen ahead (reporting on one at the Third Avenue Bridge on a hot summer Sunday, in which "hundreds of cars were backed up over a two-mile radius," the *Times* reported that "the snarls were intensified as motorists tried to make U-turns to get out of the jam"); frantic lane switching that drove up accident rates on all major routes; attempts to find new ways through the maze (reported *The New Yorker,* never one of Moses' favorite publications, anyway:

> We've become increasingly aware that the best way to avoid highway congestion is to duck the proud network of parkways in Westchester and Long Island and take to the traffic-lighted, non-cloverleaf-intersected roads of our youth. . . . What have man and Moses wrought? Answer? A boomerang).

With the numbness not yet having had a chance to set in again and the pain, still fresh, more intense than ever, there was an upsurge in the question of how best to alleviate it. Awareness was escalating, too. Now there was general awareness among urban planners and some segments of the public that something else might be just as important as roads—might, in fact, be more important. By 1952, there was in at least three New York newspapers, the *Times,* the *Tribune* and the *Post,* at least the beginning of emphasis on the need to improve and add mass transit facilities as well as roads. There was even a beginning of the realization that the construction of highways alone might be "boomeranging," defeating its own ends, a realization Lewis Mumford was later to summarize in a 1955 series of articles in *The New Yorker*, "The Roaring Traffic's Boom": "The prevalent conception" is that "the main purpose of traffic is to enable a maximum number of citizens to derive all possible benefits from the use of automobiles," Mumford said. But that isn't the purpose of transportation at all. "Transportation—I blush to utter a truism now so frequently ignored—is a means and not an end. . . . Like any other tool, it must be used for some human purpose beyond the employment of the tool itself. . . ." He said that "before we cut any more chunks out of our parks to make room for more automobiles or let another highway cloverleaf unfold, we should look at the transformation that has taken place during the last thirty years in Manhattan."

Ever since the nineteen-twenties the municipal and state authorities have been plunging blindly from one grandiose traffic scheme to another, without showing any striking understanding of the problems they were trying to solve. . . .

For a whole generation, New York has become steadily more frustrating and tedious to move around in, more expensive to do business in, more unsatisfactory to raise children in, and more difficult to escape from for a holiday in the country. (The subway rides grow longer and the commuting trains carry their passengers from more distant suburbs, until as much time is spent in transporting the human carcass as is gained by diminishing the work week . . . the distant dormitory areas of New York describe ever wider arcs.) By 1975 . . . it will be impossible to build enough highways to accommodate the weekend exodus, just as it is already impossible to provide enough internal traffic arteries to handle Manhattan's present congestion. . . .

But your one-eyed specialists continue to conduct grandiose plans for highway development, as if motor transportation existed in a social vacuum, and as if New York were a mere passageway or terminal for vehicles, with no good reasons of its own for existence. To these experts, a successful solution of the traffic problem consists of building more roads, bridges and tunnels so that more motorcars may travel more quickly to more remote destinations in more chaotic communities, from which more roads will be built so that more motorists may escape from these newly soiled and clotted environments. . . . Instead of curing congestion, they widen chaos.

. . . the private motorcar [is] a method that happens to be, on the basis of the number of people it transports, by far the most wasteful of urban space. Because we have apparently decided that the private motorcar has a sacred right to go anywhere, halt anywhere, and remain anywhere as long as its owner chooses, we have neglected other means of transportation. . . . The major corrective for this crippling overspecialization is to redevelop now despised modes of circulation—public vehicles and private feet. . . . An effective modern city plan would use each kind in its proper place and to its proper extent.

Mr. Robert Moses . . . uses the word "regional planning" as a swearword, to indicate his abiding hatred of . . . comprehensive and forward-looking policies, just as he invokes the term "long-haired planner" to designate anyone who turns up with a proposal that does not fit into his own set of assumptions, most of them by now manifestly inadequate and badly out of date. . . . *Think!*

A handful of thinkers like Mumford were even beginning to venture a revolutionary opinion: that automobiles—and highways—should be barred from certain central areas of the city, that some congested avenues and streets should, instead of having their roadways widened for cars, be closed to cars and turned into "pedestrian malls." Some, in fact, were beginning to postulate a more revolutionary opinion still: that major arterial through highways had no place in the interior of a city at all, that a city could not endure as a good place to live if they were built in any number within its borders.

This awareness was by no means pervasive. If the *Times,* the *Tribune* and the *Post* were beginning to emphasize the importance of mass transit vis-à-vis highways, little of the same emphasis could be found in the city's other daily newspapers. For several of these, in fact, a frequent practice when the need for a transportation analysis was felt was to ask Moses to write it, his articles appearing in the *News* and *Journal-American,* for example. (The *Journal-American* was, of course, part of the Hearst chain, and in 1952 Hearst newspapers were conducting a nationwide campaign for "new and better roads.")

But the awareness was spreading. After July 1951, when the Regional Plan Association published the results of "investigations . . . to determine the amount, extent and trends of commuting . . . to central New York," facts and figures were available to document the effect of two decades of neglecting mass transit facilities in favor of highways. A few months earlier, Moses, issuing a lavish four-color brochure, had boasted that in "our reports in milestones of progress . . . issued on important occasions . . . when something has happened which is worth telling about," "we rely on illustration rather than technical explanations" which "are bound to be dull, statistical [and] boring." The RPA's "Bulletin Number 77," black-and-white, was statistic-crammed—but to anyone interested in why New York's congestion was really increasing so rapidly, it was not boring but startling. The common assumption—previously held not only by Moses but by press, politicians and many urban planners—was that congestion was increasing because the population around New York was increasing at a tremendous rate, and therefore commuting into New York must be increasing at a tremendous rate. Estimates of the number of commuters had ranged from 500,000 to 1,500,000. The fact—a fact documented for the first time in Bulletin 77—was that although the population was increasing just as fast as people thought it was (the number of families in the counties surrounding New York had increased by 50 percent between 1930 and 1950), the commuting wasn't. There had been 301,000 commuters coming into the city daily in 1930; in 1950, there were 357,000—an increase of only 19 percent. The difference was not in the number of people coming into and out of New York every day, but in *how* they were coming. The number of rail commuters had actually declined, from 263,000 in 1930 to 239,000 in 1950; 38,050 persons had commuted by automobile in 1930, 118,400 persons commuted by automobile in 1950. While the number of commuters was up 19 percent, the number of automobile commuters was up 321 percent. And, the RPA statistics showed, the trend was continuing—and accelerating. The gap between use of rail and road was widening month by month. The failure to maintain existing railroad lines in a condition that would persuade even their present riders to keep using them, much less to attract new ones, the failure to construct new lines into newly developed areas, while building new highways into those areas, was driving more and more commuters off the railroad and onto the highway. The effect on the city of the widening gap could only be disastrous.

> The automobiles required to transport the equivalent of one trainload of commuters use about four acres of parking space in Manhattan, eight times the area of the Grand Central main concourse.
>
> Every trainload of commuters shifting to automobiles requires automobile parking space about equal to the effective parking capacity of one side of Fifth Avenue from Washington Square to Sixty-eighth Street [3 miles].

The lesson to be gleaned from the statistics was clear even though they did not include statistics on the intracity shift in subway to automobile use, statistics that would have made the lesson even more dramatic. The trend must be reversed. Emphasis must be shifted from road building to railroad building. The lesson was scanted by most of the press—the RPA report received one-day play in most of New York's papers—but in 1954 it was repeated in more popular form by a *Times* series, and thereafter there was at least a general awareness of it in most of the more detailed transportation stories in the New York press. And, as in the previous decade, it sometimes seemed—from the sharp tone of letters-to-the-editor compared to editorials—that awareness was growing faster among the public than in the media supposed to educate the public or among the politicians supposed to lead the public: almost as if the people of New York and its suburbs—forced to spend hours daily being exposed to the harsh lessons of urban transportation, trapped daily in a classroom on the realities of urban transportation, a classroom in which the reality of what was being taught was worsening so fast that numbness had not yet caught up to it—were learning the lessons for themselves. Mumford was not the only person pleading with public officials to *Think!* Many men and women who had never opened a planning textbook in their lives were, by the early 1950's, repeating in their own words the great planner's plea. People were learning for themselves. By 1940, most urban planners had come to understand that roads were not good *per se,* that a highway was not an unqualified boon for mankind. By the early 1950's, much of the general public appeared to understand this, too, even if the press did not. There was general awareness of the need for a dramatic change in the region's transportation policies. Mumford, unsatisfied though he was at the rate of mobilization of public opinion ("The majority of the American people . . . remain strangely quiet and passive about the matters that should concern them most"), saw hope now that Moses' "irrational" plans could be changed. Pointing out that "the things that spoil life in New York and its environs were all made by men, and can be changed by men as soon as they are willing to change their minds," he now saw hope that men would do so.

But for New York, only one mind mattered, and that mind would not change.

As Moses' first postwar mileage had been opening, he had been as confident of the wisdom of his policies as he had been when he announced them in 1945. "Today we are well underway to a solution of the traffic problem," he had boasted in 1948. Now, in 1954, with considerable new mileage open, the problems were worse than ever, but the confidence was diminished not a whit. All that was necessary, he said—and believed—was more of the same.

The roads he had been building had all been conceived by him in 1930. Now, for the first time, he expanded his highway plan. New arterials should be built paralleling old arterials already built, he announced—a Sheridan paralleling the Major Deegan and Bronx River and Harlem River and Hutchinson River and Henry Hudson that already ran down through the Bronx, a Nassau paralleling the Van Wyck southeast through Queens. Arterials should be built into sections of the city into which no arterials now ran, a Prospect and Cross-Brooklyn Expressway into the teeming heart of that borough, for example. And arterials should reach out from the city into its suburbs, a Long Island Expressway all the way out deep into still-rural Suffolk, for example. And, of course, the "series of east and west crossings in Manhattan" which he had so long advocated should be begun; it was during this period that he was forcing the Port Authority to start the Lincoln Tunnel link that would give him a wedge on the Mid-Manhattan Crossing along Thirtieth Street. As to what to do with the cars when they got to the city, he had no doubt that his proposed multistory, "off-street" parking garages—"two, three, four stories or whatever height they have to be"—would solve *that* problem; the "success" of the first "publicly financed" off-street garage in the city's history, Triborough's seven-story Battery Park Garage—it was filled to capacity almost from the day it opened—proved that. "When we get the expressways . . . you will see how they will take care of most of this through or cross-town traffic," he said in a lengthy 1952 question-and-answer session with *U. S. News & World Report,* which identified him as the "recognized authority" on the future of America's cities. ("Q. But in city streets . . . are off-street garages the answer? A. Yes . . .") As for the use of city money for mass transit construction, he fought such proposals to their death, and when, in 1952, some state legislators suggested that Triborough take over the city's subways and use its surplus to improve them, Moses rushed back from a Virgin Islands vacation to declare that there was no surplus because "all our future revenues are pledged to our bondholders"—who, he said, would never permit the Authority to become involved in deficit-producing operations. (In that same year, the General Electric Company announced that its Urban Traffic Division had "costed out" rapid transit on auto-highway center malls and that if provision for tracks was made in the original highway design their cost would be one-tenth of providing them later. Moses' reply? "The cost of acquiring additional width and building for rapid transit would be prohibitive and hundreds of families would be dislocated.")

Not all planners fully understood yet that if Moses' proposals were carried out, New York would become a place not for people but for cars, spread out by the hundreds of acres on monstrous parking fields, cars piled up seven stories high or more—to "whatever height they have to be"—cars that would bring their roar and the fumes of their "foul exhausts" into its every corner. But they did understand fully—by 1952 there was a general understanding among urban planners, an informed consensus—that Moses' plans made no sense unless they were supplemented by mass transportation.

There was some applause in the press for Moses' proposals—these were the years in which he was enjoying general editorial support for a proposal to create a City Parking Authority with unprecedented power over the city's streets—and a rather remarkable lack of understanding of some of the subtleties of transportation politics. A *Herald Tribune* editorial said that Triborough's 1951 annual report

> ought to give every citizen of New York a bit of a thrill. Business is booming. . . . Traffic is everywhere exceeding the experts' predictions. . . . If the present volume keeps up, all the bridge bonds will be retired by 1957 and all tunnel bonds by 1963. When that happens, every bridge and tunnel so successfully built and operated by the Triborough Authority will become the free and unencumbered property of the people of New York City. . . . Good work, gentlemen.

Only the *Post* gave more than scant attention to the problems of the thousands of tenants being evicted for Moses' highways. While press applause was by no means as enthusiastic as it would once have been, and editorials more and more frequently expressed doubt about the city's transportation policies, they never linked those policies with the man responsible for them. There was no direct attack on Moses, no threat of any real seriousness to his power. And with that power, he laid out the new routes, obtained the state and federal commitments for them, had the blueprints drawn—started them down the road to completion.

And in 1954 he took a further step—one that sealed the city's future.

40. *Point of No Return*

THE SILVER STREAM of quarters and dimes and nickels on which Moses' power was based was flowing faster and faster. By 1952, with 120,000,000 vehicles per year using Triborough's facilities, the Authority's annual revenues stood at $28,300,000—an increase of 453 percent over prewar levels. And since operating and maintaining its bridges and tunnels cost little, and not even Moses could spend enough on parties, luncheons, brochures, ribbon cuttings and advance planning to make a dent in such income, most of the revenue was surplus: after paying all bills and interest, the Authority's surplus for 1953 alone was $21,000,000. Capitalized—multiplied in terms of the amount of revenue bonds that could be sold because of it—its total surplus was worth, at 1953 interest rates and bond-market conditions, close to half a *billion* dollars. The man who had once had to beg bankers to give him three million dollars for the Henry Hudson Bridge (one deck at a time) now could obtain from bankers five hundred million—and the bankers would fight for the chance to give it to him. Moses now had available to spend on public works in the city far more money than the city had available to spend.

The very size of that surplus, however, made it a source of danger as well as opportunity. Were the attention of public and politicians to be focused upon it, they might demand that it be used, in the spirit of the law creating the Authority, to retire its outstanding bonds and remove its tolls (the *Herald Tribune* editorial demonstrated how easily such a demand could spring up—especially if it was ever realized that all the bonds could be retired, and toll booths torn down, not in some distant future but within six years) or to ease the subway deficit and the need to raise subway fares (the alarming speed with which the legislators' demand that Triborough bail out the subways had caught fire—before Moses had rushed back from the Virgin Islands to stamp it out with the statement that there was no surplus—was an indication of its appeal). Either course—bond retirement or subway bail-out—would strip Moses of his accumulating millions. He had realized back in the Thirties that authorities could be a means to immense achievement and a source of immense personal power—but only if their revenues were spent on new public works as fast as they were earned, only if, in other words, he kept building as fast as possible. The editorials and resolutions of the Fifties only demonstrated again the correctness of that insight. Triborough's money had to be spent—and it had to be spent fast.

There was, however, a problem, a problem that could be solved only by rapprochement with his old foe, the Port of New York Authority. Vast as his resources might be, they were nowhere near as vast as his dreams. Ground was already broken for the Coliseum; he was going to have to pour $43,000,000 into that gaping hole at Columbus Circle. The Throgs Neck Bridge must get under way as soon as possible; for that span he would need $92,000,000. He had already allocated $90,000,000 to get work under way on the Long Island and Prospect expressways and the East River Drive extension up to the Triborough Bridge. Almost half the half billion was already committed. Then there were the other roads, envisioned decades before and still unbuilt. Their cost was measured now in the hundreds of millions of dollars. And the bridge which he had conceived of as the crowning glory of his career, the supreme monument to the life of Robert Moses, a bridge whose construction would take close to five years, was not yet even begun—and Moses was, after all, already sixty-five years old; who knew when time, so long on his side, might turn on him with the Narrows Crossing not yet begun? And the Narrows Crossing would (without approaches, just for the bridge structure alone) cost $345,000,000. And how about the new parks he wanted to create, the old parks he wanted to reshape? Jamaica Bay, which was to be his park masterpiece, Jamaica Bay, which was to be *his* creation, not merely his reworking of an Olmsted creation, Jamaica Bay, which was to be the greatest urban waterfront park in the world, was not even begun. There was so much yet to do! Even the monumental wealth of Triborough was nowhere near enough to do it. Wealth far greater was almost within his grasp. The proposal—even then in preparation in Washington—for a Federal Interstate Highway System, for which the federal government would pay 90 percent of the cost, a state only 10 percent, would make $50 billion available to construct 41,000 miles of such highways during the next ten years. Moses had been working quietly with top Eisenhower aide Sherman Adams and with General Lucius D. Clay, chairman of a key presidential committee studying highway needs, on details of the program—the scope of it, in fact, was his: $50 billion over ten years were his figures—and had succeeded in obtaining a key revision in the program: although Eisenhower was adamant that the new highways were not to be toll roads, Moses had obtained the inclusion of a clause saying they could link up with toll facilities; if he could build the bridges, the federal government would pay for the highways connecting with them. But to be eligible for inclusion in the interstate system, highways had to be interstate; they had not only to connect with highways in another state but to form with those highways a highway *system* interstate rather than local in character. Given the geographical location of New York City, that state could only be New Jersey—and in the portion of New Jersey closest to New York, the highway-building power was the Port Authority.

There were additional incentives for rapprochement. Since O'Dwyer had handed it Idlewild in 1946, every ensuing confrontation between the two giant "public benefit corporations" had resulted in a Moses victory; during the reign of Impy, in fact, he had forced the Port Authority to agree to reserve $13,000,000 for his Mid-Manhattan Expressway as the price for permission to enlarge the Lincoln Tunnel. But the situation had changed. Wagner Junior ("For a man who's been a friend of your father's, you have . . . a sense of humility, of respect") had just become mayor, and the Port Authority's chairman had been one of his father's closest friends, campaign treasurer for his 1926 senatorial race, in fact. Howard S. Cullman was as adroit as Moses at playing on the Mayor's feelings. Wagner, astute judge of men that he was, was fully aware of what Cullman was doing. "I always knew when he wanted something," the Mayor would recall years later of his fellow Yale graduate. "He'd take me to lunch at the Players Club and he'd talk about the '26 campaign and about Yale." But Wagner let him do it anyway; nothing—not even an awareness of how men used it to play on him—could lessen the "respect," and Wagner was not the man in any case to offend, or even confront, a Port Authority board that included, besides tobacco tycoon Cullman and tugboat tycoon Eugene F. Moran, banking barons S. Sloan Colt of Bankers Trust and Bayard F. Pope of Marine Midland Trust. For Austin Tobin, Wagner had little use; the Mayor's keen eye saw through his attempt to act as arrogant as Moses. ("Moses and Tobin? Oh, Moses is tougher. And smarter. Once you get away from standing at the bridge and taking in quarters, what Tobin has is that board. When I first came in, Austin used to go around calling me 'stupid.' Then I ran in to him at a party, and I said—with a smile—'Austin, you wanna get anything through, you better stop calling me "stupid."' He never called me 'stupid' again, and Howard apologized to me for his behavior.") But the board—coupled with the "respect"—was enough. Cullman's hold over the Mayor was quickly apparent to City Hall insiders—and to Moses. Without the Mayor in his corner, the Port Authority was too big and too powerful to fight. Fighting such a foe could be not only bloody but unprofitable. Cooperation might be profitable. With Port Authority help, he would be able to get there first for the federal cash in the 1950's as he had in the 1930's. Immediately upon passage of the Interstate Highway Act, he would be able to present to Washington a proposal for a complete, unified system of highways joining, across authority bridges and tunnels, New York and New Jersey and, through New Jersey, linking up with other highways and other states, a proposal ready to go, planned, blueprinted, costed out, approved, ready for ground breaking, while the proposals of other cities were still in the talking stage, years away from even a possibility of implementation.

Cooperation might, moreover, allow him to tap not only the federal but the Port Authority cashbox.

That cashbox, so long empty, was full now, thanks to the postwar traffic boom, fuller even than Triborough's; its 1953 surplus—its real surplus, not the one reported to the public—was $29,000,000; Triborough's surplus was worth $500,000,000 in new bonds; the Port Authority's was worth $700,000,000. Long on cash, moreover, the Port Authority was short on dreams. The visionaries who had created it were long gone from its councils; Julius Henry Cohen had been replaced by money men like Cullman and Colt and Pope whose eyes were brightened by the balances in the Authority's ledgers, not by the potentialities for improving the common weal that those balances represented. The purpose for which the Authority had been created—the development of an *over-all* transportation system to knit together a great port—had been lost sight of for years. Plans the Authority had aplenty, of course, but unrelated plans, plans for individual projects, joined by no link other than the fact that their construction would return the agency profit. It had more money than Moses but no more than a fraction of his creative vision. As Wagner put it, "Once you get away from . . . taking in quarters, what Tobin has is that board"—and the board's first concern was that Tobin take in more quarters each year than the year before. What Moses had after the quarters was dreams. Moses may have seen—his actions suggest he saw—an opportunity to put the Port Authority surpluses at the service of those dreams, to persuade his erstwhile rival to build first those of its planned projects that would help to realize his vision. The stakes were too high—the chance for profit in both accomplishment and power too big—not to cooperate with his old enemy.

Sometime late in 1953 or early 1954, over luncheon at Randall's Island, he broached to the Port Authority board a plan of staggering scope. At succeeding luncheons at which Tobin represented the board, all did not go smoothly. The plan was Moses' plan—what he was proposing *they* build would turn out to be the bypass route around New York which he had conceived in 1930 and which he had been building in bits and pieces ever since —and he lost no opportunity to make clear that it was his plan, and that anyone who questioned any of its details didn't know what he was talking about. At one luncheon, Tobin jumped up from the table, said, "I don't have to sit here and be insulted like this," and stalked out. But, as it turned out, Tobin *did* have to sit still and be insulted; his boss, Cullman, persuaded by a super helping of Moses' charm that they were again the close friends they had been in the Al Smith era, ordered him to. For, if Moses had reasons to be anxious to cooperate, so did the Port Authority's businessman board.

Having plumbed, in a ten-year series of disputes, the depths of Moses' power in Albany, the Port Authority knew that, deep though theirs ran, his ran deeper. Having attempted to get a string on Hulan Jack, the puppet borough president of Manhattan, the key borough in their plans, they had learned that all the strings were firmly in Moses' hands. Wherever they wanted to go in Manhattan, moreover, they found running along its shore, like a barricade in their path, the Henry Hudson Parkway, over which, as Park Commissioner, Moses had absolute control. They wanted to build a new bridge across the Hudson at 125th Street—such a bridge required connections with the parkway, and, for maximum effectiveness, with Moses' proposed Upper Manhattan Expressway across 125th Street and, via that expressway, with Moses' Triborough Bridge on the other side of Harlem. They wanted to double-deck the George Washington Bridge—double-decking required new connections to the parkway. Moreover, with bridge traffic already cramming the streets of Upper Manhattan near the bridge, the 75 percent increase double-decking would generate could be handled only by construction of a Trans-Manhattan Expressway to the Bronx—with, at its far end, a bridge link to the Cross-Bronx, and with links to the Major Deegan and Harlem River expressways running along the banks of the river far below. City and state had given Moses a veto power over all such bridges and expressways. A power struggle would be bloody. Asked years later who would have won, Wagner would tell the author with a slow smile, "It would have been a hell of a struggle—with that board." And what businessman wants blood when he can have profit? What businessman wants blood when he can end loss? Three Port Authority bridges—the Goethals, Bayonne and Outerbridge spans connecting Staten Island and New Jersey—had been losing money every year for twenty years, earning, in 1953 alone, half a million dollars less than the interest on the bonds that had been floated to build them. Only the construction of the Narrows Crossing that would connect Staten Island to the rest of the city and open it up to large-scale traffic would turn those money losers into money makers. And Moses, thanks to his takeover of the Tunnel Authority, held sole legislative authorization to build the crossing.

Triborough's surpluses were, moreover, not the only surpluses being eyed by politicians. The pressure on the Port Authority to aid mass transit was, in fact, even greater than the pressure on Moses, because the five near-bankrupt railroads whose lines ended at the Hudson were pleading for rail connections across the river, and because the Port Authority's refusal to spend money on such connections was weakened by its original legislative mandate, which clearly envisioned it doing so. The New Jersey Legislature was, in fact, even then in the process of establishing a Metropolitan Rapid Transit Commission, with a prestigious board of its own, and the Legislature had pointedly given the MRTC the responsibility of producing an "over-all coordinated plan for transportation." The Port Authority had to get its surpluses committed—and it had to get them committed fast. Doing so was difficult on the basis of individual projects. A far-reaching road and bridge program would obviously be easier.

Lastly, the Port Authority saw, as Moses saw, that, in the broadest view, they had an identity of interest. In the terms used by Dun and Bradstreet—the terms in which the Port Authority board and Austin Tobin thought—"the success of toll facilities . . . is largely dependent upon the adequacy and convenience of the approaches and connecting highways. Thus, like the ever widening ripples from a stone dropped in the water, every improvement in this system of highways, even at some distance from the . . . facilities, is likely to increase to some extent the traffic on those facilities." A huge new metropolitan region highway network would increase traffic on all bridges and tunnels, theirs as well as Moses'. And such a network could be obtained most easily by—probably, given the immensity of its cost, only by—making it part of the Interstate Highway System, and it could most easily—perhaps only—become part of that system through cooperation. In February 1954, the Port Authority agreed to work with Triborough on a "Joint Study of Arterial Facilities," and on January 16, 1955, the results—sixty-two pages long, hard-bound, four-color, glossy paper, summed up by Moses, who wrote its introduction and whose name, not by coincidence, was listed first among its sponsors—were released to the press.

The "Joint Study" announced that the two authorities "recommend and are prepared to proceed" immediately with three "bridge projects": building the Throgs Neck and Verrazano and double-decking the George Washington. It laid out a system of new arterial highways extending to and from these bridges: a "Bergen County Expressway" on the New Jersey side of the George Washington Bridge and a depressed "Trans-Manhattan Expressway" (really a westward extension of the Cross-Bronx Expressway) on the New York side; a "Clearview Expressway" on the south or Queens side of the Throgs Neck Bridge and a "Throgs Neck Expressway" and "Cross-Bronx Expressway [Eastern] Extension" on the north or Bronx side; a "Clove Lakes Expressway" on the Staten Island side of the Narrows Bridge to link it up with the Goethals and Bayonne spans, and a "Seventh Avenue Expressway," really an extension of the Gowanus Parkway (which was itself now incorporated into the Brooklyn-Queens Expressway), on the Brooklyn side. It recommended that these roads be built immediately with federal and state funds, along with the long-discussed "Mid-Manhattan Elevated Expressway" linking the Lincoln and Queens-Midtown tunnels and the long-discussed "Lower Manhattan Expressway" linking the Holland Tunnel with the Williamsburg and Manhattan bridges. And it recommended for "future construction" a vast new system of expressways across every borough of the city and stretching out into the suburbs, some that Moses had advocated previously and some that he had only recently envisioned: in Queens, a "Long Island," "Ridgewood-Maspeth" and "Nassau"; in the Bronx, a "Sheridan" and "Bruckner"; in Brooklyn, a "Bushwick," "Prospect" and "Cross-Brooklyn"; in Staten Island, a "West Shore," "Richmond" and "Willowbrook"; and, finally, an "Upper Manhattan Expressway" that would cross the island "in the vicinity of 125th Street" to link the Triborough Bridge on the island's east shore with another bridge, a "Hudson River Bridge," which would touch down at 125th Street on the island's west shore, consideration of which should be "deferred until the George Washington Bridge, Narrows Bridge and Throgs Neck Bridge projects have been completed and the traffic patterns at that time can be studied."

The "Joint Program" was nothing more nor less than a business arrangement, with the businessman who could bring to the new partnership the most of the crucial material—power—getting the most out of it. The arrangements for the Narrows Bridge are one proof of this. Moses did not have the money to build the bridge that he envisioned as his supreme monument. But he had the power to build it. The Port Authority was as anxious as Moses to see the Narrows Bridge built, and the Port Authority had the money to build it. But it did not have the power. So under the "Joint Program," the Port Authority agreed to pay for the construction of the bridge—under a contract which said that although the Port Authority would pay for it, the Authority would have nothing else to say about it. The Triborough Authority would lease the great span from the Port Authority, operate it, maintain it and control it absolutely—and would have the right to buy it as soon as it had accumulated enough cash to do so. Moses would, in other words, be building the bridge with his erstwhile rival's money—which would leave him with the money to build another bridge, the Throgs Neck. To get the Narrows Bridge built, moreover, the Port Authority had to give up another bridge that *it* had been anxious to build; it had to allocate for the Narrows span the money it had been planning to spend on the 125th Street span, and formally agree to "defer" that span indefinitely.

The "business" basis for the Joint Program is demonstrated more forcefully still by the program as a whole. As a result of the construction of the Narrows Bridge, use of the Port Authority's three Staten Island spans increased 172 percent—an increase that in terms of tolls collected came, in 1970, to about $5,500,000 per year. As a result of the double-decking of the George Washington Bridge, use of that bridge increased 75 percent—an increase that in terms of tolls collected came, in 1970, to about $11,000,000 per year. The Port Authority's profit from the Joint Program in hard cash was thus about $16,500,000 per year. By 1970, Triborough was collecting $11,000,000 annually in tolls on the Verrazano Bridge, $7,500,000 on the Throgs Neck Bridge—a hard cash profit of $18,500,000 per year. Given the added assets of power that Moses put into the partnership, both parties came out just about even. The two giant authorities were dividing the potential profits from the city's traffic as if congestion were a large and succulent pie. And Moses, who got the slice he wanted, was ecstatic. Talking to a reporter about the Narrows Bridge just before the Joint Program was released, he was again the young man "burning with ideas," unable to contain his enthusiasm. Unable to sit still, striding around his office with smiles breaking through the studiedly aloof mask he habitually wore now, forgetting to fold his arms and gesturing enthusiastically, he told the reporter that at last, after so many years, the Narrows Crossing is no longer "an academic dream."

"There's going to be a bridge pretty soon—the bridge of my dreams," he said. "It's going to be the most important single piece of arterial construction in the world. It will be the longest suspension bridge in the world, and the tallest. . . . It will be the biggest bridge, the highest bridge, and the bridge with the greatest clearance. It's all superlatives when you talk about this bridge . . ."

Although he didn't talk to reporters about them, Moses had additional reasons for elation. The 1955 deal between the Port and Triborough authorities sealed, perhaps for centuries, the future of New York and its suburbs. And it sealed the future on his terms.

In the background behind Moses marched a mighty division: the giant automobile manufacturers out of Detroit, the giant aluminum combines, the steel producers, the rubber producers, fifty oil companies, trucking firms in the hundreds, highway contractors in the thousands, consulting engineers, labor union leaders, auto dealers, tire dealers, petroleum dealers, rank upon rank of state highway department officials, Bureau of Public Roads bureaucrats, congressmen, senators—all the selfish interests whom author Helen Leavitt was to label "The Highwaymen." That coalition was always behind him; it was no accident that he was the recipient in 1953 of a $25,000 award from the General Motors Corporation for the best essay in a nationwide contest on "How to Plan and Pay for Better Highways," that some of Triborough's most lucrative franchises were held by oil companies, that the three automotive giants would later plow tens of millions of dollars into his World's Fair at a time when other major companies were shying away from it. In the sense that he was America's, and probably the world's, most vocal, effective and prestigious apologist for the automobile, that he designed highway networks not only for New York but for a dozen cities, that by his success in building expressways in the city he did more than any other single urban official to encourage more hesitant officials to launch major highway-building programs in *their* cities, and that, by building them to new, high standards, he did more than any other single urban official to set the early standards for urban expressway design—he was the spearhead, the cutting edge, of this Panzer division of public works. But thanks to the Joint Program, he was not forced to rely on any distant division. He was the spearhead of—he marched at the head of—his own elite local regiment. The Joint Program represented profit—profit from bonds, deposits, contracts, premiums, retainers, jobs, payoffs, bribes, grease. It enlisted behind him all those forces in the city—banks, unions, contractors, venal politicians, venal or shortsighted public officials—who put profit from public works above the public interest or the public trust. And in the New York of the mid-twentieth century, those forces could bend the city's government to their will. The Joint Program represented profit on a scale hitherto undreamed of by even the greediest among them. The highways and bridges recommended in the Joint Program represented not millions of dollars but hundreds of millions—in 1968, with some of the most expensive items in the program not yet underway, $1,817,701,607 had been spent on it.* Moses did not have to urge these men on. The Retainer Regiment followed him eagerly.

And the regiment marched in lockstep. The incentives offered to it by the Joint Program insured against the slightest break in its ranks. With the release of the over-all program for the metropolitan region, protests from the ranks no longer concerned him. He could simply threaten, as he did again and again in the years to come, that if any part of the program was eliminated or even altered in any way whatsoever, he would see to it—by withdrawing from the program his Triborough Authority funds or his influence in Albany and Washington—that the entire program would be discarded. A borough president might be allowed to oppose a neighborhood-wrecking highway in public but in private, where it counted, he could

---

* Moses and Triborough PR men referred to the study recommendations as a "$600,000,000 program"—although the cost of the major projects listed came alone to $740,000,000. The $740,000,000 figure may be discarded as safely as the $600,000,000 figure, however; none of the individual cost estimates bore more than a passing relationship to reality.

not take the action that would have meant genuine opposition: the invocation in Board of Estimate executive session of his veto power over projects in his own borough. John Cashmore might publicly assail Moses' plan to run a twelve-lane approach to the Narrows Bridge through the heart of Bay Ridge instead of on a more logical route along the shore, but he had to privately okay Moses' route to the other members of the "Borough Presidents' Union." If he did not do so, Moses made clear, there would be no Narrows Bridge—and no $345,000,000 in bonds and contracts. Moses' technique may have been a bluff, but officials who remembered how he had once canceled $23,000,000 worth of projects in the Bronx because Jimmy Lyons balked at the Bruckner Expressway had too much at stake to call it. Occasionally—very occasionally—a public official might shy away from a politically dangerous proposal, but whether he was a borough president, a Mayor or a Governor, he was quickly reined back into line. Into his office would pour the phone calls from the other members of the regiment, the phone calls that symbolized the behind-the-scenes, subtle, selfish pressure that spelled power in New York City. After the release of the Joint Program, the city didn't have a chance of rejecting the deal that had been arranged. And that deal, worked out by this lover of the bridge and the highway, meant that the city would, for long years to come, build bridges and highways—and nothing else.

In January 1955, the two authorities had a combined immediate fund-raising capacity of about a billion and a quarter dollars.

A billion and a quarter dollars could have built a wonderful mass transportation system for New York and its suburbs. Triborough's share alone—the close to $500,000,000 that could have been raised from the sale of revenue bonds backed by its annual surpluses—would in 1955 have been more than enough to completely modernize the desperate Long Island Rail Road, giving it sleek, gleaming cars, new, powerful modern locomotives much faster than the old ones—and straighter tracks so that those locomotives could attain the speeds they were capable of. Triborough's share would, in 1955, also have been more than enough to build atop the tracks at central locations in Queens and Nassau County multilevel parking garages so that thousands of commuters could drive to them, park and simply take an elevator down to their trains, and in still sparsely developed Suffolk County to acquire sufficient land for, and to build at a number of central locations, entire huge modern commuter parking terminals. Triborough's share would have been more than enough to build not only new modern switching yards so that passengers would no longer be forced to change trains at Jamaica, but a new East Side LIRR terminal in Manhattan. It would have been enough also—especially if right-of-way was obtained along the median strip of the Long Island Expressway—to build a whole new rapid transit line to supplement the three existing Long Island Rail Road lines, a line with tracks so straight that trains could speed passengers into and out of the city at eighty miles per hour. It would have been more than enough, in short, to build what would in effect have been a whole new Long Island Rail Road, a modern railroad capable of meeting the mass transportation needs of a modern metropolitan area, and of attracting to mass transportation enough highway users to go a long way to solving the area's highway needs as well. The cost of such a system—impossibly expensive in 1974—would, in 1955, have been not $500,000,000 but $200,000,000.

The Port Authority's share alone—more than $700,000,000—would have been more than enough to build a modern trans-Hudson rail loop that would connect New Jersey and Manhattan via two new under-river tunnels, one at the Battery and one at Fifty-ninth Street, and would provide transfer stations to all the New Jersey railroads and all major New Jersey highways in the area, speeding 140,000 commuters, shoppers and theater-goers per day not just into Manhattan but to wherever in those Manhattan business and commercial districts they wanted to go—there would be stops at Cedar, Canal, Houston, Eighth, Fourteenth and other streets all the way north to Columbus Circle—and removing tens of thousands of cars from New Jersey highways, the trans-Hudson vehicular tunnels, the West Side Highway and Manhattan streets, so that those commuters who still used them would have easier trips also. The cost of such a system would, in 1955, have been about $300,000,000.

If what was left over after the completion of the Long Island Rail Road modernization and the trans-Hudson tubes—about $700,000,000—was used on the city's subway system, it would have been more than enough to build the long-proposed and desperately needed Second Avenue Subway, *and* to build a tunnel across the East River through which a branch of the Second Avenue line would extend out to Queens to provide adequate subway service there, *and* to build extensions of the existing subway lines in Queens to provide service to the hundreds of thousands of residents of eastern Queens who were miles from the nearest subway, *and* to extend the Nostrand Avenue Subway in Brooklyn three miles along Flatbush Avenue to a new, modern terminal that would serve the growing Mill Basin area that possessed no rapid transit facilities at all, *and* to construct a new plaza and grade-crossing elimination project at DeKalb Avenue that would eliminate switching delays which caused the most severe bottleneck in train service between Brooklyn and Manhattan—the total cost of these improvements in 1955 came to $600,000,000. And there were other alternatives. If, instead of spending part of it in the suburbs, the two authorities devoted their total revenue-raising capacity—$1,200,000,000—to the subways instead of commuter facilities, it would have been sufficient to give the city a completely modern subway system—the total cost of a complete modernization was estimated by the Transit Authority in that year as $1,187,000,000. (Even if only that portion of the capacity left after commuter improvements was used for subways, it might still have been sufficient to give New York a modern subway system, for during the decade following the

Joint Proposal, the two authorities' annual revenues from tolls rose so much faster than expected—for their forecasters never understood, and therefore never took fully into account, the phenomenon of traffic generation—that their wealth far outstripped even their most optimistic expectations, and the amount available for mass transit facilities, if their total resources had been devoted to such facilities, might well have been not a billion and a quarter dollars but more than two billion dollars.) The two authorities had it in their power in 1955 to make it possible for the people of the New York metropolitan region to travel around that region quickly, cheaply and pleasantly. They had it in their power in January 1955 to change the way the region's millions lived.

Instead, as a result of Robert Moses' Joint Program, the two authorities, with three major exceptions—Triborough's Coliseum; the Port Authority's substantial expenditures for airports, and for a 1960 takeover of the Hudson and Manhattan Railroad—spent their money on facilities for the automobile. Triborough spent, once the Coliseum expenditures were subtracted, 100 percent of its resources on the automobile. During the decade following the formulation of the Joint Program, Triborough spent $755,000,000 on the bridges, tunnels and highways advocated in that study—and not a cent on anything else.

The authority funds that the Joint Program committed to facilities for motor vehicles widened more indirectly the disparity between public investment in such facilities and public investment in mass transit that was fostered by the Program. During the following decade—1955 to 1965—federal and state governments spent on new highways in the metropolitan area—the new highways recommended in the Joint Program—about $1,200,000,000. They spent not a cent on mass transportation. New York City's own contribution to Moses' new highways is more difficult to calculate, hidden as so much of it is—owing to Moses' wiles—under hundreds of "sewer," "street opening," "gas" and "lighting" items that bear no indication that they would not have been necessary had it not been for highway construction—but the city's expenditure for new facilities for motor vehicles almost certainly tops $500,000,000. During the decade following presentation of the Joint Program, therefore, public investment in new highways in and around New York was about $2,700,000,000. The public investment in new mass transportation facilities was a small fraction of this amount. During this decade, 439 miles of new highways were built—and not one mile of new railroad or subway. In 1974, people using subways and railroads in and around New York were still riding on tracks laid between 1904 and 1933, the last year before Robert Moses came to power in the city. Not a single mile had been built since.

Because there were no subways or railroads into many newly developed areas, their residents could use mass transit only by first making their way to the old rail lines—often a journey in itself. More than half of all suburban "rail commuters" and "subway riders" from outlying areas of the city had to take a bus or car ride—often of considerable length—to the nearest subway or railroad station.

At rush hours, the scenes at subway stations in the greatest city in history's richest and technologically most advanced civilization were incredible. At a hundred stations, the traveler arrived each morning at the head of the stairs leading down onto the loading platforms to see beneath him, overflowing them, lapping precariously full to their very edges, a sea of humanity—a sea into which the traveler had no choice but to hurl himself.

To get inside the trains, men and women pushed and shoved like irritable animals, rushing for seats as animals rush for a food trough, for without a seat they would have to stand—body crushed against body, strangers' smells in their nostrils, strangers' breath in their faces—in a press so dense that there could exist in it neither comfort nor dignity nor manners. Writers called subway cars "cattle cars"; they said people were crammed into them "like sardines"; and such nonhuman images were apt. For the crowding in New York's subways—crowding to which hundreds of thousands of human beings were subjected day after day, year after year, for all the years of their working lives—was inhuman. Although most office workers were not due at work until nine o'clock, on any weekday morning one could see around the subway stations in the outlying areas of the city—past the chain-link fences of the giant parking lots on Woodhaven Boulevard near the giant new Lefrak City housing development in Queens, for example—long lines of men and women, during fall and winter huddling in their coats against the too early morning chill, hurrying for the stations at seven forty-five or even seven-thirty, willing to forgo a half hour or more of sleep, willing to gulp down a coffee and danish at the office instead of breakfasting at home, to avoid the worst of that degrading ordeal. By eight, it was already too late. As one observer described the scene at that hour:

> . . . the parking lots around the Woodhaven Boulevard station are filling up rapidly as cars stream from the expressway. Buses filled to capacity pull up and disgorge their passengers. Now the subway platform is packed six deep with people waiting impassively. As the local arrives, they surge forward, merging, pushing, straining. Some clutch newspapers, but they cannot move, much less read. At Roosevelt Avenue, the express trains arriving from Jamaica, Kew Gardens and Forest Hills are jammed to the doors, but somehow more bodies squeeze inside. By eight-thirty the crowd at Woodhaven Boulevard backs up the stairs. Those in the rear files must wait for one and perhaps two locals before they can wedge themselves aboard.

Crowded though they were, the Queens subway lines were not as crowded as the lines running down from the Bronx along the east side of Manhattan. Since shortly after World War I, the city had been promising to build a Second Avenue Subway to service those areas. Lying in the bottom drawer of the desk of a city engineer whose job dealt with subway design was a set of plans. "My father [a civil servant in the same department] gave me these plans when I came into the business" in 1929, he would tell friends. They would unroll the plans—and the friends would laugh at seeing they were plans for "The Second Avenue Subway." After World War II, the city, having torn down the old Second Avenue El, which serviced a portion of the same area, repeated its promise. In 1955 (in the process of tearing down the Third Avenue El, which serviced part of the same area), the city promised that construction was imminent. But in 1965, the subway would still not be built—or even begun. And the thousands of passengers who had used the two old elevated lines had to pack into the already crammed Lexington Avenue IRT line. By 1965, the average car in the southbound express, designed for an "absolute maximum" capacity of 120 passengers, was jammed during the morning rush hour with some 170 passengers, which, as one study indicated, "is just about the maximum short of suffocation."

There were available in 1955, the year of the authorities' Joint Program, technological innovations which could have increased not only subway capacity but subway speed. Not one of any significance was instituted. The rides were as long as ever—longer, for the lack of available operating funds forced continual cutbacks in express service.

The cars into which subway riders were crammed were cars thirty and forty years old in 1955, and due for replacement. Such replacement would have been possible with the authorities' surplus. They were not replaced—and in 1965, almost 20 percent of New York's subway cars had been in use for more than half a century. In winter, because of their ancient, malfunctioning heating systems, subway cars were cold; in the summer—particularly on the IRT, built in 1904, because in 1904, construction techniques to ventilate subway tunnels had not yet been invented—they were so swelteringly hot that one writer compared a ride on them to incarceration in the Black Hole of Calcutta.

Not only were new cars not purchased; the old ones were not repaired. It was about 1956 that there was instituted on the New York City subway system, because of lack of funds, a policy of "deferred maintenance"—a phrase which, translated into practice, meant that brakes and signals and switches were inspected less frequently, that wheels were ground round to keep rides smooth less frequently, that electrical relays which should have been replaced every five years were replaced every thirty years, that the vast system was sometimes completely "out" of light bulbs to replace burnt-out signals, alcohol to keep switches from freezing, and other basic supplies.

So superbly engineered and maintained had the system been previously (New York had once been enormously proud of its subways) that it took years for this systematic neglect to take its toll, but, every year after 1956, every criterion of subway performance—on-time runs, individual car breakdowns—disclosed that the toll was steadily mounting. By the late 1960's, the day of full reckoning had arrived: 17,070 runs had to be halted during a single eight-month period; forty-five cars were breaking down on an *average* day; forty trains were derailed in a single year.

By the time Robert Moses left power, the *Times* could report that on a system that had for decades been called—accurately—"the safest subway in the world," there have been more serious accidents . . . in the last ten years than on any other major subway system in the world; in the last year, there have been more accident injuries than on any other system.

During a single seven-month period, there were four major accidents; in one, an empty IND local—being operated from the third car because the brakes in the first two cars no longer worked—smashed into a crowded local near Roosevelt Avenue, killing two persons and injuring seventy others; in another, a clogged South Bronx catch basin—cleaning machines had not been replaced as they wore out—turned IRT tunnels into gigantic storm sewers as water cascaded down air shafts and stairways, trapping 30,000 passengers for up to three hours in subway tunnels where the temperature reached 100 degrees in a disaster in which one woman died and 150 passengers suffered heat prostration. During this same seven-month period, four separate fires in subway tunnels under the city—caused at least in part by equipment that an investigating grand jury was to call "inherently dangerous and defective"—sent thousands of "terrified, smoke-blinded passengers stumbling out into the subterranean murk to grope their way to emergency exits and reach the street above via manholes." One blaze—toll: one dead, fifty felled by smoke poisoning—went unreported for long minutes: the motorman's radio was out of order.

Less dramatic than the injury toll—but wearing on the tens of thousands of subway riders who were never involved in a major disaster—was the daily toll imposed by calculated neglect. The floors of New York's subways were filthy, and the grime was mixed with scattered pages of newspapers, candy and gum wrappers and, for emphasis, an occasional blob of spittle or a smear of vomit that no one had yet wiped up. Subway walls were covered with verbal filth; the scenery amid which the New Yorker traveled around his city was a vast mosaic of FUCK and SUCK and COCK and CUNT.

Knowing that they could no longer rely for safety on brakes and signals, the operating authorities responsible for the subways responded to each major disaster by placing more and more of their reliance on caution; trains crept where once they could have safely speeded, and ground to a halt at the slightest possibility of danger ahead. Consequently, the time New Yorkers were forced to spend daily, shivering or sweltering on those bumpy, jolting, filthy trains, grew longer and longer. Where once the average trip from the city's outskirts to its center had been forty or forty-five minutes, now it was an hour or more. When Robert Moses came to power in New York in 1934, the city's mass transportation system was probably the best in the world. When he left power in 1968, it was quite possibly the worst.

With money, you could buy almost anything in mid-twentieth-century New York. But you couldn't buy a decent trip to and from work. Wealthier families might move to the suburbs, but Moses' Joint Proposal of 1955 had sealed the fate of the metropolitan region's nine suburban commuter railroads. In 1955, some of those railroads were still healthy—the New Haven, profitable, clean and punctual, had just purchased scores of gleaming new cars; the Penn Central's Harlem and Hudson divisions were, one commentator said, "a model of how to keep 42,000 daily commuters happy"—but others were teetering precariously on the brink of financial disaster; the Long Island, the commuter line most directly in Moses' line of fire, had, in fact, been shoved over the brink; it had plunged into bankruptcy in 1949 and had been kept alive—barely alive—thereafter only by a series of state tax concessions.

Moses' Joint Program expressways siphoned off the railroads' customers precisely as the planners had predicted. The railroads were private corporations, in existence for the sole purpose of showing a profit. To show one, they would have had to compete successfully with the public authorities that were their competitors. But while the authorities' toll-charging facilities were subsidized by hundreds of millions of dollars of connecting highways, by freedom from taxes on their hundreds of millions of dollars of real estate and on their income, the railroads enjoyed no such subsidies, and were trapped as well by mounting labor costs, minimal to authorities operating only low-maintenance bridges and tunnels. Every railroad attempt during this decade to obtain meaningful subsidies was defeated by New York's local "highwaymen," the banks, construction unions, contractors, engineering and bonding and building-supply firms and politicians who reaped profit from Moses' highways, a coalition led by Triborough's chairman, who, as its prestigious public spokesman, on one occasion assured Congress that no subsidy was needed because "there is little need for an expansion of railroad commuter facilities in the New York metropolitan area," and, on another, when an impartial private study called a subsidy imperative, dynamited it by assuring the public that the major problem was simply that the railroads were not as efficient, prudent, practical and businesslike as the public authorities—stating: "These railroads have got to be more ingenious. . . . bailing out busted, lazy and backward private enterprises is [not] the business of government." (Moses added that mass transportation needs could be met on highways as well as on railroads. "A great deal of passenger traffic today consists of carpools," an "immeasurably more convenient" and less expensive system, he said.)

Unable to compete with the authorities, the railroads grew poorer as their rivals grew richer. Even those which in 1955 had been showing profits, by 1959 or 1960 were showing losses—bigger losses every year. By the early 1960's, those who still possessed any money in the bank were living off it just to stay alive—and were rapidly consuming the last of it. They had no alternative but to raise fares and cut back service, moves that touched off a self-defeating cycle: each fare increase and service cutback drove railroad passengers to the highways. (The Long Island Rail Road increased fares five times during ten years; after each increase, the railroad collected a million fewer fares per year.) A decade after the Joint Proposal, with millions of new potential customers, the commuter railroads were providing substantially less service: the Long Island Rail Road, which during the 1920's had run between fifty and sixty trains per hour into Manhattan, in

1965, with Long Island's commuter population up more than 200 percent, ran between twenty and thirty.

The service that was provided in 1965—or 1968, the year Robert Moses left power—should be chronicled in depth. Otherwise, future urban historians will dismiss oral and daily press descriptions of that service as exaggeration.

The Long Island Rail Road, for example, was, in the words of one reporter, "the kind of train that, if smaller, would make your little boy cry if he found it under his Christmas tree." With its creaking, rickety 1900-vintage coaches, it resembled the comic strip "Toonerville Trolley." Humorist Russell Baker, naming it "The Looneyville Trolley," said that it

> was nationally recognized as the worst railroad of any kind in the entire country. Railroad buffs from all over the world came to New York to look at it. A few would even have ridden on it in spite of the warnings of medical science, except that they made the mistake of going to the station when the time-table said the Long Island would be there and, therefore, could never find it.

But if the Long Island was a joke, it was a bitter joke. Its riders laughed because, as one of them, Al Cassuto of Woodmere, put it, "What else can you do but laugh? If you don't you'll go crazy."

Living standards on affluent Long Island were high even for America. The homes of many Long Island Rail Road commuters were large, luxurious, thickly carpeted, richly draperied, crammed with the most modern appliances for cleanliness and cooking. The vicissitudes of climate were eliminated for them not only in their homes—no county in America had so many centrally air-conditioned homes as Nassau—but in their automobiles, all of them heated, most of them air-conditioned. These automobiles—the automobiles out of which Long Islanders stepped every weekday morning to board the Long Island Rail Road—symbolized the degree to which the affluence and technological genius of America had given its people a life cushioned against physical discomfort.

Then the train arrived, and the Long Islanders climbed aboard.

The linoleum on the floors of the coaches into which they stepped was cracked and split, impacted with layers of grime. Paint was flaking off grimy walls. The windows, so thickly smeared with grime that you could hardly see through some of them, were filled with spider webs, and with the lacy spread of thin cracks radiating out from holes smashed in them and never repaired. Some of the holes were covered with bits of cardboard held on with tape; others gaped jaggedly.

The seats were ripped and humped. Their springs were sprung. Their backs sagged limply backwards. Sitting in those seats meant sitting in dirt. If you rested your arm on a windowsill, your coat sleeve came away covered with dust. You sat with your feet among wads of chewed-up gum on which the spittle had long since dried, among gum and candy wrappers, sheets of newspapers, fragments of ice-cream cones and, occasionally, discarded hunks of food. It was a good idea not to let your eyes focus on the floor. You might see drobs of spittle, or fat bugs scuttling by your bright and shiny shoes. Yet men pushed and shoved for those seats, for those who didn't get them had to stand, and standing on the Long Island's swaying, lurching coaches wasn't easy.

Particularly because one might have to stand for quite a long time. Even when it was running on time, the Long Island Rail Road was slow—incredibly slow. And the railroad seemed almost never to be running on time. There were days, in fact, on which, because of equipment malfunction in the LIRR's main Pennsylvania Station terminal, every Long Island train was late. There were days on which every Long Island train was *hours* late; some commuters couldn't remember when last they had been on time. In tabulating the number of delayed trains, the LIRR did not even bother counting those delayed less than ten minutes. Even so, the daily figures were not unremarkable. Here is one day's record:

Trains canceled yesterday—one; commuters affected—1,000. Trains more than ten minutes late—187; total time lost—74 hours, 15 minutes; commuters affected —140,250.

Getting a seat was not total victory. Getting an end seat was what counted. Many of the LIRR seats had been designed for three people—but they had been designed half a century before, when people were smaller. There wasn't enough room for three people. Sitting in even an end seat was indignity; it was sitting with your shoulder and thigh tight against a stranger's shoulder and thigh, pressing into him at every lurch, pushing against him while opening a newspaper or reaching into a pocket for your train ticket, surreptitiously taking advantage of shifts in his position to gain an extra quarter inch of room for your leg or arm. But sitting in the middle was indignity doubled. The person sitting there was crushed from both sides, leaned into from both sides, without room to make an unrestricted movement of any kind. "Of all the things I hated about the Long Island Rail Road," says one woman, "the worst was sitting in the middle on those seats. You'd have men pressing against you on both sides. They didn't mean anything by it. Some of them were sleeping and lying all over you. But it made me feel dirty. Standing at rush hour—it was the same thing. There'd be men leaning all over you. But being stuck in the middle on those seats was worse. There was never a time it happened that I didn't get off the train feeling dirty." It was no wonder that the first two persons to reach the three-man seats took the two end positions, and that when a third arrived, invariably the one sitting on the outside, closest to the aisle, would, instead of politely sliding over to make room for the new man on the outside, stand up and let him by to take the middle seat, careful not to look him in the eye.

In winter, the trips were cold. Heating equipment half a century old and haphazardly maintained could not be expected to work well. Not that even modern, well-maintained equipment could have kept heated a coach in which it seemed that every other window either had a hole in it or could not be shut tightly. A reporter who took a thermometer onto an LIRR train one winter day—not by any means the coldest day of the winter—found that the temperature aboard was 29 degrees. Men who in home and office enjoyed temperature controlled to the precise degree, had to travel between home and office huddled shivering in their coats.

And winter was, perhaps, better than summer. The crush in the cars kept the temperature up, and in winter that was a help. In summer, it was not, and help was needed, since 70 percent of the LIRR's ancient rolling stock did not have air-conditioning equipment. Men who tried frantically to open windows—one could watch them tug on them furiously every few minutes on a long summer ride home—found them stuck fast. A reporter who took a thermometer onto a jam-packed LIRR train one summer day—not by any means the hottest day of the summer—found that the temperature aboard was 98 degrees. Men who would not have dreamed of living in a home or working in an office that was not air-conditioned, rode each day between home and office sweltering, the sweat forming in their armpits and crotches and running down their backs and legs.

Long Island Rail Road trains did not always run late. Sometimes they did not run at all. Year by year, as already old equipment grew older, the number of trains that simply broke down on the track increased. It was no longer unusual to see a train arrive in Jamaica being pushed along by another train. The number of trains that didn't even make it out onto a track increased. By 1964, it was not unusual for the railroad to cancel ten trains per day. One train, the 7:45 A.M. from Babylon to Brooklyn, did not appear for 102 consecutive days; would-be passengers named it "the Phantom."

Long Islanders' lives were cushioned—approximately twenty-two hours out of every twenty-four—by all the material wonders the twentieth century could provide. For those other two hours—two hours that could with accuracy have been called "Robert Moses' Two Hours," for he had made them what they were—they lived like nineteenth-century Russian peasants.

There comes a time, H. L. Mencken said, when every normal man is tempted "to spit on his hands, haul up the black flag and begin slitting throats." The LIRR's conductors were not responsible for conditions on the railroad. The commuters knew that—rationally. But the conductors were a visible symbol of the railroad's management on which the commuters could vent their frustration. Men normally rational found themselves snarling and cursing conductors, refusing to show them their tickets; as a result, men who would not have been able to conceive of themselves being arrested suddenly found themselves in that state. "Arrested!" as one reporter put it: "Portly, balding, mild-mannered, 53-year-old Seymour Cummins, district sales manager, commuter, family man. Seymour Cummins, of all people, being led off the train by two policemen, one on each arm, as his wife watched in disbelief." By 1968, the year Robert Moses left power, commuters were, as one writer put it, "so . . . surly that the conductors occasionally choose, like prudent lion tamers, not to enter the cage." One freezing evening, at Jamaica, while commuters huddled in downstairs waiting rooms because the waiting rooms near the tracks upstairs were unheated, a malfunctioning public-address system prevented them from hearing announcements of incoming trains. Storming upstairs in sudden senseless fury, 250 commuters began pounding on the glass walls of the announcer's booth, trying to get at the terrified occupant—they had broken the glass when police arrived to pull them away. On another freezing night, a train broke down some miles from the nearest station. Its passengers got off and began throwing rocks at it. Similar incidents occurred again and again. One evening in Penn Station—with 150 rush-hour trains running late—a fifty-eight-year-old bank employee from Bayside, enraged because a conductor would not open the doors to let him on a train that had loaded but had been standing for close to half an hour on the platform, reached through the window to the engineer's booth, grabbed something and refused to let go. And when the railroad police rushed up to pull him away, suddenly, as one police sergeant put it, "this place was wall-to-wall people, thousands of people"—pulling at the policemen, punching them. "It was a riot down there," the sergeant said. "It was actually a riot." And it was testimony to the rage to which conditions on New York's railroads could drive men.

Actual physical violence was, of course, unusual, and therefore it is not in violence that the true toll of commuting on the Long Island Rail Road should be computed. It is in the norm—to which the violence is only occasional, violent punctuation—the norm that endures day after day, week after week, year after year, for tens of thousands of commuters (the LIRR carried 80,000 daily), that the toll of commuting should be computed.

The true extent of this toll can perhaps be described in psychiatric terms. The chairman of the Nassau County Mental Health Board, in one of the first detailed studies of the subject, discovered a "commuter syndrome," "a mild state of chronic stress resulting from internalized rage and frustration due to the uncertainty of disrupted schedules." It was most serious in commuters who were "business executives, overly worrying, driving, ambitious and aggressive types. . . . Such a person, who preserves his valuable time by living to a tight schedule, is tremendously vulnerable, psychologically speaking, to transportation failures." But the commuter syndrome, the study found, was not present only in executives. Three out of every four commuters tested suffered from its symptoms.

Chronically.

But it did not take a psychiatrist to compute the toll. A layman could do it—by asking commuters in a relaxed setting—a cocktail party, perhaps—about commuting and then taking note of the contrast between the answers he gets from young men—or men recently moved to a new home on Long Island—and those he gets from older men.

A young man might say, as twenty-six-year-old Michael Liberman of Dix Hills did one evening, "People's lives revolve around the railroad. You can spend five hours a day on it, and then you're just too tired to work." He might say, as thirty-six-year-old Allen Siegal of Roslyn did one evening, "I think we're out of our minds to do this. The trip home is worse than eight or nine hours at the office." Men who have been commuting for years, however, generally do not go into detail. Nor do they complain much. Their standard reply—one so standard that the questioner can hear it a dozen times in a dozen conversations—apparently sincere, is: "Oh, you get used to it after a while."

The implications of that reply should be considered.

"Get used to it!" Accept as part of your daily existence two or three—or more—hours sitting amid dirt, crammed against strangers, breathing foul air, sweating in summer, shivering in winter. Accept that you will be doing this for a substantial portion of every working day of your life, until you are old. *"Get used to it!"* One has to think about what those words, so casually uttered, really mean. One has to realize that the man uttering those words has accepted discomfort and exhaustion as a part—a substantial part—of the fabric of his life. Accepted them so completely that he no longer really thinks about them—or about the amount of his life of which they are, day by day, robbing him. *We learn to tolerate intolerable conditions.* The numbness that is the defense against intolerable pain has set in—so firmly that many of the victims no longer even realize that the pain *is* pain.

One should listen to the wives of these men—to be more precise, the younger wives—say, as Mrs. Mary Severine of Huntington, whose husband, Louis, was general manager of advertising for the American Broadcasting Company, says: "We never plan anything during the week. There's got to be something more in life than Saturday night." Older wives do not talk much about it. After enough years, they don't complain that "there's got to be something more in life than Saturday night." They just forget that there ever was.

And then, to comprehend the full toll of commuting, one should try to imagine—for no one has yet arrived at an objective method of measuring it—the total human cost, individual cost times 80,000, of commuting under such conditions. It may be that the cost—the total toll in human terms—is too large to be imagined. But if one makes the effort nonetheless, and obtains even a glimpse of its dimensions, one can get a glimpse of the true cost of Robert Moses' transportation policies on Long Island.

And Long Island was not the only New York suburban railroad on the track toward chaos. It was only the first of many making that journey. When Moses had first come to power in the suburbs—in 1924—New York's suburban railroads had been in good shape. As late as 1955, when he formulated his Joint Program, most of them had still been in fair shape. By the time he left power in 1968, they were all as much of a bitter joke as the Long Island. The New Haven Railroad had in 1955 been a model of punctuality, cleanliness and profitability. In 1968, as one headline put it, ON THE NEW HAVEN, L.I.R.R. LOOKS GOOD. By 1968, moreover, with the annual surplus of Moses' Triborough Bridge and Tunnel Authority running more than $30,000,000 per year, every suburban railroad in the New York metropolitan area was either bankrupt or teetering on the brink.

The massive migration to the city's outlying precincts and to the suburbs beyond had created hundreds of thousands of new commuters. Had the subways and railroads been extended into these regions and improved with the Authority funds available in 1954, they would have been used by many of these commuters. Had they been merely maintained at even their old levels, with their old fares—not improved, just maintained—they would at least have kept those riders they already had. But, disintegrating, they did not. After the Joint Program, the number of rides taken annually on New York's subways and commuter railroads declined by almost two million per year. Commuters by the tens and hundreds of thousands had been forced onto the highways and bridges Robert Moses had laid out under the Joint Program and had been building ever since. And it was on those highways and bridges—the creations of a single individual, public works sprung from that individual's private creative vision, financed and approved as a result of his unique political genius, driven to completion by his savage drive and unswerving will—that the effect of that single individual's policies on the 12,000,000 individuals who lived in the New York metropolitan region was most clear.

Those highways and bridges were awesome. The transportation network built by Robert Moses after World War II ranks with the greatest feats of urban construction in recorded history. Possibly it outranks them all. Possibly it is history's greatest feat of urban construction. The longest tunnel in the Western Hemisphere, the longest suspension bridge in the world, the largest and most complex traffic interchanges ever built—these were all merely segments of that achievement. Its over-all scale can perhaps best be grasped by a single statistic: mileage. The "urban" highways—controlled-access through roads within cities and the heavily populated surrounding suburbs—built in America during the quarter century following the Second World War dwarfed any urban highway or system of highways built in any country in the world any time in recorded history. In 1964, when Robert Moses completed his major highway building, there were completed or well under way in the New York metropolitan region 899 miles of such highways—627 built by him, many of the rest, most of which were in New Jersey, built as a result of the Joint Program he worked out with the Port Authority. No other metropolitan region in America possessed 700 miles of such highways. No other metropolitan region possessed 600 miles—or 500. Even Los Angeles, which presented itself to history as the most highway-oriented of cities—which was, in fact, not a city in the older sense in which New York was a city but a collection of suburbs whose very existence was due to highways—possessed in 1964 only 459 miles of such highways. No city in America had more than half as many miles of such highways as New York. But nothing about his roads was as awesome as the congestion on them.

Nineteen fifty-five was also a turning point for New York and its suburbs because that was the year construction started on the Long Island Expressway.

Long Island, that vast, empty, beautiful open area beyond the city line that Moses had looked upon in 1923, had since been covered—thanks largely to his parkways, his starving of its railroads, his initiation and encouragement of industry-excluding zoning—with a formless, unfocused sprawl of subdivisions, mile upon endless mile of land-gobbling, single-family, large-lot developments that were not only destroying the very assets that he prized—its openness, its spaciousness, its beautiful North Shore hills and South Shore marshes and wetlands, its ocean and bay and sound—but were replacing it with communities that were not communities, that had no "downtowns," none of the focal points that alone make meaningful community development possible and that were so spread out that a trip to anywhere—store, church, school, movie, business—generally required a car, so that the lives of its residents were eaten up by the difficulties in getting from one place to another. The construction of the expressway offered a chance to reshape the Island, to free its people from the tyranny of the automobile.

Just laying two rapid transit tracks down the expressway's center mall would have done the job. Without them, expressway-fostered development would follow the same pattern as the development fostered previously by Moses' parkways, and for the same reasons: its users would be arriving at their exits in the evenings in cars; it would not make that much difference to them if their homes were located miles from an exit; having been driving for an hour or more, it wouldn't matter much to them if they had to drive for another fifteen or twenty minutes. They would be accustomed to driving, oriented to cars—and their homes would therefore spread out widely over the land. But men arriving on high-speed rapid transit would feel as men arriving home on the subways felt. Many would want to be able to walk home; more important, they would not be car-oriented in general; they would want to live in neighborhoods rather than subdivisions—you would therefore have, as you had in New York City, high-density development—apartment houses, private homes on small plots—in the central corridor up which the expressway was to run. (As was proven by Long Island's existing apartment-house development: concentrated almost exclusively within a block or two of major LIRR stations in communities such as Great Neck, Roslyn, Mineola, Hempstead, Rockville Centre, Freeport and Baldwin.) Higher population densities make feasible the construction of theaters and large department stores, of museums and reference libraries, and people living in or near the central corridor would therefore be able to reach these facilities—and their churches, doctors, dentists and their son's Boy Scout troop meetings—on foot or in buses (for high densities support convenient local bus service). For people living in the central corridor, it would not be necessary to get into cars every time they left the house. Automobile usage for the Island as a whole would, at a stroke, be dramatically slashed. In terms of transportation alone, building rapid transit on the Long Island Expressway would immensely improve the lives of millions of people.

And there were other terms of improvement as well. Long Island's central corridor also contained both the Northern State Parkway and the LIRR's central line. Building the expressway would lure industry to that corridor; industry was already attracted to it because of the LIRR line. (Planners had long been urging that that lure be strengthened by improving the LIRR and linking its Brooklyn terminal to the New Jersey railroads, a move that would make it immensely more attractive to freight shippers; their hopes would finally be dashed by Moses' refusal to consider an alternative location for the Verrazano Bridge that would have made such a link feasible.) As industry moved to Long Island's spine, so would its workers, and there would be enough of them who wanted to live close to their jobs to further increase those densities—and the apartment houses and variety of services those densities would support. The Island, now without a focus, would be given one. Its over-all development would, at a stroke, be made more orderly: people who wanted to live in apartments or near stores or jobs or rapid transit to New York would live in the center of the Island instead of having to live like everyone else in sprawling subdivisions. People who preferred larger homesites to convenience would live farther away from the center. Densities would therefore get lower and lower the farther one moved from the center. People who wanted open space would have been able to find more of it—larger lots for their houses, more parks and woods preserved, for they would no longer be so valuable to developers; people who wanted open space, in other words, would be able to find more of it on Long Island at the same time that people who wanted a more urban type of life could have found that, too. The concentration of population down the center of the Island would preserve at least some of the Island's beauty away from the center.

Building rapid transit on the Long Island Expressway was not only the best way to rescue Long Islanders from the automobile but the only way. The Island's transportation problem was complicated by one unblinkable geographical fact: Long Island *was* an island, connected by Moses to the mainland at only one end. Its other end stuck out into the Atlantic Ocean, connected to nothing. It was a cul-de-sac, a dead end. It might be a gigantic dead end—116 miles long, an average of 12 miles wide, it contained 1,404 square miles—but it was a dead end nonetheless. Manufacturers wanting to import raw materials or ship out finished products had only one way to go, and so did commuters heading for the great corporate headquarters lumped together on Manhattan Island, housewives heading for Manhattan's museums, art galleries and theaters—anyone who wanted to leave the Island for any purpose whatever. As an industrial mortgage broker put it: "You can't think east; it's got to be west. Your raw materials have to come in from the west; your finished products have to go out to the west. And the west is New York, and New York is congestion." In 1955, Long Island's population was already 6,200,000, greater than that of forty-one states. But forecasters were predicting that by 1985 the population would be at least 8,500,000. Forecasters agreed, moreover, that little of this increase would come in Brooklyn and Queens, the part of the Island within the city limits, and relatively little in western or central Nassau County—most of the land on Long Island for a distance of thirty miles out was already substantially covered with homes. The increase was going to come in the rest of Long Island—the eighty additional miles stretching out to the east, eighty miles that were in 1955 still to surprising extent the scrub-oak and pine barrens and far-stretching potato fields they had been in 1923 but into which Moses was planning to lay, not only for the expressway but for extensions of the Northern and Southern State parkways, broad swaths of concrete, giant cloverleafs among the potato fields. The Regional Plan Association was predicting conservatively that the population of Nassau and Suffolk—less than a million and a half in 1955—would be more than four million in 1985. Onto Long Island's potato fields was going to be dumped a population the size of Philadelphia. Without local jobs, this population was still going to be largely dependent on Manhattan, on the west. There would not only be many more people living on Long Island; these people would have to travel much farther to their jobs. The intracounty roads—local roads, mainly north-south roads—of Long Island's two suburban counties were already clogged with their present traffic. How were they supposed to handle the traffic generated by two and a half million more people?

And it wasn't on the north-south roads that the most serious problems were going to occur but on the roads to the great city to the west. In 1955, there were an estimated 600,000 individual car trips across the city line eastward or westward every twenty-four hours. In 1960, the RPA was predicting, there would be an estimated 800,000; in 1970, an estimated 1,000,000; in 1985, the last year for which projections were made, an estimated 1,400,000. How were roads ever going to handle such traffic?

In particular, how were they going to handle the traffic during morning and evening rush hours?

Employment-location forecasts showed that in 1985 about half of all Nassau and Suffolk wage earners were still going to be commuting daily to New York because that was where the jobs were going to be. The only difference in the situation was going to be that, because of the deterioration of the Long Island Rail Road and the diffusion of population away from its lines, a far greater proportion of commuters was going to be commuting by car. In 1955, out of 250,000 wage earners living in Nassau and Suffolk, 115,000 commuted to New York, 40,000 by automobile (joining 50,000 from Queens—see footnote, page 946). In 1960, according to the most conservative forecasts, there were going to be about 125,000 commuters crossing the city line heading west in the morning rush hour and crossing it heading east in the evening rush hour—about 50,000 in cars; in 1970, there were going to be 160,000 commuting—70,000 in cars; in 1985, 215,000 commuting—90,000 in cars. And these were just the commuters from beyond the city line. How about the commuters from Queens—an estimated 90,000 car commuters by 1985 piling onto the same east-west roads at the same time as the 90,000 from the suburban counties?

Attempting to handle traffic in such volume by building highways just didn't make sense. In 1955, there were 90,000 drivers commuting from Nassau, Suffolk and Queens, and existing highways couldn't come near handling them. Now you were talking about adding another 90,000 drivers. The capacity of an expressway lane, under optimum conditions, was only 1,500 cars per hour. You would have to build sixty lanes of new highway just to keep up with the increase in traffic, not to catch up with the deficit in lanes already existing. The Long Island Expressway would be six lanes, three in each direction. Its maximum rush-hour capacity would therefore be 4,500 cars. Forty-five hundred cars out of 90,000! Building the Long Island Expressway, expending on it hundreds of millions of dollars of public money, would hardly make even a noticeable dent in the Long Island commuting problem. Building a dozen Long Island Expressways wouldn't make a noticeable dent. And how about when that traffic reached the central city? The streets of Manhattan and downtown Brooklyn were already jammed, filled to overflowing with cars and trucks. Now you would be piling into them 90,000 additional cars. Congestion in city streets had already reached intolerable levels. To what levels was it going to be escalated? You couldn't possibly solve Long Island's transportation problems—or the city's—by building roads. You couldn't possibly even come near solving those problems by building roads. Trying to solve them by building roads just didn't make sense. Building the Long Island Expressway didn't make sense.

But building the Long Island Expressway with rapid transit on the center mall—rapid transit that could carry 40,000 passengers per hour, 40,000 passengers who would arrive in Manhattan without cars to be parked—made sense. Says Lee Koppelman, executive director of the Nassau-Suffolk Regional Planning Board: "By the time the Long Island Expressway was planned, we planners had been screaming for years about the need for mass transportation. By this time, the suburbanization—the urbanization in parts—of Long Island had already occurred. We saw the forces, we saw the problems, and we were talking about the problems, and we all knew we had to have mass transit on that road. It was obvious. In terms of commutation, you have to say, 'How can you make this road work so I don't have to build six more Long Island Expressways?' and there was only one answer. We all knew that if there was no mass transit on that road, it would be a disaster. Without mass transit, the road was guaranteed—*guaranteed*—to fail before it was built."

"Mass transit doesn't only mean trains, you know," Koppelman says. "It can mean buses."

Buses do not have the capacity of trains. But they have enough to make a difference. "Every bus," as Koppelman puts it, "can be the equivalent of fifty automobiles." And if an expressway is designed for buses as well as automobiles—if one lane, slightly wider than the normal lanes, is reserved exclusively for buses by separating it from the others by a divider and if the width and turning radii of entrance and exit ramps are made big enough to facilitate their use by the big vehicles—hundreds of buses can use that lane in an hour, theoretically as many as 800, conservatively 400. The capacity of that lane becomes 20,000 people per hour, about thirteen times greater than it was before. Designing and reserving for buses two of the Long Island Expressway's six lanes—one in each direction—would be the equivalent of building a new eight-lane expressway right next to it.

But such capacity can be attained from buses only if a lane is designed and reserved exclusively for them. If it is not, if buses are forced to creep along in the general traffic flow, they no longer offer the faster trip that, along with the comfort of letting someone else drive, would overcome for substantial numbers of commuters the disadvantages represented by the higher immediate, out-of-pocket expense of a bus trip and the fact that the nearest bus stop might be inconveniently far from their offices. Too few commuters would be lured out of their cars onto the buses to significantly alleviate expressway congestion. If Moses wouldn't build rapid transit on the Long Island Expressway, planners pleaded, at least let him build it with lanes for buses. Moses refused even to consider the suggestion.

Making provision for mass transportation on the Long Island Expressway was in many ways not only Long Island's chance but its last chance.

Mass transportation systems work only if they are able to transport masses—people in numbers sufficient to pay the system's cost, to justify the immense public investment that created it. Such systems work only if there is high-density development around them. They do not work in an exclusively low-density subdivision landscape. Low-density subdivision had already inundated two-thirds of Nassau County. But the rest of Nassau and most of vast Suffolk still lay largely unsubdivided—unshaped; great chunks of Long Island were in 1955 still a *tabula rasa* on which a design for the future could be etched with the lessons of the past in mind. For these areas—close to a thousand square miles of land—there was still time to insure a different, better, type of development—a different, better, life for the millions of people who would one day be living on that land. But there wasn't much time. With the population of the two counties increasing at the rate of almost 100,000 per year, each year the tide covered almost five miles more of the Island. If a change was to be made in the development pattern, it must be made at once.

Once the Long Island Expressway was built, no change would be possible. Construction of the great road would open the entire Island to development. As it pushed through new farm country—even before it pushed through the country, as soon as the announcement was made that the push was imminent—that country would fill up with subdivisions. The pattern of development—a pattern too low in density to support rapid transit—would be fixed. (And, of course, the land would become too expensive for the creation of the huge commuter parking terminals.) The time was now, before the expressway was built, to insure not only that rapid transit would be provided but that it would be used by enough people to ease the transportation burden from the backs of all the people on Long Island. It would not be possible once the expressway was built. Build the Long Island Expressway with mass transit—or at least with provision for the future installation of mass transit—and Long Island might remain a good place to live and play. Build the Long Island Expressway without mass transit and Long Island would be lost—certainly for decades, probably for centuries, possibly forever.

* * *

When planners proposed rapid transit on the expressway, Moses replied by saying it was "impossible"—and by refusing to discuss the matter. The chairman of the newly formed Metropolitan Rapid Transit Commission knew from personal experience—twice, after all, Charles H. Tuttle had had Robert Moses on the witness stand before him under oath—the value of independent investigation of Moses' assertions. Going outside the Moses sphere of influence—over the New Jersey border to Philadelphia and the firm of Day & Zimmerman, Inc.—he found consulting engineers who didn't depend on Moses for a living and commissioned them to find out if *this* Moses assertion was true.

The MRTC could not afford a complete study. Day & Zimmerman therefore analyzed the cost and effect of placing rapid transit not on the entire eighty-five miles of the expressway but only on a seven-mile stretch in Queens, from Marathon Parkway near the city line running west to Corona, where the tracks could link up with one of several existing subway lines and follow its tracks into Manhattan. This limitation placed the rapid transit proposal in the worst possible light, maximizing its right-of-way cost, for Queens was built up far more heavily than the less heavily populated suburbs, and minimizing its effect, since while in the suburbs development could still be influenced by rapid transit, with higher densities near the line so that traffic on it would be increased, in Queens the pattern of development was already set.

Even in the worst possible light, however, the proposal looked good.

One Day & Zimmerman alternative, for example, was to lay tracks down the expressway center mall from Marathon Parkway into Corona, leave the expressway at Flushing Meadows Park, cut across its northeastern corner to link up with the IRT Flushing subway near its 111th Street station and follow that line (which "has ample capacity to accommodate" the added traffic) to Times Square. The total cost of building such a line—the total cost of the additional forty feet of expressway right-of-way, of bridges at grade separations, of electric substations, of eleven large, modern passenger stations with parking garages at the eleven major avenues intersecting with the expressway within that seven-mile stretch, of every piece of moden rapid transit equipment desirable—would be only $20,830,000.

Benefits to the public would be as large as costs to the public would be small. Day & Zimmerman calculated these benefits only for the small section of northeastern Queens directly involved and for adjacent northern Nassau County. But even for this limited area, the figures were staggering. From it, in 1955, 158,500 persons traveled into Manhattan and back on an average weekday, 85,000 by automobile, 59,500 by bus and 14,000 on the Port Washington branch of the Long Island Rail Road.* The vast majority of these commuters would be able to save significant amounts of money

* The Day & Zimmerman figures do not fit in with figures for over-all commuting from Queens, Nassau and Suffolk furnished by the Regional Plan Association and the Nassau and Suffolk Planning Boards (the two counties then each had its own planning

and time—in Queens up to twenty-five minutes, in Nassau up to forty minutes—by using the proposed rapid transit system instead. Based on surveys of the commuters, on analyses of traffic patterns and on other surveys done in similar situations in other cities, "initially about 17 percent of general commuter traffic from the area would use the proposed rapid transit line in the initial year of operation." And 17 percent of 158,500 is 27,000. Twenty-seven thousand commuters who now jammed available means of transportation to New York twice a day would be removed from those means of transportation, freeing them for other users—and their own trips would be made vastly cheaper and faster, as much as forty minutes each way faster.

The effect on the jam-packed buses from the area would be dramatic. Some 19,000 of the 27,000 passengers diverted to the new rapid transit would be bus passengers. The effect on the jammed Long Island Rail Road would be less dramatic but still meaningful. Some 1,500 passengers of the 27,000 passengers diverted would be LIRR passengers. And as for the highways—most notably the Long Island Expressway, which the vast majority of commuters from this area would use once it was opened—close to 6,500 of the 27,000 persons diverted would be persons who drove their cars into and out of Manhattan every weekday.

These figures were conservative—far too conservative, most planners felt. The figures would, moreover, increase year by year, as the area's population increased and as the percentage of the population using the rapid transit line increased as more commuters became aware of its advantages.

But even the initial, ultraconservative figures had remarkable implications. Robert Moses was planning to spend $500,000,000 for an expressway that would increase the one-way automobile-carrying capacity of Long Island by a maximum of 4,500 automobiles or buses per hour—during the two-hour peak period, by a total of 9,000 automobiles or buses. For $20,000,000—one twenty-fifth of that cost—he could reduce the automobile-carrying capacity *needed* by 6,500 automobiles and 400 buses. He could do as much for Long Island by spending $20,000,000 as by spending $500,000,000—if he spent it on rapid transit.

And these figures represented the advantages of building rapid transit on only seven miles of the Long Island Expressway, seven miles out of eighty-five.

No study was ever done of the cost of building such a line on the other seventy-eight miles of expressway, so much of it in 1955 still open farm country, but the best-informed estimate is that the cost—including large terminals in key locations—would, if the job had been done in 1955, have

---

board). For example, while the figure for the over-all number of commuters by car from those three counties was given at the time as 90,000, the Day & Zimmerman figures show 85,000 commuters from northeastern Queens and northern Nassau County alone. The reason for the discrepancy is that the over-all figures are not based on detailed studies, while the Day & Zimmerman figures are—and that the figures for automobile commuting from Queens, Nassau and Suffolk should actually be higher than 90,000.

been no more than half a million dollars per mile. Building a rapid transit line the length of the Long Island Expressway would almost certainly have cost less than $100,000,000—one fifth of the cost of the expressway without rapid transit.

To save Long Island, it was not absolutely necessary for rapid transit to be built into the Long Island Expressway in 1955. But it was absolutely necessary for provision for rapid transit to be built in. The right-of-way for the tracks had to be acquired and the necessary heavier foundations had to be sunk beneath the center mall. As long as those two steps were taken, tracks could be installed on the expressway with a minimum of expense and inconvenience in the future. Fail to take those steps and, as with the Van Wyck Expressway ten years before, the expense of acquiring the land—now so cheap—would be enormous, so enormous, in fact, that it would probably be prohibitive financially—by Day & Zimmerman's estimate $15,000,000 per mile—and politically: not only would building rapid transit on the shoulders of the road require the acquisition of additional right-of-way and cause public outcry from the owners of that land and from thousands of others whose adjacent homes would be blighted by a nearby roalroad, but rebuilding the expressway's foundations would require the closing of several lanes for years, causing immense public inconvenience. The cost of making provision for rapid transit would, in 1955, be minimal in terms of the expressway's over-all cost: acquiring 240 feet of land instead of 200 feet and building heavier foundations would cost, for the whole eighty-five-mile length of the expressway, perhaps an extra $20,000,000. The expressway was going to cost $500,000,000 anyway. For $20,000,000 more—for an increase in the cost of only 4 percent—you could take the step that would insure that the expressway would one day be able to fulfill the function for which it was built. Fail to spend that 4 percent, and the expressway would never be able to fulfill the function for which it was being built. And that money was available: if Moses couldn't persuade the city or state to put it up, he could put it up himself—Triborough had the $20,000,000 readily available.

The Day & Zimmerman study, the first independent analysis of the long-term effects of a Moses highway proposal during the thirty years that Moses had been building highways, represented a serious threat to Moses. His opponents were usually unable to refute his facts and figures with figures of their own. When he told press and public a proposal was "impossible," there was no choice but to accept that statement. Now there would be. And if editorial writers learned how simple it would be to provide rapid transit on the expressway, there might well be a public outcry for that provision.

Moses knew how to handle threats.

While Day & Zimmerman were studying, he started building—getting the expressway under way with $20,000,000 in Triborough funds so that he wouldn't have to wait for state or city allocations. Even while the MRTC consultants were attempting to determine the advisability of making provision for rapid transit on the expressway, Moses was building the expressway without any such provision. By the time the firm reported its findings to the MRTC, it had to report also that the findings no longer mattered. Because of "actual construction work" done on the expressway "since the conception of the rapid transit study plans," the firm stated, placing rapid transit on the expressway would now "require complete revision of the expressway plans and the economic waste of the substantial construction work completed. . . . Construction of a rapid transit line on this highway" is no longer "practicable." Discussion of the question no longer served any useful purpose. Not surprisingly, there wasn't any—at least not any of significance. The Day & Zimmerman report was one of the best-kept secrets in New York planning history. The city's newspapers carried scarcely a word on it. *Newsday,* the Long Island daily, never mentioned it. The public never knew of the ease with which rapid transit could be built on the Long Island Expressway. Long Island never found out about the report that spelled out a way by which Long Island could have been saved. The Long Island Expressway was built without rapid transit—and without provision for rapid transit in the future. And as each section of the superhighway opened, it was jammed—with traffic jams of immense dimensions. One man's dream became a nightmare—an enduring, year-after-year nightmare—for tens of thousands of other men. Year by year, the huge road bulled its way eastward, through Queens, across Nassau County, deeper and deeper into Suffolk; it would take fifteen years to build it out to Riverhead. And as each section opened, as each piece of Moses' largest road-building achievement fell into place, the congestion grew worse. The Long Island Expressway's designed daily capacity was 80,000 vehicles. By 1963, it was carrying 132,000 vehicles per day, a load that jammed the expressway even at "off" hours—during rush hours, the expressway was solid with cars, congealed with them, chaos solidified. The drivers trapped on it nicknamed Moses' longest road "the world's longest parking lot."

Part of Moses' solution to congestion on his biggest road was to make it bigger. By 1962, while he was presiding over opening ceremonies on stretches of the expressway in Nassau County, Andrews & Clark were frantically redesigning stretches of the expressway that had been opened in Queens just a few years before. Even before its eastern stretches were laid down, its western stretches were being hacked up. In 1966, while state highway crews were building it deep into Suffolk County at its eastern end, other crews were rebuilding it at its western end: construction of a single, monster interchange—its cost $75,000,000, more than all the highways Moses had built before the war—at the most congested spot on the expressway, its intersection with the Brooklyn-Queens Expressway, got under way in that year. "My God," Lee Koppelman told a friend one night in 1966, "they shouldn't be doing that. If they've got $75,000,000, they should be spending that $75,000,000 on bus service—building a bus lane and parking areas where commuters could pick up the buses. Building that interchange isn't going to change a damn thing. If you eliminate one interchange problem, all you're going to be doing is shifting the bottleneck east of the interchange, further out in Queens. So then they'll probably decide to widen it east of the interchange in Queens. And all that'll do is shift the bottleneck east to where the widening stops." Koppelman was right. By 1970, on a five-mile stretch directly to the east of the Brooklyn-Queens Expressway interchange, work had begun on carving four additional lanes of expressway out of the grass slopes bordering the expressway. Final blueprints were being prepared for a similar "widening" for the next five-mile stretch to the east—and for providing still more capacity by cantilevering service roads out over the highway.

The continual construction made the traffic jams even worse while it was going on. And, the men planning the highway knew, it would be going on for decades. Not only was the expressway going to have to be widened deep into Suffolk; at every point where it intersects with another major road—Moses' Van Wyck and Clearview expressways or Grand Central, Cross Island and Northern State parkways, for example—giant new interchanges are going to have to be built. Although the public didn't know it, "improvements" under design in 1974 would not be completed until the end of the century "at the earliest." Men who had been suffering for years on Moses' road, who had been trapped every working day of their lives in those terrible, life-eroding traffic jams, would be freed from that trap only by growing too old to work.

Long Island planners could tell when the Throgs Neck Bridge opened by their charts of traffic volume on the Island's highways: with the opening, the volume, climbing steadily month by month anyway, made a sudden, sharp jump. The bridge itself was jammed, and the traffic using it did not mean less traffic on the Bronx-Whitestone Bridge paralleling it across Long Island Sound two miles to the west. For two years, there was a substantial decrease in Bronx-Whitestone traffic, and then, inexorably, it began, even while traffic on the new bridge to the east kept climbing, to creep back to its former levels. Moses' solution: build another bridge across Long Island Sound to the east, a huge "Sound Crossing" between Oyster Bay and Rye. Presumably, when that bridge was completed, there would be another bridge to *its* east—and then another, and another. Moses would, if he had his way, cover the Sound with bridges as the Tiber was covered with bridges in Rome.

(The Throgs Neck Bridge at least was two miles away from the Bronx-Whitestone. On the other, south, side of Long Island, Moses was building a "Captree Causeway"—a name later changed to "Robert Moses Causeway"—connecting Captree, the easternmost end of the Jones Beach barrier beach, with the Fire Island State Park—whose name would later be changed to "Robert Moses State Park." Traffic on that bridge was, immediately upon its opening, so intolerable that within two years Moses had begun building another bridge parallel and next to it—and exactly sixty-eight feet away.)

With the opening of the Verrazano-Narrows Bridge, which within two years of its opening in 1964 was carrying 21,000,000 cars per year, a traffic level Moses had not believed it would attain until 1980, traffic volume on Long Island experienced not a jump but a huge surge. With congestion reaching new levels, Moses said the solution was to build a huge new Cross-Brooklyn Expressway, starting near the point where the bridge touched down on Long Island. For that, of course, he needed state, city and federal approval. But no one's approval was needed to enable him to do what he wanted on the bridge itself. He built on it a second deck that would almost double its capacity.

Robert Moses was, after all, mortal, Lee Koppelman kept reminding himself —"even if sometimes it didn't seem that way"—and, one day, either death or old age would end Moses' decades of power. And, Koppelman believed, it would not take long after that day for bus service to be instituted on all Long Island's major highways, not only on its expressways but on 200 miles of parkways.

The young planner cherished that belief until, driving along the old Wantagh Parkway one day, he happened to notice something he had never noticed before.

"I was coming up to one bridge across the parkway," he would recall, "and just as I was about to go under it, I noticed how low it seemed to be. I took a good look at the next bridge, and goddammit, it *was* low! I pulled over and measured it with my arm at the curb, and I could see that it wasn't any fourteen feet high. At the next exit, I got off and found a store and bought a yardstick and got back on the parkway and measured the next bridge. At the curb it was eleven feet high. And I didn't have to go and measure all the other bridges. I knew right then what I was going to find. I knew right then what the old son of a gun had done. He had built the bridges so low that buses *couldn't* use the parkways!"

The Wantagh Parkway had, of course, never been rebuilt since it had opened in 1929. Most of Moses' other parkways were being rebuilt to handle the greatly increased traffic loads on them. As he drove back to his office, Koppelman was hoping that the rebuilt bridges, the overpasses that carried intersecting local roads over the parkways, would be higher. But, at the office, when he pulled out the design drawings he had been sent by the Long Island State Park Commission, he saw at a glance that his hopes had been false. The new bridges were several feet higher in the center—over the two "fast" lanes, one in each direction, of the expanded six-lane parkways—than the original bridges, because, as Koppelman was later to realize, Moses didn't want unadorned straight overpasses over his beautiful early roads, and curving an overpass over a wider expanse necessitated greater clearance beneath it. But the clearance at the curb was precisely the same beneath the new overpasses as beneath the old: eleven feet.

Most buses were about twelve feet high. They could not use the curb lane or, because the design of many overpasses kept the rise in clearance toward the center of the road very gradual, the lane next to it. They could in theory use the center lane, the "fast" lane in each direction, but not in practice: no practical bus-fleet operator would dare take the risk of hours of delay that would be involved in routing his buses down a road in which only one lane was available for their use. If an accident or an overheated car or repaving—or any of the hundred other causes that blocked lanes—blocked that one lane, any buses on the road would be trapped at the next overpass until it was opened again. In practice, no practical bus operator would run his buses on any road on which the clearance at the curb wasn't at least fourteen feet. "I sat there looking at that goddamned drawing—I'll never forget it," Koppelman says. "And I realized that the old son of a gun had made sure that buses would *never* be able to use his goddamned parkways."

"The building of the bridges is an example of his foresight and vision," Sid Shapiro says in his quiet way. "I've often been astonished myself that he was so right in those days, and not only so right but so indispensably right. Mr. Moses had an instinctive feeling that someday politicians would try to put buses on the parkways, and that would break down the whole parkway concept—and he used to say to us fellows, 'Let's design the bridges so the clearance is all right for passenger cars but not for anything else.' All the original bridges were designed with nine feet of clearance at the curb. Later we went up to eleven feet, but that has the same effect. Well, yes, buses *could* use the center lane, but that's an impractical thing. No bus would do that. Mr. Moses did this because he knew that something might happen after he was dead and gone. He wrote legislation [clauses prohibiting the use of parkways by "buses or other commercial vehicles"] but he knew you could change the legislation. You can't change a bridge after it's up. And the result of this is that a bus from New York couldn't use the parkways if we wanted it to." A quiet smile broke across Shapiro's seamed face, and he almost laughed as a pleasant recollection crossed his mind. "You know," he said, "we've had cases where buses mistakenly got on a parkway—we had this on the Grand Central Parkway several times, I remember—buses from a foreign state, I suppose, and the first bridge stopped them dead. One had its roof rolled up like the top of a sardine can."

"Foresight and vision." Apt, if the vision was one man's private vision. Building parkway bridges low was indeed an example of Moses' foresight in trying to keep intact his original concept, the bright and shining dream he had dreamed in 1924—of roads that would be not just roads but works of art, that would be "ribbon parks" for "pleasure driving." Building the parkway bridges low was indeed an example of Moses' foresight in trying to keep intact his original concept of the area through which those roads ran—lovely Long Island—as a serene and sparsely populated suburban setting, a home for the relatively small number of people wealthy enough to live there, a playground for the larger but still restricted number of people wealthy enough to drive there and play in the parks he had built there.

The vision was no longer relevant. It no longer bore any relation to reality. Reality was no longer a Long Island that was a sparsely populated playground, but the residence of millions of people. Moses' parkways now had to perform a function, getting tens of thousands of commuters to and from work. The Southern State Parkway—4,000,000 cars in 1940, 20,000,000 in 1950, 26,000,000 in 1955, 30,000,000 in 1957—was the most heavily traveled highway in the entire world—and probably the most congested: engineers clocking traffic in 1967 found that on the first five-mile stretch of road, from the toll booths in Valley Stream out to Lynbrook, the "speed range" at which traffic moved during a rush hour never, for more than the briefest of periods, got above sixteen miles per hour—and often was as low as three miles per hour, about as fast as the people driving could have walked. The parkways had a different function now from that of the great open road on which Moses had envisioned cars breezing along. But Moses still had absolute control over parkways. And whether or not that vision had any relation to reality, he used that control to insure that it would endure far beyond his own lifetime, long "after he was dead and gone." Thanks to his foresight, it was—as late as 1974, decades after the reality had changed—his vision and not reality that governed the shaping of the parkways, and that therefore prevailed over that portion of the lives of its users that they spent on it.

For how long would it continue to do so?

Well, Sid Shapiro had been overstating the case, of course, when he said, "You can't change a bridge after it's up" and that therefore buses would never be able to use the Long Island parkways. A bridge can be rebuilt. When, in 1969, a five-mile stretch of the Northern State Parkway was rebuilt, in fact, it was rebuilt with bridges with a fourteen-foot clearance because doing so would make the job eligible for federal funds, and, as Shapiro put it, "on that section, you have the Long Island Expressway right next to it, and buses wouldn't want to use a parkway where they have an expressway, so it doesn't really matter."

But that was one stretch of parkway out of 200 miles of parkway on Long Island. And on the rest of those 200 miles, it would not be true that "it doesn't really matter"—and Shapiro said, sitting there complacently on the terrace in the bright sun, there were no plans in existence to rebuild bridges along the rest of those 200 miles, and he felt that probably they would never be rebuilt. Asked what would happen if bus operators did decide that they wanted to use the Northern State instead of the expressway, he said, "Well, they can use it for a five-mile section. But then they'll have to get off."

Never? Shapiro was probably overstating the case. Sometime in the future, surely, the Long Island State Park Commission would be in the hands of men with a different philosophy from that of Robert Moses and Sid Shapiro, and they would want the bridges rebuilt. Maybe not in the near future, for Shapiro's successors as the commission's top administrators were already hand-picked and groomed, but sometime in the future. Well, Sid Shapiro said, you see, those bridges cost about $750,000 per bridge. "And," Sid Shapiro said slowly, in his quiet, sly voice, "there are 204 bridges on those parkways, you know." Robert Moses had condemned to monstrous traffic jams not merely the present generation of users of his parkways but generations to come.

He had condemned *all* Long Islanders—for generations to come.

In the 1970's, after the fall of Robert Moses, public officials would be talking about modernizing the existing mass transportation facilities on Long Island and building new ones. Handsome four-color brochures—designed to win voter approval for the bond issues in the billions that would be required to finance these improvements—assured voters that the expense would, if not end, at least substantially alleviate traffic congestion on Long Island.

But building them wasn't going to be that easy.

Moses had been asked to reserve space on the Van Wyck Expressway. Reserving it would, at the time, have cost only $1,750,000. And if Moses had spent that money, it would now, in the 1970's, be possible to construct all the high-speed rail links involved for less than $10,000,000.

In 1968, with congestion on the Van Wyck and at Idlewild (now John F. Kennedy) Airport even more intolerable than F. Dodd McHugh had predicted, no sooner was Moses out of power than the decision was taken to build a rapid transit line to the airport. But because Moses had not reserved space, that line would now cost—not in official estimates but in truth—$300,000,000. And even for that amount, it would not be possible to obtain many of the advantages McHugh had envisioned. The cost could be kept down to $300,000,000 only by eliminating from the plans the subway linkup between downtown Brooklyn and central and northern Queens, as well as all local service that would have increased the rapid transit capacity of the Queens-to-Manhattan line; the astronomical cost of local stations made it impossible even to contemplate including them. Moses' refusal to listen to McHugh had probably deprived New York of those advantages forever.

The cost of the airport link even in its stripped-down version was so high that no man could say with any certainty when it would be built. The official charged with building it announced in 1968 that construction would be completed by 1971. In 1969, he announced that construction would be completed by 1972. In 1970, he admitted that, as the *Times* put it, "his agency had no funds available" to build it. "When asked when the line would be completed, he said that he hoped it would be built in 1973, but that it would be safer to say 1974." It would have been safer—and more accurate—to say that he didn't have any idea when it would be built, for that was in fact the case. The money to begin construction was still not in hand.

It was possible to predict with some certainty that the airport rapid transit line would, eventually, be built—if for no other reason than that the cost was within the ability of the Port Authority to pay, and the Port Authority, losing money because of traffic congestion (travelers' eagerness to avoid the airport was considered the primary reason for a year-by-year decline in patronage beginning in 1969), could be expected to come up with the money if no one else would. It was not possible to make such a prediction about the other desperately needed Long Island mass transportation improvements, projects that could have been built with such relative ease years before, if, at that time, Moses had consented to reserve space for them or to allow Triborough Authority funds to be spent on them.

The increase in the cost of the land needed for parking areas and terminals of new dimensions had added tens of millions of dollars to the cost of modernizing the Long Island Rail Road. The further improvements made necessary in the intervening years if the railroad was to attract new passengers from the mass of automobile users on Long Island had added tens of millions of dollars more. And inflation had caused these additional costs to multiply. In 1954, when, before the imposition of the Joint Program, Triborough funds for the modernization had been available, the modernization would have cost $200,000,000. In 1970, after Moses' fall, the cost was $1,500,000,000. While public officials talked vaguely about that sum being raised by a combination of bond issues and contributions from new mass transit allocations that would hopefully be made someday by the federal government, in fact money that would allow expenditures of that dimension on a single rail line was nowhere in sight on Capitol Hill—and even while local officials were trying to find it, inflation and further land development were causing that cost to rise by more than $50,000,000 per year. Home construction on the land around the LIRR lines meant that certain of the changes indispensable for a true modernization program—straightening and elevating the tracks to permit high-speed train operation—were, politically, immensely difficult. No man could predict with any real certainty that improvements of significant scope—not the patchwork supplying of new cars and improvement of repair and maintenance facilities that was going on in the early 1970's, but the transformation of the LIRR into a truly modern eighty-mile-per-hour carrier—would be carried out during his lifetime. No man could predict that they could be carried out within his children's lifetime.

As for building a *new* rapid transit line on Long Island, no man could predict with any certainty that it would *ever* be built. Most planners who had studied the prospects felt, as Lee Koppelman felt, "they'll never do it."

And even if the mass transit lines were built, they weren't going to help the transportation situation on Long Island nearly as much as the public officials believed—or, to be more precise, nearly as much as they told the public they believed.

Four-color brochures may have been assuring voters that if the mass transit improvements they had planned were built, they would, if not end, at least substantially alleviate traffic congestion on Long Island.

But stark, unadorned black-and-white charts, graphs and computer print-outs stacked on tables or taped to the otherwise bare walls in a small cinder-block room, hardly more than a cubicle, in a red-brick building set back off the Veterans Memorial Highway in Hauppauge, Suffolk County, Long Island, told a very different story.

The building contained the executive offices of the Nassau-Suffolk Regional Planning Board, and the little room, down a hall from Koppelman's, was the office of John F. (Jack) Sheridan, Koppelman's transportation analyst. And the charts, graphs and print-outs, thick stacks of numbers and lines, represented the first analysis of transportation on Long Island—how the 2,500,000 residents of Nassau and Suffolk counties got to work, to the supermarket, to school, to wherever they went when they left their homes; when they went there; how frequently they went there; why they went there by the transportation means they used instead of by some other means—ever done in meaningful depth.

One of the charts, a map really, showed traffic levels on the nine major east-west routes in Nassau and Suffolk counties: from top to bottom (north to south) Route 25-A, the Long Island Expressway, Northern State Parkway, Hillside Avenue, Jericho Turnpike, Hempstead Turnpike, Southern State Parkway, Merrick Road and Sunrise Highway. Various levels were made graphic by different colors—purple for congestion. On the right-hand side of the map—the side showing eastern and central Suffolk County—the map was a blaze of different colors, but in the center of the map, western Suffolk and eastern Nassau, one—purple—was beginning to dominate. And in the left-hand section of the map—central and western Nassau County—there were eight purple lines. Only Jericho Turnpike was operating with any leeway at all. The other eight roads had no capacity at all left for additional traffic.

Another chart showed—by means of curves representing the relationship between time and distance traveled during that time—the delays on those east-west roads at those levels of traffic. The curves rose terribly steeply on Long Island's pre-Moses roads—25-A, Hillside, Jericho, Hempstead Turnpike, Merrick Road, Sunrise Highway—on which traffic is slowed by traffic lights and intersecting streets. But they rose almost as steeply on Moses' roads, the roads built—at a colossal public investment—to free the public from traffic lights and intersecting streets. Moses' "modern" rebuilt Southern State Parkway, for example, paralleled the "obsolete" Merrick Road and Sunrise Highway. The curves showing time and distance covered in that time for each of those roads ran almost parallel, rising and falling together. "Until you get out to Wantagh," Jack Sheridan says, "there's no advantage to the Southern State Parkway over the Sunrise Highway [or Merrick Road]. Which is a pretty horrible thought."

But those charts, graphic displays of the present, were not the most disturbing things in that cinder-block room. That distinction is reserved for computer print-outs giving projections of the future. Their figures were not transposed onto the charts and graphs. For in order to contain them, the charts and graphs would have to be too big. Some 560,000 cars a day went "through the Long Island corridor"—crossed the city line from Nassau into Queens—in 1968. By 1985, 1,400,000 cars a day will be trying to go through that corridor. The roads available to handle them were jammed to capacity and far beyond capacity. And the load they will be asked to handle will, just seventeen years later, be twice as big.

There were print-outs more disturbing still. Some, for example, dealt with "modal split": planners' jargon for the percentage of travelers which can be persuaded to change, or split off from, their present mode of travel to another—in Long Island's case, from highways to mass transit. The print-outs show that, on Long Island, optimistic predictions to the contrary, there is little possibility of any significant modal split at all.

If travel on the Long Island Rail Road was revolutionized—if the railroad was given modern rolling stock; if travel time was cut in half; if new, more convenient stations were strategically located throughout Manhattan—if all these improvements were accomplished, a highly unlikely feat because it would cost two and a half billion dollars—the modal split induced would be no more than 10 percent. Sixty-five percent of commuters from Nassau and Suffolk counties used the LIRR in 1968; spend two and a half billion dollars and you could increase that percentage only to 75 percent.

The numbers are more depressing than the percentages. Some 85,890 Long Island–Manhattan commuters used the LIRR in 1960; revolutionizing the railroad would increase that number to 156,700 by 1985, an increase of 70,810 riders. The Island's population was going to increase by 1,548,000 between 1960 and 1985. The number of commuters to Manhattan was going to increase not by 70,810 per day but by 81,000 per day. The LIRR's additional riders would not be riders diverted from the highways. The expenditure of two and a half billion dollars would reduce the load of commuters the highways would have to carry not at all. The load would be increased—by more than 10,000 per day. Even after that expenditure, those nine east-west roads, already jammed so far beyond capacity, would be asked to carry daily almost 10,000 more cars.

And far more than 10,000 more cars. For the above figures were only for Manhattan-bound commuters. Hundreds of thousands of other Nassau and Suffolk residents were going to be commuting to jobs on Long Island by 1985, hundreds of thousands *more* than in 1960. The daily average of all "work trips by all travel modes" by residents of Long Island in 1960—work trips to Manhattan or anyplace else—was 680,020. *By 1985, it would be 1,225,500.* And the modal split induced among the non-Manhattan trips by the modernization of the Long Island Rail Road would be infinitesimal. The number of daily work trips to non-Manhattan locations would be rising by 549,780. The number of those trips by rail would be increasing by 1,420. Long Island's east-west roads, already jammed so far beyond capacity, would—even if two and a half billion dollars were spent revolutionizing the Long Island Rail Road—be asked by 1985 to carry every day not only 10,000 more cars bound for Manhattan but tens of thousands of additional cars bound for jobs in Brooklyn, Queens, the Bronx, and within Nassau and Suffolk counties. Spending even the immense sum of two and a half billion dollars on mass transportation on Long Island would not help the highway problem on Long Island to any significant degree.

No mass transportation improvement could help that problem to any significant degree. In 1963, for example, Nassau County undertook an in-depth study of the possibilities of fast and frequent bus service. The expense would be immense, the county found. And the over-all modal split accomplished in journeys to work—the proportion of transportation to and from jobs now accomplished by car that could be turned into bus trips—would be no more than 5 percent and perhaps as low as 2 percent. Nassau County could beggar itself to provide mass transportation—and still manage to lure off the roads perhaps no more than one car out of every fifty.

And all the trips above represent only work trips. How about nonwork trips—all the other journeys (to supermarket, to bowling alley, to tennis or swimming or golf or bridge club, to school, to friends', to movies, to restaurants, to dinner, to doctor, to dentist) that when added together come to a total that dwarfs even the immense total of work trips and that are, on Long Island, to an overwhelming extent trips made by car? In Sheridan's office are maps covered by incredible masses of lines representing the total of such trips on highways and streets on Long Island, and computer print-outs totaling such trips for towns and villages and unincorporated areas. The complexity of such figures is immense, but the bottom line is clear: the modal split that would be effected by improvements in mass transportation on Long Island is infinitesimal. Highways and local streets in Nassau and Suffolk were handling a heavy load of traffic in 1960. By 1985, the load those highways and streets would have to handle would be more than twice as heavy. And no improvements that could be made in mass transportation at any expense that could conceivably be borne by state, city, counties or public authorities could lighten that load much. "You see," Jack Sheridan says, "if we had had subway lines, or rapid transit lines, we would have had high density along those lines. But since there was no mass transit, the development took place according to the way the automobile dictated it. And that meant low density, very low density. To have feasible mass transit routes, you have to have sufficient density. And we don't. And, except perhaps in central Nassau, we're not going to for any foreseeable future. Because of the highway, because of the pattern of high highway use developed by the lack of mass transit before, we're faced with this problem now, and right now we just can't get around it." And it is a problem to which a solution—if there is a solution—lies only in a future distant enough so that sufficiently large areas of Long Island will have density high enough so that putting mass transit lines through them will make a difference in the Island's transportation picture. That day, in 1974, seems decades—generations—away.

VII

THE LOSS OF POWER

41. *Rumors and the Report of Rumors*

HIGHWAYS WERE, of course, only one field of Robert Moses' activity. There was also housing—most notably the vast amount of housing he was building as director of the Mayor's Slum Clearance Committee. And a few isolated but perceptive observers were beginning to notice clues to something very disturbing about slum clearance.

For Hortense Gabel, it was rumors.

Mrs. Gabel, a small, painfully nearsighted lawyer, was a reformer with a healthy helping of the reformer's penchant for idealism and the worship of such liberal heroes as Franklin D. Roosevelt ("My father's chief rival") and Stephen S. Wise, the crusading rabbi who had founded the American Jewish Congress, for which, at the age of thirty-four, she was working as a volunteer. Her involvement with housing had begun—in 1948—at a dinner party at the home of the rabbi's daughter at which, to Mrs. Gabel's surprise, the rabbi was the only person present besides the daughter's husband and her own.

"I had thought it was a purely social evening," she recalls, "but they told me that there was about to be organized a 'New York State Committee on Discrimination in Housing'—we didn't even have the courage to say 'against'; it wasn't until later that this got changed—which was an outgrowth of the fight on Stuyvesant Town. They told me that the American Jewish Congress was contributing space and had been persuaded to do some funding. And I said, 'Oh, you mean against discrimination in *public* housing.' And—I'll never forget it—he smiled, and he said, 'No, Hortense. *Housing*.' And I sat there in a kind of stunned silence. It was such a breathtaking thing that you could dream that someday Negroes might have the chance to live wherever they wanted to. It was like getting drunk—that there was a world leader like Rabbi Wise who could even dream of thinking that we would have a ghetto-less country."

But "Horty" Gabel was a reformer with a difference: she *listened* to the people she was supposed to be helping (later, a city housing official, she would be described as the only one "who really has a close relationship with the Negro community"). And during 1951 and 1952, when Robert Moses and the press were cheering Moses' gigantic new Title I slum clearance or "urban renewal" program, the director of the Committee Against Discrimination in Housing, leaving her office—a tiny ten-foot-by-fourteen-foot cubbyhole on the top floor of an ancient loft building—attended meetings of Negro and Puerto Rican organizations in the evenings, and her ears picked up the first whispered rumors about what was going on on the Title I sites—rumors so terrible that she went up to visit the sites for herself, on a trip that would lead her to say years later:

"I've visited a lot of bad slums, but I never saw any worse than the Title I slums when the developers started milking them. I remember I went into a building on the Godfrey Nurse site,* and, as any woman instinctively does, when I went into a bathroom, I glanced into a mirror to see if my hair was straight. And when I looked at the mirror, or where the mirror ought to be, I found myself looking straight into the next apartment."

For Lawrence Orton, it was statistics.

During his decades on the City Planning Commission, Orton had learned to cast a wary eye on Moses'. And he had a sense that there was something wrong—very wrong—with the statistics that the Coordinator was issuing (and that the press was reprinting without the slightest attempt at verification) to demonstrate that every consideration was being shown to families being relocated from Title I sites, that he was not only obeying but going beyond the federal requirement that these families be relocated in "decent, safe, and sanitary dwellings." "In order to set at rest any fears," Moses had announced in his brochure on the Manhattantown† project that would require the razing of six square blocks of tenements and old apartment houses on the Upper West Side, "families are assured that relocation help will be readily available and there is a frank desire to be of maximum assistance in carrying out the individual wishes of each family." If they wanted to move into the new, modern apartments being erected on the site, they would be given "preferential status" in applying, he promised. If they preferred to find their own new apartments, they would be assisted by "personal counseling" from a trained relocation firm, which, he said, was compiling a citywide listing of vacancies, and by "financial assistance" from the developers—at the minimum, "moving expenses plus the first month's rent in new quarters." And families still unable to find new apartments did not have to worry; they—all relocated Title I site families, in fact—could always move into low-income public housing projects, which would represent an improvement in their living quarters anyway; their applications would be given "first priority." Each of Moses' statements was backed up by columns of statistics in the stylish brochures issued in a steady stream by the Mayor's Slum Clearance Committee which the Coordinator headed. For example, the statistics on family income, family size and a

* From 132nd to 135th streets, between Fifth and Lenox avenues. The name of the project was later changed to "Harlem."

† Later renamed "West Park."

half dozen other indices proved, he said, that more than a quarter of the families presently living on the site—998 out of 3,628—would be able to afford to live in the proposed Manhattantown development at anticipated rentals. Orton's years of dealing with housing problems told him that that statistic was false. No tenement tenants he had ever met could afford Moses' anticipated Title I rentals. Orton could not *prove* that statistic false without a detailed analysis of the financial situation of the Manhattantown site tenants. But what bothered him even more were the statistics on public housing. Orton knew all too well that existing public housing was already fully occupied. Familiar with city building plans, he had been under the general impression that there was little new low-income housing scheduled for imminent construction, and checking, he found that his impression was all too correct: the total number of public housing units scheduled for construction during the next year or two was a mere fraction of the number of tenants Moses was telling the world that he was going to move into those units. Analyzing Moses' soothing statistics, Orton was able to see—all too well—how the Coordinator had arrived at them. "With every project—Title I or some expressway or whatever—he would say, 'Don't worry about the people living there. If they don't want to go anywhere else, we've always got room for them in public housing.' But what he was doing was using the same public housing vacancies for many projects. The same vacancies that were alleged to be available for one project had already been allocated for a previous project—or perhaps ten previous projects." Orton began to wonder exactly what Moses was planning. Tens of thousands of persons were now living on urban renewal sites. Where was the Coordinator planning to put them?

For Walter Fried, it was garbage cans.

Strolling the brownstone-lined side streets of his neighborhood—the neat, solid, stolid, middle-class West Side around Ninety-fourth Street and West End Avenue, where he lived—during the winter of 1952 and the spring of 1953, the regional counsel of the Federal Housing and Home Finance Agency had had a sense that it was changing somehow. "Some of the buildings began to seem a little seedy, a little run-down," he recalls. But it was a vague sense. "There wasn't anything really dramatic that you could put your finger on. You had a feeling that the whole neighborhood was beginning to show signs of disrepair, but there was nothing specific."

And then one day, Fried suddenly realized that, without taking note of it, he had, for some time, been seeing something quite specific indeed: in front of some of the brownstones "there were more garbage cans than there should have been." And Fried's housing expertise told him the significance of that fact.

"You'd walk past a four-story brownstone," Fried says. "Those brownstones had always been inhabited by—at most—four families. But in front of that brownstone now there might be four large garbage cans. The garbage for four families is not anywhere near four large cans, not when the garbage was being picked up every day, as it was at the time. So you knew that there were many more people living there now than there had been before. And you knew what that meant: the landlords were breaking up the apartments inside into smaller apartments, so the same space that had been occupied by a family of five might now be occupied by twelve people. When you saw that many garbage cans you knew that this building was being run now as a tenement for very poor families, or even as a rooming house."

When the heat of the New York summer arrived, expertise was no longer required to tell what was happening. The evidence of change was out in the open: leaning on the windowsills of the brownstones-turned-tenements, sitting on their stoops, crowding the benches on the islands in the middle of Broadway, people, poor people, Negro and Puerto Rican people, people in such numbers that the Broadway benches, long crowded anyway with Jewish grandmothers and grandfathers, were now crowded as never before. It wasn't just the fact that these people didn't have white skin that disturbed the older residents of the West Side; it was that they obviously didn't have money either; it was that so many were obviously drunk or on drugs. And it was that there were so many of them. With the first hot day of 1953, the West Side was—all at once—not just a racially mixed neighborhood, but a much poorer neighborhood, and a much more crowded one. And, month by month, its deterioration accelerated. "Ninety-fourth and Ninety-fifth streets between West End and [Riverside] Drive—nice, quiet blocks before—became a shambles," Fried recalls. "It had been happening for months, probably, but in the heat it was intolerable to stay inside those places, so now it began to spill out into the streets. You began to notice the hopheads, the alcoholics. Every night, the city ambulance was out. The cops would come screaming down the streets . . ."

Trying to think back and determine what major change on the West Side had caused so drastic a crumbling of a neighborhood that for decades had stood so solid, Fried could think of only one: the $54,000,000 Manhattantown urban renewal project between Central Park West and Amsterdam Avenue and between Ninety-seventh and 100th streets. And recalling dates, he realized that the deterioration of his neighborhood, some blocks away from Manhattantown though it was, had begun not long after Moses had turned over the six-square-block site to the developers. Fried began to direct his walks toward the site, and with every block that he drew nearer, conditions worsened. Blight was obviously spreading out from Manhattantown. In little more than a year, the streets immediately adjacent to the development—always poor and predominantly Negro but, previously, with well-maintained buildings—had become a slum, a teeming, seething hive of humanity—a place of squalid, run-down, dilapidated tenements so overcrowded that children had to sleep in shifts, of doorways filled with drunks and narcotics addicts and gutters filled with garbage. Obviously, Fried saw, the area had been inundated with a flood of new residents. And there was no place these residents could have come from so suddenly and in such numbers but Manhattantown. A project designed—at immense cost—to clear up a localized, six-block-square slum infection was instead causing that infection to spread over many more than six other blocks.

Trying to figure out why, Fried began to have suspicions disturbing to this long-time admirer of Robert Moses. Federal law required families on urban renewal sites to be relocated in a considerate, humane manner. Every block of the area through which Fried was walking brimmed over with indications that the families on the Manhattantown site were simply fleeing from their homes into the nearest available shelter, no matter how inadequate. What was Moses doing on that site anyway?

Fried's job required frequent tours of the city. Now, his eyes sharpened by the West Side experience, he began to realize that he had been seeing, in different settings, similar symptoms. Traveling through the Rockaway Peninsula one cold winter day, he had happened to pass the sprawling colonies of summer bungalows in Arverne. He had passed those bungalows before in winter, and they had always been vacant, for the flimsy little structures, each barely big enough to accommodate a single family, provided little protection from the cold and damp. This time, to his shock, he had found all the bungalows filled—there were several shivering Negro and Puerto Rican families in each. He had heard disturbing rumors about tenants from other Title I sites being dumped by the hundreds into vacant tenements in a section of Brooklyn called "Brownsville." What was Moses doing on *all* his Title I sites?

By 1953, many New York liberals concerned with housing were asking that question, and some—such as Hortense Gabel and Stanley Isaacs—began going to the sites to see the answer for themselves. They returned horrified. "Stanley came back sick, just sick," an associate recalls. "He said, 'They're hounding those people out like cattle.' " These liberals began to understand that something terrible was going on on some of the Title I sites, not the sites turned over by Moses to organizations such as the Rockefeller-backed Morningside Corporation* or the ILGWU, but the sites he had turned over to corporations hastily set up by Democratic clubhouse politicians allegedly fronting for bigger politicians—something whose shape they were only beginning to dimly glimpse through the curtain of Moses' assurances, but something whose shape was huge and frightening in its implications not only for New York's poor but for the city as a whole. If Moses simply hounded the people living on those sites out of their homes without finding them new homes, these liberals realized, they would have no choice but to flee to other slums, to further crowd tenements already horribly overcrowded, to live in their cellars, their basements, in apartments without kitchens or bathrooms, in tiny rooms carved out of rooms that had been tiny before they had been made tinier to receive them. That would make conditions in the city's existing slums—conditions already bestial, inhuman

* The Morningside Corporation had enlisted Orton's help to create a humane and compassionate relocation program.

—even worse. And the residents of Title I sites numbered not in the thousands but in the tens of thousands. Crowd as they would into slums, there would not be enough room in the slums for them. So they would move into areas adjacent to the slums, into areas in which landlords, without incentive to keep up their property anyway because of the slums' proximity, would see an opportunity for financial profit and take it by breaking up large apartments into small and by cutting down on maintenance and repairs. The slums would spill over their boundaries, spreading into blocks as yet untouched by blight. Moreover, some slum dwellers hounded from their homes would flee into "soft" areas of the city such as Brownsville, neighborhoods in which there were a large number of vacancies. These vacancies would now be filled in a rush by the dispossessed of the ghetto. The policy Moses might be pursuing would create new slums. The city must be alerted to what was happening, these liberals felt; the public must be educated to the facts about what was really happening; the people must be aroused.

But the public was not educated or aroused, because the only medium through which it could be educated or aroused—its press—was not interested. The liberals wanted the press to get the facts behind Title I, but the press made no move to get them.

It was the *Times* that counted, and Isaacs and other reformers with entree to its editors repeated the attempts made by reformers like McAneny and Windels in other generations: they attempted to persuade the *Times* to send out reporters to ascertain if the statements Moses was making —and that the *Times* was printing as if they were fact—were actually factual. And the results were the same that McAneny and Windels had achieved: a single entry in a log on Title I developments kept by a reformer with entree, Elinor G. Black, tells the story:

> Called *N.Y. Times*. Illson [reporter Murray Illson] called back Sat. Said it would be better if we made a "statement." *Times* not a "crusading paper. . . ."

The *Tribune* or the *Daily News* would have helped. But when reformers talked to *Tribune* editors, they found that the paper's refusal to attack Moses, while, as Orton says, "not anything like the open secret it was at the *Times*," was just as firm. As for the *News*, it was to fulfill its responsibility to the public by exposing "Communists" in the Housing Authority; says Orton, "If you came in with any information that might be derogatory to Moses, the *News* wouldn't give you the time of day." Among the city's other dailies, only Dorothy Schiff's *Post* told readers there might be another side to the Title I story besides Moses'.

All right, these liberals said. If the press refused to go out and get the facts for itself, they would get the facts for it.

They were able to do so, in large part, because Orton had "gone underground" with the City Planning Commission's "Master Plan unit" when Moses had eased Bennett in as the commission's chairman two years before. The unit's offices on the fifteenth floor of a Park Row office building were only just across City Hall Park from commission headquarters in the Municipal Building, but the distance was, apparently, sufficient for security; "Bennett never once set foot in the place," Orton says, smiling. More important, the chairman hardly ever inquired as to what the unit was doing, and never pressed Orton to expand on his uncharacteristically evasive answers. As a result, Orton says, "my boys just vanished so far as the rest of the city government was concerned. This was a subversive activity—a real, authentic, fifteenth-story job. No one gave us anything to do. So we could do whatever we wanted." And now they began doing what no one had ever done during the twenty years during which Robert Moses had been building public works in New York City: finding out how many people were being evicted from their homes to make way for them, what was happening to those people—and what was happening to the city as a result.

The difficulties were immense. Moses' relocation statistics had always been accepted. No city agency or newspaper had ever computed them even roughly for itself. There were probably over-all statistics in existence, of course, and brought together in one place—but the place was Randall's Island, and Randall's ruler kept the long rows of filing cabinets there locked. Many of the statistics were kept in the City Bureau of Real Estate, but the Bureau was under Moses' thumb; it was after attempts to obtain its statistics—supposedly public records—that Orton, ordinarily so punctilious in speech, said with real passion one evening: "The Real Estate Bureau was a stench in my nostrils." What statistics were available—often in obscure files, in other city agencies, of whose existence the unit would never have known were it not for Orton's encyclopedic knowledge of every corner of city government—were patently too low; Moses kept them low by refusing to count the actual number of people being evicted (instead he multiplied each "dwelling unit" by an "average" family size so small as to bear no discernible relation to reality), and by simply ignoring the existence of "doubled-up" families and boarders (of whom there are always a significant number in low-income areas) as well as of people living in rooming houses or hotels. (There is considerable evidence to suggest that the counts thus arrived at even after these omissions were arbitrarily reduced still further when Moses felt they sounded too high.)

Orton's unit could not repair these deficiencies. With the buildings in which these uncounted tenants had lived demolished and the tenants moved away, there was no longer any way of obtaining a record of their existence. Yet the unit did come up with a rough compilation: during the seven years since the end of World War II, there had been evicted from their homes in New York City for public works—mainly Robert Moses' public works—some 170,000 persons.

This total was almost certainly far too low. Orton, leaning over backwards as always to be fair and to make sure that the figures would "stand up" no matter what devices Moses employed to discredit them, leaned too far. He permitted his unit to make some adjustment in "official" figures, but not nearly enough to make them accurate. And he permitted his boys to include as "public works" only projects public *in toto*. He did not permit them to include projects such as Stuyvesant Town, Peter Cooper Village, Riverton and Concord Village although he should have, for though the money that built them was supposedly private money, the tax abatement that Moses arranged for them would, when totaled over the years, insure that the public investment in them would dwarf the private, and the powers that Moses utilized to make possible not only their construction but the assemblage of their sites—eminent domain, street closings, utility easements—were all public. (The number of persons relocated for Stuyvesant Town alone was, by Moses' own figures, 12,000.) But the 170,000 figure was eye-opening enough. Robert Moses had, in just slightly more than seven years, moved from their homes more people than *lived* in Albany, Phoenix, Little Rock, Sacramento, Tallahassee, Topeka, Baton Rouge, Trenton, Santa Fe, etc. In terms even of huge New York, the unit was to report, this was "an enforced population displacement completely unlike any previous population movement in the City's history."

If the number of persons evicted for public works was eye-opening, so were certain of their characteristics.

Their color, for example. A remarkably high percentage of them were Negro or Puerto Rican. Remarkably few of them were white. Although the 1950 census had found that only 12 percent of the city's population was nonwhite, at least 37 percent of the evictees (Moses' own figures) and probably far more were nonwhite.

And their income. The income of evictees not only for slum clearance projects but for *all* Moses' public works including expressways was far below the citywide average. In 1951, the Federal Bureau of Labor Statistics found that $4,083 was needed for a family of four to maintain a minimum standard of living for a year. Only one out of every four of the evicted families earned $4,083 per year; 20 percent earned less than $2,000 per year.

Liberals had long suspected that most of the people evicted by Moses were poor people, and particularly poor Negroes and Puerto Ricans, hampered in apartment hunting not only by poverty but by discrimination. The "Orton Survey" confirmed these suspicions. Moses was throwing out of their homes precisely those people who were least able to find new homes.

And the manner in which he was throwing them out was worth noting, too.

Because it was so difficult for these people to find decent homes on their own, the government of their city—the government which had authorized their eviction from their old homes—had solemnly promised them help. Its highest legislative body had pledged that "tenants will not be evicted from the site of a public improvement unless and until quarters equivalent to those occupied are available." Moses, ostensibly the instrument of that government, had, for seven years, created the impression that he was honoring that pledge; he had stated that a "minimum of inconvenience" was involved in relocation. Orton's staffers found that a substantial number of families had been moved "two or more times" to other buildings "within the site"—had been shuttled from one building about to be demolished to another, and then to another, and perhaps yet another. For seven years, Moses had been giving the impression that the bulk of the low-income families displaced by his public works had been accommodated in public housing projects. In reality, the unit found, the percentage of displaced families that had been admitted to public housing was pathetically small. Moses had been giving the impression that he had taken great pains to insure every evictee "decent, safe, and sanitary" living quarters. When the Planning Commission staffers obtained access to files on tenants for whom relocation responsibility had been "discharged," they found that more than a third of the files—for some projects, more than half—were marked: "Disappeared—whereabouts unknown." *Disappeared!* Moses *couldn't* know that the living quarters into which his projects had forced tens of thousands of persons were "decent, safe, and sanitary." He couldn't know *what* the new living quarters were like. He didn't even know where those living quarters *were*.

Orton's handful of staffers, without sufficient time to trace the individual families involved in relocation, were unable to locate those missing families. But it was all too obvious that they had moved either to other sections of the ghettos, doubling up with other families, causing further overcrowding in those already intolerably overcrowded slums, or to adjoining areas, creating slums out of once decent neighborhoods. Robert Moses' slum clearance program might be creating new slums as fast as it was clearing the old.

If this picture of the past was disturbing, it paled before the picture of the future. Orton's staffers had assembled—for the first time—"statistics on the volume of tenant displacement we may expect in the foreseeable future." During the previous seven years, 170,000 persons had been evicted: a rate of about 24,000 per year. But Moses' slum clearance program was only now moving into high gear. During the next *three* years, 150,000 persons were scheduled for eviction: 50,000 per year. These people were mostly low-income Negroes and Puerto Ricans. If future relocation was carried out as past relocation had been carried out, it would increase overcrowding in existing slums, and create new ones faster than before. The city's relocation practices should be changed—taken out of the hands of the Moses-dominated Slum Clearance Committee and Housing and Triborough authorities—in the name of common humanity, Orton's report said. And these practices should be changed in the name of the city's own interest. If they were not, the vast urban renewal programs, the unprecedented expenditure of public funds, which the city was undertaking to improve its future, would wreck that future instead. Orton's statistics proved that without a doubt.

The Women's City Club went beyond statistics.

Even Moses could hardly call these civics in skirts "radicals." Charter members could recall that during the national debate on women's suffrage, opinion within the club had by no means been unanimous. In 1953, the club's "liberalism" was still the narrow-gauged, less militant liberalism of the 1930's. But its membership rolls included women who had been campaigning for better housing for decades, and they were worried because, under Moses' procedure, relocation was being handled not by the city but by a private real estate firm. The club decided to do what no newspaper, government agency or other civic group had done before: study relocation on a Title I site (they selected Manhattantown) in detail—on the site.

No whispers prepared the club's young women for what they found. As one observer was later to describe it:

> Manhattantown looked like a cross section of bombed-out Berlin right after World War II. Some of the tenements were still standing, broken windows gaping sightlessly at the sky, basement doors yawning uncovered on the sidewalks; and surrounding them were acres strewn with brick and mortar and rubble where wreckers and bulldozers had been at work.

And in the buildings—the ruins of buildings, the shells of buildings—people still lived. Visiting those people—entering those shells of buildings, shrinking perhaps past the huddled wreckage of a man that lay in the doorway, stepping into a dim hallway filled with the stench of urine and vomit and, in its shadows, a vague menace, stumbling up unlit flights of stairs that had steps missing, grasping for a banister that wasn't there—was an unnerving experience for these women. Mrs. Elinor Black recalls a man on the street shouting earnestly as she opened the door to one tenement: "Don't go in there, lady! It's not safe to go in there!"

But it was an educational experience. For the people living in the ruins of Manhattantown taught the good ladies of the Women's City Club something about slums that they hadn't learned in their textbooks. In the textbooks, "slums" were synonymous with "dirt" and "blight." But, recalls Mrs. Black, "the thing that hit me was that most of the apartments you went into were well kept, clean." Time after time, City Club volunteers would walk off the filthy street, up the filthy stairs, down a filthy hall, and knock on the door of an apartment—and when the door to that apartment was opened, behind the frightened face peering out ("Oh, they were always frightened," one of the volunteers said. "They always thought you were from the developer or the city") was a room neat and clean. "What hurt the most," Mrs. Black says, "was just the feeling of people trying to make a decent place for their family to live in these conditions." It is possible to read through scores of textbooks and tracts on housing conditions written in the 1940's and early 1950's without finding even a hint of the fact that many of these women volunteers, who had read the textbooks, now learned for the first time: to the people who lived in them, slums were *home*.

The people who lived in those buildings Robert Moses was tearing down were not just passing through. The Puerto Ricans, a small fraction of the area's population, were relative newcomers, of course (although by 1953 13 percent of its Puerto Ricans had lived there for more than ten years), but among the Negro and white families, more than half had lived in their apartments for several decades. Women's City Club members who had been taught that "slum" connoted "transients" sat and listened as one family after another informed them that they had lived in their building "since it was built"—thirty or forty (or, in one case, fifty-four) years before. The people of the area knew each other. Shopkeepers said hello to their customers when they happened to pass them on the street. The Manhattantown area was a slum area. Its people were poor; the average weekly income was sixty dollars per family. Its buildings were old; there hadn't been a new building constructed in it in twenty-five years. Most of them were overcrowded with families of five or six members jammed into apartments that should have held no more than three or four, and many were dilapidated. But the area also was stable, settled, friendly. Its people had a sense of community, of neighborhood, that some of the members of the Women's City Club realized, driving home at night to their luxurious homes in the sterile suburbs, they wished *they* had. The textbooks didn't speak of "advantages" in talking about slums, but, the more perceptive of these women realized, the Manhattantown "slum" had advantages. There were no playgrounds in it, of course, but there was Central Park. "Most families," the club's report would conclude, "seemed to be well satisfied with the neighborhood facilities—with the good bus and subway transportation, the good shopping facilities and nearness to the heart of the city." It was a racially integrated area—a fact very important to the Negro families, not only because they wanted their children to grow up with white children but because they knew, as the City Club was to report, that "services such as garbage and snow removal, schools and shopping were far better in non-segregated areas." And the area didn't have some of the disadvantages associated with slums. Drugs, for example, were already a scourge in slums like Harlem; the junkie was a rarity here. The buildings in which they lived might be dilapidated and overcrowded, but they were palaces compared to buildings in Harlem. Most important—to the families who lived here and were trying to bring up their children "decently"—rents were low, low enough so that they could do so. Three-quarters of the 400 families interviewed were paying less than $50 per month. The average rent per room was $10 per month. In other areas of the city—including most slum areas—rents were much higher, so high that low-income families had to skimp on clothes and food for their children in order to pay them. The more perceptive of the women learned that, while the people who lived in the Manhattantown area did not have much in life, what they did have their neighborhood gave them,

And they learned about the helplessness of the poor in the city, a helplessness so much greater than even the helplessness of the lower-middle-class people of East Tremont.

The old people—the old people alone—dreaded "the room," the single furnished box, four walls and no more, in which they might have to live out their days if they lost the tiny apartments with their own toilet and cooking facilities for which they now managed to scrape up the rent each month. "I would die if they put me in a room," one old man told the nice young woman in the well-tailored dress who had come to ask him questions. Parents of young children dreaded "Harlem," the name by which they referred not only to Manhattan's great black slum but to black slums not yet identified by names such as "Brownsville" or "Bed-Stuy"—the "Harlem" in which their children would have to sleep with them in the same room, the

"Harlem" in which they would have to live with cockroaches and rats, the "Harlem" in whose schools their kids wouldn't learn, and in which the drug pushers would be waiting for them, the "Harlem" in whose streets the garbage lay piling day after day, the "Harlem" whose landlords would squeeze them dry. One question on the Women's City Club questionnaire was where the family being interviewed would like to live. Mother after mother, seeing the abyss before her and her children, answered with a reply that was a cry for help out of the depths of fear: *Anywhere. But not Harlem.* But, the club's volunteers knew, unless someone helped these people, unless someone kept the city's promise to find them "decent, safe, and sanitary dwellings . . . within [their] financial means," "the room" and "Harlem" were where they were going to have to go.

For, the volunteers came to realize, these people had no choice.

Color barred the Negroes and Puerto Ricans among them from most nonslum neighborhoods. Poverty barred the whites among them from most nonslum neighborhoods. Stated the Women's City Club report: "One tenant reported visiting real estate offices almost daily for the past year but whatever listings appeared were always prohibitive in price." The size of many of the area's families—25 percent contained five or more persons—cemented the bars in place. Said one tenant: "We have six children. I looked and looked everywhere, but apartments don't want so many children." Many landlords, able to pick and choose among tenants because of the housing crisis, didn't want any children. Asked one mother bitterly: "Am I supposed to drown them?" Most of the families interviewed—not all; a number which the interviewers found surprisingly large expressed real affection for their neighborhood—did not fool themselves into thinking that their neighborhood was ideal. They were living there because they had no place else to go. Their only alternative was the abyss.

And it was because the volunteers realized this that they were filled with indignation when they found out how Moses was "helping" these people.

Moses had stated that evicted families who wanted to move into the new apartments to be built on the site would be given "preferential status" in applying. In reality, Mrs. Black learned, they were being discouraged from applying at all. No applications were being accepted for Manhattantown and none would be until most of the families now on the site were gone.

Not that Moses' precaution was really necessary. The evicted families had been paying an average of $10 rent per room per month. The rent in Manhattantown was going to be—if Moses' figures could be believed—$34 per room per month, about $100 for even a small three-room apartment. Out of 400 families interviewed, exactly one said it could afford to pay $100 per month rent. The families being displaced "cannot even consider the possibility of applying for the new project displacing them. Where will [they] go?"

Not, in any numbers, into public housing. Moses had stated that Title I-displaced families would be given "first priority" in applying for such housing. Priorities meant little, however, because the public housing Moses was building had, with its lack of apartments for large families or single people (*"Build, build, build! There was never any thought as to what he was building!"*) little relationship to the needs of the displaced people. As to whether any priority was in fact given to these people, almost 300 of the 400 families interviewed wanted to get into public housing—a check by the Women's City Club three years later would show that only fifty had made it.

Promising "personal counseling," the compilation of a citywide list of available "decent, safe, and sanitary dwellings . . . within the financial means" of the families to be displaced—and "financial assistance," at least moving expenses plus a month's rent, to enable them to move into them—Moses had stated that "in order to set at rest any fears, families are assured that relocation help will be readily available and there is a frank desire to be of maximum assistance in carrying out the individual wishes of each family." The notice to move that the families actually got was a little more curt. Not even mailed to the individual families but tacked up in the entrances to their homes, it said:

DEMOLITION OF THIS BUILDING WILL BE STARTED AT ONCE.

TENANTS MUST VACATE.

FOR INFORMATION, CALL RELOCATION OFFICE, COR. OF WEST 100TH STREET.

When they called, or went in person, there were no "personal interviews," no "counseling." There was no information on finding apartments. The citywide listing of vacancies? No listing of *any* vacancies was available. There was no help in finding apartments. "I looked everywhere and couldn't find anything," one man told an interviewer. "Now, I don't know where else to look. And when I ask them for help, they just say they can't help me." Maximum assistance? In that relocation office, there was not even minimum mercy. "I'm 74 and too sick to look and no one helps you," one woman said. The Women's City Club interviewer's report on the "T Family" reads:

Mr. T was injured in accident and is now unable to walk stairs. He must attend the rehabilitation clinic daily. Mrs. T is disabled and has difficulty getting around. The son is recovering from polio and the boarder who lives with them is blind. They cannot look for other quarters. No one is helping them.

Financial assistance? The assistance for which the developers were being given a million dollars by the city? Except in rare instances, these impoverished people could not even obtain reimbursement for the moving expenses which they were being forced to incur through no choice of their own. Not only were they forced to move out of their homes, they were forced to pay for the moving. What was available—for most of the people who had lived on the site—was a single piece of advice: Get out—and get out fast. Returning stunned from the "cor. of West 100th Street," one man said he had been told to "be out in ten days." The inducement offered them to move—not in ten days, of course; that was just a scare tactic, to soften them up and make sure they wouldn't be too insistent on their rights—was somewhat more subtle than those mentioned in Moses' glowing brochures.

The developers owned the tenements now—and they simply stopped maintaining them. Said the report:

> Typical of the statements made by . . . tenants were the following comments: "No repairs are ever made." "There are large holes in the walls and floors where rats come through." "The toilet bowl has been broken for a long time but they won't fix it." "The plaster is coming down over the stove. If I bake a pie, the plaster comes right down into it!" One interview carried the terse report: "Baby screamed. Rat in crib."

Reading the filled-in questionnaires piled in her office, Elinor Black wrote "The bewilderment of people being forced out of their homes and their inability to cope with problems beyond their control was most evident." Also evident, recorded in the handwriting on those questionnaires, was apathy: "I have no money to move, so why should I waste time looking. I'll just wait—God and faith will find something for me." Despair: "I walked from 109th Street to 23rd Street and couldn't find a thing for us. The rents are too high. There's nothing to do." And, most of all, hatred and bitterness, hatred and bitterness at the vague, unseen force that was doing this to them, a force they identified only as "the city": "The city doesn't care about us. We're just nothing as far as they're concerned." Bitterness and hatred that would have been understood so well by Alfred E. Smith, who once, standing in the well of the Assembly Chamber in Albany, had asked, "What must be" the "feelings" of the widowed mother "when she sees these children separated from her by due process of law . . . ? What can be the feelings in the hearts of the children themselves . . . to know what the State's policy was with respect to their unfortunate condition?"

Now those feelings were understood by the Women's City Club. "God and faith will find something for me," an old Negro woman had said. God and faith would have to, realized the trim young matron who had interviewed her. The city wasn't going to. Robert Moses wasn't going to. And if any of the volunteer interviewers had any doubts as to whether the hatred and bitterness were justified, those doubts vanished when they moved on to the next step: finding out what had actually happened to the residents of buildings already demolished, people whose Title I-caused future was no longer a matter of conjecture but of reality.

Finding out wasn't easy. The developer—Moses' "reliable bidder"—refused to talk to them, as did the Relocation Office, as did, for weeks, the director of the city's Real Estate Bureau, the official charged on behalf of the city with the responsibility for seeing that the developer and the relocation firm gave the evicted tenants the "decent, safe, and sanitary dwellings" that the city had promised them. And when he finally consented to see them and they asked him where the tenants had moved to, he said he didn't know. He had never checked, he said.

They checked. Fifty of the 400 families, of course, had been placed in public housing, although they found that many of these "lucky" evictees, desperately lonely for their friends from the old neighborhood, felt as did one aged woman who said, "If they put the old house back, I'd move in again, even though I had to make my own hot water and heat." The others were more difficult to trace. Some had left no forwarding address deliberately, "to avoid creditors or payment of rent, or because of fear of the law or governmental agencies," as the Women's City Club report put it; others because, unable to speak English and inexperienced in even the basics of city life, they had left one not with the Post Office but with a neighbor or with the building superintendent—who had later also moved. The club's volunteers tried to trace them. They walked the streets of the bombed-out Manhattantown site trying to find someone who knew the family for whom they were searching, combed school registration records throughout the city, hunting for the names of the family's children. But "after all feasible tracing methods had been exploited," the club said in a follow-up report, new addresses could be obtained for only 167 of the original 400 families.

These were probably the people among the 400 who were best off. But even among them, the circumstances in which they were found were illuminating.

The volunteers found some of them on the West Side, in the area around Manhattantown, in the brownstones-turned-tenements. Wrote one volunteer:

> Some places were much worse than what the family had left. For example, a family of two moved from a four-room standard apartment with all utilities, central heating and hot water, private bath and toilet into a three-room apartment in poor condition, with no central heating, no refrigeration, tiny bath in kitchen and a hall toilet. Another family of three moved from four standard rooms to a six-room "railroad flat" with not a single enclosed room, holes in the floor and ceiling plaster falling.

The volunteers found many of these families in the cellars of these tenements—in dark and dampness. "It's all right," one woman said when asked about her "present quarters," "but I have arthritis now, which is not good, living in a basement." The volunteers found many of the old people in the furnished rooms of these tenements—the "rooms" that the old people had dreaded; some of them had been living with their children and grandchildren when the volunteers had met them before, but they were living alone now because the "new quarters" their family could find were too small.

For such apartments, moreover, the tenants were almost invariably forced to pay more rent than they had been paying before—often much more, often enough more to "seriously affect" the family's "standard of living."

These people were the lucky ones among the evictees that the club's volunteers could locate. They had managed to stay out of Harlem. Others had not. It was "Harlem" these families had dreaded. But it was in Harlem that the volunteers found them.

Seeing these people, perhaps the best off among the evicted families, the volunteers could picture the others. They could picture the basements in which they must be huddled, the railroad flats into which they must be crammed, the loneliness in which they must be living, deprived of the friends of years. During their visits to these families, they had gotten to know some of their children—and the fears their mothers had harbored for their future if they had to bring them up in Harlem. They could picture the lives of the children now.

And, the volunteers found, it was not the evictees who had moved to Harlem who were worst off. It was those who had moved— who had, utterly unable to find apartments, *been* moved—to new apartments "on-site," to the shells of buildings in the bombed-out Manhattantown site to which the developer would not send a painter or plumber, much less an exterminator; one volunteer recalls glancing into a kitchen and recoiling in disgust from the sight of a ceiling literally alive with vermin. Moses' "reliable" developer had moved some of these families not once but several times, shoved them from one building that was about to be torn down into another whose demolition was still a while off, and then, when it came time for *that* building to be demolished, moved them again—hitting them with a rent increase each time. The Women's City Club volunteers saw very clearly the implications for the city of such relocation tactics. After months of research, they knew with absolute certainty that the Title I program as being administered by Robert Moses was creating new slums as fast or faster than it was clearing old ones. But, after the exposure to concentrated human misery which they had undergone, it was the implications not for the city but for individual human beings that tore at their hearts. In writing the report, Elinor Black leaned over backwards to keep it fair and understated—leaned over backwards so far that at times the stance of the report was almost ludicrously tilted. But, despite the understatement, at times the emotion these women felt seeped through. The Moses-approved relocation policy, Mrs. Black wrote, "does not adequately meet" the demands either of the law or "of human decency." The City Planning Commission's Master Plan unit had uncovered the statistics that disproved Moses' claims. The Women's City Club volunteers had gone beyond the statistics to document the falseness of the claims in terms of human misery. The misery was now documented, quantified, broken down into individual cases and, with the issuance of the first Women's City Club report in March 1954, printed in black and white, as was the draft of the Master Plan unit report. A complete picture of what was really happening in Title I was ready for presentation to the city at large.

But the city did not see that picture.

In part, it did not see that picture because of Moses.

With the Master Plan unit's relocation report completed, Orton's chief aide, Henry Cohen, and Hortense Gabel, two liberals with a taste for political stratagem, began to plot ways to get the report before the public. They drafted a resolution requesting the Planning Commission to study "the relocation problem created by . . . public improvements"—"ordering us," in Orton's words, "to do what we had already been doing." Introduced, in March 1953, by Isaacs in the City Council and Wagner and Halley in the Board of Estimate, it was adopted with little discussion; it was not the kind of measure to which a politician could easily object in an election year and Moses did not get excited about studies that would take months, if not years, to complete—if indeed, thanks to his monopoly of available statistics, it could ever be completed at all. It may even have been his plan to see that the Commission deferred taking any action on the request until it was forgotten. But when the study was mentioned at the next commission meeting, Orton blandly said—while Stuart Constable, jolted out of the ostentatiously nonchalant slouch he habitually affected in imitation of "RM," bounced abruptly upright in his chair—that it was already completed and ready for adoption.

Cohen and Mrs. Gabel were convinced that a study bearing the official imprimatur of the City Planning Commission would receive prominent play in the press. Moses may have feared so, too. For six months, every attempt by Orton or his two allies on the commission, Bloustein and Livingston, to make the study official was defeated, 4–3, by Moses and *his* three allies, engineer Robert G. McCullough (of the Cross-Bronx Expressway), Queens real estate operator Charles Sturla and chairman Bennett (who was, of course, secretly organizing one profitable Title I syndicate himself). A series of 4–3 votes even defeated every attempt to place the study on the commission's calendar for formal consideration.

And while Moses was stalling the study, he was rewriting it. Some key statements were removed entirely. Others were modified subtly—just enough to change their meaning. "In some cases," the study had read, "the tenants were obliged to find their own new quarters." Now the study read: "In some cases, the tenants voluntarily found new quarters." Others were modified less subtly. New, false statistics were inserted; one set "showed" that the living conditions of an overwhelming majority of relocated tenants had been improved by relocation. And in the "Introduction" and "Recommendations" chapters of the report, the chapters from which Moses knew the press generally selects its material, the whole tenor of the document was changed. Relocation procedures in the past, it now said, had been "a noteworthy achievement for which credit is due." And "the outlook for the next four years . . . to be brighter than in the past." Those who had been in charge in the past should be left in charge in the future. The major recommendation of the report was a smoke screen added by Moses to draw attention away from the tenant relocation that was its ostensible subject—a proposal to finance public housing by a two-dollar-per-year tax on every telephone in the city. When, after sixteen major civic organizations joined in demanding the report's release and after the *Post* had been telling its readers for weeks about THE REPORT MOSES SUPPRESSES and the *Times* and *Herald Tribune* had finally begun to report the conflict on the commission (and after Impellitteri's defeat by Wagner had made it obvious that the report could not be bottled up indefinitely), the commission in December 1953—more than nine months after it had been written—adopted a "Tenant Relocation Report," it was not the report as originally presented but the report as rewritten by Moses, although so furious were Orton, Bloustein and Livingston that Bennett found it politic to allow them to append a minority report including most of the original points.

The smoke screen on the Women's City Club report was thrown up by Samuel I. Rosenman, Moses' lawyer, who was also, for $250,000, Manhattantown's, and who now proved that he was worth the money, putting at the service of his "developer" client not only his immense prestige that made his name a byword for integrity in New York but also the talent for words that had made him a valued speech writer for two Presidents. Rosenman's statement defending Manhattantown, Inc., possessed rhythm, punch—everything but truth. "The Women's City Club report, based upon an erroneous premise, does not reflect the situation as it existed at the time of the survey. It also does not reflect the situation as it exists today. . . . Relocation has not progressed at as rapid a rate as we had hoped. Although it has been slow, it has been successful. We consider it successful, because without imposing unnecessary hardships on tenants, a larger number of slum, substandard and insanitary buildings have been cleared and have been demolished. Within the near future, new, safe, sanitary buildings will rise on the land thus cleared." And if it did not possess truth, it was so intricately woven a tissue of half-truths and misleading statistics that sorting out fact from fiction would be an almost impossible chore for anyone without firsthand knowledge of the situation.

A reporter trying to find out the facts would now have to choose between two conflicting sets. He could not know that one of the sets—the one bearing the imprimatur of an adviser to Presidents and president of the Association of the Bar of the City of New York—was false.

And reporters were not trying to find out the facts. Their publishers and the editors who carried out the publishers' wishes made sure of that. If one reason the city did not get to see the true picture of what was going on on the Title I sites was Moses' strategy, another—more important—reason was that the press was not trying to see behind that strategy.

Mrs. Gabel feels that the draft relocation report she helped write—the draft that ended up as the Planning Commission's minority report—was a significant document in the history of urban renewal in New York City because it was "the first major relocation exposé," "the first public report, the first official report by any governmental agency, that even hinted obliquely that Moses wasn't God." But Mrs. Gabel was wrong. The facts presented in the minority report—and their implications for the future of the city—were as significant as she felt. But the report's impact on the city was not. It was an exposé without exposure. The public at large hardly knew about it—because it was hardly told about it. Although reporters, told by Orton that Moses' telephone-tax proposal was a strictly diversionary tactic, had his statement confirmed by Bennett's confession, when they questioned him closely, that "details . . . had not yet been worked out" (they never would be, either), the *Times, Herald Tribune* and *Daily News* all led with this proposal. The *Times* did not even bother to mention the relocation controversy until the seventh paragraph, and then quoted, at greater length than it devoted to any other quote in the report, a "reply" to the minority report inserted in the report by

Moses that implied—falsely—that the real purpose behind their report was to move "about 20 percent of the entire City population"; and said, "No wonder the radicals would like to get hold of tenant relocation." (The first that "the radicals" knew of Moses' "reply" was when they read about it in the newspapers the next day. Bennett, they charged, had locked up all the commissioners' copies of the report so that they couldn't get to see it—and hence couldn't answer it.) Of the city's daily newspapers, only the *Post* devoted any substantial space to the relocation facts so laboriously uncovered. The reformers had provided the city's press with facts that disproved the statements by Moses and other city officials from the Mayor on down that the press had been printing for months. If the city's press was unable—or unwilling—to obtain for itself ammunition to shoot holes in the curtain of secrecy surrounding the relocation of tenants on the vast Title I sites, it no longer had to do so. The ammunition had been stacked up, ready for its use, by others. But the press did not use it. The fate of poor people had never been news in New York City; it still was not news. Housing had always been a field whose complications discouraged the press from delving beneath its surface; thanks to Moses' strategy, moreover, the official report, the report the press was almost obligated to carry, now said that there was nothing wrong, or even worth discussing, with the relocation program—there seemed no reason to delve beneath the surface. The suspicions of the press, which would normally have been aroused by the rumors of "deals" and involvement by high-level politicians in a program calling for a vast write-down by the taxpayers, were lulled by the fact that this program was being run by apolitical Robert Moses; his legend draped over Title I a comforting, concealing cloak. The relocation report was never, except in passing, to be referred to in print again. Title I coverage continued to be predominantly a reprinting of Moses' statements and of "facts" from his brochures. As for city policy, just one week after the report's release, Hortense Gabel appeared before the Board of Estimate as a representative of seventeen civic groups protesting Moses' plans for his Washington Square Southeast Title I project. She appealed to the Board not to approve the project until it had at least studied the report. "Sheer, unadulterated bunk," Moses said. The Board approved the project.

On October 1, 1954, an event occurred that should, by all normal standards of newsworthiness, have been eminently newsworthy.

For months, investigators of the Banking and Currency Committee of the United States Senate had been looking into Manhattantown's books and, despite the frantic juggling which those books had undergone, had been able to come up with a detailed picture of the "reliable bidder's" financial operations—and on October 1, in a public hearing held in New York, it placed that picture on public exhibition.

The hearing was marked by remarkable lapses of memory on the part of Manhattantown's ostensible founder, Samuel Caspert, a Democratic clubhouse figure to whom Moses had seen fit to hand over, on behalf of the City of New York, 338 apartment houses and tenements housing thousands of human beings. Under questioning by committee general counsel William Simon, Caspert was unable to recall even whether there had ever been a written document—any kind of prospectus, formal or informal—telling prospective stockholders the financial details of the project in which they were investing. And whenever it seemed that Simon had Caspert firmly on the hook at last, there were deft interventions to get him off—by his counsel, Judge Samuel I. Rosenman—interventions that were made easier by the deference with which Simon treated this prestigious public figure. But despite the evasions, denials and interventions, by the time Senator Prescott Bush, a Republican from Connecticut, gaveled the hearing to a close late in the afternoon, it was a matter of public record—because it was a record of an official Senate committee hearing, privileged public record, so that any newspaper could print it without worrying about the possibility of libel damages—that more than two years before, the Mayor's Slum Clearance Committee had handed over to Caspert and Company six square blocks of Manhattan real estate, worth $15,000,000, for $1,000,000. It was a matter of public record that as of October 1954, the month of the hearing, Caspert and Company were required to have all 338 buildings demolished—but that about 280 buildings were still standing, their tenants still paying rents. It was a matter of public record that not one brick had been laid for any new buildings—and that not one piece of financing for new construction had been obtained. It was a matter of public record that, in the more than two years since Moses' committee had turned over the slum clearance project to his "reliable bidder," that bidder's major activity had been not to clear those slums but to milk them. And so were the replies of Simon and Senator Bush—made near the end of the hearing, when the transcript indicates that they had come to the conclusion that Rosenman had pushed them around enough—when, after Simon had hinted that perhaps that was all Caspert and Company had ever intended to do, that the developers of the slum clearance project were trying to clear those slums as slowly as possible so as to continue making money from them as long as possible, Rosenman denied there was "any intention not to go ahead with this project":

Mr. Simon. . . . the contract required that the new buildings be completed in four years [and more than two years] have gone by, and only one-sixth of the demolition has been done, and none of the new construction has been done, which is a fact that speaks for itself.

Senator Bush. The thing the committee is curious about, Judge, is whether the attractiveness of the operation that these people have been engaged in hasn't perhaps delayed the construction of these buildings, which is what the Federal Government is interested in.

And although Rosenman replied to those statements by protesting that "there is no such attractiveness . . . it is far from attractive," the truth of the judge's protests was also a matter of public record, a record based on Simon's questions, the evasions of Caspert and his partners—and the stark facts entered into that record by committee investigators. That record showed that the profits made off the hapless human beings in the buildings still standing on the Manhattantown site were so huge that Manhattantown's thirteen stockholders had been able to receive from the company—in addition to regular "partners' drawings"—special payments made under a variety of devices apparently designed to conceal the "attractiveness" from investigators: one partner, for example, receiving through a "construction company" that had no office of its own and only two employees, himself and his secretary, $42,000 (although no construction had been done), and through a "management company" another $38,000; another partner, for example, receiving $26,000 in "legal fees"; another partner receiving $48,000 for accounting and auditing work; a group of partners receiving profits of $153,000 paid to a dummy "management firm" they had set up—as Simon put it, "different people got cut in for a piece of different things but when it was all over everybody got a ride on one of the horses." And the record also showed that the profits the partners had already reaped, large as they were, were small compared to the profits the partners were planning to reap in the future. One partner, a close friend of Moses' ally, Bronx Boss Charlie Buckley, was in line for $375,000 for architectural services. So huge were Manhattantown's profits that they had been spread around—among stockholders' fathers, stockholders' sons, stockholders' daughters, as well as stockholders' uncles, aunts, nieces, nephews and assorted in-laws. And spread around liberally. The brother of the stockholder who had received $42,000 for "construction" and $38,000 for "management" himself received $30,000 as Manhattantown's "comptroller." In one transaction—just one of many spread on the record by the committee to demonstrate how money was siphoned off from the parent corporation into the pockets of its partners and their relatives—Caspert had skimmed off for himself and his family $115,000 in less than a year. He set up a separate corporation headed by his son-in-law. Manhattantown sold the son-in-law's corporation all the gas stoves and refrigerators in the tenements for $33,000—and then rented them right back from the corporation, paying it in effect for the privilege of using what had been its own appliances. And Manhattantown paid so well—paid rental fees so high—that in less than a year the son-in-law's corporation earned, after all expenses, $115,326.37. At the end of the year, Manhattantown bought back the stoves and refrigerators for the same amount it had sold them: $33,000. Financially, Manhattantown had wound up right where it had started—but the son-in-law's firm had pocketed $115,326.37. By the end of the hearing, it was a matter of public record not only that in more than two years the slum clearance project had cleared hardly any slums, not only that no progress was being made in providing the new housing that the project was designed to provide—but that everyone involved in the project was getting rich.

Here, by any customary newspaper definition, was *SCANDAL.* A major city administration program in which, it was now revealed, a $15,000,000 slum had been turned over, for a mere fraction of its worth, to promoters who were milking it of hundreds of thousands of dollars, profits documented, down to the dollar, by federal probers—here was scandal of the first magnitude in a town in which allegations of twenty-dollar bribes to a few building inspectors were found worthy of big black headlines. Moreover, juicy as had been the revelations of the Senate hearing, the hearing held the promise of far juicier revelations to be uncovered. There was the clear scent of far bigger scandal in the air. Manhattantown was one Title I project; there were ten others then under way in the city—one of them, in fact, also run by Samuel Caspert and friends. To reap that harvest of headlines, newspapers would normally have sent into the fertile fields of Title I their best gleaners, their ace investigative reporters.

By customary practice, moreover, New York's papers would have brought into the picture an element the Senate hearing had not—the name of the city official responsible for the turning over of the slum to the promoters: the chairman of New York's Slum Clearance Committee. Rosenman let slip the name of that official only once—in the hearing's fifth and last hour—when he could not avoid using it in identifying for the record a report addressed to that official. In all the sixty-six pages of the hearing transcript that is the only time his name appears. In referring to the authorities responsible for turning over the slum to Manhattantown, it was always "the city." The city's press would customarily not have been so vague. They would have identified the official, printed his name in big, black headlines, used his photograph, questioned him, examined his answers to their questions with printed suspicion. By the time a normal press investigation of Title I had been completed, his name would have appeared in a hundred headlines, his picture would have stared from a hundred front pages, the public would have been reminded a hundred times that he was the man responsible for Title I, in the public mind his name would have been ineradicably linked with its failures, its abuses—and with "*SCANDAL*," the noun which had spelled the doom of so many officials' careers.

But the Manhattantown revelations hardly touched Robert Moses at all. The fear and awe in which he was held by reporters, rewritemen, copy editors and city editors was never more evident than on the day following the Senate hearing on Manhattantown and in the days that followed. Robert Moses had conceived the Manhattantown project. He had directed its planning. He had selected the cast of characters who ran it. He had shifted the cast around when the political winds in the city shifted. It was a Robert Moses project from beginning to end. The *Times* story on Manhattantown did not mention Robert Moses once. The other papers followed suit. His name was hardly mentioned; no editorials called for his removal. There might have been scandal in Manhattantown, but Manhattantown's creator was unscathed by it.

And because he was, Manhattantown and the Title I program of which Manhattantown was a part were largely unscathed, too.

The *Times* did not do another story on Manhattantown in the months that followed, but that might have been expected: the *Times* was not a paper of inquiry, and inquiry would have been necessary for follow-up stories. But what was not to be expected—from the customary behavior of the press in New York—was that no other papers would undertake any inquiry either. Not one investigative reporter was assigned to probe further into Manhattantown or Title I. Some reporters wanted to, but were refused permission, in some cases probably because of their publishers' admiration for Moses, in most cases simply because it seemed to editors a waste of time: where Moses was involved, they felt, there would be no scandal to be found; trying to find it would be a misuse of manpower that could be more profitably employed investigating politicians or bureaucrats. The creators of the Moses myth believed in what they had created. The myth still glowed, as strong as ever—with a glow that blinded New York to the shabby reality of what was going on on the Title I sites.

During the following eighteen months—the rest of 1954, and all of 1955, and the spring of 1956—there were, as there had been since 1952, continual rumors about Title I, continual protests about individual Title I projects, continual questions about the whole shape and scope and direction of Title I and about the individuals to whom Moses had handed over so much of this program that was going to reshape the city. More and more people and groups were hearing these rumors, making these protests, asking these questions. The Women's City Club made a new, follow-up survey of relocation practices at Manhattantown, and other investigations were made by at least five other public and civic agencies: the 108-year-old Community Service Society, the one-year-old City Wide Committee on Relocation Problems, the Mayor's Committee on Housing, the City Administrator's office and Walter Fried's Federal Housing and Home Finance Agency. The results of all received only cursory treatment from the press. By the end of 1955, Stanley Isaacs was being joined in his repeated pleas for an investigation of Title I by several maverick city councilmen. All of those pleas were buried in Council committee, and in the newspapers. The myth that shielded Title I—and other Moses public works projects; 1953 and 1954 were, after all, the years in which he was ousting from their homes the 1,530 families of East Tremont who could find a voice for their cries only in the New York *Post*—from public view stayed firmly in place. The movement to reveal the truth about Moses' projects had been an underground movement, a movement led not by the City Planning Commission's majority but by the rebel commissioner Orton and his "fifteenth-story undercover" band of researchers, not by the city's reform housing "establishment" but by the new, boat-rocking Hortense Gabel. As late as April 1956, it was still an underground movement. "We were still voices crying in the wilderness," Orton recalls. "We couldn't get anyone to listen to us." A *World-Telegram and Sun* reporter managed to write a two-part series on relocation—a pallid, surface description that left the impression that all was generally well—without mentioning, even once, the man most responsible for relocation. Before the city could begin to see the truth about Moses' programs, his legend would have to be exposed for the lie it was. Before the people would be willing to look at Moses' programs straight on, they would have to look at Moses straight on, and before the public could do that, there would have to be an issue that would show him so clearly for what he was that there could be no mistake.

42. *Tavern in the Town*

THAT ISSUE might never have arisen if some engineer hadn't left his blueprints lying around during lunch hour.

He left them in a little glen in Central Park, a grassy, tree-shaded hollow between Sixty-seventh and Sixty-eighth streets about three hundred feet in from the stone wall along Central Park West that Frederick Law Olmsted had built to mark the line where the city would end and serenity begin, where, among "country roads and scenery," the city dweller could "forget for a time the rattle of the pavements and the glare of brick walls."

Robert Moses had made forgetting more difficult. Before 1934, the glen, shielded from Central Park West to the west by higher ground, had faced, across bridle path and West Drive (kept curved and narrow by Olmsted to discourage auto traffic and shielded from the glen by heavy shrubbery), Jacob Wrey Mould's classic little sheepfold and, beyond it, the broad "Green" or "Sheep Meadow" on which the wooly white Southdowns grazed placidly under the eye of sheepdog and crook-carrying shepherd. After 1934, the new Park Commissioner threw out sheep and sheepdog and shepherd, converted the sheepfold into the "Tavern-on-the-Green," built a parking lot behind it, and, to provide "more convenient access" to the restaurant, cut a new road, an extension of Sixty-seventh Street, into the park past its front door, where he widened the pavement into a large parking circle; thereafter, the view to the south from the glen was asphalt and automobiles. He straightened and widened the West Drive, decimating the shrubbery shield in the process, and thereafter the herds to the east were not meandering sheep but thundering cars. On the high ground to the west, there were now swings and slides, and asphalt and a tall black iron fence—one of the perimeter playgrounds the Park Commissioner had built to "intercept" children who wanted to use the park.

Yet, within its sheltering border of trees and bushes, behind its shield of high ground, the glen still offered at least a measure of refuge from the city, particularly for mothers with small children. Its big trees, huge boulders and expanses of grass made it a perfect place for kids to play. On a typical day, the glen was a picture—an urban version of a pastoral landscape—of kids throwing baseballs or footballs, kids scrambling up boulders, kids climbing trees or lying behind them in coonskin caps (1956 was television's Davy Crockett era) bang-banging their six-shooters or Texas long rifles at each other or ambushing the automobiles heading past along the West Drive. And as the kids played, their mothers sat chatting on a row of benches situated between glen and playground so that they could keep an eye on both at the same time—sat among trees and grass and quiet. "You know, at that time in your life, your life centers around your children," says one. "We *lived* in that little spot in the park. We took our kids twice a day—once wasn't enough, for God's sake! I remember once being in that playground in the snow—freezing! That little spot in the park was really the center of our neighborhood. And it was beautiful, tranquil. You know, in a city like New York, a spot like that is really precious."

Then, on April 9, 1956, a sunny spring Monday, one of the mothers, Roselle Davis, sitting on a bench watching her four-year-old son, Earl, play in the playground, noticed below her in the glen a group of men with surveying equipment and blueprints. The sight didn't disturb her. "I thought they were planning some sort of improvement for the playground," she recalls. But walking home at lunchtime, she noticed that although the men had gone for lunch, the blueprints were still spread out on the grass. Out of curiosity, she bent down to read them—and saw their title: "Detail Map of Parking Lot."

Returning to the playground after lunch, Mrs. Davis related her discovery to other mothers—among them Augusta Newman, wife of Arnold Newman, a world-famous photographer who possessed a healthy sense of moral indignation. "I wasn't sure that anything could be done about it, and I sort of forgot about it," Mrs. Newman recalls. "But that evening we went to a party or something, and in the cab coming home, I said to my husband, 'You know, Roselle told me today that they're building a new parking lot for the Tavern-on-the-Green in that spot in the park where the boys play,' and he—unlike me—said: 'They can't do that!' " Although it was after midnight, he telephoned Mrs. Davis for more details and then telephoned Sixty-seventh Street's most famous resident, the elderly novelist Fannie Hurst, to solicit her help in writing a petition. In addition to his eye for social injustice, Newman had one for public relations. He was aware that because Sixty-seventh Street contained the literarily oriented residence hotel, the Hotel des Artistes, and a row of studio duplexes designed for artists, complete to two-story windows letting in north light, it was the home of a quota of "names" from the artistic, literary and show-business world high even for the West Side. Two of the most famous illustrators of the Thirties, Floyd Davis and Gladys Rockmore, lived in No. 1 West 67th Street, along with oceanographer William Beebe. Roselle Davis and her husband, painter Stuart Davis, lived in No. 15, as did dancer Pearl Lang. No. 33 housed, in addition to the Newmans, newscaster Raymond Gram Swing, publisher Jason Epstein, photographer Philippe Halsman, sculptor George Lober and illustrator Dean Cornwell. Ludwig Bemelmans lived in No. 39, the Yiddish actor Joseph Buloff and playwright Samuel Raphaelson in No. 40, violinist William Kroll in No. 50. Around the corner on Central Park West lived composer Harold Rome. The hotel's residents included Howard Chandler Christie, who had painted the nude-filled murals in its Café des Artistes (he took the sun every morning on a park bench near the glen, nodding politely to the mothers walking by), and Mae Murray, the Merry Widow herself: the woman who had once been Hollywood's most glamorous star lived in the hotel in an attic formerly a chambermaid's room. When the petition was written, Newman got a healthy number of high-caliber names on it—and then sent his wife and Mrs. Davis out soliciting signatures from mothers at the playground. Trying to telephone the Park Commissioner, he received a customary Moses brush-off, but he mailed him the petition, signed with twenty-three names, with a copy to Mayor Wagner. The newly appointed deputy mayor, educator John J. Theobald, just recently recruited from his Queens College presidency by Wagner, to whom the Mayor referred the matter, did nothing about it on Wednesday—and gave no indication that he was contemplating doing anything about it ever. But another one of the mothers happened to be the wife of a *Herald Tribune* reporter, Richard C. Wald. By Thursday, Wald had realized that the story he had been told by his wife might be of interest to a wider audience, and even though Stuart Constable, the pompous Park Department executive officer whose bushy walrus soup-strainer had earned him the nickname "Mustache," tried to make him understand that this parking lot he was making such a fuss about would be less than an acre, a meaningless fraction of 1 percent of 843-acre Central Park, it was printed in Friday morning's edition. By eleven o'clock, Theobald had decided that the thing to do was to hold a meeting between representatives of the mothers and of Moses that afternoon, and, unable to reach Moses, asked one of the Commissioner's secretaries to have him call back and tell him what time would be convenient for him or one of his "top people."

Local protest over a park "improvement" may have been a new story to Theobald, but it was an old one to Moses—old and boring. Ever since he had become Park Commissioner he had kept such protest to a minimum by keeping the "improvements" secret, so that, often, before the neighborhood concerned knew there was an improvement planned it was already under way, and by ignoring protest and going ahead with the "improvement" as if it didn't exist. Scores—hundreds—of mothers' committees and chambers of commerce and civic associations and taxpayers' associations and merchants associations and block associations had objected to one plan or another for a parking field or a baseball diamond or a playground or a highway in some city park, and Moses' method had almost invariably proven effective. Not a week before, in fact, Flushing mothers had begged him not to destroy "the only spot of green" anywhere near their neighborhood by cutting down about forty "fine old trees" to turn little Weeping Beech Park just south of Northern Boulevard into a paved playground. He had simply ignored the plea: the trees were down now and the paving machines complacently at work. On the seismograph on which Moses recorded public tremors, in fact, the Tavern-on-the-Green protest had barely registered. Twenty-three mothers? He had just finished evicting hundreds of mothers rather than shift a section of his Cross-Bronx Expressway a single block! He was at that very moment in the process of displacing *five thousand* mothers for Manhattantown, *four thousand* for Lincoln Center! A parking lot, and a tiny parking lot at that! He had just finished building a

Coliseum! The only aspect of a protest that concerned him at all was the play it might receive in the press, and there seemed no reason for concern on that score. The city's big dailies seldom gave more than token coverage to local protest, anyway. Not one had carried so much as a line on Weeping Beech Park. His rapport with the press—the *Post* excepted, of course—was at one of its all-time peaks, now that the Coliseum Title I project in which publishers were so interested was completed: the editorial board of the one paper that had printed the story on the Tavern-on-the-Green protest was that very morning deciding to run the next day an editorial lauding the Coliseum as "stimulating evidence" of his "tremendous progress" in Title I. Most of the dailies were preparing to take the occasion of the Coliseum's formal opening in two weeks to heap encomiums on its creator; the *Times,* in fact, was going to publish a special 72-page "New York: Coliseum City" magazine section on opening day, with Moses commissioned to write an article on "What the City Means." Writers of letters-to-the-editor might be more and more critical, but as for editorial writers, the writers who counted, after thirty years of lionization by their pens, he was still their lion; just a month before, two key ones had taken time out from their ordinary duties to review his just-published *Working for the People,* and, perhaps because of the difficulty of finding favorable things to say about that nonbook, had devoted most of their reviews to its "author," the *Trib*'s L. L. Engelking calling him "the selfless servant of the people," William Ogden of the *Times* calling him "one of the great public servants of our time." The only element of the protest worth noting at all was that Theobald had dared to suggest that it be given a hearing; this refugee from the campus needed a lesson. Not Moses but one of Moses' secretaries returned Theobald's call—by reading him a memo from her boss. Picking up his telephone expecting to find Moses on the other end, the startled deputy mayor heard a woman's voice saying: "We are not prepared to attend any conferences. I do not think the deputy mayor should get into matters of this kind which are the concern of commissioners until the commissioners have answered letters." The mothers' would be answered next Tuesday; until then, let them wait; "we would suggest to Dr. Theobald that he *not* see these people until after we have answered their letter." Even as Moses' secretary was reading his memo promising an answer, moreover, Moses was issuing an order that would make the answer—and the protest—meaningless. Early Tuesday morning—before the mothers would have received their mail—a bulldozer was to tear up the glen. His letter would not placate the mothers, of course, but that would no longer matter. By the time they read his explanation of why it was necessary to destroy the glen they were fighting for, there would no longer be any point in fighting for it. It wouldn't be there. This protest would be disposed of as he had been disposing of protests for thirty years.

But this protest was different.

It was different partly because the protesters were well educated and heeled, possessed of both the sophistication to know the best methods of fighting Moses and the money to implement those methods. There hadn't been a single lawyer among the 1,530 East Tremont families in the path of the Cross-Bronx Expressway near Crotona Park, but there were plenty of lawyers—good ones—among the hundred or so families near Central Park West and Sixty-seventh Street whose children played in the little glen, and many of them were willing to take the case for nothing. And those families could afford to raise the money for the substantial other legal expenses for a full-scale fight against the city.

This protest was different because the issue behind it was unusually clear-cut. Protests on housing invariably involved arguments based on differing and involved philosophies to which there were always two—and often twenty—sides. Protests on highways were complicated by a myriad of arcane engineering considerations. Protests involving parks were generally simpler, but usually when Moses tore up part of a park for a nonpark purpose, the purpose was clearly a public one—a highway, for example—so that the issue was complicated, and in presenting it the press was also hampered by its necessary reliance on "expert opinion," most of which was controlled by Moses. But there was nothing complicated about *this* issue. No expert opinion was necessary to decide the rights and wrongs of tearing up a park for a parking lot that would benefit only a private restaurant—an expensive restaurant at that. New York's press was enthusiastic only on clear-cut issues—and here was one that was very clear-cut.

This protest was different because Moses' responsibility was unusually clear-cut. Because of the nontraditional role, a role outside the normal democratic processes, that he played in Title I and highways, his responsibility was difficult for the public to understand—particularly because the press, which did not appear to fully grasp it either, never explained it adequately. But his responsibility here was clear and direct; no newspaper had to make the connection.

But the primary difference in this protest had nothing to do with philosophy or governmental roles; it was due to the simple physical fact of the parking lot's location: the park in which it was located was Central Park.

Central Park was something very special to New York. It was special because it sat, spacious and green and beautiful, at the very heart of the concrete city, because more New Yorkers used it than any other park, because it was practically the back yard for an astoundingly high proportion of the city's wealthiest and most influential individuals, because for most of these users—and for hundreds of thousands of others, inhabitants of the otherwise all but greenless center of the most densely inhabited island in the world—it was their *only* park. It was special to New Yorkers interested in park history because of its beauty and historic significance as the first and most influential of American landscaped parks. It seemed little less than a miracle to them that in this greediest of cities 843 acres of the most valuable real estate had somehow been set aside—and preserved for a hundred years—as a public resource.

It was special, also, because journalists had made it special. For a hundred years, newspapers had paid more attention to Central Park than to all the city's 710 other parks, large and small, combined. Central Park had, like a President, become news in itself. Central Park had become a symbol, a symbol that evoked universal and positive emotions in New Yorkers; it had become the symbol of beauty, open space, peace, fun—of everything parks meant to a city. "Of all the city's wonders," the city's historians said, "Central Park ranks first in the affection of New Yorkers." If all parks were holy to New Yorkers, Central Park was the holy of holies—a thing that must be preserved. Every attempted "invasion" of Central Park for a nonpark purpose, no matter how small, was a cause to which an editorial writer's response was almost Pavlovian; in the hundred years since its creation, a thousand editorials had proclaimed that every foot of it was "sacred." Even during the 1930's, when it had been all adulation for Moses in the press, protests over Moses' remaking of parts of Central Park had been treated with seriousness. That they hadn't been more serious was due to Moses' success, because of his ability to use great forces of WPA workers without going through normal city governmental channels, in rushing through his remaking in secrecy; to the fact that Tammany-induced decay in the park had reached a point at which any change could hardly help being an "improvement"; to the fact that his baseball diamonds and playgrounds were, after all, "park purposes," even if not the purpose for which Central Park had been intended. But these conditions no longer existed. There was no WPA and no Tammany—and not even Robert Moses could make the city believe that the Tavern-on-the-Green parking lot was a "park purpose." Moses' reputation as a defender of parks, the keystone of his whole image, had endured because what he was doing to parks—like paving over the beautiful Van Cortlandt Park marshes for the Major Deegan Expressway—had been carried out largely in secrecy because the press had never focused public attention on it. Only a year or so earlier, a group of Sutton Place mothers, every bit as well educated and quite a bit richer than the Central Park West mothers, had been unable to get any publicity for a baby-carriage picket line they threw up to protest his rape of their East River Drive playground at Forty-ninth Street. But there could be no secrecy about anything he did in Central Park, a half acre of which meant more to the city's press than 150 acres of Van Cortlandt. Moses' image as park defender was still intact only because the public had never been given a close look at his park controversies. But at any substantial controversy in Central Park, the press would give the people a very close look indeed.

And there was going to be a very substantial controversy in Central Park.

In April, the leaves over the little glen were still only a pale-green haze, not yet thick enough to obscure the view of the ground from Elliott and Elinor Sanger's twelfth-floor apartment directly across from the glen at 75 Central Park West. And when, at about seven o'clock Tuesday morning, April 17, 1956, Elinor Sanger awoke and went into the bathroom and glanced out her large bathroom window, she saw a large bulldozer ripping at the ground to tear out the roots of the trees.

The Sangers were friendly with Stanley Isaacs, so Mrs. Sanger did what people who knew Stanley Isaacs always seemed to do when they were confronted with injustice: she called him for help. "Get the women out there, and call the newspapers and television," Isaacs said. "I'll be right over." "What are you going to do?" Mrs. Sanger asked. "I don't know," said the dignified, white-haired attorney, then in his seventies. "But if I have to, I'll lie down in front of the bulldozer."

As it turned out, he didn't have to. Mrs. Sanger telephoned Augusta Newman, who began frantically calling other mothers, and telling them to call others. Within minutes, astonished doormen saw thirty or forty women running down Sixty-seventh Street and along Central Park West, yanking along dogs and little children and wheeling baby carriages. ("The baby carriages were my idea," Augusta Newman says. "I thought they would make a good picture. After all, we *are* in the business, you know. And anyway, most of the mothers *had* to bring their children. They didn't have maids. Their husbands were going to work. Who were they going to leave them with?") Running into the glen, where the bulldozer was snorting and grinding away, they began somewhat hesitantly—leaving plenty of room between it and them—to move to a position that would later be somewhat loosely described as "in front of it." The driver, an employee of a small private contractor to whom Moses had given the parking lot construction job, cut his engine. "He was a very nice man," Mrs. Newman recalls. "He told a policeman [who had just come running up to see what was going on], 'I'm not going to do a *thing* as long as those ladies are standing here.' " When Isaacs arrived, he saw, beneath the trees, the earth-moving machine stopped, its driver standing beside it, a line of mothers and baby carriages, and, moving up close to them, policemen who, summoned by the first, had sped up in several patrol cars.

It was a tableau that—complete to Isaacs' presence—might have been lifted intact from a score of earlier Moses battles. But within a few minutes a new element had been added to it, an element that had been conspicuously missing from the earlier tableaus—and that was to make April 17, 1956, the watershed of Moses' career. Following Isaacs' instructions, Elliott Sanger had telephoned more than a score of newspapers, radio stations and television stations to ask them to send men to the scene. And they did.

A hundred neighborhood representatives had asked radio stations, television stations and the big citywide daily newspapers to cover their protests against Robert Moses projects. If they were lucky, two or three sent a man; often only the *Post* did; often even the *Post* didn't bother. Lillian Edelstein had managed to get three mayoral candidates and an audience of four hundred people to the rally in JHS 44 in East Tremont; in that audience there had been not a single reporter or photographer. But on this Tuesday morning there came, driving into the Tavern-on-the-Green's parking circle, jumping out and running over to the little glen, shoving microphones and triple-folded copy paper into the faces of the mothers and the bulldozer driver, reporters and photographers from the *Post*—and from the *Herald Tribune,* the *World-Telegram and Sun,* the *Journal-American,* the *Daily Mirror,* from the *Times,* the newspaper with the greatest prestige in the country, and from the *Daily News,* the newspaper with the largest circulation in the world, even from the Brooklyn *Eagle,* from WMCA, WOR, WABC, WNBC, WHN, WINS, WNEW, from WCBS-TV, WNBC-TV, WABC-TV, WOR-TV and WPIX-TV. A hundred local protests against some plan or other of Robert Moses' had been carried out, so far as the public was concerned, in secrecy, the secrecy so necessary to Moses' success. This local protest against this Robert Moses plan would be carried out in a spotlight, the brightest spotlight on earth—the spotlight thrown by the massed mass media of the city that was the communications center of the civilized world.

Within hours, every major radio station in New York was telling its listeners the story of the mothers, the baby carriages and the bulldozer. That evening, the story was on every major television newscast. The next day, a picture of mothers and children lined up defiantly between the menacing machine and a large tree was displayed prominently in every newspaper in town.

By the weekend—with Moses trying to trick the protesters by taking no action on Wednesday, giving reporters the impression that he would await the results of a Thursday conference between Theobald and the mothers, and then ordering the bulldozer back into action Thursday morning, only to have it turned back again by sentries because the mothers had set up a rotating schedule that kept the glen guarded from 7 A.M. to dark, trying vainly again on Friday with a new bulldozer operator bearing assurances that all he wanted to do was "move some topsoil around"—the story was on page one. It would stay there for weeks.

For this story had everything.

It had "names." Lillian Edelstein couldn't get one quote in the *News*; the *News* begged Fannie Hurst for a quote ("Central Park stands 'as a heartbeat of the asphalt city.' Yet 'we see trees sacrificed to a restaurant and a night club' "). And it had more than "names." It had trees, too—especially since the week in which Moses had chosen to cut down the ones in the glen happened to be National Arbor Week. Said a front-page *World-Telegram* box: "School children have been memorizing 'Woodman, spare that tree/Touch not a single bough . . .' And up in Central Park, Park Commissioner Robert Moses observed the week in his own unique way by sending ax-wielding workmen . . . to chop down a stand of maples to make way for a parking lot." And it had more than "names" and trees—it had *Central Park.* By the second week, several papers had found the catch phrase they were looking for: "The Battle of Central Park." It had more than just names and trees and Central Park. It had bulldozers, a word that by the mid-1950's carried enough emotion-laden and unpleasant overtones to keep a story going all by itself. And it had more—much more. It had mothers. Parks and trees might be "motherhood issues," but this was more than a motherhood issue: *this* was MOTHERHOOD! The press saw this—and made the most of it. It was "Moms-vs.-Moses" in the *News,* and "The Brigade of Mothers" in the *World-Telegram,* and "Park Moms" in the *Post,* and "Fighting Park Moms" in the *Journal-American* and "the embattled mothers of Central Park" in the *Herald Tribune*; as the headlines blasted out at New York five and six a day, day after day, the words that leaped from them, bold and black, were not only magic words like "parks" and "trees" and "bulldozer" but the most magic word of all. And the stories under the headlines were stories about mothers engaged in that most holy of mothers' wars, a battle to protect a place for their children (their "tots," their "kiddies") to play, a "mothers' battle to keep the grassy, wooded section a haven for their children away from the concrete and clatter of the city streets," as the *World-Telegram* put it. There was nothing unique or even unusual in the "Battle of Central Park." But because the site of this battle was Central Park, the press had begun looking at it—and had seen elements so sensational that it couldn't, even if it wanted to, tear its fascinated eyes away. The tactics Moses was using were the tactics he had been using for thirty years—but now the press was reporting them, and a whole city was watching them. The things Stanley Isaacs was saying now were the same things he had been saying for thirty years. The only difference was that now people were listening to them. Now, when he spoke, a dozen microphones were held up before his face, amplifying his words, as Moses' had been amplified for thirty years, until they were loud enough for a whole city to hear them. This time, his tightly reasoned letters-to-the-editor were quoted in editorials and in news articles, front-page news articles. When Moses replied with the argument he had been using against Isaacs ever since he had helped drive him out of his borough presidency with it in 1938, the *Daily Mirror* picked up the attack as usual ("the claque complaining about Robert Moses is headed by Stanley Isaacs, who, when he was president of the Borough of Manhattan, gave employment to Simon Gerson, who was a Communist . . ."), but for once—the first time—the *Mirror*'s voice was a lone voice. For once, when Isaacs tried to explain to the press the philosophy behind Moses' projects and what was wrong with that philosophy, the press paid heed to the explanation—even on the editorial page of the newspaper that had been Moses' staunchest defender for thirty years and whose principal stockholder believed "there has never been as great a public servant." Exactly what happened in the editorial conferences of *The New York Times* is not known, although certainly Mrs. Sulzberger's love for Central Park—the original concept of pastoral, serene Central Park—the love which she had previously subordinated to her admiration for Moses, had something to do with it, and possibly so, too, did the fact that by 1956 the brilliant conservationist John Oakes was taking a more active role on the editorial page; on April 20, the *Times* carried an editorial that, while it perpetuated the Moses myth, also contained statements that were, coming from the *Times,* especially remarkable, as remarkable as the editorial's title: ONLY A HALF ACRE—BUT.

If this were land somewhere else there would be nothing to get excited about. But Central Park is different. To New Yorkers, and especially those who live near the park, it is sacred land. To use it for anything but park is like insulting the flag.

After fighting all these years against all the causes that were offered to invade it, why should New York at this late date give up a half acre for the personal convenience of eighty carloads of people having chicken dinner in the Tavern?

Those who protest do so belatedly. We plead guilty, like the rest, to tardiness. This is regrettable. But the principle on which protest is based is no less valid, and ordinarily Mr. Moses would be its chief defender against those who would destroy a blade of park grass. Let the diners at the Tavern ride there in taxicabs. . . .

Things had gone far enough. When the Coordinator struck again, he struck with picked troops, not some contractor's hired hands but uniformed Park Department veterans, men loyal to the Sycamore Flag (and to the promise of overtime pay for the unusual mission on which he was dispatching them), and he sent them into the field under the personal command of an aide whose enthusiasm for such missions was a legend in the Department: the hard-bitten commander whom other men called "Mustache."

He struck in secrecy—in after-midnight darkness, when the enemy's sentries had been withdrawn for the night. At 0130 hours on April 24, when only a few scattered lampposts and a three-quarter moon broke the gloom of the battlefield—Constable had prohibited the use of any other lights—a hand-picked Park Department platoon headed by a gardener first class moved into the glen, hammered steel stakes into the ground around its perimeter and wired to them a "snow fence" of wooden slats, about four feet high, strung on wires. It was not until the fence was in place—and painted, to make it look all the more official—that the more easily spotted mechanized equipment was brought up, and then the bulldozer was moved into position inside the fence on a flat-bed truck so that its noisy treads would not have to be activated until the moment it went into action. To insure against leaks, not even the Police Department had been told what was going on; it was not until about 3 A.M., when a patrolman, summoned by a stroller on Central Park West who had heard a mysterious hammering coming from the park, arrived and saw—to his shock—shadowy figures moving about in the darkness, that a call was made by Constable to police higher-ups—and then it was made to request the immediate dispatch of reinforcements in sufficient force to repel any counterattack and of both sexes, so that newspaper photographers would not be able to take pictures of any mothers who had to be hauled away being hauled away by men. When, shortly before six, an early-morning horseman came cantering along the bridle path, he suddenly saw, through a mist that shrouded what had always been an empty glen—a bulldozer, a truck and a platoon of green-uniformed "parkies" inside a fence, and, in a ring around the fence, thirty-one policemen and policewomen under the command of an inspector and two captains. (The sight so startled his horse that it reared and almost threw him.) By the time daylight revealed the scene to the apartments above, and the first of the mothers came running into the park, the bulldozer had pushed over a big maple tree and Park Department axmen were chopping it into small pieces. And when the mothers tried to reach the machine, the policemen joined hands and politely but firmly stopped them at the fence. These were not mothers to whom more violent protest would have been even a possibility; they did not even consider fighting the policemen; there was nothing they could do except stand outside the fence and cry as the trees came down.

And the media went wild.

"It was a dirty, lousy stab in the back," Mrs. Sanger said—and that was how the media played it. "The Brigade of Mothers lost their battle at the Tavern-on-the-Green in Central Park today after the city mounted a sneak attack under cover of darkness," said the lead in the *World-Telegram*. Other papers painted the Park Commissioner as a bully as well as a sneak; the lead in the *Post* said sarcastically that he "routed a small band of women and children. . . . It was a brilliant victory." Rewritemen rose to what for them was almost poesy in describing the "sylvan victims" felled on the "hillside on which he plans to build a beautiful asphalt-surfaced parking lot." "Sweet-smelling sticky sap ran as the chips flew," mourned the *World-Telegram*.

On its editorial page, the *Post* raged ("Who else but Bob Moses would have been audacious enough to proceed in this fashion before the issue could even be debated before the City Council? . . . Who other than Moses would have been capable of so arrogantly saying, 'The public be damned'?") and added a prediction: "Politicians live in awe of him and journalists treat him with . . . nervous reverence. . . . But we think the man has finally overreached himself. Before this is over, at least a few more city dignitaries (and editorial writers) may finally say out loud that Robert Moses can be wrong." And the *Post* was right. For the first time, its outrage was echoed in other editorial voices.

And the words didn't hurt nearly as much as the pictures.

As the trees had begun tumbling before the bulldozer, a well-dressed, elderly woman, the hair beneath her stylish little cloche white, had run up to the fence and the policemen and stood there crying, trying to wipe the tears from her face with a handkerchief balled up in her white-gloved hand. Beside her stood a much younger woman, one of the young mothers, with the hands in *her* white gloves clenched and on her face an expression in which was mingled sadness and indignation. As the two women stood there, oblivious to everything but the trees falling in front of them, a dozen photographers snapped their picture—and the next day those women were weeping on the front page of every newspaper in town except the *Herald Tribune,* in which they were weeping on the split page, and the *Times,* which limited itself to views of the over-all scene. As the Newmans had run out the door that morning with their four-year-old son, David, Arnold Newman had, at the last moment turned back, snatched up the boy's toy rifle and carried it to the park, where he had handed it to him. ("We were in the business, you know," Augusta Newman explains, grinning.) Other men in the business also knew a great prop when they saw one—and the next day the "little soldier in the park war" was sitting pointing his gun, which seemed longer than he was, through the fence at the bulldozer while, beside the small, pathetic figure, a burly policeman stood looking studiously away from him with genuine shame on his face, across five full columns of the front page of the *Journal-American*.

And these were only two pictures—two out of a dozen with drama and pathos. The *News* alone used seven the next morning, one on page one, three on page three, three in the centerfold. Out at New York leapt scenes of a workman raising his ax next to a tree while three big policemen restrained one diminutive mother stretching her hands out toward the tree as if to protect it from the blade, of mothers turning away from the line of policemen in tears, of little boys peering through the fence slats at the bulldozer rooting at a tree while beside them a policeman stood sad-faced guard, of one dismembered tree, a sawn-through cross-section of its trunk very white in the picture, being loaded in sections onto a truck, of Stuart Constable striding past mothers and baby carriages with a self-satisfied little smirk on his face that, combined with the walrus mustache, made him look like nothing so much as the villain come to foreclose the mortgage in *The Old Homestead*—pictures worth not a thousand words but a million. And these pictures were flashed before the public not only in still life but in motion—on evening television newscasts on which they were, if possible, even more dramatic.

The outrage the press expressed was echoed by the public. Letters not by the hundreds but by the thousands poured into newspapers and the offices of public officials; on a single day, Mayor Wagner received close to four thousand. And if the public was outraged, they knew precisely whom they were outraged at. A single day's selection from a single newspaper shows the tone: in the *Journal-American* of April 26:

> I have always admired Commissioner Moses, but he certainly pulled a boo-boo on that Central Park deal.
>
> —Ex-Moses Fan

> So the great Moses had to stoop to pulling a sneak attack at night to outmaneuver the embattled Central Park mothers! What's the matter, didn't he have the courage to face them in the daylight? Of all the low-down tricks, that's just about the lowest in my book.
>
> —Mrs. C. Brown, Bronx

> Those pictures of mothers weeping as they watched bulldozers tearing down beautiful trees and destroying a children's playground for, of all things, a parking lot for restaurant patrons, made me want to weep, too. Shame on you, Commissioner Moses!
>
> —Disgusted

"Sneak!" "Shame!" "*EX*-Moses Fan!" Thirty years before, Robert Moses had leapt onto the front pages in a single bound—in stories that portrayed him as a fighter for parks, as a faithful, selfless public servant, a servant whose only interest lay in serving, as a hero. This portrait, painted in an instant, had survived for thirty years and had hardened into an image that had withstood, without so much as a crack, a dozen explosions that would have shattered the image of the ordinary public figure. Now, in a single day, over a single dispute—a dispute over a hollow in the ground and a few trees—that image had cracked. Not wide-open, of course. Large parts of it remained untouched; it was still an image untarnished by scandal, untainted by compromise; Robert Moses was still the public official uninterested in money, unwilling to truck with bureaucrats or truckle to politicians. But for the first time he had been portrayed to the public at large not as a defender but as a destroyer of parks and as an official interested not in serving the people but in imposing his wishes upon them. The image would never be whole again. Tuesday, April 24, 1956, the day that Robert Moses sent his troops into Central Park, was Robert Moses' Black Tuesday. For on it, he lost his most cherished asset: his reputation. The Moses Boom had lasted for thirty years. Now it was over.

Surveying the battlefield on Tuesday night, Moses may have had at least one consolation. In one respect, at least, the Battle of Central Park appeared to have ended as his battles usually ended. However Pyrrhic his victory, it was still victory: press and public might yell, but the trees were coming down; his bulldozers were in operation, and no one in the city government was going to stop them, a fact that became clear on Thursday when Wagner's press secretary said, "Commissioner Moses has the right to do what he is doing. We have the right to stand behind the Park Commissioner," and the City Council shunted a Stanley Isaacs resolution demanding action off to a committee which scheduled a hearing for the following week—by which time the trees would all be down and the grass would be covered with concrete. (Moses declined the committee's invitation to attend. No councilman but Isaacs seemed to feel there was anything wrong with that.) On the judicial front, there was a development on Thursday that may have been of interest to students of the law concerned with the influence of public opinion on the judicial process. In 1934, with Moses at the peak of his popularity and the voice of the press a chorus in his praise, the five justices of the Appellate Division had heard an appeal for an injunction in a case (Moses' move against Jimmy Walker's Casino) turning on precisely the same basic question, the extent of Moses' authority over physical changes in Central Park, and had held, quickly and unanimously, that that authority was absolute. In 1956, with the voice of the press a chorus against him, State Supreme Court Justice Benjamin J. Hecht granted the mothers' request for an injunction halting work pending a full hearing the next morning. Justice Samuel H. Hofstadter, who presided over this hearing (and who could hardly have been unfamiliar with the Casino case, since as a state senator he had chaired the "Seabury Committee" that broke up the "Walkerian Court"), quoted poetry (" 'The tree depicts divinest plan.' That is why I am taking cognizance of the trees") and paid a personal visit to the site—accompanied by half a hundred reporters, photographers and TV cameramen. And when he completed the visit, he continued the temporary injunction pending a hearing on whether or not to make it permanent—a hearing that would be held before another judge. But Moses knew what the law said; he had, after all, written it. He was confident that this setback was only temporary and would soon be ended. He told Corporation Counsel Peter Campbell Brown that he wanted the hearing scheduled immediately; if by any chance he lost, he said, he wanted the case appealed at once. To a newsman who asked if there was any possibility of a compromise, he replied: "No, no, nothing of that sort."

But even this consolation of victory was to be denied him. There were two points in the Tavern-on-the-Green battle on which the Commissioner was extremely vulnerable—and now Stanley Isaacs remembered one and discovered the other.

One was the resemblance between this fight and the one over the Casino. The mothers' attorney, Louis N. Field—probably at Isaacs' suggestion—looked up the Casino fight in the *Times* and found Moses' statements justifying his decision to tear down that old park landmark—that only restaurants with "reasonable" prices "within the reach of persons of average means" belong in public parks. The fact that Moses had never believed this argument—that he had used it because it was the only one available—did not matter. What mattered was that he had used it, and his words could be quoted against him. And when Field pointed out that at the Tavern a "simple hamburger and a glass of beer would cost $4.50," the press took up his point eagerly: soon stories were informing the public about the Tavern's alternating "society" orchestras, about the fashion shows "attended by women in fur capes" while "several chauffeur-driven Cadillacs waited" at the door, and about the "non-economy prices" that only "well-to-do residents . . . could afford"; as one story put it: "Dinner and tip for two came to nearly $23. There was another $5 at the bar for two drinks each. It's not a place to go the day before pay day." And the press coverage produced the fallout that could be expected. Soon, for example, the Rev. Dr. Ralph Curry Walker, of the Madison Avenue Baptist Church, was inveighing against the Tavern in sermons, and announcing that he would ask the Protestant Council of the Five Baptist Associations to adopt a resolution opposing the parking lot, because it would tend to encourage the sale of intoxicating liquor in a park.

The second issue—discovered by Isaacs—was the nature of the financial arrangement between Moses' Park Department and the restaurant's owner, old Moses favorite Arnold Schleiffer. Schleiffer paid the city only 5 percent of his gross income to operate a restaurant in the renovated sheepfold. This was a pittance compared to the rent most restaurant owners paid their landlords—even if Schleiffer had paid it all.

And, Isaacs discovered, he hadn't.

Studying Schleiffer's contract, the councilman found a provision that allowed the restaurateur to "improve" (repair and renovate) his restaurant and deduct the cost of the improvements from his rent payments. Checking with the Comptroller's office, he found that the restaurateur had made full use of that provision. In one four-year period, for example, the gross income of the Tavern-on-the-Green had been $1,786,000. On that income, Schleiffer should have paid the city about $90,000—a low enough figure. Instead, he spent more than $80,000 on "improvements." On a gross income of $1,786,000, he had paid the city only $9,000—half of 1 percent. Out of every thousand dollars that he collected, he handed the city a lone five-dollar bill. Isaacs had heard rumors that Schleiffer, who had been operating on a shoestring when he was first taken into the Moses empire, was now a man of considerable wealth. After he saw those figures, the councilman had no trouble believing those rumors. Moses had made the concessionaire rich. And he had made him rich at the city's expense.

The arrangement with Schleiffer was a typical Moses arrangement, no different from scores in effect for more than twenty years with the favored concessionaires who were so integral a part of his empire—no different, in fact, from the others in effect with Schleiffer, who, unknown to Isaacs, operated half a dozen other park concessions. There was nothing illegal about it. Moses certainly was not making a dime from it; he even insisted, to Schleiffer's voluble dismay, on paying for every meal he ate there. He favored it partly because it allowed him to circumvent the city's budgetary requirements for capital improvements—and mainly because by giving the concessionaires huge profits he was in a position to ask them to throw huge parties, the lavish dinners and receptions that were an integral part of his way of power. At many of his most elaborate receptions—receptions for guests in the hundreds or thousands—the Tavern-on-the-Green had provided not only plates, glasses, silverware, tablecloths, napkins and the finest of food and liquor but waiters and busboys and bartenders and chefs. The Board of Estimate would never have approved the expenditures for such parties, of course. It would have felt the city had more pressing needs that might be met with the thousands—tens of thousands—of dollars involved. But under this arrangement, the Board had nothing to say about them.

For more than twenty years, Moses had been boasting that he had ended all favoritism to concessionaires, and for more than twenty years, the press had been repeating and amplifying that boast, and ignoring Isaacs' attempts to present them with the facts that would have disproved it. But this time, when Isaacs talked, the press was listening. And when he provided facts on the Tavern-on-the-Green concession arrangement, reporters gobbled them up.

Suddenly there were editorials in a tone that had never been used in relation to Moses before. "At issue now is the Park Commissioner's latitude in dealing with concessionaires," the *World-Telegram* said. "The financial arrangements between the Tavern-on-the-Green and the city coffers need a lot more explaining than anyone has been willing to provide so far." PARK WINDFALL: TAVERN PAYS ONLY 1/3 RENT, headlines blared. PARK TAVERN

YIELDS CITY ONLY 2%; MOSES DUCKS COUNCIL HEARING. MOSES DROPS CURTAIN ON TAVERN PARK DEAL. "Windfall!" "Ducks!" "Deal!"—words that spelled scandal. The editorials, headlines—and stories—were oversimplified, so oversimplified as to be misleading. But whereas Moses had always used his image to make the press's bent for oversimplification work for him, now that bent was working against him. In the sense in which the public understood words like "windfall" and "deal"—illegalities, payoffs, bribes—there was no scandal in the Tavern-on-the-Green affair. But the press made it appear that there was. During more than thirty years of public service, the name of Robert Moses had never even been brushed by so much as the hint of scandal. But the hint of scandal was brushing it now.

He apparently did not realize at first the threat to his name in the controversy over the insignificant parking lot. He saw no need to change plans for a vacation; on the very morning on which Hofstadter issued his injunction, Moses was boarding the Italian luxury liner *Cristoforo Colombo* with Mary for a twenty-four-day trip to Spain. Reporters rushing to the dock to get his reaction found him smiling and relaxed. "We're just going to go right through with the action," he said. "We will pursue this to the last court." And those had, in fact, been his private instructions to Corporation Counsel Peter Campbell Brown.

But he realized it at last. His crossing was sunny, but, behind him, the storm he had expected to blow itself out raged harder than ever. For the press was being given a continuing supply of fresh meat on which to feed. Constable, trying as usual to out-Moses Moses, refused outright to provide reporters with detailed figures on the Tavern modernization program of which the parking lot was a part—a mistake that Moses would never have made, for not only were the figures public record, but they were available to the reporters in the City Comptroller's office. Reporters demanded that Wagner order the Park Department executive officer to release them—and a flustered Mayor did, telling his press secretary to deliver the order to Constable personally. The figures revealed nothing new, but the fact that the Mayor had ordered them released made a front-page story in the *Times* ("Mayor Wagner directed the Park Department yesterday to produce detailed figures . . ."). When they were produced, Wagner pointed out that "there was nothing to hide." But the press didn't concentrate on that statement. Reporters had pressed the Mayor as to whether the Board of Estimate would investigate the concession arrangement. Only after he had run out of evasions did he reply at all, and then he did so as circumspectly as possible: "I think we will discuss it. No doubt we will discuss it." But the press blew his words up into far more than they meant: a six-column headline across page one of the *World-Telegram* blared: MAYOR DEMANDS AIRING OF PARK TAVERN FINANCE. Such press coverage, and the continuing public response —letters poured in and were printed by editors day after day—coupled, possibly, with Moses' absence, encouraged politicians to make statements on the issue. And each statement made another meal for the press. One can almost see, day by day, the realization dawning among reporters and headline writers that even though the public official involved was Robert Moses, this story could be handled like any other story. Day by day, their pens grew sharper. Appearing on WCBS-TV's "Let's Find Out," Wagner was asked about the financial arrangement. "There is nothing illegal about it," the Mayor said: Moses had "clearly" been acting within his powers under the City Charter. He went out of his way to defend the Park Commissioner; the controversy had been "rather amusing," he said, because "he has been the toughest one, if you remember, about holding on to park space and trying to acquire more." When reporters pressed him as to the possibility of Board action on the arrangement, he gave the minimal response possible; the Board would "review" the possibility of requiring bidding on all city concession contracts. But what the headlines said the next day was: MOSES' WINGS DUE FOR A CLIP and WAGNER AND CITY WEIGH CURB ON MOSES. Corporation Counsel Brown had asked Wagner if he should go ahead with the appeal of Hofstadter's decision as Moses had asked. Do whatever Moses wants, the Mayor told him—and the ensuing appeal provided still more fresh meat—as well as fresh evidence of the interaction of public and judicial opinion. In 1934, when another Corporation Counsel had appealed the decision of a lower-court judge, the five justices of the Appellate Division had agreed unanimously that while the powers that the law granted to Moses were far too broad, the law as it stood was perfectly clear: they had no choice but to overrule the lower court's decision. In all relevant respects, the law was the same—but this time the five justices unanimously upheld the lower court. (When Brown argued that the restaurant was open to anyone, one of the justices said: "You mean anyone who can afford it. I'm not complaining about my salary, but I can't afford $5.85 steaks"—"MORE THAN I PAY," SAYS JUDGE.) The criticism began to spread from the one isolated Tavern incident to the legend as a whole: "What I have not seen commented on," said one letter writer in the *World-Telegram*, pointing out that in Van Cortlandt Park alone more than 150 acres had been devoted to traffic use, "is the general policy of the commissioner. . . . He seems to feel that as long as money can be saved by the use of park property, instead of condemning private land, any invasion of the parks is justified." Federal officials, long silent, released statements critical of the handling of Title I in New York. "The Battle of the Tavern-on-the-Green has already had a salutary effect on the city," the *Post* commented. "Men have begun to feel that it is safe to question Robert Moses." Moses had been receiving daily reports of the controversy in Spain. Returning—the circles under his eyes bigger and darker than when he had left three weeks before—he tried to smile for the photographers who had boarded a pilot's boat and crowded onto the *Cristoforo Colombo* as it was still steaming up the harbor toward its berth, posing him at the rail of the big liner, but the pictures showed a smile so forced that it was more of a grimace. Twenty-four days alone with the wife whose advice had helped him out of tight spots before had had some effect: he made an obvious effort to contain himself, greeting reporters genially and telling them, "I don't intend to get excited about this matter.

There is an enormous acreage in Central Park and this discussion is all over one-half an acre and the taking down of four [sic] trees." When reporters asked him about the price of a steak at the Tavern, he said, "I don't know anything about the price of steaks at the Tavern," and, still containing himself, added, "I'm not going to let them get my goat or get disturbed about it. I have other things to do. I don't propose to get excited about it. I know something about New York and its people, and I'm sure they all appreciate what we have done in the city." Turning to the skyline the liner was moving past, he said, the face creaking into a smile again: "Isn't this a wonderful city?" But the questions continued, questions of the kind that no reporter had asked Robert Moses since the gubernatorial campaign of 1934. And the outcome now was the same as the outcome then. For twenty-four days, bile had been rising in his gorge. Now, in a rush, it spilled over. "Oh, who are these critics anyway?" he demanded. "Troublemakers. A small, noisy minority. You have Mr. Isaacs and the Citizens Union and these childless women howling about their non-existent children. Take a woman like Fannie Hurst. Where are all her children? I've never heard of her having any children." He had been making similar attacks for years, but never had they been handled as these were handled. Not only the *Post* —"It had not previously occurred to most Americans that they had to give birth before disputing Robert Moses"—but other newspapers treated his words as the outburst of a cranky old man, almost as a joke not worth taking seriously. His victims even got what so many past victims had been denied: a chance to reply. Watching Moses on television, the Newmans suffered over the insult to the elderly woman they had persuaded to join the fight. "I don't know how Fannie Hurst took it, but I took it very badly," Augusta Newman would say. "Perhaps she had always wanted children and couldn't have any . . ." When reporters called for comments, Arnold Newman called Moses' statement "a proper greeting from a man with a concrete mind and a non-existent heart," and his wife invited the Park Commissioner up to "visit my non-existent children . . . aged four and six"—and these rebuttals were played high, as was the fact that the request for an injunction had been brought in the name of Mrs. Norma Rosen, "mother of two." On reaching his office that afternoon, moreover, Moses must have known that worse was to come. Waiting on his desk was a copy of a memo from Brown to Wagner summarizing a private conference the Corporation Counsel had held with Field. According to the memorandum, at that conference the mothers' attorney had noted that he had not yet revealed in court many of Moses' more damaging statements made under oath in the Casino case, or the full details of Moses' arrangements with many park concessionaires. "In the event of a trial," Field had said, "he would be compelled to amend his complaint to raise these issues and to present data 'that would undoubtedly tend to perpetuate the publicity received in the press and might prompt challenge to other activities of Commissioner Moses.' " Moses knew what his statements, and those arrangements, were. For one thing, he had authorized Schleiffer to spend $48,000 for a separate corridor for guests at plush private wedding parties. He must have known how his statements and arrangements would look in print.

He did what he had never done—at least publicly—before. He backed down.

Brown was anxious to drop the case. "Moses in the dock—that would be the number-one show in town no matter what else was playing," the Corporation Counsel would say years later. "What was number one in 1956 —*My Fair Lady*? *My Fair Lady* would be the number-two ticket if Moses was in the dock. And he was going to look bad. Everybody loves moms. You can't beat that. I had great respect for him, the greatest respect, for him and for his accomplishments. My regard for him was really without limits. And I didn't want to see that." To avoid that, Brown had worked out an arrangement under which Moses might save at least a little face, and by June 7 he had privately obtained Field's consent to it. The city would use a series of delaying tactics to keep the case from coming to trial, without announcing that it was being dropped, which would have been a formal admission of defeat. Then, after a suitable period of delay—long enough, hopefully, for the furor to die down a bit—Moses would announce that he had decided to give the mothers the play space they wanted by building another playground—on the site on which he had wanted to build the parking lot. This would enable Moses to avoid announcing that he was dropping the parking lot plan and simply leaving the park the way the mothers wanted it—and it would also enable him to avoid the charge that he had destroyed trees for no purpose at all. Field would be privately notified of what was going on so that he would not press the case.

Walking over to Moses' office in the State Office Building at 270 Broadway, across City Hall Park from his own in the Municipal Building, Brown stopped by Wagner's for last-minute orders, but received only one: keep him out of it; the Mayor was almost frantically anxious to avoid any confrontation with his Park Commissioner. At 270 Broadway, Brown found that Wagner was not the only key figure in the dispute who wanted to keep involvement limited; Brown was accustomed to finding Moses surrounded by his retinue whenever he arrived at the Coordinator's office. This time, when he was ushered in, Moses was alone.

"I just told him that a trial would be the kind of thing that wasn't going to do anyone any good," Brown recalls. "And I said if you do this [build the playground], it will show you're even a bigger man than people know you are." Then, according to a memo Brown sent Wagner the next day,

> Commissioner Moses agreed that if the litigation should continue, a trial would be held and unfavorable publicity would result. . . . Commissioner Moses was agreeable to an adjournment to avoid an early trial, with the possibility of ultimately disposing of the case without further litigation.

Attempting to save face, Moses allowed no hint that the case was being dropped to sneak into the press. Instead, the Corporation Counsel's office kept requesting delays—none of which Field objected to. Then, six weeks later, on July 17, after an unannounced meeting in which Brown signed on behalf of the city a stipulation that the city would build the playground, and Field signed one that in that event the suit would be dropped,

Moses' aides distributed a press release announcing that he had decided to build a playground rather than a parking lot. The Tavern-on-the-Green fight—"the Battle of Central Park"—was over. The man who never retreated had retreated at last.

But he had not retreated in time.

The amount of face saved was infinitesimal. The press treated his announcement as the barely conditional surrender it was: MOSES SURRENDERS TO MOTHERS; MOSES LOSES HIS PARK BATTLE; MOSES YIELDS . . . MOTHERS WIN—over a *Post* editorial, ONE FOR OUR SIDE. The aura of invincibility, the aura that had been so important to him in the past, the aura that had lasted for thirty years, was gone, destroyed in a day just as the aura of infallibility had been destroyed.

And this was the least of what the Battle of Central Park cost Robert Moses.

He had allowed himself to remain too long in the glare of a spotlight strong enough to show him as he was. The city had finally gotten a good look at the man behind the legend. Part of the legend still remained unilluminated. Even after the Battle, Robert Moses was still, in the public consciousness, a man uninterested in money, a man who ignored bureaucrats and politicians, who was above political considerations. He was still the Man Who Got Things Done. Those elements of the Moses myth remained untouched.

But other elements had been destroyed. No one who had followed the Battle closely could believe any longer that Robert Moses was in public life solely to serve the public. It had been all too obvious that what he wanted was to be not the public's servant, but its master, to be able to impose his will on it.

That was one crack in the image. There were others. Moses' public appeal had always been based largely on his identification with the magic word "parks." In the public mind, he had always, first and foremost, been the Robert Moses of Sunken Meadow and Jones Beach, the fighter for and defender of open space and grass and trees and sun and surf and brine for urban masses. The halo placed on his head by the Timber Point fight thirty years before had now been knocked off.

He was, moreover, identified by the Tavern-on-the-Green fight with the bulldozer. By the mid-1950's, the bulldozer had quite specific connotations in the public mind. Now the name of Moses had those connotations, too.

The aura of infallibility was gone also. If Moses was the Man Who Got Things Done, implicit was the assumption that the things that he got done were things that *should* be gotten done. He had always been portrayed as a man who was right. Now, in a single, dramatic tableau, he had been shown to be utterly, unmistakably wrong.

Most important, the aura of incorruptibility was gone. It was gone unfairly, for nothing he had done for the Tavern-on-the-Green was illegal, and by the standards by which the public judges morality in politics, what he had done for the restaurant was only faintly immoral. But it was gone nonetheless. The breath of scandal had tarnished this incorruptible public figure only slightly. But slightly was enough. His image had once dazzled even most of the reporters and editors hardest to dazzle. Now it no longer shone quite so brightly. The press could look at Robert Moses and at his operations and methods as they would look at the operations and methods of an ordinary public official.

And they looked.

"That Tavern-on-the-Green thing, that was such an insignificant thing," Sid Shapiro would say, years later, looking back on his idol's career. "It was such a meaningless little thing. I don't know to this day what the hell those people got so excited about.

"But it was—I don't know—it was just never the same after that."

43. *Late Arrival*

> *The Great Statesman McKee is a synthetic character which never actually existed on sea or land, puffed up by the press . . . and now in the process of deflation. There is a large amount of unfairness to the individual in this process, but in the end it arrives at the truth.*
>
> —ROBERT MOSES, 1933

AT ABOUT THE TIME that the "Battle of Central Park" was ending, investigative reporter Gene Gleason of the *World-Telegram and Sun* was winding up his latest assignment. His editors, trying to think up a new one, asked him if he had anything in mind. Yes, he said, he had.

Robert Moses.

The Tavern-on-the-Green concession contract spelled immense profits for someone, Gleason explained. And that was just one contract; Moses in his many different governmental roles was the author of scores—hundreds, probably—of contracts. *World-Telegram* rewriteman Fred J. Cook recalls the reporter saying: "This is the most powerful SOB in the city. If this is so bad at the tip of the iceberg, there must be more."

The *World-Telegram* was not one of the New York dailies aggressively dedicated—from the publisher's office on down—to the idealization of the Coordinator. Moses' relationship with publisher Roy W. Howard was more cordial than close; his overwhelmingly favorable coverage in Howard's newspaper was more a function of his secret, favor-cemented relationship with the paper's veteran chief political reporter, Murray Davis. Still, because of the image of Moses the Incorruptible, prior to the Battle of Central Park, Gleason would have been told to go hunt up another idea. Now city editor Norton Mockridge told him to go ahead, and asked him in what field of Moses' far-flung operations he would like to begin looking.

A number of considerations motivated Gleason's reply: he would have liked to begin with the power of the public authorities, "but," Cook recalls, "it was recognized that that would be a terribly tough nut to crack," both because no one had done any groundwork on the authorities' place in government and society on which a reporter could draw and because "the records were super-secret" and the ultimate documentation necessary for exposés—the records that confirm an investigator's hunches in black and white—would therefore be unattainable. Some groundwork had been done on Moses' Title I Slum Clearance Committee, however; Gleason's interest had been piqued some months before by a series on Manhattantown by the *Post*'s Joe Kahn, who, happening to pass the renewal site, had seen in the middle of it a large parking lot, had begun wondering, "Why should they have a parking lot if they were going to build housing?," had dug out the clips on the 1954 Senate "Caspert hearings" and had written a series pointing up the fact that almost two years after those hearings—and more than four years after Moses had turned over the site to Caspert's "reliable" developers, who had been milking it ever since—the only development was the parking lot. Reading the two-year-old transcript of the Senate hearings, the hearings all but ignored by the New York press, Gleason realized, as Cook put it, that "it had the makings of a scandal; it was obvious." The investigator told Mockridge that he wanted to look into Title I.

His first look was not particularly searching or perceptive. He uncovered few facts not already in print somewhere else—in Kahn's series or in individual "human interest" features on the eviction of some impoverished tenant, in one-shot articles on the protests of the residents of Moses-threatened neighborhoods, in the relocation studies made by the Women's City Club and Lawrence Orton's "undercover" City Planning Commission unit.

But new facts were not necessary. Plenty to document the true shape of the Moses version of urban renewal were already available—had been available for years—in hearing transcripts or in club or commission pamphlets, rich nuggets of news just lying around waiting for someone to pick them up, put them together—show them not as isolated incidents but as part of a pattern—and print them.

And on July 30, 1956, just a month after the conclusion of the Battle of Central Park, the *World-Telegram and Sun* began printing them.

For all its omissions, this first series on Title I—researched by Gene Gleason and written by Fred J. Cook—painted a disturbing picture of the way New York City was being reshaped. It showed, as no one had previously shown, the relationship between the fact (previously written about in any real depth only by Kahn) that on many Title I sites no development had taken place in the four years since the city had handed them over to private interests and the fact (brought out in the Caspert hearings but never before documented in all its shocking details by anyone) that Moses' system financially encouraged failure to develop. It showed that the "slum clearance" program was clearing not just slums but healthy, pleasant residential and business sections—and was not building anything to replace them. If it did not contain the real "dynamite" that a little digging would have uncovered—the fact that Robert Moses, the man who allegedly refused to deal with politicians, had turned over a billion-dollar program to shady politicians—it contained ample documentation of Cook's disturbing conclusion:

> It is a system under which neighborhoods actually have deteriorated; it is a system under which the number of apartments, already inadequate, has been reduced for years to come. It is a system . . . beginning again the cycle of overcrowding and bad housing that creates slums.

Most importantly, while previous media coverage had almost invariably referred to Title I as the "city's" program, Cook made sure that readers understood it was the city's Slum Clearance Committee, Robert Moses, chairman. If Gleason and Cook did not disclose—because they did not understand—that Moses was not only the official in charge of Title I but the official in *sole* charge, that neither Mayor nor any other elected official of the city but he and he alone made all final decisions in regard to this program that was supposed to reshape the city—they nonetheless nailed the responsibility for Title I's failures to his door more firmly than it had ever been nailed before. Moses' name may still not have been in headlines about the failures, but at least—at last—it was in print.

If the editors of the *World-Telegram and Sun* realized the significance of the series, they concealed that realization well. Only one of its parts even made page one. And there were other indications that while the Moses image may have been tarnished, it still retained enough glitter to intimidate, that the editors were regretting having given Gleason the go-ahead on Robert Moses, that, having taken the plunge at last, they were trying to make an about-face in mid-air. Apprising Moses of the series' contents in advance, they gave the Coordinator space each day to attack—in a separate article—their own newspaper's stories. Moses' name was, moreover, conspicuous by its absence from the headlines over the Gleason-Cook revelations of faults in his program; it appeared only in the headlines over his own articles praising that program. Not only did the *Telly*'s editorial writers not praise the series, they didn't even mention it.

But still, the most significant fact about the series was that it ran at all. Investigative reporters quickly become aware of a phenomenon of their profession: information so hard to come by when they are preparing to write their first story in a new field suddenly becomes plentiful as soon as that first story has appeared in print. Every city agency has its malcontents and its idealists and its malcontent-idealists—officials and aides and clerks and secretaries unhappy with the philosophy by which it is being run or the payoffs that are being made within it—who have been just waiting, for years, for the appearance of some forum in which their feelings can be expressed. When they realize that there is one at last—when they see that first story—they cannot get their information to its writer fast enough. Scores of city employees—men and women angry for personal or philosophical reasons at the inside workings of the Moses empire—and hundreds if not thousands of city residents whose homes or neighborhoods had been destroyed for his

Title I projects, and who then had watched vainly for years for the projects to be built, had been looking for such a forum. They had been desperate for one. They had almost given up their hopes of finding one. With the exception of the *Post*, they had never had one, and the *Post* had exposed his philosophy rather than his payoffs, the "scandals" on which so many officials and residents were convinced they had information. Now, with the appearance of the first Gleason-Cook series, these people were convinced that at last such a forum had appeared. And the two journalists' telephones began humming with calls—some anonymous, some not, some from private individuals, many from officials up to and including a liberal Bronx congressman—revealing the secrets of the Moses operation: the politicians who were the real interests behind his "front men" developers, the deals that had been made with city agencies to immunize those developers from health laws. Along with the calls came letters; out of one envelope fell a clipped-out newspaper ad for Pratt Institute Housing in Brooklyn with a name circled: "rental agent—Samuel Caspert." As soon as Gleason picked up the clipping, he realized what its sender was trying to tell him: Manhattantown was not the only development that Moses had turned over to that phony developer. On the day the series ended, Cook summarized future leads that should be dug into; Mockridge, passing the rewriteman's memo along to managing editor Richard Starnes, scribbled on it: "RS—Seems we've got some material for more stories—Shall we go ahead?" RS said yes, and Gleason was soon holding conferences with city officials.

With virtually only one exception—Hortense Gabel—even the most cooperative of these officials were wary of Moses' power. All interviews had to be completely off the record, of course; Gleason could not find a single official willing to be quoted. Because most were afraid to have the reporter seen in their offices and many, believing their phones were tapped, refused to talk to him over the telephone, Gleason met them, after dark, in their automobiles or in out-of-the-way bars. One was so terrified that a key memo might find its way into print and thereby reveal his cooperation that he read the document to the reporter—but refused to let him touch it. Without access to the records of the Slum Clearance Committee, information about the involvement of key politicians could not be documented, and therefore could not be printed. But there was plenty of other material that could be checked. Finding that the newspaper clipping tip on Pratt checked out, Gleason reported on August 28, 1956, that the key figures in that operation were also Caspert and Company, and that instead of developing the site they were milking it as they had Manhattantown. Returning to the "bombed-out" Brooklyn neighborhood in January 1957, Gleason came back with notes from which Cook wrote a story about a ninety-two-year-old woman huddling in blankets and an overcoat in an apartment in which a thermometer registered 40.5 degrees and about a mother who hadn't been able to give her two little boys a bath all winter because there hadn't been any hot water, about complaints being ignored not only by the developers but by the City Health Department: "We have yet to see an inspector around here." Some of the anonymous phone calls were coming from an aide in the City

Comptroller's office; in April, one call from this source informed Gleason that the Pratt "developers" weren't paying their real estate taxes to the city, hadn't been for almost three years and, now that they had milked the project for "millions," were planning to pull out and turn it back to the city. When Gleason ran this story, he had to include in it denials by Spargo and Lebwohl, speaking for Moses, but it was soon confirmed by an announcement from the developers. Then Gleason's informant told him that other Title I developers were also not paying taxes. Presenting himself in the Comptroller's office, Gleason demanded to see the tax records, and on April 24, 1957, working from Gleason's notes, Cook revealed that while developers had reaped fortunes from Title I projects, "the city is holding the bag . . . to the tune of nearly $1 million in delinquent taxes and interest."

The play of these stories was still not big. To Gleason's and Cook's disgust, the articles on Pratt ran only in the Brooklyn edition. And a giant must still be treated as a giant: there had been headlines for almost a year now in the *World-Telegram* on Title I exposés but Moses' name was seldom in those headlines. His name was seldom in the stories, in fact, partly because of his success in letting Spargo, Lebwohl and Brooks speak for him; it was not until the fourteenth paragraph of the April 24 revelations on the tax delinquencies of the developers selected by the Slum Clearance Committee that the name of the chairman of that committee was mentioned. The city's other dailies were in general picking up the Gleason-Cook stories only to allow Wagner to deny them, the Mayor soothingly reassuring the public that everything was going along fine in Title I. Even in the *Post*, Title I revelations were few and far between. And as for the *Times*, bellwether and fashion setter for the city's press, in January 1957, the day after Gleason had revealed that tenants on the Pratt site were freezing in their apartments, and that the Health Department was doing nothing about it because of a secret agreement with the Slum Clearance Committee, the *Times*, practically apologizing for running the story at all ("It became an issue yesterday because of allegations in a newspaper"), stated straight-facedly that "the Department of Health reported yesterday that tenants awaiting relocation from slum-clearance sites had been getting more heat and better sanitary services as a result of its crackdown on five developers"; and repeated without qualification the following lie:

> Robert Moses, chairman of the slum clearance committee, said his agency, which is in charge of Title I development, had made no deal with the Health Department. He said he had told all developers they must obey all city regulations.

The *Times* did, on May 26, run one long story on Title I; the headline read: CITY LEADS NATION IN SLUM CLEARING.

Then there ensued a development more difficult for editors to play small.

In June, Moses was informed by Spargo and Lebwohl that Manhattantown, Inc., whose tax arrears had now topped $600,000 and were rising every day, had, because its officers had been siphoning out the money as fast as it came in, none available to pay the taxes any time in the foreseeable future; that there was also no money in sight to pay the interest on the $2,000,000 mortgage Moses had persuaded the city to give them, let alone the amortization; that there was no money in sight to build any of the buildings the corporation had, more than five years before, contracted to build on the six-block site Moses had turned over to it—that, in short, there was no possibility at all that his "reliable bidders" could go ahead with the project. Moses had no choice. On June 11, the Slum Clearance Committee asked the Board of Estimate to institute foreclosure proceedings and take back the property in the name of the city so that it could be turned over to a new sponsor.

The move was made, through Corporation Counsel Peter Campbell Brown's office, as quietly as possible. The *Times*'s initial play of the story was not designed to make any noise, either; the revelation that a corporation to which the city had turned over 338 buildings worth $15,000,000 for only $1,000,000, a corporation which didn't even bother to pay its city taxes, a corporation which had for five years been collecting rents on those buildings, was now saying that it could not develop the site after all, was found worthy by the *Times*'s editors of five paragraphs on page fourteen. But the rest of the press was less discreet. Every charge Gleason and Cook had been making for so many months had turned out to be true, and most newspapers played it that way. As Cook was later to write: "The scandal that Moses and Wagner had kept denying for a year was there at last for everyone to see, confirmed in eight-column headlines." Gleason was even allowed a very personal moment of triumph. For months he had been trying in vain to obtain an interview with Wagner. Now Wagner had no choice but to hold a press conference on Title I, and Gene Gleason was there.

Every time the Mayor attempted to excuse the fiasco by blaming it all on the promoters, saying they had misled the city, Gleason would remind him that the facts had been in print—over and over again—for almost a full year; as Cook put it, "it had all been there in black and white for city officials to read, and they had done nothing except to deride the revelations. How did the Mayor explain that?" In the climactic moment:

> "We were misled," Mayor Wagner confessed, unhappily.
>
> "You mean to say you were conned for five years?" Gleason asked.
>
> "Well, if you want to put it that way—yes, I guess you could say we were conned for five years," the Mayor acknowledged.

For a few days, the press focused on Title I—even the *Times* moved the story onto its front page—although in no newspaper was Moses linked directly and repeatedly with the scandal being unfolded. The *Times* article announcing that new sponsors were replacing the original "reliable bidders" of five years before on several Title I projects said: "The changing ownership . . . is regarded in building circles as the squeezing out from the slum clearance program of some of the early promoters who had little construction know-how." Neither the *Times* nor any other paper asked why these "promoters" had been allowed into the program in the first place—or who had allowed them in. Nonetheless, Gleason and Cook were confident that there would be at least curtailment of Moses' powers and quite possibly the Mayor's acceptance of the resignation that Moses was continually offering him. Deep as they had probed into corruption in city government, they had not probed deep enough; they still did not understand the fundamental reality of Moses' relations with that government and the venal machine of which that government was in crucial respects no more than an extension. They did not understand the extent to which the machine depended on Robert Moses, the extent to which he was its feeder, the supplier of the raw meat of patronage and contracts, of premiums and fees, of the whole stew of "honest graft" on which it battened. They did not understand that he was the only feeder possessed of enough food to satisfy its ravenous appetite. They did not understand that the machine *needed* Robert Moses, needed him at least as much as he needed it, that the county organizations of which the borough presidents (and in 1957, the Mayor) were only representatives could not do without him. The two reporters' expectation was not unreasonable. Ordinarily, the tainting of a city program with scandal and failure—scandal of immense proportions, failure five years in duration—would result in at least curtailment of the powers of the mayoral subordinate heading that program, lest the public outcry turn against the Mayor. Their expectation was just based on a false premise: that Robert Moses was really the Mayor's subordinate. They did not understand that, as a matter of practical politics, the Mayor could not discipline, demote or remove Title I's administrator.

And so they were surprised at ensuing developments.

Moses—or, rather, Moses' spokesmen, Spargo, Lebwohl and Brooks; the Coordinator was keeping his lowest profile ever—announced that a new sponsor, William Zeckendorf's Webb & Knapp, Inc., was willing to take over all Manhattantown's debts, including its liabilities to the city, and build the project. Gleason and Cook realized that by changing owners without foreclosing on the old ones first, Moses was allowing Manhattantown, Inc., to escape from the project, which they had been milking for five years, with no financial penalties whatsoever. But the advantages for the city were undeniable, not only because of the avoidance of lengthy foreclosure proceedings but because, in obtaining Zeckendorf, the city was trading in a promoter for a genuine developer. And letting Manhattantown go scot free was something that was only to be expected; whatever the nature of the political muscle that had allowed the corporation to milk a sizable slum for five years while the city turned a blind eye to tax arrears, that muscle was certainly strong enough to keep the city from taking any genuine punitive action against it.

But then some of the details of the takeover arrangement to which Moses had agreed—and on which he had apparently sold the Mayor and the Board of Estimate—were leaked to light, not by Moses' tight-sealed

Slum Clearance Committee, of course (as usual, that group deliberated in secret), but by City Hall.

Under the arrangement, Webb & Knapp would not merely insure Manhattantown's principals against any liability to the city. It would buy out the two principal stockholders—Seymour Millstein and Jack Ferman (Caspert having prudently sold out before the company's collapse)—for $533,250, and put them on Webb & Knapp's payroll as "consultants" for five years at a fee of $30,000 per year, a total of $150,000 more. These two men, key figures in Manhattantown since its inception, were not merely being allowed, after five years of delay—five years during which they had made fortunes—to slip quietly into the night without punishment. They were being paid hundreds of thousands of dollars to do so. And this money was not for *all* their stock. Under the Moses-approved arrangements, Ferman and Millstein would be given sizable stockholdings—between them a total of 32 percent—in Webb & Knapp's Manhattantown subsidiary. "The developers who hadn't developed," Cook wrote, "would be entitled in the future to nearly one-third of the profits" of the developer who *did* develop.* The cast of characters in the Manhattantown story was, moreover, getting a significant addition. The Moses-approved contract did not, of course, contemplate any reduction in Democrat Samuel Rosenman's $250,000 retainer. But it added another $75,000 legal fee—to Daniel J. Riesner, president of the National Republican Club.

Outcry in the press—the afternoon press, primarily—apparently panicked the administration. During the executive session of the Board of Estimate at which the new contract was scheduled to be approved (Moses was not present; he was presiding at a Long Island ribbon cutting at which Herbert Bayard Swope "conferred" on him the title of "Doctor of Human Betterment"), reporters waiting outside the closed doors heard voices raised in argument for three and a half hours after Spargo, Lebwohl and Brooks went in. Emerging harried, Wagner said the Board had refused to okay the contract—and when, in several days, it was resubmitted, Riesner's fee had been cut in half and Ferman's consultantship had been eliminated entirely. Gleason and Cook were not impressed by the fact that Ferman was now going to be paid "only" $300,000 and Riesner "only" $37,500, particularly after Gleason drew from a perspiring Wagner an admission that he did not know what legal services—if any—Riesner had ever performed for Manhattantown. "This was plain trafficking . . . in huge square-block chunks of city real estate that had been made available to [favored insiders] at knock-down prices by the taxpayers' millions," Cook wrote. Attempting to put a better face on the arrangement, Wagner then declared with firm and earnest mien that Ferman and Millstein "will be out as sponsors of Title I projects"; they would, he said, never be allowed to benefit from the program in the future. "It sounded good if you didn't think," Cook was to recall, "but it seemed to reporters who did that the words, even as the Mayor uttered them, had a hollow ring. Weren't Ferman and Millstein going to benefit in the future?" Of course they were, to the tune

---

*** Ferman said he actually lost money.**

of 32 percent.* The developers who hadn't developed were still being rewarded for not developing; they were just not being rewarded as much.

And as the various arms of the city government quick-marched through the various steps necessary to the formalization of this arrangement, Gleason and Cook realized that the arrangement was a *fait accompli*, no matter how diligently they and their fellow journalists alerted the public to its injustices. The total result of their torturously obtained exposés would be to give to the milkers of Manhattantown a substantial extra helping of pure cream. As for Robert Moses, as the revelations faded away it became apparent that his powers over slum clearance were to be curtailed not a whit. Their exposés—and the resultant action—had, really, changed nothing, Cook was to write. "It disturbed no fundamental realities. Robert Moses still ran the show. Projects still reeked of political influence."

And if anyone had any doubt of the truth of Cook's observation, proof was not long in coming.

On the basis of its previous behavior, New York's press could not be expected to take much interest in the relocation details of Lincoln Center, the Title I project that best revealed the vast breadth of Moses' creative, city-shaping imagination. (With his first realization of the possibilities in Title I had come what he was later to describe as a "vision of a reborn West Side, marching north from Columbus Circle, and eventually spreading over the entire dismal and decayed West Side.") The Coliseum at the Circle had been the first encampment in that march, and no sooner had he built it than three coincidences had combined to show him the next leg. Sitting beside him on a dozen daises, Fordham president Father Laurence J. McGinley was repeatedly mentioning to him that the university desperately needed a midtown campus but was unable to afford midtown real estate prices; Ruth Baker Pratt and other opera lovers kept mentioning to him at dinner parties that forcing the Metropolitan Opera to perform in its ancient, inadequate building on Thirty-ninth Street was scandalous; and then he read in the papers one morning that Carnegie Hall had just formally notified the New York Philharmonic that its lease would not be renewed after 1958. From the three coincidences, his mind leapt to a grand conception: razing eighteen square blocks of slums stretching north from the Coliseum and rearing on their ruins a huge, glittering cultural center that would house—in grandeur—not only university, opera and Philharmonic but a dozen other related institutions. By 1957, his plan for the Lincoln Center for the Performing Arts included not only a four-square-block Fordham campus, a Philharmonic Hall and a new Metropolitan Opera House but a ballet center, a repertory theater, a high school of the performing arts, a library and museum of the performing arts, a new home for the famed Juilliard School

* Wrote Cook: "Asked how he squared this indubitable fact with his new [statement], Mayor Wagner showed a little irritation and answered a bit peevishly: 'Well, I think Webb & Knapp was lucky to get that much interest [a 68 percent stockholding] in it. They have control.' "

of Music, and such related facilities as 4,400 units of housing, a public school and playground, an underground parking garage, a firehouse, a park with bandshell for outdoor concerts, a headquarters for the American Red Cross and the Fiorello H. La Guardia High School, "not to speak," as Moses put it, "of the neighboring offices of *The New York Times*." Newspapers were filled with artists' renderings of the magnificent cultural institutions to be erected where, for the most part, shabby tenements now stood; by its traditional standards, the press could not be expected to be very interested in the fact that 7,000 low-income families and 800 businesses were going to have to be displaced from the site—or in the charges being made that despite the fact that, as reformer I. D. Robbins put it, "there . . . are plenty of funds available" under various housing acts "to enable the planner to establish the first truly balanced neighborhood in New York," Moses was not making even a pretense of creating new homes for the families displaced; to replace the 7,000 low-income apartments being destroyed, 4,400 new ones were being planned—4,000 of them luxury apartments.

By its traditional standards, however, the press might be expected to be interested in several financial facts about Lincoln Center: although Moses had received an offer from certain reputable housing developers of $9.58 per square foot for land, he was selling the land to other, favored, developers for $7.00 per square foot; while the city was acquiring the rest of the huge site by blanket condemnation proceedings, it had for some unexplained reason found it advisable to take the building at 70 Columbus Avenue, owned (under a trust established by Democratic moneyman and Charles Buckley intimate Joseph P. Kennedy) by Robert F. Kennedy and three of his sisters, Jean Kennedy Smith, Eunice Kennedy Shriver and Patricia Kennedy Lawford, not by condemnation but by purchase—for $2,500,000, a price so high that while the land under the buildings adjacent to the one owned by the Kennedys was worth $9.58 per square foot, the land under theirs became worth $62.88 per square foot.

And those facts were to be brought to the press's attention—by public statements by a public official. For Housing and Home Finance Agency Administrator Albert M. Cole, over-all federal administrator of Title I, who had been chafing for years over Moses' administration of Title I in New York, Lincoln Center was the last straw. In April, Cole had attempted to go over Moses' head, refusing to provide funds for the giant cultural complex until the city's Mayor and Board of Estimate met with him to decide "broad policy questions" about Title I's future in New York. Wagner let him know who would decide that future: "Would suggest your representatives meet with Slum Clearance Committee," the Mayor telegrammed. The press had backed Moses, and Cole had been forced to back down. Now, with the Manhattantown mess spread on the record, Cole, believing that some of the glitter might have rubbed off the Moses legend, and that the time might be ripe to curtail his powers, decided to try again. He demanded new appraisals of the Lincoln Center real estate, by "independent" appraisers. And when Moses refused, Cole charged publicly that during the HHFA's ten-year existence "the agency has had more trouble with Mr. Robert Moses than with any other single individual in all the cities of the United States." Title I's "many difficulties" in New York, he stated, were due to Moses' "unique method" for selecting housing sponsors, and his refusal to consider changing it. "It has been our documented and arduous experience that Mr. Moses misrepresents what the housing agency is doing or trying to do; he will not take the trouble to ascertain the facts; his obscurities are misleading, and he is inflexibly bent on following his own course whatever may be the outcome." Threatening to cut off all Title I aid to the city unless the method was changed, Cole again asked Wagner and the Board to intercede.

Moses' response was his usual offer to resign. "Any further statements on this subject will of course have to come from the Mayor," he said.

Wagner could not make his statement fast enough. Within an hour after Moses' offer to resign, the Mayor rejected it—in a late-afternoon press release which contained a political version of a Freudian slip as to his reasoning. "I have every confidence in Bob Moses. . . . Mr. Moses has made great contributions to the City of New York, *and the people are well aware of this*" (italics added). And proof of the political wisdom of the Mayor's course arrived with the morning papers, so much more important to a politician than the PM's. Wagner, by rushing, had just barely beaten them to the punch. Said the *Herald Tribune*:

> True enough, the course of Title I slum clearance has been far from smooth. But such deficiencies ought to be a challenge to renewed effort at getting things done.
>
> . . . New York has been committed from the beginning to the Bob Moses way of getting things done. . . . Washington should take notice that this city will not drop its construction pilot.

The New York Times responded to Cole's challenge with perhaps its clearest statement ever of its principal owner's feelings about Robert Moses.

> Mr. Cole had better face the fact, as F.D.R. had to, that New York City is not going to drop Bob Moses as a public servant as long as he is willing to keep working for the city. La Guardia, O'Dwyer, Impellitteri, Wagner—none of them, as Mayor, could get along without him. To be sure, it's possible to find a mistake and a failure here and there. But look at the long, long record of successes. You don't bench a Babe Ruth because he strikes out once in a while. You consider the home runs and the batting average.
>
> Maybe some other system would have worked better here, on urban renewal, than the "unique" New York system. That can only be a matter of speculation. What we do know is that, in general, New York's slum clearance progress has been unequalled and that, in the memory of living man on the New York scene, there has never been the equal of Bob Moses for getting things done. The Federal Government is not going to change Mr. Moses. It had better try to get along with him, for that is the way we will travel farthest fastest for the public good.

"Moses could push a button and the calls would pour in . . . ," Lutsky says. "Calls from the people who really mattered." Now Moses pushed that button. People in New York who had access directly to the White House used that access. Father McGinley and other key figures in the Catholic Archdiocese, key union leaders, key bankers, John D. Rockefeller 3d himself—all were on the phone to Washington. "The amount of pressure he put on was just unbelievable," Cole says. "He just murdered me in there." A "compromise" was hastily announced: the HHFA would accept a new appraisal—by Moses' own appraisers, the same men who had made the original appraisals. Meanwhile, the HHFA was "reserving" for Lincoln Center the $27,000,000 for which Moses had asked.

It was a striking display of power. After the Lincoln Center episode, Gleason and Cook realized bitterly that Moses still had too much power to be touched by the federal government just as he had too much power to be touched by the city government. Even more bitter was their realization that, despite their attempts to shatter his image, it still endured, looming over New York almost as brightly as ever.

Part of the Moses myth—the part that portrayed the Park Commissioner as the park defender—had been cracked away by the Battle of Central Park. But the heart of the myth—the part that portrayed Moses as a man above politics and corruption—had not. Thirty years—and thousands upon thousands of newspaper articles—had gone into the creation of that myth. No single series of exposés in a single newspaper was going to destroy it, particularly not when that series, while revealing corruption in a Moses-run program, shied away from connecting that corruption with Moses personally. Gleason and Cook had hoped that other papers would pick up their revelations, repeat them, launch full-scale investigations of their own. Instead, when it came to the crunch, editorials had likened Robert Moses not to Boss Tweed but to Babe Ruth. Gleason and Cook knew that reporters on every paper in town wanted to dig into the Moses empire; they knew therefore that the decision not to dig—and to support Moses against the federal government—had been made at higher levels. Gleason and Cook could see that Moses' relationship with publishers and top editors was as close as ever. Not only had they been the recipients of his charm and his favors, they had been the key figures in making the Moses myth; they had a psychological vested interest in it. To dispatch investigators to dig into it would be an admission on their part that they had been wrong—had been wrong for years. That was not an admission that, in the absence of evidence a lot stronger than Gleason had been able to uncover, they were prepared to make. Some of them would permit their papers to print derogatory items about Moses if such items were breaking news; they would not allow their reporters to dig up such items and make them news. And without such digging beneath the surface of that image, the image would endure.

They may have chipped it, they realized, but it was still there.

Still they kept working—despite new obstacles.

> . . . the heat was really on [Cook says]. City officials with whom we had been able to talk previously flew into rages at the sight of us—and later let us know, privately, that they had had to put on an act either because spies had been planted at their elbows or because they felt their offices were bugged, their phones tapped. The reporting half of this team sometimes found strange men

trailing after him when he made his rounds of the municipal offices; and the little guys in the scandal-packed bureaus—the men who had fed us with tips—asked us never to try to get in touch with them again, even at their homes at midnight. They all felt that their phones were tapped, that they were being watched.

They were working almost alone. "There was a time (and it lasted for almost three years) when we were virtually the only writers in New York focusing a critical spotlight on the [Title I] program," Cook was to write. And while he may have exaggerated the length of time involved, the rest of his statement was accurate. Only stripmining before, Gleason was digging deep now, his way lighted by a long line of anonymous tips, and he was beginning to unearth evidence that the city's whole political structure was tied in to Title I; photostats of canceled checks for Manhattantown's insurance premiums were placed in his hands, and Cook was thereupon able to write: "Manhattantown began with Sam Caspert in a political clubhouse. Caspert was a vice president of Robert Blaikie's Democratic Club on the Upper West Side. . . . Blaikie handled the insurance.* . . . Many of the original investors, officers and employees of Manhattantown came out of Blaikie's political club." Residents of Gramercy Park protested that their neighborhood wasn't a slum; they couldn't understand why it had been designated for slum clearance—Gleason and Cook informed them that their own assemblyman, who in public was opposing the project, was in private the organizer of the real estate syndicate to whom Moses had awarded it, the revelation marking "the first time that an elected public official had been closely identified with Title I operations." And each tip about politics and corruption established more clearly the link between them and the living legend who was supposedly above them; by March 1958 the circle had tightened to a point at which Gleason and Cook were able to print that "Moses Man" William S. Lebwohl, the director of Moses' Slum Clearance Committee, was a stockholder in the Nassau Management Company, a real estate firm that had been set up on a shoestring just three years before—and that during those three years it had collected, largely for tenant relocation on Moses' slum clearance and highway projects, fees totaling $2,250,000. They were able to print that a brochure published by the firm to lure potential investors into purchasing its stock contained endorsements not only by Lebwohl but by two other "Moses Men," Slum Clearance Committee assistant director Samuel Brooks and Housing Authority chairman Philip J. Cruise. And they were even able to reveal the ties between this corporate recipient of Moses' largesse and Tammany Hall: the firm was so generous a contributor to the Hall that its president had been invited by the Democratic State Committee to serve as vice chairman of the annual party dinner; all relocation contracts had been funneled through the City Real Estate Bureau, and that bureau was headed by a boutonniered front man for Carmine De Sapio, Percy Gale, Jr. And the two reporters acquired—and

* "But only, Blaikie says, because Caspert came to him in desperation after four other brokers had refused to help him."

printed—evidence of an even closer link between the man supposedly above politics and the archetypal politician: De Sapio representative Gale was a member of Moses' Slum Clearance Committee. But Gleason and Cook were the only reporters investigating Title I now. The *Post* faithfully reported the controversy—mostly tenant protests—over the various Title I sites, but was doing no original investigative work of its own. Gleason and Cook needed the prestigious AM's; having recanted their apostasy, however, these papers were showing no inclination whatsoever to repeat it. "All through this time," Cook says, "we were shooting our shots practically alone."

Enthusiasm for their work was not exactly rampant even on their own city desk. Their editors, unenthusiastic about making the *World-Telegram* a voice of dissent amid a chorus of praise, kept downplaying Moses' connection with the revelations of political influence, the connection that had to be made, clearly and strongly, if the public was, amid the complexities of Title I, to grasp it. In the Gleason-Cook article revealing that the Gramercy Park slum clearance project had been given to an assemblyman, for example, there was not a mention of *who* had given the assemblyman the project; Moses' name never appeared. Cook's paragraphs making what the rewriteman considered the key point of the Nassau Management scandals—that a Robert Moses aide had received immensely lucrative contracts from Robert Moses without competitive bidding—were edited out of his copy day after day. Lebwohl and Brooks were identified as "city officials" although what they really were were Moses officials. The contracts involved in the stories were described as "city contracts" although not the city but Moses had awarded them. "The guts were cut out of those stories," Cook says. Moreover, as Cook puts it, "the paper began to get more and more weary of this. There was no real pressure from [publisher] Howard. It was just 'Who the hell understands this stuff?' 'It's too goddamn complicated for the public to understand.' 'The public doesn't care.' In essence it was 'When are you guys gonna start doing something else?' I'd write a great story and I'd come in the next day and it'd be on page twenty-seven." The myth that surrounded Moses had been created on page one. It was on page one that the myth would have to be destroyed. Stories on page twenty-seven would never do it.

Knowing this as they did, the two years following the Manhattantown exposé was a time of terrible frustration for Gene Gleason and Fred Cook. Moses' manipulations may have been on page twenty-seven; his triumphs were on page one. Despite revelations that would have destroyed the career of the typical public official, during these two years this public official rammed through, over the opposition of protesting neighborhoods, approval for new expressways, for two great new bridges, the Throgs Neck and the Verrazano, together with the neighborhood-destroying bridge approach routes he wanted; killed, over the efforts of Brooklyn Dodgers owner Walter O'Malley, plans for a City Sports Authority that might have kept the Dodgers and Giants in New York, and began happily to plan the housing projects that he had wanted on the sites of the Polo Grounds and Ebbets Field all along; presided with a grim smile of triumph at ribbon cuttings marking the opening of the Harlem River Drive and a dozen other public works projects and sat in his limousine laughing at protesters burning him in effigy. It was during these years, in fact, that there were named after him two dams, two parkways, two parks and a bridge. While those two "guttersnipes" had been trying to blacken his name, it had, instead, been enshrined, forever, in concrete and steel and imperishable pieces of the public domain. "You know, once you get headlines, you get people coming to you," Cook says. "But when the paper itself begins to lose interest, doesn't play these things, the well sort of dries up, you know." It was drying up now. There were fewer and fewer tips. And Gleason and Cook were finding it harder and harder to check into what tips there were. "The desk was just tired and bored with it, and it wasn't making a public impact. The paper couldn't afford this investment in time indefinitely. Other things'd come up that they'd want us on. They couldn't spare us for Title I any more. By the time 1959 came around—the early winter of '59—we were pretty much dead."

To understand what Gleason and Cook did then, it is necessary to understand Gleason and Cook.

Gleason was *Front Page*. Big, brawny and boisterous, with a crooked Irish grin and a nose that must have been broken at least once in his thirty-two years, he looked the part—complete to the collar of his trench coat, which was invariably turned up. And he acted it. Hard-drinking, he talked loudly in barrooms about the big stories he was working on, the big men he was going to unmask; the sacred profession of journalism was to him the newspaper game, and he played it with a swagger. Cook could always tell when Gleason had dug up a good item. "He'd be licking his chops. He'd come in with a bounce and a grin and turn down the aisle and—'Hey, we got a good one today!' "

But Gene Gleason was driven by more than an urge for self-dramatization. Injustice, the little guy being trampled on by powers too big for him to fight—those were the stories that interested him. And in trying to pin them down and get them into print, as fellow *World-Telegram* staffer John Ferris wrote, "nothing halts him. Time is of no consequence: he will work 24 hours without thought of rest. Weather never daunts him: he has sloshed through rain, crawled through snow, braved bitter cold and sweated through oppressive heat. He is tough physically . . . and tough mentally." Covering a revolt by Transit Authority motormen against powerful TA union boss Mike Quill, he sensed that the motormen's headquarters was being bugged and warned them. Following his advice, they found a hidden microphone from which a wire led out the window; police summoned to the scene were conspicuously uninterested in discovering where the wire led; Gleason climbed out the window into a freezing, windy winter night to follow it over treacherous, ice-covered roofs himself. The ice forced him to give up that night, but the next day, when no one expected him, he was back, found policemen rolling up the wire and uncovered the fact that the Transit

Authority had planted the bug with apparent police connivance. Wrote Ferris: "No one awes him. The story comes first." And when he couldn't get that story, when he had to watch injustice and do nothing about it, Gene Gleason took it personally. Wrote Murray Kempton: "He seemed to me out of another time, and I must confess that with him I was never sorry that I was so middle-aged. If I took things the way Gene Gleason did, I wouldn't sleep at night. He is a big fellow and a young one, but, when I first met him, the first thing I thought was here is a man who doesn't sleep at night."

Fred J. Cook kept his coat collars flat and his voice low. He was not a reporter but a rewriteman—the quintessential rewriteman, so accustomed to seeing the world through the earpiece of a telephone headset and notes taken by other men that he felt no need to see it for himself; not once during the more than three years during which he was writing about Manhattantown did he get into a subway and take the twenty-minute ride that would have enabled him to see Manhattantown; he never once visited the site of that development. "I was tied to the desk all the time . . . one story after another . . . the grind in there was such that at the end of the day I just wanted to get out of there." But he had the gift of turning notes into prose; during the fifteen years he had sat at a desk in the *World-Telegram*'s rewrite bank—in 1959 he was forty-eight—Fred Cook had earned a reputation as a fast man with a good word. "Fred Cook was a master writer," Joe Kahn says. No reporter who saw Manhattantown described it nearly as well as Cook did without seeing it.

And you could be quiet and tied to a desk and still care. During the 1950's few journalists—even the most liberal—criticized the FBI; in a brilliant article for *The Nation,* Cook criticized the FBI. At the very height of the storm of invective against Alger Hiss, Cook wrote a book defending Alger Hiss. And by 1959, Cook had gotten to care quite deeply about Title I. Years later, questioned about his reasons for pursuing a story his editors would have been happy to see him drop, Cook, speaking in a low, calm voice, would tick off reasons founded in intellect—that he felt he had failed to make the public understand the importance of the issues involved, that other newspapers had failed in their responsibility by refusing to pick up their stories, that "we were sure there was a bigger scandal there, and we hated to see it die without further effort being made on the thing." "You mean there was no feeling of injustice involved on your part?" an interviewer would ask. "Yeah," Cook said, his voice betraying surprise that the other man should have not understood that. "I used to get these phone calls. I remember there was this druggist . . . He had a little store in the Washington Square area for twenty-five years, and all they were offering him was $750 for his fixtures, and he had just paid $15,000 for them, and when he tried to get to see someone about them, they wouldn't even listen to him. . . . There were dozens of calls like that. Dozens. They were too small fry for anyone to listen to them. I had this deep sense of injustice. I felt I knew Moses. The son of a bitch doesn't give a good goddamn about people, and he never did. The power brokers only care about power and who the hell the little human beings are who get trampled in their game doesn't mean a hoot in hell to them." The measure of Cook's caring was the stories he had been writing. "The *Telly* had a real skeleton staff compared to the *Times* or the *Trib*," he would recall. "There were never enough guys on the rewrite bank, and you were always writing too much every day anyway. There were always other stories to do—breaking stories. They never wanted to give me any time for these. So I had to just keep them going myself, as a side effort so to speak."

Gleason and Cook possessed a full share of journalistic competitiveness. They had won awards for their stories, the "exclusives" they had dug up or written themselves, and they wanted more awards—and therefore more exclusives. Their paper, hitting the newsstands each afternoon within minutes of the *Post* and *Journal-American*, was part of a fierce three-way competition. But now, frustrated, knowing that, unless they did something drastic, "we were dead" as far as further exposures of Title I and Robert Moses were concerned, Gleason and Cook decided that the only way to keep it going was to share their hard-dug material—to give it to a competitor.

The choice of whom to give it to was an obvious one. Only the *Post* would give Gleason's information the play it deserved and invest the time and energy necessary to dig out its own, and there was a *Post* reporter, thirty-one-year-old William J. Haddad, who had already proven, in sensational exposés of City Building Department malpractice, that he possessed all Gleason's toughness and tenacity—in addition to the rare ability to discern patterns in seemingly unrelated facts, to identify the locus, not just the symptoms, of corruption.

Luckily, Haddad and Gleason were already friends. Gleason gave him information, and Haddad was soon writing stories based on it. The *Post*'s stories had the effect on Gleason's city desk that he had known it would; his editors got interested in Title I again—even more so because Gleason was able to provide them with new leads, given him by Haddad. For Haddad quickly arrived at the same realization as Cook and Gleason. "We found out very early that it had to be a joint effort," he says. "It would never *go*—it would rise and die in one paper—unless another paper picked it up. Then the TV would pick it up and then the political authorities would start to react—that was the carbohydrate that made it work." Soon, like two flamenco dancers spurring each other to wilder and wilder efforts, Haddad and Gleason were both helping and striving to outdo each other, their stories picking up and taking off from each other's and hitting harder and harder. As the tempo accelerated, moreover, the tipsters joined in again, a whole chorus of disgruntled bureaucrats who realized that this time there was a real chance that someone would print their information.

With its two competitors playing a scandal in banner headlines day after day, the third afternoon daily couldn't ignore it even if its top executives would have liked to: soon the *Journal-American* was printing Title I stories. Then, tentatively at first, then more and more boldly, readers were given a chance to read about Title I in the morning as well: the *Trib* was in.

But the pooling continued. In fact, there soon sprang up a circle at whose heart were Haddad and Gleason but which included also Woody Klein of the *Telly*, the *Journal-American*'s Marty Steadman, Peter Braestrup of the *Herald Tribune*—and a reporter from the underground, thirty-one-year-old Mary Perot Nichols; born a Philadelphia Main Line Wasp, she had moved to the East Village, begun crusading against Moses' proposed road through Washington Square Park, and had seen at a glance truths about Moses' whole method of operation that no one, seemingly, had understood before; her only journalistic connection was *The Village Voice,* but her observations in it were in many ways the most penetrating printed up to that time. These reporters would meet almost daily with Hortense Gabel, the one city official willing to openly help them. There was no one "important" at that table. "We were chipmunks," Hortense Gabel would recall. "[Moses] wouldn't even know who we were. There was no one important even in journalism." But they met daily, an underground movement, to force the city's journalistic establishment to do what they wanted.

In any assessment of their motivations, their age is important. Everyone in the circle was in his late twenties or early thirties. Recalling those days, years later, Haddad would say with a rueful smile: "Our motives? It was us against the world, us against them—the city, corruption, unmovable forces. We were young enough to breathe that kind of air then." Moreover, these young idealists hadn't even been born when Robert Moses had been on the front pages battling the robber barons to open Long Island to the masses. They had been only infants when Jones Beach was dedicated. In 1934, when Robert Moses had revitalized New York City's park system, to the city's cheers, Gleason had been only seven years old, Haddad six. The Robert Moses they knew was not the Robert Moses of the beautiful parks and the beautiful parkways—the parkways that were going to solve traffic problems. The Robert Moses they knew was the Robert Moses of the Tavern-on-the-Green and Manhattantown and those damned expressways he insisted on building even though everybody knew the city should be building subways instead, and for which he evicted thousands of helpless families; their impression of him was of an arrogant, dictatorial old man who, if not corrupt himself, had certainly managed to surround himself with a lot of corrupt people; like the Newmans, they were too young to have seen him as great; they saw him only as crotchety, old—and wrong; their perception of the Coordinator was unclouded by the preconceptions that had clouded reporters' eyes in the Twenties and Thirties, that he was the selfless, incorruptible, apolitical public servant *sans peur et sans reproche*. They saw him as he was.

The members of this journalistic cabal were also too young to be afraid. Those rare reporters of the Thirties and Forties who might have contemplated investigating the Moses empire had been very conscious of what had happened to reporters who had tried it before. But it had been a long time now since Robert Moses had broken a reporter, so long that Haddad and Gleason didn't even know that he ever had. Haddad, the spiritual heir of Milton Racusin, a *Herald Tribune* reporter who a decade earlier had investigated the Moses empire and written a series on it but had seen the series killed (and had been forced to personally apologize to Moses to boot), had never even heard Racusin's name, much less the story of how his career had been wrecked.

If the age explanation was simple, the psychological was not. The motives that inspired these young reporters to take on "the most powerful SOB" in the city were as mixed as are the motives of all investigative reporters. One cannot talk to some of them for long without knowing that competitiveness was a spur, and in varying degrees there was present also at that table the desire for personal self-glorification, as well as the simple desire to drag down someone bigger than they. But, with most of them at least, so was a spur of a purer metal. "Can't somebody do something about the son of a bitch?" Gleason had shouted to Cook in frustration one day, and behind that shout was the outrage, the "sense of injustice," that had built up in him and in his partner over what Moses and the city's other power brokers were doing to "the little human beings . . . who get trampled in their game." "To me," Kahn says, "he was the personification of a certain arrogance against the average man. I don't think he ever cared about how many hearts he had to break to Get Things Done. And so I felt he *had* to be stopped. And there wasn't anyone else to stop him but us." If most young men of intelligence and drive are ambitious, not all of them put that intelligence and drive at the service of justice as had a Gene Gleason or a Bill Haddad. And they kept chipping away at the image of Robert Moses. After thirty years of building up that image, the press had begun chopping it down.

It was triumph as usual for Moses as 1959 opened. Having celebrated his seventieth birthday on a Christmas vacation in Barbados, he was greeted upon his return after New Year's by reporters trooping into his office to commemorate the occasion with interviews and stories reporting, as stories had reported on his sixtieth birthday and his sixty-fifth, that time had left no visible mark upon the man who the *Long Island Press* reiterated in 48-point Bodoni was still "Public Friend No. 1"—and by news that the success of the largest bond issue in history had been assured by a syndicate of the biggest investment bankers on Wall Street and that the three-quarters of a billion dollars that would bring his Niagara dream to fruition was therefore in hand. The submission of his reappointment as State Power Authority chairman touched off anger in the State Senate Chamber. "He has held every public official who has ever disagreed with him up to ridicule and scorn," one senator said. "I don't call that greatness, but a desire to do away with the democratic processes." Another said he had "never encountered an arrogance that could even approach that of the man we are asked to approve." But the lopsidedness of the margin by which the nomination was approved after such denunciation—50 to 6, with several of the senators who had joined in the denunciation casting their votes for confirmation—was proof that his power in Albany was as great as ever. And when, shortly after his return, he announced a series of huge new Title I projects, the announcements were greeted by the press with customary uncritical acclaim. All was as it had always been.

But by the beginning of February, Haddad was poking holes in those announcements ("Only twenty families out of 1,420 now living on the site of the Title I Gramercy Park slum clearance project will be able to afford the rents for the new housing units") and by the middle of February, Haddad had one of his own to make.

It had a hard-hitting lead ("Sidney J. Ungar is a man of position and property. . . . His property, a *Post* investigation revealed today, includes some of the city's worst slums") and a hard-hitting headline (THE SLUM PROPERTIES OF AN ANTI-SLUM LEADER) and plenty of facts to back them up. Ungar, Moses' choice for sponsor of the Riverside-Amsterdam urban renewal project, had indignantly and volubly denied the tip Haddad had gotten that he was a slumlord. "As a native New Yorker whose entire life has been devoted to the welfare of the people of the city, assuming leadership in philanthropic, religious and communal activities, I have for many years been fighting the real battle for improvement of housing," said his press release. He had threatened to sue for "several million dollars" if the *Post* said different; if Haddad didn't believe him, he said, the reporter could just go and look at his buildings. But Haddad had done what Ungar had evidently not expected him to do: he went and looked.

The quotes from Ungar's tenants ("My son Stephen—he's six—is in the hospital. A rat bit him between the eyes. I tried to fix the rat holes here, but the rats cut right through. I complained but no one did anything to fix them." "I have no water, hot or cold . . . the bathroom ceiling is falling down . . . rats all over the building . . . sewers backing up . . . dumbwaiter packed with garbage . . . cellar flooded") made great copy, and the pictures that confirmed the quotes made great pictures, and the fact that Robert Moses was giving a lucrative slum clearance project to a slumlord, and a politically well-connected slumlord at that (Haddad discovered, and printed, Ungar's financial backing of campaigns of both Wagner and Hulan Jack), made a great story, and the *Post* not only played it to the hilt but emphasized that it was a *Post* exclusive. And after that story had appeared, the *World-Telegram*'s editors, afraid of falling behind in a story that had once been (exclusively) theirs, hastily reassigned Gleason to Title I, and he began coming up with revelations of his own. And soon the *Post* was picking up the *Telly*'s stories and the *Telly* the *Post*'s—and the editors of each paper, afraid that when the rival paper hit the stand that afternoon they would find themselves outplayed, were playing these revelations as editors had so seldom played revelations about Robert Moses' mistakes: big. And just in case their interest might slacken, Haddad and Gleason, while ostensibly—for the benefit of their bosses—fiercely competing for new exclusives, were actually dividing them up, one and one. And by March, Joe Kahn was on the story, too, and Kahn was writing it as it should be written: in his leads, for the first time consistently in any paper, it was no longer "The Mayor's Slum Clearance Committee" but "Robert Moses' Slum Clearance Committee." Anxiously leafing through the paper every day to see where his latest story had been played, Haddad no longer had to leaf far; it was a rare day on which the latest Title I exposé was not the lead on page seven or five or three. Day by day, the reporter watched Title I march off the inside pages of the *Telly* and the *Journal* and the *Trib* and onto the split pages and then onto page one. For generations, people thrown out of their homes by Robert Moses had been complaining about his ruthlessness. Now, at last, their complaints were in headlines: NOWHERE TO GO AND 30 DAYS TO GET THERE; "TO GET US OUT, THEY MOVE VERY QUICKLY." In 1953 the Women's City Club had issued reports disclosing that Moses had been shifting tenants in "slum clearance" sites to other buildings on the site like gypsies. The reports had been ignored. In 1954, a minority report of the City Planning Commission had made similar revelations. That report had been ignored. But now, in 1959, when J. Clarence Davies, Jr., new, independent head of the city's Real Estate Bureau, made the same report, it was CITY ADMITS SHIFTS FROM SLUMS TO SLUMS. "The press of the city, awake at last!" Fred Cook exulted, and he was right. The press had not been awakened by its owners (with the exception of Mrs. Schiff, of course) or by its top editors (with the exception of the *Post*'s James Wechsler, of course). It had been awakened by its reporters, not by its famous reporters but by young unknown staff writers scheming together to force publishers and editors to do what the young men felt was their duty. But it was awake.

And then came an issue that required no reportorial scheming to become a big story, for it was too much of a natural—as much a natural as the Tavern-on-the-Green fight that had begun the deflation of the Moses image. This story had the same key setting as that fight (its locale was, in fact, just a short stroll away)—the sacred turf of Central Park; some headline writers were, in fact, to dub it "the Second Battle of Central Park." It had issues as simple and clear-cut, black and white, starkly dramatic. And if it did not have mothers and baby carriages, it had something almost as good.

W. Shakespeare.

44. *Mustache and the Bard*

MR. MOULDER. *In connection with the work that you are doing at the present time, do you have the opportunity to inject into your plays or into the acting or the entertainment supervision which you have, any propaganda in any way which would influence others to be sympathetic with the Communist philosophy or the beliefs of communism?*

MR. PAPIROFSKY. *Sir, the plays we do are Shakespeare's plays. Shakespeare said, "To thine own self be true," and various other lines from Shakespeare can hardly be said to be subversive or influencing minds. I cannot control the writings of Shakespeare. . . .*

MR. AHRENS. *We are not concerned with the plays and you know we are not, and there is no suggestion here by this chairman or anyone else that Shakespeare was a Communist. That is ludicrous and absurd. That is the Commie line.*

—HEARINGS OF THE HOUSE COMMITTEE
ON UN-AMERICAN ACTIVITIES, JUNE 19, 1958,
TESTIMONY OF JOSEPH PAPIROFSKY (PAPP)

WHAT PRESS AND PUBLIC were never told about the Second Battle of Central Park—and, because of the viciousness of the tactics Moses employed in his campaign to win it, would probably not have believed if they *had* been told—was that he did not want it and had no part in bringing it about. Of all the battles the old lion had fought, this was the one for which he had least stomach.

Robert Moses loved Shakespeare—he could recite whole scenes—and he loved the idea of presenting Shakespeare in Central Park. He had never met Joseph Papp, but he liked his style. When, in 1956, the boyish-looking CBS stage manager had asked for permission to present free productions of Shakespeare in the little amphitheater Moses had built in 1936 at Corlears Hook on the waterfront on the Lower East Side, Moses had asked around about him, and had been impressed with what he was told: slight, dark-haired Joe Papirofsky had grown up in Brooklyn's brawling

Williamsburg "surrounded by terror . . . I got beat up regularly . . ." and by poverty. To help his trunkmaker father pay the rent, he hauled garbage, hawked newspapers, sold pretzels, plucked chicken feathers and shined shoes ("I never thought I'd get the black out of my fingers"); his mother stuffed cardboard in the holes in his own. Then, at the age of twelve, he discovered the public library and Shakespeare, memorizing "vast tracts" of the plays. In the Navy during the war, he produced shows on the decks of aircraft carriers. Mustered out, he used the GI Bill to attend not college but the Actors Laboratory. While working in 1953 as a television stage manager (CBS-TV changed his name because Papirofsky was inconveniently long for the credits), he finally implemented an idea he had cherished for years: his life had been changed by books—free books, the only kind he could afford; poor people were as entitled to free theater as free books. Begging pittances from foundations to rent the basement of a church on the Lower East Side and pay the salaries of promising young actors, he began to put on Shakespearean plays, productions that, critics began to notice, were not only free but good. Moses had been suspicious that Papp might be trying to use the amphitheater as a money-making device, but from all reports Papp was genuine; when theater critic Walter Kerr advised him to charge admission because people appreciate more what they pay for, he had replied that "if I had had to pay . . . it is doubtful that I would have read the plays of Shakespeare," adding that it was because people had to pay for theater tickets that most New Yorkers had never seen a live professional production. "I believe," he said, "that it is of the utmost importance to have a public theater—a theater for everybody —yes, everybody; for those who can afford it and those who cannot." Moses would ordinarily have agreed with Kerr, but he had built the amphitheater because Al Smith had told him that, as a youth on the Lower East Side anxious to become an actor, he could never afford a theater ticket, and in the intervening twenty years no one had ever evinced the slightest interest in producing plays in it. No one, in fact, had ever evinced much interest in producing *anything* in it; the amphitheater generally stood empty and unused. Papp's proposal would put the structure at last to use—the use for which Moses had intended it. When Park Department executive officer Stuart Constable argued that poor people wouldn't appreciate Shakespeare and that the tough kids in the neighborhood would break up the show, Moses told Mustache: "Oh, let him have it." It was in fact Moses who gave Papp his first big boost; the big foundations would not consider even modest grants without an "expression of interest" from the Park Commissioner; Papp wrote the Commissioner asking for one and got it.

During that first season in that little amphitheater on the East River, two things had become apparent—one, the moment the lights went up and the spectators saw the façades of an Italian Renaissance town and, through an ingenious series of arches and doorways, an entire cast made an entrance in full regalia, and from the audience came a single, thrilled, breathless "Ahhh!"; the other when the reviews came in—one, Papp was right, the city's poor *would* appreciate Shakespeare; two, Papp's productions were *good,* considering the youth of his actors and the paucity of his budget, amazingly good. Moses liked audacity—and, as the more perceptive of his aides had previously noticed, this man who had never had the son he so badly wanted often revealed a certain tenderness toward audacious young men. When, the following year, Papp had shown up at the Arsenal with a plan to bring the Bard to the whole city, via a mobile stage that would be transported from park to park on a truck scrounged from a boyhood chum, Moses' reaction to Constable's doubts had been a gruff: "Oh, let him do it." He had placed at Papp's disposal Park Department equipment and employees, a car and chauffeur. And when, in 1957, Papp had asked to present plays in Central Park, Moses had said okay, as long as he didn't charge admission and try to make money out of his shows.

If the Commissioner had doubts as to the wisdom of his decision, the reviews for the first Central Park season must have come down heavily on Papp's side. While holding down a full-time job as CBS stage manager, he had managed to produce, on a shoestring so frayed that he was sometimes opening productions without money on hand to pay for more than two performances (a gamble that always seemed to pay off in sufficient contributions for a full run), productions that were hailed as not just good but great; Papp's Central Park *Romeo and Juliet,* Kerr said, was "in many respects the best *Romeo and Juliet* I have ever seen." Papp was continually asking Moses to allow him to solicit voluntary contributions from the stage. Moses, through Constable, was continually refusing; Papp was continually making the solicitation anyway. Before one performance, a police sergeant told Papp, in a friendly way, "If you go on tonight, I'll have to pull you in." "Well, then, we'll go out on the street [Central Park West]," Papp said. "That's Park Department property, too," the sergeant said. "Across the street?" Papp asked. "And," the producer recalls, "he said that was all Park Department property, too, except the northwest corner." So Papp stationed men on that corner with big baskets. Watching Moses carefully to gauge the depth of his outrage at this defiance, Sid Shapiro was astonished to see a grin of delight sneak across RM's face. The Park Commissioner always politely refused Papp's invitations to attend—what was he supposed to do? Sit on a blanket?!?—but he had had himself driven past the scene and had been pleased with the spectators' orderliness. He had been very pleased with published reaction to the plays. After two years, New York was having a love affair with its Shakespeare Festival. A queue began to form three hours before the distribution of tickets began at 6:15 each evening; for every performance, it seemed, the lawn was filled, hundreds of standees crowded up to the fences in the back, and hundreds of other persons had to be turned away from what *Horizon* magazine called "This Blessed Plot, This Shakespeare in the Park." Observers noted that, as *Horizon* put it, "drawn from all classes and income groups, the Central Park spectators have an almost Elizabethan buoyancy and verve which are a startling contrast to the spiritual vacuity of Broadway's mink matrons and expense account aristocrats. . . . [They] come not out of duty but out of desire." And the spectators included people whose opinions Moses listened to; theatrical people like his neighbor Cornelia Otis Skinner and Port Authority chairman Howard S. Cullman were telling him excitedly about the brilliance of the productions and of the unknown young actors and actresses whom Papp was discovering and persuading to work for forty dollars a week; Cullman was particularly impressed by a young fellow who had gotten his first big role in Papp's production of *The Merchant of Venice*, George C. Scott. Moses' favorite magazine, *Saturday Review*, pointed out that "because the . . . Festival performance drew 2,100 persons into the park each evening, a whole section of Central Park was transformed from a threatening jungle into a tranquil gathering place for healthy entertainment." At a party thrown for Papp and his cast by the Tavern-on-the-Green ("Schleiffer had gotten quite a business out of it," Papp notes), "Constable came over to me and said, 'Don't worry about next season. I talked to Mr. Moses about it and he's going to raise the money himself.' " And Moses fully intended to do so; shortly thereafter, Papp received a letter from the Commissioner whom he had never met saying that he had already contacted Cullman about forming a committee to raise the $50,000 needed for another season, and that Papp could stop worrying. In March 1959, when Moses left for a three-week Barbados vacation, the producer believed that everything was set.

Papp and Constable had never gotten along well, however. Two men could hardly have been more dissimilar than the intense, idealistic, informal young producer and the paunchy, mustache-tugging executive so pompous that even mild Bob Wagner cursed when he mentioned his name. "Look at that title," Papp says. "Executive Officer. The whole thing was a military operation." Constable, for his part, had found Papp suspiciously liberal; he was unable to rid himself of the sneaking suspicion, based largely on the fact that Papp was Jewish, that the young producer was making money out of the Festival somehow. During Moses' vacation, the friction between their personalities produced sparks, and someone finally brought to Constable's attention a fact of which the Moses organization had not previously been aware: that the year before, testifying before the House Committee on Un-American Activities, Papp, while denying that he was presently a Communist, had refused to say whether he had ever been one, and had refused to identify friends who had. (He had been fired by CBS-TV for this stand, winning reinstatement only after a fight by the Radio and Television Directors Guild.)

To as passionate a Red hater as Stuart Constable, this revelation was enough to confirm all his suspicions—and he was sure it would have the same effect on RM. So sure was he, in fact, that, without checking with his absent boss, he took a step designed to drive Papp out of the park: in March —just three months before the Festival was to begin—he informed the producer that the Park Department could not afford the extra maintenance expense caused by the Shakespeare Festival, that the Festival would have to reimburse the Department for that expense and that, since the Festival had no funds with which it could guarantee reimbursement, it would be allowed to put on plays only if it charged admission. There would, Mustache said, be no more free Shakespeare in any city park.

None of the political commandments ingrained in Robert Moses by his Gamaliel had been ingrained more deeply than the rule stating that an executive gives subordinates absolute loyalty and support, and Moses' belief in this particular commandment was reinforced by the iron bands of his personality. He had, to a remarkable degree, consciously made his "muchachos" extensions of himself: admitting to outsiders that one of them was wrong would be almost like admitting that he himself was wrong. Moreover, Moses' loyalty to the Moses Men—his refusal, no matter how harshly he might abuse them in private or in front of other members of his clique, to let anyone else criticize them at all—had become within the circles in which he moved an integral part of the Moses legend. Wagner aide Warren Moscow was to verbalize what everyone in city and state government believed: "Every [Moses] deputy could count on the absolute support of his boss, if his position was ever challenged by any outsider." That legend was terribly important to Moses. He could not bear to have it defaced. He was its prisoner. Just three months earlier, in the seventieth-birthday interviews of which he had taken advantage to refurbish it, he had made a point of saying that his men "know I'll always stand up and take the public beating for them." He could not now publicly overrule one of them.

On Moses' return from Barbados, Papp attempted to contact him to persuade him to overrule Constable. He would not come to the phone. Then Papp wrote him, asking about the $50,000 he had promised to raise, money which would, Papp believed, enable him to reimburse the Park Department and make the season possible even under Constable's conditions. "I didn't hear from him and I didn't know about the money, and I began pressing," Papp recalls. "And finally I got a letter from him. Very terse. Very cavalier. No money. And we were planning a whole damn season on his word." A Papp letter pleading for a personal interview drew only a reply setting out for the record the "reasons" for the Park Department ruling: that fencing was necessary "for control" of crowds, that "adequate sanitary and dressing facilities" for the actors were needed and, most important, that the lawn on which the audience had sat must be paved over and seats provided because "we can't maintain grass, and serious erosion problems would soon face us unless the area is paved." Fifty thousand dollars wouldn't begin to meet the cost, Moses wrote; $100,000 to $150,000 would be needed. Certain that he could reason with Moses if he could only talk to him, Papp wrote again pleading for a face-to-face meeting. He had just read a Moses article on Irish playwright Sean O'Casey, Papp said, and "I feel certain that a genuine rapport can be established because I know that a man who can write with such depth of feeling about O'Casey will certainly understand the dilemma of our organization. I appeal to you to make it possible for this meeting to materialize." Moses replied that "this matter is entirely in the hands of Stuart Constable. . . ." Constable had mentioned an admission charge of a dollar; Papp said he would consider that price scale;* Constable immediately replied that he had changed his mind: two dollars would be necessary. Only

* Whether Papp would actually have charged admission will never be known; he and his board of directors were themselves reconsidering, and, during the period in which his letters and Constable's were crossing, the board went on record against any admission at all.

then did Papp grasp the fact that the real issue was not price but political philosophy—Constable was determined that no plays produced by a Red like Joe Papp would be allowed in the parks—and that there was no hope of intervention from Constable's boss.

If Constable's bloodhounds had been thorough, they would have told him that he was dealing with a fighter, one not ashamed of his past and not afraid to go to the public with a cause. Winning reinstatement at CBS hadn't been easy, after all; Papp had in fact been the first television figure fired as a result of the Un-American Activities Committee hearings ever to do so. Mustache was, moreover, dealing—as would become apparent in later years—with an opponent who knew exactly *how* to go to the public, with a public relations genius of the first magnitude, of Moses magnitude, in fact. Closing down his Shakespeare Festival for a full year would mean that the foundations which had been supporting it would lose the habit, and that the company of actors and production personnel he had so painfully brought and held together would fall apart. Even the meager momentum so tortuously built up in four years of effort would be lost; the New York Shakespeare Festival that was his dream might have to close forever. With his back against the wall, the young producer did what a young state park official with *his* dream menaced and *his* back against the wall had done thirty-five years before: he went to the press. And Joseph Papp went as Robert Moses had gone—not with a defense but with an attack.

"Erosion?" he told reporters. "Do people sitting and watching a play create more of an erosion problem than football, softball, soccer and similar sports encouraged in the parks at no cost to the players?" Perhaps, he said, "the park situation would be improved by more 'soil erosion' caused by the gathering of 2,000 people each night in an area where three years ago only squirrels dared to congregate." Papp spiced his attack—and emphasized what it was that Moses was depriving the city of—with a device that couldn't miss: quotes from the Bard. He won the heart of one reporter who asked why he had decided to fight Moses' ban instead of giving in, by asking her in return "Whether 'tis nobler in the mind to suffer the slings and arrows of outrageous fortune, or to take arms against a sea of troubles, and by opposing end them." Moses himself smiled when he read that—"He had never met him, but you could tell he was getting to like the guy," Shapiro says—but he stood up for Constable, although there was a decidedly unwonted gentleness in the press release in which he replied:

> I have considerable respect for Mr. Papp's singleness of purpose, but can't adopt it as a principle and shall certainly not direct Mr. Constable to do so.
>
> While the present park administration is in charge, Mr. Papp will have to put his enterprise on a workable basis or go elsewhere. I believe I have the Mayor's confidence. Mr. Constable has mine.

And when the young producer replied to this by attacking again—"To abandon our policy of free admissions would result in disenfranchising the very people we are anxious to serve"—he obtained the results the young Moses had once obtained: unanimously favorable reviews, the *Herald*

Tribune calling Moses "short-sighted," the *World-Telegram* saying he was being "not merely inconsistent but capriciously unreasonable."

That did it. Moses may have been pulled into the fight reluctantly, but he knew he was in one now. And he fought with his customary enthusiasm—and methods. There was behind-the-scenes pressure put on officials whose support Moses needed by the men who he knew could put it on best (former Police Commissioner George V. McLaughlin was in a position to put it on Police Commissioner Stephen P. Kennedy; McLaughlin to Kennedy: "I am . . . taking the liberty of suggesting that you cooperate . . ."). There was the behind-the-scenes innuendo of the type that Jack Madigan believed had worked so well with Mrs. Sulzberger in the matter of Inwood Hill Park (Moses to Corporation Counsel Charles Tenney: "The place is dark and impossible to police adequately. How many couples on the grass came for Shakespeare and how many for other purposes I don't know"). And there was behind-the-scenes innuendo of the type that had worked so well on opponents during the 1940's.

Constable had never revealed the real reason for his hostility toward Papp, but Moses did. On April 23, 1959, a personal message from the Park Commissioner was delivered to Wagner and other key city officials by a Triborough messenger who had been instructed to place it in no one's hands but theirs: "As a result of recent experiences we have looked him up more carefully. He turns out to be a typical of the breed. He took the Fifth Amendment twelve times in June, 1958, before the House Un-American Activities Committee." And when behind-the-scenes innuendo did not achieve the desired result—several borough presidents were hinting at support for Papp—Moses moved it onto center stage.

It wasn't really erosion he was concerned about, he told reporters; it was "muggers, degenerates and pickpockets" preying on the audience. "This was a disorderly type of performance," impossible to police properly, he said. In his mail one morning he had found a three-page letter attacking Papp's "Communist" background and questioning his "probity" in accounting for the donations he collected. The letter contained no proof of these charges, and after Moses was through with it, it contained no signature either. He cut the signature off, turning it into an anonymous communication. Then he had copies made and mailed them to anyone—editors, officials, politicians—he thought might be interested, along with either a covering note stating ominously: "What he [the anonymous writer] says is true and there is a lot more to it," or a longer letter, such as another one to Corporation Counsel Tenney, stating: "Papp . . . adopts the old left wing technique of the agitator among artistic and so-called liberal groups, the big lie, etc. He was a communist of long-standing, affiliated with all the radicals, took the Fifth Amendment again and again, etc."

But it wasn't the 1940's any more. It was not even the early 1950's; the Senate hearings that had put an end to the McCarthy era had occurred in 1954. The tactics that had driven Stanley Isaacs out of his borough presidency and Rex Tugwell out of New York City backfired when the press learned about them now, especially after Constable, asked by Bill

Haddad if the letter did not smack of McCarthyism, replied: "What's wrong with McCarthy?" The letter produced the desired effect in the *Daily Mirror* and *Daily News* ("Back Big Bob, Mr. Mayor. Papp . . . has used the smear tactics you'd expect from one who took the Fifth Amendment") but nowhere else; the *Post*'s anger ("The letter . . . was the kind of reckless assault no man with any claim to decency would utilize") was echoed even by *Newsday* ("Perhaps . . . Jove has nodded").*

And Papp kept attacking—eloquently.

Dear Commissioner Moses:

. . . Perhaps in politics you have learned that by standing the truth on its head you can get enough people to believe a lie. . . . You were responsible for circulating a letter questioning . . . my political background, and my probity in handling festival funds. . . .

The letter represented your second position for denying the Festival the use of Central Park. Your first was soil erosion. . . . In position number three, you called the operation a disorderly type of performance.

May I bring to your attention the remarks of a prominent critic who described the Central Park audiences this way, "the long patient line of people hoping to get into an amphitheatre that seats 2,300 is a humbling sight for anyone who believes in the theater. The alert attention of the people who do succeed in getting in chastens anyone familiar with sophisticated audiences." . . .

Every civic minded organization has . . . expressed the opinion that Shakespeare in the Parks has had a civilizing effect rather than a disorderly one. One letter writer said "Thank you for making the park safe again." To keep Shakespeare out of the park because certain elements "might prey on the audience" is to say that we discontinue all gatherings of people in the park and leave it as a haven for crime. It is my conviction that the more activity in the parks, the less lawlessness.

I think everyone is growing tired of the distortions, outright fabrications and anonymous allegations put out by your office. No new excuse you can conjure up will stop us from pressing for the right to continue the free presentation of Shakespeare in Central Park.

In the court that mattered most to Moses—the court of public opinion—the Second Battle of Central Park, like the first, was a battle he couldn't win. Like the first battle, the second leapt onto the front pages with the initial exchange of salvos, and stayed there, getting the full New York media spotlight, for weeks. And in that spotlight Moses was again portrayed as villain. Media oversimplification had made that first fight "Moses Against Mothers." It made this fight "Moses Against Shakespeare"—*free* Shakespeare at that. FREE FESTIVAL DIES—MOSES CHASES SHAKESPEARE OFF PARK GRASS; THE BARD VS. THE COMMISSIONER—those were the headlines. Papp

---

* A *Post* editorial writer also contributed the following ditty, which ran as an editorial: *My name is Robert Moses, I'm Commissioner of Parks;/On the subject of free Shakespeare I have a few remarks:/If the people of this city want this theater on my grass,/They'll have to pay two bucks a head to get a Moses pass./Now it is clearly logical that those who disagree/Are probably subversive, or at least a threat to me./That's why I took it on myself to McCarthyize Joe Papp;/ Who questions my sagacity gets purged right off the map.*

even borrowed a pose from Arnold Newman: during the Tavern-on-the-Green fight, the photographer had posed his son leaning sadly against a symbolic Central Park snow fence; Papp posed leaning sadly against one, too.

The press was questioning Moses' statements now—and Moses could not endure questioning. When he said the Festival had harbored crime, reporters checked, and wrote stories like the one that said, "You can't prove it by the police records," which showed that there had, during two summer-long Festival seasons, been only two crimes on or near its site. Not only editorial writers but theater critics attacked him, as did columnists from Hedda Hopper and Leonard Lyons to Eleanor Roosevelt, his ancient and bitter enemy writing, "I cannot help wishing that his decision might be changed." The erosion really involved in the fight now was the erosion of Moses' most priceless property, his name—the continuation and acceleration of the decay that the Tavern-on-the-Green fight had begun three years before; newspapers were filled with letters like the one that said: "As a child I could visualize poor Mr. Moses working valiantly with pick and shovel, long after everyone else had gone home to bed, just so that I could have a place to play. Today we have to be practical and make it pay." During the 1930's and 1940's, schoolchildren had attached thousands of signatures to memorials praising Moses; now a delegation from Lafayette High School, unable to get in to see Wagner, handed Warren Moscow a petition with 1,500 signatures asking the Mayor to overrule the Park Commissioner. During the 1930's and 1940's, high schools had voted Moses "the most admired New Yorker"; now, when Helen Hayes, appearing at a high school as a member of a panel on "Commissioner Moses' move to abolish free Shakespeare," said, "Abolish Mr. Moses!" the students cheered. There was a telling indication of how much he feared what was happening. During the most severe crises of Robert Moses' career—the period in the Order Number 129 fight when it seemed likely that he would lose, for example—his iron constitution had suddenly betrayed him; each time he had been hospitalized during his adult life, it had been during such a crisis. Now he was hospitalized again, for eleven days, with an illness whose precise nature was carefully concealed, but which was variously described as "a bad cold," "a respiratory infection," "viral pneumonia," "pleurisy" and "nervous exhaustion." Pictures of him leaving the hospital for further rest in Babylon show a man gaunt, hollow-cheeked, with sunken eyes and, under them, circles so dark they seemed almost bruises—a man who suddenly looked, for the first time, old.

Although it would still not reveal completely the true nature of the relative power positions of Robert Moses and Robert Wagner, the spotlight focused on the Second Battle of Central Park by the massed New York media would make that relationship clearer than it had ever been before, for the press, able at last to look critically at Robert Moses, now wanted his decision reversed, and looked to the Mayor to do so—as was only natural, since it still conceived of Moses as the Mayor's subordinate.

Aiding in this development was a strategic decision of Papp's. "I made the Mayor responsible, really," the producer would recall, partly because "I think he would have liked to help us, he had been helpful to us before," primarily because "I felt that if only I could push the confrontation [between the Mayor and Moses], make the Mayor take responsibility," he would, because of the public opinion on the issue, have no choice but to overrule Moses. "Moses has had his say," he declared publicly. "The public has had theirs. It's now up to you, Mr. Mayor, to . . . insist that the Festival be permitted to operate free in Central Park . . ." Papp's plea was picked up by the press. "Is Bob Wagner or Bob Moses the Mayor of New York?" the *Post* demanded.

Luckily for Wagner, city hospital workers were on strike, and he was able to keep very busy trying to arrange a settlement. "He would rather be in the hospital strike twenty-four hours a day than this," Warren Moscow would recall. But the strike could not last forever, alas, and eventually the Mayor could no longer avoid reporters' queries.

Papp's intuition about Wagner was correct: the Mayor liked the idea of free Shakespeare in the park; he thought Moses' stand wholly unreasonable; he knew that the real source of the "Moses-Papp" feud was Constable, and, detesting Constable, he would have loved to overrule him. Moscow, always antagonistic to Moses, saw in this fight a chance to achieve a break between him and Wagner. But, Moscow came to realize, "Wagner was seriously handicapped" by his fear of the political power of the Catholic Church; if there was one man in the city sure to be influenced by Moses' innuendoes that Papp was a "left-winger," it was Francis Cardinal Spellman. And, of course, for both political and personal reasons it was wholly unfeasible for Wagner to fire Moses—and Moses made it clear that if the Mayor wanted to let Papp use Central Park, that was what he would have to do.

Infuriated that the Mayor would dare even contemplate intervening, Moses refused even to accept his telephone calls. Every time the Mayor's secretaries called Moses' office, they were told that the Park Commissioner was "in the field" and couldn't be reached.

Moses' stance subjected the Mayor to the largest doses of humiliation he had had to swallow since he had been caught between the press and Moses on Manhattantown three years before; not understanding that the Mayor couldn't fire his Park Commissioner, the press made it seem that he was afraid to. After the first day on which he had to confess that he had been unable to reach his appointee, Wagner promised reporters he would reach him the next day. When he was unable to, the *Post* addressed some advice to him: HOW TO FIND THE PARK COMMISSIONER. When he was still unable to the next day, the headlines began to read: MAYOR STILL SEEKS TO REACH MOSES. Even the *Times* found the spectacle worthy of a front-page story that began: "Mayor Wagner continued to search for Park Commissioner Robert Moses yesterday. . . . At the end of the day, the Mayor's quest was still unrewarded." At a press conference the following morning, Wagner "appeared irritated when asked if he had got in touch with Mr. Moses. 'I have many more important things to worry about,' he said, adding on a note of impatience: 'I'll get in touch with Mr. Moses.'" He didn't, however, and the heat was taken off only by Moses' hospitalization, which for eleven days made the Mayor's dilemma less obvious. Leaving the hospital, however, Moses was asked if he intended to confer with Wagner about Papp. His reply consisted of one word: "No." It was not until more than a week later that Wagner was able to announce that Moses had agreed to meet him for lunch and to promise, in response to reporters' questioning, that he would certainly bring up the anonymous letter. At the lunch, held at a neutral site—ironically, the Players Club, founded by the great Shakespearean actor Edwin Booth—the two men dined alone (Moscow was told to wait outside in the Mayor's limousine) and the precise details of the conversation are unknown. But, says Moscow, "when he came back [to the limousine], it was perfectly obvious that he had never had a chance to open his mouth." (The Mayor would himself later admit that the anonymous letter had never been mentioned.) "Riding back in the car with him, I said, 'What are you going to do?'

"He said, 'I don't know.'

"I said, 'Well, you're not going to fire him, are you?'

"He said, 'No, I'm not.'

"I said, 'Then you have to support him.'

"He said, '*You* say that?'

"I said he had no choice if he wasn't to look very weak indeed. So I drafted the statement. . . ." Released as fast as the Mayor could have it mimeographed, it said: "Although I can't approve of all the ways this has been handled, the only alternative would be to get a new Park Commissioner. I wouldn't consider that for a moment. He's too valuable a public servant."

The Mayor had surrendered, and that was the way the press played the story. MAYOR GIVES IN TO MOSES ULTIMATUM was the *Herald Tribune* headline. And the press did not minimize the loss to the city. Said the *News*: BILL SHAKESPEARE LOSES OUT AS WAGNER SUPPORTS MOSES. The Shakespeare Festival was eventually to be saved—and, as Moscow puts it, "we [the Wagner administration] were rescued"—only by the courts, and by certain of Moses' actions puzzling to those who believed he really wanted the Festival killed.

Turning from City Hall to the courthouse, Papp was rebuffed by a lower court, which reaffirmed the unconditionality of the Park Commissioner's power over parks, but the Appellate Division said he could not exercise it in "arbitrary and capricious" fashion, and ruled he had done so in the Papp case; the court declined to order Moses to issue a permit to the Festival but, in a somewhat ambiguous decision, said he must set "reasonable conditions" under which the Festival could reimburse the city for any expenses.

The Appellate Division ruling was a long way short of signaling defeat for Moses, of course. He could have appealed, and precedent suggests he would have won an appeal: every time similar cases had climbed the judicial ladder past Supreme and Appellate courts to the Court of Appeals rung, where the clamor of popular opinion grew faint, that tribunal had ruled that the law—his law—was clear: his power in parks was absolute. Even had his appeal been denied, moreover, its filing alone would have insured that there would be no Festival in 1959 at least. It was, in fact, within Moses' power to kill the Festival for the year even without an appeal. The Appellate Division had left the definition of "reasonable conditions" up to him; it would have been simple for him to justify conditions—a cash bond to guarantee reimbursement of the $100,000 to $150,000 he had estimated the Festival cost the city, for example—impossible for a shoestring producer to meet.

Instead, Moses said he would "of course abide by the court's decision," and said $20,000 would enable the performances to go on under "makeshift arrangements"—which, it turned out, would be almost precisely the same arrangements as had prevailed in the past. He himself asked the Board of Estimate to provide the funds so that Papp wouldn't have to raise them. The Board members, caught between Shakespeare and Spellman, tried to placate both sides, assailing Papp ("I want it clearly understood that in my vote for this item there is no approval of a creature named Papp," Jimmy Lyons said. "I hope that in the future Mr. Moses will find someone whose Americanism is unquestioned") but voting him the money, which, as it turned out, wasn't needed after all. Two philanthropists had previously offered Wagner donations of $10,000 apiece, and the Mayor announced that this money would be used instead. Although rehearsals began immediately, there was time remaining for only one production instead of three, but that production, *Julius Caesar,* was hailed as a triumph, with theater critics taking care to remind their readers whom it was a triumph over. With several broad avenues of legal action still wide open before Moses, this man, who never overlooked even the narrowest legal byway, declined to pursue them and consigned himself to the humiliation of defeat.

One explanation is that Moses realized that his previous position was disastrous for his public image, and wanted the fight ended as soon as possible—at any cost. Another, advanced by Moscow, always quick to see the basest motives behind Moses' every action, is that Moses believed the $20,000 figure was high enough to kill the Festival. According to this theory, Moses thought that Papp couldn't raise the money himself and believed that the Board of Estimate, afraid of Catholic reaction, wouldn't give it to him.

Not only the smallness of the figure Moses set but subsequent events do not support these theories, however. For Moses, who never forgave and never helped someone he considered his enemy, did not act that way with Joseph Papp. Needing trucks, lights and other heavy equipment for his production and unable to afford to buy or rent it, Papp asked the Park Department for it. Constable would have refused the request, but felt he'd better ask RM about it. "Oh, give it to him!" was the order. Moses would not see Papp in person—fifteen years later he would still never have met him—but after the season closed, Papp got a letter from him. The young producer had always wanted a theater for his production; the letter said that the Park Department was going to build one for him.

Raising the money for that theater took three years—it might never have gotten built at all if publisher George Delacorte had not contributed $150,000 of the necessary $400,000—and Papp was never consulted to the extent he wished on design, but for Moses to allow someone outside his organization a say in design was too much to expect. The crucial point was that Robert Moses built a showcase for the talents of the young man whom he had publicly been fighting so viciously. Papp would not agree with this interpretation. Warren Moscow, who saw the fight from Wagner's angle, would not agree. But Sid Shapiro, the aide closest to Robert Moses, found it difficult to avoid the sneaking suspicion that the fight, into which, Shapiro knew, Moses had been dragged only by the hysteria of a subordinate, was one fight that RM was not at all sorry to lose. There were times, in fact, when Shapiro found himself wondering if RM had not wanted to lose it.

Whatever the reason it ended the way it did, his fight with Robert Moses was one of the best things that ever happened to Joe Papp. By making him the hero of the city's wealthy liberals, it gave him the money—both from private contributions and, after the Fifth Amendment flurry had faded from public consciousness, from a Wagner-prodded city government—to make free plays a major element of the city's cultural life. By 1965, when Wagner left office, the city was giving Papp $420,000 a year, to add to $1,900,000 he had received since the Moses fight from private sources, and Papp's troupes were playing the Bard not only in the Delacorte Amphitheater but in the schools and, from ingenious theaters-on-wheels, in streets and parks all over New York. Papp was to become so big that when, in 1972, *Newsweek* did a cover story on him, his fight with Moses thirteen years before was worth no more than a few lines. But that fight had been the turning point in Papp's career. "It was the greatest publicity the Festival could have had," he himself says. The Park Commissioner whom Joe Papp never met, who was identified in the public mind as his enemy, was also his greatest benefactor.

But the Second Battle of Central Park was not one of the best things that ever happened to Robert Moses.

Occurring at a time when Moses' reputation was trembling in the balance, it helped tip that balance against him, not only by again demonstrating his contempt for the public but by demonstrating, even more clearly than the First Battle of Central Park, his dominance over the Mayor who was supposedly his superior, his exemption from the normal democratic processes. Stanley Isaacs had been asked on television, "Do you feel that the Mayor allows Moses to have his own way?" "Does anyone doubt it?" the elderly councilman had replied. The public had never understood before which one of the two men was really boss. But after the daily barrage of headlines dramatizing the Mayor's inability even to persuade his Park Commissioner to return a telephone call, the public understood now.

Moreover, the fight over Shakespeare in the Park made Moses a villain not only to the public but to the press. Constable's arrogance toward reporters, an arrogance they assumed had been ordered by Constable's boss, and in particular his ousting them bodily one day from the Arsenal—a public building—had infuriated not only the reporters involved but their editors, and it had given their publishers a new insight into the man who was so charming to them at dinner parties.

Before the Papp fight, press scrutiny of Robert Moses had been the work of Hortense Gabel's "chipmunks," a handful of young, mostly unknown reporters. There had still been many editors and reporters unwilling to face the falseness of the image they had helped create. There had still been newspapers—most notably, of course, the *Times*—that had shrunk back from the investigations into Title I. Those newspapers concerned with circulation and the headlines that could boost it understood better now that probing Moses' operations would yield headlines. Those newspapers concerned with their responsibility in a free society understood better now that Moses' operations not only could but should—must!—be scrutinized. It was during the Papp fight that the *Times* decided to do its own investigation of Title I, assigning hardworking Wayne Phillips to the task. The fight documented to the newspaper establishment what rebel reporters like Gleason and Cook and Haddad and Kahn had been trying to explain for years.

The media's new awareness was particularly significant because it is so strongly influenced by the images that are its own creation. For years, articles about Robert Moses had been researched, written and played in the light of the image of Robert Moses as hero. Now Robert Moses was a villain. If the press was to obtain information of the kind it had previously downplayed, now it would upplay it—mercilessly.

And a vast new store of that information quickly became available.

45. *Off to the Fair*

In May 1959, New York's Citizens Union, the most prestigious organization of the civic reformers from whose ranks Robert Moses had sprung but who had long since disowned him, sent his Slum Clearance Committee a list of questions about Title I sponsors. And the press not only demanded answers but, when Moses supplied them, played them as no Moses statement had ever been played.

The tone of Moses' reply to the Union was one of indignation that such questions should be asked of him, and of assurance that his answers would lay all doubts to rest. But that was not the way it worked out. To a question asking who had proposed the Manhattantown and Pratt developments, for example, Moses replied by naming Congressman Franklin D. Roosevelt, Jr., and various civic organizations. In previous years, the press would have printed that statement at face value. Now several papers pointed out that, as the *Post* put it, the reply "makes no mention of the fact that Samuel Caspert, a Tammany politician, was the prime mover in" both "sponsoring groups." Moses' admission that the sponsors had been selected without competitive bidding, and that Caspert and Company had been given Pratt despite years of failure to produce at Manhattantown, was emphasized, not buried.

Such admissions sounded sinister enough, but it was Questions 5 and 6—or, rather, Moses' answers to those questions—that were to prove most damaging. Question 5 was: "Were written reports made to the Mayor's Slum Clearance Committee, reviewing the qualifications of the various bidders?" Question 6 was: "If written reports were made, are they in the files of the Slum Clearance Committee, and may they be inspected by responsible persons or groups"—in particular the press? Of course written reports were made, Moses replied indignantly. Of course they were in the committee's files. And of course they "may be inspected by responsible groups or persons." The *Post*'s Haddad and Kahn and the *Telly*'s Gleason promptly said they wanted to inspect them. They could hardly believe it; they were going at last to get a look at Robert Moses' files—the files no outsider had ever looked at before. "It was a great day, the day he said we could look at those files, I'll tell you that," Haddad says. "A great day!"

About the reasons for Moses' reply—one of his greatest tactical blunders—it is possible only to speculate.

He may simply have felt he had no choice. A mayoral-appointed committee was no public authority whose records could be concealed behind the excuse that they were the records of a private corporation: they were clearly public records, open to the public by law. The people demanding them were, moreover, people who would hold him to that law: the reformers had never hesitated to take him to court, and against their money and free legal talent his customary stalling and expense-incurring legal maneuvers would not work; eventually, no matter how many appeals were instituted, there would be a final legal decision that the records must be opened. If he fought, he would lose. Losing—and losing to the men he hated above all others—would, for this man who hated to lose, be bad enough. And a refusal to open his books would make it seem as if he had something to hide. For this man to whom his public image was so dear, such a stance would be intolerable.

He may simply not have known what was in those files. His preoccupation for almost five years with the massive power dams at Massena and Niagara had forced him to delegate authority for Title I far more than for any other enterprise; perhaps he was simply unaware of the extent to which Shanahan, Spargo and Lebwohl had made political pull or financial tie the main qualification for Title I sponsorships. And even if he did know—and he must have been aware of at least some of his aides' manipulations, he must have had *some* idea of what was in those files—he appears not to have fully realized how those manipulations would look to the public. Insulated from the public for decades, insulated moreover by a coterie to whom such manipulations were standard procedure, he appears not to have understood how deeply revelation of Title I's secret scorecard would shock the other, larger, world outside.

Had he time to think about the situation, this realization might have come to him, but he had less time to think than ever. With barely six weeks before the opening of the great Massena dam, which Queen Elizabeth II and Vice President Richard M. Nixon were scheduled to attend, the dam was far from completed; the contractors had to be driven, and a thousand last-minute details had to be overseen, and, with the pages of that huge calendar on the wall over his head falling inexorably one by one, Moses was working fourteen, sixteen, eighteen hours a day. Bill Chapin was to remember the last months before the Massena opening, with the telephone awakening him and his boss's voice rasping over it sometimes at midnight and sometimes at 5 A.M. and sometimes during the hours between, as months of unmitigated exhaustion, and Bill Chapin was fifty-five. Robert Moses was seventy. Incredibly, he showed not a sign of fatigue—he seemed as tireless at seventy as he had been at thirty. But there was little time to spare for administration of the city park system, where the Papp episode was a time-consuming irritant, for the eleven major state park expansion projects he was undertaking on Long Island, the four major expressways he was ramming through the city, the two great suspension bridges, one under way, the other in the final stages of planning—and certainly not for consideration of the best way to handle the impudent Citizens Union request.

He may simply have felt that he could conceal most of the scorecard.

Whether with or without his knowledge, the files would, when reporters got to see them, be stripped virtually clean of revealing material; he may have believed that it was possible for his aides to remove all of it. Moreover, reporters had investigated his operations before. In almost every case, his reputation had insured that editors had not given the reporters the time necessary to investigate in the necessary depth. In the rare cases in which reporters—such as Milton Racusin—had nonetheless uncovered some of his secrets, his influence with publishers had been sufficient to get the stories killed or toned down. He may have heard so much about investigations that he no longer worried about them. And, as would later become apparent, he had not realized the crucial change that had occurred: the tarnishing of his reputation to a point at which reporters would now be given the time to make their investigations thorough, and at which the facts they uncovered would now be examined and played by the same standards as facts revealed about other public officials, standards which placed a premium on sensationalism. For years every fact he fed the press had been grist for a mill whose end product was something sweet to him. He appears not to have realized until he saw the play of his replies to the Citizens Union that now any facts the press uncovered were going to be grist for a mill that could grind out only bitterness. And that realization came too late. He had already put himself on record publicly. He tried to draw back, stalling for two weeks while Triborough counsel Lebwohl told the reporters who telephoned every day that the records were still being "assembled." But with editorials reminding the public of his promise to make them available, he could not stall indefinitely. On May 29, 1959, Haddad and Kahn (Gleason apparently did not call that day), telephoning Lebwohl, were sullenly told to come ahead.

"Christ, we were just dying to get to see that stuff," Haddad recalls. "And of course there was nothing there."

After he and Kahn had arrived at the Triborough Authority's Randall's Island headquarters, Lebwohl kept them waiting "for hours" before sending a secretary to escort them into a small narrow room, walls painted institutional green, in the middle of which was a narrow conference table on which had been piled stacks of file folders. The moment when the two reporters flipped open the first one was historic; Robert Moses had been in public office for thirty-five years, and this was the first time that any reporter had gotten a look at his files. Historic but not significant. The folders were bulging with papers, but these papers turned out to be building plans, brochures, formal memoranda written for the record—in Haddad's words, "all pro forma stuff." They could find no information of significance—particularly not about the individuals in whom they were most interested: the sponsors. The next day, after being kept waiting for hours again, the two reporters asked Lebwohl where this information was, and were referred to Spargo. Haddad recalls their meeting with Triborough's general manager vividly—"that little shit sitting in that big office eating a bowl of soup" while feeding them only evasive answers. "What qualified a sponsor to become a sponsor—that was all we were asking," Kahn recalls. "We didn't even suspect that a sponsor might be someone who had never built something and had no money or financial backing to build anything." But they could get no answers to their questions and the files yielded none and seemed likely to yield none. "They had stripped them completely," Haddad recalls.

"But for some reason," Kahn says, "we kept looking. It was just like police work. You write down every name you come across, and that night when you get back to the office, you check it in the clips, just in case you'll find something."

"We were tilting at windmills," Haddad says, and the accuracy of the image seems demonstrated by their mount. The giants they were trying to pull down from their castles—Moses, Shanahan, Rosenman, Goldwater—had big black Cadillacs; so did Haddad—a Cadillac he had bought for twenty-two dollars.

"It was ancient," the young reporter would recall. The windows rolled up and down—sometimes; generally they remained firmly in whichever position they happened to be. The *Post* copy girls whom Haddad squired became accustomed to getting very wet in the rain. The window problem was, however, insignificant compared to the overheating problem; recalling the Title I investigation years later, Joe Kahn recalls more vividly than the stories he wrote the difficulty in keeping the engine cool while researching them. The trip back downtown to the *Post* office from Randall's Island was too far for the vehicle, which "just managed to make it to Sixty-fourth Street," where there was a gas station at which they could obtain enough water to keep the engine cool as far as the Downtown Athletic Club, whose friendly doorman would run inside for water whenever he saw them coming. The overheating problem was complicated by the hood problem, which resembled the window problem: it frequently wouldn't go up. Once, carried away by enthusiasm, they tried to make it all the way back to their office without stopping for water. The car boiled over in the Battery Park underpass, and the hood stuck fast. Passing motorists gaped as the two reporters tried to cool off the car by throwing pails of water on the closed hood. Every morning they would pull up to Triborough headquarters in that sputtering car—apprehensive; "it looked like a military fortress, and they had guards all around"—and alight, looking in their shabby sports jackets like the $140-a-week reporters they were (in deference to their surroundings, Haddad wore a tie, but this attempt at respectability was somewhat undermined by his inability to button his collars; he had bought the wrong size shirts), and walk inside, to sit waiting for hours for Lebwohl's pleasure and then be shown into the narrow little room by a flunky who made no attempt to conceal his contempt, to begin hours of plowing through meaningless documents, hoping that somewhere in those files they would find information enabling them to prove that the Moses image was a false image.

And then one day they found it.

It was in one of the file folders relating to a Title I project which had received almost no publicity at all: one called "Mid-Harlem." In that folder, apparently overlooked by whoever had stripped it, was a letter ("just this long," Kahn would recall, holding up his fingers an inch or two apart) from a man applying to be one of the sponsors, together with a note indicating that his application had been approved. The man's name was Louis I. Pokrass. Haddad seemed to recall hearing that name during his days with the Kefauver Crime Committee, but he couldn't recall in what connection. Back in the office that night, however, he pulled Pokrass' clip file—and "as soon as I saw those clips, I said, 'Holy Christ! Joe! Look at this!' " "This" was clips on Kefauver Committee hearings in which it had been disclosed that in his previous business dealings Louis I. Pokrass had had as secret partners underworld kingpins Frank Costello, Meyer Lansky and Joe Adonis.

"That was the one that did it," Kahn says. "Pokrass was the guy that crumbled him. When organized crime got into the picture, that blew the lid off." *Frank Costello* was a name that, to the average newspaper reader, threw off reverberations as powerful in one context as *Robert Moses* did in another. And the story in which this Costello associate figured was as simple and dramatic as most previous slum clearance stories had been complicated and obscure. With the first *Post* headline on June 30, 1959, on the new revelation —COSTELLO PAL GOT TITLE I DEAL—Moses' urban renewal program was scandal in a way in which, despite three years of previous exposés, it had never been scandal before. Overlooked by Moses' file strippers among the bland minutes and reassuring brochures in the "Mid-Harlem" file folders had been another single sheet of paper—not even a full-size sheet of paper but a handwritten note—containing dynamite enough not merely to chip but to blast a substantial hole in the Moses image. The handwriting on the note was Tom Shanahan's, and what the note said was that he had been made aware of a "delicate situation" involving Pokrass—and the date on the note was several weeks before the Slum Clearance Committee had approved Pokrass' application. Gleason either came across that piece of note paper himself or was fed it by Haddad, and with the first *World-Telegram* headline the following day—BANKER HAD WARNING ON COSTELLO PAL—the scandal had an added, significant dimension: not only had Robert Moses' committee approved an associate of racketeers as a slum clearance sponsor, it had done so although Moses' key colleague on the committee had known he was an associate of racketeers.

Of all the charges that might have "crumbled" the image of Robert Moses, none could have been more unfair. He had never met Pokrass; if he had ever heard his name, he did not recall it. He certainly had no idea that one of his sponsors had had underworld connections. To him, the Mid-Harlem sponsors were "Colonel Bennett's group"; it was represented by the former judge, State Attorney General, Democratic gubernatorial candidate and, as chairman of the City Planning Commission, his obedient lackey, Colonel John J. Bennett. Moses had left the investigation of the syndicate behind Bennett entirely to Shanahan—Mid-Harlem was one of the projects over which he had delegated the banker complete authority. But

Kahn was right. By giving the Title I program underworld overtones, the Pokrass story was the one that crumbled him.

Not only reporters but other persons hostile to the Coordinator suddenly, for the first time, began trying to find other evidences of underworld "infiltration" of Title I, and an aide in the Comptroller's office soon found one: in the payroll records filed in the office by the Washington Square Village Corporation, he told Gleason, there appeared, as a temporary night watchman, the name of Vincent (the Chin) Gigante, a former boxer who had been accused—and then acquitted—of being the "hit man" in a "contract" put out on Costello by other Mafia figures; he had, a year before, ambushed the underworld overlord in his apartment-house lobby, but had only grazed him with a pistol shot. REVEAL THUG HELD TITLE I VILLAGE JOB, the *World-Telegram* blared.

"Could any charge be more grotesque?" Moses demanded. Hardly. The Chin had not been hired by the Title I committee. He had not been hired by the sponsor to whom the committee had awarded the "Village job." He had not even been hired by the contractor to whom the sponsor had awarded the construction work on the job—not that the identity of men on the contractor's payroll would have been scrutinized by the sponsor anyway, much less by the committee. He had been hired by one of the contractor's subcontractors. "The inference is that this committee should not have permitted his employment and, having stood idly by while this atrocity went on, is guilty of association with mysterious gangsters," Moses said. "This committee has no responsibility for the help employed by contractors for sponsors and could not conceivably have . . . And in any event, as a matter of fairness and decency, is Mr. Gigante, who was acquitted of failure to take good aim at Mr. Costello, when out of jail not entitled to find work of some sort to keep him out of further mischief?" Such witty ridicule would once have turned back any charge; the reporter responsible would have been hastily reassigned. Now, he was reinforced. A whole platoon of investigative reporters rode out on the slum clearance trail.

The trail was marked by anonymous tips and by other scattered pieces of information overlooked in Moses' files—marked clearly enough so that these reporters could see now where it was really leading. Abandoning side trips like the search for underworld connections, they stuck now on the main road that led them at last to the truly significant secret behind Title I, the secret that would destroy the heart of the Moses legend.

Haddad led the pack, for he had the gift of seeing patterns, and he saw them in the seemingly innocuous material—minutes, memos, letters, notes—scattered before him on the narrow table in the little room. One, for example, was woven around press agents. Reading through endless reams of documents, Haddad noticed that two names kept reappearing in files relating to different projects: William J. Donoghue and Sydney S. Baron. He didn't know who Donoghue was, but Kahn, with his encyclopedic knowledge of city politics, did: a press secretary for both O'Dwyer and Impellitteri and a key Tammany insider. And everyone knew who Baron was, of course:

Carmine De Sapio's personal publicist. Pulling up his tie as far as it would go to conceal his opened shirt collar, Haddad walked with Kahn onto the ankle-deep carpets of the silken-draperied, sliding-paneled room—adorned with just one photograph: that of a man with dark-tinted glasses—that was Sydney Baron's office, and wrung from him an admission that he had formed an "association" of Title I sponsors that paid him $1,500 a month. He swore that he had "never received a fee" from individual sponsors, but federal audits—leaked to Haddad now by Walter Fried, who had chafed so long at his inability to curb Moses—revealed that he lied. And one sponsor told the reporters: "It would be fantastic to tell you we hired Baron for any other reason than his influence." And Kahn and Haddad made clear where that influence came from, identifying Baron as "Tammany's and Carmine De Sapio's press chief." The same story was repeated with Donoghue.

Gleason, thundering hard at Haddad's heels, had received a tip about a ninety-two-acre tract at Clason Point on Long Island Sound in the Bronx that had been selected for a slum clearance project to be called "Soundview" even though it was not a slum at all but a community of 245 neat, well-tended bungalows: the tipster said that Moses' Slum Clearance Committee had agreed to purchase the tract for a million dollars although its present owners had recently purchased it for half a million—thereby giving those owners a quick half-million-dollar profit before they even began to build the "high-rent" apartments that the committee had approved for the site. According to the tipster, the land was held in the name of a "dummy" owner, and it would be worth Gleason's while to find out who the real owner was. The deeds on file in the Bronx County Courthouse showed the owner to be a Miss Helen Nugent, who Gleason guessed at once was a secretary in some lawyer's office.

But whose office? Who was Miss Nugent a dummy for? Who was making the half million—and the millions more that were to come? Gleason learned that her employer was the law firm of Goldwater & Flynn. Goldwater denied that he had any financial interest in the project, maintaining he was only the attorney for the real owners. But he refused to reveal their identity, and the *Telly*'s head (played above a picture of neat bungalows captioned "This Is a Slum?") noted that the "MYSTERY WOMAN'S" BOSS was "DEM BIGWIG" Goldwater, and under that head, Fred Cook, writing the hell out of the story, said that the Soundview "deal" represented "a clear $500,000 windfall to political insiders," and soon he and other newspapers were noting that Ed Flynn's old partner was still a power in Bronx politics under Flynn successor Charles Buckley—and that he and his son represented not only Soundview but two other controversial Title I projects.

"Influence." "Dem Bigwig." "Tammany." "Political Insiders." De Sapio. Buckley. The Boss of Manhattan and the Boss of the Bronx were somehow involved—deeply involved—in a Moses program. Following the trail left by those overlooked documents in Moses' files, the hard-riding reporters had come at last upon the secret that would destroy the heart of the Moses legend: the fact that this man who supposedly scorned politicians had allowed the top echelon of New York's politicians to reap fortunes from his Title I program. And they led their readers to the secret—with stories that, linking Moses to politicians, were as accurate as earlier stories linking him to the underworld had been unfair. A letter to the *Times* showed that at least one reader was grasping the significance of these revelations. It was a letter such as had never before been printed about Robert Moses. "Robert Moses," the letter said, "is a boss like De Sapio himself."

And of course the deeper the reporters delved, the more there began to come into focus the shadowy figure of the man who formed the key connection between Moses and the machine, and the clearer that connection became.

Haddad had been hearing about Shanahan for years, of course. During his earlier investigations into the Building Department and Housing Authority, he had learned that, as he puts it, "the word was out that if you wanted to do any kind of work with the city you had to put your money in Federation—I mean, it was no secret. Everyone you talked to seemed to know it." And hardly had a surly Moses aide dumped the first batch of Slum Clearance Committee minutes in front of him when he noticed that the committee was taking many decisions "on report and recommendation of vice chairman." Among these decisions, he noticed, were many of those on the selection of sponsors. What, he asked Lebwohl, was the vice chairman's role in the selection process? Well, Lebwohl replied, he "qualifies" them. And what, Haddad asked, did that mean? He "uses his bank to check the financial responsibility of potential sponsors, at no cost to the committee," Lebwohl replied. "He determines who is the most qualified." And, Haddad asked, did the committee always accept Shanahan's recommendation? Usually, Lebwohl replied.

The discerner of patterns saw the pattern then. "Moses was up in the clouds as far as Title I was concerned," he says. "He was the grey eminence. Shanahan was the administrative force. Gradually we began to find out that Shanahan was making all the decisions." For weeks, however, the vice chairman's approval of the Pokrass designation was the only newsworthy decision he and Kahn could directly lay at his door. Then, one day one of the anonymous calls—"You answer every one; you're always hoping that this is the one that will blow the whole thing open"—told Kahn that one sponsor approved by Shanahan not only had deposited huge sums of money in Shanahan's bank but had also, when he received his first commitment from the FHA for a $3,000,000 loan, borrowed the money from Shanahan's bank, and was currently negotiating with the FHA for a $10,000,000 loan, which he was also planning to make from Shanahan's bank. The caller told Kahn that the FHA guarantee made these loans prime, risk-free business on which the bank would make more than a million dollars in interest—and that, since the guarantee applications had been made to the FHA, his tip could be verified. Getting the hint, Haddad went to the FHA—and verified it, and began at last to break the Shanahan story.

Shanahan flatly refused to talk to reporters, or to let them see any of

Federation's records, but with the story breaking, Haddad's phone was hot with tips—that Moses had deposited millions of Triborough funds in Shanahan's bank; that slumlord Ungar's sponsorship had been approved by Shanahan after he offered to deposit $700,000; that Shanahan was a director of at least one Title I company. Checking these tips, Haddad found they checked out. And his stories identified Shanahan to the public, not as the "banker" or "philanthropist" that newspapers had called him in the past but in the role that made him important to Moses: "a fund-raiser and campaign treasurer for the Democratic Party . . . and a close friend of Tammany leader De Sapio."

The band of eager young reporters was meeting at the corner table in Blake's Artists and Writers Bar almost every evening now. They had it down to a system. "The only way to keep it going was to keep the papers goosing each other," Haddad would reminisce years later. "If nobody picked it up, we were dead. So we'd leave a little piece out of a story, and give that piece to Gene or Woody so they'd have a new lead, and they'd do the same for us. Sometimes, I'd even give them carbons of my stories, so they'd have it right in their desk. Their editor would say, 'Check this out,' and they'd have it right there."

Each day now they could see their strategy working. The *Post,* of course, had always played Title I revelations as they should be played. James Wechsler "helped you in the same way that a magazine editor or a book editor helps you—a real kind of involvement, of suggestion, of criticism, of rewriting," Haddad recalls. "The editorial support—you couldn't ask for better placement in the paper, you couldn't ask for better editorials." As for Wechsler's boss, "There was constant pressure on Mrs. Schiff," Haddad would say. "But she never buckled." Years later, he could still recall sitting with Kahn in the city room one night, hour after hour, while, upstairs, in Mrs. Schiff's office, she and Wechsler were, the reporter knew, receiving telephone calls from her good friend Sam Rosenman and from other friends she respected assailing her for printing their previous stories and asking her not to print any more—while in front of them was the story he had just written for the next day, even more hard-hitting than the previous stories had been—waiting for the decision on whether the paper would run it, and Wechsler coming down finally and saying: "Just be sure you're thorough. We're not going to stop anything you write."

And now, thanks to the "chipmunks'" strategy, the editors of the *World-Telegram* were—at last—enthusiastic, too, even if their enthusiasm was based less on principle than on concern that they not be beaten by a competitor. Gleason and Cook and Woody Klein didn't have to sell editors on new material now; the editors were begging for it. Title I was page one now, not only in the *Post* but in the *Telly*—and, more and more, in the *Journal-American.* "First they started picking up our stuff, and then Marty Steadman, a good, tough reporter, started developing some of his own. And one day, they had an eight-banner. They were in, too!"

"We knew, to really break it open, the *Times* and the *Trib* had to start picking it up," Haddad says. Now Peter Braestrup rejoined Haddad, Gleason, Klein and Steadman (Kahn, too competitive to share, would never come and Cook had no time to) at the corner table: the *Trib* was in.

Of all the factors that had kept Moses' popularity intact for thirty-five years, none was more important than the support of the newspaper whose principal stockholder felt "there has never been as great a public servant." During the first months of 1959, despite all the Title I exposés by other papers, he had continued to enjoy that support. "There was a time . . . ," Cook would write, "when . . . we could practically guarantee that any critical article of ours in the afternoon would bring a featured, official denial in *The New York Times* in the morning." While the *Times* may not have been a crusading newspaper, however, it was a newspaper of record—proud of being *the* newspaper of record. And now the records were open. Formal press conferences were being held—not only by the Mayor but by Monroe Goldwater and Sidney Ungar. If the *Times* had wanted to ignore the Goldwater and Ungar revelations, it would have been difficult for it to do so. After the Papp incident, moreover, there seemed to be less of a desire on the part of the paper's editors to do so—Charlie Grutzner, who had some years earlier been pulled off the housing beat because his articles angered Moses, was put back on it, and Wayne Phillips was assigned to an in-depth investigation. Haddad knew a new era was dawning when he picked up the *Times* on the morning of June 1, 1959, and read—on page one—"The redevelopment plan proposed by Robert Moses for the Soundview slum-clearance project calls for the payment of nearly $400,000 [sic] for land that the owners had offered for nothing."

The entrance of the *Times*, with its ample space, immediately gave the Title I exposés a new dimension and depth. The daily running stories in the PM's averaged about 800 words; a four-part series that the *Times* began on June 26 ran 8,000; although the impression would later exist that that series had contained many new revelations, it contained hardly any that Haddad or Gleason hadn't uncovered before; all that had happened was that, by bringing them all together in a unified form, Phillips had shown the city the over-all picture of its slum clearance program, and by so doing had shown it in all its shocking dimensions.

The entrance of the *Times* also gave the Title I exposés a new respectability, the cachet conferred by the newspaper's reputation for accuracy. Political officials suddenly became willing to comment. Stanley Isaacs and a young, movie-star-handsome congressman named John V. Lindsay had been assailing Moses' practices for months, but now politicians joined the parade in force—and each comment made a new article, kept the story rolling, kept momentum building.

In every city room in New York, now, the phones were, in Haddad's words, "jumping off the hook." Many of the tips coming over them were checking out into stories. "The thing was feeding on itself now, getting bigger and bigger," Kahn says. "It was the greatest time of my life," Haddad recalls. "We were making 140 bucks a week—and it was just great."

For months—years, really—all the months and years in which the Title I exposés had been building up, it had been a young man's war, a guerrilla action carried out by what Kahn called "newspapermen who weren't part of the newspaper establishment," and an action that had, moreover, been ridiculed by older, cynical, tired reporters. Haddad and Gleason first noticed the change when they stopped by Room 9, the City Hall Press Room. The older reporters were noticeably more friendly now. Then they became more helpful. Looking up from the Room 9 desk at which he was sitting one day, Haddad found one standing over him, waiting to fill him in on details of political alliances of New York. When Gleason had first been interrupting Wagner's staid, friendly, gentlemanly press conferences with embarrassing questions—and refusing to let evasions go unchallenged—many of the older reporters had been openly hostile to him, believing he was disturbing their "rapport" with the Mayor, some of them going so far as to ask other questions on less controversial topics so as to change the subject. Now, when Gleason—joined by Haddad—began pressing the Mayor for answers, there were no interruptions—and even some follow-up questions from the older men. Pressing particularly hard about Goldwater's conduct in Title I, Gleason roused Wagner to anger. "You can just get out of this room," he said. From the other reporters, there came a low murmur of disapproval. "You can't do that, Mayor," a voice said clearly. Gleason stayed. The next day *World-Telegram* city editor Norton Mockridge ordered up John Ferris' admiring story on Gleason, and the story included the line: "No one awes him." Haddad knew for sure that the times were changing in the city rooms on that long night when he sat waiting for hours for Mrs. Schiff's decision on whether to run the story he had written for the next day. He noticed that an elderly former photo editor, who had advanced to a more exalted editorship and now considered laying out pictures beneath him, was waiting around, too, hours past his time to go home. Finally, Haddad asked him why he was staying. Oh, the old newspaperman said embarrassedly, as offhand as if he did such things all the time, I might as well stick around to do the picture layout on it if it goes.

Bigger and bigger now, the stories were also closer and closer—to Robert Moses.

Haddad and Kahn had noticed Donoghue's name on the payrolls of Title I sponsors. Now they learned that it was also on the payrolls of Moses' public authorities. Showing up on the payrolls of shady sponsors, they told the public, was "Robert Moses' personal publicist."

Many of the anonymous tips concerned Lebwohl, the Moses aide whose Moses-enriched "relocation" firm had hounded from their homes thousands of families in the way of the Cross-Bronx Expressway and other Moses projects.

"We had good information that Lebwohl was chummy with an architect close to Charlie Buckley" who had been given many Title I contracts, Kahn recalls. They interviewed him.

After we had hammered away at [Lebwohl] for about an hour, he finally admitted that he and the sponsor patronized the same health club. "If you pass a man going across the gym, is that a crime?" he asked. "I can't control the membership of a private health club."

"But isn't it true that you eat with him later and he picks up the check?" Lebwohl was asked.

"Not all the time," was the answer—the one we had been waiting for.

Leaving Lebwohl's office, Kahn noticed that Haddad, usually so "fiery and tough," looked pensive. Finally the younger reporter asked him if he felt they should use the interview. "Why not?" Kahn said. "You're not suddenly getting soft, are you?"

"No, it's not that," Haddad said sadly. "It's just that all during the time you were throwing the questions, I couldn't take my eyes off the photograph of his wife and kids on the desk."

Kahn had noticed the photos himself—and he had known Lebwohl for a long time. "A reporter," he was to write, "is human and he is moved by what he sees and hears as much as other people." But, he was to add, "in the end he must live with himself. . . . I'm sorry, I told Bill. I felt for the Lebwohl family as much as he did, but—it had to be done. And it was." And Kahn's stories about Lebwohl identified him not as a "city official" but as he should have been identified all along: "Robert Moses' right arm." The circle of scandal was drawing closer around the man who had never been linked with scandal.

And then it drew tighter still, with what Cook termed "the first peep that has been obtained into the workings of the private consultant's role—one that Mr. Spargo frequently fills." Item by item now, the investigators were finding out about the supreme bloodhound, the man "who always kept notes"—that his salary as Triborough general manager was $40,000, as high as the Mayor's; that in addition to that salary he had received "on the recommendation of Mr. Robert Moses" $35,000 in consultant's fees from the Nassau County Bridge Authority, and, from Moses' own State Power and Jones Beach authorities, a total of $243,000 in additional fees; that, while serving as director of the Slum Clearance Committee, he was a director of Shanahan's Federation bank, which had made secret profits on slum clearance deals. Moses' identification with Lebwohl had gotten his name out of the back paragraphs of these "scandal" stories and into the leads; his identification with Spargo got it into headlines—headlines over profiles identifying Spargo as MR. MOSES' MAN, eight banners in the *Telly* and *Journal*, big screamers in the *Post*—TIE MOSES AIDE TO BOND FEE; FEES PAID TO MOSES OFFICIALS FOR BRIDGE BONDS; the $243,000 revelation put Moses' name—in a story that reeked of scandal—on the front page of *The New York Times*. Shanahan wasn't just a "banker" any more; he was MOSES' BANKER AIDE. After decades of building up an empire based on the raw material out of which newspapers produced scandal, Robert Moses' name was in eight banners of scandal at last.

He kept it there himself. Unable to endure even the hint of criticism, he simply could not ignore attacks aimed at his associates. He had to respond, and he did so almost frantically, trying to answer each charge, his messengers rushing replies marked "For Immediate Release" to newspaper offices sometimes within an angry hour of the time those newspapers hit the stands.

But response was a self-defeating tactic now. Its primary effect was to bring himself, hitherto only a figure behind the Shanahans, Spargos and Lebwohls, front and center, thereby accomplishing what the reporters, despite all their efforts, had not previously been able to accomplish: to make himself, rather than them, the primary target.

Moreover, to Moses response meant attack. Since it was primarily the press making the charges he was opposing, he attacked the press. As usual, he attacked on all fronts. Haddad soon became aware that investigators were checking into his whole life history, trying, the reporter believed, to find some "handle" that could be used against him. Reporters were trying to cover the meetings of the Slum Clearance Committee in Triborough headquarters now. Moses saw to it that they were not told what time the meetings would be over, so they had to wait in the lobby downstairs—his guards would not permit them up to the second floor, where the meetings were held—for hours so that they would not miss the participants emerging. Previously, reporters up at Randall's Island would be invited to the sumptuous lunches at which Moses would charm them; now not only were they not invited, but when Moses learned that, afraid to leave the island and travel all the way back to Manhattan for lunch, they had been making do with Cokes and candy bars from the vending machines in a corridor off the lobby, he had the door to the corridor locked. Wagner may have been bullied at his press conferences; Moses was not. The Coordinator, fresh from his lunch, strode into the room in which reporters were waiting, hungry and thirsty, after one four-hour committee meeting. ("He was," Gleason reported in a memo to his office, "licking his chops—literally.") Would it perhaps help if the reporters were allowed to see the committee's agenda so they could know what topics the committee had discussed? "No," Moses said. The reporters waited for him to say something else. He said nothing. Finally, the reporters began asking other questions. Gleason asked one in his bullying style. "Jesus, [Moses] seemed to tower when he came out of his seat," Haddad recalls. Moses had two words for Gleason: "Get out." The other reporters tried the technique that had worked with Wagner, saying unless Gleason stayed they would all go. Without another word, Moses rose and strode from the room. The press conference was over. Moses' main fire was directed over reporters' heads, of course. Triborough's messengers were deluging publishers and their top editors with personal complaints. Moses was soon taking the fight to the press on a dozen different fronts.

But fighting the press is a battle that no public official can win, for the battleground is not just of the press's choosing—it *is* the press. His attacks would be played as the media wanted them played. Moreover, attacking a particular newspaper—and because the articles were to a great extent exposés that were breaking in one paper at a time, his attacks were often against a specific newspaper—was practically the surest guarantee that that newspaper would attack him again in its turn. The story that had enraged

Moses may have been written by an individual reporter, but it was not the reporter alone who would have to bear responsibility for it and defend it to the publisher or chief editor. Lower-ranking editors—with stories of such significance, editors on several levels—would have had to approve it. Therefore, when Moses attacked a newspaper publicly or in a private letter to its publisher, a lot of people on that newspaper had to justify themselves. And the most effective method of justification was to find other things wrong with the Title I program—and to write more stories. Many key newspapermen in New York had previously had a vested interest in preserving Moses' image; now many of these same journalists had a vested interest in destroying it. What was needed was discreet silence—the wait until the storm was over—and silence was one commodity it had never been within Moses' power to deliver.

The self-defeating nature of Moses' tactics was demonstrated in developments on the *Times* front.

Even after Grutzner and Phillips had begun breaking—and receiving good play on—Title I revelations, the paper's attitude toward its long-time hero was decidedly schizophrenic. Moses attacked the reporters personally—to one Phillips piece he replied on June 22, "The *Times* reporter is either very befuddled or deliberately malicious"—and the *Times*'s handling of his replies embittered other reporters, one of whom, Gay Talese, was to write in his history of the paper:

> . . . his letters of objection did not appear in the "Letters to the Editor" space, where they belonged; instead they were published on various days within the news columns as *news,* being prefaced by an explanatory paragraph, appearing under a news headline, and being given immediate and serious play. This not only raised readers' doubts about the credibility of the series, but it also took some of the edge off the series, which the reporter had carefully researched for months—and which was accurate and objective, if not totally satisfactory to Moses in all of its detail and interpretation.

When, on June 25, Moses used his familiar resignation gambit on Wagner, the *Times*'s editorial response was its traditional one: "Our confidence in Mr. Moses as an honest, incomparably able public servant is unshaken. His resignation from any office would be an irreparable loss. Where is his equal?"

But as Moses continued to attack—criticizing even straight running news stories on breaking developments—the *Times*'s ardor began almost visibly to cool. When Grutzner helped break the Gigante story, Moses replied, "This is one of those 'startling disclosures' promised by the *Times* over the radio in the morning to solicit new readers." Grutzner's city-room editors responded by okaying his submission of a list of written questions to Moses. Moses tried to go over their heads. "I immediately protested to Orvil Dryfoos, president of the *Times*, about innuendoes in those questions," he says. The result, in Moses' own words:

> In spite of a placating reply by Managing Editor Turner Catledge, the *Times* continued in this vein, printing slanted, inaccurate and misleading stories. . . . a

reporter needled a Federal housing official into declaring that prior approval of the Bellevue South project had not been obtained. I wrote to Dryfoos again, pointing out that . . . "this is not the kind of journalism we have been led to expect from a great newspaper." Additional reporters were assigned, and I was soon presented with the fruit of their labor—a new questionnaire of the kind ordinarily addressed to Appalachian thugs, dope peddlers, etc. Since, as I wrote Dryfoos, they were "directed only at baiting me in the hope that your staff can cash in on some more sensationalism," I decided not to answer them.

He tried to go over everyone's head—reporters', editors', president's—in July, following an incident that occurred during a vacation, an incident that, were he susceptible to humiliation, would have been deeply humiliating. He described it in a letter to his old and close friend Arthur Hays Sulzberger, the *Times*'s publisher.

Yesterday afternoon, following a series of similar phone calls from the *Times* addressed directly and indirectly to officials in Puerto Rico and the Virgin Islands, a reporter from *El Mundo* interrupted Mary and me at the San Juan airport to ask grossly insulting questions, one of which was what I had to say about relations with the "underworld" in connection with Title One housing in New York. I was able to glance at some of the questions on a yellow sheet which this reporter said were telephoned from the *Times*. The word "underworld" was definitely and unmistakably on this sheet. There were several people around who heard this. Officials in the area told me of similar phone questions aimed to embarrass me. Fortunately, the only effect of these questions on the people who invited me down was to lower the prestige of the *Times*.

This response worked for a while. Sulzberger apologized, and shortly thereafter invited Moses, as he did every summer, to visit Iphigene and himself at their country home. "A lot of water has gone under the bridge . . . ," the publisher wrote, "but I hope it hasn't washed the bridge away." "The bridge is pretty damn rickety, what with the flood of abuse and bilge we have been subjected to, but we shall drop in," Moses replied. For some weeks thereafter, the *Times*'s Title I play, while substantial, appeared considerably toned down.

But what he had done could no longer be undone. The *Times*'s coverage of Title I had been balanced on a razor's edge. His efforts had tipped the balance—against himself. As the revelations in other papers continued, the *Times* began to pick them up again, and to play them bigger and bigger. Not only Phillips and Grutzner but their immediate superiors, and some not so immediate, were now in the same boat as their counterparts on the *Herald Tribune* and the *Journal-American* and the *World-Telegram*: once they had had a vested interest in building Moses up, now they had one in tearing him down, in finding new material that would support earlier articles. If new material was to be available to these newspapers now, they would do their best to join the *Post* in giving it proper play. And as the telephone tips, and the anonymous letters, and the public statements, and the federal and city audits poured in to all these different city rooms, these reporters and editors had all the material they needed. They were not chipping away any longer at the towering Moses image, they were chopping away at it—with great roundhouse swings of the media ax—chopping away day after day, week after week, month after month. First, it had been Moses' programs that had been under attack. Then it had been his aides. And now, finally, it was he himself.

"The Great Statesman McKee is a synthetic character which never actually existed on sea or land, puffed up by the press . . . and now in the process of deflation," Robert Moses had written once. "There is a large amount of unfairness to the individual in this process, but in the end it arrives at the truth."

His observation had been accurate—and it was never better proven than by his own case.

The Incorruptible, Uncorrupting, Apolitical, Utterly Selfless Public Servant Moses had been a synthetic character, largely puffed up by the press. That character had endured for thirty-five years. But in 1959 the process of deflation by the press—a process that had been going on intermittently for several years—had begun in earnest. In that process there had been a large amount of unfairness. But that process had in the end arrived at the truth. At the beginning of 1959, the Moses image had stood in most of its glory, intact except for a few small chips. At the end of 1959, it lay in unsalvageable ruins. Popularity, Al Smith had warned him, was a slender reed. Now the reed was broken.

But popularity was no longer a significant factor in Moses' power equation. His power rested not on a reed but on a rock.

Unaware of the full extent of the power of the public authority, the press did not understand this. It assumed that he could be fired or forced to resign like any other mayoral appointee. But Wagner couldn't do that. Personality made it difficult, both because of the Mayor's respect for men of his father's generation ("You don't fire your father," he was to tell a young anti-Moses aide, Tim Cooney. "Never forget that, Tim. You don't fire your father") and because of other Wagnerian traits. Paul Screvane, asked if the Mayor might not have done it, just laughs. "Do you know Wagner?" he says. "Wagner never fired anyone in his life unless the fellow was convicted of a crime. And when you think of him firing a giant like Moses, it's just inconceivable. . . . Moses might have been a thorn in his side. Wagner may have wanted him out. He may have wanted to get the press off his neck. But Wagner would *never* have fired Moses." Politics made it impossible. Whether or not the calmly canny Mayor was already contemplating snatching the reins of party power out of De Sapio's hands, or whether he was only concerned with keeping Tammany's horses in line, he needed what Moses—and to a large extent Moses alone—could give him: the contracts and fees on which lived the machine and the other economic forces—banks, unions—which conferred political power in New York. In 1959 this provender was stacked higher than ever in the larders of Moses' authorities: with $92,000,000 worth of contracts for the Throgs Neck Bridge about to be let, $345,000,000 worth of bond issues for the Verrazano-

Narrows Bridge firmed up and ready to be sold, and $100,000,000 worth of new bridge-connecting expressways ready to be approved as soon as Moses gave the word to the federal highway officials under his thumb, the Mayor had half a billion reasons to keep him friendly. Firing Moses would cut his—the Mayor's—tie to the source of funds which kept men loyal to a mayor. And to such men no rationale would excuse such an action. What was he supposed to do? Tell Pete Brennan and Van Arsdale that, because of a little heat from the press, they would have to get along without $100,000,000 worth of expressway jobs?

Firing Moses would not, moreover, remove Moses from power. Far from it. Moses' power was largely beyond a mayor's reach. Wagner could fire him as Slum Clearance Committee chairman, Park Commissioner and Construction Coordinator. He couldn't fire him from his five state posts, which gave Moses so much power in a city dependent on Albany, or from his Triborough Authority chairmanship, which gave him so much of his money; he had handed Moses a fresh six-year term just a year before. Moses would still have those posts no matter what Wagner did.

He dare not even antagonize Moses, lest Moses, in anger, throw his money and power on the side of the Mayor's enemies; he could not risk hinting, even in private, that he might not object if Moses resigned just one —the Slum Clearance Committee chairmanship—of his many posts, lest the hint ignite Moses' always smoldering anger. Despite innumerable provocations, Wagner, in dealing with Moses, had been swallowing his pride for years. He would have to go on swallowing it.

Had the press access to records more revealing than those of the Slum Clearance Committee—Triborough's records—they might have understood this; it would have been difficult not to had they known that the whole Democratic machine, the leaders of all five county organizations, on which Wagner depended, were on Moses' payroll—and that they were all in line for pay boosts: that not only Shanahan and, through Shanahan, De Sapio, the Manhattan leader; but Steingut, the Brooklyn leader, and Roe, the Queens leader, and Buckley, the Bronx leader, had, in one form of fee or contract or another, made money out of Triborough's projects in the past and were expecting to make more money out of Triborough's projects in the future. Even without those records, there were plenty of symbols around that should have made the press understand the extent to which Wagner's power rested on Moses' money. Two men involved in the Title I picture were Shanahan and Goldwater. Were Shanahan and Goldwater friends of Moses' only? Hardly. They were friends also of Wagner's. In his last three campaigns for public office, they had been his two key fund raisers. In the case of Shanahan, the press had discovered a fact even more blatantly symbolic: it was not just Moses who had been depositing huge sums in Shanahan's bank; Wagner had, too.

But the press, without access to Triborough's records or understanding of Triborough's power, portrayed to the public a misleading picture of ensuing developments.

In part, too, the press's misunderstanding was merely the wish's predilection to be father to the thought. Having exposed wrongdoing, the crusading reporters wanted it stopped—stopped, moreover, by some official action that would have the effect of placing the imprimatur of official verification on the revelations they had made. While editorial writers demanded action, reporters kept asking Wagner what action he was planning to take. Wagner had no choice but to say he was certainly going to take some, but he kept his statements as low-key and vague as possible, and, when pressed for specifics, never gave any. All the Mayor was doing was trying to ride out the storm; he had no intention of doing anything that might arouse Moses' ire. But the press read into Wagner's remarks hints that action was imminent. And when none occurred, they misinterpreted the reason, portraying for their readers a Mayor who wanted Moses out but was constantly—and inexplicably—being faced down by him; they portrayed conflict where none existed, created a drama of confrontation between two men who were actually conspirators. The depth of the misunderstanding was shown in a remark by one of them: "You could only push Bob Wagner so far. When it came to protection of the political body, he could be very tough indeed. And protection of the political body was what it had come to here." This observer was right about Wagner's toughness, but wrong about what it required. He thought protection of the Mayor's "political body" required Moses to go. Actually, it required him to stay. There was never any real chance that Wagner would force Moses out—as, years after the fact, himself long retired from office, he told the author quite frankly (although he was less frank about the reasons). After circling warily about the issue for hours, finally obviously weary of answering the same questions over and over, Wagner said in exasperation: "Look, I didn't push it. . . . Never in any way did I ever induce anyone to intercede with him or to hint to him [that he should resign]. And I never would have." Wagner would probably have liked Moses to resign, so long as he did so on a friendly basis. But if Moses didn't want to go, he would not have had to.

Reading what they wanted into Wagner's every innocuous remark, reporters continually assured their readers that the Mayor was going to "crack down" on Moses, "pull up the reins," "cut his power." And therefore the reporters—and those readers who wanted Moses' power cut—were to be repeatedly disappointed.

Misunderstanding and consequent disappointment can be read clearly between the lines of the Cook-Gleason recapitulation, in "The Shame of New York," of the events that followed their Soundview revelations.

> . . . the Mayor authorized a deputy to tell the press [that] the Soundview project was as good as dead. It had been up before the Board of Estimate, and the board hadn't liked the looks of that $500,000 markup in land value. The Mayor was positive that the board wouldn't think any better of it now.
>
> Taking the Mayor at his word, residents in the bungalow colony danced in the streets that night—a celebration that, as the sequel was to show, was decidedly premature. For, though Mayor Wagner had begun to announce, in his City Hall press conferences, that "I am the Mayor," there is now rather abundant evidence that the statement isn't to be taken as literally as the late Frank Hague's "I am

the law." The project may have been dead in the mind of Robert (I am the Mayor) Wagner, but it definitely wasn't dead in the mind of Robert (The Great Doer) Moses. A few weeks after the Mayor had announced Soundview's demise, Moses gave out a list of eight projects for which he wanted the City Planning Commission to put up $10 million for advance planning. The list included Soundview. Moses was questioned at once: Wasn't Soundview, on the Mayor's own admission, supposed to be dead? The reply: "You can bet your life it's alive."

(And so it proved to be. Checking quietly with the Mayor to find out if he wanted the project or not, HHFA administrator Fried was told flatly that he did.)

The "showdowns" repeatedly predicted by the press somehow never occurred. Once, anti-Moses Wagner aides, desperate to force the Mayor's hand, leaked a Moses resignation ultimatum. MOSES READY TO QUIT, the headlines read. MAYOR WEIGHS FULL INQUIRY. At his next press conference, Wagner tried to laugh off the threat: pressed to the wall, he finally said he would have a "long talk" with Moses at the Massena opening the next day. (Would he give Moses' resignation offer "serious consideration"? a reporter asked. Certainly, the Mayor said.) WAGNER AND MOSES WILL CONFER ON TITLE I DISCLOSURES TODAY, the *Times* headlined, telling its readers that the "talk may affect the administration of New York City's slum clearance." Actual developments at Massena hardly merited headlines, however. Moses took the Mayor's wife and two sons to meet Queen Elizabeth, the Moseses and Wagners had dinner together, the next day the two men toured the Robert Moses Power Dam and then went for a swim together. On Wagner's return to the city, he said blandly that Moses had given "no indication" that he wanted to resign. What about the "serious consideration"? Wagner replied with a single sentence: "Bob Moses is a good public servant." Had the two men really discussed Title I at all? Wagner said they had but when asked about the discussion replied, "Nothing . . . specific."

When Moses said that the controversy about Title I had made the program a "dead duck" in New York, Citizens Union, City Club—and a dozen editorials—demanded Wagner fire him. "It is no longer a question whether anyone should be asked to resign," a Citizens Union statement said. There was no sense having a vital program headed by someone who didn't believe it could accomplish anything more. Reporters told their readers that there was a serious possibility that Moses might leave, that "officials around City Hall" were already speculating on "who will take his place." Wagner said he was sure Moses wasn't serious; of course Title I had a great future in New York. Moses, informed of Wagner's statement by reporters, said, "I don't care what the Mayor says. . . . I still say Title I is a dead duck." Shanahan issued a statement agreeing with Moses.

Publicly humiliated, Wagner displayed an anger new to reporters. Face flushed, pounding his desk, the Mayor said, "If people can't implement the policies of this administration, they have lost their usefulness. If they feel Title I is a dead duck, then they can't be helpful. I'm the Mayor, and . . . I will not have anyone on any committee if they cannot be helpful. I'm going to . . . stop a lot of this nonsense." The Mayor "indicated he might put the axe to both Moses and Shanahan," the *Daily News* reported. But the *News* summed up Wagner's next press conference in the headline: FIRE MOSES? WAGNER DUCKS.

A single incident should have illuminated the true nature of the relationship among Moses, Shanahan and Wagner. After a new series of revelations about the banker's manipulations, the Mayor had his press secretary tell reporters that he was spending the day at his summer home in Islip but was certainly "dissatisfied" with Shanahan and would question him personally as soon as possible. Returning to City Hall the next day, Wagner implied that he had not yet spoken with the vice chairman. But reporters discovered that Wagner had not really been spending the previous day at his home but at the Deepdale Golf Club in Manhasset, golfing and having a long, convivial dinner with Shanahan. Even after this discovery, however, the press kept playing events as if Wagner really wanted Moses to resign.

Press coverage was misleading in its interpretation not only of Wagner's attitude but of Moses'. It portrayed the Mayor as wanting to get rid of Moses as head of Title I, and that portrayal was false. But it also portrayed Moses as wanting to remain as head of Title I.

And that portrayal was also false.

Acting as intermediary between the two men, Deputy Mayor Paul O'Keefe was speaking to Moses frequently now, and he was suddenly startled, he recalls, to find himself with the clear impression that, despite the fact that Moses had never said anything directly, "the housing job wasn't life and death to him." Months earlier, two very astute judges of human nature had come to an even stronger conclusion. "Moses called a meeting when all the shit was hitting the fan," Peter J. Brennan says. "Van and I went up to the island." On the surface, the meeting was one of Moses' customary mobilization-of-forces lunches. "Jack Straus [of Macy's] was there, and a lot of other guys who counted," Brennan says. "[Moses] indicated that too many cry-babies were being listened to, and he reviewed his program to show he was doing it right." Over dessert, Brennan recalls, "he indicated that if there wasn't the proper kind of support, he wanted out." The two labor leaders grinned at the familiar Moses ultimatum, but, reviewing during their return trip downtown other statements Moses had made during lunch, they came to a startling conclusion: "This time he really meant it. He wanted out." They were right. For the first time in his life, Robert Moses was willing to surrender some of his power.

Moses would never, of course, have allowed himself to be forced out under fire. But during the summer of 1959, a graceful exit had materialized: the proposed New York World's Fair.

The World's Fair presidency held several attractions.

Some were personal—poignantly personal. His daughter Jane had cancer. She needed two major operations and long, expensive, recuperative periods. The circumstances of her divorce had, moreover, left partly on her father the burden of her support. Jane's daughter, Caroline, had reached college age as a brilliant, arrogant girl in whom he saw much resemblance to himself; his granddaughter must have the best schooling, and tuition costs were rising—and after college he wanted her to go to Oxford as he had gone. Jane's son, Christopher, would be ready for college soon. And now Mary's arteriosclerosis and arthritis had advanced to a point where the seventy-four-year-old woman was increasingly unable to care for herself. Doctors told Moses that she must either be placed in a nursing home or given around-the-clock nursing care: it was a depressed Robert Moses—as depressed as Sid Shapiro had ever seen him—who told his loyal aide one day that such care, combined with the cost of the extensive medication his wife would require for the rest of her life, would cost $24,000 a year.

To meet these harrowing bills, Robert Moses had, in cash reserves, practically nothing. For all the years of his adult life, he had been short of money. During the last five years, for the first time, his salary from his numerous public offices had risen above a pittance, with his pay as Park Commissioner having been raised to $25,000 and his appointment as State Power Authority chairman giving him an additional $10,000 annually. After taxes, however, the $35,000 total shrunk to about $22,000—little enough for a man maintaining an apartment on expensive Gracie Terrace as well as a summer home in Babylon, especially when combined with the Moses prodigality with money, and with his absolute refusal to leave himself open, by using his expense accounts for personal needs, to the type of pressure he exerted on others. That prodigality had exhausted most of his inheritance and even that relatively small portion of the $100,000 consultants' fees from other cities that he had kept for himself. Seventy-one years old, Robert Moses, the Robert Moses whom the press persisted in describing as "independently wealthy," was, so far as cash was concerned, all but penniless.

Accepting the World's Fair presidency would change that. The Rockefellers were prepared to participate in the Fair quite actively, and in preliminary discussions with his counsel, Samuel Rosenman, the salary of $100,000 per year plus $10,000 in expenses had been mentioned—as had a seven-year contract. (The contract finally worked out between Moses and the Fair Corporation gave him $75,000 per year plus $25,000 per year in expenses for seven years, mid-1960 through mid-1967, and thereafter an annuity of $27,500 per year for an additional seven years, 1967 through 1974. The money to guarantee the payment of this sum—a total of $892,500—was to be taken off the top of the Fair Corporation's receipts and placed in a special escrow account. Smaller—but still lucrative—salary and annuity arrangements were made for many Moses Men.) He would, at a stroke, be assured of freedom from the financial problems with which he had been living for so long.

Some of the Fair's attractions were philosophical. Try as he might to get away from that fact by using urban renewal funds for universities and cultural centers, "Title I" meant primarily housing, and housing had never engaged his enthusiasm as had parks and highways—which may have been why he had delegated it so completely to someone else. It was a cluttered, complicated field—one in which the grand conceptions of which he was capable never emerged as cleanly as in the uncluttered beauty of a bridge or beach.

But, as always with Robert Moses, neither personal finances nor philosophy but power and reputation were apparently the determining factors. Although he never spelled out his feelings in detail even to his top subordinates, he did drop enough hints to show them at least vague outlines of his thinking.

In his view—and, as always where power was concerned, his view was to prove perceptive—soon there wasn't going to be that much power in Title I in New York any more. He had meant what he said when he called the city's program "a dead duck"; HHFA officials had been trying for years to slash drastically the city's disproportionate share of funds; now, with his reputation so badly smeared, he believed they would do so with a vengeance; what new projects were built, moreover, would be built by genuine real estate builders like Zeckendorf, not by the type of promoters whose projects could give him political power.

There was going to be power in the World's Fair—immense power. Sitting in on preliminary meetings of the Fair Committee, he had seen that Fair spending—for pavilions, for example—would be on a national and international scale. To ease access to Flushing Meadows Park—he had determined that the Fair was going to be held in that park—a vast network of new Queens highways, $120,000,000 worth of new highways, would be needed. As his keen eye for power had seen in 1945 that housing was the field to enter, now it saw that the World's Fair was the field to enter; the Fair grounds were going to be the prime locale of power in New York.

He could not keep his Title I job and take the Fair job. He could not in fact keep any of his formal city jobs. The city's Code of Ethics was quite specific about that; the spectacle of a paid official simultaneously holding a paid job with a private corporation might be too grotesque to surmount, even for his oft-proven ability to get laws or codes changed, and he was not in as strong a position as he had been in the past to get laws changed. But there was little power in his formal city jobs, anyway. Power was not derived from a park commissionership whose annual budget was so small that no new park development of any real size could even be contemplated; it certainly was not derived from his membership on the City Planning Commission, which he no longer dominated. His informal city job as Construction Coordinator, in which he measured his resources in tens of millions of dollars, gave him power, but, thanks to the vagueness with which that job was defined, he had thought of a way in which he could keep that job. Power was derived from his Triborough Authority job, in which he measured his resources in hundreds of millions of dollars. He would be able to take the Fair job and still keep that. Power was derived from his chairmanship of the State Power Authority, in which his resources were also measured in the hundreds of millions, and he could take the Fair job and still keep that—as well as his other state posts: the Long Island State Park Commission presidency, the Jones Beach and Bethpage State Park authorities and State Council of Parks chairmanships. His appetite for power was undiminished. Shortly he would be seeking to take over the development of atomic energy in the state because he saw that this was the new field into which money might be poured—his method would be the advocacy of laws placing all such development under his State Power Authority—but by trading in his city jobs for the Fair presidency, he would be giving that appetite more, not less, on which to feed.

As for his precious reputation, Title I was wrecking it—and would continue to wreck it as long as he stayed connected with that operation. Unjustified though it may have been, there had been too much scandal attached to it. There was always going to be massive relocation involved, and the media's bleeding hearts made anyone in charge of massive relocation look bad.

The World's Fair would be a chance to start in a new field with a clean slate—in a field which needed no clearing for there wasn't a single protesting tenant in all Flushing Meadows' 1,400 acres. The Meadows were a blank slate, almost as *rasa* a *tabula* as Jones Beach had been—Jones Beach that had brought him glory. The Fair was, moreover, a chance to write something glamorous, spectacular on that slate. For how could a World's Fair not be glamorous and spectacular? Even that incompetent clotheshorse Grover Whalen had reaped wonderful publicity before his mismanagement had turned the 1939 Fair into a source of ridicule. There would be no mismanagement under *him*; the Fair would give his name back all its old luster. With its intonations of international amity and good will, it was a cause that would put its leader again firmly "on the side of the angels."

A World's Fair was, moreover, no local event. It was big news nationally, to some extent all over the Western world. That was no small consideration to a man to whom fame was a spur. Moses' fame had been in general limited to New York and nearby states. His sips of national fame had been few and far between. Here was a chance to get himself a real swallow.

In his last consideration, he was motivated by a more obscure consideration. He had long seen the parallels between his own career and that of the man who, in the modern world, ranked closest to him as a city-builder, Baron Georges-Eugène Haussmann (whom Moses was fond of referring to as "the brawny Alsatian"), and he knew that it was not the Bois de Boulogne but the great Universal Exposition held in Paris in 1867 that had given Haussmann his greatest contemporary glory. "I think Bob thought the World's Fair would be the crowning achievement of a long career," Paul Screvane says.

Informed of Moses' oblique hints, the Mayor got the message. In a series of meetings during the week of August 10, meetings at which Wagner had a representative, final arrangements were made for Moses to take the Fair post. On August 20, the Mayor announced that he was appointing a management consultant, J. Anthony Panuch, to "reorganize the city's housing picture." Moses could not take the Fair post until the Legislature approved a law he had drafted exempting officers of the Fair Corporation from the city's Code of Ethics, and the Legislature did not meet until January, and so Panuch had to keep studying the situation for months. When opposition developed in the Legislature, he had to delay his report until it was crushed. On February 20, with all the details ironed out, Moses wrote Panuch that he wanted to leave the housing field because he was going to be heading the Fair, and on March 9, Panuch issued a report recommending that all agencies involved in the city's housing program—including the Mayor's Committee on Slum Clearance—be combined into a single, new agency. And Moses announced that he would resign as committee chairman and as Park Commissioner, member of the City Planning Commission and member of the City Youth Board on May 23. He recommended that the office of City Construction Coordinator, which he said was "no longer necessary," be abolished. Official liaison with the state and federal highway agencies should be carried on by the chairman of the Triborough Bridge and Tunnel Authority, and the Mayor should officially designate him as that representative.

Moses' enemies never understood what was going on. They believed that the appointment of Panuch was a desperation move by a Mayor determined to force Moses out by reorganization if he couldn't get him out in any other way—Haddad and Kahn called the appointment "pushing the Panuch button," but the conclusive proof that Moses left voluntarily was the way he did it.

He left in triumph. There were the editorials of praise, of course, and the letters. Wagner's said:

> For well over a quarter of a century in city service, and for nearly forty years in state service, you have . . . come closer to being the irreplaceable man than any other in the history of our city government.
>
> Our consolation in your leaving lies in the fact that we have had you so long. The city will long remember your work in its behalf. . . .
>
> You helped give to our city excitement and color, as well as concrete highways. Your severest critics of yesterday will say in years to come, "He may have been a headache but he never was a bore." I, for myself, would rather quote the title of that song, "Thanks for the Memory."

An even more revealing index of the depth of that triumph was the crowd in the grand ballroom of the Hotel Commodore on May 3, and the identity of the people who made up that crowd. In April, business, political and union leaders—a cross-section of the elite among New York's power establishment—had received invitations to a testimonial banquet (proceeds to charity) in honor of Robert Moses. The price for the tickets was a hundred dollars a plate, and the invitations had been sent not to corporations, which might purchase whole tables and give away the tickets, but to individuals, who would have to bear the cost of their loyalty themselves. Moreover, they would, if they bought tickets, be honoring an individual who had for months—almost a year, in fact—been linked by headlines with "scandal." Yet the invitations bore the names of a sponsoring committee that included not only Tom Shanahan, Carmine De Sapio and Sydney Baron but a score of other prominent politicians, businessmen and union leaders. None of them had asked for anonymity. Not one of them was in any way ashamed to be connected with a ceremony honoring the headlines' target. In fact, they were proud of it; many of them asked Shanahan for a chance to speak. And no one invited wanted to be left out. No matter what other plans the recipients of the invitations may have had for the evening—and most of these men had schedules booked far longer in advance than the three weeks before the dinner—they dropped those plans, and came. Expecting a normal number of turn-downs, the committee was astonished to find that all but a handful of invitations had been accepted; on the evening of May 3, the Commodore ballroom was jammed to the doors with 1,044 guests. More than a thousand persons had been willing—eager—to pay a hundred dollars for the privilege of honoring a man whom the press had been attacking mercilessly for months. And when, speaker after speaker having praised him, Robert Moses arose to accept a gift of gold cuff links from Shanahan, those men jumped to their feet and cheered. Sid Shapiro says he will never forget that moment. "Everybody was there," he says. "Everybody. And you should have seen them. They were standing there applauding and yelling like a bunch of schoolboys." And the men standing and yelling for Shapiro's idolized "RM" were the men RM would have wanted standing and yelling for him, not the establishment of the political, banking, union and construction fields in which he moved, but the elite of that establishment, the *crème de la crème* of New York's influentials.

And more important than leaving in triumph, he left with power. Wagner announced that Newbold Morris would be Moses' successor as Park Commissioner, the second citywide Park Commissioner in the city's history. The press hailed Morris—or, to be more precise, Morris' image, which, created in the La Guardia era, had been that of a young, independent reformer. But it wasn't his independence that had gotten Morris—now fifty-eight, still goodhearted but bumbling, ineffectual and so nervous that rumors were adrift about his drinking habits (and very anxious indeed to return to city employment)—the job; rather the qualification was his awe—a hero worship that amounted to utter subservience—of Robert Moses. A subject of City Hall jokes even in the La Guardia days, those feelings had dimmed not at all—as some spectators at the dedication in 1963 of a bust of Fiorello La Guardia at La Guardia Airport would see. Recalls Henry Barnes: "Morris made a speech and at the end of it he gave an Italian phrase which he had obviously studied very hard to get just right. Moses was the next speaker. He got up and said, 'I had no idea that Newbold was smart enough to speak Italian,' and then he starts off into a whole run of Italian, very fluent, shrugging his shoulders and everything. Just deliberately to humiliate Newbold like that, and Newbold wasn't in too good shape at the time—it was just vicious." But what astounded Barnes was that after the ceremony Morris came up to Moses and "tried to talk to him—just groveling for a word from the master." At his swearing in as Park Commissioner—which Moses did not bother to attend—he called his predecessor: "A giant in public works who will be remembered long after we are gone." With almost the entire Park Department hierarchy of Moses Men left intact under him, Morris was Park Commissioner only in name. Robert Moses was still running the Department exactly as he had run it before—as anyone having much business with the Department soon found out. Whenever Joe Ingraham called Morris in the evening with a question, the new commissioner would—no matter what the subject—say, "I want to think about it. I'll call you back in a few minutes." Ingraham would wait a minute or two and then telephone Moses' private number. Almost invariably that number would be busy—and when Morris called back, he would give Ingraham a statement that Moses' old reporter confidant could tell came direct from Moses, as verbatim as if the new commissioner had copied down and repeated what the old commissioner had told him to say word for word. "He just wouldn't move unless Bob Moses told him to move and when," Barnes says. "I argued with him one time about something and he said, 'Well, Bob Moses feels this way about it.' I said, 'Who's the Park Commissioner?' He said, 'Well, Bob Moses built the parks . . .' " Once he dared to make a statement on his own—and accepted (almost eagerly) a public spanking. He said that unless Westchester County stopped barring New Yorkers from its parks, the city might have to obtain entrance for its residents by legislative fiat. Upon reading his successor's quote, Moses said, "I am afraid Newbold was a bit impulsive. His demand that all parks everywhere must be open to everybody has a superficial charm which won't stand analysis." Reporters telephoned Morris for a comment, which was: "Mr. Moses is absolutely correct. I am impulsive." As Screvane says, by naming Morris as Moses' successor, "[Wagner] *knew* he was keeping [the Department] in Moses' hands."*

At first, reporters, not understanding the conditions under which Moses was resigning his city jobs, assumed that Moses was losing his power over roads, but soon Ed Katcher of the *Post* was writing that "Commissioner Moses, New York's longest-running municipal feature, is not, after all, vanishing entirely from the local administrative scene. . . . He will continue to represent the city on the federal and state arterial highway programs." On the day he resigned, Peter Kihss of the *Times* took the trouble to do a little figuring of the cost of the arterial program and such other Moses projects under way as the Verrazano and Throgs Neck bridges and the Niagara power, park and parkway project and wrote that "a rough check indicated that Mr. Moses . . . still retained other jobs by which he was presiding over $2,800,000,000 in projects to make over the city and state."

The only power Moses lost by his multiple "resignations" was in housing—a power he was glad to give up anyway. In parks and roads he was still in charge. And to replace the power he had lost in housing, he had been given command of a new project loaded with power.

He left in triumph—because he wasn't really leaving at all. Furthermore, no one could ever make him leave. Thanks to his control of one city and

* Wagner confirms Screvane's statement, even if he does so in more tactful terms. "Bob wanted Morris," the Mayor says. Why? "Frankly, I think Bob knew he would have an influence on him."

three state public authorities, he had anchored himself in a position so secure that no one could take his power away from him. Only he could lose it for himself; his career, booming to new heights in the eighth decade of his life, could be checked only by his own personality. Only Robert Moses could lose Robert Moses his power.

And he did.

46. Nelson

THERE WERE DIFFERENCES between the sixth Governor under whom Robert Moses was serving and the previous five.

The key difference could be defined in dollar signs. His ranch in Venezuela, five times as large as the combined boroughs of New York City; the Rockefeller family estate in Pocantico Hills, six times as large as the principality of Monaco and containing, for the family's private use, seventy separate structures—these were only symbols, two among innumerable, of the fact that Nelson Aldrich Rockefeller and his sister and four brothers were probably the richest family on earth. Lehman and Harriman had been rich men. Harriman sometimes gave the impression of possessing almost unimaginable wealth, and he did: perhaps as much as fifty million dollars. But the riches of Rockefeller dwarfed those of Harriman. Those of Nelson Rockefeller alone were perhaps five times greater than Harriman's, but because the Rockefeller family holdings are unified, interlocking, and because the Rockefeller brothers work closely together, he had at his command a fortune whose size has never been publicly calculated but whose visible portions alone have been estimated* as high as five billion dollars—one hundred times larger than Harriman's.

"The very rich are different from you and me," Fitzgerald wrote. Rockefeller was different from the very rich—and the difference extended to politics. In financial terms, Lehman and Harriman might be major contributors to their state party; the Rockefellers *were* their party, to such an extent that Theodore H. White called it "almost a dependency of the Rockefeller family, like the Rockefeller Foundation or the Rockefeller University. . . . the family and its friends had picked up every deficit of the statewide Republican Party in every campaign; and, on occasion, Nelson Rockefeller could pull out of his inside pocket a little folded paper, typed in blue, which reminded him precisely of the total the Party had cost their family over the years, a very large figure indeed . . ." Are banks key in political financing? There is scarcely a bank in New York State with which the Rockefellers do not have some link, direct or hidden. As for the state's largest bank, the Chase Manhattan Bank that is probably the most powerful financial institution anywhere on earth, Chase is, as White notes, "the last great bank controlled by an individual family—the Rockefellers." Are utilities key in

* By Ferdinand Lundberg, whose estimate seems the most thorough.

political financing? So large are the Rockefeller shareholdings in the state's largest utility, the Consolidated Edison Company, that White says they are "probably the controlling shareholdings." The dominance of the Rockefellers over the whole politically powerful Wall Street financial community was symbolized by the fact that former Governor Dewey, powerful in that community in his own right, was David Rockefeller's lawyer (to be more precise, in fact, he was *one* of David Rockefeller's lawyers) and by the ease with which, deciding in 1958 to enter New York politics at the top, Nelson Rockefeller took the gubernatorial nomination away from the previous Wall Street favorite for the job, former GOP national chairman Leonard W. Hall. "I bet on money—not just any kind of money but old money," one veteran New York politician says. "New money buys things; old money calls notes." In politics in the Empire State, the Rockefellers held enough notes to achieve any aim; their power was as close to an absolute as had ever existed in New York.

But the difference could not be defined strictly in dollar signs. Harriman used wealth to obtain the prize, but, having won it, he did not know what to do with it. Nelson Rockefeller knew exactly what to do with it. He may have bought his way into the game; once in it he played it like a master—as if he had been raised in the Fourth Ward instead of Pocantico Hills—played it with zest and verve in public and, in private, with a ruthlessness that was a reminder that his bloodline ran direct from the grandfather who had created the greatest monopoly the world had ever seen by mercilessly crushing every competitor—played it, in fact, with a ruthlessness that reminded some politicians of Robert Moses. Of the men who had been Governor over Moses, only Smith and Roosevelt had possessed such onstage and backstage capabilities in combination.

Nelson Rockefeller possessed, moreover, a particular type of imagination possessed neither by Smith nor by Roosevelt. It was not the original, creative, shaping imagination of a Robert Moses. But Rockefeller did possess an appreciative imagination of a high order, an ability (rare in itself) to grasp and judge the inspirations of other men—to see them as their creators saw them while they still existed only in their creators' minds. He could see—not only visualize but judge and assess the value of, and determine to bring to reality—proposed physical developments. He had always been the Rockefeller most interested in art and architecture and housing. Bored by a routine executive job as a young man, a biographer reports, his imagination was fired by Rockefeller Center, the complex of office buildings his father was building in midtown Manhattan. At the age of thirty, he became its president: "Nelson . . . enjoyed his job—especially when it allowed him to don a hard hat and preside over ceremonies celebrating construction progress." He had the imagination of the builder.

On the grand scale. Hardly had he become Governor when he was undertaking a vast expansion of the state's educational plant—large, beautiful new campuses all across the state. Soon his architects were planning a "State Mall," a complex whose four mammoth office buildings would tower over a rebuilt Albany. Money was no consideration. To finance such immense physical improvements, he resorted to a variety of "backdoor" financing plans (most of them modeled on Moses' public authority concept) that allowed the state's voters no say over them and that preserved the illusion of a "balanced budget"—and even so, during Rockefeller's Governorship, the state budget would increase by more than 300 percent and the state debt would quadruple. He was a builder on a scale on which no previous Governor had been a builder. He was, in fact, a builder on Moses' scale.

His arrogance was also on the Moses scale.

Behind it lay what White calls "a strange, pietistic sense of responsibility," a serene sense that because his motives are pure, his decisions are right. "He was rough," White writes. "His enemies called him, quite simply, the most ruthless man in politics. But what in other men would be simple arrogance was in Rockefeller the direct and abrupt expression of motives which, since he knew them to be good, he expected all other men to accept as good also." Behind it lay principles: in the midst of his run for the presidency in 1964, a run that needed Southern support, he insisted on giving substantial donations to activist Negro civil rights groups. Behind it lay sheer stubbornness: once his mind was made up, he would not change it. And behind it lay the assurance, based on a lifetime as a member of America's closest counterpart to a royal family, that what he wants he will get.

His arrogance was easy, charming, gracious—the arrogance of a man handed at birth the power to enforce his will. It was not the hard, glittering, abrasive arrogance of a Robert Moses who had had to fight and scheme for that power. But it was equally unshatterable. Nelson Rockefeller was rough, all right. He was a threat to Robert Moses far more dangerous than any that had previously existed in Albany. Moses had defied and overawed all Al Smith's successors in the Executive Chamber. The threat to resign—his ultimate ultimatum—had brought them all to heel. But the man in the Executive Chamber now was not a man who would be willing to heel. And, perhaps most important so far as Moses was concerned, Rockefeller would, moreover, be an opponent—the only opponent Moses had met, since he conceived and gained the powers of the public authority—on whom there was no handhold. Governor Dewey had deeply resented both his power and his arrogance, and Dewey had been ruthless and shrewd. But Russ Sprague and King Macy and the banks had been the way to exert pressure on Dewey, and Moses had been in a position to make Sprague and Macy and the banks exert that pressure. Governor Harriman had sought at first to curb him. But De Sapio and Rosenman and the unions had been the way to exert pressure on Harriman, and Moses had been in a position to make De Sapio and Rosenman and the unions exert that pressure. But when Rockefeller had come to the Governorship, there had been no way to exert pressure on him except through the unions, and the Governor had early struck up his own alliances with them to make himself exempt even from that pressure. "In the Empire State," Theodore White writes, "Nelson Rockefeller was beholden to no one; no crevice of weakness or obligation could be found. . . ." "Moses could push a button," Lutsky says, "and in would come the calls"—from men who wielded immense power. But there was no power that Nelson Rockefeller could not deny.

There were so many avenues that Moses could use to get to someone. But not one of them led to Nelson Rockefeller. Survey the whole vast cast of characters on the New York political scene and there was only one man who could with impunity confront—and defeat—Robert Moses.

The man who was now Governor.

It is not so difficult to see the arrogance and strength in Nelson Rockefeller. One has only to see that big jaw set once to know it. Penetrate the slightest bit beneath that charm and the tough stubbornness is there, not the surface crustiness of a Harriman but the real iron. Robert Moses, once the keenest reader of personalities, should have been able to read that of his new Governor like a book.

But Moses had long since ceased being interested in personalities. He believed that even a Governor's had no significance for him. If this newest Governor disliked him, so what? Dewey had disliked him. And anyway, he didn't think Nelson disliked him. In fact, he was sure Nelson liked him—liked him and admired him.

He had been an ally of Nelson's father in many projects; the two men had laid out the Palisades Interstate Parkway together during his long days driving through John D. Rockefeller, Jr.'s, vast tract along the Hudson. He had been an ally of Nelson's brothers. He had envisioned and obtained the land for Lincoln Center, for whose construction John D. Rockefeller 3d had raised a large share of the money. David Rockefeller, whose Chase Manhattan Bank presidency gave him a vast stake in Lower Manhattan, had always been one of the strongest supporters of his Lower Manhattan Expressway. Laurance Rockefeller had drawn often on his beachfront expertise in developing his Dorado Beach resort in Puerto Rico. He had been an ally of Nelson himself; not only had they worked together in bringing the United Nations to New York, but in 1948 Nelson's International Basic Economy Corporation, building housing projects, factories and supermarkets in Venezuela, had retained him, at a fantastic fee (which, of course, he distributed to his "muchachos"), to lay out a highway program for Caracas. (So pleased had Nelson been with the Caracas–La Guaira toll highway and other arterials that were a monument to that consultantship that in 1950, with IBEC expanding into Brazil, Moses and muchachos had been retained to lay out a comprehensive city plan for São Paulo, and year after year Nelson asked him to return there to check on its implementation.) A long history of alliances counted for a lot in Moses' world. The admiration of the younger man—fifty when he became Governor to Moses' seventy—who wanted to get things done for the older man who had got so many things done, was well known. When the incoming Governor accepted his recommendations on several appointments—including that of Burch McMorran as Superintendent of Public Works—and vetoed the bill that would have forced Moses to shift his Verrazano Bridge approach out of Bay Ridge, Moses began to speak of "Nelson" (he would never address him as Governor, as he had never addressed Roosevelt, Lehman, Dewey or Harriman as Governor; for Robert Moses, there would always be only one Governor) with an affection that was almost paternalistic.

In the early months of Rockefeller's Governorship there had been one area of friction. William J. Ronan, a former professor of government at NYU who had begun working for Rockefeller in 1956 as executive director of a temporary state commission Rockefeller was heading, and had thereafter—thanks, in the opinion of some observers, to a remarkable capacity for obsequiousness to the Governor—advanced to become a steadily more important member of his inner circle of advisers. In 1957, as staff director of another temporary state commission, Ronan had recommended curbing the "potentially dangerous" power of public authorities. Moses had told reporters, "I don't take this seriously," and his power in Albany had insured that he didn't have to. But Ronan had irritated him. A tall, bespectacled, jowly, smooth-spoken man, he seemed typical of the "impractical" academics, men who were afraid to do anything except by committee, whom Moses despised. While demolishing the commission's recommendations, he had taken time out to deliver Ronan a gratuitous public spanking, charging that the recommendations had "emanated from an ambitious professorial mind." With his patron in the Governor's chair, Ronan had evidently been emboldened to try for a small measure of revenge; shortly after taking office, Rockefeller had appointed him chairman of a "task force" to reorganize the state government, and one of the recommendations of the task force was that Moses' State Council of Parks be abolished and authority over state parks be given in fact as well as theory to the Department of Conservation. Moses blasted the "Ronan Report"—and Rockefeller had evidenced a distinct unwillingness to get into any conflict with him; nothing further was heard of the parks recommendation.

Nonetheless, tension began to build between Moses and the Governor. Observers who saw them both frequently believe it could not be avoided. Two men so arrogant, so accustomed to getting their own way in everything, could not long be in contact without friction—particularly when both men were grand-scale builders. So acute an observer as Perry Duryea says he "could just see Rocky thinking that there wasn't enough room in one state for a Robert Moses and a Nelson Rockefeller both clicking on all six." Rockefeller's first great programs of public improvements, moreover, had concerned—perhaps deliberately—areas outside Moses': education, for example. But they were beginning now to intrude more and more on Moses' turf—turf that had been his, and his alone, for close to forty years. Rockefellers had always been interested in parks; their creation was part of the family's heritage. Understanding the need to acquire as much as possible of the state's remaining open space before it was swallowed up by the developers' bulldozers, by 1960 the Governor was discussing the matter in depth with his brother Laurance, a dedicated conservationist who had established the Virgin Islands National Park and a foundation to coordinate conservation efforts, and had chaired a presidential Outdoor Recreation Resources Review Commission. This did not cause too much friction with Moses; when Laurance mapped out a state park-land acquisition program and Rockefeller adopted it, Moses campaigned for the $100,000,000 bond issue referendum that made it possible. But no such harmony was possible with the Governor's feelings about mass transportation. With an insight still rare among government officials in 1960, the Governor had seen that if congestion was ever to be eased in and around urban areas, the emphasis on building more and more highways must be replaced by a balanced transportation system—in which emphasis must be shifted, gradually but steadily, to mass transportation.

Dinner with Nelson Rockefeller sometimes had a new feature now, Theodore White relates:

> . . . he might, immediately after coffee, haul out the red cardboard folders in which he carries his papers, and spread out on the floor the state's master program for parks—explaining in detail his plan for Troy, Syracuse, Utica, as if he were rearranging the furniture in his living room. . . . Lounging by a poolside, he might suddenly set off on a gorgeous imaginary tour of New York City, Long Island and the lower Hudson Valley as they would be twenty years hence when his transportation program was finished: in his imagination, high-speed trains darted from Riverhead, Long Island, seventy-five miles away, to downtown Manhattan in less than an hour. Subways served the great airports.

For almost forty years, public physical development in New York State had been shaped pre-eminently by the vision of one man. Now there were two.

"Transportation was becoming one of Nelson Rockefeller's crusades—you know, like health became one of his crusades and housing became one of his crusades," says one long-time political observer. "And when Nelson Rockefeller had a crusade, it was *Nelson Rockefeller's* crusade. He was going to get credit for it. And Moses, being the way he was, could never be part of a transportation setup identified with Rockefeller."

Moreover, Rockefeller had delegated authority for explorations into transportation needs to Ronan, who was rapidly becoming his closest adviser. And while in Moses' presence the ex-professor was always, Moses' aides say, "sucking up" to Moses (Moses would scarcely deign to speak to him), Moses' men began to hear reports that Ronan was constantly working to "poison" the Governor's mind against Moses. A confrontation was inevitable. And when it occurred, Moses' personality led him—forced him—to make a mistake.

The confrontation came over age, and was caused in part by another aspect of Moses' personality—the overriding vanity which kept him from wearing a hearing aid although his deafness had worsened until he could no longer discern clearly the words of a man only a desk-width away.

His age had become the sorest of subjects with Moses, who disregarded it utterly himself, still working the endless schedule he had been working for half a century, still swimming far out into the ocean on the roughest days, and who expected others to disregard it as well—to such an extent that he seemed to regard every reference to it as a personal affront.

The heart of the soreness was the relationship of age to his power. All state employees were required by law to retire at the age of sixty-five. The Governor was empowered to request the board of the State Retirement System (which, of course, invariably honored his requests) for a one- or two-year extension in exceptional cases, and Moses had been receiving such extensions since he had turned seventy. But whereas Harriman had gone out of his way to offer two-year extensions well before his birthday and without being asked, Rockefeller had been less gracious. "Each [extension] was to the annoyance of Bob Moses because the Governor would keep him waiting until just before his birthday," Sid Shapiro recalls. "RM had consulted his attorneys, but they told him there was no way of getting around this. And every week, he'd say, 'Did that thing come yet?' You'd call the Governor's office and ask about it and the answer would be, 'It's in the works. Don't worry.' But legally, if the thing didn't come through by the day his birthday arrived, he'd have to retire." Equally disturbing, each extension was for one year, not two, so that Moses had to go through the whole humiliating experience every December. Worse still, during the last two years, the Governor had become more and more insistent on discussing an "orderly transition" which he felt had been made necessary in the overall direction of the state park program because the acquiring and developing of parks under the $100,000,000 program would take probably two decades. "Rockefeller had had discussions with Moses about Laurance taking over"—moving up from vice chairman to chairman of the State Council of Parks—Shapiro recalls. The Governor had even made a public statement about it—with Moses sitting right behind him on the speakers' platform. In a speech opening Lake Welch Beach in Harriman State Park on June 15, 1962, Rockefeller had said that his brother was "Bob Moses' greatest disciple" in recreation. "New York State is fortunate to have Laurance Rockefeller following in the footsteps of Robert Moses." And observers glancing quickly at Moses to gauge his reaction had seen him smiling pleasantly.

"Here," Shapiro says, "maybe Mr. Moses' hearing difficulties enter into the picture—lots of times in the last few years, he'd come back and say, 'I had a good talk with So-and-so,' and he'd even write a letter confirming it [the details of the agreement he thought had been reached] and then the guy would write back saying, 'We never agreed to that!' " On public occasions, Moses was often unable to hear what speakers were saying. He may have been smiling pleasantly after Rockefeller's remark at Lake Welch Beach because he hadn't heard it. "They had agreed that Laurance would be Mr. Moses' successor," Shapiro says. "RM *had* agreed to do this." But, Shapiro says, Moses was evidently under the impression that the changeover would take place in some vague, indefinite—and certainly long-distant—future, while the Governor thought they were talking about an imminent changeover, and was becoming increasingly impatient at the delay.*

---

* Shapiro's impression that the two men were talking at cross purposes is confirmed by several insiders. Peter J. Brennan, for example, says that "we knew it was coming—the Governor said that Moses had . . . agreed to surrender" the chairmanship—and were puzzled by conversations with Moses in which he seemed to envision holding on to it for many years to come.

In 1962, the weeks before Moses' seventy-fourth birthday on December 18 dwindled down, and there was still no extension from Rockefeller. The two men were scheduled to meet on the morning of Tuesday, November 27, at the Governor's brownstone office at 22 East Fifty-fifth Street to cover a wide-ranging agenda of public works problems, and Moses decided that he would have to bring up the subject at that meeting. He prepared with his usual tactical wizardry, arranging to have lunch that day with Jack Flynn, publisher of the *Daily News,* and his top editors, who could be counted on to support him in any controversy—and making sure that the Governor knew about the lunch.

What happened at that meeting is not known. Only the two men were present, and neither one will go beyond the official statements they were later to issue in discussing it. But there was a witness, albeit a biased one, to its conclusion, for that conclusion took place not in the Rockefeller brownstone but outside on Fifty-fifth Street. That witness was Sid Shapiro.

"We drove in to Fifty-fifth Street, just the Boss and I and the chauffeur," Shapiro says. "We had an appointment for lunch with Jack Flynn of the *News*, so he asked us to drive around and come back in an hour and pick him up. Then he gets out of the car and goes inside.

"When we came back, I witnessed an astonishing scene. The Boss comes out of the building and there's the Governor coming out after him and tugging at his arm, really pulling at him, trying to get him to come back inside and let's discuss it. Moses pulls his arm away from him and gets inside, saying, 'Come on, let's go,' and we pull away, leaving the Governor of the State of New York just standing there on the sidewalk, and there are members of the public standing around and staring at this scene."

Driving downtown, Moses, Shapiro says, "tells me this story of what happened inside, and he made me promise not to tell a single soul." When he had brought up the matter of the extension, he said, Nelson Rockefeller had, in his charming, gracious, assured manner, picked up a paper lying on his desk, let Moses see that it was the extension for his presidency of the Long Island State Park Commission and held it up in his hand—his left hand, Moses said, dramatizing the scene with his customary vividness—while saying, referring to the chairmanship of the State Council of Parks, "Now, Bob, don't you think now is the time for Laurance to take over?" Moses reacted to what he viewed as a naked threat—the Governor would not sign the paper he was holding aloft and thus allow him to retain the Long Island post unless he surrendered the statewide chairmanship—with hot rage. Keeping one post without the other, he said, was "out of the question"; if the Governor wanted him to resign one, he would—but he would resign the other, too. In fact, he would resign all posts connected with parks, the Bethpage and Jones Beach authorities chairmanships, too. In fact, perhaps the Governor would also like him to resign his other state job—the Power Authority chairmanship—since he seemed to feel he had too much to do. Of course not, the Governor said, all he was talking about was the Parks Council chairmanship. He would be happy to sign extensions allowing Moses to keep the other posts. "Out of the question," Moses said. The Power

Authority was a different field, but all state park work was interconnected; the only way he would resign one of the park posts was to resign them all.

Suddenly, he told Shapiro with a grim smile, Nelson had seemed a lot less sure of himself. Let's not make any final decision on anything now, the Governor had said. Let's meet again—for lunch—before the December 18 deadline. How about December 14?

Then, perhaps thinking of the luncheon to which Moses would be heading as soon as he left, the Governor, Moses was to write, "asked, I might say ordered, that I should not inform anyone of our conversation."

"I told him," Moses was to write, "I would accept no such order and make no such agreement . . . since I would have to make a public explanation." He told Shapiro that he had said, "Give me my coat and hat and let me get out of here"—and, snatching them up, had stalked out of the room and out of the house and onto the street, before the startled passers-by, the Governor hurrying after him and tugging his arm all the while.

This description of the conversation—coupled with Rockefeller's anxiety during the scene Shapiro had just witnessed—made Shapiro sure that RM had won. The Governor, he felt, would react as Governors—and Mayors—had always reacted to Moses' threat of resignation with "public explanation"; he would back down and let Moses keep all his posts. Moses' demeanor at the *Daily News* made the Moses Man more certain still. RM was gleeful, almost gloating over his victory—and he and Reuben Maury, the paper's chief editorial writer, concocted a ploy that they felt would make that victory more certain still: at Rockefeller's next press conference, the *News*'s Albany reporter James Desmond would ask the Governor if he planned to keep Moses in his posts. The question would take Rockefeller by surprise, they figured; he would certainly not want to announce without preliminaries that he had asked for Moses' resignation; he would have no choice but to say of course he planned to keep Moses in all his posts.

After he and RM returned to Randall's Island, Shapiro was more certain of victory than ever. The Governor's office had been calling and calling, one of Moses' secretaries said as soon as he walked in the door of his office. Moses was supposed to call back the minute he got in. While Shapiro was sitting there, Rockefeller's office telephoned three more times. "Mr. Moses wouldn't come to the phone. He figured if the Governor was calling him, he must have won, and he wouldn't talk to him. The last time his [Moses'] secretary says, 'The Governor is on the phone himself!' and Mr. Moses wouldn't take it. He had figured he had won."

And he might have, too. Rockefeller certainly had given no indication of wanting a full-scale showdown. The Governor himself was to say that during their brownstone confrontation "I urged him not to resign" his other posts "but simply to allow a transition to take place in connection with the State Council . . ." He had several times previously asked Moses to allow that "transition" to take place, and every time that Moses had refused, he had backed down. From the demeanor that Moses and Shapiro describe, there is certainly reason to believe he would, at the December 14 luncheon he had suggested, back down again. But Moses' arrogance led him to push the Governor too far. He sought to make him surrender, not gracefully but unconditionally—by using his ultimate weapon, the ultimatum that had never failed him before. Still refusing to take telephone calls from the Governor, he replied to him by firming up his threat, putting it in writing—and extending it. If the Governor wanted him to resign one state post, he wrote in a letter delivered to Rockefeller the next morning, Wednesday, November 28, he would resign all—not only the park posts but the chairmanship of the State Power Authority. He was, he said, already making arrangements to do so. And he made clear that there was no room for compromise at all.

"I shall of course meet you at lunch on December 14, but you have made your position abundantly clear. Meanwhile I am making tentative arrangements . . . to resign from the Long Island State Park Commission . . . Perhaps the simplest thing would be to resign as head of Power also so that you can make other arrangements to meet your program in this field."

There are indications in Moses' letter that even as he was writing it, he may have realized that he was going too far. He modified it several times, and as it emerged, Shapiro points out, "it wasn't *exactly* a resignation, if you look at the wording"—notably the words "tentative" and "perhaps." Still, it was in all essential respects the typical Moses ultimatum.

This time, however, the ultimate weapon misfired. After thirty years of issuing that defiant challenge, he had issued it to a man who would take him up on it. On the day after he received Robert Moses' resignation, Nelson Rockefeller accepted it. "I hope you will continue" in the Power Authority post, Rockefeller said. As for the others, "I note that you are making arrangements to resign from the Long Island State Park Commission. This is a decision which I accept with regret."

And now the events which Moses had set in motion conspired against him.

Neither his nor Rockefeller's letter had yet been released to the press (a circumstance which, incidentally, led Shapiro to hope that the Governor's, as well as Moses', was a bluff). Rockefeller had not held a press conference since Moses had arranged his Desmond ploy. But with one newspaper privy to the impending crunch between the state's Governor and its most famous official, the media rumor mill had begun to grind, and Moses' secretaries were reporting enough inquiries from other reporters so that he knew that it was only a matter of a short time before it hit the press. John Wingate broadly hinted at the situation in his WOR-TV newscast on Thursday evening. According to Shapiro, Moses realized now that the planted question designed to make the Governor retreat might well have the effect of forcing him to make his decision public, and thus irrevocable. But it was no longer feasible to have Desmond not ask the question. If he didn't, some other reporter would. And then, on Friday afternoon, Moses learned that Rockefeller had scheduled a press conference for that very night. Shapiro says that Moses realized that if Rockefeller was asked about the rumors, the Governor would have to reveal the resignations—and the acceptance. If it was the Governor who revealed them, it would appear to the public that the Governor had initiated them—that the Governor had asked him, Robert Moses, to resign. The Governor might even be pinned down by the reporters and have to say so directly. It would look as if he, Robert Moses, had been fired! To Moses—to whom public image was so terribly important—such loss of face would be intolerable. He had to get himself out of that position, had to make clear that, in the case of most of the resignations anyway, he had offered them, not been asked for them. The Governor had said he could keep the Power Authority chairmanship. He would resign that job, too! And he would have to make clear that he was in the right. He would reveal to the public what he felt was the reason the Governor had wanted him to resign—not his vigor or competence but out-and-out nepotism—although, for good measure, he would also intimate that there might be a hint of politics involved as well. And he would reveal the humiliating way in which, after decades as a faithful public servant, the Governor had been treating him for the past two years.

Hastily, almost frantically, drafting a statement, he got it into the hands of the press before the Rockefeller press conference. And if the mere fact of his making the resignations public was not enough to make his split with Rockefeller, and his loss of all state power, irrevocable, the text of the statement was.

> Last Tuesday morning . . . Governor Rockefeller . . . asked me flatly and with no preliminaries to resign immediately as chairman of the State Council of Parks so that he could put his brother Laurance . . . in my place. . . .
>
> I . . . told him that I would resign as president of the Long Island State Park Commission, also an unpaid position, since it is in that capacity that I sit on the Council. The Governor asked me to remain. . . . I told him this was out of the question. . . .
>
> I asked the Governor whether he wanted me to retire as head of the Power Authority, since he seemed to think I had too much to do. He said no. . . .
>
> Under the circumstances, I shall retire from all state park work on January 1 and from the Power Authority. . . . There has been a vacant trustee position for some time on the Power Authority. With my retirement, there will be two, and the term of the only Democratic member expires in the spring. I may add that on two previous occasions there was a long humiliating period of delay in signing extensions of my trusteeship and that the last two extensions were reduced from two years to one.

In a statement issued by his office, Rockefeller paid the required obeisance to Moses' "long and brilliant career and leadership." "There is no one who has done more to develop parks, not only in this state but anywhere in the nation, than has Commissioner Moses, and the people of this state will forever be indebted to him," he said. The Governor tried—at great length—to make the voters understand that he had not sought to end Moses' career but only to insure an "orderly transition of leadership" in one phase of it, a phase that "will take years to fully develop." He pointed out at length that Moses was giving up the other posts voluntarily. But contained in the statement was cold Rockefeller anger: "It is regrettable that in his statement of resignation to the press, Mr. Moses has made an invidious reference to my brother Laurance. Laurance Rockefeller . . . has been associated with the state park system since his appointment by Gov. Herbert H. Lehman in 1939 as a member of the Palisades Interstate Commission." The resignations were regretted. But they were accepted. All of them.

"I don't think Mr. Moses realized what he was doing in the rush that day," Sid Shapiro says. "I don't think he really expected the Governor to let him resign [from all the park posts] and I don't think he ever expected him to let him resign from the Power Authority. When he did realize it, I think it broke his heart." Moses' statement had gotten him the kind of headlines he wanted—the *Times,* for example, gave his nepotism charge a big page-one headline—but at a terrible cost.

At one stroke, he had cost himself five jobs—five on top of the four city jobs he had lost two years before. Once, he had held twelve separate posts. Now he was down to two—the chairmanship of the Triborough Bridge and Tunnel Authority and the presidency of the World's Fair—three if one counted his informal (and, of course, still enormously powerful) designation as city representative on arterial highways.

And it wasn't the number of jobs he had lost so much as what jobs they were. "The Long Island parks—well, they were the thing he had done first, you know," Shapiro says. "He loved Long Island more than any other place. And Jones Beach and the rest of those parks—well, they were his baby. It mattered so much to him that they be kept beautiful—just as he wanted them—and that he be able to expand them the way they should be expanded. Nothing else mattered as much to him as those parks. And now he had lost them."

And not only had he lost control of his first great dream, he had lost a huge hunk of his power. His power had been derived partly from popularity and mostly from money—money that he had sole discretion to spend. The popularity had vanished some years back, but its loss had not mattered much so long as he didn't lose the money. But the money came from his network of four public authorities. Now, at a stroke, three of them were gone—including the biggest of them all, the State Power Authority that, with both Robert Moses Power Dams completed at last, was beginning to generate tens of millions of dollars in annual revenue.

To reporters, he said firmly that the matter was closed. "There is nothing I am doing about it," he said with a broad smile, announcing that he was leaving for a previously planned vacation in Puerto Rico—ironically, at Laurance's Dorado Beach Hotel. (MOSES TAKES OUSTER CALMLY, headlines said.) But behind the scenes he was maneuvering almost frantically to attempt to retrieve his mistake. His emissaries were working on anyone who had Rockefeller's ear; Van Arsdale and Brennan were soon asking the Governor to let Moses withdraw his resignations, even if that withdrawal meant that Moses would have to eat public crow.

A man closer to the Governor, however, had guessed the futility of such attempts. "[Moses] got friends of mine to come to me and ask me to try to persuade Rockefeller to let him take it back," recalls Thomas E. Dewey. "I must have had a dozen phone calls from people I knew. But I had made a discreet inquiry, an indirect inquiry; Rockefeller wasn't going to let him take it back. I felt sorry for him." For what might have been the one reason for Rockefeller to let Moses withdraw his resignations—not his Parks Council resignation, perhaps, but his others—did not, to his surprise and that of political insiders, exist. The expected storm of protest had not materialized. Robert Moses had been fired. And hardly anyone had really cared.

Citing "nepotism" as its cause, the *Daily News* reacted to the ouster with outrage, as did the *Journal-American* (WE NEED HIM!) and conservative columnists. "No public official in any part of the country is comparable to Robert Moses in his devoted and unending and mostly uncompensated public service for nearly half a century," George E. Sokolsky declared. "No man can be trusted with major affairs who asks such a man as Robert Moses to resign. . . ." But in the rest of the media there was only a brief flurry of editorials, and the editorial that mattered never came. Moses must have known he had lost when, on December 2, he turned at his breakfast table to the editorial page of *The New York Times* (which only three years before had said: "You don't bench Babe Ruth") and read: "The most incredible of all the prodigious qualities of Robert Moses has been his ability to sustain, long after most other men retire, a superhuman burden of responsibilities. . . . He has conquered every obstacle in four decades of public service, except the ability to make himself immortal. . . . We hope that, after the verbal skyrockets sputter out, he will recognize the wisdom of the Governor's suggestion that it was time—indeed, past time—to begin planning for an orderly transition of authority. . . . No government function can be made so dependent on a single individual that he becomes the indispensable man."

The young reporter assigned to cover the otherwise vacant *Newsday* city desk Saturday afternoon and Sunday morning—the paper had no Sunday edition then—found waiting for him a memo from an editor telling him to compile a summary of all the statements that the editor was sure would be pouring in for a big story on reaction in governmental circles to be written by state political editor Stan Hinden Sunday night for Monday's paper. But all Saturday there was exactly one such statement—a brief one from Democratic state chairman William H. McKeon charging the Governor with "cavalier treatment." Telephoning around for comment Sunday evening, Hinden found politicians rather reluctant to make any, and those they did make were carefully hedged. Aside from a few Democratic county chairmen backing McKeon, of a score of public officials telephoned, only Newbold Morris ("I can't believe it") was willing to go on record with the type of public statement the editor had expected. Pragmatists all, politicians had grasped at once the basic reality of the situation: the Governor, the man with the power, was the man they didn't want to offend. As for the public at large, aside from a spate—a brief spate—of letters-to-the-editor, there was hardly any reaction at all.

In political circles the illusion of Moses' popularity with the voters had lingered long after the reality was gone, partly because in those circles, many of whose members were making money off him, that popularity was undimmed, partly because politicians were close enough to him to be overawed by his personality so completely that they could hardly conceive of his falling into public disrepute. For decades, Governors had dreaded what would happen if they had to be the one to fire Bob Moses. Now one Governor had fired Bob Moses.

And nothing had happened.

The next meeting of the State Council of Parks was the first in thirty-eight years over which Robert Moses had not presided. It was the first meeting of the State Council of Parks *ever* over which Moses had not presided.

At that meeting, his successor read a eulogy with, observers say, obvious feeling. Then resolutions were adopted unanimously to change the names of not one, but three separate state parks, one at Niagara, one at Massena and one on Fire Island, to "Robert Moses State Park."

At a time at which the naming of public works after individuals had not reached the floodtide it was later to assume, this was an almost unprecedented honor. It is doubtful that any individual below the rank of President had ever had three separate major public works named after him at the same time. Coupled with the eulogy, it made the January 22, 1963, meeting of the State Council of Parks one of unparalleled tribute to Robert Moses. But Robert Moses had not presided over that meeting.

More important, he had not been present. For only the heads of the various regional park commissions could attend, and he was no longer the head of the regional park commission he had headed for thirty-eight years, the park commission that represented his youthful, and cherished, and most nearly perfect dreams.

During the following years, Robert Moses never admitted even once—not even to his closest friends; not even to Shapiro—how much the loss of the presidency of the Long Island State Park Commission meant to him. But people who knew him saw through his assumed indifference.

His successor as commission president, Perry Duryea, Jr., son of an old associate and an admirer himself, speaks of the "great emotional strain" that the seventy-four-year-old commissioner went through when discussing the parks with him. "He always considered the Long Island State Park Commission as his base," Duryea says. "Long Island was, after all, the place he knew best. This was really the Moses baby above everything else." Says Joe Ingraham: "He would never let on, but you could see it in everything he said—they broke his heart when they took that away from him."

Not only pride but politics prevented Moses thereafter from displaying open resentment. Having had a taste of Nelson Rockefeller once, he was not anxious for another one. He was, shortly, to swallow his pride and make up with the man who had so grievously injured him. At the dedication of the Alexander Hamilton Bridge two weeks after the firing, reporters were watching to see Moses' reaction when Rockefeller appeared. Moses' reaction was to throw his arms around Rockefeller and to go out of his way to praise him during his speech. (Rockefeller threw his arms around Moses, and praised him, too.)

47. The Great Fair

THE NEW YORK WORLD'S FAIR of 1964–65, huge and spectacular though it was, could not capture the imagination of the man who was in charge of it. To him—preoccupied with immortality, creator of public works that would endure for centuries—two years, the total duration of the Fair, was but a watch in the night. He saw the Fair only as a means to other ends.

One of these ends was a dream, a dream out of his youth that had remained bright in his old age—a dream of a great park, the greatest in New York City, the greatest within the limits of any city in the world, the ultimate urban park, *rus in urbe* supreme, a park worthy of being named "Robert Moses Park." He had been fighting for that dream close to forty years, using first one expedient and then another to inch it, step by painstaking step, closer to reality, and after forty years it was still nowhere close. The Fair, he realized at once, might at last be the means to achieve it. For the site of the Fair, like the site of the dream, was the Flushing Meadows.

Nature had presented the meadows as a gift to the city—three miles of marshland too low-lying and waterlogged for any developer to fill in, so that as the ugly man-made tide called "slurb" swept eastward across Queens, engulfing in cheap subdivisions the fields and woods on the higher land bordering the meadows, it broke and ebbed around that marsh, leaving the meadows undivided, whole, still available for the common weal.

Man, in the person of Tammany Hall and a character named Fishhooks McCarthy, had done his best to squander that gift. Although the meadows were city-owned "park land," for years the Forty Thieves on the city's old Board of Aldermen had allowed Fishhooks' Brooklyn Ash Removal Company to use them as a gigantic dump for the burning of the garbage of all Brooklyn; by the 1920's, 110 railroad carloads of the offscourings of the Borough of Churches, transported on private railroad tracks used exclusively by Fishhooks' firm, were being dumped daily onto the meadows, and a once beautiful marshland was covered with foothills of filth (one, nicknamed "Mount Corona," towered nearly a hundred feet in the air) infested by rats that, Moses was to say, were "big enough to wear saddles," and by swarms of fur-bearing creatures so numerous that nearby shanty dwellers eked out livings trapping them and selling them to fur dealers. The once lovely Flushing River had become an open sewer. At night, burning refuse from the Flushing Meadows dumps, and from those on Riker's Island just beyond, glowed and flamed dramatically; during the day, the scene was ugly enough to inspire the creative mind. It inspired F. Scott Fitzgerald, who in *The Great Gatsby* described it as

> a valley of ashes—a fantastic farm where ashes grow like wheat into ridges and hills and grotesque gardens, where ashes take the forms of houses and chimneys and rising smoke, and finally, with a transcendent effort, of ash-gray men, who move dimly and already crumbling through the powdery air. Occasionally a line of gray cars crawls along an invisible track, gives out a ghastly creak, and comes to rest, and immediately the ash-gray men swarm up with leaden spades and stir up an impenetrable cloud . . .

And it inspired Robert Moses.

From the 1920's, the Flushing Meadows had fired Moses' imagination. Part of the inspiration had been their size, of course: they were 1,346 acres, a Central Park and a half. Part had been their location: they lay almost precisely at the geographic center of New York; as the city's population shifted, moving steadily eastward, its population center was moving steadily closer to those meadows, too—a park there, Moses felt, would be a true "Central Park" to the whole city. For a man with a vision so broad that it required vast open spaces for realization, here was a vast open space—at the city's geographic and population center. And in some way the very ugliness of the meadows seemed to furnish inspiration, too. They, and the Riker's dump beyond, were "a cloud of smoke by day and a pillar of fire by night," he was to write. Rereading Isaiah, he came across "Give unto them beauty for ashes"—after that, his dream had a slogan. He would turn what may well have been the ugliest part of New York City into its most beautiful.

As with all Moses' dreams, this one kept expanding. By 1930, on the maps he prepared for the Metropolitan Park Conference, there was green—the green that symbolized future park land—not only over the Flushing Meadows but, extending eastward from the meadows in a continuous corridor right along the spine of Queens all the way out to the city line, not just a park but a string of three parks (Kissena, Cunningham and Alley Pond) connected by strips of greenery—parks designed to serve not only the single-family-home Queens of the present generation but the high-rise Queens he foresaw for future generations.

But it was to be a tough dream to realize. No project on which Robert Moses had ever embarked was to document more definitively his statement: "It takes more than a good idea to make a great public improvement. The fact is that such things happen when there are leaders available, ready and eager to take advantage of the logic of events. Even then the whole result is accomplished only by a series of limited objectives, over a surprisingly long period of years." No project was to demonstrate more dramatically that of all the qualities which enabled him to build public works of the first magnitude, none was more important than the simple fact that he endured, that he stayed in power not for years, but for decades.

Because it took decades.

He began trudging through the park, actively planning it in detail, in 1934, walking through the valley of ashes, trudging, as he put it, over "thirty years of the offscourings, the cans, cast-off baby carriages and umbrellas of Brooklyn," among the ash-gray men carrying spades, followed by a group of men without spades—Madigan, Howland, Andrews, Latham, Shapiro, Chapin. Soon there were transoms and plumb lines among the spades, and then blueprints, for, searching for a way to extend the Grand Central Parkway to the Triborough Bridge, he had determined—and the engineers had confirmed—that the way could be along the western edge of the meadows. For a while thereafter he hoped that the parkway could lead to the park, that the road might prove the key to unlocking the monumental expenditure of public funds necessary for the realization of so monumental a vision. With La Guardia in, Tammany was out—and so, too, was Fishhooks; state funds were available to build the parkway, and, cynical as he had become about the ability of the legislative leaders in Albany to see the public interest, he could not believe that even they would allow him to build a road along which motorists would have to drive through hills of garbage; he was sure that once he got the parkway built he could get state money to build a park around it. But he had underestimated Albany; the Legislature would give funds for a road and nothing else; the Grand Central Parkway and a narrow right-of-way on either side of it was all he was able to build on the meadows. He moved 50,000,000 cubic yards of rubbish, but they made in Mount Corona only a narrow pass; recalls Rodgers, "Motorists still had to pass through the dark wall of refuse before coming out on the broad prospects of meadow and bay." "For a while," Moses would recall ruefully, "we fondly hoped to cover" the garbage "with a thin layer of topsoil and to plant, at a price which would not subject us to indictment," but obtaining even the topsoil strained his ingenuity to the limit; planting was out of the question. As for the great park, "We studied every possible means of acquiring the whole meadow, but this dream seemed too big for the vision and means of the City in the face of competition of so many other urgent enterprises."

Then, he says, in words that reveal that inside Robert Moses the Power Broker there was still a Robert Moses the Dreamer, "the miracle happened—the idea of a World's Fair."

Not the 1964–65 World's Fair, the 1939–40. The mind that could grasp an idea in an instant, expand it, fill in its details, see its relation to other ideas, lunged at that idea of the Fair as it fell from George McAneny's lips. "By God that's a great idea!" he had said, pounding the table; he would sell it to La Guardia, and he himself "would stop at nothing to help"—if the Fair was held on Flushing Meadows, and if "from the beginning the project was planned so as to insure a great park" on the meadows after the Fair closed.

Moses thought he had taken out every possible form of insurance. His park commissionership made him in effect the Fair Corporation's landlord; the lease he drew up—and, as additional insurance, embodied in legislation he had passed in Albany—provided that the improvements necessary to make the meadows usable be permanent, not temporary, improvements, and that they be installed in conformance with his plan for the park—right down to the creation of a boat basin at the north end of the site and two lakes at the south: thousands of trees were planted and thousands of yards of underground utility lines laid according to the landscape design for the park, not the Fair. The first $4,000,000 of Fair profits, moreover, were to be used —as a spark to kindle further state and city contributions—to create a park. Making the meadows usable proved to be immensely more difficult than even the most pessimistic of his engineers had foreseen—it was at the Flushing Meadows, for example, that there were encountered, for the first time on such a large scale in the metropolitan area, "mud waves" of a force that ripped loose foundations and pilings. A new drainage system for the entire Flushing area—which included placing a branch of the Flushing River in a conduit as large as a tube of the Holland Tunnel—had to be created; cleaning up pollution in Flushing Bay required two giant sewage treatment plants. Even for Moses, the list of other basic improvements required was "endless"; even he had to call their total cost—$59,000,000—"staggering." But Moses got the money from Albany and, with La Guardia's help, from Washington. He even got an additional million dollars—which La Guardia found somewhere in the city budget after Moses promised him that the building would have plenty of the Mayor's favorite architectural element, glass bricks—for an Aymar Embury-designed permanent, pillared New York City Building housing an ice- and roller-skating rink ("You could get a lot of building for a million then," Moses would recall ruefully). And then he saw all his precautions made meaningless by Grover Whalen's inefficiency; the $4,000,000 was supposed to come out of the Fair's profits, and there were no profits; the 1939–40 New York World's Fair ended with a deficit so large that it could repay its backers only thirty-three cents on the dollar. By 1940, federal funds had dried up; the city was broke; all during the five years of World War II the Flushing Meadows remained a park mostly in name only, littered with debris from the buildings of exhibitors who had had enough money to dismantle their structures but not enough to truck the remains away, grass and trees dying, rats starting to reappear—all that was left was a skating rink and, underground, invisible, tens of millions of dollars' worth of utilities that would provide a foundation for a park—if ever there should come another chance to build it.

One "event" in which Moses saw the "logic of using it to progress a park" had been a highway, another had been a World's Fair. It took a leader with his single-mindedness to see such logic in the third, which occurred five years after the Fair; other men might see the formation of the United Nations in 1945 as a chance for peace, he saw it as a chance for a park. Persuading Secretary-General Trygve Lie to use the City Building until UN headquarters in Manhattan could be completed, he got $2,000,000 from the enthusiastic Board of Estimate to "remodel" it—and enough of that money found its way into remodeling around, rather than in, that building to develop scores of acres near it according to the park plans he had stored away for so many years now.

Another five years, and another event—and the same Park Commissioner still around to take advantage of its "logic." With the population of

Queens burgeoning in 1951, the Board of Estimate approved a huge new storm sewer for the borough. When Moses had finished taking a hand in its planning, it was running along a route linking Alley Pond, Cunningham and Kissena parks, enough land along it had been condemned so there could be at least a strip of park land all the way from Flushing Meadows to the city line, arrangements had been made to fill the gash made for the sewer with Sanitation Department fill according to plans drawn up by the Park Department—and after decades of dreaming about a Queens park corridor, the land for it was at last in his hands.

And when, in 1959, he had first heard that men were planning another World's Fair, he believed that the chance had come to turn the great Queens dream—Flushing Meadows Park, the corridor, the three other parks along it—into reality at last. That was the key attraction for him in assuming the Fair presidency. He admitted this fairly frankly in public. "Visitors to such an exposition," he wrote, "carry away indelible impressions, lively lessons, enduring satisfactions and pleasant memories, but what finally remains in the ground when the pageant has faded, the brickbats have been removed by the wreckers and scavengers, and the park planners have gone to work is of more concern to the next generation than any spectacle, however gorgeous." In private, he was more frank. "I don't think RM really ever cared about the Fair—not in the sense he cared about Jones Beach, say," Sid Shapiro declares. "What he cared about—what he was always talking about—was what the Fair could do for parks."

The Fair could do what he had wanted to do for so long. The "chain of urban parks," he said, would be "the ultimate residuary legatee of the Fair." And he was sure the legacy would be large enough. Hardly had he assumed the presidency when the engineering firms of his two most trusted park consultants—W. Earle Andrews of Andrews & Clark and Gilmore Clarke of Clarke & Rapuano—were costing out the full-scale development of the chain. The figure came to about $56,000,000, and his financial consultant, Jack Madigan of Madigan-Hyland, assured him the Fair's surplus would be far higher. He went on record with a confident promise: "The Fair will . . . finish the Flushing Meadow and Corridor program without cost to the city. . . . The Fair management is committed without reservation to . . . presenting to the City an integrated chain of urban parks which will serve as a model to rapidly growing municipalities everywhere. . . . We [will] build a heritage for all time." There was even a timetable, laid out park by park, and guaranteeing—unconditionally—completion by "the summer of 1967," less than two years after the Fair was to close. The Fair would be the instrument by which the dream he had cherished for almost forty years would be transformed into reality—reality grand enough and beautiful enough to bear his name.*

* There was a further piece of evidence to prove that Moses' interest was not in the Fair but in the parks that would follow it. Mass transportation was desirable—crucially important, in fact—for a fair to which people would come by the tens of thousands each day. And Moses was expecting to draw heavily on the city's poorer families, many of which did not have automobiles. But it was not desirable—

As he expected to be identified with it. One of the bankers he appointed to its finance committee would soon be suggesting that "the new park must be called Robert Moses Park." Moses did not demur. It was an open secret among his aides that the suggestion was just what RM had in mind.

The realization of a dream was one end to which the World's Fair represented a means; there were two others—power and popularity.

On the single square mile of former garbage dump that would be the actual Fair grounds, a single mile over which Robert Moses possessed sole jurisdiction, there would be spent—by state and federal governments on highways, by city government on other improvements, by state, federal and city governments and private corporate grants on exhibits—well over a billion dollars. A single item in the first estimate prepared by his office of the money that would be poured into the site gave some idea of the dimension of spending he had in mind. That item was: "Miscellaneous—$55,000,000." He made sure that that billion wasn't wasted. He distributed it where it could bring the greatest return in power.

Maintenance—cleaning, repairs, garbage collection and disposal—was obviously going to be a huge item at the Fair. Of all maintenance companies in New York, none was better connected politically than the Allied Maintenance Corporation. On March 9, 1964, there went out from Fair headquarters a memo: "Constable to All Participants: Allied . . . has been designated by the Fair Corporation as the only refuse and garbage collectors at the Fair." Exhibitors would no longer be allowed to pick and choose among maintenance firms to get the best rates; Allied had been given a monopoly. (Allied used that monopoly to the hilt, charging rates so inflated that during the Fair's first season alone the company was to collect from helpless exhibitors more than $10,000,000.)

Commissions on the insurance that would be required of exhibitors would come to more than $3,000,000. Carmine De Sapio, despite his break with Wagner, still possessed considerable behind-the-scenes political power,* particularly, through his ally state Democratic chairman Michael J. Prendergast, in the State Capitol, where Moses now needed power more urgently than he had in decades. De Sapio was known to look fondly on an insurance agency named Campo & Roberts. And Article XVII of the Fair's General Regulations for Exhibition—with which all exhibitors were bound by con-

---

in Moses' view—for a great park, because he did not want his great parks to be open to low-income people, particularly the Negro and Puerto Rican people who made up so large a percentage of the city's lower-income families. So Moses vetoed the Transit Authority's proposed new subway extensions to the Fair.

* Writes Warren Moscow: De Sapio "kept the loyalty of a substantial bloc within the Tammany executive committee, although other members had gone down to defeat with him. He had many friends in the business community whom he had helped in their dealings with the city, and who did not choose to run away from him now that he had been defeated." And one of those friends, of course, was Thomas J. Shanahan.

tract to comply—required that ". . . insurance must be procured from insurance companies approved by the Fair Corporation," and only one company, Campo & Roberts, was approved.

Mayor Wagner protested. But in a competition with De Sapio, Wagner was handicapped: he was honest. Commissions wouldn't buy him. The Mayor could have asked Moses to give Fair-oriented insurance to firms operated by his supporters but for another handicap: his unshakable resolution never to give Moses something the Coordinator could hold over his head by asking him directly for a favor. He had Deputy Mayor Paul Screvane, the key liaison between the Mayor and Moses on the Fair, raise the subject, and Screvane recalls: "Moses would say—as he said on other things that came up during the Fair—'Well, for Christ's sake, let him ask for it. I can't do anything for him if he doesn't ask.' I used to go back and tell Wagner to name the guy he wanted to get the insurance, but he wouldn't do it." Finally, "there was a meeting at Gracie Mansion, just the three of us," Screvane recalls. Previously, the Deputy Mayor says, Wagner had been "incensed. If, when he had the confrontation with him, he had spoken the way he spoke in private, Moses would have changed the insurance." But Wagner wouldn't. Finally, "[Moses] asked Bob if Bob had someone—'Give me a name!' But Bob wouldn't tell him."*

Insurance commissions were only one of a thousand fees created by the Fair, and it sometimes seemed as if every one of them was distributed according to a single criterion: the amount of power it could purchase for Robert Moses. Others might see the Fair as a chance to foster "peace through understanding," or to boost the occupancy rate of New York hotels, or to increase sales in New York department stores; Moses appears to have seen the Fair as a gigantic gravy train on which he could ride back to the power he had left behind. In those early days, the Fair's future appeared as golden as the statue of the Moroni angel atop the Mormon Pavilion; ticket sales were going even better than expected; money was flowing in at a rate exceeding Madigan's most optimistic estimates; Moses was soon boasting that there might be even more money available than he had thought.

Soon everyone was scrambling to get on board. One Fair Corporation executive, speaking of an "attitude of affluence" at Flushing Meadows, says, "There was Moses talking about all those millions of dollars in advance sales. And the unions and Allied said, 'Why should we try to hold costs down? If a guy's making so much dough, why shouldn't we get some of it?' "

And Moses helped them on. Lavish spending had always been part of

---

* Here is Wagner's recollection of this issue: "I didn't see after my battle of 1961 why De Sapio should have the insurance. I said, 'Bob, I hear De Sapio's got an interest in the insurance.' I never got a straight answer. I know from other sources that he did, but I never got a straight answer."

Asked why Moses felt an alliance with De Sapio would be more profitable than an alliance with him, the Mayor replied by recalling a song once sung by reporters at an Inner Circle dinner, whose key lines, Wagner says, were: "Mayors Come and Mayors Go/But Old Man Moses, He Just Keeps Rolling Along."

his life style; he certainly wasn't going to change that style now. Unions were allowed—encouraged—to charge exhibitors rates unusual even for New York; carpenters, for example, received—not as overtime but as normal pay—$23 an hour. The $10,000,000 that Allied was to reap from individual exhibitors during the Fair's first season alone might have seemed sufficient for even so politically well-connected a firm, but the contract Moses signed with Allied on behalf of the Fair Corporation was, in that year alone, to hand the company an additional $12,000,000. The Fair Corporation's original budget for security had been a lavish $5,000,000 a year. But Moses wanted security laid on with an eye not just for safety but for show. A whole platoon of Pinkerton guards, dressed in elaborate uniforms with white gloves and white ascots, was assigned as an honor guard at Fair headquarters so that when foreign ambassadors or heads of state drove up, Moses could greet them with suitable panoply. During the Fair's first year of operation alone, Moses spent almost $10,000,000 for "security." He liked to reward his allies on an imperial scale. Politically well-connected PR man Tom Deegan, with his statement that "I . . . expect to continue to serve without any fees or expenses of any kind" still warm on the record, was given an annual fee of $100,000 and expenses that included a $1,000-a-month suite at the Waldorf and a $572 monthly salary for a chauffeur. And that was just Tom Deegan personally. The Thomas J. Deegan Co., Inc., received from the Fair an additional $350,000 per year. Not that the Deegan firm was responsible for the whole Fair public relations effort. The firm owned by Bill O'Dwyer's canny PR man—and still well-connected political insider—Bill Donoghue received $400,000 per year. Then there was Ed O'Brien and Murray Davis—and a list of former newspapermen that ran to the dozens. The listed Fair Corporation expenses for public relations for its first season alone ran to $2,772,542.49. Moses had always liked to pick up checks in the grand style. This predilection was indulged. So that VIP visitors—every politician, it seemed, from New York State or City, their relatives, influential businessmen, architects, engineers, contractors and *their* relatives, Moses' whole Yale class of 1909, dozens of neighbors from Babylon, scores of his acquaintances, and of Constable's, Spargo's, Shapiro's, of everyone connected in any way with the Fair administration—would not be forced to tour the Fair grounds on foot with the hoi polloi, the Fair Corporation purchased a fleet of white sedans, and set up a chauffeurs' pool in which there were often scores of men sitting around waiting for their next assignment. The chefs and waiters necessary for Moses to host at luncheons in his accustomed style were laid on. As for the scores of cocktail parties and other receptions he hosted, " 'economize' was a dirty word," one Fair Corporation executive recalls. During the Fair's first season, the bill for "Reception, travel and *subsistence* [italics added] expenses" was $706,053.51. During its first year, the Fair Corporation spent on operating expenses alone $33,299,000—double the original budget. And those expenses do not include the helping hand Moses offered to allies in trouble: one of his Triborough concessionaires had bitten off, in a concession called "The Belgian Village," more than he could financially chew; he needed $750,000 in cash, and he needed it fast. Although there was very little chance that it would ever be seen again—and in fact it never was—the Fair Corporation lent him the money.

Moses wanted a full passenger list aboard this most luxurious of all gravy trains not only so that he could have the largest possible audience for his hospitality but because, more important, a passenger's acceptance of his ticket would couple his fortunes to Moses', make him his ally, help him retain and increase the power he had begun to lose. He wanted power—and to get it he selected his passenger list with care. "Why don't you come aboard?" O'Brien and Donoghue were asking, and Joe Kahn says, "Sometimes it seemed as if everyone who mattered was." The unions, thanks to the exclusive, padded contracts, were already snug in their berths. The banks, thanks to $29,000,000 in Fair Corporation bonds were snug in theirs. And now, in response to Moses' invitations, a substantial portion of the city's power elite scrambled aboard—contractors (the names on the big signs beside the excavations on the Fair site—Tully & Di Napoli, Hendrickson Bros., Corbetta, Slattery, Johnson, Drake & Piper, De Lillo, Gull—were a roster of political clout); engineers (Shumavon & Buckley; Parsons, Brinkerhoff; Tibbetts, Abbott, McCarthy, Stratton—and one new name: Blauvelt Engineering, a firm with a new partner, George E. Spargo); architects; suppliers. The legal fees—immense legal fees—went to Sam Rosenman and, with the help of Moses-authored legislation exempting the Fair from the city's Code of Ethics, the law firm that former city administrator Charlie Preusse had just resigned to join. The vice president in charge of international affairs was Charles Poletti, called "Governor" because he had once served a twenty-nine-day term in that post as Lehman's interim successor; the head of the United States Pavilion was Triborough commissioner and powerful realtor and political insider Norman K. Winston; lucrative concessions were handed out to men like Howard Cullman and George P. Monaghan, who had been replaced as State Harness Racing Commissioner when the State Investigation Commission revealed that contractors who, on his recommendation, had been given contracts by the harness tracks had repaired his home—for free. The lucrative contract for the Fair's souvenir program went to Henry Luce's Time, Inc.; other benefits from the Fair went to a subsidiary of John Hay Whitney's Whitney Communication Corporation Holding Company.

The World's Fair gave Robert Moses a billion dollars to spend on power, and he got his money's worth.

Proof of that was forthcoming within a very short period of time after he became Fair president. Some bankers, remembering the 1939–40 fiasco at Flushing, were reluctant to purchase Fair bonds unless the Fair could show some operating capital of its own first. Moses asked the city to come up with some. There were plenty of objections—from liberals, including city councilmen (Stanley Isaacs was, of course, among them) who said that the city had more urgent needs on which to spend money—but not from the people who counted. The Council and the Board of Estimate and Mayor hastily approved an allocation of $24,000,000 to the Fair whose purpose had supposedly been to earn the city money, and the $24,000,000 was only the visible portion of the city's contribution. Whenever Moses needed more money—and he needed it often—he went back to the city for quiet contributions. The total city contribution to the Fair is hidden under scores of innocuous items, but one estimate, possibly conservative, was that it topped $60,000,000.

The Fair got him power; popularity was something else again. The universal exposition should have restored much of the universal affection in which he had once been held, both because its loudly proclaimed end as a great park should have reminded that portion of the public old enough to remember that Robert Moses was primarily a "park man," and because a "fair" was a cause almost as much on the side of the angels as parks, an event the press would normally cover in a blithe, carefree, favorable vein. It should, in fact, have in a way broadened his popularity, making it national in scope, giving him coast-to-coast publicity. The Fair should have rehabilitated Robert Moses' reputation and expanded it. Instead, the Fair destroyed it.

It was his own fault. In love with power, he could not give it up. To accept this new, bigger, construction post, it had been necessary for him to trade in a smaller—Title I—but he would not even consider giving up anything else. At the same time that he was undertaking to build the largest exposition the world had ever seen, therefore, he was simultaneously building the world's largest hydroelectric facility, the world's largest suspension bridge and the world's largest metropolitan arterial highway system—as well as building another huge suspension bridge, acquiring thousands of acres of new Long Island parks,* battling on a dozen fronts to win approval of one new highway down Fire Island and two across Manhattan, giving general direction to city and state park programs, and administering a $60,000,000-a-year corporation: six-bridge, two-tunnel Triborough; and a $65,000,000-a-year corporation: the State Power Authority. Title I had been his first failure, and part of the reason had been the fact that he had simply had too much else to do. Now, thanks to his reluctance to relinquish power, he was stepping into the same trap. He was moving into a new field, one in which he possessed no expertise—and he was allowing himself no time to acquire any.

Nor would he hire himself any. His "muchachos" had built and administered highways, bridges, tunnels and parks; they had never built or administered a World's Fair. Yet he would not allow outsiders into his operation; long-time Moses Men comprised the Fair's entire upper echelon, its top-level executive staff included not a single person with exposition experience. The man he assigned to sell space in the industrial area was J. Anthony Panuch, whose sole qualification appears to have been the fact that his housing reorganization report praised Moses; Panuch, as one critic was to

* It was not until 1962—after he had been running the Fair for two years—that Rockefeller would blast him free of some of these responsibilities.

note, "had never sold anything in his life." (Two years later, Moses was to fire him; he "couldn't do the job," he was to say. "A nice fellow, but he couldn't do the job.") The emissary to foreign governments was not the diplomat needed but Governor Poletti.

Most important, perhaps, he simply was not especially interested in this mammoth enterprise he had undertaken to create and direct.

In all his public life, only one field he had entered—public housing—had failed to ignite the imagination that, when ignited, could blaze so fiercely. Now there were two. The Fair would catch his imagination later, but not at the beginning—and it was at the beginning that he made a mistake that would later be ineradicable. He was not at that time interested in the Fair itself, so he was not interested in Fair pavilions, and they were temporary structures, anyway; this man who built for the centuries could not be interested in structures that would last two years. The great end he had in mind—a great park—would in fact be endangered by any construction the Fair Corporation undertook itself: most financial analyses of the 1939–40 World's Fair agreed that a prime cause of its fiscal disaster had been Grover Whalen's willingness to build pavilions because there was an exciting idea behind them—and then find that he couldn't recoup the Fair's investment through rentals. Moses was determined not to repeat that mistake. Practically the first major decision made about the Fair by this master builder was that he was going to build as little of it as possible; he would, of course, build its interior roadway system and do the landscaping (because they would later become part of the park), but of the more than 200 exhibition pavilions, the Fair Corporation would build exactly three—a small administration building, one small Fair Corporation-operated pavilion and an 18,000-seat auditorium for athletic events and outdoor attractions—to be constructed to the cheapest possible specifications.

Uninvolved emotionally in the pavilions as he was, he had an additional financial reason to remain aloof: because rents from his exhibitors would go to his park, he wanted them set as high as possible, and exhibitors weighing high rents would want complete control over their own architecture. He decided therefore to give it to them; each exhibitor would have virtual carte blanche in his pavilion's design and construction. "A fair begins with its buildings," a critic wrote, stating that by his decision Moses had in effect "taken himself out of the fair business." Soon he was to take another step in that direction. Prior to Moses' installation as its president the Fair Corporation had appointed a "Design Committee" of five distinguished architects—Wallace K. Harrison, Edward Durrell Stone, Gordon Bunshaft, Henry Dreyfuss and Emil Praeger—to develop a central theme and plan. To give the Fair unity, they proposed housing all its exhibits in a single doughnut-shaped pavilion a mile around and 1,800 feet in diameter, which would be constructed by the Fair Corporation and in which exhibitors would rent slices. Moses knew something about the design that none of its supporters—including, apparently, the Design Committee—knew: since he had studied the life of Haussmann, he knew that the doughnut-shaped building had been used at a previous World's Fair, Haussmann's Universal Exposition of 1867. He turned the proposal down, reiterating that there would, by design, be no central plan of any type.

So uninterested was he that he wasn't even interested in the layout of the Fair. Hardly had he accepted the Fair presidency when he commissioned the Port Authority as the Fair's agent in selling the 2,000,000 square feet of rentable space set aside in the transportation area; the only instructions given to the Port Authority executive to whom this responsibility was delegated were: "Here are eighty acres. You develop a master plan and sell them." Another commission—a lucrative one—for selling space in the "industrial area" was given to an agent of John Hay Whitney.

Even his critics had always had to admit that organization was Robert Moses' strong point. The Fair would be disorganized, its 200 pavilions a disorganized hodgepodge of 200 different sizes and shapes. Lack of a theme, a sense of unity, was a weakness of the first magnitude. All great expositions of the past "seem," as one critic was to put it, "to have some reason behind them." Uninterested in a great exposition—interested only in a great park—Moses seemed to feel he could have one without the other.

The Fair destroyed Moses' reputation also because he had to have his own way about everything, even in a field to which he was the newest of newcomers. He could have his own way in New York, but in putting on a World's Fair, he had to deal with other states and countries—and his arrogance antagonized them.

Dealing with scores of foreign nations would have been difficult enough in any circumstances. Governments were constantly falling, Cabinets changing—no sooner had one agreed to join the Fair than a new one was in power. Sukarno would participate only if Indonesia's pavilion was placed precisely midway between the United States' and Russia's to symbolize its neutrality. West Berlin wanted its exhibit symbolically situated on a traffic island beside that of the United States. (Poletti finally persuaded it to accept a less isolated site—one that was still right across from its protectors'.) Moses made such dealings impossible.

Most European nations were members of the Bureau of International Expositions, a Paris-based body set up in 1928 to regulate their number and nature. The B.I.E. had at least two rules incompatible with Moses' desire for a huge profit: Fairs could not run for more than six months, and could not ask foreign exhibitors to pay ground rents. "None of [these] obstacles was insuperable," as one observer wrote; there was, in fact, a plethora of precedent for the quiet bending of such rules with tacit B.I.E. approval—some of it established by the 1939–40 World's Fair, which had obtained B.I.E. sanction despite its duration and ground rent. While Robert Kopple, the originator of the idea for the Fair (forced out by Moses when he took over), had been running the Fair, several countries had begun planning "informal" but lavish exhibits ostensibly sponsored by national Chambers of Commerce but actually financed by government funds.

But Moses had made these obstacles insuperable. Arriving at B.I.E. headquarters in Paris to find them unimpressively modest and B.I.E. officials unwilling to pay immediate and formal obeisance to his demands, he departed muttering audibly about "three people living obscurely in a dumpy apartment in Paris." To the press he bluntly announced, "We . . . are not subject to any rulings." He must have thought he was talking to the New York State Legislature. The B.I.E. directors, however, were not on his payroll; they responded not only by refusing the Fair its official sanction—a step which need not have hurt—but by taking the highly unusual step of formally requesting its members not to participate—which hurt plenty. Within weeks, Britain, which had been planning to participate, announced it wouldn't—and so did three-fourths of the British Commonwealth, along with France and Italy. Of all the major European countries outside the Iron Curtain, only one—Spain—defied the B.I.E. and accepted a Moses invitation; with one press conference, he had made his World's Fair a fair without Europe.* Out of all the world's more important nations, in fact, the Fair obtained exactly six government-sponsored pavilions: Indonesia, Egypt, India, Japan, Mexico and Pakistan. And as Poletti was indiscreetly to put it, "It's pretty hard to have a World's Fair without a lot of international participation."

His loss of reputation was his own fault primarily because the image he created for the Fair was one of controversy.

A World's Fair was not a bridge that the public had no choice but to pay to use, it was a show to which the public had to be persuaded to purchase tickets. The key to the Fair's success was, therefore, public relations. It had to be portrayed to the public in attractive colors, as something gay, glowing, exciting. Moses understood this—intellectually. The hard-sell public relations effort he launched was perhaps one of the most extensive ever undertaken on behalf of any enterprise except a presidential election. Movies were made, speakers sent out, equipped with elaborate slide presentations, to urge Kiwanis, Rotary and Elks clubs from coast to coast to "Come to the Fair"; television, radio, magazine and newspaper ads were laid on so lavishly that Moses' Fair Corporation would eventually spend a total of $3,260,963 on public relations. And this was no more than a drop in the promotional bucket; the Fair would be featured in tens of millions of dollars of paid advertising by such giant corporate exhibitors as Ford, General Motors and IBM. The Travelers Insurance Co. alone staged elaborate "Come to the Fair" presentations in eighty-three cities.

But Moses' PR men, aware of his desire for national publicity, did everything they could to influence the press to play the Fair in terms of its boss. The Fair Corporation's own publicity was built around Moses, of course; the *Time* and *Newsweek* and *Look* cover stories had not only the Unisphere but RM on their covers; *Life*'s story was entitled "Everything Coming up Moses." The hour-long CBS network show on the Fair was largely devoted to Moses' career; the local CBS-TV show was "The Man Who Built

---

* There would be pavilions named for European countries, but they would be cheap-jack jobs financed by private promoters.

New York." And because Fair publicity was built around Moses, it was wasted; the Fair's over-all image was not of a scene of gaiety but of a scene of strife and uneasiness and rage.

Moses' decades-long honeymoon with the press of New York City was over, of course. Criticism in Dorothy Schiff's *Post* was harsher than ever. Even *Newsday* publisher Alicia Patterson, her admiration for the man unstinted, could not go on supporting the man's transportation policies. *Newsday* revealed her ambivalence; even as Jack Altschul was being relieved of his duties as city editor for two weeks to enable him to research thoroughly an admiring three-part series entitled "Wizard of the Fair," its editorial page was saying: "The commissioner's arguments lack the good old Moses logic." The editorial was incorrect: the logic of Moses' arguments was the same old Moses logic—it was the editorial understanding of that logic that had been altered. The *Times* it was a-changing. Iphigene Sulzberger's opinion of this "man of vision," this "giant," had not changed, but she was as scrupulous as ever in her determination not to interfere too overtly in the paper's news coverage and editorial policy, and with Moses' old friend Arthur Hays Sulzberger crippled and increasingly out of touch with the paper now and Moses' relationship with Orvil Dryfoos friendly but not nearly as close, her scrupulousness hurt now, as an incident in 1961 revealed. A review of Lewis Mumford's latest book referred to Moses as an example of city planners whose concentration on highways was destroying needed open space around cities. Mrs. Sulzberger wrote a letter to the editor of the *Book Review* taking "exception" to that sentence and noting that "I have worked very closely with Mr. Moses for almost thirty years and I would like to testify that he has never considered a roadway merely as a means of transportation, but he has always made them into parkways using every bit of acreage possible for parks and playgrounds." But the significant point about the letter was not that Mrs. Sulzberger wrote it, but that writing it—a mild letter at that—was all she had done. Similar criticism of Moses would soon be running in the *Times* again, in book reviews and in the paper's news sections. With the accession to the publishership of Arthur Ochs (Punch) Sulzberger in 1963, such remarks increased in number. "Moses would complain to poor old Sulzberger on his sickbed, and Sulzberger would call in Punch, and the editors closed ranks and they started looking for other things to prove that Moses was not worthy of the praise, over-all," Shapiro says. Most important, the editorial-page editor of the *Times* was no longer Charley Merz of 1 Gracie Square and the morning rides downtown but John Oakes. Even while Dryfoos was publisher, Oakes had been attacking Moses' emphasis on highways at the expense of mass transit and parks. After the publisher's death on May 25, 1963, Oakes went further than he ever had before, spelling out the paper's change of heart in an editorial on Moses' 1963 push for the Lower and Mid-Manhattan expressways: "As a newspaper we have previously endorsed those crosstown expressways, and we stand by that earlier endorsement. But we must admit to a growing disenchantment with great urban highway and expressway schemes." Particularly irritating to Moses was the new refusal of the *Times* to print every letter he wrote it. "That really infuriated him," Ingraham recalls. "He really thought everything he wrote should be printed."

But there was a powerful predisposition in the press toward a favorable, cooperative attitude toward the Fair, a predisposition based greatly on financial considerations. Most of the New York papers were desperate for revenue—it would not be long after the Fair's close that the *Herald Tribune, World-Telegram* and *Journal-American* died—and the Fair was a source of substantial revenue, both through special Fair "'supplements" crammed with advertising from Fair exhibitors and contractors, and through increased advertising, aimed at Fair-bound tourists, by hotels and restaurants. There was, moreover, civic pride: the press was part of the city's establishment; in the circles in which the publishers moved, the *New York* World's Fair was not an event to be derided. And a fair was a fair. "There was nothing to be against," as Joe Kahn says. "What was there to be against? Did you ever hear of a fair or a circus that people were against?" No editor or publisher wanted to be the one to cast the first knock. All Moses had to do was ignore or roll with the criticism of his other activities, and as the Fair began to dominate headlines and editorials, that criticism would fade before a tide of praise. The honeymoon may have been over, but a divorce was by no means inevitable—particularly on the grounds of a World's Fair.

But Moses made it inevitable. He did not ignore the press or roll with its punches. He did not forgive it.

Rationally, logically, he knew that, for a public figure, fighting the media is a battle he can only lose; he was, in fact, constantly expounding this axiom to his aides. But it had long since ceased to be reason or logic that dictated his actions. It was emotions, feelings, passion—the complex, fierce personality to which, for decades, he had become accustomed to giving free rein. That personality made it impossible for him to ignore criticism. During 1961 and 1962, he was embroiled in battle on several non-Fair fronts—Henry Barnes, the Fire Island road, the Lower Manhattan Expressway. Press coverage was noticeably restrained, editorial criticism rather light. But no matter how glancing the attack, Moses seemed impelled to retaliate massively—by public attack on the paper involved and the press as a whole, and by private complaint to editors about reporters, and to publishers about editors.

And his attitude carried over to the Fair.

He scheduled press conferences because he realized, intellectually, that the Fair needed the publicity, and because, rationally, he felt sure he could charm the reporters into friendliness. But when he found himself in the same room with these men and women who had attacked him, reason fled before rage. He went out of his way to show his contempt for them; the face he turned on them was one of disdain; his answers were sarcasm and scorn. He lectured them—and he antagonized them. It would have been easy to make them allies; he made them enemies instead.

Any real chance of a reconciliation vanished on August 5, 1962, when he began lecturing the press in public as well as private.

The first lecture might, according to Sid Shapiro's post-mortem analysis of why the *Times*'s old-line Sunday editor decided to sponsor it, have been called "The Lester Markel Lecture to Show Mrs. Sulzberger That She Was Making a Mistake in Allowing New Editors to Be Brought In." For whatever reason, Markel invited Moses to write an article for his Sunday magazine giving his view of the press.

Moses accepted.

> The power of the press, radio and television to make or break any man in public life . . . is awesome and often grossly unfair [he wrote]. The press, for the ostensible purpose of keeping it honest, has done much to make public employment dangerous and unattractive. . . .
>
> Many a good official has been frightened or flattered by idle gossip, random criticism or attack. . . . Aaron and Hur do not hold up his arms so that his side may gain the victory. . . .
>
> There is a type, fortunately rare, which is indifferent to the ordinary decencies and proprieties, skilled in eavesdropping, glued to keyholes, willing to embarrass families and friends, a species to whom nothing is sacred. Such reporters, if they could, would wire and violate the confessional. . . . I sometimes wish we had a few Gorgases to keep yellow journalists off our necks so that we would be free to do our work. . . .
>
> Perceptive journalists sense that the public has tired of hearing Aristides called "The Just," and therefore yell for his ostracism. . . .
>
> There is a notable tendency in the press to cut officials to one size in a sort of bed of Procrustes, to put on spiked shoes and cleats and to jump on victims when they are down, like a mob at the fights shouting with such glee when an aging champion is beaten up and dethroned. There is also a potent minority of jackals and vultures who hang around the outskirts and hover over trouble spots to discover a wound or blood and then close in or swoop down for the kill. . . .
>
> Cleverly and dramatically reflecting public opinion is one thing. Planting suspicion, poisoning minds, rousing the mob spirit, quoting out of context—these are cute tricks far removed from straight honest reporting. . . . Critics build nothing. The only excuse for a critic is to toughen the hides of his victims. . . .

Jackals. Vultures. Yellow journalists. "There is only one way to get the press united and that is to attack it," Joe Kahn says. Now Moses had attacked it. The reporters who had to cover the Fair every day, the reporters he had insulted at first to their editors, then to their publishers, then to their faces, then to the public, were now his enemies. If he gave them material with which to tear him down now, they would use it for all it was worth.

And he gave it to them by lying.

He had been twisting facts for years, shielded by the secrecy which the courts had erected around his public authorities. But the World's Fair was a private corporation whose records were open, one, moreover, which was, because of its need for public support, forced to operate in the public eye. The press could look at the World's Fair—and he had made it willing and determined to look.

Joe Kahn looked first.

Moses was deluging city desks with Fair brochures and "Progress Reports." The *Post* reporter began to read them with care. "I don't like to say it was a natural antagonism against the man and the men around him," he says. "But I guess it was. And it was natural, being the kind of reporter I am, to be suspicious—particularly when you have these suspicious characters around, guys like Rosenman—I mean he was the lawyer for all these guys who tried to fuck everyone—you had to be suspicious when you saw he was involved. And you know, you started reading those brochures, and you could see he [Moses] had the same old crew in." Kahn began to look "for tie-ins and conflicts of interest and that kind of thing"—and soon he was telling *Post* readers about the $10,000,000-a-year restaurant business that Moses had handed to two Fair directors for a pittance rental without competitive bidding, and was feeding Stan Opotowsky, writing a series titled "Who-Do-You-Have-to-Know Or: How to Do Business with the City," information about the lucrative arrangements with Deegan and Donoghue and Preusse and Constable and Spargo and Shanahan and Rosenman.

From Moses' public relations offices was coming a steady stream of announcements of states, foreign countries and prestigious private exhibitors who had "agreed" to sponsor pavilions. Kahn began to check into those announcements. "I couldn't call Panama, for Christ's sake—the *Post* would have gone out of its mind. So what I did was I called the embassies here. And I wrote to every Governor whose state was supposed to be in. I was never assigned to the World's Fair. Nobody in his right mind would assign me to a thing like this—it took too much time. So I was doing it all on my own, at the same time that I was doing my regular assignments. I was doing it all myself. God, I remember now. I never told anyone what I was doing. A terrible, awful job." But it began to produce results. Moses had announced a huge Hall of Medicine and Health, to be sponsored by the American Museum of Health. When Kahn telephoned the Museum's chairman, he said the Museum had decided not to sponsor the exhibit. Moses had said that California was sponsoring an exhibit; Kahn checked, and Governor Pat Brown said California was not. Soon there were other stories: PUERTO RICO DROPS OUT OF '64 FAIR; VIRGIN IS. DROPS PLAN FOR PAVILION.

The city's other papers were reluctant to pick up this new theme at first. As late as the spring of 1963, the general play given to the World's Fair in New York's press was still upbeat. But Moses took care of that.

The first of a new series of press conferences on "the Fair's progress" was held on June 27, 1963. The prepared statement with which Moses opened it had evidently started out to be a plea for cooperation: "We are not shrinking violets or sensitive plants and constructive questions won't irritate us," he said. "Let's be working partners in bringing the world to New York." But it turned into a statement with the Moses touch: "We at the Fair build. The Press in its many manifestations reports. Who am I to explain our respective missions and to acknowledge our dependence upon you? . . . We are entitled to the support of all decent citizens. . . . Error is the besetting sin of journalism, perhaps occasionally acknowledged in the Confessional but almost never publicly."

The reporters found, moreover, that their questions were not considered constructive. He had planned the main news of the day to be the fact that ground was being broken for a Sudanese Pavilion, and the fact that the Fair was coming along on schedule. "Do not, we ask, overemphasize the absentees," he had said in his statement. The reporters persisted in asking about the empty spaces on the map behind him and how much missing rental they represented. He began to get angry. The reporters asked him about the fees paid to Preusse. "That is not a subject that comes under the category of the Fair's progress," Moses said. The reporters walked out fuming, and the *Herald Tribune*'s lead the next day was that the Fair's "economic prospects . . . were trimmed yesterday." Its article enumerated every unoccupied plot. The Sudanese Pavilion barely made the last paragraph.

To attack, there was for Robert Moses only one response: counterattack. A few days later, a group of Queens civic leaders were touring the Fair. Greeting them, Moses noticed reporters nearby. "This is a highly critical community," he rasped. "I think we have more critics than we are entitled to for our size. They foul the city's nest and are always more interested in what is going wrong than in what is going right."

A luncheon that had been planned to "clear the air" with the new editors who were taking over the places once held by his friends at the *Times* did little to convince them of his reasonableness.

Public officials lunching with *Times* editors almost invariably do so at the *Times*; even Presidents come to them. Not Moses; if they wanted to see him, he told Ingraham, who was arranging the luncheon, they would have to come to him. They agreed to do so, and eight or nine—"the very top, Daniel and Salisbury were there," recalls Ingraham—journeyed out to Flushing Meadows one day. Ingraham says he was brought along "to explain things to them," but explanations were to prove superfluous. Moses made things perfectly clear.

"Moses started sounding off and made some reference to his job as City Construction Coordinator and the power it gave him," Ingraham says. "So Frank Adams [*Times* city editor] asked, 'How far does your jurisdiction as Construction Coordinator extend—the way you put it, it would seem that if a road starts in Florida, you have jurisdiction over it as long as it ends up here.' "

"I consider that an insulting question," Moses said. Leaping out of his seat, he stalked out of the room—"leaving nine top executives of *The New York Times* absolutely flabbergasted." For a while they sat there, stunned, waiting for their host to return. Gradually they began to realize that he wasn't going to. Says Ingraham: "After a while, we just got up and went home."

Moses paid the price for the pleasure of giving his emotions rein.

In every announcement, the press found something to carp at. When the Administration Building opened, they emphasized not that the first structure for the Fair had been completed, but that it had cost a million dollars instead of the expected $600,000. When landscaping on the site began, they noted that it began "well after the promised Spring of '62." Did

Moses proudly announce that the city had agreed to construct a $3,500,000 Science Museum? "A far cry from the multimillion-dollar Federal Science Pavilion erected by the United States at the Seattle Fair."

Press conferences were the stage for the most overt encounters, of course. At every press conference there would be mounted behind Moses a huge map of the Fair. He wanted to talk about the exhibits that had filled in spaces since the last press conference—the new exhibits that had been signed up. They insisted on asking him about the spaces that remained empty. Why was the Fair having so much difficulty persuading states and nations to exhibit? He would get angry, and blast the press for making an issue out of something he considered unimportant; the blast would be the biggest news of the day.

He couldn't let anything alone. He had to fight with everybody, and fight publicly.

Negotiations with H. L. Hunt, the eccentric Texas oil magnate who had offered to rent 152,000 square feet and erect a complex of thrill rides and the other amusement attractions the Fair so badly needed, together with several restaurants, were probably doomed from the start, since Hunt was as accustomed as Moses to having his own way. But since the negotiations had never been a matter of press interest, their termination did not have to make the front page of *The New York Times*. Moses put it there—after disagreements over the "standards" of the rides, which Moses felt might be too "gaudy," had reached the point where Moses ordered Hunt's check for more than a million dollars returned—with a full-scale statement to the press that arrangements had been "mutually terminated." Hunt, who had previously been happy to go quietly, felt called upon to make his own—eight-page—statement denying that there would have been any gaudiness and that there had been anything mutual at all about the termination, saying that he would have been happy to be part of the Fair despite Moses' "vacillating and capricious moods and . . . emotionally-arrived-at decisions" until Moses had flatly declared he was "out." All of which not only increased the air of controversy around the Fair, but emphasized the difficulty Moses was having in providing traditional amusements for the Fair. Moses wanted a $25,000,000 Federal Pavilion at the Fair, but his reaction—in public statements, press releases and testimony before congressional committees—was one of such outrage that anyone, even a United States senator, should raise any questions at all about a Robert Moses demand, that Senator Paul Douglas of Illinois called him "one of the most competent and irritating men in the history of the United States." Before Moses arrived in Washington, the request, with President Kennedy solidly behind it, had been regarded as assured of passage. By the time Moses left, it was all but dead, and only White House intervention saved it in scaled-down dimensions. Not satisfied with what he had thus wrought, Moses proceeded to make new public attacks on congressional stinginess.

In a dozen such incidents, Moses created controversy where none was necessary, handing reporters fuel, fuel he had made them anxious to use.

And when they used it, turning it into stories, he attacked them for using it—thereby making more stories. It was attack and counterattack, and attack and counterattack, in a war of words that escalated and escalated and escalated again. As opening day grew closer, the Fair, thanks to its president, was surrounded by furor. There was the racial controversy—there was, of course, not a single Negro or Puerto Rican on the Fair's 200-person administrative staff, and not many more even in menial posts around the Fair Administration Building until Screvane managed to ease some in, and the protests of Negro civil rights groups were met by Moses with scant courtesy. And there was the religious controversy: every one of the major religions in America was represented at the Fair, save one, and Jewish leaders were increasingly perturbed by the absence of any representation of their faith (some of them seeming to feel that the Fair was not especially anxious to have any); their feelings were not especially assuaged by the fact that when Israel decided it could not afford a national pavilion (after learning that the cost of its pavilion was more likely to be $3,000,000 than the $1,250,000 Moses had promised), Moses attacked Premier David Ben-Gurion. There was the controversy over unions—the press dubbed it "The Great Garbage Controversy"; foreign exhibitors were shocked by $17-an-hour-per-man garbage-collector rates; after enraged Spanish Pavilion officials refused to hire Allied Maintenance crews and tried to hire their own, teamsters refused to pick up the pavilion's garbage, and the Spaniards threatened to dump it into the Unisphere pool. And then the controversy over art; Moses turned down repeated requests by artists' societies for a pavilion to display American art because no one came up with the high rental he demanded. Then there was the opening-on-time controversy. Instead of simply admitting that a few exhibits and some landscaping would not be ready on Opening Day, which would have made this a not-very-newsworthy item, Moses kept insisting—although he knew differently—that everything would, which allowed the press to do daily stories on the items which were behind schedule.

Moses was raging at the press now. If these jackals and hyenas thought they could attack with impunity, he'd show them how wrong they were. Blasting the "assorted dyspeptics, grouches, grumblers, hit-and-run writers and talkers who hint broadly that our fair will be artless, boycotted, funless, foodless, constipated, strangled and tasteless," he told 1,400 members of the Fifth Avenue Association gathered to honor him in October 1963 that he had decided that "if your natural weapon is the broadax, you should not affect the rapier"—and, dropping the more delicate weapon, he swung the ax more and more frequently; by the start of 1964, it seemed that every speech on whatever occasion—the opening of a new pavilion, the dedication of the Unisphere, welcoming a delegation of New England Governors to the Fair—was an occasion for a vicious denunciation of the news media. Some of the controversies he won and some he lost, but all had the same result: more publicity about strife and disunity at an event whose slogan was "Peace Through Understanding." He had turned a skirmish with the press into a full-scale war—and he had been its leading casualty.

Out of the Flushing Meadows—an expanse of flat, barren, almost unadorned land not two years before—there took shape now a square mile of forms out of the past like the thatched replicas of African tribal huts housing tree-house restaurants, of forms out of the future like the hulking massiveness of the United States Pavilion and of traditional fairground adornments such as the curving, looming dark walls of the Hall of Science, the little, brightly colored cable cars swinging in procession overhead and the clusters of white balloons that marked the Brass Rail hot-dog stands scattered throughout the grounds—a flag-lined, fountained scene that may have been disorganized and hodgepodge but that was also somehow vital and vivid, not trend-setting certainly but gay and alive, a scene certainly not boring, a scene that may not have titillated the sophisticated taste of New York intelligentsia but that would have thrilled the general public. But in the public perception of the Fair—the perception created by the media—this scene was not foreground but background. There loomed before it the figure of its creator, dominating the scene, muting its gaiety, casting a dark shadow across its brightness, a figure not inviting but hostile, a figure of arrogance and controversy and rage. With the opening—on time—of the Fair, the wind of controversy died away for a while. But the whirlwind was still for the reaping.

The first hint of the great storm to come was the daily attendance figures. Every day that the Fair was open, its expenses were $300,000—on top of the $30,000,000 it had spent prior to Opening Day. To pay these expenses—and to fulfill his promise to repay the city its $24,000,000 loan, and to have the necessary $29,000,000 left over for his great chain of parks—the daily attendance had to average 220,000. Moses had confidently predicted it would. There would, he boasted, be many "quarter million days." But the controversies he had spawned had come home to roost. Attendance on Opening Day, April 22, 1964, was 49,642. Moses ascribed that to overdramatization of a civil rights protest auto stall-in and to chill, drizzly weather. But attendance the next day, clear and warm, was 88,130. On the first weekend there were crowds each day of 170,000. But during the following week, the fatal figures read: 45,000; 53,000; 38,000.

Wait until May, when the weather turns warm, Moses said. During the entire month of May, there was not a day on which attendance reached the break-even 220,000. On only seven days did it reach 200,000. On five days it did not even reach 100,000. Attendance for June was scarcely higher.

Wait until July, when the schools let out, and parents can bring their kids, Moses said. All through July, the Fair waited—in fair weather—for its first quarter-million day. It never came. On only five days did attendance reach 200,000. By the end of July, according to Moses' "conservative" forecasts, 25,000,000 persons should have paid their way into the Fair. The actual number was 15,000,000. With attendance thus off by 40 percent, so was revenue from admissions and parking fees, and from the Fair's percentage of concessions and restaurant income. The Fair was not earning the profit Moses had expected. It was not earning enough even to pay its bills.

It took Moses a long time to realize the implications of those attendance figures, partly because for a long time no one told him about them. His shrewd money men, Spargo and Madigan, were not part of the team handling the Fair's day-by-day financial administration. That team had been brought over from Triborough; its head, Erwin Witt, the Fair's Comptroller, had been Triborough's comptroller. Comptrolling for Triborough had been a notably undemanding job. The monopoly enjoyed by the Authority made its revenues easily predictable and inevitably increasing; during Witt's years as comptroller, the Authority had never once been in serious financial straits. The extravagance and wastefulness of its spending—extravagance not only condoned but encouraged by its chairman—had bred within the Authority an attitude toward money of carelessness and disregard.

And it showed.

At the Fair, Witt had made a mistake worthy of a first-year accounting student. He had credited *all* the advance discount sales to the first year's income, thereby making the Fair's balance sheet look far better than it should, for the balance sheet did not reflect a fact that would become apparent during the second season—that 15,000,000 persons who would be attending during the second season would not be paying to do so. Had attendance been as high as predicted, there would have been so much money that the mistake would not have been fatal. But it was fatal now: the money had been spent, and no more was coming in.

And after Moses' aides finally *did* realize the implications of the attendance figures, they still took a long time to tell RM about them. For they were afraid to tell him. Knowing the blind, punishing rages—and, in some cases, the ostracism, the severance from power and prestige and money—with which RM greeted bad news, not only Witt but the executives to whom Witt reported, the Constables and Shapiros, stalled for weeks before breaking the news. The only one of Moses' aides with enough guts (and money) to tell the Boss the unpleasant truths was George Spargo, then chairman of the Fair's finance committee. Spargo had been working for Moses for thirty years and was closer to Moses than any other aide. Unlike the other Moses Men, he was close to the Boss personally as well as professionally; they double-dated together; Spargo had introduced him to the woman who was to become his second wife. By any standard—including the one that, in the Triborough empire, really mattered: the money that Moses had let him make—Spargo was Moses' favorite. When Spargo told Moses the truth about the Fair's finances, Moses fired him on the spot. "We don't want any negative thinking around here," he said in an explanatory memo to the staff. Then he summoned Witt to his office. The comptroller was a short, mild-mannered, white-haired man of sixty-five with a history of heart trouble whose wife had recently died. His session with Moses lasted for almost three hours and he returned from it pale and trembling. "He was never the same again," one of his secretaries says. Within days, he had suffered a heart attack—from which he never recuperated. He underwent open-heart surgery, did not recover from it and died.

When—sometime in late August or early September, it appears from his memos—Moses at last began to realize the seriousness of the situation, it was too late to remedy it. The money had been spent—$30,000,000 before the Fair opened and perhaps $30,000,000 more since April 22, a total of perhaps $60,000,000. He had expected the Fair to have earned $90,000,000 by this point. It had earned perhaps $35,000,000. He had been able to spend the extra money because he had also had in the till about $25,000,000 worth of tickets sold but not used. But because these would be used during the Fair's second season, income during that season would be very small. There would be very little new money coming in—and so much had already gone out. Frantically, he tried to cut back expenses, but what could he cut? The contracts with the insurance companies, with Deegan and the engineering firms, were already signed, and had to be paid by the month. So did the annuity contracts. Interest on the notes was mounting daily. He took some measures, issuing a memo—perhaps the first of its kind ever sent out of Robert Moses' office—ordering a "drastically reduced budget" for maintenance and security, and an effort to reduce expenses in all areas. The Allied and Pinkerton forces were cut back to levels at which they should have been all along—about half of what they had been. But other areas resisted economy; as Peter Brennan puts it, "The unions had been built up to this high level. They resisted cutbacks." And the economies were, simply, too late. He had paid out $60,000,000. He couldn't get it back.

Attempting to conceal the truth from the press, Moses' aides consistently inflated daily attendance figures. A special handsomely—expensively—printed Interim Report announced that the Fair had been a "financial success" and as of August 31 had a balance of $12,700,000 cash on hand. But when he tried to sneak an $8,600,000 appropriation through the Board of Estimate, Mary Perot Nichols of *The Village Voice* spotted it, and began to speculate publicly that the Fair might be in financial difficulties. Following her lead, other reporters spotted other clues, although the conclusion drawn was only that the Fair was not making as much money as Moses had predicted; no one, all through 1964, guessed the truth in its full extent.

Moses appears not to have known its full extent himself. Certainly his aides, having seen what happened to Spargo and Witt, were not going out of their way to tell him about it. "You've got to remember," says one city official, "that everyone out there was scared to death. Moses *made* all those people and he can destroy them. He doesn't want to hear that *his* Fair is going badly. He's always regarded criticism, however constructive or well meant, as a personal attack. All he wants to hear is, 'Yes, RM.' The result was that his own people allowed him to live for months in a fool's paradise."

It had to end, however. The Fair was not a public authority. When its money ran out, there would be no legislative appropriation to put more in its till. When its money ran out, it would be out of money. There was going to have to be a day of reckoning.

It came in December.

The bank presidents who, with Spargo gone, made up the Fair's finance committee had become increasingly worried over the vague rumors they were hearing and over Moses' evasions when they asked for hard facts and figures, and he had finally agreed to appoint an outside auditor. The expert named—Henry J. MacTavish, a retired vice president of the Chase Manhattan Bank and trusted aide to David Rockefeller—was met on his first day on the job in November by a typical Moses attempt to bring him into camp: a full serving of charm and the promises of future financial rewards—if, the implication was clear, he behaved himself. Moses escorted him around the Fair Administration Building to meet the other officers, gave him a spacious office near his own, promised him all the secretarial help he could use and escorted him into a meeting of the Fair executive committee, where it was moved that he would be appointed the Fair's financial vice president—on January 1, after his study was completed.

But MacTavish was not a Moses man but a Rockefeller man. A tall, tough Scotsman, he was, moreover, a hard-nosed analyst of balance sheets who understood all too well what he found in the Fair's. By standard accounting methods, he found, the Fair, as of October 31, 1964, had, not a surplus of $12,700,000, but a deficit of $14,000,000.

Charm having failed, Moses essayed intimidation, summoning MacTavish to a meeting at which, according to a non-Moses Fair official, he hoped to make the Rockefeller man back down. In the midst of receiving estimates and projections from his department heads, Moses turned to the Scotsman and said—"almost casually," this official recalls—"By the way, Mr. MacTavish, do you want to say anything?" The official recalls that "MacTavish shifted his legs, looked Moses in the eye and said: 'Are you sure you want me to speak now?' " Certainly, Moses replied. He had no secrets from his boys. But again MacTavish hesitated, asking: "Do you want me to say what I have to say before this group?" Perhaps lulled by MacTavish's hesitancy into believing he had won, Moses said firmly: "I do." And then, the official recalls: "MacTavish let him have it. He ripped all the estimates and projections to shreds, and when he was all through he leaned back, smiled and said, 'As of today, Mr. Moses, we're insolvent.' "

Reality, which Moses had been attempting for months to dodge, had struck him full in the face.

MacTavish's secretary was fired (according to one report, she was later rehired), the executive committee voted to revoke his nomination as financial vice president and he received a handwritten memo from Constable instructing him that, in accordance with Moses' wishes, "under no circumstances" was he to attend the Fair employees' Christmas party. Even this ultimate proscription, however, failed to break his spirit. Moses said flatly that "under no circumstances" was he to make any copies of his formal report or to show it to anyone before Moses had approved it, but MacTavish defied the order and on December 10 sent a copy to George Moore, president of the First National City Bank and Spargo's replacement as finance committee chairman. Moses was frantic to keep the bad news from the press, but the bankers who had lent their names and reputations to the Fair were growing worried about what would happen to their own prestige if the Fair went down. This was particularly true of Moore, whose bank, unlike most of the others, had never been a leading beneficiary of past Moses bond issues. One conversation between Moore and Moses was described this way:

Moore: Bob, we've found bills of six and seven figures that weren't booked. We just can't continue without reliable information.

Moses: George, your figures are wrong. You don't know what you're talking about.

Moore: Bob, I've been in the banking business all my life and if there's one thing I know it's a column of figures.

At an executive committee meeting on January 12, 1965, Moore demanded specific, audited, information. "Moses said to wait until next month. Moore said he couldn't continue this way. Moses accused Moore of trying to sabotage the Fair. 'If you don't like it,' Moses shouted, 'you can get the hell out.' "

Moore did, taking a majority of the finance committee with him. Moreover, he did so publicly, informing reporters that he was resigning "because of the way finances are being handled." "You know," he said, "back in June they said they would have a $50,000,000 surplus. What has happened to that surplus? What? I don't know."

Reporters had been writing for months that the Fair was in financial difficulties. Moses had publicly branded them hyenas, jackals, yellow journalists—in effect, liars—for saying so. Now the truth—that the Fair was in financial difficulties far worse than any reporter had imagined—was out in the open. The meat eaters of the media fell upon the feast with a will—and tore the already bleeding carcass of the "greatest single event in the history of the world" to bits.

Moses was flying frantically around the world trying to round up new exhibits that would enable his Fair to break previous fairs' second-year fall-off pattern—and he was spectacularly successful, obtaining from the Vatican a $600,000 Gutenberg Bible, the Pope's bejeweled coronation tiara, and Michelangelo's statue of St. John; winging on to Madrid to present a Fair medal to Franco and obtain new major Spanish works of art for the Spanish Pavilion; arranging for a Churchill Pavilion containing a film of Sir Winston's life, thirty of his paintings and a comprehensive collection of Churchill memorabilia. Disaster was staring him in the face now; to stave it off, even navels must be enlisted: no longer were he and Constable screening out "tawdry" shows and auditioning the ones allowed in to make certain that female dancers did not display belly buttons or cleavage; in 1965, there would be nine discotheques featuring go-go dancers, and their bras were creeping further down nightly; in 1964, Moses had insisted that bras be put on "Les Poupées de Paris" and that sexy posters be taken off the front doors of that show; in 1965, the girl taking tickets outside was spilling out of her bikini—"to make the show's point perfectly clear," its promoter explained. Moses would not admit he had surrendered but, as one reporter put it, "everywhere there is evidence of the Moses compromise—more scantily-clad girls, carnival-style booths and games . . . 69 new bars, gorillas Toto and Gargantua II." For opening day of the second season, spectacular pageantry was arranged—a parade with eighteen bands, four thousand marchers and thirty-one floats, speeches by Vice President Humphrey and West German Chancellor Willy Brandt, an eight-mile run from Central Park Arsenal to the Singer Bowl by Olympic marathon champion Abebe Bikila. Over and over Moses repeated that 1965 would be "a new Fair, a new show"; when he said "Come to the Fair" now, he was almost pleading.

But what the press was emphasizing now were the juicy quotes Moore was giving out (a photo of the bank president clapping his hand to his forehead in an ostentatious gesture of dismay accompanied a national magazine's story on the Fair), while the financial revelations from the first outside audits and Abe Beame's investigation made the financial picture look worse and worse: on January 26, in receipt of preliminary audit figures, Moses announced that the Fair would be unable to repay the city its $24,000,000 "loan" but that the $23,000,000 in investor-held notes would be paid in full. But two weeks later, the final audit revealed the full extent of the gap between Moses' $12,700,000 "surplus" and reality—some $30,000,-000; the Fair had actually finished the first season with a deficit of $17,540,-000. It was obvious to Beame's auditors that the Fair was not going to be able to repay its notes in full—and the press headlined that fact. The memos waiting for Moses every morning on his desk showed the situation to be even more desperate than that. Now that the auditors had finally discovered all the unpaid bills, the Fair did not have enough money to pay them; on December 31, the exposition, which had taken in $80,000,000, had $639,000 in cash, unpaid bills of $3,000,000, and $4,000,000 more in bills due before opening day, with no revenue expected until that day. Moses sent aides to ask the major exhibitors to prepay rents not due until after the opening, and some did; he threw into the pot $400,000 being held in escrow to guarantee his salary and ordered other aides with escrow accounts to do the same. But there was still a shortfall and the press found out about it, and about another development in relation to it that made it a bigger story still—not only was the Fair not going to be able to reopen without a new loan, but it was having difficulty obtaining one. An executive of one of the banks approached—holder of millions of dollars' worth of notes that might now become worthless, in danger of losing still more money on the Fair because loans to marginal exhibitors were going bad—intimated to Fred Ferretti of the *Herald Tribune* that the reason his bank would not make the loan was that Moses was still in charge; the intimation was false to begin with, and Ferretti played intimation as fact with a *Herald Tribune* exclusive, played under the most damaging headlines yet—LOAN TO FAIR: NOT IF MOSES IS KEPT ON—and the rest of the press jumped on that story in headlines such as FAIR'S CHOICE: MOSES OR MONEY. Even on the day the Fair got the loan it needed, *Newsday* could, truthfully, say: "Few days at the Fair contain good news only. The bad news yesterday was that one of the most popular foreign buildings, the Indonesian Pavilion, is being shut down by President Sukarno because of increasing bitterness in U.S.-Indonesian relationships." Exhibitors insisted on pleading for a reduction in the admission price, at least during evening hours; when they could not obtain an audience with Moses, they went to the press. Day after day the headlines about the Fair were not about new exhibits but about prices and deficits and money.

The general aura of financial difficulties that now surrounded the Fair, moreover, made it feasible for reporters to dredge up all the rumors they had been hearing for three years—the incredible contracts with Allied and Pinkerton and the unions, the huge salaries paid to the consultants. Beame, working with reporters and hunting for publicity, demanded the Fair books so he could audit them; Moses refused to produce them, but the courts ordered him to. And as, over a period of months, Beame's auditors delved deeper and deeper into them, new facts came out—to surround the Fair not only with an aura of inefficiency and financial difficulties, but with an aura of scandal, an aura linked with Moses himself.

Soon Moses himself was at the center of these charges, for reporters had discovered the escrow account set up to insure his salary (the account had been replenished by gate receipts after the Fair opened for the second season). Headlines told the public that Moses had been guaranteed a salary of $100,000 per year.* That salary was then near-incredible for a public servant; the Mayor's was only $40,000 per year. There was, moreover, the "escrow account"; the public may not have understood it, but there was something sinister about the way the press played it. It made him seem greedy, money-hungry, taking a huge personal profit out of an institution that had been supposed to provide the city with parks and educational money but was not doing so. The last surviving portion of the Moses image was destroyed. No one had ever said he was personally interested in money. Now they had. Of the image of Robert Moses, that had stood glittering and pure for thirty years, there was now not a single part left untarnished.

He became an object of derision, almost of scorn, to the reporters he had derided and scorned for so long.

Every desperate move he made to try to save the Fair was ridiculed. When he raised the admission price, *Newsday*'s lead said: "Visitors to the World's Fair in 1965 will have to pay an additional fifty cents to reach 'Peace Through Understanding.' " When he asked for an end to "controversy" and more expressions of confidence in the Fair by Wagner, while simultaneously criticizing the Mayor for withholding them in the past, *Newsday*'s headline said: PEACE-MAKER MOSES OPENS NEW FRONT.

The *Herald-Tribune* had a whole stable of brilliant young columnists. At times, they almost seemed to be taking turns taking potshots at the sitting target that the old man had become. Dick Schaap wrote a whole—hilarious—column on the impossibility of reaching him on the phone, and when he visited Franco wrote: "Moses' mission to Madrid is another indication of his keen public relations sense. Franco is practically an American folk hero. His firm democratic stance cannot be questioned. No one could be more deserv-

---

* Actually, of course, it was $75,000 per year, plus $25,000 in expenses—plus the seven-year $27,500-per-year annuity.

ing of the World's Fair's Gold Medal, unless, of course, it is Robert Moses himself."

He tried to roar back at his critics. "Those who can, build. Those who can't, criticize," he said. But his invective, once so feared, was now ridiculed. "There was a time when the verbal jousting of Robert Moses enlivened and sharpened civic controversy," said a *Times* editorial. "In defending his handling of the World's Fair, however, Mr. Moses' sorties suffer from petulance, and what is worse, they are ineffective. He would be wise to pack in his rusty lance."

When the suggestion came that he resign as president of the Fair, the press was confident it would be adopted.

The suggestion came from the top. Mayor Wagner was increasingly worried about the situation at the Fair and afraid that its failures might tar his administration. He believed the solution was for Moses to resign and be replaced by an administrator not tied to the unsuccessful policies of the past and thus more amenable to changing them. Other officials besides the Mayor were afflicted with the same worries. Between the two seasons, Governor Rockefeller and Senator Javits were also working quietly to persuade Moses to resign. For years he had been threatening to resign from one post or another, confident that no one would take him up on the threat. Now people were asking him to resign.

He would have liked to. Knowing the true financial picture, he knew that, bad as the publicity had been, it was going to get worse. And there was a more serious threat—one that was never to receive any publicity at all. Unknown to press and public, the Internal Revenue Service had begun an intensive, in-depth audit of the Fair to determine if it had adhered to the restrictions that went with the various tax exemptions it had been accorded. The investigation would not be completed for months—there is some question whether it was in fact pressed to a conclusion, there was never any public report of its findings, and Moses was, years later, to write in his memoirs that it "resulted in a clean bill of health"—but it would have been a man supremely unconcerned about his reputation who would not be concerned about the results of such an investigation, and Moses was not such a man. He thought he saw one way to leave so that no one could say he had been forced out: to accept a call to a higher duty, a bigger job. With the United States preparing to surrender all control of the Panama Canal, there was increasing talk in Washington of building a new canal in Colombia. Moses asked Bernard Gimbel to take steps to bring him the assignment. "Moses thought he could do a cheaper, higher-quality job with less political pressures than anyone else," Gimbel says. Gimbel contacted New York Democratic committeeman Edwin Weisl, an intimate of President Johnson, and Weisl contacted the White House. But although no formal word was passed back, it became apparent that Moses wasn't going to get the job. "It's a sad thing," one of the Moses Men would say. "Bob is old and tired. He feels he can't resign, but he can't get out any other way."

And no one could make him. Wagner sent emissaries in relays, beginning with Screvane, who made breakfast overtures. The first was discreet. "I told him that I thought he should resign because he had built this thing that everyone had said couldn't be done, and now he should let the day-to-day handling of it be done by someone else," that mere management was not a job worthy of Robert Moses. The second was more to the point. "I told Bob, 'You know damn well I'm fond of you and I think you've done a great job, but here we are—things aren't going well and we're going to be deeper in the hole next year. We need a fresh start.' " The second emissary was financier John A. Coleman, Al Smith's old breakfast companion, whom Wagner selected in the hope that their shared love for the dead Governor might give Coleman a unique leverage. The third was a committee of bankers, the men who had $23,000,000 in notes, and millions more in loans to individual pavilions, at stake in the Fair. There were further discreet hints from Rockefeller and Javits.

But when Screvane made his first suggestion, Moses "said something to the effect of 'I never expected *you* to say a thing like that—it smacks of disloyalty.' " When he made his second, "he started smacking the table. The words just poured out. I don't remember exactly what he said but there was no way he was going to be forced out." With Coleman, he was friendly but firm. With the bankers, he was firm. "They're all very courageous—until they face him," Wagner says with his quiet smile. "They would be so brave—'We *will* do this, we will *tell* him'—and then. . . . It's his personality. He overawed them."

Then there were attempts to force him out. "We tried every way short of going to court to get him out of there," Screvane says. The Fair board of directors or its executive committee had the power to oust him, and the members of that board, once his allies, were all falling away from him now. Additional pressure was brought. Recalls Wagner: "The banks had a big investment. I said, 'Well, you bankers—you're the ones that have to . . . get the committee on your side.' Oh, 'We can do it. We can do it.' Well, they found out they couldn't do it."

Now was the time for the dossiers. Screvane knew what was going on. "On at least twenty occasions when we were on the same side, Bob would say, 'Well, goddammit, if he doesn't go along, I'll destroy the son of a bitch!' And sure enough, when the vote came, the fellow would go along." Other members of the executive committee were making money from the Fair concessions he had given them, and didn't want to chance upsetting the arrangements. Others may have recalled that, when the Fair was over, Moses would still be head of Triborough and the arterial program. They went along, too. Others supported Moses out of loyalty, or conviction that he was still the best man for the job—any job. Whatever the reason, Screvane says, "we wouldn't have the votes." The same reality that the press had failed to grasp about Title I was still at work here. Not public opinion—not even the opinion of a Mayor and Governor—but raw power would determine whether Moses stayed on as president of the Fair, and of power he still had more than enough. On the Fair board were dozens of the most powerful men in the city and state. Moses handled them like unruly children. At one meeting,

Senate minority leader Joseph Zaretzki tried to interrupt the Moses-dictated agenda by rising to a point of order. Moses smashed the gavel down. "You're out of order." "You can't do that," Zaretzki said. "I'm speaking to a point of order." Moses curtly nodded to the next-scheduled speaker, Fair executive vice president General William Potter, who began reading his report while Zaretzki was still speaking, drowning him out because he had a microphone while Zaretzki did not. Not one member of the board raised a voice in protest. On February 24, there were more than seventy-five reporters and photographers on hand for a meeting of the Fair executive committee, but there were also on hand scores of nightstick-wielding Pinkertons to herd them away from the Fair Administration Building and into the Press Building, where, it was announced, a briefing would be held later. At the briefing, Potter announced that the twenty-one-member executive committee had given Moses a "unanimous" vote of confidence. One reporter who checked found out later that only nine committee members had actually voted; five had not shown up and seven had abstained. But the nine votes had been for Moses; when the Fair's second season was opened, he was still in charge.

But holding on to the Fair did Moses little good. The second season was worse than the first. There was the continuing drumfire of audit revelations, and when the press managed to tear its attention away from those, it focused not on attractions but on attendance, and it was all too clear that in that area this Fair was to be no different from its predecessors; day after day, the gate count ran below that of corresponding days the previous year. The press headlined the attendance and wrote crisis stories about it and its consequences—failing exhibitors, increasing lack of maintenance—which further discouraged people from attending, and, blaming it on Moses' decision to increase prices, laughed at it, a *Newsday* column saying: "In truth, Moses must be credited with a striking improvement over last year's World Fair. He has . . . done away with the Fair's most unpleasant feature—people."

He twisted and turned, seeking a way out of the nightmare that kept looming closer every day as the end of the Fair grew closer, cutting maintenance and security forces to the bone, firing employees by the hundreds, slashing salaries, eliminating expense accounts. He began arranging quiet Park Department allocations for Flushing Meadows Park, set Triborough executives to work figuring out how much of the Authority's money could be spent on the Fair site. But the damage had been done long before—when he had authorized the spending of the tens of millions collected before the Fair opened. It could not be corrected now. His worst fears were becoming reality. His auditors told him there would be no money to repay the city the $24,000,000 it had advanced, no money to create the great new chain of parks that had been the main reason he had taken the Fair job in the first place, no money even to create the "Robert Moses Park" on Flushing Meadows of which he had dreamed—he was, he realized, going to be in the same humiliating position in which that wastrel skirt chaser Grover Whalen had found himself: unable to repay more than a few cents on the dollar of the notes the Fair had floated, perhaps unable even to demolish the buildings of exhibitors who had gone bankrupt and could not demolish them themselves, so that the principal monument to this enterprise which he had believed would resurrect his reputation and reburnish his name would be heaps of moldering wreckage and debris.

Absolute disaster was staved off by the last three weeks.

Going into those weeks, the total attendance for the second season had not been the 37,500,000 that would have enabled the Fair Corporation at least to break even for the season, but only 17,000,000. The Fair Corporation, practically penniless, was paying its bills from week to week. With schools back in session and the weather turning chilly, there was no logical reason to expect any dramatic change in the lack of public interest that had prevailed for two years.

But as October began and the press began reminding the public that the Fair was in its last month, crowds suddenly began pouring in as if the populace of New York had suddenly realized that, despite all the adverse publicity, they wanted to see the exposition, and take their children to see it—and as if, having seen it once not through Fred Ferretti's eyes but their own, they liked it, loved it in fact, and came back during the short time remaining as many times as possible. For two years, Moses had been waiting—practically in vain—for "quarter million days." Now, suddenly, there was one such day after another, and then—for the weekends of three weeks—half million days, as on six triumphant Saturdays or Sundays, 500,000 persons paid their $2.50 and pushed through the turnstiles. During its final three weeks, 7,000,000 persons came to the Fair, pouring into the Fair Corporation's barren exchequers, through admission and parking fees and concession percentages, more than $13,000,000. If attendance had continued at its pre-October pace, the corporation would have had a deficit of more than $24,000,000; as it was, its deficit was reduced to only about $10,000,000. On closing day, his auditors informed Moses that there was $11,580,000 in the bank to be used either to repay the $23,000,000 in notes or for the restoration of Flushing Meadows Park.

The bankers and other noteholders expected that he would use this money to repay his debts. But Moses had other priorities—and he announced them with his usual flourish. At a post-Fair executive committee meeting attended by several bankers who were among the largest noteholders, a Fair official announced that the corporation had a surplus of $11,600,000. The committee applauded, the bankers looking rather relieved. But then Moses stood up. There was just one thing, he said. He wasn't going to use any of the $11,600,000 to pay them. The money was going to restore the Fair site and create the park. At least two of the investment bankers, W. H. Morton of W. H. Morton & Co. and Frederic H. Brandi, president of Dillon, Read & Co., leaped to their feet to protest. Moses favored them with one of his prize glares; the big head tilted back, and it was down his nose that he was looking at the bankers when he replied that he did not feel any particular sense of responsibility to noteholders "who ride around in big limousines with telephones in the back."

By the bankers' code, Moses was committing the original sin: losing them money. They instituted legal action to compel him to use the money to pay his debts. But they were helpless. Eventually they were, in a compromise, to receive a total of $3,000,000—bringing the total return on their $30,000,000 investment ($7,000,000 had, of course, been prepaid) to $10,000,000—or about thirty-three cents on the dollar, ironically just about the same as Grover Whalen had repaid his investors.

The money left—$8,600,000—wasn't enough for the $29,000,000 chain of parks, of course, just as it wasn't enough to repay the city's $24,000,000. But it was enough—together with $6,576,000 from Triborough coffers, various quiet Park Department allocations, and enough money from the Heckscher Foundation to create a zoo—to enable the Fair Corporation to demolish the pavilions of bankrupt or impoverished exhibitors, to clean up the Fair site and to do at least a little park work on Flushing Meadows. The park he was able to build there may not have been the great park he had envisioned, but at least it was a park—with a Hall of Science, the Federal and New York State pavilions, the columned skating rink—and a Unisphere to remind future generations of Robert Moses' World's Fair.

Looming over the whole park from beyond its northern end was the Shea Stadium that was his answer to the Colosseum of the Caesars. And the park was of course surrounded by his great roads, the cloverleafs and broad ribbons of concrete that to him represented beauty and that were his trademark; they tied up the park with neat, clean, sweeping borders, delineating the outskirts so sharply that from the air the green was sliced off by gray as sharply as by a knife, nothing left over on the edges, nothing frayed, making it a landscape by Moses, bearing his signature as plainly as if he had scrawled it into the concrete in giant letters. And he considered the landscape beautiful. On the day, filled with pageantry, he gave the Flushing Meadows back to New York, he said in a statement entitled "Beauty for Ashes": "The Fair cannot entirely complete this great work so that nothing further will be required. Every step, however, follows an ultimate plan which is realizable in the not distant future. . . . We believe it is no exaggeration to say that two World's Fairs have ushered in, at the very geographical and population center of New York, on the scene of a notorious ash dump, one of the very great municipal parks of our country."

Public monies spent under Robert Moses' direction during preparations for the 1939–40 World's Fair to make the Flushing Meadows a feasible park site came to $58,842,000. For the 1964–65 World's Fair, Robert Moses' Fair Corporation spent on permanent park improvements $22,256,000. Robert Moses' Triborough Bridge and Tunnel Authority spent on permanent park improvements $6,576,000. The City of New York spent $31,000,000. The State of New York spent at least $12,000,000 (and probably far more). The federal government spent $12,000,000. The public monies spent during this Fair on permanent improvements to make Flushing Meadows a park thus came to a total of at least $83,832,000. For the two Fairs, the total was at least $142,674,000. And no one even suggested it be named after him.

In computing the balance sheet for the 1964–65 World's Fair in relation to what its president had hoped to get out of it, its effect on his popularity must weigh heavily indeed on the debit side.

The methods he had employed in building and running the World's Fair were not new. He had been using them for forty years. The only thing different was that this time the world had seen them. Formerly he had employed these methods behind the cloak of public authorities which kept the public from seeing these methods. The Fair had given the world a look at his methods.

And by so doing, the Fair had destroyed what was left of the legend of Robert Moses. The great universal exposition that had been supposed to rehabilitate his popularity had instead destroyed the last of it—and destroyed it beyond repair. When the Fair came to a close on October 17, 1965, Robert Moses was revealed to the public in all his egotism, arrogance and ruthlessness. He was, in fact, portrayed, in the press's emphasis on the $100,000 a year in salary and expenses and the escrow account, as something worse than he was—greedy for money. He was in public disrepute so great that his name had become a symbol for things the public hated.

For the ordinary public official in a democracy, such a state of affairs would have meant loss of power. If he had been an elected official, he would have been ousted from office by the public at the next election. If he had been an appointed official, he would have been ousted from office by the official who had appointed him—probably not in a matter of months but in a matter of weeks if not days.

But Robert Moses was an official of a public authority. The public had no voice in whether or not he stayed in office. The power he wielded in the position to which the Mayor had appointed him made him, once in power, virtually immune to the Mayor's authority—as the new Mayor entering office shortly after the Fair drew to a close was soon to find out.

Mary Moses' worship of the husband who was her hero and her obsessiveness with public recognition of his greatness had grown more noticeable. Once an architect, meeting her at a party, mentioned casually to her that he had been one of the young architects who had worked for the Park Department under WPA. "Anybody who is of any importance in the city has worked for Mr. Moses at one time or another," she replied haughtily. Her response to the increasing criticism of her husband during the 1950's was violent, so violent that friends felt it helped worsen her fast-failing health. Says Becky Vollmer: "Her whole life was Robert. Once they went to dinner at the Sulzbergers—this was during the Fifties, when there first started to be criticism—and Iphigene got Mary to one side and said, 'Mary, why does Robert antagonize people so terribly?' Mary was wild! As if Iphigene Sulzberger thought Robert deliberately antagonized people! It was just that some people refused to understand!" Mrs. Moses was, in her early sixties, an old woman. Her "nervous troubles" had not been solved, leading to further hospitalizations in the Payne Whitney Psychiatric Clinic, and she developed severe arthritis, which led to her increasing confinement in a wheelchair.

"Someone *had* to order his shirts, see that he had money, take care of him," his daughter Jane says. For a while, Jane herself did so. She was now divorced and living at her parents' Babylon home. Moses, so youthful and vital, showed little sign of advancing age. One could mark the developments in Moses' career by the women he selected as companions. During his reforming, idealistic period he had been in love with Mary, an idealistic reformer. During his alliance-with-the-North-Shore-robber-barons period, he had been publicly affectionate with a North Shore robber baroness. As a politician involved with Tammany Hall, the relationship most subject to gossip among his aides and acquaintances was a canny, tough female city commissioner. Within the tight little Triborough empire, social affairs were commonplace; now, one of Moses' secretaries recalls, they began "getting Mary II to go along with the Boss." Mary Grady—Mary II as she became known in the empire—was a secretary twenty-eight years younger than Moses. Soon their friendship was an open secret. Joe Ingraham became aware that "at every party Moses attended, Mary Grady would be there in the background." Moses had never taken a vacation without Mary I, but in 1952 she was too ill to accompany him to Florida; after that he began taking Mary II instead.

His wife was affected with heart trouble and what a friend calls "all the ailments of old age." She was confined more and more to the Thompson Avenue house in Babylon now; he lived more and more in the Gracie Terrace apartment in the city. It wasn't, emphasize the Vollmers who had known them for years, that he was "mean" to her—whenever he saw her he was as courteous and friendly as ever; he would often drive out to Babylon on a Sunday to have lunch with her. And it was for her that he made what for him was a supreme sacrifice: his reputation for being above money; it was, after all, at least partly to pay for her round-the-clock nursing care that he had subjected himself to public criticism by accepting the "$100,000 a year" World's Fair post. The Vollmers feel that there was a reason why Mary entered her final decline in 1959: "it was quite noticeable that she got worse when the real criticism of him began," Becky says. "I don't think she could stand it. . . . It was just that he turned his back on her. He was able to withdraw, to turn his back, on personal problems. . . . He withdrew from Mary—she could be at a hospital and he would be at a party someplace at the same time acting the same as ever, as if nothing was wrong."

Mary Sims Moses was virtually completely bedridden after 1962. She lived in Babylon, her husband mostly in New York. She died on September 5, 1966, at the age of eighty-one. Her obituary in the *Times* said—accurately—"From the day she exchanged a reformer's role for that of a housewife 51 years ago, Mrs. Moses was content to remain in the shadow of her husband . . ."

Less than a month later, her husband, seventy-seven, married Mary Grady, forty-nine.

48. Old Lion, Young Mayor

He paweth in the valley, and rejoiceth in his strength; he goeth on to meet the armed men. . . . He saith among the trumpets, Ha, ha; and he smelleth the battle afar off, the thunder of the captains, and the shouting.

—JOB, 39:25

FOR TWENTY YEARS, mayoral candidates had been vying for Moses' support. In the 1965 campaign, none of the three candidates had. On the contrary, they had all criticized him. The conservative candidate, an admirer, had been muted in his criticism, but the two major candidates had attacked his park, transportation and housing policies—everything, it seemed, that he had done or was planning to do for New York. And the one who had been elected was the one who had meant it. Hardly had he been elected when John V. Lindsay appointed as Park Commissioner Thomas P. F. Hoving, author of a White Paper on Parks that had attacked Moses' policies.

But there was no real power left in the Park Department, hadn't been for years. The real power was in highways, and the two posts Robert Moses held were in that area, the only two posts he had left—chairmanship of the Triborough Bridge and Tunnel Authority (his term did not expire until June 30, 1970, eighteen months after Lindsay's was to expire) and city arterial highways representative. Lindsay said he could take those posts away, too. Well, that was all right. Moses didn't mind him saying that. That was of a piece with his rhetoric during the campaign, and a new Mayor had to pay at least lip service to that rhetoric after his election.

But the funny thing was that John Lindsay really believed he could.

Robert Moses knew different. He had lost enough power so that a tough, canny Mayor, skilled in the ways of New York politics, could have given him a hard fight, but his shrewd old eyes had taken their measure of John Lindsay the first time the two men had ever sat down and talked, and he knew that Lindsay wasn't the Mayor to do it. Shortly after his election, the handsome young Mayor-elect had invited him down to his pre-inaugural headquarters at the Hotel Roosevelt for a discussion. Leaving for the meeting, Moses had been tense—a barometer of his feelings had been the fact that he had accepted Lindsay's invitation instead of making Lindsay come to him—but returning he was smiling and relaxed. "If you elect a matinee-idol Mayor," he told aides, "you're going to get a musical-comedy administration."

Lindsay had talked about "the power brokers in our city" but, when pressed by reporters, had never identified them ("Who are the power brokers? They know who they are" was his reply)—possibly because, as he was to demonstrate during his mishandling of the first crisis to confront him, a transit strike, he didn't really know who they were. He was going to find out though—the hard way. During the pre-inaugural period, his bright, eager young aides had been working out the transportation merger that his Transportation White Paper had so blithely proposed during the campaign. It sounded so easy to these articulate, cocky young men. The Transit Authority had a deficit which was imposing an intolerable burden on the city's financial structure, the Triborough Bridge Authority had a surplus—what could be more logical than to use the one to offset the other? The philosophy of the new administration was, at the time, militantly pro-mass transit, anti-automobile—taking away Triborough's funds with which the Authority would otherwise build new automobile facilities and using them to improve the subways dovetailed with that philosophy, particularly if the new agency were to raise tolls on Triborough's bridges and place them for the first time on non-Authority bridges so as to further discourage automobile traffic into the city, a proposal toward which the new administration was leaning. All they were doing, Lindsay's aides could feel, was finally putting into force the proposals reformers such as Citizens Union and City Budget Commission study groups had been advocating for years. What was hard about it? Both authorities, Transit and Triborough, were controlled by the city, weren't they? And John Lindsay *was* the city now. The ignorance of some of these men concerning the true nature and powers of public authorities would have been ludicrous if it had not been the city's future that that ignorance was jeopardizing. Lindsay was, moreover, full of confidence—overconfidence—and optimism about his ability to run the city; he was going to be another La Guardia, with one exception—La Guardia had never gone on to be President as he was sure *he* was going to; lest anyone miss the comparison with the Greatest Mayor New York Had Ever Had, Lindsay had hardly been inaugurated when he had La Guardia's portrait moved out of another spot in City Hall and into his office, along with La Guardia's desk,* and was, in an interview with A. M. Rosenthal of the *Times,* making "it clear that he doesn't intend to be the chairman of the board. He intends to run the city. 'I would call it a style not of tight control but of total supervision . . .' " Lindsay was going to be in complete charge. A man who stood in their way, who was a dinosaur out of another age—how old *was*

* It was not the desk of the Little Flower but what happened to it that was the more descriptive symbol of the Lindsay administration; during La Guardia press conferences the man behind it had dominated the room; so unable was Lindsay to control the photographers he was constantly summoning to his office that during one picture session, less than a week after the desk had been moved in, several climbed onto it and it caved in.

the old bastard, for God's sake? *Seventy-seven?* Christ!—a cranky, cantankerous, ludicrous figure, they did not consider an obstacle at all; because they laughed at him, they thought everyone laughed at him, or at least anyone whose laughter was worth anything. They mistook his deafness for senility, seemed to think they were dealing with an old man, but they were reformers themselves or men parroting the phraseology of the reformers. And Robert Moses had been taking care of reformers for forty years. It wasn't rhetoric that was going to determine control of the transportation program in New York City, it was resolutions—the bond resolutions, the contract covenants of the Triborough Bridge and Tunnel Authority. It wasn't polemics that were going to count in any confrontation; it was power. John Lindsay and his glib young aides had the polemics; the grim old ruler of Randall's Island had the power. More, he knew how to use power. There was a phrase he employed in discussing Lindsay's merger proposal that had a certain significance. It was, he said, "ripper legislation." "Ripper legislation" —a phrase denoting legislation passed to remove an official from power indirectly when it is impossible to do so directly—was a phrase out of another age; it had not been in general use since the 1920's. The significance lay not in the phrase but in the fact that the man using it was still around—in power—forty years later. He was still around because he had managed to hold on to power for decades. These men with their first taste of power laughed at him; he had not only tasted power but held it longer than many of these men had been alive. Did Lindsay think he had the ability to outsmart Robert Moses? Robert Moses had outsmarted *La Guardia*. From the very same post from which Lindsay was trying to remove him, a President of the United States, at the peak of his popularity and power, dedicated to his destruction, had tried to remove him—and that President had failed. These rash young men thought he was only Robert Moses of the World's Fair and Title I; he was also Robert Moses of Timber Point and Jones Beach and Hither Hills, of the Northern State Parkway and the Triborough Bridge and the Cross-Bronx Expressway and the Bay Ridge Approach. He was Moses of Massena, Moses of the Niagara Frontier. This was their first real battle; he came to it scarred with the wounds of a hundred battles—battles he had won. LINDSAY MAPS PLANS TO SLASH MOSES' POWER, the headlines read. Moses sat in his lair up on Randall's Island and grinned—the grin of the old lion.

On January 13, 1966, Lindsay announced that legislation creating a new, centralized transportation authority that would merge Triborough with the Transit Authority and make its surplus available for subway operation, and empowering him to name the chairman of the new agency, would shortly be sent to Albany. A reporter asked him if he foresaw any difficulty getting the Legislature to pass it. No, he said with a confident smile, he didn't. At another press conference several days later, he said he had "no reason to believe" that Moses "will not go along" with the plans. Did the Mayor have any reason for his opinion? a reporter asked. No, he said with his boyish, winning grin, he had "not seen anything definitive from Mr. Moses" but "I have not seen any signs of hostility from Mr. Moses" either. "Don't start fights where there aren't any." Lindsay's aides—including legal aides—were just as confident in private. Moses was beaten, they told reporters, and he must know it; his era was over; whether he liked it or not, he was going to go. Not one of the brigade of lawyers striding so confidently through the corridors of City Hall appeared ever to have heard of bond covenants.

They were to hear of them shortly, however. On January 20, there was delivered to all newspapers and radio and television stations in New York a "memorandum in opposition" to the Lindsay proposal signed by Moses and his two Triborough co-commissioners. The memorandum included a legal opinion by former Corporation Counsel Preusse, Triborough counsel Lebwohl and one of the nation's most respected experts on municipal bonds, Franklin S. Wood, of Hawkins, Delafield & Wood: "The holders of bonds are . . . the beneficiaries of independent contractual obligations by . . . the Authority. Any attempt to alter these contractual rights by legislation designed, perhaps, to divert pledged revenues would be plainly invalid. Article 1, Section 10, of the United States Constitution forbids any state to 'pass any . . . Law impairing the obligation of Contracts.' . . . The appropriation of Authority moneys to such a purpose would contravene . . . provisions of the New York State and United States Constitutions." Such legalisms were not meat for the media; it all but ignored them, playing up the accompanying Moses broadside, which said merger proposals "are poorly advised, spring from panic and not logic, solve no problems and create additional ones." (The indifference of the media was a shame; emphasis on and explanation of this point could have begun at last the education about the political realities behind the powers of public authorities that the public had been needing for thirty years.)

Incredibly, the new administration still didn't get the point—as it didn't get the point of some other hints in Moses' statement, such as his comment that "Triborough is the only agency with the personnel or funds to perform [highway] planning and coordination. If Triborough is destroyed, the city is likely to lose, at least in the next five years while alternative planning and administrative forces are developed, hundreds of millions of dollars of federal and state highway aid. The effect of such loss upon the city, its construction industry and its labor forces, will be catastrophic." That statement was a rallying call to the forces that exerted so large a degree of control over the Legislature, which alone could effect the merger Lindsay was so blithely predicting, but the new administration appeared not to understand this. It was through not only his Triborough chairmanship but his informal post as city arterial highways representative that Moses represented to the "construction industry" and "labor forces" hundreds of millions of dollars of federal and state highway aid. Remove him from the arterial post and half of his remaining power, already so drastically reduced, would be gone—and removing him from that post would not require legislative action; removal could be accomplished merely by sending him a letter. But, incredibly, while Lindsay wanted Moses out of the arterial post, he did not understand its importance; believing the Triborough chairmanship to be all that mattered, he thought the letter could wait—and it waited, all through the ensuing fight. Joining a walk-in against a Moses highway, the Richmond Parkway through the Staten Island Greenbelt, Lindsay aides made a pretty picture, particularly "briskly striding Commissioner Hoving," who explained to reporters that his multicolored hiking outfit was "multinational," with the red ski cap from Austria, the white turtleneck sweater from Ireland, the purple scarf from Iceland, etc. "This [parkway fight] is a classic case of conservation versus modern times," he said—and he, like the other aides along, had not the slightest doubt that modern times would win. Shortly before the final draft of the merger proposal was completed, Lindsay made the gesture of sending transportation aide Arthur E. Palmer to see Moses and ask him personally to resign, but the tone in which Palmer couched the request was as condescending as his attitude—Palmer was told to make it clear to Moses that he was being given an opportunity to resign to save the face he would lose by being forced out—and it was only a gesture anyway; the new Mayor all too obviously felt he was being charitable, that Moses had no choice but to go. Palmer was to recall that "from the beginning and during all this," Lindsay never had "the slightest" respect for Moses or comprehension of Moses' powers. "[Lindsay's] attitude was—what he used to say was 'For Christ's sake, throw the old bastard out on his ear!' "

Interestingly enough, it was Palmer, an older, quieter man despised by Lindsay's glib young men because he didn't talk as fast or (they thought) think as fast as they, who first grasped the facts in the situation—possibly because he had had the face-to-face meetings with Lindsay's opponent which the new Mayor's other aides had not.

There were three meetings. One was at Randall's Island, one was at Moses' Gracie Terrace apartment and one was at Moses' favorite booth in the Oak Room at the Plaza. None was at Palmer's office, or at any place he suggested—because Moses made it quite clear that if the Mayor's new man in transportation wanted to meet him, he would have to do so at Moses' convenience. Moses' utter indifference to whether or not the meeting ever took place was hardly like the attitude of a desperate old man. Palmer found it, in fact, rather unsettling. Further unsettling was Moses' reaction to Lindsay's generous offer to let him save face. He wasn't in the least interested even in discussing it. Instead, he gave Palmer lectures. "The conversations consisted of monologues during which he was giving me messages—some of which I got at the time, some of which I got later, some of which I don't think I've ever gotten"—messages about power in the city and how he controlled it, that "the Mayor didn't have the power to unhorse him, that he wasn't going to be intimidated, that he didn't propose to change his program, which included the Bushwick Expressway, the Lower Manhattan Expressway, etc., that others had tried that scheme before, that there were a dozen other devices he could use, that he was prepared to cooperate with the Mayor, but only on his own terms." Palmer, who was by no means as dense as Lindsay's aides considered him, may not have gotten all the messages, but he got enough. When he reported Moses' refusal to resign to Lindsay, the Mayor asked him, "Well, do I fire him or not?" Palmer replied, he recalls, that "according to the [Triborough] statute, you haven't got the power to fire him." Palmer's honesty apparently ended his rapport with the Mayor; Lindsay appeared, Palmer was to recall, to cool toward him from that moment on. But Moses' message was apparently beginning to sink in—accompanied by other unpleasant facts of political life which Lindsay was beginning to learn. At a subsequent meeting, Palmer recalls, he received indications of a diminution in Lindsay's confidence, including one conversation in which the Mayor enunciated, as though he had learned it for the first time, a virtual playback of Palmer's own words: "Don't forget, Moses has a lot of credit cards outstanding, and he's not going to be an easy guy to get out." Soon there were stronger indications. Someone in the administration had apparently read the bond covenants; the legislation as submitted to Albany no longer made any mention of the Triborough surpluses; all that was now proposed was a merger of the two authorities. And before the news of this Lindsay concession was released to the press, Palmer was dispatched again to Moses—not this time as an act of charity but to try to make a deal based on their assumption that Moses still thought Lindsay would try to appropriate the surplus as well as merge the authorities: since Moses was always stressing the sacredness of the bond covenants, and saying that they revolved around the surplus, Palmer was to offer to do what Lindsay now knew he had no choice but to do anyway—leave the surplus intact—if Moses would agree to cease his opposition.

Nothing revealed the inability of the new administration to comprehend Moses' power or his motives more clearly than did this offer, for it failed to take into account either the fact that Moses was really interested in keeping not surpluses but power or the fact that he had the political clout to keep power without making any concessions at all. Moses' reaction—delivered in the Oak Room—was, in Palmer's recollection, to make his previous messages plainer, as if he had just realized that, in the person of John Lindsay, he was dealing with a pupil even slower than he had thought.

"You keep asking me to cooperate with your Mayor," he said. "How can I cooperate with anyone who's proposing to break" the bond covenants? Palmer said, "Mr. Moses, if you would cooperate, I don't think any breaking of the covenants would be necessary."

Leaning across the table at Palmer, Moses said: "I wouldn't cooperate with that goddamned whippersnapper no matter what he did! He'll come and go; Triborough is going to be around for a long time!" Palmer, after a pause, replied: "What you're really saying, Mr. Moses, is that these talks are really fruitless."

At last, someone had gotten the idea. Moses leaned back with a smile. "Yes," he said, "that's about what I'm saying." On February 26, John Lindsay had to make a trip to Canossa. He had telephoned Moses for a meeting; certainly, Moses replied, he would be glad to meet the Mayor—at Randall's Island or Gracie Terrace. If the Mayor wanted to see him, the Mayor would have to come to him. And when, on February 26, Lindsay came to Moses' apartment, Moses replied to his attempts to negotiate the issue by grabbing up a yellow legal pad and scribbling out on it a "revision" of the legislation Lindsay was proposing. The details of the "revision" are unknown, but both Moses and Palmer, to whom Lindsay gave the yellow piece of paper, are agreed on its purport: while it would create the "Transportation Administration" about which Lindsay had been talking, it would leave not only Triborough's surpluses but its independence untouched—along with the powers of its chairman and Moses' continuation in that post. It would leave Moses in power as firmly as before. And when Lindsay attempted to discuss the proposal, Moses wasn't interested in discussing it. The Mayor could take it or leave it. At last, Palmer recalls, the Mayor seemed to understand that Moses was sure he could win any showdown.

Lindsay thought Moses was wrong. As the Legislature moved closer to taking up his proposal, he and his aides were aggressively, boastfully confident that the old bastard's day was about over.

In part, their optimism was based on the outcome of a meeting with Governor Rockefeller. At the meeting, held over dinner in the Governor's Fifth Avenue apartment, the merger plan had been presented to Rockefeller and several of his aides, including his counsel, Sol Corbin, and a tall, burly man dressed in evening clothes whom Richard M. Rosen, Lindsay's legislative aide, thought at first was one of the butlers but who was introduced to him as Bill Ronan (he left early to attend a formal dinner elsewhere). So naïve was the team representing the city that it wasn't until, after they left Rockefeller's apartment, they decided to go to Sardi's for a drink to discuss what had happened—the handsome young celebrities were very big at Sardi's—that they realized, as Rosen puts it, "that we had been talking to Dr. Ronan about a plan that would have deeply affected the area he was interested in," that we had been "giving a proposal that would compete with the things he was doing. We had felt, we admitted to one another, a little silly saying when you get your state things together, it'll fit right in with what we're doing. As if we were trying to pull the wool over his eyes. . . . No one's pulling the wool over Bill Ronan's eyes." Nonetheless, they were lulled by the Governor's attitude. One member of the Lindsay team, who would discuss the meeting only on condition not only that he not be quoted about it but that the author never reveal to anyone, anytime, that he had ever agreed to talk to him about *anything,* says: "The Governor was very favorable. My recollection is that the Governor said he would support [the Lindsay merger proposal]. My recollection is that the Governor said he could put it through quickly." Palmer says, "[Rockefeller] went over the legislation and he undertook to get it passed. We all had dinner together and parted great friends." Rosen says, "There was never—at any time—a pledge of support, but we thought the Governor liked the proposal conceptually, as an idea." (Neither Rockefeller, Ronan nor any of the Governor's other aides would discuss the meeting.) Lindsay certainly appears to have believed he had the Governor's support. And even if he had doubts about the Governor's word, the doubts would not have worried him overly; "to tell the truth," one of Lindsay's aides recalls, "we thought we could win up in Albany without it; to tell you the truth, we had no doubts about it." Interviewed by newsmen, mayoral legislative aide Rosen allowed himself to be just a little pontifical. "The way you handle legislators is with power," he said. And, he made clear, there was no doubt that the Mayor of New York had the power in any matter so vital to the city's future.

Everyone in Albany seemed to know what was going on with regard to John Lindsay's transportation legislation. Everyone but Lindsay's man in Albany, city legislative representative Rosen. The three leaders who made the decisions for the Legislature were Assembly Speaker Anthony Travia, Assembly Minority Leader Perry B. Duryea, Jr., and Senate Majority Leader Earl Brydges. (Senate Minority Leader Joseph Zaretzki had little real power.) Moses "came to me personally—and through friends—and said, 'Look, you don't want this to happen to me, do you?' " Duryea recalls. "And I said, 'No'—look, you don't have a Bob Moses come along in a state every day, and you don't just kick him out. Jim Evans [one of Moses' men in Albany] came to me and asked what could be done. I said, 'I don't like removing a guy by legislation. If [Lindsay] wants him out, let him be ballsy enough to do his own dirty work.' And I convinced Brydges. But I also told Evans that I was of the minority party and that he'd better get to Travia if he wanted to save Moses." By the time the proposed legislation came up for a public hearing, Travia had been gotten to—perhaps by Wagner (whose support had made him Speaker), perhaps by a promise by Moses to eliminate from his highway plans a proposed Cross-Brooklyn Expressway through Travia's district, perhaps by Travia's county leader, Stanley Steingut of the City Title Insurance Co., perhaps by a simpler reason: Travia's contempt (shared by Duryea, Brydges and other legislators) for Lindsay as an intellectual lightweight who combined a truly astonishing ignorance of how things got done in Albany with an arrogance that led him to lecture them, privately and publicly, on how to do their jobs. Travia, Duryea and Brydges could have swung the entire Legislature to their side if they had needed to do so, but the Legislature was on their side already—and if there were any recalcitrants, the leaders had allies. "Christ," one senator was to say years later, "I still remember that one: that was the first time I ever got a call from Harry Van Arsdale himself. Himself! Not his lobbyist. Harry Van Arsdale! Christ, everyone was calling—the banks, the leaders, you name it. There was enough muscle against that thing to have beaten *anything*." (This is the quote of Lindsay's man Rosen on the subject: "I discussed the bill with the legislative leaders and their reaction was generally favorable, a good response to the ideas that were presented.")

"They were playing games with Lindsay that year," says one reporter, a good one, covering Albany in 1966. "They kept saying, 'Amend it, amend it.' He'd make the amendments they asked. Then they'd ask him to make some more. I mean everyone knew what was going on. I myself heard some guy [legislator] say to Rosen in the corridor, 'You're forgetting about that bill for this year, aren't you?' The guy was trying to hint to him, you know? But Rosen didn't even understand what the guy was trying to tell him. He started to seriously discuss with the guy why it wasn't really dead, why the Mayor—*'THE MAYOR!'*—was determined—*'DETERMINED!'*—to have it passed."

The contract out on the bill was executed with finesse. Travia told Rosen one day that a joint session of the Senate and Assembly Rules Committees would hold a public hearing on the proposed legislation. Recalls Rosen: "Travia . . . said to me, 'All we want up there is the Mayor and one other person—there'll be one or two people there from the other side. It'll be a friendly little thing, casual.' The only reason we're having it at all, I was told, was that it was required by law." Rosen passed the message along to Big John, who appears to have seriously believed that a joint session of the two most powerful committees of the Legislature, a session on a proposal to remove Robert Moses from power, would indeed be little more than a formality. On the morning it was scheduled to be held, the Mayor flew up from New York, accompanied by only two aides, Corporation Counsel J. Lee Rankin and Executive Assistant Corporation Counsel Norman Redlich—neither of whom had even done much research into the matter to be discussed. Rosen met the three men at the airport, drove them straight to the Capitol and, before leaving in the press room transcripts of the statement the Mayor was going to make at the hearing, escorted the three men into the Assembly Parlor, in which the hearing was to be held—so that the Mayor was already in the Parlor when Rosen, in the press room, had his moment of truth.

It came in the form of a handout, lying on the big table opposite the press-room door on which public relations men for the various legislative committees leave stacks of handouts for reporters' use. As Rosen put his stack down, he saw it lying there, and picked it up and read it. It was a handout announcing the public hearing, and the names of the speakers who were to appear at it. "A friendly little thing, casual?" It was billed as the biggest event of the day—and, Rosen saw as his eyes followed the type down, the billing was justified. Appearing for the Mayor's proposal would be one person, the unknown Redlich. Appearing for the other side would be, in addition to Moses, two former Governors, Dewey and Poletti; one former Mayor, Wagner; one former counsel to Presidents and possibly the most prestigious Democratic attorney in the state, Rosenman; Brennan of the construction workers, Guinan of the transport workers and others of the state's most powerful labor leaders; a representative of its most powerful bank (although David Rockefeller had sent a spokesman rather than appearing himself); its most powerful investment bankers; its largest stock brokerage firm; its leading and most powerful bond attorneys—and a platoon of representatives of other power groups ranging all the way from the Transit Authority to the Automobile Club of America. It was a lineup of most of the most powerful forces in the state—and it was a lineup arrayed against his boss. It was at that moment, all in a flash, Rosen recalls, that he realized that Lindsay had been led into a carefully concealed trap—one from which there was no escape. "I didn't realize what had happened until I saw the handout. Then I said, 'Travia's fucked us.' "

Running back to the Assembly Parlor, Rosen whispered these tidings to his boss. Even without this news flash, however, Lindsay was getting the message for himself. For as he stood in the Assembly Parlor, ready for the friendly, casual little get-together, jamming through the doors came television cameramen, radio and newspaper reporters and photographers—by the dozen. And mixed among them, in addition to Travia, whom the Mayor had expected to see, were Duryea, Brydges—and a half dozen other key legislative leaders.

Then the old lion came into the room.

The crowd, which had been milling around, parted to let him through, and he was suddenly face to face with his enemy.

Lindsay half turned away, almost as if to pretend he hadn't seen Moses, but as the photographers rushed up, the Mayor plunged his hands into his pockets and his face creased in a forced smile. A broad, wide grin broke across Moses' face, and for a moment the two men stood there, one young, handsome, dressed in a gold-buttoned blue blazer, precisely knotted striped rep, nervousness showing through the mask on his face; the other old, lined, bald, tough, wearing a dark suit with jacket unbuttoned and plain dark tie pulled askew—and utterly relaxed. The photographers asked for a handshake; Lindsay hesitated; sure, Moses said, and as Lindsay took his hand and Moses looked into his handsome face, the grin broadened into a smile of real delight. Then, abruptly, while Lindsay was still standing straight and still and keeping the smile glued on, Moses yanked his hand loose and whirled to walk away. There was command in that gesture; the circle around them parted—followed by his entourage, he strode through it and slouched down casually on a red leather sofa against a wall. The sofa seated four, but no one took the other seats; "at least three [aides] were standing behind him—standing!—as he sat alone on that long sofa," says reporter Sidney Schanberg of the *Times*. When Schanberg approached him, "he answered a couple of questions and then he got churlish and turned to Ed O'Brien and he said, 'Ed, I want to hear this testimony.' Meaning, 'Get rid of this shit!' " Then he looked up inquiringly, and another aide hurriedly ran over and whispered in Travia's ear. The Speaker had been chatting with his own aides. He stopped abruptly, caught Duryea's eye, walked with him over to the hearing table and, even before sitting down, began pounding the gavel.

Lindsay was the first at the lectern set up at the left end of the long table. Normally so poised, the Mayor stared down with almost painfully obvious nervousness at the full battery of microphones before which he had been lured. "He read [like] a schoolboy reciting his graduation speech," Schanberg says. Slouched on the couch, leaning on one hand, the other, big and still powerful, gripping his knee, Moses listened intently for a few minutes, even putting on the glasses with the concealed hearing aid so that he could be sure he heard. For a few minutes he was impassive, his lips pressed tightly together. But as he heard what Lindsay was saying, they turned up in a small smile. As the Mayor continued and it became apparent that he had no new cards to play, the smile widened a bit. And when the Mayor got to his attack on Moses' proposed new highways, and said, "Under my administration, these proposals will never be accepted," Moses began to laugh, hastily putting a hand up to his face to hide the laughter when he saw a photographer lifting a camera in his direction. On receipt of Rosen's message, Lindsay, Rankin and Redlich had hastily decided that the best thing to do was to "get the Mayor out of there" as fast as possible; recalls one of those men, "The Mayor testified and said he had to go and 'If there are any questions, Mr. Redlich will answer them.' " Then he headed out the door. Moses was obviously having real difficulty keeping from laughing out loud. If Albany was a jungle, with many of the principal beasts of prey gathered in the Assembly Parlor that day, an observer could, just by watching Robert Moses, have known that it was *his* jungle. He may have been an old lion, but John Lindsay wasn't the young lion to take his jungle away from him.

"And then," as one observer recalls, "there followed the parade of the power brokers."

Moses led off, as was fitting—relaxed, at home, reading his speech without looking up, speaking in bored tones, making his points effortlessly. When some of the rank-and-file assemblymen present asked him a few mild questions, he answered—in Schanberg's phrase—"like you're peasants." After a short while, he had had enough of it; he swung away from the lectern.

The other power brokers followed. All the points necessary to be made were made, by the people best suited to make them—the lawyers that the proposed merger was illegal; the investment bankers that it would destroy the "businesslike" nature of public authorities and would thereby make it impossible for them to raise money for needed public improvements ("No one will buy a long-term revenue bond if the management of the project operates at the beck and call and whim of elected officials"); former government officials that the man proposing it didn't know anything about government (John J. Gilhooley, not only a Transit Commissioner but a former Assistant Secretary of Labor, calling it "a political power grab . . . inanely conceived and ineptly drafted" legislation by "rank amateurs" in City Hall); politicians that the man proposing it was power hungry (it was, said Wagner, who had refused all previous overtures to attack his successor, but had trotted out his prestige at Moses' command, nothing more than "a reach for power"); the AAA that it would unfairly penalize motorists who had paid for highway facilities "through the tolls and taxes they have paid"; the union leaders that it was just plain bad. Worst of all, speaker after speaker emphasized, Lindsay's plan would deprive the public of the services of Robert Moses. "Make no mistake," Poletti said, "this arrogant and shameless ripper legislation . . . sponsored by Mayor Lindsay is intended primarily to get rid of Bob Moses." "I have not, nor shall I ever join the pack that is currently snapping at the heels of Robert Moses," Gilhooley said. "His achievements are beyond the reach of the peashooters now attacking him . . . he will be honored by anyone who reads or writes the Twentieth Century history of the State of New York." But it wasn't what the speakers said that mattered, but what they represented. They represented power, enough power to defeat anyone in the state—even a Mayor of New York City—and to defeat him easily. As the perceptive Schanberg was to put it, "The hearing was a pro forma charade. It was like the Green Bay Packers playing a high-school team. Lindsay never had a chance." Moses didn't stay around to review the parade of power brokers he had marshaled—and there was no reason why he should. Lindsay should have—he might have lost face, but he would have learned something—he would have learned the identity of those "power brokers" he was always talking about. His foe had lined them up and paraded them before him.

With his customary attention to detail, Moses had even arranged for a series of mopping-up actions to follow the hearings. On the following day, Brennan launched a new, all-out attack on Lindsay, charging the new Mayor with "sitting on $3 billion worth of construction projects" by putting "politics ahead of people." The construction projects listed, of course, were almost all Robert Moses projects. And the day after *that,* the Chase Manhattan Bank supplemented its previous opposition to the merger proposal by announcing that if the Legislature should adopt it, it would, as trustee of $379,300,000 worth of Triborough bonds, sue to invalidate the legislation; a legal brief designed to demonstrate the illegality of such a contract-breaking move was being filed with the Legislature's Rules Committees by the bank's law firm—Dewey, Ballantine, Bushby, Palmer and Wood. (The *Times* carried this story on page seventy-three; in terms of political realities in New York State, it was the story, above all the merger stories, that should have been on page one.) All bases were covered; when the *Times* editorialized that it was sure the merger would be legal, Franklin S. Wood wrote the editors a letter concluding dryly: "Your . . . opinion . . . will not, we think, be shared by most lawyers." But Moses' precautions were superfluous, a case of overkill. The Lindsay merger proposal had been dead long before—as soon as it was made, in fact. The actual murder had been delayed until the public hearing only to add to his humiliation.

(By the way, Travia told reporters during a mid-afternoon recess, the legislation should never have been sent up to Albany in the first place without a home-rule message from the City Council; he didn't see how that had happened: the Legislature could not consider it without such a message.

(That was rubbing it in, some listening legislators said, unable quite to hide their smiles. Travia had, of course, known all along that a home-rule message was required. Everyone had known. He could have mentioned the fact to Rosen previously. He must have forgotten to do so.)

The bill was dead—although Lindsay did not have the sense to let it die quietly. He telephoned Rockefeller for support, instructed Rosen to "get to work" on the legislators. But the support from the Governor was somehow never forthcoming. The Mayor announced to reporters that it had "never occurred to anyone that it would be necessary to have a home-rule resolution" but that "now" the Legislature was trying to "buck-pass" the matter back to the City Council. When he asked the Council for the home-rule message, the request never even got out of committee.

The Parade of the Power Brokers had, to anyone interested in the nuances of true power in New York State, been a good show. It was to be the last Robert Moses ever produced. The imperial guard would never charge for him again.

On July 11, 1966, he had arranged a celebration to mark the thirtieth anniversary of the opening of the Triborough Bridge. There were crowds—3,500 children rounded up from housing projects and by the Police Athletic League and bused to Randall's Island for the occasion—and pageantry—officials used silver shears to snip a ribbon at the Queens end of the span and then rode in a twelve-car motorcade (eleven limousines led by Moses in a 1936 Ford touring car driven by Omero C. Catan of Teaneck, New Jersey, who on July 11, 1936, when the great bridge first opened, had been the first driver to cross) to Randall's Island, where bands played and speeches were given—and a sumptuous luncheon in Triborough's state dining room (3,500 box lunches were there for the children)—and brochures—a magnificently printed, boxed volume recording the Authority's achievements entitled *Thirty Years of Accomplishment*. In his speech, Moses effectively disposed of the Triborough surpluses Lindsay was always talking about, announcing that he had "committed" $40,000,000 in Authority funds for improvements to Authority-owned bridges (no city approval needed), such as a new toll plaza for the Triborough and a complete reconstruction of the Cross Bay, and $8,000,000 to the Park Department for new playgrounds. With Austin Tobin of the Port Authority taking the opportunity to tell reporters present that he was planning to open bids for the World Trade Center shortly despite the fact that Lindsay had not yet approved the project, the ceremony was turned into a demonstration by the city's two great rump governments that they were planning to proceed in future as they had in past—without being bound by the wishes of City Hall.

To keep the bridge clear for the motorcade, all other traffic had been barred from the Queens span, and as the officials cut ribbons, thousands of Manhattan-bound motorists were kept waiting for half an hour behind them in broiling heat while Triborough Bridge and Tunnel Officers ignored the angry protest, not allowing them on the bridge until the motorcade had completed a markedly leisurely trip to Randall's Island. And there was praise enough even for Moses, Austin Tobin lauding his "great gifts of intellect, imagination, courage and dynamic energy—as well as his instinct for the jugular," Queens Borough President Mario Cariello telling the children that "New York City would never be what it is today" had Moses been born in South America, Australia or at the North Pole. But the celebration ended on a distinctly sour note: while Moses was still bidding his guests farewell, a messenger from the Mayor's office handed an aide a letter for Moses, and the aide gave it to Moses, and Moses, ripping it open, saw that it was a letter dismissing him as arterial highways representative.

The Mayor had taken this step—which he should have taken before the merger fight—after it was over, too late to help him in it—but he had taken it. Once Robert Moses had held twelve government jobs simultaneously; now he was reduced to one, the chairmanship of the Triborough Authority. And within the week, Lindsay had moved to give himself a toehold even in Moses' last stronghold; Commissioner Tracy's term had expired on June 30; the Mayor appointed Transportation Administrator Palmer in his place.

The Palmer appointment had no effect on Moses' power. The primary purpose of putting him on the board, Lindsay had told him, was to "protect the city's interest by saving as much of the surplus as possible." But Palmer proved unable to accomplish anything. "The first time I voted 'No' on a proposal, Moses got up and walked around and gave me a half-hour speech, how I didn't understand how these things were done. . . . It was probably the first 'No' vote in the history of Triborough. And the staff . . . was also appalled—they had never seen Moses confronted before." But the vote on the issue was 2–1, with the other Commissioner, realtor and Democratic financier Norman K. Winston, voting with Moses. Palmer says he had been told that Winston might be ready to be wooed away from Moses, but their first talk indicated that that was wrong; Winston was ready to follow the chairman unquestioningly on every decision. And that, of course, made Palmer's opposition academic. He consistently voted against Moses proposals—and always lost, 2–1. He was not even able to stop Moses' "commitment" of an additional $20,000,000 of surplus to the building of a second deck on the Verrazano Bridge, a project to which Lindsay was adamantly opposed.

As for Lindsay's other move—the ending of Moses' designation as arterial highways representative—that would have slashed Moses' power greatly if it had stuck, but whether it would have or not is by no means certain.

By the end of the year, Lindsay was beginning to display signs of an awareness of the need for accommodation with the labor power brokers he had scorned, and they were determined to keep at least some of Moses' highways alive and well and driving toward inauguration—and the best way to do that, they were convinced, was to keep Moses in charge of them. Moreover, if the Mayor wanted to build any highways at all, he had little choice. Only Moses had the plans for major expressways, and only Moses had the money for further plans; an astonished and dismayed Lindsay was informed that to plan a completely different arterial program would take five years, and would cost, in either fees to consultant engineering firms or salaries for a sufficient number of civil service engineers, $7,000,000 a year—an amount there was absolutely no chance of the financially strapped city ever raising. Moses, moreover, had far more leverage even than those contained in the rolls of blueprints piled on Triborough's shelves; he had Triborough's money—for of course the Authority would, in the next year or two, have millions—

tens of millions—of dollars of capitalizable income that had not been committed for specific projects.

One estimate of the money available for this purpose over the next three years was $250,000,000. This money could be used to pay part of the costs of highway projects; in fact, many highway projects would not be feasible without sizable Triborough contributions. No man with $250,000,000 to spend on public works in a financially strapped city desperate to build public works could possibly be frozen out of public works negotiations with federal and state governments; in reality he would, whether designated as arterial representative or not, still be that representative in fact if not in name, until he could be replaced as Triborough chairman. He could not be replaced as chairman until June 30, 1970, and by that time there might well be a new Mayor, one who wouldn't want to replace him. While Moses' removal was headlined by the press—which speculated, week after week, that he might soon be removed from power entirely by the Mayor—Lindsay's latest gestures were in many ways as futile as the others the Mayor had made against Moses.

By this time, however, it didn't matter to Moses what Lindsay did. Someone much smarter than the Mayor—the Governor who had already stripped so much of his power away from him—was moving against him now, trying to remove him, once and for all, from the last of the power he had held for forty years.

49. The Last Stand

ROCKEFELLER HAD BEEN laying his transportation plans out for eight years. Now they were ready. Ronan had filled in the details. Lindsay's attempt to take over the transportation setup had been the final factor in determining the Governor to move to implement them. If there was going to be a takeover, it was going to be *his* takeover. And therefore, the Governor seemed to feel, it was time for Moses to go.

To implement his grand conception, the Governor needed money, a particular kind of money—seed money.

It was, of course, impossible, in so inflationary an era, to calculate with precision the cost of the network of highways, mass transit facilities and airports of which he was dreaming. If he had even a rough estimate, moreover, he made sure it was never revealed honestly to the public—for a very sound political reason when dealing with a Legislature in which upstate conservatives played a prominent role: it was almost unimaginably huge. One estimate, probably far too low, was that, if begun in 1968, it would cost $6.4 billion in the next five years alone. Much of this money Rockefeller had to obtain from the federal government, but federal contributions were determined in some cases by state and local participation in the funding. That meant local money. In almost all cases federal contributions were dependent on state and local planning—Nelson Rockefeller had learned what Moses knew: that it was the state with plans, not vague proposals but detailed blueprints, ready when new federal appropriations became available, that got the federal money. And certain pieces of the grand conception could not be built by the federal government at all, because the only way to make their building feasible was to make them toll or revenue-producing facilities, for which federal expenditures were prohibited.

But state and local money on the scale the Governor needed was simply unavailable: eight years of his massive spending had reduced the state to a condition in which it was all but impossible for him to meet the constitutional requirement that he balance its budget annually; costs were outrunning revenues even for current programs; state revenues could simply not support a major new one. A $500,000,000 highway bond issue passed some years before was all but exhausted in 1966; if a new one wasn't approved, highways would have to be built out of current revenues—which meant that, in effect, no major new highways would be built. As for local money—New York City money—deficits stared him in the face everywhere: Transit

Authority deficits, Long Island Rail Road deficits, Penn Central Railroad deficits, the city itself so broke that it had to borrow money each year just to pay current bills—everywhere, that is, but in the accounts of the two giant public authorities, Port and Triborough. Port, armored by the fact that he had to win approval from the New Jersey Governor and Legislature for anything he wanted that agency to do, was, for the immediate future at least, beyond his reach. And that left just one place to turn.

The Triborough Bridge and Tunnel Authority had $110,000,000 in cash and securities on hand—a surplus that was growing at the rate of almost $30,000,000 a year. A surplus that would grow much faster if Triborough's tolls were raised—and Rockefeller was already secretly considering raising the tolls. A capitalizable surplus—worth, over the next five years, even if current tolls were not raised perhaps half a billion dollars. He needed that money. He wanted it. And Moses, adamant that he and he alone would decide how it was to be used, stood in his way.

And more important than money was personality. There were Ronan's and Moses', of course—the personality of the cool, cautious, bankerly corporation man versus that of the bold, slashing, imaginative creator; an exceptionally perceptive politician and reader of men who had plenty of time to read those two (and who was to have a ringside seat during the ensuing struggle), Assembly Speaker Perry Duryea, says, "They were too antagonistic to work together in *any* setup." And there were Rockefeller's and Moses'. When Moses was in a picture, he dominated it; any transportation improvement in which he played any sort of a key role would, in the public's eye, be *his* improvement, not the Governor's.

"So," as Duryea says, "Rocky wasn't satisfied with what happened in '62. He really had to knock him out of the box."

And Moses had so little left to fight back with.

Once he had had so much. With income from the State Power, Jones Beach and Bethpage authorities as well as from a State Park Commission and Parks Council as well as the City Park Department, Triborough's annual surplus had been only one piece of a very large pie. More important than the size of the pie had been the fact that it was divided into so many pieces. More important than the amount of money at his command was the fact that this money came from so many different and varied sources, that he had held simultaneously twelve different government jobs—some state and some city. A Governor contemplating removing him from those under his control would have to reckon with the fact that, because Moses' authority chairmanships had staggered six-year terms, he could do even that only over a period of years. And he had to reckon with the fact that, not only during those years but thereafter, Moses would still be holding many powerful city posts, that "you'd have to fight him on so many different fronts." Moses had been able to prop up each post with others, to use each as leverage to make the others more powerful than they would otherwise have been. The position in which he had once stood had been all but unassailable. But he had, by resigning in anger from his state posts, knocked out many of the props himself. Now all the props were gone. His single remaining post stood alone. And he now had only $30,000,000 a year left to fight with—a significant sum but not when measured against the resources of the state that were the resources at his foe's command, and a sum even less significant because it was derived from only one post, his last post, so that men who choose up sides on the basis of money could see clearly that if he lost that post, he would have nothing left to give them—a factor which made them reluctant to take his side. If Robert Moses had still possessed twelve jobs—if "Triborough" had still consisted of twelve arms—Nelson Rockefeller might have found, as Harriman and Dewey and Roosevelt had found, that it was unfeasible to cut off one of them. But now "Triborough" consisted only of Triborough. A Governor could lop off that arm with the assurance that if he did so, Moses would have none left at all.

Moses' lone position might still have been secure, for it rested on the solid rock of the Triborough bond covenants, the contracts sacred under law. Not even a Governor, backed by the Legislature and armed with the full authority of the state, could break those covenants, for if he tried, bondholders could sue, and the courts would surely uphold them.

Except for one consideration. While in theory even a single injured bondholder could sue, in practice no individual bondholder would. In the first place, the legal costs of so complicated a suit would, even in the preliminary steps, be enormous—far beyond any injury the bondholder might have suffered or any damages he could realistically claim. More important, a bondholder contemplating an individual suit would be faced with a legal reality: suing as an individual would be viewed by a court as an admission that only he was hurt—why weren't other bondholders suing?—so that the bondholders, or a substantial number of them, would have to sue as a group. To cover such a possibility, an agent had been appointed, in the contracts, to protect the bondholders' rights—to, if necessary, sue on their behalf. The contracts had appointed a bondholders' trustee.

And the trustee was the Chase Manhattan Bank, and the Chase Manhattan was the only large bank in the United States still controlled by a single family.

The Governor's.

"After the 1966 Legislature had wound up its business without passing our bill and had gone home, we began to get straws in the wind that the Governor and Ronan had plans of their own for taking over transportation," Arthur Palmer says. Lindsay was in no position to object, desperate as he was for a way out of the continual financial crisis posed by the subways (and for a way to avoid a second fare increase—Lindsay had already raised it from fifteen to twenty cents—before he had to run for re-election in 1969). Moreover, neither the Mayor nor his aides seem to have grasped the extent of the power Ronan was negotiating away from the city. By January 4, 1967, Rockefeller was confident enough of city cooperation to ask Legislature and voters to approve a $2,000,000,000 bond issue for highways, mass transit facilities and airports throughout the state and to begin planning a "coordinated," "balanced," "regional approach"—with far greater emphasis than ever before on mass transit—to transportation in the metropolitan region, merging and incorporating in Ronan's Metropolitan Commuter Transportation Authority all the region's public transportation agencies: the New York City Transit Authority, the Manhattan and Bronx Surface Transit Operating Authority (MABSTOA), the Long Island, Penn Central and New Haven railroads, the Staten Island Rapid Transit Service—and the Triborough Bridge and Tunnel Authority.

Rockefeller had a lot riding on approval—not only the plan itself, which had fully captured his imagination, but a consideration considerably more mundane: driven to the wall by the state's worsening financial crisis, the Governor had, through various budgetary devices, discharged his legal obligation to balance the budget by including in anticipated "revenues" a substantial amount—according to some sources $49,000,000, according to others $51,000,000, according to still others $89,000,000—in money from the bond issue for which he was still asking approval. If it were not approved, the resultant deficit would prove highly embarrassing. The Governor was, moreover, planning to use bond issue monies to help in future budgets. If it were not approved, the state would be in for a truly hair-raising tax increase, one that would reinforce his image as a wildly spending liberal among the Republican conservatives across the country whose support he needed for his planned 1968 presidential bid.

The emphasis on mass transit insured media support for the plan in the metropolitan area, and, with leading politicians, Democratic and Republican, endorsing it, legislative approval was assured. Approval in the November referendum, however, was more doubtful. Widespread voter resentment against higher taxes had in recent years caused the rejection of many bond issues; the Governor was worried about the so-called silent vote. Resentment on the part of upstate conservative voters against the Governor's free-spending, high-taxing policies was flooding toward a crest that would spill over in the conservative legislative revolt two years later. In an off-year election, with most voters apathetic and the turnout small, passage of controversial bond issues is traditionally difficult when the only voters who turn out in force are those opposed to specific transportation projects. Results of Rockefeller-commissioned polls were highly discouraging. With the issue in the balance, Rockefeller was afraid that Moses would tip it against him.

The powerful construction labor unions were still solidly behind Moses, for Van Arsdale and Brennan knew that vast allocations were of little use in creating jobs unless the crushing of local opposition and the planning and blueprinting that had to take place before men could actually be put to work was ramrodded through, and their meetings with Ronan had convinced them that he was not a ramrod—if indeed he was even competent, which the two union leaders doubted. "You need a man who knows how to put a show on the road," Brennan was to say. "We had to keep Moses in there." More important, Moses still possessed his name—which, while a symbol around Washington Square of all that was hated, was a symbol of something quite different in Queens and Staten Island. Moses would continue to have the voters' ears, the Governor knew, because he still had the *News* and *Newsday,* the papers with the largest circulation in New York City and on Long Island; in its editorial on the Governor's proposal, for example, the latter had said: "Essential is the participation of Bob Moses in the new agency. His experience will be invaluable." Most important of all, Moses still possessed, unimpaired by his seventy-eight years, the instrument that had gotten him power in the first place: his powerful, supple intelligence. Alone now, Robert Moses began doing what he had done when he had been trying to find a way out of the West Side Improvement financial impasse, when he had conceived the possibilities of the public authority—at so many crises during his career: jotting down figures on a yellow legal note pad.

Ronan's public relations men had been feeding the press figures showing that the unification would end the city's traditional subway deficit crisis. Several years later, Duryea, no friend of Ronan's, could still recall them with a wry grin: "The surplus from Triborough would be $30 [million] a year, the surplus from MABSTOA would be about $5 [million], the Long Island [Rail Road] would either break even or have a surplus of about $1 [million], and these surpluses would be just enough to make up the Transit Authority deficit."

But Moses found that the merger wouldn't come close to making up the transit deficit. Calculating the present and future cost of union contracts then being negotiated and union contracts that would have to be negotiated within the next year or two, increasing maintenance costs and future debt service, he concluded that MABSTOA and LIRR would have not small surpluses but tremendous deficits, and that the Transit Authority's deficit was growing so fast that no conceivable combination of contributions from other agencies could make it up. The primary rationale that the Governor was using to sell the plan to the conservative upstate voters—that it would free the state once and for all from the annual worries about New York's subway problem—wasn't true at all.

And that was only one small point proved by Moses' figures.

Since he had become Governor, Rockefeller had created several giant "public authorities" that were bastards of the genre because their revenue bonds would be paid off not out of their own revenues but out of the general revenues of the state.

No one outside the Governor's confidential staff had ever figured out what the total debt service on all these bond issues was going to be when they were all sold and paying interest simultaneously. Only one other state official, the quietly independent Democratic Comptroller, Arthur Levitt, was interested in doing so—teams of his auditors had just begun calculating that very point.

Moses did it alone. He would never discuss what he found. But Duryea—his last friend in power and the one he took most fully into his confidence at this stage in his career—did, in an interview in 1969: "Three years ago, the state had budgeted for debt service 25–30 million. Last year, it was 40 million and this year 47. Well, Moses had a projection that if all the authorities Rocky was proposing went through, the debt service in 1972—this was the year of total sale—would be 500 million." Rockefeller's proposals would load down present and future taxpayers of the state with a staggering debt. In addition, Moses had done the simple multiplication necessary to figure out something all the reporters and editorial writers who had written about the $2,500,000,000 Metropolitan Transportation Authority bond issue had apparently never bothered to figure out—at least not one of them had mentioned the point: how much that bond issue was going to cost the taxpayers in interest. The answer was more than $1,000,000,000. A billion dollars in interest! By the time Moses finished figuring, Duryea says, "he had some numbers that were devastating."

The implications were enormous. "If he had ever gone screaming to the public . . . ," Duryea says. Moses not only possessed devastating numbers; he could devastate with them. While other opponents of the bond issue had no money to put their case before the public, Moses, with the resources of Triborough still behind him, did, and his prestige alone guaranteed him a full hearing in the media; let him take those numbers to the public with his vast and efficient public relations apparatus, and he could well wreck Rockefeller's grand conception.

And he was prepared to do so. "Only two or three of us knew of these figures," Duryea says. "But we knew that Moses was ready to blow the Governor's transportation" referendum with them. "They had to get him on board so that he wouldn't scream and holler."

Before delivering his "State of the State" message, the Governor and Ronan had had at least one conference with Moses at which they attempted to enlist his support. They failed; he flew off to a vacation in the Bahamas still an opponent. While he was there, Ronan drafted, and airmailed to the old warrior honing his rapier down there in the warm sun, some modifications designed to mollify. They did not; during the three weeks he stayed away following the Governor's speech, reporters checked with Triborough daily to try to talk to him, and as soon as he returned, he had a statement for them. He was too smart to play his trump on the first hand; it was not empty victory but power in the new transportation setup that he wanted. He did not reveal his figures. But he gave the Governor an inkling of the intensity of the opposition he was prepared to provide. It was uncompromising. The merger proposal was "absurd," he said. "Grotesque. It just won't work. . . . They don't know what they are driving at." And the opposition made major stories in every metropolitan area newspaper. On March 9, 1967, Moses met with Rockefeller in Rockefeller's Fifty-fifth Street townhouse. And two days later he announced that the Governor's plan—the "absurd," "grotesque" plan—was "indispensable" and that he was supporting it. "We believe the Governor is on the right track, that only a bold approach can succeed, and for our part shall cooperate to this end." (Said Ronan: "This is welcome news.")

The reason Moses gave for his 180-degree change of heart was that "after considerable discussion, the Governor included in his proposal a paragraph on protecting the rights of Triborough bondholders." Actually, however, nothing new of any major significance to the bondholders had been added to the proposal. Levitt and Duryea knew the real reason: the Governor had bought Moses' support with the only coin in which Moses was interested —power, a promise that he would have it under the revised transportation setup. "I know for a fact that Rockefeller felt he had bought Moses' support," Duryea says. "How [do I know]? I know because one Monday in Albany—it was at one of those Monday-morning so-called leadership conferences—Rockefeller announced that Moses would support his transportation unification program. I said, 'What'd you give him?' And Rockefeller said, 'A promise that he wouldn't be thrown in the ashcan,' that he would be given something substantial in the MTA reorganization." Levitt had even more conclusive proof. To gain maximum impact for his "figures," Moses knew they should be released by someone other than himself, someone who could not be accused of having a personal stake in the defeat of the transportation proposal. On March 8, the day before his conference with the Governor, he had telephoned Levitt, who recalls: "He called me up and said, 'I want to see you. I have figures . . . and I want you to use them and blast Rockefeller.' The very next day, I had to go to Fifty-fifth Street for a meeting of the state pension fund. I didn't know what room to go in, and I was wandering around from room to room, trying doors, and I opened one, and there, to my surprise, was Moses and his whole coterie. I said, 'What are you doing here?' He said, 'Oh, waiting to see the Governor.' I said, 'Where are those figures?' He said, 'Oh, I'll send them to you,' in a hedging tone of voice. And the next day he comes out for MTA. I never got the figures."

Van Arsdale and Brennan knew the reason, too. Rockefeller had also told it to them. The day after Moses' announcement of support, Brennan—previously conspicuously silent on the Governor's proposal—chimed in with his. The *Times* story announcing the arrival on board of the powerful unionist contained a sentence whose source was apparently Brennan himself: "It was learned . . . that Governor Rockefeller had offered Robert Moses a seat [on the MTA board] . . . as well as continued direction" of Triborough. Brennan himself confirms that Rockefeller had given "Van and I" that impression: "The Governor said he would have an important part [for Moses]." Not satisfied with that vague statement, the two unionists asked Rockefeller precisely what that meant. He told them he had given Moses what Moses wanted: "He told us Moses wanted a part of the construction." "Will he have a part?" Brennan asked. "And the Governor said, 'Oh, absolutely. We know his talents, his ability, and we want to use them.' " Rockefeller was careful to leave the same impression with the public. The Governor told reporters that each of the authorities, while being merged, would "retain [its] identity and be under the administrative direction of an executive head in charge of operations," who, the *Times* reported, "would possibly have the title of president of the agency." *President of Triborough*—that sounded even better than "Chairman."

Moses appears to have had no doubt that the Governor would keep his promise. His statement announcing his support of the referendum had stated: "If the verdict is favorable, all the talent and goodwill available must be recruited to realize the exceedingly complex, long-term improvements." He had no doubt that that talent would, in the fields of highways and bridges, continue to be his own. And with that assurance in hand, he proceeded during the seven months prior to the referendum to prove that he would violate any principle—even that most sacred one to which he had always sworn allegiance, the sacredness of the bondholders' covenants—to keep power. He outdid himself in support of the referendum; when Rockefeller didn't contact him, he called the Governor's office to ask for an appointment so that he could learn how he could best be of assistance in persuading voters, and following that meeting, he lied for the referendum (although he knew that bond revenues were slated for approach roads to his proposed Long Island Sound Crossing, he told the press: "Statements . . . that the pending transportation proposition is to be tapped to pay in whole or in part for the Long Island Sound Crossing . . . are wholly irresponsible and malicious. Not a cent of state subvention, aid or credit is required. . . ."); poured money behind it, using Triborough funds to pay for a full-scale advertising campaign ("Traffic—Commuter—Transit Delays Got Your Goat? Don't Sit And Grumble. Get Out And VOTE!"), plastering Triborough's toll booths with huge "VOTE YES!" signs—and repeatedly flattered the Governor so enthusiastically and obsequiously ("Governor Rockefeller has . . . guts"; "It takes a lot of courage and faith to ask the voters to approve a $2.5 billion . . .") that at times he seemed to be almost desperately trying to reassure Rockefeller that the Governor wouldn't have to worry about his loyalty after the reorganization, that he could be a loyal member of his team.

After an almost equally frantic statewide campaign by Rockefeller, the referendum passed, but there remained another, equally important reason to keep Moses on board. There was still the possibility of a legal fight over whether the Triborough bond covenants would be violated by the merger of the Authority into a larger authority—a question which, it seemed likely, could, if pressed, be resolved only one way: in the bondholders' favor.

Any party to a contract can bring suit if he feels it has been violated. There were two parties to the contracts that were the Triborough bonds—the Authority and the bondholders, represented by the trustee Chase Manhattan Bank.

Prior to his March 9 meeting with Rockefeller, Moses had prepared to have the Authority bring suit; he had instructed Sam Rosenman to gear up for a full-scale, no-holds-barred legal battle. But after his March 9 meeting with Rockefeller, he had Rosenman stand down, at least in part; the attorney, on behalf of Triborough, joined Dewey, representing Chase Manhattan, in attacking the proposal to use the Authority's surpluses, but let the former Governor carry the load, following through only pro forma, and he dropped opposition to the merger, the part that would have deprived Moses of power—because, of course, Moses believed Rockefeller had promised him power after the merger as well. "I understand that he had a promise that he would be part of the MTA board," Dewey was to recall. "I don't think Rosenman would have been so cooperative with the MTA if Moses hadn't thought that he'd have a place."

Of the circumstances surrounding the final removal of Robert Moses from power, the key one—the resolution of the suit against the merger that, if successful, could have kept him in power—remains shrouded in mystery.

Two things are clear. One: that, in the opinion of almost every legal expert on municipal and public authority bonds, if the suit had been prosecuted vigorously, it would have been successful—the merger would have been voided. Until all its $367,200,000 bonds had been redeemed, the Triborough Bridge and Tunnel Authority would have remained an independent, autonomous agency, and if the Authority chose not to redeem its bonds, it would have remained independent and autonomous indefinitely. Two: that the suit was not prosecuted vigorously. Why the suit was not prosecuted vigorously is not known.

Chase Manhattan had certainly given the impression that it intended to press the suit to the limit when it was filed in June 1967. The retaining of Dewey as counsel seemed proof enough of that, and the bank's initial sixteen-page, thirty-six-count complaint instituting the action seemed determined. Transfer of the Authority's surpluses or income to the Metropolitan Transportation Authority would, the bank's complaint stated, cause the bondholders the bank represented "irreparable injury, for which they have no remedy at law." Both state statute—the New York public authorities law—and the Authority's contract with its bondholders forbade such a financial merger until all bonds were paid off and the contract thus voided, the complaint stated. An administrative merger was similarly illegal, the brief stated, forbidden by Federal and State Constitutions and state law as well as bond covenants, and was injurious to bondholders because the aims and interests of the TBTA and those of the MTA contained a basic, irreconcilable conflict: "Triborough must facilitate the use of its projects by motor vehicles whereas the MTA and the TA must facilitate the use of their respective train and subway service systems, thereby diverting traffic from Triborough bridge and tunnel projects."

Following passage of the referendum, the suit was resumed, but all through December and January, intensive negotiations were being carried out between representatives of Governor Nelson Rockefeller and those of his brother David, Chase Manhattan's president and absolute boss. And the suit was finally settled not in court, open or closed, but in the Governor's Fifty-fifth Street townhouse, shortly after 9 A.M., February 9, 1968, at a fifty-minute meeting attended by the two brothers, each attended by one aide, Dewey for David and Ronan for Nelson. At this meeting, a three-page stipulation previously drawn up by attorneys for both sides was signed by Nelson Rockefeller on behalf of the State of New York and David Rockefeller on behalf of the Chase Manhattan Bank. Following the meeting, the stipulation was taken to the chambers of the judge who would have been sitting on the case had there been a case—State Supreme Court Justice William C. Hecht, Jr.—and sealed, not to be seen by any outsider or newspaperman. Under the stipulation, the Governor's family's bank dropped all opposition to the Governor's transportation merger, the merger under which the Triborough board—Robert Moses, chairman—was supplanted by the MTA board—Dr. William J. Ronan, chairman. The point that Moses had always believed would keep him in power, therefore, was not contested—even by Moses. On his instructions, Rosenman agreed on behalf of Triborough that the merger was constitutional and legal. The crucial point was not contested by anyone.

What Chase got in exchange is not known, although it continued to head syndicates—as it had in the past—that underwrote and purchased tens of millions of dollars in state bonds, immensely profitable to banks.

Even such a bonus would probably not have persuaded the normal bank—run by a board of directors responsible to a multitude of stockholders—to abrogate its legal obligations, thereby leaving itself open to stockholder action. A bank controlled by a single family could do so, however. In the entire United States, only one bank large enough to be a trustee for $367,200,000 in bonds is still family controlled. What was necessary to remove Moses from power was a unique, singular concatenation of circumstances: that the Governor of New York be the one man uniquely beyond the reach of normal political influences, and that the trustee for Triborough's bonds be a bank run by the Governor's brother.

Why did Moses choose to rest his future on Rockefeller's word? At least part of the answer is probably understood by the perceptive Duryea, who says he had little choice but to do so. "He didn't have much left to fight with any more," the Speaker says. And probably another part is provided by Shapiro, who, asked why his boss had not exacted a promise in writing, says: "I suppose because he couldn't really believe that they wouldn't want him in the picture at all. I mean, they wanted the bridge [Sound Crossing] built, didn't they? They wanted the program pushed, didn't they? And he was the only one who could push it like it should be pushed. He just couldn't understand that they might not feel like that, I suppose. I mean, it had always been like that before . . ."

Rockefeller's promise to Moses had served its purpose well. It had kept Moses quiet for almost a year, persuaded him not to oppose Rockefeller's transportation merger or the referendum which had funded it. The Governor's promise had, moreover, persuaded Moses to withdraw the lawsuit which might have invalidated Rockefeller's transportation merger. It had enabled Rockefeller to use his name.

And now, having used his name, having gotten everything out of him that he could, the Governor threw him away.

* * *

Up until the very day on which the crucial stipulation was signed and sealed, all was honey between the Governor and the old man, now seventy-nine. On February 9, the day it was signed, Moses still believed he had a firm promise that he would have a substantial role in the new setup, possibly as president or executive head of Triborough, certainly as a member of the MTA board. Then, with less than three weeks before the merger was to take effect, the mask dropped away.

Immediately following the stipulation signing, Moses telephoned the Governor for an appointment. He got one—and when they met, Rockefeller apparently repeated his promise. Moses says that the Governor "told me I would be appointed to the MTA and would have the title of president or something of the sort at the head of Triborough under the general supervision of the MTA." But, Moses says, "Dr. Ronan did not like this." Perry Duryea says that "Moses asked me—really to intercede—with the Governor and Ronan to attempt to guarantee that he would get a meaningful position. He didn't ask me himself; he had someone else [Shapiro says it was he] ask me if we could get together and I went to his apartment in New York. He had met with Ronan and Rockefeller the week before and he left that meeting with a very bad taste in his mouth. He felt the Governor hadn't given him the time he deserved. The Governor was in and out of the room, the conference was interrupted. It was left that Ronan would call him in a week. And he hadn't heard from Ronan. And the deadline . . ." The deadline—the date for the merger—was midnight, February 29. At 12:01 A.M., March 1, the Triborough board would go out of existence. He would be out of a job—out of power completely.

Duryea felt sorry for Moses. "It was his dream to be part of the new transportation setup," the Speaker says. "He still felt the drive and the involvement, the old fire horse when the bell clangs. Here was this great new thing going forward—he wanted to be part of it." Duryea agreed to intercede on the old man's behalf, and thereafter, no more than a day or two at most before the merger took effect, Ronan contacted Moses.

He offered Moses a post as "consultant" to the Triborough Bridge and Tunnel Authority. The post, he said, carried with it a salary of $25,000 a year and continued use of his limousine, his chauffeurs and his secretaries. Moses would be in charge of "coordinating" Triborough's present construction program, and his "primary responsibility" would be the Long Island Sound Crossing.

Whether Moses could bring himself to question Ronan further about the "details" of this offer himself, or whether he had an intermediary do it, is not known, but with each answer he received, his humiliation must have deepened. For there were no further "details." That offer was all there was. He had thought he had been promised a seat on the MTA board; there was no mention of such a seat now; during the next day or two, in fact, Ronan announced the names of the nine members of the board of the agency that would be responsible for all intrastate public transportation in the New

York metropolitan region—the name of Robert Moses was not among them. Moses had thought he had had a promise of Triborough's "presidency," or at least its chief executive officer, whatever the precise title might be; Ronan did not make any mention of such a promise now; in fact, when Moses or his intermediary asked Ronan directly about it, Ronan replied that there *would* be a chief executive officer—but it would be Joseph F. Vermaelen, Moses' chief engineer. Vermaelen, and Lebwohl, and the rest of Moses' team, would report directly to the MTA staff.

Analyzing the offer only deepened the humiliation. "Coordinating" Triborough's current construction program was a meaningless phrase: that program consisted only of a relatively minor reconstruction of the Cross Bay Bridge and the adding of a second deck on the Verrazano—and those projects were already under way. The Sound Crossing would be a great project, but no one knew when it would start—and it would probably not start soon. And that was only one project—one for a man accustomed to directing dozens. "Don't take all Bob's toys away," Moses' wife had begged the Governor. Well, the Governor hadn't. He had left him one—or, to be more precise, the promise of one. When the implications of what Ronan was saying sank in, Moses realized that he was being allowed, almost as a gesture of charity, to keep the perquisites of office—the car, the chauffeurs, the secretaries—but not so much as a shred of power. He could if he wished stay on at the Authority he had created and made strong and great, but not only would he no longer be in charge of it, he would no longer have any say in its affairs. Even the men around him, his muchachos, the men who had looked to him for leadership for so many years, would now be reporting to someone else.

The offer was a slap in the face. But there was no other offer. The fatal deadline of March 1 was upon him; he had no choice but to accept it; on the very last day before the merger was to take effect, he did so. His statement to the press, issued the following day, the day the Triborough Bridge and Tunnel Authority, the last remaining arm of once twelve-armed "Triborough," became a unit of the Metropolitan Transportation Authority, was one sentence long:

"The Metropolitan Transportation Authority has offered me an advisory post in the metropolitan transportation enterprise, and I have accepted."

More poignant than his statement on the day of the merger was his attitude.

Ronan had scheduled for that day a ceremonial tour of some of the Transit Authority and Triborough facilities by the members of the MTA board. Believing he would be one of them, Moses had invited Ronan and the board to lunch with him at Randall's Island, and Ronan had accepted. Now, though he sat at the head of the big table in the big dining room as he had sat there at a thousand lunches during the thirty-four years he had been head of Triborough, he had to know that he was sitting there only by sufferance, that he, who so loved to be the gracious host, was in reality not the host of that luncheon at all, that he was only a guest himself. The very cost of the lunch would have to be approved by someone else—by this college professor whom he had once derided as "sophomoric" but who had, he felt, weaseled his way into power, not by accomplishment, not by achievement, not by the honorable means by which he felt he had attained power, but by, he felt, "ass kissing" his way around Nelson Rockefeller.

Worse—much worse for him who had always delighted, gloried, in giving free rein to his feelings—he could not let his feelings show. If he were ever to have any power at all again—if he were ever to actually get to build even the Sound Crossing they had held out to him as a pittance—he would have to get on the good side of this man who had stripped him of power. Ronan, he felt—at least his aides say so—had defeated him not in a fair fight but by lying to him and betraying him. But he would have to make friends with Ronan. Reporter Richard Witkin, who covered the changeover for the *Times*, noted that: "Mr. Moses . . . seemed to go out of his way yesterday to take a back seat to Dr. Ronan. . . ."

The *Newsday* story, which noted that "Moses, who once held fourteen [sic] public positions simultaneously, appeared to defer yesterday to Dr. William J. Ronan," noted also that the Authority adopted a new emblem, a two-tone blue "M" that would appear shortly on all its trains and other facilities, and said, "During the last four decades the same capital letter might have been used as a symbol of domination of the area's planning scene." But it couldn't any longer. The age of Moses was over. Begun on April 23, 1924, it had ended on March 1, 1968. After forty-four years of power, the power was gone at last.

50. Old

IT WASN'T the spring and summer just ahead that worried the men who loved Robert Moses, but the months beyond.

"He had just as much energy as ever," Harold Blake said. "And what was he going to do with it now?" Said Arnold Vollmer: "The idea of this great mind having nothing to do now—that's the most awful thing." Said Vollmer's wife, who had also worked for Robert Moses: "It's horrible. For him, that would be hell." Spring and summer would cloak horror in sun and breezes and the chance to do in full measure the things he had always been pressed for time in doing, not only to swim (yes, he still hurled himself headfirst into big Atlantic breakers at seventy-nine, still swam far out to sea, still stayed in so long that his men, determined that there should always be someone in the water with him, were forced to perform this safety precaution in relays, young steers unable to keep up with the old bull) but to fish and sail his beloved Great South Bay and to tramp for hours along its beaches and wetlands, to steer the *Sea-Ef* himself instead of hunching over papers in the stern while Captain Pearsall steered, to cruise the bay in the late afternoon watching the gulls soar up from the marshes as the four-o'clock breeze stirred the reeds—to be the "South Shore Boy" he liked to call himself. But the fall and winter beyond, the months when the bay froze, the months when there was nothing Robert Moses wanted to do except work, the months when that "great mind" would be churning restlessly, searching insatiably for material on which to feed, those months loomed bleak and terrible. What, Blake and Vollmer and Sid Shapiro asked each other, was RM going to do then? If they could just get the Boss through the winter, they told each other, perhaps by that time the Governor would give the go-ahead for the Sound Crossing. Ronan might become panicked by demonstrations of his incompetence as administrator and builder—demonstrations which, in their view and that of labor leaders, engineers and contractors who had to deal with him, had already begun to pile up—into realizing that he needed Moses if he was to get the Governor's construction programs rolling.

It was not, however, necessary to wait until cold weather for the effect of powerlessness upon Robert Moses to become apparent. That year, winter came in spring. Near the end of April, less than two months after the chairman had become consultant, he was visited by the author at the summer cottage he was renting at Oak Beach. Because he did not then know the details of Triborough's absorption into MTA, and because there had been no official announcement that Moses had been utterly removed from power, the visitor did not know there had been so dramatic a change in the status of his host. But he saw at once that there had been a dramatic change in the host. He wrote on his note pad: "The eyes are definitely more rheumy today. He seems somehow just more shrunken, too." During the interview, Moses had sent his chauffeur on an errand, and the chauffeur had not returned when the interview was completed. Moses asked the visitor to drive him down to Captree, where a boat—a big cabin cruiser belonging to Adam Carp, a consulting engineer who had grown rich on Moses fees—was standing ready to take him out for blues. And as they walked down the steps of the cottage to the author's car, Moses did something that made him feel for an instant that the man walking behind him was not Robert Moses but Paul. The author had, unknown to Robert Moses, spent time with his dead brother. Paul Moses had managed to keep his chin up even in discussing the misfortunes of his life, but sometimes, drifting into reveries during lulls in the conversation, he had—unconsciously, it seemed—uttered a phrase, a sigh, almost a moan, that hinted at the depths of the melancholy within him: a painful, reflective sighing: "Oh ho ho ho. Oh ho ho ho." The author had speculated that so unusual an expression might be inherited from their father. But in all the times he had previously talked with Robert Moses, the author had never heard *him* make that sound of discouragement and something close to despair.

But he made it now.

For Robert Moses had lost none of his ability to look into other men, and he had apparently looked into William J. Ronan. RM's aides were sure he would shortly get the assignments he had been promised. Shortly after the author talked to Moses at Oak Beach, Harold Blake, Moses' male secretary, assured him, "They want him to get done with the current TBTA program as fast as possible so he can help expedite the over-all MTA program. I think Ronan wants him to help cut the red tape." But Moses appears from the first to have known what was really in store for him. According to Blake, Ronan almost never telephoned his predecessor, who was still sitting in his office up at Triborough—hoping to hear from him. Moses sent him memos on matters he felt needed Ronan's attention. Some Ronan passed to lower-level aides for replies. Others were simply ignored. The new MTA chairman did not bother even to acknowledge their receipt. Moses' aides understood that they were no longer to report to him. They had not, however, fully understood that they were not to talk to him—at least not about Triborough matters. But, following the takeover, this was quickly made clear to them. Says one: "A couple of times, I mentioned to RM some things that [Ronan's aides] had told me to do, and he didn't like [the instructions] at all, and he telephoned Ronan to complain. And word came back to me that [Ronan] didn't like that *at all.* And I mean, what could I do? You couldn't say to Mr. Moses: 'Now don't talk to anyone about this.' It was easier just not to tell him what was going on." Soon his former aides were avoiding his office. Said Blake: "It's sad to see a guy who used to be in charge of a place still there but not in charge any more."

And there was to be no start on the Sound Crossing in 1969—or 1970 or 1971 or 1972.

There were various excuses from Rockefeller's office—in 1969, the bond market was soft and the issue couldn't be floated at feasible rates; in 1970, there was a gubernatorial campaign, and, with the affected sections of Long Island and Westchester up in arms against the bridge, the Governor didn't want to be put on the spot; in 1971, it was financing problems again; in 1972, a legislative campaign and the Governor didn't want to damage Republican chances to hold control of the Legislature—with each delay, Moses was assured that next year would be the year the big project got under way.

Moses was fooled by the fact that Rockefeller himself wanted the great bridge built. He was fooled by the fact that the Governor had promised publicly as well as privately that Moses would be the one to build it: once, as a sort of test, Moses leaked to a reporter the fact that he had been promised the job, the reporter contacted Ronan's office and Ronan himself said that that was indeed the case. He was fooled most of all by the fact that it was simply inconceivable to him that he would not be allowed to build it: he had conceived it, chosen its precise location and the routes of its approach highways, he had directed the planning and blueprinting, he had, in a sense, since it was Triborough's money that would back the bonds that would pay for it, raised the money for it; it was no more than one more link in the chain of bridges linking the island with mainland—Triborough, Whitestone, Throgs Neck—that he had planned decades before and had been building ever since. It was *his* bridge! To let someone else build it and take credit for it would be an injustice of an enormity he seemed unable to grasp. It took a long time for realization to sink in.

But, as the years passed, it sank in, all right. It gradually became clear to him that they weren't going to give him the job. The Governor wanted the bridge built, he came to understand, but he would not let Moses build it; it might, considering the public and private promises, be too raw to assign the direction of the huge task to anyone else, so he would simply wait to get the five-year job started until Moses, aging, was no longer able to embark on it. It gradually became clear to Moses that the Governor and Ronan weren't going to give him *any* job—that, despite all their promises, they were not, ever, going to give him anything to do, that they were just waiting for him to grow old and die or go quietly away somewhere.

Then the old man grew desperate. He had almost no leverage left, except for the fact that Ronan couldn't get things done, and there were people around who, for their own purposes, wanted things to be gotten done. He used this leverage frantically. Recalls Brennan:

"I've had other people—professional architects, the engineers—come to me and say, 'Gee couldn't you do something? . . . Bob is going crazy that they're shelving him!' They don't say they were asked to talk to me, but . . . they were."

He talked to Brennan and Van Arsdale himself. He tried to put on a good front, but the two hard-eyed unionists saw through it. "He tells us he could have been on the [MTA] board, [that he turned it down himself because] he wanted to be free to do construction. But maybe that's just his pride. He's nothing; he's a consultant. And he's not even being consulted with." What Robert Moses, once so arrogant and powerful, was doing was begging, begging them to help him get a little of his power back. He had been reduced to pleading—and he was, to these men who had known him when, almost pathetic in his pleas.

He's getting edgy [Brennan says]. He tells you that he knows he's being kept out of things. He's mad at dragging things out like they're doing. He tells us that things should be under way now. And meanwhile costs are going up. He complains that these people have no guts. He talks about the program, about his frustrations that things aren't moving—how they should be doing this or that on the bridge, taking borings or whatever. He never talks in terms of getting him back in; it's in terms of the program . . . It wasn't on the basis of him but getting the job done. . . . He's taking this very hard. He's a hard, crusty old guy, but he's sensitive.

Brennan and Van Arsdale responded as Moses had hoped they would, and so did various contractors, engineers and architects who had entree to Rockefeller or Ronan. For they were afraid that without Moses, public works would never again be constructed in the New York area on the scale that had made some of them rich and others of them powerful. "As far as the MTA is concerned, there's nothing moving—no doubt about it," Brennan said in 1970, more than two years after Ronan had taken over. "There's no roads being built. There's nothing being built." Speaking of Ronan, the red-faced, white-haired, blunt unionist tries to keep the contempt out of his voice, but it keeps seeping in. "Ronan tells us that the planning on the Second Avenue Subway and tunnel is in the hands of the city and that it's being held up by the Mayor and the City Planning Commission. He says the MTA is ready to move on it as soon as the city lets them. As soon as the city lets them! Jeez! And that would be a billion two. Or Ronan tells us it's a billion two."

So they fought for him. Said Brennan late in 1968: "We—I say *we*, people in the industry, those of us who know Moses and have been trying to keep his hand in these things, feel there is no question there's people trying to sidetrack him. We're hoping they'll realize he's needed. It's silly to take him and put him on a shelf. We've been talking to the Governor and Ronan . . . The architects, the engineers, the contractors have been talking. . . . We're going to try hard.

"But," Brennan said, "it's going to be tough. He's not in the power position he used to be in. . . . The Governor says that he put Ronan in there, and Ronan is boss. Bill Ronan says, 'Oh, we want to use Bob once we get going.' We say, 'What do you mean "once you get going"? You need to plan now, assign guys to things.' When we press him, [the] answer is then very vague. So I can see that it's just a snow job. They want him to get tired and to go away and get lost.

"But I say: 'Forget it! This guy don't blow away!'

"And the sad thing is that a lot of people who like Bob Moses are saying he's too old and it's not a bad idea to ease him out because of that. But he's not too old. He's got fantastic ideas on housing!"

The old man was reduced to publicly praising Ronan and his boss—in 1969, at a time at which Moses and his aides were privately ridiculing Ronan's failures to get the MTA program moving, and the deterioration of the Long Island and other commuter railroads under his direction, Moses said publicly, "As to Nelson Rockefeller, he's no cautious Calvin Coolidge. . . . He has put his reputation on the line. The people voted for his two and a half billion program. They could not have expected instant results. . . . So put away your flying bottles and slingshots and give Bill Ronan a break." He tried to take advantage of every opportunity to see them in person—at dinners or dedication ceremonies, for example—to engage them in conversation and try to make friends with them. The Governor was always charming in return—often these two men would stand chatting in public with their arms around each other. Ronan's manners with the old man left something to be desired. He let the boredom he felt show. Watching Moses try to curry Ronan's favor once, Harold Blake muttered bitterly about the MTA chairman's "smug, college-professor look," but then added with resignation in his voice, "He [Moses] wants to stay in public life, so what do you do? Swallow your pride."

But nothing he could do helped. Rockefeller and Ronan stayed bland, and the bridge stayed unbuilt, and Moses' memos still went unanswered.

He had to suffer also what was for him perhaps the ultimate humiliation. He had to know that people knew that he no longer had power.

Because his power had never come from anything as clear-cut and publicly understandable as an election, it took a long time for even many political insiders to realize that he had lost not only some power but all. More than a year after the MTA reorganization, Jack Lutsky, now a judge, was told that Moses was out of power completely, and he refused to believe it. He telephoned Lebwohl to check and, hanging up, said with a wondering sigh: "You're right." But eventually they all realized it. He could see pity in the eyes of those of them who, like Lutsky or Wagner, were capable of pity. "I feel sorry for him," the former Mayor said one day after sitting next to him on a luncheon dais. "He enjoyed power so much. He should have become a private citizen. At least then he could have spoken out." He could see contempt in the eyes of others. When, at a dinner party, he would launch into one of the interminable monologues about past accomplishments to which people had once listened with respect, people grew bored. There were a thousand little hurts. Once he invited Bronx Borough President Herman Badillo, whom he had never met, to lunch on Randall's Island. Badillo called him "Bob." For just an instant, the big head went back in the old haughty gesture with which he would once have withered any guest who dared to use that familiarity without invitation. Then one could almost see him remembering that he needed any ally he could get. The head came down, and he went on with the conversation.

Piled on humiliation, frustration.

Age was not a consideration in Moses' thinking. "He absolutely refused to talk about the birthday," reported a *Daily News* reporter interviewing him on the occasion of his eighty-first. " 'Birthdays are a nuisance,' he said. 'Birthdays are to forget.' " "He was always talking about De Gaulle and Adenauer and how they were older than him, and age wasn't affecting *them*," Shapiro recalls. And Moses had an example closer to home if he wished to use it; his grandmother, Rosalie Silverman Cohen—the "Granny Cohen" of family legend whom he so closely resembled in manner—had been intellectually alert until the very day she died at the age of ninety-three.

Physically, the years had left their mark: the deafness was very bad indeed; he now required eyeglasses for reading although he whipped them off whenever a visitor came into the room; liver spots had mottled the olive skin; he had a paunch now. But it was not a large mark; above the paunch, the shoulders were still broad, the chest deep, the arms muscular—incredibly muscular for a man in his eighties. His physical presence was still dominating; wrote the *Daily News* reporter:

> He's a big man, not so much in height and weight as in presence, and even now, on the eve of his eighty-first birthday, he's got enough vitality and power to become the instant center of attention when he walks into a room. . . . Even now, it's easy to see why they called Robert Moses a giant.

Mentally, there was no mark at all. Aside from his deafness, said a former associate who hadn't seen him for twenty years, "he hasn't changed at all." His mind had lost little of its monumental capacity, its voraciousness for knowledge—all knowledge. Books were piled in heaps around the Oak Beach cottage, and in a single pile a visitor saw the latest Simenon, Rattay's *History of Long Island Hurricanes*, O'Casey's *The Plough and the Stars* and an old, worn Boswell's *Johnson*, so old and worn that it might have been the very volume through which the young Bob Moses had first begun to idolize Dr. Johnson at Yale. One afternoon, Moses' chauffeur delivered to the door Mary I's sister, Emily Sims Marconnier, carrying three books for him. None was particularly good, she said, although Mary Renault's *The Mask of Apollo* wasn't bad. ("Well," he said, with his warm, charming grin, "let's see how bad they are.") The following evening, the chauffeur returned the three books to Mrs. Marconnier—all read. More and more of his *Newsday* columns were columns of literary criticism, some of it very perceptive indeed.

His intelligence was still a creative, shaping intelligence. Still roaming vigorously the length and breadth of the metropolitan region, it still saw in everything, as it had seen on the walks with Frances Perkins almost sixty years before, "ways to make it better." Moreover, freed at last of the crushing day-to-day political and administrative responsibilities, that intelligence was free to contemplate, to reflect. Moses' imagination—in shackles so long to responsibility and ambition—was loosed again to dream and plan in leisure as it had dreamed and planned half a century before, when, with all other planners baffled by the urban recreation problem, it had, looking at Long Island, conceived a revolutionary solution. Within one year after his ouster from power, Robert Moses possessed what he had not possessed during the years in which he had been building housing: a unified, comprehensive housing program.

It would be simple in concept. Because the principal barrier to urban renewal programs was tenant relocation, new housing should be built where there were no tenants: in vacant areas of the city. After it was built, tenants from slum areas should be moved out of the slums—out of whole slums at once—into the new development. The areas they had vacated, now empty, should be razed, and new housing should be built there. Then residents of another slum area should be moved into *that* new housing, their area razed and rebuilt, tenants from still another slum moved in—until all the city's slums had thus been replaced with modern housing. Dedicating Co-Op City, the 15,382-apartment community, largest apartment development in the United States and largest cooperative apartment community in the world, that he had played a key role in conceiving and organizing, he offered, as a "visible, palpable, large-scale demonstration of the efficacy" of his plan, a proposal for an "Atlantic Village" at Breezy Point that would dwarf even Co-Op City, providing schools, shopping centers, playgrounds and a three-mile-long public beach, as well as 50,000 modern apartments looking out over the ocean, while, incidentally, solving the city's dilemma over what to do with that valuable long piece of beachfront, hitherto fought over by park and housing advocates as if the building of one would preclude the building of the other. Financing? "Ingenuity and boldness" would solve that problem, as it had on the West Side Improvement, he said; he had several alternate methods already worked out. And after the buildings were opened, into them should be moved 50,000 Bedford-Stuyvesant families, then that "ghetto area should be rebuilt and, by repeating this process, in ten years there will be no more ghettos."

Moses had a citywide program worked out—right down to specific sites (among them, Welfare Island, air rights over the Sunnyside Yards of the Long Island Rail Road and a vast, unused tract of Bronx park land near the Whitestone Bridge) and costs: five billion dollars could clean up every slum in the city in ten years. It was a typical Moses plan: no consideration of the city investment required to provide facilities for these new, isolated communities, or of whether the city could afford such investment, no concern that by isolating low-income people by the tens of thousands he would be creating new ghettos. But he did not see these flaws. His plan was large enough in scope to deal with the immense slum problem, the only plan that was. He was sure it would work—he was as enthusiastic as a boy about it. And he could not restrain his impatience with those who criticized it: the "Lindsay people" have "had their chance to solve this problem with their scattered sites and vest-pocket things. None of these fancy words are going to solve the housing crisis—only lots of new houses will solve it, and this is the way to get lots of new houses . . ." He was so anxious to be given a chance to prove he was right.

Housing was not the only area in which he had plans. In every conversation now, as Vollmer put it, "there is this concern growing for so many things left undone, so many things to be done." What people didn't understand was that everything he had done was part of a plan, a dream—a plan planned and a dream dreamed decades before. Large parts of the plan were realized, but larger parts were not—including some of the most beautiful, some of the ones he most wanted to realize, some of the public works he had been trying to build for decades. His cottage might face the Robert Moses Causeway and Robert Moses State Park; these were two achievements that should have been enough to content any man. But what he saw when he stood on the porch of the cottage and stared out was not the bridge and the park but the road, the great Fire Island highway, that the bridge and the park had been supposed to bring closer to reality, the road still unbuilt. His dream had not been merely of an Ocean Parkway and a Belt Parkway that ran along the water for forty miles; his dream, dreamed so clearly in 1924, had been of a great Shorefront Drive all the way from Staten Island to Montauk Point—160 miles. A drive whose heart would be the Fire Island Road bordered on the one hand by bay and on the other by ocean, a highway along which people could drive almost literally among boats and waves—the most beautiful drive in the world. That road would be built one day; he had no doubt about it—and he wanted it to come while he could see it, he wanted to build it himself so that he could be sure it was built right. He had built parks in the city, but the greatest waterfront park—the Jamaica Bay Development that he had conceived of in 1924—was still not built. He had reserved for future generations so many great tracts of Long Island land—the Marshall Field Estate that had been renamed Caumsett State Park, the Southside Sportsman's Club that had been renamed Connetquot State Park—but it wasn't enough. There were so many more country clubs and big estates that must be saved from the developer's bulldozer and preserved for the public. And despite his pleas to his successor on the State Council of Parks, Laurance Rockefeller; to Duryea's successor as head of the Long Island Commission, A. Holly Patterson; to county officials of Nassau and Suffolk; to philanthropists—to anyone who would listen—no one was doing anything to preserve them. He had built great urban highways—more great urban highways than any man in history—but where were the greatest of the highways, the expressways across Manhattan Island, that would complete the expressway net and alone make it workable? There were a hundred big things left to do, and a thousand small: he had put Lincoln Center together for the Rockefellers and then they had goofed up by not providing ramps and wider roadways from the West Side Highway; "they don't grasp [the problem], they don't even remotely grasp it," he said one day; he could take care of it in a couple of months—and if it wasn't taken care of, you were always going to have an access problem there. The walls of his office on Randall's Island were covered with pictures of his achievements—pictures of bridges and dams illuminated at night—and through the window behind him could be seen the solid concrete and steel of the Triborough Bridge. But the office was dominated by a huge map of New York City. And while that map was crisscrossed with the solid lines that represented achievements built—highways, bridges, tunnels—on it also were lines, many lines, that were not solid but broken: lines representing achievements not yet built, dreams yet to be turned into reality. As he sat at his desk, that map, its width wider than his armspread, its height taller than a man, stared back at him, reminding this man to whom accomplishment was so important that there was so much yet to accomplish. There was visible behind his urge to keep building an element almost of desperation; the public was doubting the wisdom of his creations—the way to convince them was to complete the system, to build more highways, more bridges, more housing—to build, build, build in a frantic attempt to rescue his reputation. But there was behind the urge also genuine creative drive, a drive undimmed by eighty years of life, the shaping impulse of the shaping man—and a drive supported by the arrogance which since his youth had told him in a voice that would not be denied that he had the answer to the problem, that he knew what to do. If only he were to be allowed to do it.

What made his situation more frustrating still was that the problems that needed solving were not being solved. His city, the city that he thought of as a product he had created, was, he felt, being destroyed by the men who had succeeded him in power. Hoving and August Heckscher, grandson of his early benefactor and Hoving's successor as Park Commissioner, had had their opportunity to institute their park policies designed to "return the parks to the people"; after five years of such a return, the parks were ruined, in as bad shape as he had found them when he took over from Tammany Hall. Little new housing was being built, the slums were getting worse. *No* highways were being built; supposedly this was because the money was being spent on mass transportation, but at the rate mass transit facilities were being built, they would never solve any transportation problems—if indeed most of them were built at all. Democracy had not solved the fatal dichotomy; he did not see the problem as a dichotomy but only as a failure on the part of public officials to understand the realities of the situation—that the public say on public works must be limited, and, in general, ignored, that critics must be ignored, that public works must be pushed ruthlessly to completion.

Understanding this, convinced that he had the plan for the salvation of New York, he schemed and twisted and turned to get the power to do it: ass-kissing pompous double-chinned Ronan and his arrogant boss, asking allies—fewer each year as more and more architects, engineers and contractors were pulled into the Rockefeller-Ronan orbit—to "intercede" for him. Frantically he tried to get the United Housing Foundation interested in the "Atlantic Village" project—and to put him in charge. In one desperate ploy to do this, he planted an interview with the *Daily News* which appeared

—under the hopeful headline GREATEST URBAN RENEWAL EVER: REENTER BOB MOSES—in a story favorable to the plan and closed with a broad hint of who should run it.

> Moses, whose only job at present is that of consultant, . . . was asked during the interview whether he might consider himself just the nonpolitical man for the job.
>
> "Will you take any direct part in this project?" he was asked.
>
> "Nobody has asked me," he replied.

Nobody did. His agile mind, always so quick to find avenues to power, twisted and turned and darted at every one that he felt might open up—and, with the city's Mayor and the state's Governor unalterably opposed to him, found them all closed. Rockefeller and Ronan kept him firmly on the shelf; his impatience, the same terrible impatience he had had as a young man, turned into frustration, a deep gnawing, terrible bitterness. As this man, who had measured off his life in days each of which was vital, looked back on weeks in which nothing had occurred to advance his plans—as weeks turned into months—as he realized that he had been seventy-nine when he lost power and that he was now eighty-two (or eighty-three or eighty-four), he fell into violent rages. His conversation revealed, more and more, foreboding of the ultimate. He had thought Oak Beach would be his Elba. Was it to be instead his St. Helena? Was he to die without ever getting the chance to build another bridge, to redeem his name?

He could have used the time to write, and publishers approached him with substantial offers for an autobiography. But he had not the patience to write, nor the desire—and, it may be, other considerations militated against it as well: a key to Moses' ability to buy men had been his ability to keep the purchase secret, and the sellers' confidence that he would do so. He could hardly write a story of his life without going at least to some extent into the machinations by which he had obtained power, and were he to reveal them, men whom he would need to get power back might shy away from him. He did come up with a book, published in 1970 by McGraw-Hill: *Public Works: A Dangerous Trade*. But this was not really a book at all, and it was certainly not by Robert Moses. A vast volume—952 pages—90 percent of it consisted of documents already in the public record: reprints of speeches, press releases, brochures, reports, newspaper and magazine articles on his triumphs, letters to and from prominent persons. And most of the remainder was written not by Moses but by members of his staff. There was no triumph in its publication; it was extensively reviewed, but reviewers treated it for what it was—a nonbook.

He could not sit still. Reading in the afternoon, he would jump up from his chair, yank on his old corduroy jacket and stride out onto the long wooden porch outside the Oak Beach cottage, pacing back and forth, sometimes for an hour and more, grim and restless. Urged on by desperate secretaries and associates and wife, he took vacations, but he didn't enjoy them. He was always anxious to get back—lest some chance for power pass him by. But upon his return, no chance would come. Things he had once enjoyed doing were less and less solace to him now. For no matter what he did, he could not get away from himself. To this man who had consecrated his life to Getting Things Done, to the getting and exercising of power, hell was the continued urgent, desperate, insatiable need for accomplishment and power—combined with the inability to satisfy even a little part of that need.

His muchachos did all they could to make life pleasant for him—most of his muchachos; most of them loved Robert Moses. Some of them loved Robert Moses only for what Robert Moses could do for them, and he couldn't do anything for them any more—he had made up with George Spargo after the World's Fair and given his engineering firm contracts, but the loyal Harold Blake was to comment bitterly one day that "Mr. Moses doesn't see much of George Spargo any more. And Spargo was closer to Mr. Moses than anybody."

Thanks to Sid Shapiro, who was still general manager and chief engineer of the Long Island State Park Commission, the big corner table in the Marine Dining Room at Jones Beach was reserved for Moses and his party every Saturday and Sunday, and the chef would cook up something special (whatever Moses wanted; if it wasn't in stock at the restaurant, a patrol car would be sent screaming up to the mainland to get it), and whenever Moses went to the Marine Theater—which was frequently—there would be the introduction by Guy Lombardo and the spotlight and the unfailingly generous applause from the crowd above, and the opportunity for him to look unutterably bored by it all. The *Sea-Ef* was kept always ready for him, gassed, manned and stocked by the commission.

Driving around the parks and parkways was still pleasant, for the senior officers at every facility were men who had served with RM when he had been the commission's president, and they treated him with the respect he remembered. *Everybody* connected with the commission, in fact, treated him with respect. When the author drove him down to meet Adam Carp, Moses told him to park in an area marked "No Thoroughfare." After he left, the author was sitting there jotting down notes when a Long Island State Park Commission patrolman loomed in his window. "Don't you see the sign?" he asked with the usual LISPC arrogance. "Well, you see, I drove Mr. Moses down . . . ," the author began. "Oh," the cop said, straightening, and started to walk away without a word. Then he returned. "Thanks for telling me," he said. "I'd be out of work and my children would be starving."

There were bright spots in his life. On July 3, 1970, a handsome monument in a large plaza on the Lincoln Center campus of Fordham University was unveiled—a bronze bas-relief of Moses, executed by sculptor Albino Manca, mounted on a handsome three-sided slab of green marble over the words, chiseled and gilded in gold:

ROBERT MOSES

MASTERBUILDER

FRIEND OF FORDHAM

Terence Cardinal Cooke blessed the monument, Nelson Rockefeller gave the principal address, calling Moses a man who "built his own greatness," and as the Reverend Michael P. Walsh, president of Fordham, announced that the plaza would be named after him, long lines of state officials, Fordham priests and old Moses Men stood applauding with warm smiles on their faces until Moses had to bow his head to hide tears.

To a man whose sensitivities had been rubbed as raw as Moses', however, there were unfortunate ironies even in this honor. In praising Moses, Rockefeller had, perhaps indelicately, alluded to the fact that up to now in the city "no public work has borne his name." Despite Fordham's touching and appreciated gesture, of course, that was still the case. This gesture wasn't an honor from the public, the public he had served so long and so selflessly at such great self-sacrifice, but from a private institution. His name was immortalized in concrete and steel and park land from one end of the state to the other. But it was on no public work in the city in which his efforts had been concentrated.

It had been supposed to be on one, but it wasn't.

And a plaza on a college campus wasn't quite the same thing as Flushing Meadows Park.

There were other bright spots. He was Man of the Year for the Salvation Army and the Masons and the Society of Civil Engineers—for a dozen organizations—between 1968 and 1972. A junior high school in Babylon was named after him—the tenth structure to bear his name. There were the ceremonies attendant on the completion of the public works that had been launched before the end of his Triborough chairmanship—in 1968 the huge new park on the landfill he had added to Randall's Island, in 1969 the lower level of the Verrazano Bridge, in 1970 the reconstruction of the Cross Bay Bridge—ceremonies that gave him the opportunity to make speeches, and, now able to devote the necessary time to them, he delighted in writing them, so that their phrases had again the felicity and force of his speeches as a younger man. There were moments of triumph, such as his speech at the annual dinner of the Building Trades Employers Association in the Grand Ballroom of the Waldorf-Astoria Hotel in 1969, when, after Roger Corbetta of Corbetta Construction introduced him ("a great man, a great builder, a man of history . . . this great dirt mover . . . this master builder"), the hundreds of men in the audience rose to their feet and cheered and cheered for long minutes. The *Daily News* gave good play to his pronouncements; when, in 1969, former Secretary of the Interior Stewart Udall, urging the infusion of "young blood" into city planning, criticized "the jaded planning of Robert Moses" and said it had made New York an example of how not to conduct urban planning, the *News* replied, "We'd just like to observe that when Udall can show a list of accomplishments—in power, transportation and conservation—one tenth as long as Moses', it will be time enough for him to shoot off his yap." During the mayoral election of 1969, he backed the ultraconservative Democratic candidate, Mario Procaccino (he preferred the more intellectual Republican candidate, John J. Marchi, also a conservative, but his endorsement, as always, was dictated by practicalities; he wanted a winner—someone who could return him to power—and he felt no Republican candidate could win in New York), jeering at Lindsay as "the glass of fashion and the mould of form"—and an utterly incompetent Mayor—and declaring, "We are sick of amateurs who are not dry behind the ears." And the endorsement was in headlines on page one of the *Times* as it had been in elections past.

But the bright spots became fewer and fewer.

The Cross Bay Bridge rebuilding was Robert Moses' last major construction project, the last with which he could occupy even a little of his time; and its opening celebration was the last at which he would be a leading figure. The requests to have him speak slowed from a torrent to a trickle, and by 1972 had dried up almost entirely. The mail, once so huge a bundle three times a day, fell off to almost nothing. There were continual discourtesies and humiliations. On May 22, 1969, the city dedicated Damrosch Park at the Guggenheim Band Shell at Lincoln Center. Damrosch Park had been conceived by Robert Moses. He had battled for the inclusion of the 2.34-acre open space in the Lincoln Center project when everyone else involved had opposed such "waste" of land. He had persuaded the Guggenheim and Damrosch families to donate the necessary funds. But he received only a form invitation to the opening ceremonies. Not only was there no invitation to speak, there was no place for him on the platform. He watched the ceremonies (presided over by Park Commissioner August Heckscher, whose primary contribution to Damrosch Park had been the approval of plans calling for lampposts on which the bulbs would be set thirty feet above the ground, too high for any of the Department's bulb-changing equipment to reach) from a bench near the rear of the audience. (Noticing him sitting there, Heckscher asked him to come up and sit in a chair that happened to be vacant on the platform; no thanks, Moses replied.) He was preoccupied with immortality now; in one *Newsday* column, he said he was convinced that "the finest short story ever written" was Anatole France's "The Procurator of Judea," which ends with Pontius Pilate saying, "Jesus? Jesus? Of Nazareth? I do not believe I can recall the name." And what roused him most to fury was the attempt of Lindsay and his bright young men to paint him as responsible for all the city's ills. Some of that criticism was unfair—predicated upon the ignorance of the new administration about the city it was supposed to be governing. Once, for example, the Mayor criticized Moses for laying concrete through Alley Pond Park, which he implied had been a wonderful rustic nature spot before Moses came along and ruined it. Moses had ruined a hundred rustic nature spots in New York City, but Alley Pond Park wasn't one of them. There hadn't *been* an Alley Pond Park until Moses came along and built it up out of an inaccessible, reeking marsh; the concrete Lindsay was talking about, the Cross Island Parkway, had been put through it at the same time. On another occasion, Lindsay said, "The Moses approach, where you take a bulldozer and mow people's houses down, just doesn't work in this city any more. We get more done by working on smaller sites in cooperation with the community." Get more done! In his first four years in office, the total housing production of the Lindsay administration consisted of fewer units than Moses had been accustomed to produce every single year! But it was the reason Lindsay kept using his name that hurt Moses most; in some way he was totally unable to comprehend, his name, which had once been a symbol of the good in urban life, had become a symbol of the bad; when Lindsay's Housing Administrator, Jason R. Nathan, wanted to blast some new housing proposal, he simply said it was an example of "The Moses Approach." Of all things, his reputation was now dearest to him—and it was his reputation that this incompetent Mayor was destroying.

And after a while, he couldn't even fight back.

Always he had broadcast his views through mass mailings—of his letters, his memos, his press releases, his brochures—to hundreds if not thouands of influentials in city and state, mailings mimeographed by Triborough personnel or printed with Triborough funds, mailed with Triborough stamps.

Whether or not it was "made clear" to him—as so many humiliating new restrictions on his activities were "made clear" to him by Ronan's men in the months after the MTA takeover—that Triborough printing and stamping privileges were no longer to be available to him in quantity, or whether it was simply that he was too proud to go on using resources that had not been offered to him, the fact remained that shortly after the MTA takeover, Moses' mailings were being addressed by hand and stamped with stamps purchased by him.

Doing it that way was too much of a load even for three secretaries and his wife, who chipped in to help. The evidence was not on the front of the envelopes, which were typed as cleanly and neatly as ever. But on the back, the return address was printed on roughly by a stamp. Even that did not help enough. The mailings were reduced in size and then reduced again.

Then, however, after another while, the work load was no longer such a problem, for there was almost nothing to mail. The principal ingredient of the mailings had been reprints of Moses' speeches and the column he wrote once a week for *Newsday* and syndication. Requests for him to speak were fewer in 1969 than they had been in 1968 and fewer still in 1970. By 1972, they were down to a handful. When his friend Harry Guggenheim sold *Newsday* to the Los Angeles Times Mirror Company in 1970, the column was discontinued. Now he had no public platform at all from which to voice his views, or to reply to the criticism continually being heaped upon him.

The column had, moreover, given him something to do. Now he had absolutely nothing to do. He grew terribly nervous; his big hands kept playing around his head, his fingers moving restlessly over his forehead; he kept putting his glasses on and taking them off. His fingers drummed on the table; sitting, he would squirm nervously; he would jump up every few minutes and pace for a minute or two, sit down, jump up and pace again; he was almost desperate for something to do.

It was principally for this reason that when the *Daily News* asked him to host a new television interview series, "New York Closeup," on its WPIX-TV station, he agreed. He was not quite attuned to the blandness required in the medium—as he demonstrated conclusively even before his first program, at a press conference called by WPIX-TV at the Overseas Press Club to announce the new show. Asked why Moses, who had no experience on TV, had been selected as host, the station's president, Fred M. Thrower, intoned: "There is no one in New York better suited to make an important contribution to New York and to television in the public affairs field." When reporters turned to Moses, he said, with a grin, as the *Times* reported, " 'To tell the unvarnished truth' he was being hired because the various networks have decided to devote more time to public affairs in response 'to a demand on the part of Congress, the F.C.C. and others' "—a remark which prompted the *Times* reporter to remember that WPIX's license was being challenged by a rival group, and that the F.C.C. was scheduled to hold hearings on the two applications shortly.

The programs were a fiasco, partly because Moses refused (except for a brief, embarrassing attempt) to wear a hearing aid, and as a result could not hear his guests' replies to his questions, partly because he was not interested in the replies anyway and took up most of the program lecturing at the camera. After some twenty programs, he and the station jointly agreed to discontinue the series.

His mind was as active as ever. Ideas still churned out of it. To occupy his days, he agreed now to see people he had never seen before because he had felt they just wanted to pick his brains, use his ideas themselves and "get a fee out of it"—consultants from other countries and cities with specific problems on which they wanted his advice. And his imagination leaped as nimbly at these problems as the mind of the young Robert Moses had leaped at problems half a century and more before. "The other day," Blake recalls, "some man called who had been hired to do a study of what uses to make of Alcatraz Island. I mentioned it to him, and he starts to think, hmmm, 'Alcatraz—the problems are very similar to Ellis Island, very interesting . . .' And boy he was off to the races. He must have talked for an hour." One day a delegation of sixteen Japanese urban planners showed up to discuss a plan for, as Blake recalls it, "linking up some little island to the mainland." Moses began asking questions. Then the yellow legal pad was pulled across his desk and a pencil was in his hand. For more than two hours, the sixteen Japanese sat transfixed as that pencil flew, and the big hand pounded the desk, and the big man jumped up and paced as the ideas took hold. On their way out, one of the Japanese said almost reverently: "A great man. A great man." There were so many ideas about things closer to home that needed doing—new parks for Long Island, new highways, his planned bridge. But now not only could he do nothing about his ideas, he couldn't even tell anyone about them.

He lived on slim hopes—that Procaccino would defeat Lindsay and that Brennan and Van Arsdale could persuade Procaccino to return him to power, that Rockefeller would at last see through Ronan's obsequious flattery to what Moses felt was the incompetence beneath, that Rockefeller would win the presidency in 1968 and go to Washington, leaving Lieutenant Governor Malcolm Wilson in the Governor's chair (Malcolm Wilson is a great admirer of Mr. Moses', you know, Harold Blake, would say), that Rockefeller would be given a Cabinet position by Nixon in 1972, and thus place Wilson in the Governor's chair. But in 1974, when Rockefeller resigned and Wilson did become Governor, the only post offered to Moses was a meaningless one as a housing "adviser" to the Governor; Rockefeller apparently still had enough influence to keep him out of any significant assignment.

The Moses Men were growing old. "He had so many people serving with him, and I see in my mind all these faces, dim now, like ghosts, and his face vivid, outlasting all of them," Sid Shapiro had said. RM had outlived one generation of aides. Now he was starting to outlive another. One after the other, they died. His bankers died: the younger one had gone first—Shanahan had been dead for years; in 1969, George McLaughlin died, too. When an interviewer asked about the remaining aides, Shapiro said to him sadly: "You're talking about a bunch of white-haired old men now, you know. I remember when we were all young, out there at Belmont Lake . . ."

As long as Shapiro himself was still around and in administrative charge of the Long Island State Park Commission, of course, the other deaths did not matter too much. Shapiro could still provide Moses with all the amenities that gave his life what happiness it had. This most loyal of men held on to the end, past the age when he might have retired, to make things easier for RM. He held on even after he was told he had cancer. He held on until his pain and weakness made it impossible for him to work even occasionally any longer, and then, on April 12, 1972, he retired. Hoping for a while he might recover, he moved into a house on Oak Beach, right near that of the man he had served and worshipped for fifty years—his companionship was undoubtedly welcome, but the commissioners of the Long Island State Park Commission were by now all men whom Moses knew only slightly, and as Shapiro's replacement they selected not the Moses Man next in line, Frank Champ, but an official of the National Park Service, and now there was no longer the deference to Moses in the parks he had created, or the introductions at the Marine Theater; even the corner table at Jones Beach was no longer waiting. And after July 20, 1972, when Shapiro died, even the companionship of his oldest and most loyal aide was gone.

Robert Moses, preoccupied with immortality, had no sons. He had three grandsons, two by his daughter Barbara, one by his daughter Jane. The one Barbara had named after him was mentally retarded. For her other son, John Olds, a Princeton graduate who married an heiress and became a banker, he had no use.

Jane's son, Christopher Collins, was a tall, handsome youth with a broad, engaging grin and an easygoing nature. Unlike Jane's daughter, Caroline, a tall, brilliant girl who won honors at Oxford before getting married, from the time he began school, his grades were a problem, and he displayed no marked interests except in girls and surfing; he loved to spend the summers on the beach at Gilgo. "He's too good-looking for his own good," Jane said.

But Robert Moses loved Chris. He doted on him, taking him with him everywhere. He taught him to fish and sail. With her husband long since "out of the picture," he was supporting Jane, of course, and he saw that the boy always had plenty of pocket money. When Jane lost her temper with Chris over his grades, Chris would reply, "Gramps never says anything." Instead of an Ivy League university, he wanted to go to little Chapel Hill College in North Carolina; Jane was appalled, but Moses told her, "Oh, let the boy go where he wants." When his first report card came back with straight C's, he said, with a grin, "Well, at least he's consistent."

In 1967, as a senior at college, Christopher Collins' attitude changed. His report card came back all A's. "I don't think RM was any prouder of the Verrazano Bridge than he was of that report card," Sid Shapiro says. When Chris said that he wanted to study law at Stanford, Moses helped him get in.

On December 11, 1968, driving home to Long Island from California as a passenger in a car driven by a Stanford friend, Christopher Collins, twenty-one, was killed when the car veered off the road and smashed into a concrete culvert.

Once he had had battalions to boss and on which to demonstrate his administrative ability; now he had only his secretaries and chauffeur, so he did so on them. He was harsh and abrupt and arrogant in talking to them, and about them; explaining how he had gotten caught the day before in a traffic jam, he said: "The chauffeur took the wrong route—he always takes the wrong route if he's left alone, and I never interfere: that's his business; he's the chauffeur; if you don't like it, you get another chauffeur . . ." He became a name dropper, trying consciously to lard his conversation with the names of great men he had known.

Still he lived on—year after year, vital and alert, imaginative and energetic, but with nothing to do with his vitality, his imagination and his energy except to bottle them up, feeding on himself.

His name had faded from the headlines in New York City long before. For a while after *Newsday* no longer published his column, its reporters still telephoned him for comment on stories involving public works on Long Island, and played his statements prominently, as did the *Long Island Press*. But as time went on that all but stopped, too. This man who for decades had read the newspapers first thing every morning no longer found his name in them except on rare occasions—and on those occasions almost invariably in a derogatory context, as a man who had been responsible for housing and highway mistakes. He had built Jones Beach and Sunken Meadow State Park, and Heckscher, and the Massena and St. Lawrence power projects—but no one remembered those. He was forgotten—to live out his years in bitterness and rage.

In private, his conversation dwelt more and more on a single theme—the ingratitude of the public toward great men. And once, invited by the Church to speak at the dedication in Flushing Meadows Park of the Excedra, a huge, marble bench for reflection donated by the Roman Catholic Diocese of New York, he gave vent to his feeling in public. Turning to a high church official who was also an old friend, his voice booming out over the public address system, he said:

"Someday, let us sit on this bench and reflect on the gratitude of man."

Down in the audience, the ministers of the empire of Moses glanced at one another and nodded their heads. RM was right as usual, they whispered. Couldn't people see what he had done?

Why weren't they grateful?

NOTES

DEBTS

The main trouble with clichés is that their constant reiteration has worn them out, so that they no longer possess their force and meaning. Every author, it seems, thanks his wife and his editor. How then to express adequately the thanks I owe to mine?

Ina Joan Caro provided support and encouragement and many keen critical insights, and took care of our home and son while I wrote—and she did so for seven years. She typed the massive manuscript—typed some chapters over and over—without one single word of complaint. But she also tracked down and interviewed the farmers dispossessed for the Northern State Parkway during the 1920's and the residents of Sunset Park displaced for the Gowanus Parkway during the 1930's—no small task. Searching through scores of libraries, the morgues of a dozen deceased newspapers and endless rows of filing cabinets of ancient, crumbling city records, she found a hundred pieces of information that enriched this book. For some months during which I was physically unable to do my own research, she did it for me. I believe there are few if any persons in this city who possess her knowledge of where to find information about it, and this knowledge was of immense help to me. If there is a way to express adequately thanks for such long years of such gracious selflessness, I do not know it. Only I will ever know how much it meant to me.

In an era during which perceptive editorial criticism seems to be harder and harder for an author to come by—and in which detailed editing of even short manuscripts is rapidly becoming a lost art—my editor, Robert Gottlieb, not only gave this terribly long manuscript detailed editing but improved it with brilliant perceptions. Despite the grinding pressures of his responsibilities as president of Knopf, he lavished on it, week after week and month after month, his time, his energy and his genius as an editor. No one who is not an author can understand what this has meant to me, and not all authors can, either—only those who have Bob Gottlieb for their editor.

On a book of this size, the difficulties of production loom ominously large. A hundred problems fell on Katherine Hourigan of Knopf, who solved every one—and who furnished much perceptive editorial criticism of her own.

Among the many other people at Knopf to whom I am indebted, I must thank especially Martha Kaplan, Nina Bourne, Fran Lipton and Betty Anderson. Others who contributed in large measure were Priscilla Worland Burton, my research assistant; Lynn Nesbit, my agent; and Andrew L. Hughes, who provided literary as well as legal advice. Two institutions were helpful: the Carnegie Corporation, which provided a grant that helped me get started, and the New York Public Library, which, by providing working space in its Frederick Lewis Allen Memorial Room, helped me get finished.

It is unfeasible for me to thank individually every person I interviewed; there are hundreds of them—a total of 522 interviews were conducted (some persons were interviewed several times); the names of those especially helpful are listed in the "Selected Interviews" section. Some, however, gave particularly generously of their time and knowledge.

First among them are Lawrence M. Orton and Lee Koppelman. Larry Orton, a member of the City Planning Commission for thirty years, possesses an incredible store of knowledge about New York City—he put it at my service. Lee, executive secretary of the Nassau-Suffolk Regional Planning Board, did the same for my chapters on Long Island.

Lillian Edelstein, leader of East Tremont's valiant fight against the Cross-Bronx Expressway, was endlessly helpful in my attempt to describe what a modern highway can mean to a city neighborhood; William Exton and Robert C. Weinberg were helpful in describing a dozen fights against a dozen Moses projects; Augusta Newman was the definitive source for the Tavern-on-the-Green battle.

Four reporters who during the 1950's brought to light for the first time many of the facts about the Moses empire turned over to me their insights and, where possible, their files. These trailblazers were Fred J. Cook, William Haddad, Joseph Kahn and Mary Perot Nichols—who also, as a Park Department official during the Hoving era, secured me access to Department files that helped illuminate the Moses era.

The Oral History Project of Columbia University was a source of immensely helpful material.

R.A.C.
New York City
January 31, 1974

A NOTE ON SOURCES

From its inception, Robert Moses did his best to try to keep this book from being written—as he had done, successfully, with so many previous, stillborn, biographies.

After I had been researching it for more than a year, however, he apparently realized that it would be written despite him. He agreed to sit for a series of interviews with me, and, over a period of some months, seven interviews—long hours in length; one lasted from 9:30 A.M. until evening—took place in his summer cottage at Oak Beach, on the far end of the "Jones Beach" portion of the Long Island barrier beach, where Robert Moses sat talking, framed, through a picture window, by the Robert Moses Causeway and Robert Moses State Park. "Interviews" is a less appropriate term than "monologues," for Moses permitted few questions, none on sensitive subjects, and when the time came that I had no choice but to ask some (for, having interviewed others involved in the subjects in question and having examined the records—many of them secret—dealing with them, it was necessary to reconcile the sometimes striking disparity between what he told me and what they told me), the series of interviews was abruptly terminated. Nonetheless, the long hours alone with Robert Moses have enriched the book immensely, not only in the many incidents and anecdotes he related that turned out to be accurate, and in the masterful word pictures he drew of all but forgotten eras (to hear Robert Moses talk about the Legislature's "Black Horse Cavalry" of the 1920's is to *see* the Black Horse Cavalry), but because, as is always the case when a reporter can spend enough time with a subject, the subject reveals more of himself than he knows. All unknowing, Moses told me, I believe, much that he didn't realize he was telling me. The subject of this book is, therefore, the first source that I must cite.

I must thank him as well. If his monologues, shying from the sensitive as they did, were in a sense lectures on the philosophy and art of Getting Things Done in a democratic society, they were nonetheless the lectures of a genius. Having been an investigative and political reporter for some years, I have naïvely believed that I knew something about the innermost fabric of decision-making in New York City and New York State, and not a little about government and politics in general. All that I knew was as nothing besides what I learned from this unique Gamaliel.

During the era of cooperation, moreover, Moses relaxed the rule, hitherto rigid throughout his empire, that no one was to talk to me, and allowed certain of his aides to do so. Most importantly, he allowed Michael J. (Jack) Madigan and Sidney M. Shapiro to do so. Madigan worked hand in glove with Moses for thirty-five years. Although an engineer who headed the engineering firm most closely identified with Moses in the public mind, his real importance to Moses was in his secret role as architect of the intricately crafted bond issues that made Moses' public works possible. If the Moses empire had a treasurer, Madigan was the man. Shapiro was even more important to me. If the empire had a prime minister, it was he. General manager and chief engineer of the Long Island State Park Commission, he worked for Moses for more than forty years, the last twenty or so as his closest and most trusted aide. With Shapiro, I spent more than a hundred hours. Besides showing me what the "royal tour" for a Moses guest meant—and I am grateful for, if still somewhat incredulous at, that experience—he talked to me freely, having obtained my promise not to quote him directly or indirectly. He agreed, however, that his death would void that promise, and he died on July 20, 1972. It is thanks to Shapiro more than to any other single source that I came to understand Moses' attitude toward Negroes, toward "that scum floating up from Puerto Rico" that was befouling his parks, toward what "RM" called the "lower classes"—as well as Moses' reasoning on such questions as mass transit vs. highways. As to why Shapiro spoke so openly, promise or no promise, I have, after much speculation over intriguing possibilities, concluded that perhaps the primary reason was that he did so simply because he believed what Moses believed—believed it so fervently that he could see nothing wrong with it, and could not understand how anyone of "real intelligence" could see anything wrong with it. Forty years in the insulation of the Moses inner circle had taken its toll.

One further note of detailed explanation on a particular source may be of interest to some readers. When, in the Notes that follow, I cite the "Secret TBTA Files," I refer to the secret files of the Triborough Bridge and Tunnel Authority, kept under lock and key to this day on Randall's Island, barred for forty years to inspection by public or press, none of whose contents has, to the best of my knowledge, ever been revealed. It was some of those files, made available to me, that became the primary source of the information in this book on such political payoffs as insurance premium commissions to selected legislators. In those files—the legendary Moses dossiers—are the frankest of memos on who's getting what, and why.

Several other collections of documents which, so far as I can determine, have never been consulted before by any writer, have been of use in my research.

The voluminous personal files of W. Kingsland Macy, State Republican Chairman from 1930 to 1934, Suffolk County Republican Chairman from 1927 to 1960, and a power in New York State politics for thirty years, were discovered by the author in the cellar of the Macy mansion in West Islip, Long Island. They are referred to in the Notes that follow as the "Macy Papers."

Other perhaps virgin collections of documents consulted include the internal memoranda of the New York City Park Department during the twenty-six years of Robert Moses' commissionership. These files, made available to the author through the cooperation of Mary Perot Nichols, are stored in the dank recesses below the Seventy-ninth Street boat basin near the West Side Highway. They are referred to as the "Park Department Files." Other collections include the letters, memos and informal diaries of reformer William Exton, which detail his battles during the 1930's against the West Side Highway and such other Moses projects as the remodeling of Washington Square Park. The "Exton Papers" are kept at his family's home in Millbrook, Dutchess County. The internal memoranda and draft reports of the State Reconstruction Commission, of which Moses was chief of staff in 1919, were preserved for half a century by commission staffer John M. Gaus at his home in Utica, together with a vast collection of forty years of unpublished reports on Moses projects by planning and reform organizations. This huge compilation—the result of Gaus's enduring fascination with his first boss long after he himself became a Harvard professor and respected political scientist—is referred to as the "Gaus Papers."

The memos on the Title I scandals of the 1950's written by Gene Gleason and other New York *World-Telegram* reporters to rewriteman Fred J. Cook and various editors and kept by Cook in his home in Interlaken, New Jersey, were given to the author by Cook. These are referred to as the "Cook Papers." Various other documents relating to Title I given to the author by Stephen G. Thompson, then on the staff of the New York *Herald Tribune*, are referred to as the "Thompson Papers." Letters, memos and secret internal documents relating to Moses' 1964–65 World's Fair—obtained, and painstakingly filed and cross-referenced, by New York *Post* reporter Joseph Kahn—were given to the author by Kahn. These are referred to as the "Kahn Files."

In 1966, 1967 and 1968 audits were made of the Triborough Authority and of Moses' Long Island State Park Commission, Bethpage State Park Authority and Jones Beach State Park Authority by auditors on the staff of State Comptroller Arthur Levitt. In addition to the published "audit reports," there were made available to the author some of the unpublished—and, since the published reports were heavily edited at Moses' insistence, far more revealing—work sheets of the auditors. These are referred to as the "Levitt TBTA Audit" and the "Levitt LISPC Audit."

Of the manuscript collections cited, the following mayoral papers are at the Municipal Archives and Reference Center, 23 Park Row, New York City: La Guardia Papers, O'Dwyer Papers, Impellitteri Papers and Wagner Papers. The Alfred E. Smith Papers are at the New York State Library in Albany. The Franklin D. Roosevelt Papers and the Henry Morgenthau, Jr., Diary are at the Roosevelt Library in New Hyde Park. The Henry L. Stimson Papers are at the Sterling Library, Yale University.

The "Black Papers" refer to the vast collection of questionnaires and reports on displaced tenants on Moses' Title I sites compiled by Mrs. Elinor Black in her capacity as chairman of the housing committee of the Women's City Club. The "Edelstein Papers" refer to the documents collected by Mrs. Lillian Edelstein during her fight against the Cross-Bronx Expressway. They are now back in her possession at her new home near Boston. The "Gabel Papers" refer to a few documents Hortense Gabel gave the author from her tenure as Deputy State Housing Rent Administrator, the "Kopple Papers" to a collection of memoranda and files given the author by Robert Kopple, the true creator of the 1964–65 World's Fair, the "Zeckendorf Papers" to copies of letters and memos relating to the creation of the United Nations Headquarters given the author by William Zeckendorf.

The Joseph M. Price Papers are at Butler Library, Columbia University. The Maurice P. Davidson Papers are in the possession of the Davidson family.

The Oral History Project is at Columbia University.

More than one hundred brochures written or edited during a period of more than forty years by Robert Moses and published by one of his public authorities or the Mayor's Slum Clearance Committee or the New York City Park Department were given to the author by Sidney M. Shapiro. There is no one location in which the numerous other Moses brochures can be found, but most are located in the New York Public Library or the La Guardia, O'Dwyer, Impellitteri or Wagner Mayoral Papers.

SELECTED INTERVIEWS

There were 522 interviews conducted for this book. The list below identifies persons interviewed who are cited frequently in the Notes that follow. Persons cited infrequently are identified in the chapters in which the citations occur.

The persons on this list are described not by their most well-known position but by the role they played in their relationship to Robert Moses. Adolf A. Berle, Jr., for example, is described not as a Roosevelt Brain Truster but as Fiorello La Guardia's first City Chamberlain, the role in which Moses dealt with him.

The dates in parentheses are the dates of the interviews. While dates are not given in the chapter notes for interviews with persons cited infrequently, all these interviews took place between March 1, 1967, and February 3, 1972.

ADAMS, DOLIE MCWHINNEY: Assemblyman Thomas McWhinney's daughter (Mar. 23, 1967)

BARNES, HENRY: City Traffic Commissioner, Wagner era (Feb. 14, 15, 1968)

BEN SCHEIBER, ISRAEL: vice president of Madison House (July 13, 20, 1967)

BERLE, ADOLF A., JR.: City Chamberlain, La Guardia era (Nov. 22, 23, 1967)

BINGER, WALTER D.: Stanley Isaacs' Borough Works Commissioner, La Guardia era (Dec. 22, 1967; Jan. 15, 1968)

BLAKE, HAROLD: Moses secretary (1969, 1970)

CARR, MARY: secretary to Al Smith and Belle Moskowitz (Feb. 16, 1967)

CHANLER, WILLIAM C.: La Guardia Corporation Counsel (Dec. 14, 1967)

CHAPIN, WILLIAM S.: Moses aide (Apr. 24, May 8, 1968)

CHILDS, RICHARD S.: president of the New York State Association; chairman of the Citizens Union (Feb. 21, Mar. 3, 10, 1967)

CLARK, ERNEST J.: long-time Moses engineering consultant; president, Andrews & Clark (May 10, 17, 1968)

CLARKE, GILMORE: long-time Moses architectural consultant; president, Clarke & Rapuano (Apr. 5, 1967)

COLEMAN, JOHN A.: financier, key adviser to O'Dwyer and Wagner (Feb. 7, 1967)

COLLINS, JANE MOSES: Moses' daughter (1968, 1969, 1970)

CONDELLO, VICTOR F.: city legislative representative, O'Dwyer, Impellitteri eras (1969)

COONEY, JOAN GANZ: *Sesame Street* producer (July 10, 1968)

COONEY, TIMOTHY J.: Wagner aide (Aug. 14, 1968)

COSTIKYAN, EDWARD N.: Democratic district leader, reform leader of Tammany Hall, Wagner era (July 16, 1968)

CULLMAN, HOWARD S.: Port Authority chairman (Feb. 7, 8, 1967)

DAVISON, F. TRUBEE: assemblyman, campaign chairman for Moses' gubernatorial campaign (May 1, 1967)

DEWEY, THOMAS E.: Governor (Apr. 25, May 7, 1968)

DURYEA, PERRY B., JR.: State Assembly Speaker, president of Long Island State Park Commission, Rockefeller era (Apr. 27, 1968)

DYKMAN, JACKSON A.: Moses' Yale classmate and attorney for contractors, La Guardia era (July 22, 1967)

ERNST, MORRIS L.: noted attorney, reformer, social acquaintance of Moses (Nov. 7, 1967)

EVARTS, JEREMIAH: Assistant Corporation Counsel, La Guardia era (1968)

EXTON, WILLIAM, JR.: reformer (Jan. 25, Feb. 11, 12, 1968; May 1969)

FEARON, GEORGE R.: State Senate majority leader, Lehman era (May 5, 1967)
FINKELSTEIN, JERRY: City Planning Commission chairman, O'Dwyer era (May 1, 1968)

GAUS, JOHN M.: noted political scientist, staffer on Moses' Reconstruction Commission (Apr. 14, 19, 26, 27, 1967)
GOLDWATER, MONROE: partner, Goldwater & Flynn, behind-the-scenes Democratic power, La Guardia, O'Dwyer, Impellitteri, Wagner, Lindsay eras (Dec. 20, 27, 1967)
GREENBERG, NETTIE: Moses secretary (1969)
GULICK, LUTHER H.: staffer, later official at the Bureau of Municipal Research (Mar. 2, 27, 1967)

HALL, LEONARD W.: assemblyman, chairman of Republican National Committee (May 9, 1967)
HALLETT, GEORGE: secretary, Citizens Union, La Guardia, O'Dwyer, Impellitteri, Wagner, Lindsay eras (Oct. 30, Nov. 4, 1967)
HELLMAN, MRS. HILDA E.: Moses' cousin (Jan. 23, 1968)
HIGGINS, RITA: Belle Moskowitz's secretary (Apr. 1, 1967)
HOGAN, ANN: Al Smith's secretary (Apr. 10, 1967)
HOVING, THOMAS P. F.: City Park Commissioner, Lindsay era (1969)
HOWELLS, MRS. ELMER B.: friend of Moseses (Apr. 15, 1967)

IMPELLITTERI, VINCENT R., Mayor (Apr. 22, 1968)
INGRAHAM, JOSEPH T.: *New York Times* reporter, transportation editor (Apr. 18, 24, 25, 26, 1968)
ISRAELS, CARLOS: Belle Moskowitz's son (Feb. 20, 21, 1967)

JOHNSON, ELIAS A.: Moses' Yale roommate (July 21, 22, 1967)

KAPLAN, H. ELLIOT: head of State Retirement System and civil service expert (July 7, Aug. 16, 19, 1967)
KAPLAN, SAUL: counsel to Assembly minority leader Irwin Steingut, Lehman, Dewey, Harriman eras (1969)
KERN, PAUL J.: La Guardia law secretary and later President of the Municipal Civil Service Commission, La Guardia era (Jan. 19, 23, 1968)

LATHAM, WILLIAM: Moses aide (Nov. 1, 2, 1967; Jan. 1968)
LAZARUS, REUBEN A.: New York City legislative representative, Smith, Roosevelt, La Guardia eras; counsel and municipal affairs consultant to Senate majority leader and other Albany posts thereafter (Feb. 6, Oct. 20, Nov. 7, 8, 1967; Apr. 21, 1968)
LEVITT, ARTHUR: State Comptroller, Rockefeller era (1968, 1970)
LUTSKY, JACOB: Assistant Corporation Counsel, La Guardia era; legal aide to the Mayor, O'Dwyer, Impellitteri, Wagner eras (May 8, 15, June 25, 1968)

MADIGAN, MICHAEL J. (JACK): long-time Moses engineering consultant; president, Madigan-Hyland (May 2, 9, 16, 1968)
MARCONNIER, EMILY SIMS: Moses' sister-in-law (June 29, 1967)
MAYES, RICHARD: Democratic leader of Oyster Bay Town (June 2, 1967)
MCGOLDRICK, JOSEPH D.: City Comptroller, La Guardia era (May 2, Dec. 17, 18, 20, 1967; Jan. 19, 20, 1968)
MCMORRAN, J. BURCH: superintendent, State Department of Public Works (Apr. 29, 1968)
MEYERS, GENERAL HARRY L.: Moses aide (Sept. 25, 1968)
MILBANK, JEREMIAH: Moses' Yale classmate, GOP financier (July 21, 1967)
MOLONEY, EDWARD J.: State Department of Public Works official, Dewey era, later a Moses consultant (July 2, 5, 1968)
MORSE, MRS. HAROLD: Mary Moses' friend (Feb. 21, Aug. 11, 1967)
MOSCOW, WARREN: *New York Times* reporter, La Guardia, O'Dwyer, Impellitteri eras; Wagner aide, executive director, City Housing Authority, Wagner era (Dec. 3, 1967; Jan. 14, 15, 1968; Mar. 15, 1970)
MOSES, PAUL EMANUEL: Robert Moses' brother (Dec. 30, 31, 1966; Jan. 16, Feb. 4, 5, 9, 10, 11, Mar. 16, 29, 30, 1967)
MOSES, ROBERT (May 26, June 11, 16, July 25, Sept. 21, 1967; Apr. 20, 27, 1968)

O'KEEFE, PAUL: Deputy Mayor, Wagner era (1969)
ORTON, LAWRENCE M.: City Planning Commission member and vice chairman, Smith, La Guardia, O'Dwyer, Impellitteri, Wagner, Lindsay eras (Apr. 21, Dec. 22, 1967; Oct. 3, 8,

1968; Mar. 15, 1971; Nov. 17, 18, 19, Dec. 27, 1972; Mar. 8, Apr. 17, June 3, 1973)

PALMER, ARTHUR E., JR.: Lindsay transportation administrator, Lindsay appointee to Triborough board (June 23, 27, 1968)

PRICE, ROBERT: Lindsay strategist and Deputy Mayor (June 25, 1968)

PROSKAUER, JOSEPH M.: member of Smith's "Kitchen Cabinet" (Feb. 24, 1967)

RABINOWITZ, AARON: realtor, State Housing Board member, Al Smith era; Democratic financier (Feb. 27, 1967)

REID, LLOYD B.: City Traffic Commissioner, O'Dwyer era (June 16, 1968)

RODRIGUEZ, CHARLES F.: various positions under James J. Lyons in Bronx borough president's office, La Guardia, O'Dwyer, Impellitteri, Wagner eras (May 1, 20, 1968)

ROSEN, RICHARD M.: city legislative representative, Lindsay era (June 25, 1968)

SCREVANE, PAUL R.: Deputy Mayor, City Council President, Wagner era (Oct. 21, 1968)

SHAPIRO, SIDNEY M.: Moses aide (nineteen interviews, 1968–69)

SINGSTAD, OLE: general manager, New York City Tunnel Authority (Jan. 10, 17, 1968)

SULZBERGER, IPHIGENE OCHS: *New York Times* (Dec. 11, 1967)

TALLAMY, BERTRAM D.: superintendent, State Department of Public Works, Dewey era; federal highway administrator, Harriman, Rockefeller eras (May 14, 1968; 1970)

TAPPAN, HAZEL: Moses secretary (1969, 1970)

TRUEX, JAMES: Harriman aide (July 7, 1968)

TUGWELL, REXFORD G.: City Planning Commission chairman, La Guardia era; would-be Moses biographer (Jan. 16, 1968)

VOLLMER, ARNOLD AND REBECCA: Moses aides (July 6, 1968)

WAGNER, ROBERT F., JR.: Mayor (Jan. 26, Feb. 2, 3, 1972)

WARNER, ALBERT L.: Albany correspondent for Brooklyn *Eagle, New York Times,* Smith era (May 9, 1967)

WARNER, EMILY SMITH: Al Smith's daughter (Mar. 25, 26, 1967)

WEEKS, GEORGE L., JR.: Islip Town Historian (Apr. 14, May 2, 1968)

WEINBERG, ROBERT C.: reformer, urban planner (May 2, 1968)

WILLIAMS, ARTHUR B., SR.: Moses aide (Oct. 3, 1967)

WINDELS, PAUL: La Guardia Corporation Counsel (Nov. 8, 9, 10, 1967)

SELECTED BIBLIOGRAPHY

A bibliography for this book would be another book in itself, and an exercise in pedantry to boot. The following list includes only those books specifically cited in the Notes that follow, and I include this list for one purpose alone: so that in the Notes I can use abbreviations.

ALLEN, FREDERICK LEWIS: *The Big Change.* New York: Harper & Row; 1952.

ALLEN, ROBERT S.: *Our Sovereign State.* New York: Vanguard; 1949.

ALLEN, WILLIAM H.: *Al Smith's Tammany Hall.* New York: The Institute for Public Service; 1958.

——— AND EDA AMBERG: *Civic Lessons from Mayor Mitchel's Defeat.* New York: The Institute for Public Service; 1921.

AMORY, CLEVELAND: *The Last Resorts.* New York: Harper & Brothers; 1948.

ANDERSON, MARTIN: *The Federal Bulldozer.* Cambridge, Mass.: MIT Press; 1964.

ANDREWS, WILLIAM LORING: *The Iconography of the Battery and Castle Garden.* New York: Scribner's; 1901.

———: *New York As Washington Knew It.* New York: Scribner's; 1905.

BACON, LEONARD: *Semi-Centennial.* New York: Harper & Brothers; 1939.

BARD, ERWIN W.: *The Port of New York Authority.* New York: Columbia University Press; 1942.

BARUCH, BERNARD: *My Own Story.* New York: Holt, Rinehart & Winston; 1957.

———: *The Public Years.* New York: Holt, Rinehart & Winston; 1960.

BELLUSH, BERNARD: *Franklin D. Roosevelt as Governor of New York.* New York: Columbia University Press; 1955.

BIRD, FREDERICK L.: *A Study of the Port of New York Authority.* New York: Dun and Bradstreet; 1949.

BIRMINGHAM, STEPHEN: *Our Crowd.* New York: Harper & Row; 1967.

BLAKELOCK, CHESTER R.: *History of the Long Island State Parks.* West Islip, N.Y.: The Long Island Forum Press; 1959.

BOLT, ROBERT: *A Man for All Seasons.* New York: Random House; 1962.

BRANDT, LILLIAN: *An Impressionistic View of the Winter of 1930–31 in New York City.* New York: New York Welfare Council; 1932.

BUREAU OF PUBLIC ROADS: *When All Roads Led to Rome.* Washington, D.C.: Bureau of Public Roads; undated.

CARO, INA JOAN: "Building a Public Works Project in a Democracy: The Verrazano-Narrows Bridge" (Unpublished Master's thesis, 1973).

CATLEDGE, TURNER: *My Life and the Times.* New York: Harper & Row; 1971.

CLARK, RALPH H.: *Four Years' Journey with Yale 1909.* Privately published; 1967.

COHEN, JULES HENRY: *They Builded Better Than They Knew.* New York: J. Messner; 1946.

CONNABLE, ALFRED, AND EDWARD SILBERFARB: *Tigers of Tammany.* New York: Holt, Rinehart & Winston; 1967.

COSTIKYAN, EDWARD N.: *Behind Closed Doors.* New York: Harcourt, Brace & World; 1966.

CUNEO, ERNEST: *Life with Fiorello.* New York: Macmillan; 1955.

DAHLBERG, JANE S.: *The New York Bureau of Municipal Research: Pioneers in Government Administration.* New York: New York University Press; 1966.

DOIG, JAMESON W.: *Metropolitan Transportation Politics and the New York Region.* New York: Columbia University Press; 1966.

EAST, JOHN BENTON: *Council-Manager Government: The Political Thought of Its Founder, Richard S. Childs.* Chapel Hill, N.C.: University of North Carolina Press; 1965.

EBERLEIN, HAROLD B.: *Manor Houses and Historic Homes of Long Island and Staten Island.* Port Washington, N.Y.: Ira J. Friedman; 1928.

ELLIS, DAVID M., JAMES A. FROST, HAROLD S. SYRETT, AND HARRY F. CARMAN: *A Short History of New York State.* Ithaca, N.Y.: Cornell University Press; 1957.

ELLIS, EDWARD ROBB: *The Epic of New York City.* New York: Coward-McCann; 1966.

FARLEY, JAMES A.: *Behind the Ballots.* New York: Harcourt, Brace; 1938.

———: *Jim Farley's Story: The Roosevelt Years.* New York: Whittlesey House, 1946.

FELKER, CLAY (ed.): *The Power Game.* New York: Simon & Schuster; 1969.

FITZGERALD, F. SCOTT: *The Great Gatsby.* New York: Charles Scribner's Sons; 1951.

FLYNN, EDWARD J.: *You're the Boss.* New York: Viking; 1947.

FOWLER, GENE: *Beau James.* New York: Viking; 1949.

FREIDEL, FRANK: *Franklin D. Roosevelt: The Ordeal.* Boston: Little, Brown; 1954.

———: *Franklin D. Roosevelt: The Triumph.* Boston: Little, Brown; 1956.

GARRETT, CHARLES: *The La Guardia Years.* New Brunswick, N.J.: Rutgers University Press; 1961.

GERVASI, FRANK: *The Real Rockefeller.* New York: Atheneum; 1964.

GILDER, RODMAN: *The Battery.* Boston: Houghton Mifflin; 1936.

GLUCK, GEMMA LA GUARDIA; edited by S. L. Schneiderman: *My Story.* New York: David McKay; 1961.

GRAHAM, FRANK: *Al Smith, American.* New York: G. P. Putnam's Sons; 1945.

GRAHAM, GEORGE A.: *Education for Public Administration.* Chicago: The Committee on Public Administration; 1961.

GULICK, LUTHER H.: *The National Institute of Public Administration: An Adventure in Democracy.* New York: The National Institute of Public Administration; 1928.

GUNTHER, JOHN: *Inside U.S.A.* New York: Harper & Row; 1951.

HAMBURGER, PHILIP: *Mayor-Watching and Other Pleasures.* New York: Rinehart; 1958.

HANDLIN, OSCAR: *Al Smith and His America.* Boston: Little, Brown; 1958.

HAPGOOD, NORMAN, AND HENRY MOSKOWITZ: *Up from the City Streets.* New York: Grosset & Dunlap; 1927.

HAVEMEYER, LOOMIS: *My Student Days at Wall Street.* Privately published; 1963.

HERNDON, BOOTON: *The Sweetest Music This Side of Heaven.* New York: McGraw-Hill; 1964.

HOOVER, EDGAR M., AND RAYMOND VERNON: *Anatomy of a Metropolis,* Cambridge, Mass.: Harvard University Press; 1959.

ICKES, HAROLD L.: *The Secret Diary of Harold L. Ickes.* Vol. I: *The First Thousand Days, 1933–1936.* New York: Simon & Schuster; 1953.

ISAACS, EDITH: *Love Affair with a City.* New York: Random House; 1967.

JACOBS, JANE: *The Death and Life of Great American Cities.* New York: Random House; 1961.

JENKINS, SHIRLEY: *Comparative Recreation Needs and Services in New York Neighborhoods.* New York: The Research Department, Community Council of Greater New York; 1963.

JONES, JOHN F.: *The Jones Family, Descendants of Major Thomas Jones, 1665–1726, and Allied Families.* New York: Tobias A. Wright; 1907.

JOSEPHSON, MATTHEW: *The Robber Barons.* New York: Harcourt, Brace; 1934.

——— AND HANNAH JOSEPHSON: *Al Smith: Hero of the Cities.* Boston: Houghton Mifflin; 1969.

KAPLAN, H. ELLIOT: *The Law of Civil Service.* Albany, N.Y.: M. Bender; 1958.

KIELEY, JOHN B.: *Moses on the Green.* University, Ala.: University of Alabama Press; 1959.

KLEIN, WOODY: *Lindsay's Promise.* New York: Macmillan; 1970.

LA GUARDIA, FIORELLO HENRY: *The Making of an Insurgent: An Autobiography, 1882–1919.* New York: Lippincott; 1948.

LEAVITT, HELEN: *Superhighway–Superhoax.* Garden City, N.Y.: Doubleday; 1970.

LEWINSON, EDWIN R.: *John Purroy Mitchel: The Boy Mayor of New York.* New York: Astra Books; 1965.

Lewis, Arthur B.: *The Day They Shook the Plum Tree*. New York: Harcourt, Brace & World; 1963.

Lie, Trygve Halvdan: *In the Cause of Peace: Seven Years with the United Nations*. New York: Macmillan; 1954.

Limpus, L. M., and B. W. Leyson: *This Man La Guardia*. New York: Dutton, 1938.

Lipson, Leslie: *The American Governor from Figurehead to Leader*. New York: Greenwood Press; 1939.

Lowe, Jeanne R.: *Cities in a Race with Time*. New York: Random House; 1968.

Lundberg, Ferdinand: *America's Sixty Families*. New York: Citadel; 1937.

———: *The Rich and the Super-Rich*. New York: Lyle Stuart; 1968.

Lynch, Richard M.: *Alfred E. Smith: An Anthology*. New York: Vantage; 1960.

Manley, Seon: *Long Island Discovery*. Garden City, N.Y.: Doubleday; 1966.

Mann, Arthur: *La Guardia: A Fighter Against His Times*. Philadelphia: Lippincott; 1959.

———: *La Guardia Comes to Power: 1933*. Philadelphia: Lippincott; 1965.

Matz, Mary Jane: *The Many Lives of Otto Kahn*. New York: Macmillan; 1963.

Mitgang, Herbert: *The Man Who Rode the Tiger*. Philadelphia: Lippincott; 1963.

Mockridge, Norton, and R. H. Prall: *The Big Fix*. New York: Holt; 1954.

Moger, Roy W.: *Roslyn—Then and Now*. Roslyn, N.Y.: Roslyn Public School; 1965.

Moley, Raymond: *27 Masters of Politics*. New York: Funk and Wagnalls; 1949.

Morris, Joe Alex: *Those Rockefeller Brothers*. New York: Harper & Brothers; 1953.

———: *Nelson Rockefeller: A Biography*. New York: Harper & Brothers; 1960.

Morris, Newbold, in collaboration with Dana Lee Thomas: *Let the Chips Fall*. New York: Appleton-Century-Crofts; 1955.

Moscow, Warren: *Politics in the Empire State*. New York: Alfred A. Knopf; 1948.

———: *What Have You Done for Me Lately?* Englewood Cliffs, N.J.: Prentice-Hall; 1967.

———: *The Last of the Big-Time Bosses: The Life and Times of Carmine De Sapio and the Rise and Fall of Tammany Hall*. New York: Stein and Day; 1971.

Moses, Robert: *The Civil Service of Great Britain*. New York: The Faculty of Political Science of Columbia University; 1914.

——— [for the Committee on the State Park Plan]: *A State Park Plan for New York*. New York: New York State Association; 1922.

——— [for the Committee on the State Park Plan]: *The State Park Plan for New York—Revised to Show Progress to Date*. New York: New York State Association; 1924.

———: *Four Years of Park Progress*. New York: The City of New York, Department of Parks; 1938.

———: *Six Years of Park Progress*. New York: The City of New York, Department of Parks; 1940.

———: *Flushing Meadow Park, Tenth Anniversary*. New York: The City of New York, Department of Parks; 1949.

———: *Working for the People*. New York: Harper & Brothers; 1956.

———: *La Guardia: A Salute and a Memoir*. New York: Simon & Schuster; 1957.

———: *Flushing Meadow-Corona Park: A Family Park*. New York: New York's World Fair 1964–65 Corporation; 1962.

———: *A Tribute to Governor Smith*. New York: Simon & Schuster; 1962.

———: *Public Works: A Dangerous Trade*. New York: McGraw-Hill; 1970.

——— and Carl H. P. Thurston (eds.): *Yale Verse*. New Haven: Yale Publishing Association; 1909.

Mumford, Lewis: *The Highway and the City*. New York: Harcourt, Brace; 1963.

Nevins, Allan: *Herbert H. Lehman and His Era*. New York: Charles Scribner's Sons; 1963.

——— and John A. Krout (eds.): *The Greater City: New York, 1898–1948*. New York: Columbia University Press; 1948.

Owen, Wilfred: *The Metropolitan Transportation Problem*. Washington, D.C.: Brookings Institution; 1966.

Perkins, Frances: *The Roosevelt I Knew*. New York. Viking; 1946.

Phillips, Cabell: *From the Crash to the Blitz: 1929–1939*. New York: Macmillan; 1969.

Pierson, George W.: *Yale College: An*

Educational History, 1871–1921. New Haven: Yale University Press; 1952.

POLING, JAMES (ed.): *The Rockefeller Record.* New York: Thomas Y. Crowell; 1960.

PRINGLE, HENRY F.: *Alfred E. Smith: A Critical Study.* New York: Macy-Masius; 1927.

PRITCHETT, VICTOR S.: *New York Proclaimed.* New York: Harcourt, Brace & World; 1965.

PROSKAUER, JOSEPH M.: *A Segment of My Times.* New York: Farrar, Straus; 1950.

RANKIN, REBECCA B. (ed.): *New York Advancing: A Scientific Approach to Municipal Government; An Accounting to the Citizens by the Departments and Boroughs of the City of New York, 1934–1935, F. H. La Guardia, Mayor.* New York: Municipal Reference Library; 1936.

———: *New York Advancing: The Result of Five Years of Progressive Administration in the City of New York, F. H. La Guardia, Mayor.* World's Fair Edition. New York: Municipal Reference Library; 1939.

———: *New York Advancing: Seven More Years of Progressive Administration in the City of New York, 1939–1945.* Victory Edition. New York: Municipal Reference Library; 1945.

REED, HENRY H., AND SYLVIA DUCKWORTH: *Central Park: A History and a Guide.* New York: Clarkson N. Potter; 1966.

RETHI, LILI, AND EDWARD M. YOUNG: *The Great Bridge.* New York: Farrar, Straus & Giroux; 1965.

RIORDON, WILLIAM L.: *Plunkitt of Tammany Hall.* New York: Dutton; 1963.

RODGERS, CLEVELAND: *Robert Moses: Builder for Democracy.* New York: Holt; 1952.

RODGERS, WILLIAM H.: *Rockefeller's Follies.* New York: Stein and Day; 1966.

ROSENMAN, SAMUEL I.: *Working with Roosevelt.* New York: Harper & Row; 1952.

SAALMAN, HOWARD: *Haussmann: Paris Transformed.* New York: Braziller; 1971.

SAYRE, WALLACE S., AND HERBERT KAUFMAN: *Governing New York City.* New York: Russell Sage Foundation; 1960.

SCHLESINGER, ARTHUR M., JR.: *The Age of Roosevelt.* Vol. I: *The Crisis of the Old Order.* Boston: Houghton Mifflin; 1957.

———: *The Age of Roosevelt.* Vol. II: *The Coming of the New Deal.* Boston: Houghton Mifflin; 1959.

———: *The Age of Roosevelt.* Vol. III: *The Politics of Upheaval.* Boston: Houghton Mifflin; 1960.

SCHREIBER, HERMANN: *Merchants, Pilgrims, and Highwaymen: A History of Roads Through the Ages.* New York: G. P. Putnam's Sons; 1962.

SHERWOOD, ROBERT: *Roosevelt and Hopkins.* New York: Harper & Brothers; 1950.

SILVER, ARTHUR: *Jews in the Political History of New York City, 1865–1892.* New York: Yeshiva University (unpublished thesis).

SOBIN, DENNIS P.: *Dynamics of Community Change: The Case of Long Island's Declining "Gold Coast."* Port Washington, N.Y.: Ira J. Friedman; 1968.

STILES, LELA: *The Man Behind Roosevelt: The Story of Louis McHenry Howe.* Cleveland and New York: World; 1954.

STOKES, ISAAC NEWTON PHELPS: *The Iconography of Manhattan Island, 1498–1909.* 6 vols. New York: Dodd, Mead; 1915–1928.

STRUNSKY, SIMEON: *No Mean City.* New York: Dutton; 1944.

TALESE, GAY: *The Bridge.* New York: Harper & Row; 1964.

———: *The Kingdom and the Power.* New York and Cleveland: World; 1969.

THOMPSON, BENJAMIN F.: *History of Long Island from Its Discovery and Settlement to the Present Time.* Port Washington, N.Y.: Ira J. Friedman; 1962.

TIECK, WILLIAM A.: *Riverdale, Kingsbridge, Spuyten Duyvil—A Historical Epitome of the Northwest Bronx.* Old Tappan, N.J.: Fleming H. Revell Company; 1968.

TUGWELL, REXFORD GUY: *The Art of Politics.* Garden City, N.Y.: Doubleday; 1958.

ULMANN, ALBERT: *A Landmark History of New York.* Port Washington, N.Y.: Ira J. Friedman; 1969.

WARNER, EMILY SMITH: *The Happy Warrior.* Garden City, N.Y.: Doubleday; 1956.

WEEKS, GEORGE L., JR.: *Isle of Shells.* Islip, N.Y.: Buys Brothers; 1965.

WHALEN, GROVER: *Mr. New York: An Autobiography.* New York: Putnam's; 1955.

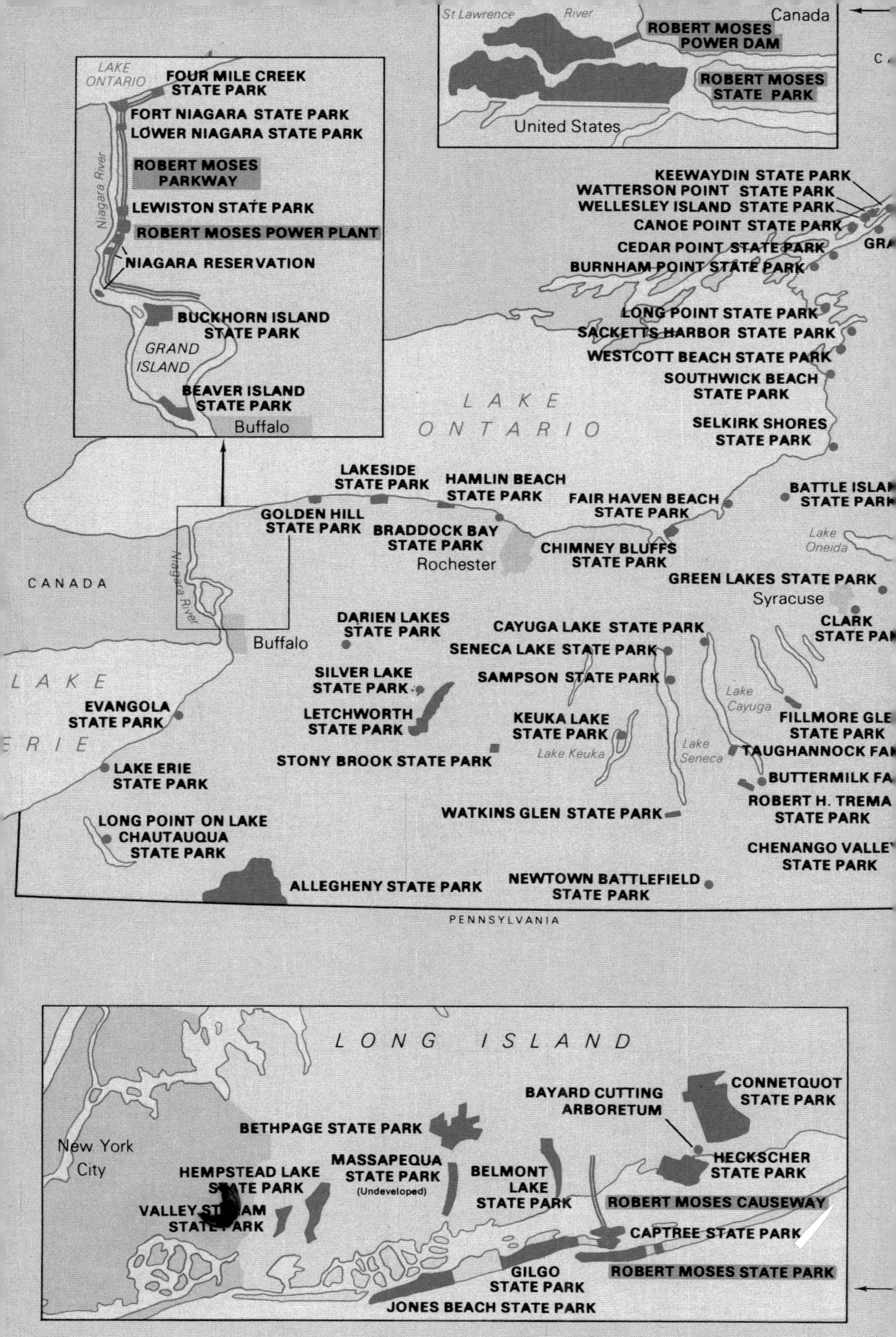

St Lawrence
River
Canada
ROBERT MOSES
POWER DAM
ROBERT MOSES
STATE PARK
United States
LAKE
ONTARIO
FOUR MILE CREEK
STATE PARK
FORT NIAGARA STATE PARK
LOWER NIAGARA STATE PARK
Niagara River
ROBERT MOSES
PARKWAY
LEWISTON STATE PARK
ROBERT MOSES POWER PLANT
NIAGARA RESERVATION
BUCKHORN ISLAND
STATE PARK
GRAND
ISLAND
BEAVER ISLAND
STATE PARK
Buffalo
KEEWAYDIN STATE PARK
WATTERSON POINT STATE PARK
WELLESLEY ISLAND STATE PARK
CANOE POINT STATE PARK
CEDAR POINT STATE PARK
BURNHAM POINT STATE PARK
LONG POINT STATE PARK
SACKETTS HARBOR STATE PARK
WESTCOTT BEACH STATE PARK
SOUTHWICK BEACH
STATE PARK
LAKE
ONTARIO
SELKIRK SHORES
STATE PARK
LAKESIDE
STATE PARK
HAMLIN BEACH
STATE PARK
FAIR HAVEN BEACH
STATE PARK
GOLDEN HILL
STATE PARK
BRADDOCK BAY
STATE PARK
Lake
Oneida
CHIMNEY BLUFFS
STATE PARK
Rochester
CANADA
Niagara River
GREEN LAKES STATE PARK
Syracuse
CLARK
DARIEN LAKES
STATE PARK
CAYUGA LAKE STATE PARK
Buffalo
SENECA LAKE STATE PARK
LAKE
SILVER LAKE
STATE PARK
SAMPSON STATE PARK
Lake
Cayuga
EVANGOLA
STATE PARK
LETCHWORTH
STATE PARK
KEUKA LAKE
STATE PARK
STATE PARK
ERIE
Lake Keuka
Lake
Seneca
STONY BROOK STATE PARK
LAKE ERIE
STATE PARK
WATKINS GLEN STATE PARK
ROBERT H. TREMAN
STATE PARK
LONG POINT ON LAKE
CHAUTAUQUA
STATE PARK
STATE PARK
ALLEGHENY STATE PARK
NEWTOWN BATTLEFIELD
STATE PARK
PENNSYLVANIA
LONG ISLAND
CONNETQUOT
STATE PARK
BAYARD CUTTING
ARBORETUM
BETHPAGE STATE PARK
New York
City
HECKSCHER
STATE PARK
HEMPSTEAD LAKE
STATE PARK
MASSAPEQUA
STATE PARK
(Undeveloped)
BELMONT
LAKE
STATE PARK
VALLEY STREAM
STATE PARK
ROBERT MOSES CAUSEWAY
CAPTREE STATE PARK
GILGO
STATE PARK
ROBERT MOSES STATE PARK
JONES BEACH STATE PARK

Goldwater and Luther H. Gulick. They, former city legislative representative Reuben A. Lazarus and Moses aide Sidney M. Shapiro, saw the scene at the public swearing in. For further details, see "Notes," Chapter 34.

Mumford quote: Interview with author. **250,000:** City Planning Commission, *Tenant Relocation* (see "Sources," Chapter 41).

1. *Line of Succession*

SOURCES

Books and newspapers:

Birmingham, *Our Crowd*; Rodgers, *Robert Moses*; Silver, *Jews in the Political History of New York City, 1865–1892*; issues of *The Jewish Messenger* and *The Jewish Times*, 1897.

Author's interviews:

The description of RM's home life and of his parents and grandparents has been drawn from interviews with his cousin Mrs. Hilda E. Hellman; with two of his sisters-in-law, Emily Sims Marconnier and Louise Benjamin Moses; with another of his relatives who wishes to remain anonymous and shall be identified as "confidential source"; from eleven interviews with his brother, Paul Emanuel Moses; as well as from interviews with Madison House trustees and staffers who worked with Bella and Emanuel Moses and who knew the "Moses boys," including Israel Ben Scheiber, Ruth Larned, Georges Friedlander and Ann and Louis Lubin; from interviews with RM's Yale classmates who spent considerable time at the Moses home, including Edward O. Proctor, Malcolm T. Dougherty and Elias ("Five A") Johnson.

NOTES

No middle name: Birth certificate, Connecticut State Department of Health. **Reason for its omission:** PEM, confidential source.

Bernhard Cohen: Mrs. Hellman, PEM; obituary, *NYT*, May 17, 1897; *The Jewish Messenger*, May 21, 1897. *Jewish Times* editorial, Sept. 24, 1875, quoted in Silver, p. 64.

Rosalie Silverman Cohen: Hellman, PEM, confidential source. **Bella and Emanuel Moses:** Rodgers, pp. 1–2; Mrs. Hellman, PEM, Louise Moses, Emily Marconnier, Ben Scheiber, Larned, Friedlander, the Lubins, Proctor, Johnson. Quote is from Ben Scheiber.

Life on Dwight Street: RM, PEM, and two of the children who played with the Moses boys there, Edward F. Andrews and Mrs. Paul Sperry.

"I didn't like New York": RM quoted in Rodgers, p. 2.

Settlement House movement: I am indebted to Birmingham, pp. 289–97. Quotes are from his book. **Madison House:** *Forty Years of the House on Madison Street*, a privately printed pamphlet; Larned, the Lubins, Friedlander. **Bella at Madison House:** Ben Scheiber, the Lubins, Friedlander, Larned. First staffer quoted is Ben Scheiber, second Larned. The head worker in the story is Ben Scheiber.

The Moseses' financial situation: PEM, confirmed by confidential source.

"Oh, Dad": Dougherty, who also remembers the "solace" quote.

"Robert Moses is Bella Moses' son": This statement, repeated so often it is part of the family tradition, was made to the author by Mrs. Hellman, PEM, Louise Moses and confidential source.

2. *Robert Moses at Yale*

SOURCES

Books, newspapers and pamphlets:

Rodgers, *Robert Moses*. A picture of Yale in that era is furnished in George W. Pierson, *Yale College: An Educational History, 1871–1921;* and in such memoirs written by Yale men as *Semi-Centennial* by RM's classmate Leonard Bacon; as well as in the *Yale Daily News* and the *Yale Courant*, various issues, 1905–09; and in pamphlets published by the class, including *Who's Who in 1909* (the Freshman Blue Book) and the "Class Histories" published at graduation and at ten-year intervals thereafter, down to 1959. (RM contributed articles of personal reminiscence to the 1949 and 1959 Class Histories.) In addition, classmate Ralph H. Clark wrote, and privately published, an instructive reminiscence: *Four Years' Journey with Yale 1909* (1967).

Author's interviews:

With thirteen of RM's surviving classmates: William R. Babcock, Alexander C. Campbell, Ralph H. Clark, Malcolm T. Dougherty, Jackson A. Dykman, Elias ("Five A") Johnson, Robert L.

Levy, Paul G. Merrow, Jeremiah Milbank, Edward O. Proctor, E. C. M. Richards and two who prefer to remain anonymous, as well as with George Gordon Hyde '10 and two other members of the swimming team who prefer to remain anonymous.

NOTES

A tightly sealed society: Figures from *Who's Who in 1909;* the classmate is Dougherty. The fact that no Jew had ever made a Senior Society was a piece of common knowledge mentioned by several of RM's classmates. Bacon, p. 47.

Age: The 1909 Class History shows the average age at graduation to have been twenty-two years, nine months. RM was twenty years, six months. **"Regarded as a young boy":** Campbell.

"Almost a recluse": Dykman.

Closing his door: Rodgers, p. 9. The Mohegan Lake alumnus is Campbell.

Never won a race: RM himself, Richards, Hyde, examination of *Yale Daily News.* He lost one race, the fifty-yard crawl in a meet against CCNY, "by a few inches" in the "excellent time of 27 and 1/5 seconds" (*Daily News,* Dec. 7, 1908).

Poetry: "Song of the Arctic Nereid," *Courant,* Dec. 1907, p. 12; "Fragments," Nov. 1908, p. 34.

Idealism deep, reading for its own sake: Johnson, his roommate, in particular. **"Durstig Geist":** Dougherty.

Europe: Dougherty was his companion. "Mona Lisa" quoted in full in Rodgers, p. 8.

Samuel Johnson; Tinker's "fire": Pierson, p. 427. RM credits Tinker with doing more than anyone else to, as Rodgers puts it, "arouse and stimulate his interest in literature and writing."

Officers chosen on merit: Johnson, Proctor. **Social recognition for academics:** RM editorial in *Courant,* Feb. 1909.

Walter Camp episode: "He regarded [it]": Bacon, quoted in Rodgers, p. 5. Bacon feels that RM's courage was "really magnificent." RM's version of the episode, given to the author, in an interview July 25, 1967, is confirmed by classmates' recollections, and *Courant* and *Daily News* articles. **RM's editorials:** *Courant,* Jan. 1908, pp. 294–99 (italics added), Jan. 1909, p. 219; *Daily News,* Nov. 23, 1907.

"Made the threat public": *Courant,* Jan. 1909, pp. 219–20. **"Quite a thing":** Hyde.

Swimming-team episode: See "Notes," Introduction.

Yale Verse: The classmate was Carl H. P. Thurston, editor of the *Yale Literary Magazine.* A front-page review in the *Yale Daily News,* of Feb. 10, 1909, praised the volume, which was sold in New Haven bookstores for $1.25, saying: "The . . . selections are complete and represent painstaking efforts on the part of the editors."

Professor: Emerson D. Fite, quoted in Rodgers, p. 6.

Bull sessions: Johnson, Dougherty, Proctor, private sources.

Senior Council: *Yale Daily News,* Feb. 11, 1909.

Class Day Committees: *History of the Class of 1909,* Yale College (1909). **"Frankly":** Dykman. The Class History sneered at the *Courant* also, saying (p. 9): "Six men entered the competition for places on the *Lit* and five of them were elected. The other one did not get anything accepted. . . . He made the *Courant."*

"In our little world": Bacon, p. 47. He also said: "That the imbecile anti-semitism of half-grown boys should have cramped his form in any respect is no compliment to our respective intelligence." The attitude of RM's coterie is expressed by Proctor, who says: "He was outstanding, one of the better members of the class. He would certainly have been in a fraternity if he had not been a Jew." Another member of the coterie, James McConaughy, is quoted by Rogers (p. 6) as saying: "In an undergraduate group where fraternity membership counted largely, he gained a position of acknowledged leadership . . . although himself not a fraternity man. . . . He was known for his brilliance and his independence. He was a great arguer and a fine conversationalist." The last, poignant word on his college career was spoken by RM at his class's fiftieth reunion in 1959, at which he was the principal speaker, and said, as if in passing: "Nor shall I stress at this late date the minor tragedies of college life, now muted, and shall merely suggest that those who were not the fortunate, whose doors the social forces of the time passed by, forget these childish tragedies and reflect how trivial they now seem in perspective. I would assume that on our fiftieth anniversary there are no outsiders."

3. *Home Away from Home*

SOURCES

The principal sources for this chapter are Rodgers, *Robert Moses*; the author's interviews with PEM and with Malcolm T. Dougherty; and Moses, *The Civil Service of Great Britain.*

NOTES

American Club: *The Oxford Times*, Dec. 1909 (no more precise date available). The two speakers are identified only as "S. C. Custer" and a "Dr. Smyth."

Yale Alumni Weekly: Mar. 3, 1911, Vol. 20, p. 583. **"Universally loved":** RM's Oxford classmate Hugh R. Norton to Sandra G. Turner (author's research assistant), Nov. 10, 1967.

Swimming and water polo: *The Oxford Year Book*, 1911, 1912. How bad the water-polo team was is indicated by the score by which it lost to Cambridge under RM's captaincy: 21½ to ½. The players admired RM, however. Not only was RM the first American ever to captain the team, he was the first American ever to play on it, and when the second, Wilburt Davison, tried out for it in 1913, several players told him: "You're the second American ever to play on the team, and if you're as good as the first one, you'll be all right." Davison to author, Apr. 11, 1967.

Yale Alumni Weekly: Mar. 3, 1911, Vol. 20, p. 584.

Affectations and letters to mother: PEM.

Congress on Race Problems: Dougherty; Rodgers has a toned-down version (p. 10). RM himself, in an interview with the author, told the story with glee.

Thesis: "excremental eloquence"; p. 47; "masterly vindication": p. 53; civil service as instrument for social reform: pp. 260–61; patronage "intolerable": p. 44; "far-sighted": p. 212; admires class differentiation: pp. 241–45 (interestingly, RM entitled the chapter in which he discussed this point "The Question of Intellectual Aristocracy"); "false democracy": p. 266; "this difficult question": p. 243; "The writer believes": p. 202; "remorseless exercise": p. 269; plea to his own country: pp. 246–70; "We must decide": p. 266 (his decision had already been made; "We *must* discriminate at the start on the basis of education": p. 264); faith in Wilson: p. 269.

4. *Burning*

SOURCES

Books, pamphlets and articles:

Dahlberg, *The New York Bureau of Municipal Research*; Graham, *Education for Public Administration*; Gulick, *The National Institute of Public Administration*; Lewinson, *John Purroy Mitchel*; Rodgers, *Robert Moses.*

Of dozens of articles on the BMR the most useful were: William H. Allen, "Training Men and Women for Public Service," *Annals*, May 1912; John M. Gaus, "The Present Status of the Study of Public Administration in the United States," *The American Political Science Review*, Feb. 1931.

Among the many pamphlets published by the BMR that give the flavor of the Bureau, the Training School and the reform sentiment of the era are: *Training School for Public Service, Annual Report* (1913); *Training School for Public Service, Program of Courses and Field Work* (1916–17); *Announcement of the Training School for Public Service* (1918).

Author's interviews:

The description of the attitude of the students at the Training School and of RM's activities and attitudes at the school and at the BMR is drawn from interviews with him—and from interviews with the following men who were at the BMR at the same time he was: Charles Beavers, Arthur E. Buck, Philip H. Cornick, Luther Gulick, Arch Mandel, Lewis Mayers, L. E. Meador, Chester E. Rightor. Other information derives from interviews with PEM, Emily Sims Marconnier and RM's Yale classmate Edward O. Proctor.

Oral History Reminiscences:

William H. Allen, Mrs. Genevieve B. Earle, Luther Gulick, Frances Perkins, William Jay Schieffelin, Laurence A. Tanzer, Leonard M. Wallstein.

NOTES

Beard quote: In Dahlberg, p. 39.

History of BMR: Dahlberg (discussion of budget, pp. 149–200). **Bruère quote:** Dahlberg, pp. 4, 37; Gulick.

Ahearn investigation: Dahlberg, pp. 17–19, 27; Lewinson, pp. 34–44.

A sense of mission: Graham, p. 136; Gulick, pp. 12–13.

"A new literature": Gulick.

"A place was waiting": RM.

"The system of the future": RM Ph.D. thesis, p. 263.

Atmosphere at Training School and attitude of other students toward RM: Gulick, Beavers, Buck, Cornick, Mandel, Mayers, Meador, Rightor; Perkins OHR, Vol. III, pp. 360–61.

"How would I sum up?": Cornick. **"You couldn't walk in":** Gulick. **"The man best educated":** Elias Johnson. Unfortunately RM's report cards cannot be found.

RM and Riverside Park: RM; Perkins OHR, Vol. III, pp. 362–63.

Lashing advisees: Gulick.

Might be fired shortly: Buck, Cornick; Perkins OHR, Vol. III, p. 360.

Mary Louise Sims: Her sister, Mrs. Marconnier; Rodgers, p. 20. **"Very much in love":** PEM and various social friends; the quote is from Edward O. Proctor. **Meeting in the library:** They were there so much several BMR students told the author she was the librarian.

"Mitchel took fire": Allen OHR.

RM appointment to Civil Service Commission: Allen OHR.

5. *Age of Optimism*

SOURCES

The situation in the NYC civil service in 1914 is described in RM's *Detailed Report* to the commission, July 8, 1915, a copy of which the author located by chance in the library of the Institute for Public Administration; the situation is also described in the Annual Reports of the Executive Committee of the New York Civil Service Reform Association, 1914–23 (1918 and 1920 are missing); it was also described by H. Elliot Kaplan in a series of interviews with the author. RM's fight to implement his reorganization plan is detailed in newspapers in 1915, 1916 and 1917, although in detail only in the *World* and the Brooklyn *Eagle*, and in Allen and Amberg, *Civic Lessons from Mayor Mitchel's Defeat.* A transcript of one of the meetings at which Moskowitz, James and RM attempted to persuade municipal employees to support the plan, including RM's earnest pleas, is found in "Discussion of Employees' Service Rating," *The Municipal Engineers Journal,* May 1917. Kaplan, Lewis Mayers, Arthur E. Buck and Mrs. Luther Steward are among those who watched RM speak at those meetings. RM's feelings over his defeat show clearly in a paper, "Standardization of Salaries and Grades in Civil Service," read on Dec. 29, 1916, to the American Political Science Association convention in Washington, D.C., reprinted in *The American Political Science Review*, 1916, pp. 296–314. Lewinson, *John Purroy Mitchel*, Graham, *Education for Public Administration*, and Kaplan, *The Law of the Civil Service*, as well as Rodgers, *Robert Moses*, were also helpful, as was Francis E. Leupp, "Civil Service Reform and Common Sense," *Atlantic Monthly*, Jan. 1914, and Raymond Moley, in an interview.

Other interviews with: Charles Beavers, Moses' friend George Gove, Mary Moses' friend Mrs. Harold Morse, PEM, Edward O. Proctor.

NOTES

"We expect great things": Ordway quoted in *NYT*, May 16, 1914.

Attempt to fire Spencer: *NYT*, July 1, 1914.

Steward and Kaplan quotes: Mrs. Steward, Kaplan.

RM's first advice to commission: "Discussion of Employees' Service Rating."

Newspaper leak: The article is in Brooklyn *Eagle*. **Details of leak:** Apr. 7, 1914. **RM's feelings:** RM.

Working under RM: The feeling of the older men expressed by, among others, Buck. **"He worked all of us hard":** Beavers. Buck, among others, gives details of RM at work on this report.

Detailed Report: Quotes from pp. 5–11 (italics added). RM's aide is Mayers, who recalls RM disagreeing violently with the conventional theory that appointees to higher-level policy-making positions should be exempt from competitive examinations. RM told Mayers: "The higher up you get, the more need there is for working out rules."

RM's view on need to "eliminate" positions: Kaplan.

RM on the human element and public discussion: His "standardization" paper, *The American Political Science Review,* 1916, pp. 312 and 306, respectively.

"Clearly discernible": Mayers. **"No reason why it cannot":** PEM.

RM's confidence in Mitchel: Mayers, Buck, PEM.

"Pioneer work": Annual Report of the Executive Committee, 1916. **Moskowitz and James quotes:** "Discussion," p. 157. **Mitchel's promise:** *NYT*, Sept. 14, 1915.

RM and Mary: Yale classmate Proctor; Rodgers, p. 20. A friend, Mrs. Lorraine Fishel, who was visiting RM's sister, Edna, at Lake Placid, recalls that his campaign to get her interested in mountain climbing suffered a setback when, halfway up a heavily wooded mountain one morning, miles away from the path down, the couple became confused by an unexpected heavy fog. Realizing they were lost, RM told Mary to sit down and wait while he located the path. But by the time he found the path, he had forgotten the way back to Mary, and she stayed lost until, late in the day, the fog lifted.

The couple's poverty and idealism: Mrs. Harold Morse.

Walking with Gove: Gove.

Mocking BMR: Mayers. **"Very little doubt":** Private source. **"Here was this tall, handsome character":** Buck.

Tammany waiting: Kaplan. **Moses volunteering:** Mayers. **"Reclassification became Moses":** Kaplan. *NYT* articles, 1915–16, detail the circulating of petitions and the building up of anti-reorganization sentiment.

Moskowitz compromising: Moskowitz, "Old and New Problems of Civil Service," *The Annals of the American Academy,* 1915, pp. 153–67 (italics added). RM's refusal to consider compromise is related by Kaplan, Mayers and others.

The defeat of RM's plan: *NYT,* Brooklyn *Eagle,* Sept. 1915–Oct. 1917; Kaplan, Mayers; RM's paper to the American Political Science Association (this paper, nineteen pages in length, is a step-by-step description of the fight over the plan—and, in its frankness, provides a remarkably clear picture of its author's feelings at the time).

"Nothing . . . more ridiculous": RM's paper, p. 312.

Cleveland's shift: Graham, p. 138; *World,* Oct. 14, 1917.

"Feet in the trough": Allen and Amberg, p. 62. **The Kingsbury story:** Lewinson, p. 171. Allen and Amberg detail Mitchel's cooperation with ward leaders. **"His concern was for the city":** Lewinson, p. 117.

New York Central giveaway: Allen and Amberg, pp. 20ff.

Not "dry and dull": RM's paper, pp. 297–98. **Still confident:** p. 313. **Mass meetings:** An article describing one is *NYT,* Jan. 21, 1917.

Hylan quote: Brooklyn *Eagle,* Jan. 23, 1918. **His destruction of civil service:** Annual Report of the Executive Committee, 1921.

"Need for executive support": RM's paper, p. 310. **"It is futile":** p. 313.

Declining army commission: The reason he did so is not known. Asked about it by the author, RM replied that he "really wanted" to accept, "but I couldn't afford it—I had a wife and two children . . ." The Hog Island episode and being forced to return to the Bureau are from this interview.

Contemporaries had moved on: *Announcement of the Training School for Public Service* (1918). **RM on line in Cleveland:** Moley interview.

Food Commission: *Announcement.* **RM's domestic problems:** Mrs. Harold Morse; confidential source. **Confused and worried:** PEM was struck by the change in his brother's demeanor.

"A typical Tammany politician": Ernest Willvonseder, quoted in Rodgers, p. 23.

6. Curriculum Changes

SOURCES

Chapters 6 through 15 take place during Alfred E. Smith's Governorship. The general background of this Governorship—and the biographies of Smith and Belle Moskowitz—are drawn from:

Books and articles:

Allen, *Al Smith's Tammany Hall;* Baruch, *My Own Story* and *The Public Years;* Bellush, *Franklin D. Roosevelt as Governor of New York;* Cohen, *They Builded Better Than They Knew;* Ellis, Frost, Syrett and Carman, *A Short History of New York State;* Farley, *Jim Farley's Story* and *Behind the Ballots;* Freidel, *Franklin D. Roosevelt: The Triumph;* Handlin, *Al Smith and His America;* Hapgood and Moskowitz, *Up from the City Streets;* Josephson and Josephson, *Al Smith;* Lynch, *Alfred E. Smith;* Moley, *27 Masters of Politics;* Moses, *A Tribute to Governor Smith* and *Working for the People;* Pringle, *Alfred E. Smith;* Proskauer, *A Segment of My Times;* Warner, *The Happy Warrior.* Other sources are Rodgers, *Robert Moses,* and Dahlberg, *The New York Bureau of Municipal Research.*

Out of innumerable magazine articles, especially informative were Christian Gauss, "How Governor Smith Educated Himself," *The Saturday Evening Post,* Aug. 30, 1930; Dennis Lynch, "Friends of the Governor," *North American Review,* Oct. 1928; Ann O'Hagan Shinn,

"Alfred E. Smith: A Personal Impression," *The New York Times Magazine,* Oct. 22, 1922, and "Belle Lindner Moskowitz," *The Survey,* Feb. 1933.

Author's interviews:

With Smith's daughter, Emily Smith Warner, and Mrs. Moskowitz's son, Carlos Israels; with the three surviving high-level members of his administration: RM, Joseph M. Proskauer and Reuben A. Lazarus; with his three surviving secretaries: Mary Carr, Rita Higgins and Ann Hogan; with intimates, associates and/or friends: Dolie McWhinney Adams, Howard S. Cullman, John A. Coleman, Mrs. Eva Garson (Newman) Levy, Aaron Rabinowitz and Lindsay Rogers; with the widows of two associates: Justice Florence Shientag and Mrs. Raymond Ingersoll; with legislators who dealt with Smith: George R. Fearon, Leonard W. Hall, Ellwood M. Rabenold and three who declined to be identified; with reporters who covered Albany: Albert L. Warner, Leo O'Brien and Ernest K. Lindley; with two reformers who observed the Albany scene closely: George Hallett and Robert S. Binkerd; as well as with Reconstruction Commission staffers Arthur E. Buck and John M. Gaus and with RM's daughter Jane Moses Collins and Luther Gulick.

Documents:

Smith, FDR, Gaus and Macy Papers.

Oral History Reminiscences:

William H. Allen; Mrs. Genevieve B. Earle, between 1908 and 1913 a BMR staffer; State Senator Martin Saxe; William Jay Schieffelin; reformer John Lord O'Brien; Frances Perkins; Lewis H. Pink, chairman of the State Housing Board; Lawson Purdy, civic leader and first board chairman of the RPA; Frederick C. Tanner; Laurence A. Tanzer, counsel for the Factory Investigating Commission; Norman Thomas; reformer Leonard M. Wallstein.

NOTES

No one had studied her career: No one has studied it yet. This remarkable woman has been all but forgotten. An evaluation of the significance of the closing of the dance halls is in *NYT,* Nov. 23, 1914. For a description of typical halls, *NYT,* May 28, 1915. **"She understood . . . perfectly":** Cohen, pp. 246–47. (Cohen was the employers' attorney.)

Dr. Moses said he would; first meeting with Smith: RM; Israels.

"Bob Moses was never to learn why": RM.

Belle believing Smith best hope; the University Club incident: Israels.

Belle suggesting a "Reconstruction Commission": Smith often told this story to intimates, two of whom, Proskauer and Cullman, repeated it to the author.

1915 **BMR study:** Best is Dahlberg, pp. 93–122.

Reconstruction Commission: The basic source is the *Report of the Reconstruction Commission to Governor Alfred E. Smith on Retrenchment and Reorganization in the State Government,* submitted Oct. 10, 1919. Three commission staffers who worked for Moses interviewed in the spring of 1967: Arthur E. Buck, John M. Gaus and one who prefers to remain unidentified. Gaus saved many internal commission memos, including many from RM.

RM and Mrs. Moskowitz: RM. **Phrase struck out:** In fact, *Reconstruction Commission Report,* p. 42: "Adjustments will not be made by cutting of salaries or by the wholesale elimination of positions." **"The council will remain":** *Reconstruction Commission Report,* p. 23. **"A real divergence":** Buck. **"She was the boss":** Gaus. **Calling her names:** Gaus; confidential source.

RM memos: RM to Channing Schweitzer, May 2, 1919, Gaus Papers; Gaus. **Leaving commission in his hands:** RM.

Smith's speech: Hapgood and Moskowitz, p. 220. **"You had to like him":** Buck.

RM's corrections: The report quoted is one of Gaus's on the State Labor Department, Gaus Papers. **RM at work:** Gaus, Buck, confidential source.

Gaus to Schweitzer: May 13, June 13, 1919, Gaus Papers.

RM to the chart maker: RM to Sedley H. Phinney, Apr. 3, 1919, Gaus Papers.

RM on weekends: Perkins OHR, Vol. III, p. 365. Jane Moses Collins (RM's daughter).

BMR report: Quoted in Dahlberg, p. 99.

"The only serious argument": *Reconstruction Commission Report,* p. 12. **"No other way":** pp. 7, 8 (italics added). **"One of the possible benefits":** pp. 34–35. **Various recommendations:** pp. 3–12, 36–37, 316–19.

"I wrote the report": RM. **Rough-drafts comparison:** Gaus Papers. **Beard episode:** Gulick, Buck, confidential source; Dahlberg says (p. 105), in an overstatement

of her own that reveals the bitterness BMR alumni feel over RM's attitude: "Dr. Beard contributed in large part to the writing of the Commission's final report."
"He was so angry": Gulick.
Stimson: Henry L. Stimson to George Wharton Pepper, Nov. 26, 1919, Stimson Papers.
Smith's speeches: Hapgood and Moskowitz, pp. 224–25.
RM's letter: To Stimson, Mar. 7, 1920.
"He thought fast": Gaus.
Smith inviting RM home: Emily Smith Warner.
"Al Smith listens to me": Ernest Willvonseder, quoted in Rodgers, p. 23.

7. *Change in Major*

SOURCES

For Al Smith's biography, see "Sources" for Chapter 6. Biographical details about Richard Spencer Childs are from East, *Council-Manager Government.*

Author's interviews:
Robert S. Binkerd, Richard S. Childs, John A. Coleman, Howard S. Cullman, PEM, Emily Smith Warner.

NOTES

Friendship between Smith and RM; barbershopping: Coleman, Cullman, Emily Smith Warner. **"They were opposites":** Coleman.
Change in RM: The author's interviews with Childs, PEM and Binkerd; Perkins OHR. RM's growing pro-Smith partisanship is, of course, documented in newspaper articles. But the basic source is the author's examination of the nineteen issues of the *State Bulletin* of the New York State Association, which RM wrote and edited in 1921, 1922 and 1923. These issues were kindly given to the author by Childs.
Childs biography: East, *passim*. **Childs offering job to RM:** Childs, RM. **"The embodiment":** Childs, confidential source. **Davenport:** *State Bulletin*, Mar. 30, 1922. **"The principle is the important thing":** *State Bulletin*, Aug. 1921. **Seemed the very model:** Perkins OHR. **"Cheap political trick":** Confidential source.
RM's attacks on Miller: *State Bulletin*, Jan. 4, 1922, p. 5; July 22, 1922, p. 5; Miller replies: *NYT*, Feb. 15, 1922; New York *Herald*, July 27, 1922; *Herald* editorial, July 28, 1922. **Laughing at reformers:** Childs, Binkerd, confidential source.

8. *The Taste of Power*

SOURCES

See "Sources" Chapter 6. Some material on Jimmy Walker is from Fowler, *Beau James.*

NOTES

Jimmy Walker in Albany: Fowler, *passim*; RM interviews with author; Rabenold; RM, "Cinderella Man in City Hall" (review of *Beau James*), *NYT*, Apr. 10, 1949. **Al Smith in Albany:** See "Sources," Chapter 6.
Prisons: *RM*. Best summary of Smith's prison reforms: Hapgood and Moskowitz, p. 300.
Grade crossings: RM; RM to Smith, Feb. 20, 1924, Smith Papers. **RM's forms:** RM to Smith, Jan. 30, 1924, Smith Papers.
He liked the taste: Lazarus, Israels; even the secretaries in Smith's office, while charmed by the Governor's handsome young aide, noticed it: Carr, Higgins and Hogan.
"The best bill drafter": Proskauer, Israels.
"What do you want?": RM; Proskauer and Lazarus heard the Governor pressing RM to accept various jobs, and RM refusing.

9. *A Dream*

SOURCES

Books, pamphlets, articles and documents:
Moses, *Dangerous Trade,* pp. 75–153; Rodgers, *Robert Moses,* pp. 31–57. The increased public need for parks and roads, and the lack of them, is detailed in newspapers and magazines during the 1920's (particularly valuable are an article in the *NYT,* Dec. 19, 1926, by Raymond Torrey, and "A Plea for Parks and Park Trails," a speech he delivered to the American Institute of Park Executives, Oct. 31, 1926); in reports and minutes of one of the leading reform organizations struggling with the problem, collected in *Annual Reports and Minutes of the American Scenic and Historic Preservation Society, Jan. 7, 1921–Feb. 14, 1927*; in *Progress Report of the Highway Bureau of the Long Island Chamber of Commerce,* Feb. 2, 1928. By far the most detailed and vivid de-

scriptions are by RM himself: *A State Park Plan for New York,* Dec. 1922; *The State Park Plan for New York—Revised to Show Progress to Date,* Jan. 1924; "State Regulation of Private Forests in the Adirondack Park," *State Bulletin,* Mar. 5, 1932; "State Lands for Municipal Parks and Playgrounds," *State Bulletin,* Sept. 15, 1932; and *Annual Reports of the Long Island State Park Commission to the Governor and Legislature of the State of New York,* 1924–1930.

Other sources consulted:

Allen, *The Big Change*; Amory, *The Last Resorts*; Birmingham, *Our Crowd*; Blakelock, *History of the Long Island State Parks*; Eberlein, *Manor Houses*; Fitzgerald, *The Great Gatsby*; Jones, *The Jones Family*; Josephson, *The Robber Barons*; Lundberg, *America's Sixty Families*; Manley, *Long Island Discovery*; Matz, *The Many Lives of Otto Kahn*; Moger, *Roslyn*; Sayre and Kaufman, *Governing New York City*; Sobin, *Dynamics of Community Change*; Thompson, *History of Long Island*; and Weeks, *Isle of Shells.*

Smith Papers.

Author's interviews:

As noted under specific topics.

NOTES

Population: Sayre and Kaufman, p. 18.

Westchester and Palisades situation: RM, *A State Park Plan for New York,* esp. pp. 18–26.

Long Island: The population of Nassau County was 126,120 according to the 1920 federal census, of Suffolk County 110,246. **Geological history:** Manley, pp. 15–27; Weeks, pp. 1–14; *Some of Town of Islip's Early History* (Bay Shore, N.Y.); RM, *Annual Report of the LISPC,* 1926, pp. 9–10; Fitzgerald, p. 301.

The baymen: Manley, pp. 1-14. **Cholera episode:** Manley, p. 202; author's interviews with bay families. **Ku Klux Klan:** Author's interviews with RM; his aide Sidney M. Shapiro; Islip Town Historian George L. Weeks, Jr.; old LI newspaperman Lloyd Record; and Gladys Vunck, W. Kingsland Macy's private secretary.

The robber barons: Books by Josephson and Lundberg.

Life on the Gold Coast: Books by Eberlein, Sobin, Moger and Amory (mainly for Mrs. Belmont, pp. 203–12); "Long Island in the Year of Our Lord 1932," *Fortune,* June 1932; Harvey Aronson, "Once upon a Gold Coast," *Newsday,* Apr. 6, 1968; author's interviews with Mrs. Etienne Phipps Boegner, Leonard W. Hall, F. Trubee Davison, LI newspaperman C. H. MacLachlan, Oyster Bay Democratic leader Richard Mayes; 1920's Oyster Bay Town Clerk Charles Ransom, long-time LI restaurateur Paul Reinhardt, Winthrop heir Robert Payne. The best picture of the day-to-day life on the Gold Coast is found in *The North Shore Almanack,* the area's weekly newspaper. **Phipps Estate:** "Old Westbury Gardens" (tour brochure); interviews with Mrs. Boegner. **Kahn Estate:** Josephson, p. 333 (for information about the creation of the mountain). Other descriptions of Kahn estate are found in Matz, pp. 20, 150, 233–34; Birmingham, p. 320. **The barons' selfishness; allowing public roads to fall into disuse:** Sobin, p. 98. **Pratt and LIRR:** Sobin, p. 99. **Sands Point:** Harold M. Morse to RM, Apr. 16, 1923; Smith to Secretary of Commerce Herbert Hoover, Apr. 23, 1923; George Gordon Battle to Smith, May 1, 1923; Hoover to Smith, May 8, 1923; Graves to RM, June 20, 1923; RM to Smith, Morse to Smith, Aug. 30, 1923. All in Smith Papers. Interview with Mrs. Morse. **Glen Cove:** Ransom, Reinhardt. **Cold Spring Harbor:** Sobin, p. 99; MacLachlan. **Lloyd Neck and Eatons Neck:** Hall. **Huntington:** MacLachlan, who obtained the precise figures during a survey he did for a local newspaper of which he was editor. **The barons' political power; 49 members:** Hall. **No state roads:** Hall.

Four hours: Transcript of joint hearing before Senate Finance and Assembly Ways and Means Committee, at Albany, Feb. 11, 1925; testimony by Assemblyman John Boyle, Jr. **Cemetery acreage:** A private survey prepared for W. Kingsland Macy by his secretary, Gladys Vunck, Dec. 19, 1925.

The South Shore: Allen, pp. 29–30; "Idle Hour," tour brochure of Vanderbilt Estate in Islip. **Timber Point Club:** "The Timber Point Club," club introductory brochure; author's interviews with Gladys Vunck, and with TPC members Horace Havemeyer, Jr., Robert Livingston Hollins and Buell Hollister, Jr. **Population:** New York Telephone Co. estimate, 1922.

RM's inspiration: RM. **Exploring the parks:** Also Israels. **Getting lost on the bay:** Also Mrs. Lorraine Fishel. **Tramping the barrier beach with him:** Also Mrs. Harold Morse, confidential sources. **Major Jones:** Jones, *passim;* Blakelock, p. 39.

Statewide situation: Moses, *A State Park Plan*; ASHPS, minutes of various meetings. The Forest Preserve, not a park in the true sense of the word, and Palisades Interstate Park, an interstate park and privately funded, are not included in this tabulation.

Revolutionary: The largest previous bond issue for parks floated anywhere had probably been $10,000,000, and that had been, in New York, for the Forest Preserve, not a true park. **"To provide for permanent improvements" and for "parkways":** Moses, *A State Park Plan*, pp. 6–7. **"Hailed by park planners":** See, for instance, "Summary, Third National Conference on State Parks, Turkey Run State Park, Indiana, 1923," printed by the conference.

Smith: "lacked TR's zest," "red flannel underwear": Rodgers, p. 33. **Responded to graphic presentations:** Perkins OHR. **Sinking in chair and "Bob, you win":** Rodgers, pp. 33–34; Childs.

Mail pouring in: His secretaries, Carr, Higgins, Hogan; Ingersoll and Hunt letters and scores of others, Smith Papers. If there was an editorial opposing the message, it is not in Smith's files. **Chairman of the National Conference:** John Barton Payne to Smith, Jan. 18, 1924, Smith Papers. **Albany reporter:** Warner.

RM tramping around LI again: RM. The friend was Israels. Townsend Scudder, Jr., heard about the walks from his father, a great walker who could keep up with RM—for a couple of hours. **Whitman:** "Paumanok." **RM on Montauk:** *Annual Report of the LISPC*, 1926, pp. 9–10. **Knew his plans too small:** Moses, *The State Park Plan for New York—Revised to Show Progress to Date.*

Smith offer of commission presidency: RM.

10. *The Best Bill Drafter in Albany*

SOURCES

This chapter is based on the author's interviews with F. Trubee Davison and on detailed analyses by W. Kingsland Macy's lawyers of the bills Davison introduced for RM (see Chapter 11) and by Marvin Shiebler, secretary of the Suffolk County Taxpayers Association, in a memo to Macy found in Macy Papers and in Committee of Citizens of Suffolk County, "State Parks," undated but apparently Feb. 1925. The author's interviews with RM were helpful on some points.

NOTES

"The more spigots": *Reconstruction Commission Report* (see "Notes," Chapter 6), p. 8.

Parks no exception: *Reconstruction Commission Report*, pp. 8–9, 21.

"Appropriation" method had never been used: Shiebler, "The Long Island Park Program," Jan. 30, 1926, p. 2; "Important Notice," Apr. 12, 1926 (two broadsides put out by the Committee of Citizens of Suffolk County).

RM impatient: RM to Graves, Apr. 12, 1924, Smith Papers.

11. *The Majesty of the Law*

SOURCES

Books:

Talese, *The Kingdom and the Power*; Warner, *The Happy Warrior*; see also "Sources," Chapter 6.

Author's interviews:

Leonard W. Hall, William Latham, Richard Mayes, Robert Payne, Joseph M. Proskauer, P. G. Rasweiler, Sidney M. Shapiro, Iphigene Ochs Sulzberger, Albert L. Warner.

NOTES

RM's overhead expenses: Attorney General Albert Ottinger, press release, reprinted in *NYT*, May 18, 1925. **Exempting friends:** Graves to RM, May 5, 1924, Smith Papers.

Fire Island State Park: Blakelock, *The Long Island State Parks.*

Smith calling Hayes: RM. **Drinking beer:** RM, Shapiro.

One day's hunting: Deer Range stockholder Percy R. Pyne II statement in *NYT*, Jan. 9, 1925.

Threatening the farmers: Author's interview with P. G. Rasweiler, confirmed by RM to Graves Oct. 29, 1926, Smith Papers, and by Shapiro, who boasted about taking the surveys from the adjoining farm. Also Robert A. Hug "and neighbors" to Smith, Oct. 25, 1926, Smith Papers. **Threatening the Timber Pointers:** Havemeyer quote from newspaperman Lloyd Record, who heard him. **"Mr. Moses told me":** Macy's testimony under oath in examination before trial in Brooklyn Supreme Court, related in *NYT*, Oct.

27, 1925. **Threatening the North Shore robber barons; seeing the surveyors and being threatened with appropriation:** Davison, Hall, Mayes, Payne, Latham. **Stimson to Smith:** May 18, 1925, Smith Papers. **"Teach a lesson":** Incident recounted in Old Westbury landowner Henry M. Earle to Smith, June 23, 1926, Smith Papers. **"I felt awful":** Davison. **Lawyer's opinion:** Marvin Shiebler to Robert P. Griffing, Nov. 13, 1925, Macy Papers.

Taylor Estate fight: Timber Pointers' contentions in court briefs—for example, "Pauchogue Land Corporation, Plaintiff, against Long Island State Park Commission, and Robert Moses, Townsend Scudder and Clifford L. Jackson, individually and as Commissioners of the Long Island State Park Commission, Defendants"—"Brief on Behalf of Plaintiff-Appellant"; "Appellant's Reply Brief"; and "Record on Preliminary Injunction for Submission to the Finance Committee of the Senate and the Ways and Means Committee of the Assembly." **Smith's advisers believe he won't sign:** Tone of Graves to RM, Oct. 9, 1924, and of RM to Smith, Oct. 10, 1924, Smith Papers. **The closed hearing:** Virtually all Smith biographers give accounts of this hearing, which became a legend in New York State, but all these accounts have Smith treating Havemeyer's remark as a joke. The account the author believes to be accurate comes from RM, in interview with author, and is confirmed by Carlos Israels' and Joseph Proskauer's recollections of what Belle Moskowitz and Smith, respectively, told them the next day.

W. Kingsland Macy: The "observer" was Alva Johnston, who profiled Macy for *The New Yorker*, Sept. 12, 1931; quotes are from pp. 26 and 25. Of many newspaper profiles of Macy, the most detailed are S. J. Woolf, *NYT Magazine*, May 17, 1931, and Brooklyn *Eagle*, Sunday Magazine Section, Jan. 4, 1931.

Troopers on property: Pyne in *NYT*, Jan. 9, 1925. **$25,000 limit and Macy's refusal to view the fight in purely business terms:** Havemeyer to Macy, Apr. 28, 1925; Jan. 5, 1926; Macy to Havemeyer, Apr. 28, May 5, 6, 1925; Jan. 5, Dec. 23, 1926, Macy Papers.

Furman finds illegal: "Order to show cause," issued by Mr. Justice George H. Furman, Judge of the County Court of Suffolk County, Dec. 30, 1924. **Macy refusing to show reporter around:** Macy note to Miss Vunck, undated, Macy Papers. **"The amateur in politics":** RM. **"The defendants have proceeded . . . illegally":** Van Siclen, "Injunction Order," quoted in *NYT*, Feb. 18, 1925. Van Siclen, "Order of Preliminary Injunction," Feb. 17, 1925, p. 2.

Senate Finance Committee hearings: *NYT* and *HT*, Feb. 12, 1925. **RM's edited transcript:** Copy found in Macy Papers.

Smith veto message and legislative fight: From three newspapers, *NYT*, *HT* and Brooklyn *Eagle*, various issues, Apr. 2–June 27, 1925.

Macy-RM face-to-face confrontation: Macy statement issued May 5, 1925; Pauchogue Land Corporation "Complaint" in "Record on Preliminary Injunction," p. 13.

RM stalling: Among those who said so were Justices Van Siclen and Dike. Van Siclen commented, "The suit should have been tried long ago" (*NYT*, May 28, 1925). Dike was to blast the "dilatory tactics of the Commission," adding that RM's actions seem to show "a studied effort to affront the court" (Brooklyn *Eagle*, Oct. 19, 1925).

Macy's confidence: Macy to Havemeyer, May 5, 1925, Jan. 5, 1926, and others, Macy Papers. **Wait, Smith said:** Proskauer.

NYT editorial: Feb. 17, 1925. **"The bible":** Talese, p. 7. **NYT slanting Van Siclen story:** Handling of Ottinger story, May 18, 1925; editorial on Ottinger charge, May 18; the paper stated as a fact that the Governor was "willing to make any reasonable compromise . . ." (June 5, 1925); a June 14 article contains such phrases as "The Governor believes in parks. He loves them. . . . Not long ago he motored over Long Island, where [park] plans have precipitated bitter opposition by certain wealthy residents." Another article (Jan. 12, 1925) began: "Whatever may be the outcome of the controversy between the Long Island State Park Commission and the group of men opposing purchase of the George C. Taylor property on the Great South Bay, an examination on the ground indicates that the property in many respects is ideal for a public park . . ." Not only does the article make no mention of the opponents' contentions that the park was too far from New York City, too inaccessible to public transportation, etc., for a park; it ignores their contention, later proved true, that developing it would take, in terms of public expenditures of the time, an enormous expenditure: "seemingly it could be developed at no very great expense," the

article states, and it is obvious from the article, although it never says so, that that statement is based entirely on RM's estimate of that expense.

Adolph S. Ochs: Helping RM preserve the Saratoga Battlefield: RM to State Comptroller Morris S. Tremaine, Aug. 8, 1928, Smith papers. His interest in parks: Talese, pp. 79, 96–97. The publisher's intense interest in parks occasionally proved an embarrassment to RM; once, while the Governor was visiting Sulzberger at the publisher's Lake George home, RM wrote Smith a letter about new park plans, delicately hinting to Smith that he not tell Ochs about them lest they find their way into the pages of the *Times* before they were finalized; RM to Smith, Aug. 8, 1924, Smith Papers. **Iphigene "thrilled":** Iphigene Ochs Sulzberger interview with author. **Warner:** Interview. **Ochs's Park Association award:** *NYT,* Dec. 25, 1931.

RM's secret visit to Ward and Mastick: RM.

Citizens Union statement: *NYT,* June 23, 1925. **Price:** Smith telegram to Price, June 25, 1925, Smith Papers. **Roulstone's tour:** *NYT,* June 21, 1925.

Record speed of veto; Knight and Walker quotes: NYT, June 27, 1925. **"Sealed orders":** Smith quoted in *NYT,* June 26. **"Too much pressure":** Mastick, *NYT,* June 26. **"My career would end":** *World,* June 27.

Bitter facts; options lost: *Annual Report of the LISPC,* 1925, p. 47. **Deciding to call Heckscher:** RM. **Smith-Heckscher conversation:** Related in numerous biographies of Smith, including Josephson, p. 333.

Court fight: Tuttle, *HT,* Sept. 13, 1925. **Smith tried privately to persuade Macy:** Macy to Smith, Sept. 12, 1925, Macy to Heckscher, Oct. 11, 1925, Macy Papers.

RM under oath: *NYT, HT* and Brooklyn *Eagle*; court transcripts. Goldsmith memorandum in *NYT,* Sept. 12, 1925.

Jones Beach: Babylon *Leader,* issues of July 18, 25, Aug. 15, 1924; Amityville *Sun,* Aug. 8, 1924; *Long Island Sun,* Nov. 20, 1924. **RM's feelings:** RM.

12. *Robert Moses and the Creature of the Machine*

SOURCES

The general picture of corruption on Long Island is drawn from interviews with Richard Mayes, Nassau County Democratic leader in the 1920's and 1930's; Eugene Hurley, a shrewd attorney who opposed RM in court continually during the 1930's; James B. Cooper, Jr., editor of the Babylon *Leader*; Leonard W. Hall, a GOP assemblyman at the time; Dolie McWhinney Adams, Thomas McWhinney's daughter; Paul Reinhardt, an Oyster Bay restaurateur and intimate of politicians; three of RM's key aides at the time, Sidney M. Shapiro, William Latham and one who prefers to remain unidentified; the author's casual conversations with old-time Long Island politicians during several years as a reporter for *Newsday,* the Long Island newspaper. There are various newspaper articles on one aspect or another that came to light. But the most graphic over-all picture is probably that provided by RM's own articles in the *State Bulletin,* 1921, 1922 and 1923.

The on-the-record court fight is contained not only in numerous newspaper articles but in the court records cited in the "Notes" for Chapter 11. The behind-the-scenes maneuvering is detailed in the Macy Papers, in the Smith Papers, in an interview with Gladys Vunck, Macy's personal secretary, and in a confidential interview with one of Moses' aides.

Other information was supplied in interviews with Israel Ben Scheiber, William S. Chapin, Gilmore Clarke, Mrs. W. Kingsland Macy and Mrs. Harold Morse.

The compromise reached in Albany is discussed in newspapers and explained in the Macy Papers, in the Smith Papers and in interviews with Miss Vunck and RM.

NOTES

Hewitt offering to sell: Hewitt to RM, Dec. 31, 1924, Smith Papers. **RM's refusal:** Lutz to Smith, June 24, 1925, Smith Papers. **RM refused to give inside information on highway routes to Smith's friends:** Francis Pettit, one of them, to Smith, complaining, Mar. 21, 1925, Smith Papers.

Doughty and Booth & Weston: Hurley, Shapiro; confirmed by confidential sources.

Giving Hempstead Town politicians access to LISPC plans: Smith to Gen. George W. Goethals, Mar. 30, 1926, Smith Papers; *NYT,* Dec. 12, 1925, gives details of formation of the joint commission to plan Jones Beach. **Moses be-**

coming friendly with McWhinney: Adams.

Lawyer forming corporation: Nassau County Clerk's Office, Certificate of Incorporation, Index No. 5415, Year 1926. **The only land it ever purchased and sold:** Nassau County Clerk's Office, Records of Purchases of Real Property—Onslow Estates (microfiche). The specific purchases and sales involved can be found in the County Book of Deeds—Liber No. 1075, p. 48; 1086, p. 5; 1101, p. 355; 1118, p. 251; 1128, p. 37; 1168, p. 247; 1181, p. 163; 1197, p. 160; 1235, p. 443; 1227, p. 379; 1517, p. 89. Also helpful were interviews with Hurley and confidential source. **Contracts to Weston and Hendrickson:** Hurley, Mayes, confidential source; various newspapers, various issues, 1927–29.

Doughty's friendship: Hall, Hurley, confidential interviews. The alliance between Moses and Doughty—and with Doughty's nephew and successor, J. Russel Sprague—was to be an open secret of Long Island politics for the next forty years.

Compromise in Albany: Wadsworth's orders: RM. The maneuvering is detailed in RM's interviews and the Smith Papers, the attempt to stop it in the Macy Papers. **Macy got his first hint:** Macy to Charles D. Hillies, Republican national committeeman, Apr. 4, 5, 1926, Macy Papers. (In one letter Macy raged: "The entire program of the Long Island State Park Commission is moving forward through a number of small and apparently unimportant bills in spite of . . . promises to the contrary.") He might have known earlier that he had been betrayed had he read, in a Brooklyn *Daily Times,* Feb. 19, 1926, account of one of his trips to Albany, an article evidently leaked to the paper by RM: "The joke is said to be that while the Long Islanders were in secret session at some hotel here [in Albany] on the best methods to block the Taylor estate park development, Governor Smith was fixing his signature to the appropriation bill, included in which is an appropriation for the park at East Islip." Macy-Hutchinson confrontation recounted in Macy to Hutchinson, Feb. 20, 1926.

Hidden appropriations for development of LI parks: It is impossible to locate all of them in state budgetary bills, or in the 1926 *LISPC Annual Report* or anything else RM wrote in this period—or in any newspaper. But they are detailed in a memorandum prepared by the Suffolk County Taxpayers Association, Apr. 4, 1926, entitled: "Long Island State Park Commission Program by Piece-meal Legislation," Smith Papers.

Smith inviting Hewitt and Hutchinson to LI: RM.

Trial before Strong: *NYT* and *HT,* May 18, 26, June 4, 8, 1926.

Bella and Emanuel: Israel Ben Scheiber, who was the social worker.

For both sides weren't equal: "A business affair": Havemeyer to Macy, Apr. 28, 1925. **"Ramifications":** Macy to Havemeyer, Jan. 5, 1926. **Printing bill:** Macy to Havemeyer, Apr. 23, 1928. **Stenographic bill:** Macy to Havemeyer, Dec. 23, 1926. **$10,000 bill:** Havemeyer to Macy, Apr. 28, 1925. **"My limit":** Havemeyer to Macy, Jan. 5, 1926. **Macy's determination to carry on alone:** Macy to Havemeyer, Jan. 5, 1926. **$43,192.61:** Havemeyer handwritten memo attached to letter to Macy, May 1, 1928. **Macy being dunned:** Martin A. Schenck, for Davies, Auerbach & Cornell, to Robbins (Macy's personal attorney), Apr. 22, 1929. The author cannot locate any definitive final total of Macy's court costs, but they appear to have been about $74,000. All of the documents cited above are in the Macy Papers.

Macy: See note, Chapter 11. **RM the only person he wanted to see:** Mrs. W. Kingsland Macy.

The lessons RM learned: Interviews with RM, Shapiro, Latham, Chapin and other RM aides.

Planning Jones Beach: RM, Shapiro, Gilmore Clarke, Mrs. Harold Morse.

13. Driving

SOURCES

Books:

Moses, *Dangerous Trade*; *Working for the People*; and *The State Park Plan for New York—Revised to Show Progress to Date*; Rodgers, *Robert Moses.* See also "Sources" for Chapter 6.

Author's interviews:

Dolie McWhinney Adams, Richard Boyce, Gilmore Clarke, Morris Ernst, James J. Flynn, Mrs. Elmer B. Howells, William J. Junkamen, William Latham, Michael J. Madigan, Mrs. Harold Morse, Sidney M. Shapiro, Mae Smisek.

NOTES

The need for haste: RM. **RM in action:** Junkamen, Clarke, Flynn, Latham; con-

fidential sources; Mrs. Morse. **Outings:** Dolie McWhinney Adams, Mae Smisek. **"No side":** Morris Ernst.

Inspiring designers: Shapiro, Clarke, Latham, LISPC official Richard Boyce.

Jones Beach: Rodgers, pp. 50–56; Shapiro. **$20,000:** Rodgers, pp. 54, 55; confirmed by Michael J. (Jack) Madigan, one of the firm's foremen. **Guggenheim:** Rodgers, pp. 52–53.

Babylon election: RM's feelings: RM, Shapiro, confidential source. **Coolness toward Mary in town:** Mrs. Howells. **RM threats:** LISPC press release, Apr. 12, 1928. **Finding the weak spot:** RM, confirmed by confidential source and Babylon Town Supervisor Joseph Warta. **Without warning, "Judases!":** Babylon *Leader*, Mar. 16, 1928; confidential sources. **No tolls:** RM letter to *Leader*, published Mar. 3, 1928. **Cooper's feelings:** His editorials in *Leader*. **State employees voting:** *Leader*, Apr. 16, 1928; Suffolk County Taxpayers Association press release, Apr. 17, 1928. The release states: "The State Park Commission . . . had at least ten automobiles in operation at this election. . . . It was further reported by the inspectors of election that many young men, unknown to them, had been brought in these cars and demanded the right to vote." Strangely, the release states, the registers customarily provided by the Town Board for poll inspectors to check the qualifications of voters were not provided this time. "There were no challengers at the polls and no one to decide upon the qualifications to vote of the young men brought to the polls in state automobiles, upon this occasion."

"Scandalous": *Leader*, Apr. 6, 1928.

"A vote of confidence": LISPC press release, Apr. 4, 1928, Macy Papers.

9,700 acres: *NYT*, Nov. 3, 1928. Overall progress from newspaper stories, spring and summer, 1928; *Annual Report of the LISPC*, 1928.

Editorials: *NYT*, *World*, Dec. 20, 1928.

State parks: Moses, *Dangerous Trade*, pp. 119–31; Moses, *Working for the People*, pp. 149, 167–80; Moses, *The State Park Plan for New York—Revised to Show Progress to Date* (1924). Attendance soared in the upstate parks as well as on Long Island: during the summer of 1928, 3,000,000 persons visited the new state parks in the Niagara and Allegheny regions, a million more than had visited them in 1925.

14. Changing

SOURCES

Books:

Graham, *Al Smith*; Moses, *A Tribute to Governor Smith*; see also "Sources," Chapter 6.

Author's interviews:

Howard S. Cullman, Leonard W. Hall, Carlos Israels, Joseph M. Proskauer, Ellwood M. Rabenold, Emily Smith Warner.

NOTES

No one bother to reply: On July 6, 1925, RM to Graves, he made one such suggestion, calling the writer a "crackpot"; on Oct. 2, 1924, he called another a "nut"; the increasing frequency of the suggestion that no reply be made is documented by letters in the Smith Papers.

Twomey story: Related by Hall; it was also related to the author by two other legislators of the era, who prefer to remain anonymous.

Park philanthropists' philosophy: *Annual Reports and Minutes of the ASHPS, Jan. 7, 1921–Feb. 14, 1927.*

Moses had let them believe: RM's statements and press releases of this period continually reiterate that the State Council of Parks would be only an "advisory body." The fact that the old men believed him is shown not only in their speeches and general support of his bills, but, specifically, in *Minutes* of society meetings, p. 460, for example.

"The height of impertinence": Staley to Kunz, quoted in society *Minutes*, p. 1431. The *Minutes* also show their growing realization of the significance of his bylaws.

Letchworth State Park: Society *Minutes*, Apr. 26, 1926, p. 1716; one trustee says there that the park should be kept as "a shrine" to nature. Another, p. 1487, quotes Wordsworth's "one impulse from a vernal wood . . ." Through a series of manipulations and behind-the-scenes bureaucratic ploys, backed in the crunch by Smith's power, RM eventually succeeded in ousting the defiant society trustees and in transforming Letchworth Park along the lines he envisioned.

Niagara and Clearwater: Obituary, Kingston *Leader* and Kingston *Daily Freeman*, Sept. 23, 1933; *NYT*, Sept. 24, 1933. **"Your views are just":** RM to Smith, Dec. 17, 1924, Clearwater to RM, Dec. 12, 1924, Smith Papers. **Wilcox:** Obituary, Buffalo *Evening News*

and *NYT*, Jan. 27, 1930. **Knew he was dying:** De Forest to Smith, June 22, 1926, Smith Papers. **Schoellkopf's cooperation:** "Transcript" cited below, p. 163. **Clearwater swaying Treman:** Society *Minutes*. **RM embarrassed:** "Transcript" cited below, p. 21; on p. 45, RM says, "We have made ourselves ridiculous at Albany." **Dispute over parkway:** "Transcript," pp. 16–32: RM's real worry, although he never states it in so many words, is revealed by a statement he makes on p. 25. **Doctors gave him no chance:** Wilcox to Smith, June 22, 1926, Smith Papers.

RM moving against the old men: Three documents are central—a 210-page "Transcript, Joint Conference, Special Committee of State Council of Parks and State Reservation at Niagara, July 15, 1926" (hereafter referred to as "Transcript"); "Report of Special Committee Appointed by the State Council of Parks to Examine and Report on the Matter of a Connecting Parkway from the State Reservation at Niagara across Grand Island, and Upon the Matters Referred to in the Letter of His Excellency, Hon. Alfred E. Smith, Governor of the State of New York, dated June 3rd, 1924, Adopted by the State Council of Parks at a Meeting Held on July 24th, 1926, at Binghamton" (hereafter referred to as "Report"); Wilcox's last letter to RM, Aug. 5, 1926 (hereafter referred to as "Wilcox Letter"). These documents were found in a sealed manila folder in the Smith Papers that had apparently never been opened. The folder is identified only as "200-276-2."

Wilcox believes RM wrote "Smith" letter: "Wilcox Letter," pp. 5, 6; the original draft cannot be found in the Smith Papers, but if RM did not actually write it, and Smith send it out substantially unchanged, over his signature, it would be the only such letter from Smith on the subject of parks, out of hundreds the author examined in the Smith Papers.

June 26 Parks Council meeting: The Niagara Commission's resolutions are contained in "Minutes, State Reservation at Niagara," attached to Wilcox to Smith, June 22, 1926, Smith Papers. **Moses never even told the council of their existence:** Wilcox to Lutz, Aug. 21, 1926, Smith Papers. **"The stenographer was told to omit things":** "Wilcox Letter," p. 7. In the "Transcript," there are "discussions off the record," on pp. 93 and 164; the unreported "argument" is on p. 132.

Not an investigation: "Transcript," p. 7. **RM's interruption:** p. 11. **"Just one minute":** p. 153. **Downer's "I have no fault to find":** p. 155, repeated on p. 166. **"What if it was, Mr. Moses?":** p. 164.

"The opportunity is slipping": Wilcox to Smith, Aug. 4, 1926, Smith Papers. **Sure Downer would be fair:** "Wilcox Letter," p. 8. **Downer's exoneration.** "Report," pp. 4–5. **Report not distributed:** "Wilcox Letter," pp. 3–9.

Letter to Lutz: Wilcox's innocuous letter is in Smith Papers; RM to Wilcox Aug. 4, 1926, Smith Papers. **"In Wilcox's view":** "Wilcox Letter."

"Commission not functioning": RM to Smith, May 25, 1927, Smith Papers. **De Forest to Smith:** No date visible, Smith Papers. **Clearwater's letter:** Clearwater to Smith, Mar. 28, 1927, Smith Papers. **RM convinces Smith:** RM to Smith, May 25, 1927, Smith Papers. (Smith sent the letter embodying the changes, a letter written by RM, same date.)

Al Smith stuck: "I am very sure": De Forest to Smith, no date visible, Smith Papers. **"You idiot!":** Graham, p. 139. **Smith on Mills and the barons:** *NYT*, Oct. 26, 28, 1926. **Emily's analysis:** Interview with author. **Parks were an improvement he could see:** Perkins OHR and several interviewees made this comment. **Smith didn't realize how drastic . . . :** Emily Smith Warner.

"We could have done nothing without him": Moses, *A Tribute to Governor Smith*, pp. 17–18; Israels, Proskauer. **"I wonder what Bob's doing tonight":** Cullman. **"A tie":** Cullman.**"You could tell":** Rabenold.

15. *Curator of Cauliflowers*

SOURCES

Books:

Dahlberg, *The New York Bureau of Municipal Research*; Freidel, *Franklin Delano Roosevelt: The Ordeal* and *Franklin Delano Roosevelt: The Triumph*; Handlin, *Al Smith and His America*; Hapgood and Moskowitz, *Up from the City Streets*; Lipson, *The American Governor*; Moscow: *What Have You Done for Me Lately?*; Pringle, *Alfred E. Smith*; Rodgers, *Robert Moses*; Schlesinger, *The Age of Roosevelt*, Vol. I: *The Crisis of the Old Order* and Vol. III: *The Politics of Upheaval*; Warner, *The Happy Warrior*. See also "Sources" for Chapter 6.

Author's interviews:

Israel Ben Scheiber, William S. Chapin, Richard S. Childs, Ernest J. Clark, Jane Moses Collins, John A. Coleman, Perry B. Duryea, Jr., Mrs. Hilda E. Hellman, Mrs. Elmer B. Howells, Carlos Israels, John Krumenacker, William Latham, Richard Mayes, Robert Payne, Joseph M. Proskauer, Mrs. Helen Roth, Jimmy Roth, Sidney M. Shapiro, Bertram D. Tallamy, Hazel Tappan, Emily Smith Warner.

NOTES

State reorganization: Three books—Dahlberg, pp. 93–112, Hapgood and Moskowitz, and Lipson—describe it in detail, as did Richard S. Childs in interviews with the author.

Al Smith said so: Quoted in Warner, p. 173. His daughter herself says, "In his own belief the work he did in reorganizing the state government stood first" among all his achievements, p. 173. **"Against the tide of the Twenties":** Freidel, *Triumph*, p. 11; Handlin, p. 186. **Roosevelt was to say:** Schlesinger, *Politics*, p. 520. **Lippmann:** To Smith, Nov. 6, 1925, Smith Papers. **Wagner:** Hapgood and Moskowitz, p. 218. **"The great classic":** Lipson, p. 90.

Secretary of State: RM to be a "Deputy Governor": Brooklyn *Eagle*, Jan. 25, 1927. An unidentified GOP senator is quoted as saying: "We were given to understand by the Governor that the new Secretary of State job is to be the most important of them all." **Politicians raged:** Pringle, p. 258. **"The most hated man in Albany":** Israels. **Wanted to formalize the arrangement:** Hapgood and Moskowitz, p. 186. **"None of the objectors":** *Eagle*, Jan. 21, 1927; see also Feb. 2, 1927. **Brown postcard and Thompson reply:** Quoted in *Eagle*, Jan. 24, 1927. **Relatives commenting:** Hellman. **Bella's comment:** Ben Scheiber, the Madison House head worker to whom she made the comment when he brought her the news.

Boxing: W. O. McGeehan's "Down the Line" columns in the *Tribune* in 1927 furnish many humorous anecdotes about the Annie Oakley controversy. Quote is from his column of Mar. 24, 1927. **Farley:** *NYT*, Feb. 19, 1927. **"Any decision should be unanimous":** RM quoted in Rodgers, p. 65. **"Frankly admitting":** *Tribune*, Jan. 20, 1928.

Put RM in charge of Cabinet; made RM personally responsible: RM, Proskauer, Coleman.

He set his life into a hard mold: Shapiro, Latham, Jane Moses Collins, Mrs. Howells, Miss Tappan, Lazarus, Israels, Childs, confidential sources. **Duryea:** Interview with author. **A woman:** Confidential source. **One executive:** Latham. **Secretaries:** Confidential sources. **"Loved that bay":** Mrs. Howells. **"He wasn't so tense then":** Latham. **Picking men, chain of command:** Shapiro. **Chapin afraid to leave desk:** Chapin. **Observer:** Moscow, p. 205. **Tallamy:** Tallamy. **Overcoming Shapiro's shyness:** Shapiro. **Suicide:** The name of the aide involved, a young assistant counsel of the LISPC, is withheld at the request of a friend because, forty years later, his mother still suffers from the recollection. **Executives' homes:** One row of homes is on a secluded, difficult-to-reach street in Belmont Lake State Park, south of the Southern State Parkway.

The satisfaction of working for him: Although this was a theme repeated to the author by many architects and engineers, it was stated especially forcefully and perceptively by Ernie Clark, president of Andrews & Clark, in an interview with the author. **Summary of achievements under Smith:** Rodgers, pp. 58–64. **Firing the engineer:** Coleman. **The two speeches:** Transcripts made by stenographer Lloyd Record on commission for W. Kingsland Macy (found in Macy Papers) of speeches by RM before the Eastern Long Island Real Estate Board at the Canoe Place Inn, Hampton Bays, June 16, 1927; and before the Long Island Real Estate Board at the Montauk Manor, Montauk, Sept. 9, 1927.

"Whether the commissioners . . .": RM quoted in *Tribune*, Feb. 4, 1927.

Bathhouses: Perkins OHR, Vol. III, p. 367. **Speeding motorcade:** RM denied the charges of speeding, but residents of the villages still remember the incident, and articles in the Babylon *Leader* (for example, Aug. 12, 1927) and the Brooklyn *Daily Times* quote people who saw it. **Cooper editorial:** Aug. 5, 1927.

Compromising with the barons: Latham, Richard Mayes, Robert Payne; FDR to Francis P. Garvan, Apr. 9, 1929, FDR Papers.

The Roths: The author's interviews with Mrs. James J. (Helen) Roth and Jimmy Roth. The feelings of other farmers were obtained by Ina Joan Caro from John Krumenacker, who owned an adjoining farm. The author also interviewed RM's aide William Latham, who handled the engineering under which the route was shifted. Latham recalled vividly

the negotiations with De Forest. He couldn't remember the farmers at all.

"Bob, it's over": Warner, p. 205; Handlin, pp. 112–36. **RM ran the state for Smith:** Proskauer, Cullman, Warner. **Screened out hate mail:** Warner.

16. The Featherduster

SOURCES

The relationship of the three men—Smith, Roosevelt and Moses—before and during FDR's Governorship is described —from widely varying points of view but never in sufficient depth—in Bellush, *Roosevelt as Governor*; Farley, *Behind the Ballots* and *Jim Farley's Story*; Handlin, *Al Smith and His America*; Proskauer, *A Segment of My Times*; Rodgers, *Robert Moses*; Warner, *The Happy Warrior*; as well as in Flynn, *You're the Boss*; Freidel, *Franklin D. Roosevelt: The Ordeal* and *Franklin D. Roosevelt: The Triumph*; Ickes, *The Secret Diary of Harold L. Ickes*, Vol. I: *The First Thousand Days*; Perkins, *The Roosevelt I Knew*; Rosenman, *Working with Roosevelt*; Schlesinger, *The Crisis of the Old Order*; Stiles, *The Man Behind Roosevelt*; Moley, *27 Masters of Politics*; Sherwood, *Roosevelt and Hopkins*. But the primary sources used for these chapters are the Smith, FDR and Morgenthau Papers; the Reuben A. Lazarus, George Van Schaick and Frances Perkins OHR's (Miss Perkins is franker in her OHR than in her book); interviews with observers of the Albany scene at the time, including Adolph A. Berle, Jr., Carlos Israels, Michael J. Madigan, Lazarus, Proskauer and Albert L. Warner—and RM himself, who discussed Roosevelt with some tact in *Dangerous Trade* but whose hatred spilled over in "Why I Oppose the Fourth Term," *The Saturday Evening Post*, Oct. 17, 1944, and in interviews with the author. These sources —taken all in all—present a picture of the Smith-Roosevelt conflict that suggests more strongly than do any of the Roosevelt biographers, except, possibly, Freidel, a picture of the older Governor as wronged.

NOTES

FDR's relationship with Smith circle: Schlesinger; Freidel, *The Triumph*; Handlin, pp. 138–40. **Eleanor and the teapot:** Freidel, *The Ordeal*, p. 200. **FDR telephoning RM:** RM, Israels. **"Pissroom":** Albert Warner. **"Featherduster," "a harmless bust":** Schlesinger, pp. 323, 331. **Haughtiness in Albany:** Schlesinger, p. 338. **"Happy Warrior" speech:** This story was related to the author by Proskauer and RM in interviews. Carlos Israels says that Belle Moskowitz had told it to him, and Emily Smith Warner says she was told it by her father. **"Showy but harmless"; Mrs. M worried:** Proskauer.

"Secretary and valet": Rodgers, p. 39; RM, Madigan; the incident, although not the exact wording of what RM said to FDR, is confirmed in Smith Papers. **FDR "cared deeply about nature":** Schlesinger, pp. 334–35. **1922 proposal:** Freidel, *The Ordeal*, p. 149. **FDR's plans for the Taconic region:** In great detail and with great enthusiasm, in various letters to Smith, most notably Dec. 3, 1926, Smith Papers, **"Splendid project":** FDR to Smith, Dec. 3, 1926, Smith Papers. **RM's feelings:** Confidential source. **"Absurd and humiliating":** FDR to Smith, Dec. 3, 1926, Smith Papers. **"I suggest you write him":** RM to Smith, Dec. 23, 1926, Smith Papers; Smith did so, sending the letter out, over his signature, exactly as written, Jan. 10, 1927. **"No function left":** FDR to Smith, Dec. 30, 1927, Smith Papers. **Revealing letter:** FDR to Smith, Jan. 30, 1928, Smith Papers. **"I know of no man":** Smith to FDR, Feb. 3, 1928, Smith Papers.

Roosevelt nominating Smith: Freidel, *The Ordeal*, p. 243. **"It's a pity":** Perkins OHR Vol. III, pp. 40–41. **Decision to urge FDR to run:** Freidel, *The Ordeal*, pp. 250–56; Emily Smith Warner; RM. **RM to Emily at the convention:** Warner, p. 239. **Rosenman:** Schlesinger, pp. 283–85; Freidel, *The Ordeal*, pp. 261–62. **RM to Perkins:** Perkins OHR Vol. I, p. 422; Vol. III, p. 40. **"Vicious":** Confidential source. Berle told the author RM "always talked badly about Eleanor Roosevelt. **Roosevelt to Perkins:** Perkins OHR, Vol. III, pp. 11, 372. **"Real hatred":** Lazarus.

He meant it: Most of Roosevelt's biographers take Smith's post-1928 disclaimers of presidential ambitions at less than face value, but the author's interviews with such Smith intimates and observers of both men as, among others, Smith's daughter, Proskauer, Lazarus, Cullman, John A. Coleman and RM, have led him to conclude that this assessment is unfair. He feels the definitive word on the subject is provided by the recollections of Edward J. Flynn (in *You're the Boss*) and James A. Farley (in *Behind the Ballots*, written while

Farley was still friendly with Roosevelt). **"Same team":** Proskauer, p. 64. **Roosevelt had pledged to continue Smith's work:** Freidel, *The Ordeal,* pp. 261-63. **He "forgot":** Schlesinger (pp. 386–87) gives a different, more pro-FDR interpretation of this period.

"Generally, for that is what we said": Freidel, *The Triumph,* p. 12.

Roosevelt's character: Moley, pp. 36–44; Sherwood, p. 9; Handlin, p. 144.

Conflict over RM: "That was the way it was set up": RM. **RM meeting with Roosevelt:** RM.

Letter of resignation: RM to Roosevelt, Dec. 18, 1928, printed in *NYT,* Dec. 19. **FDR reply:** *NYT,* Dec. 20, 1928. **Editorials:** *World, NYT,* Dec. 20, 1928.

Roosevelt pursuing Flynn: Flynn, pp. 74–77. The fact that Flynn never devoted much time to the job rankled RM, who had wanted it to be one of continuing importance, and he told the author that one day, at least a year after his appointment, Flynn arrived at the building in which the Secretary of State's office was located, and didn't know what floor it was on.

FDR's "wistful smile": Quoted in Freidel, *The Triumph,* p. 20. **RM stalking out:** RM, confirmed by Albert Warner, who was covering the inauguration for the *NYT,* and by Lazarus.

17. The Mother of Accommodation

SOURCES

Books:

Farley, *Behind the Ballots*; Flynn, *You're the Boss*; Handlin, *Al Smith and His America*; Josephson and Josephson, *Al Smith: Hero of the Cities*; Rodgers, *Robert Moses*; Sobin, *Dynamics of Community Change.* See also "Sources" for Chapter 16.

Author's interviews:

Howard S. Cullman, Eugene Hurley, Reuben A. Lazarus, Ann and Louis Lubin, Sidney M. Shapiro, Emily Smith Warner.

Oral History Reminiscence:

Frances Perkins.

NOTES

Northern State Parkway fight: The author's understanding of the veiled phrases in the correspondence from the FDR Papers was aided by Sidney M. Shapiro, who offered the assistance with the stipulation that he not be named unless he died (which he has since done), and by two confidential sources, one on RM's staff. It was when the author attempted to question RM about the $10,000 Kahn "gift" that RM broke off the interviews and refused further cooperation with this book. **Clark and RM writing to FDR at Warm Springs:** FDR refers to Clark telegram in FDR to RM, Nov. 23, 1928, FDR Papers.

FDR backing RM at first: Conversations referred to in Clark to FDR, Mar. 29, 1929, FDR Papers.

Hutchinson and Hewitt telegram to RM: Mar. 21, 1929. **RM defiant:** RM to FDR, Mar. 21, 1929, FDR Papers. (The crucial sentence: "Mr. Kahn generously offered to buy three of four small pieces of land owned by farmers who could not afford to dedicate.") **"Will not make a creditable chapter":** Clark to FDR, Mar. 29, 1929, FDR Papers.

Clark ultimatum: ". . . while we are ready and anxious to arrive at some adjustment and agreement, in the event that this cannot be done, there seems to be nothing to do but to fight the matter out to a conclusion by presenting the matter carefully on its merits. It would be too bad if we have to go through a long controversy on this subject. But what is there to do . . . ," Clark to FDR, Oct. 23, 1929, FDR Papers. **Actual cost $2,250,000:** Sobin, p. 105. **RM has to promise no parks:** Shapiro, Hurley, confidential source.

"A bond on your signature": Lazarus. **A new routine:** RM, Emily Smith Warner.

Begging Lutz: FDR to Lutz, Jan 17, 1931, FDR Papers. **LI Democrats:** Nassau Democratic leader Krug to FDR, Sept. 14, 1930, FDR Papers.

"An old school boyfriend": FDR to RM, Apr. 23, 1930, FDR Papers. Among other humiliations the Governor had to suffer over the question of patronage was one that occurred when he began running for the presidency in 1932. A key Massachusetts supporter wrote him asking for a promotion for a relative on the LISPC staff, FDR wrote RM, and RM replied, in a letter to FDR's secretary, James J. Mahoney, "I think the efforts of this young man to get himself some sort of special preference through political channels in Massachusetts is wholly improper. . . . The best thing this young man can do is to take his medicine and be glad that he has a job of any

kind." Buckley to FDR, Apr. 9, 1932; FDR to RM, Apr. 12, 1932; RM to Mahoney, Apr. 19, 1932, FDR Papers.

Fort Schuyler: A long series of letters from FDR to the Army and from influentials to FDR in "Fort Schuyler" folder, FDR Papers. **Straus speech:** *NYT*, June 24, 1932.

Executive budget fight: The definitive discussion is in Freidel, *The Triumph,* Chapter 4. **RM's advice:** RM to Mark Graves, State Budget Director, Oct. 15, 1931, FDR Papers.

Jones Beach: Attendance: Newspapers and *Annual Report of the LISPC,* 1929. **Biehl:** *NYT,* Aug. 18, 1931. **Englishman:** Rodgers, p. 56. **"You will feel like a heel":** *Shell Progress.* **"Magical":** Rodgers, pp. 188–89. **"No concessions"; attendance:** Relevant *Annual Reports of the LISPC.* **"More than doubled":** *Annual Report of the LISPC,* 1930, p. 6.

$75,000: RM. **Ocean highway:** RM quoted in *NYT,* June 25, 1930. **The Smith sisters:** RM to FDR, Aug. 17, 1931; Waldridge, another Fire Island landowner, to RM, Aug. 21, 1931, FDR Papers. **Typical RM threat to resign:** RM to FDR, Nov. 10, 1930, FDR Papers. **Typical FDR backing away:** FDR to RM, May 9, 1933, FDR Papers.

Inviting Lehman and not FDR: Shapiro. **FDR tour:** *HT,* Aug. 4, 1930. **"Best money ever spent":** FDR quoted in *NYT,* July 27, 1931.

Valley Stream grade-crossing elimination: Worst one on LI: *NYT,* Apr. 15, 1931. **FDR signing the petition:** *NYT,* July 27, 1931. RM's work on the problem detailed in correspondence with FDR, Aug. 1, 1931–May 2, 1932, FDR Papers. **"I must ask to be relieved" and FDR's reply:** May 9, 1932 FDR Papers.

Torrey incident: Torrey's account of it in Torrey to FDR, Oct. 5, 1929, FDR Papers. RM's statement, issued Oct. 16, 1929, said, "There is a good deal of picturesque exaggeration in Torrey's reference to my language and conduct," but does not deny any specific point in Torrey's account. Newspaper accounts, which quote witnesses of the incident and contain the RM and FDR quotes, in *NYT* and *HT,* Oct. 7, 1929. **Among his closest friends:** Ann and Louis Lubin. **Reducing Torrey's salary, ASHPS position.** ASHPS *Minutes,* p. 1784.

Distaste for public: Perkins OHR. **Bridges low:** Shapiro. **"Dirty":** Shapiro, Windels. **Permits, "flagging," pool temperature:** Windels, Kern. **FDR investigation:** Mills to FDR, Aug. 24, 1932; Gorton to Cross, Sept. 2, 1932, FDR Papers.

"Badge of poverty": Daniel Mitchell of Enfield Falls to FDR, no date, FDR Papers. **"Legitimate kick":** FDR to RM, Aug. 19, 1930, FDR Papers. **"I do not care to be associated":** RM to FDR, Aug. 22, 1930, FDR Papers. **FDR's veto:** *NYT,* Mar. 22, 1932.

Special assignments: Among them was bulldozing through a bridge bypass to carry Northern Boulevard around Roslyn that had been stalled for years by the opposition of Roslynites to State DPW plans; thinking up a solution for frequent brush fires in Suffolk County pine barrens (RM's solution was the building of watchtowers staffed by an augmented state forest ranger force); and investigating a series of rapes at Girl Scout camps in Palisades Interstate Park.

"Do you know, by God": Josephson and Josephson, p. 435. **Walker humiliating Smith:** Cullman, confidential source. **Farley and Flynn:** Farley, *Behind the Ballots, passim*; Flynn, *passim.* **"He felt . . . hurt":** Perkins OHR. **RM's recollections:** In interview with author. **"A fight to the death":** Josephson and Josephson, p. 440; best account of Smith's defeat in Farley, *Behind the Ballots,* pp. 78–79, 80–95.

18. New York City Before Robert Moses

SOURCES

Books:

Lillian Brandt, *An Impressionistic View of the Winter of 1930–31 in New York City*; Ellis, *The Epic of New York City*; Garrett, *The La Guardia Years*; Mann, *La Guardia Comes to Power*; Mitgang, *The Man Who Rode the Tiger;* Rankin, *New York Advancing, 1934–1935*; Rodgers, *Robert Moses*; Schlesinger, *The Age of Roosevelt,* Vol. II: *The Coming of the New Deal.*

Author's interviews:

With two La Guardia officials, Paul J. Kern and Joseph D. McGoldrick; Iphigene Ochs Sulzberger; and Park Department officials John Mulcahy and Samuel White.

NOTES

New York during the Depression: Ellis, pp. 532–33; Brandt, p. v. **Schoolteacher and nurse:** Quoted in Brandt, pp. 6, 8, 18. **Clinics:** Brandt, p. 10. **"Everywhere**

there seemed": Gellhorn, quoted in Schlesinger, p. 272.

Seabury investigation: Ellis, Mann, Mitgang books. **"This is how we make Democrats":** Ellis, p. 540.

City's debt: Harold Phelps Stokes, article in *NYT*, May 28, 1933; Rankin, p. 39.

"Engineers" without diplomas: Kern. **"The city did not get"; subway:** McGoldrick. **Schools:** Garrett, p. 57.

Strangling: *NYT*, *HT*, various issues, 1931–33. **West Side Highway:** See RM brochures, quoted, Chapter 25. Also Stephen G. Bick to *NYT*, Oct. 24, 1933. **Conditions on Queensborough Bridge:** *NYT*, Aug. 8, 1930, July 18, 1933. **Henry Hudson Bridge:** RM's brochures. **Narrows tube:** Ina Joan Caro, "Building a Public Work in a Democracy: The Verrazano-Narrows Bridge (unpublished M.A. thesis), pp. 13–28. **Triborough history:** Many articles; for example *NYT*, Aug. 15, 1934. **A dozen accidents a day:** *NYT*, Dec. 25, 1933.

Parks: Brooklyn Park Department: *HT*, Apr. 11, 1934; June 26, 1934. **Beach front rented out:** *HT*, Jan. 11, 1931; *NYT*, Feb. 28, 1934; Mrs. Sulzberger, PD official John Mulcahy. **Not a single structure, statues:** Park Association survey quoted in *NYT*, June 6, 1934; also *NYT Magazine*, July 15, 1934. **Bryant Park:** *NYT*, Feb. 3, 1932; July 23, 1932; Nov. 26, 1932; *HT*, Feb. 17, 1934. **Central Park:** Eugene Kinkead and Russell Maloney, "Profiles—Central Park," *The New Yorker*, Sept. 13, 20, 27, 1941. **Zoo:** *The New Yorker*, Dec. 1, 1934. **"A player standing on line":** *HT*, Jan. 26, 1934. **"You couldn't tell the difference":** Mulcahy. **Curtaining off toilets:** PD official Samuel H. White. **Chopin nocturne:** *The New Yorker*, Sept. 20, 1941. **Hoovervilles:** Various newspaper articles, 1932–33; *HT*, Apr. 27, 1934. **Lack of park land:** *Architectural Forum*, Dec. 1936, p. 503. **No parks in slums:** Author's study of borough park department maps, pre-Moses. **One reformer:** Allen Jacobs to *NYT*, printed Mar. 8, 1931. **"The wistful faces":** Dorothy Bromley in *NYT*, May 6, 1934.

Casino: *The New Yorker*, Sept. 20, 1941; various newspaper articles, 1932–1933.

Pleading with officials for roads: RM. **Triborough Bridge:** RM quoted in Rodgers, p. 98.

RM's plan: Metropolitan Conference on Parks, "Program for Extension of Parks and Parkways in the Metropolitan Region," Feb. 25, 1930. Among those watching in the audience who recall details of his appearance are Paul Windels (La Guardia's Corporation Counsel), Shapiro, Madigan and Childs. **Lack of cooperation from city officials.** RM.

Lehman's admiration for RM: Confidential sources. **State Emergency Public Works Commission:** Rodgers, pp. 76–77. **City wasting Triborough funds:** Rodgers, p. 98.

City's financial situation worsening: Garrett, pp. 142–50.

19. To Power in the City

SOURCES

Books and documents:

Garrett, *The La Guardia Years*; Mann, *La Guardia Comes to Power*; Mitgang *The Man Who Rode the Tiger*; Moscow, *What Have You Done for Me Lately?*; Rodgers, *Robert Moses*; and the collections of personal papers of three key Fusion figures—Maurice P. Davidson, W. Kingsland Macy and Joseph M. Price.

Oral History Reminiscences:

Joseph M. Price, Paul Windels.

Author's interviews:

Adolf A. Berle, Jr., Richard S. Childs, Paul J. Kern, William Latham, Reuben A. Lazarus, Michael J. Madigan, Joseph D. McGoldrick, Sidney M. Shapiro, Iphigene Ochs Sulzberger, Paul Windels.

NOTES

Seabury hearings: Mitgang, pp. 158–310. **O'Brien's gaffes:** Mann, p. 90. **Reformers viewing RM paternally:** Tone of letters and memos in Price and Davidson Papers; Childs, Windels.

"Only partially valid": Garrett, p. 20. **McGahen:** Quoted in Mann, p. 81.

Wald: Lillian Wald to RM, Oct. 30, 1936, Price Papers. **Didn't know details of those triumphs:** The author's conclusion from his interviews with Childs, McGoldrick and other reformers and from his study of Price and Davidson Papers. **"High purpose":** Childs. **"Starry-eyed":** Windels. **Favorable publicity:** "No man has gotten more praise recently," the Brooklyn *Eagle* noted on Jan. 14, 1933. **"If Moses ran, they believed":** New York *Evening Post*, July 15, 1933. **RM contacted by Price, assures him he will accept nomination; an almost unani-**

mously favorable response: Draft of proposed Price press release (never released), undated but probably May 18, 1933, Price Paper. See also *WT*, July 6, 1933.

Seabury's opinion of RM: RM; Garrett, p. 101; Mann, p. 83; Mitgang, pp. 316–18; Price press release: "Statement of Reason for Joseph M. Price's Withdrawal from Fusion Conference: Judge Seabury's Objections to Robert Moses's Availability as Mayoral Candidate" (unreleased and undated but probably July 1933), Price Papers; Price to reformer Richard Welling, July 18, 1933, RM to Price, July 29, 1933, Price Papers.

Seabury biography: Mitgang book; Mann, pp. 38–46.

"Reserve all personal liberty": RM. **"I am not a candidate":** RM quoted in *NYT*, July 12, 1933. **RM feels Seabury will back him:** RM. **Five reformers:** The judges were John C. Knox and Clarence J. Shearn, the business executive Richard C. Patterson, Jr., vice president of NBC. **Davidson on Straus:** Davidson Papers, memo entitled: "Wanted: A Mayor," pp. 54–59. **LaG "standing in the wings":** Davidson Papers, quoted in Mann, p. 79. **LaG biography:** See "Sources" for Chapter 23. **Reformers' attitude toward him:** Mann, pp. 67–72. **Seabury's attitude:** Mann, pp. 72–75, 80. **18 for RM, 5 for LaG:** Price Papers.

Seabury-Davidson lunch: Seabury quoted in Davidson, "Interview as Recorded," p. 26, Davidson Papers. **RM tells Price not to nominate him:** RM. **O'Ryan episode:** Mann, pp. 84–85. **"Sit down, Sam":** Mann, p. 86.

RM's participation in campaign: Windels. His statements: *NYT*, Oct. 26, 28, Nov. 3, 1933.

WT editorial: Nov. 4, 1933. **"Sidewalks of New York":** Windels gave the order to play it; Windels.

"It was like he owned the United States": Marie La Guardia quoted in Mann, p. 20. **Driving around on Sundays:** Kern. **Hated lawyers:** Kern, Lazarus. **LaG feared Smith:** Windels. **"I told the Mayor":** RM in *NYT Magazine*, Aug. 16, 1936.

"I'm appointing the best man": Mrs. Sulzberger. **Drafting his own bill:** Raymond P. McNulty to LaG, Dec. 27, 1933. Letter obtained from confidential source.

Neither man considered the Triborough appointment particularly significant: Windels, Lazarus, RM, Madigan. **"No man is big enough":** Senator Thomas F. Burchill, quoted in *NYT*, Jan. 16, 1934. **RM tells LaG not to worry:** Lazarus. **"The finger":** Moscow, p. 199. **Reformers influencing legislators:** *NYT*, Jan. 10; *HT*, Jan. 17, 1934. **"No possible conflict of interest":** LaG quoted in *NYT*, Jan. 7, 1934. **"Nothing to get excited about":** RM quoted in *WT*, Jan. 6, 1934.

CWA was ruining the parks: Summary, Rodgers, p. 83. **Marine Park:** *HT*, Feb. 1, 1934.

Orchard Beach: *NYT* and *HT*, Feb. 28, 1934; Shapiro, Latham. **The notebook:** "Pattern for Parks," *Architectural Forum*, Dec. 1936. **"His orders just poured out":** Shapiro. **RM standing at Orchard Beach:** Latham, confidential source.

20. One Year

SOURCES

Books, articles and documents:

The basic source for this chapter is the hundreds of articles on Robert Moses, his rebuilding of New York City's parks and his building of parkways and the Triborough Bridge that appeared on almost a daily basis, month after month, in New York's newspapers during 1934.

Rodgers, *Robert Moses*; Moses, *Dangerous Trade*; Phillips, *From the Crash to the Blitz*; Rankin, *New York Advancing, 1934–35*, pp. 127–36; Moscow, *What Have You Done for Me Lately?*; Talese, *The Bridge*; Reed, *Central Park*; WPA, *New York Panorama*; PWA, Moses, "Report on Accomplishments of Park Department in First Two Years of Fusion Administration," 1936 (hereafter referred to as "Two Years"); Moses, *Four Years of Park Progress*, 1937 (hereafter referred to as *Four Years*). Triborough Bridge Authority, "The Triborough Bridge, a Modern Metropolitan Traffic Artery, July 11, 1936"; "Fifth Anniversary of the Opening of the Triborough Bridge," July 11, 1941.

"Pattern for Parks," *Architectural Forum*, Dec. 1936; "Robert (Or-I'll-Resign) Moses," *Fortune*, June 1938; Hubert Herring, "Robert Moses and His Parks," *Harper's*, Dec. 1937; Moses, "Municipal Recreation," *American Architect and Architecture*, Nov. 1936; Moses, "The Changing City," *Architectural Forum*, Mar. 1940; *The New Yorker*'s 1941 series on Central Park.

Park Department Files; La Guardia and Davidson Papers.

Author's interviews:

With ten of RM's top aides—William S. Chapin, Ernest J. Clark, Gilmore

Clarke, James A. Dawson, Richard Guthridge, William Latham, Michael J. Madigan, Sidney M. Shapiro and two who cannot be identified; three of his personal secretaries—Hazel Tappan, Nettie Greenberg and one who cannot be identified; nineteen architects who worked for the Park Department—Simon Brines, Isaiah Ehrlich, Harry Gould, Richard Korchien, David Levine, Irving Levine, George Levy, Joshua Lowenfish, Janet Patt, Bernie Rosen, Allen Saalberg, Carl Schilling, Clarence Stein, Robert Weinberg, Henry Wright, Michael Zimmer and three who prefer not to be identified (most of the interviews with these architects were conducted by Mrs. Priscilla Worland Burton); Mrs. Lidia Nelson, executive secretary of the Architects Emergency Committee; also Adolf A. Berle, Jr., John A. Coleman, Howard S. Cullman, Emily Smith Warner, Paul Windels.

NOTES

The weeding out: Dawson, Latham, Madigan, confidential source. **Confronting CWA:** PD Files, LaG Papers, Latham.

Proportion of architects and engineers out of work: W. A. Shoudy, "The Engineer and the Depression," *The Nation,* Sept. 13, 1933; Talbot Faulkner Hamlin, "The Architect and the Depression," *The Nation,* Aug. 9, 1933. **"When you got inside":** Clark. **Scene at Arsenal:** Interviews cited above.

"I see to it": RM quoted in Brooklyn *Eagle,* May 9, 1935. **The firings:** *NYT* and *HT*, Feb. 1, 1934. **Scenes among laborers:** Interviews cited above. **"We expect the men to work":** RM quoted in *NYT*, Feb. 1, 1934 (italics added). **The winter of '34:** Phillips, pp. 317–18, says: "For brutish, man-killing, soul-destroying weather the years between 1934 and 1938 probably cannot be matched in the climatological annals of the United States." **Embury:** article in *NYT*, Feb. 27, 1934. **Tablecloth:** Clarke.

Every structure: Rankin, pp. 127–136; "Two Years"; *Four Years.* **Park benches:** "Topics of the Times" in *NYT*, May 18, 1934. **Bryant Park opening:** *HT*, Sept. 9, 1934. The speaker was John Finley, a leading conservationist. **Central Park:** *The New Yorker,* Sept. 13, 20, 27, 1941; Dorothy Dunbar Bromley, "New Vistas Open for Manhattan's Oasis," *NYT Magazine,* Apr. 15, 1934. **Creating new parks:** Latham, Shapiro. **RM asked LaG:** PD Files, LaG Papers. **Chrystie-Forsyth:** *NYT*, Feb. 1, 1934; cost tabulation: *Architectural Forum,* Dec. 1936. **Unappropriated state lands:** Moses, *Dangerous Trade,* p. 3; Shapiro. RM's awareness of their potentiality as city parks is documented in Smith Papers as far back as 1927 (RM to Smith, Apr. 23, 1927). **Red Hook swampland:** RM to LaG, Mar. 26, 1934, LaG Papers. **War Memorial Playgrounds:** *HT* and *NYT*, Mar. 2; *NYT*, Mar. 20, 23; Berle, in interview with author, contended that *he* conceived the switch from monument to playgrounds, but this contention is not supported by evidence in the LaG Papers. **Two tennis courts:** RM to LaG, Mar. 26. **Consolidated Gas:** *NYT*, Dec. 1. **Rothstein estate:** RM to Delehanty, July 23; Delehanty to RM, July 25; RM to LaG, July 27; LaG to RM, Aug. 5; Earle Andrews to La Guardia aide Lester Stone, Sept. 27; Stone to Andrews, Oct. 1; LaG Papers. **Rockefeller:** *NYT*, June 23, 1935. **Dreier-Offerman:** "Two Years," p. 2.

The city cheered: "New Deal": *NYT*, Feb. 11, 1934. **"100 Days":** Brooklyn *Eagle,* May 6. **"An urban desert bloom":** *WT*, Dec. 14. **"Hercules":** *NYT*, Mar. 20. **NYT editorial:** Sept. 13. **Murray Davis interview:** *WT*, Jan. 30. **"The people own the parks":** *HT*, May 26. **"2, 4, 6, 8":** *HT*, Dec. 3.

Smith begging FDR for leases: RM.

Central Park Zoo: Smith asking RM to improve Zoo: RM, Emily Smith Warner. **Bear pacing:** *HT*, Apr. 22, 1934. **Smith had had no hint:** Warner. **Smith visiting the Zoo at nights:** Coleman, Cullman, Warner. **CWA cramping RM's style:** PD Files. **"Gay and amusing":** *Fortune,* June 1938. **"The finest eating view":** *Architectural Forum,* Dec. 1936. **Attendance:** PD Files.

Triborough Bridge: Statistics (dwarfed any other single enterprise he had undertaken; the ultimate cost would be $60,-300,000, more than the combined total he had spent during the previous ten years on the construction of all his Long Island projects; comparison of anchorages with pyramids, etc.; "to make the girders," etc.): Public Works Administration, "Case No. 1: New York—Bridge," pp. 226–31. **Enough concrete for four-lane highway:** 1936 TBA brochure, p. 21. **"Largest vertical-lift bridge":** *HT*, July 12, 1936. **"Largest batch," 5,000 men working at site, etc.:** "Case No. 1," pp. 226–31; *HT*, July 12, 1936. **Description of islands:** WPA, *New York Panorama,* pp. 77, 421; *NYT*, Apr. 21, 1946; *HT*, Feb. 6, 1935. **Scene from air in 1934:** The author is indebted to H. I. Brock,

who described it in *NYT Magazine,* Apr. 28, 1935. The image of the streets rushing together is his. **The only hope:** RM. **85%:** Windels. **Moses' traffic studies:** Madigan. **Lanes too narrow:** RM in *NYT,* Apr. 12, 1934, interview. **Hearst deal:** RM's contention that this is the reason for placing the Manhattan approach at 125th Street is supported in Moscow, p. 197, and by Windels, first Triborough counsel under RM. **Burkan's only interest:** RM, Windels, confidential source. **"I sent for the chief engineer":** RM quoted in Rodgers, p. 98. **Othmar Ammann:** For a biographical sketch, see Talese, pp. 31ff. **Loeser "a Prussian and a Nazi":** RM quoting LaG in *Dangerous Trade,* p. 164. **The most experienced bridge builders:** *NYT,* Feb. 28, 1934.

Cost reduced from $51,000,000 to $30,000,000: Burkan in *NYT,* Apr. 4, 1934. **Moses' plans for using the money:** RM, Shapiro, Windels. **The forgotten lease:** *HT,* July 26. **Washburn Co.:** *HT,* Oct. 12; *NYT,* Oct. 30.

$6,000,000 loan: *NYT,* July 7. **Con Ed.:** Confidential source. **Another trip to Washington; LaG finding another $1,300,000;** LaG Papers.

Wanting a huge stadium: RM interview in the New York *American,* Apr. 22, 1935.

Central Park Casino: Restaurant owners' offers: *NYT,* Mar. 19, 1936. **Charpontier:** *NYT,* Dec. 26, 1935. **"Not going to confer":** *NYT,* Feb. 21, 1934. **Advised by Windels:** Windels. **Court fight:** Various newspapers, Mar. 12, 13, 27, 1936. **"The right to do":** *HT,* Mar. 25, 1936. **Carew's decision:** *NYT,* Mar. 27, 1936. **RM's answer; Appellate Court's reversal:** *NYT,* May 2, 1936.

21. The Candidate

SOURCES

Books:

Freidel, *Franklin D. Roosevelt: The Triumph*; Mitgang, *The Man Who Rode the Tiger*; Moscow, *Politics in the Empire State*; Moses, *Dangerous Trade*; Nevins, *Herbert H. Lehman and His Era*; Schlesinger, *The Age of Roosevelt,* Vol. II: *The Coming of the New Deal.*

Author's interviews:

With RM's campaign chairman, F. Trubee Davison, and Long Island Democratic leader Richard Mayes, and with Senate Majority Leader George R. Fearon, Joseph D. McGoldrick, reporter Warren Moscow, Joseph M. Proskauer, Aaron Rabinowitz, Emily Smith Warner and Paul Windels.

NOTES

"More or less forced on me": Moses, *Dangerous Trade,* p. 882. **"He encouraged me":** Davison. **"He was hungry for it":** Windels. **The barons' domination of the Republican Party:** Davison, Windels; Freidel and Moscow books. **Snell:** Schlesinger, p. 480. A picture of the Old Guard's thinking was obtained from interviews with Davison and Mayes, and from the Macy Papers. **"Anybody who amounted to anything":** Moscow, p. 71, **W. Kingsland Macy:** Freidel.

"That was all we had to hear": Davison. **What was wanted was a front man:** Davison, Mayes; Macy Papers.

North Shore Almanack: Sept. 27, 1934. **"No one questioned" and crucial meeting:** Davison. **"None can say":** Buffalo *Evening News,* Sept. 29, 1929. **"One of the most hectic":** Rochester *Times-Union,* Sept. 20, 1934. **"At last!":** *WT,* Sept. 29, 1934. **RM had written most of the platform himself:** Davison.

"Some kind of a record": Windels. **"A fearful row":** Davison. **Rabinowitz dinner party:** Rabinowitz. **Feeling of RM's old associates:** Rabinowitz, Proskauer, McGoldrick.

First press conference: *WT,* Oct. 2, 1934; *HT,* Oct. 3, 1934, is best. **LaG "support":** One typical headline, in *NYT,* Oct. 2, 1934, said: "Moses Confident of La Guardia Aid." He also said, when cornered, "The Mayor doesn't talk much politics. He doesn't to me."

Upstate tour disaster: *WT,* Oct. 25, 27, 1934; Fearon, Davison. **Campaign plans:** Davison.

First speech: Best in Brooklyn *Eagle,* Oct. 5, 1934. The Union League Club had recently called for a "justifiable war upon the New Deal theorists" (Mitgang, p. 332). **Disparaging remarks about Jews:** Windels heard them.

Threatened to sue Jewish Encyclopedia: Confidential source. **McGoldrick's shock:** McGoldrick. **Shuls in the Bronx:** When the author—thirty-five years after the gubernatorial campaign—interviewed Bronx Jews for the "One Mile" chapter, many vividly recalled Moses "trying to say he wasn't Jewish."

"These stuffed shirts": *WT,* Oct. 5, 1934. **"I am a liberal":** RM at press conference reported in *HT,* Oct. 3, 1934.

RM on Lehman: *Dangerous Trade,* p. 878; RM interview. **Donating million to depositors:** RM.

"Moses Calls Lehman Weak": *HT,* Oct. 10, 1934. **"Stupid":** *American,* Oct. 14. **"Puppet":** *Post,* Oct. 16. **"Respectable front":** *NYT,* Oct. 24.

Lehman handled Moses just right: Proskauer, Davison. And Moses knew it: "I made an honest campaign and pulled no punches, which meant little in view of Governor Lehman's strategy, dictated by clever campaign managers, to keep out of range and avoid any real infighting," he wrote in *Dangerous Trade,* p. 883. **Speech in Binghamton:** Text in *HT,* Oct. 25, 1934. **"Cannot dispose of":** Brooklyn *Eagle,* Oct. 5, 1934.

Court of Claims corruption: *NYT,* Oct. 26, 1934. **City Trust report:** *HT,* Oct. 14. In an interview with the author, RM admitted this charge was false. **O'Connells:** RM quoted in *WT,* Nov. 1. **Accusing Lehman of being utilities' ally:** Full text of charge in *HT,* Oct. 25. **"Scrupulous":** Nevins, p. 153. **O'Ryan:** *NYT,* Oct. 28. **Cluett's campaign manager Charles E. Cole:** *WT,* Nov. 2; McGoldrick. **WT editorial:** Nov. 3. **Libel insurance:** Davison.

RM on Farley: *HT,* Oct. 31, 1934. **On O'Connor:** *HT,* Oct. 30; *NYT,* Nov. 3. **On Seabury:** *HT,* Nov. 4. **On Copeland:** *HT,* Oct. 24. **On Tremaine:** *HT,* Oct. 24. **On Straus:** *HT,* Oct. 27. **Straus's friends:** Rabinowitz. **On Murray:** *HT,* Oct. 16 (italics added). **Flynn reply:** *HT,* Nov. 3.

RM and Smith: The source has asked that he not be identified. **Smith's feelings:** Emily Smith Warner. **Dinner party:** Proskauer, who was the host. **One observer:** McGoldrick. **Reporter:** Julian Grey Mason in *The North Shore Almanack,* Oct. 11, 1934. **"He made no gestures":** *WT,* Oct. 28. **How he affected audiences:** McGoldrick, who sat behind him on the platform during speeches. **"More attacks on personalities":** *NYT,* Nov. 4.

Election results: *HT* called it: "The greatest defeat the Republican Party has ever suffered in this state. . . . Mr. Moses . . . suffered the worst defeat of all Republicans who ever ran for Governor in this state." **Political reporters astonished:** Moscow interview.

"An attempt to swim up Niagara": RM interview in *HT,* Nov. 7, 1934. **Lehman on RM:** Rodgers, p. 224. **"He was terribly sensitive":** RM.

22. Order Number 129

SOURCES

Books, articles and documents:

Ickes, *The Secret Diary of Harold L. Ickes,* Vol. I: *The First Thousand Days, 1933–1936* (Ickes furnishes more details, however, in "My Twelve Years with F.D.R.," *The Saturday Evening Post,* June 26, 1948); Moses, *Dangerous Trade*; Rodgers, *Robert Moses*; Schlesinger, *The Age of Roosevelt,* Vol. II: *The Coming of the New Deal.*

La Guardia, Price and FDR Papers.

William D. Guthrie, "Opinion of Counsel as to the Legality of Order No. 129 issued under date of December 26, 1934, by Hon. Harold L. Ickes, Secretary of the Interior, as Administrator of the Federal Emergency Administration of Public Works, if intended or held to be applicable to the pending Loan Agreement dated September 1, 1933, between The United States of America and the Triborough Bridge Authority" . . . March 11, 1935.

Oral History Reminiscences:

Frances Perkins, Joseph M. Price.

Author's interviews:

Howard S. Cullman, Reuben A. Lazarus, Sidney M. Shapiro, Paul Windels.

NOTES

"I don't trust him": FDR quoted in Frances Perkins OHR, Vol. III, p. 372.

LaG's thinking: Windels, Lazarus.

"LaG regretted the situation": Ickes, pp. 148–49. **RM threatens to resign from both positions:** RM later revealed he had said this to LaG; *NYT,* Jan. 4, 1935.

Berle telegram: Mar. 1, 1934. FDR replied the next day: "I love your suggestion that Bob Moses' real name is the duc d'Enghien. Also, though I do not mind your calling me Caesar, I hate your suggestion about Napoleon! As a matter of fact, the case of your friend, the duc, is in no sense a personal one . . . ," FDR Papers. **Roosevelt "implacable":** Ickes to Burlingham, Aug. 13, 1948, quoted in Moses, *Dangerous Trade,* pp. 181–82. **Farley and Howe urging FDR on:** Ickes, p. 148. **LaG stalling, Ickes threatening:** Ickes, p. 229. "It seems that Moses is a bitterly persistent enemy of the President's, and the President has a feeling of dislike of him that I haven't seen him express with respect to any other person," he diaried. **"He would make promises":** Ickes, p. 267; Windels. **"Naturally I had to declare a truce":** Ickes, p. 229. **A further threat.** He wrote this in his diary on Nov. 23, 1934 (p. 229).

"Almost the incarnation": Schlesinger,

p. 282. **"A modern Horatius":** Rodgers, p. 100. **Ickes telephoning LaG:** Ickes, p. 229.

Order Number 129; assurance it would not apply to Post: Windels. **"The President helped me draft this order," and discussed it personally with LaG:** Ickes, p. 268. **LaG shows order to RM:** RM, Windels, Lazarus. **RM's narration:** Statement issued Jan. 3, 1935, printed in newspapers the following day.

"I had to lie": Ickes, p. 268. **One of his advisers:** Lazarus. **Resolutions:** LaG Papers; various newspapers. **"Our Mayor has . . . crawled":** Edward M. Chase, Mar. 4, 1935, printed in *HT*, Mar. 5. **"A crooked course":** Ickes, p. 268.

"I need steel": LaG quoted in *HT*, Jan. 5, 1935. **Shouldering through reporters:** *NYT*, Jan. 9, 1935. **Reasonable men; "at least Post is on the high seas":** LaG in, for example, *HT*, Jan. 5. **"Making a martyr out of him":** Ickes, "My Twelve Years with F.D.R.," p. 83. **"At PWA headquarters":** *HT*, Jan 17, 1935.

The definitive word: Burlingham to LaG, Feb. 15, 1935, Price Papers. **Price and FDR:** Price to FDR, Jan. 30, 1935; FDR to Price, Feb. 2, 1935; Price Papers; FDR Papers. **The mail tally:** FDR Papers. **Burlingham to FDR:** Feb. 22, 1935, Price Papers. **"Almost a national issue":** Ickes, "My Twelve Years with F.D.R.," p. 82. **Krock:** *NYT*, Jan. 25, 1935. **Lippmann:** *HT*, Jan. 24, 1935.

Huey Long: *HT*, Mar. 7, 1935. An in-depth series on RM in *PM*, by John K. Weiss, says that one reason FDR backed down is that Long threatened to release RM's figures on Farley.

"An arbitrary and capricious fiat": Guthrie brief, p. 13. **Price:** Quoted in Rodgers, p. 102. Price also related the conversation he said he had with the President to Windels and Lazarus. **"The President, I know":** Ickes, p. 291. **Secret meeting between FDR and LaG:** No account of this can be found in the *Secret Diary*, but Ickes states that it took place in "My Twelve Years with F.D.R.," p. 83. **Hiding behind the shades:** Windels. **The letter stratagem:** Ickes, "My Twelve Years with F.D.R.," p. 83. The letters made public are quoted in the press, Mar. 12, 1935. **Smith stepping in:** RM, Cullman; Ickes, p. 317. **Ickes reminiscing to Burlingham:** "A dozen years after the dedication of the Triborough Bridge," RM wrote in *Dangerous Trade* (p. 181), "I received [from Burlingham] a letter which threw some additional light on the impact of Mr. Ickes' curious character." RM then quotes the Ickes-Burlingham letter, dated Aug. 13, 1948. **Rodgers:** p. 105. **"In the saddle":** Windels.

Sara Delano Roosevelt Park: Windels, Shapiro.

Triborough Bridge opening ceremony: "It is very small indeed": Ickes, p. 623. **"I understand that there will be a national hookup":** Ickes to FDR, June 23, 1936, FDR Papers. Handwriting on the letter, probably that of Marvin McIntyre, mentions that RM had previously invited FDR. **FDR's memo:** FDR to Ickes, June 25, 1936, FDR Papers. **RM promises not to introduce the President, gives him six minutes:** Windels. **Ickes overwhelmed by RM's charm:** Ickes, pp. 636–37.

23. In the Saddle

SOURCES

Books, articles and documents:

Catledge, *My Life and the Times*; Cuneo, *Life with Fiorello*; Fowler, *Beau James*; Garrett, *The La Guardia Years*; Gluck, *My Story*; Ickes, *The Secret Diary of Harold L. Ickes*, Vol. I: *The First Thousand Days, 1933–1936*; La Guardia, *The Making of an Insurgent;* Limpus and Leyson, *This Man La Guardia;* Mann, *La Guardia: A Fighter Against His Times* and *La Guardia Comes to Power*; Morris, *Let the Chips Fall*; Moses, *Dangerous Trade, La Guardia: A Salute and a Memoir* and *Working for the People*; Rankin, *New York Advancing: 1934–35* and *World's Fair Edition* and *Victory Edition*; Rodgers, *Robert Moses*; Talese, *The Kingdom and the Power*; Tugwell, *The Art of Politics*; Whalen, *Mr. New York*; WPA, *New York City Guide* and *New York Panorama*; Zinn, *La Guardia in Congress.*

Among scores of magazine articles and reports, in particular: Hubert Herring, "Robert Moses and His Parks," *Harper's*, Dec. 1937; Moses, "Municipal Recreation," *American Architect and Architecture*, Nov. 1936; Moses, "The Changing City," *Architectural Forum*, Mar. 1940; New York City Park Department, *Park Progress* reports, 1937, 1939, 1941; "New York's Mr. Moses," *Commonweal*, Mar. 14, 1941; "Pattern for Parks," *Architectural Forum*, Dec. 1936; "Robert (Or-I'll-Resign) Moses," *Fortune*, June 1938; Triborough Bridge Authority, "Fifth Anniversary of the Opening of the Triborough Bridge," June 11, 1941; O. G. Villard, "Great Public Servant," *The Nation*, Oct. 17, 1934.

Davison, Exton, La Guardia, Morgenthau and FDR Papers. Park Department Files.

Oral History Reminiscences:
Charles C. Burlingham, Stanley M. Isaacs, Marie Fischer La Guardia, Reuben A. Lazarus, Newbold Morris, Paul Windels.

Author's interviews:
Adolf A. Berle, Jr., Walter D. Binger, William C. Chanler, Ernest J. Clark, Gilmore Clarke, Jackson Dykman, William Exton, Jr., George R. Fearon, William McD. Griffin, Joseph T. Ingraham, Saul Kaplan, Paul J. Kern, Jacob Lutsky, Michael J. Madigan, Joseph D. McGoldrick, F. Dodd McHugh, John Mulcahy, Lawrence M. Orton, Wallace Sayre, Sidney M. Shapiro, Florence Shientag, P. Fearson Shortridge, Ole Singstad, Iphigene Ochs Sulzberger, Rexford G. Tugwell, Robert C. Weinberg, Samuel White, Paul Windels.

Author's correspondence: William Fellowes Morgan, Nov. 18, 1967.

NOTES

"Treated his commissioners like dogs": Tugwell, pp. 96–97. **Peering between fingers:** Lazarus, Windels. **"Boners":** Garrett, p. 130; Lazarus. **"If you were any dumber":** Moses, *La Guardia*, p. 30. **Turnover unprecedented:** Tugwell, p. 97. **Firing secretary:** Lazarus. **Sealing commissioners' files:** McGoldrick, confidential source.

LaG-RM relationship: General picture from interviews with Berle, Binger, Chanler, Kern, Lazarus, Madigan, McGoldrick, Orton, Sayre, Shientag, Tugwell, confidential sources. **Sending Andrews:** Lazarus, Windels. **"Come to blows":** Confidential source. **RM's nicknames for LaG:** Madigan, Lazarus, Windels. **"His Grace":** McGoldrick, Windels. **Resignation threats:** Kern, Lazarus, McGoldrick, Windels. **LaG dropping investigation:** Dykman.

Astoria ferry: By coincidence, *The New Yorker* had a writer on the very ferry which found its slip being destroyed when it returned, and Madigan was in Kracke's office when the first call to Kracke came in: *The New Yorker,* Aug. 1, 1936; Madigan. Other descriptions of event: *NYT, HT,* July 23, 1936. **Later developments:** *NYT,* July 30, 1936; *HT,* Aug. 1. **RM's earlier attempts to force action:** RM to Kracke, Feb. 4, 1936; Kracke to RM, Feb. 10; RM to Kracke, Feb. 11; Kracke to RM, Feb. 14; RM to Kracke, Feb. 18, June 9; RM to Wharton Greene, resident project engineer, Triborough Bridge Authority, July 23; all in PD Files.

Burlingham on "brutalities": Quoted in Mann, *La Guardia Comes to Power,* p. 30. **"Nurtured that like a plant":** Mrs. LaG OHR. **"You'd see the two of them":** Madigan. **"That's the way you get things done":** Shientag.

Playing on LaG's enthusiasm for engineering; constantly pressing him to go on tours: The LaG Papers are filled with RM invitations; Madigan states that RM realized—and deliberately played on—LaG's enthusiasm. **"Stood like a child":** Kern. **Chinning himself on the fence:** Picture in PD Files. **Watching lift span hoisted:** *HT,* May 4, 1936. **"The greatest engineer in the world":** *HT,* July 26, 1936, for example.

Playground openings: The LaG Papers contain sheafs of photographs taken by RM's photographers to remind the Mayor of the scenes of which he had been the centerpiece. RM even had the photographers take pictures, from directly in front of the platform, of the faces of listeners staring up at the Mayor and sent those to LaG, too, to heighten the effect. John Mulcahy and Samuel White, two Park Department officials, outlined for the author the elaborate preparations that went into these openings; White was in charge of the chrysanthemums, which he would have loaded onto trucks the minute a ceremony was over and rushed to another ceremony that the Mayor was scheduled to attend later that day. Of innumerable newspaper accounts of these events, those in *NYT,* July 27, 1935 (the "Babe Ruth opening"), and July 21, 1937, and in *HT,* July 16 and Aug. 12, 1934, are particularly detailed. LaG's unmitigated delight in the pageantry was related to the author by, among others, Kern. **Glowering at the organ grinders:** Shapiro.

Swimming pools: "Moses," *Fortune,* June 1938. **Hopkins quote:** *NYT,* July 3, 1936. **"The best thing":** RM to LaG, May 26, 1936, LaG Papers.

RM and the press: The author, as a reporter for *Newsday* during the 1960's, observed personally the lengths RM went to in order to charm and entertain *Newsday*'s publishers and key editors and reporters. **Left-wing leaflets:** Shapiro. **Merz:** Ingraham. Ingraham believes—and Shapiro's reply when the author questioned him about the statement was a wordless, sly smile—that RM selected the building

next to Merz's deliberately, wanting one where he could casually "drop in" on Merz, but feeling that moving into the very same building would be too obvious. **Emphasis on reporters:** Shapiro explained how RM learned this from Mrs. Moskowitz.

NYT; Ochs: See "Notes," Chapter 11. **Sheehy had never been in Central Park:** Mrs. Sulzberger. **Giving him the scroll:** *NYT* and *HT*, Jan. 19, 1935. **Her view of RM:** Mrs. Sulzberger. **Not that she always agreed:** Mrs. Sulzberger. **"Iphigene gave us many arguments":** Madigan. **Great lawn:** *DN* charged, on Feb. 7, 1935, that "he did knuckle under to Iphigene Ochs Sulzberger (daughter of Adolph Ochs), the landscape architects and wealthy residents in the matter of the lower reservoir site in Central Park. . . . Moses resurrected the 'Great Lawn for Play' scheme at [their] behest. These people were acting in good faith. They honestly believed that the parks should be for trees, shrubs and rich or middle class people, just as we honestly believe that they should be for children and poor people primarily." Shapiro confirms that it was Mrs. Sulzberger's feelings that were decisive.

Taking her to Inwood Hill: Madigan. **The quarrel:** Mrs. Sulzberger to RM, Dec. 23, 1935; RM to Mrs. Sulzberger, Dec. 24, 1935—both printed in *NYT*, Dec. 25, 1935. **"Now you tell her you're sorry":** Mrs. Sulzberger. **Public apology:** Mrs. Sulzberger to RM, Jan. 2, 1936, printed in *NYT*, Jan. 4.

Influence on NYT: Talese, pp. 15–16; Catledge, p. 222. **NYT's special treatment of RM:** Author's analysis of articles and editorials. **Mrs. Sulzberger visiting LaG's office:** Mrs. Sulzberger.

LaG "didn't dare" fire him: Kern. **"What'll the Times say?":** Windels, Lazarus. **"Stop interfering":** Numerous letters from RM to LaG aides, mostly to Deputy Mayor Henry H. Curran, who had been assigned as liaison with various departments, in LaG Papers, particularly in folders marked "Parks, Department of—1934" and "Parks, Department of —1935." **Threats to resign:** For example, RM to LaG, June 9, 1934, LaG Papers. **Let him have his way:** Numerous letters in LaG Papers, PD Files. **Coney Island tract:** Brooklyn *Eagle*, date missing; *HT*, June 22, 1934. **Other reasons why it was unfeasible for LaG to crack down on RM:** Analysis by Windels, Lazarus, Berle, Jacob Lutsky, Kern, McGoldrick. **"You've got to understand":** Lutsky.

Size of federal contribution: Deputy Comptroller William E. Wilson to LaG, Oct. 17, 1937, LaG Papers (a complete tabulation requested by the Mayor).

RM's relationship with State Legislature: Interviews with Fearon, Kaplan, Lazarus, Windels and various legislators who wish to remain anonymous. **Patronage; "a practical fellow":** Kaplan, confirmed by various confidential sources. **Upstaters distrusted LaG:** Windels, Lazarus. **RM making himself the broker:** Typical letter showing this—one of many in LaG Papers—are RM to LaG and RM to Fearon, Jan. 12, 1934. **An inoffensive bill:** Lazarus.

24. Driving

SOURCES

See "Sources" for Chapter 23. Also, author's interviews with Richard S. Childs and Jeremiah Evarts.

NOTES

Municipal Art Commission: Charter, Section 637. **Submitted on very day:** Childs; *HT*, Jan. 2, 1937.

Insinuations about Corporation Counsel: RM to Windels, May 8, 1936, LaG Papers.

Stepping up the pressure: Telegrams between Windels and RM, May 7, 1936, LaG Papers. Not only Windels but McGoldrick, Lazarus, Sayre and several confidential sources described RM's use of this technique to the author.

Matthewson episode: *NYT*, June 21, 1934; *HT*, June 22, 24, 28; *NYT*, Dec. 22.

Kern episode: Almost a member of the family: Windels. **"I was a Moses fanatic":** Kern. **Refusing to allow RM to circumvent regulations:** Kern, Sayre. Among many conflicts documented in the LaG Papers, one specific issue—RM's attempt to have the WPA pay several employees $90 per month as "electrician foremen" at the same time that the city was paying them $150 per month as civil service "public address operators" —is unfolded in Nov. 10, 1938, George Spargo memo (recipient not indicated); RM to LaG, Nov. 11, 1938; LaG to RM, Nov. 16, 1938; Dayton to LaG, Nov. 29, 1938; LaG Papers. **Lying to LaG about Kern:** The lie is documented in RM to LaG, Feb. 1 and Apr. 7, 1938; LaG to RM, Apr. 12, 1938; RM to LaG Apr. 29, 1938; LaG to Kern, Kern to LaG, Apr. 29, 1938. The last was furnished to the author by Kern; the others are in the

LaG Papers. **"Disowning him":** Sayre. **"Communist" investigation; "OGPU":** RM quoted in *NYT* and *HT*, Nov. 21, 1939. **"A good Roman Catholic":** Kern. **Father Coughlin:** *Social Justice*, Sept. 11, 1939. William O'Dwyer joined in the attack; during his first campaign for mayor—against LaG—in 1941, he pointed to Kern as proof that LaG had filled his administration with "left-wingers." **Council investigation:** S. Burton Heath, "Investigation by Innuendo," *Survey Graphic*, Oct. 1941. **"Don't let Kern set up an OGPU in New York":** RM to LaG, Oct. 14, 1939, LaG Papers. **LaG's fear of being called "Communist":** Windels, Lazarus, McGoldrick, Kern, among others. **Fired him:** Sayre is also convinced that the "Communist" charge was the underlying reason. **"His hatred of me":** Kern. **No more interference:** O'D, Impy, Wagner Papers.

Bullying commissioners: Chanler. **Refusing to attend luncheons:** McGoldrick. **Having one aide in each department designated:** One with whom RM did this was Jeremiah Evarts, an Assistant Corporation Counsel; Chanler, Evarts, Lazarus.

Chrystie-Forsyth: Windels; *WT*, Dec. 14, 1934. **Driving wedges:** First—$3,600,-000—estimate is *NYT*, Sept. 12, 1934. Others come from various articles and RM brochures over the years. **Deceptions: "Not a penny":** New York *American*, Mar. 22, 1935; **$250,000:** Apr. 11, 1935; **$8,000,000:** July 7, 1935. **Single press release on Zoo has two estimates:** And *NYT*, Mar. 9, 1934, included them both in the same story without mentioning or attempting to explain the discrepancy.

Just as one borough president learned never to trust: McGoldrick, sitting on the Board as Comptroller, saw this happening again and again; McGoldrick. **"Graceful malice":** "Moses," *Fortune*, June 1938. **"A couple of jobs":** Lazarus. **"Brazen attempt":** *NYT*, June 9, 1939.

No provision for baby carriages: Weinberg, interview and various memos to Exton, 1936, 1937, Exton Papers.

RM pleading with WPA: RM to WPA Regional Administrator Brehon Somervell, July 3, 1937, is only one of a hundred such letters in PD Files. **$2,500 for clocks:** Somervell to RM, July 23, 1937; RM to Somervell, July 27; RM to LaG, Aug. 7; LaG to RM, Aug. 9; all in LaG Papers.

A standard playground design: Weinberg was one WPA-paid Park Department architect who was always trying to make innovations, and was invariably rebuffed by his superiors, who told him frankly that *their* superiors, top "Moses Men" such as Andrews, Latham and Stuart Constable, would not even consider irritating RM by deviating from the standard design.

Playgrounds into animal cages: Latham, Shapiro, various correspondence in PD Files.

Vest-pocket parks: "That's a little job": Confidential source. **Refuses 1936 Transportation Board offer:** RM to Kern, July 7, 1936, LaG Papers. **No parks in slums:** The Park Department's own maps, in PD Files, show this, as does "New York Youth Tells Its Story" (for which, see "Sources," Chapter 25). **Reformers' views:** Exton, Orton, Weinberg. **Negro immigration:** Description, and of Harlem during the 1930's, in WPA, *New York City Guide*, pp. 52, 132–40, and WPA, *New York Panorama*, pp. 257–64, and in "Harlem," *Fortune*, July 1939. **$850 per year; "slave market":** "Harlem," *Fortune*. **Not a single bank, not a new school:** *New York Panorama*, p. 147. **One clinic, one hospital:** *New York Panorama*, pp. 147, 262, 263. **Maternity death rate:** *New York Panorama*, p. 258. **"The question of what will happen":** *New York Panorama*, p. 151.

"Easily accessible": RM, "Parks and Recreation in Harlem," Oct. 6, 1944, LaG Papers. **Three acres the smallest:** RM, *NYT*, Mar. 11, 1934. The definitive statement from him that he built parks in slums—that he had, in fact, given them more attention than other areas of the city—was the Oct. 6, 1944, statement, after a grand jury investigating slum conditions criticized the city's failure to provide adequate recreational facilities in slums.

"We shall provide one playground": RM to Alderman Conrad A. Johnson, Mar. 21, 1934, LaG Papers.

Reformers and the implications of his park policies: Exton, Orton, Weinberg; Minutes, City Club Park and Recreation Committee, 1934–36.

25. Changing

SOURCES

Books, articles and documents:

Moses, *Dangerous Trade* and *Six Years of Park Progress*; Rodgers, *Robert Moses*; Ickes, *The Secret Diary of Harold L. Ickes*, Vol. I: *The First Thousand Days*,

1933–1936; Strunsky, *No Mean City*. See also "Sources" for Chapter 23.

The basic sources for the history and financing of the West Side Improvement are three long brochures edited and to large extent written by RM and published by the Henry Hudson Parkway Authority: "Opening of the Henry Hudson Parkway and Progress on the West Side Improvement," Dec. 12, 1936; "Opening of the West Side Improvement," Oct. 12, 1937; and "Completion of the Henry Hudson Bridge and Henry Hudson Memorial Park," May 7, 1938.

The basic sources for the effect of the Improvement on Inwood Hill Park, Spuyten Duyvil and Riverdale—and the differences in the effect on these locales of the proposed alternate route—are James E. Briggs, Sproul Braden, William S. Ladd and Lawrence M. Orton, "Planning Northern Riverdale," Sept. 23, 1930; Regional Plan Association, "Proposed Parkway Connecting a Drive with Van Cortlandt Park—to Mr. Weinberg, Confidential," June 1934; The Rev. William A. Tieck, *Riverdale, Kingsbridge, Spuyten Duyvil—A Historical Epitome of the Northwest Bronx*; Robert C. Weinberg to William Exton, chairman, Parks and Recreation Committee, City Club, "Report to the Committee in regard to design of portions of the Henry Hudson Parkway and other matters of Park design of recent date," Dec. 4, 1939.

For the recreation needs of the poor and the effect of RM's policies, "New York Youth Tells Its Story," transcript of the testimony given at hearings held by the City Council's Committee on Youth Welfare, May 13, 17, 31, 1938; American Youth Congress, "The Case for the Use of Schools as Recreation Centers," 1938; Shirley Jenkins, *Comparative Recreation Needs and Services in New York Neighborhoods*.

Author's interviews:

Walter D. Binger, William C. Chanler, William Exton, Jr., William Latham, Michael J. Madigan, Joseph D. McGoldrick, Lawrence M. Orton, Sidney M. Shapiro, Robert C. Weinberg and confidential sources.

Interviews on matters other than the West Side Improvement with Israel Ben Scheiber, John A. Coleman, Mrs. James B. Cooper, James B. Cooper, Jr., Howard S. Cullman, Melvin Daus, F. Trubee Davison, Rev. C. Edward Harrison, Joseph T. Ingraham, Nettie Greenberg, F. Dodd McHugh, Emily Smith Warner.

NOTES

Antagonizing people: Beal: *NYT*, Mar. 3, 1934. **Architects:** *HT*, Feb 18. 1934. **Exton:** Exton.

Pearl Bernstein: Her biography, *NYT*, Dec. 27, 1933. **RM to Kern:** Apr. 25, 1934, and Oct. 1, 1935, LaG Papers; Kern.

"You're just a swabbie": Ingraham and Ben Scheiber, both present, were among those squirming. **Fist fights:** Ingraham. **Swinging at Isaacs:** Binger, McGoldrick.

False charges against Weinberg: Exton, Orton, Weinberg. **Wrecking the Leader:** Mrs. James B. Cooper, James B. Cooper, Jr.; confirmed, with a sly smile at this proof of the unwisdom of getting in RM's way, by Shapiro—and by a check of the *Leader*'s legals.

Columbia Yacht Club: History: *HT*, Mar. 27, 1934. **Their only request:** Chanler, as Assistant Corporation Counsel, handled most of the negotiations for RM. Says Chanler: "One fellow, a former Tammany surrogate, an old fellow, called me and said, 'They're trying to take our club in May or June and we know they're not going to start building until October. The fleet is coming in July. Let us stay through then and we'll be glad to go after that.' I spoke to Moses about it. He said they had to be evicted at once. I said, 'Why?' He said, 'Because they were rude to me.' Well, he was the client and we didn't have much choice. We did kick them out, but I didn't like it much." **Parks "for the people":** RM quoted in *NYT*, Apr. 20, 1934. **"A social racket":** *HT*, Apr. 24. **"Influence," "interesting fact":** *NYT*, Apr. 21. **"No lease":** *HT*, Apr. 27. **Check photostat and club's side:** *NYT*, Apr. 27. **Levy ruling:** *NYT* and *HT*, May 3. **Steam shovels:** *HT*, Apr. 29. **Electricity:** *HT*, Apr. 30. **"Steam-shovel government":** *NYT*, May 1. **"The whole question":** *NYT*, May 4. **Charging a quarter:** *HT*, June 13. **"Because they were rude to me":** Chanler.

And the dream unrolled: An over-all description of RM's accomplishments during this period is found in his biannual *Park Progress* reports; *in* Moses, *Dangerous Trade*, pp. 1–74, 161–90; in Rodgers, pp. 82–95, and in the magazine articles cited in the "Sources" for Chapter 23. **5,000 acres:** *Six Years of Park Progress*, pp. 12–15. **Adding to Manhattan:** *Six Years*, p. 14.

Distribution of playgrounds uneven: Author's analysis of a huge map, labeled "Playgrounds—Present and Future," pre-

pared by RM for LaG, dated Oct. 1939, LaG Papers; Shirley Jenkins, *Comparative Recreation Needs.*

"We have to work all day": "They were begging": Harrison interview with author, Feb. 17, 1969. **Playground supervisors:** Daus. **"The police just keep the kids moving"; "Harlem is a poor section":** "Junior City Government of New York to Hon. Fiorello H. La Guardia," Aug. 31, 1937, LaG Papers. **"Caged tigers":** Father Bishop. **"The fact is that":** RM, "Parks and Recreation in Harlem, Past, Present, and Future," Oct. 6, 1944. **United Parents Association:** Its study quoted in *NYT*, Brooklyn *Eagle*, Mar. 2, 1941. **Grand jury:** *HT*, Nov. 28, 1943. **Took fourteen years:** Bishop's letters-to-the-editor, to the *NYT*, none of which the *NYT* printed, were found in the Stanley Isaacs Papers, 1950 **NYT article:** May 6. **RM sowing playgrounds:** *NYT*, Apr. 24, 1935.

Swimming pools: Under his prodding: Latham; "Patterns for Parks," *Architectural Forum,* Dec. 1936. **"You know how RM felt":** Confidential source. **"They don't like cold water":** Windels told the author that RM said this to him. That this was RM's view is confirmed by confidential source. Shapiro, who echoed RM's views, told the author confidentially that "you can pretty well keep them out of any pool if you keep the water cold enough." **Never once mentioned:** Author's survey of *NYT, HT* and Brooklyn *Eagle,* 1934–39.

Stadium empty: Attendance figures nowhere to be found, but McGoldrick, who, as Comptroller, had to study the stadium's finances, recalls its emptiness.

"Three weeks": Windels. RM's solution: Moses, "New Parkways in New York City," Summer, 1936. **Planners' doubts:** Orton, Planning Commission staffer F. Dodd McHugh; doubts find a voice in *HT* editorials such as Aug. 18, 1936, and articles such as Nov. 22, 1936, and *NYT*, Jan. 2, 1938.

Triborough: Ickes, p. 637; Hugh Johnson column in *WT*, July 15, 1936; LaG and Hopkins, *HT*, July 12, 1936; *NYT* editorial July 11, 1936; *NYT* article, July 10, 1936; Valentine, *HT*, Aug. 12, 1936.

"Cross-country traffic jam": *HT*, Aug. 18, 1936. **Ingersoll:** *NYT*, Sept. 19, 1937. **RM said he knew what to do:** "Moses Is Building a City of the Future," New York *Sun*, Jan. 8, 1938.

"Today we are well on our way": RM, introduction to "Northern and Wantagh State Parkway Extension," published Dec. 17, 1938, by the LISPC and the New York State DPW, pp. 2, 3. **Enthusiastic applause:** Brooklyn *Eagle*, Dec. 18, 1938. **Ammann speech:** *NYT*, Nov. 19, 1936. **Traffic counts:** All traffic counts on Triborough facilities from TBA, "Fifth Anniversary." The counts on other bridges from various newspaper articles. Orton recalls the experts' puzzlement. **RPA's plea for transit on Bronx-Whitestone:** *NYT*, June 28, 1936.

Gowanus Parkway: The picture of the Sunset Park neighborhood and of the effect on it of the parkway is drawn from interviews with a score of residents of the neighborhood conducted by Ina Joan Caro; and from WPA, *New York Panorama*, pp. 68, 87, 115–16, and WPA *New York City Guide*, p. 468. **NYT editorial:** Nov. 1, 1941. **Brooklyn borough president:** John Cashmore, quoted in *Eagle*, Nov. 2, 1941. **Board of Estimate had been under the impression:** McGoldrick. **1,300 families:** *NYT*, July 9, 1940. RM frightened many of them away by sending them an initial notice which gave them ten days to move.

West Side Improvement: The three brochures cited in the "Sources" provide the basic information on RM's plans. They do not provide information on the cost of those plans. That information can be found in no public document, nor in any newspaper or magazine. Because he feared that his plans would not be approved if their true cost was known—or even hinted at—he never let even a hint get out. The highest figure he ever put on them was $24,000,000—a fraction of their true cost. The total—$109,000,000—which the author uses is to be found nowhere. The author has compiled this figure by adding together and analyzing a multitude of figures in letters, confidential memoranda obtained from PD Files, from the LaG Papers and a confidential source, and from interpretation of these data by Jack Madigan and Sidney M. Shapiro. The brochures will be identified by the dates on which they were published.

$109,000,000 already spent: Various newspapers, 1932–33. **Railroad in no position to pay:** Railroad bonds in general were in so precarious a position during the Depression that in July 1938 the Banking Department would remove more than $3 billion of them from the list of legal investments for savings banks. **They watched RM:** Madigan, Shapiro. **New York Central financing:** *NYT*, Mar. 30, Apr. 16, 1934; explanation of the facts

behind the stories, and maneuvering with Lehman: Madigan.

Using railroad's landfill: Shapiro.

"RM has this mind": Shapiro.

Seventy-ninth Street boat basin: Shapiro, Madigan. **Ickes suggesting grade crossings:** Quoted in *NYT*, Nov. 17, 1934. **RM whipsawing LaG and CWA:** RM; various memos, PD Files.

State aid for railroads, etc.: Shapiro.

Whipsawing the Board of Estimate for $10,000,000: *NYT*, Apr. 27, 1934; *J-A*, *NYT*, *HT*, June 19–21, 1934, contain misleading RM figures. **Whipsawing the CWA for $20,000,000:** Madigan.

Selecting the new route through Fort Tryon and Inwood Hill; bankers' caution: RM, Madigan. **Not a single new issue:** Brochure, Dec. 12, 1936. **Madigan biography:** Madigan; Moses, *Dangerous Trade,* pp. 919–20. **Madigan's inspiration:** Madigan.

Inwood Hill Park: WPA, *New York Panorama,* p. 28 ("perhaps the finest," p. 28); Exton. **"Only a few trees":** RM in *NYT*, Mar. 23, 1935.

Spuyten Duyvil: Tieck, *A Historical Epitome.* **A "village":** *HT*, June 23, 1935. **"It will be the end":** Francis C. Williams to *HT*, July 11, 1935.

The alternate route: Exton, Weinberg, Orton, and McGoldrick, whom Exton escorted along it. **Weinberg to Exton:** Dec. 4, 1939, Exton Papers. **RM would not allow anyone else to do any planning:** An "Ad Hoc Committee for Planning Northern Riverdale" conceived a plan for running the parkway through the Marble Hill shanty town and for accommodating the increased residential development that would be brought to Riverdale anyway by careful zoning. The plan was printed as "Planning Northern Riverdale." But RM would not discuss it with the community group, and the City Planning Commission he dominated would not take it up seriously: Orton.

Van Cortlandt Park: The biology teachers' protest and the response from RM's aide is described in Jeanne Morse to Exton, Apr. 6 and June 15, 1939, Exton Papers.

"It didn't require much brains to see": Weinberg. **RM's values:** They emerged clearly during his interviews with the author. **"Laughing at you":** Exton. **McGoldrick was convinced:** McGoldrick.

Building the bridges too low for buses: Why he did so on LI: Shapiro. **Doing so on the Henry Hudson Parkway:** Farley report paraphrased in Chapin to RM, Feb. 2, 1936 (given to author by Shapiro). RM reply in memo to Board of Estimate, Feb. 27, 1936, LaG Papers. **"He would brook no change":** McGoldrick.

RM's charge against Weinberg; Seligman called Exton in: Weinberg, Exton, McGoldrick. **City Club committee report:** *Sun*, Mar. 22, 1935. **Mrs. Sulzberger to RM:** May 24, 1935; printed in *NYT*—in a story on the West Side Improvement—May 28, 1935. **City Club disowning report:** *NYT*, Mar. 23, 1935.

Cutting down trees before public hearing: *NYT*, *Sun*, Mar. 17, 22, 1935. **"He knew how to handle them":** Madigan. **RM's boast about "ingenious device":** Moses, *Dangerous Trade*, p. 187.

$34,000,000 vs. $6,000,000: *NYT*, *HT*, *Sun*, various issues between Apr. 27 and June 20, 1935. **LaG wanted it built before election:** Madigan.

The overnight bridge: *WT*, July 12, 1935.

Reasons for RM's reluctance to talk to Exton: Madigan.

Henry Hudson Bridge opening: RM, Madigan. **In the moonlight:** Rodgers, p. 88. **On Madigan's yacht:** Madigan. **"This, then, is the Hudson waterfront":** Quoted in Moses, *Dangerous Trade,* p. 188.

"The most beautiful drive in the world": *DN*, Oct. 12, 1937. **"Always the man in the car":** *NYT*, Oct. 10, 1937. **Strunsky:** *NYT*, Oct. 9, 1937. **"The poet Wordsworth":** Strunsky, *No Mean City,* p. 165. **RM promises it will eliminate jams:** For example, in *Bronxboro* (a local newspaper), Dec. 1936. **Only twenty-six minutes:** RM, brochure, May 7, 1938, pp. 10–11. **"A veritable motorist's dream":** *J-A*, Oct. 12, 1937. **"Much more":** *Sun*, Oct. 12, 1937. **"A fountain":** *J-A*, Oct. 13, 1937.

Statistics: Primarily the three brochures. **"The most extensive alteration":** *NYT*, Oct. 10, 1937. **Cost:** *NYT*, June 26, 1941.

Built Harlem recreational area only because LaG insisted: Windels.

Gigantic viaducts: Peter Blake, "How to Destroy a City," *HT*, Mar. 13, 1964. "Monstrous misstatements," RM called Blake's opinions, in the brochure he issued in reply, *The Expanding New York Waterfront*, Aug. 1964.

Traffic on the Henry Hudson Bridge: A chart detailing it day by day—prepared for RM by one of his aides—was sent by RM to LaG and was found in the LaG Papers.

"Motorists launching gaily": *NYT* editorial, Nov. 2, 1937. **1938, 1939, 1941 traffic counts:** "Fifth Anniversary." **26,000,000; traffic cut in half in 1956:** TBTA Annual Report, 1956.

Scrapbooks: *NYT*, Oct. 3, 1936. **Richmond HS Arista:** *HT*, Nov. 14, 1936. **McCarren Park opening:** Brooklyn *Eagle*, Aug. 1, 1936. **Park Association comes to him:** *HT*, Jan. 19, 1936. **Price comes to his apartment:** *NYT*, May 22, 1937. **Rename West Side Highway:** *HT*, July 3, 1935. **Dinners:** Descriptions of two typical affairs at which RM was honored are *NYT*, Apr. 4 and Dec. 7, 1937. **"Never in the history of philanthropy":** Moses, *Dangerous Trade*, p. 50; confirmed by F. Trubee Davison interview. Jesse Jones later confided confidentially that one member of the RFC had voted to give the money for the planetarium thinking it was a cafeteria. **Award from 16 organizations:** *NYT*, May 26, 1935. **Typical newspaper supplements or series:** William P. Vogel, *PM's Weekly*, Aug. 3, 1941, for example, or Floyd Taylor, "Danger! Man at Work," *WT*, Jan. 3–8, 1938.

Harper's: Herring, "Robert Moses and His Parks," Dec. 1937. **Time:** Oct. 17, 1938. **The Saturday Evening Post:** "From Dump to Glory," Jan. 15, 1938. **Architectural Forum:** "Pattern for Parks," Dec. 1936. **Fortune:** "Robert (Or-I'll-Resign) Moses," June 1938.

Boston award: *NYT*, Feb. 5, 1942. **Reading speeches over telephone:** A description of him doing so in *NYT*, Feb. 5, 1942. **Stored in packing cases:** Nettie Greenberg. **Shore and Beach Preservation Society:** *HT*, Sept. 12, 1939. **Hartsfield:** Brooklyn *Eagle*, May 26, 1939. **More miles of through highways than in next five largest cities combined:** Statistics furnished by BPR Library.

"Kidnap Robert Moses": "Pattern for Parks," *Architectural Forum*, Dec. 1936. **Engineers from other cities applying his principles:** Among those who told the author that highways in their cities were laid out on RM's principles were Lloyd Reid, then chief engineer of the Michigan Highway Department, and Bertram D. Tallamy of Buffalo. **British urban planners:** *HT*, Apr. 17, 1943.

Suggested as Republican nominee: Among many articles mentioning the possibility—and suggesting that he would be a good choice for 1940—*Harper's*, Dec. 1937, "Robert Moses and His Parks." *The Saturday Evening Post* commissioned him in 1936 to write two articles as a spokesman for the national GOP—"To My Party," Jan. 25, and "End of Santa Claus," June 27.

No room for dissent: Hotel Pennsylvania dinner: Apr. 4, 1937. **Kiwanis luncheon:** *NYT* and *HT*, Mar. 18, 1934. **"We owe much":** Moses, *Six Years of Park Progress*, p. 56. **"We'll undoubtedly":** McGoldrick.

Al Smith: Interviews with Coleman, Cullman, Emily Smith Warner, confidential sources. **"A slender reed":** Warner.

26. Two Brothers

SOURCES

Author's interviews:

With Dolie McWhinney Adams, Jane Moses Collins, Joan Ganz Cooney, Mrs. Hilda E. Hellman, Mrs. Elmer B. Howells, Joseph T. Ingraham, William Latham, Michael J. Madigan, Emily Sims Marconnier, General Harry L. Meyers, Mrs. Harold Morse, Lawrence M. Orton, Elwood Rabenold, Sidney M. Shapiro, Florence Shientag, Mae Smisek, Iphigene Ochs Sulzberger, Rexford G. Tugwell, Rebecca Vollmer. Interviews in connection with Paul E. Moses are noted below.

NOTES

Paul's personality: A composite drawn from the author's interviews with Mrs. Hilda E. Hellman, Emily Sims Marconnier and two other members of the Moses family who prefer to remain anonymous; with Paul's wife, Louise Benjamin Moses; with his stepdaughter, Dr. Patricia Kendall Lazarsfeld; with four of his friends: Joseph Lewin, Mrs. Carl Proper, Louis Schulman and one who prefers to remain anonymous; with six officials of the La Guardia administration who knew him: Paul J. Kern, Reuben A. Lazarus, Joseph D. McGoldrick, Paul Windels, Wallace S. Sayre, and one who insists on remaining anonymous; with one of Robert Moses' aides, who insists on remaining anonymous; and with Mayor Robert F. Wagner, Jr., Jan. 26, 1972. The author got to know Paul Moses during eleven long interviews, Dec. 1966–Mar. 1967.

Lexicon: Lazarsfeld. **Most knowledgeable:** Windels. **"Genuinely friendly":** Confidential source. **RM knew servants only as servants:** RM. **Paul knew them as people:** PEM. **Romance at Princeton:** PEM, confidential source. **Con Ed:** PEM.

Llanerch Pool: PEM, but he didn't want to talk about it much. The most complete account comes from Dr. Lazarsfeld, who, as a teen-ager, spent several summers working there. The most complete account of its finances comes

from an affidavit by PEM filed Oct. 24, 1941, in "In the matter of Louise B. Moses, Plaintiff, against Paul E. Moses, Defendant," Supreme Court, County of New York. **Hounded by creditors, sued by own lawyer:** PEM affidavit, March 8, 1943.

Reconciliation with mother: PEM, Lazarsfeld, Mrs. Proper. **Con Ed:** PEM, Windels. **Believed they were still friends:** PEM.

Never went to see his mother: Mrs. Hellman. **She refused to see him:** Confidential family source.

Her will: File 1463, Liber 1446, p. 93, Surrogate's Court, County of New York.

"I'm trying all this time": PEM. **Explanation for mother's decision:** PEM.

RM unable to pay tuition: confidential sources. **Bill for $10,000:** RM to FDR, date missing, FDR Papers. **"More than she could afford":** RM to LaG, Mar. 31, 1936, LaG Papers.

Down to $1,000,000: PEM, confirmed by *NYT*, June 4, 1930. **"Advances":** PEM. **Net worth down to $690,422:** PEM, confirmed by *NYT*, May 15, 1931. **$50,000 to charity:** In fact, she left $40,000 (including $20,000 to Madison House) and $10,000 to a friend.

LaG administration officials: Interviews with author. **"While it is nobody's business":** RM to LaG, Mar. 19, 1934, LaG Papers. **In charge of 33-man staff:** *HT*, Apr. 29, 1936. **No firm would hire him:** PEM.

The Moses prodigality toward money: Account of his free-spending habits from Lazarsfeld. **Llanerch Pool finances, living on $25 a week:** Depositions by Davidson Sommers, Oct. 22, 1941; by Louise Benjamin Moses, Oct. 22, 1941; by PEM, Oct. 24, 1941; Supreme Court, County of New York, "In the Matter of Louise B. Moses, Plaintiff, against Paul E. Moses, Defendant."

He wasn't getting a cent: PEM, confidential source. These accounts are confirmed by various documents submitted to Surrogate's Court, County of New York, "In the Matter of the Judicial Settlement of the Account of Proceedings of ROBERT MOSES, EDNA M. HURT, WILFRED A. OPENHYM . . . as Trustees for Paul E. Moses, under Paragraph Sixth of the Last Will and Testament of Bella Moses, Deceased." These documents include "Affidavit of Services of Attorney-Trustee under Section 285 of the Surrogate's Court Act" (affidavit filed by Openhym, July 16, 1941); "Memorandum in Support of Objections Filed by Paul E. Moses, Life Tenant" (Oct. 27, 1941); and "Memorandum on Behalf of Accounting Trustee" (filed by Openhym, Sept. 5, 1941). Also "Schedule K—Statement of Commissions Due Upon This Accounting" and "Schedule F-1—Statement of Distribution of Income to Paul E. Moses, the Life Beneficiary of the Trust" (filed by Robert Moses, Edna M. Hurt and Wilfred A. Openhym, Mar. 11, 1941).

"He had some sort of independent income": Schulman. **"Damned strange":** Confidential source.

Visitors to his apartment: Schulman, Lewin, confidential sources.

Hanging around City Hall: Mayor Wagner, Schulman, Orton.

The two gifts from RM: PEM; confirmed—as are the subsequent events—by a confidential source in RM's office.

RM's treatment of his sister: PEM; confirmed by confidential source.

Tugwell biography: Tugwell, Shapiro. **"Thanks particularly":** RM to *PM*, Sept. 4, 1946.

Attitude toward relatives: Confidential sources.

RM at home: Jane Moses Collins, Mrs. Marconnier, Ingraham, Shapiro, Madigan, Mrs. Howells, among others. **"He never acted busy":** Mrs. Howells. **"No side":** Adams.

Robert and Mary: Above interviews, but particularly interviews with Mary's close friend Mrs. Harold Morse. **Her sister:** Mrs. Marconnier. **The captain's sister:** Mrs. Mae Smisek.

"Bob's on one of his rampages": Latham. **Markel incident:** Mrs. Vollmer. **"Those of us who are privileged":** Kaltenborn, "Introduction" to Rodgers, *Robert Moses*, p. xvi.

"A mouse": Confidential source. **Florence Shientag:** Interview with author. **"Mary was a darling":** Mrs. Sulzberger. **The one interview:** *WT*, Nov. 2, 1934. **Joan Ganz Cooney:** Interview with author. **"An alcoholic": Arsenal party:** Mrs. Hellman. **Hospitalized:** Shapiro, General Meyers.

27. Changing

SOURCES

Books and documents:

Mann, *La Guardia: A Fighter Against His Times*. La Guardia Papers.

Author's interviews:

For Tunnel Authority fight, with the Authority's chief engineer, Ole Singstad, deputy chief engineer William McD. Griffin, general manager P. Fearson Shortridge, and with Reuben A. Lazarus and Walter D. Binger. (All three Authority commissioners are dead.)

For Housing Authority fight, with Adolf A. Berle, Jr., Paul J. Kern, Reuben A. Lazarus, Joseph D. McGoldrick and Paul Windels.

NOTES

"Leave the son of a bitch off": Lazarus. **RM attempted to have bill killed:** Lazarus, Singstad. **Overtures to Singstad:** Singstad. **Ickes adamant:** Singstad, Windels. **RM sought delay:** Singstad, Windels, Lazarus; *NYT*, Apr. 15, 19, 20, 21, 30, May 6, 8, 12, 1936.

RM interested in housing because that was where the money was: Windels had a private luncheon with him at this time at which, he says, RM's thinking was obvious. RM had made almost no public statements on housing up to this time. **LaG's personal interest in housing:** Mann, p. 140.

No one suspected the truth: Windels, Berle. RM's housing proposal was detailed the next morning in *NYT*, and *HT*, Nov. 23, 1938.

Cutting him off the air: When questioned about it, LaG at first said blandly (*NYT*, Nov. 24, 1938) that it had been due to a "misunderstanding": WNYC, the Mayor said, was prohibited by law from incurring expense in broadcasting "private" functions; the station had set up the equipment under the impression that the speech was a Park Department function; when it discovered that was not the case, it had no choice but to cancel it. "It's a pity," the Mayor said. "If some responsible person had only telephoned me at my home I would have been glad to arrange for the broadcast." Reported the *Times*: "Mr. Moses has no comment to make." On June 24, 1939, LaG indirectly admitted having ordered the cutoff (*HT*).

Maneuvering on the committee: Windels. **Orders McGoldrick not to pay the bill:** McGoldrick.

LaG convinced RM seeking personal power: Windels, Kern, Lazarus, McGoldrick. With McGoldrick, in particular, LaG made his feelings about "priorities" clear. **Cuts off two park projects:** They were RM's plans for a huge new "Soundview" park in the Bronx and for a complete renovation of City Hall Park. For a feeling of the real acrimony developing between LaG and RM at this time, see LaG to RM, Oct. 27, Nov. 30, 1938, LaG Papers. In a development whose outcome was significantly different from the past, RM personally insulted Corporation counsel Chanler (RM to Chanler, Nov. 2, 1938), Chanler protested to LaG (same date), LaG demanded that RM apologize (Nov. 26), RM refused (Dec. 1, 1938)—and LaG cut off the Soundview appropriation. All in LaG Papers. **Tells McGoldrick and Morris to take harder line:** McGoldrick.

28. The Warp on the Loom

SOURCES

Books, articles and documents:

Bard, *The Port of New York Authority;* Bird, *A Study of the Port of New York Authority;* Cohen, *They Builded Better Than They Knew*; Garrett, *The La Guardia Years*; Nevins, *Herbert H. Lehman and His Era.*

Temporary State Commission on Coordination of State Activities (William J. Ronan, Director of Studies), "Staff Report on Public Authorities under New York State," hereafter referred to as "Ronan Report."

Edward T. Chase, "Lindsay Challenges the Port Authority," *The Reporter*, June 30, 1966. William S. Fairfield, "The New York Port Authority: Guardian of the Tollgates," *The Reporter*, Sept. 29, 1953.

Charles Haydock, "Municipal Authorities: Their Backgrounds and Postwar Possibilities," an address before the Pennsylvania Municipal Association, Harrisburg, Nov. 1943.

Reuben A. Lazarus, "Public Authorities," 1965 or 1966 (unpublished).

William S. Lebwohl (TBTA counsel), "Memorandum—Power of Port Authority to Construct Third Tube of Lincoln Tunnel," Mar. 23, 1951.

Author's interviews:

Reuben A. Lazarus, Michael J. Madigan, Joseph D. McGoldrick, Lawrence M. Orton, Sidney M. Shapiro, Paul Windels.

NOTES

History of authorities: Primarily Haydock, Bird and Lazarus. **Named "Author-**

ity": Cohen, p. 290. **Jimmy Walker:** Lazarus, who was asked by Walker to draft the legislation for it. **Port Authority:** Cohen, pp. 289–90. **All authorities created in a single pattern:** Haydock, Bird, Bard. **Port Authority members expect its tolls to be eliminated:** Cohen, pp. 262–63. **First "general bond":** Bird, pp. 17–19; Bard, p. 248.

But RM's thinking was changing: The entire following discussion of RM's thinking is based primarily on the observations of two men who were privy to it—Paul Windels, first counsel of the Triborough Bridge Authority under RM, and Jack Madigan, RM's most trusted financial confidant—and one man who was not: Reuben A. Lazarus, who had to analyze RM's handiwork for LaG and whose bill-drafting genius made him perhaps the man best able to do it. The author is indebted to these three men for the substantial amounts of time they gave him in helping him to follow the intricacies of the authorities' enabling legislation.

Carrying and maintenance charges on Henry Hudson: Madigan. **Traffic counts:** TBTA Annual Reports. **Revenues could be used in only one way:** Lazarus, "Public Authorities." **Bankers willing to settle for lower coverage:** Madigan. **LaG's new firmness:** See last note, Chapter 27. **Albany drying up:** Nevins, pp. 172–74. Early in 1938, in fact, the Governor, showing a new firmness toward RM, vetoed bills that would have authorized state contributions for construction of RM's proposed Cross County, Southern, Pelham, Hutchinson River and Marine parkways, stating, "It is clear that the state in its present financial condition cannot possibly, with safety, assume [such] large financial operations." *NYT*, Apr. 12, 1938. Legislative leaders said they could see no time in the foreseeable future when these parkways could be started. Brooklyn *Eagle*, Apr. 17, 1938. **City's financial difficulties:** Garrett, pp. 142–51. RM in interview with author summed up this view of the difficulties, and the fact that there was no reasonable possibility of the city's being able to finance his dreams.

Money he would be free to use: Windels, Madigan, Lazarus, Shapiro. Author's analysis of the Triborough acts RM wrote, plus interviews. **City had no alternatives:** The above interviews, plus McGoldrick, Orton.

Powers of a different type: Interviews and analysis cited above. The Lebwohl memo, although written in 1951, shows RM's thinking at work.

State cannot interfere with bonds: Best statement, Lazarus, "Public Authorities," p. 4.

He had to conceal his purposes from everyone: Lazarus, Windels. The various devices he used are shown in sections of bond resolutions of RM's various authorities. While Lazarus, Windels and Madigan assisted the author in understanding them, the following section is the author's own interpretation of the enabling legislation creating the various Moses authorities, and he assumes full responsibility for its conclusions. **Fiscal agent:** Ronan Report, pp. 466–72, 478.

"To be a caretaker": RM. **Authority officials traditionally unsalaried:** Cohen, p. 289; Ronan Report, p. 116. **"If I may be permitted":** TBTA, "Fifth Anniversary of the Opening of the Triborough Bridge," June 11, 1941, p. 6. **Jones Beach, Jacob Riis:** Ronan Report, p. 462.

LaG's awakening: RM to LaG, Apr. 7, 1938; LaG to RM, Apr. 11, 1938; RM to LaG, Apr. 12, 1938; LaG Papers. **Description of LaG's thinking:** Windels, Lazarus, McGoldrick.

29. *"And When the Last Law Was Down . . ."*

SOURCES

Books, articles and documents:

Andrews, *The Iconography of the Battery and Castle Garden* and *New York As Washington Knew It*; Bolt, *A Man for All Seasons*; Garrett, *The La Guardia Years*; Gilder, *The Battery*; Isaacs, *Love Affair with a City;* Lewinson, *John Purroy Mitchel*; Nevins and Krout. *The Greater City*; Moses, *Dangerous Trade*; Pritchett, *New York Proclaimed*; Stokes, *The Iconography of Manhattan Island*; Talese, *The Kingdom and the Power*; Ulmann, *A Landmark History of New York*; Wilson, *New York Old and New*; WPA, *New York City Guide* and *New York Panorama.*

New York City Tunnel Authority brochure comparing a bridge and a tunnel, referred to hereafter as "Singstad brochure."

Triborough Bridge and Tunnel Authority, "The Brooklyn-Battery Bridge," Jan. 22, 1939; "Is There Any Reason to Suppose They Are Right Now?," 1939; "A Preposterous Scheme: The Regional

Plan Association's Alternate to the Brooklyn-Battery Bridge," 1939; "Brooklyn-Battery Bridge: memorandum in support of revised application to War Department for approval," May 24, 1939; "Brooklyn-Battery Bridge: appeal from decision of Secretary of War Woodring denying a permit for construction," Oct. 19, 1939.

A complete record of the Moses-La Guardia maneuverings and machinations can be found scattered and misfiled throughout the La Guardia Papers, but particularly in Box No. 842, folders labeled "Brooklyn-Battery Tunnel—1935–39" and "Tunnels—Brooklyn-Battery Tunnel—1940–45," and Box No. 2643—"Tunnel Authority—Brooklyn-Battery Bridge."

Oral History Reminiscences:
Stanley M. Isaacs, George McAneny, Frances Perkins.

Author's interviews:
Walter D. Binger, Richard S. Childs, William Exton, Jr., William McD. Griffin, Reuben A. Lazarus, Joseph D. McGoldrick, Lawrence M. Orton, Sidney M. Shapiro, P. Fearson Shortridge, Ole Singstad, Rexford G. Tugwell, Paul Windels.

NOTES

Bypass route costs: True costs, different from newspaper figures, in RM to LaG, Sept. 3, 7, 1938, and in suggested draft by RM of LaG to Ickes, undated, LaG Papers. **The Mayor would have to allow him to take over the Tunnel Authority:** RM to LaG, Sept. 8, 1938, LaG Papers. **$39,000,000 to $43,000,000 and various LaG maneuverings:** McGoldrick.

Tunnel becomes bridge: TBTA, "The Brooklyn-Battery Bridge," Jan. 22, 1939. **"The finest architecture":** RM introduction to TBTA, "Three Decades of Progress," 1966. **"A vehicular bathroom":** Moses, *Dangerous Trade*, p. 220. **"A hole in the ground," taking LaG out on yacht:** Shapiro.

"He's going to bankrupt the city": McGoldrick quotes Frank Taylor, the last pre-Fusion Comptroller, as telling him this upon McGoldrick's appointment to the post in 1934.

The capital budget situation was even more ominous: McGoldrick's feelings were based on these figures: In Oct. 1938, the money left to the city under the state ceiling was only $70,943,125—and $55,568,056 of this amount was already committed for future expenditures on projects, mostly Moses', already under construction. The Comptroller believed that the city's assessed valuation—the base which determined the debt limit—would increase in 1939 to a point at which the margin left under the limit would rise to $126,683,125, but this was only a prediction, not a certainty, and he and the Mayor had, moreover, agreed, when he first took office, that a reserve of at least $45,000,000 must be left in the debt limit at all times to pay for preventive maintenance to the city's physical plant, for unexpected major repair work and for other emergencies. If this principle was adhered to, the total amount available to the city for new expenditures in 1939 would, McGoldrick estimated, be $26,583,125. And the forecast for 1940 was even gloomier; obligations already assumed by the city for payment in that year assured that the total available for capital outlays would be under—well under—$20,000,000.

McGoldrick's feelings, LaG's agreement with him: McGoldrick. **"Reluctant as I am":** *NYT*, Oct. 12, 1938. **RM's attack:** *NYT*, Oct. 13, 1938. **Board of Estimate session:** *NYT*, *HT*, Brooklyn *Eagle*, Oct. 14, 1938; McGoldrick.

A ten-story building: *NYT*, Jan. 26, 1939. **Almost to Rector Street:** *HT*, Mar. 19, 1939. **Corporation breaking off negotiations:** Tom Brown, manager of downtown office of Cushman & Wakefield, Inc., to LaG, June 5, 1939, LaG Papers.

History of Lower Manhattan: Books by Gilder, Nevins and Krout, Stokes, Ulmann. **They had had to watch as cobbled slips . . . :** WPA, *New York Panorama*, pp. 204–18. **"The vocabulary of thrift":** Henry James, quoted in Pritchett, p. 6.

History of the Aquarium: Books by Stokes and Ulmann; WPA, *New York Panorama*, pp. 21, 24, 39, 53, 92, and *New York City Guide*, pp. 49 ff. The most complete history is Gilder book and McAneny OHR. Gilder's book contains pictures of the fort in each of its incarnations. **Lafayette:** Gilder, pp. 148ff. **Attendance at Aquarium:** Gilder, pp. 233–36; *HT*, Feb. 7, 1941; McAneny OHR. **Reformers' feelings of effect of the bridge on the park:** Letters-to-the-editor, *HT*, throughout 1939; McAneny OHR; Binger, McGoldrick, Windels.

McAneny biography: Lewinson, pp. 85–88; obituaries, *NYT*, *HT*, July 31, 1953; Garrett, pp. 92–93; McAneny OHR. **Could have had Fusion nomination:** Various newspapers, 1917. **"A sort of**

moral background": Talese, p. 174. **Wrinkled:** Binger, Childs. **World's Fair:** McAneny OHR.

Isaacs biography: Isaacs' book; J. M. Flagler, "The Public Be Served," *The New Yorker*, Dec. 12, 19, 1959; obituaries, *NYT* and *HT*, July 13, 1962; Binger.

"Maybe, idolizing him": Confidential source.

Isaacs sent him letters; he didn't reply: Isaacs to LaG, enclosing copies of letters to RM, Jan. 25, 26, 1939, LaG Papers. **Disturbed but not worried:** Binger, Windels.

Costs: TBTA, May 24, 1939, brochure vs. Singstad brochure. **"Without a nickel":** RM, introduction to TBTA brochure. **Ammann's "guidance":** Exton, one of the two representatives (the other is dead); Windels. **$21,500,000:** Isaacs to LaG, Jan. 26, 1939; to RM, Jan. 28, 1939; RM to Isaacs, Feb. 1, 1939; LaG Papers. Binger. **"On the basis of real cost":** Singstad brochure.

The two drawings: Both were printed in *HT*, Feb. 6, 1939. **Morning newspapers:** *NYT*, *HT*, Feb. 14, 1939. **Planning Commission hearing:** *NYT*, *HT*, Brooklyn *Eagle*, Feb. 16, 17, 1939. **Decision:** Mar. 2, 1939. **The commission did not make even a pretense:** Orton. **Eating up the track in Albany:** Brooklyn *Eagle*, Mar. 1, 8, 9, 1939; *HT*, *NYT*, Mar. 1. **Isaacs noticed a point:** Binger; Isaacs demanded a ruling from State Attorney General John J. Bennett on whether a home-rule message was required—Bennett said it was.

Foot-stamping fury: McGoldrick. When LaG learned about the buried clause from Isaacs, he called in the Comptroller and Reuben Lazarus and had McGoldrick produce from his files a copy of RM's letter of Sept. 8, 1938, promising it wouldn't cost the city "a nickel" and then exploded. McGoldrick, Lazarus. A copy of RM's letter is in the LaG Papers, together with this prescient attached memo from the Mayor to McGoldrick, dated Sept. 28, 1938: "Please keep this copy in your permanent files. As we are in agreement that no part of this cost could be absorbed by the city, I think the time will come when we may need this letter for useful reference." **A ray of hope:** McGoldrick, Singstad, Windels.

"Central Committee's" activities: Description in "Minutes of Victory Luncheon, Central Committee of Organizations Opposing the Battery Toll Bridge, Held at Architectural League, 15 E. 40th St., New York, N.Y., July 20, 1939," LaG Papers. **Burlingham's conversation with LaG:** Singstad and Windels are among those to whom "CC" related it. **Gave Tunnel Authority permission to lobby:** Lazarus, Singstad; Robert F. Wagner, Sr., to LaG, Mar. 13, 1939, LaG Papers.

"A brief delay": *NYT*, Mar. 11, 1939. **"It seems clear now":** *HT*, Mar. 20, 1939.

Telegram from Key West: RM to LaG, Mar. 9, 1939, LaG Papers. **"The same old tripe":** *NYT*, Mar. 27, 1939.

City Council hearing: *NYT*, *HT*, Brooklyn *Eagle*, Mar. 28, 29, 1939. **Feelings of reformers:** Binger, Exton, McGoldrick, Windels. **Civil service architects vs. consultants:** The analysis, by George Curran, showed that on major public works designed by civil service employees, design costs were 3.2 percent of the total, while on public works designed by consultants, such costs were between 6 and 7.5 percent. **"If there was an argument raised":** Exton. **A surplus of $4,000,000:** See Chapter 31. **"I was afraid":** McGoldrick. **"Shock":** That word was used by, among others, Childs, Exton and Windels.

"A happy smile": *NYT*, Mar. 29, 1939. **"The tunnel is dead":** RM quoted in Brooklyn *Eagle*, Apr. 5, 1939. **"And when the last law was down":** Bolt, p. 66.

"Call Eleanor": Windels. **"My Day":** *WT*, Apr. 5, 1939. **Burlingham's letters-to-the-editor:** *HT*, Apr. 6, June 2, 1939. **RM's answer:** *HT*, June 5.

"In graveyard confidence": Burlingham to FDR, Apr. 10, 1939, FDR Papers. **RM assured of favorable report:** RM; also RM quoted in *NYT*, July 19, 1939. **"Speak to the President":** Watson to Schley, Apr. 26, 1939. On the same day, moreover, Woodring memoed FDR: "I have checked into the proposed Battery Bridge project, New York City, without disclosing the fact C. C. Burlingham had written you. If you desire, I shall be glad to discuss this project with you after the Chief Engineer has received the field report and before any final action is taken thereon by the War Department." FDR Papers. **The engineers suddenly evasive:** Hall to RM, May 2, 1939, quoted in *Dangerous Trade*, p. 204. RM's whole side of this controversy, pp. 202–07, in section titled "Enter Mrs. Roosevelt."

"The President pulled down his lip": Frances Perkins OHR, Vol. III, p. 371. **"Personal and Confidential":** Watson to FDR, May 18, 1939, FDR Papers. **Woodring announcement:** *NYT*, July 18, 1939. **"Rage and ridicule":** *HT*, July 18.

Air Force experts: RM. **RM's hint that FDR was behind it:** *NYT*, July 18, 19. **The President said firmly:** *NYT*, July 19. **"No doubt this squares up accounts":** RM quoted in *NYT*, July 18. **LaG's gratification:** Lazarus.

"Any mention": The author mentioned it in an interview with RM and drew this reaction. **Eleanor Roosevelt's denial:** "My Day," *WT*, May 13, 1939. **"Oh, she was in the middle of it":** RM. **"Increasingly unprintable":** Lazarus. **"A review of 'My Day'":** Moses, *Dangerous Trade*, p. 202.

$12,000,000 pill: The complicated financing that went into the final arrangements—so different from newspaper accounts—is detailed in RM to LaG, Nov. 6, 1939 (which contains RM's plea to charge tolls); Singstad to LaG, Nov. 21, 1939; RM to LaG, Nov. 30, 1939; unsigned and unaddressed memo dated Jan. 18, 1940; Jesse Jones to Alfred B. Jones, Mar. 9, 1940; Fearson Shortridge to LaG, Mar. 12, 1940; Morton McCartney (chief, self-liquidating projects division of RFC) to RM, Nov. 20, 1940. All in LaG Papers.

Victory Luncheon: See "Minutes" cited above.

30. Revenge

SOURCES

Books:

Rodgers, *Robert Moses*; White and Willensky, *AIA Guide to New York City*.

See also "Sources" for Chapter 29.

NOTES

"If the roof leaks": Robert Forman to *HT*, Mar. 1, 1941. **Reformers' feelings:** From interviews with many, and from their OHR's, particularly McAneny. Among those interviewed who consented to be quoted are Binger, Exton, McGoldrick, Orton, Weinberg and Windels.

Whole columns of letters-to-the-editor: *HT*, for example, printed nine on Mar. 1, 1941.

RM states tunneling will undermine: For example, *NYT*, May 13, 1941. **Exton checks:** Exton, confirmed by Singstad and Binger, and by Singstad to Exton, Feb. 15, 1941, Exton Papers. **170 feet:** Isaacs' successor as Manhattan borough president, Edgar J. Nathan, Jr., in letter to *NYT*, Mar. 16, 1943. **It was going to fall down; "a joke":** Binger. **"No history worth writing about":** RM in *HT*, Feb. 25, 1941. **"Why must this ancient thing be torn from us?":** Exton to *NYT*, Feb. 17, 1941. **Not even certain of new location:** Confidential source. In fact, LaG shortly thereafter announced *he* had decided the new location would not be in the Bronx; *HT*, May 2, 1941. **Demolition not the issue:** *NYT*, *HT*, Sept. 12, 1941.

Palma switch: *NYT*, May, Sept. 12, 1941; **Morris switch:** May, Sept. 12, 1941.

No construction company would bid: Actually one bid was submitted in 1942, but it was a false bid, submitted to save RM embarrassment. **Suit:** McAneny OHR; Binger, Windels. **"With the unleashing":** *HT*, Feb. 25, 1941. **Burlingham visiting the Aquarium:** Binger. **McAneny's fight:** McAneny, Isaacs OHR's; Binger, Exton, Windels. **"The successful conclusion," "most gratifying":** *NYT*, Oct. 8, 1949. **"McAneny beat Moses":** Isaacs OHR. **"Now it is a monument":** White and Willensky, p. 10. **"The ten-year battle":** Rodgers, p. 94.

31. Monopoly

SOURCES

Documents:

"Excerpt from Minutes of a Meeting of the Port of New York Authority held Thursday, Sept. 25, 1941"; "Special Report of the Staff to the Construction Committee on Mr. Ole Singstad and the Acquisition of the Properties of Anjou Realty Corporation and Nord Holding Corporation"—both these documents attached to RM to LaG, Nov. 10, 1941, LaG Papers.

"Re: Ole Singstad" (this is the title of a letter from Alfred B. Jones to LaG, Mar. 20, 1942, which constitutes the Tunnel Authority investigation of the Anjou and Nord companies).

Author's interviews:

Howard S. Cullman, William McD. Griffin, P. Fearson Shortridge, Ole Singstad, Paul Windels, confidential sources.

NOTES

RM recommends halt in tunnel work: *HT*, Oct. 6, 1942. **Not steel at all:** William H. Friedman in *HT*, Oct. 6. **LaG's furious statement:** *HT*, Oct. 7. **WPB stopping production:** *NYT*, Oct. 13, 1942.

"Doing the right thing": RM quoted in *HT*, Oct. 18, 1942.

Tunnel Authority financial situation: Various "Tunnel Authority" folders in LaG Papers; Shortridge, Singstad. **RM's analysis of that situation:** Various letters in LaG Papers; typical is RM to LaG, June 7, 1945. **"Mess":** For example, RM to LaG, Dec. 4, 1940, and RM to Jones, Sept. 29, 1945; LaG Papers.

Singstad's brother-in-law's real estate transactions: Minutes of Port Authority meeting of Sept. 25, 1941, and staff report that was presented to that meeting. **Power struggle:** Singstad, Windels. **"He was afraid":** Windels. **"Great regret":** Alfred B. Jones reported this to RM, July 16, 1943, LaG Papers. **"The Singstad story":** RM to LaG, Nov. 10, 1941. LaG Papers. This and subsequent communications indicate that RM had given the Mayor an oral version of the affair. RM quoted Cullman about the alleged $50,000 in Nov. 10, 1941, letter. **Madigan's overture to Singstad:** Singstad, Windels. Madigan would not discuss it, but Lazarus says he knew about the overture.

RM recommends Cullman: The recommendation was made secretly, and cannot be found, but a green slip dated Feb. 10, 1943, and filled out by one of LaG's secretaries to indicate the nature of the document for filing purposes can be found in LaG Papers, Box 710, folder marked "Parks—Feb., 1943."

Friedman to LaG: June 15, 1945. **LaG reply:** June 18, 1945. **Buried newspaper articles:** For example, *HT*, July 26, 1945.

RM firing Shortridge: Shortridge.

32. *Quid Pro Quo*

SOURCES

Books:

Garrett, *The La Guardia Years*; Gunther, *Inside U.S.A.*; Morris, *Let the Chips Fall*; Moses, *La Guardia: A Salute and a Memoir*; Moscow, *Politics in the Empire State.*

Author's interviews:

Walter D. Binger, Joseph D. McGoldrick, Paul Windels.

NOTES

LaG's desk: Gunther, p. 580. **Pressing his back:** Morris, p. 204. **"I guess I'm tired":** To Gunther (p. 588).

DN straw poll: Garrett, p. 285. **Analysis of his problems:** McGoldrick, Windels; Garrett, pp. 275–99; Morris, pp. 202–03; Moscow, p. 28.

RM's one public statement: *HT*, Oct. 22, 1945. **Men who knew Moses:** McGoldrick, Windels. **WJZ announcement:** Various newspapers, Nov. 2, 1945. O'D describes his first conference with RM—at the Links Club—in his OHR, pp. 246–247: "I . . . asked [Moses] if he'd be winning . . . [Moses] said, 'Well, of course, I might tell you that I'm bound to make two speeches for one of your opponents . . .' "

"It's true": *HT*, Nov. 2, 1945. **Press reaction:** *Post*, Nov. 2; *DN*, Nov. 3; *HT*, Nov. 3.

"So shrunken": Moses, *La Guardia*, p. 44. **Engineers Club scene:** Binger.

33. *Leading Out the Regiment*

SOURCES

Books, articles and documents:

Allen, *Our Sovereign State*; Connable and Silberfarb, *Tigers of Tammany*; Costikyan, *Behind Closed Doors*; Doig, *Metropolitan Transportation Politics and the New York Region*; Felker (ed.), *The Power Game*; Flynn, *You're the Boss*; Garrett, *The La Guardia Years*; Gunther, *Inside U.S.A.*; Hamburger, *Mayor-Watching and Other Pleasures*; Isaacs, *Love Affair with a City*; Leavitt, *Superhighway–Superhoax*; Lowe, *Cities in a Race with Time*; Lundberg, *America's Sixty Families* and *The Rich and the Super-Rich*; Mockridge, *The Big Fix;* Moscow, *Politics in the Empire State, What Have You Done for Me Lately?* and *The Last of the Big-Time Bosses*; Morris, *Let the Chips Fall*; Moses, *Dangerous Trade*; Nevins and Krout, *The Greater City*; Riordon, *Plunkitt of Tammany Hall*; Rodgers, *Robert Moses*; Sayre and Kaufman, *Governing New York City*; White, *The Making of the President 1964.*

Austin J. Tobin, "Public Relations and Financial Reporting in a Municipal Corporation," May 23, 1951.

Fred J. Cook and Gene Gleason, "The Shame of New York," *The Nation*, Oct. 31, 1959.

Office of the State Comptroller, Division of Audits and Accounts, "Report on Audit of Certain Financial and Operating Practices, Triborough Bridge and Tunnel Authority," Jan. 10, 1967; also a preliminary draft of this audit report never released to the public; also audi-

tors' work sheets (all hereafter referred to as "Levitt TBTA Audit").

Office of the State Comptroller, Division of Audits and Accounts, "Draft Report" on LISPC, Jones Beach and Bethpage authorities; also auditors' work sheets (all hereafter referred to as "Levitt LISPC Audit").

Certain files of the TBTA made available to the author on a confidential basis (hereafter referred to as "Secret TBTA Files").

TBTA Annual Reports, 1946–67.

Oral History Reminiscences:

Stanley M. Isaacs, Reuben A. Lazarus, George McAneny, William O'Dwyer.

Author's interviews:

Henry Barnes, Harold Blake, Peter J. Brennan, Peter Campbell Brown, William Chapin, Ernest J. Clark, Ernest Cohen, Albert M. Cole, John A. Coleman, Victor F. Condello, Fred J. Cook, Joan Ganz Cooney, Timothy J. Cooney, Edward N. Costikyan, Howard S. Cullman, Thomas E. Dewey, Perry B. Duryea, Jr., Julius C. C. Edelstein, Jerry Finkelstein, Walter S. Fried, Hortense Gabel, Monroe Goldwater, Nettie Greenberg, William J. Haddad, Mrs. Rudolph Halley, Vincent R. Impellitteri, Joseph Kahn, Saul Kaplan, Edna F. Kelly, William Latham, Reuben A. Lazarus, Arthur Levitt, Jacob Lutsky, Michael J. Madigan, Michael J. Merkin, J. Burch McMorran, Edward F. Moloney, Warren Moscow, John Mulcahy, Mary Perot Nichols, Paul O'Dwyer, Paul O'Keefe, Lawrence M. Orton, Jackson Phillips, Charles F. Rodriguez, Dwayne Saunders, Louis Schulman, Paul R. Screvane, Sidney M. Shapiro, Philip Shumsky, Charles Stark, Bertram D. Tallamy, James Truex, Robert F. Wagner, Jr., Arthur B. Williams, William J. Zeckendorf.

More than a score other interviewees —Moses men, Wagner men, city officials, state officials, federal officials— have requested anonymity.

NOTES

Construction Coordinator: Not one of the Assistant Corporation Counsels: Condello. **Citizens Union protest:** *NYT* (Feb. 6, 1946) noted that, at a Board of Estimate session, "a letter from . . . the Citizens Union protesting that the bill gave too much power to one person and superseded the Charter, went unheeded." **O'D's belief that it would be "purely administrative":** *Post*, May 2, 1946. The one paragraph which the *Times* devoted to the Board's approval of the bill was the next to last in a story on Feb. 5. **Using innocent phrase as authorization:** Rodriguez, Lutsky. **Lying for twenty years:** Edelstein.

RM's relationship with Bureau of Public Roads: Du Pont to RM, Jan. 25, 1954, Wagner Papers; Tallamy. **Their idol:** Author's interviews with Tallamy and various BPR officials who declined to be identified. **"Under federal law":** Lutsky.

Taking over housing: Although its membership changed from time to time, the Moses Men who gave him control of the Housing Authority board for most of the 1946–58 period were Thomas F. Farrell, its chairman from 1946 to 1950; Philip J. Cruise, its chairman from 1950 to 1958; Thomas J. Shanahan, its vice chairman from 1948 to 1958; and William Wilson, a long-time Moses consultant who was a board member from 1952 to 1957. Among top Authority officials who were loyal "Moses Men" were Assistant to the Chairman Gerald J. Carey, Director of Development James A. Dawson, Director of Planning Samuel Ratensky and Director of Personnel Joseph Rechetnick. **Controlled it absolutely for a decade:** Moscow, its executive director for two years, Orton, Lazarus, confidential sources; the author's analysis of communications between RM, the Authority and O'D, Impy and Wagner, from the respective Mayoral Papers. One of the few public attempts to reveal the extent of RM's influence was made by former Authority Chairman Langdon Post in 1947, when he said, "The City Housing Authority, by law, has five members. But the sixth and really important member seems to be Bob Moses." *Post*, Sept. 5, 1947.

Dewey liked to boast: Interview with author. **RM cursing him:** State DPW official Arthur B. Williams, confidential sources.

Harriman sitting silently: Joan Ganz Cooney, among others. **"Get tough with Moses":** Truex; confirmed by several confidential sources. **Suggesting dam be named for RM:** Chapin, Latham, Shapiro.

The extra carbons: Shapiro, confirmed by confidential sources.

Control of District Ten: Most of the DPW engineers who spoke with the author declined to be identified. Among those who agreed were McMorran, Maloney, Tallamy and Williams and their stories are confirmed by, among others, Barnes, Clark, Latham and Shapiro.

Macy, in Macy to Dewey, Oct. 30, 1947, Macy Papers, complains about RM's domination of the District.

RM recommending McMorran: McMorran. **RM's evaluation of McMorran:** *Dangerous Trade*, p. 298. **RM's absolute veto power:** Tallamy, McMorran, Maloney. **States had final say:** Leavitt, pp. 166–167.

The machine: Moscow, *What Have You Done for Me Lately?* and *Last of the Big-Time Bosses*; Connable and Silberfarb, pp. 292ff.; Garrett, pp. 303–36; Cook and Gleason, "The Shame of New York." **"A vast, corrupt organization":** *HT*, quoted in Gunther, p. 561. **Judgeships sold:** Garrett, p. 307. **Democrats bringing in Republicans:** "Shame"; Morris, p. 220; Moscow, *Politics in the Empire State*, p. 136; *What Have You Done for Me Lately?*, pp. 56–57. **How this device stymied investigations:** "Shame," p. 289.

The Tweed Ring: Penn Station: Moscow, *What Have You Done for Me Lately?*, p. 147. **Plunkitt:** Connable and Silberfarb, pp. 158–59. **"Honest graft":** Moscow, *Politics in the Empire State*, pp. 213–15; *The Last of the Big-Time Bosses*, esp. p. 51. **Al Smith quote:** Allen, p. 89. **"A king's ransom":** Lazarus OHR.

He had the money to pay it: These figures come primarily from the author's analysis of Comptroller's Reports, 1946–63. The housing figures come also from various confidential sources in the City Comptroller's office and in RM's hierarchy, and from City Planning Commission, "Public Works Progress Report," 1949, and "Planning Progress, 1940–50," Mar. 15, 1951, and from analysis of Authority figures by Orton and confidential sources in the Comptroller's office; and from the Housing Authority's "Project Data —Dec. 31, 1972." DPW funds come also from various DPW reports, 1946–63, and from RM's "Arterial Progress Reports," particularly Nov. 8, 1965, pp. 2–31. Slum Clearance funds from various Slum Clearance Committee "Title I Progress" reports, particularly July 15, 1957, and Oct. 26, 1959. **Three and a half billion dollars dispensed in the city:** According to "Comptroller's Reports," see above, $3,684,114,-923 between 1946 and 1960. **Triborough traffic and income figures:** TBTA Annual Reports, 1946–68.

Difficulty in auditing TBTA: Confidential sources. **1,400 editorials:** Tobin, "Public Relations," p. 8. **Feelings of politicians:** None willing to be quoted; among those who observed their feelings are Lazarus, Lutsky, Orton, Rodriguez. **"The natural locus of corruption":** Costikyan, p. 297. He said: "It is not a particular group of people that is the magnet which attracts corrupters. Power, and power alone, attracts. The natural locus of corruption is *always* where the discretionary power resides. It follows that in an era when political leaders exercised basic power over the government officials whom they controlled, the locus of corruption was in the offices of the political bosses—Tweed, Croker, Kelly, and the rest. But as power has shifted from the political leader to the civil servant and the public officeholder, so the locus of corruptibility and of corruption has shifted." Rodriguez, in an interview, gave a very perceptive view of this situation to the author, as did Haddad, Kahn, Lazarus, Lutsky and others.

Triborough insurance: On slum clearance project: Blaikie had it first: "Shame," p. 290. **Lost it to De Sapio broker:** Lazarus. **Over-all pattern:** Secret TBTA Files, including RM to Spargo, Dec. 4, 1953; Spargo to RM, Dec. 8, 1953. **$500,000 per year:** Moscow, in interview, said he was told this by De Sapio. The figure is confirmed by those figures available in the TBTA files. **Brokers had to do no work for it:** Spargo to C. J. Reid, Dec. 3, 1954. **Shifting policies to broker "friend of Tom Shanahan's":** Spargo to RM, Dec. 8, 1953, Secret TBTA Files. **For a decade:** Levitt TBTA Audit, pp. 113–31. **De Sapio:** The friend was Moscow, and Moscow related this to author in an interview. **Some to a broker close to the leader:** The broker was Timothy W. Foley, Inc., and Levitt TBTA Audit, p. 114, shows that the Foley company received premiums totaling $121,000. Later De Sapio was believed to be close to Campo & Roberts, Inc. Levitt TBTA Audit shows that that firm received premiums on Verrazano-Narrows Bridge insurance beginning Nov. 9, 1959; a very incomplete early total of the premiums it received from this one project is $57,-000. Campo & Roberts received hundreds of thousands of dollars in premiums on other Moses projects. Screvane interview and see "Notes" for Chapter 45. **Steingut:** Levitt TBTA Audit, p. 116. **No "government business":** *NYT*, June 17, 1968. **Roe:** Spargo to Roe, June 2, 1968, Secret TBTA Files. **Crews:** Spargo to RM, Dec. 28, 1953, Secret TBTA Files. **Stephens:** RM to Spargo, Dec. 4, 1953; Spargo to RM, Dec. 8, Secret TBTA Files; Lazarus.

Triborough legal fees: Rosenman's boost from RM: Moses, *Dangerous Trade*, p. 705. **Jimmy Hines' assemblyman:** Lazarus. **$250,000 fee:** Transcript, "Hearings, U. S. Congress, Senate Banking and Currency Committee," Vol. 49, p. 3131 (New York City, Oct. 1, 1954). Rosenman also represented a syndicate to which RM was planning to hand an immensely valuable Title I site adjacent to the Lincoln Center development for "a group of theaters" (*Dangerous Trade*, p. 520). Why this plan fell through is unclear. Rosenman was also to reap a small fortune from RM's 1964–65 World's Fair (see Chapter 45). **Preusse:** See Chapter 45.

"Because Tobin doesn't give me anything": Lazarus. **Rosenman's trip:** *NYT*, Feb. 25, 1957. The *Times*'s profile of Rosenman on this occasion called him, in an unintended double-entendre, "Proconsul of Power."

Shanahan: Biography: *J-A*, Aug. 3, 1954; *NYT*, Sept. 2, 1956; July 3, 1959; *Post*, Aug. 26, 1959; "Shame," pp. 294–305. Interviews with Cook, Finkelstein, Goldwater, Haddad, Kahn, Lazarus, Merkin, Moscow, Screvane, Wagner and numerous confidential sources. **"He went on face value":** Merkin. **Hatred of "Commies":** Moscow. **"One of the most notorious":** Edelstein. **"Ethically . . . left something to be desired":** Moscow. **"We all knew":** Goldwater. **No mention:** Connable and Silberfarb book. **$27,978:** Levitt TBTA Audit, p. 114. **Fees for banking services:** Levitt TBTA Audit, pp. 148, 150. **$15,000,000 deposit:** Work sheets for Levitt TBTA Audit, undated and unnumbered. **$48,963,000:** Levitt TBTA Audit, p. 149. **Bank couldn't cover it:** Confidential source. **Shanahan and Housing Authority:** Moscow. **RM delegated him slum clearance power:** Goldwater, Haddad, Kahn. **"A part of my deal":** Unidentified sponsor quoted in "Shame," p. 294. **$20,000,000:** Number of shares given by Merkin. **Housing Authority projects were the projects Moses wanted:** Author's analysis of TBTA files, O'D, Impy and Wagner Papers; interviews with RM, Chapin, Coleman, Gabel, Goldwater, Impellitteri, Lazarus, Lutsky, Moscow, Mulcahy, Orton, Rodriguez and numerous confidential sources. **"Utmost importance":** RM to Impy, Feb. 11, 1953, Impy Papers. **Buckley phone call:** Rodriguez. **State senator:** Confidential source.

"Only one way to hold a district": Quoted in Riordon, p. 25. **Wagner to Screvane:** Wagner, Screvane. **Dossiers:** Ingraham, Lutsky. **Getting Salmon a job:** RM to Cashmore, date lost, Wagner Papers.

"Silence to the grave": Confidential source.

Banks: The best analysis of banks' relationship to New York politicians is the *HT*'s "Our Sideline Legislators" series by Richard L. Madden and Martin J. Steadman, Aug. 1963. The best analysis of banks' relationships with one politician is a series of articles on State Senator Edward J. Speno in *Newsday* by an investigating team headed by Bob Greene, 1969. The best analysis of banks' power in general is Lundberg, *The Rich and the Super-Rich*. This section—as well as the following sections on unions and contractors—is drawn in large part from the author's own observations as a political and investigative reporter for *Newsday*. **Banks needed authority bonds:** Interviews with Jackson Phillips, director of municipal research, Dun and Bradstreet; Dwayne Saunders, vice president, Bank Investment Division, Chemical Bank; Ernest Cohen, director of research, State Banking Department; Madigan; confidential sources. **"Supply and demand":** Madigan. **RM's feelings:** Madigan; they remained unstated but were obvious in the author's interviews with RM. **15% reserve:** Levitt TBTA Audit, p. 22. **"We all knew":** Confidential source. **RM offered bankers more than safety:** The additional incentives he offered by such devices as unnecessarily high interest rates were explained by Phillips and other bankers, and confirmed by Levitt TBTA Audit, pp. 18–37, 147–50, and by comments deleted from the audit at RM's demand but made available to the author. **Private placement:** Madigan.

Chase had the most: White, p. 83. **"There's a dictator":** O'Dwyer OHR. **Largest single recipient:** Levitt TBTA Audit, p. 32. **Chemical Bank:** *NYT*, Oct. 25, 1968. **"We bought a ton":** Saunders. **Remaining divided up:** Levitt TBTA Audit, pp. 32ff. **Rockefeller to RM:** May 25, 1960, quoted in Moses, *Dangerous Trade*, p. 73. **"Pushing hard":** Rodriguez.

"Replacing graft": Rodriguez. **History of the organization:** Connable and Silberfarb book.

"Get the names in": Costikyan. Saul Kaplan says legislators who wanted summer jobs for children or relatives in state parks had only to ask.

Cardinal Spellman's opinion of Eleanor Roosevelt: Moscow, *Last of the Big-Time Bosses*, p. 122, relates the Cardinal attacking Mrs. Roosevelt personally and being ordered to call on her at Hyde

Park and "make up"—an order delivered by Pope Pius XII after Ed Flynn had flown to Rome to see him. **Swapping pieces of land:** RM. **Fordham:** See Chapter 36. **Church interceding for him:** Numerous interviews.

The store for Macy's: Barnes.

"All Moses had to do was push that button": Rodriguez; virtually the same words were used by Lutsky—and by many other politicians in interviews.

Borough presidents: Moscow, "Political Machines Have Lost Their Grip," *The Saturday Evening Post,* Apr. 12, 1947; *What Have You Done for Me Lately?,* pp. 57ff. **Tammany's 30,000:** Moscow, *What Have You Done for Me Lately?,* p. 57. **Power running both ways:** Connable and Silberfarb, pp. 182ff. **Cook:** "Shame," p. 262. For an over-all analysis of the shifts in their power, see Sayre and Kaufman, pp. 638–39. **Effect of the new scale of construction:** The most incisive analysis the author has heard was given by Rodriguez, who worked for both an "old" BP—Jimmy Lyons—and a "new," Herman Badillo. **"On the chessboard":** Sayre and Kaufman, p. 652. **Control of the streets:** Sayre and Kaufman, pp. 629–30. **"Unwritten law":** Moscow, Rodriguez, among others. **"Commanding position":** Sayre and Kaufman, p. 631. **New realities:** Costikyan, Moscow, Rodriguez, Lazarus, Wagner, among others; confirmed by the author's analysis of major public works proposals—and their ultimate disposal—between 1946 and 1960. **Stepping into the vacuum:** Rodriguez described how RM's offers looked from Lyons' angle. Moscow, who dealt with all the BP's on Wagner's behalf, saw it happening, too. Also interviews with Barnes, Chapin, Cullman, Latham, Lazarus, Madigan, Screvane, Shapiro, Tallamy, Wagner. **"Push a button":** Confidential source. **RM disciplining Lyons:** Moscow, *What Have You Done for Me Lately?,* pp. 201–02; *NYT,* Mar. 12, 1953. **"Center of gravity":** Sayre and Kaufman, p. 626. **Forcing Board to approve Narrows Bridge approaches:** Moscow; Ina Joan Caro, "The Bridge" (unpublished M.A. thesis). **Require redemption:** The total value of Triborough facilities was set at that figure by Dun and Bradstreet.

"A foreign, sovereign state": Confidential source. **Lutsky:** Interview. **No attempt to modify it:** Author's analysis of program.

34. Moses and the Mayors

SOURCES

Books, articles and documents:

Anderson, *The Federal Bulldozer*; Connable and Silberfarb, *Tigers of Tammany*; Costikyan, *Behind Closed Doors*; Felker (ed.), *The Power Game*; Flynn, *You're the Boss*; Garrett, *The La Guardia Years*; Gunther, *Inside U.S.A.*; Hamburger, *Mayor-Watching*; Lie, *In the Cause of Peace*; Mockridge, *The Big Fix*; Moscow, *What Have You Done for Me Lately?* and *The Last of the Big-Time Bosses*; Morris, *Let the Chips Fall*; Moses, *Dangerous Trade*; Nevins and Krout, *The Greater City*; Rodgers, *Robert Moses*; Zeckendorf, *Zeckendorf.*

Fred J. Cook and Gene Gleason, "The Shame of New York," *The Nation,* Oct. 31, 1959. Philip Hamburger, "The Mayor," *The New Yorker,* Jan. 26, Feb. 7, 1957.

Moses, "Construction Schedule for Arterial Highways and Parkways," Nov. 26, 1945.

Moses, "Report to the Mayor, Board of Estimate, City Planning Commission and City Council by the City Construction Coordinator on Progress and Proposed Revision in the Program of Essential Postwar Public Improvements, New York City," Apr. 15, 1946.

Moses to O'Dwyer, Memorandum "on the necessity for immediate agreement by the Board of Estimate on the City's improvement program in the years 1947, 1948 and 1949," Apr. 10, 1947. These two reports are the most valuable out of the great mass of O'Dwyer Papers.

City Planning Commission, "Planning Progress, 1940–50, City of New York," Mar. 15, 1951.

O'Dwyer, Impellitteri, Wagner and Zeckendorf Papers.

Oral History Reminiscences:

Stanley M. Isaacs, Reuben A. Lazarus, George McAneny, William O'Dwyer.

NOTES

—O'DWYER

Author's interviews:

For the O'Dwyer period: Charles Abrams, William S. Chapin, John A. Coleman, Victor F. Condello, Howard S. Cullman, Thomas E. Dewey, Jerry Finkelstein, Monroe Goldwater, Saul Kaplan, Jacob Lutsky, Michael J. Madigan, Joseph D. McGoldrick, Warren Mos-

cow, Paul O'Dwyer, Lawrence M. Orton, Sidney M. Shapiro, Paul Windels, William J. Zeckendorf, confidential sources.

O'D biography: Gunther, pp. 559–65; Hamburger, pp. 84–114; Moscow, *What Have You Done for Me Lately?*, pp. 31–34, and *Last of the Big-Time Bosses,* pp. 64–65, 85–89; Nevins and Krout, pp. 115–24. **"Little did the boys know":** Hamburger, p. 108. **O'D and Moran:** *NYT*, May 2, 1951; Dec. 19, 1952; "Shame," pp. 266–69; Fulton Oursler, "The Remarkable Story of William O'D," *Reader's Digest,* May 12, 1952; Morris, pp. 215–23. **Trying to withdraw:** Moscow, *What Have You Done for Me Lately?*, p. 32. **In Mexico:** Hamburger, p. 99. **Grand-jury charges:** *NYT*, Oct. 30, 1945.

O'D's relationship with RM: $1,565,000,000 price tag: Moses, "Report . . . by the City Construction Coordinator on . . . Postwar Public Improvements." The report given to the Mayor-elect was a draft of the one published the following April.

No money available: Moses, "Report," p. 5; McGoldrick; various newspapers, Dec. 1945–Feb. 1946. **"I tell you":** O'D quoted in Hamburger, pp. 96–97. **Then Moses appeared:** Moses, "Construction Schedule for Arterial Highways and Parkways," Nov. 26, 1945. **Housing:** *NYT*, Mar. 6, June 2, 1946; *Post*, Nov. 7, 14, 15, 1945; *HT*, Dec. 20, Dec. 21, 1945. **Airports:** Spivack in *Post*, Jan. 29, 1946.

"Deferred" and "nondeferrable" lists: Codified in Apr. 15, 1946, "Report."

RM wants to be named to Housing Authority: His boldest attempt was to come some months later in a series of leaks to the *DN*, climaxed in *DN*, Oct. 25, 1946.

"Bob Moses represented to me": O'D OHR, p. 87.

"Municipal extortion": NYC Consumer Council statement, quoted in *NYT*, Feb. 20, 1946. **Isaacs pointed out:** In letter printed in *HT*, Feb. 24, 1947. **"Give-away":** McGoldrick interview with author; McGoldrick quoted in *Post*, Mar. 22, 1946. **La Guardia radio broadcast:** *NYT*, Jan. 7, 1946. **Lazarus Joseph:** *HT*, Feb. 20, 1946. **Democrats demand O'D ask for more state aid:** For example, *NYT* and Brooklyn *Eagle*, Feb. 24, 28.

RM threatens to "reveal some facts": *Post*, Mar. 22, 1946. **Naked display of power:** Moscow. **O'D empowers RM to represent him:** *NYT*, Feb. 18. **Joseph on third floor, RM on second:** *HT*, Feb. 18. **City's business entirely through RM:** Condello, the city's legislative representative; a confidential source who represented Dewey in the negotiations; Kaplan, Assembly minority leader Steingut's counsel; Lazarus, on the scene in an unofficial technical capacity; Moscow, covering City Hall for the *Times.* See also *HT*, Mar. 29. **The deal:** Interviews cited directly above. *NYT*, *HT*, and Brooklyn *Eagle*, various issues, Feb.–Mar. 1946, have the details although they did not know the significance of RM's role. **RM did not represent their position:** *NYT*, Feb. 19. **O'D did not apply pressure:** *NYT*, Feb. 20.

RM's commission: Approval of Tunnel Authority takeover: *NYT*, Apr. 24, 1946; **of increase in bonds and new bond interest rates:** *HT*, Mar. 5; **of Airport Authority:** Various newspapers, Mar. 27; **of housing:** *NYT*, June 2; **$22,000,000 bonus:** *NYT*, Feb. 20.

Analysis of deal results: Isaacs OHR, pp. 248–60; interviews cited above. The few public analyses came only much after the fact—for example, *Post*, Mar. 16, 1950.

"Pick your members": O'D OHR, p. 871. **Why members selected:** Shapiro. **"I never spoke":** O'D OHR, p. 871. **McLaughlin, Meyer appointments:** O'D OHR, p. 583. **Appointments in other key agencies:** O'D OHR, p. 546.

"Strong man": *NYT*, Jan. 8, 1946. **"Oberbürgermeister":** LaG radio speech quoted in *NYT*, Dec. 29, 1945. **RM boasts:** *Christian Science Monitor* article quoted in *Post*, May 21, 1946. **"Matters pending":** Corcoran to O'D, May 29, 1946, O'D Papers. **Laughing it off:** O'D interview in *Post*, May 22, 1946.

O'D getting angry: *Post*, May 2, 1946; Lutsky, Moscow, Orton. **Spargo:** Moscow. **"Trouble-shooting" squad:** *NYT*, May 27, 1946. **O'D calls Orton:** Orton. **RM losing on Planning Commission:** Orton. **Stop worrying:** McAneny OHR; Windels.

Idlewild: RM planning 600 percent rise: *PM*, Mar. 19, 1946. **Lunch at Randall's Island:** *HT*, July 10, 20. **The bonds could not be sold:** *NYT*, July 22. **Port Authority announcement:** *HT*, Dec. 19. **Press accuses O'D:** Various newspapers, July 1946. **O'D gives Port Authority airports:** *NYT*, Aug. 3. **Cancellation of $1,178,250 contract:** O'D Papers.

Liberal organizations: *Post*, June 24. **28,000:** *NYT*, June 24, 1946. **"The biggest story":** *PM*, July 28. **O'D considering enlarging Planning Commission:** Acting Corporation Counsel John J. Bennett to O'D, Dec. 28, 1946, O'D Papers. **RM's**

access to O'D restricted: Confidential source. **RM asks deputy mayor:** RM to Corcoran, Nov. 22, 1946, O'D Papers. **Herzstein reply:** Herzstein to RM, Nov. 25, 1946, O'D Papers. **"Tell the gentleman";** Coleman, who was present, in interview with author.

O'D desperate for money, trying to oust Rogers: Moscow. **$3,000,000:** Abrams. **Parking garages:** O'D Papers; various newspapers, Dec. 3, 1946.

State awards falling off: Author's analyses of newspaper articles and editorials, July–Dec. 1946. **Mid-Manhattan captures O'D's fancy:** Hamburger, p. 101. **RM-Rogers joint announcement:** *NYT*, Oct. 15, 1946. **"Capital . . . still in City Hall":** Citizens Union quoted in *NYT*, Dec. 16. **RM no comment:** *NYT*, Dec. 3. **Scene on ground floor:** *HT*, Dec. 3. **O'D's thinking during this period:** Some clues from Coleman, Cullman, Lutsky, Madigan, Moscow, confidential sources.

United Nations: "The one great thing": O'D OHR, p. 191. **Appointed RM chairman:** *HT*, Dec. 3, 1945. **RM fatherly toward Nelson Rockefeller:** RM, Shapiro. **UNO opened on site RM had selected:** Moses, *Dangerous Trade*, p. 485. **Maneuvering among different cities:** Lie, pp. 107–14; *Dangerous Trade*, pp. 485–91; Zeckendorf, p. 68; O'D OHR, p. 192. **Needed a "gesture":** O'D OHR. **Lie personally awed by RM:** See next paragraph of Notes. **"Unless they came up":** Lie, p. 112. **"Fervently":** Zeckendorf, p. 69. **"Working on Mr. Rockefeller":** O'D OHR, p. 191. **"Tense and exciting":** Lie, p. 113. **For every snag, a knife:** Zeckendorf interview. **"Would you sell it?":** Zeckendorf, p. 70. **Arranging the housing:** *Dangerous Trade*, pp. 435, 485. **Housing:** *NYT*, *HT*, Apr. 28, 1946. **$32,000,000:** O'D OHR, pp. 191–93.

"My deepest thanks": Lie to RM, Dec. 14, 1946, quoted in *Dangerous Trade*, p. 490. **"One of the greatest men of our time":** Lie quoted in *NYT*, Dec. 17, 1949. On the occasion of his retirement as Secretary-General, Lie wrote RM, "Day by day, the United Nations Plaza acquires the appearance which you must have had in mind all along. . . . New York City is indeed fortunate that it has in you so imaginative and dynamic a planner and builder." Lie to RM, Apr. 14, 1953, quoted in *Dangerous Trade*, p. 500. **Rockefeller letter:** *Dangerous Trade*, p. 490. **O'D letter:** *Dangerous Trade*, p. 495.

RM memo on highways: RM to O'D, July 21, 1947, O'D Papers. **O'D tolerated no further delays:** *NYT*, July 17, 1947, was the first sign. **Contracts to Federation-linked firms:** Author's analysis of contract awards, through confidential sources. **Joseph dispute:** *HT*, *Sun*, Nov. 21, 1947. **"Tuesdays":** O'D quoted in Hamburger, p. 101. **Few mornings:** Coleman. **Use of entree:** Lutsky.

"The city's too big": Hamburger, pp. 91, 110. **"The scene":** Paul O'Dwyer. **"All decisions that mattered":** Orton. **HT editorial:** Dec. 26, 1947. **"On contracts, I'd rely":** O'D OHR, pp. 546–57. **"He has both":** O'D OHR, pp. 182–83.

RM apprised O'D: He knew because Senator Taft was consulting him at every step, RM interview with author; Rodgers, p. 154. **Allowed him to name most committee members:** It included, besides RM, three long-time RM allies—his former aide, Philip J. Cruise; John C. Reidel, chief engineer of the Board of Estimate; and Corporation Counsel John P. McGrath—and one opponent: Lazarus Joseph.

Power of a new immensity: Anderson book. **May 1949 speech:** Rodgers, p. 234. **RM instrumental in draft movement:** Coleman and confidential sources. **Supporting O'D:** For example, a "Battle Page" he wrote for *DN*, Oct. 24, 1949. **Predicted solutions:** *NYT*, Oct. 15. **Windels quote:** *NYT*, Oct. 13. **"If there is anything certain":** *HT*, Sept. 13. **"We're talking about housing":** *HT*, Oct. 19. **RM's support helpful:** Moscow. **Quintessential ribbon-cutting campaign:** For example, *NYT*, *HT*, Oct. 15, 19, 20, 25, Nov. 3, 8. **Spargo to O'D:** Nov. 22, 1949, O'D Papers.

Finkelstein: Finkelstein interview, confirmed by Orton. **Proof that Orton was right:** "Request of the City Planning Department for 1950–51," Feb. 1, 1950. pp. 1, 8, 13, 115. **Per capita:** "Request," p. 7. **Duplication:** "Request," p. 4. **Lunch with RM:** Finkelstein. **Sent Hodgkiss:** Handwritten notes in ink on Hodgkiss to RM, Mar. 28, 1950, O'D Papers. **"A last protest":** RM to O'D, Mar. 29, 1950, O'D Papers. **Went public:** *NYT*, Feb. 8, 1950.

A lot of old men: McGoldrick, Orton; *NYT*, Feb. 2, 1950; Nathan Straus to *NYT*, Mar. 2, 1950; George Hallett to O'D, Mar. 10, 1950, O'D Papers. **NYT editorial:** Feb. 8, 1950. **O'D pushed the Board:** Orton.

"O'D loved Moses": Finkelstein. **Other commission members support Finkelstein:** Orton. **UN site:** *NYT*, May 11, 1950. **Playgrounds:** Deputy Mayor William

Reid to Finkelstein, Apr. 1, 1950, O'D Papers.

Real public hearings: *HT*, Aug. 8, 1950. **Realtors' support obtained:** Finkelstein, Orton.

Washington Square: *NYT*, May 11, 1950; *HT*, Apr. 12, 1950; Rodgers, pp. 274–75.

O'D's campaign contributions: *NYT*, various issues, 1951–52. **"Real pressure," Moran burning retirement papers:** Moscow, *What Have You Done for Me Lately?*, pp. 32–33.

—IMPY

Author's interviews:

For the Impellitteri period: Victor F. Condello, Howard S. Cullman, Jerry Finkelstein, Monroe Goldwater, Mrs. Rudolph Halley, Vincent R. Impellitteri, Reuben A. Lazarus, Jacob Lutsky, Michael J. Madigan, Warren Moscow, Lawrence M. Orton, Charles F. Rodriguez, Sidney M. Shapiro.

NOTES

RM in South America unaware: RM, Madigan, Shapiro; during this period his private memos to aides and in the O'D Papers show him utterly unaware that the Mayor might be planning to resign.

How Impy was chosen: Moscow, *Last of the Big-Time Bosses,* p. 63, says that the "Green Book" story was actually one devised to cover up the fact that Thomas (Three Fingers Brown) Luchese had ordered the ticket shifted around to make room for Impy, but three participants present at the last-minute reshuffling—RM, Lazarus and one confidential source—confirm that, improbable as it sounds, the "Green Book" version has it precisely the way it happened. Impy possessed, in fact, the ninth-longest name in the entire "Green Book," *NYT*, Aug. 27, 1950. **"The perfect Throttlebottom":** Moscow, *Last of the Big-Time Bosses,* p. 97.

RM's endorsement: *NYT*, Oct. 25, 1950; Moscow calls Impy's obtaining of that endorsement a "coup," in *Last of the Big-Time Bosses,* p. 97. **"Even I"; leading Impy around by the hand:** Lazarus OHR, pp. 405–06. **Campaign analysis:** Moscow, *What Have You Done for Me Lately?*, pp. 34–35.

"All I have is three votes": For example, *NYT*, Oct. 10, 1953. **"You think they'll come?":** Condello. **Too timid:** Lazarus. **Humming with the choir:** *NYT*, Oct. 10, 1953. **"You got any ideas?":** Moscow interview. **Wringing his hands:** A vivid picture of the Mayor at Board of Estimate executive sessions is painted by Condello, Lutsky, Moscow and various other members of the Impy administration who wish to remain unidentified.

"RM is actually running this town": Lazarus showed the author this entry in his diary. **RM dropping by at nine:** Impy's daily schedules, many of which were found in his papers, show that he generally left ninety minutes for his sessions with RM. **"I didn't want them interrupted":** Impy interview with author. **"Marching orders":** Wagner, Moscow. An example of the peremptory tone Moses used with Impy is a letter he wrote him on Nov. 2, 1951: "My suggestion therefore is that you call Bob Wagner [then Manhattan borough president] and tell him that the hearing should be held by the Committee and not independently by him, and, of course, he should be present. This hearing should be held at City Hall in the room in which the Board of Estimate executive meetings are held, on Thursday, Nov. 8th, at 3 P.M." Impy Papers. **"No use boring you":** RM to Impy, Dec. 7, 1950, Impy Papers. **"Moses' word was law":** Condello. Moscow (*Last of the Big-Time Bosses,* p. 97) says Impy left "policy-making in the hands of Moses and the city's Bureau of the Budget," but Impy Papers clearly reveal that whenever the two disagreed, RM won by threatening to resign unless Impy ordered the Budget Bureau to do what he wanted. For example, memo, "Telephoned by Office of Commissioner Moses for Mayor Impellitteri," Aug. 14, 1951; and RM to Impy, Sept. 13, 1951, states: "The Budget director had withheld from the calendar . . . items [for] related repairs agreed upon with the United Nations. . . . If this item is to be deleted or is to be the subject of debate and controversy I should like to be relieved of all future responsibility for completing the UN Program." **Recommendations and blackballings:** RM to Impy, Mar. 28, June 13, Dec. 6, 1951, on over-all reorganization of the Board of Education, with which RM ostensibly had no connection, and May 4, Sept. 16, 1952, Impy Papers.

Secret "understanding": Condello, confidential sources.

Point-by-point "suggestions": RM to Impy, June 27, 1953, Impy Papers.

Shelter Cottage: RM to Impy, Mar. 9, 1951, Impy Papers.

Rezoning study: Finkelstein, Orton. **Finkelstein and Impy letters:** *NYT*, Oct. 5, 1950. **"Dear Vince":** RM to Impy,

handwritten note, Dec. 4, 1950, Impy Papers. **RM recommends Bennett—and has Impy give Reidel a salary increase:** RM to Impy, Dec. 20, 1950, Impy Papers; confidential sources. **Rodgers:** Shapiro. **Forcing out the young planners:** Orton, confidential sources; memos in "City Planning Commission" folder in Impy Papers; for example, Jan. 29, 1953. **Fate of rezoning report:** Orton. **"Now the city's built up":** O'D OHR, p. 580. **RM was back in control:** So sure of Bennett was he that he didn't even object when—after eleven years—the commission finally published an annual report. The reason for his lack of objection becomes clear in the opening paragraph of Bennett's introduction: the report will deal, the chairman says, with "the steady progress of planning in New York City and the translation of the plans into public betterment. . . . One measure of this progress was presented in the report of . . . the City Construction Coordinator." "Planning Progress," p. 5.

Halley: Mrs. Halley. **Lyons:** *NYT*, Mar. 13, 1953. **"Taken for granted":** Moscow interview.

Summary of trends in Impy administration: Peter Kihss, *NYT*, Aug. 10–14, 1953; Moscow, *Last of the Big-Time Bosses.*

—WAGNER

Author's interviews:

For the Wagner period: Robert F. Wagner, Jr.

Wagner appointees, advisers or friends: William F. R. Ballard, Henry Barnes, Peter J. Brennan, Peter Campbell Brown, John A. Coleman, Victor F. Condello, Timothy J. Cooney, Edward N. Costikyan. Howard S. Cullman, Perry B. Duryea, Jr., Julius C. C. Edelstein, Hortense Gabel, Monroe Goldwater, Luther Gulick, Saul Kahn, Reuben A. Lazarus, Jacob Lutsky, Warren Moscow, Paul O'Keefe, Lawrence M. Orton, Charles F. Rodriguez, Philip Shumsky, Paul R. Screvane. Eleven Wagner appointees, advisers or friends preferred to remain unidentified.

RM aides or associates: William S. Chapin, Ernest J. Clark, William Latham, Michael J. Madigan, Sidney M. Shapiro, Arnold Vollmer, Arthur B. Williams. Four RM aides or associates preferred to remain unidentified.

Reporters: Fred J. Cook, William J. Haddad, Joseph Kahn, Mary Perot Nichols.

NOTES

Unforgettable evenings: Wagner, RM, Cullman. **His interest in city planning:** Hamburger, *The New Yorker*, Jan. 26, 1957. **Insisted on using his own contractors:** One on whom Wagner insisted, to RM's displeasure, was Del Balso, whom RM, in a 1950 letter to Wagner, calls "your contractor" (O'D Papers). **"Bubblehead":** The author has been unable to locate a copy of the letter, but many people around City Hall, including Lutsky, recall reading it. **"I'm not going to let Moses":** Among those whom he told he was going to "rein in" Moses were Coleman, Cullman, Goldwater, Gulick, Lutsky, Moscow. **"A source close":** *Post*, Nov. 6, 1953. **The second leak:** *Post*, Nov. 18, 1953.

Good Government strategy: Gabel, Orton. **Left the interview believing:** Orton.

The swearing in: Among those watching who noted RM's anger were Coleman, Cullman, Lazarus and Shapiro. **Typing up own form:** Lutsky, Shumsky. **Moscow:** *What Have You Done for Me Lately?*, p. 196. The *NYT* article on the swearing in, attempting to account for the fact that RM was sworn in publicly for only two posts but was later listed as having been sworn in for three, quotes Wagner as saying, "There is one more coming up but the necessary papers are not ready," but none of the persons the author interviewed recall the Mayor making such a statement, none of the other newspapers mentions it (all, in fact, say the announcement of RM's third appointment following the ceremony came as a complete surprise), and several other liberals, listening to the ceremonies over the radio—such as City Planning Commissioner Lawrence M. Orton—told the author that Wagner "passed right on" to the next appointee and that they began cheering because they thought they had won.

Authority to "represent" the city: RM to Wagner, Jan. 5, 1954; F. V. Du Pont, Federal Commissioner of Public Roads, to RM, Jan. 25, 1954; Wagner Papers.

Mitchell-Lama fight: Moscow, *What Have You Done for Me Lately?*, pp. 203–04; Moscow, Orton. **RM's "own" housing program:** Orton to RM, Oct. 11, 1955, Wagner Papers; *NYT*, *HT*, various dates, 1954.

"My friend, Bob Wagner": *HT*, Feb. 24, 1954. **"He has been heard to say":** Hamburger, *The New Yorker*, Feb. 2, 1957.

Port Authority: Cullman, Wagner.

Housing Authority: *NYT*, Jan. 9, 1954; Moscow, confirmed by Wagner. **Cruise's swearing in:** *Post*, Jan. 10, Feb. 11, 1954. **"Well, I made my deal":** Wagner quoted by O'Keefe, in interview. **McMurray friendly to Shanahan:** Moscow, O'Keefe, confidential sources. **Cruise making his divorce:** Moscow, Shapiro, confidential sources.

Screvane: Interview with author. **RM showing up late:** Costikyan. **Gracie Mansion receptions:** Confidential sources. **"He does a lot of his work":** Unidentified source quoted in Hamburger, p. 82. **RM dominated the relationship:** Among many, Barnes, Brown, Chapin, Cooney, Moscow, Screvane.

Wagner's attempt to gain fifth Housing Authority vote: Moscow. **Day-to-day Authority affairs still dominated by RM:** Confidential sources on Authority staff. **Edelstein:** In interview with author. **Wagner never interfered with Title I:** Lutsky, who was supposedly the Mayor's "watchdog" on the committee; confidential sources.

Wagner surrendering to resignation threat: Goldwater, for example, told the author that the Mayor agitatedly telephoned him for advice after many threats; each time, Goldwater says, he told Wagner that Moses' popularity made it necessary to give him his way—and each time, Goldwater says, Wagner took his advice. For a typical threat—and Wagner surrendering to it—see RM to Wagner, Sept. 1, 1954, and Epstein to RM, Sept. 3, 1954, Wagner Papers.

35. *"RM"*

SOURCES

Books and documents:

Herndon, *The Sweetest Music This Side of Heaven*; Lewis, *The Day They Shook the Plum Tree*; Rodgers, *Robert Moses.*

Office of the State Comptroller, Division of Audits and Accounts, "Draft Report" on LISPC, Jones Beach and Bethpage authorities. This report was compiled by auditors in the office of State Comptroller Arthur Levitt and never publicly released. It is referred to in the Notes as "Levitt LISPC Audit."

Author's interviews:

Harvey Aronson, Bernie Bookbinder, Henry Barnes, Ernest J. Clark, Ralph Clark, Jane Moses Collins, Perry B. Duryea, Jr., Nettie Greenberg, Edgar L. Hazleton, Joseph T. Ingraham, Joseph Kahn, Lee Koppelman, William Latham, Reuben A. Lazarus, Jacob Lutsky, Michael J. Madigan, General Harry L. Meyers, Lawrence Orton, Sidney M. Shapiro, Mae Smisek, Hazel Tappan, Bertram D. Tallamy, Arnold Vollmer.

NOTES

Authority meeting: Rodgers, p. 179. **First play in years:** Ernest Clark. **Mary's chores:** Jane Moses Collins, Shapiro. **Asking for a dollar:** Ingraham. **The manila envelope:** Shapiro. **"A dynamo":** Greenberg. **The letters:** Tappan, Greenberg.

RM on the Sea-Ef: Mae Smisek, daughter of the captain. **Dictating at 7 A.M.** Madigan. **Propped up in bed:** Tallamy.

"You're just a swabbie": Shapiro. **Throwing the inkwell:** Confidential sources.

Bringing breakfast to Mary: Jane Moses Collins. **"Protecting" him in relays:** Latham. **From Palms to Pines:** Vollmer.

Learned Hand letter: A copy given to author by Shapiro. **"He never got tired":** Confidential source.

Hetty Green bequest: Lewis, p. 311, says he "merely endorsed his $10,000 check and turned it over to charity the day he received it!" This recollection does not conform with that of Shapiro, Madigan or several confidential sources. **Used commissions to buy other men:** Madigan; confidential sources.

"A feeling of isolation": Bookbinder. **Air-conditioned car:** Lazarus. **Three personal chauffeurs:** Shapiro. **That car alone:** Meyers. **Telephoning Randall's Island; captains on call; network of pools:** Meyers, Smisek, Ingraham.

Frenzy in the offices: Author's observations. **Subservience:** Barnes, Kahn.

RM's hospitality: The author was a recipient, and part of the following section is drawn from his personal observations. The scope and the cost to the public of this hospitality RM dispensed is found in Levitt LISPC Audit. **Boardwalk Restaurant:** Levitt LISPC Audit, Sec. A, pp. 8ff. **New Boardwalk Restaurant:** Levitt LISPC Audit, Sec. D, p. 6.

Marine Stadium: Not for general public: Shapiro. **Rearranging his schedule:** Author's observation. **Phony "vote":** Author was standing with Shapiro when he made the comment. **Attendance figures:** Levitt LISPC Audit, Part II, unnumbered

pages. The audit also states that, between 1967 and 1971 alone, "it cost the Authority almost $1,600,000 more than the revenues it received to present entertainment. . . . This does not include our estimate of $574,000 for the amortization of the cost of the facilities. . . . We believe these subsidies would be better expended on entertainment which would be more attractive to a larger segment of the public."

Guy Lombardo: Levitt LISPC Audit, Part II. **Other producers would have paid:** Shapiro, Ingraham. **"One bottle of Scotch":** Herndon, p. 220. However, to cite one item out of many found by the auditors, Guy personally received a "producer's fee" which, in 1964 for example, was $51,000 and a fee "paid . . . for use of his band for dancing in excess of the amounts paid to band," which, for 1966 alone, was $70,000. **Costs to taxpayers:** Levitt LISPC Audit, Part II, unnumbered pages; Sec. D, p. 6.

Limousines, etc.: See "RM's hospitality" above. **Wainwright:** Confidential source. **Typical tour:** Schedule provided to author. **Yale class:** Ralph Clark. **Planners' tour:** Koppelman. **Niagara excursion:** Aronson. **"How could you turn the guy down?":** Lutsky. **Bookbinder's pass:** Bookbinder.

Made disagreement difficult: Many of his guests—most perceptively, Orton—noted this.

"In the year 1999": RM. "What will New York Be Like in 1999—Not so Different" *NYT Magazine*, Feb. 6, 1949.

"Make him give his name": *HT*, *NYT*, Sept. 27, 1958; Shapiro. **Left because furious:** Shapiro. **Beach grass:** Hazleton; confirmed by Shapiro. **Trujillo:** RM related this story—with pride—to John Lord O'Brien and others.

Jones Beach: RM, "From the Bridge" column, *Newsday*. **Bronx-Whitestone:** RM, "From the Bridge" column, *Newsday*. **Waterfront:** RM, "The Expanding New York Waterfront" (brochure), Aug. 1964. **"The City Builder must have":** RM, quoted in *NYT Magazine*, Jan. 19, 1941. **"The ancient truth":** RM quoted in *NYT*, Mar. 7, 1948.

Compares himself to Lincoln: *HT*, Nov. 21, 1943; *HT*, May 15, 1946. And in the Rodgers biography of RM on which RM worked so closely: "Moses believes, like Lincoln, that government should do those things which the people cannot do for themselves" (p. xxvi); Shapiro.

Bay Shore teacher: Ralph Housrath said this to Aronson.

Refuses to consider hearing aid: Meyers; author's observations.

Golf: RM to *NYT*, Apr. 22, 1944.

36. The Meat Ax

SOURCES

Books and articles:

Bureau of Public Roads (BPR), *When All Roads Led to Rome*; Leavitt, *Superhighway–Superhoax*; Moses, *Dangerous Trade*; Rethi and Young, *The Great Bridge*; Rodgers, *Robert Moses*; Rose, *Public Roads of the Past*; Saalman, *Haussmann: Paris Transformed*; Schreiber, *Merchants, Pilgrims*; Talese, *The Bridge*.

Ernest J. Clark, "The Cross-Bronx Expressway" (mimeographed); "Roads and Highways," *Encyclopædia Britannica*, 1958 edition; Theodore H. White, "Where Are Those New Roads?," *Collier's*, Jan. 6, 1956. "Longest Lighted Submarine Tunnel," *American City*, July 1950. R. Thruelsen, "New York's Deepest Tunnel," *The Saturday Evening Post*, Mar. 25, 1950.

Clay Committee hearings, Oct. 7–8, 1954, transcript. (A committee appointed by the President to study U.S. highway needs; General Lucius D. Clay, chairman.) Moses, "Construction Schedule for Arterial Highways and Parkways," Nov. 26, 1945; "Openings—Federal State City Arterial Construction Program" (Report to Hon. Vincent R. Impellitteri), Oct. 14, 1950.

Author's interviews:

Many Bureau of Public Roads officials, among whom the only ones willing to be identified are former Federal Highway Administrator Bertram D. Tallamy and former BPR chief Francis Turner; former State DPW head J. Burch McMorran, former DPW officials Arthur B. Williams, Sr., James Truex, Edward Moloney and many unwilling to be identified; Moses' engineering consultants Ernest J. Clark, Michael J. Madigan, Arnold Vollmer and others unwilling to be identified; Moses staffers William S. Chapin, William Latham, Sidney M. Shapiro and others unwilling to be identified.

The author is indebted to Ernie Clark and members of Andrews & Clark, Inc., consulting engineers, for numerous days spent touring and studying the engineering of the Cross-Bronx Expressway.

NOTES

The Royal Road and Herodotus: Schreiber, pp. 10–24. **The "silk roads" and the Khan's post roads:** Schreiber, pp. 25–63. **The highways of Rome:** BPR, *passim*; quotes from Alfred Leger (*Les Travaux Publics et les Mines et la Métallurgie aux Temps des Romains*, Paris, 1875) in BPR, after pp. 2, 4, 42. **Roads on a different scale:** BPR, Rose and Schreiber books; *Encyclopaedia Britannica*. **Eighty acres:** Clark. **Haussmann:** Saalman book.

No one dared lay superhighways through a city; Their mileage would not add up: BPR Library.

Cross-Bronx Expressway: Ernie Clark of Andrews & Clark, its principal designer, interviews and his "Cross-Bronx Expressway" speech; Chapin, Madigan, Moloney and other engineers involved in its planning and construction who wish to remain anonymous. **"I never knew there were trees like that":** Bronx resident Edward J. Korn. **Hardly mentioned it; a new word necessary:** Clark, "Cross-Bronx Expressway." **Visualizing it:** Clark, Madigan, Chapin, confidential source.

Van Wyck: Rodgers, p. 179. **Cost of highways:** Average and total from Moses, "Arterial Progress," Nov. 8, 1965. The $40,000,000 mile is the mile discussed in the next chapter.

Verrazano statistics: TBTA, "Spanning the Narrows," Nov. 21, 1964, pp. 22–38.

Brooklyn-Battery Tunnel statistics: "Longest Lighted Submarine Tunnel"; Thruelsen, "New York's Deepest Tunnel."

Moses Men and the agencies: Chapin, Clark, Madigan, McMorran. **Amending state law, bond issues, etc.:** Moses, introduction to "Openings—Federal State City Arterial Construction Program," p. 6. **Persuading Congress to finance roads linked to toll facilities:** Madigan, Tallamy, Turner, confidential sources. **Persuading state to pick up city costs:** McMorran, Tallamy. **Korean steel:** *NYT*, various articles, 1951; editorial, Oct. 8, 1951. **Copper strike:** *NYT*, various articles, 1952.

Shuffling properties: With Catholic Church: RM. **With Con Ed:** Madigan. **Major Deegan exchange:** *NYT* and *HT*, Oct. 31, 1949.

"Toy building blocks": The reporter was Walter Lister, Jr., *HT*, Jan. 22, 1950. **"Absolutely crazy":** RM. **Marguerite Hotel:** Shapiro.

Moley: Foreword to *Dangerous Trade*, p. xi.

"Can't make an omelet": RM flaunted this slogan for more than two years on signs posted over the Long Island Expressway at the site of the 1964–65 World's Fair. **"Meat ax":** *Dangerous Trade.*

37. One Mile

SOURCES

Books, brochures, reports, engineering studies and documents:

Moses, *Dangerous Trade.*

Edelstein, Impellitteri and O'Dwyer Papers.

Bronx Borough President, "Route Study for Development Plan—Cross-Bronx Thruway," Jan. 1944.

Arthur Katz, "A Neighborhood Organizes to Fight City Hall—A Case Study in Community Organization," circa 1960 (a report written, apparently for his own pleasure, by the executive director of the East Tremont Neighborhood Center).

Moses, "Construction Schedule for Arterial Highways and Parkways," Nov. 26, 1945; "Construction Schedule for Arterial Highways and Parkways" (Report to Hon. William O'Dwyer), June 10, 1946; "City of New York Public Works Program Progress Report," Jan. 1, 1949; "Openings—Federal State City Arterial Construction Program" (Report to Hon. Vincent R. Impellitteri), Oct. 14, 1950; "George Washington Bridge Approach—Highbridge Expressway Interchange," May 5, 1952; "Deegan Expressway—Cross-Bronx Expressway—Long Island Expressway," Nov. 4, 1955; "Cross-Bronx Expressway—Alexander Hamilton Bridge–George Washington Bridge Bus Station—Opening," Jan. 17, 1963.

New York City Board of Estimate, Minutes, "Hearing in the Matter of Authorizing a Proceeding for Acquiring Title to Cross-Bronx Expressway, Section 2, from Anthony Avenue to Longfellow Avenue," Nov. 18, 1954, pp. 14176–79; Dec. 2, 1954, pp. 15354–60.

New York City Community Planning Board No. 6, "The East Tremont Story," 1962.

Author's interviews:

With 127 past and present residents of East Tremont.

Lillian Edelstein provided the most detailed account of the fight against the expressway.

Especially helpful in describing the pre-expressway neighborhood were Mrs. Dorothy Beltzer, Mrs. Nora Brown, Samuel and Katherine Coe, Arthur Clark, Mrs. Esther Gassel, Saul Janowitz, Sol Kleinman, Lee Koppelman, Edward J. Korn, Mrs. Helen Lazarcheck, Isidore Malek, Louis Meltzer, Lillian Roberts, Cele Sherman, Fannie Silverstein, Charles Smith, Dominick Tesone and Mrs. Frances Twersky.

Especially helpful in describing the changes wrought in the neighborhood by the expressway were Mrs. Vivian Dee, Bert Gumpert, Arthur Katz, Harry Keifetz and Bernard Lambert.

Among politicians, engineers and others involved in expressway decisions: Ernest J. Clark, Joseph T. Ingraham, Warren Moscow, Lawrence M. Orton, Charles Rodriguez, Robert F. Wagner, Jr., Bernard Weiner and many who would talk only on condition that they remain unidentified.

NOTES

The neighborhood: The picture of it is drawn from the 127 interviews and from the Community Planning Board's "East Tremont Story." **60,000:** This is an estimate. The population of the entire area covered in the "East Tremont Story" is 129,000 but 49,500 are Italians to the north in the Belmont neighborhood, so Tremont's population would be 79,500. East Tremont is 75 percent of the land area; 75 percent of 79,500 is 60,000. According to the "East Tremont Story," 44,000 of the 60,000 are Jews. **"A feeling of crowdedness":** "Story," p. 22. **"Simchas" in the neighborhood," "myriad of social systems," "each had his following":** "Story," pp. 11–13.

RM calls them "slums": Moscow recalls RM persuading the Board of Estimate by calling the neighborhood that.

An urban staging area: "Story," pp. 3–22, which includes "a chronological picture of the in and out movement of the various cultural and ethnic groups." **Negroes being integrated into neighborhood:** Smith. **7 in Elsmere Gardens:** Katz. **Population figures on nonwhites:** "Story," p. 18.

Survey for new Y: Lambert, its executive director.

Money nowhere in sight, privately figuring on 18 months: Analysis of memos and letters in Impy, Wagner Papers. **"To shake 'em up a little":** Shapiro. **Subsequent notice:** RM, "Memorandum to Owners and Tenants on Cross-Bronx Expressway between Longfellow Avenue and University Avenue," Dec. 15, 1952.

Section 3: Mrs. Edelstein; *Post*, various articles, Feb. 7, 1949–June 6, 1953. **"Not fit for rats":** *Post*, Feb. 7, 1949. **"A right":** *Post*, Nov. 16, 1952. **"None of the families . . . has been turned into the street":** RM, quoted in *Post*, July 17, 1951. **Waiting six years:** *Post*, Nov. 16, 1952. **"Knew of no one":** Edelstein quoted in *Post*, June 6, 1953 (italics added). **"A nightmare":** *Post*, June 6, 1953.

Weiner study: Weiner; see map, p. 864.

Mrs. Edelstein's telephone call: Edelstein.

Lyons in favor of their route: Lyons quoted in *Post*, Bronx edition, Feb. 23, 1953. **"You have from time to time remarked":** RM to Lyons, Feb. 21, 1953, Impy Papers. **Resignation threat:** RM to Impy, Mar. 10, 1953, Impy Papers. **"A damnable lie":** Lyons quoted in *Post*, Bronx edition, Mar. 13, 1953. **Board of Estimate hearings:** Various newspapers, Apr. 24–May 14, 1953. **Tallamy letter:** Tallamy to RM, May 5, 1953, Impy Papers.

How much more Moses' mile would cost: Robert G. McCullough, Report to Board of Estimate, Apr. 15, 1953 (Board Calendar, pp. E687-1-4). Maps printed in *WT*, *Post*, Sept. 7, 1954.

Wagner had appeared receptive: Edelstein, Janowitz, Katz. **Moscow's Board of Estimate statement.** Transcript, Board of Estimate, Calendar, in No. 48, May 14, 1953; Katz, p. 19. **Letter to ETNA; promise in writing:** Moscow to William Cohen, May 18, 1953, copy from Mrs. Edelstein; Moscow to ETNA, Katz, p. 20. **"I will vote against any resolution":** Katz, p. 20. (The press did not cover the rally.) **Oct. 14 rally:** Katz, p. 20. **Why, certainly, Wagner replied:** Wagner to Edelstein, Oct. 27, 1953, in reply to Oct. 26. **"In December?":** Edelstein.

Wagner intended to keep promise: Confidential source. **Repeated it:** Janowitz.

A direct order: Moses, *Dangerous Trade*, pp. 210–11.

Gerosa switch: Katz, p. 21.

Kahn's articles: *Post*, May 9, 1954, reprints Wagner's letter of Aug. 5, 1953; also *Post*, May 12, 1954, July 21, 1954, Nov. 28, 1954.

Hodgkiss-Wagner exchange: Katz, p. 22. **Epstein:** Katz, p. 23.

Planning Commission hearing: *Post*, July 15, 1954.

Wagner visibly moved: Edelstein; Katz, p. 23. **"Every member":** Wagner

quoted in *Post*, Sept. 22, 1954. **McCullough's trick:** Katz, p. 22; Katz, Edelstein, confidential source. **Wagner orders Epstein to oversee:** *Post*, *WT*, Nov. 19, 1954; Edelstein.

Final hearing before McCullough: Katz, pp. 22–23; Edelstein; *Post*, Nov. 28, 1954. McCullough's report, dated Nov. 12, 1954, attached to Board of Estimate, Calendar No. 4, "Hearing in the Matter of Authorizing a Proceeding . . . ," Nov. 18, 1954. **"Not the slightest":** RM. **Epstein:** See below. **"Very uncomfortable":** Katz. **Epstein's switch:** Edelstein, Katz.

Showdown Board meeting: Katz, p. 23; **Lyons:** Quoted in *Post*, Nov. 21, 1954. **"So fast":** Edelstein.

Why did Epstein switch?: RM. **"Very little real hardship":** RM. **NYT one paragraph:** Nov. 2, 1954.

What Spargo told Ingraham: Ingraham.

Nassau Management: Fred J. Cook and Gene Gleason, "The Shame of New York," *The Nation*, Oct. 31, 1959, pp. 300–01. **Its East Tremont office:** Interviews with residents cited in "Sources." **Cymrot:** *Post*, Jan. 12, 1955. **Dispossess notices:** *Post*, May 6, 1955. The residents' description of the deterioration of East Tremont during relocation is supported by many articles by Joe Kahn and Abel Silver in the *Post*, by articles in the *WT* and the *Bronx Press-Review*. **Tesone:** Quoted in *Post*, May 17, 1956, and interview with author. **11 children:** *Post*, Sept. 22, 1955.

38. *One Mile (Afterward)*

SOURCES

See "Sources" for Chapter 37.

NOTES

Underestimated cost: Comparison of figures in various RM brochures cited in "Sources" for Chapter 37. **Traffic too heavy for Washington Bridge:** Madigan, Clark. **$250,000,000:** RM, various brochures.

It was shaking: Clark, the engineer in charge.

Landlords: Lambert, Katz. **In 1960 still 25,000:** "East Tremont Story," p. 5.

Bronx Park South: Lambert, Dee, Korn. **"I got to get my kids out of here"; "Are you the man from the welfare?":** Present residents of East Tremont to author.

39. *The Highwayman*

SOURCES

Books, articles, brochures, reports and documents:

Bureau of Public Roads (BPR), *When All Roads Led to Rome*; Doig, *Metropolitan Transportation Politics*; Jacobs, *The Death and Life of Great American Cities*; Mumford, *The Highway and the City*; Wood, *1400 Governments*.

F. Dodd McHugh, "Draft of 'Master Plan for New York City Airports,'" and the City Planning Commission's final report, issued Dec. 19, 1945.

Regional Plan Association: "New York's Commuters—Trends of Commuter Transportation in the New York Metropolitan Region 1930–1950," July 1951; "Spread City," 1962; "The Future of Westchester County," Mar. 1971.

RM brochures listed in "Sources" for Chapter 37, identified by date, and "Arterial Progress," Nov. 8, 1965.

Author's interviews:

Planners Lee Koppelman, Joseph McC. Lieper, F. Dodd McHugh, Lawrence M. Orton, John Sheridan, Stanley G. Tankel, Robert C. Weinberg, Paul Windels.

NOTES

Gray two-door sedan: *NYT*, July 4, 1945.

RM's response: *HT*, Sept. 6, 1945.

"The postwar highway era is here": RM, "Construction Schedule," Nov. 26, 1945.

Planners' feelings: Koppelman, Lieper, McHugh, Orton, Tankel, Weinberg, Windels; numerous Mumford articles in *PM*, *The New Yorker*; for example, *PM*, May 12, 1946; *The New Yorker*, Mar. 19–June 16, 1955. RPA, "Spread City," "The Future of Westchester County." **Susquehanna:** Wood, p. 12. **Nathan:** Sept. 3, 1945. **2 out of 3 residents:** Leigh Denniston, *HT*, Sept. 12, 1945. **1,500 per hour; 40,000 per hour:** Out of many varying figures on the capacity of expressway and rapid transit, the author has selected those derived from a careful study made by the Nassau-Suffolk Regional Planning Board in 1968; various documents made available to him by Koppelman.

Press screaming for action and liked RM's plans: For example, *HT* editorial, Jan. 1, 1951; *HT* editorial, Aug. 27, 1947;

NYT, Feb. 20, 1946; *HT*, Nov. 26, 1945; *NYT*, Nov. 4, 11, 1945.

Mumford: *PM*, May 12, 1946. **"Why not bar?":** Letter from Lester E. Waterbury to *NYT*, Oct. 22, 1945. **Williams:** Quoted in *NYT*, Jan. 24, 1947.

Take one simple step: Among the many planners arguing—at the time—for the city to do this were McHugh, Orton and Windels.

"Smart aleck": RM to Salmon, Aug. 12, 1942.

Van Wyck Expressway: This section drawn from McHugh and Orton interviews; from McHugh's draft version of "Master Plan for New York City Airports," written Oct. 10, 1945 (pp. 10–14 deal with mass transit to Van Wyck); and from the "Master Plan" actually adopted by the City Planning Commission on Dec. 19, 1945 (the watered-down Van Wyck discussion is on p. 7). McHugh arrived at the 3,220 figure by taking the average load per vehicle arriving at other airports at peak periods—3.1—and dividing 10,000 by that figure. **Widen Belt and Conduit:** "Master Plan." **$30,000,000:** Figures in various Moses brochures vary from $28,600,000 (RM brochure, Oct. 14, 1950) to $36,785,000 (Nov. 8, 1965). $30,000,000 was the figure McHugh was given at the time. **McHugh's resignation:** McHugh, confirmed by Orton.

Vision of LI: "The Future of Nassau County," address by RM before members of the Nassau Bar Association, Mineola, L.I., June 30, 1945. **"Traffic will run pretty smoothly":** RM to *HT*, Sept. 6, 1945, among others. **Typical RM prediction:** In 1950, for example, he said: "When this [his current arterial] program is fully realized—say, five years from now—we shall have reduced congestion and produced a free flow of traffic except at peak periods everywhere in the city . . ." (RM brochure, Oct. 14, 1950, p. 6.) **"We shall deserve":** RM, *NYT Magazine*, Apr. 29, 1951. **Statius, Claudius:** Leger, quoted in BPR, Fig. V. **1949 article:** RM, *NYT Magazine*, Feb. 6, 1949. **"No network":** RM, Oct. 14, 1950, brochure, p. 6.

Van Wyck jams: *NYT, HT, Newsday*, various articles, 1950–72.

"One of man's greatest": Cardinal Spellman, quoted in *Dangerous Trade*, p. 219; *NYT* and *HT*, May 26, 1950. **BBT traffic prediction and actuality:** TBTA Annual Reports. **"Another pleasant surprise":** TBTA Annual Report, 1951. **No drain-off on other bridges:** *NYT*, May 29, 1950. **Queens-Midtown worse:** TBTA Annual Report, 1951. **Triborough, Whitestone Bridge figures:** TBTA Annual Reports. **New Jersey figures:** RPA, "New York's Commuters," pp. 3, 5, 6, 7, 11. **Lincoln Tunnel, crosstown clockings:** *NYT*, Aug. 11, 1951.

Protests in 1920's: *NYT* and *Tribune*, various issues, 1924, 1925, 1926. **Howl during 1930's:** *NYT* and *HT*, various issues, 1938, 1938, 1939.

Geometrical: RPA, various bulletins. **NYT clocking on West Side Highway:** July 26, 1948. **U-turns:** *NYT*, Sept. 17, 1951. **"Boomerang":** *The New Yorker*, Mar. 10, 1951. **Awareness escalating:** *NYT, HT, Post*, various issues, 1952, 1953. The *Post* was ahead of the other two; it was the only New York newspaper, during this period, which was giving its readers a glimpse of the "costs" to the public involved in the eviction for highways of thousands of families. Other papers were ignoring this aspect of highways all but completely. **"Transportation . . . a means and not an end":** Mumford, "The Roaring Traffic's Boom," *The New Yorker*, Mar. 19, Apr. 2, 16 and June 16, 1955.

RM brochure: Oct. 14, 1950, p. 3. **RPA bulletin:** "New York's Commuters." **People were learning for themselves:** Author's analysis of scores of letters-to-the-editor in *NYT*, *HT*, Brooklyn *Eagle*, *Post, WT, J-A* and *DN*, various issues, 1952–55.

"Today we are well underway": RM, *Post*, July 28, 1948. **He had no doubt:** *U. S. News & World Report*, Aug. 8, 1952. **General Electric:** *NYT*, Jan. 23, 1952. **RM's reply:** RM to *NYT*, Feb. 11, 1952.

"Good work, gentlemen": *HT* editorial, Mar. 16, 1951. **Never linked policies with the man:** Articles in every NYC newspaper during this period lamented over the traffic problem without linking it to RM's policies.

40. Point of No Return

SOURCES

See "Sources" for Chapter 39. Also:

Books, reports, studies and documents:

Hoover and Vernon, *Anatomy of a Metropolis*; Leavitt, *Superhighway–Superhoax;* Moses, *Dangerous Trade*; Owen, *The Metropolitan Transportation Problem*; Whalen, *New York: A City Destroying Itself.*

Dun and Bradstreet, Inc. (D&B), "Municipal Credit Survey—TBTA," Dec. 30, 1955; June 24, 1957; Mar. 18, 1958; Apr. 30, 1959; Apr. 14, 1960; "Municipal Credit Report—TBTA," Nov. 9, 1961; Feb. 12, 1963; May 13, 1963; Apr. 22, 1964; Sept. 30, 1966. Day & Zimmerman, Inc., "Report No. 5849-C to Metropolitan Rapid Transit Commission on Comparative Studies of Proposed Alternate Rapid Transit Plans for Northern Queens County and Vicinity, Long Island, N.Y., Including Effects upon Other Transit Operations," Philadelphia, Pa., Jan. 31, 1957. Day & Zimmerman, Inc., "Report No. 5849-Bi to Metropolitan Rapid Transit Commission on Expanded Comparative Studies of Proposed Alternate Rapid Transit Plans for Staten Island, New York, via the Proposed Narrows Bridge, Including Effects upon Other Transit Operations," Philadelphia, Pa., Nov. 29, 1956. New York State Metropolitan Commuter Transportation Authority (MCTA), "LIRR Modernization Program—Technical Memorandum No. 3, Travel Volume Projections," Feb. 1967.

Jackson Phillips, director of municipal research for Dun and Bradstreet, "Postwar Default Experience of Municipal Bonds," testimony prepared for the Joint Economic Committee of the House of Representatives, Dec. 1966. Port of New York Authority and TBTA, "Joint Study of Arterial Facilities, New York–New Jersey Metropolitan Area," Jan. 1955. TBTA, various prospectuses for bond issues, of which the most illuminating is "$100,000,000—Narrows Bridge Revenue Bonds, Third Series," Feb. 14, 1963.

Author's interviews:

Henry Barnes, Ernest J. Clark, Howard S. Cullman, Lee Koppelman, Joseph McC. Lieper, Jacob Lutsky, Michael J. Madigan, J. Burch McMorran, Edward Moloney, Warren Moscow, Lawrence M. Orton, Jackson Phillips, Charles F. Rodriguez, Paul R. Screvane, Sidney M. Shapiro, Walter Sheridan, Bertram D. Tallamy, Robert F. Wagner, Jr., Paul Windels.

NOTES

Faster and faster: The number of cars and trucks passing through Triborough's toll booths had reached 39,000,000 in 1941. In 1946, the first full postwar year, the number was 49,000,000. In 1947, the number passed 50,000,000; in 1948, 60,000,000; in 1949, 70,000,000. In 1950, the Brooklyn-Battery Tunnel opened; in that year, the Authority's traffic count was 90,000,000. In 1951, it was 110,000,000; in 1952, 120,000,000. From TBTA Annual Reports. **Most of revenue was surplus:** In 1952, TBTA's annual expenses were only about $4,000,000, about the same as the annual interest on its bonds. TBTA, Annual Report, 1952. **Surplus worth half a billion:** Surveys of TBTA by D&B listed in "Sources;" Madigan, Phillips.

Bonds could be paid off within six years: In 1953, TBTA had $215,000,000 in outstanding bonds, but $27,000,000 in cash in its General Fund could be applied to them, leaving a balance of $188,000,000. Its surplus in that year was $21,760,000; it was rising every year, but even if it stayed the same, $25,000,000 a year would pay off the bonds in seven years. (D&B,)

Dreams greater than resources: TBTA, Annual Reports, 1952–54. **RM's thinking:** Shapiro, but, without being stated specifically, it also comes through in many articles and brochures he wrote at this time.

Interstate Highway System; working with Adams and Clay: RM, Madigan, Shapiro; Leavitt, p. 30. **$50 billion over ten years his figure:** RM, "How to Plan and Pay for Better Highways," Aug. 1953, quoted in *Dangerous Trade*, p. 281, when, as RM notes on p. 280, "the recommendations since adopted were novel, disturbing and controversial." See also his testimony before the Clay Committee, Oct. 7, 1954, largely a restatement of the 1953 essay. Although historians of the Interstate System such as Leavitt do not credit RM with a formative role in planning the administration of this system, such a role emerges from discussions with such BPR administrators as Francis Turner and Bertram D. Tallamy and from RM's correspondence with Clay, such as RM to Clay, 1955, quoted in *Dangerous Trade*, p. 294. Madigan and Shapiro, who spent months in Washington in 1954, 1955 and 1956—along with Hodgkiss and other Moses Men—working with congressional proponents of the System and with staffers of Clay's Advisory Committee in a National Highway Program, confirm the Turner and Tallamy impression of RM's crucial role. **Key revision:** Madigan; a discussion of negotiations on the point contained in numerous internal TBTA memos made available to the author, including Hodgkiss to RM, Aug. 20 (or 26—date unclear), 1955.

Rapprochement with Port Authority: RM, Cullman, Wagner and numerous TBTA, Port Authority and Wagner administration officials who prefer to remain unidentified. Also Lieper, Madigan, Orton, Phillips, Tallamy, Windels. **Wagner on Cullman and Tobin:** Wagner.

Port Authority finances: Port Authority Annual Report, 1954. **Worth $700,000,000:** Cullman, quoted in *NYT*, Mar. 12, 1954, as saying the Authority would be able to finance this much worth of new projects in the next ten years. **Short on dreams:** Orton.

RM broaching his plan: Cullman, Orton. **Port Authority thinking:** Cullman, Madigan, Orton, Shapiro, Wagner, confidential sources. **Pressure on Port Authority:** Doig, pp. 80–139. **"Ever widening ripples":** D&B, Apr. 30, 1959, p. 30. **Port Authority profit from "Joint Program":** Port Authority Annual Reports, 1966–70. **TBTA profit:** TBTA Annual Reports, 1956–70.

"The bridge of my dreams": RM, quoted in *J-A*, Dec. 10, 1954.

In lockstep: Observers behind the closed doors of Board of Estimate executive sessions such as Lutsky, Moscow, Rodriguez, Screvane and numerous confidential sources. **Cashmore:** Moscow.

Triborough's share would have modernized LIRR: The cost of doing everything necessary to modernize the LIRR except buying the land for the new terminals and parking garages and building a new line down the LIE—of buying new cars and high-speed locomotives and rebuilding the trackage; of building the new switching yards—was set at $60,000,000 in 1954 by a special state commission. The cost of building an 80-mile-per-hour rapid transit line down the center of the LIE was estimated at $85,000,000 by the State DPW. The cost of the land for the new terminals and garages was not estimated at any time during the 1950's, but it would have been relatively minor, considering the relative cheapness of land in Suffolk and western Nassau counties. In 1965, a state Special Committee on the LIRR (the so-called Ronan Committee) estimated the cost of a full-scale modernization program—with, as far as can be determined from its hazy wording, provision for only a few terminals—at $200,000,000: Special Committee, *A New Long Island Rail Road*, Feb. 1965. A full fifteen years after 1955—on July 6, 1970—*Newsday* could report that "the Metropolitan Transportation Authority . . . sees the full program of LIRR modernization as a 20-year, *$500,000,000* project" (italics added). It is of interest—although many factors clouded the picture—that when the state purchased the LIRR from the Pennsylvania Railroad in 1965, the total cost of its rolling stock and all other physical facilities amounted to only $65,000,000.

Port Authority's share would have built trans-Hudson loop, etc.: Metropolitan Rapid Transit Survey, *Report of the Project Director*, sets the "capital requirements" figure at $345,000,000 (p. 39). Several sources involved, in fact, believe this figure was set at its upper limits and that the loop could have been built for less.

Subway system: Various newspaper articles, 1953, 1954, 1955. A figure of $587,000,000 was given in NYC Transit Authority, Report, 1953–54, p. 25.

$1,187,000,000: NYC Transit Authority, Report, 1953–54, pp. 10–36; also see Reports for 1957–58. *NYT*, July 14, 1955. **East River tunnel and extension into Queens:** "The proposed subway tunnels from 76th Street to Astoria [in connection with the Second Avenue Trunk Line Plan] provide the key to the solution [of additional transit service to Queens and LI]. The Astoria extension has been proposed to run to the LIRR at Woodside and thence along the LIRR to Rego Park and a connection to the subway line at the Rockaways. *The cost* of the branch from mid-Manhattan to Woodside *has been estimated at $110 million*" (italics added). (MRTC, "Staff Report," pp. 20, 21.) The cost of modernizing the Port Washington branch of the LIRR and linking it up with the city subway at Woodside or Long Island City—the total capital cost, including new cars—would have been $47,000,000. (Day & Zimmerman report cited below under "Long Island Expressway.")

Expenditures under Joint Program: All figures from "Arterial Progress," Nov. 8, 1965, pp. 26–31. (See Appendix "A.")

"The parking lots": Whelan, p. 82.

Plans from father: Robert Olmsted, quoted in *DN*, Aug. 29, 1969.

Black Hole: Solarz in *NYT*, Feb. 7, 1970.

Ancient cars; deferred maintenance; toll mounting: *NYT*, *DN*, *Post*, various articles, 1964–72. 45 **cars break down per day:** *NYT*, Feb. 6, 1970. **"There have been more serious accidents":** *NYT*, July 29, 1970. **"Terrified, smoke-blinded":** *DN*, "Our Staggering Subways."

"There is little need": RM quoted in Hoover and Vernon, p. 130. **"Busted, lazy":** RM, quoted in Doig, p. 151.

Baker: *NYT*, Feb. 5, 1970. **LIRR lateness record:** "Track Record," *Newsday*, various issues, 1970.

Long Island Expressway: A chance to reshape LI: Koppelman, Barnes; Nassau-Suffolk Regional Planning Board, various publications; the following discussion is based on extensive interviewing of locational consultants, trucking and bus company and business firm presidents, Nassau and Suffolk County public officials and staffers of the Nassau-Suffolk Regional Planning Board and the Regional Plan Association that the author conducted in 1965 for a *Newsday* series he wrote entitled "Suffolk the Sick Giant." **Car trips:** MCTA, "LIRR Modernization Program—Technical Memorandum No. 3." **Buses:** Koppelman, Barnes, bus company executives. **The seven-mile stretch:** Day & Zimmerman, "Report No. 5849-C." **The other 78 miles:** Barnes, Ingraham, confidential sources. **$15,000,000 per mile:** Day & Zimmerman, "Report No. 5849-C." **They had to report:** Day & Zimmerman, p. 47; Lieper. **Traffic load:** *Newsday*, various articles. **Solution—make it bigger:** Clark; confidential sources in DPW. **Koppelman told a friend:** The friend was the author.

41. *Rumors and the Report of Rumors*

SOURCES

Books, articles, brochures and documents:

Lowe, *Cities in a Race with Time;* Moses, *Dangerous Trade*; Talese, *The Kingdom and the Power*.

Fred J. Cook and Gene Gleason, "The Shame of New York," *The Nation*, Oct. 31, 1959.

City Planning Commission, *Tenant Relocation Report*, Jan. 20, 1954. Mayor's Slum Clearance Committee, "Manhattantown Slum Clearance Plan," Sept. 1951. Women's City Club of New York, *Tenant Relocation at West Park*, Mar. 1954; *Manhattantown Two Years Later*, Apr. 1956 (Manhattantown was the original name for "West Park"). "Hearings, U. S. Congress, Senate Banking and Currency Committee," Vol. 49 (New York City, Oct. 1, 1954).

Elinor Black Papers, including the "Relocation Questionnaires" filled out by displaced residents of the Manhattantown site, and the "Black Log," an informal record of her activities on their behalf.

Author's interviews:

Algernon and Elinor Black, Fred J. Cook, Walter S. Fried, Hortense Gabel, William J. Haddad, Joseph Kahn, Lawrence M. Orton, Robert C. Weinberg.

NOTES

Rumors: Gabel. **The only one:** *NYT*, Apr. 3, 1962.

Statistics: Orton. **Federal requirement:** "Contracts for financial aid shall be made only with a duly authorized local public agency and shall require that . . . there are or are being provided . . . at rents or prices within the financial means of the families displaced from the project area, decent, safe, and sanitary dwellings equal in number of and available to . . . displaced families and reasonably accessible to their places of employment . . ." Sec. 105c, Title I: Slum Clearance and Community Development and Redevelopment, National Housing Act of 1949. **"To set at rest":** RM, "Manhattantown Slum Clearance Plan," p. 17. **Columns of statistics:** "Plan," p. 18. **RM's statistics false:** See below.

Garbage cans: Fried.

"Like cattle": Isaacs quoted in Lowe, p. 83.

Liberals' feelings: Liberals Elinor and Algernon Black, Gabel, Orton, Weinberg.

"Not a crusading paper": Black Log. **HT, DN:** Orton.

"Going underground": Orton. **The Bureau was under RM's thumb:** "Shame," pp. 300–06. **RM kept count too low:** Author's comparison of City Planning Commission Report figures with RM's figures. **170,000 evicted:** CPC Report, p. 40. **Orton leaned too far:** Author's analysis of figures in CPC Report for Manhattantown, pp. 46–47, compared with figures from on-site investigation by Women's City Club members, in the club's two brochures. **12,000 for Stuyvesant Town:** Moses, *Dangerous Trade*, p. 433.

Their color: CPC Report, p. 42. **Their income:** Report, p. 47. **Evicting people least able to afford new homes:** The 1950 census reported that 29 percent of the city's nonwhite families—almost one out of every three—were living in accommodations listed as "substandard."

The city's pledge: Summarized in CPC Report, p. 1. **Shuttled within site:** Report, pp. 50–51. **Few into public housing:** Report, pp. 48–49. The actual percentage

was 27.1, Report, p. 47. **Disappeared:** Report, p. 37; "43% of all relocatees moved to an unknown address." **Were doubling up or moving into border areas:** Gabel, Orton.

50,000 per year: CPC Report, p. 43. **Practices should be changed:** Report, pp. 31–34.

Veteran women campaigners for better housing: The club's board of directors, for example, included Mrs. Elinor Black, Stanley Isaacs' wife and daughter and Mrs. Nathan Straus, wife of the federal housing administrator.

"Bombed-out Berlin": "Shame," p. 286. **Experiences of Women's City Club volunteers:** As they recorded them for Mrs. Black on the "Relocation Questionnaires" preserved in the club's files.

Length of Puerto Ricans' tenancy: *Tenant Relocation at West Park*, p. 8. **"Since it was built":** A phrase repeated on relocation questionnaires. **Average income:** *Tenant Relocation*, p. 6. **Buildings old, overcrowded:** *Tenant Relocation*, pp. 1, 7. **But area friendly:** Interview forms; Mrs. Black. **Volunteers envious of sense of neighborhood:** This emerges clearly in some of the interviews. **"Well satisfied":** *Tenant Relocation*, p. 8. **Average rent:** *Tenant Relocation*, p. 7.

"I would die": Unnamed resident, quoted in *Tenant Relocation*, p. 5. **Anywhere. But not Harlem:** Questionnaires.

Color and poverty barred them from most areas: *Tenant Relocation*, pp. 5, 8–10; quotes, p. 10, p. 5.

No applications being accepted: "Interview, Nov. 25, 1952. Dr. Wortis, Mrs. Black at the Bureau of Real Estate, 10 to 11:15 A.M.," Mrs. Black's notes, Black Papers. **300 of 400 wanted public housing:** *Tenant Relocation*, p. 9. **Only fifty:** *Two Years Later*, p. 19.

The notice: *Tenant Relocation*, p. 2. **No help available:** pp. 10–11; questionnaires. **Typical:** p. 7.

Finding out wasn't easy: Mrs. Black's Log records her efforts. **Difficulty in tracing tenants:** *Two Years Later*, pp. 7–8. **Only 167:** *Two Years Later*, p. 8. **Probably the best off:** Isaacs to Black, Feb. 21, 1956, Black Papers. **Quotes from relocatees:** Questionnaires.

"Seriously affected": *Two Years Later*, p. 27. **Could picture:** Mrs. Black. **From one building to another:** *Tenant Relocation*, p. 10; "Shame," p. 263. **Leaned over backwards:** After reading her report, Isaacs wrote her, "You are too much of a lady and far too gentle to make the emphatic comments that some of the facts that you have uncovered really deserve. . . . I am really tired of the way that what has been done so badly has been covered up so effectively," Isaacs to Black, Feb. 21, 1956, Black Papers. **"Human decency":** *Tenant Relocation*, p. 13.

City Planning Commission report: Infighting: Gabel, Orton, confidential source. **Resolution:** Board of Estimate calendar, No. 363, Mar. 12, 1953. **Constable's shock:** Orton. **Bennett reaping profit:** See "Notes" for Chapter 43. **RM's rewriting:** The "Minority Report" gives some examples, p. 33. **"The outlook":** "Minority Report;" pp. 4–5. **Civics demand:** Lowe, pp. 83–84. **The report RM suppresses:** *Post*, Dec. 11, 1953; *Post*, *NYT*, *HT*, Dec. 14, 1953.

Rosenman's statement: "Hearings" transcript, p. 3151.

"Moses wasn't God": Gabel. **Bennett's confession:** *NYT*, Jan. 21, 1954. **Papers led:** *NYT*, *HT*, *DN*, Jan. 21, 1954. **Bennett locked up copies:** Orton, confidential source. **Only the Post:** *Post*, Jan. 21, 1954. **Why press didn't cover:** Cook, Gabel, Haddad, Kahn, Orton; Talese, pp. 99–101, gives the *Times*'s general handling of RM. **Gabel before Board:** *NYT*, 1958. **"Bunk":** RM, quoted in *Post*, Jan. 28, 1954.

Senate hearings: Caspert testimony: "Hearings" transcript, Vol. 49, pp. 3097, 3133. **Example of Rosenman's interventions:** p. 3103. **Rosenman-Simon-Bush exchange:** pp. 3139–40. **Profits huge:** pp. 3118–43; *passim*. For individual profits, see charts pp. 3144, 3146. **"Different people":** Simon, on p. 3129. **$375,000:** p. 3129. **Comptroller renting appliances:** pp. 3123–24, but best summing up is done by Cook in "Shame," p. 287.

Didn't mention Moses once: *NYT*, Oct. 2, 1954.

Reporters refused permission: Cook, Kahn tell of them.

Six agencies investigating: Lowe, p. 82.

Pallid series: *WT&S*, May 9–10, 1955.

42. Tavern in the Town

SOURCES

Books, pamphlets and documents:

Isaacs, *Love Affair with a City*; Kieley, *Moses on the Green*; Reed and Duckworth, *Central Park*.

Moses, "Statements by Mr. Arnold Newman et Al., Concerning Reconstruction of the Tavern on the Green," Apr. 17, 1956.

Wagner Papers, esp. various files in Box 1943—"Community Activities," and Box 1944—"Tavern on the Green."

Author's interviews:

Peter Campbell Brown, Jacob Lutsky, Warren Moscow, Arnold Newman, Augusta Newman, Elliott Sanger, Elinor Sanger, Arnold Schleiffer, Sidney M. Shapiro, Robert F. Wagner, Jr., and the two auditors in the City Comptroller's office, Alfred A. Fried and Samuel Shafran. Also several confidential sources.

NOTES

(All dates 1956)

"Country roads . . . rattle of pavements": Andrew Jackson Downing, quoted in Reed and Duckworth, p. 15.

"Beautiful, tranquil": Augusta Newman. **Mrs. Davis' discovery:** *HT*, May 6. **"They can't do that!":** Augusta Newman. **Brush-off:** Arnold Newman. **Wald story:** *HT*, Apr. 13.

"Working for the People" reviews: *NYT*, Mar 11; *HT*, Mar. 18. **Giving Theobald a lesson:** "Telephone Message from Commissioner Moses, 11:04 A.M., Friday, April 13," Wagner Papers.

RM's thinking: Author's analysis of his interviews with RM, Shapiro.

"Of all the city's wonders": Reed and Duckworth, p. 1.

Calling Isaacs: Sangers. **Mothers and baby carriages:** Augusta Newman. **"In front of it":** *HT*, Apr. 18. **Tableau:** Pictures in various newspapers, Apr. 17, 18.

RM trying to trick the protesters: Kieley, p. 4; *NYT*, *DN*, Apr. 21.

"Move some topsoil": *NYT*, Apr. 21.

"A heartbeat": Hurst quoted in *DN*, Apr. 23. **Front-page box:** *WT&S*, Apr. 24. **Newspaper coverage:** *NYT, HT, Post, DN, Daily Mirror, J-A, WT&S*, various issues, Apr. **"The claque":** *Daily Mirror*, May 29. **Isaacs' letters:** *NYT*, Apr. 26 for example.

The April 24 raid: All papers. Best is *Post*, Apr. 24, by William H. Rudy. **"Stab in the back":** Elliott Sanger, quoted in *HT*, Apr. 24. **"Sylvan victims":** *J-A*, Apr. 25. **"Who else?":** *Post*, Apr. 25. **The pictures:** Various newspapers, Apr. 24, 25. **"Little soldier":** *J-A*, *Daily Mirror*, Apr. 25. **Constable's smirk:** *DN*, Apr. 25.

"Moses has the right": William Peer, quoted in *NYT*, Apr. 2. **Council:** Kieley, p. 4; *NYT*, Apr. 27, 28. **Hecht:** *NYT*, Apr. 27. **Hofstadter:** Various papers, Apr. 28–May 3. **Quoting poetry:** *Post*, Apr. 22. **RM to Brown:** Brown. **"No, no":** *DN*, Apr. 27.

Probably at Isaacs' suggestion: Isaacs was suggesting the move to everyone who would listen. For example, Isaacs to Wagner, Apr. 17, 1956, p. 2: "I remember well the time when he closed and razed the Casino in the Park. I wish someone could extract from the newspapers of that day all that he then said to justify his act—which, incidentally, I approved." Wagner Papers. **"Society" orchestras, etc.:** *Post*, Apr. 25, 30, *HT*, *DN*, May 23.

"Schleiffer arrangement: Isaacs quoted in *HT*, May 2. **Paid only $9,000:** "Statement," Office of the Comptroller, undated, Wagner Papers; Shafran. **No different from other arrangements:** Unsigned memo "To: Leo Larkin, Asst. Corp. Counsel," from "Office of Comptroller, June 20, 1956," which lists other concessionaires and their rental arrangements with city. Wagner Papers. **Paid for every meal:** Schleiffer, various Tavern waiters. **Why RM favored this arrangement:** What he said publicly was that he favored it because under it the concessionaire pays for improvements to property that "the city owns . . . in the end" (*HT*, May 2).

"At issue now": *WT&S*, Apr. 30. **"Park Windfall":** *J-A*, May 1. **"Only 2%":** *Post*, May 1. **"Drops Curtain":** *Post*, Apr. 26.

Didn't realize the threat: Shapiro, confidential sources. **"We're just going":** *HT*, May 3. **Private instructions:** Brown.

Constable's refusal, Wagner's order: *Post*, May 1, 2; *NYT*, May 2. **"Nothng to hide":** Wagner quoted in *NYT*, May 5. **"Mayor Demands Airing":** *WT&S*, May 4. **"Let's Find Out":** *NYT*, May 21. **"Moses' Wings":** *DN*, May 21. **"Wagner and City":** *Post*, May 21. **Wagner conversation with Brown:** Brown. Wagner told the author he did not recall the conversation. **"What I have not seen":** L. O. Rothschild to *WT&S*, May 9. **Federal officials:** *Post*, Apr. 14; *NYT*, Apr. 16. **"Salutary effect":** *Post*, May 8. **Circles, grimace:** Pictures in *Daily Mirror, WT&S*, May 27. **Shipboard interview:** Various papers, May 27. **Newmans' feelings:** Newmans. **"A proper greeting":** Newman quoted in *Post*, May 27. **"Mother of two":** *WT&S*, May 28. **Memo:** Brown to Wagner, May 14, Wagner Papers.

$48,000: "Statement," Office of the Comptroller; *HT*, May 5.

"Moses in the dock": Brown. **Face-saving arrangement:** Brown, confirmed by memos, Brown to Wagner, May 9, 14.

Field agreed to let Moses save face. Reported the *Post* (July 18): "Asked what caused Moses to change his mind, Field says: 'I did not ask him and he did not tell me. . . . It's all closed and on a friendly basis.' " **Brown's conferences with Wagner, RM:** Brown. **"Commissioner Moses agreed":** Brown to Wagner, June 8, Wagner Papers.

Surrender headlines: Various papers, July 18.

Destruction of the myth: It was striking to the author that in interviews with persons who dealt with RM primarily after the Tavern fight, these persons spoke of him in terms emerging from that fight—in contrast to persons who dealt with him only before the fight. **"Never the same":** Shapiro.

43. Late Arrival

SOURCES

Books, articles, brochures and documents:

Anderson, *The Federal Bulldozer*; Lowe, *Cities in a Race with Time*; Moscow, *The Last of the Big-Time Bosses* and *What Have You Done for Me Lately?*; Moses, *Dangerous Trade*.

Fred J. Cook and Gene Gleason, "The Shame of New York," *The Nation*, Oct. 31, 1959.

Cook, Gabel and Thompson Papers.

Author's interviews:

Albert M. Cole, Fred J. Cook, Walter S. Fried, Hortense Gabel, William J. Haddad, Joseph Kahn, Jacob Lutsky, Mary Perot Nichols, Lawrence M. Orton, Stephen C. Thompson, Robert F. Wagner, Jr.; numerous federal, city and state housing officials, Moses aides and journalists who declined to be identified.

NOTES

Gleason's thinking: Cook. **Kahn series:** *Post*, May 23–25, 1956. **First Gleason-Cook series:** *WT&S,* July 30–Aug. 4, 1956. **Editors intimidated:** Cook. RM's articles appeared Aug. 1, 2, 3. **Phone tips pouring in:** Cook, "Memo for Nort," Aug. 3, 1956, Cook Papers. **Clipped-out ad:** Attached to undated, untitled memo, Gleason to Cook, Cook Papers. **Future leads:** Cook to Mockridge, Aug. 4, Cook Papers.

Interviews with city officials: Cook, Gabel, Thompson; Haddad would later have similar experiences. **92-year-old woman:** *WT&S*, Brooklyn edition, Jan. 17, 1957. **Comptroller's aide:** Gleason, "Memo re Title I," Apr. (date unclear), 1957. **"The Department of Health reported yesterday":** *NYT*, Jan. 24. **Manhattantown foreclosure:** "Shame," p. 291. **Five paragraphs:** *NYT*, June 13. **"We were conned":** *WT&S*, June 13, and editorial, same date. **In no newspaper:** Various papers, June 14–21. **"The changing ownership":** *NYT*, June 19.

Gleason and Cook confident: Cook; "Shame," p. 291. **Zeckendorf:** "Shame," pp. 291–92; Cook. **Board of Estimate session:** Various papers, June 21, 22, 26, 27, 1957. **"Human Betterment":** Swope quoted in *NYT*, June 22. **"Plain trafficking," "It sounded good," "disturbed no . . . realities":** "Shame," pp. 291–92.

Lincoln Center: RM's grand conception: *Dangerous Trade*, pp. 516–33; author's interviews with RM. **"Not to speak":** p. 528. **$9.58 vs. $7.00:** *Architectural Forum,* Oct. 1957. **Kennedy property:** *WT&S*, Oct. 9, 1957; RM's reply (*Dangerous Trade*, p. 525): "Ambassador Kennedy was not interested in selling the building, preferred to keep it, and was induced to agree upon a very reasonable option price primarily as a matter of public service. . . . Far from representing a handout . . . this was getting for the City and Federal government far more than the usual written-down price for the area. . . . The story that the city lost or will lose money because of overpayment . . . is malicious and wholly without basis in fact."

Cole attempting to go over RM's head: *HT*, Apr. 8, 14, 18, 1957. **Wagner's telegram:** *HT*, Apr. 19. **RM's offer to resign, Wagner rejects it:** *NYT*, July 27. **Editorials:** *HT*, *NYT*, July 29. **McGinley, Rockefeller, etc.:** Cole, Fried. **"Compromise":** *NYT*, Aug. 9. **Gleason and Cook realization:** Cook.

"The heat was really on"; "There was a time": "Shame," p. 292. **Photostats:** Cook Papers. **"Manhattantown began":** "Shame," pp. 289, 290. **Gramercy Park:** *WT&S*, Oct. 8, 1958, which produced a flyer circulated in the neighborhood: "It's Our Own Assemblyman Who Wants to Kick Us Out of Our Homes." **Nassau Management:** Many *WT&S* articles, summarized in "Shame," pp. 300–01. **"Alone," "guts cut out":** Cook, confirmed by author's comparison of Cook's rough drafts with articles actually printed: Cook Papers.

Gleason: Cook, Haddad, Kahn, Thompson, but the definitive word was Murray Kempton's, *Post*, Nov. 25, 1959. **"Nothing**

halts him": *WT&S*, June 23, 1959. See also *Time*, Dec. 7, 1959. **Hidden mike:** "Shame," pp. 280–84. **Cook:** Haddad, Kahn, Thompson. **"Sense of injustice":** Cook.

Giving it to Haddad: Cook. **Helping each other:** Cook, Haddad, Kahn. **"Chipmunks":** Gabel. **"Our motives?":** Haddad. **The RM they knew was not the RM of the beautiful parks:** This fact emerged quite clearly from the author's interviews with Cook, Haddad, Nichols and Thompson. **"He had to be stopped":** Kahn.

Public Friend No. 1: *Long Island Press*, Jan. 4, 1959; interviews: *NYT*, Jan. 7, 1959. **Senate confirmation:** *HT*, Mar. 21, 1959. The two senators quoted were John Cooke of Buffalo and Robert C. McEwen of Ogdensburg.

"Only 20 families": *Post*, Feb. 16, 1959. See also Mar. 31. **Ungar:** *Post*, Feb. 14, 1959. **"Nowhere to Go":** *Post*, Mar. 20. 1959. **"City Admits Shifts":** *Post*, Apr. 11, 1959. **"Awake at last":** "Shame," p. 292.

44. *Mustache and the Bard*

SOURCES

Books, articles, transcripts, documents:

Moscow, *What Have You Done for Me Lately?*

Robert Hatch, "This Blessed Plot, This Shakespeare in the Park," *Horizon*, Nov. 1960. H. Hewes, "Public Theatre: New York Shakespeare Festival," *Saturday Review*, Mar. 8, 1958. J. Sack, "Good Earth," *The New Yorker*, July 4, 1959.

Robert Brustein, "O, For a Draught," *The New Republic*, Sept. 12, 1960.

J. M. Flagler, "Onward and Upward with the Arts," *The New Yorker*, Aug. 31, 1957.

"The Public Fights for Life," *Newsweek*, Mar. 22, 1971.

Joseph Papp, "The Price of This Ticket Is Responsibility," *HT*, Mar. 16, 1958.

Charles Michener, "Papp's Universal Theater," *Newsweek*, July 3, 1972.

"Testimony of Joseph Papirofsky (Papp), Accompanied by Counsel, Ephraim London," House Committee on Un-American Activities, June 19, 1958.

Wagner Papers, primarily Box 1944—"Jan.–June, 1959."

Author's interviews:

Howard S. Cullman, Warren Moscow, John Mulcahy, Paul O'Keefe, Joseph Papp, Sidney M. Shapiro, Robert F. Wagner, Jr. Also one Moses aide who declined to be identified.

NOTES

(*All dates 1959 unless otherwise noted*)

Could recite whole scenes: Author heard him do so. **Liked his style:** Cullman, one of those he asked, recalls RM questioning Cornelia Otis Skinner at length about Papp at a dinner party, and being impressed; also Shapiro, confidential source.

Papp biography: Magazine articles cited above, but mostly Papp interview with author. **"If I had to pay":** Papp in *HT*, Mar. 16, 1958. **Why RM built amphitheater:** RM. **"Oh, let him have it":** Shapiro recalls the incident. **Gives Papp "expression of interest":** Papp.

A certain tenderness: Shapiro; the author noticed this quality of RM's in discussions about Thomas P. F. Hoving, among others. **Gave Papp car, etc.:** Papp. **Kerr:** Quoted in *The New Yorker*, Aug. 31, 1957, p. 56. **Papp and the sergeant:** Papp. **Sit on a blanket:** RM's feelings described by Cullman, Shapiro, confidential source. **Horizon articles:** Nov. 1960. **Saturday Review:** Mar. 8, 1958. **Constable assurance:** Papp, confirmed by tone of later RM-Papp correspondence, Wagner Papers.

Didn't get along with Constable: Papp, Shapiro, confidential source. **Papp's testimony:** "Testimony of Joseph Papirofsky (Papp)," pp. 2549–58.

Without checking: Moscow, pp. 205–06. **No more free Shakespeare:** Papp to "Members of the Fact Finding Committee of the Entertainment Unions," Mar. 11, Wagner Papers.

"Every deputy": Moscow, p. 205. **Birthday interview:** *NYT*, Jan. 7. **Papp trying to contact RM:** Papp. **"Very cavalier":** RM to Papp, Mar. 18, Wagner Papers. **"Erosion problems":** RM to Papp, Mar. 1959, Wagner Papers.

"I feel certain": Papp to RM, Mar. 25, Wagner Papers. **"Entirely in the hands":** RM to Papp, Mar. 26, Wagner Papers. **Papp says he will consider:** Papp to Constable, Mar. 30, Wagner Papers, but Papp to Constable, Apr. 7: "We regret that it is impossible. . . . The whole idea of charging came up for re-examination yesterday by . . . our Board of Directors."

Papp's desperation: Papp. **Press conference:** *HT*, Apr. 16. **RM's reply:** Park Department press release, Apr. 15. **Papp attacks again:** Papp to RM, May 4,

Wagner Papers. **Editorials:** *HT, WT&S*, Apr. 30.

McLaughlin: McLaughlin to Kennedy, May 1, attached to Constable to Wagner, May 6, Wagner Papers. **Tenney:** RM to Tenney, Apr. 28, Wagner Papers, in which RM also states: "The artistic quality of the performers may be left to the judgment of others. Certainly they don't represent professional standards."

"A typical of the breed": RM to Wagner, Apr. 23, Wagner Papers. He circulated copies of Papp's testimony before the House Un-American Activities Committee to some key city officials; turned over to the author was a transcript with the following note to Bronx Borough President Lyons attached: "Dear Jim: Here's the lad who has been putting on the heat in Central Park." **Unsigned letter:** *Post*, Apr. 29.

"Muggers," etc.: *DN*, May 2. **"What's wrong with McCarthy?":** Constable, quoted by Haddad, *Post*, Apr. 29. **Editorials:** *Daily Mirror*, May 21; *DN*, May 8; *Post*, Apr. 29; *Newsday*, May 1. **Papp's eloquent letter:** Papp to RM, May 4, Wagner Papers.

"You can't prove it": Post, May 6. **Hopper:** *Post*, Apr. 27. **Lyons:** *Post*, May 13. **Eleanor:** "My Day," in *WT&S*, Apr. 21. **"As a child":** Roger West to *Post*, May 7. **1,500 signatures:** *Post*, May. 7. **"Abolish Mr. Moses!":** *Post*, May 20. **Pictures leaving hospital:** *DN*, May. 2.

Papp's strategy: Papp. **"It's now up to you":** Papp to Wagner, May 5, Wagner Papers. **Post editorial:** May 6. **"He would rather be":** Moscow.

Wagner detested Constable: Wagner told the author, "He was a pompous ass. . . . He antagonized a lot of people. He thought he came down with the word from Olympus." **Wagner's feelings:** Moscow.

Wagner's humiliation: Various papers, Apr. 17–May 2. Here is an example of the newspaper play by Judith Crist on p. 1 of the Apr. 21 *HT*: "For the fifth consecutive day yesterday Mayor Wagner reported that he was unable to get in touch with Park Commissioner Robert Moses. . . . Undaunted, the Mayor indicated that he hopes to reach Mr. Moses eventually." **NYT story:** Apr. 21. **"Appeared irritated":** *WT&S*, Apr. 21. **"No":** *DN*, May 2. **Players Club lunch:** Moscow. Statement in press, May 12.

Lower Court: *NYT*, May 19, June 3. **Appellate Division:** *NYT*, June 18. **"Of course abide":** *NYT*, June 19. **Two philanthropists:** Florence Sutro Anspacher and the Edward L. Bernays Foundation. **"Julius Caesar" hailed:** Judith Crist in *HT*, Aug. 4, for example, said: "Moses . . . missed a good show."

"Oh, give it to him": Shapiro and confidential source, who agree on what RM's true feelings were. A one-sentence letter agreeing to put Park Department equipment at Papp's disposal was sent to him by RM, July 6, Wagner Papers. **One of the best things:** *Newsweek*, July 3, 1972, p. 54.

"Does anybody doubt it?": Isaacs quoted in *NYT*, Apr. 27. **The public understood now:** Among the many editorials pointing this out: *Post*, Apr. 16; *NYT*, Apr. 18; *HT*, Apr. 16; *WT&S*, Apr. 17.

45. Off to the Fair

SOURCES

Books and articles:

Lowe, *Cities in a Race with Time*; Moscow, *What Have You Done for Me Lately?*; Moses, *Dangerous Trade*; Talese, *The Kingdom and the Power*.

Fred J. Cook and Gene Gleason, "The Shame of New York," *The Nation*, Oct. 31, 1959.

Cook and Wagner Papers.

Moses, "The Fair and the Building Congress" (a speech delivered to the New York Building Trades Congress), May 4, 1961.

Author's interviews:

Henry Barnes, Peter J. Brennan, Albert H. Cole, John A. Coleman, Jane Moses Collins, Fred J. Cook, Timothy J. Cooney, Thomas E. Dewey, Walter S. Fried, Monroe Goldwater, William J. Haddad, Joseph T. Ingraham, Joseph Kahn, Robert Kopple, Jacob Lutsky, Michael J. Madigan, Warren Moscow, John Mulcahy, Mary Perot Nichols, Paul O'Keefe, Joseph Papp, Paul R. Screvane, Sidney M. Shapiro, Robert F. Wagner, Jr.

NOTES

(*All dates 1959*)

Citizens Union questions and answers: Various papers, May 11, 21. **"A great day!":** Haddad.

Haddad, Kahn and the files: Haddad, Kahn. **"Delicate situation":** Shanahan memo, Feb. 24, 1957, copied by Gleason; Cook Papers. **To RM, sponsors were Colonel Bennett's group:** RM, press release, July 3; Moses, *Dangerous Trade*,

pp. 456–57. **Had left investigation to Shanahan:** Confidential source. **Gigante:** "Benson Memo to City Desk—Subject: Vincent Gigante," undated, Cook Papers. **"Grotesque":** *NYT*, July 4.

Donoghue and Baron: Haddad, Kahn; *Post*, June 26; Gleason, "Memo—Re: Hall developers, et al.," Jan. 21, 1956.

Soundview tip: Cook.

Shanahan: Haddad. **"Answer every one":** Kahn. **FHA loans, Ungar's $700,000:** *Post*, various articles. **"A fund-raiser":** *Post*, June 16; *WT&S*, July 11.

Wechsler and Mrs. Schiff: Haddad, Kahn. **"There was a time":** "Shame," p. 292. **Change in older reporters:** Cook, Haddad, Kahn, confidential sources. **"You can't do that, Mayor":** Haddad, confidential source.

"Personal publicist": *Post*, June 26. **Interview with Lebwohl:** Kahn, "Some Stories I Didn't Write," *Page One of 1972*, pp. 41–42.

Spargo: *WT&S*, July 22, Aug. 24; *Post*, June 18, July 22, 27, 28, Aug. 24; *HT*, Aug. 24; *NYT*, June 30. **"Mr. Moses' Man":** *Post*, Aug. 26. **Front page:** *NYT*, Aug. 23. **RM's response:** On June 21, for example, he issued two separate statements, rushing the first to city desks and telegraphing the second: *NYT*, June 22.

Investigators checking Haddad: Haddad, Kahn, confidential source. **Locking off the vending machines:** Kahn. **"Licking his chops":** "To Fred Cook from Gene Gleason," undated memo, Cook Papers. **"Get out":** Haddad.

"Befuddled": *NYT*, June 23. **"As news":** Talese, pp. 99–101. **"Our confidence":** *NYT* editorial, June 25. **"Startling disclosures":** *NYT*, July 1, 4. **Editors okayed submission:** Confidential source. **"I . . . protested":** Moses, *Dangerous Trade*, pp. 460–61. **RM to Sulzberger:** Letter quoted in *Dangerous Trade*, p. 461. **Sulzberger's invitation:** Quoted in *Dangerous Trade*, p. 461. **Play toned down:** For example, when, on July 29, Wagner responded to another Moses resignation ultimatum with another concession, the *Times* editorialized: "We need, occasionally and more often, to turn away from fault-finding and examine with appreciation the extent to which New York is being rebuilt. . . . Among the good news . . . is the word that Mr. Moses—hard to live with but impossible to do without—will still be in there pitching."

Fire RM?: Cooney, Screvane; confirmed by Coleman, Goldwater, Lutsky, Moscow, O'Keefe, confidential sources. **Needed RM:** Author's analysis. **RM's estimates:** Moses, "The Fair and the Building Congress." **Press misunderstanding:** Various papers, July, Aug., Sept., but best summarized in "Shame," pp. 297–300. Quote is p. 298. **"And I never would have":** Wagner. **"Checking quietly":** Fried. **"Moses Ready to Quit" and then Massena:** *NYT*, June 27, 28. **Citizens Union statement:** *NYT*, July 10. **"Who will take his place?":** *DN*, July 12. **Wagner sure RM not serious:** Lutsky. **"A dead duck":** *NYT*, July 4. **Pounding his desk:** *WT&S*, July 9. **"Indicated . . . the axe":** *DN*, July 9. **"Wagner Ducks":** *DN*, July 10. **Golf Club incident:** *HT*, July 3.

Not life and death: O'Keefe, Brennan.

RM's thinking: Interviews with Brennan, Jane Moses Collins, Cullman, Dewey, Ingraham, Madigan, O'Keefe, Screvane, Shapiro, Wagner and others with whom he consulted or who were attempting to analyze his thinking at the time—plus the author's interpretation of remarks RM made to him. **Atomic power:** Moses, *Dangerous Trade*, pp. 407–10. **Haussmann:** RM's recognition of the importance of the Fair in Haussmann's career emerges clearly from speeches he made in 1959–60.

Resignation announcement: *Long Island Press*, May 22, 1960. **Wagner's letter:** *NYT*, May 10, 1960. **Grand-ballroom dinner:** *NYT*, Apr. 22, 1960.

Morris' hero worship: Barnes, Ingraham, Mulcahy. Also Papp, who says: "He hero-worshipped Moses. You could just tell it from the things that he said. He was a poor, sad man, like a little boy." **Humiliating Newbold:** Barnes. **"A giant":** *Post*, May 19, 1960. **Phone episodes:** Ingraham, confirmed confidentially by another reporter. **The public spanking:** *NYT*, July 15, 1960.

Katcher's article: *Post*, May 9, 1960. **Kihss's article:** *NYT*, May 24, 1960.

46. Nelson

SOURCES

Books, articles and documents:

Gervasi, *The Real Rockefeller*; Lundberg, *America's Sixty Families* and *The Rich and the Super-Rich*; Morris, *Nelson Rockefeller: A Biography* and *Those Rockefeller Brothers*; Moses, *Dangerous Trade*; Poling, *The Rockefeller Record*; Rodgers, *Rockefeller's Follies*, White, *The Making of the President—1960, 1964* and *1968*.

Frank Lynn, "The Rockefeller Years," *Newsday*, Apr. 14–18, 1969; David Nevin, "Rockefeller: The Old Avidity Is Gone," *Life*, Mar. 29, 1968.

Nelson A. Rockefeller, "The Story of Rockefeller Center," address at the luncheon of the New York Building Congress, Nov. 10, 1937.

La Guardia and Wagner Papers.

Author's interviews:

Harold Blake, Peter J. Brennan, William S. Chapin, Ernest J. Clark, John A. Coleman, Thomas E. Dewey, Perry Duryea, Jr., Jerry Finkelstein, Leonard W. Hall, Joseph T. Ingraham, H. Elliot Kaplan, Arthur Levitt, Jacob Lutsky, Michael J. Madigan, J. Burch McMorran, Paul R. Screvane, Sidney M. Shapiro, Bertram D. Tallamy, Hazel Tappan, Robert F. Wagner, Jr., William J. Zeckendorf and various sources who would talk only on guarantees of anonymity.

NOTES

Rockefeller's wealth: Lundberg, *Sixty Families*, pp. 6, 424–28; *The Rich*, pp. 592–631; White, *1960*, pp. 79, 87, 217; *1964*, p. 65. **Vs. Harriman:** Lundberg, *The Rich*, p. 136. **$5 billion:** Lundberg, *The Rich*, p. 158.

"Almost a dependency": White, *1968*, p. 226. **"The last great bank":** White, *1964*, p. 65. **"I bet on money":** Quoted in White, *1964*, p. 68.

Ruthlessness similar to RM's: This comparison was made, over and over, to the author by men who are afraid to be quoted. Among those willing: Shapiro (if he was dead), Dewey, Zeckendorf.

"Enjoyed his job": Rodgers, p. 25. **The imagination of the builder:** Duryea. **Backdoor financing:** Lynn series; Levitt in *NYT*, Jan. 30, Aug. 18, 1970.

"Strange, pietistic": White, *1960*, p. 182. **"Rough":** *White, 1964*, p. 77. **Civil rights donations:** White, *1964*, p. 74. **"No crevice":** White, *1968*, pp. 224–28. **"Button":** Lutsky.

RM sure Nelson liked him: RM, Dewey, Shapiro. **Palisades Parkway:** Moses, *Dangerous Trade*, p. 137. The closeness of the relationship between RM and John D. Rockefeller, Jr., is documented in LaG to RM and RM to LaG, Nov. 15, 1934, LaG Papers. **Dorado Beach:** *Dangerous Trade*, pp. 819–20. **South America:** Brochure, *Dangerous Trade*, pp. 791–806; Clark. **Fantastic fee:** $100,000, Madigan says.

Spanking Ronan: He called the report: "Impractical ideas edged with malice which emanated from an ambitious professorial mind." *HT*, Feb. 22, 1957. **"Task Force" recommendations:** Recommendation 19: "The Department of Conservation should be assigned the responsibility for the management of state parks now delegated to the regional state park commissions and the State Council of Parks. The commissions should be reconstituted as advisory councils to regional park directors appointed by the Commissioner of Conservation."

Discussing parks with Laurance: Nelson Rockefeller quoted in *NYT*, Dec. 2, 1962. **Red cardboard folders:** White, *1968*, p. 225. **Becoming a crusade:** Confidential source. **"Sucking up":** Shapiro, Blake. **Poisoning:** Stan Hinden, *Newsday*, Dec. 1, 1962.

Tension over retirement extensions: Shapiro, Blake; confirmed by H. Elliot Kaplan, head of the State Retirement System. **Lake Welch speech:** *HT*, June 16, 1962; Shapiro, Chapin.

The meeting at the brownstone: Shapiro. **"Asked, I might say ordered":** RM statement, Nov. 30, 1962. **RM at DN:** Confidential sources. **Ploy:** Shapiro, confidential sources. **Rockefeller trying to call him:** Shapiro, Tappan. **"I urged him not to resign":** Rockefeller statement, Nov. 29, 1962.

Firming up his threat: RM to Rockefeller, Nov. 28, 1962. **Modifying it:** Shapiro. **Rockefeller accepted it:** Rockefeller to RM, Nov. 29.

The events conspiring, RM's feelings: Shapiro, confidential sources. **RM's statement:** Nov. 29, 1962. **Rockefeller's statement:** Nov. 30.

"It broke his heart": In his memoirs, RM says, in the only such admission he ever made on any subject, so far as the author could find, that his resignation was offered "perhaps impetuously, as I look at it now." *Dangerous Trade*, p. 154.

"There is nothing": RM quoted in *DN*, Dec. 2, 1962.

"Calmly": *DN*, Dec. 2, 1962. **Maneuvering:** Brennan, Dewey.

"Nepotism": *DN*, Dec. 1, 1962. **Sokolsky:** In "These Days," *Long Island Press*, Dec. 6. **No statements:** The new reporter was the author. **Hardly any public reaction:** Various newspapers, Nov. 30–Dec. 7.

State Council of Parks meeting: *Newsday*, Jan. 23, 1963. **"Emotional strain":** Duryea. **"They broke his heart":** Ingraham. **Bridge dedication:** Various newspapers, Jan. 18, 1963.

47. The Great Fair

SOURCES

Books, brochures, articles and documents:

Moscow, *The Last of the Big-Time Bosses*; Moses, *Dangerous Trade, Flushing Meadow–Corona Park: A Family Park* and *Working for the People*; Rodgers, *Robert Moses*; Talese, *The Kingdom and the Power.*

John Brooks, "Diplomacy at Flushing Meadow," *The New Yorker*, June 1, 1963.

Martin Mayer, "Ho Hum, Come to the Fair," *Esquire*, Oct. 1963.

Mary Perot Nichols, "Private Opinion," *The Village Voice*, Apr. 4, 1963–Mar. 11, 1965, particularly Apr. 4, Dec. 5, 1963; Nov. 26, Dec. 17, 1964; Mar. 11, 1965.

Chris Welles, "The Big Bash That Is Running Short of Cash," *Life*, May 14, 1965.

Metropolitan Conference on Parks, "Program for Extension of Parks and Parkways in the Metropolitan Region," Feb. 25, 1930.

New York World's Fair 1939–1940 Corporation, "Minutes of Executive Committee, Dec. 4, 1935–June 24, 1941."

City of New York, Park Department, *Report to the World's Fair Committee of the Board of Estimate and Apportionment on the Acquisition and Development of the World's Fair Site,* 1935.

Moses, "After the Fair—Flushing Meadows Park," Apr. 30, 1939.

Building Trades Employers' Association, Inc., "Builders of New York and the New York World's Fair 1964–65," Mar. 16, 1961.

New York World's Fair 1964–1965 Corporation, *Flushing Meadow and Beyond,* Jan. 20, 1964.

New York World's Fair 1964–1965 Corporation, "Progress Reports," eleven reports, issued at intervals, Jan. 16, 1961–March, 1964.

Peat, Marwick, Mitchell & Co., NYWF 1964–1965 Corp., Financial Statements and Schedules, Dec. 31, 1964.

City of New York, Office of the Comptroller, Third Supplemental Report on New York World's Fair 1964–1965 Corporation, "Covering Operations from Inception to December 31, 1966," Oct. 26, 1967.

Kahn Files. Kopple Papers. La Guardia Papers, particularly Box 687, Folder "Parks Dept. F." Wagner Papers, particularly Box 5570, folders marked "World's Fair—1961" (all years in these folders).

New York World's Fair 1964–1965 Corporation, various internal memos and other documents made available to the author by confidential sources.

Speeches: Moses, "The Fair and the Building Congress," May 4, 1961; "Statement by RM," May 4, 1961.

Oral History Reminiscence:

George McAneny.

Author's interviews:

Robert Alden, Henry Barnes, Harold Blake, Peter J. Brennan, Ernest J. Clark, Gilmore Clark, John A. Coleman, Timothy J. Cooney, Howard S. Cullman, Thomas E. Dewey, Perry B. Duryea, Jr., Fred Ferretti, Joseph T. Ingraham, Joseph Kahn, Robert Kopple, Jacob Lutsky, Michael J. Madigan, J. Burch McMorran, Harry L. Meyers, Mary Perot Nichols, Paul O'Keefe, John Sattler, Paul R. Screvane, Sidney M. Shapiro, Robert F. Wagner, Jr., Bernard Weiner.

NOTES

(The author covered the Fair and investigated its finances during 1965 as a reporter for *Newsday*. Many of the observations in this chapter are those made by him at that time.)

Wanted it named after him: Madigan, Shapiro.

History of FM Park and RM's dreams for it: Moses, "The Saga of FM," *FM-Corona Park*, pp. 7–24; Metropolitan Park Conference, "Program," pp. 10, 12. **"A cloud of smoke":** Moses, *Dangerous Trade*, p. 541. **1930 maps:** Metropolitan Park Conference, "Program," p. 16. **Rereading Isaiah:** RM interview with author; he used the slogan in numerous speeches. **"It takes more than a good idea":** RM, quoted in Rodgers, p. 110. **"Dark wall":** Rodgers, p. 112. **"For a while," "the miracle":** Moses, "The Saga," p. 8. **"By God":** McAneny OHR. **"Stop at nothing":** Moses, "The Saga," pp. 8–9.

Every form of insurance: RM; RM to La Guardia, memos, letters, Jan. 4, 1936–Sept. 18, 1939, La Guardia Papers; Park Department, *Report to the World's Fair Committee of the Board of Estimate,* 1935. **Mud waves:** Weiner. **$59,000,000; "staggering":** Moses, "The Saga," p. 11. **"A lot of building":** RM.

"Of more concern": "residuary legatee"; "a heritage": Moses, Introduction, *FM and Beyond*, p.5. **$56,000,000:** *FM and Beyond*, p. 4. The applicable items

are "Demolition—$2,000,000; Restoration of Park—$5,000,000"; "Reimbursement to the City for Construction—$24,000,000"; "Balance available for Flushing Meadows and Corridor Improvements, of which $23,000,000 is required to complete the program, leaving a possible balance of $2,725,000—$25,725,000." **Timetable:** W. Earle Andrews, Gilmore Clarke, "Report of Consultants," *FM and Beyond*, pp. 7–9. **In private:** Shapiro, Madigan, private sources. After an interview with Moses, Martin Mayer wrote that "Moses says that the thing that interests him most is the park, which will remain in perpetuity" (*Esquire*, p. 183). **Banker's suggestion:** George S. Moore to RM, Feb. 24, 1963, quoted in Moses, *Dangerous Trade*, p. 605.

A billion: Moses, "The Fair and the Building Congress." **"Miscellaneous—$55,000,000":** WF Progress Report No. 1, Jan. 16, 1961, p. 5. **Constable memo:** "To: All Participants," Mar. 9, 1964, Kahn Files. **$10,000,000:** Peat, Marwick audit, Schedules 1, 2, 3. **$3,000,000 insurance premiums:** Audit, Schedules 2 and 3 for WF Corp. through end of 1964—$2,280,710. **Campo & Roberts:** Screvane, confidential sources; Moscow, p. 195. Discussion leading up to the approval was not extensive. Recalls one Fair official: "Moses just said it would be Campo & Roberts and that was that." **Wagner:** Interview with author. **Screvane:** Interview with author.

"Attitude of affluence": Confidential source; Wells, *Life*, pp. 142, 144. **Unions encouraged:** Brennan, Screvane, confidential sources. **$12,000,000 more for maintenance:** Peat, Marwick audit, Schedules 1, 2, 3. **$10,000,000 for security:** Audit, Schedule 3. **Deegan's statement:** *Post*, Nov. 27, 1963. **His fees and expenses:** Audit, Schedules 1, 2, 3; *HT*, Feb. 7, 1965. **Donoghue and other PR costs:** Audit; *NYT*, Sept. 3, 1965. **Entertainment:** Author's observations. **"A dirty word":** Confidential source. **$706,053:** Peat, Marwick audit. **$33,299,000:** Audit has $35,508,822. **Belgian Village loan:** *NYT*, May 8, 1964. **"Why don't you come aboard?":** Among the people asked was the author, whose articles were angering RM, and Kahn. **Legal fees to Rosenman and Preusse:** In 1965 alone, the WF Corporation paid $47,297.11 to Rosenman's firm, $299,525.73 to Preusse's, Whitman, Ransom and Coulson. (Comptroller, "Third Supplemental Report," p. 40.) The Fair's total legal fees came to $2,243,128.65. Of this amount, the bulk went to the Rosenman and Preusse firms. Preusse to RM, Apr. 27, 1960; RM to Preusse, Apr. 28, Wagner Papers. *Post* Nov. 27, 1963. Some size of the figures involved is indicated by a single bill from Preusse's firm, Whitman, Ransom and Coulson—$116,996,31. *HT*, Feb. 7, 1965.

Lucrative concessions: To Monaghan: *Post*, Nov. 27, 1963. **To Cullman:** He was given a slice of the Terrace Club at the Fair. **Luce and Whitney:** Mayer, *Esquire*, p. 180; *Post*, Nov. 27. **$24,000,000 allocation:** Nichols, *Voice*, Dec. 17, 1964. **Actual figure $60,000,000:** Comptroller's Report; also worksheets of Comptroller's auditors.

No outsiders: A roster of upper-echelon Fair officials can be found in WF Progress Report No. 1, pp. 53–55. The list of "Administration" and "Consultants" includes such long-time Moses Men as Constable, Witt, Andrews, Clarke, Farrell, Edward C. Maguire, Robert G. McCullough (of the Cross-Bronx Expressway), A. K. Morgan, Shapiro. **Panuch "never sold," "couldn't do the job":** Mayer, *Esquire*, p. 180.

Determined not to repeat Whelan's mistake: RM; Potter, quoted in Mayer, *Esquire*, pp. 179, 180. The critic is Walter McQuade, *The Nation*, p. 357. **Design Committee proposal and RM's turndown:** Summary in Mayer, p. 180. The clearest statement of the reason RM was determined not to have a single building is in a confidential letter to Wagner, Dec. 17, 1959, Wagner Papers: "We need a park there." **Haussmann:** Moses, *Dangerous Trade*, p. 549. **Commissioning Port Authority:** Mayer, p. 180.

Disorganization: Among the critics who commented on this. The one quoted is *NYT*, May 3, 1964.

Sukarno: Brooks, *The New Yorker*, p. 56. **West Berlin:** Brooks, p. 48.

BIE: Obstacles not insuperable: Kopple; Deegan to Wagner, Nov. 5, 1959, Wagner Papers. Brooks, *The New Yorker*, p. 42. **Precedent:** Brooks, p. 42. **"Informal" exhibits being planned:** Kopple. **"Three people living obscurely":** *NYT*, Sept. 11, 1963. **"Not subject":** Kopple. **BIE's retaliation:** Summary in Mayer, *Esquire*, p. 179. **"It's pretty hard":** Poletti quoted in Mayer, p. 182.

Extensive public relations effort: Detailed in *Post*, Nov. 14, 1963. **Fair publicity deliberately built around RM:** PR men O'Brien and Davis discussed this in author's presence during the Fair.

Newsday's ambivalence: Altschul series, editorial May 11, 1962.

Mrs. Sulzberger's letter: *NYT*, May 7, 1961. **"Mr. Moses would complain":**

Shapiro. **Expressways editorial:** *NYT*, June 15, 1963. **"Infuriated":** Ingraham.

Predisposition to be favorable: Kahn.

RM's attitude at press conferences: Alden, Ferretti; author was present at some. **"The Lester Markel Lecture":** Moses, "Moses Meets the Press—Head On," *NYT Magazine,* Aug. 5, 1962. **"Only one way":** Kahn.

Kahn's crusade: Kahn. **Opotowsky article:** *Post*, Nov. 27, 1963. **California:** Lucien C. Haas (Brown's press secretary) to Kahn, Mar. 29, 1963, Kahn Files. *Post*, July 30, 1963. **Puerto Rico, Virgin Is.:** *Post*, Mar. 18, 29, 1963.

"Foul the nest": RM quoted in *NYT*, July 24, 1963. See also his speech "The Fair, the City and the Critics," Oct. 13, 1964, on "avant-garde critics and left-wing commentators, . . . jaded publishers [who] befoul everything."

NYT editors' luncheon: Ingraham, confidential source. **Carping on Administration Building opening:** Various newspapers, Jan. 12, 1961. **On landscaping:** *NYT*, Aug. 28, 1963. **On Science Museum:** *NYT*, Apr. 10, 1963; Oct. 9, 1963. **Press conferences:** *NYT*, Sept. 15, 1964.

Fighting with H. L. Hunt: *NYT*, Oct. 10, 19, 25, 1963. RM's version in *Dangerous Trade*, pp. 587–91. **Douglas:** *HT*, Sept. 13, 1961. **Request had been assured of passage:** *HT*, Mar. 14, 1962. *NYT*, Apr. 18, 1962. **RM all but killed it:** *HT*, Sept. 13, 1961. **Attacks Congress:** *NYT*, Sept. 21, 1961, Mar. 11, 1962.

Racial controversy: *NYT*, Mar. 12, 1962, June 19, 1963, Apr. 10, 1964; Screvane. **Religious controversy:** Moses, *Dangerous Trade*, pp. 579–87. In 1965, RM was awarded the Jordanian Kawkob (Star of Jordan) decoration of the First Order, for "contribution to understanding and friendship of nations." **Garbage controversy:** Welles, *Life*, p. 138. **Art controversy:** *NYT*, Nov. 18, 1963. **Opening-on-time controversy:** *NYT*, Feb. 28, 1964.

Daily expenses $300,000; $30,000,000 spent before opening day: Peat, Marwick audit, p. 3, Schedules 2 and 3. **Needed 220,000 per day:** Author's calculation based on internal Fair memos. **Daily attendance figures:** "Daily Turnstile Count," internal WF Corp. memo.

Witt's mistake: Peat, Marwick audit, p. 3. In *Dangerous Trade,* RM wrote: "It is clear that I relied too much on . . . the late Erwin Witt, who proved honest but timid and weak" (p. 606). **Afraid to tell him, firing Spargo:** Welles, *Life*, p. 144. **"Never the same again":** Confidential source.

"Drastically reduced budget": Welles, *Life*, p. 146. **His dilemma:** Brennan. **Allied, Pinkerton cut back:** *Newsday*, Feb. 2, 1965.

Inflating attendance figures: The author, as a reporter covering the Fair, was given the "official" figures by Fair PR men, but the true figures by a bank president with whom RM was negotiating for a loan to keep the Fair afloat and who had insisted on being given RM's personal "Daily Turnstile Count." **"Financial success":** *NYT*, Oct. 14, 1964. **Mary Nichols spotted it:** *Voice*, Dec. 17, 1964. **"A fool's paradise":** Welles, *Life*, p. 146.

MacTavish episode: Welles, *Life*, pp. 146–48; confirmed by Spargo to RM, Feb. 1, 1965, and Witt to RM, Jan. 20, 1965 (given to author by confidential source). **Moore-RM conversation:** Welles, p. 148. **Moore resignation:** *NYT*, Jan. 19, 1965.

RM rounding up new exhibits: *NYT*, Feb. 5, Feb 18, Mar. 10, Apr. 21, 1965. **Almost pleading:** For example, Moses, "The Fair, the City and the Critics," Oct. 13, 1964, spends nine pages cataloguing "slanted headlines," etc., but ends: "We badly need the press. . . . With . . . agreement on main objectives, differences in detail will be entirely consistent with mutual respect, and there will be a new dawn when the Fair reopens next April. Why not try this formula?"

Moore photo: *Life*, May 14, 1965, p. 13. **Can't repay loan:** RM, in *NYT*, Jan. 27, 1965. **$17,540,000 deficit:** Peat, Marwick audit. **Can't repay notes:** *NYT*, Feb. 6, 1965. **Dec. 31 financial situation:** Peat, Marwick audit; *HT*, Jan. 24, 1965; Witt memo, Feb. 15, 1965, Schedule II, WF Corp. internal document. **Threw in escrow account and other desperate measures:** *Newsday*, various articles, Dec. 1964. **Loan difficulties:** Nichols, *Voice*, Dec. 17, 1964; *Newsday*, Feb. 20, 23, 1965. **Ferretti's overplay:** *HT*, Feb. 22, 1965. **Newsday article;** Mar. 13, 1965. **Beame:** *NYT*, Nov. 24, 1964; *HT*, Feb. 1, 3, Sept. 10, 1965. **Escrow stories:** *HT*, Jan. 21, 1965.

Newsday ridicule: Jan. 13, 1965. **Schaap:** *HT*, Jan. 14, 1965.

NYT editorial: Feb. 7, 1965.

Wagner's feelings and resignation moves: Wagner, Screvane, Coleman; the author's interviews at the time with city and state officials who demanded anonymity. **IRS investigation:** Moses, *Dangerous Trade*, p. 606. **Panama Canal:** Gimbel, quoted in Welles, *Life*, p. 150. **"A sad thing":** McMorran.

Screvane's overtures: Screvane. **Coleman's:** Coleman. **Bankers':** Wagner, confidential sources. **Executive committee maneuvering:** Screvane, Wagner, Shapiro, confidential sources. **Gaveling Zaretzki:** *HT*, June 23, 1964. **Feb. 24 meeting:** *Newsday*, Feb. 24, 25, 1965. **One reporter:** The author.

Newsday column: Mike McGrady, May 11, 1965. **His auditors told him:** One Fair official, not a Moses Man, was feeding the author the daily memos on the situation being circulated within the Fair Administration Building; see, for example, *Newsday*, Mar. 15, 1965.

Last-minute attendance boom: Various newspapers, *NYT*, Oct. 14, 1965. **$13,000,000:** Internal WF Corp. memos.

RM meeting with bankers: *NYT*, Oct. 18, 1965. **Legal action and compromise:** *NYT*, Nov. 17, 1965. **Triborough funds made available:** *NYT*, Sept. 1, 1965. **Quiet Park Department appropriations:** Nichols, *Voice*, Dec. 17, 1964; Morris to Felt, Mar. 8, 1962, Wagner Papers ($675,000 for trees). **"One of the very great municipal parks":** Moses, *Dangerous Trade*, p. 543. He also called it "the city's finest park": *Newsday*, Oct. 18, 1965. **$142,674,000:** Moses, *FM-Corona Park*, p. 33.

48. *Old Lion, Young Mayor*

SOURCES

Books and documents:

Klein, *Lindsay's Promise;* Moses, *Dangerous Trade*.

Levitt TBTA Audit (see "Sources," Chapter 33).

TBTA, "Memorandum in Opposition to Legislation Providing for the Merger of TBTA with the New York City Transit Authority and Other Transportation Facilities," Jan. 21, 1966.

Author's interviews:

Henry Barnes, Harold Blake, Peter J. Brennan, Thomas E. Dewey, Perry B. Duryea, Jr., Thomas P. F. Hoving, Joseph McC. Lieper, J. Burch McMorran, Edward J. Maloney, Arthur E. Palmer, Jr., Robert Price, Richard M. Rosen, Sidney Schanberg, Sidney M. Shapiro, Bertram D. Tallamy, Robert F. Wagner, Jr., Norman K. Winston.

NOTES

(*All dates 1966 unless otherwise noted*)

"Matinee idol": RM was to repeat this in print later; the first time he said it was to his aides that day: Blake, Shapiro, confidential source.

"The power brokers": Klein, p. 95.

It sounded so easy: *NYT*, Jan. 14, 15. **Moving LaG's portrait:** *NYT*, Feb. 19. **Their feelings about RM:** Hoving, Price, Rosen, confidential sources. **RM's feelings about them:** RM. **"Lindsay Maps Plans":** *Post*, Dec. 10, 1965. One RM aide remembers RM grinning grimly when he read that headline.

Lindsay confident: *NYT*, *Newsday*, Jan. 14, 18. **Lawyers ignorant of bond covenants:** The author spoke to several administration officials, including some in the Corporation Counsel's office, who were attorneys. Their ignorance of the covenants and their significance was striking. All would talk to the author only on guarantees of anonymity.

"The holders": Wood, Preusse and Lebwohl, Memorandum of Law, "Memorandum in Opposition," p. 9. **"Poorly advised":** RM quoted in *NYT*, Jan. 21. **Media all but ignored:** All area newspapers, Jan.–Feb.

Rallying call; and they saw it as such: Brennan, Tallamy. **Didn't understand importance of arterial post:** Price; interviews with anonymous Lindsay confidants. **"Briskly striding Commissioner Hoving":** *NYT*, Jan. 30. **Palmer being sent to RM:** Palmer. **Their three meetings:** RM, Palmer concur fully on their details. **"You haven't got the power":** Palmer, Price. **Legislation no longer mentioned surpluses:** Senate Intro. 795, Print 798 by Mr. Conklin compared with Senate Intro. 419, Print 419 by Mr. Mackell. **"That goddamned whippersnapper":** Palmer.

Lindsay-RM meeting: RM, Palmer.

Boastfully confident: Various newspapers, Feb. 22–Mar. 10. **The Rockefeller apartment meeting:** Palmer, Rosen, confidential sources who also were present. **Lindsay believed he had Rockefeller's support:** Palmer, Price, Rosen. **"The way you handle legislators":** Rosen quoted in *NYT*.

"Harry Van Arsdale": Confidential source. **Rosen's quote:** To author, in interview, June 25, 1968. **Playing games:** Schanberg. **Seriously believed:** Palmer, Price, Rosen, confidential sources.

The hearing: Brennan, Dewey, Palmer, Rosen, Schanberg, Shapiro, confidential sources who were present; *Newsday, DN, NYT, Long Island Press, HT,* Mar. 11, 12. **The handshake:** Photos in *Newsday, HT*. **"No one will buy":** Robert Christie, vice president of Dillon, Read & Co.,

principal manager for all TBTA bonds. **"Pro forma charade":** Schanberg.

RM arranging mopping-up actions: Shapiro, Brennan; *HT*, Mar. 13. **Chase:** *NYT*, Mar. 13. **Editorial:** *NYT*, Mar. 12. **Wood reply:** Wood to *NYT*, Mar. 18. **By the way:** *Newsday*, Mar. 12; confidential sources. **Lindsay telephoning Rockefeller, instructing Rosen:** Rosen. **"Never occurred":** Lindsay quoted in *NYT*, May 14, **Rockefeller support not forthcoming:** Reported *NYT* on Mar. 16: "Over and over at the news conference the Governor praised 'John Lindsay's courage and forthrightness in stepping up to meet the city's problems.' But just as many times, he counseled the Mayor on the wisdom of compromise in the face of opposition."

Thirtieth-anniversary pageantry: *NYT*, *Newsday*, July 12. **The letter:** *NYT*, July 13.

Lindsay's instructions to Palmer: Palmer. **Unable to accomplish anything:** Palmer, Winston. **Winston for RM on everything:** RM, Winston.

Signs of awareness: *NYT*, June 18, July 14; Brennan, Palmer, confidential sources. **Would take five years:** Lieper. **Lindsay's astonishment:** McMorran, Moloney, Palmer, Price, confidential sources. **$250,000,000:** Levitt TBTA Audit (pp. 2–3) shows surplus running about $29,-000,000 per year. TBTA Annual Report, 1966, p. 13, shows cash, investments and receivables as $142,000,000. The combination of the two figures would, by the end of 1969, at then current interest rates, have enabled Triborough, by refinancing its outstanding bond issues, to raise an additional $250,000,000 for construction.

49. The Last Stand

SOURCES

(Certain crucial details of this chapter were supplied to the author by banking sources who would, out of fear of Gov. Rockefeller, agree to talk only on guarantees of anonymity.)

Books, articles and documents:

Moses, *Dangerous Trade*.

Frank Lynn, "The Rockefeller Years," *Newsday*, Apr. 14–18, 1969.

Levitt TBTA Audit (see "Sources," Chapter 33).

Author's interviews:

Harold Blake, Peter J. Brennan, Thomas E. Dewey, Perry B. Duryea, Jr., Joseph T. Ingraham, Lee Koppelman, Arthur Levitt, Joseph McC. Lieper, Michael J. Madigan, Arthur E. Palmer, Jr., Jackson Phillips, Richard M. Rosen, Sidney M. Shapiro, Arthur V. Sheridan, Robert F. Wagner, Jr., Franklin S. Wood.

NOTES

$6.4 billion: *NYT*, Mar. 8, 1967. **State's financial condition:** Lynn, "The Rockefeller Years." **$110,000,000 on hand, $30,-000,000-per-year surplus:** Levitt TBTA Audit, pp. 2–3. **Rockefeller's thinking:** Brennan, Dewey, Duryea, Levitt, Shapiro, confidential sources.

So little to fight back with: Ingraham, Shapiro, Madigan, Wagner.

"Straw in the wind": Palmer, Rosen, confidential sources. **Didn't grasp extent of power:** Author's impression from interviews with Lindsay aides, most of whom insist on anonymity. **Driven to the wall, planning to use bond monies in budget:** Levitt; *Newsday*, Mar. 21, Oct. 22, 23, Nov. 8, 1967. **Tax increase:** *NYT*, May 2, Nov. 7, 1967. **Voter resentment:** *NYT*, Nov. 7, 1967. **Afraid RM would tip it:** Brennan, Duryea. **"Essential is the participation":** *Newsday*, Mar. 14, 1967.

RM's figures: Duryea, Levitt, Shapiro, confidential sources.

First Rockefeller-Ronan conference with RM: Jan. 5, 1967. **Letter to the Bahamas:** *World-Journal-Tribune*, Mar. 12, 1967; Shapiro. **Statement on return:** *NYT*, Jan. 22, 1967. **RM and Rockefeller meet:** *NYT*, Mar. 11, 1967. **Nothing new:** Ingraham, Shapiro. **Rockefeller had promised RM power:** Duryea, confirmed by another leader present; Levitt, confirmed by Shapiro, who was one of the coterie; Brennan. **"It was learned":** *NYT*, *DN*, Mar. 12, 1967.

No doubt: Blake, Madigan, Shapiro. **Asks for appointment; "not a cent"; "guts," "a lot of courage and faith":** RM, "Why New York Needs That Transportation Bond Issue," *Newsday*, May 26, 1967, quoted in *Dangerous Trade*. **Rosenman:** Confidential source. **"He had a promise":** Dewey.

Suit would have been successful: Phillips, Wood, confidential sources. **Chase brief:** *NYT*, July 1, 1967.

Meeting of the two brothers: *NYT*, Feb. 10, 1968. The author has been unable to obtain a copy of the stipulation. He did, however, hold detailed discussions with two individuals who did—

Ingraham, who obtained a copy only by promising he would never quote from it directly but would use it only for background (and who, in fact, never used it for anything at all), and a confidential source. The author's discussion of the stipulation is based on what they told him. **On his instructions, Rosenman agreed:** Confidential source; *World-Journal-Telegram*, Mar. 12, 1967; *NYT*, Mar. 20, 1967.

All was honey: Shapiro. **The Governor "told me":** Moses, *Dangerous Trade*, p. 257. **Duryea's intercession:** Duryea, Shapiro. **Ronan's offer:** *NYT*, Feb. 29, 1968. RM's salary was later raised to $35,000. **RM's feelings:** Shapiro, Wagner. **Articles:** Witkin, *NYT*, and *Newsday*, Mar. 2, 1968.

50. Old

SOURCES

Books and articles:

Moses, *Dangerous Trade.*

Moses, "From the Bridge," *Newsday* column.

Author's interviews:

Harold Blake, Peter J. Brennan, Jane Moses Collins, Perry B. Duryea, Jr., Jacob Lutsky, Michael J. Madigan, Charles F. Rodriguez, Sidney M. Shapiro, Arnold Vollmer, Robert F. Wagner, Jr.

NOTES

Still swam: Author saw him do it.

Ronan's incompetence: Brennan, Shapiro, confidential sources.

"A couple of times": Confidential source.

RM fooled by Governor on Sound Crossing: RM's desire for it to be built—and his rationalizations as to why it wasn't—are summed up in *Dangerous Trade*, pp. 262–75; also "From the Bridge," Dec. 23, 1967, and Jan. 4, 1969. **Desperate:** Brennan, Ruryea, Shapiro. **"No Calvin Coolidge":** RM, speech to "Fall Guy" luncheon, Garden City Hotel, Jan. 24, 1969, quoted in *Dangerous Trade,* pp. 258–59. **Governor charming, Ronan not:** The author saw this on several occasions. Blake's muttered comment was to the author on one occasion at which Ronan all but snubbed RM, the opening of the "Sunken Meadow" addition to Randall's Island, July 11, 1967.

Lutsky: Telephoned Lebwohl during interview with author. **"Sorry for him":** Wagner. **Badillo incident:** Rodriguez.

"Birthdays are to forget": *DN*, Dec. 16, 1969. **"Hasn't changed":** Confidential source.

Housing program: *DN*, Apr. 30, 1969. **"Atlantic Village" proposal:** *Dangerous Trade*, pp. 478–80. **Citywide program:** Discussed it with author.

So much left to do: RM to author in interviews.

"Dangerous Trade" written by staff: Author saw the drafts submitted by various staffers.

Fordham dedication: *NYT*, July 4, 1970. **Building Trades dinner:** Author present. **"We'd just like to observe":** *DN* editorial, 1969. **"The glass of fashion":** RM, quoted in *NYT*, Oct. 13, 1969.

Damrosch dedication: *NYT*, May 23, 1969; Moses, *Dangerous Trade*, pp. 532–33. **"The finest short story":** Moses, "From the Bridge" column, *Newsday*, 1969. **Alley Pond Park:** *NYT*, Sept. 8, 1969. **Lindsay's accomplishments in housing:** For example, *NYT*, July 5, 1969, Jan. 11, 1971.

Slim hopes: RM to author; Blake, Shapiro.

RM's attitude toward John Olds, Christopher Collins: Jane Moses Collins, Madigan, Shapiro. It was apparent in RM's interviews with author; he referred to John scornfully as "the banker," waving his hand disdainfully. **Christopher's death:** *Newsday*, Dec. 13, 1968.

Chauffeur, name dropping: To author. **Why weren't they grateful?:** The author was present at the Excedra ceremony.

INDEX

D

H

O

T

U

PHOTO CREDITS

Arnold Newman: *Section III: plates 4–5, 6.*

New York Daily News Photos: *Section I: plates 6 (top), 8 (top and center), 13 (top and center), 14 (center), 15 (bottom right). Section II: plates 1, 2–3 (all but bottom right), 4, 6, 7, 11 (bottom left), 12 (bottom), 13 (top right and bottom right), 14 (top right), 16. Section III: plates 2 (bottom right), 3 (top right), 7 (center right and bottom right).*

Wide World Photos: *Section I: plates 3 (top), 7 (bottom), 10 (top right and bottom right), 12 (top and center). Section II: plates 10 (center), 11 (bottom right), 13 (center), 14 (bottom), 15 (top and bottom left).*

The New York Times: *Section I: plate 10 (bottom left), plate 16 (bottom).*

Power Authority of the State of New York: *Section I: plate 10 (top left). Section II: plate 10 (top and bottom), Section III: plate 7 (bottom left).*

United Nations: *Section III: plate 13 (top left).*